Praise for

FDR

"Miraculous . . . a careful, intelligent synopsis of the existing Roosevelt scholarship . . . and a meticulous re-interpretation of the man and his record . . . At last we have the biography that is right for the man."

—*The Washington Post*

"Magisterial . . . The author's eloquent synthesis of FDR's complex and compelling life is remarkably executed and a joy to read. . . . This erudite but graceful volume illuminates FDR's life for scholars, history buffs and casual readers alike."

—*Publishers Weekly* (starred review)

"[A] remarkable, sympathetic biography . . . [Smith] does a fine job."

—*The New Yorker*

"Compelling . . . richly researched . . . one of those monumental works that . . . does not lose sight of the individual at its heart."

—*The Denver Post*

"An outstanding biography of 'the most gifted American statesman of the twentieth century' . . . an exemplary and highly readable work that ably explains why FDR merits continued honor."

—*Kirkus Reviews* (starred review)

"A marvelous book."

—*The Dallas Morning News*

"Especially deft . . . Smith vibrantly captures the complete drama of an American original."

—Newark *Star-Ledger*

"An intricate network of personal detail . . . deeply moving."

—*The New York Sun*

"Smith's towering new biography brings the great man to vivid life once more, offering us a valuable chance to ponder again the crucial mystery of leadership."

—JON MEACHAM, author of *Franklin and Winston* and *American Gospel*

"[Smith] is an accomplished biographer, and he lays out in the most charming prose the dynamics of a gifted politician."　　—*The Washington Times*

"This page-turner is the best single-volume biography available of America's thirty-second president. Essential."　　—*Library Journal* (starred review)

FDR

JEAN EDWARD SMITH

RANDOM HOUSE TRADE PAPERBACKS

NEW YORK

Published in the United States by Random House Trade Paperbacks, an imprint
of The Random House Publishing Group, a division of Random House, Inc., New York.

RANDOM HOUSE TRADE PAPERBACKS and colophon are trademarks
of Random House, Inc.

Originally published in hardcover in the United States by Random House, an imprint of
The Random House Publishing Group, a division of Random House, Inc., in 2007.

Grateful acknowledgment is made to HarperCollins Publishers, Inc., for
permission to reprint brief excerpts from *Working with Roosevelt* by Samuel I. Rosenman,
copyright © 1952 by Harper & Brothers. Copyright renewed © 1980 by
Dorothy R. Rosenman, Robert Rosenman, and James R. Rowen. Used by permission.

Unless otherwise noted, the photographs in this work are courtesy of the Franklin D.
Roosevelt Presidential Library and Museum, Hyde Park, New York.

LIBRARY OF CONGRESS CATALOGING-IN-PUBLICATION DATA

Smith, Jean Edward.
FDR / Jean Edward Smith.
p. cm.
Includes bibliographical references and index.
ISBN 978-0-8129-7049-4
1. Roosevelt, Franklin D. (Franklin Delano), 1882–1945.   2. Presidents—United
States—Biography.   I. Title.
E807.S58 2007   973.917092—dc22   2006043087
[B]

Printed in the United States of America

www.atrandom.com

4 6 8 9 7 5

Book design by Simon M. Sullivan

To the memory of my parents,
Eddyth and Jean—proud Mississippians
devoted to Franklin Roosevelt

He lifted himself from his wheelchair
to lift this nation from its knees.

Preface

THREE PRESIDENTS DOMINATE American history: George Washington, who founded the country; Abraham Lincoln, who preserved it; and Franklin Delano Roosevelt, who rescued it from economic collapse and then led it to victory in the greatest war of all time. Elected for an unprecedented four terms, Roosevelt proved the most gifted American statesman of the twentieth century. When he took office in 1933, one third of the nation was unemployed. Agriculture lay destitute. Factories were idle, businesses were closing their doors, and the banking system teetered on the brink of collapse. Violence lay just beneath the surface. The Hoover administration had deployed tanks and tear gas to drive a bedraggled remnant of World War I veterans (the Bonus Marchers) from Washington but otherwise appeared incapable of responding to the crisis.

Roosevelt seized the opportunity. He galvanized the nation with an inaugural address ("the only thing we have to fear is fear itself") that ranks with Lincoln's Second Inaugural, declared a banking holiday to restore confidence in the nation's banks, and initiated a flurry of legislative proposals to put the country back on its feet. Under FDR's energetic leadership the government became an active participant in the economic life of the nation. More important, he restored the country's confidence. Roosevelt revolutionized the art of political campaigning, revitalized the Democratic party, and created a new national majority that included those previously cast aside. His fireside chats brought the presidency into every living room in America. And what may be more remarkable, he did this while paralyzed from the waist down. For the last twenty-three years of his life, Franklin Roosevelt could not stand unassisted.

The literature on the Roosevelt era is immense. Virtually every major participant has written his or her memoirs, scholars have filled library shelves with analytic studies, and the nation's most prolific writers have addressed the New Deal, the Second World War, and the outsize personalities who dominated American life in the 1930s and '40s. Biographies of Franklin Roosevelt are only slightly less numerous than those of Washington or Lincoln, and there is little that has not been said, somewhere, about the president. These works are easily accessible to the student of history, yet are seldom consulted by the general public. In recent years, biographies of lesser figures—Truman, MacArthur, Eisenhower, the numerous Kennedys—have shaped popular perceptions of the period. Rummaging through the life of Eleanor Roosevelt has become a cottage industry. As a result, Roosevelt himself has become a mythic figure, looming indistinctly out of the mist of the past.

The riddle for a biographer is to explain how this Hudson River aristocrat, a son of privilege who never depended on a paycheck, became the champion of the common man. The answer most frequently suggested is that the misfortune of polio changed Roosevelt. By conquering adversity he gained insight into the nature of suffering and found new sources of strength within himself. That is undoubtedly true. But it does not go far enough. FDR's effort to recover from polio took him to Warm Springs, Georgia. Year after year at Warm Springs he was exposed to the brutal reality of rural poverty. All around him he saw hardworking people who were "ill-housed, ill-clad, ill-nourished." Roosevelt's patrician instincts rebelled, and he began to formulate the economic ideas that came to fruition in the New Deal. As governor of New York when the Great Depression hit, FDR was the only state chief executive to organize extensive relief efforts. "Modern society, acting through its government," he said, "owes the definite obligation to prevent the starvation or the dire want of any of its fellow men and women who try to maintain themselves but cannot."

Roosevelt was too talented to be confined by the circumstances of his birth. His devotion to his career and his conviction that he was a man of destiny far outweighed any tribal loyalty. A social conservative by instinct and upbringing, he did more to alter the relationship between ordinary citizens and their government than any other American. And he shaped our notion of the modern presidency. In that sense Roosevelt was a natural. He was not especially gifted in any field except politics. But in politics he had no equal.

Roosevelt knew the Democratic party better than anyone. It was said he could draw a line on a map from the East Coast to the West Coast and name every county the line intersected. In most counties he knew the Democratic leader and one or two officeholders as well. And he kept close watch on party patronage. His appointments were calculated not only to reward, but co-opt. As his first secretary of war, he appointed Utah isolationist George Dern. For secretary of state he chose conservative Tennessee senator Cordell Hull— a sheet anchor to protect the administration from carping redneck legislators. His vice president, hard-drinking John Nance Garner of Texas, former Speaker of the House, solidified southern support. To dole out federal money at the Reconstruction Finance Corporation, FDR chose conservative Texas banker Jesse Jones. When the Securities and Exchange Commission came into being, he appointed Joseph Kennedy to head it. "It takes a thief to catch a thief," *The Washington Post* chortled.

FDR's administrative style was a legendary mixture of straightforward delegation, flowchart responsibility, Machiavellian cunning, and crafty deception. James MacGregor Burns called him a lion and a fox. Frances Perkins, FDR's long-serving secretary of labor, said Roosevelt was "the most compli cated human being I have ever known." He kept major decisions in his own hands, played his cards close to his chest, and enjoyed the consternation of opponents when his maneuvers were revealed. "I'm a juggler," Roosevelt told Treasury secretary Henry Morgenthau, Jr. "I never let my right hand know what my left hand is doing." Occasionally he overreached. His wrongheaded 1937 Court-packing scheme boomeranged badly, as did his ill-considered intervention in Democratic senatorial primaries in 1938. He made mistakes. Some were catastrophic, such as his 1937 decision to slash federal expenditures, precipitating the "Roosevelt recession" of 1938–39.

Roosevelt expected cabinet officers to run their own shows, but did not hesitate to enter the arena when an issue interested him. He handled the nation's diplomacy largely through Undersecretary of State Sumner Welles, a fellow Grotonian, and often ignored Secretary Hull. The Navy he ran through the chief of naval operations, Admiral William D. Leahy, who had skippered FDR's yacht when Roosevelt was assistant secretary of the Navy. When he decided to replace Douglas MacArthur as Army chief of staff in 1934, he sent the general on an inspection tour of Hawaii and then announced his successor while MacArthur was en route.

Roosevelt relished being president. His buoyant energy and unshakable optimism transmitted itself to everyone he met. After the lusterless Warren G. Harding, the dour Coolidge, and stuffy Herbert Hoover, FDR seemed like a breath of fresh air in the White House. His self-assurance was exactly what the country needed. With the possible exception of Ronald Reagan (who voted for FDR four times), no president has been more serene in the conviction that whatever happened, everything would turn out all right. "Take a method and try it," he once said. "If it fails, admit it and try another. But above all, try something." Social Security, unemployment compensation, stock market regulation, the federal guarantee of bank deposits, wages and hours legislation, labor's right to bargain collectively, agricultural price supports, rural electrification—all of which we take for granted—did not exist before FDR.

As commander in chief, Roosevelt was better prepared than any president before him, save Washington and Grant. For eight years under Woodrow Wilson he had been the number two man in the Navy Department. He understood how the services operated and did not hesitate to assert presidential authority. When war clouds gathered in 1939, he passed over the Army's senior leadership and named George C. Marshall chief of staff. As the situation grew tense in 1940, he reached out to the Republican party and named the redoubtable Henry L. Stimson secretary of war and Frank Knox of the *Chicago Daily News*, who had been Alf Landon's running mate in 1936, secretary of the Navy. When war came, he turned to hard-bitten Admiral Ernest J. King to fight the fleet and recalled Admiral William Leahy to be his own chief of staff. To manage military procurement, it seemed natural to select Army engineers who had worked closely with Harry Hopkins and the WPA: Brehon Somervell and Lucius Clay.

Roosevelt nudged the nation toward a war footing. He pressed passage of the Lend-Lease Act to provide aid for embattled Britain, reestablished the draft (its extension carried by only one vote in the House of Representatives), and, probably in violation of the Constitution (and certainly contrary to statute), traded fifty seaworthy destroyers to Great Britain for base rights in the Western Hemisphere. What he did not do is connive with the Japanese in the attack on Pearl Harbor.

Roosevelt did not pay as much attention as he should have to the deteriorating situation in the Pacific in 1941; he allowed hawkish subordinates too much leeway, and he muffed a possible summit meeting with the Japanese prime minister. The administration recognized that Japan might attack in December 1941, but it did not expect the assault to come at Pearl Harbor, which the military believed to be impregnable.

FDR can be criticized on a number of issues. He ignored racial segregation, he did not rush to admit the victims of fascism to America's shores, and he could be cavalier about the protection of civil liberties in wartime. But there is absolutely no evidence that he was complicit in the events of December 7, 1941.

Roosevelt's wartime leadership resembles that of Lincoln. As in 1933, he restored the nation's confidence. Under FDR's hands-on direction, the United States became "the arsenal of democracy." Britain was saved from defeat, the Soviet Union was provided the materiel it required, and by 1943 American armed forces had assumed the offensive. Roosevelt's wartime diplomacy paved the way for the defeat of the Axis powers and the establishment of a world order based on the rule of law. His relations with Winston Churchill and Joseph Stalin suggest statecraft at its finest. On the other hand, his treatment of Charles de Gaulle was petulant and continues to roil Franco-American relations. It would also be fair to say that FDR did not fully comprehend the difficulties that would arise in containing communism in postwar Europe, nor did he fathom the sea change at work in China. The United States was a third-rate military power when World War II began. When it ended, America was the most powerful nation in history.

Roosevelt's personal life has been obscured by his accomplishments. The "children's hour" every evening at which the president mixed martinis for his guests, the poker games with cabinet cronies, the weekly sojourns on the presidential yacht *Potomac,* and his personal relations with family and friends warrant extended treatment. Roosevelt enjoyed life to the full, and his unquenchable optimism never faded.

Not to be overlooked are the four women who played crucial roles in FDR's life: his mother, Sara; Lucy Mercer, the woman he loved; Missy LeHand, the woman who loved him; and his wife, Eleanor. After Eleanor discovered FDR's affair with Lucy in 1918, their relationship became more professional than personal—an armed truce, in the words of their son James. They remained together for a variety of reasons, and Eleanor became a national personality in her own right. But her impact on the president's life was tangential. She and FDR moved in different circles, each with a separate entourage, and only at formal levels did their paths converge. I say this as an unabashed admirer of Mrs. Roosevelt. She has been deservedly canonized because of what she stood for, yet we overlook the fact that she was a political liability for the president in the 1930s and '40s. FDR did not need reinforcement among liberal and minority voters, where Eleanor was most highly regarded; he needed the votes of the white South, the Middle West, and the Great Plains, where for many she was anathema. Eleanor Roosevelt is a truly great American, not least because she was her own person. But she did not flourish until after the president's death.

The most important figure in Roosevelt's life was his mother, Sara. As an only child, Franklin grew to maturity in the warmth and security of single-minded maternal devotion. Sara shaped him, supported him, and transmitted to him the unshakable confidence that characterized his presidential leadership. Seven of Sara's ancestors landed with the *Mayflower*. Unlike the cautious Hudson River Roosevelts, the Delanos were swashbuckling sea captains, global traders, and risk takers. Her father, Warren Delano, made a fortune in China in the 1840s exporting tea, then a much larger one in the 1860s in the opium trade. Sara lived two years in China, was educated in France and Germany, and as a young woman was courted assiduously by New York's most eligible bachelors, including the irrepressible Stanford White. As a friend remarked, "she had a gift for saying the right thing at the right time, and she could say it in several languages." Sara gloried in her Delano heritage and molded FDR in that tradition. "My son Franklin is a Delano," she often said. "He is not a Roosevelt at all."

Sara held the purse strings. She supported Franklin generously, bestowed on him and Eleanor an elegant New York town house (which she staffed and furnished), remodeled and enlarged the Hyde Park residence to accommodate her son's political ambitions, and, when Franklin thought of leaving Eleanor for Lucy in 1918, intervened decisively to keep the couple together. Sara's wealth freed Franklin from earning a living and allowed him the luxury of pursuing a political career unencumbered by financial worry. "Nothing," said Eleanor, "ever seemed to disturb the deep, underlying affection they had for each other."*

Like Sara, Lucy Mercer has not been given her due. "Every man who ever knew her fell in love with her," wrote Jonathan Daniels, a keen observer of the Washington scene. Lucy was everything Eleanor was not. Beautiful, warm, affectionate, she gave Franklin the attention he craved. Her voice had "the qual-

---

* A close parallel to Sara's role vis-à-vis Franklin is that of her contemporary Mrs. Arthur MacArthur and her son Douglas. Military scholars are well aware that when Douglas was a cadet at West Point, Mrs. MacArthur took an apartment nearby to be with him. Less well known is that for two years during FDR's time at Harvard, Sara took an apartment in Boston to be near him.

ity of dark velvet" and her impeccable manners made her a most agreeable listener. Lucy's mother was once described by the *Washington Mirror* as "easily the most beautiful woman in Washington society," and her father, a founder of the Chevy Chase Country Club, was descended from Charles Carroll of Carrollton, a signer of the Declaration of Independence. The family had fallen on hard times, and Lucy was working as Eleanor's social secretary when Franklin met her in 1914. Their relationship blossomed slowly. By the summer of 1917, with Eleanor at Campobello, the two had become an item of Washington gossip. Alice Roosevelt Longworth, the tart-tongued daughter of TR (and Eleanor's cousin), encouraged the romance and sometimes invited the pair for dinner. "Franklin deserved a good time," she was quoted as saying. "He was married to Eleanor."

The affair broke off in 1918, but Lucy and Franklin remained close throughout the president's life. She surreptitiously attended each of his inaugurals in a closed White House limousine provided by the Secret Service, met with FDR often in the 1940s, and was with him when he died at Warm Springs.

Missy (Marguerite) LeHand, a quietly competent, attractive young woman of twenty-three, joined FDR's team during his vice presidential campaign in 1920 and remained at his side until she suffered a debilitating stroke in June 1941. She was not only Roosevelt's personal secretary ("F.D." as she and only she addressed him) but his constant companion and attendant—a surrogate for both Eleanor and Lucy. When Roosevelt cruised off the Florida coast for months at a time in the 1920s in an attempt to regain his health, it was Missy who accompanied him. It was Missy, not Eleanor, who went with him to Warm Springs; it was Missy who presided over his office; and it was Missy who served as hostess when FDR entertained. Neither Eleanor nor Sara objected to the arrangement, and Roosevelt's friends took it in stride. Missy was deeply in love with FDR, and the president, if not in love, certainly preferred her company to all others'. She died without knowing that the president had made her the beneficiary of one half of his estate in gratitude for her commitment.*

---

* FDR's will, dated November 12, 1941, provided that his papers, personal property (paintings, china, furniture, silver), and the house at Hyde Park be given to the United States government. The balance of his estate (investments, land, inheritance from Sara) was to be placed in trust, one half of the income to be paid to Eleanor, the other half to Missy, with the children and grandchildren enjoying remainder interests. Missy died in July 1944 and

Sixty years after his death, it is high time Roosevelt be revisited. The Great Depression, the New Deal, the Second World War are fading memories. The extent to which the United States was threatened is scarcely remembered. The national sacrifice is forgotten. All the more reason to recall that cheerful man who could not walk, who could not stand unassisted, yet who remained serenely confident as he calmly guided the nation into a prosperous, peaceful future.

JEAN EDWARD SMITH
Huntington, West Virginia

---

did not benefit from the president's bequest, but the will was never amended. When it was probated and made public in June 1945, the press reported the financial details minutely but chose not to mention the provision pertaining to Missy. Last Will and Testament of Franklin D. Roosevelt, Franklin D. Roosevelt Library, Hyde Park; *The New York Times*, June 7, 1945; *United States News*, October 4, 1946.

Contents

FDR

ONE

HERITAGE

Some thought the Roosevelts were entitled
to coats of arms. Others thought they were
two steps ahead of the bailiffs from an
island in the Zuider Zee.

—ALICE ROOSEVELT LONGWORTH

THE ROOSEVELTS WERE an old but relatively inconspicuous New York family. Their wealth derived from Manhattan real estate, the West Indian sugar trade, and thrifty investment. The men in the family married well: indeed, much of the Roosevelt inheritance descended on the maternal side. Yet for six generations the family had produced no one of significant stature. Suddenly, in the seventh generation, this "dynasty of the mediocre" (in the words of the *New York Herald Tribune*) erupted with not one but two of the most remarkable men in American history.[1]

The common ancestor of Franklin and Theodore Roosevelt—"our *very* common ancestor," as TR phrased it—was Claes van Rosenvelt, an obscure Dutchman who landed in New Amsterdam in the 1650s.[2] His only son, Nicholas, was a prosperous miller. He in turn fathered two sons: Johannes, the progenitor of the Long Island branch of the family that produced Theodore; and Jacobus, founder of the Hudson River strain from which Franklin descended. Johannes's heirs were merchants and traders. The descendants of Jacobus—James in English—remained closer to the soil, farming initially in upper Manhattan, then living the life of gentleman farmers along the Hudson.

James's son Isaac (Franklin's great-great-grandfather), a sugar refiner, was briefly active in the Revolutionary cause, helped draft New York's first constitution, and proved a solid but silent member of the Federalist phalanx led by Alexander Hamilton at the state convention that ratified the United States

Constitution. With Hamilton he founded the Bank of New York and served as its president from 1786 to 1791.

The Roosevelts avoided flamboyance, moved cautiously, and did not become involved in public affairs unless they had to. As charter members of the city's original elite they enjoyed inherited social status, a self-contained lifestyle, and a profound sense of entitlement. Isaac's son James (1760–1847) went to Princeton, followed his father into the sugar-refining business, dabbled at banking, bred horses, and in 1819 purchased a substantial tract of land fronting the Hudson north of Poughkeepsie. There he built a large house, which he called Mount Hope, and assumed the life of a country squire. His son, another Isaac (1790–1863), also went to Princeton, trained as a physician at Columbia, but declined to practice medicine. The sight of blood was unbearable to him, and he could not tolerate the sound of suffering.[3] Instead, Isaac turned inward. He lived with his parents at Mount Hope, where he devoted himself to raising exotic plants and breeding horses. A charitable relative described him as having "a delicate constitution and refined tastes." The fact is, Dr. Isaac was a recluse, a hypochondriac paralyzed with fear of the everyday world.[4]

To the family's surprise, Dr. Isaac, at the age of thirty-seven, announced his intention to marry Mary Rebecca Aspinwall, the sprightly eighteen-year-old daughter of their neighbors, the John Aspinwalls. For three generations, the Hudson River Roosevelts had been a family of declining enterprise, content to husband the money they inherited. That was not the case with the Aspinwalls, a hearty, acquisitive, seafaring family from New England. Together with their partners, the Howlands, the Aspinwalls dominated the shipping industry in New York. Their clipper ships, including the record-breaking *Rainbow,* were familiar in the ports of every continent, and the firm easily adjusted to the advent of steam. The discovery of gold in California in 1848 proved an even greater bonanza for the company, which held a monopoly carrying passengers and freight between the East and West coasts via its steamship lines and the Panama Railroad—which it had pioneered.

Rebecca Aspinwall brought Yankee vigor to the sluggish Roosevelt gene pool. "Thus the stock kept virile and abreast of the times," FDR wrote in a Harvard essay on the family.[5] The infusion was overdue. Dr. Isaac had no house of his own, and it was to his parents' home at Mount Hope that he took his bride in 1827. The following year a son was born, christened James in the Roosevelt

tradition of alternating "James" and "Isaac" for the firstborn son from generation to generation. James, the president's father, was the third of that name in
the line. Not until four years after James's birth did Dr. Isaac establish a home
of his own. At Rebecca's insistence, and with a generous dollop of Aspinwall
money, he purchased a large plot of land immediately across the Albany Post
Road from Mount Hope and constructed a rambling gabled house with deep
verandas. He named it Rosedale and planted shrubbery so thickly that the
house was forever shrouded in shade. As one chronicler of the family has written, "it was a quiet place, quietly furnished, quietly lived in," and it was here
that James grew up, an only child for the first twelve years of his life.[6]

Franklin's father was not only a Roosevelt but an Aspinwall. After graduat-
ing from Union College in 1847 and before matriculating at Harvard Law
School, he asked his parents' permission to undertake a European grand tour.
Dr. Isaac objected. Wandering through Europe would be dangerous, he told
James. Sickness and disease lurked everywhere, and there were unmistakable
signs of political unrest. But Rebecca supported the idea, and eventually Dr.
Isaac yielded. From November 1847 until May 1849, Franklin's father traveled
through western Europe and the Holy Land. Family legend has it that while in
Italy he briefly joined the redshirted legion of Giuseppe Garibaldi, fighting for
Italian unification. FDR was fond of reciting the tale:

> He became close friends with a mendicant priest—spoke only Latin with
> him—and the two of them proceeded on a walking tour in Italy. They
> came to Naples and found the city besieged by Garibaldi's army. They
> both enlisted in this army, wore a red shirt for a month or so, and tiring
> of it, as there seemed to be little action, went to Garibaldi's tent and
> asked if they could receive their discharge. Garibaldi thanked the old
> priest and my father and the walking tour was resumed by them.[7]

Upon his return from Europe, James entered Harvard Law School, graduated in 1851, was admitted to the New York bar, and for two years clerked with
the prosperous Wall Street firm of Benjamin Douglas Silliman.[8] In the meantime Grandfather James died, leaving the bulk of his estate, including Mount
Hope and a fashionable New York brownstone, to his young namesake.
Wealthy now in his own right, James chose not to practice law but devote himself to managing his investments and living the life of a Hudson River grandee.

On April 23, 1853, at the age of twenty-five, he married Rebecca Brien How-land, a daughter of his mother's first cousin and an heiress to another shipping fortune. They set up house at Mount Hope and later in the year sailed for England, establishing a pattern they would follow for the remainder of their lives. Slightly less than two years later a son was born, James Roosevelt Roosevelt, inevitably known as "Rosy," the president's half brother.

James Roosevelt was a cautious investor who deployed his inheritance skillfully. But the Aspinwall spirit of adventure was not completely extinguished. He bet heavily on what West Virginians call the dark industries—coal and railroads—and for a few years his investments prospered. James became a director of the Consolidated Coal Company, the largest bituminous coal enterprise in the country, and the Delaware and Hudson Railroad and briefly served as president of the Southern Railway Security Company, a holding company that controlled most of the railroads south of the Potomac. But the Panic of 1873 intervened, the consortiums to which James belonged lost heavily, and he was soon shunted into the role of a passive investor.

Exactly what James did during the Civil War remains a mystery. He was only thirty-two when General Pierre G. T. Beauregard fired on Fort Sumter, yet he made no effort to join the struggle. FDR claimed his father served as a member of the Sanitary Commission, providing aid for wounded soldiers, yet documentary evidence is lacking.[9] Theodore Roosevelt, Sr., James's cousin and contemporary (and TR's father), did not serve either, and was embarrassed by it for the rest of his life. James never gave it a second thought.[10]

In the summer of 1865, while the Roosevelts were touring the Swiss Alps, Mount Hope burned to the ground. The cause remains unclear. Tenants blamed a faulty flue, yet there was a suspicion of arson. With the exception of an antique tea service and several Roosevelt heirlooms, all the family papers and possessions were destroyed. James and Rebecca were devastated but could do nothing. Rather than return immediately, they chose to remain in Europe for another year, wintering in the Saxon capital of Dresden. The richness of the city's art treasures, its musical tradition, and its cosmopolitan sophistication attracted a large colony of foreign residents. In 1865, more than two hundred English and American families called Dresden their home.

Around the corner from the Roosevelts lived General and Mrs. George B. McClellan, the young Napoleon who had met his political Waterloo the year before, running as the Democratic candidate against Abraham Lincoln. The general had gone into what he called winter quarters in Dresden and would remain abroad for the next three years. At thirty-nine, McClellan was just two years older than James, and the two hit it off from the start. A common interest in railroading broke the ice. As superintendent of the Illinois Central, McClellan had been the highest-paid railroad executive in the United States when the Civil War began.[11] And they were both Democrats. Originally, the Roosevelts had been Federalists, then Whigs. When the Whig party fell apart over the issue of slavery, TR's branch of the family, staunchly abolitionist, went Republican. The Hudson River clan preferred the moderation of James Buchanan and became Democrats.[12] James voted for Stephen A. Douglas in 1860 and backed McClellan in 1864. Party loyalty was something the Roosevelts took seriously, and James found special pleasure discussing politics with the party's most recent nominee. For the next eight months they managed to take a stroll or have a smoke almost every day. "I see a good deal of General McClellan, and like him very much," James wrote his brother, John, at Christmastime.[13]

The Roosevelts left Dresden May 17, 1866, a year to the day after they had departed from New York. Five months later, after meandering from Karlsbad to St. Moritz to Paris, London, and Liverpool, they were home. James chose not to rebuild Mount Hope and sold the land to the State of New York as the site for the state mental institution. With the proceeds he hoped to buy the opulent estate of John Jacob Astor III at Rhinebeck, but when the price proved more than he could afford, James settled for a lesser property just over the boundary from Poughkeepsie in Hyde Park.

This was Brierstone, a 110-acre estate that belonged to railroad executive Josiah Wheeler. The property was partially wooded and sloped to the river bank. The house was not large as Hudson River manors went—there were only seventeen rooms—and it was in poor repair. But the view of the river was majestic. And there was a lovely rose garden surrounded by a tall hemlock hedge. Wheeler had never taken to farming, and the fields had been neglected. The fences were down, and the outbuildings required immediate attention.

James was in his element. Within less than a year the manor house, renamed Springwood, had been put in order. Indoor plumbing was installed, new carpets laid, draperies hung, and furniture purchased to replace that lost at Mount Hope. James placed great store on restoring the fields to productivity and eventually would expand the farm to almost a thousand acres. To maintain a monthly cash flow, he purchased a sizable herd of dairy cattle from the Channel Islands—Jersey, Guernsey, and Alderney—but his primary interest was trotting horses. By the 1870s Springwood had become one of the leading stables in the East. In 1873 James's magnificent gelding Gloster, foaled at Springwood, set a new trotting record for the mile at two minutes, seventeen and a quarter seconds. That autumn, former governor Leland Stanford of California, president of the Central Pacific Railroad and founder of Stanford University, bought Gloster from James for $15,000. The horse was shipped west, but before it could race again it was killed in a train wreck. (Gloster's tail, mounted on a wooden plaque, hung in FDR's White House bedroom.)[14] After the Panic of 1873 James withdrew from the trotting world, although he continued to maintain a stable of horses at Springwood and rode daily until shortly before his death.

Life at Springwood took on the affectations of an English country manor. A none-too-kind acquaintance observed that James patterned himself on the Whig leader Lord Lansdowne "but what he really looked like was Lord Lansdowne's coachman."[15] James prided himself that the estate broke even and undertook a modest role in community affairs—commodore of the local yacht club, vestryman at St. James' Episcopal Church, the Hyde Park school board, the board at the state mental hospital. In 1871 he was elected as a Democrat to a two-year term as one of the town supervisors. Three years later party officials asked him to run for the State Senate. "James went to a political meeting," Rebecca wrote in her diary on October 18, 1874. "I was dreadfully afraid he would be nominated . . . but he got home safely." In an autobiographical sketch written toward the end of his life, James said, "I have always refused to accept any nomination for Public Office, repeatedly refused nomination for Congress, State Senate and Assembly."[16]

The Roosevelts divided their time between Springwood, an elegant town house at 15 Washington Square in New York City, and long vacations abroad. When in the city, whether on business or for the social season, James frequented the Union League, the Metropolitan, the Century, and the University clubs. Travel was facilitated by a private railroad car, the *Monon,* which stood on a siding off the main Hudson River line, a few hundred yards from Springwood.* The outside world rarely intruded. As a reflective biographer has writ-

---

* TR's daughter Alice often joked that the difference between the Oyster Bay Roosevelts and

ten, James "seems to have enjoyed business much as he had enjoyed trotting. It was a challenge and worth working at, but it never ran his life."[17]

Sorrow came gradually. In 1875 Rebecca's health began to fail. The symptoms of heart disease were unmistakable. Doctors ordered her to stop climbing stairs. James installed elevators at Springwood and the house in New York, but the symptoms grew worse. In August 1876 James took Rebecca aboard his yacht for a cruise on Long Island Sound, hoping the sea air would ease her cough. Shortly after they got under way, she suffered a massive heart attack. James put in at New York harbor and carried her home to Washington Square. She died there on the twenty-first of August and was interred at Hyde Park.

Two years after his mother's death, Rosy was graduated with honors from Columbia. Following the path laid out by his father and grandfather, he became engaged to the debutante of the year, Helen Schermerhorn Astor, the daughter of Mrs. William Astor, the fabled arbiter of New York society.[18] Rosy was enormously attractive, exceedingly sociable, and utterly without ambition, save to live a life of privilege. Insofar as the Astors were concerned, he represented unassailable Knickerbocker lineage and the prestige that attached to the families of original settlers. Regardless of their lack of accomplishment, the Roosevelts were prominent members of New York's old guard, and a Dutch pedigree still counted for much among the city's social elite.

Rosy and Helen were married in the autumn of 1877. Helen brought with her a trust fund of $400,000 (roughly $7 million today) and a mansion on Fifth Avenue.[19] Rosy shelved plans to study law and like father and grandfather settled in to manage the matrimonial estate. He and Helen bought a smaller property adjacent to Springwood, where betwixt the social season in New York and annual pilgrimages to Europe, the couple enjoyed the leisure their wealth permitted.

James had been forty-eight when Rebecca died. After a suitable period of mourning he commenced a one-sided courtship of his favorite cousin, Anna "Bamie" Roosevelt, TR's older sister. Bamie was just twenty-two and by all odds the most talented of the Long Island tribe. Alice Roosevelt Longworth insisted that if Bamie had been born a man, she, not Theodore, would have become president. Bamie was fond of James, appreciated his company, but never

those from Hyde Park was that her family traveled in a borrowed railroad car while the Hyde Park clan owned one. Linda Donn, *The Roosevelt Cousins* 88 (New York: Knopf, 2001).

considered him a romantic interest. When he proposed marriage in early 1880, she was stunned. Not wishing to hurt him directly, she passed the proposal to her mother, Mittie, who, being an old friend of James, let him down gently.[20]

Perhaps because she felt sympathy for James, Mittie now played matchmaker. Two months after his proposal to Bamie had been rejected, she invited James to a small dinner party at the Roosevelt home on West Fifty-seventh Street. Bamie and her sister Corinne were there, along with an old family friend, Richard Crowninshield of Boston. So was a young woman whom Bamie introduced as one of her closest friends, Sara Delano. James was captivated. Sara was twenty-six, one of five spirited daughters of Warren Delano of Newburgh known to New York society as "the beautiful Delano sisters." Tall at five feet ten, slender, with a sophisticated manner and a regal carriage, Sara was the very image of the ideal American beauty popularized by Charles Dana Gibson. Her expressive eyes and chiseled features set her apart from those who were merely pretty. A strong chin suggested substance and determination. In a word, Sara had what the English called "presence."

James responded as Mittie had anticipated. "He talked to her the whole time," she told Bamie after the guests departed. "He never took his eyes off her."[21] Whether James had met Sara before is unclear. The Delanos were every bit as grand, much richer, and far more accomplished than the Roosevelts.[22] Like the Aspinwalls and Howlands, they were an adventurous seafaring family and traced their lineage to the *Mayflower*. The Pilgrim who chartered the ship, seven of its passengers, and three signers of the Mayflower Compact were Delano forebears.[23] Sara's paternal ancestor Philippe de la Noye was reputedly the first Huguenot to land on American soil, arriving in Plymouth in 1621.[24]

Sara's grandfather, the first Warren Delano, went to sea at nineteen, became a merchant captain in his early twenties, pioneered clipper ship trade with the Orient, and retired to the whaling industry in New Bedford. Her father, Warren II, born in 1809, apprenticed himself to importing firms in Boston and New York, and at the age of twenty-four sailed for China as supercargo aboard the clipper *Commerce*. At Canton he secured a junior position in the tea-exporting firm of Russell, Sturgis and Company, later Russell and Company, the largest American firm in the China trade. At thirty-one he was a senior partner, heading the firm's operations in Macao, Canton, and Hong Kong. Two years later, having been in China nine years and amassing a considerable fortune, he returned to the United States on home leave, where he met, courted, and married Catherine Robbins Lyman, the eighteen-year-old daughter of Judge and Mrs. Joseph Lyman of Northampton, Massachusetts.

The bride and groom sailed for China on December 4, 1843, and remained there another three years. Warren continued to run Russell and Company, increasing its profits with each successive season. At the end of 1846 he resigned his post and returned to America to stay. His twelve years in China had netted a fortune of more than a million dollars. With that, he entered an exclusive circle of not more than a dozen Americans.[25]

In New York, Warren threw himself into business with the same force and vigor that had paved the way for success in the Orient. He invested heavily in New York waterfront property, railroads, Tennessee copper mines, and coal in Pennsylvania, where a mining town near Wilkes-Barre was named Delano in his honor. He owned clipper ships and paddle steamers, including the first boat on the Sacramento River servicing the California goldfields. By the early 1850s he was well on his way to earning another million.

Befitting their wealth, Warren and Catherine lived at Colonnade Row on Lafayette Place, nine unusual Greek Revival houses linked by a common portico.[26] Washington Irving lived in one, as did John Jacob Astor, the founding father, widely regarded as the richest man in America. So did Warren's younger brother Franklin, who had recently married Mr. Astor's granddaughter Laura. Franklin Delano, "Uncle Frank" as Sara called him, and for whom FDR was named, was also in the shipping business but had recently retired to manage his wife's immense trust fund.

Warren and Catherine summered annually at Danskammer Point, six miles above Newburgh on the west bank of the Hudson. In 1851, after much looking, they purchased a sixty-acre estate four miles downstream. The brick and stucco house was modest, but had a commanding view of the river and the Hudson Highlands. Warren named it Algonac and immediately set to convert it into a rural sanctuary for his growing family. Already there had been five children, and eventually there would be eleven, of whom Sara, born September 21, 1854, would be the seventh.[27]

To redesign Algonac, Warren engaged Andrew Jackson Downing, the premier landscape architect in America, who was then laying out the grounds of the White House, the Capitol, and the Smithsonian Institution in Washington. Downing converted the house at Newburgh into an Italianate villa of forty rooms and added a large square tower and deep verandas, as well as a compatible gatehouse, several barns, greenhouses, and stables. Plantings were designed to provide bloom or greenery year-round, and at Warren's direction a broad lawn was constructed, sloping down to the river. The house was furnished with equal attention to detail, emphasizing Warren's years in China. To tend the estate required a permanent staff of ten, with temporary help hired as needed.[28]

The Delanos prospered at Algonac, and Warren's business affairs flourished.* That is, until the summer of 1857, when without warning the giant Ohio Life Insurance and Trust Company, the second largest bank east of the Mississippi, abruptly closed its doors. Panic struck the nation's financial community. Years of wild speculation in railroads, coal mines, and real estate had vastly inflated stock prices. The market dropped 50 percent overnight. Banks suspended specie payment, thousands of businesses closed, commodity prices plummeted. Federal troops were called out to protect government buildings. In San Francisco, the fledgling banker William Tecumseh Sherman went under. In Missouri, Ulysses S. Grant was driven off his farm. Across America prosperity turned sour. Tens of thousands of people lost everything they had.

Warren Delano was caught in the downdraft. He was always an aggressive investor, and the collapse in stock prices found him dangerously overextended. For two years he fought to remain solvent as one after another of his investments failed. He cut back spending, sold the townhouse on Colonnade Row, and even tried to sell Algonac. All to no avail. In January 1860, at the age of fifty, Warren Delano faced bankruptcy.

"Warren has various projects, mostly impractical," wrote his brother Ned. "One is to go to China to do business five years and return with a fortune."[29] Which is precisely what he did. Leaving his family at Algonac, Warren sailed for Hong Kong, where he organized another trading empire. This time it was not tea but opium—open, notorious, and far more profitable—a business not strictly legal, but nevertheless one conducted with the acquiescence and cooperation of Chinese authorities.[30] Warren supplied medicinal opium to the War Department to alleviate the suffering of Union wounded, but that was scarcely his only market. "I do not pretend to justify the prosecution of the opium trade in a moral or philanthropic point of view," he wrote his brothers from

---

* Throughout his life, FDR used "Algonac" as a code word to mean that everything was all right, "superfine, splendid et pas cher." See FDR to SDR, June 7, 1905, 2 *The Roosevelt Letters* 21, Elliott Roosevelt, ed. (London: George G. Harrap, 1950).

China. "But as a merchant I insist that it has been a fair, honorable and legitimate trade; and to say the worst of it, liable to no further or weightier objections than is the importation of wines, Brandies, and spirits into the UStates, England & c."[31]

By 1862 Warren's fortunes had improved to such an extent that he brought his family to join him. "I suppose it was altogether terrifying to my mother to give up her beautiful home and its peaceful security," Sara observed, but if so, her mother said nothing about it.[32] Warren leased Algonac to Abbot Low, the patriarch of another great mercantile family, and from Low chartered the *Surprise,* one of the sleekest, fastest clippers on the China run, to transport his family. For seven-year-old Sara it was the journey of a lifetime: four months at sea on a 183-foot square rigger with only her family and the crew. It was more like a yacht than a ship, Sara recalled. Seventy-five years later, she would entertain her great-grandchildren at Springwood by singing sea chanteys she learned from the sailors.[33]

Down the river hauled a Yankee clipper,
And it's blow, my bully boys, blow!
She's a Yankee mate and a Yankee skipper,
And it's blow, my bully boys, blow!

For FDR, his mother's trip to China was another family legend he could not resist embellishing. Two days out of New York, *Surprise* sighted a steamer to leeward that the captain feared might be a Confederate privateer. It proved to be a British mail packet bound for Bermuda. For the president, it was the dreaded *Alabama.* "I have a copy of the log of the clipper ship my Mother and her Mother went to China on," he wrote to Felix Frankfurter in April 1942. "They passed the Confederate commerce destroyer *Alabama* in the night but were not seen."[34] The fact is, the *Alabama* was lying unfinished in a shipyard near Liverpool when *Surprise* set sail from New York and did not put to sea until July 1862, by which time the *Surprise* had rounded the Cape of Good Hope and was in the Indian Ocean. The president often told the story of his mother's narrow escape from the *Alabama,* and none of his friends corrected him. It was part of FDR's charm: a good story was sometimes preferable to an accurate one. The president kept a wooden model of the *Surprise* on the table behind his desk, and two paintings of the ship hung on the wall of his study.

In 1864 Sara and three older children were sent home to resume their schooling. Two years later they rejoined the family in Paris. Warren Delano had succeeded far beyond his expectations in China and toyed with the idea of residing permanently in Europe, perhaps on an estate in the Pyrenees. "I should want it to be isolated from our countrymen or others who would speak English habitually, and I should want to organize my household as to combine the real comforts and proper luxuries of life with a system of order and regularity of studies, duties, exercise and recreation."[35] Finding nothing to suit him, Warren settled for an opulent Right Bank apartment in Paris overlooking the Avenue de l'Impératrice (now the Avenue Foch). It was the time of the great Paris Exposition and construction of the Eiffel Tower. Sara recalled seeing the crowned heads of Europe as they passed her balcony. Even more impressive was the sight of Count Otto von Bismarck, the German chancellor, walking alone and unattended from exhibit to exhibit.[36]

From Paris the Delanos moved to Dresden and took a commodious apartment on the Christianstrasse, near where the Roosevelts wintered the year before. Sara attended a local school, where she studied German and music, and formed a lasting appreciation for the masterpieces at the Dresdner Gemäldegalerie. In the summer of 1868 most of the family went home to Algonac while the older children remained in Germany to complete their studies. Sara attended finishing school in Celle, a medieval city north of Hannover, where she lived with the mayor's family. Summers were spent on the island of Rügen in the Baltic and the Harz Mountains. In June 1870, as hostilities threatened, the children returned to Algonac aboard the *Westphalia*, the last passenger vessel to leave a German port before the Franco-Prussian War. Sara had been away from home for almost eight years, and abroad for six.

Under Warren's tutelage, life at Algonac was a disciplined round of reading, letter writing, and entertaining, interlaced with the New York social season, archery, boating, and riding. From the age of eighteen, Sara was a regular at the balls, cotillions, and dinners of the city's most fashionable families. Rita Halle Kleeman, Sara's friend and biographer, reports that she was an avid dancer and could waltz an evening away to the Vienna melodies of Johann Strauss or experiment with popular new steps such as the Galop and the Boston.

If Sara fell in love, it was with the young Stanford White, whose aunt lived nearby. "Stanny" was a frequent visitor at Algonac and apparently fascinated Sara. In 1876 he commenced to court her seriously, and Sara responded. White was one year older, but at twenty-three his prospects looked dismal. Boastful, boisterous, and irreverent, he had been working for five years as one of several underpaid draftsmen for the great Boston architect Henry Hobson Richardson. Yet, as White's biographer noted, beneath the offputting exterior lay a gargantuan capacity for work and a contagious obsession with beauty.[37] Aside from Sara, few recognized it. Warren Delano despised White, called him "the red-headed trial," and found nothing that would recommend him as a son-in-law. When Sara persisted, Warren urged her to go abroad and reconsider. Ever dutiful, Sara agreed to visit her sister Dora in Hong Kong, where Dora's husband was now the senior representative of Russell and Company. Sara was away nine months. When she returned to Algonac in September 1877, she had come around. White called once more, but whether he was received by Mr. Delano or saw Sara is unclear. The romance was over. But as one member of the Delano family later recorded, "Sara loved only one man in her life, and that man was Stanford White."*

It was three years after Stanford White that Sara met James. For James it was love at first sight, and he set out on a resolute courtship. Sara's motives are less clear. James was fifty-two, she was twenty-six—the same age as James's son, Rosy. She was also two inches taller. Her father had objected to Stanford White, but James satisfied basic Delano requirements: sufficient wealth so as not to be suspected of fortune hunting, demonstrated maturity, and impeccable lineage. He was also kind, considerate, handsome in an elderly way, and, unlike White, very much a gentleman. That settled it for Sara. The age difference would take care of itself. So too the height. Above all, at twenty-six—old by Victorian standards—she might never have another opportunity. It required someone as bold as Stanford White, or as secure as James, not to be intimidated by Sara. Writing to her son on the eve of his first run for the

---

* Seven years later White married Bessie Springs Smith of Smithtown, Long Island. By then McKim, Mead and White had become the leading architectural firm in America, setting the pace in both public and private building, and driven by the manic energy of Stanford White. Warren Delano's forebodings to the contrary, White became exceedingly wealthy. But on one point Warren may have been correct: White was probably unsuitable as a husband. His philandering was notorious, and in 1906 he was shot and killed by a jealous husband, Harry Thaw, while watching the floor show at the rooftop restaurant at Madison Square Garden—which White had designed. Paul R. Baker, *Stanny: The Gilded Life of Stanford White* 33–34, 372–373 (New York: Free Press, 1989).

presidency, she acknowledged as much. If not for James, Sara wrote, "I should now be the 'old Miss Delano' after a rather sad life."[38]

Having made her decision (Warren reluctantly approved), Sara was steadfast in her devotion. The couple were married in an understated ceremony at Algonac on October 7, 1880. After vows were exchanged and a brief reception, the bride and groom departed in the Delano carriage for Hyde Park. At Milton, roughly halfway, the Roosevelt coach awaited. The wedding couple took their seats, and James grasped the reins and drove the remaining distance to Springwood.

The Roosevelts spent the next month together at Hyde Park before embarking on an extended honeymoon in Europe. Twice when James went to New York on business, Sara returned to Algonac, and twice the Delanos visited Springwood. Throughout their married life, James and Sara always journeyed to Algonac for family celebrations: Christmas, Thanksgiving, birthdays, and anniversaries. In that respect, the Delano tie prevailed.

On November 7, 1880, the Roosevelts sailed for Europe aboard the White Star liner *Germanic*, the newest ship on the Atlantic run. They spent the next ten months abroad, visiting friends and relatives, enjoying the leisure of first-class travel as they slowly toured Italy, France, Germany, Switzerland, the Low Countries, and the British Isles. On Sunday morning, August 21, 1881, the Roosevelts attended services at Saint Peter's Cathedral in York. Sara reported in her diary that she nearly fainted, "giving James a little fright." She was already four months pregnant, and it was time to return to Springwood. On September 1 they boarded the *Germanic* again, and ten days later they were back in the United States. It had been a perfect honeymoon. "James was wonderful in the way he did it all and we have had such happy days," wrote Sara. "He has been untiring and thoughtful of everything."[39]

TWO

MY SON FRANKLIN

I have always been a great believer in heredity.
—SARA DELANO ROOSEVELT

FRANKLIN DELANO ROOSEVELT was born late in the evening of January 30, 1882. Sara was in labor twenty-six hours and narrowly survived an overdose of chloroform administered by a solicitous country doctor. That night, in the diary Sara kept, James wrote, "At quarter to nine my Sallie had a splendid large baby boy. He weighs 10 lbs., without clothes."[1] For the next two months the baby went unnamed as James and Sara delicately struggled for control. Roosevelt tradition dictated the boy be named Isaac. By naming Rosy after himself twenty-eight years earlier, James had disrupted that tradition. He now wished to restore it by naming the baby in honor of his father. Sara, who was expected to defer to her husband's wishes, declined to do so in naming her son. She detested the name Isaac. Before the child was born she had decided that if it were a boy, he would be named for her father: Warren Delano Roosevelt. The to-ing and fro-ing continued through February. Eventually James gave way. His commitment to Roosevelt tradition was no match for Sara's determination.[2]

Sara's father was delighted. The baby, he wrote, was "a beautiful little fellow—well and strong and well-behaved—with a good-shaped head of the Delano type."[3] But there was a problem. A brother of Sara's had recently lost a young son who had been named Warren Delano IV. Out of sympathy, Sara agreed it would be untimely to name her baby Warren as well. "We are disappointed, and so is Papa," she wrote, "but of course there is nothing to say."[4] As an alternative, Sara proposed to name the baby for her favorite uncle, Franklin Delano, who had married Laura Astor and lived a few miles north at a baronial estate known as Steen Valetje in Barrytown. Her father worried that some might think the name was selected "with an idea of possible advantage" since Uncle Frank and Aunt Laura were childless, but Sara brushed the objection aside.[5]

Franklin Delano Roosevelt was christened on March 20, 1882, at a small family ceremony in the chapel of Hyde Park's St. James' Episcopal Church. Nelly Blodgett, one of Sara's closest friends since childhood, was godmother. There were two godfathers: Will Forbes, Sara's brother-in-law (Dora's husband), and Elliott Roosevelt, the younger brother of Sara's friend Bamie and TR, and soon to be the father of Eleanor. Had he lived, Elliott, in addition to being Franklin's godfather, would also have become his father-in-law.

The world appeared remarkably peaceful when FDR was christened. The "Concert of Europe," in place since the Napoleonic wars, provided unprecedented international stability. Christianity, capitalism, and colonialism cemented the cohesion of the Great Powers. German unity had been achieved by Bismarck without rending the fabric of consensus, and few shed a tear for the demise of the papacy's temporal authority in Italy. In Britain, Queen Victoria ruled majestically in the fifth decade of her seemingly endless reign. Emperor Franz Josef was well into his fourth decade on the Hapsburg throne; Republican France appeared to have found its footing; and north of the U.S. border a newly autonomous Dominion of Canada greeted the United States as a full-fledged North American partner.

Beneath the veneer of calm, passions stirred uneasily—a dangerous portent of what lay ahead. In 1881 President James Garfield and Czar Alexander II of Russia were both victims of political violence: Garfield slain at the hand of a madman in Washington; Alexander killed by a terrorist bomb on the streets of Saint Petersburg. The rapid pace of industrialization, the dislocation of families from rural to urban settings, massive immigration, unspeakable working conditions, labor unrest, and pestilential slums darkened the horizon.

This was a time of enormous growth in the United States. The population, which stood at 35 million at the close of the Civil War, had jumped to 53 million—a 51 percent increase in little more than fifteen years. The American birthrate, 39.8 per thousand in 1882, was almost twice that of Great Britain and three times that of France. Immigration had soared to 800,000 people annually. In the year of FDR's birth, more than a quarter of a million potential new citizens arrived from Germany and an almost equal number from Scandinavia and the British Isles.[6]

America's gross domestic product (GDP) had doubled since 1865 and was now the largest in the world: one third larger than Britain's, twice that of France, and three times as great as Germany.[7] The production of steel, less than twenty thousand tons in 1867, totaled almost 2 million tons in 1882. Coal production had tripled. On the negative side, more than five hundred miners lost their lives in deep-pit accidents each year.[8]

Within a decade of FDR's birth, the electric light, the telephone, and the automobile were invented. The continent would be spanned by not one but six transcontinental railroads. This was the age of Social Darwinism and robber barons: Jay Gould, Collis P. Huntington, and William Vanderbilt in transportation; the steel trust of Andrew Carnegie; John D. Rockefeller and Standard Oil; and the mother of all trusts, the great sugar trust of Henry Havemeyer. Chester Arthur was in the White House, the Republicans controlled the House, the Democrats the Senate, and civil service reform, a belated reaction to the assassination of President Garfield, was just around the corner.

Few of the worries of American life intruded at Springwood. FDR grew up in a privileged, carefree environment of comfort and security. "In thinking back to my earliest days," he said many years later, "I am impressed by the peacefulness and regularity of things both in respect to places and people. Up to the age of seven, Hyde Park was the center of the world."[9]

Families as wealthy as the Roosevelts usually entrusted newborn babies to the care of experienced nurses and old family retainers. Not Sara. As soon as she recovered from childbirth, she insisted on doing everything herself: "Every mother ought to learn to care for her own baby, whether she can afford to delegate the task to someone or not." And although a wet nurse was available, Sara nursed Franklin for almost a year.[10]

Mittie Roosevelt, who had introduced James to Sara two years before, spent a week at Hyde Park in June 1882. To her son Elliott she wrote, "I held your dear little godson and enjoyed him intensely. He is such a fair, sweet, cunning little *bright* five-months-old darling baby. . . . Sallie [is] devoted and looks so very lovely with him, like a Murillo Madonna and infant."[11]

Sara was determined to raise Franklin as a Delano—which meant to raise him as she had been raised under the benign discipline of her father. When the Roosevelts made their first pilgrimage to the Delano ancestral home in Fairhaven, Massachusetts, FDR was placed in the same hooded cradle in which his grandfather had slept seventy-three years earlier. Warren Delano eventually had seventeen grandchildren, yet none of the others was ever permitted such indulgence.[12]

Because of Franklin's difficult birth, Sara was advised to avoid a second and possibly fatal pregnancy. The Roosevelts, like many couples in the nineteenth century faced with a similar problem, adopted abstinence as a remedy, and from time to time that led to marital tension.[13] Sara, still young and energetic, found solace arranging and organizing the life of her little son. No moment of Franklin's day was unscheduled or unsupervised. Awake at seven. Breakfast at eight. Lessons until eleven. Lunch at noon. More lessons until four. Two hours of play followed by supper at six and bed by eight. It was the formula her father had imposed on the large Delano brood, and Sara instinctively adopted it. It was a loving regimen but a regimen nonetheless. A less tractable child might have rebelled, but Franklin never did.[14]

Initially, FDR was schooled at home by Sara. At six he attended an impromptu kindergarten on a neighboring estate. Then began a series of governesses and tutors at home. FDR was drilled in Latin, French, German, penmanship, arithmetic, and history. Sara organized the study plan, and a tutor either deferred to her wishes or departed. One of the most gifted tutors was a young Swiss woman named Jeanne Rosat-Sandoz, who, in addition to drilling Franklin in modern languages, attempted to instill a sense of social responsibility. Mlle. Sandoz believed in economic reform and the Social Gospel; she did her utmost to arouse in FDR a concern for those less fortunate. Years later Roosevelt wrote her from the White House, "I have often thought that it was you, more than anyone else, who laid the foundation for my education."[15]

Learning at home deprived FDR of the rough-and-tumble of public school, but it saved him from inept or mediocre teaching. His mind was continually challenged. While public school children his age were learning their ABCs in English, he was mastering them simultaneously in French and German. At the age of six his German was such that he could write his mother *auf Deutsch*:

[TRANSLATION]

Dear Mama!

  I will show you, that I can already write in German. But I shall try always to improve it, so that you will be really pleased. Now I want to ask you to write me in German script and language.

                                        Your loving son
                                        Franklin D.R.[16]

Sara was determined to keep her son from being spoiled by too much attention yet at the same time wanted to show her affection. "We never subjected the boy to a lot of don'ts," she wrote. "While certain rules established for his well being had to be rigidly observed, we were never strict merely for the sake of being strict. In fact, we took a secret pride in the fact that Franklin instinctively never seemed to require that kind of handling."[17]

James, already in his mid-fifties when FDR was born, was content to leave the disciplining to his wife. Little Franklin was his partner, his inseparable companion with whom he rode, hunted, and sailed. Looking back at her own childhood, Sara noted that "Franklin never knew what it meant to have the kind of respect for his father that is composed of equal parts of awe and fear. The regard in which he held him, amounting to worship, grew out of a companionship that was based on his ability to see things eye to eye, and his father's never-failing understanding of the little problems that seem so grave to a child."[18]

Like many an only child, FDR spent most of his time in the company of adults, and it was assumed he would act like an adult. Sara believed that children "had pretty much the same thoughts as adults" but lacked the vocabulary to express them. To remedy that she read aloud to Franklin daily. *Robinson Crusoe*, *The Swiss Family Robinson*, and *Little Lord Fauntleroy* were favorites. The downside of being captivated by *Little Lord Fauntleroy* was that Sara kept Franklin in dresses and long curls until he was five. Then he graduated to kilts and full Scottish regalia. Not until he was nearly eight did he wear pants in the form of miniature sailor suits Sara purchased in London. Staying at Algonac one weekend, he proudly wrote his father, "Mama left this morning, and I am to have my bath alone." He was then almost nine and evidently had never taken a bath by himself before.[19]

Another consequence of living on a rural estate under the close supervision of his parents was that FDR had few playmates. Occasionally small visitors were invited for the day, but none was permitted to stay overnight. The young, well-bred Whitney sisters were invited several times. Many years later, when both sisters had grown old, their parents died within weeks of each other, subjecting them to a double inheritance tax. The sisters had long since lost touch with their former playmate, but Isabel, the older, a stouthearted Republican, swallowed her pride and wrote to FDR in the White House, asking for an appointment. The president, who relished meeting old acquaintances, agreed to see her and listened patiently to her grievance. Roosevelt said he was terribly sorry, but it was a New York law and even the president could not change it. Isabel rose angrily and shook her cane. "You were always a nasty little boy, and now you are a nasty old man."[20]

The birth of a son did not deflect the Roosevelts from their annual journey to Europe. On Easter morning 1885 the family, including three-year-old Franklin, were returning from England on their favorite White Star liner, the *Germanic.* Suddenly a violent storm arose, plunging the ship into total darkness. As wave after wave broke over the bow, the vessel began to founder. In their cabin on the main deck, the Roosevelts feared the worst.

"We seem to be going down," said Sara.

"It does look like it," James replied.

When the water in their cabin became ankle-deep, they prepared to abandon ship. "I never get frightened and I was not then," Sara remembered. She took her fur coat from its hook and wrapped it around Franklin. "Poor little boy," she told James. "If he must go down, he is going down warm." Miraculously, *Germanic* remained afloat. The water never reached its boilers, the storm subsided, and the ship limped back to Liverpool for repairs.[21]

Travel was an integral part of FDR's childhood. In 1887, when he was five, his parents spent the winter in Washington, D.C. James was heavily invested in a syndicate to construct a sea-level canal across Nicaragua linking the Atlantic and Pacific, in direct competition with the French effort of Ferdinand de Lesseps in Panama. The purpose of the trip was to enlist the support of Congress and the Cleveland administration in negotiations with Nicaragua. The Roosevelts rented the fashionable town house of the Belgian minister at 1211 K Street N.W. and entered the Washington scene with gusto. "Every one is charming to us," wrote Sara. "Even Franklin knows everybody."[22]

Several times the Roosevelts visited the Clevelands in the White House. James had contributed generously to Cleveland's gubernatorial campaign in New York and even more lavishly to his 1884 presidential run. The president pressed James to accept a diplomatic post, preferably as minister to Holland, but James declined. He did, however, secure for Rosy an appointment as first secretary to the American legation in Vienna. Rosy too was a loyal Democrat, had given handsomely to the Cleveland campaign, and could pay most embassy expenses from his wife's fortune. James objected to Rosy's frivolous lifestyle in New York and convinced Cleveland that an appointment overseas would be beneficial.

Before leaving Washington in the spring, James and five-year-old Franklin called on the president to say good-bye. James found Cleveland more care-worn than ever. At the close of the interview the massive Cleveland, a great walrus of a man, put his hand on FDR's tiny head: "My little man, I am making a strange wish for you. It is that you may never be president of the United States."[23]

Many years later Sara was asked if she had thought her son would ever become president. "Never," she answered. "The highest ideal I could hold up before our boy [was] to grow to be like his father: straight and honorable, just and kind."[24]

In addition to their annual sojourns in Europe, the Roosevelts spent almost every summer on Campobello, a slender, rockbound island in Canadian waters off the coast of Maine. James and Sara were so taken with the invigorating sea air and the congenial social life that in 1883, a year and a half after Franklin was born, they bought four acres and built a summer home. "Sometimes," Sara wrote, "James sails with some of the gentlemen and then I work or read German or French aloud with several people here who care for these languages."[25] Franklin learned to sail at Campobello, navigating the rocks and tides and treacherous currents of the Bay of Fundy. And it was at Campobello that he began to dream of Annapolis and a naval career. "I've always liked the navy," he said shortly after becoming assistant secretary of the Navy in 1913. "In fact I only missed by a week going to Annapolis. I would have done so, only my parents objected."[26] It was James, not Sara, who objected. For Sara, FDR's love of the sea was natural. "The Delanos have always been associated with the sea, and I have always been a great believer in heredity," she said.[27] The Roosevelts, on the other hand, were a landlocked clan, and James wanted Franklin trained to take over the family's business affairs.

As country gentry had done for generations, FDR learned to ride at an early age. At two he was sitting atop a pet donkey in the Roosevelt paddock; at four he was riding out each morning with his father to oversee the estate; at six he was given his own Welsh pony, Debby, on the understanding he care for her himself. He was also held responsible for the care for his dog: initially a spitz puppy; then a huge St. Bernard named Nardo, followed by an even larger Newfoundland called Monk, and finally a red Irish Setter whose full name was Mr.

Marksman. Caring for the pets was designed to instill responsibility, but as Roosevelt remembered, it was a herculean task.[28]

As a child Roosevelt collected stamps and developed a passionate interest in ornithology. At the age of ten he was given his mother's already formidable postage stamp collection, which she had started when she was five and her father was in China. Over the years FDR would tend it meticulously, eventually amassing a collection of well over a million stamps mounted in 150 matching albums. Admiral Ross McIntire, the White House physician, estimated that Roosevelt spent well over two thousand hours while he was president tending his collection.[29] Franklin's impressive collection of stuffed birds, all of which he shot himself, is still displayed in glass cases in the entrance hall at Hyde Park. His grandfather Delano rewarded his attainments as an ornithologist with a life membership in the Natural History Museum of New York. FDR often referred to the occasion on which the certificate was presented to him as the greatest thrill of his early life.[30]

The Roosevelts were serious about religion but took the Episcopal faith for granted. Young Franklin was expected to attend Sunday service at St. James', and he did so without objection. In that sense his belief was instinctive. Nevertheless, he remained committed to his boyhood church until his death, serving first as junior vestryman, then as vestryman, and finally as senior warden. After he became president, vestry meetings were usually held at Springwood and would often extend into the early morning hours.[31]

Religious faith provided one of the sources of FDR's unflagging optimism. Deep down he possessed serene confidence in the divine purpose of the universe. He was convinced that however bad things might be at the moment, they were bound to come out all right if he remained patient and put his faith in God. Once asked by Eleanor whether he believed everything he had learned in church, Roosevelt replied that he had never really thought about it. "I think it is just as well not to think about things like that too much."[32]

On November 1, 1890, James suffered a mild heart attack. He lived ten more years but became increasingly frail. The impact on Franklin was severe. James had always been his active companion, but less and less would that be the case. Instead, he was someone to care for and look after. That brought Franklin and Sara even closer together. Before 1890, European travel had been a pleasant diversion for the Roosevelts. After James's heart attack they considered it a necessity. The warm mineral baths at Bad Nauheim were thought to be particularly beneficial for heart patients. James and Sara first went there in 1891; they returned five times in the next seven years. James believed intently in the healing powers of the baths, and Sara and Franklin came to share his enthusiasm—which may help explain FDR's subsequent attachment to the mineral waters at Warm Springs.

It was in Bad Nauheim that FDR attended school for the first time. Remembering her own experience in Dresden and Celle, Sara insisted that nine-year-old Franklin be enrolled in the local Volksschule to improve his German. Proud of his ability to cope in a foreign setting, Roosevelt enjoyed it immensely. "I go to the public school with a lot of little mickies," he wrote his young cousins in America. "We have German reading, German dictation, the history of Siegfried, and arithmetic . . . and I like it very much."[33] His German schoolmaster, Christian Bommersheim, remembered FDR as a child in a blue sailor suit. "His parents put him in my class [and] he impressed me very quickly as an unusually bright young fellow. He had such an engaging manner, and he was always so polite that he was soon one of the most popular children in the school."[34]

In the summer of 1896, in Bad Nauheim with his parents once again, FDR went on a cycling tour of Germany with his tutor. Each of them had an allowance of four marks a day, which meant they lived largely on bread and cheese and slept in small country inns or farmers' houses. Several times the pair were arrested for minor traffic infractions, and each time Franklin, whose command of German was excellent, talked their way out of a fine. In the autumn FDR would be entering Groton, and as a final treat his parents took him to Bayreuth for Wagner's Ring Festival. "Franklin really appreciated it far more than I thought he would," Sara wrote her sister Dora. "He was most attentive and rapt during the long acts and always sorry to leave, never for a moment bored or tired."[35]

America's confidence in FDR depended on Roosevelt's incredible confidence in himself, and that traced in large measure to the comfort and security of his childhood. As his daughter, Anna, put it, "Granny [Sara] was a martinet, but she gave father the assurance he needed to prevail over adversity. Seldom has a young child been more constantly attended and incessantly approved by his mother."[36]

FDR's mind was developing. He read rapidly and retained facts easily, a trait that would become more pronounced in the years ahead. He was fluent in French and German and already possessed an uncanny ability to assimilate what he observed. But Roosevelt was not a reflective thinker, nor an original thinker. He learned by doing. And the extensive traveling he did with his parents—he went to Europe eight times in his first fourteen years—exposed him to a wider range of experience than most boys his age. He was small for his age—five feet three, 105 pounds—but his physical growth had yet to begin. All in all, he looked forward to entering Groton—two years late, as it were, most boys entering at the age of twelve.

After the safe harbor of Springwood, Groton was a challenge for Roosevelt. For fourteen years he had been the center of attention of two doting parents. Now he was one of 110 adolescent boys living in an almost monastic setting. Each new boy faced such problems, but for Franklin they were compounded, entering as he was in third year, without any real experience of organized schooling. If he was concerned, he did not show it. "I am getting on finely both mentally and physically," he reported in his first letter home.[37]

The founder and headmaster of Groton was the Reverend Endicott Peabody, a man of immense personal magnetism, who had studied for the ministry in England and the Episcopal Theological Seminary at Cambridge, Massachusetts. His first church was at Tombstone in the Arizona Territory at the time of Wyatt Earp and Doc Holliday, just after the shoot-out at the OK Corral. A large, vigorous, uncomplicated man with the build of an athlete, Peabody fit right in on the frontier. "Our parson," clucked the *Tombstone Epitaph*, "doesn't flirt with the girls, doesn't drink beer behind the door, and when it comes to baseball, he's a daisy."[38]

But Peabody's overriding desire was to create a church-affiliated boarding school for the sons of America's establishment. In 1883, with the financial assistance of family friends, including J. P. Morgan, Peabody realized his dream and founded Groton on ninety acres of donated farmland thirty-five miles north of Boston. The school was small: six classes of not more than twenty boys each. Tuition was $500 a year. That was about twice what the average American family had to live on.[39] And there were no scholarships. Morgan served on the board of trustees, as did Phillips Brooks, the Episcopal Bishop of Massachusetts, and William Lawrence, dean of the Episcopal Theological Seminary. The contrast between the rawness of Tombstone and the refinement of Groton seems extreme, yet there is no better measure of the breadth of Peabody's character.

Groton's purpose, as the rector saw it, was to cultivate "manly Christian character, having regard to moral and physical as well as intellectual development." He believed in religion, character, athletics, and scholarship—roughly in that order. And character was formed by discipline and obedience. Especially obedience. "You know," Averell Harriman (Groton '09) once said to his father, the rector "would be an awful bully if he weren't such a terrible Christian."[40]

Groton was an immediate success and within ten years had become the most exclusive school in America. Wealthy fathers, disgusted with the soft living their offspring enjoyed, flocked to send their sons to a school where boys would be trained not only intellectually but morally and physically as well. Some of the most successful men in the country had never been to college, but they were good judges of character, and they recognized that Peabody was their type of man. They welcomed the opportunity to place their sons under his care.

Life at Groton was Spartan. Each boy lived in a six-by-ten-foot cubicle with a bed, bureau, rug, and chair. All were standard issue. There was no closet, wall hangings were prohibited, and there was a curtain instead of a door because Peabody frowned upon too much privacy. Mornings began at 6:45 with an icy shower in a communal washroom. Breakfast, chapel, and three morning classes followed with clockwork precision. Dinner, the main meal, was served at noon, followed by two afternoon classes and athletics. Another frigid shower, the evening meal (for which official school dress was required), chapel, and study hall, following which the Rector and Mrs. Peabody shook the hand of each boy and wished him good night.

Despite his pampered upbringing, FDR adjusted handily to the rigor of Groton. Twice a week for the next four years he wrote to his parents, and never once did he complain about his experience. In a sense, except for the cold showers, he was substituting one disciplined regime for another. Autumns were filled with football excitement, edging on to the Christmas season, culminating in the unforgettable reading of Dickens's *Christmas Carol* by the rector's father.[41] In winter, skating and sledding substituted for team sports; with spring came baseball, tennis, swimming, and golf. At vacation time most boys reacted like sailors on shore leave. Franklin was an exception. If he got into mischief, there is no record of it. School vacations were invariably spent at Hyde Park. Summers he usually went to Campobello, where he enjoyed nothing so much as sailing his twenty-one-foot knockabout, *New Moon,* which his father had given him.

Groton's curriculum was classical, taught with great attention to detail. Peabody himself taught sacred studies and set the tone of the school. He saw Groton as a large family with the rector as paterfamilias. Leading the school athletic teams, Peabody personified the muscular Christianity in which he believed. Football was his favorite. To Yale coach Walter Camp he wrote, "I am convinced that football is of profound importance for the moral even more than for the physical development of the boys."[42] As one graduate put it, the boys loved him and feared him, and from him they learned determination and to be unafraid. Roosevelt said the influence of Peabody and his wife meant more to him than that of any other people, "next to my father and mother."[43]

FDR had little difficulty academically. He had been well prepared and within a month of his arrival stood fourth in a class of nineteen, a position he more or less maintained. As Peabody recalled, Roosevelt "was a quiet, satisfactory boy of more than ordinary intelligence, taking a good position in his form but not brilliant. Athletically he was too slight for success. We all liked him."[44] Athletic success was central to real distinction at Groton, and, as Peabody noted, FDR was too small. He was also inexperienced, never having played a team sport before. He was assigned to the second worst of eight football teams and the worst baseball squad, but his enthusiasm never wilted. When hit in the stomach by a line drive, he wrote his parents that it was "to the great annoyance of that intricate organ, and to the great delight of all present."[45] In his final year Roosevelt won a school letter as equipment manager of the baseball team. He also won the Latin and Punctuality Prizes and was a dormitory prefect and a member of the school choir and the debating society.

FDR's four years at Groton provided a transition from the snuggery of familial warmth at Hyde Park. He accepted Peabody's premises and made them his own: competition is healthy, success comes from effort, reward is based on performance, religious observance and moral probity are indispensable to a productive life. "Playing the game" came naturally to FDR. When graduation came, he was sorry to leave. "What a joyful yet sad day this has been," Franklin wrote his parents. "Scarce a boy but wishes he were a 1st former again."[46]

In one sense, Roosevelt never left Groton. The experience was indelible.

"More than forty years ago," he wrote to the old rector in 1940, "you said, in a sermon in the Old Chapel, something about not losing boyhood ideals in later life. Those were Groton ideals—taught by you—I try not to forget—and your words are still with me and with hundreds of others of 'us boys.' "[47]

FDR entered Harvard in the autumn of 1900, along with sixteen of his eighteen Groton classmates. The university was rigidly stratified in those years. Students from socially prestigious families, most of whom had attended East Coast private schools, lived off campus in sumptuous residence halls on Mt. Auburn Street known as the Gold Coast. Young men who were less well-off, usually high school graduates from middle- and working-class backgrounds, made do with considerably more modest accommodations in university housing within the Yard. Roosevelt, together with his Groton classmate Lathrop Brown, took a three-room corner suite in Westmorly Court, the newest of the Gold Coast edifices, and with Sara's help furnished it in an opulent style so firmly prohibited by Rector Peabody. By Harvard standards, FDR's $400-a-year suite was luxurious. He and Brown lived there for the next four years, surrounded by fellow Grotonians and other preppies.

Only rarely did men from the Gold Coast and the Yard interact. Except for friendships that grew out of common interests in the classroom or on the athletic field, there were few opportunities for students of different backgrounds to come into social contact. Professors decried the division of the campus, and Endicott Peabody railed against "the gap between Mt. Auburn Street and the Yard," yet not until the development of the house system in the mid-1920s did Harvard achieve anything approaching social integration of the student body.[48]

Under President Charles W. Eliot, appointed in 1869 and still in firm control when Roosevelt entered, Harvard stood in the vanguard of university reform. Scholarship, not "teaching," became the order of the day. Education was defined exclusively in intellectual terms and had little concern for character development or the protection of private morality. Faculty were appointed on the basis of their research, and students, after a few required courses in the first year, were free to enroll in whatever they wished. Eliot believed a student could choose his courses better than anyone else and that all nonvocational subjects had equal value. He also believed students should make their choice based on the professor teaching the course, not the course description.[49]

Harvard's emphasis on intellectual advancement attracted brilliant scholars. William James, Hugo Münsterberg, and Josiah Royce held chairs in philosophy; the great Shakespearean scholar George Lyman Kittredge adorned the English Department along with George Pierce Baker, founder of the "47 Workshop" for playwrights, and Charles Townsend Copeland, the matchless "Copey" for generations of Harvardians. In the newly established Government Department, A. Lawrence Lowell held forth; Frank W. Taussig lectured in economics; Nathaniel Shaler, the nation's preeminent geologist, headed the Lawrence Scientific School; and Christopher Columbus Langdell was dean of law.

For students, the elective system and its corollary, voluntary attendance at classes, were enormously liberating. FDR and his Groton classmates had taken the equivalent of the required freshman courses during their sixth-form year and therefore were allowed to skip the mandatory curriculum entirely. Not only did that mean they could graduate in three years instead of four, but they could choose whatever courses they wished. Roosevelt hewed closely to fact-heavy courses in economics, government, and history. "I took economics courses in college for four years and everything I was taught was wrong," the president quipped in 1941.[50] FDR took his studies seriously—unlike many Gold Coast habitués he took no "football courses"—and though he won no honors, he was never in academic difficulty. Thanks to the elective system, he avoided courses in philosophy and theory, which might have meant trouble. Throughout his life Roosevelt remained mystified by abstract thought, and Harvard did nothing to lessen that.

In late autumn of his first year, FDR received disturbing news from Hyde Park. His father had suffered a severe heart attack. Then a second one. Sara took James to their New York apartment so he might be nearer his doctors, but his health continued to deteriorate. On December 8, with his family at his bedside, James died. "All is over," Sara wrote in her diary. "At 2:20 he merely slept away. Dr. Ely was in the apartment and called, but it was too late. As I write these words I wonder how I lived when he left me."[51] James left an estate of roughly $600,000, or slightly less than $14 million in today's currency. Franklin and Rosy were each provided a trust fund, with Springwood passing to Sara. Two years before, on the death of her own father, Sara and her siblings had each inherited $1.3 million from the Delano fortune. That would amount to more than $28 million now, and it became the primary source of FDR's family wealth.

Roosevelt spent the spring of 1901 in close touch with Sara. That summer, with the memory of James hanging heavily, they chose not to return to Campobello but to travel to Europe. The Roosevelts spent ten weeks abroad, returning in late September just in time for FDR to return to college. First, it was off to the fjords of Norway on the Hamburg-Amerika Line's elegant cruise ship *Princessin Victoria Luise*—and a chance encounter near the Arctic Circle with the kaiser, William II, who invited them aboard his yacht. Sara found the emperor impressive and energetic but not so kind as she remembered his grandfather, William I, whom she had once seen in Paris. Later they visited Dresden so Sara might show Franklin where she had lived and gone to school as a child. They spent a week with Aunt Laura Astor Delano, Uncle Frank's widow, at the Beau Rivage on the shore of Lake Geneva. In Zurich they stayed at the same hotel in which Sara had stayed on her honeymoon. In Paris, their last stop, they learned that President William McKinley had been shot while visiting the Pan-American Exposition in Buffalo. Twelve days later, as they passed the Nantucket lightship on their way home, they received the news by megaphone: "President McKinley died last Saturday." Cousin Theodore was president of the United States.[52]

Back at Cambridge, FDR threw himself into a round of frenetic activity. After a grueling competition in freshman year, he had been elected to the editorial board of *The Harvard Crimson*, the undergraduate newspaper. For the next three years, the *Crimson* would be his central interest, often requiring four to six hours a day to ready the paper for publication. Along with membership on the editorial board went prestige and responsibility. Franklin gloried in both. He represented the paper at the Yale bicentennial celebration, an occasion notable in retrospect for the presence on the platform of President Theodore Roosevelt, Princeton president Woodrow Wilson, and FDR. In his third year, Roosevelt was elected managing editor of the *Crimson* and worked even harder. Administrative responsibility came naturally. He handled the staff adroitly and was always able to cajole crusty Cambridge printers into opening the forms and remaking a page for last-minute submissions by tardy college journalists. "In his geniality was a kind of frictionless command," his co-editor, W. Russell Bowie, recalled.[53]

At the end of his third year, Roosevelt was elected editor-in-chief (president) of the *Crimson*. He took his degree in June, but remained for a fourth year to discharge his editorial responsibilities. His professors advised him to enter graduate school. "Great fight in my mind between it and Law School, but latter too much with outside duties," FDR recorded in his diary.[54] That fall he enrolled as a graduate student in history but had no intention of pursuing a degree. "The paper takes every moment of time," he informed his mother in early October.[55] As Arthur Schlesinger noted, editing the *Crimson* crowned FDR's Harvard career. Both at the time and in retrospect, it was extremely important to him.[56] In later years he enjoyed joking with reporters that he was a former newspaperman. Visiting Portland, Oregon, as the assistant secretary of the Navy in 1914, he told a press photographer that he too had been "a reporter in Boston ten or twelve years" before and had often lined folks up for the camera.[57]

Sara, meanwhile, found life at Springwood oppressive without James. "I try to keep busy, but it is all hard," she confided to her diary the following spring.[58] Sara stepped into James's role—managing the estate, supervising the workmen, handling business affairs—and for the most part made do. FDR returned to Springwood for Christmas, but in contrast to previous years the celebration was muted. In January the social season accelerated. On the first weekend in the new year, Franklin journeyed to Washington to attend the gala coming-out party given by TR and his wife, Edith, for their daughter, Alice, at the White House. It was the premier social event of the season. FDR spent three crowded days in Washington attending formal dinners, a reception at the Austrian Embassy, and the dance itself, held in the East Room. There was also tea with Cousin Theodore, lunch at Cousin Bamie's house on N Street, and a second private talk with the president. "One of the most interesting and enjoyable three days I have ever had," Franklin wrote Sara.[59]

FDR returned to Cambridge, and soon afterward Sara joined him. The winter at Hyde Park had become too melancholy. She took an apartment in Boston and discreetly joined the social and cultural life of the city. Sara wanted to be "near enough to the University to be on hand should [Franklin] want me and far enough removed not to interfere with his college life."[60] Franklin seemed delighted. He came frequently to dine and sometimes spent the night. The following winter Sara returned to Boston for another three months. She participated vicariously in FDR's success and cushioned whatever disappointment came his way. "His father and I always expected a great deal of Franklin," she once said. "After all, he had many advantages that other boys did not have."[61]

Socially, FDR's dance card at Harvard was fuller than most. He kept a horse and a runabout, and there was scarcely a weekend when he was not attending a dinner or a party somewhere in the Boston area.[62] He was not admitted to Porcellian, the most prestigious of the final clubs, but he did make Fly (Alpha Delta Phi) and Hasty Pudding, served as librarian of each, and began his life-long habit of collecting naval Americana. Years later, with typical hyperbole, he told a distant relative that his failure to make Porcellian was "the greatest dis-appointment he ever had."[63] Yet, as his roommate, Lathrop Brown, noted, "Franklin was not a typical club man of his generation. He had more on his mind than sitting in the Club's front window, doing nothing but criticizing the passers-by. His not 'making' the Porcellian meant only that he was free of any possible restraining influences of a lot of delightful people who thought that the world belonged to them and who did not want to change anything in it."[64]

Roosevelt received his degree from Harvard in 1903. But in the tradition of the Ivy League he was always a member of the Class of '04. At graduation he was elected permanent chairman of the class committee, the linchpin of alumni affairs. Roosevelt won no prizes and did not make Phi Beta Kappa, yet he had prospered intellectually. His university experience imparted renewed confidence and enhanced the innate optimism that James and Sara had so carefully nourished. As one biographer has written, "At Groton, Roosevelt learned to get along with his contemporaries; at Harvard he learned to lead them."[65]

THREE

KEEPING THE NAME IN THE FAMILY

Nothing is more pleasing to the eye than a good-looking lady,
nothing more refreshing to the spirit than the company of one,
nothing more flattering to the ego than the affection of one.

—FRANKLIN D. ROOSEVELT

LESS THAN A YEAR after graduating from Harvard, FDR married Anna
Eleanor Roosevelt, his fifth cousin once removed, the orphaned daughter of
his godfather, Elliott—a tall, striking young woman variously described by an
adoring New York press as "beautiful," "regal," and "magnificent," with "greater
claim to good looks than any of the Roosevelts."[1] Franklin was an impressionable twenty-three. Eleanor was twenty: the same age her mother had been, yet
still innocent of the birds and the bees. As she later informed her son James,
the kiss she and Franklin exchanged at the close of the wedding ceremony was
their first in more than two years of courtship.[2]*

Throughout his adult life FDR relished female companionship. Yet he was
late discovering it. At Springwood for fourteen years his contact with the opposite sex was limited. At Groton he relied on his mother to organize his social

---

* Eleanor's cousin Alice, who was the same age yet far more worldly, reports trying to impart the facts of life to Eleanor, but "I almost came to grief. . . . She suddenly leapt on me
and tried to smother me with a pillow, saying I was being blasphemous. So I shut up and I
think she probably went to her wedding not knowing anything about the subject." Michael
Teague, *Mrs. L: Conversations with Alice Roosevelt Longworth* 57 (New York: Doubleday,
1981).

Eleanor was not alone in her naiveté. Corinne Robinson Alsop, ER's younger cousin, remembered having once been kissed by a boy in the stable of her family's home in Orange,
New Jersey. "It frightened me to death, and I discussed with my intimate friends whether I
would immediately have a baby." Alsop Family Papers, Harvard University.

life: "I wish you would think up some decent partner for me for the N.Y. dance, so that I can get someone early, and not get palmed off on some ice-cart."[3] At Harvard he was on his own but hesitated to take an unguided step. "What do you think of my taking M.D.R. [Muriel Delano Robbins], Helen [Roosevelt], and Mary Newbold to see the Harvard–West Point game Saturday afternoon?" he asked Sara. "If you approve make arrangements as to trains."[4]

Gradually, his diffidence faded. By the end of sophomore year FDR was charming and relaxed, eager to ingratiate himself with the eligible young women of upper class Boston and their families. This was 1902—the apogee of Victorian restraint. Unlike John F. Kennedy and his classmates in the 1930s, who took a direct approach, the men of FDR's generation were oblique. In refined circles contact with the opposite sex was strictly chaperoned. Touching was risqué, kissing stretched the limit, and premarital sex was absolutely prohibited. There were two outlets: the company of loose women who traded in sex, or marriage. For someone of FDR's straitlaced upbringing, the former was unthinkable.* As a consequence Franklin proposed not once but three times to young women who caught his attention at Harvard.

FDR's first love in Cambridge was Frances Dana, granddaughter of both Richard Henry Dana (*Two Years Before the Mast*) and Henry Wadsworth Longfellow. Reportedly, Sara talked her son out of marriage because Miss Dana was Catholic and thus unacceptable to the Protestant Delanos and Roosevelts.[5] After Frances, FDR was smitten with Dorothy Quincy, daughter of an equally prominent Brahmin family. Then Alice Sohier, the exceptionally beau-

---

* FDR's resolve was reinforced by the behavior of his nephew Taddy (James Roosevelt Roosevelt, Jr.), the son of Rosy and Helen Astor. Almost three years older than Franklin, Taddy dropped out of Harvard in 1900 to marry Sadie Messinger, a habitué of the Haymarket Dance Hall in New York, better known by her trade names, "Dutch Sadie" and "Sadie of the Tenderloin." The press had a field day (to the chagrin of the Roosevelts and Astors); Rosy tried to have the marriage annulled, but Taddy, who had just turned twenty-one and come into half ownership of his late mother's Astor legacy, held tight. After a brief stay in Florida, Taddy and Sadie returned to New York, where they took two rooms over a garage in which he repaired automobiles. They remained together until Sadie's death in 1940. Taddy never touched his legacy and on his death in 1958 left his millions to the Salvation Army. FDR blamed Taddy for bringing on James's fatal heart attack in 1900. "One can never again consider him a true Roosevelt," he wrote Sara. "It would be well for him not only to go to parts unknown, but to stay there and *begin* life anew." FDR did not see or speak with Taddy again. Letter, FDR to SDR, October 23, 1900, FDRL.

tiful daughter of an old North Shore family. Alice's mother was an Alden, a Massachusetts clan that predated the Delanos, and her father was an astute New England businessman with a town house in Boston, an estate in Beverly, and summer homes in Maine and New Hampshire. At some point in 1902 Alice and Franklin discussed marriage. FDR was twenty; Alice just seventeen. Having been an only child, Roosevelt told Alice he wanted a large family—at least six children. That evidently alarmed Alice, who later told a friend she had decided not to marry Franklin because "I did not wish to be a cow."[6] The bond between FDR and Alice was not severed that easily, however. They continued to see each other, and in the autumn of 1902 Alice's parents sent her to Europe—an insurance policy against teenage infatuation. Many years later, FDR put a different gloss on their breakup:

> Once upon a time when I was in Cambridge, I had serious thoughts about marrying a Boston girl and settling down in the Back Bay. . . . By the grace of God I took a trip at that time, meeting a number of real Americans, *i.e.* those from the west and south. I was saved, but it was an awfully narrow escape.[7]

As with many of FDR's stories, fact and fiction mingle freely. It was Alice, not he, who backed away from marriage, and it was she who undertook the decisive trip in 1902.[8]

In the wake of Alice Sohier's departure for Europe, Franklin met Eleanor. Each autumn, New York society launched the social season with a gala horse show at Madison Square Garden. For so long as there had been a horse show, the Hudson River Roosevelts had been prominent participants, sometimes showing, sometimes judging, but always in attendance. November 17, 1902, was no exception. The family box, now maintained by FDR's half brother, Rosy—a connoisseur of coachmanship and fine carriages—literally bulged with Roosevelts: Franklin, Rosy's daughter Helen, her cousin Eleanor, Helen's fiancé, Theodore Robinson (another cousin), Mary Newbold, a neighbor from Hyde Park, and assorted uncles and aunts from Long Island and Connecticut. After the show, Rosy took the young people to dinner at Sherry's, New York's most fashionable restaurant. "Dinner with James Roosevelt Roosevelt, Helen Roosevelt Roosevelt, Mary Newbold and Eleanor Roosevelt at Sherry's," FDR recorded in his diary—his first reference to Eleanor.[9] Two weeks later he lunched with Eleanor and his niece Helen in New York, and two weeks after that, in the city with Sara for last-minute Christmas shopping, he slipped away for tea with Eleanor.

The two were together again in Washington for the nation's New Year's festivities. FDR stayed with Cousin Bamie on N Street; Eleanor with TR's daughter Alice in the White House. On New Year's Day they stood in the "inner circle" to watch Cousin Theodore shake hands with thousands of well-wishers who filed through the East Room. They took tea with Alice and Mrs. Roosevelt, dined with the president in the state dining room, then attended the theater, where, Franklin noted, he "sat near Eleanor. Very interesting day."

A month later, Eleanor was among those Rosy invited to celebrate Franklin's twenty-first birthday at Sherry's, an affair FDR described as "very jolly." In late June, Eleanor came to Springwood for a four-day weekend, one of a group of six young people and accompanied by her maid. Three weeks later there was another house party, which Eleanor attended, again accompanied by her maid. On Saturday, July 7, after a quiet afternoon lounging on the lawn, Franklin took the group for a dinner cruise aboard the *Half Moon*, the family's motorized sailing yacht. "Franklin was at his best aboard his boat," his cousin Corinne Robinson remembered—"handsome at the tiller, a splendid sailor and completely confident."[10] That evening, after the others had gone to bed, Franklin wrote in his diary that the day had been great fun. "E is an angel." Once again FDR was in love.

Whether this was vouchsafed to Eleanor is unclear. Franklin may have written and she may have replied, but no early letters survive. In 1937, when she was at work on the first volume of her autobiography, Eleanor burned all of Franklin's letters, finding his youthful avowals of constancy too painful to reread.[11] FDR carefully preserved Eleanor's letters to him, but none date from this period. In the Victorian era correspondence between a young man and a young woman was not undertaken lightly. As Eleanor later recorded, "It was understood that no girl was interested in a man or showed any liking for him until he had made all the advances. You knew a man very well before you wrote or received a letter from him . . . and to have signed one in any other way than 'very sincerely yours' would have been not only a breach of good manners but an admission of feeling which was entirely inadmissible."[12]

Eleanor's cramped view reflected an upbringing even more sheltered than FDR's. Her mother, Anna Rebecca Hall, died of diphtheria when Eleanor was only eight. Less than two years later her father, Elliott, succumbed to alcoholism. From the death of her mother until her marriage to Franklin, Eleanor was in the care of her maternal grandmother, first at the Hall estate at Tivoli on the Hudson, then at boarding school in England. Apart from vacations, when she occasionally met a Roosevelt cousin, she was virtually removed from the company of men. In material terms, Eleanor was well provided for. But a nunnery novitiate would have met more men than she did.

Franklin saw Eleanor off and on during the summer of 1903, always well chaperoned, and that autumn he invited her to Cambridge for the Yale game, traditionally the last football game of the season. After the game, Eleanor went to Groton to visit her younger brother. FDR followed the next morning and spent Sunday with Eleanor. As they strolled along the bank of the Nashua River, Franklin proposed and Eleanor accepted: "A never to be forgotten walk," FDR noted that evening. Eleanor said, "It seemed entirely natural."[13]

The next weekend Franklin journeyed to Fairhaven, Massachusetts, to observe Thanksgiving with the Delanos. When he took his mother aside and broke the news, Sara was stunned. "Franklin gave me quite a startling announcement," she wrote in her journal. Sara did not object to Eleanor, whom she knew well and had often entertained at Springwood. She simply believed Franklin too young. Her father had been thirty-three when he married and had already established himself as a major player in the China trade. He could offer something to his wife. FDR was still in college. He would not enter law school until the following fall. He was largely dependent upon his mother for support, and had she wished, Sara very likely could have forbidden the marriage. Instead, she extracted a commitment from Franklin and Eleanor that they would keep their engagement secret for a year, not see each other unless properly chaperoned, and keep sufficient distance so as not to arouse suspicion. Sara played for time. She knew from experience how fragile young love could be. Twenty-seven years before, her own romance with Stanford White had dissolved when they were kept apart, and a year now might cool the couple's ardor. For their part, Franklin and Eleanor believed the interval of a year would erode Sara's resistance. They accepted the arrangement and resolved to make the best of it.

Franklin and Eleanor shared a common heritage. Both were Roosevelts. But Eleanor's maternal forebears placed her in a celestial constellation of Livingstons and Ludlows, Ver Plancks and Stuyvesants—families who traced their provenance to letters patent from either the monarchs of Restoration England or the Dutch East India Company. Eleanor's grandmother, many generations removed, was Amy Stuyvesant, sister of Peter Stuyvesant, Director General of the New Netherland colony.[14]

In the struggle for American independence, few families, save perhaps the Adamses of Massachusetts and the Lees of Virginia, could duplicate the patriotic contribution of the Livingstons of New York, whose ranks included signers of both the Declaration of Independence and the Constitution, a U.S. Supreme Court justice, and two secretaries of state.[15] Chancellor Robert Livingston, one of the nation's most distinguished jurists, administered the presidential oath of office to George Washington in 1789. His granddaughter Elizabeth (Eleanor's great-grandmother) eloped to marry Edward Ludlow, scion of an equally prominent Hudson River family, Tory rather than patriot, and among the wealthiest in America. Edward Ludlow founded New York City's premier real estate holding company, and in 1861 his daughter, Mary Livingston Ludlow (Eleanor's grandmother), married Valentine Hall, Jr., heir to an even larger commercial fortune. The Halls had six children, of whom Eleanor's mother, Anna, was the eldest.[16]

On the paternal side, Eleanor's father, Elliott, was the younger sibling of Bamie and TR, children of Theodore Roosevelt, Sr., and his wife, Mittie.* Just as the Aspinwalls and Delanos had infused new vigor into the Hyde Park bloodline, so Mittie, an enchanting southern belle from Cobb County, Georgia, added more than a soupçon of spice to the Long Island clan. One of fourteen children and stepchildren of Martha and James Stephens Bulloch, Mittie was a vivacious hostess and daring horsewoman who enchanted New York society. Her friends in Georgia later claimed that TR inherited "his splendid dash and energy" from his southern mother.

Eleanor's parents enjoyed a fairy-tale romance: Elliott, the playboy prince charming; Anna, the beautiful maiden swept off her feet. Yet this fairy tale ended tragically. Unlike his brother and sisters, Elliott was fatally flawed. To this day the pathology is uncertain. Whether Elliott suffered from epilepsy or mental illness, or was driven to excess by unbridled self-indulgence, cannot be positively determined.[17] What is clear is that he could not handle the rigors of

---

* Bamie, whose real name was Anna (Bamie was short for "bambino") was born in 1855; TR in 1858; Elliott in 1860; and a fourth child, Corinne, in 1861.

formal education, dropped out of St. Paul's at sixteen, spent a year or so out West hunting and fishing, and returned to New York just before the death of his father in 1878. The elder Roosevelt left each of his four children approximately $125,000, which would have provided an annual income of about $8,000—more than twenty times that of the average American family. When their mother, Mittie, died in 1884, each received an additional $65,000. That afforded each child an annual income of about $14,000. A simple monetary conversion equates that with an income of roughly a quarter of a million dollars today, but the money went much further in the 1880s because there was no income tax.[18]*

Elliott remained in New York for two years after his father's death, playing polo, drinking heavily, and leading the sporting life of a well-connected bon vivant. A note from TR to their mother, written during a hunting trip with Elliott in 1880, provides a glimpse:

> As soon as we got here he took some ale to get the dust out of his throat; then a milk punch because he was thirsty; a mint julep because he was hot; a brandy mash "to keep the cold out of his stomach;" and then sherry and bitters to give him an appetite. He took a very simple dinner—soup, fish, salmi de grouse, sweetbread, mutton, venison, corn, macaroni, various vegetables and some puddings and pies, together with beer, later claret and in the evening, shandigaff.[19]

In the autumn of 1880 Elliott set out on a leisurely world tour, highlighted by several months of big-game hunting in India.[20] He returned to New York in March 1882, tried his hand halfheartedly at real estate, and within months met

---

* With the exception of a brief period during the Civil War, there was no federal income tax until 1894, when a Democratic Congress amended the Wilson-Gorman Tariff Act to provide for a general tax of 2 percent on incomes above $4,000 (28 Stat. 509, 553 [1894]).

The following year, a sharply divided (5–4) Supreme Court struck down the income tax as unconstitutional. *Pollock v. Farmers' Loan and Trust,* 157 U.S. 429 (1895). "We are reversing one hundred years of error," said Chief Justice Melville Fuller, speaking for the Court. Fuller's reference was to the Supreme Court's earlier decisions in *Hylton v. United States,* 3 Dallas (3 U.S.) 171 (1796), and *Springer v. United States,* 102 U.S. 586 (1881), both of which would have sustained the tax. As a result of the Court's decision in *Pollock* a federal income tax was not instituted until after adoption of the Sixteenth ("Income Tax") Amendment to the Constitution in 1913.

and fell in love with Anna Rebecca Hall, widely acclaimed as the most glamorous debutante of the year. They became engaged the following Memorial Day at a house party given in their honor by Laura Delano (Sara's youngest sister) at Algonac, and were married December 1, 1883. *The New York Herald* described the wedding as "one of the most brilliant social events of the season." Percy R. King, a childhood friend, was Elliott's best man; James and Sara were among the guests.[21]

The Long Island Roosevelts were delighted. Anna, they hoped, would provide Elliott with the motivation to make something of himself. And for two years the couple prospered. Elliott went to work for the Ludlow real estate firm on Lower Broadway, Anna ordered her dresses from Palmer in London and Worth in Paris, and the couple maintained a well-staffed brownstone in New York's fashionable Thirties. Repeatedly Anna was singled out in the city's society pages for her classic, captivating beauty.[22]

Elliott, like FDR's half brother, Rosy, was a mainstay of the hard-drinking horsey set: polo at Meadowbrook, riding with the hounds in cross-country steeplechase, the annual hunt ball, tennis and sailing at Bar Harbor and Newport. A keen observer of the New York scene called Elliott "the most loveable Roosevelt I ever knew," adding that "if personal popularity could have bestowed public honors on any man there was nothing beyond the reach of Elliott Roosevelt."[23]

On October 11, 1884, a daughter was born, Anna Eleanor Roosevelt, named after both mother and father. For Elliott, his daughter was "a miracle from heaven." In 1889 she was joined by a brother, Elliott, Jr., and two years later by a second brother, Hall, named for his maternal ancestors.[24]

By then the marriage had all but collapsed. Always prone to excess, Elliott's drinking was out of control, compounded by frequent recourse to laudanum and morphine—painkillers to thwart whatever demons stalked him. Unable to handle even the most routine assignments, he resigned from his uncle's firm. An extended sojourn in Europe ended with Elliott confined to a Paris sanitarium to dry out. His mental deterioration was so great that TR and Bamie, with Anna's reluctant approval, brought suit in New York court to have him adjudged insane and place his remaining property, estimated at $170,000, in trust for his wife and children. "It is all horrible beyond belief," said TR.[25]

News of the Roosevelt family squabble splashed across the front pages of New York's press. ELLIOTT ROOSEVELT INSANE, bannered the *Sun*. DEMENTED

BY EXCESSES, said the *Herald*.[26] Elliott fought back with a letter to the editor of the European edition of the *Herald,* asserting he was in Paris merely for the "cure at an establishment hydrotherapeutique."[27] In January 1892 Theodore traveled to Paris to confront Elliott. He and Bamie would drop the suit, he said, if Elliott would place most of his assets in trust, submit to additional treatment for alcoholism in the United States, return to work, and spend two years on probation apart from his family. It was a Spartan regimen for someone as undisciplined as Elliott, yet TR was relentless. After a week of browbeating and intimidation, Elliott yielded. "Thank heaven I came over," Theodore wrote Bamie. Elliott, he said, was "utterly broken, submissive, and repentant. He signed the deed for two-thirds of *all* his property, and agreed to the proba- tion. . . . He was in a mood that was terribly touching. How long it will last of course no one can say."[28]

Elliott's philandering did little to improve matters. Three months after he left New York for Europe, Katy Mann, a young servant girl employed by Anna at their Long Island estate, informed the family she was pregnant with Elliott's child. When Elliott denied the accusation, Katy threatened legal action and public scandal. The Roosevelts initially sided with Elliott. "Of course she is lying," said TR. But when they met with Katy and saw the baby, they gave up the fight.[29] The Roosevelt lawyers initially offered $4,000; Katy demanded $10,000; and eventually that sum was placed in trust for her son, defiantly named Elliott Roosevelt Mann. According to the Manns, the child never re- ceived a dime, the money apparently looted by Katy's lawyers.[30] Whatever may have happened to the funds, there is no doubt that Elliott Roosevelt Mann was Eleanor's half brother.*

While in Paris, Elliott, unknown to Anna, took up with a sophisticated American expatriate, Mrs. Frances Bagley Sherman of Detroit. They lived inti- mately for six months, and when TR forced Elliott to leave France, Mrs. Sher- man was heartbroken. "How could they treat so noble and generous a man as they have?" she asked.[31]

---

* After FDR was elected president in 1932, Elliott Roosevelt Mann and Katy wrote Eleanor to congratulate her. ER replied, "I was very interested to receive your letter and to learn that you were named after my father. . . . I shall hope sometime to see both you and your mother." No invitation was ever extended, nor was any further correspondence from the Manns answered by ER. Blanche Wiesen Cook, 1 *Eleanor Roosevelt* 65n. (New York: Viking Penguin, 1992).

Elliott returned to the United States in February 1892, underwent treatment for alcoholism in Chicago, then moved to Abingdon, Virginia, to manage the vast Appalachian estate of his brother-in-law, Douglas Robinson. Anna meanwhile moved the family uptown to a new and more comfortable mansion in the East Sixties and did the utmost to provide her children a normal life. She declined to sue for divorce, hoping that Elliott would recover. But she was frequently depressed, and shattering migraines immobilized her for days at a time. "I know now that life must have been hard and bitter and a very great strain on her," Eleanor wrote many years later. "I would often sit at the head of her bed and stroke her head. . . . As with all children, the feeling I was useful was perhaps the greatest joy I experienced."[32]

In early November, Anna entered the hospital for surgery to relieve her headaches. She recovered from the operation but soon contracted diphtheria. On December 3, she lost consciousness. Four days later she died, her health broken by two years of anguish and disappointment.[33] Six months after Anna's death, Eleanor's three-year-old brother, Elliott, Jr., also died from diphtheria.

In Abingdon, Elliott fell off the wagon almost immediately. One evening, drunk and naked, he toppled a kerosene lamp and burned himself badly. Friends in Abingdon urged TR to come down, but he refused. "It would be absolutely useless," he said.[34] Elliott attended Anna's funeral, drank immoderately, sang bawdy songs, and was quickly ushered out of town. He returned to New York surreptitiously in the autumn of 1893, rented a house near Riverside Park under the name of Maxwell Eliot, and took up with another married woman, a Mrs. Evans, who, like Mrs. Sherman in Paris, found him irresistible. He was now consuming half a dozen bottles of hard liquor daily. In May he spent the night in a police lockup, too drunk to tell his cabbie where he lived. "He can't be helped," TR wrote Bamie. "He must simply be let go his own gait."[35] On August 13, 1894, seized by delirium tremens, Elliott attempted to jump from his parlor window, fell back in convulsions, and lost consciousness. He died the next evening.

Eleanor's autobiographical writings depict a lovable, caring father and an austere, self-absorbed mother. Those were the memories of an impressionable young child. But as Blanche Wiesen Cook, ER's preeminent biographer, points out, Eleanor was off the mark: "She did not relate to her mother's bitter situation, even in adulthood, after she knew the facts. And she never acknowledged the sacrifice her mother had made for her, an act of love that allowed Eleanor to maintain her romantic image of her father."[36]

Unlike FDR, Eleanor was a solemn child. As a youthful relative remembered, she "took everything—most of all herself—so tremendously seriously."[37] After Anna's death, Eleanor and her brother went to live with Grandmother Hall, dividing their time between the Halls' stately brownstone on West Thirty-seventh Street and the estate at Tivoli in upstate New York. "Our household," said Eleanor, "consisted of a cook, a butler, a housemaid, and a laundress." In the country, there were additional coachmen, servants, and tutors. Grandmother Hall was only forty-eight at the time, and, as Eleanor remembers, discipline was strict. "We were brought up on the principle that 'no' was easier to say than 'yes.' "[38]

Eleanor was tutored in French, German, and music. She studied piano, attended classes in dancing and ballet, and was taken regularly to the theater. Her uncles taught her riding, jumping, lawn tennis, and how to shoot. As one biographer has noted, the six years Eleanor spent with Grandmother Hall were a time of healing. She became the center of attention. From her grandmother Eleanor derived "a new sense of belonging. Out of the chaos of her parental home, Eleanor felt for the first time secure and wanted."[39]

Isolated as she was at Tivoli, there was little opportunity for Eleanor to meet or play with other children. One exception was Alice Roosevelt, TR's daughter, whose mother had died after giving birth and who was being raised by Bamie. "I saw a lot of Eleanor as a child," said Alice. "We both suffered from being deprived of a parent. But whereas she responded to her insecurity by being do-goody and virtuous, I did by being boisterous and showing off."[40] Alice agreed that many aspects of Eleanor's childhood were unhappy. "But she had a tendency to make out she was unattractive and rejected as a child, which just wasn't true. She made a big thing about having long legs and having to wear short skirts. Well, as far as I was concerned, I envied her long legs and didn't notice her short skirts, if indeed they were short. She was always making herself out to be an ugly duckling but she was really rather attractive. Tall, rather coltish looking, with masses of pale, gold hair rippling to below her waist, and really lovely blue eyes."[41]*

* James Kearney, an early biographer, suggested that when Eleanor wrote *This Is My Story* in 1937 she deliberately emphasized the unhappy aspects of her childhood because she wished to identify with the "agonizing insecurity and aspirations of American youth in the thirties." *Anna Eleanor Roosevelt: The Evolution of a Reformer* 6 (Boston: Houghton Mifflin, 1968).

When Eleanor turned fifteen, Grandmother Hall sent her to boarding school in England. Anna, before she died, had asked that Eleanor be sent abroad, preferably to Allenwood; and Bamie, who had studied under the school's headmistress in France, strongly supported the choice. Located in Wimbledon Park on the outskirts of London, Allenwood was in some respects the female equivalent of Groton: a pioneering school that offered the daughters of England's elite a liberal education emphasizing social responsibility and personal independence. Marie Souvestre, the founder and headmistress, was the daughter of the French philosopher and novelist Émile Souvestre. A committed feminist, she believed passionately in educating women to think for themselves, to challenge accepted wisdom, and to assert themselves. These were subversive doctrines to patriarchal Victorians, yet Allenwood succeeded, in no small measure because of the sparkling erudition of Mlle. Souvestre. Liberal intellectuals—Joseph Chamberlain, Henry James, the Stracheys and the Webbs—considered her a soul mate. Beatrice Webb said her intellectual rigor forged the future for a generation of young women.[42] Like Endicott Peabody at Groton, Marie Souvestre *was* Allenwood. And for the thirty-five girls enrolled, Allenwood *was* Marie Souvestre.

Eleanor flourished at Allenwood. The school was conducted entirely in French, and Eleanor was perfectly bilingual. "I remember the day she arrived at school," said one classmate. "She was so much more grown up than we were, and at her first meal, when we hardly dared open our mouths, she sat opposite Mlle. Souvestre, chatting away in French."[43] Eleanor quickly became the most popular girl in school. She excelled in French, German, and Italian, wrote superb essays, and made the first team in field hockey. Marie Souvestre wrote Mrs. Hall, "She is the most amiable girl I have ever met; she is nice to everybody, very eager to learn and highly interested in her work."[44]

For the next three years Eleanor continued to sit opposite Mlle. Souvestre.* During school breaks she traveled with her to Europe: "One of the most momentous things that happened in my education," said Eleanor.[45] Other times

---

* Sitting opposite the formidable Marie Souvestre, then in her seventies, was considered the place of honor. According to ER, "The girl who occupied this place received [the head-mistress's] nod at the end of the meal and gave the signal, by rising, for the rest of the girls to rise and leave the dining room." Eleanor Roosevelt, *Autobiography* 26 (New York: Harper & Brothers, 1961).

she toured the continent with her Aunt Tissie, Anna's younger sister. Tissie was married to the wealthy art collector and portrait painter Stanley Mortimer, lived most of the year in Paris, and introduced Eleanor to a style of living enjoyed only by Europe's most affluent.[46] Photographs of Eleanor at the time show a tall, slender young woman with soft brown hair coiffed in a pompadour and dressed in current Paris fashions. "Entirely sophisticated, and full of self-confidence and *savoir-faire*," said an admiring classmate.[47]

Marie Souvestre's goal was to make her students "cultivated women of the world," and Eleanor blossomed under her tutelage. If ER had a fault, it was her seriousness. "Totty [as Eleanor was known] is so intelligent, so charming, so good," said Mlle. Souvestre. "*Mais pas gaie, pas gaie.*"[48] For her part, Eleanor was despondent when at eighteen it was time to return to New York to make her social debut. "Mlle Souvestre had become one of the people I cared for most in the world and . . . I would have given a great deal to have spent another year on my education."[49] Later Eleanor said, "Whatever I have become had its seed in those three years of contact with a liberal mind and a strong personality."[50] Throughout the remainder of her life, ER kept a framed portrait of Marie Souvestre on her desk. And when the headmistress died in 1905, Eleanor and Bamie served on her memorial committee.

Allenwood ranked as the most emancipated women's school of the era. Yet it was totally deficient in preparing young ladies to deal with a world of men. Marie Souvestre and Aunt Tissie taught Eleanor the finer points of cosmopolitan behavior, how to present herself, how to dress. Yet her three years at Allenwood were as cloistered as the previous five with Grandmother Hall at Tivoli. At the age of eighteen, Eleanor had never dated, had rarely talked to a young man alone, and as a practical matter had seldom been in mixed company. Her mind had been finely honed, she brimmed with self-esteem, but she was naive beyond despair.

Eleanor's lack of worldly experience appealed to Franklin. "A more sophisticated woman would have scared the daylights out of him," said his son Elliott.[51] It is not surprising Franklin was drawn to Eleanor. Aside from being young, attractive, and smartly dressed (ER's wardrobe was meticulously put together by Aunt Tissie), Eleanor had an air of serious intelligence about her: a genuine interest in what took place around her. Her years at Allenwood imparted a maturity that FDR adored.[52] She was also a Roosevelt and the favorite niece of Cousin Theodore, who was not only president of the United States but

Eleanor's godfather. By marrying Eleanor, FDR would acquire even greater access to the man he most admired. Her financial endowment was taken for granted. Eleanor was not rich like the Astors, but her trust fund provided an annual income of about $8,000 ($160,000 today), which was considerably more than Franklin's, the principal of which was still administered by Sara.

The Roosevelt children, Anna and Elliott, believed that Eleanor "set out to win Father more than he tried to woo her. . . . She was stunned by the thought that here was a handsome man who would not only look at her but seek her companionship. She poured her heart out to him, undoubtedly the best listener she had ever met."[53] Eleanor wrote Franklin every evening to ensure that he did not forget her. "Oh! Darling I miss you so and I long for the happy hours which we have together. I am so happy. So very happy in your love dearest, that all the world has changed for me."[54] Eleanor often signed herself "Little Nell," the nickname her father had bestowed, and she addressed Franklin as "Boy Darling," "Dearest Boy," and occasionally, "Franklin Dearest." For the most part, Eleanor's nightly letters during their secret engagement were reports on the day's happenings, but, as one biographer notes, they "were as full of love as any letters she would ever write."[55]

In September 1904 Franklin entered Columbia Law School. He lived with Sara in an imposing town house his mother rented at 200 Madison Avenue, directly across from the marble mansion of J. P. Morgan. "I am anxious to hear about the first day [at Columbia]," Eleanor wrote from Tivoli, "and whether you found any old acquaintances or had only Jew Gentlemen to work with!" Ethnic identity was delineated more sharply at the time, and Eleanor shared the traditional prejudices of Knickerbocker society. Her friend and biographer Joseph Lash reports that FDR's class at Columbia "showed 21 Jewish names in a class of 74." Lash also notes that ER's comment did not prevent her from teaching part-time at Rivington Street Settlement House on the Lower East Side, where most of her pupils were recent Jewish and Italian immigrants, nor did it "inhibit her solicitude for them."[56] FDR sometimes met Eleanor at Rivington House and once, when a child in her class became ill, accompanied her to the tenement in which the child lived. "My God," Franklin said, "I didn't know anyone lived like this."[57]

On October 11, Eleanor's twentieth birthday, FDR presented her with a gift he had chosen at Tiffany's "after much inspection and deliberation": a large diamond engagement ring. It suited Eleanor perfectly. "You could not have found a ring I would have liked better," she wrote. "I love it so I know I shall find it hard to keep from wearing it."[58] After eleven months, the subterfuge was wearing thin. Later that month Eleanor and Franklin were houseguests at a family party given by Aunt Corinne and Douglas Robinson in Orange, New Jersey. "E. and F. are comic," noted young Corinne, Jr. "They avoided each other like the black plague and told beautifully concocted lies and deceived us sweetly in every direction. . . . I would bet they are engaged." FDR played the scene with such aplomb that Corinne told him he had a very deceitful nature. Eleanor was equally opaque. Three days later she and Corinne, Jr., went driving. "Neither of us mentioned Franklin," Corinne wrote, "but I think he was on both our minds."[59]

The engagement was announced on December 1 and was followed by a blizzard of congratulatory letters. "I never saw the family so enthusiastic in my life," wrote Lyman Delano. Grandmother Hall was thankful Eleanor was "going to marry such a fine man." Alice Roosevelt, who would be Eleanor's maid of honor, thought the news "too good to be true." Bamie said she loved Franklin not only on his own account but because "his character is like his father's [who was] the most *absolutely* honorable upright gentleman we ever knew."[60]

From the White House, Uncle Theodore wrote Eleanor that only in married life is "the highest and finest happiness to be found. I know you and Franklin will face all that comes bravely and lovingly." To FDR he wrote:

Dear Franklin,

We are greatly rejoiced over the good news. I am as fond of Eleanor as if she were my daughter; and I like you, and trust you, and believe in you. No other success in life—not the Presidency, or anything else—begins to compare with the joy and happiness that come in and from the love of the true man and the true woman, the love which never sinks lover and sweetheart in man and wife. You and Eleanor are true and brave, and I believe you love each other unselfishly; and golden years open before you. May all good fortune attend you both, ever. Give my love to your dear mother.

Your aff. cousin
Theodore Roosevelt[61]

The wedding was set for March 17, 1905, and Franklin asked Endicott Peabody to preside. "It would not be the same without you," he told the rector.

Eleanor requested Uncle Theodore stand in for her father and give the bride away. TR was delighted. He suggested that the wedding be held "under his roof" at the White House and insisted on handling all the arrangements. That was TR's style, but it was more than Eleanor and Franklin had bargained for. It was eventually agreed that the wedding would be held in New York under Grandmother Hall's auspices on a date when the president could attend. March 17—Saint Patrick's Day—was the first available.

Before the wedding, Franklin and Eleanor took time to attend Uncle Theodore's inauguration. In November 1904 TR had defeated his Democratic opponent, the conservative Alton B. Parker, chief judge of the New York Court of Appeals, by 2.5 million votes—a landslide in which Franklin cast his ballot for the Republican ticket.[62] Addressing the annual Jackson Day Dinner of the Democratic Party in 1938, FDR said, "My father and grandfather were Democrats and I was born and brought up as a Democrat. But in 1904, when I cast my first vote for president, I voted for the Republican candidate, Theodore Roosevelt, because I thought he was a better Democrat than the Democratic candidates. If I had to do it all over again, I would not alter that vote."[63]

On March 4, 1904, Franklin and Eleanor sat just behind the president and his family at the east front of the Capitol and heard TR's characteristic call for vigor and effort, "without which the manlier and hardier virtues wither away."[64] Afterward they went to the White House for lunch with the president, watched the parade with him, and went to the inaugural ball that evening in the atrium of the old pension building.

The wedding was held in the twin town houses of Eleanor's great-aunt, Elizabeth Livingston Ludlow, and her daughter, Cousin Susie (Mrs. Henry) Parish, at 6–8 East Seventy-sixth Street. The formal drawing rooms of the two houses opened into each other and could accommodate two hundred guests, an elegant yet understated New York setting often used by the family on ceremonial occasions. Outside, on Fifth Avenue, the Saint Patrick's Day parade wound its way northward, the Ancient Order of Hibernians filling the air with "The Wearing of the Green." Moments before 3:30, the clatter of carriage horses signaled the arrival of the president, top-hatted and buoyant, a shamrock in his lapel, to give the bride away. As the orchestra commenced the wedding march from *Lohengrin,* Eleanor's six bridesmaids descended the circular staircase. Each wore a white silk gown, its sleeves embroidered with silver roses, with a demiveil and three silver-tipped ostrich feathers (the Roosevelt crest) in her hair. The six ushers wore tie pins with three Roosevelt feathers depicted in diamonds. Franklin and Lathrop Brown, his Harvard roommate who was standing in for Rosy as best man, wore formal morning attire.[65] The bride's satin wedding gown was covered with Grandmother Hall's rose-point Brussels lace, which Eleanor's mother had worn at her wedding. Her veil was secured with a diamond crescent that had belonged to her mother as well. As fate would have it, March 17 was also Anna's birthday.

When Reverend Peabody asked, "Who giveth this woman in marriage?," TR answered emphatically, "I do!" Hands were joined, rings and vows exchanged, and the rector pronounced Franklin and Eleanor man and wife. The president reached out to kiss the bride. "Well, Franklin," he exclaimed, "there's nothing like keeping the name in the family." TR then strode off to find the refreshments and the guests followed in his wake. Franklin and Eleanor trailed along. "We simply followed the crowd and listened with the rest," said Eleanor.[66] TR had upstaged the stars of the wedding and stolen the audience. Even the cutting of the wedding cake failed to attract many onlookers until the president was persuaded to come and get a slice. As TR's daughter Alice observed, "Father always wanted to be the bride at every wedding and the corpse at every funeral."[67]

FOUR

ALBANY

Frank, the men that are looking out of
that window are waiting for your answer.
They won't like to hear that you
had to ask your mother.

—ED PERKINS (DEMOCRATIC CHAIRMAN OF
DUTCHESS COUNTY) TO FDR, 1910

FDR LED A PERILOUS LIFE as a first-year law student. His classmate General William Donovan, who headed the Office of Strategic Services during World War II, later said that Roosevelt's most prominent characteristic at Columbia was his "daring"—a remarkable observation from a man who won the Medal of Honor leading New York's "Fighting Sixty-Ninth" in the Meuse-Argonne.[1] What Donovan meant was that after Groton and Harvard, Franklin had enormous confidence in himself—perhaps overconfidence—and he never let law school interfere with his personal life.

Following his wedding on Saint Patrick's Day, he and Eleanor departed for Springwood and a week's honeymoon. That contributed to the seventy-three absences FDR recorded his first year and helps explain why he initially failed two of his seven courses (contracts and civil procedure). "It certainly shows the uncertainty of marks," he wrote Sara. "I expected much lower marks in some of the others and failures in one, and thought I had done as well on the two I failed as in those I passed with B."[2] A Columbia professor saw it differently. Franklin, he said, had little aptitude for the law and "made no effort to overcome that handicap by hard work."[3] After studying haphazardly over the summer, FDR took makeup exams in contracts and civil procedure and easily passed both. His final grades were three Bs, three Cs, and a D, which placed him roughly in the middle of his class.[4]

FDR's attitude toward law school was similar to Ulysses S. Grant's view of West Point: it was a hurdle but should not be taken too seriously. At West Point, Grant—who also had enormous confidence in himself—read novels instead of field manuals and spent his free time painting in the studio of his art professor. At Columbia, FDR led an exhausting social life and wrote doggerel about his instructors:

> REDFIELD ON BLEATING*
> BAH! BAH! BAH!
> We are little bored sheep
> That have lost their way
>   Bah! Bah! Bah!
> Gentlemen lawyers off on a spree
> Wrong from here to eternity
> God ha' mercy on such as Redfield
> . Bah! Bah! Bah!

During the summer between first and second year, Franklin and Eleanor undertook a second honeymoon in Europe, much as James and Sara had done twenty-five years earlier. In England they dined with Whitelaw Reid, a long-time Hudson River neighbor and publisher of the *New York Tribune*, who had just taken up his duties as ambassador to the Court of St. James. In Scotland, visiting friends of Eleanor's parents, they had dinner with Sidney and Beatrice Webb. "They write books on sociology," Eleanor wrote Sara. "Franklin discussed the methods of learning at Harvard with the husband while I discussed the servant problem with the wife."[5] While in Scotland the honeymooners were asked to open a village flower show. Franklin did the honors. He was fortunate, he said, "in having had a Highland nurse, so that I passed my early years with kilts on the outside and oatmeal and scones on the interior." With a perfectly straight face FDR went on to tout the advantages of American vegetables: "Instead of water, we cook them nearly always in milk, and this, of course, makes them more nutritious, besides bringing out the flavor."[6]

---

* Written in pencil by Roosevelt on the flyleaf of his copy of Professor Henry S. Redfield's *Selected Cases on Code Pleading and Practice in New York*. Redfield was one of two professors who failed FDR.

From Scotland the couple went briefly to Paris, and from there to Milan, Verona, and Venice. Then the Dolomites, Switzerland, and the Black Forest. Their continental excursion lasted more than three months: Eleanor, Baedeker in hand, resolutely examining the monuments and masterpieces of Europe; Franklin, enjoying himself at the expense of one and all. In Venice, Eleanor pronounced the Titians on display "not among his best." Franklin loped ahead through the galleries of what he called the "Academica de Belly Arty" (Accademia dei Belle Arti) briefly perusing the paintings —"chiefly indecent infants sitting or falling off clouds—or sacred apostles trying to keep the sun out of their eyes."[7] In Cortina, Eleanor went to bed early and FDR attended the hotel dance alone. To Sara he wrote, "The hotel maids, cooks, and some of the villagers did a *Schuhplattler*—the native dance. It beats a cake walk and a court quadrille all to pieces. . . . I danced with Mme. Menardi [the proprietress], and talked to the cook and smoked with a porter and had the time of my life."[8]

In St. Moritz they stayed with Aunt Tissie and her husband, Stanley Mortimer, who summered there regularly. Then back to Paris for an extended stay with Aunt Dora (Sara's sister) and Uncle Paul Forbes, who had made the City of Light their permanent home.[9] They were entertained by Cousin Hortense Howland, a sparkling Parisian who was the sister-in-law of FDR's father, James, by his first marriage, and whose salon was described by Marcel Proust in *Remembrance of Things Past*. "You would have laughed if you could have heard Mrs. Howland flatter Franklin," wrote Eleanor.[10] While in Paris, Franklin and Eleanor had their fortunes told by a French clairvoyant. "E. is to inherit a fortune," FDR wrote Sara, "and I am to be President of the U.S. or the Equitable, I couldn't make out which."[11] Harvard friends seemed to be everywhere. One evening Franklin and his classmates took Eleanor and Aunt Dora to a naughty French farce. Eleanor was shocked. "I confess my Anglo-Saxon sense of humor was somewhat strained," she remembered.[12]

Throughout the trip Franklin teased Sara about his and Eleanor's purchases and the money they were spending. From London he wrote that they stayed in the Royal Suite at Brown's Hotel for £1,000 a night (actual cost £36). In Paris he reported buying "thousands of dollars worth of linen. . . . Eleanor got a dozen dresses. . . . I am getting Eleanor a long sable coat and a silver fox coat for myself." From Venice, "3 or 4 old tapestries and a Tintoretto—the latter in his best style. . . . Also an old library—about 3000 books—and had them shipped to London." Back in Paris, "I got some Rembrandt engravings and a cunning little sketch by Claude Lorraine." At one point he suggested they were planning to expand the trip into a tour around the world—"It is only a step or two." At another he suggested buying the woodwork and mosaic floor tiles from an old Venetian palace: "It can be got for about $60,000. If you care to have it cable me."[13]

From Europe the newlyweds pressed Sara to find a house for them, preferably the rental property of their Dutchess County friends the Drapers, at 125 East Thirty-sixth Street—just three blocks from Sara's Madison Avenue address. "It is just the right situation and size for us," wrote Franklin. "Our one hope is to hear very soon that you have got it for us. It would be so nice to feel that all is settled before we return."[14] Eleanor wrote Sara, "you are an angel to take so much trouble about the house, but I am glad you are going to see it and I do hope you will take it if it is possible."[15] When Sara replied that she had taken the house for two years, Eleanor was delighted. "We are so glad and think you have done wonders for us. It is very nice that the work can be begun before we get home . . . and we will get settled so much sooner than if we waited to choose a house on our return."[16]

The Draper house was temporary. At Christmas 1905, Sara informed Franklin and Eleanor that she was building a town house for them. "A Christmas present from Mama—number and street not yet quite decided." The following year Sara bought an expensive plot on East Sixty-fifth Street just off Park Avenue and hired a well-known architect, Charles A. Platt, to draw plans for two adjoining houses—one for herself and one for Franklin and Eleanor— similar to the Ludlow-Parish houses on East Seventy-sixth Street. The drawing rooms and dining rooms of the two houses opened into each other, there were connecting doors on the upper floors, and a common vestibule. Construction began in the spring of 1907 and was completed the following year. Sara retained title to both houses, and upon her death in 1941 FDR sold them to the Hillel Foundation of Hunter College for a modest price.[17]

Franklin, who loved to design things, immersed himself in the construction of the houses and worked constantly with the architect, the builder, and the decorators. Eleanor was consulted but chose not to become involved. "Instead of taking an interest in these houses, one of which I was to live in, I left everything to my mother-in-law and my husband."[18] One evening shortly after they moved in, Franklin found his wife in tears. This was not her home, she sobbed. She had not helped plan it, and it was not the way she wanted to live. FDR was bewildered. Why hadn't she said something before? he asked. They had gone over the plans together—why hadn't she spoken up?[19]

As Eleanor recalled the incident, "he thought I was quite mad and told me so gently, and said I would feel different in a little while and left me alone until I should become calmer."[20] FDR avoided further friction simply by refusing to recognize that a problem existed. That was a trait he would hone to an art form in public life. "If something was unpleasant and he didn't want to know about it, he just ignored it and never talked about it," said Eleanor. "I think he always thought that if you ignored a thing long enough it would settle itself."[21]

In the summer of 1909 Sara gave Eleanor and Franklin a second house—a thirty-four-room, three-story, seaside "cottage" nestled on ten acres of prime Campobello shoreline. The expansive house, constructed along the lines of the Arts and Crafts Movement, had been built in 1898 by the Hartman Kuhn family of Boston and stood next to the Roosevelt house, separated by a tall hemlock hedge. This time Sara transferred full title to Franklin: "a belated wedding gift," as she expressed it. For Eleanor the house was a godsend, the first dwelling she felt she owned. Mrs. Kuhn had left all the furnishings, linen, crystal, and silver, and ER spent weeks rearranging things. "I have moved every room in the house around," she wrote Franklin, "and I hope you will like the change." Eleanor never tired of the place. "There was no telephone . . . no electricity," she remembered. "There was a little coal stove on which you did all your cooking, and the lamps sometimes smoked, and you went to bed by candlelight. But it had great charm."[22]*

---

* Except for the wicker furniture, there was little rustic about the Kuhn-Roosevelt "cottage." In addition to the extensive manicured lawns extending to the water's edge, there were four full baths, two butler's pantries, seven fireplaces, and a full-size laundry. It required a staff of eight to operate. After FDR contracted polio, the cottage was used sparingly. In 1952 the house and all of its furnishings were sold to the financier Armand Hammer. Hammer carefully restored it, installed electricity, and offered Eleanor full use whenever she wished. After ER's death in 1962 Hammer donated the property to the U.S. and Canadian governments, which jointly established the Roosevelt Campobello International Park. See Jonas Klein, *Beloved Island: Franklin and Eleanor and the Legacy of Campobello* (Forest Dale, Vt.: Paul S. Eriksson, 2000).

Financially, Franklin and Eleanor were well provided for. Between them, they had trust-fund income of a little over $12,000—the rough equivalent of $240,000 after-tax dollars one hundred years later.* Yet their combined incomes were insufficient to support their lifestyle. Eleanor and Franklin were not members of the fastest, richest set in New York, but they lived in three different houses at various seasons of the year, always employed at least five servants, maintained a large yacht and numerous smaller boats, automobiles, and carriages, dressed in fashion, belonged to expensive clubs, traveled extensively, and gave generously to political and charitable causes. Sara subsidized the shortfall. As her grandson Elliott recalled, "Granny was generous to a fault. Whenever Father needed help, he had only to ask for it, and he usually had no need to ask, because Granny anticipated what he or Mother wanted and was ready with a check, cash or a gift in kind."[23]

Midway through his third year at Columbia, Franklin took the grueling eight-hour New York bar examination and passed handily. He was immediately admitted to practice and at that point dropped his courses at Columbia and never took a degree. Twenty-two years later, Roosevelt, then governor of New York, was invited to address the Columbia Law School Alumni Dinner. Columbia's president, Nicholas Murray Butler, sat next to him, chatting affably. At some point Butler was overheard joking with FDR on his failure to obtain an LL.B. "You will never be able to call yourself an intellectual until you come back to Columbia and pass your law exams." Franklin flashed his famous grin: "That just shows how unimportant the law really is."[24]

The young Roosevelts spent the summer of 1907 relaxing at Campobello and Hyde Park. Anna, their firstborn, was a one-year-old toddler. Eleanor was pregnant once more, and their second child, James, named for FDR's father, would be born in December. In their first ten years of marriage, Franklin and Eleanor would have six children, one of whom would die in infancy.† Later, Eleanor would write, "For ten years I was always just getting

---

* FDR received approximately $5,000 annually from the trust fund his father established. ER's inheritance produced a little over $7,000, the principal invested primarily in New York Central Railroad stocks and bonds, administered by Cousin Henry Parish, vice president of the Chemical Bank.

† Anna Eleanor (May 3, 1906); James (December 23, 1907); Franklin Delano, Jr. (March 18, 1909–November 8, 1909); Elliott (September 23, 1910); Franklin Delano, Jr. (August 7, 1914); and John Aspinwall (March 13, 1916).

over having a baby or about to have one, and so my occupations were considerably restricted."[25]

Unlike Sara, who handled every detail of FDR's childhood, Eleanor delegated the raising of her children to a succession of nurses and caregivers. "I had never any interest in dolls or little children," she wrote, "and I knew absolutely nothing about handling or feeding a baby." Having heard that fresh air was good for babies, Eleanor ordered a small chicken wire cage constructed and, placing Anna in it, hung the contraption out a rear window at the town house in New York. It was on the north side of the building, cold and shady, and the baby often cried, but Eleanor paid no attention. Finally, an irate neighbor threatened to report the Roosevelts to the Society for the Prevention of Cruelty to Children. "This was rather a shock for me," Eleanor recalled, "for I thought I was being a very modern mother."[26]

Years later Eleanor acknowledged that she had been completely unprepared to be a practical housekeeper, wife, or mother. "If I had it to do over again, I know now that what we should have done was to have no servants in those first few years. . . . However, my bringing-up had been such that this never occurred to me, and neither did it occur to any of the older people who were closest to me. Had I done this, my subsequent troubles would have been avoided and my children would have had far happier childhoods."[27]

For his part, Franklin, like his father, left the child rearing to his wife. "Father's attitude on nurses and other household affairs was strictly hands off," said his son James.[28] When the children were older, FDR enjoyed roughhousing with his "chicks," taking them riding at Hyde Park, and sailing at Campobello. "Father was fun," said Anna. "He would sometimes romp with me on the floor or carry me around on his shoulders."[29] The children adored "Pa," who seemed much warmer than their straitlaced mother. He was like a favorite uncle who entertained them, while Eleanor was the disciplinarian.*

---

* Even within the family, FDR kept his feelings largely to himself. After the death of their infant son Franklin, Jr., in 1910, Roosevelt quietly joined the board of the New York Milk Committee, to help combat infant mortality. Franklin, Jr., had been bottle-fed, and the death rate for bottle-fed infants in the city was extremely high—over a thousand babies died in Manhattan alone the summer Franklin, Jr., fell ill. The trouble was traced to unpasteurized or adulterated milk drunk from unsterilized bottles. The Milk Committee ran a chain of storefront milk stations in the poorest sections of the city, which provided pure milk and free medical advice to mothers unable to afford either. See Geoffrey C. Ward, *A*

In September 1907 Franklin joined the distinguished Wall Street firm of Carter, Ledyard and Milburn as one of five unsalaried apprentices. "I know you will be glad to start," wrote Sara. "Try to arrange for systematic air and exercise and keep away from brokers' offices, this advice free gratis for nothing."[30]

Carter, Ledyard and Milburn was one of the most prestigious law firms in the nation. It had a large general practice and was executor of the Astor estate, but its major source of income was corporate law, at which it had few equals. James Carter, the firm's founder, was so highly respected at the appellate bar that the attorney general of the United States engaged him to argue the government's case before the Supreme Court in *Pollock v. Farmers' Loan and Trust* in 1894, the great income tax case.[31] Louis Cass Ledyard, an intimate of J. P. Morgan, played a vital role in arresting the Wall Street Panic of 1907, served as counsel for both the Morgan Bank and United States Steel, and later represented the American Tobacco Company in antitrust litigation before the Supreme Court.[32] John G. Milburn, the third senior partner, was counsel for John D. Rockefeller's Standard Oil cartel in an equally well publicized antitrust suit in 1911.[33] Milburn himself had clerked for Grover Cleveland in his Buffalo law office, and it was at Milburn's home in Buffalo that William McKinley died after being shot by an anarchist in 1901.[34]

FDR had little passion for the law, but he was a fast learner blessed with an avuncular, ingratiating personality. "He had a sanguine temperament, almost adolescent in its buoyancy," a fellow clerk recalled.[35] Franklin wrote Sara that he was a "full-fledged office boy." Like his fellow apprentices, he kept dockets for the partners, looked up cases for them, answered calendar calls, recorded deeds, and ran all manner of errands. After a while he took on minor cases in the municipal courts, and during his second year he was made managing clerk in charge of municipal cases.* The following year he moved on to the firm's admiralty division, one of the nation's most lustrous. As numerous observers have noted, there was always a whiff of the sea at Carter, Ledyard. Cass Ledyard succeeded J. P. Morgan as commodore of the exclusive New York Yacht Club,

---

First-Class Temperament: The Emergence of Franklin Roosevelt 102–103 (New York: Harper & Row, 1989).

* FDR proved adept at the law when he chose to apply himself. Legend at Carter, Ledyard and Milburn holds that when Franklin was managing clerk he was one day sent by John Milburn to municipal court to settle eight or nine minor suits against the American Express Company,

and Edmund L. Baylies, head of the admiralty section, was president of and principal fund-raiser for the Seamen's Church Institute. Franklin became a director of the institute and a member of the Yacht Club. But even the laws of the sea had little appeal for FDR. He was perpetually good-humored and energetic but made little secret of his desire to move on.

Grenville Clark, a Harvard classmate who was a fellow clerk at the firm, recalled FDR in those early years. "We were a small group," said Clark, "and in our leisure hours sometimes fell into discussions of our hopes and ambitions. I remember him saying with engaging frankness that he wasn't going to practice law forever, that he intended to run for office at the first opportunity, and that he wanted to be and thought he had a real chance to be President. I remember that he described very accurately the steps which he thought could lead to this goal. They were: first, a seat in the State Assembly, then an appointment as Assistant Secretary of the Navy , , , and finally the governorship of New York. 'Anyone who is governor of New York has a good chance to be president,' he said.* I do not recall that even then, in 1907, any of us deprecated his ambition or even smiled at it as we might have done. It seemed proper and sincere and moreover, as he put it, entirely reasonable."

Clark went on to say that FDR not only had made politics his profession for thirty-five years "but had adopted that profession deliberately and constantly enjoyed it, just as one enjoys a game that one has always liked and learned to play well."[36] FDR's friend Cornelius Vanderbilt, Jr., made the same point somewhat differently. Had Franklin not gone into politics, said Vanderbilt, he would have been "just another corporate lawyer, summering in Newport and hibernating on Wall Street."[37]

---

one of the firm's principal clients. Milburn instructed FDR to take $1,000 from the cashier and pay what was necessary. Later that afternoon the firm's cashier reported to Milburn that Roosevelt had just come back and returned the $1,000. Milburn immediately called Franklin into his office and demanded an explanation. "Oh," said Roosevelt. "When they called the cases, I tried them all and won." Francis M. Ellis and Edward F. Clark, Jr., *A Brief History of Carter, Ledyard & Milburn* 115–116 (Portsmouth, N.H.: Peter E. Randall, 1988).

* At first blush, FDR's statement appears somewhat grandiose. Until his election in 1932, only three New York governors had been elected president: Martin Van Buren (1836), Grover Cleveland (1884 and 1892), and TR (1904). But from the perspective of 1907, when FDR was speaking, his assertion warrants greater credence. New York cast almost 10 percent of the total electoral vote, and three of the last six presidential victors had indeed been New York governors.

Political lightning struck in the summer of 1910. As FDR remembered it, he was kidnapped off the streets of Poughkeepsie—"one of the first cases of deliberate kidnapping on record"—and taken to the Dutchess County policemen's picnic. "On that joyous occasion of clams and sauerkraut and real beer I made my first speech, and I have been apologizing for it ever since."[38]

Hyperbole aside, the Democratic leadership of Dutchess County did indeed make the initial overture to FDR. But never was a victim more eager to accompany his abductors. Because of the large working-class vote in Poughkeepsie, Dutchess County was one of the few Democratic strongholds in upstate New York.* And for a political novice seeking entry to the state legislature, there were few opportunities so golden.

The first feelers were extended by Judge John E. Mack, the district attorney of Dutchess County and one of three members of the Democratic party's executive committee. Mack had been a friend of FDR's father, James, and owned a 100-acre farm in Clove Valley where he raised prizewinning peonies. In the folksy manner of upstate New York he called himself "a Dutchess County farmer who does a little lawyering on the side." Beneath the folksiness lay cunning political instinct. Mack was virtually unbeatable at the polls. He endeared himself to his Irish and Italian constituents in Poughkeepsie by not prosecuting public drunks provided they sign a release asking him to lock them up for six months should they be arrested again. Mack's rationale was based on the theory "All dogs get one bite." And it was a surefire winner in the immigrant community. He courted the rural vote equally assiduously by prosecuting chicken thieves for the more serious crime of burglary rather than petty larceny. Mack prided himself on being able to hear the political grass grow beneath the soil, and in the early summer of 1910 he engineered an excuse to call on FDR at Carter, Ledyard and Milburn. Some documents, it seems, needed Sara's signature. Rather than mail them, he thought he'd drop them by personally.

FDR received Mack warmly. When their business was completed, the talk turned to politics. The Democrats were in trouble in Dutchess County, Mack told Franklin. The incumbent Democratic assemblyman, Lewis Stuyvesant

---

* In the 1909 election, the Democrats won all countywide offices and twenty of the twenty-seven town supervisors. See Alfred B. Rollins, Jr., *Roosevelt and Howe* 18 (New York: Alfred A. Knopf, 1962).

Chanler of Barrytown, wanted to retire. A descendent of John Jacob Astor on his maternal side, Chanler had been elected lieutenant governor in 1906. In 1908 he won the party's gubernatorial nomination, only to lose the election to Charles Evans Hughes. After exposure to statewide politics, Chanler was bored with being a mere assemblyman and was thinking of stepping down. If he did, would Franklin consider running? FDR could scarcely believe his good fortune. The Second Assembly District was as safe a Democratic seat as any outside the Solid South. Nothing would please him more, he told the judge. Mack casually suggested that FDR spend some time on weekends in Poughkeepsie getting to know local Democrats and let it go at that. There was no offer, merely an inquiry.*

Two weeks later, Edward E. Perkins, president of the First National Bank of Poughkeepsie, who was also the Democratic state committeeman for Dutchess County, invited Franklin to a dispersal sale of high-grade Guernseys on the Reece farm in Wappinger Falls. They could run down and pick up some good ones, said Perkins. On the way home, after inspecting the cattle, Perkins confirmed to FDR that Lewis Chanler did not wish to run again. Would Franklin be interested? "I'd like to talk to my mother first," Roosevelt replied.

They drove on to Poughkeepsie and pulled into a parking spot in front of Perkins's bank. "Frank," he said, "the men that are looking out that window are waiting for your answer. They won't like to hear that you had to ask your mother."

"I'll take it," said Franklin.[39]

If the New York legislative seat was certain for the Democrats, why was the party leadership so eager to bestow it on a neophyte like FDR? The decision was not as bizarre as it might appear. For the men who ran the county, a seat in the New York Assembly was small potatoes. The important offices were sheriff, tax assessor, county clerk, the various town supervisors, the judges and

* On election eve in November 1932, Roosevelt received a letter from Edwin De Turck Bechtel, a leading partner at Carter, Ledyard, who had been a fellow clerk with FDR at the firm and had been in the bullpen with him when Judge Mack discussed Dutchess County politics. "It thrills me," Bechtel wrote, "to realize that your decision in 1910 as you sat at your old roll-top desk at 54 Wall Street and the political principles which you chose then and have always followed should have led to such a marvelous goal." Enclosed with the letter were photostats of two pages from the ledger FDR kept as managing clerk "as a reminder of old times." Legal Papers, Roosevelt Family Papers, FDRL.

prosecuting attorneys—positions that levied taxes, spent money, and enforced the law. The assembly seat was a low-paying, part-time job in Albany. Second, while Poughkeepsie was safely Democratic, the rural areas of the county tilted Republican. It was useful to have someone on the ticket who could appeal to conservative voters in the countryside. In 1910, all New York counties employed the party-column ballot. Straight-ticket voting was the rule, and successful party leaders always sought a balanced ticket: a name or two on the ballot that would reassure the district's farmers and small-town residents. At the national level, that traditionally dictated the choice of presidential running mates (FDR's 1932 selection of John Nance Garner, for example), and the same calculus applied at county level. The Roosevelt name was a tremendous drawing card, and a Democratic Roosevelt on the ticket might galvanize the rural voters of Dutchess County. Finally, electoral campaigns were expensive—even in 1910. And FDR (or at least Sara) had deep pockets. "I guess several people thought that I would be a gold mine," Franklin said later, "but unfortunately the gold was not there." Not quite true. When party fund-raisers came calling, the Roosevelts eventually coughed up $2,500—about $50,000 in current value, a substantial sum for a seat in the state legislature.[40]

Sara had little difficulty with Franklin's decision. Her father had gone to China twice with nothing in his pocket, and twice he had returned with a fortune. The risks of political life, the winner-take-all aspect of a campaign, and the high-stakes rewards appealed to her Delano instincts. TR had started small and made it to the White House. Sara had no doubt that her son was as gifted as his Oyster Bay cousin, and she understood the advantage her personal fortune gave to FDR. She would have preferred that he make a brilliant career at the law; she would have been even more pleased if he had chosen to be a country squire like James; but if Franklin wanted politics, she resolved to make the best of it. As her friend Rita Halle Kleeman put it, "All her life Sara had been accustomed to accepting the decisions of the men in the family whom she loved and respected. From the moment she heard Franklin make his simple, sincere declaration of principles, she accepted his decision and knew that it was wise."[41] And when Sara embraced a decision, she did so without reservation. Within days she was referring to the surrounding countryside as "Franklin's district."[42]

Many years later, sitting at Springwood on election night awaiting the presidential returns, Sara reflected on that first campaign. "I shall never forget it," she said. "I was one of the few sympathizers Franklin had among his own people. Many of our friends said it was a shame for so fine a young man to associate with 'dirty' politicians. Some of them hoped he would be defeated for his own sake and learn a lesson. I knew only that I would always be proud of him [and] I was indeed happy when he won."[43]*

Franklin discussed the matter with Eleanor, and she too was delighted.[44] But he did not ask her approval. "I listened to all his plans with interest," she said later. "It never occurred to me that I had any part to play. I felt I must acquiesce in whatever he might decide and be willing to go to Albany if he should be elected."[45]

A greater question mark for FDR was cousin Theodore. TR had just returned from a twelve-month safari in East Africa ("I hope every lion will do his duty," J. P. Morgan quipped on the eve of TR's departure) and was beginning to thrash around in the politics of the Empire State. If he should campaign in Dutchess County and say anything remotely disparaging about his Democratic kinsman, it would end Franklin's political career before it began. FDR hesitated to approach the former president directly but with Sara's encouragement laid the problem before Bamie, who visited Campobello that summer. As FDR hoped, Bamie wrote to her brother immediately. "Franklin ought to go into politics without the least regard as to where I speak or don't speak," TR replied on August 10. "Franklin is a fine fellow," he told Bamie, although he wished he were a Republican.[46] FDR correctly interpreted the former presi-

---

* Sara, understandably, was never happy with the rough-edged politicians and less-than-couth newsmen FDR brought to Springwood, nor with the mannish social workers Eleanor escorted in the 1920s, but she was always gracious to them. "I have always believed that a mother should be friends with her children's friends," she gamely put it. The one exception was Louisiana senator Huey Long, whom she could not abide. In the autumn of 1932, Senator Long visited Hyde Park to discuss campaign strategy with FDR. (The Kingfish had personally intimidated the wavering Arkansas and Mississippi delegations to keep them in line on the crucial third ballot at the Democratic convention, and Roosevelt owed him.) Always a flamboyant dresser, Long was attired in a loud checkered suit, orchid shirt, and a watermelon pink necktie, which was garish even for him. FDR received Long affably and invited him to lunch, where they continued their conversation, leaving the other guests to talk among themselves. During a momentary lull in the conversation, Sara could be heard sotto voce from her end of the table: "Who is that *awful* man sitting on my son's right?" When asked later by newsmen about his opinion of FDR, Long said, "I like him. But by God, I feel sorry for him. He's got even more sonsofbitches in his family than I got in mine." T. Harry Williams, *Huey Long* 601–602 (New York: Alfred A. Knopf, 1969).

dent's reply as a green light. When TR spoke before a throng of 40,000 well-wishers at the Dutchess County Fair later that autumn, he refrained from mentioning either Franklin or his Republican opponent.

FDR's fledgling campaign ended before it began. In mid-September, three weeks before the Democrats held their nominating caucus, Lewis Chanler announced for reelection. He was not stepping down. The Assembly might be dull, but it was far livelier than no office at all. Franklin felt snakebitten. He went to Mack and Perkins and threatened to run as an independent. Mack knew Roosevelt was serious. "Why not run for the Senate?" he asked. For a second time, FDR could scarcely believe his good fortune. The State Senate seemed far more attractive than the Assembly, although the odds of winning were slight: Mack put them at one chance in five. The Senate seat comprised Dutchess, Putnam, and Columbia counties, the three counties stacked one above the other along the east bank of the Hudson. The district was thirty miles wide and ninety miles long, and, with one exception, no Democrat had won the seat since 1856.[47] The Republican incumbent, Senator John F. Schlosser of Fishkill Landing, was a well-known lawyer, seasoned campaigner, and president of the State Volunteer Firemen's Association. His 2-to-1 margin of victory in 1908 made him appear invincible. Roosevelt was undeterred. Youth and inexperience melded with the patrician confidence instilled at Springwood, Groton, and Harvard. Franklin exuded confidence in victory from the first day of the campaign.

"I accept this nomination with absolute independence," FDR told the Democratic caucus in Poughkeepsie on October 6. "I am pledged to no man; I am influenced by no special interests. . . . In the coming campaign, I need not tell you that I do not intend to stand still. We are going to have a very strenuous month [and] we have little to fear from the result on November eighth."[48]

Roosevelt opened the campaign with a rally on Bank Square in the center of Fishkill Landing, the home of Senator Schlosser, the idea being to cause as much consternation as possible. The Democratic organization could be counted upon to deliver the votes in Poughkeepsie and the other towns in the district, so Roosevelt carried his fight to the countryside. Election day was only a month away, and to cover the three counties he rented a fire-engine red, open-top Maxwell touring car. To drive the car, which had two cylinders and no windshield, FDR engaged Harry Hawkey, an itinerant Poughkeepsie piano tuner with an encyclopedic knowledge of backcountry roads gleaned from years of calling on customers. The cost for car and driver was $20 a day, a fee few legislative candidates could afford.

The idea of campaigning by automobile was risky. Cars were still luxury items in rural New York, and to use one might remind voters unnecessarily of Franklin's silk-stocking pedigree. Far more serious was the possibility of an accident. Farmers didn't like automobiles because they frightened their horses. In fact, New York law gave the right-of-way to horse-drawn vehicles. "When we met a horse or a team—and that was about every half mile or so," said FDR, "we had to stop, not only the car but the engine as well."[49] But the experiment proved a whopping success. Wheezing along at the dazzling speed of twenty miles an hour, Roosevelt crisscrossed the district as no candidate had done before. The flag-draped little car soon caught people's attention.* Even the mandatory horse stops worked to FDR's advantage. Farmers were duly impressed with the candidate's deference, and Franklin used the halts to chat up the teamsters and anyone else in the vicinity.

For companionship, and to learn the tricks of the campaign trail, Franklin invited Richard E. Connell, the editor of the *Poughkeepsie News-Press* and perennial Democratic nominee for Congress, to accompany him. Connell was a gifted stump speaker in the florid style of William Jennings Bryan and began each of his orations by referring to his audience as "My Friends"—a phrase Roosevelt quickly adopted as his own. It was also Connell who advised FDR to discard the pince-nez he had worn since Groton. Made him look snooty, said Connell.

For four exhausting weeks, Franklin, Connell, and Hawkey spent day after day on the dusty back roads of Dutchess, Putnam, and Columbia counties, giving the same speeches as often as ten times a day. They spoke from the porches of general stores, atop hay wagons, in dairy barns, at village crossroads, sometimes standing on the backseat of the old Maxwell itself—any place where a group of farmers could be brought together. "I think I worked harder with Franklin than I ever have in my life," said Hawkey afterward.[50]

FDR was having the time of his life. Nothing seemed to lessen his enthusiasm for jumping into a crowd, pumping hands, and making friends. He was "a

---

* Twenty-two years later, FDR would capture the nation's attention by flying from Albany to Chicago to accept the Democratic nomination for president—the first presidential candidate to use an airplane during a campaign.

top-notch salesman," a Hyde Park housepainter, Tom Leonard, remembered. "He wouldn't immediately enter into the topic of politics when he met a group. He would approach them as a friend and would lead up to that . . . with that smile of his."[51]

No roadside gathering was too small for Franklin. He startled a gang of Italian railroad workers repairing track near Brewster by leaping from his car into their midst, chattering away in what they slowly realized was his own version of Italian—a cross between textbook French and the Latin he had learned at Groton.[52]

Occasionally Roosevelt's enthusiasm got the best of him. Campaigning in the Harlem Valley on the eastern edge of the district late one afternoon, he stopped in front of a small-town saloon, rushed inside, and invited everyone to have a drink. "What town is this?" he asked the bartender. "Sharon, Connecticut," said the man pouring drinks. FDR paid up, passed out campaign buttons, and told the story on himself for years.[53]

As the campaign wore on, Judge Mack recognized that FDR was a natural. His speech making was still awkward, but he had an uncanny ability to persuade his audience. Women's suffrage did not come to New York until 1917, but an increasing number of ladies began to attend Franklin's rallies, especially those in the evening. "They came to see as well as hear the handsomest candidate that ever asked for votes in their district," said Mack. "Franklin was so good looking he might have stepped out of a magazine cover."[54]

Roosevelt was his own campaign manager. He ordered up 2,500 campaign buttons, designed 500 posters for storefront windows throughout the district, and personally wrote checks to pay for advertisements he placed in each of the twenty-four county newspapers, ranging from the Amenia *Times* to the Wappinger *Chronicle*. His platform was entirely personal and avoided substantive issues that might trigger opposition. "I want to represent you, the people of these counties, and no one else," he told an October rally in Hudson. "I am pledged to no man, to no special interest, to no boss. I want to stay on the job representing you twelve months of the year."[55] Later, he would write with disarming candor, "During the campaign . . . I made no promises in regard to particular legislation."[56] Instead, he identified himself with good government and blasted away at the "rotten corruption of the New York legislature and the extravagant mismanagement of the State administration."[57]

Nineteen-ten proved to be a banner year for the Democrats. Riding a wave of protest against the complacency of the Taft administration in Washington, the party picked up ten seats in the United States Senate and more than half the governorships (including Princeton president Woodrow Wilson in New Jersey) and won a majority in the House of Representatives for the first time since 1892. The GOP debacle was greatest in New York, where the party lost the governorship, both houses of the legislature, and two thirds of the seats in Congress.

FDR was a direct beneficiary of the Democratic landslide, which, in New York at least, was partially attributable to Cousin Theodore's reentry into political life. In a preview of the 1912 presidential election, TR took up the cudgels for reform, lambasted the party's old guard, and split the GOP down the middle. The issues were tailor-made for TR. Governor Charles Evans Hughes had been locked in a bitter struggle with Republican regulars and old-line Democrats over electoral reform. Hughes sought to introduce direct primaries for party nominations to state office—an innovation that threatened the power of both the GOP bosses in Albany and the Tammany leadership in New York City. But Hughes was elevated to the Supreme Court before the battle was won. When the bosses combined to defeat the measure, Teddy jumped into the fight. At the Republican state convention in Saratoga on September 27, TR wrested control of the party apparatus from the old guard, forced the nomination of his friend Henry L. Stimson for governor, and dictated a reformist platform. Party regulars responded by sitting on their hands during the election.

Franklin capitalized on the Republican split. He lashed out at political bosses in both parties, fighting alongside his illustrious cousin against graft, privilege, and corruption. Asked at a farm rally whether he supported Governor Hughes's policies, FDR replied, "You bet I do. I think he is one of the best governors the State has ever had."[58] Since his opponent, Schlosser, had voted against the election reform bill, the lines were drawn. The cadences of political rhetoric came naturally to Roosevelt: "I don't know who Senator Schlosser represents," he told a gathering at the Quaker meetinghouse in Clinton Corners. "But I do know that he hasn't represented me and I do know that he hasn't represented you."[59]

The Republicans initially paid no attention to FDR. But as the campaign drew to a close, panic set in. In the final week, Hamilton Fish, who represented

Dutchess County in Congress,* attacked Franklin as a carpetbagger who lived in Manhattan, not Hyde Park. His automobile campaign, said Fish, was nothing more than a cheap "vaudeville tour for the benefit of the farmers."[60] The *Poughkeepsie Eagle,* which had otherwise ignored FDR, now railed against his ties to big business: "Franklin D. Roosevelt represents just the opposite of what Theodore Roosevelt stands for. The *News-Press* reports him as managing clerk of the firm of Carter, Ledyard and Milburn of 54 Wall Street. It is well for the electors of this Senatorial District to bear in mind that this firm are the lawyers for some of the great trusts which are being prosecuted by President Taft's administration, such as the Standard Oil Co., and the Sugar Trust."[61] Schlosser, who had conducted what amounted to a front-porch campaign, joined the fray with a vituperative attack on FDR's patrician origins and dandified appearance. Roosevelt responded by renewing his attack on Schlosser's subservience to the GOP bosses in Albany. "I had a particularly disagreeable opponent," FDR remembered years later. "He called me names . . . and I answered in kind. And the names I called him were worse than the names he called me. So we had a joyous campaign."[62]

FDR closed out the race with an election-eve rally in Hyde Park. With Eleanor and Sara at his side, he told his fellow townsmen, "You have known what my father stood for before me, you have known how close he was to the life of this town, and I do not need to tell you that it is my desire always to follow in his footsteps."[63]

November 8, election day, dawned gray and rainy—a good omen for Democrats, who always prayed for bad weather upstate to keep the Republican faithful indoors. FDR voted early and returned to Springwood to await the results. As the returns trickled in that evening, it quickly became apparent that the state and the nation were undergoing one of those defining moments when political power passes from one party to the other. The Democrats swept everything in sight. Republican Henry Stimson suffered a crushing defeat for governor, Richard Connell upset Hamilton Fish in the race for Congress, and Roosevelt carried more than two thirds of the precincts in the Twenty-sixth

---

* Hamilton Fish [II] was the son of *the* Hamilton Fish, who served successively as governor of New York, U.S. senator, and Grant's secretary of state for eight years. Fish II served in Congress for only one term (1909–1911) and is the father of Hamilton Fish, Jr., who subsequently held the seat from 1920 to 1945 and delighted in tweaking FDR.

Senatorial District, defeating Schlosser 15,708 to 14,568—an unprecedented Democratic majority.

But it was not just the Democratic avalanche that propelled FDR into office. He outspent Schlosser five to one; he outcampaigned and outorganized him by an even greater margin; and he led the entire Democratic ticket.[64] He ran almost as well in the countryside as he did in Poughkeepsie, carried Hyde Park 406–258, and defeated Schlosser on his home turf in Fishkill.

Sara watched the returns as avidly as Franklin, proudly noting the results in her firm Delano hand on a sheet of personal stationery: "Franklin carried Poughkeepsie by 927 . . . carried Hudson by 499 . . . Fishkill 128 . . . Second Assembly district of Dutchess 900." Sara was not surprised. "I have always thought Franklin perfectly extraordinary," she once said, "and, as I look back, I don't think he has ever disappointed me."[65]

At the age of twenty-eight, Roosevelt had found his calling. He passed out two dozen expensive cigars to friends and relatives and settled in to savor his victory. It was a singular personal triumph. He had run strongly in the rural reaches of the district, where party professionals had thought he had little chance. And the pros took notice. When "Big Tim" Sullivan, the Tammany wheelhorse who represented the Bowery in the Senate, heard that TR's cousin was going to be a colleague, he told friends, "If we've caught a Roosevelt, we'd better take him down and drop him off the dock. The Roosevelts run true to form, and this kid is likely to do for us what the Colonel is going to do for the Republican party, split it wide open."[66]

New York legislators earned $1,500 a year. The session rarely lasted more than ten weeks, and most members either commuted or stayed in one of the half-dozen tourist-class hotels and boardinghouses that catered to transient lawmakers. Hyde Park was sixty-five miles from Albany on the main Delaware & Hudson rail line and FDR might have easily commuted, yet he chose to convert his election victory into a full-time career as a state senator. Skeptics might argue it was a rich man's hobby: Franklin could not have established himself in the capital without his trust-fund income and Sara's largesse. But FDR was committed. As he told the voters in Hudson, he intended to stay on the job in Albany "twelve months of the year."

In mid-November Franklin went to Albany to find a suitable house. "I suppose I must have gone [with Franklin] and looked at the house which we took, though I have no recollection of doing so," Eleanor said many years later.[67]

What the Roosevelts found was a massive three-story brownstone in the Flemish Renaissance style favored by wealthy moguls living upstate. The house was situated on a one-acre lot at 248 State Street, virtually in the shadow of the capitol. "It is quite a big house with a piazza and a big yard . . . and built more like a country house," Eleanor wrote to her friend Isabella Ferguson in Tucson.[68] Franklin called it "palatial." Sara said it was "a fine house that could be made comfortable."[69] The large downstairs rooms provided ample space for entertaining, and there was an enormous paneled library at the rear and more than enough room on the second and third floors for their three children, the children's nurses, and a household staff of six. The rent was $400 a month—$4,800 annually, or more than three times FDR's senatorial salary. Later the Roosevelts moved into even larger quarters at 4 Elk Street, known as "Quality Row" for the affluent Albany families that lived along it. That mansion had been built by Martin Van Buren when he was governor—the first New York governor to reach the White House—and reflected Little Van's penchant for lavish living.

The legislature convened on January 4, with the Democrats in control of both houses. The Assembly was led by the thirty-seven-year-old Alfred E. Smith, a seven-term veteran from the Lower East Side, son of an Irish mother and an Italian-German father, a vital cog in the Tammany organization who despite an eighth-grade education had demonstrated a political savvy that catapulted him ahead of a legion of better-educated, more seasoned legislators. In the Senate, the organization turned to thirty-three-year-old Robert F. Wagner, son of a Wiesbaden printer, who had landed in New York at the age of nine, not speaking a word of English. Smith and Wagner exemplified the spirit of urban reform that characterized Tammany in 1911, though FDR had yet to recognize it.

The first order of business was the election of a United States senator. The term of Chauncey Depew, the Republican incumbent, expired March 4, 1911. Under the Constitution, U.S. senators were chosen by state legislatures, and in New York it was done in joint session: 150 assemblymen and 50 state senators, a total of 200 votes, of which a majority (101) was required to elect. Since there were 114 Democrats in the legislature, it was a foregone conclusion that Depew's successor would be named by the Democratic caucus.

Tammany's candidate was William F. Sheehan, known throughout the state as "Blue-eyed Billy," the former political boss of Erie County, lieutenant governor, and assembly speaker who was now practicing law in New York City as the partner of Judge Alton B. Parker, the 1904 Democratic presidential nominee. Sheehan had amassed a considerable fortune in and out of politics, and his current legal practice reflected the ultimate in white-shoe respectability. He was director of a dozen or so public utility companies and, with the conservative Judge Parker, embodied the alliance between big business and machine politics. Sheehan raised money from his clients for the Democrats; Tammany spent the money and remembered from whence it came.

But the caucus was far from unanimous. Sheehan was anathema to old Cleveland Democrats—men like Franklin's father, upstate WASPs who abhorred political bosses in principle yet as a practical matter were far more hidebound and conservative. Their candidate was Brooklyn attorney Edward M. Shepard, counsel for the Pennsylvania Railroad, an intimate of J. P. Morgan who had long been active in the cause of good government but could scarcely be called a liberal crusader. The fact that Sheehan was Irish Catholic and Shepard a Yankee Episcopalian was of more significance than many would openly admit.

Franklin sided with the Cleveland crowd. "Sheehan looks like [Tammany's] choice," he noted in his diary in early January. "May the result prove that I am wrong! There is no question in my mind that the Democratic Party is on trial, and having been given control of the government chiefly through up-state votes, cannot afford to surrender its control to the organization in New York City."[70] Like Theodore when he first entered the legislature, FDR was itching for a fight. It was a matter of publicity and power, not policy or substance. The issue for Franklin was "bossism," and the contest for U.S. senator was the first target of opportunity that came into view. Whether Sheehan was more progressive than Shepard was immaterial.

Under party rules the decision of the caucus was binding. A majority of the caucus was fifty-eight votes, and if party discipline prevailed—and it invariably did—those fifty-eight determined how all 114 Democrats would vote on the floor. That gave Tammany the whip hand. The New York City organization controlled far more than the fifty-eight votes required, and Charles F. Murphy, the astute Tammany chieftain, confidently expected to put Sheehan in the Senate come March.* Yet there was a loophole. When asked by FDR, Al Smith con-

* Charles Murphy, who headed Tammany Hall from 1902 until his death in 1924, was the antithesis of his ham-handed predecessors. Known variously as "The Quiet Chief," "Silent

firmed that only those Democrats who attended the caucus were bound. If a member was absent, he was not bound by the caucus's decision.[71]

Both parties scheduled their caucuses for nine o'clock on the evening of January 16. The Republicans met briefly and unanimously named Depew. But when the Democrats called their meeting to order, twenty-three members were absent. Those present voted sixty-two for Sheehan, twenty-two for Shepard, and seven for D. Cady Herrick, a former candidate for governor. The caucus formally nominated Sheehan, but only ninety-one Democrats had attended—ten fewer than the 101 votes required to elect.

While the Democrats caucused, twenty-one of the absentees convened nearby in the Ten Eyck Hotel. Some favored Shepard, some favored other candidates, but all were agreed that they would not support Sheehan. A brief press release explained they did not wish their individual votes smothered by the caucus. "The people should know just how their representatives voted . . . and any majority should be credited to the representatives in the Legislature and not someone outside that body"—a blast at Tammany in general and Charles F. Murphy in particular.[72]

The legislature met in joint session the next morning. When the ballots for U.S. senator were tabulated, Sheehan had ninety-one votes from the Demo-

---

Charlie," or simply "Mr. Murphy," he had a cleansing effect on both the organization and New York politics.

The son of an Irish tenant farmer, Murphy saved enough money driving a Blue Line horse trolley to open a saloon (the first of four) known as Charlie's Place on Second Avenue, where he learned politics doling out favors to the neighborhood. He rose quickly through the Tammany ranks, attributable in part to his gentlemanly discretion and in part to his innate political instinct, to become the most powerful Democratic leader in the state.

Reform was in the air when Murphy took control of Tammany, and he put the organization at the head of the parade. As he saw it, reform had too many ramifications to be left to the reformers. Under Murphy, Tammany became the most potent force for effecting economic and social change in New York. It supported Republican governor Charles Evans Hughes in the creation of a Public Utilities Commission, as well as laws regulating banking, insurance, and tenement housing. It pioneered legislation for old-age pensions, workman's compensation, and five-cent transit fares. Robert Wagner would later refer to Murphy's Tammany as "the cradle of modern liberalism." Nancy J. Weiss, *Charles Francis Murphy, 1858–1924: Respectability and Responsibility in Tammany Politics* 27–38 (Northampton, Mass: Smith College, 1968); Alfred Connable and Edward Silberfarb, *Tiger of Tammany: Nine Men Who Ran New York* (New York: Holt, Rinehart and Winston, 1967); Charles LaCerra, *Franklin Delano Roosevelt and Tammany Hall of New York* 43–46 (Lanham, Md.: University Press of America, 1997).

cratic caucus, all eighty-six Republicans voted for Depew, and the remaining Democratic votes were split among a number of sentimental favorites.* No candidate had received the 101 votes required for election. For the next ten weeks battle lines hardened and the legislature ground to a halt. "Never in the history of Albany have 21 men threatened such total ruin of machine plans," the veteran newsman Louis Howe reported in *The New York Herald*.[73] The rebels "are the talk of the capital," said *The New York Times*. "They are not radicals. They speak with moderation, and have made clear that while they will resist to the last any attempt at coercion, they are keenly alive to the necessary processes of government by party."[74]

FDR was not the instigator of the insurgency or even its prime organizer. Yet he quickly emerged as its spokesman and informal chairman. He was always available to the press, he had no political baggage from past campaigns, and he was articulate and self-confident. "There is nothing I love as much as a good fight," he told *The New York Times* on January 22. "I never had as much fun in my life as I am having right now."

The name Roosevelt fascinated reporters bored with statehouse routine. Comparisons with TR were inevitable. The *New York Post* told its readers that Franklin had "the strong insurgent tendencies of the family."[75] The *American* reported, "His face is boyish, but those who remember Theodore Roosevelt when he was an Assemblyman say the Senator bears a striking likeness to the Colonel."[76] According to the *New York World*, FDR was "of spare figure and lean intellectual face, suggesting a student of divinity rather than a practical politician."[77] The *New York Globe* depicted a matinee idol: "Tall, with a well set up figure, he is physically fit to command. His face is a bit long but the features are well modeled, the nose is Grecian, and there is a glow of country health in his cheeks. . . . It is the chin, though, aggressive and somewhat prominent, that shows what a task the leaders in Albany have if they have thoughts of making this young man change his mind. His lips are firm and part often in a smile over even white teeth—the Roosevelt teeth."[78]

. FDR's house, just one block from the capitol, became insurgent headquarters. It was our "harbor of refuge," said Kings County assemblyman Edmund R. Terry.[79] Every morning the insurgents gathered in the Roosevelts' library,

---

* Edward M. Shepard 14, Judge Alton B. Parker 6, former governor Herrick 2, State Supreme Court justice James W. Gerard 2, and Martin W. Littleton 2.

walked together to the legislature, cast their votes against Sheehan, returned after the session, went out again for supper, and came back for a long evening of drinks and cigars. The sessions were as much social as political. "There is very little business done at our councils of war," FDR confided to a *Times* reporter. "We just sit around and swap stories like soldiers at a bivouac fire."[80] There were shouts and laughter and a blue haze of cigar smoke that engulfed everyone and everything. The smoke became so pervasive that Eleanor eventually moved the children to the third floor so they might breathe more easily.

The fight against Sheehan gave Eleanor her initial taste of political life. "It was a wife's duty to be interested in whatever interested her husband, whether it was politics, books or a particular dish for dinner. That was the attitude with which I approached that first winter in Albany," she said later.[81] Eleanor watched proceedings from the Senate gallery, entertained the insurgents at home, prepared their drinks and snacks, and forged some unlikely friendships. Veteran Tammany pols like Tom Grady and Tim Sullivan—who had little use for Franklin—found Eleanor delightful. "Be with the insurgents, and if needs be with your husband every day in the year but this," wrote Grady to ER on Saint Patrick's Day. "But this day be with us."[82] Eleanor's understanding of the personal aspects of politics seemed instinctive. She softened Franklin's self-righteousness and made him appear less arrogant. When Lord Bryce, Great Britain's ambassador to the United States, addressed a joint session of the legislature, ER stepped forward and hosted a massive reception where Tammanyites, insurgents, and Old Albany society mingled freely. That first year in the state capital was a seminar in practical politics, and Eleanor enjoyed every minute. As one of her most sympathetic biographers has written, "Franklin's entrance into politics saved them both from the kind of ordinary upper-class life, vapid and fatuous, that ER associated with society—at least that part of society where she had never felt welcome, comfortable, or understood."[83]

Tammany exerted maximum pressure on the insurgents. Pet projects were shelved, patronage dried up, hometown constituents were mobilized, local newspapers counseled against delay, county chairmen, bankers, and prominent businessmen threatened to withdraw support. More than once, FDR had to raise funds for his colleagues to pay off mortgages called suddenly by their banks.[84] When intimidation failed, the Sheehan forces turned to favors and inducements. Al Smith did not say "to get along, you have to go along," but the capital was rife with rumors of judicial posts and other perks offered to the rebels. Charles Murphy journeyed to Albany to meet with FDR; Sheehan and his wife had lunch with Franklin and Eleanor—all to no avail. At the end of March the rebels still held out. The legislature had been in session ten weeks, and not one measure of substance had been enacted.

Both sides were becoming restive. Governor John Dix, in despair for the state budget, called for Sheehan to withdraw. A number of compromise candidates emerged, and finally Charles Murphy settled on State Supreme Court justice James Aloysius O'Gorman, a former Tammany sachem (underboss) and longtime president of the Friendly Sons of St. Patrick. O'Gorman had been on the bench for ten years and his reputation for integrity was unassailable. Unlike Sheehan and Shepard, he had no ties to the corporate world or big business. Yet he was far more a creature of Tammany than Sheehan had ever been. He would be hard for the rebels to accept, but even harder for them to reject.

When Smith and Wagner promised there would be no reprisals, the insurgents broke ranks. A majority voted to accept O'Gorman. FDR sought to hold out, but with his troops thinning, further resistance was futile. He embraced the inevitable: "We would have taken Justice O'Gorman at the very beginning and been perfectly satisfied," he later told the *Times*.[85]

On the afternoon of March 31, 1911, when the rebels filed into the chamber for the final vote, jubilant regulars let out a raucous cheer. There were cheers and more cheers, and then an Irish voice burst into song: the rhythmic anthem of the New York City organization: "Tam-ma-nee . . . Tam-ma-nee." The regulars joined in, chorus after chorus, including the improvised

Tam-ma-nee, Tam-ma-nee
Franklin D., like Uncle "The,"
Is no match for Tam-ma-nee;
Tam-ma-nee, Tam-ma-nee

Eventually order was restored and the clerk called the roll—the sixty-fourth ballot for U.S. senator. When his name was called, Roosevelt stood to explain his vote, struggling to make himself heard above an undercurrent of hisses. "We have followed the dictates of our consciences and have done our duty as we saw it. [Hisses.] I believe that as a result the Democratic Party has taken an upward step. [Groans and hisses.] We are Democrats—not irregulars, but regulars. [Silence]. I take pleasure in casting my vote for the Honorable James A.

Gorman. [Tepid applause.]"[86] The results were predictable. One hundred twelve Democrats voted for O'Gorman; eighty Republicans for Depew. The insurgency was broken. All but three of the twenty-one members who had rebelled with FDR would be defeated in upcoming elections.

The fight against Sheehan became another myth Roosevelt could not resist embellishing. Two days after the vote in Albany, Franklin addressed the YMCA of Greater New York and claimed victory. "I have just returned from a big fight," he announced. "A fight that went sixty-four rounds. This fight was a free-for-all . . . and many of the other side got good and battered. . . . The battle ended in harmony, and we have chosen a man for the people who will be dictated to by no one."[87]

Over the years the public forgot how ignominiously the insurgents had been beaten and remembered only that Sheehan had not been elected. This became gospel for FDR, who never tired of retelling the tale of his first political victory.* "Do you remember the old Sheehan fight of 1911?" he asked a long-time friend in 1928 when he was running for governor. "When the final Murphy surrender came, the flag of truce was brought to me by Assemblyman Alfred E. Smith and State Senator Bob Wagner. What a change has taken place all along the line."[88]

FDR harvested a bumper crop of national publicity from the Sheehan fight, and for some he became a youthful symbol of political reform. The Cleveland *Plain Dealer* tabbed Franklin as TR's successor: "May it not be possible that this rising star may continue the Roosevelt dynasty? Franklin D. Roosevelt is, to be sure, a Democrat, but this is a difference of small import. In other respects, he seems to be thoroughly Rooseveltian."[89] In North Carolina, Josephus Daniels, editor of the Raleigh *News & Observer*, wrote an editorial praising FDR's stand against Tammany entitled "A Coming Democratic Leader."[90] In Trenton, New Jersey's reformist governor Woodrow Wilson took notice, and TR wrote his congratulations: "Just a line to say that we are really proud of the way you have handled yourself."[91]

---

* Judge Joseph M. Proskauer, one of Al Smith's closest advisers, said party professionals in New York always laughed a little at FDR for the Sheehan affair. "According to the gospel, FDR won a great victory. But the victory was that instead of getting Sheehan, who was a pretty good upstate lawyer, [Tammany] withdrew him and nominated O'Gorman, whom they would much rather have nominated in the first place." Interview, Judge Joseph M. Proskauer, Columbia Oral History Project, Columbia University.

The downside of the Sheehan struggle was that FDR was tagged as anti-Catholic and anti-Irish—a label that proved hard to shake. The Reverend Patrick Ludden, the Roman Catholic bishop of Syracuse, claimed that Franklin and his colleagues reflected a resurgence of "the old spirit of Knownothingism" that prevented Catholics, especially Irish Catholics, from getting ahead.[92] Daniel O'Connell, political boss of Albany for several generations, put it more pungently. Franklin, he said, "was a bigot. He didn't like Tammany. He didn't like poor people. He was a patronizing son of a bitch."[93] FDR's denials were more fervent than convincing. Both he and Eleanor shared the anti-Irish, anti-Catholic prejudices of their time and class.* Franklin would learn tolerance, and over the years he and the nation's Irish pols would use each other for their mutual benefit. But their affection never ran deep. James A. Farley, who served FDR for a dozen years as campaign manager and party chairman, had as one of his tasks to persuade his fellow Irish leaders that they could work with Roosevelt in spite of what they might have heard about his youthful anti-Catholicism. Farley did a superb job, but he was never personally convinced. Later he lamented that his relationship with FDR had been purely professional. "Strange as it may seem, the President never took me into the bosom of his family, although everyone agreed I was more responsible than any other single man for his being in the White House."[94]

A lasting legacy of the Sheehan fight was the Seventeenth Amendment to the Constitution, providing for the direct election of U.S. senators by the voters in each state, not the legislatures. In April 1911, the New York legislature took up a bill previously introduced by Roosevelt instructing the state's congressional delegation to support such an amendment. The direct election of senators was popular with the progressive movement throughout the country and had been one of the planks in the Democratic platform. FDR led the debate in the State Senate, which on April 20 passed the measure 28–15. Four days later the Assembly adopted it 105–30. The Democrats in both houses voted solidly in favor, most Republicans against. The Sheehan battle, taken to-

---

* ER's feelings never completely changed. "Franklin was always surrounded by Catholics," she told her friend Irine Sandifer in 1960. "They were determined to see that he was always surrounded." Irine Reiterman Sandifer, *Mrs. Roosevelt as We Knew Her* 86 (Silver Spring, Md.: privately printed, 1975). Also see James MacGregor Burns and Susan Dunn, *The Three Roosevelts* 143, 196–197 (New York: Grove Press, 2001).

gether with similar struggles in New Jersey and Illinois, launched a groundswell of popular sentiment behind the amendment. Congress adopted it by the required two-thirds vote on May 13, 1912, and upon ratification by three quarters of the states, it became part of the Constitution on May 31, 1913. (New York was the fourth state to ratify, acting January 15, 1913.)

Fighting "bossism" came naturally to FDR. He challenged Tammany over a bill to reorganize the State Highway Commission, pressed for adoption of a direct-primary bill, and struck a puritanical pose against such Tammany-endorsed measures as Sunday baseball, legalized prizefighting, and betting at the racetrack. "Murphy and his kind must, like the noxious weed, be plucked out root and branch,"[95] he told an audience in Buffalo. These stands were popular with Roosevelt's churchgoing constituency of upriver farmers and small-town businessmen. But they ignored the economic issues of the day, failed to address the growing problems of industrialization, and tagged Tammany with an out-of-date label more appropriate to the days of the Tweed Ring than the progressive leadership of Murphy, Wagner, and Smith.* As one legislative veteran put it, FDR's ideas in 1911 were "the silly conceits of a political prig [devoid] of human sympathy, human interests, human ties," a characterization with which most members would have agreed.[96]

---

* FDR's view of Tammany eventually caught up with the times. When Charles Murphy died in 1924, Roosevelt said feelingly, "In Mr. Murphy's death, the New York City Democratic organization has lost probably the strongest and wisest leader it has had in generations. . . . He was a genius who kept harmony, and at the same time recognized that the world moves on. It is well to remember that he had helped to accomplish much in the way of progressive and social welfare legislation in our state." Weiss, *Charles Francis Murphy* 21; LaCerra, *Franklin Delano Roosevelt and Tammany Hall* 61.

FIVE

AWAKENING

I was an awfully mean cuss
when I first went into politics.
—FRANKLIN D. ROOSEVELT

FRANKLIN WAS LITTLE LIKED in Albany. Most of his colleagues found him insufferable. Al Smith wrote him off as a dilettante—"a damn fool" who thought more about political appearances than substantive legislation. Robert Wagner saw him as a stage dandy interested only in publicity: "Senator Roosevelt has gained his point. What he wants is a headline in the newspapers. Let us proceed to our business." The elderly Tom Grady, who had served in the legislature with TR, thought Franklin the more obnoxious of the two. Even the genial Tim Sullivan, a man of exceptional warmth and kindness, believed him to be "an awful arrogant fellow."[1]

Frances Perkins, fresh out of Mount Holyoke and Columbia Graduate School, was often in Albany lobbying on behalf of labor. She knew the Roosevelts socially in New York City and traveled in the same circles. No one who saw FDR in those years, she wrote, would have been likely to think of him as a potential president.

> I have a vivid picture of him operating on the floor of the Senate: tall and slender, very active and alert, moving around the floor, going in and out of committee rooms, rarely talking with the members, who more or less avoided him, not particularly charming (that came later), artificially serious face, rarely smiling, with an unfortunate habit—so natural that he was unaware of it—of throwing his head up. This, combined with his pince-nez and great height, gave him the appearance of looking down his nose at most people.

I think he started that way not because he was born with a silver spoon in his mouth and had a good education at Harvard, but because he really didn't like people very much and because he had a youthful lack of humility, a streak of self-righteousness, and a deafness to the hopes, fears, and aspirations which are the common lot.[2]

The fight against Sheehan provided national publicity for Roosevelt. But it exposed his social indifference. On March 25, 1911, while the legislature was still deadlocked, fire broke out in the Triangle Shirtwaist factory, which occupied the three top floors of a New York City loft building just off Washington Square. The flames spread quickly. The doors to the only stairwell were chained shut, ostensibly to prevent theft, and there was no fire escape. Forty-six employees fell or jumped to their deaths on the sidewalk below; one hundred perished in the inferno. All but fifteen were girls and young women between the ages of sixteen and thirty-five. In the trial that followed, the company was absolved of responsibility and collected $64,925 in insurance damages. Twenty-three families of the dead sued and received an overall total of $1,725. That amounted to $75 for each life lost.

The Triangle Shirtwaist fire, the worst factory fire in New York history, exposed the evils of unregulated working conditions. "This calamity is just what I have been predicting," said the city's fire chief.[3] Rose Schneiderman of the Women's Trade Union League put it more pejoratively: "The life of men and women is so cheap and property is so sacred, it matters little if one hundred and forty-six of us are burned to death," she told a protest rally at the Metropolitan Opera House.[4] Political leaders in Albany took up the cry for reform. The legislature immediately established a Factory Investigating Commission with Robert Wagner as chairman, Al Smith as vice chairman, and Frances Perkins as chief investigator. Over the next three years the commission would produce a flood of thirty-two bills that came to serve as models of industrial reform throughout the nation. Franklin Roosevelt stood on the sidelines. He said nothing about the Triangle fire and took no part in the legislative effort the tragedy produced.

One of the principal pieces of social legislation to come forward at the 1911 session was a bill to limit the workweek of women and children to fifty-four hours. The measure was being held up in committee, and Democrats were divided. Every vote was important. Miss Perkins approached Roosevelt to ask his support and was dismissed abruptly: "No, no. More important things. More important things. Can't do it now. Can't do it now. Much more important things."[5]

Thanks to help from Tammany stalwarts like Big Tim Sullivan and The MacManus ("the Devil's Deputy from Hell's Kitchen"), Miss Perkins got the measure to the Senate floor a year later on the final day of the session. Under the rules, an absolute majority—twenty-six votes—was required for passage, and the supporters were two votes shy. At the last moment, Tim Sullivan and his cousin Christy, whom Miss Perkins managed to call back from the night boat that was about to take them down the Hudson to New York, crashed through the chamber door to cast the two decisive votes. "It's all right, me gal," Big Tim thundered. "The bosses thought they were going to kill your bill, but they forgot about Tim Sullivan."[6] Pandemonium erupted on the floor. The Senate was swept by a tidal wave of emotion. Callous old politicians found themselves weeping. And at the back of the chamber, Frances Perkins was weeping too.[7]

Franklin was absent when the bill passed. "I remember being considerably disappointed because Roosevelt wouldn't do anything about the 54-hour bill," said Perkins. "I took it hard that a young man who had so much spirit did not do so well in this, which I thought a test, as did Tim Sullivan and The MacManus, undoubtedly corrupt politicians."[8]*

Whether he could not remember, or whether he simply wanted to cover his tracks, FDR's version of that night varies substantially—another example of

---

* Sullivan ran the gambling and prostitution rings south of Fourteenth Street in Manhattan, and he thrived on the intensely personal side of politics. Every year on his mother's birthday, he distributed tickets entitling each of the two thousand children in his Bowery constituency to a free pair of shoes, and he could always be counted upon in the legislature to support measures that would benefit the poor.

Sullivan served one term in Congress but left in disgust because it was too far removed from the voters and too anonymous. "There's nothing in this Congress business," he told a reporter. "They know 'em in Washington. The people down there use them as hitching posts. Every time they see a Congressman on the street they tie their horse to them."

When Sullivan died in 1913, twenty-five thousand people, including three United States senators and twenty members of the House of Representatives, followed his casket to the grave. Charles F. Murphy and the mayor of New York headed the pallbearers. The high requiem mass was celebrated by Monsignor Kearney, rector of the old St. Patrick's Cathedral. Sullivan's estate, estimated at $2 million to $3 million dollars, was placed in trust for charitable purposes. M. R. Werner, *Tammany Hall* 508–510 (New York: Greenwood Press, 1968).

excluding unpleasant facts from the record. Campaigning for governor in 1928, Roosevelt told a labor rally in Manhattan, "One of the first measures that we started in 1911 was the fifty-four-hour law for women and children in industry. In those days a fifty-four-hour law was considered the most radical thing that had ever been talked about."[9] Several years later, Roosevelt ratcheted up his involvement, telling reporters how he and Robert Wagner had been called Communists because they had worked for a fifty-four-hour-a-week law. "It is an old story," said FDR, "but like an elephant, I have a long memory."[10]

The most blatant reinterpretation was provided by Roosevelt's principal aide and general factotum, Louis Howe, writing for *The Saturday Evening Post* in 1933. In Howe's version, FDR not only supported the bill but played the central role in its passage. It was "young Senator Roosevelt," wrote Howe, who held the Senate floor with a filibuster while Sullivan was summoned from the night boat. When told by runners that Big Tim refused to return, Roosevelt is supposed to have said, "Tell him he has to and I said so."[11]*

FDR's early record on women's suffrage was little better. Although his district included Vassar College, a hotbed of feminism, Roosevelt initially hewed to the negative attitude of his farming constituency. Under relentless pressure from campus militants, he took cover in public opinion. "I am trying to get the sentiment of Dutchess County," he wrote Anna Dayley, a Poughkeepsie attorney, in February 1911, "and I shall be guided very largely by the result."[12] At the end of May, he was still equivocal. "I am not opposed to female suffrage," he allowed, "but I think it is a very great question whether the people of the state as a whole want it or not."[13]

The following year, when the issue of a constitutional amendment for women's suffrage was before the legislature, FDR came out in favor. Always fond of a good story, Roosevelt enjoyed telling how he had been convinced by the glamorous suffrage lobbyist Inez Milholland, who perched on his desk in the Senate chamber and dazzled him with Vassar wiles and lawyerly argu-

---

* Howe, who covered Albany for years for the *New York Herald,* knew his account could not be disproved because the *Senate Journal* recorded votes only and not speeches. But four New York City newspapers, three Albany papers, and one from Poughkeepsie covered the debate. Five mentioned the Sullivans being called back, but not one mentioned Roosevelt taking part. *New York Herald, The New York Times, New York World, New York Tribune,* Albany *Knickerbocker Press,* Albany *Daily Argus,* Albany *Evening Journal,* Poughkeepsie *Daily Eagle,* March 30, 1912.

ments. Milholland was often described as the high priestess of the suffragist cause, and, as FDR would have it, she persuaded him that suffrage was "the only chivalric position for a decent man to hold."[14]

Eleanor supported women's suffrage reluctantly. Throughout her life she refused to concede Milholland's role. Nevertheless, Franklin's conversion left her stunned. "I had never given the question serious thought," she wrote, "for I took it for granted that men were superior creatures and knew more about politics than women did. I realized that if my husband was a suffragist I probably must be too [but] I cannot claim to have been a feminist in those early years."[15]

FDR's attitude toward Prohibition was equally equivocal. Never averse to bending an elbow himself, he nevertheless accumulated a perfect voting record in the Senate, according to the Anti-Saloon League. In January 1913, he actually introduced a local option bill for the League and became the subject of a laudatory editorial ("An Advocate of Christian Patriotism") in its national magazine.[16] In this instance, Franklin appears to have been too clever by half. Prohibition was anathema in New York City, and his opponents never tired of tying him to it. Down through 1932 the story persisted that whatever Roosevelt might say, there was a voting record to prove he was "dry" at heart.[17]

Following the path blazed by TR, conservation of the state's natural resources turned Roosevelt progressive. It was as chairman of the traditionally somnolent Forest, Fish, and Game Committee in the Senate that FDR found his voice as a progressive spokesman. He spearheaded the successful fight to update and codify New York's fish and game laws but lost a bitter battle with the timber industry to enact a similar code to protect the state's forests. Franklin's bill for the "Protection of Lands, Forests, and Public Parks" imposed drastic restrictions on harvesting timber—including a clause to restrict cutting trees below a minimum size on private property.

The state's timber producers descended on Albany in droves, charging that to tamper with private ownership was unconstitutional. For Roosevelt, it was baptism in a battle he would often revisit. "The same old fight is going on up here," he wrote to a friend in February 1912, "between the people who see that the Adirondacks are being denuded . . . and those [timber interests] who succeeded in getting for nothing what they would have to pay well for today. Nobody here has any desire to confiscate property and the bill before my Committee is a conservation measure only."[18] But few believed that. Any attempt to regulate what private landowners could do with their property galvanized the gods of free enterprise. Roosevelt failed to get his bill out of committee. A related bill that FDR introduced to permit the state to flood its own forest lands to provide reservoirs for public power died in the Assembly.

When the fight over the timber bill was at its height, Roosevelt was invited to give the keynote address to the progressive People's Forum, meeting in nearby Troy. By this time his concern for conservation had morphed into an awareness of the perils of excessive individualism. The speech comes as close as FDR ever came during his early years in politics to providing a philosophical explanation for his actions. Impatient with abstract ideas, he adroitly translated contentious concepts into phrases his audience could relate to—a preview of the mature Franklin D. Roosevelt. No one was better than FDR at simplifying a complex issue and translating it into words the average American could understand.

The course of modern history, he suggested, had been a struggle for individual liberty. "Today, in Europe and America, the liberty of the individual has been accomplished." What was now required was a process by which that liberty could be harnessed for the betterment of the community. "Competition has been shown to be useful up to a certain point and no further. Cooperation, which is the thing that we must strive for today, begins where competition leaves off." FDR avoided the term "community interest" as too socialistic. He eschewed "brotherhood of man" as too sentimental. Instead, he defined cooperation as "the struggle for the liberty of the community rather than the liberty of the individual" and said it was "what the founders of the republic were groping for."

The answer was regulation. But don't call it regulation, said Roosevelt. "If we call the method *regulation,* people will hold up their hands in horror and say 'unAmerican' or 'dangerous.' But if we call the same process *co-operation* these same old fogeys will cry out 'well done.' "[19]

FDR's embrace of a regulative role for government led him to Trenton and Woodrow Wilson, the fast-rising leader of the progressive wing of the Democratic party. In 1910, the year Franklin was elected to the Senate in Albany, Wilson was rescued by New Jersey Democrats from a difficult situation at Princeton and elected governor.* Wilson proved more adept at state politics

---

* Thomas Woodrow Wilson, Princeton class of 1879, received his Ph.D. from Johns Hopkins in 1885, was appointed to the Princeton faculty in 1890, and became president in 1902.

than academic infighting ("The reason academic politics are so vicious is because the stakes are so small" is often attributed to Wilson) and in his first four
months as governor cajoled the legislature into enacting a spectacular series of
reform measures including a direct primary law, a corrupt-practices act, a bill
establishing a strong public utilities commission with rate-setting authority,
and an employer's liability law. The speed with which Wilson pushed the measures through the statehouse provided a lesson in leadership that made him
the odds-on favorite among progressive Democrats for the party's 1912 presidential nomination.

Roosevelt was but one of many Democrats who journeyed to Trenton to
meet Wilson. The get-together served a common purpose: Wilson was interested in the delegate vote count in New York; FDR was eager to join the Wilson
campaign at its inception. They met in Wilson's office in the autumn of 1911.
How many votes could he count upon from New York? the governor asked.
The prospects looked bleak, FDR replied. New York had ninety votes at the
convention and perhaps a third might support Wilson. But like the Democratic legislative caucus in Albany, the state operated under the unit rule. Charles
Murphy would control the delegation, and Murphy's candidate, who was likely
to be anyone other than Wilson, would get all of New York's ninety votes.[20]

Late that afternoon FDR and Wilson resumed their conversation on the
train back to Princeton, where Wilson lived. As they sat opposite each other in
a Pennsylvania Railroad day coach, the short ride to Princeton Junction gave
the man who would become the twenty-eighth president of the United States
and the man who would follow twelve years later as the thirty-second an opportunity to appraise each other. At fifty-five years of age, Wilson was the

---

His first few years as president were punctuated by a flurry of educational reforms, but by
1906 his welcome had worn thin. He alienated alumni by attempting to abolish the eating
clubs on Prospect Avenue, and his academic certitude turned faculty against him. In
1909–10 he lost a showdown battle with Dean Andrew West '74 over the location and role
of the graduate school (Wilson wanted it in the midst of the campus; West preferred a bucolic location). Trustees, faculty, and important donors sided with West, and Wilson recognized that his authority as president was fatally compromised. New Jersey Democrats had
been urging him to run for governor, and after West's triumph Wilson had little choice. He
accepted the party's nomination in September 1910. Arthur S. Link, "Woodrow Wilson," in
A Princeton Companion 512–515, Alexander Leitch, ed. (Princeton, N.J.: Princeton University Press, 1978).

beneficiary of a sudden wave of popularity. But he remained cold, stern, and professorial—a dour Presbyterian academic born to southern privilege who believed God was guiding his every step. Crisply articulate, inflexible, and dedicated to principle, his firm belief in right and wrong evoked in Franklin memories both of his father, James, and, more poignantly, the Reverend Endicott Peabody. Peabody lacked Wilson's brilliance but shared his righteous certitude. Wilson's academic writings suggested a highly theoretical approach to the daily cut and thrust of politics, yet this was belied by his stunning pragmatism as governor.[21] He was not a man approached easily; he was concerned more with issues than personalities; yet his grasp of political reality was indisputable. Years later, writing from the oval office, FDR drew on his own political experience to contrast Wilson with his early role model, Cousin Theodore. As Franklin saw it, TR lacked Wilson's depth "and failed to stir, as Wilson did, the truly profound moral and social convictions." Wilson, on the other hand, failed where TR succeeded in arousing popular enthusiasm over specific events, "even though these events may have been superficial."[22]

In FDR, Wilson saw a tall, young (Roosevelt was twenty-nine), ebullient Harvardian, somewhat full of himself, a shade too eager, not unlike many young men he had met at Princeton. He was smooth, bordering on glib, yet he spoke truthfully and reported the New York situation accurately. He would be of little help at the convention, assuming he was a delegate, but he was a Roosevelt and a Democrat, and obviously shared a commitment to reform. If Wilson got the nomination—a very big "if" in the autumn of 1911—the young man sitting opposite would be most useful building an organization in New York that could help carry the state in November. If TR became the Republican candidate, a Democratic Roosevelt would be even more valuable.

In the ensuing months, Wilson's political fortunes eroded. His honeymoon with New Jersey legislators ended abruptly—the governor had shed none of his sanctimonious rectitude—and early backers lost interest. Supporters on Wall Street, who saw Wilson as a conservative counter to the populism of William Jennings Bryan, became disenchanted with his increasingly progressive agenda and were now working actively against him.[23] Campaign funds dried up, and other candidates, led by House Speaker Champ Clark of Missouri, entered the field.[24]

The political tide was running strongly against Wilson when New York Democrats convened for their nominating convention in New York City on

April 12, 1912. FDR organized a dinner for Wilson supporters at the Belmont Hotel the evening before. He invited close to a hundred upstate delegates, but fewer than twenty replied and of those only three accepted. Murphy dominated the convention from start to finish. A slate of ninety uninstructed delegates was chosen, Tammany held a decisive majority, and Roosevelt was pointedly passed over, as either delegate or alternate.[25]

If Franklin was discouraged he did not show it. Following a month's vacation in the Caribbean with his brother-in-law Hall Roosevelt (at TR's request, Colonel George Goethals gave them a VIP tour of the Panama Canal), FDR accepted the chairmanship of the New York State Wilson Conference, a splinter group of disaffected Democrats, including William Gibbs McAdoo, Henry Morgenthau, Sr., and, to everyone's surprise, Senator James Aloysius O'Gorman. The organization was paper thin but provided cover for Roosevelt to organize a rump of 150 Wilson supporters to attend the Democratic National Convention in Baltimore—an offset to the official New York delegation under Murphy. FDR's team set up headquarters in the Munsey Building across from the convention and bombarded delegates with manifestoes urging Wilson's nomination. No Democrat—save Madison and Buchanan—had ever won the White House without the electoral vote of New York, and winning New York, they asserted, required a progressive candidate. Senator O'Gorman interceded with the Democratic National Committee to obtain seats for the Wilson Conference in the gallery, where they chanted incessantly for Wilson.[26] Franklin obtained credentials from the sergeant at arms who admitted him to the convention floor. These were countersigned by Joseph E. Davies, the pro-Wilson national committeeman from Wisconsin who many years later would serve as FDR's ambassador to the Soviet Union.

The 1912 Baltimore convention was Roosevelt's first exposure to national politics and he reveled in the excitement. He spent hours working hotel lobbies and dining rooms, shaking hands and touting Wilson's virtues. Reporters and delegates alike flocked to meet the Democratic Roosevelt. One was Josephus Daniels, editor of the Raleigh *News & Observer*, who had been a fan of FDR since "Blue-eyed Billy" Sheehan had been denied a seat in the U.S. Senate. Daniels was also the Democratic national committeeman from North Carolina and a prominent fixture in the Wilson campaign. "Franklin and I became friends at that convention," Daniels wrote later. "It was a case of love at first sight."[27] Another new friend who would play an important role in FDR's political life was the taciturn Tennessee congressman Cordell Hull, an old-school Appalachian liberal who drove the Wilson bandwagon in the South.

The Democratic convention operated under the two-thirds rule, a tradition that not only gave the South veto power over the nominee but also ensured that voting would continue for at least several days. In 1912, there were 1,088 delegates; 545 constituted a majority, but two-thirds (726) were required to nominate. Most states voted under another historic relic, the unit rule: all votes from a state must be cast for a single candidate. This smothered individual delegates' preferences and gave each state organization effective control of the vote count. Balloting began June 28. After the roll of the states was called, Champ Clark led with 440 votes; Wilson was second with 324; Judson Harmon, the conservative governor of Ohio, had 148; and Congressman Oscar Underwood of Alabama trailed with 117.* The New York delegation, in a holding pattern, cast its ninety votes for Harmon. Murphy preferred Clark but was waiting for the opportune moment to swing the Empire State's vote and start a stampede that would put his candidate across.

The summer of 1912 was one of the hottest on record in Baltimore, and the delegates sweltered through roll call after roll call. On the tenth ballot Murphy decided the time had come and threw New York's support to Clark. That gave the Speaker a majority, but he was still well short of the 726 votes required. Nevertheless, his momentum appeared unstoppable. At that moment William Jennings Bryan rose from his seat in the Nebraska delegation to address the convention. The "Great Commoner" had three times led the party to defeat, but he retained the affection of many southern and western delegates, and his voice had lost none of the resonance that electrified convention after convention. "So long as the ninety wax figures of the New York delegation vote for Clark," said Bryan, he was withdrawing his support and casting his vote for Wilson. Bryan's intercession derailed the victory train. For the next dozen ballots Clark's strength hovered around 550; then it began to erode. On the thirtieth ballot Indiana's favorite son, Governor Thomas R. Marshall, withdrew

* The remaining 59 votes were split among a variety of favorite-son candidates, including Governor Thomas R. Marshall of Indiana (31). William Jennings Bryan, who was not a candidate but who hovered over the convention like Banquo's ghost, received one vote. Congressional Quarterly, *Guide to U.S. Elections* 148 (Washington, D.C.: Congressional Quarterly, 1975).

and shifted the Hoosier State's 31 votes to Wilson, who pulled ahead 460–455. With each succeeding ballot Wilson gained strength. On the forty-third ballot, four days after the voting started, Illinois switched its 58 votes from Clark to Wilson, and the landslide began. Three ballots later, Wilson was nominated with 990 votes. Tammany voted for Clark to the bitter end. Governor Marshall was later rewarded for his switch with the vice presidential nomination.[28] Bryan would become Wilson's secretary of state. FDR, who did little but lead cheers and organize demonstrations, made ready to work for Wilson in the coming election. WILSON NOMINATED THIS AFTERNOON, he wired Eleanor at Campobello. ALL MY PLANS VAGUE. SPLENDID TRIUMPH.[29]*

The day after Wilson was nominated, FDR called on the governor at his summer residence in Sea Girt, New Jersey. With Murphy temporarily persona non grata, Franklin sought and obtained the candidate's permission to organize pro-Wilson New York Democrats to fight the November election. Two weeks later, at a much-ballyhooed press conference in New York City, Roosevelt proclaimed the Empire State Democracy, a grassroots progressive movement with a national agenda. Backed by Ralph Pulitzer's *New York World*, the *Sun,* and a sprinkling of upstate papers, the movement quickly picked up speed. "We are not a small minority," Franklin told a second organizational meeting of two hundred Democrats at the Hotel Astor on July 29. "We are a big majority." If state party leaders cannot release themselves from their bondage to Tammany, he said, then "true party loyalty demands that bondage be broken by the rank and file. If this be party treason, let those who are responsible for such conditions make the most of it."[30]

The Republicans meanwhile were self-destructing. TR and President Taft traded barbs throughout 1911 and then broke irrevocably in February 1912. The issues were initially political. TR pressed a reform agenda; Taft preferred the status quo. But the dispute soon became personal. Taft denounced Teddy and his supporters as "neurotics" who sought to "pull down the pillars of the

---

* Wilson attributed his nomination to divine intervention. "I am a Presbyterian and believe in predestination. It was Providence that did the work in Baltimore," he told his campaign manager, William F. McCombs. McCombs, who had worked round the clock to secure Wilson's victory, was understandably taken aback. "I must confess I felt a chill . . . because I thought that if he attempted to apply that Predestination doctrine to the extreme, the Democratic campaign might find itself very much in the ruck." William F. McCombs, *Making Woodrow Wilson President* 180–181 (New York: Fairview Publishing Co., 1921).

temple of freedom." TR dismissed Taft as a "blackguard," a "fathead," and a "puzzlewit" with an intellect slightly less developed than a guinea pig's. "My hat is in the ring and the fight is on," he told a crowd of cheering supporters on February 21, 1912.[31]

The GOP convened in Chicago in mid-June. Taft forces controlled the convention machinery; TR commanded the party's rank and file. "It is a marvelous thing" wrote Franklin, "that [Cousin Theodore], acting with the support of untrained militia, has succeeded in overcoming the well-organized opposition of the trained soldiers of the Republican Party."[32] Almost, but not quite. The credentials of some two hundred delegates were contested, and the Taft forces prevailed in virtually every case. That ensured the president's renomination. TR charged that the deck had been stacked and dramatically instructed his delegates to walk out of the convention. "We stand at Armageddon, and we battle for the Lord," said Theodore, with his penchant for understatement. Seven weeks later TR accepted the nomination of the newly formed National Progressive party and, as Arthur Schlesinger, Jr., observed, took the social conscience of the Republican party with him. Claiming to be "as fit as a bull moose," he posed a threat of unknown dimensions to both parties.[33]

Woodrow Wilson believed his election was preordained.[34] His campaign staff was less convinced. And with TR added to the race and threatening to siphon off a sizable portion of the progressive vote, all bets were off. The rupture of the Democratic party in New York now took on alarming proportions. If Taft had been the only opposition, FDR's Empire State Democracy and half a dozen other splinter groups could have been tolerated. Wilson could oppose bossism and let the devil take the hindmost. But now every vote counted, and the Wilson campaign could not afford to alienate Tammany and the regular party organization. For his part, Charles F. Murphy was a constant Democrat. Candidates come and go, but the party continues. He had no difficulty supporting the ticket, even though he had opposed Wilson at the convention.

Wilson and Murphy made no explicit deal. But FDR soon found himself outmaneuvered. The issue came to a head in early October, when the state Democratic party met in Syracuse to nominate its candidate for governor. Murphy supported another term for the complacent John Dix and had the votes to win, though it would likely split the party. Wilson opposed Dix and demanded an open convention. The delegates, he told *The New York Times,* "must be left free from personal control of any sort."[35]

With barely a month before the election, neither Wilson nor Murphy could afford a total break. So while Wilson continued to attack the New York machine publicly, Colonel Edward M. House, his principal adviser and alter ego, negotiated with Murphy to find a compromise candidate: "some unobjectionable Tammany man . . . who could not bring discredit upon the party," as House expressed it.[36] The charade that followed was carefully choreographed. For the first three ballots Tammany dutifully supported Dix. On the fourth, Murphy shifted his support to Congressman William "Plain Bill" Sulzer of New York City, a public champion of progressivism who had been a Tammany insider for years. Sulzer was exactly the type of common denominator behind whom the party could unite. As with Sheehan two years before, Murphy lost the battle over Dix but won the war.[37]

Sulzer's nomination appeared open and above board. House's role was not revealed. Wilson claimed victory and hailed the "freedom of action which the convention exercised."[38] The party split was healed, the Empire State Democracy dissolved, and FDR said he was proud to be a Democratic regular. "I believe in unity," he told the *Times*.[39] The only discordant note was sounded by Thomas Mott Osborne, the financial angel of the Empire State Democracy. Wilson, he said afterward, was "perfectly willing to put the ten commandments to a vote and reject them if the vote were adverse."[40] Senator Robert Wagner called Osborne a poor loser.[41]

FDR's practical education continued. He began to appreciate that life in the political arena involved more than bossism and good government. He saw House negotiate with Murphy and recognized how expendable he himself had been. He also recognized that he had to get through the eye of the Democratic needle and be renominated for his Senate seat. After that he faced a general election against not just a single Republican opponent but a Bull Moose acolyte of Cousin Theodore as well. Franklin saw the handwriting on the wall and made peace with Tammany. As one scholar expressed it, FDR became a Democratic regular and a Tammany irregular.[42] There were even rumors that if a Democratic victory in the gubernatorial race had been in doubt, Murphy would have held his nose and backed Roosevelt—just as the Republicans had nominated Theodore in 1898 to avoid defeat.*

* An unsigned Tammany memorandum from a member of the State Senate, perhaps Tim Sullivan, to Charles Murphy, makes the case for an alliance with FDR: "I would rather an or-

After FDR pulled in his horns he was nominated unanimously by the Democratic caucus in Poughkeepsie. Past differences were brushed aside, and Franklin once again hired Harry Hawkey's red Maxwell convertible to barnstorm the district. But before the campaign commenced, Roosevelt was struck down with a particularly virulent attack of typhoid. Eleanor, who was also hit, but not as seriously, blamed the drinking water aboard the steamer returning from Campobello.[43] Franklin's political career appeared to have come to an abrupt end. He could not possibly win a three-way race without mounting a strenuous backcountry campaign similar to the one he had waged two years before. But he was feverish and bedridden. To make matters worse, he had been stricken in New York City, not Hyde Park, and the old carpetbagger accusation was certain to resurface. In desperation, Franklin asked Eleanor to send for Louis Howe.[44]

Eleven years older than FDR, Louis Howe was the Albany reporter for the *New York Herald*. A veteran newsman with a hopeless addiction to politics, Howe gloried in an atmosphere of racetracks, gambling casinos, and the ornate watering holes of East Coast society. He was barely five feet tall, emaciated, his face scarred by a childhood bicycle accident. A malodorous Sweet Caporal cigarette dangled perpetually from his lips, the ashes falling randomly on his rumpled three-piece suits. Even when freshly scrubbed, which was not often, he looked dirty and unkempt. Howe took perverse pride in his appearance, claiming to be one of the four ugliest men in New York. "Children take one look at me on the street and run."[45] A fellow reporter once called him a "medieval gnome," and Howe accepted the designation with delight. For most people, Louis Howe was an acquired taste. But he was blessed with superabundant energy, uncanny political insight, and a penchant for intrigue. His cynical view of human nature rarely left him disappointed. And he was always broke. His job with the *Herald* was seasonal and provided a precarious living at best. As a result, he hired himself out as a ghostwriter whenever possible, but the

ganization man were elected, but we can't win with an organization man. . . . My reasons for favoring Mr. Roosevelt are as follows: First—He is a young man, who would go up and down the state capturing a great army of young men. . . . Second—The name Roosevelt would mean at least 10,000 votes to the Democratic ticket. Third—He is worth several million dollars, and could finance his own campaign, if necessary. Fourth—He is independent and is known throughout the state as a man who will fight for what he believes to be right." Manuscript, Senate files, FDRL.

pickings in Albany were slim. "I'm in a hole," he wrote FDR after Wilson's nomination. "If you can connect me with a job during the campaign, for heaven's sake help me out."[46]

Howe leaped for joy when Eleanor's message arrived. He had admired Franklin's fight against Sheehan, provided valuable advice to the insurgents on legislative strategy, and interviewed Roosevelt at length for the *Herald*—FDR's first exposure to the national media. "Almost at that very first meeting," Howe said later, "I made up my mind that nothing but an accident could keep him from becoming President."[47] Howe needed a hero, and Roosevelt—who in personal appearance and patrician background was everything Howe was not—fit the bill. FDR, for his part, needed practical political guidance, and Louis Howe provided it. Except for a basic attachment to the Democratic party, Howe was indifferent to ideology. Yet he was an astute tactician with a litmus ability to distinguish a sound political move from one that was likely to cause trouble. Roosevelt became virtually unbeatable once Howe joined his entourage. It was a symbiotic relationship in which each supplied what the other could not.

Franklin turned his Senate campaign over to Howe. For the next six weeks Howe became FDR's surrogate. He moved to Poughkeepsie, decorated Harry Hawkey's Maxwell with Roosevelt banners, and hustled the countryside for votes. He was as energetic as Franklin had been two years earlier, but he focused more sharply on specific constituencies. To win the farm vote, Howe devised a scheme to protect farmers from New York City commission merchants, the middlemen who pocketed the difference between what the farmer got for his crop and what the consumer paid. Howe pointed out that if reelected, Roosevelt would become chairman of the Senate Agriculture Committee. There he would ensure passage of an agricultural marketing act with real teeth in it. Howe mailed hundreds of personal letters over FDR's signature informing farmers of the proposal. Each letter contained a stamped, self-addressed envelope for the farmer's reply. Similar letters promised apple growers that Franklin would introduce a bill to standardize the size of barrels, another sore spot for farmers whose apples were often measured in oversized barrels. Shad fishermen were assured that license fees on the Hudson would be lowered. Altogether, Howe dispatched more than eleven thousand letters on FDR's behalf.[48]

No voter was left uncourted. Howe took out full-page newspaper advertise-

ments, unprecedented in upstate races, in which Roosevelt pledged his support for women's suffrage, identified with the concerns of the workingman,
and bashed the Republicans for standing pat. Howe worked at the end of a
long leash. FDR was consulted, but often after Howe had already acted. "Here
is your first ad," he wrote the bedridden Roosevelt in late October. "As I have
pledged you in it I thought you might like to know casually what kind of a
mess I was getting you into. . . . Your slave and servant, Howe."[49]

FDR turned his checkbook over to Howe and soon found himself overdrawn. Expenses were heavy, and Howe, evidently unfamiliar with check writing, always added the amount of the check to the balance rather than
subtracting it.[50] FDR met most of the expenses from his personal funds, including Howe's salary of $50 a week. Overall the race cost about $3,000,
roughly twice the salary of a state senator.[51] A few friends loaned Franklin
money for the campaign. "I pray your mother is as wealthy as reported so I can
get some of the money back," wrote FDR's Hyde Park neighbor Jefferson Newbold.[52]

Howe scoured the district, promising in Franklin's name whatever would
win votes. "I'm having more fun than a goat," he wrote FDR in early November.[53] Everyone was pleased except Eleanor and Sara, who were put off by
Howe's habits, particularly his addiction to high-powered Sweet Caporals.
"Remember, I was still a Puritan," Eleanor said many years later.[54] Howe ran
the campaign so effectively that FDR's absence was rarely noted and never
commented upon by his opponents.* Voters for the most part remained unaware that Roosevelt was ill—a forerunner of the campaigns Howe would conduct when FDR ran for governor and president, in which many voters never
realized the candidate could not walk.

In the final week of the campaign, Jacob Southard, Franklin's Republican
opponent, attacked FDR as anti-Catholic—an unfortunate legacy of the 1911
fight against Sheehan. Howe enlisted a number of Catholic friends to put out
the fire. He told Franklin not to worry. "Everyone is happy and singing the

---

* In what surely ranks as one of the greatest examples of chutzpah of modern politics,
Howe, over FDR's signature, wrote the voters of Columbia County on November 1 to attack
Franklin's Republican opponent for not having visited the county during the campaign.
FDR, meanwhile, was still flat on his back on East Sixty-fifth Street. FDR to [Voter's name],
November 1, 1912, FDRL.

doxology."[55] Howe was as good as his word. Without ever setting foot in his district, Franklin won by a larger margin than he had two years before.[56]

FDR's victory was part of a Democratic sweep. Wilson defeated TR by 2 million votes and Taft by almost 3 million.* In the electoral college, Wilson carried forty of the forty-eight states with 435 votes, Roosevelt carried six states with 88 votes, while Taft carried only Utah and Vermont for a total of 8 votes. The Democrats added 61 seats in the House of Representatives, giving them a lopsided 291-127 majority, and regained control of the Senate for the first time since 1895.[57] In New York, Tammany's "Plain Bill" Sulzer easily won a three-cornered race for governor and the Democrats regained control of both houses of the legislature. FDR led the ticket in the Twenty-sixth Senatorial District, running 700 votes ahead of both Wilson and Sulzer. "Congratulations on your deserved and notable victory," wrote FDR's Dutchess County friend John Walker. "When a bull moose and an elephant are both outrun by a man sick-a-bed it would seem 'Manifest Destiny.' "[58]

Franklin returned to Albany in January 1913, still so frail and pallid that Eleanor worried about his ability to carry on. "I'm very well and taking care of myself," he wrote reassuringly. "Wearing rubbers, brushing my teeth, etc., etc." As Howe had predicted, FDR became chairman of the Senate Agriculture Committee and the ranking member of Forest, Fish, and Game. "This isn't bad," he wrote Eleanor. "I am particularly glad that the other members of Agriculture gave me control of the committee as against our N.Y. City friends."[59]

Roosevelt evidently assumed he would be joining the Wilson administration when it took office on March 4. Instead of the opulent houses they had rented in previous sessions, he and Eleanor took a two-room suite at the Ten Eyck Hotel. They commuted to Albany Tuesday through Thursday while the children remained at the town house on East Sixty-fifth Street.

The first hint that FDR might go to Washington came on January 13, 1913, when he received a telegram from Joseph Tumulty, Wilson's private secretary, summoning him to Trenton for a conference with the president-elect.[60] Pa-

---

* The final returns showed Wilson with 6,293,152 to Theodore Roosevelt's 4,119,207 and Taft's 3,486,333. Eugene V. Debs, the Socialist candidate, received 900,369, mostly in the West, where agrarian unrest was rampant (he received 16.5 percent of the vote in Nevada and 16.4 percent in Oklahoma). Congressional Quarterly, *Guide to U.S. Elections* 284 (Washington, D.C.: Congressional Quarterly Inc., 1975).

tronage matters were discussed, and Tumulty pressed Roosevelt on his willingness to join the administration. Tangential evidence suggests that FDR expressed his preference for the number two post in the Navy Department.* No
formal offer was extended, yet Eleanor recalled that in the weeks leading up to
the inauguration Franklin was confident he would be going to Washington.
Whether he would become the assistant secretary of the Navy was less clear.[61]

Wilson chose his cabinet primarily to reward the faithful, repay obligations,
and punish his opponents. Little attention was paid to professional expertise
or even a modest awareness of the subject matter of each portfolio. William
Jennings Bryan had never been outside the United States when he became secretary of state. Lindley M. Garrison of New Jersey, the secretary of war, knew
precious little about the military but had a distinguished record as a conservative jurist and was given as hostage to the strict-constructionist wing of the
party.[62] When Garrison departed the cabinet in 1916, he was succeeded by
Newton D. Baker, the mayor of Cleveland. Baker too knew little about the
Army but had played a key role in swinging Ohio behind Wilson at a crucial
moment in Baltimore.[63]

As secretary of the Navy, Wilson chose North Carolina newspaper editor
Josephus Daniels. Daniels, from landlocked Raleigh, knew even less about the
Navy than Garrison did about the Army, but he had been a vital Wilson sup-
porter in the South and was on friendly terms with the president-elect.†
William Gibbs McAdoo of New York, whom Wilson tapped to be secretary of

---

* Michael Francis Doyle, a young Philadelphia lawyer active in both the Wilson and Bryan
presidential campaigns, was informed by Bryan shortly after the election that Wilson
planned to appoint him assistant secretary of the Navy. After FDR's visit to Trenton, Bryan
advised Doyle that Roosevelt had his eye on the position and urged Doyle to withdraw,
which Doyle did. Frank Freidel, interview with Michael Francis Doyle, October 17, 1947,
cited in Freidel, *Franklin D. Roosevelt: The Apprenticeship* 155 (Boston: Little, Brown, 1952).
† Daniels was initially concerned about his lack of nautical knowledge but rationalized his
acceptance by recalling that he had been a successful newspaper editor without understanding linotype machines or rotary presses. Horatio Nelson, after all, had been a poor sailor,
and, as Daniels would have it, Napoleon had had "no practical experience handling troops."
Daniels remained at the Navy Department for the entire eight years of the Wilson administration. Afterward he relished retelling the query put by a newsman to longtime Republican congressman Martin B. Madden of Illinois: "Can a civilian direct the Navy if he
had no experience in Naval affairs?" Madden answered, "Daniels did." Josephus Daniels,
The Wilson Era: Years of Peace—1910–1917 122–123 (Chapel Hill: University of North Carolina Press, 1944).

the Treasury, was a distinguished New York lawyer and railroad executive and would later become Wilson's son-in-law. But he had no background in finance. He was selected primarily because he was a prominent anti-Tammany Democrat who had worked vigorously for Wilson's election. His appointment sent an important message to the New York Democratic organization.

As attorney general, the logical choice was Louis Brandeis, widely regarded as the nation's leading advocate of judicial reform. Instead, Wilson repaid his debt to Tennessee's Cordell Hull and appointed James C. McReynolds from the Volunteer State. A decent lawyer who had served in TR's Justice Department, the ultraconservative McReynolds was scarcely a crusader for reform and had little in the way of national reputation. He proved the least congenial of Wilson's original appointees and was soon elevated to the Supreme Court, where he would later prove an implacable foe of Franklin Roosevelt and the New Deal.[64]

FDR made certain he was not overlooked. He and Eleanor took rooms at Washington's Willard Hotel on March 1, three days before the inauguration. Located at Fourteenth Street and Pennsylvania Avenue—less than two short blocks from the White House—the Willard had been a favorite with visiting politicians for decades. Lincoln had stayed at the old Willard before his inaugural, Grant had stayed there when he went to Washington to assume command, and virtually every subsequent chief executive had stayed at the Willard at one time or another. In 1913, most members of the incoming administration were among its guests, and Wilson attended a gala banquet there on the eve of his inaugural.[65]

On his first day at the hotel, FDR met the incoming Treasury secretary, William Gibbs McAdoo, with whom he had worked closely during the campaign. McAdoo was busy assembling his team at Treasury and asked Franklin if he would like to be either assistant secretary or collector of customs of the Port of New York. Both were prime appointments, particularly the collector's post, which would have provided FDR with a vast patronage base were he interested in running for statewide office in New York. Roosevelt was appreciative but noncommittal. McAdoo's offer was too good to turn down, but he still hoped for the post at Navy. Two days later, on the morning of the inauguration, Roosevelt ran into Josephus Daniels in the cavernous lobby of the Willard.

As Daniels recalled, FDR was bubbling with enthusiasm: "as keen as a boy to take in the inauguration ceremonies." Franklin congratulated Daniels on his appointment. Daniels responded by offering Roosevelt the appointment he sought: "How would you like to come to Washington as assistant secretary of the Navy?" Franklin beamed. "It would please me better than anything in the world," he told Daniels. "All my life I have loved ships and have been a student of the Navy, and the assistant secretaryship is the one place, above all others, that I would like to hold." Roosevelt said McAdoo had asked him to join Treasury, "but nothing would please me so much as to be with you in the Navy."[66]

The symbolism of the appointment was apparent. Daniels noted in his diary that Franklin's "distinguished cousin TR went from that place to the Presidency. May history repeat itself."[67] The Raleigh *News & Observer,* announcing FDR's posting, proclaimed, "He's Following in Teddy's Footsteps." Cousin Theodore, who at this point despised Wilson even more than Taft, penned a short note: "It is interesting that you are in another place which I myself once held. I am sure you will enjoy yourself to the full as Ass't Secty of the Navy and that you will do capital work."[68]

Before sending FDR's nomination to the Senate, Daniels, as custom required, consulted New York's Democratic senator, James Aloysius O'Gorman. O'Gorman owed his place in the Senate to FDR, and he assented readily. The Senate, he said, would confirm the appointment promptly.[69] Out of courtesy Daniels also touched base with the Empire State's distinguished senior senator, Republican Elihu Root. Root, who had served as secretary of war under McKinley and secretary of state under TR, had just been awarded the Nobel Peace Prize. As Daniels recalled, a queer look came over Root's face when he mentioned FDR. "You know the Roosevelts, don't you?" Root asked. "Whenever a Roosevelt rides, he wishes to ride in front." Root told Daniels he knew Franklin slightly and the appointment would be fine, "though, of course, being a Republican, I have no right to make any suggestion." Daniels replied that he wasn't worried about FDR and that he wanted a strong man as assistant secretary. "A chief who fears that an assistant will outrank him is not fit to be chief."[70]

After the inauguration FDR returned briefly to Albany to wind up his affairs. He paid a courtesy call on Senate leader Robert Wagner and asked whether he thought it was wise to go to Washington. "Go, Franklin, go," Wagner said, delighted to have Roosevelt in the nation's capital rather than Albany. "I'm sure you'll be a big success down there."[71]

SIX

ANCHORS AWEIGH

---

*As a member of the Wilson administration, Roosevelt
noted Wilson's personal difficulties with the
politicians, his remoteness and isolation from them.
Taking state committeemen to luncheons to listen to
and mollify their grievances was one of the chores
Franklin undertook. He unbent, laughed with them,
swapped yarns. FDR was good at this. He learned to
be a politician.*

—FRANCES PERKINS

THE WILSON ADMINISTRATION commenced on a high plane of moral rectitude. Mrs. Wilson canceled the inaugural ball as too frivolous for so solemn an occasion; the president, an avid golfer, declined membership in the Chevy Chase Country Club because it was too exclusive; and incoming Secretary of State William Jennings Bryan initiated the era of grape juice diplomacy by refusing to serve alcohol at state functions.[1] Wilson had campaigned under the banner of the New Freedom, which promised "the emancipation of the generous energies of the people," primarily through states' rights, free competition, and tariff reform.[2] But for the Virginia-born Wilson, the New Freedom was for whites only. The first southerner elected president since Zachary Taylor, Wilson immediately segregated the government's workforce. Black Republican appointees in the South were discharged and replaced by whites, and within six months government workers in Washington who had worked side by side for years found themselves separated by race.[3] "Public segregation of civil servants, necessarily involving personal insult and humiliation, has for the first time in history been made the policy of the United States government," lamented W. E. B. Du Bois, who, unlike most black leaders, had supported Wilson.[4]*

After sixteen years in the wilderness, the Democrats had returned to power—not old-school, high-caste, hard-money Cleveland Democrats but a coalition of agrarian populists, urban workers, middle-class progressives, and all ranks of southerners, who voted Democratic for the same reason most blacks voted Republican: Abraham Lincoln, Emancipation, and the Civil War.[5] The southern tilt of the Democratic party was more pronounced than ever, and with the GOP hopelessly divided, it was the South that called the tune.[6]

To head the Navy, Wilson had chosen Josephus Daniels, the populist editor of the Raleigh *News & Observer*, who had managed his campaign publicity in the South. Partially to achieve regional balance, Daniels chose FDR as his assis-

---

* Wilson, like many white southerners, believed segregation to be divinely ordained. As president of Princeton he barred the admission of blacks and later told Sambo stories in cabinet meetings. When challenged about segregation in the federal government, he defended it as a means of reducing tension. "It is as far as possible from being a movement *against* the Negroes," he wrote Oswald Garrison Villard of *The Nation*. "I sincerely believe it to be in their interest." In a similar message to H. A. Bridgman, editor of *Congregationalist and Christian World*, Wilson said, "I think if you were here on the ground [in Washington], you would see, as I seem to see, that it is distinctly to the advantage of the colored people themselves."

There is no doubt that was Wilson's view. There is also no doubt that virtually all black leaders were disappointed by it. "When the Wilson Administration came into power," wrote New York's *Amsterdam News*, "it promised a 'new freedom' to all people, avowing a spirit of Christian Democracy. But on the contrary we are given a stone instead of a loaf of bread; we are given a hissing serpent instead of a fish."

The NAACP was equally critical. In a public letter to Wilson published in *The New York Times*, the association asked, "Shall ten million of our citizens say that their civil liberties and rights are not safe in your hands? To ask that question is to answer it. They desire a 'New Freedom,' too."

Ironically, Wilson had appealed for black votes in 1912 and had actually won the largest number ever given to a Democratic presidential candidate. But the anti-Negro bias of the administration caused most blacks to return to the Republican Party, where they remained until FDR ran in 1932.

Arthur S. Link, *Wilson: The Road to the White House* 3, 502 (Princeton, N.J.: Princeton University Press, 1947); Josephus Daniels, *The Cabinet Diaries of Josephus Daniels* 195, 234, 321, 414, 493, E. David Cronon, ed. (Lincoln: University of Nebraska Press, 1963). WW to OGV, July 23, 1913; WW to HAB, September 8, 1919, Woodrow Wilson Papers, Library of Congress. *Amsterdam News*, October 3, 1913; *The New York Times*, August 18, 1913.

tant secretary, and the president submitted Franklin's nomination to the Senate on March 12, 1913. He was confirmed unanimously five days later. No hearings were held. Roosevelt, who had been waiting anxiously, promptly took the oath of office. It was March 17, his eighth wedding anniversary, and he immediately wrote Eleanor, who was at home in New York with the children:

> *My own dear Babbie:*
>
> *I didn't know until I sat down at this desk that this is the 17th of happy memory. In fact with all the subdued excitement of getting confirmed and taking the oath of office, the delightful significance of it all is only beginning to dawn on me. My only regret is that you could not have been with me but I am thinking of you a great deal.*[7]

The desk at which FDR wrote was the same mahogany behemoth Cousin Theodore had salvaged from a Navy storeroom sixteen years earlier. Festooned with hand-carved warships bulging from the side panels, it had originally been made for Gustavus Fox, the Navy's assistant secretary during the Civil War. TR had been thirty-eight at the time he was appointed; Franklin was barely thirty-one—the youngest assistant secretary in the history of the Navy, twenty years junior to Secretary Daniels, half the age of most flag officers, and forty-five years younger than Admiral George Dewey, hero of the battle of Manila Bay, the ranking officer on active duty.

Government was small in 1913, and the entire Navy Department was housed on two floors of the old State, War, and Navy Building, adjacent to the White House. An architectural monument in more ways than one (the stone walls were four feet thick), the opulent Second Empire style of the building epitomized the conspicuous consumption of America's Gilded Age.[8] Roosevelt's office on the third floor was almost as large and ornate as the connecting corner office Secretary Daniels occupied. Both enjoyed large French doors opening onto a balcony that overlooked the South Lawn of the White House, which FDR could see easily when seated at his desk.[9]

"Dearest Mama," Franklin wrote after he settled in. "I am baptized, confirmed, sworn in, vaccinated—and somewhat at sea! For over an hour I have been signing papers which had to be accepted on faith—but I hope luck will keep me out of jail." Absentmindedly, he signed the handwritten note to his mother with his full official signature, "Franklin D. Roosevelt." Sara noted the gaffe and did not miss a beat: "Try not to write your signature too small," she joked. "So many public men have such awful signatures."[10]

The Navy that Daniels and Roosevelt took charge of in 1913 had mastered the transition to modern weaponry but was hobbled by an administrative structure substantially unchanged since 1842. The fleet consisted of 259 ships, including 39 battleships and heavy cruisers, manned by 63,000 officers, sailors, and marines, with an annual budget of $144 million—roughly 20 percent of all federal expenditures.[11] The British Admiralty ranked it third in the world (behind Great Britain and Germany), but the numbers concealed the antiquated design of most of the American vessels.[12] The fleet was also divided into three independent formations (Atlantic, Pacific, and Asiatic), each with a separate command structure. Promotion was strictly by seniority, advancement was slow, and there was no overall commander analogous to Britain's First Sea Lord.

The barnacled logistical apparatus, originally patterned after the administrative boards of the Admiralty in the age of sail, had proved impervious to change. The department was organized into eight quasi-independent bureaus (Navigation, Ordnance, Equipment, Steam Engineering, Construction and Repair, Yards and Docks, Supplies and Accounts, Medicine and Surgery), each headed by a powerful chief who was legally responsible to Congress, not the secretary of the Navy or, for that matter, the president. The bureau chiefs, most of whom were admirals who had held their posts for years, conducted their business in splendid isolation from one another and with little regard for the department as a whole.[13] They often duplicated one another's work, competed furiously for appropriations, and steadfastly resisted any organizational change that would diminish their authority.

In 1903 Secretary of War Elihu Root brought the Army, which had a similar structure, reluctantly into the twentieth century. The power of independent branch chiefs such as the adjutant general and the chief of engineers was broken, a general staff system established, and the entire uniformed service brought under the command of a single military head, designated chief of staff to the secretary of war. As president, TR had attempted to reorganize the Navy along similar lines but had been defeated by congressional opposition precipitated by the bureau chiefs.[14]

Because of the autonomy of the bureaus, the Navy was considered the most difficult cabinet department to administer.[15] FDR was a vocal critic of the free-standing bureaus—they worked at cross-purposes to the department, he told the House Budget Committee in 1919—but it was not until after the attack on Pearl Harbor that he succeeded in bringing them under executive control.[16]

Roosevelt's duties as assistant secretary were not defined by statute.[17] Traditionally, the secretary of the Navy worked with the president on policy matters, dealt with Congress, and watched over the fleet. The assistant secretary handled the Navy's business affairs, rode herd on the bureaus, supervised civilian personnel, and negotiated contracts. But, as FDR said, "I get my fingers into just about everything and there's no law against it."[18] When TR had occupied the post, he had taken advantage of Secretary John D. Long's one-day absence from the department to flash the historic signal to Commodore Dewey to move against the Spanish fleet in the Philippines, and Franklin, whenever Daniels was away, enjoyed twitting reporters about potential parallels.[19] "There's another Roosevelt on the job today," he would say with a grin. "You remember what happened the last time a Roosevelt occupied a similar position?"[20]

Daniels and Roosevelt made an odd couple. Yet they served together harmoniously for virtually the entire eight years of Wilson's presidency. The strengths of one complemented the weaknesses of the other, and FDR learned from Daniels the folksy art of Washington politics. The fact is, Josephus Daniels was the only person to whom Franklin Roosevelt was ever directly subordinate. It was Daniels who made the decision to appoint him; it was Daniels who brought him to Washington; and it was Daniels who treated him as a father might treat a prodigal son whenever FDR wandered off the reservation. Daniels's motives were primarily political. Aside from regional balance, the name Roosevelt was solid gold in every wardroom in the fleet. Daniels also recognized that an energetic assistant with an amateur's knowledge of the sea would make his job easier. And though he did not know FDR well, he had liked him from their very first meeting and saw in him the future of the Democratic party.[21] Roosevelt, who throughout his life called Daniels "Chief," never forgot the debt he owed him.[22] Upon taking office in 1933, one of FDR's first acts as president was to appoint Daniels ambassador to Mexico, a post in which he served with distinction until 1941.[23]

FDR cut a splendid figure as assistant secretary: tall, athletic, well spoken, enthusiastic. Daniels called him "as handsome a figure of an attractive young man as I had ever seen."[24] The secretary, by contrast, was short, pudgy, slow-moving, and deliberate. Always slightly rumpled, he nevertheless dressed with studied southern formality—a tailored black frock coat in winter, white linen and seersucker in the summer. His pleated shirts were always white, his ties always black, and his high-top shoes always well polished. He wore broad-brimmed hats to shield his face from the sun and to the uninitiated looked like a stock figure from central casting.[25]

Courtly and modest, Daniels had an amiability that concealed an iron will and a remarkably wide-ranging intelligence. He was a tireless worker, a shrewd judge of people, and a longtime rebel against established authority. He suspected that what every admiral told him was wrong, and, as one observer noted, nine times out of ten he was correct.[26] Daniels could be as stubborn as a country mule, and he was also without fear. Two months after taking office he went for a training flight with Lieutenant John H. Towers, the pioneer Navy aviator, in a rudimentary open-cockpit, 75-horsepower flying machine at the breathtaking speed of sixty miles an hour—the first high-ranking government official to fly in an airplane. Asked by President Wilson why he had risked his life in such a contraption, Daniels said it was his duty to sign orders for naval officers to fly and "I would not assign any man to any duty I would not try myself."[27]

Daniels and William Jennings Bryan were intimate friends of long standing. They were also the two most radical members of Wilson's cabinet. For seventeen years they had worked to free the common man from the clutches of trusts, railroads, robber barons, and whatever other vested interest appeared on the horizon. Daniels served as Bryan's publicity director in each of his presidential campaigns, and the two shared a contempt for anything that smacked of wealth and special privilege. Together they sought to promote the values of an old-fashioned, rural, small-town America: pacifist, prohibitionist, and religiously fundamental. They opposed sin with the same vehemence that they opposed the plutocracy of the Republican party and often found it difficult to distinguish between the two.

Daniels brought these values to the Navy Department and aroused the wrath of the naval establishment in so doing. TR thundered that Wilson was guilty of "criminal misconduct in entrusting the State Department and the Navy Department to Bryan and Daniels."[28] While Bryan sought to paper the world with arbitration treaties, Daniels dreamed of disarmament, saw the Navy in terms of Wilsonian neutrality, and was more concerned with the welfare of the enlisted men entrusted to his care than building battleships or expanding the officer corps.[29]

In 1913 the Navy Department was its own little world. Henry L. Stimson, Taft's outgoing secretary of war, said it receded from the realm of logic "into a dim religious world in which Neptune was God and Mahan his prophet."[30] That did not deter Daniels. He defined civilian control as civilian command and with Wilson's support exercised it relentlessly. Daniels abolished the board of four admiral aides that stood between him and the department; limited the term of bureau chiefs to four years; and required deskbound officers to put to sea. He visited naval facilities from coast to coast, often breaking ranks to shake hands with enlisted men lined up for inspection; overrode reluctant admirals and ordered the fleet to cross the Atlantic in winter; and took issue with hallowed naval nomenclature that called left "port" and right "starboard." At Daniels's direction, FDR signed General Order No. 30 on May 5, 1913, requiring that directional instructions to the helmsman henceforth be given as "right" and "left."

Daniels also jettisoned the Navy's choker-collar uniforms, took engineering officers out of dress whites, and instituted a promotion system based on merit. But his overriding concern was to break down what he considered artificial barriers between officers and enlisted men. He opened the Naval Academy to enlisted applicants, added civilian instructors to the faculty, and sought to make every ship a floating "university" so that sailors would be better prepared to return to civilian life.[31] Daniels halted the practice of serving wine in the officers' mess, not only because he believed in temperance but because he thought it undemocratic. If enlisted men could not drink aboard ship, neither should their officers.[32] He also banned the issue of condoms to sailors going on shore leave. "It is equivalent to the government advising these boys that it is right and proper for them to indulge in an evil which perverts their morals."[33]

FDR was on an inspection trip to the West Coast when Daniels's temperance directive came down, but he supported it strongly. "The wine order is . . . on the whole absolutely right. It took nerve to do it, but tho the Secy will be unpopular in a small circle for a while, it will pay in the end."[34] There is no record of his response to Daniels's order pertaining to condoms.

Initially FDR thought Daniels a hopeless hayseed who would be over-whelmed by Washington politics. But as he watched the secretary seize control of the Navy Department, socialize with congressional committee chairmen like South Carolina's irascible "Pitchfork Ben" Tillman,[35] and deal intimately with Wilson in the White House, he changed his opinion.[36] Two incidents in the spring of 1913 confirmed that judgment. The first dealt with command authority. The State of California had recently adopted legislation forbidding Japanese citizens from owning land in the state.[37] On May 9 Japan lodged a vigorous protest with Washington. Wilson rejected the note, tempers flared, and relations deteriorated. Senior military and naval officials believed war to be inevitable. On May 14, the Joint Board of the Army and Navy, chaired by Admiral Dewey, with General Leonard Wood, the Army chief of staff, serving as vice chairman, unanimously recommended that the Navy immediately move the three large battle cruisers of the Asiatic fleet (*Saratoga*, *Monterey*, and *Monadnock*) from their station on the Yangtze River to the Philippines and that additional reinforcements be dispatched to Hawaii and Panama. Secretary of War Lindley M. Garrison approved the recommendations on May 15, and the following day two New York newspapers carried sensational stories that the Army and Navy were preparing for war.[38]

Daniels was outraged. He had not signed on, he disapproved of the recom-mendation, and he saw the press leak as a deliberate attempt to force his hand. He told his operations aide, Rear Admiral Bradley A. Fiske, that there would be no movement of ships without his or the president's order. Daniels said he did not think war was inevitable and that such a move by the Navy would scuttle efforts to achieve a negotiated settlement. He said that in his view the board had exceeded its authority, but he would lay the matter before the president.

Wilson backed Daniels, and that should have ended the discussion. But the admirals, accustomed to having their way under Taft and TR, appealed the de-cision. Wilson came down hard. It was the duty of the military to follow or-ders, not to challenge them, he told Fiske. The president thereupon ordered the Army and Navy Board not to meet again without his express authoriza-tion. The war scare subsided, and the board remained in limbo for the next two and a half years until, with World War I lapping at America's shores, Daniels recommended that it be reconvened.[39]

The second key event for FDR involved the Navy's contracting authority. Daniels hated monopolies, and the collusion among American steel companies bidding for Navy contracts aroused his special ire. FDR enjoyed telling how in the spring of 1913 he was present when Daniels met with representatives of Bethlehem, Carnegie, and Midvale Steel, each of which had submitted an identical bid for the armor plate to be used in constructing the battleship *Arizona*. Daniels threw the bids out and asked the companies to submit new figures by noon the next day. "I loved his words," FDR recalled, reflecting on the pained expressions of the businessmen as they left and his and Daniels's pleasure at their distress. But at noon the next day the steel men returned with exactly the same figures. Daniels threw those out as well and told FDR to take the next train to New York and meet with Sir John Hatfield, the leader of a British steel consortium who had just arrived in the United States. Hatfield submitted a substantially lower bid, which the American companies agreed to meet. Daniels told Congress that the Navy had saved $1,110,084 (roughly 10 percent of the total cost) as a result.[40]

For the first six months FDR led a bachelor's life in Washington, living first at the Willard, then at the Powhatan Hotel, an aging landmark at the corner of Eighteenth Street and Pennsylvania Avenue, little more than a block from his office. He joined the ultraexclusive Metropolitan Club (Wilson was not tendered an invitation), the Army-Navy Club, the University Club, and the Chevy Chase Country Club— these in addition to the New York clubs to which he already belonged: the New York Yacht Club, the Knickerbocker Club, the City Club, the Racquet and Tennis Club, and the Harvard Club—to all of which he paid dues regularly.[41] Eleanor was in New York with the children, then at Campobello for the summer. Franklin visited for the July Fourth weekend and ordered one of the Navy's largest battleships, the 22,000-ton *North Dakota*, to stand off Eastport, Maine—just across the narrow strait from Campobello— for the Independence Day celebration. The Roosevelts entertained the officers on the island, and FDR, who relished the pomp and ceremony attached to his office, later went aboard ship. He would not dress formally, he told the captain, but would appreciate the seventeen-gun salute to which he was entitled since his Campobello neighbors would expect it.[42]

Shortly thereafter, FDR ordered the destroyer *Flusser* to take him to the naval base at nearby Frenchman's Bay for an inspection. The *Flusser* was commanded by Lieutenant William F. Halsey, Jr., the famous Bull Halsey of World War II. Roosevelt asked Halsey's permission to pilot the ship through the treacherous Lubec narrows between Campobello and the mainland. With some misgiving, Halsey agreed. Handling a 700-ton destroyer under full power is a lot more complicated than sailing a pleasure boat. According to Halsey, "a destroyer's bow may point directly down the channel, yet she is not necessarily on a safe course. She pivots around a point near her bridge structure, which means that two-thirds of her length is aft of the pivot, and that her stern will swing in twice the arc of her bow. As Mr. Roosevelt made his first turn, I saw him look aft and check the swing of our stern. My worries were over. He knew his business."[43]*

Back in Washington, Franklin found the city hot and humid. Congress and the Supreme Court were adjourned, but in the executive branch it was business as usual. "The Secretary and I worked like niggers all day," he wrote Eleanor in late July. Daniels was preparing to go on vacation for two weeks and would leave FDR in charge. "He has given me carte blanche and says he will abide by my decisions."[44]

"I think it is quite big of him to be willing to let you decide," Eleanor replied. "It shows great confidence."[45]

Roosevelt could not have been happier. "I now find my vocation combined with my avocation in a delightful way," he wrote an old Harvard chum, Charlie Munn.[46] Socially, FDR had also arrived. Years later he liked to joke that Washington society provided three diversions: "the saloon, the salon, and the Salome." The "saloon" was a house where drinks flowed freely; the "salon" a house where artists and intellectuals congregated; the "Salome" was Roo-

* FDR met many young officers during his eight years as assistant secretary and did not forget them when he became commander in chief. Lieutenant Commander William D. Leahy was skipper of the Navy's Dolphin, the official yacht of the secretary and assistant secretary. Leahy became chief of naval operations in 1937, was later FDR's ambassador to Vichy France, and served as the president's personal chief of staff throughout World War II. Admiral Husband E. Kimmel, commander in chief of the Pacific fleet at Pearl Harbor, had been Roosevelt's naval aide in 1915. Lieutenant Emory S. Land, who later chaired the nation's Maritime Commission, served in that post as well. Lieutenants Harold Stark and Chester Nimitz, both CNOs (Nimitz after Roosevelt's death), were well known to FDR during World War I. The naval historian Robert Greenhalgh Albion wrote that as president, FDR always kept a copy of the Navy Register close at hand and knew most senior officers personally. "Some were remembered favorably, a few unfavorably, and some were not remembered at all." *Makers of Naval Policy: 1775–1941* 385 (Annapolis: Naval Institute Press, 1980).

sevelt's term for "a mansion where the music was soft, so were the sofas, and the ladies were very pretty." Franklin was welcome at all three.[47]

As a member of Wilson's subcabinet and as a Roosevelt, Franklin was readily accepted by Washington's cave-dwelling social establishment. His good looks, natural friendliness, and buoyant optimism made him a much-sought-after dinner companion. Bainbridge Colby, later secretary of state, thought him "the handsomest and most attractive man in Washington."[48] British diplomat Nigel Law found him "the most attractive man whom it was my good fortune to meet during my four years in America."[49] Yale football coach Walter Camp called him "a beautifully built man, with the long muscles of an athlete."[50]

Franklin was a frequent guest at the home of Cousin Alice and Nicholas Longworth, fashionable leaders of Republican society in exile. Longworth had been given a two-year sabbatical from Congress by the voters of Cincinnati, but that did little to dampen his hospitality or stanch the flow of booze and gossip for which he and Alice were famous.[51] TR's old friends such as the British and French ambassadors, Sir Cecil "Springy" Spring-Rice and Jules Jusserand, made a point of seeking Franklin out, as did Massachusetts senator Henry Cabot Lodge.* Harvard friends seemed to appear from nowhere; FDR entertained many of them cruising down the Potomac on the *Sylph*, the smaller of two yachts the Navy maintained for the president. Weekends were sometimes spent at Doughoregan Manor, the baronial Maryland estate leased by his old Harvard roommate, Lathrop Brown, who had just been elected to Congress as a Democrat from New York's silk-stocking First District on the Upper East Side.

---

* As a young diplomat Cecil Spring-Rice served as best man at TR's wedding to Edith Carow in 1886 and always had a warm spot in his heart for the president. "You must always remember that Roosevelt is about six," he gently reminded a friend when TR was in the White House. Jusserand, for his part, had once skinny-dipped with TR in the Potomac near Chain Bridge wearing only his gloves. "We might meet ladies," he informed the president when asked about his attire. Lodge and TR had maintained a mutual admiration society since the Republican National Convention in 1884, co-authored three books, and shared a view of America's muscular role in the world. Edmund Morris, *The Rise of Theodore Roosevelt*, 249–250, 357 (New York: Coward, McCann & Geoghegan, 1979); *Theodore Rex* 512–513 (New York: Random House, 2002).

For lunch, FDR usually dined at either the Metropolitan Club or the Army-Navy Club, both of which were within easy walking distance. Several times a week, and most weekends, he would hoist his golf bag over his shoulder and clamber aboard the Connecticut Avenue streetcar for the long ride to Chevy Chase. "Yesterday P.M. I golfed and went to the Department in the evening," he wrote Eleanor. "Today I have played 45 holes and am nearly dead!"[52] Roosevelt was a natural long-ball hitter and, according to the author Don Van Natta, Jr., one of the best presidential golfers to play the game.[53] Sometimes FDR would join a congressional foursome at Chevy Chase, and in later years he was often paired with the junior senator from Ohio, Warren G. Harding, who was as easygoing and likable as Roosevelt himself.[54]

In the autumn of 1913 Eleanor and the children joined Franklin in Washington. They moved into the handsome four-story brick town house owned by TR's sister Bamie (Eleanor's aunt and FDR's cousin) at 1733 N Street, N.W., six short blocks up Seventeenth Street from the Navy Department. Bamie and her husband, Rear Admiral W. Sheffield Cowles, had lived there when the admiral was stationed in Washington, and both Eleanor and Franklin had stayed in the house on their various visits to the capital when TR was president. In 1901 TR himself lived there briefly while Ida McKinley, the president's widow, vacated the White House. Later, as president, TR visited so frequently that the press began to call it the Little White House. "We're really very comfortably settled now in this dear, bright house," Eleanor wrote her friend Isabella Ferguson. "I feel very much at home, chiefly because Auntie Bye [Bamie] lived here."[55]

It was a snug fit. In addition to the three children (Anna, James, and Elliott), Eleanor brought a car and chauffeur from Hyde Park, four servants, a nurse, and a governess. Four years later, after the addition of two more children (FDR, Jr., and John), the Roosevelts moved to much larger quarters at 2131 R Street, a double town house some sixty feet wide that Bamie also owned.[56] Franklin and Eleanor paid the expenses in both houses but lived rent-free. Bamie and her husband were comfortably ensconced at "Oldgate," the Cowles estate in Farmington, Connecticut, and were content simply to have their Washington homes remain in the family. Meanwhile, FDR leased his New York town house on East Sixty-fifth Street to Thomas W. Lamont, a senior partner (and later chairman) of J. P. Morgan & Co.

Nineteen-thirteen was the first year for federal income tax under the Sixteenth Amendment. The rate was 1 percent, graduated to 6 percent for those with incomes above $500,000 a year. Dividends were not taxed. FDR's returns for the eight years he was in Washington show a gross income that averaged slightly more than $20,000 annually. (To convert to current dollars, multiply by 18.) Five thousand dollars came from his salary as assistant secretary, another $5,000 from rent on the New York town house, and the remainder from interest and dividends. FDR invested primarily in high-dividend-paying banks, railroads, and General Electric. After deductions and exemptions, his federal tax bills averaged somewhat less than $200.[57]*

It was as assistant secretary of the Navy that FDR established his enduring relationship with Louis Howe. Two days after he was sworn in, Franklin asked Howe to join him at the Navy Department (evidently he had made the offer before leaving Albany). "Dear Ludwig," he wrote. "Here's the dope. Secretary— $2000—Expect you April 1 with new uniform."[58] Howe telegraphed his acceptance instantly: "I am game but it's going to break me."[59] In truth, Howe had never made so much money, nor with more security. He hurried to Washington, bringing his family with him, and rented an apartment in the 1800 block of P Street, two blocks from the Roosevelts. Every morning at 8:15 sharp he would call for Franklin, and the two would walk to the Navy Department. FDR's son Elliott fondly remembers his father "striding down Connecticut Avenue with Louis hurrying along at his side. The two of them looked uncannily like Don Quixote and Sancho setting out to battle with giants."[60]

Howe was more than a secretary. Later he joked that when he arrived in Washington he knew so little that for the first several days he was reduced "to blotting Franklin's signature."[61] Within weeks he was on top of the job. Howe became the junior member of a two-man firm dedicated to furthering FDR's career. As one biographer has written, Howe and Roosevelt played politics like doubles partners played tennis and their goal from the beginning was the White House.[62] For Howe the decision was simple: he loved power. Eleanor, who later developed a great affection for Howe, said, "Louis had enormous in-

---

* FDR received his pay from the Navy Department every two weeks. Initially, he took it in cash and put the money in his pocket. "I don't know where it went, it just went. I couldn't keep an account with myself. After about six months of this, certain complaints came back from home about paying the grocery bill. And so I began taking my salary by check and putting it in the bank and taking perhaps five dollars cash for the week and putting it in my pocket—trying to anyway." Elliott Roosevelt and James Brough, *An Untold Story: The Roosevelts of Hyde Park* 66 (New York: G. P Putnam's Sons, 1973).

terest in having power, and if he could not have it for himself, he wanted it through someone he was influencing."[63] Roosevelt, for his part, found in Howe an extension of his own persona who automatically operated in his interest without requiring hands-on control. Howe had no agenda of his own. The veteran journalist John Gunther put it best when he wrote, "If FDR had come out for the Devil, it wouldn't have mattered much to Louis Howe."[64]

Ostensibly, Howe's duties involved labor relations, special investigations, and speechwriting. He also took charge of patronage, handled Roosevelt's correspondence, made appointments for his boss, wheedled postmasterships for deserving upstate Democrats, and kept his finger on the pulse of New York politics, building an organization to challenge Tammany when the time came. He thought up myriad projects for Roosevelt to sponsor and insofar as possible took the blame for whatever went wrong. He mastered the intricacies of the Navy's bureaucracy with remarkable swiftness. As Daniels put it, Howe "knew all the tides and eddies in the Navy Department, in the administration, and in the political life of the country. He advised [FDR] about everything. His one and only ambition was to help steer Franklin's course so that he could take the tide at the full. He was totally devoted. He would have sidetracked both President Wilson and me to get Franklin Roosevelt to the White House."[65]

FDR was never a friend of paperwork. He had an exceptional ability to absorb information and was able to make decisions rapidly, but his attention span was short. Paperwork was Howe's strength. He read quickly, wrote quickly, and had a way with words that was lucid and convincing. He had a newsman's ability to distill essential facts from vast amounts of information and make the most wearisome details appear interesting. Howe's mordant sense of humor, his distrust of piety, and his biting cynicism also appealed to FDR. Roosevelt's personal letters to Howe, often in a jocular German, express an instinctive rapport. "*Lieber Ludwig,*" he would write. "*Hier bin ich, mit grosser Gesundheit und Vergnügen,*" which translated means "Here I am in great health and having loads of fun."[66] FDR benefited personally as well. Howe, who loved to bet on the ponies and visit establishments less than genteel, knew much about life that Roosevelt never had the opportunity to learn. Howe shared those experiences and made Franklin more worldly. Frances Perkins once wrote that FDR's Harvard education was a political handicap.[67] In many respects Louis Howe was the antidote.

Howe, the older man, always called Roosevelt by his first name and spoke out whenever he thought FDR was mistaken. "Louis Howe was a damned smart able man and the best advisor Roosevelt ever had," said Admiral Emory S. Land, "because he had the guts to say 'no.' "[68] Few people could have talked to FDR the way Howe was overheard on the telephone: "You damned fool! You can't do that! You simply can't do it. . . . If you do it, you're a fool—just a damned idiotic fool." Howe said jokingly that his principal function in Washington was to provide "toe weights to keep Franklin's feet on the ground," and FDR accepted Howe's advice, usually without question.[69]*

As assistant secretary of the Navy, Roosevelt's impact on the policies of the Wilson administration was minimal. But his duties in the Navy Department were significant, and, more important, his eight years in Washington provided a proving ground where he learned the realities of national politics. Under the tutelage of Daniels and Howe, FDR came to appreciate the diversity of the Democratic party, the need to accommodate regional politicians, and the importance of small favors and public gestures. Howe taught Franklin how to deal with organized labor. As assistant secretary, FDR had supervisory responsibility for the Navy's vast civilian workforce—tens of thousands of workers at Navy yards across the country. Howe insisted that Roosevelt handle labor relations personally. Time and again he would usher union leaders and delegations of workmen into Franklin's office to chat with "the Boss." Always a good listener, FDR was at his best in these exchanges. "I want you to feel that you can come to me at any time in my office," he was soon telling union spokesmen, "and we can talk matters over. Let's get together for I need you to teach me your business and show me what's going on."[70]

Much to the discomfiture of the Navy's stiff-as-starch officer corps, the assistant secretary's office became the clearinghouse for labor's complaints. FDR took the workers' concerns seriously, and whenever possible used his author-

---

* FDR's son James reports a rare instance in which Roosevelt overruled Howe. It was 1932 in Chicago, en route to accepting the Democratic nomination. "I squeezed into the car which carried Father to the hotel. Louis Howe rode in the back seat next to Father, and immediately there began one of the most incongruous performances I have ever witnessed. Louis had strong objections to parts of Father's proposed acceptance speech and he began arguing with him even as the car was rolling in from the airport. Pa listened with one ear— all the while smiling and waving at the wildly cheering crowds. Finally, Pa exploded: 'Damnit, Louie, *I'm* the nominee.' " James Roosevelt and Sidney Shalett, *Affectionately, F.D.R.* 225–226 (New York: Harcourt, Brace, 1959).

ity to settle their grievances. "The laboring men all liked him," Daniels remembered. "If there was any Groton complex, he did not show it."[71]

Roosevelt's contact with union leaders filled a large gap in his political education. Many with whom he worked became lifelong friends and supporters. When he stepped down as assistant secretary in 1920, FDR could boast with only slight exaggeration that there had not been a single strike or work stoppage on his watch.[72] Eleanor said later that thanks to Louis Howe, FDR's experience overseeing the nation's Navy yards was largely responsible for having made her husband "more than just a very nice young man who went out in society and did a fair job but was perfectly conventional about it."[73]

Dealing with Congress proved equally instructive. FDR learned that informal favors granted graciously often counted for more on Capitol Hill than cogent arguments and party loyalty. Constituents routinely asked congressmen to run interference with government departments, and the Navy was no exception. Sometimes a sailor wanted an early discharge, sometimes compassionate leave, forgiveness for misdeeds, and so forth. Roosevelt did his best to fulfill every reasonable request that came from the Hill, and many of those that were not so reasonable as well.*

When Republican senator Henry Cabot Lodge, the ranking member of the Naval Affairs Committee, sought a promotion for his nephew, Roosevelt com-

---

* Occasionally a request was beyond the pale, especially if it ran against Daniels's puritanical instincts. In 1915 Congressman Lathrop Brown, FDR's Harvard roommate, wrote to request that a young friend named Donald Clapham be allowed to enlist in the Navy. Clapham had gone astray with a young woman, had been convicted of stealing $38, and had received a suspended sentence. Howe replied to Brown on FDR's behalf:

> Now, about your young friend . . . who appears to be one of nature's noblemen and to have nothing against him except that he has broken most of the Ten Commandments. I am willing to admit that if we bar from the Navy every gent who has become mixed up with a beautiful female we would have to put most of our ships out of commission and I am afraid we might lose an admiral or two, but in this case the young man was unfortunately caught with the goods. You have run against one of the secretary's strongest antipathies. And while I know Mr. Roosevelt will speak to Mr. Daniels about the case again, I honestly do not think he has a chance on earth. Do you want one of those "we are doing everything on earth to get this done because of the affection for the Congressman" letters or not? Will send you a masterpiece that will convince your friends that Mr. Roosevelt is sitting on Mr. Daniels' doorstep every night waiting for a chance to make one more plea when he comes home to supper, if that will ease the strain any.

Louis Howe to Lathrop Brown, September 21, 1915, FDRL.

plied.[74] When Massachusetts congressman George Tinkham asked that a young sailor, Josef Paul Zukauskas, be discharged because boxing manager John Buckley thought he had promise, FDR did so promptly. Zukauskas later fought professionally as Jack Sharkey, "the Boston Gob," and took the heavyweight title from Max Schmeling in 1932. Sitting in the Oval Office many years after that favor had been done, FDR told Frances Perkins that what congressmen wanted most was to have "a nice jolly understanding of their problems rather than lots of patronage. A little patronage, a lot of pleasure, and public signs of friendship and prestige—that's what makes a political leader secure with his people and that is what he wants anyhow."[75]

Other department responsibilities molded Roosevelt. The Navy was frequently called upon to maintain order and protect American interests in the Caribbean. For years he enjoyed telling how an agitated William Jennings Bryan raced into his office one afternoon in 1914 shouting, "I've got to have a battleship. White people are being killed in Haiti, and I must send a battleship there within twenty-four hours."

Roosevelt told Bryan that would be impossible. "Our battleships are in Narragansett Bay and I could not get one to Haiti in less than four days steaming at full speed. But I have a gunboat somewhere in the vicinity of Guantanamo and I can get her to Haiti in eight hours if you want me to."

"That is all I wanted," said Bryan. The secretary of state turned to leave, then stopped. "Roosevelt," he said, "when I talk about battleships, don't think I mean anything technical. All I meant was that I wanted something that would float and had guns on it."[76]

The situation in Haiti to which Bryan was responding was not unlike that which had erupted in the Dominican Republic ten years earlier. Because of widespread corruption in the collection of customs revenue, the Dominican Republic had found itself unable to pay the interest on its foreign debt. European powers had threatened to intervene, at which point Cousin Theodore had stepped in and assumed responsibility under color of the Monroe Doctrine.* The United States initially established a fiscal protectorate over the re-

---

* The "Roosevelt corollary" to the Monroe Doctrine, announced by TR in his annual message to Congress on December 6, 1904, provided that "Chronic wrongdoing, or an impotence which results in a general loosening of the ties of civilized society, may in America, as elsewhere, ultimately require intervention by some civilized nation, and in the Western

public and, when unrest did not abate, transformed that into a military occupation that continued until 1924.

In Haiti, the nation's finances had collapsed and France and Germany threatened to assume control to protect their investors. The Haitian government initially refused American assistance, riot and revolution followed, and in 1915 Wilson ordered Daniels to intervene. Marines were dispatched from Guantánamo to Port-au-Prince, and Haiti, like the Dominican Republic, became an American protectorate. Daniels staunchly opposed long-term occupation of the island, and gradually FDR embraced Daniels's position.[77] In his inaugural address in 1933, FDR replaced the Roosevelt corollary with what he called the "Good Neighbor" policy toward Latin America. Subsequently, at Montevideo in December 1933, the United States joined the nations of the Western Hemisphere in pledging that "No state has the right to intervene in the internal or external affairs of another."[78] The following year the United States formally renounced its right to intervene in Cuba under the Platt Amendment,[79] and FDR withdrew the last American marines from Haiti—nineteen years after the occupation had begun.

Hemisphere the adherence of the United States to the Monroe Doctrine may force the United States . . . to the exercise of an international police power." It was a unilateral blank check that allowed the United States to intervene in Latin America and became the bedrock of America's hemispheric policy from 1904 until 1930, when it was repudiated by Secretary of State Henry L. Stimson on behalf of the Hoover administration. The Monroe Doctrine, said Stimson, was "a declaration of the United States versus Europe, not the United States versus Latin America."

SEVEN

WAR

These dear, good people like W.J.B. [William Jennings Bryan]
and J.D. [Josephus Daniels] have as much conception of
what a general European war means as [four-year-old] Elliott
has of higher mathematics.
—FRANKLIN D. ROOSEVELT, AUGUST 2, 1914

AFTER A YEAR as assistant secretary, FDR grew restive in Washington. While he relished the ceremonial trappings of his office and reveled in the proximity to national power, he was still a pale second to Secretary Daniels and relegated to department housekeeping rather than the grand strategy and high politics to which he aspired. Much of the day-to-day work in the Navy Department he found tedious. He could recommend, but final authority rested with Daniels. Senator Elihu Root had recognized the trait: Roosevelts were accustomed to ride in front. A southern wit like Addie Daniels, Josephus's wife, would simply have said that Franklin was getting too big for his breeches.

Through Louis Howe, FDR kept tabs on New York politics. The state Democratic party was in more than the usual disarray, and Franklin maneuvered to exploit the confusion. If further advancement in Washington was temporarily blocked—as it clearly was—he would rekindle his career by seeking statewide office in New York. Roosevelt's perspective was clouded by Potomac myopia, the affliction of self-importance that often causes senior Washington officials to overestimate their significance in their home states, and in FDR's case he assumed that the governorship of the Empire State was within easy grasp.

"Plain Bill" Sulzer, who had been Tammany's handpicked choice for governor, had run afoul of the organization and was removed from office in October 1913. He was replaced by the reliable Martin H. Glynn, a Democratic stalwart from Albany. But the heavy hand of Tammany had tainted the impeachment process and made Glynn vulnerable. He was also Catholic, the first of that faith to occupy the governor's chair, and whether a Catholic could win a statewide election in 1914 was far from clear. In addition, New York had recently enacted the direct-primary law for which FDR had worked so diligently in the legislature. As Franklin saw it, that would limit Tammany's ability to dictate the party's nominee and open the way for a candidate with strong grassroots support—support that the name Roosevelt virtually ensured. Finally, FDR envisioned himself as the anointed candidate of the Wilson administration, departing Washington with the president's blessing to smite the Murphy machine on behalf of political reform.

Wilson's support was crucial to FDR's campaign. Yet throughout late 1913 and early 1914 the president refused to commit himself. He may have savored the thought of a reform victory in New York, but he needed the votes of the state's Tammany-dominated congressional delegation to put the New Freedom legislative program across. Howe launched a series of trial balloons for FDR in the New York press and did his utmost to hint at Wilson's support, but it was wishful thinking.[1] In March 1914, Roosevelt tried to force Wilson's hand. Ralph Pulitzer of *The New York World* had asked FDR to write an article for his paper on the political situation in the Empire State. Franklin asked Wilson for guidance. Could he have five minutes of the president's time to discuss the matter?[2] Wilson declined. Instead, he sent FDR a brief note advising him to say nothing. Events in New York were still unfolding, said the president, and "the plot is not yet clear."[3] That was scarcely the vote of confidence Roosevelt needed to challenge a Tammany incumbent in the primary.

When Franklin dispatched intermediaries to canvass Cousin Theodore's support, the result was equally disappointing. TR said he admired his young Hyde Park relative but was too busy mending fences with liberal Republicans to offer a Progressive endorsement.[4] The final blow to FDR's gubernatorial aspirations was administered by Congressman John J. Fitzgerald of Brooklyn, the powerful chairman of the Appropriations Committee and the Tammany spokesman in the House. Unless Wilson disavowed self-appointed critics of Tammany within the administration, said Fitzgerald, he and twenty other New York Democrats would find it difficult to support the New Freedom legislative agenda.[5] That finished FDR. Wilson issued a public statement saying he had the highest regard for Mr. Fitzgerald and certainly did not endorse the characterization of Tammany congressmen as "representatives of crooks, grafters, and buccaneers"—campaign rhetoric that had become a staple for FDR.[6]*

Roosevelt recognized the impossibility of his quest and put an upbeat spin on the outcome. "Thank God," he wrote Eleanor, "the governorship is out of the question."[7] To the *Times* he denied that he had ever been a candidate: "When I said I was not a candidate and would not accept the nomination, I did not say it in diplomatic language, but in seafaring language, which means it."[8]

The reason for FDR's jauntiness soon became apparent: an even more desirable statewide office was available. In May 1913 the Seventeenth Amendment, providing for the direct election of senators, was added to the Constitution. Senator Elihu Root's term was expiring, and Root, who had opposed the amendment in Senate debate, announced that he would not seek reelection.[9] That provided an opportunity FDR had not anticipated. The venerable Root was one of the most distinguished members of the Senate—secretary of war under McKinley, secretary of state under TR, recipient of the Nobel Peace Prize in 1912. Had Root run, he would have been unbeatable. Now the race was wide open. Even better, there was no Democratic incumbent to contest the nomination. Franklin could barely contain his excitement as he broke the news to Eleanor that he planned to seek both the Democratic and Progressive nominations for the U.S. Senate. "I really would like to be in the Senate just so as to get a summer with my family once every three or four years."[10]

FDR's 1914 flirtation with elective office was interrupted by events in Sarajevo, far off in the Balkans. On the morning of June 28, Austrian archduke Franz Ferdinand, heir apparent to the Hapsburg throne, and his wife, Sophie, Duchess of Hohenberg, were shot and killed by a nineteen-year-old Bosnian terrorist while riding in an open car in downtown Sarajevo. The assassin, Gavrilo Princip, one of seven young Bosnian co-conspirators, believed that by killing the archduke he would liberate Bosnia from Hapsburg captivity.[11] The

---

* In 1916, Wilson sealed his bargain with the New York regular organization when he tapped Martin H. Glynn to give the keynote address at the Democratic convention in Saint Louis, and it was Glynn, in that speech, who coined the slogan "He kept us out of war." In 1921, as a private citizen, Glynn introduced Prime Minister David Lloyd George to the Irish leader Eamon De Valera and brokered the deal that established the Irish Free State. *The New York Times,* October 7, 1923.

Serbian government was implicated in the assassination, and the Austrians demanded satisfaction. Germany backed Austria and gave Vienna a blank check to proceed as it wished. Diplomatic demands escalated, armies mobilized, governments miscalculated, and events took on a life of their own. The Concert of Europe, elaborately crafted by Viscount Castlereagh and Count Metternich one hundred years earlier and embellished by Otto von Bismarck and Benjamin Disraeli in the 1870s, came crashing down like a house of cards. The year before his death, Bismarck had predicted that "some damn foolish thing in the Balkans" would ignite a general war in Europe. Princip provided the spark that set things off.[12]*

On July 23, more than three weeks after the assassination of Franz Ferdinand, the Austrian government, believing itself ready for war and confident of German support, presented Serbia with an ultimatum couched in language carefully crafted to make it all but impossible for Belgrade to accept.[13] The Serbian reply, deliberately evasive, was rejected by Vienna on July 25, and both nations mobilized. Austria declared war on Serbia on July 28; Russia mobilized to support Serbia on July 30; France mobilized to support Russia the following day; and Germany called up its reserves immediately afterward.[14]† Last-

---

* Instability in the Balkans traced to the collapse of the Ottoman Empire and the defeat of Turkey by Russia in 1878. At the ensuing Congress of Berlin, Serbia, Romania, and Montenegro became independent states and Austria was given a mandate to occupy Bosnia and Herzegovina. In 1908 Austria unilaterally repudiated its occupation mandate and annexed the two provinces directly into the Austro-Hungarian Empire, precipitating the Annexation Crisis of 1908. Austria prevailed, but the reaction of the south Slavic people to the annexation was unforgiving.

Two minor Balkan wars in 1912 and 1913 redistributed the remaining territory of Turkey in Europe among Bulgaria, Greece, Romania, and Serbia. The ensuing treaties of London (May 30, 1913), Bucharest (August 10, 1913), and Constantinople (September 29, 1913) appeared to resolve all outstanding issues except the annexation of Bosnia and Herzegovina by Austria, which continued to rile Serbian irredentist sentiment. When Franz Ferdinand was assassinated, both Serbia and Austria welcomed the showdown, which both believed would be decisive. A balanced account is provided by Fritz Fischer in *Germany's Aims in the First World War* 51–57 (New York: W. W. Norton, 1967). Also see Gordon A. Craig, *Germany: 1866–1945* 302–338 (New York: Oxford University Press, 1978), and the classic study by Sidney B. Fay, *The Origins of the World War,* 2 vols. (New York: Macmillan, 1930).

† Because of the enormous military advantage acquired by the nation that mobilized first, the common law of European diplomacy held the act of mobilization tantamount to a declaration of war.

minute diplomatic efforts failed, and on August 1 Germany declared war on Russia. Locked in by military planning predicated on a two-front war, Germany declared war on France on August 3 and crossed into Belgium to outflank the French Army, which was drawn up facing the Franco-German border. The violation of Belgian neutrality brought Great Britain in on France's side, and Europe was at war.

The Central Powers believed that victory would be quick. "You will be home before the leaves have fallen from the trees," the kaiser told departing guards regiments in Potsdam the first week in August.[15] The British took a different view. "The lamps are going out all over Europe," lamented Foreign Secretary Sir Edward Grey. "We shall not see them lit again in our lifetime."[16] General Lord Kitchener, recalled from retirement by Prime Minister Herbert Asquith, said that the war "will take a very long time. No one living knows how long."[17]

FDR was fulfilling a speaking engagement for the Navy in Reading, Pennsylvania, when Germany declared war. Summoned by telegram to Washington, he jotted a quick note to Eleanor from the train: "The latest news is that Germany has declared war against Russia. A complete smashup is inevitable, and there are a great many problems for us to consider. These are history-making days. It will be the greatest war in the world's history. Mr. D. totally fails to grasp the situation and I am to see the President Monday a.m. to go over our own situation."[18] Whether Franklin was referring to the war in Europe or his political ambitions in New York is unclear, but Wilson had no time on Monday or any day that week: his wife, Ellen, was dying of cancer.[19]

With the possibility of war looming, FDR found it even more difficult to play second fiddle. His letters to Eleanor in early August brim with his own activity, in stark contrast to the lethargy he perceived around him. Inexperienced and impulsive, Roosevelt failed to appreciate Daniels's more cautious approach. The following day he wrote that upon his arrival in Washington,

> I went straight to the Department, where as I expected, I found everything asleep and apparently utterly oblivious to the fact that the most terrible drama in history was about to be enacted.
>
> To my astonishment nobody seemed the least bit excited about the European crisis—Mr. Daniels feeling chiefly very sad that his faith in human nature and civilization and similar idealistic nonsense was re-

ceiving such a rude shock. So I started in alone to get things ready and prepare plans for what *ought* to be done by the Navy end of things. . . .

These dear, good people like W.J.B. and J.D. have as much conception of what a general European war means as Elliott has of higher mathematics. They really believe that because we are neutral we can go about our business as usual. . . .

All this sounds like borrowing trouble I know, but it is *my* duty to keep the Navy in a position where no chances, even the most remote, are taken. Today we are taking chances and I nearly boil over when I see the cheery "mañana" way of doing business.[20]

Franklin told Eleanor he saw no hope of averting the conflict. "The best that can be expected is either a sharp, complete and quick victory by one side, a most unlikely occurrence, or a speedy realization of impending bankruptcy by all, and a cessation by mutual consent, but this too I think unlikely."[21]

Eleanor said she understood. "I am not surprised at what you say about J.D. or W.J.B. for one could expect little else. To understand the present gigantic conflict one must have at least a glimmering of understanding foreign nations. . . . Life must be exciting for you and I can see you managing everything while J.D. wrings his hands in horror. There must be so much detail to attend to and so many problems which must, of course, be yours and not J.D.'s."[22]

As it turned out, Daniels was more in tune with administration policy than his brash assistant secretary. On August 4, 1914, President Wilson issued the first of ten neutrality proclamations that would be promulgated during the first three months of the war. These committed the United States to complete neutrality and made it a crime for anyone to be partial beyond the "free expression of opinion."[23] Two days later Wilson told Daniels to order all officers "to refrain from public comment of any kind upon the military or political situation on the other side of the water." The Navy was instructed to "watch things along the coast," protect the neutrality of American ports, and prevent the shipment of munitions to any of the belligerents.[24] FDR was appointed to two quickly established cabinet-level committees, one to translate the principles of the neutrality proclamations into practical policy, the other to provide relief for Americans stranded in Europe by the war. He arranged for the battleships *North Carolina* and *Tennessee* to sail for the Continent loaded with gold bullion to subsidize the credit of Americans caught in the war zone and organized a coastal patrol to prevent belligerent warships from venturing too close to U.S. shores. "Most of those reports of foreign cruisers off the coast have really been *my* destroyers," Franklin proudly wrote Eleanor on August 7.[25]

FDR was consumed by the war in Europe and the Navy's responsibility. "I am running the real work, although Josephus is here," he told Eleanor.[26] But over his shoulder, Roosevelt watched what was happening in New York. The prospect of succeeding Elihu Root in the Senate was too enticing to let slip. Treasury secretary William Gibbs McAdoo, who considered himself the de facto leader of the reform wing of the Democratic party in New York, was urging FDR to run, and on August 13, following a lightning visit to Manhattan, Franklin announced his candidacy.[27] "My senses have not yet left me," he wired Louis Howe, who was vacationing with his family on the Massachusetts shore.[28]

Daniels sought to dissuade FDR. "I told him that I had a hunch he could not win in the primary, and even if he did the indications were that the Republicans would carry the State [in November]."[29] Franklin refused to be deterred. "I had no more idea or desire of offering myself as a 'white hope' than I had of attempting to succeed Kaiser Wilhelm," he disingenuously told a friend shortly after he announced. "I protested, but finally agreed to be the goat. Now I am going into the fight as hard as I can."[30] FDR was confident that the Democratic nomination was his for the taking. He remained at Campobello for the remainder of August and did not bother to appear at the campaign kickoff rally Howe organized at New York City's Cooper Union on September 2. Primary day was September 28, and thus far no opposition candidate had announced.

Early press reports indicated New York publisher William Randolph Hearst might seek the nomination. FDR wrote Howe he was "offering up prayers" that the reports were true. "It would be magnificent sport and also a magnificent service to run against him." But Hearst stepped back.[31]

In late August, Governor Glynn endorsed Roosevelt, and hope rose that Tammany would let the nomination pass by default. "The truth is that they haven't a thing to say against you," Howe told Franklin. "No one is anxious to bell the cat—particularly when they have an idea that the President occasionally pats him on the back and calls him 'pretty pussy.' "[32]

Once again FDR underestimated the political skill of Charles Murphy. On September 6, the next-to-the-last day for filing, Tammany unveiled its candidate: James W. Gerard, United States ambassador to Germany and former

State Supreme Court justice, an independently wealthy, impeccably honest adherent of the New York City organization who had already distinguished himself assisting Americans stranded in Germany by the war. Even worse for Roosevelt, Gerard had cleared his candidacy with the White House.[33] The ambassador said his duties in Berlin would not permit his return to campaign, which compounded FDR's problem. Not only did he have no visible opponent to attack, but he could scarcely pose as the administration's candidate when Wilson's personal representative in Berlin remained at his post with the president's approval. With one bold stroke Murphy undercut Roosevelt's campaign and proved why under his leadership Tammany had become so formidable.

FDR was caught unprepared. He had not expected a rival and was not ready to campaign. He crisscrossed the state several times but made little impression on the voters. Roosevelt had no particular message other than his opposition to "bossism" and he had surprisingly little grasp of the issues facing the state. "When compared to such a man as Elihu Root he cuts a sorry figure as a great statesman," commented one upstate paper.[34]

When the votes were counted on September 28, FDR was swamped by his absentee opponent. Gerard received 210,765 votes to Roosevelt's 76,888. The ambassador led FDR 4 to 1 in New York City and 2 to 1 upstate. Franklin's only consolation was to carry twenty-two of the state's sixty-one counties, including Dutchess, which he won 461–93. "I wonder if you are disappointed," his mother wrote. "I hope you are not. You made a brave fight and can now return to the good and necessary work of the Navy Department, which you have missed all these weeks."[35]

Franklin assured Sara that he was not disappointed and cheerily told the press it had been a good fight.[36] Within weeks he put a Roosevelt twist on the disaster, claiming to have carried a majority of the state's counties and losing only because of "the solid lineup of New York City," ignoring the fact that Gerard had trounced him 2 to 1 upstate.[37] Daniels, who had watched the campaign from a distance, believed the loss hurt FDR more than he cared to admit. "I refrained from telling him 'I told you so.' "[38]

As Daniels had predicted, November was a bad month for Democrats. In the general election, the GOP gained 69 seats in the House of Representatives and picked up seven governorships. In New York, Gerard, who remained at his post in Berlin, lost the Senate race to James Wadsworth of Geneseo by 70,000 votes; Glynn lost his bid for reelection as governor to Charles S. Whitman; and the Republicans recaptured both houses of the legislature.

Both Franklin and Charles Murphy learned from the debacle. Murphy recognized that while Tammany could dictate the party's nominee, it could not guarantee victory in the general election. FDR learned that running statewide was far more complicated than contesting a three-county Senate seat. He also learned he could not defy the New York City organization if he wanted the nomination, nor could he win in November without Tammany's support. Howe suggested to Franklin that it was time to make peace, and FDR needed little coaxing. Never again did he publicly criticize Tammany Hall.[39]

By 1915 Roosevelt had become a virtual regular in the New York organization. He endorsed Al Smith, Tammany's candidate for sheriff of New York County, supported Senate leader Robert Wagner for postmaster of New York City,* and posed happily with Charles Murphy at Tammany's annual Fourth of July celebration. There was even talk that FDR might head the ticket in 1916 as Murphy's candidate for governor.[40]

FDR made peace with Tammany because his political career required it. But he never forgave Gerard for having defeated him. In October 1914, Colonel House, Wilson's political majordomo, wrote McAdoo to urge Franklin to come out strongly for Gerard before the November election. Roosevelt returned the note with "NUTS F.D.R." scrawled across the top.[41] Years later, as president, Roosevelt still held a grudge. James Farley, whose job it was to keep tabs on Democratic donors, urged that Gerard (one of the largest contributors and in Farley's words "a faithful servant of the Democratic Party") be appointed ambassador to Italy. "Roosevelt was evasive," said Farley, "and William Phillips was nominated. I proposed Gerard for Paris, but William C. Bullitt was named." Eventually Farley persuaded FDR to name Gerard as his representative to the coronation of King George VI in 1937, but that was a one-shot ceremonial appearance.[42] In 1943, Eleanor attempted to make peace between the president and Gerard, but Roosevelt's answer was still no.[43]

---

* Wagner, who had his heart set on becoming a judge of the New York Court of Appeals, the state's highest court, was taken by surprise and declined the powerful patronage position of postmaster. Three years later he got his wish and was elevated to the bench, where he served until elected to the U.S. Senate in 1926. Wagner was reelected to the Senate in 1932, 1938, and 1944 and served until he resigned because of ill health in 1946.

Back in Washington, FDR turned his attention to the Navy's preparedness. From an Allied point of view, the war was not going well. The great German offensive in the West had been blunted, but the battle line was forty miles from Paris. The French government had decamped for Bordeaux, virtually all of Belgium was in German hands, and trenches stretched from Ostend on the English Channel to the Swiss border. In the East, General Paul von Hindenburg had turned back the Russian invasion of East Prussia and was moving eastward toward the Vistula. On the Serbian front, the Austrians advanced, retreated, and advanced again, taking Belgrade for the second time. The one glimmer of hope was the war at sea, where the powerful British Navy kept the German High Seas Fleet bottled up in ports along the North Sea, reluctant to risk a direct engagement.

Smarting from his defeat in the New York primary, Roosevelt was eager to resume the struggle to put the Navy on a war footing. In late October, when Daniels left Washington to inspect facilities on the Gulf Coast, FDR took advantage of the secretary's absence to release a memorandum prepared by the Navy's brass documenting the fleet's deficiencies. Thirteen battleships were laid up because the Navy lacked sailors to man them. Eighteen thousand men were needed urgently, but Congress had failed to authorize them. *The New York Times* printed the memorandum in full, much to the discomfort of the White House.[44] "The country needs the truth about the Army and Navy instead of a lot of soft mush about everlasting peace," Franklin wrote Eleanor. "I am perfectly willing to stand by [the memorandum] even if it gets me into trouble."[45]

Trouble may have come more swiftly than FDR anticipated. Daniels was not happy with his deputy's performance, and when he returned to Washington he took Franklin to the woodshed. The next day Roosevelt issued a disclaimer. "I have not recommended 18,000 more men," he told the press, "nor would I consider it within my province to make any recommendation on the matter one way or the other."[46]

On December 8, 1914, Wilson forcefully restated the administration's policy. Speaking to Congress on the state of the union,* the president counseled against turning the United States into an armed camp:

---

* Wilson reinstituted the practice of Presidents Washington and John Adams of delivering the State of the Union message in person to a joint session of Congress—a practice in desuetude since Thomas Jefferson's time.

We are at peace with the world. We mean to live our own lives as we will; but we also mean to let live. We are, indeed, a true friend to all the nations of the world, because we threaten none, covet the possessions of none, desire the overthrow of none. Therein lies our greatness.

Wilson rejected any increase in the size of the regular Army, dismissed an expansion of the reserves, and said an accelerated naval construction program would require greater study to determine precisely what type of ships should be built. "We shall not alter our attitude because some amongst us are nervous and excited."[47]

The following day Daniels assured the House Naval Affairs Committee that ship for ship the U.S. Navy was the equal of any navy in the world. He said the Navy would continue its program of building two battleships a year and requested no increase in the number of enlisted men.[48]

The committee called FDR to testify on December 16. He had plainly learned his lesson. "It would not be my place to discuss purely matters of policy," Roosevelt told the congressmen at the outset.[49] Pressed repeatedly during the five hours he was at the witness table, he steadfastly declined to discuss administration policy and did not contradict Daniels or the president at any point. In his testimony, FDR hewed closely to the facts. He had the details of every program at his fingertips and frequently cited Navy department studies to make the point that if war should come, a rapid expansion would be necessary. He was anything but shrill, and at times he was even amusing. "It is a necessity as a matter of economy that all our ships should not be in commission all the time," he told the committee. "No navy does that except that of one country."

"What country is that?" demanded several members in unison.

"Haiti," replied Roosevelt, smiling broadly. "She has two gunboats and they are in commission all the year around."[50]

FDR's testimony was a success. The *New York Herald* praised him for his promptness in answering questions and his candor. "He showed that in the short time he has been Assistant Secretary he has made a most complete study of the problems of national defense." The *Sun* said Roosevelt "exhibited a grasp of naval affairs that seemed to astonish members of the committee who had been studying the question for years."[51]

Franklin wrote Sara that the hearings had been "really great fun . . . as the members who tried to quizz me and put me in a hole did not know much about their subject and I was able not only to parry but to come back at them with thrusts that went home. Also I was able to get in my own views without particular embarrassment to the Secretary."[52]

Eleanor wrote afterward to her friend Isabella Ferguson, "War is in all our thoughts and the horror of it grows. We are distinctly 'not ready,' and Franklin tried to make his testimony before Congress very plain and I think brought out his facts clearly without saying anything about the administration policy which would of course, be disloyal."[53]

FDR was eager to see the naval war firsthand. In mid-December, immediately after his House testimony, he sought to go to London to study the workings of the Admiralty. Winston Churchill was then first lord of the Admiralty, the British equivalent of secretary of the Navy, and he was piqued that the United States had not yet entered the war. He claimed he was far too busy to receive a delegation of visiting Americans. "I have asked the First Lord as to the possibility of affording facilities to Mr. F. D. Roosevelt and a staff of United States Naval Officers," the permanent undersecretary of the Admiralty informed the American embassy on December 19. "The First Lord desires me to express his regret that the present pressure of work in the Department would render it impossible to offer the assistance necessary for the accomplishment of the object of such a visit."[54] That was FDR's only brush with Churchill until the two met four years later at a dinner given for the British war cabinet by Lloyd George. That too was unpromising.[55] Twenty-three years later, when the two statesmen met off Newfoundland to frame the Atlantic Charter, Churchill (to FDR's chagrin) had no recollection of their prior meeting.[56]

In 1915 the war at sea accelerated. On February 4 Germany declared the waters surrounding the British Isles a war zone: Allied vessels would be sunk on sight; neutral merchantmen that entered did so at their own risk.[57] Britain responded on March 1 with a counterblockade of German ports.[58] Wilson composed the United States' reply to the German announcement at his own typewriter and warned Berlin it would be held to "strict accountability" for the loss of American lives or property.[59] The response to Britain, prepared jointly by Wilson, Secretary Bryan, and Department of State counselor Robert Lansing, was milder in tone and enjoined London to treat American shipping according to the "recognized rules of international law."[60]

Wilson's effort to maintain American neutrality suffered a severe shock on May 7, 1915, when the Cunard liner *Lusitania*, the largest and fastest on the

North Atlantic run, was torpedoed in the Irish Sea and sank in eighteen minutes. Of the 2,000 persons on board, 1,198 perished, including 128 Americans. Public opinion was outraged. Newspapers railed against the "wanton murder" of helpless civilians.*

Wilson sought to calm the nation. "There is such a thing as a man being too proud to fight," he declared and dispatched a protest note to Berlin reasserting the right of Americans to sail the high seas and demanding indemnity for the loss of American lives.[61] Except for war hawks like TR, the note struck a responsive chord with the public: "a model of restraint and understatement," said *The New Republic.* "It reproduces with remarkable skill the mean of American opinion."[62] Berlin's reply, drafted with an eye to German public opinion, expressed regret, placed the blame on Cunard for carrying passengers and munitions on the same ship, and requested a delay in settling the matter until the facts could be established.[63] At the same time, and unknown to Washington, the German government ordered its U-boat commanders not to attack large passenger liners, "not even an enemy one," until further notice.[64]

The American press greeted the German reply harshly. Wilson believed Berlin was unresponsive and stalling for time. Again he pecked out a rejoinder, this time insisting that Germany renounce its "ruthless" submarine warfare and condemning the sinking of *Lusitania* as a crime against humanity.[65] Bryan, who thought the German response more than adequate, welcomed the delay Berlin requested so tempers might cool. He was certain the president's note carried the risk of war and, rather than sign it, submitted his resignation.

---

* The sinking of the *Lusitania* has intrigued historians for almost a century. The ship flew the British flag and, in addition to the passenger complement, carried 4,200 cases of cartridges and 1,250 cases of shrapnel shells. Before it sailed from New York, the German Embassy in Washington placed notices in all major newspapers warning Americans of the danger involved in traveling on a British vessel in a war zone.

The German submarine U-20, which intercepted the ship, had completed its patrol in the Irish Sea and was returning to port with only three torpedoes remaining. Captain William T. Turner of *Lusitania* had been warned of the presence of a submarine in the area and instructed to sail a zigzag course. Instead, he steered straight ahead and inexplicably reduced speed to eighteen knots, making the ship an easy target. U-20 fired only one torpedo and hit *Lusitania* on the starboard bow, just behind the bridge. The hit was followed by an enormous explosion and a massive smoke cloud. Diana Preston, *Lusitania: An Epic Tragedy* 91–241 (New York: Walker & Co., 2002); Thomas A. Bailey and Paul B. Ryan, *The Lusitania Disaster* 128–225 (New York: The Free Press, 1975); A. A. and Mary Hoehling, *The Last Voyage of the Lusitania* 102 ff (New York: Holt, 1955).

"A person would have to be very much biased in favor of the Allies to insist that ammunitions intended for one of the belligerents should be safeguarded in transit by the lives of American citizens."[66]

Bryan's resignation threw Washington into an uproar. The secretary was assailed for unspeakable treachery, weakening the president's hand and suggesting to foreign nations that the United States was divided. FDR joined the chorus. "What d' y' think of W. Jay B.?" he asked Eleanor. "It's all too long to write about, but I can only say I'm disgusted clear through. J. D. will *not* resign."[67]*

Daniels and the other members of the cabinet rallied to the president's support, as did FDR. To Wilson he wrote, "I want to tell you simply that you have been in my thoughts during these days and that I realize to the full all that you have had to go through—I need not repeat to you my own earlier loyalty and devotion—that I hope you know. But I feel most strongly that the Nation approves and sustains your course and that it is *American* in the highest sense."[68]

Wilson's longhand reply was heartfelt. "Your letter touched me very much," said the president. "Such messages make the performance of duty worthwhile, because, after all, the people who are nearest are those whose judgment we most value and most need to be supported by."[69]

In the months following Bryan's resignation, FDR toiled diligently to enhance the Navy's readiness—but always within the policy bounds Wilson and Daniels had established. Charles Murphy had taught Roosevelt the importance of disparate political alliances and Democratic solidarity: "They may be sons-of-bitches, but they're our sons-of-bitches." Daniels taught him to be a team player—a lesson TR never learned. Franklin sometimes chomped at the restraint and occasionally overstepped, but he was careful never to challenge administration policy directly.

FDR was recuperating at Campobello from a bout of appendicitis in late July 1915 when Daniels summoned him to Washington to help draft plans for the Navy's expansion.† Wilson had become increasingly worried about Ger-

---

* Twenty years later, seasoned by the responsibilities of the presidency, the revelations of the Nye Committee about the prewar machinations of America's munitions makers, and his own second thoughts, FDR recanted his harsh judgment of Bryan. To Daniels he wrote, "Would that W.J.B. had stayed on as Secretary of State—the Country would have been better off." FDR to JD, October 3, 1934, Daniels Papers, Library of Congress.

† Roosevelt suffered a sudden appendicitis attack in Washington the morning of July 1 and

many's intentions as well as his reelection chances. Public opinion, particularly on the East Coast and in the South, had become increasingly militant and the president decided it prudent to stay in step. On July 21 he instructed Daniels and Secretary of War Lindley Garrison to prepare a program for "an adequate national defense" that might be submitted to Congress when it convened in December.[70] FDR was elated. He returned to Washington in mid-August to serve as acting secretary while Daniels vacationed, and helped pull plans together. To achieve supremacy at sea, the Navy's General Board urged immediate construction of 176 ships at a cost of $600 million—the largest peacetime construction program in the nation's history. The proposal included ten battleships, six battle cruisers, ten light cruisers, fifty destroyers, and one hundred submarines, along with the sailors to man them.[71] Wilson approved the plan and submitted it to Congress on December 7, 1915. Daniels, whose peace-loving credentials were unassailable, undermined the pacifist opposition and shepherded the legislation through Congress, which authorized completion of the entire program within three years.*

For the next fourteen months the argument within the administration turned on how rapidly the United States should mobilize, not whether mobilization was necessary. FDR devised a plan for a Council of National Defense to oversee war production and took it directly to Wilson, who was unwilling to go that far. "It seems that I can accomplish little just now," Franklin wrote Eleanor. "The President does not want to 'rattle the sword,' but he was interested and will I think really take it up soon."[72] Roosevelt continued to press the project, and the council came into being in August 1916, the proposal attached as a rider to the Army appropriations bill. The council was empowered to place defense contracts directly with suppliers and draw plans for the "immediate concentration and utilization of the resources of the nation."[73] FDR played an

---

was operated on that afternoon. Daniels ordered the secretary's yacht, *Dolphin,* to take him to Campobello to recover and checked regularly on his progress. TR wired his concern, as did the Japanese naval attaché, Commander Kichisaburo Nomura. At the time of Pearl Harbor, Nomura was Japanese ambassador to the United States.

* Daniels saw preparedness as a means of preventing war; FDR looked on it as a prerequisite. Many years later Daniels recalled that Franklin on any number of occasions came into his office and said, "We've got to get into this war." Each time Daniels replied, "I hope not." Daniels, interview with Frank Freidel, May 29, 1947, quoted in Freidel, *Franklin D. Roosevelt: The Apprenticeship* 267 (Boston: Little, Brown, 1952).

important role in establishing the council and would draw on that experience in 1940, after the fall of France, when he reactivated the council's advisory panel as the first significant defense agency of World War II.[74]

Another pet project involved creation of a naval reserve. FDR was impressed with the training camp Cousin Theodore and General Leonard Wood had established at Plattsburgh, New York, to drill young gentlemen in the rudiments of military life, and he wished to establish a naval counterpart.* Initially, the going was heavy. Daniels feared the reserve would appeal primarily to rich young Ivy Leaguers and well-to-do yachtsmen and would have an upper-class bias. Franklin assured him otherwise. "You may take my word for it," he told Daniels, the reserve would be constituted "on absolutely democratic lines."[75] Daniels was won over and permitted a preliminary cruise in the summer of 1916 but procrastinated establishing the reserve itself. On September 2, with Daniels away, FDR as acting secretary ordered the creation of a Naval Reserve of fifty thousand men along with an auxiliary complement of patrol boats.[76] "Today I sprang the announcement ... and trust J.D. will like it," Franklin wrote Eleanor. "It is of the utmost importance and I have failed for a year to get him to take any action, though he never objected to it. Now I have gone ahead and pulled the trigger myself. I suppose the bullet may bounce back on me, but it is not revolutionary nor alarmist and is just common sense."[77]

Nineteen-sixteen was a presidential election year, and as a preparedness Democrat FDR was a distinct asset to the administration: a Roosevelt on display to offset the criticism of Cousin Theodore and the interventionist wing of the GOP. Wilson's chances looked dim. His narrow victory in 1912 traced to the split in Republican ranks between party regulars under Taft and progressive insurgents backing TR. But in the spring of 1916 the Colonel returned to the fold. The GOP regulars were a sordid bunch, he told friends, but "a trifle better than the corrupt and lunatic wild asses who seem most influential in

* Eleanor's brother Hall and three of TR's sons were among those who attended the Plattsburgh camp in 1915. Richard Harding Davis, the noted journalist who had immortalized TR's charge up San Juan Hill for the New York Herald, was just back from covering the war in Europe and also enrolled. Davis recalled that his squad included "two fox-hunting squires from Maryland, a master of fox hounds, a gentleman jockey from Boston, and two steeple chase riders who divided between them all of the cups the country offers." Quoted in Geoffrey C. Ward, A First-Class Temperament 309 (New York: Harper & Row, 1989).

Democratic councils."[78] Wilson's recent marriage to the Washington socialite Edith Galt, a widow considerably younger than he, also did not help his chances, coming so quickly after his first wife's death. And the preparedness issue cut both ways. While TR lambasted the administration for being too weak, many in the Middle West—where isolationist sentiment was strong—condemned Wilson for being too bellicose.

When the Republican National Convention convened at Chicago in early June, anticipation of victory was in the air. Supreme Court justice Charles Evans Hughes quickly emerged as a compromise candidate and was nominated virtually without opposition on the second ballot.[79] Twice elected governor of New York, Hughes had established a solid record of reform but had turned away from partisan politics following his elevation to the bench in 1910. His remarkable intellect and good judgment had made him the leader of the Court's liberal minority, while his stately bearing and conservative demeanor endeared him to Republican regulars. The only Supreme Court justice in the nation's history to be tapped by a major party, Hughes looked more presidential than any candidate in recent history.

On June 14, 1916, four days after Hughes was nominated, the nation celebrated Flag Day with preparedness parades throughout the country. Wilson led the Washington procession himself, a flag carried decorously over his shoulder. Civilian employees from each government department marched, and FDR headed the Navy's contingent. "The Navy Department made an excellent showing," he wrote Eleanor. "When I passed the President's reviewing stand I was sent for to join them and spent the next four hours there."[80] Press coverage the next day featured photographs of Wilson standing foursquare for preparedness, a Democratic Roosevelt beaming at his side.[81]

FDR campaigned for the ticket in New England and the middle Atlantic states. He defended the administration's preparedness record and shielded Daniels from Republican attack, suggesting that criticism of the mobilization effort was counterproductive and unpatriotic. "How would you expect the public to be convinced that a dangerous fire was in progress if they saw members of the volunteer fire department stop their headlong rush toward the conflagration and indulge in a slanging match as to who was responsible for the rotten hose or lack of water at a fire a week ago?"[82] The fire hose analogy was one of the homey metaphors FDR sometimes called up to explain the necessity for cooperation in times of crisis. In early 1940 he employed it again to support his proposal for Lend-Lease to Great Britain: "Suppose my neighbor's home catches fire, and I have a length of garden hose four or five hundred feet away. If he can take my garden hose and connect it up with his hydrant, I may help him to put out his fire."[83]

Hughes waged a lackluster campaign—TR called him "Wilson with whiskers"—but he remained the overwhelming favorite.[84] New York bookmakers quoted the final odds at 5 to 3. On election night, FDR attended a large dinner given by Henry Morgenthau, Sr., for party bigwigs at New York's Biltmore Hotel. Morgenthau chaired the Democratic finance committee, and the politicians present that evening hoped against hope the bookies had it wrong. Gloom settled in quickly. Early returns from the East showed a landslide for Hughes. Connecticut, Delaware, Massachusetts, New Jersey, New York, Rhode Island, and Vermont, all of which Wilson had carried in 1912, had swung Republican. North of the Mason-Dixon Line, only New Hampshire remained in doubt. At midnight Franklin left the Biltmore to catch the last train to Washington, certain that Wilson had lost. Newsboys were already hawking Wednesday's *New York Times* proclaiming Hughes elected in banner headlines. At press time, the Republicans had carried or were leading in eighteen states with 247 electoral votes to Wilson's 135. Two hundred sixty-six votes were needed to win, and Hughes was only 19 shy.

Results from the West were slow coming in. But when FDR reached his office the next morning, Hughes's lead had narrowed. In addition to the Solid South, Wilson appeared to be adding one after another of the states beyond the Mississippi. The Democrats campaign slogan, "He kept us out of war," had fallen on receptive ears in America's heartland. By noon the race had become too close to call. Franklin scribbled a quick note to Eleanor at Hyde Park: "Dearest Babs, [This] is the most extraordinary day of my life. Wilson may be elected after all. It looks hopeful at noon."[85] Uncertainty continued through Thursday. "Returns have been coming in every hour," FDR wrote Eleanor. "Wilson seems to have 251 votes safe. . . . It appears we have North Dakota (5 votes) and in California (13) we are well ahead, though there are still 200 districts to hear from. New Hampshire looks better and we may carry it."[86] Not until Friday morning was the California vote count complete. Wilson carried the state by 3,420 votes. That was the Democrats' margin of victory. Wilson had 277 electoral votes to Hughes 254. The popular vote was 9,129,606 for Wilson, 8,538,321 for Hughes.

Instead of making ready to leave Washington, Franklin and Eleanor settled in for another four years. "It is rumored that a certain distinguished cousin of mine is now engaged in revising his most noted historical work, *The Winning of the West*," FDR joked to an audience of party faithful immediately after the election. To Eleanor he confided, "I hope to God I don't grow reactionary with advancing years."[87]

In France, the military stalemate continued. The Allied lines were stretched thin but remained intact. Imperial Russia was on the verge of collapse and revolution loomed, but the British naval blockade was taking a dreadful toll on the German home front. Eager to drive Britain from the war, the German high command concluded that unrestricted submarine warfare—the one weapon they had not yet employed—would force the island to its knees in six months. That might bring the United States into the war, but the German military was convinced the fighting would be over before America's power could be felt. On January 9, 1917, Kaiser Wilhelm revoked his earlier edict and ordered unrestricted submarine warfare to commence on February 1. German embassies were instructed to inform their host governments on January 31, which left no time for a diplomatic protest. Foreign Minister Arthur Zimmermann dispatched an additional note to the German ambassador in Mexico City:

We shall endeavor to keep the United States neutral. In the event of this not succeeding, we make Mexico a proposal of alliance on the following basis: Make war together, make peace together, generous financial support, and an understanding on our part that Mexico is to reconquer the lost territory in Texas, New Mexico, and Arizona.[88]

On February 3, following the U-boat sinking of the freighter *Housatonic*, Wilson went before Congress to announce that he had severed diplomatic relations with Germany.[89] FDR was inspecting the Marine occupation of Santo Domingo at the time and received an urgent message from Daniels to return to Washington immediately.[90] "No one knew anything for certain except that the German Ambassador, Count von Bernstorff, had been given his passports and it seemed probable that the United States and Germany were already at war," Roosevelt recalled. "As we headed north on our way to Hampton Roads no lights were showing, the guns were manned and there was complete radio silence."[91]

When FDR arrived in Washington, he found it was business as usual. Wilson hoped that by breaking relations he would convince Germany to rescind its submarine campaign, and the administration settled into a period of watchful waiting. But the president's hopes were soon dashed. By the end of February German U-boats had sunk an unprecedented 781,500 tons of Allied shipping. Reeling under the impact, the British Admiralty furnished the U.S. Embassy in London a decoded copy of Zimmermann's January telegram to his ambassador in Mexico City.* The embassy passed the message to Washington, and on March 1, 1917, an infuriated Wilson released it to the press. A wave of anti-German sentiment swept the country, and the United States inched closer to war.

With hostilities looming and Daniels out of town, FDR as acting secretary asked Wilson for permission to bring the Atlantic Fleet north from Guantánamo Bay so that it could be fitted out for war. Wilson declined. "I want history to show," Roosevelt remembers the president saying, "not only that we have tried every diplomatic means to keep out of the war; to show that war has been forced upon us deliberately by Germany; but also that we have come into the court of history with clean hands."[92]

Daniels shared Wilson's view. "If any man in official life ever faced the agony of a Gethsemane," he wrote later, "I was that man in the first four months of 1917."[93] Not surprisingly, Daniels became the whipping boy for interventionists in the GOP, the Navy League, Wall Street, and the steel industry, as well as the jingoist press, all of which clamored for immediate entry into war. Also, not surprisingly, FDR was praised extravagantly. "Secretary Daniels has been criticized for four years," wrote Washington's *Evening Star,* "but there has been little, if any criticism of his assistant, for the simple reason there has been little to criticize."[94] When an old Harvard friend wrote to suggest that he assume Daniels's position, FDR stood by his chief:

---

* British Naval Intelligence intercepted Zimmermann's message and quickly decoded it but did not pass it on to the American embassy in London until February 23. Ambassador Walter Hines Page immediately flashed it to the State Department, which was able to verify its authenticity by checking it against American cable intercepts. The United States had the coded German message on file but had not bothered to decipher it. Once its authenticity was established, Secretary of State Lansing, Bryan's successor, passed the telegram to Wilson.

I am having a perfectly good time with many important things to do and my heart is entirely in my work.

Personally I have no use for a man who, serving in a subordinate position, is continually contriving ways to step into his boss's shoes and I detest nothing so much as that kind of disloyalty.

Franklin said he had "worked very gladly under Mr. Daniels and I wish the public could realize how much he has done for the Navy. I would feel very badly indeed if friends of mine should unwittingly give the impression that I was for a minute thinking of taking his place at the head of the Navy."[95]

The German U-boat campaign soon resolved whatever tension existed between FDR and Daniels over the speed of mobilization. On March 18 the steamships *City of Memphis, Illinois,* and *Vigilancia* were all torpedoed, the *Vigilancia* without warning. Two days later, Wilson placed the question of war before his cabinet. Daniels was the most reluctant, but in the end, with tears in his eyes, he voted to make the recommendation for war unanimous. "I had hoped and prayed that the hour would not come, but the attitude of the Imperial German Government left us no other course."[96]

Wilson called Congress back from recess and on the evening of April 2 asked for a declaration of war. The House chamber was packed to capacity that evening as the Senate, the Supreme Court (in a departure from tradition), and the cabinet joined the 435 members of the House.[97] The galleries were crammed with those fortunate enough to get tickets. FDR sat with Daniels on the House floor, Eleanor in the diplomatic gallery. Setting the tone for the evening, the president was escorted up Pennsylvania Avenue to the Capitol by a mounted battalion from the 1st Cavalry, stationed at Fort Myer. He was greeted by thunderous applause when he entered the chamber. Virtually every member was on his feet cheering, led by the towering figure of the chief justice of the United States, Edward D. White, a seventy-two-year-old Louisianian who had fought for the Confederacy and had long supported the Allied cause.

Wilson spoke clearly, without bombast or excess. Our quarrel was not with the German people, he said, but with their government, which had "thrown to the winds all scruples of humanity." America's object was not conquest but peace and justice—a war "without rancor and without selfish object," a war without revenge. "The world must be made safe for democracy."

His pastoral Presbyterian voice reverberating through the chamber, Wilson asked Congress to recognize that a state of war "has been thrust upon us." He requested authorization to draft 500,000 men and bring the Navy to full combat readiness. "There is one choice we cannot make, we are incapable of making. We will not choose the path of submission." He ended by paraphrasing the words of Martin Luther. America was privileged to spend her blood for the principles she treasured. "God helping her, she can do no other."[98]

The House chamber erupted in frantic applause. A few members—Senator Robert La Follette of Wisconsin, Senator George Norris of Nebraska, Senator James K. Vardaman of Mississippi, Representative Jeannette Rankin from Montana—sat silent. But Wilson carried the day. Senator Henry Cabot Lodge, an inveterate foe of the administration who hated Wilson with a passion, approached the president as he made his way out of the chamber. "Mr. President, you have expressed in the loftiest manner possible the sentiments of the American people."[99] FDR told the press that Wilson's speech would be "an inspiration to every true citizen no matter what his political faith."[100] Eleanor said she "listened breathlessly and returned home still half dazed by the sense of political change."[101]

Daniels pronounced the most eloquent benediction: "If I should live a thousand years, there would abide with me the reverberation of the fateful ominous sound of the hoofs of the cavalry horses as they escorted Mr. and Mrs. Wilson back to the White House."[102]

EIGHT

LUCY

---

*You were a goosy girl to think or even pretend to think
that I don't want you here all the summer, because
you know I do! But honestly you ought to have six
weeks straight at Campobello.*

—FRANKLIN TO ELEANOR, JULY 16, 1917

WHEN CONGRESS DECLARED war on April 6, 1917, the United States was a second-class military power.[1] The Army, relegated to showing the flag in Latin America and pursuing Mexican banditti, consisted of 108,399 men, a third of whom were on garrison duty in Panama, Hawaii, and the Philippines. The various state militias, recently formed into a National Guard, added but another 200,000, and there was no organized reserve.[2] The Navy numbered slightly more than 60,000 in all ranks, with a mere 197 ships on active service.

Within six months the Navy's strength expanded fourfold. By war's end nearly half a million men had joined the fleet and the number of ships exceeded two thousand. During the same time, the Army grew to 2.4 million men.[3] General John J. Pershing, commander of the American Expeditionary Force, landed at Boulogne, France, on June 13, 1917. On July 4, elements of the 1st Division paraded down the Champs-Élysées. Ultimately, more than 2 million men would serve in the AEF, escorted safely across the Atlantic by the Navy's Cruiser and Transport Force.[4] Except for sporadic firings at German submarines, the U.S. Navy did not engage the enemy in World War I. But thanks to its escort duty, when the armistice was signed the Navy could boast that not one American troopship had been lost in action.[5]

FDR, who was responsible for the Navy's procurement, threw himself into his mobilization duties. He contracted for vast amounts of materiel and equipment (sometimes before Congress appropriated the money),[6] pressed for the immediate enlistment of large numbers of men, ordered training camps expanded and ship construction accelerated. "See young Roosevelt about it" became a catchphrase in wartime Washington.[7]

Roosevelt's procurement efforts were so effective that two weeks after America entered the war he received an urgent summons to the White House. In the Oval Office he found General Hugh Scott, the Army chief of staff. "Mr. Secretary," said Wilson, barely able to suppress a grin, "I'm very sorry, but you have cornered the market for supplies. You'll have to divide up with the Army."[8]

Busy as FDR was, he had no intention of fighting the war behind a desk. And though he had a wife and five young children, he was determined to see action.[9] That was the path Cousin Theodore had followed, and the old Rough Rider, who had come to Washington to volunteer his services to President Wilson, encouraged Franklin to join up.* "You must resign," said TR. "You must get into uniform at once."[10]

Neither Daniels nor Wilson would hear of it. The war placed a premium on the qualities FDR brought to his job as assistant secretary—energy, flexibility, decisiveness, and the willingness to act on a moment's notice—qualities they did not wish to lose. Daniels told Franklin he was "rendering a far more important war service than if he put on the uniform."[11] Wilson said that Roosevelt's place had already been assigned by the country. "Tell the young man to stay where he is," he instructed Daniels.[12] General Leonard Wood, who evidently heard of Franklin's desire from TR, added his voice to those urging him

---

* The day Congress declared war, TR went to Washington to ask that he be allowed to raise a division of volunteers and lead it to France. Georges Clemenceau, not yet premier, supported the proposal. The battle-weary soldiers of France needed a miracle to restore their spirits, he wrote Wilson. "Send them Roosevelt." But the president and Secretary of War Newton D. Baker, who received TR cordially, wanted no part of the idea. Wilson had decided to fight the war with a conscript army, in which there was no place for volunteers. "To make an exception of Colonel Roosevelt would have been to strike at the heart of the whole design," wrote Wilson's secretary, Joe Tumulty.

Wilson found TR more engaging than he had anticipated: "He's a great big boy. There is a sweetness about him that is compelling." But aside from the political and military risks of having TR on board, the Colonel was in poor health and half blind, and had been out of touch with military developments for twenty years. Joseph L. Gardner, *Departing Glory: Theodore Roosevelt as Ex-President* 371–373 (New York: Charles Scribner's Sons, 1973); Joseph P. Tumulty, *Woodrow Wilson as I Knew Him* 288–289 (New York: Doubleday, Page, 1921).

to remain in Washington. "Franklin Roosevelt should under no circumstances think of leaving the Navy Department," he wrote. "It would be a public calamity to have him leave at this time."[13]

Contrary to most Americans' assumptions in April 1917, the war was not going well. In Russia, the army had mutinied, the czar had abdicated, and the provisional government was fast proving powerless. On April 16—ten days after the United States declared war—Vladimir Lenin and the Bolshevik leadership detrained at the Finland Station in Saint Petersburg, smuggled from Switzerland by the German high command. In France, war weariness gripped the nation. The army might be counted on to defend French soil, but offensive operations were out of the question. In the Atlantic, unrestricted submarine warfare was taking a dreadful toll. Since February 1, German U-boats had sunk 844 Allied vessels. Nine hundred thousand tons of shipping had gone to the bottom in March, and April's total was expected to be even greater. The Germans were sinking merchantmen faster than they could be replaced. Herbert Hoover, director of American food relief in Europe, reported that British warehouses held only a three-week supply of grain: once that was depleted, the islands could be starved into submission.[14] "Unless we can stop these losses, and stop them soon, we must leave the war," said Admiral Sir John Jellicoe, Britain's First Sea Lord.[15]

It should have been obvious that the solution to the U-boat menace was to require merchant ships to sail in convoys. Yet the Admiralty stubbornly refused. Convoy duty was inglorious. The warrior ethic of the Royal Navy demanded that submarines be hunted down: a virtual impossibility given the size of the sea and the absence of radar, sonar, and long-range spotting aircraft.[16] But the mounting losses were too great to sustain. Under pressure from Prime Minister Lloyd George—who paid a dramatic visit to the Admiralty—the sea lords relented and on May 10 dispatched a trial convoy of forty ships from Gibraltar to Britain, escorted by six destroyers. All arrived safely. A second merchant convoy set out from Hampton Roads on May 29 and reached Liverpool without incident. The Admiralty recognized its error and immediately decreed that all merchant shipping to or from Britain must travel in convoy.

To provide destroyer escorts for the convoys placed an enormous strain on the Royal Navy. Several destroyer divisions—the eyes of the fleet—were withdrawn from the Grand Fleet for convoy duty, but the shortage of escort vessels remained acute. Rear Admiral William S. Sims, whom Daniels had dispatched to London, reported that unless the American fleet was "thrown into the balance," Britain and France would "be forced to dire straits."[17] FDR shared Sims's concern. A token force of six destroyers was sent immediately to the Celtic port of Queenstown (now Cobh), but it required a high-level British mission headed by former Prime Minister Arthur Balfour and then a French mission that included Marshal Joseph Joffre, hero of the Battle of the Marne, to convince Washington of the seriousness of the situation.[18]

Perhaps because he was one of the few members of the Wilson administration who spoke French fluently, FDR drew the assignment of meeting the French mission at Hampton Roads and escorting it to Washington. As a result, he had "twenty-five hours of quite intimate conversation" with the members before they saw anyone else.[19] He also met frequently with the British. In repeated discussions Roosevelt urged both delegations to press for all they needed from the United States. He also pledged to provide Britain with thirty American destroyers, although neither Daniels nor Wilson had authorized him to do so. In this instance FDR's eagerness served him well. Despite some foot-dragging by the Navy high command, in July 1917 thirty-five American destroyers were on station at Queenstown. Before the war ended, a total of 370 combat vessels had been assigned to the European command.[20]

The Balfour and Joffre missions went from Washington to New York to raise money and reinforce investor confidence. FDR's mother, Sara, went to hear Balfour speak at Carnegie Hall ("a perfect little speech") and the next morning attended a special service for the British delegation at the Cathedral Church of St. John the Divine on Morningside Heights. Franklin's halfbrother, Rosy, was a trustee of the cathedral and introduced Sara to Balfour. "He is both musical and religious, and wins all hearts, mine included," she reported. Joffre proved an even greater hit. When Sara discovered that the French hero was staying nearby at the Fifth Avenue mansion of Henry Clay Frick, she asked the marshal's aide if she might present three of Franklin's children—Anna, James, and Elliott—to him. The marshal graciously fit them into his schedule, and Sara escorted the children up the grand marble staircase at the Frick residence "to a little bedroom, and Joffre kissed all three children. Then the perfectly charming, brave Joffre spoke to me of my son in a most lovely way. I felt quite queer and rather like shedding a tear but managed to behave decently."[21] Sara asked Joffre for a photograph, which the marshal signed and which she immediately had framed and placed conspicuously on the mantel in the library at Hyde Park.

Like Winston Churchill at the Admiralty, FDR was bubbling with new ideas to confound the enemy. His most notable wartime achievement was the laying of a North Sea antisubmarine mine barrage—a chain of underwater high-explosive charges stretching 240 miles from the Orkney Islands to the coast of Norway. Roosevelt did not conceive the plan, but he promoted it so vigorously that Admiral Frederic R. Harris, the Navy's expert in construction matters, said that if not for Franklin "there would have been no North Sea mine barrage."[22]*

Long before the United States entered the war, Wilson had asked Daniels, "Why don't the British shut up the hornets in their nests? They are hunting hornets all over the farm and letting the nest alone."[23] The British had investigated but rejected the idea of constructing an antisubmarine barrier across the North Sea: the distance was too great, the water too deep, the undersea mine too unreliable a weapon, and the cost prohibitive. But Roosevelt persisted, and by October 1917 the Navy had developed a mine that did not require physical contact but could be detonated when a long, electrified antenna was brushed by a metal object. This meant that far fewer mines would be required than originally estimated and could be linked more easily. On October 3, on his own initiative, FDR authorized the manufacture of 100,000 of the modified mines. Daniels signed on, and Wilson, who despaired of London's unwilling-

---

* FDR pressed the mine barrage, oblivious to the infraction of the law of nations as well as earlier protests lodged by the United States against British and German efforts to mine the high seas. On August 13, 1914, Secretary of State Bryan had warned the British that the laying of submarine mines was in violation of Article 1 of the Hague Convention of 1907. "The Secretary of State is loath to believe that a signatory to that convention would willfully disregard its treaty obligation, which was manifestly made in the interest of neutral shipping." Diplomatic correspondence on the issue continued through the remainder of 1914 and early 1915, and on February 15, 1915, the United States sent identical notes to Germany and Great Britain expressing hope that the two belligerents "may through reciprocal concessions, find a basis for agreement . . . that neither will sow any floating mines, whether upon the high seas or in territorial waters." U.S. Department of State, *Foreign Relations of the United States, 1914,* Supplement 454–473; *1915,* Supplement 119–120; *1916,* Supplement 3–7. FDR's memo to Daniels outlining the project (October 29, 1917), as well as his letter to President Wilson (October 29, 1917), made no mention of the earlier American protests or the law of nations. 2 *The Roosevelt Letters* 293–294, Elliott Roosevelt, ed. (London: George G. Harrap, 1950).

ness to try anything new, added his formal approval two weeks later.[24] Daniels ordered Admiral Henry T. Mayo, commander in chief of the Atlantic Fleet, to London for the sole purpose of obtaining British approval, and under Mayo's unrelenting advocacy the Admiralty acquiesced. As FDR put it, the sea lords said, "We think your plan is a bit wild-eyed but go ahead if you want."[25]

In February 1918 a special convoy of two dozen vessels sailed for Scotland with 11,000 tons of TNT, 50,000 feet of wire cable, and casings for nearly 100,000 mines. The actual mining commenced in June, and by October some 70,000 mines had been sown at a cost of $80 million.[26] The war ended before the barrage could be fully tested, but at least four and possibly eight U-boats are thought to have been destroyed by it. Other estimates run as high as twenty-three.[27] Admiral Sims called the barrier "one of the wonders of the war" and partially credits it with the collapse of the German Navy's morale, but the evidence is sketchy.[28]

Joseph P. Kennedy, perhaps an unlikely source, testifies to FDR's decisiveness during the war. Kennedy was then assistant manager of Bethlehem Steel's Fore River shipyard in Quincy, Massachusetts. At the request of the Navy Department, the Fore River yard had constructed two battleships for Argentina. The ships were ready, but the Argentine government was unable to pay, and Charles Schwab, the legendary chairman of Bethlehem, refused to release them. FDR requested a meeting, and Schwab sent Kennedy to Washington in his place.

Franklin received Kennedy cordially. "Don't worry about the matter," he said reassuringly. "The State Department will collect the money."

Kennedy said that wasn't good enough. Mr. Schwab would not release the ships until they were paid for. "That's absurd," FDR replied. He and Kennedy sparred a few rounds, and then Roosevelt escorted his guest to the door. He had been happy to meet Kennedy, he said, but the Navy wanted the ships released immediately. Again Kennedy declined.

When Kennedy reported the conversation to Schwab, they agreed to ignore Roosevelt's demand, and the battleships remained securely berthed in Quincy. Less than a week later, four Navy tugboats nosed into the Fore River yard, loaded to the gunwales with combat-ready marines. As startled shipyard workers looked on, the marines took possession of the vessels at bayonet point and towed them into the harbor, where Argentine crews waited to receive them. A chastened Kennedy stood by helpless. "Roosevelt was the hardest trader I'd ever run up against," he said later. "I was so disappointed I broke down and cried."[29]

In 1917 the courtship between Tammany and FDR intensified. As assistant secretary, FDR was well placed to reward the Democratic faithful, especially those members of Congress with Navy yards in their district, and particularly someone as powerful as the Brooklyn-based chairman of the House Appropriations Committee, John J. Fitzgerald—who also happened to be Tammany's spokesman in the House. Franklin was learning the subtleties of congressional politics, and Fitzgerald was a gifted tutor. Since their set-to in 1914, FDR and Fitzgerald had become staunch allies, Fitzgerald supporting the Navy budget down the line and Roosevelt obliging the chairman with myriad personal favors. In 1915, as a sign of affection, Franklin arranged for Fitzgerald's two young sons to take part in laying the keel of the battleship *California* at the Brooklyn Navy Yard and then, with remarkable warmth, offered to join the congressman in his reelection campaign.[30] When Congress was in session, Fitzgerald stopped by FDR's office every week or so to ask a favor or two concerning the Brooklyn yard. "Usually Roosevelt would grant the requests," he recalled, "but sometimes he would say, 'The old man [Daniels] is against this and I can't do anything.' " But almost always, FDR sent the chairman away happy. "He was a very, very cooperative man," said Fitzgerald.[31]

Tammany noted Franklin's change of heart. In mid-June 1917, Congressman Daniel J. Riordan, who had succeeded to the Lower Manhattan seat vacated by "Big Tim" Sullivan, called on Roosevelt to present an invitation from Charles Murphy asking him to give the keynote address at Tammany's upcoming Fourth of July celebration, one of the grand rituals of the organization. "I guess if we can stand having you, you can stand coming," joked Riordan.[32]

FDR accepted the invitation on the spot. And so it was on July 4, 1917, that Roosevelt found himself ensconced at Tammany headquarters on Fourteenth Street, celebrating the 128th year of the organization's existence. The band of the "Fighting 69th," New York's renowned Irish regiment, provided the music; the Tammany glee club belted out the melodies, and Franklin joined the overflow audience in a lusty rendition of "Tammany Forever." It was the type of rally FDR did best, frolicking with former enemies and ingratiating himself with the Wigwam's senior leadership. The *New York Tribune* reported that Charles Murphy had invited Franklin "to give him 'the once over' " and was not disappointed in what he saw.[33] Immediately speculation arose that Roosevelt would lead the New York Democratic ticket in 1918, contesting the governorship against the two-term incumbent, Charles S. Whitman.

Back in Washington, FDR labeled the speculation "utterly wild" but kept his ear to the ground. In the autumn and winter the Tammany tom-toms beat a steady call for Roosevelt. "Your name is frequently used around New York, looking a little to the future, and it is always a pleasure to hear it," wrote the up-and-coming Jimmy Walker in November 1917.[34] Shortly afterward, John M. Riehle, a prominent Tammany chieftain who headed the National Democratic Club, publicly endorsed FDR, as did William Kelley, leader of the Brooklyn organization. When the Tammany stalwart Thomas J. MacManus (The MacManus), who had served with FDR in the legislature, offered his support, it was clear the Organization was getting its ducks in a row. Roosevelt was "a corking good man," said MacManus. "I am for him."[35]

Franklin remained noncommittal. He said he was gratified to have so many supporters and was "greatly surprised to find many of these friends in somewhat unexpected quarters," but he declined to announce his candidacy. When asked about his intentions, Roosevelt stressed the patriotic importance of his work in Washington and said it would not be right for him to leave while the war lasted. But he left the door ajar. "It would be foolish and idle for any man to say what he would or would not do in the future, particularly when the entire situation, international and political, may change overnight."[36]

In June, President Wilson added his voice to those urging FDR to run. "Tell Roosevelt he ought not to decline to run for Governor of New York if it is tendered to him," he advised Daniels.[37] But Roosevelt, with Howe's advice and Daniels's support, decided against a run for the governorship. "I have made my position entirely clear," he wrote Wilson, "that my duty lies in my present work—not only my duty to you and to the country but my duty to myself—If I were at any time to leave the Assistant Secretaryship it could only be for active service."[38] Roosevelt's motives were mixed. So long as the war continued, he believed his place was to serve the war effort, either as assistant secretary or in uniform. To abandon his post would be tantamount to desertion. He also thought 1918 would be another Republican year. Whether he could unseat a popular incumbent was far from clear. Having lost one statewide race, Roosevelt did not want to lose another. What could not be foreseen was that the war would be over by election time and the political equation would have changed. The Democrats nominated Al Smith in FDR's place in 1918, and

Smith went on to win a stunning upset victory over Governor Whitman.[39] In later years, Roosevelt claimed to have engineered Smith's nomination.* "I see that you have been called the 'best equipped' man" for governor, FDR wrote Smith on the night of the Democratic primary. "May I tell you that this is not only true, but that I trust that the people of the State will realize that this is not a mere phrase—it is based upon actual fact."[40]

As with Franklin, the war gave Eleanor the opportunity to move beyond her limited social circle. Her first four years in Washington as wife of a member of Wilson's subcabinet had been almost as circumscribed as her life had been in New York, restricted to paying formal calls and leaving visiting cards, entertaining and being entertained, while supervising a household that grew larger each year. When war came, Eleanor found herself in great demand outside that narrow world, and like Franklin she threw herself into her new role with an enthusiasm she had not experienced since her days as head girl at Allenwood. She became an indefatigable organizer of Red Cross volunteers. Scarcely a troop train could pass through Union Station without Eleanor being there with a bevy of assistants to hand out coffee, sandwiches, and hand knitted woolen socks.[41]

---

* In 1938 FDR related the episode to the Wilson biographer Ray Stannard Baker:

About the middle of June [1918] the political situation in New York flared to the front. . . . Charles F. Murphy, who had the final say in the City, and sufficient support in several large upstate cities to give him control of the convention, had come to realize that a New York City candidate would stand little chance of election if forced through by the City Organization. The secretary of Tammany Hall, Mr. Thomas Smith, came to Washington to see me with the message from Mr. Murphy that he would be very glad to support me for the governorship as there seemed no other upstate candidate who was well-known in every part of the state and who, at the same time, had a definite connection with war service. I told Mr. Smith I was extremely sorry but that I could not even consider accepting the nomination. Mr. Smith went to New York and returned a few days later to ask me to give Mr. Murphy some recommendations of upstate candidates. A careful check of the field convinced me that the best-known Democrat in the State was Alfred E. Smith. . . . It was pointed out by Mr. [Thomas] Smith and Mr. Murphy that Alfred E. Smith was not only a Tammany man but a Catholic. My reply was the demand for his nomination for Governor could well originate with upstate delegates and that in war-time, the church to which he belonged would not be raised as an issue in any community.

I communicated with many of my friends among Democratic leaders upstate suggesting to them that they should start an organized movement for the nomination of Alfred E. Smith.

FDR to Baker, October 24, 1938, Baker Papers, Library of Congress.

Despite her wide exposure, some prejudices died hard. Eleanor never felt completely comfortable with the Roman Catholic clergy and the Irish politicians with whom FDR consorted, and her tolerance for those of the Jewish faith grew slowly.* Eleanor was distressed in January 1918 when she was obliged to attend a gala given by the British Embassy to honor Bernard Baruch, then head of the War Industries Board. It would be "mostly Jews," she wrote Sara, and "I'd rather be hung than seen there." Afterward she reported, "The Jew party was appalling. I never wish to hear money, jewels, and sables mentioned again."[42]

Several months later Eleanor was surprised when FDR brought the young Harvard professor and Washington consultant Felix Frankfurter home for lunch. She found Frankfurter unappealing. "An interesting little man," she wrote Sara, "but very Jew."[43] Later she would refuse to read Maurice Low's interpretive biography of Woodrow Wilson because the author was "such a loathsome little Jew."[44] Blanche Wiesen Cook, Eleanor's elegant biographer, noted, "ER's caustic comments concerning Jews remained a routine part of her social observation for many years, diminishing as her friendship with Baruch and other Jews flourished."[45]

FDR did not have that problem. Although his half brother, Rosy, was a notorious anti-Semite, neither Sara nor Franklin's father, James, was infected with the virus. James had numerous Jewish friends, including August Belmont and Henry Morgenthau, Sr., and he told Sara on several occasions that although he was not Jewish, "if he were he would be proud of it."[46] FDR enjoyed ethnic jokes

* By 1916 Franklin had shed whatever anti-Catholic bias he might have inherited. Not only had he formed strong bonds with the Irish politicians of New York City, but many of the clergy would become his close friends, including Francis Cardinal Spellman of New York, George Cardinal Mundelein of Chicago, and especially James Cardinal Gibbons of Baltimore. Somewhat to Sara's chagrin, the Roosevelts were in fact distantly related to James Roosevelt Bayley, an Episcopal convert to Catholicism who had been Gibbons's predecessor as archbishop of Baltimore, and to Bayley's aunt, Elizabeth Ann Bayley Seton, America's first Catholic saint. In later years FDR enjoyed recounting Cardinal Gibbons's reply when asked whether he subscribed to the doctrine of papal infallibility. Gibbons acknowledged that he did, adding with a twinkle that he had met the Holy Father many times "and each time he called me 'Jibbons.' "

One might note that except for his mother and Eleanor, the three women closest to FDR during most of his adult life were his secretaries Missy LeHand and Grace Tully, and Lucy Mercer, all of whom were Roman Catholics. For the Gibbons quote, see Nathan Miller, *The Roosevelt Chronicles* 137 (New York: Doubleday, 1979).

and often told them himself, but he drew the line at sectarian slurs, especially if directed at particular individuals. And he recognized early in his career that he needed support across the religious spectrum. Henry Morgenthau, Jr., his neighbor in Dutchess County, was one of Franklin's closest friends. They shared the interests of gentleman farmers, comparing notes on everything from breeds of dairy cattle to selective timbering. "Two of a kind," FDR inscribed across a photograph of him and Morgenthau seated together in an open convertible. When he became governor, Roosevelt appointed Morgenthau chairman of New York's Agricultural Advisory Commission and then called him to Washington in 1933 to head the newly established Farm Credit Administration. The following year Morgenthau succeeded William H. Woodin as secretary of the Treasury, a post he held for the duration of the Roosevelt administration.

Throughout his career FDR drew heavily on members of the Jewish faith for their skill and expertise. Judge Samuel Rosenman joined Roosevelt's staff in 1928 as his chief aide and speechwriter and remained in that capacity until the president's death in 1945. Sidney Hillman, Ben Cohen, and David Niles were in and out of the White House, advising the president and carrying water for the New Deal. Jews constituted roughly 3 percent of the population when FDR was president, yet they represented about 15 percent of his top appointments.[47] Roosevelt set the tone with his masterly reply to a pointed query about his ancestry: "In the dim past [my ancestors] may have been Jews or Catholics or Protestants. What I am more interested in is whether they were good citizens and believers in God. I hope they were both."[48] FDR's response to the Holocaust was nuanced and complex, and certainly not everything America's Jewish community desired, but that in no way diminishes his commitment to social justice or the breakthrough that the New Deal represented. Until 1933, Washington had been run by WASP descendants of old-stock Americans. Roosevelt opened government to those of talent regardless of pedigree.

The war years also saw Franklin and Eleanor grow distant. FDR put in longer hours at the Navy Department. Eleanor was drawn increasingly into volunteer work, and their summers were spent apart, Franklin at his post in Washington, ER and the children at Campobello. After the birth of their sixth child, John Aspinwall Roosevelt, on March 13, 1916, the evidence suggests that Eleanor and Franklin adopted abstinence as the only sure means of birth control. That was common at the time. The Episcopal Church (as well as the

Roman Catholic) forbade birth control, and it was illegal in many states by statute.[49] Sara had adopted the practice after Franklin's birth, and in the refined circles in which the Roosevelts moved, contraception was almost never discussed.*

An only child, Franklin had wanted six children—the same number that had romped through Cousin Theodore's home at Sagamore Hill. That desire had been one of the reasons he had been rejected by the young Alice Sohier in 1902, before his courtship of Eleanor. Whether he mentioned this same desire to Eleanor is unclear, but she had now given birth to six children (one of whom had died in infancy), and the Roosevelts would have no more.

The Roosevelt siblings are in agreement on the matter. Anna, who was closest to her parents, said her mother told her that "sex is an ordeal to be borne." After John's birth, "that was the end of any marital relationship, period."[50] James, more circumspect, wrote, "It is possible that she [ER] knew no birthcontrol methods other than abstinence when she determined to have no more children."[51] Elliott said that from John's birth

> until the end of Father's days, my parents never again lived together as man and wife.
>
> Mother had performed her austere duty in marriage, and five children were testimony to that. She wanted no more, but her blank ignorance about how to ward off pregnancy left her no choice other than abstinence. Her shyness and stubborn pride would keep her from seeking advice from a doctor or woman friend. . . . It quickly became the most tightly held secret that we five children ever shared and kept.[52]

It was in the summer of 1916, shortly after the birth of John Aspinwall, that FDR took up with Lucy Mercer, Eleanor's part-time social secretary. ER and the children were at Campobello, and Franklin was spending another summer

---

* As Alice Roosevelt Longworth recalled, "Most of my contemporaries were far too shy even to ask their doctors about such matters. I think most American doctors at the time would have been horrified, fearing lawsuits. . . . I still have a letter written to me shortly after I was married by my sister-in-law, Nan Wallingford, who was the mother of three. In it she begged me to send her 'one of those cunning, labor-saving devices' so that she might save her 'tottering reason.' " Michael Teague, *Mrs. L: Conversations with Alice Roosevelt Longworth* 57 (New York: Doubleday, 1981).

alone in Washington. Lucy was nearby, unattached, and incredibly attractive. The long, tender love affair between Franklin and Lucy remained shrouded in secrecy until well after the president's death. Eleanor never mentioned it in her extensive autobiographical writings; Franklin said nothing; and Lucy was among the most private of persons. The families knew, the White House staff was aware, and many in the press had more than an inkling of the relationship. In those days the private lives of public persons were strictly private.[53] Journalists respected that, the public was not consumed with people watching, and the three protagonists—Eleanor, Franklin, and Lucy—conducted themselves with honor, dignity, and discretion.

Arthur Schlesinger put the romance into perspective: "If Lucy Mercer in any way helped Franklin Roosevelt sustain the frightful burdens of leadership in the Second World War, the nation has good reason to be grateful to her."[54]

Lucy Mercer came into the Roosevelt family in the winter of 1914, when Eleanor, overwhelmed by her social obligations as wife of the assistant secretary of the Navy, hired her three mornings a week to assist with correspondence and help unravel the mysteries of Washington society. Lucy was twenty-three, the impoverished daughter of high-living socialites who had recklessly spent their way through a substantial fortune. She had been raised in Washington, just a few doors from the Roosevelt home on N Street, educated at a convent in Austria, and, despite the hard times on which her family had fallen, was listed in the Social Register in both New York and Washington. She attended the same parties and dinners as the Roosevelts, was accorded the deference bestowed on aboriginal families in the District of Columbia, and found ready employment as a social secretary, a genteel calling that virtually made one a member of the family.

The Roosevelt children adored her. Anna remembered Lucy's warm smile and friendly greeting. Elliott called her gay, smiling, and relaxed. "She was femininely gentle where Mother had something of a schoolmarm's air about her, outgoing where Mother was an introvert. We children welcomed the days she came to work."[55]

Lucy was nearly as tall as Eleanor, fair, slender, and with the same blue eyes and light brown hair, but was far more graceful and at ease with herself. Alice Roosevelt Longworth recalled Lucy as "beautiful, charming, and absolutely delightful," with a really lovely face and "always beautifully dressed."[56] A friend, Aileen Tone, who held a similar position with Henry Adams, remembered seeing Lucy seated on the Roosevelts' living room floor, the family's bills, letters, and invitations spread around her in neat piles, "making order of them in a twinkle."[57] Another friend remembered her smile, "the most beautiful and winning I have ever seen."[58] Still another remembered her warm, mellow voice in contrast to the "shrill arpeggios" into which Eleanor's sometimes climbed.[59] Roy Jenkins (Lord Jenkins of Hillhead), FDR's most recent biographer, may have said it best when he described Lucy as a young lady of delicate charm, "a quintessential Jane Austen heroine, cast up one hundred years late on the shores of the District of Columbia rather than those of Dorset or Devon."[60]

Franklin was thirty-four, nine years older than Lucy, but still so youthful-looking that a cranky Wisconsin congressman ordered him to stub out his cigarette while he waited to testify before a House subcommittee, mistaking him for a junior clerk.[61] His appeal for the opposite sex was now considerable. Arthur Murray, Great Britain's assistant military attaché, spoke of Roosevelt as "breathing health and virility."[62] Bamie called him "my debonair young cousin," and her elderly husband, Admiral Sheffield Cowles, teased Franklin that "the girls will spoil you soon enough. I leave you to them."[63]

In 1915, when Franklin attended the Panama Pacific Exposition with his friend Assistant Secretary of State William Phillips, a San Francisco society matron proclaimed them "the most magnetic young men I ever saw. I had no idea that the Democratic party ever recruited that type of person."[64]* A Washington doyenne remembered FDR from his time as assistant secretary as "the most desirable man" she had ever met.[65] Alice Roosevelt Longworth, when she learned of Franklin's interest in Lucy, confessed that she marveled he hadn't strayed earlier.[66]

---

* FDR accompanied Vice President Thomas R. Marshall to officially open the 1915 Panama Pacific Exposition at San Francisco. While on the West Coast he inspected Navy installations and took his first dive in a submarine. Shortly before, the American submarine *F-4* had failed to surface after a dive off Pearl Harbor with the loss of all on board. The public was stunned, and FDR, who was worried about Navy morale, went aboard submarine *K-7* in Los Angeles. Despite heavy seas he ordered it to dive and go through its paces. Roosevelt greeted the press afterward, elated: "It was fine and for the first time since we left Washington we feel perfectly at home." *Los Angeles Tribune,* March 29, 1915; Josephus Daniels, *Years of War and After* 256; Robert F. Cross, *Sailor in the White House: The Seafaring Life of FDR* 204 (Annapolis, Md.: Naval Institute Press, 2003).

The romance began innocently enough. Franklin was again in Washington alone for the summer and continued his usual round of social engagements. Lucy was often present at those functions, and FDR, as was his wont, flirted brazenly. Lucy, who in many ways was as strong-willed as Eleanor, flirted back. One thing led to another, and soon Franklin was inviting her for cruises aboard the Navy's yacht *Sylph* and long drives in the Virginia countryside. The cruises were always well attended by a host of guests, but the drives were strictly private.

"I saw you twenty miles out in the country," Alice Longworth teased Franklin, "but you didn't see me. Your hands were on the wheel but your eyes were on that perfectly lovely lady."

"Yes, she is lovely, isn't she?"[67]

FDR was happy in Lucy's company and she very much in his. Unlike Eleanor, Lucy was uncritical in her affection and saw no need to direct his activities or admonish his behavior. She knew instinctively how to please him, to bolster rather than challenge him. Elliott recalls that Lucy had "the same brand of charm as Father, and there was a hint of fire in her warm dark eyes. In the new circumstances of Father's life at home, I see it as inevitable that they were irresistibly attracted to each other."[68]

Friends recognized that as well. A number, such as British Embassy counselor Nigel Law and Franklin's Harvard classmate Livingston Davis, often provided cover, posing as Lucy's escorts, while others, such as Alice Longworth and Edith Morton Eustis, provided safe houses for the couple to meet. "Franklin deserved a good time," said Alice. "He was married to Eleanor."[69] Alice, though she had been Eleanor's maid of honor, had little good to say about her cousin in those years, and her decision to provide succor for Franklin and Lucy was spiked with malice—perhaps because her own marriage to Nicholas Longworth had turned sour.

Edith Eustis, one of five attractive daughters of former vice president Levi Morton, was a Dutchess County neighbor of the Roosevelts and had known Franklin since childhood.[70] She admired his work in Washington and adored Lucy, a cousin of her husband, William Corcoran Eustis. Their elegant Washington mansion, Corcoran House, had been built in the earliest days of the city for Lucy's ancestor Maryland Governor Thomas Swann. It stood at the corner of Connecticut Avenue and H Street, directly across from Lafayette

Park, astride the route Franklin walked each day to and from the Navy Department.[71]*

Eleanor sensed something amiss that summer. Franklin's letters were intermittent and perfunctory, and he visited Campobello for only ten days, an aberration for someone who enjoyed the island so much as he. A polio epidemic raging along the East Coast kept Eleanor and the children at Campobello for four months instead of the usual two (the island proved to be insulated from the disease), and she did not return to Washington until after the election in November. "From a life centered entirely in my family," she wrote many years later, "I became conscious that there was a sense of impending disaster hanging over all of us."[72] The comment in her autobiography is interlaced between references to the growing menace posed by imperial Germany in late 1916, and it is easy to believe that ER was referring to the international situation. Elliott and others believe she was referring to something more personal. "By 'all of us' she meant not the country at large, but her family. She was talking about trouble much closer to home."[73]

The relationship between FDR and Lucy intensified in 1917. On June 24, ten weeks after the United States entered the war, Lucy enlisted in the Navy as a yeoman (female) and was assigned secretarial duties in the office of the assistant secretary. To believe FDR did not have a hand in the assignment is to believe in the tooth fairy. Franklin did not flaunt his infatuation with Lucy, but he made no secret of his affection for her. He began to put in longer hours at the Navy Department and often did not arrive home until after midnight.[74]

That summer Eleanor delayed her departure for Campobello as long as feasible. She and Franklin had words, there were arguments and upsets, but it was all vague. FDR was eager for her to take the children out of the Washington

---

* Corcoran House, along with the Hay-Adams houses and Decatur House, was one of Washington's most noted residences. Daniel Webster had lived there when he was secretary of state but found himself unable to support it afterward and sold it to W. W. Corcoran, founder of the Corcoran Gallery of Art. Eustis, a Corcoran grandson, was a fabled huntsman who preferred his estates in Leesburg, Virginia, and Aiken, South Carolina, to living in Washington. In 1920 he sold the house to the U.S. Chamber of Commerce, whereupon it was demolished and a new headquarters building for the Chamber was erected on the site. *Washington: City and Capital* 655–656, Federal Writers' Project, Works Progress Administration (Washington, D.C.: U.S. Government Printing Office, 1937).

heat; Eleanor was reluctant to leave Franklin alone in the city. Finally, on July 15, she packed up her family and went off to Campobello. FDR wrote her en route, part apology, part smoke screen: "[Y]ou were a goosy girl to think or even pretend to think that I don't want you here *all* the summer, because you know I do! But honestly *you* ought to have six weeks straight at Campo. . . . I know what a whole summer here does to people's nerves and at the end of this summer I will be like a bear with a sore head . . . as you know I am unreasonable and touchy now—but I will try to improve."[75]

Scarcely had Franklin written than *The New York Times* published an earnest interview with Eleanor that made matters worse. Under the headline "How to Save in Big Homes," the *Times* snidely described the Roosevelt ten-servant household on N Street as a model of wartime thriftiness: "Mrs. Roosevelt does the buying, the cooks see that there is no food wasted, the laundress is sparing in her use of soap, and each servant keeps a watchful eye for evidence of shortcomings on the part of the others; and all are encouraged to make helpful suggestions in the use of 'leftovers.' " Eleanor was quoted as saying that "Making the ten servants help me do my saving has not only been possible but highly profitable."[76]

FDR responded with biting sarcasm:

All I can say is that your latest newspaper campaign is a corker and I am proud to be the husband to the Originator, Discoverer and Inventor of the New Household Economy for Millionaires! Please have a photo of the family, and ten cooperating servants, the scraps saved from the table. I will have it published in the Sunday Times.

Honestly you have leaped into public fame, all Washington is talking of the Roosevelt plan and I began to get telegrams of congratulations and requests for further details from Pittsburgh, New Orleans, San Francisco and other neighboring cities.[77]

Eleanor was mortified. "I do think it was horrid of that woman to use my name in that way," she replied. "I feel dreadfully about it because so much is not true and yet some of it I did say. I never will be caught again that's sure and I'd like to crawl away for shame."[78] The flap ended quickly. It was ER's first experience at the hands of the press, and she had no idea how her candor could be exploited. She was never "caught again," and never again referred publicly to her household staff.*

In early August FDR came down with a serious throat infection that hospitalized him for four days. Eleanor rushed to his side and remained in Washington for almost two weeks. They evidently quarreled again, and Eleanor insisted he come to Campobello by the end of the month.[79] "I hated to leave you yesterday," she wrote on August 15. "Please go to the doctor twice a week, eat well and sleep well, and remember I *count* on seeing you on the 26th. My threat was no idle one."[80]

The precise nature of ER's threat is unknown, but the context is clear. Some authors suggest she meant to bring the children back to Washington immediately if FDR did not appear.[81] Elliott, who edited his father's papers, is more explicit: "There was no mystery; she threatened to leave him."[82]

Whatever the case, FDR made it to Campobello in time to forestall a crisis, and that autumn the Roosevelts moved into more spacious quarters at 2131 R Street. "Whether ER was consciously aware at this time that FDR spent as many hours as possible with Lucy Mercer, we shall never know," wrote Blanche Wiesen Cook. But members of the family knew, so did many of ER's Red Cross co-workers, and, in Cook's words, so did "almost everybody else of importance in Washington. Certainly on some level she knew it all, the way lovers always know, unconsciously and through every cell of their being, when somebody else has preempted some big or little piece of their beloved's heart."[83]

One important figure in Washington who had become aware was Josephus Daniels, FDR's family-minded chief at the Navy Department. On October 5, 1917, Yeoman Lucy Mercer was summarily discharged from the service "by Special Order of the Secretary of the Navy." No explanation was provided. No reason was given, and Lucy's conduct was rated outstanding. Daniels was a man who, in his son's words, "never let it be known that he knew what he did not want to know."[84] He never indicated in his diary or by word of mouth that he had ever heard of Lucy Mercer. But he could not have failed to notice the

---

* Although deeply embarrassed, ER remained resolute in her determination to save food. Elliott reports that throughout the war his mother always had a spare place set at the table for "Mr. Hoover" (Food Administrator Herbert Hoover) to symbolize for the family their need to conserve. Elliott Roosevelt and James Brough, *An Untold Story: The Roosevelts of Hyde Park* 87 (New York: G. P. Putnam's Sons, 1973).

chemistry between his assistant secretary and his comely yeoman aide, nor could he disregard the warnings flashed by his wife, who was well aware of the Washington gossip.[85]

Daniels was old-fashioned about the sanctity of marriage and the sin of divorce. When his brother-in-law, who ran the Raleigh *News & Observer* in his absence, announced his intention to divorce and remarry, Daniels peremptorily fired him and ran him out of state. The "Chief" loved Franklin as a son. He held Eleanor in deep respect. And he could recognize trouble when he saw it. A divorce would have been political suicide for FDR. Even a scandal would be hard to live down. To prevent that, Daniels evidently decided it was best for Miss Mercer to move on.

During the next six months Eleanor and Franklin saw little of each other. He continued to put in long hours at the Navy Department and saw Lucy when he could, while ER devoted every day to the Red Cross. "I loved it. I simply ate it up," she wrote later.[86] For Eleanor, her war work was an essential distraction that kept her mind occupied. Feeling alone and increasingly isolated, she instinctively turned to Sara for reassurance. The relationship between Eleanor and her mother-in-law had never been easy. But with her marriage threatened, ER found Sara a dependable ally. Sara's unyielding insistence on family tradition, her unstinting advocacy of virtue and noblesse oblige, even her deep-seated conservatism appealed to Eleanor as she faced the crisis she did not yet fully comprehend.

In the winter of 1918 Eleanor wrote Sara almost every day. She mentioned nothing directly but spoke often of the need to confide, to talk intimately: "I miss you and so do the children. As the years go on, I realize how lucky we are to have you, and I wish we could always be together. Very few mothers I know mean as much to their daughters as you do to me."[87] Sara responded with equally fulsome praise. The two women were never closer. On March 17, 1918—Franklin and Eleanor's thirteenth wedding anniversary—Sara sent a congratulatory telegram. Eleanor wrote movingly in reply:

I often think what an interesting happy life Franklin has given me and how much you have done to make our life what it is. As I have grown older I have realized better all you do for us and all you mean to me and the children especially and you will never know how grateful I am nor how much I love you dear.[88]

In the summer of 1918 FDR finally managed to get to the front in France. The Senate Naval Affairs Committee was heading to Europe, and Daniels wanted Roosevelt to get there first and correct anything that might attract its criticism.[89] Franklin chose to make the Atlantic crossing aboard the USS *Dyer*, a newly commissioned destroyer rushed into service without a shakedown cruise to escort a convoy of troopships through the war zone. He reveled in every moment, from the storm that smashed the crockery in the wardroom to an engine breakdown and the alarm bells signaling a U-boat attack that never materialized. As Roosevelt retold the story through the years, the German submarine came closer and closer until he had almost seen it himself.

In England, FDR met Lloyd George ("not very tall, rather large head, rather long hair, but tremendous vitality") and the King ("He seemed delighted that I had come over on a destroyer"); consulted with the Admiralty; spent a weekend at Cliveden with Lady Astor ("enthusiastic, amusing and talkative as always"), and spoke at a banquet at Gray's Inn.[90] In Paris he dined with President and Mme. Poincaré ("much like similar dinners at the White House except that here the wines were perfect of their kind and perfectly served"); spoke again with Marshal Joffre ("older and grayer than when he was in the United States"); and, the high point of his visit, met with the premier, Georges Clemenceau.

> I knew at once I was in the presence of the greatest civilian in France. He did not wait for me to advance to meet him at his desk, and there was no formality such as one generally meets. . . . He is only 77 years old and people say he is getting younger everyday. He seemed delighted at the present rate of progress. [T]he wonderful old man leaves his office almost every Saturday in a high-powered car, dashes to the front, visits a Corps Commander, travels perhaps all night, goes up a good deal closer to the actual battle line than the officers like, keeps it up all day Sunday and motors back in time to be at his desk on Monday morning.[91]

Roosevelt was especially impressed by French sangfroid. Despite four years of war, with the Germans literally outside the gates of Paris, they continued "the planting of the flower beds in the Tuileries and the repairing and cleaning of streets. They seem to lose their heads even less than the Anglo-Saxons— very different from what we thought four years ago."[92]

From Paris, FDR went to the front. After relieving an American naval attaché who sought to keep him out of the trenches, he pushed his party from one battlefield to the next. He saw Château-Thierry, Belleau Wood, and Verdun, was briefly under enemy fire ("the long whining whistle of a shell was followed by the dull boom of the explosion"), and came within a mile of the German lines. "Such tireless energy as Roosevelt's I have never known," said Captain Edward McCauley, Franklin's naval aide, "except perhaps for his kinsman, Theodore Roosevelt. I thought I was fairly husky, but I couldn't keep up with him."[93]

If Franklin did not see combat, he surely experienced its immediate aftermath: the shell holes filled with water, the roofless houses and splintered trees, the stench of dead horses, "rusty bayonets, broken guns, discarded overcoats and ration tins, rain-stained love letters, men buried in shallow graves, some unmarked, some with rifles stuck in the earth bayonet down, and some, too, with a whittled little cross and a tag of wood or wrapping paper hung on it and in a pencil scrawl an American name." That is the way Franklin described Belleau Wood, a memory he would cite again and again.[94]

From France, FDR went briefly to Italy, hoping to resolve the complicated command structure in the Mediterranean. In Rome he met with his naval counterparts and urged that the Italian fleet take action against the Austrians as soon as possible. At one point he questioned the wisdom of keeping the main Italian battle fleet riding at anchor in Taranto harbor for more than a year, with no drill or target practice.

"Ah," said the Italian chief of staff, "but my dear Mr. Minister, you must not forget that the Austrian Fleet have not had any either."

"This is a naval classic which is hard to beat," FDR wrote afterward, "but which perhaps should not be publicly repeated for a generation or two."[95]

From Italy back to France, then briefly to England before boarding the troopship USS *Leviathan* in Brest on September 8 for the return home. "Somehow I don't believe I shall be long in Washington," he wrote Eleanor before sailing. "The more I think of it the more I feel that being only 36 my place is not at a Washington desk, even a Navy desk. I know you will understand."[96]

Whatever Franklin's wish for active service, the Atlantic crossing of the *Leviathan* in September 1918 was certainly one he preferred to forget. Another Spanish influenza epidemic swept Europe and the United States that year, taking more than 20 million lives. *Leviathan* was hit hard. Virtually the entire ship's complement was struck down, Franklin included. Many of the officers and men were buried at sea, while Franklin hovered semiconscious in his bunk, his condition exacerbated by the onset of double pneumonia. The Navy Department kept a wary eye on *Leviathan* as it made its way to New York. Secretary Daniels telegraphed Sara of Franklin's condition, suggesting that she and Eleanor (who was in Hyde Park) meet the ship when it docked on September 19.

"When the boat docked and we went on board," Eleanor recalled years later, "I remember visiting several of the men who were still in bed. My husband did not seem to me so seriously ill as the doctors implied."[97] The fact is that Franklin's condition was still grave: he was so weak he had to be carried off the ship to an ambulance and borne up the stairs of Sara's house on East Sixty-fifth Street by four muscular orderlies. While it is possible that Eleanor's recollection may reflect her feelings at the time, it is more likely to have been colored by the bitterness that set in shortly afterward.[98]

In the course of unpacking Franklin's luggage, Eleanor discovered a neatly bound packet of love letters from Lucy Mercer. "The bottom dropped out of my world," Eleanor remembered. "I faced myself, my surroundings, my world, honestly for the first time."[99]

Family recollections differ as to what happened next. The two versions are not mutually exclusive. The Roosevelts believe that Eleanor offered to step aside so that Franklin might be with the woman he loved but that Lucy, being Catholic, could not bring herself to marry a divorced man with five children.[100] Lucy's relatives contend that she was perfectly prepared to marry Franklin but that "Eleanor was not willing to step aside."[101]

What is generally accepted is that Eleanor did indeed offer "to give Franklin his freedom." Her Aunt Maude had recently divorced, and divorce was certainly preferable to remaining where she was not wanted.[102] It is also likely that Franklin was prepared to leave. But what neither he nor Eleanor reckoned with were Sara's reaction and the counsel of Louis Howe. Both intervened decisively to hold the marriage together.

For Sara, divorce was unthinkable. If FDR really wished to leave his wife and five children for another woman and bring scandal upon the family, she said, she could not stop him. But if he did so she "would not give him another dollar," nor could he expect to inherit his beloved Hyde Park. And for Eleanor, well, it was perfectly all right for her to talk about giving Franklin his freedom, but what about the children? Who would take care of them?[103]

For Howe, it was a question of Franklin's career. Daniels would certainly have fired him, and the electorate would be unforgiving. Any hope of future elective office was out of the question. If FDR had presidential ambitions (and certainly Howe did on Franklin's behalf), he would have to choose between his career and Lucy Mercer.

Howe evidently played mediator. Sara had pulled Franklin and Eleanor back from the brink, but it was Howe, speaking separately with each, who brokered the settlement. He persuaded Eleanor that FDR could not go on successfully without her; and he convinced Franklin that to continue in politics he needed his wife.[104] FDR agreed never to see Lucy again—that was Eleanor's price for reconciliation—and with Louis Howe's help the two stitched together one of the most remarkable partnerships the world has ever known.

Franklin broke the news to Lucy but could not bear to tell her the truth. Instead, he put the blame on Eleanor: she would not agree to a divorce. Lucy said it did not matter. As a Catholic she could not have married a divorced man. Both were white lies, told by lovers to spare each other's feelings. Lucy's mother, an equally devout Catholic, had divorced and remarried, and there is little reason to believe that Lucy would not have married the man who had risked everything for her.

"She and Franklin were very much in love with each other," remembered Mrs. Lyman Cotten, Lucy's North Carolina cousin and confidante. "I know the marriage would have taken place but as Lucy said to us, 'Eleanor was not willing to step aside.' I am also sure that she thought that the religious opinions of the two could have been arranged. Nothing is easier in the Roman Catholic Church than an annulment, especially among those occupying high places."[105]

Eleanor emerged from the ordeal a different woman. "I knew more about the human heart. . . . I became a more tolerant person . . . but I think more determined to try for certain ultimate objectives."[106] Mrs. Roosevelt commenced the metamorphosis from a private to a public person. The marriage survived, but love and trust were gone. She forgave Franklin and they continued to live together, but their relationship had changed. Independent and increasingly self-confident and outspoken, Eleanor was now her own person. For her, the Lucy Mercer affair was a watershed. "I have the memory of an elephant," she told a friend. "I can forgive, but I cannot forget."[107]

Franklin, for his part, changed as well. He took care to protect his wife's feelings and to preserve outward proprieties. He would never allow anyone to criticize Eleanor in his presence. He spent more time with the children, gave up golf on Sunday mornings, and did his utmost to rebuild the marriage, albeit at arm's length. Like Eleanor, he matured and became more serious.

Historians and biographers attribute FDR's political coming of age to the searing effect of polio. Many of Franklin's friends believed his bitter disappointment in love had an earlier and equally profound effect. Corinne Robinson Alsop, Eleanor's cousin, thought that before Lucy, Franklin was without depth. "He had a loveless quality, as if he were incapable of emotion. It is difficult to describe, but to me [the affair] seemed to release something in him." Another who knew Franklin wrote that after losing Lucy he emerged "tougher and more resilient, wiser and more profound, even prior to his paralysis."[108]

There was no scandal. Not until the 1960s was FDR linked publicly with Lucy Mercer.[109] Harvard Professor Frank Freidel, writing the first multivolume biography of FDR in the early 1950s, dismissed the story in a footnote. Such rumors, wrote Freidel, "seem preposterous. They reflect more on the teller than FDR."[110] James MacGregor Burns, in his captivating *Roosevelt: The Lion and the Fox*, published in 1956, alluded to wartime rumors in Washington but refuted them in a paragraph.[111] Arthur Schlesinger, Jr., in *The Age of Roosevelt*, mentions Lucy Mercer and FDR's affection for her but resists going further.[112] The first to attempt a full account of the romance was Jonathan Daniels, FDR's presidential press aide and the son of Josephus Daniels, first in *The End of Innocence*, then in *Washington Quadrille*, published in 1968.[113] Eleanor Roosevelt confirmed the story in her long series of interviews with Joseph Lash, summarized by Lash in 1972 in his loving portrait *Eleanor and Franklin* and embellished in *Love, Eleanor* ten years later.[114]

Franklin did not see Lucy again until 1941, although they never really lost contact. In 1920, Lucy married Winthrop Rutherfurd, one of the wealthiest and by all accounts one of the most respected members of East Coast society. A direct descendent of Peter Stuyvesant of New York and John Winthrop of Massachusetts, Winthrop ("Winty," his friends called him) was an avid sportsman who divided his time between a country estate in Allamuchy, New Jersey, an elegant town house in New York, and Ridgeley Hall, his winter home in Aiken, South Carolina. In his youth, Rutherfurd was considered one of the most eligible bachelors in New York and had successfully courted and won the affection of Consuelo Vanderbilt, only to have Consuelo's mother break off the engagement and compel her to marry the ninth Duke of Marlborough.[115]

Winthrop later married another considerable heiress, Alice Morton, a daughter of Vice President Levi Morton (and sister of Lucy's friend Edith Eustis). Alice died in 1917, leaving Rutherfurd a widower at fifty-five with six children to care for. After Lucy's romance with Franklin broke off, Edith Eustis evidently brought her and Winty together, and they were married shortly afterward. He was fifty-seven, Lucy was twenty-nine.

The Rutherfurds lived together in happy contentment, dividing their time among their estates, the various social seasons, fox hunts, kennel shows, and travel abroad. Lucy helped raise the Rutherfurd children and soon had a daughter of her own. "Seldom have I seen a mother more beloved and respected than was Lucy by her stepchildren," wrote the Russian portrait painter Elizabeth Shoumatoff.[116] Lucy and Franklin maintained a formal correspondence, writing to extend greetings or condolences on special occasions. Other letters, if there were any, have been lost, destroyed, or safely sequestered. But there is no doubt the affection lingered. FDR quietly arranged for Lucy to watch each of his inaugurations from a White House limousine, and about 1940 he began calling her once or twice a week, sometimes speaking in his almost forgotten French to avoid being overheard. Lucy evidently called him as well, and the White House switchboard had standing orders to put Mrs. Rutherfurd directly through to the president.[117]

In the spring of 1941 Lucy and Franklin began to see another again. She was given the code name "Mrs. Johnson" by the Secret Service, and her name appears frequently on the White House register.[118] FDR enjoyed taking Lucy for afternoon drives through Rock Creek Park, and when Eleanor was away she would be invited by Franklin's daughter, Anna, to dine with the president. FDR, Jr., home on leave from the Navy, reports bounding into the Oval Office unannounced to find his father having his shriveled legs massaged by an unfamiliar woman whom the president introduced simply as "my old friend, Mrs. Winthrop Rutherfurd."[119]

There was "never anything clandestine about these occasions," Anna recalled. "On the contrary, they were occasions which I welcomed for my father because they were light-hearted and gay, affording a few hours of much needed relaxation for a beloved father and world leader in a time of crisis. . . . Lucy was a wonderful person. I was grateful to her."[120]

Winthrop Rutherfurd died in 1944 after a long illness, and thereafter FDR would sometimes stop the presidential train en route from Washington to

Hyde Park to visit Lucy at her Allamuchy estate. Once she accompanied him for a weekend at Shangri La, the president's Catoctin Mountain retreat (now Camp David); they spent a week together at Bernard Baruch's South Carolina estate, Hobcaw Manor; and FDR enjoyed nothing so much as driving Lucy along the meandering country roads near Warm Springs. She was with him there on April 12, 1945, and her face was the last FDR saw before he died. What attracted Franklin to Lucy? The writer Ellen Feldman sums it up nicely:

Lucy Mercer had a talent [to] make other people happy. I am not talking about giving up a career to stay at home and raise children, or nursing an aged parent, or other instances of worthy self-sacrifice. I mean a contagious genius for living joyously. Her descendants speak of the insouciance with which she met early hardship. . . . They mention her soft heart. . . . They speak of her need to make surroundings beautiful, and days bright, and loved ones glad to be alive.[121]

In the months following the president's death, Eleanor came to accept Lucy's return to Franklin's life and Anna's role in making her visits possible. Sorting through FDR's effects at Hyde Park, she came upon a small watercolor of her husband painted by Lucy's friend Elizabeth Shoumatoff. She instructed that it be sent to Lucy.[122] Anna also called. "Your telephoning the other night meant so much to me," wrote Lucy. "This blow must be crushing to you—to all of you—but I know that you meant more to your father than any one and that makes it closer and harder to bear. . . . I have been reading over some very old letters of his—and in one he says 'Anna is a dear fine person—I wish so much that you knew her'—Well, now we do know one another—and it is a great joy to me and I think he was happy this past year that it was so."[123] Anna kept Lucy's letter in her bedside table for the rest of her life.[124]

NINE

THE CAMPAIGN OF 1920

It was a darned fine sail.
—FRANKLIN D. ROOSEVELT

ON JANUARY 2, 1919, Franklin and Eleanor boarded the USS *George Washington* in New York, heading for Paris.[1] The armistice had been signed in November, and FDR was to initiate the dismantling of the Navy's vast European establishment. This included fifty-four shore installations stretching from the Azores to the Shetlands, twenty-five port authorities, and mountains of supplies, plus a vast array of claims, contracts, and government agreements arising from operations abroad. His party included Thomas J. Spellacy, a genial Irishman who was United States attorney for Connecticut, as legal adviser; and Commander John M. Hancock, chief of Navy purchasing.*

For Franklin and Eleanor it was a reconciliation of sorts—Eleanor's first visit to Europe since their wedding trip in 1905—and an opportunity to heal the hurt of the past autumn. After Eleanor discovered Franklin's romance with Lucy Mercer, she grew morose, suffered headaches, and had days when she doubted her will to live. "This past year has rather got the better of me," she wrote her friend Isabella Ferguson. "I still have a breathless, hunted feeling."[2]

Several times each week Eleanor drove herself to Rock Creek Cemetery on the outskirts of Washington to sit alone and contemplate the remarkable statue Henry Adams had commissioned Augustus Saint-Gaudens to sculpt in

---

* Hancock proved so adept at contract liquidation that soon after resigning from the Navy he joined the New York investment house of Lehman Brothers, rising to become one of its managing partners. In 1933, FDR called him to Washington to help organize the National Recovery Administration (NRA). During World War II Hancock returned to Washington to head an interdepartmental board to handle contract settlement, and he drafted the 1943 legislation on contract renegotiation.

his wife's memory. Eleanor found solace communing with that shrouded figure of grief and in later years would usually visit the cemetery whenever in Washington.[3]* Henry's wife, Clover Adams, a pioneer woman photographer, had committed suicide by drinking potassium cyanide, deeply distressed at her husband's infatuation with their friend and neighbor, Elizabeth Cameron, the beautiful young wife of Senator J. Donald Cameron of Pennsylvania.[4] To learn more about the Adamses, Eleanor gave Franklin a copy of *The Education of Henry Adams,* which had been privately printed in 1906 and had just been reissued for general purchase. They took it aboard the *George Washington,* and Eleanor read it during the crossing. "Very interesting," she noted of Henry Adams, "but sad to have had so much and yet find it so little."[5]

Four days out of New York, Franklin and Eleanor were informed by radio that Theodore Roosevelt was dead. Both were stunned. TR had just turned sixty-one and, though he had recently been hospitalized, seemed to be regaining strength for another run at the White House in 1920. The Republicans had retaken control of both houses of Congress in November, Wilson was vulnerable, there was no apparent Democratic successor, and once again the GOP appeared united. Senator Boies Penrose of Pennsylvania, a bitter critic of TR in past years, believed he would be nominated by acclamation on the first ballot.[6] The former president died of a pulmonary embolism while asleep at Sagamore Hill. "Death had to take him in his sleep," commented Vice President Thomas R. Marshall. "If Roosevelt had been awake, there would have been a fight."[7] TR was not old, said Franklin, "but I cannot help think that he himself would have had it this way and that he has been spared a lingering illness."[8] Eleanor wrote Sara that she was concerned about Aunt Edith, "for it will leave her very much alone. Another big figure gone from our nation and I fear the last years were for him full of disappointment."[9]

* On the day before FDR's inauguration in 1933, Eleanor asked her friend Lorena Hickok to pick her up at the Mayflower Hotel, where she and the president-elect were staying. Mrs. Roosevelt instructed the cab driver to take them to Rock Creek Cemetery so that she might gaze upon the statue once again. "In the old days when we lived here," said Eleanor, "I was much younger and not so very wise. Sometimes I'd be very unhappy and sorry for myself. When I was feeling that way, if I could manage, I'd come here alone, and sit and look at that woman. And I'd always come away feeling better. And stronger. I've been here many, many times." Lorena A. Hickok, *Eleanor Roosevelt: Reluctant First Lady* 92 (New York: Dodd, Mead, 1980).

Paris in January 1919 was a city of contrasts. Reminders of the war were everywhere: captured German artillery pieces lined the Champs-Élysées and the Place de la Concorde; limbless men and demobilized soldiers begged for change on fashionable street corners; and almost every other woman was dressed in black, mourning a departed loved one. Along the grand boulevards the glorious chestnut trees were gone, cut for firewood during the last desperate winter. Paris itself had been spared, but there were severe shortages of coal, milk, and bread.

Nevertheless, a festive air gripped the city. Those with money could still find wonderful clothes and jewels. The restaurants, when they could get supplies, were marvelous, and the nightclubs sparkled with gaiety. "I never saw anything like Paris," wrote Eleanor. "The scandals going on would make many a woman at home unhappy. It is no place for the boys [i.e., American soldiers], especially the younger ones. . . . All the women in the restaurant look to me exaggerated, some pretty, all chic, but you wonder if any are ladies."[10]

The Roosevelts were billeted by the Navy in a suite at the Ritz, where the lobby swarmed with foreign dignitaries sent to attend the peace conference that was about to begin. Woodrow Wilson arrived in the city the first week of January, after a triumphal tour of Great Britain and Western Europe. David Lloyd George arrived on January 11. The following day the Supreme Council of peacemakers—Wilson, Lloyd George, Prime Minister Vittorio Orlando of Italy, and Georges Clemenceau—convened for the first time.[11] They met in the ornate chambers of the French Foreign Ministry on the Quai d'Orsay, where, as host, Clemenceau presided. For the most part their discussions were conducted in English. Clemenceau, who had lived many years in the United States, spoke English fluently, and Orlando was minimally conversant.[12]

As the only head of state, Wilson was accorded a chair a few inches higher than the others, but of the four, Wilson was in the most precarious political position.[13] Lloyd George was fresh from parliamentary elections in which his coalition had won a huge majority; Clemenceau had just received an unprecedented 398–93 vote of confidence in the Chamber of Deputies; and Orlando headed a left-center government that was virtually unassailable. Only Wilson was fresh from defeat, having unwisely declared the congressional midterm elections in November a referendum on his leadership.[14] The electorate had responded by giving the GOP control of Congress for the first time since 1910.[15]

To compound his problem, Wilson had excluded the Senate from the negotiations. The American delegation, in addition to Secretary of State Lansing and Colonel House, included more than twenty academic specialists but not one member of the U.S. Senate, which ultimately would have to pass judgment on the peace treaty.* Henry Cabot Lodge of Massachusetts would soon become chairman of the Foreign Relations Committee and was on record as supporting a league of nations.[16] The personal animosity between Wilson and Lodge was notorious, but to have included him would have been an act of statesmanship from which the president would have benefited substantially. Equally damaging, Wilson had thumbed his nose at the nation's Republican leadership, almost all of whom had supported the war vigorously. William Howard Taft, Charles Evans Hughes, and Elihu Root had all endorsed the idea of a league, and their inclusion would have given the delegation a bipartisan cast.[17] Instead, Wilson chose to go it alone, convinced, as always, that his mission was divinely ordained.

The meetings of the Supreme Council were held *in camera,* and the participants' discussions remained secret. So much for "open covenants, openly arrived at," the first of Wilson's Fourteen Points. But it was just as well the sessions were closed because relations among the Big Four were tepid at best.[18] Orlando correctly perceived that he was being patronized; Lloyd George, the quintessential opportunist, had difficulty adhering to a fixed course; Clemenceau was all too fixed, obsessed with the need to provide for French security; while Wilson spoke with the dogmatic assurance of a Presbyterian elder. "What ignorance of Europe and how difficult all understandings were with him," said Clemenceau. "He believed you could do everything by formulas and his fourteen points. God himself was content with ten commandments. Wilson modestly inflicted fourteen points on us . . . the fourteen commandments of the most empty theory."[19]

FDR played no role at the peace conference. He and Eleanor remained in

* Wilson's exclusion of the Senate placed him at odds with American practice. In 1898, after the Spanish-American War, President McKinley sent a five-man delegation to Paris to negotiate the peace treaty and among the five included three senators from the Foreign Relations Committee: William Pierce Frye (R., Maine), Cushman Kellogg Davis (R., Wisconsin), and George Gray (D., Delaware). McKinley's foresight was rewarded when the Senate narrowly consented to the treaty 57–27, just three votes more than the required two thirds.

Europe five weeks, during which time Franklin devoted himself to disposing of the Navy's foreign assets. Roosevelt spoke French fluently and lubricated the discussions while Hancock and Spellacy hammered out the details.[20] "The most successful thing I pulled off in Paris," FDR remembered, was the sale of the Navy's Lafayette Radio Station near Bordeaux, the most powerful transmitter in the world at the time. The French had been dragging their feet, hoping the United States would simply abandon the installation. According to Roosevelt, André Tardieu, the French minister responsible (and later premier, 1929–30), "offered a ridiculous sum counting on the fact that the cost of dismantling and removing it would be prohibitive." Just when the meeting reached an impasse, a messenger handed a telegram to FDR that read, "Dismantle and ship station to America. [Signed] Daniels." Tardieu immediately gave in and agreed to buy the facility at FDR's asking price of 22 million francs. Roosevelt later boasted to friends that he had written the telegram himself and arranged to have it delivered to him at the meeting.[21] "This is a big success," Eleanor wrote Sara, "but don't mention it."[22]

On February 15, 1919, the Roosevelts left Paris for Brest and the return home on the *George Washington*. Among their fellow passengers were President and Mrs. Wilson, who were taking a quick break from negotiations so that the president might return to Washington to sign the final flurry of legislation passed by the outgoing Sixty-fifth Congress.[23] Wilson proudly carried with him the draft covenant of the League of Nations, which had just been completed. The president had insisted that the peace conference establish the League as its first order of business, and, with British acquiescence and French ambivalence, he had prevailed. "I like the League," Clemenceau was quoted as saying, "but I do not believe in it."[24]

Aboard the *George Washington* Wilson remained aloof and kept more or less to his cabin. "He seemed to have very little interest in making himself popular with groups of people whom he touched," Eleanor remembered.[25] One day, to FDR's surprise, the president summoned him for a discussion about the League and what it meant for the future. The invitation came out of the blue, and FDR recalled Wilson's intensity. A day or so later, Franklin and Eleanor were included in a small luncheon party given by the Wilsons. For the most part the conversation was unremarkable, though Eleanor remembered two things: Wilson said that since the war began he had read no newspapers; his secretary, Joseph P. Tumulty, clipped them for him, giving him only what was important.* The second was that Wilson had spoken with great emotion about the League. "The United States must go in or it will break the heart of the world, for she is the only nation that all feel is disinterested and all trust."[26]

The *George Washington*'s original destination had been New York, but after she was under way Wilson advised the captain that he wished to land at Boston, where he was scheduled to speak at Mechanics Hall and introduce the League. The captain adjusted course but to his horror discovered he had no charts on board for a Boston landfall. He would have to feel his way. To complicate the task, a heavy North Atlantic fog descended as the ship slanted southward along the Massachusetts coast. "I was awakened in my berth by a shuddering noise," FDR recalled. "Thinking the *George Washington* must be aground, I rushed to the bridge in my pajamas and bathrobe to discover that the ship's engines had been reversed and cut off—that was the noise—and that she lay between two jagged rocks, with little way between, facing a shoreline with a row of summer cottages. I recognized the settlement as Nahant, where I had frequently made port, and in a general way I was able to tell [the captain] where he would find Boston harbor. He then gave the order for backing the ship out of its perilous location, and proceeded safely to Boston. President Wilson, who had not been awakened, was never told what happened."[27]

Back in the United States, the Roosevelts grappled with the future. "We've had an interesting trip," Eleanor wrote her Aunt Bamie, "and F. thinks he succeeded very well with his demobilization of all possible stations in Europe. . . . He says he now expects to go into business this summer for a time so we may be in New York next year and there may be a little more time which we can call our own."[28]

---

* Eleanor was startled by Wilson's revelation. "This is too much to leave to any man," she noted of Tumulty's task in her diary. A president has a responsibility to keep himself informed. Later she wrote, "It was . . . a problem of allotting time. Franklin reserved certain periods for his study of the press, particularly the opposition press, and, at least while Louis Howe was with him, he was always closely informed on all shades of opinion in the country. This firsthand awareness of what people are doing and thinking and saying is essential to a president. When this information is filtered through other people, or selected with a view to what a few individuals think the president should know, the inevitable result is that this source of information is dangerously curtailed or misleadingly slanted. This is fatal in the formulation of far-reaching decisions." Eleanor Roosevelt, *Autobiography* 101–102 (New York: Harper & Brothers, 1961).

But first Washington beckoned. Secretary Daniels left for Europe in mid-March to attend an Allied naval conference and was gone for two months, again leaving FDR in charge. The Navy's demobilization was almost complete, and aside from adjusting to Republican control of Congress there was little other than routine housekeeping to occupy the acting secretary. Nevertheless, Daniels left detailed instructions to cover every contingency. The secretary was especially concerned that the admirals running the various bureaus not take advantage of his absence to push their pet projects through Congress. "They will probably present you with letters to sign and send to the new chairmen of the Naval Affairs Committees," he told FDR. This, Daniels said, you must not do. "It would be very well . . . for you to have a drawer and put them all in it so that we can make a study of them, and we will discuss them when I get back."[29]

Franklin was careful to stay on sides. "Ever since you left," he wrote Daniels, "things have been so quiet here as to be almost terrifying. Literally nothing has happened outside of routine work, which, however, has been positively volu minous."[30] The workload was indeed heavy. The Navy remained the only cabinet department with just one assistant secretary. Whenever Daniels or Roosevelt was absent, the entire administrative workload fell to the other. By FDR's account he worked fourteen hours a day and thrived on it. When Daniels returned in late May, Franklin wrote his old golfing partner John McIlhenny, "I have had a perfectly delightful two months, running things with a high hand and getting things done that were never done before. Last Saturday the Secretary got back and now I shall have a little leisure."[31]

If the Navy Department had returned to normal by late spring, the city of Washington was anything but. Labor unrest gripped the nation. Prices were high, jobs were scarce, and thousands of returning servicemen clamored for work. Four million Americans went out on strike in 1919, one out of every five industrial workers. Organized labor strove to expand union membership, management resisted fiercely, and both sides carried their cases to Washington. John L. Lewis and the United Mine Workers demanded that the government nationalize the coal mines immediately; mine and mill owners responded with court injunctions ordering strikers back to work. As agitation increased, violence became widespread, and Washington was not spared.

On the evening of June 2, 1919, a powerful bomb ripped the façade of the R Street home of Attorney General A. Mitchell Palmer, directly across the street from the Roosevelts'. The bomb was the work of a committed anarchist, who was blown up by his own device. Franklin and Eleanor were down the block when the bomb went off, returning from a late party. The blast shattered windows within a hundred-yard radius. Eleven-year-old James was the only Roosevelt child home at the time. Franklin raced upstairs and found him standing in his pajamas, barefoot amid the splintered glass, watching the scene below. "I'll never forget how unnerved Father was when he found me standing at the window," James recalled. "He grabbed me in an embrace that almost cracked my ribs."[32]

With James safe, Franklin went across the street to assist the Palmers, who had escaped injury. He drove Mrs. Palmer and her daughter to the home of friends and then helped police gather up pages and pages of anarchist literature scattered by the blast. "Now we are roped off," Eleanor reported to Sara the next morning. "The police haven't yet allowed the gore to be wiped up on our steps and James glories in every bone found! I only hope the victim was not a poor passerby instead of the anarchist."[33]

The following month the city was torn by a bloody four-day race riot that left fifteen dead and hundreds injured. The Washington police proved powerless, and eventually the military was deployed to restore order. "The riots seem about over today," Franklin wrote Eleanor on July 23. "Only one man killed last night. Luckily the trouble hasn't spread to R Street and though I have troubled to keep out of harm's way I have heard occasional shots during the evening and night. It has been a nasty episode and I only wish *quicker* action had been taken to stop it."[34]

The attack on Attorney General Palmer precipitated a widespread crackdown on suspected anarchists and Bolsheviks, known historically as the Red Scare of 1919–20. Primed by the Bolshevik revolution in Russia, government authorities under the attorney general's direction launched an attack on civil liberties unequaled in peacetime since passage of the Alien and Sedition Acts at the end of the eighteenth century.[35] Law enforcement officials illegally raided homes and union offices, aliens suspected of radicalism were deported, and thousands of innocent citizens were hounded for their beliefs. On a single night in January 1920 more than four thousand suspected Communists were arrested in thirty-three different cities.[36] The Palmer raids yielded almost nothing in the way of arms or revolutionaries but triggered a climate of fear that engulfed the nation. The New York state legislature, its better judgment swept away by a tidal wave of reaction, refused to seat five elected Socialists from New York City. In Washington, the House of Representatives twice refused to tender the oath of office to Socialist Victor L. Berger, elected overwhelmingly by the voters of Milwaukee.[37]

FDR showed no interest in Palmer's Red-baiting crusade. Indeed, at the same time that Congress and the New York legislature were expelling Socialists from their ranks, he upbraided Rear Admiral S. S. Robinson, commandant of the Boston Navy Yard, for discharging three machinists because they were Socialists. "Now, my dear Admiral," Roosevelt wrote, "neither you nor I can fire a man because he happens to be a Socialist. It so happens that the Socialist party has a place on the official ballot in almost every state in the union."[38]

When an old grad sought to enlist Franklin's help to cleanse the Harvard faculty of dangerous radicals (FDR was now a member of the university's board of overseers), he ignored the request. The radical in question was Harold Laski, a young instructor in the Government Department who had recently advocated nationalizing the country's railroads. "If Mr. Laski were teaching mathematics," wrote Paul Tuckerman, '78, "the argument for academic freedom would have some force . . . but he teaches our sons, not mathematics but government, and what reverence for our government and institutions can a professional Bolshevik teach? Why not clean house and get rid of this foreign propagandist?"[39] President A. Lawrence Lowell stood by Laski, and the Harvard board stood by Lowell. Laski returned to England shortly afterward to accept a position at the London School of Economics and went on to become an internationally renowned scholar and chairman of the British Labour party.

While Franklin was busy at the Navy Department, Eleanor took the first steps to make a life for herself outside the home. "Everyone is concerned about strikes and labor questions," she wrote Isabella Ferguson in September 1919. "I realize more and more that we are entering on a new era where ideas and habits and customs are to be revolutionized if we are not to have another kind of revolution."[40]

On behalf of the Red Cross, Eleanor undertook to inspect St. Elizabeth's, the nation's mental hospital in Washington, where hundreds of battle-shocked servicemen were confined. "I cannot do this," she remembered thinking to herself, but she went anyway. "*You must do the thing you think you cannot do,*" she wrote later, supplying her own emphasis.[41]

Once a week for the remainder of their time in Washington, Eleanor visited the hospital, distributing flowers and cigarettes, stopping to talk with the troubled men. When she discovered there were not enough attendants to provide proper care, she lobbied her friend Franklin K. Lane, secretary of the interior, in whose bailiwick St. Elizabeth's fell. Lane declined ER's invitation to visit the hospital—"the last thing he wanted to see was a hospital for the insane"—but he ensured that appropriations for St. Elizabeth's were increased.[42] Eleanor arranged for the Red Cross to build a recreation facility for the men, cajoled money from the Colonial Dames of America for occupational therapy, and organized a retail shop where patients could sell their handmade wares.

At the height of the Red Scare, Eleanor made her first contact with feminist organizations interested in improving working conditions for women. In late October 1919 representatives of nineteen nations convened in Washington for the First International Congress of Working Women. Because many of the delegates could not speak English, Mrs. Roosevelt and other multilingual Washington wives volunteered as translators. "It was of course, a very advanced and radical gathering," Eleanor wrote Sara, "but I found it interesting and amusing."[43]

Eleanor invited a number of the women home for lunch. The U.S. delegation included many early activists in the American labor movement: Margaret Dreier Robins, Rose Schneiderman, Maud Swartz, Julia O'Connor, Fannia Cohn, and Leonora O'Reilly. "I liked all of the women very much indeed," said Eleanor, "but I had no idea how much I was going to see of them in the future."[44]

After four months of additional negotiation, President Wilson returned to Washington on July 8 with the freshly minted Treaty of Versailles. Two days later, he presented it to the Senate. The treaty, he said, had come about "by no plan of our conceiving but by the hand of God who has led us into this way."[45]

The Senate was divided. A dozen or so irreconcilables, primarily populists from the South and West, favored rejection. Most Democrats supported the president and wished to accept the treaty outright. In the middle was a large group of Republicans led by Lodge who favored approval provided reservations to protect American sovereignty were registered. Unlike amendments, reservations do not change the text of a treaty but clarify how it will be interpreted. It is a well-established diplomatic practice for countries to add such qualifications, and if Wilson agreed, the chances were that the Senate would approve the treaty overwhelmingly. Secretary of State Lansing and the Senate's

Democratic leadership urged the president to accept the reservations, but Wilson refused.[46]

Convinced that God and the people were with him, the president chose to make a direct appeal to the electorate. On September 2, 1919, Wilson set out by special train to canvass the West. His health was failing. He had already suffered a mild stroke in Paris in April and was haggard and drawn. His face twitched, his hands trembled. During the next twenty-two days the president would travel 8,200 miles through fourteen states, delivering more than forty speeches. On September 25 Wilson spoke at Pueblo, Colorado. That evening he suffered a total physical collapse. The tour was canceled, and the president returned to the White House. The following week Wilson had a massive stroke that paralyzed his left side. For two months he hovered between life and death, barely able to scrawl a shaky signature on documents his wife presented to him. After that his mind became clear enough to follow what was happening and he was able to dictate letters. But he never fully recovered.

On November 6 Senator Gilbert Hitchcock of Nebraska, the Democratic floor leader in the fight for the League, was admitted to the president's bedside. Without the Lodge reservations, he told Wilson, he could not muster even a bare majority for the treaty, much less the two thirds required for approval. Wilson refused to accept the inevitable. "Let Lodge compromise," he told Hitchcock. Two weeks later the Senate voted on the Treaty of Versailles and the opponents won. Brought up for reconsideration at the next session, it once more failed to achieve a two-thirds majority. On March 19, 1920, the Senate formally returned the treaty to the president, noting its inability to give its advice and consent.*

Like most Democrats, FDR supported the League but did not see it as the be-all and end-all of public life. "Last spring I thought the League of Nations merely a beautiful dream, a Utopia," he told the New York Bar Association in March 1919. "But in June I went abroad [and] found in Europe not only a desire to beat the Hun but a growing demand that out of it all must come something else."[47] Three months later he warned the graduating class at Worcester

---

* The Senate's constitutional responsibility is to give its "advice and consent" to treaties by two-thirds vote. It does not "ratify" treaties. Ratification is a technical diplomatic term that applies when the president formally signs the treaty bringing it into effect, subsequent to the Senate's advice and consent.

Polytechnic Institute that "the United States would commit a grievous wrong to itself and to all mankind if it were even to attempt to go backwards toward an old Chinese wall policy of isolation."[48] But unlike Wilson he did not object to Lodge's reservations and believed the president should compromise to get the League accepted. The details were less important than the final product. "I have read the draft of the League three times," he declared, "and always find something to object to in it, and that is the way with everybody."[49]

The British, the French, and most cabinet officers shared that view. In September 1919, the British government dispatched former foreign secretary Sir Edward Grey (Viscount Grey of Fallodon) to Washington to plead with Wilson to accept the Lodge reservations. Wilson refused to receive him. When the Roosevelts entertained Lord Grey and his staff at Christmastime, they became non gratae in the eyes of the White House.[50] The consequence for FDR was negligible because by January 1920 the Wilson administration had come unglued and it was every man for himself. Colonel House was no longer consulted; Secretary of State Lansing had been dismissed; Franklin Lane resigned at Interior, as did Carter Glass at the Treasury, frustrated at their inability to communicate with Wilson. Daniels wished to resign as well but remained out of personal loyalty to the invalid president.

It was in the context of the derelict Wilson administration that FDR began to look to his political future. But he did so discreetly. "I sometimes think we consider too much the good luck of the early bird and not the bad luck of the early worm," he wrote an impetuous supporter in late 1919.[51]

Already FDR had been mentioned as a possible candidate for the U.S. Senate or the governorship should Al Smith choose not to run for reelection. But the possibility of the latter was slight, and the chance of defeating a popular Republican incumbent in the Senate, his good friend James Wadsworth of Geneseo, appeared equally remote. "I am not running for Senator or Governor or dog catcher," Franklin told a friend shortly after Christmas. "I do not personally intend to make an early Christian martyr of myself this fall if it is going to be a strongly Republican year."[52]

The idea of seeking the vice presidency, just as the possibility of running for the New York State Senate in 1910, came to Roosevelt largely by chance. On January 10, 1920, FDR received a visit from an old friend, Louis B. Wehle, a Kentucky attorney and member of the War Industries Board who had admired Franklin since their days together on *The Harvard Crimson.* The Democrats' presidential prospects looked bleak, said Wehle, but after talking to a number of party leaders he had hit upon a ticket that might win: Herbert Hoover for president, Roosevelt for vice president. Hoover was from California, FDR from New York: two states the Democrats must carry if they were to succeed. Hoover enjoyed a sterling reputation as wartime food administrator, he supported the Treaty of Versailles with minor reservations, and he was especially popular among American women, who in 1920 would be voting for the first time.[53] Like Hoover's, Franklin's wartime service as assistant secretary of the Navy had been exemplary, and he would add the luster of the Roosevelt name to the ticket. "Whether you win or lose," said Wehle, "you would make a number of key acquaintances in every state . . . that would probably lead you eventually to the presidency."[54]

Roosevelt needed no convincing. "Hoover is certainly a wonder," he allowed. "I wish we could make him President of the United States. There could not be a better one."[55] Franklin, who thus far had patterned his career on TR's, was well aware that the vice presidency had been Cousin Theodore's stepping-stone to the White House. "You can go to it as far as I'm concerned," he told Wehle. "Good luck."[56]

The following day Wehle called on Democratic kingmaker Colonel Edward House at his New York apartment. House was on the outs with Wilson but still wielded considerable influence in the party. "It's a wonderful idea," he told Wehle. "A Hoover-Roosevelt ticket is probably the only chance the Democrats have in November."[57]

Was Hoover a Democrat? Wehle called on the food administrator at his office on lower Broadway and found him noncommittal. So too did House. Like Dwight Eisenhower after World War II, Hoover was being courted by both parties and kept his own counsel. On March 6 Franklin and Eleanor dined with the would-be nominee but could not smoke him out. "Mr. Hoover talked a great deal," Eleanor wrote Sara. "He has an extraordinary knowledge and grasp of present-day problems." Evidently he did not reveal his allegiance.[58] At the end of March 1920, Hoover broke his long silence and proclaimed himself a progressive Republican: he had been registered as a Republican in California since 1898, and he had supported TR in 1912.[59] There would be no Hoover-Roosevelt ticket.

But FDR had been bitten by the vice presidential bug. Alben Barkley, Harry Truman's vice president in 1949, was fond of telling of the woman who had two sons: one became a sailor and went to sea; the other became vice president of the United States. "Neither has been heard from since."[60] "Cactus Jack" Garner of Uvalde, Texas, FDR's crusty vice president, later told newsmen the job "wasn't worth a pitcher of warm piss."*[61] For Roosevelt, it was a ticket to be punched, a way station on the road to the White House, and Wehle was correct: the nomination would bring Franklin into contact with Democrats across the country.

A successful vice presidential aspirant plays his cards close to his chest, waiting for lightning to strike. The choice of a running mate is traditionally the prerogative of the presidential nominee, and one scarcely runs for the post. But Hoover or no Hoover, FDR's credentials would have placed him on any nominee's short list: young, attractive, high-profile wartime service in Washington, liberal but not populist, probably wet but acceptable to the drys on Prohibition,† and above all a Roosevelt from New York, by far the most populous state in the Union, with forty-five electoral votes, roughly one fifth of the number required for election.

When the Democratic convention met in San Francisco on June 28, FDR had positioned himself for the nomination. The support of the New York delegation was critical, and Franklin had taken every precaution. He traveled cross-country on the Knickerbocker Express with his fellow delegates, entertained them lavishly on the battleship *New York,* anchored off Treasure Island, and volunteered to second the nomination of Al Smith, a favorite-son candidate whom Charles Murphy was using as a stalking horse until the decisive moment to shift the Empire State's ninety votes behind the winner. Franklin's entourage included his Dutchess County allies John Mack and Tom Lynch; his

---

* Newspapers sanitized Garner's comment, and "warm piss" has come down through generations as "warm spit": admittedly a four-letter word but scarcely as pungent as Cactus Jack's characterization. Garner's political insight is treated perceptively in a series of interviews with Bascom N. Timmons published in four installments by *Collier's,* February 21, March 6, 16, and 20, 1948.

† Next to the League of Nations, Prohibition was the burning political issue of 1920. The Eighteenth Amendment, banning the sale of alcoholic beverages, went into effect on January 15, 1920, a date widely celebrated by the drys and perhaps even more widely deplored by the nation's wets. As a young legislator in Albany, FDR had backed the prohibitionist cause, reflecting the sentiments of his upstate district. Thus he had a record the drys could embrace. In his personal life, Roosevelt enjoyed a drink as much as anyone. He paid no attention to Prohibition and never believed in it for an instant.

old Harvard roommate, former congressman Lathrop Brown; his law partner Grenville Emmett; and his personal secretary from the Navy Department—all of whom began to work the hotel corridors and lobbies on FDR's behalf.

Franklin took advantage of every opportunity. When a huge floodlit portrait of Wilson was unveiled during opening ceremonies, the convention erupted with a sentimental display of affection. Delegation after delegation flooded the aisles, parading around the hall, state standards held aloft. All, that is, except New York, whose delegates conspicuously kept their seats to illustrate the organization's distaste for the president. When the demonstration reached its height, FDR seized the New York standard—Murphy nodded his approval—and joined the parade, to the cheers of hundreds of delegates.*[62]

Al Smith was nominated by Tammany's Bourke Cockran, one of the most gifted orators of the day. FDR's seconding speech was brief and well received. Poised, confident, standing at a convention podium for the first time in his career, he was effusive in his praise of Smith: "I love him as a friend; I look up to him as a man; I am with him as a Democrat; and we all know his record throughout the nation as a great servant of the public."[63]

Grenville Emmett thought FDR's speech "could not have been better." Frances Perkins said Franklin was "one of the stars of the show. I recall how he displayed his athletic ability by vaulting over a row of chairs to get to the platform in a hurry. Al [Smith] always thought of this as the beginning of his friendship with Roosevelt and often referred to it as Roosevelt's real start in important public life. And so it was."[64]

Smith remained in contention for seven ballots. On the eighth, Murphy switched the bulk of New York's vote to three-term Ohio governor James Cox, a competent but colorless public servant, moderate, wet, untainted by any link to the Wilson administration, and uncommitted on the League. FDR and some nineteen upstate delegates voted for William Gibbs McAdoo, Wilson's

* In his frequent retelling of the episode, FDR invariably escalated the event: "I grabbed the standard. About half a dozen men grabbed me and we had a jolly good fight, but I got the standard and it was paraded." But Judge Jeremiah T. Mahoney, the Tammany stalwart who held the standard, reported that "FDR couldn't budge it until Mr. Murphy sort of bowed to let it go and we let it go. The whole thing probably took less than four seconds. There wasn't even an angry gesture." Frank Freidel, *Franklin D. Roosevelt: The Ordeal* 63 (Boston: Little, Brown, 1954); Judge Jeremiah T. Mahoney interview, Columbia Oral History Project, Columbia University.

son-in-law and onetime secretary of the Treasury. For the next four days the convention wavered among McAdoo, Cox, and the nation's Red-chasing attorney general, A. Mitchell Palmer. Cox gained the lead on the thirty-ninth ballot and went over the top on the forty-fourth shortly after midnight on Monday, July 6. The convention then adjourned until noon the next day, when it would meet to choose the party's vice presidential nominee.

Early Tuesday morning Cox's campaign manager, Edmund H. Moore, called the governor at his home in Dayton. Whom did he wish as a running mate? "I've been thinking about this a good deal," Cox replied, "and my choice is young Roosevelt. His name is good, he's right geographically, and he's anti-Tammany. But since we need a united front, go to see Charlie Murphy and say we won't nominate Roosevelt if he objects."[65]

Moore followed instructions. "I don't like Roosevelt," said Murphy. "He is not well known in the country, but, Ed, this is the first time a Democratic nominee for the presidency has shown me courtesy. That's why I'd vote for the devil himself if Cox wanted me to. Tell him we will nominate Roosevelt on the first ballot as soon as we assemble."[66]

When the Democrats reconvened at noon, the early roll call of the states placed several favorite sons in nomination. As the roll call continued, Florida yielded to Ohio, at which point Judge Timothy T. Ansberry, leader of the Buckeye delegation, made his way to the platform. "The young man whose name I am going to suggest," said Ansberry, "is but three years over the age of thirty-five prescribed by the Constitution . . . but he has crowded into that short period a very large experience as a public official. His name is a name to conjure with in American politics: Franklin D. Roosevelt." Indiana and Kansas seconded the nomination, the favorite sons withdrew, the rules were suspended, and FDR was nominated by acclamation.[67]

Josephus Daniels, by now the grand old man of the party, beloved by populists, Wilsonians, and big-city bosses alike, concluded the proceedings:

> I wish to say that to me, and to five hundred thousand men in the American Navy, and to five million men in the Army, it is a matter of particular gratification that this Convention unanimously has chosen as a candidate for Vice President that clear-headed and able executive and patriotic citizen of New York, the Assistant Secretary of the Navy, Franklin D. Roosevelt.[68]

Pleased with the ticket of Cox and Roosevelt, and a trifle more optimistic than the circumstances warranted, the convention adjourned sine die at 1:42 P.M. FDR's friends were overjoyed. Walter Lippmann of *The New Republic* wired his congratulations: "Your nomination is the best news in many a long day." Herbert Hoover wrote, "the fact that I do not belong to your political tribe does not deter me from offering my personal congratulations to an old friend. I am glad to see you in the game in such a prominent place, and, although I will not be charged with traitorship by wishing you success, I nevertheless consider it a contribution to the good of the country that you have been nominated and it will bring the merit of a great public servant to the front." Franklin K. Lane offered his advice: "Get plenty of sleep. Do not give yourself to the handshakers. Be wise! Don't be brilliant."[69]

On August 6, 1920, FDR resigned as assistant secretary of the Navy and headed west.[70] In the next three months he would crisscross the country twice, delivering nearly one thousand speeches and countless impromptu addresses—the most extensive campaign ever conducted by a candidate for national office.[71] Franklin wrapped himself in TR's mantle, peppering his speeches with "bully," "strenuous," and all manner of verbal tics associated with the former president. "I do not profess to know what Theodore Roosevelt would say if he were alive today, but I cannot help think that the man who invented the word 'pussy-footer' could not have resisted the temptation to apply it to Mr. Harding."[72]

Colonel Robert R. McCormick, a sometime Bull Moose and Franklin's classmate at Groton, immediately protested. On August 13 the *Chicago Tribune* called FDR "the one-half of one percent Roosevelt. Franklin is as much like Theodore as a clam is like a bear-cat. . . . If he is Theodore Roosevelt, Elihu Root is [Socialist leader] Gene Debs, and Bryan is a brewer."[73] Edith Roosevelt, TR's widow, said, "Franklin is nine-tenths mush and one-tenth Eleanor." Nicholas Longworth, Alice's husband and a man who knew something about alcohol, called FDR "a denatured Roosevelt."[74]

Franklin's advance man during the campaign was Steve Early, a blunt-spoken southern journalist who would remain at FDR's side throughout his career. His press aide was Marvin McIntyre, who had handled that job at the Navy Department and who would become another permanent fixture. Louis Howe was there, of course, as were Tom Lynch from Hyde Park and FDR's faithful personal secretary, Renah Camalier. When the campaign ran short of money, Franklin wrote a check for $5,000; Sara wrote another for $3,000. (In today's currency, that would be $50,000 and $30,000, respectively.) Roosevelt was not yet the polished campaigner he would become. But he was tireless and confident, and Louis Howe thought he was becoming increasingly eloquent. Unfortunately, he was often unfocused and prone to exaggerate his personal achievements. Early complained, "he couldn't be made to prepare speeches in advance, preferring to play cards instead."[75]

Franklin's casual approach caused a passel of trouble. On August 18, in Deer Lodge, Montana, he became carried away by his own rhetoric and claimed to have written the Haitian constitution, much as Al Gore once claimed to have invented the Internet. A week later in San Francisco, he boasted of "running Haiti and Santo Domingo for the past seven years."[76] The Associated Press picked up the stories, and Republicans had a field day. Harding said that when he became president, "I will not empower the Assistant Secretary of the Navy to draft a constitution for helpless neighbors in the West Indies and jam it down their throats at the point of bayonets carried by United States Marines."[77] John Barrett, director of the Pan-American Union, declared that Roosevelt had made a dreadful mistake. The *New York Telegraph* called him "a spoiled child to be spanked."[78] FDR denied having made the statements, but there were too many witnesses to make the denial credible.

For the most part, Cox and Roosevelt tied themselves to Wilson and the League. But the electorate was tired of both. Harding pledged "a return to normalcy," and that pledge struck a responsive chord. The November results were devastating. Harding polled 61 percent of the popular vote and trounced Cox in the electoral college 404–127. The Democrats failed to carry a single state outside the Solid South—the party's worst showing since the Civil War. The Republicans won a record 301 seats in the House of Representatives and picked up 10 additional seats in the Senate. Nowhere were the results worse than in New York, where Cox and FDR polled just 27 percent of the vote, taking Smith and the rest of the ticket down with them. Outside New York City, the Democrats did not carry a single county or elect anyone to statewide office.[79]

FDR took the defeat in stride. He telegraphed congratulations to Calvin Coolidge, Harding's running mate, and headed off to the marshes of Louisiana for two weeks of hunting and loafing. Looking back on the campaign years later, FDR told Supreme Court associate justice Robert H. Jackson that if he had not run for vice president in 1920, he would not have been nominated for president in 1932. "He created a sense of indebtedness on the part of the Democrats and made personal friends who remembered him later when his campaign manager, James Farley, went out looking for delegates," said Jackson. "Roosevelt's sense of security was such that he did not fear defeat."[80]

The 1920 campaign saw Eleanor emerge into public life. She joined the campaign train in September and for the next four weeks accompanied Franklin as he barnstormed the country—the only woman in the entourage. Unlike the Republicans, the Democrats initially made little effort to appeal to women voters.* Eleanor was relegated to playing the dutiful wife, appearing at whistle-stops to look gracious and smile adoringly while Franklin delivered the same speech over and over.[81] It was Louis Howe, not Franklin, who recognized Eleanor's potential. And it was Howe who worked her into the campaign. Repeatedly Howe would knock on her compartment door and ask her to review speeches and help plan press conferences. "I was flattered," Eleanor recalled, "and before long I found myself discussing a wide range of topics."[82]

Howe taught Eleanor about national politics, just as he had taught Franklin, and he helped her understand the importance of the press. "The newspaper fraternity was not so familiar to me at that time, and I was a little afraid of it. Largely because of Louis Howe's early interpretations of the standards and ethics of the newspaper business, I came to look with interest and confidence on the writing fraternity and gained a liking for it which I have never lost."[83]

Even more important, Eleanor and Howe developed a deep and lasting friendship. Before, she had resented his intimacy with FDR and was jealous of the role he played in her husband's life. Now she understood Howe's position and felt treated as an equal partner. Howe encouraged her political talents and helped her express them. He understood her moods and dedicated himself to bridging the distance between her and Franklin. Eleanor, for her part, discovered that Howe had many talents. Aside from an encyclopedic knowledge of

---

* The GOP had always taken a more forceful stand on women's suffrage than the Democrats, who were still captive to their southern, traditionalist base. On October 1, 1920, Harding held a special day for suffragists and then a Social Justice Day in which he called for equal pay for equal work, an end to child labor, a minimum wage, national health care, and a department of social justice—virtually the entire program of the League of Women Voters. Cox and Roosevelt let the opportunity slip by. Stanley J. Lemons, *The Woman Citizen: Social Feminism in the 1920s* 87–101 (Urbana: University of Illinois Press, 1973).

the nation's politics, he had the temperament of an artist. He painted land-scapes and portraits, sang in the choir at St. Thomas' Church, wrote poetry, and was an avid theater buff, directing and acting for the Drama League Play-ers in Washington. Howe loved the seashore, and, most endearingly, he knew when to be silent and when to speak up. As Blanche Wiesen Cook observed, "Louis Howe was the first of many intimate friends that ER grew to trust and love, with a warmth and generosity both spontaneous and unlimited."[84]

At Christmas Franklin sent each of the men who had campaigned with him a pair of gold cuff links engraved with his initials on one link and his own on the other. This was the beginning of the famous Cuff Links Club, which would meet annually on FDR's birthday to eat, drink, and reminisce about their first campaign together. The men in turn presented Eleanor with a suitably en-graved gold pin as a souvenir of the campaign, a gift she treasured.[85]

FDR had no illusions about the political future. The Democrats, he told Cox, were unlikely to return to the White House until economic catastrophe drove the Republicans out. "Every war brings after it a period of materialism and conservatism. People tire quickly of ideals." To Steve Early he joked, "Thank the Lord we are both comparatively youthful."[86]

To prepare for the political wilderness, FDR set about to restore his fi-nances. After ten years of public service his coffers were bare. And with five children attending fashionable boarding schools, plus extensive social com-mitments, membership in a half-dozen elite clubs, first-class travel, and a household of ten servants, the need to make a substantial living could no longer be ignored. The answer was Wall Street. And the opportunity came when Van Lear Black, a wealthy Democratic contributor who owned the Balti-more *Sun,* asked FDR to become vice president of his Fidelity & Deposit Com-pany of Maryland, the fourth largest surety bonding company in the United States. Roosevelt's responsibilities would be to oversee the firm's operations in New York and New England and to serve as rainmaker, bringing in new clients through his connections in government, labor, and industry.

FDR would be the firm's front man on Wall Street, for which Black agreed to pay him $25,000 a year, five times his salary at the Navy Department. It was an arrangement from which both stood to profit. The hemorrhaging of Roo-sevelt's finances would be stanched, and Black would benefit from Franklin's name on the masthead. Even more important—which both men understood implicitly—the position was a holding pattern for FDR, much as the presidency of Columbia University would be for Dwight D. Eisenhower thirty years later. It was agreed that Franklin would spend only half a day at the office, leaving him free to develop his law practice and remain active in party politics.

On January 7, 1921, Black announced FDR's appointment with a lavish black-tie dinner at Delmonico's, the favorite watering hole of the Wall Street establishment. Among the dignitaries who welcomed Roosevelt to the business world were Owen D. Young of General Electric, Edward R. Stettinius of United States Steel, Daniel Willard of the Pennsylvania Railroad, and Adolph S. Ochs of *The New York Times,* all valued clients of F & D. Within little more than a month Roosevelt mastered the business routine. He glad-handed old friends like the boxing promoter Tex Rickard and called in his chits from the days in Washington. Unions that had been recognized by the Navy Department were invited to consider having their officers bonded by Fidelity & Deposit, as were the industries contracting with the service. When Harding took office in March, FDR added Louis Howe to his staff. Like Franklin, Howe worked at both Fidelity's business and Democratic politics. As his personal secretary, FDR engaged Marguerite LeHand, a pert twenty-three-year-old who had worked during the campaign in Roosevelt's New York headquarters. Known as "Missy" because the younger Roosevelt children had difficulty saying "Miss LeHand," she too would become a permanent fixture in FDR's entourage.

As Franklin jumped into New York social life, Eleanor enrolled in business school to learn typing and shorthand. She found a housewife to teach her to cook and became active in the League of Women Voters. Her task was to keep tabs on the League's legislative agenda in both Washington and Albany, a job that brought her into contact with many of the nation's leading feminists: Carrie Chapman Catt, Minnie Fisher Cunningham, Narcissa Vanderlip, Elizabeth F. Read, and Esther Lape. Eleanor took her responsibilities with the League seriously and began to address women's groups on her own, bringing them up to date on legislative matters. She enjoyed the work, but, as she wrote Franklin from the League's national convention in Cleveland in April, "I prefer doing my politics with you."[87]

With Louis Howe's help, FDR began to stitch together an upstate organization to contest the 1922 election. This time he was careful to stress party unity. Already mentioned as a leading contender for the Democratic nomination for the U.S. Senate, Roosevelt recognized the importance of a full-blown organization effort under Charles Murphy rather than another divisive split. William Calder, the Republican incumbent, was vulnerable, but to beat him the Democrats needed a united front.*

Speaking engagements carried Roosevelt throughout the state. He also undertook a wide range of charitable and philanthropic activities. In addition to the Harvard Board of Overseers, he became a member of the executive committee of the National Civic Federation, the Near East Relief Committee, the Woodrow Wilson Foundation, and the Seamen's Church Institute. He headed a $2 million fund drive for Lighthouses for the Blind and accepted the chairmanship of the Greater New York Committee of the Boy Scouts of America. It was as chairman of the Scouts that on Thursday, July 28, 1921, FDR set sail up the Hudson for Bear Mountain and the annual Boy Scout Jamboree.

It was the type of occasion Franklin liked best. There were parades and speeches and solemn demonstrations of scouting activities. FDR posed for the newspapers surrounded by cheering boys and their scoutmasters. He served as master of ceremonies at a campfire before sailing back to the city that evening. Little did he realize that at some point during the day he had ingested a mysterious virus, incubated among the Boy Scouts, that would change his life forever.

---

* In 1922, the Democrats roared back under Murphy's leadership. Al Smith was overwhelmingly returned to the governor's office, and Dr. Royal S. Copeland, president of the New York Board of Health, easily defeated Calder for the Senate: 1,276,667 to 995,421. Congressional Quarterly, *Guide to U.S. Elections* (Washington, D.C.: Congressional Quarterly Service, 1975).

TEN

POLIO

This is the happy Warrior;
this is he,
That every man in arms
should wish to be.

—WILLIAM WORDSWORTH

AFTER EIGHT YEARS in Washington, FDR looked forward to spending the summer of 1921 at Campobello. Eleanor and the children left New York for the island as soon as school was over in June.* Franklin, who was detained by business, embarked on Friday, August 5, traveling the distance aboard Van Lear Black's oceangoing yacht *Sabalo.* "I thought he looked tired when he left," Missy LeHand wrote Eleanor. Both women hoped the brief sea voyage would revive him.[1]

---

* Moving the Roosevelt household from New York to Campobello each year was a logistical operation of considerable proportions, often involving as many as a dozen express crates, thirty or so barrels and trunks, plus a vast assortment of hand luggage. As described by FDR's son James, "First, we would proceed from New York to Boston by train—six hours if we were lucky. We would arrive in Boston in mid-afternoon and go to a certain old-fashioned hotel to rest until train time. . . . [U]sually we took the 11 p.m. sleeper, arriving next morning at Ayers Junction, Maine. There we would change to an antique train—a real museum piece—and ride to Eastport [Maine]. We would reach Eastport at noon, then transfer to a carriage, which would take us to the dock. If the tide was right, we could get off fairly quickly; if not, we had to wait to board the 'chug-chug' that took us to Campobello. We switched there to a rowboat, which took us to our own pier. Those mountains of baggage, boxes, and trunks, which had been shipped by express, came across separately on a larger ferry and were brought by horse-drawn dray to the house on Campobello." James Roosevelt and Sidney Shalett, *Affectionately, F.D.R.* 138 (New York: Harcourt, Brace & Co., 1959).

FDR arrived at Campobello Sunday evening and found their eighteen-bedroom "cottage" overflowing with guests. In addition to five children and the normal complement of servants, tutors, and governesses, Louis Howe and his family were visiting, as were several friends from Washington, including Romanian diplomat Prince Antoine Bibesco and his wife, Elizabeth, daughter of former British prime minister Herbert Asquith.

For the first time in years, Sara was not in her house next door. At sixty-seven she had resumed her prewar practice of an annual trip to Europe and on the spur of the moment had flown from London to Paris in an early twin-engine airplane. "It was five hours," she wrote Eleanor. "I had been told four hours, but I would not have missed it. If I do it again I shall take an open plane as one sees more and it is more like flying."[2]

As soon as he arrived, FDR threw himself into a frantic round of island activity: deep-sea fishing in the Bay of Fundy, afternoon sails, swimming, tennis, baseball, whatever else the children expected. On August 10, while the family was sailing, they spotted a small forest fire on one of the lesser islands. Franklin worked the boat in as close as he could—"almost on the beach," James recalled—and led Eleanor and the children ashore. They fought the blaze with pine boughs for several hours until it was extinguished. "Our eyes were bleary with smoke," said Franklin. "We were begrimed, smarting with spark-burns, exhausted."[3]

It was about four o'clock when they returned home. FDR admitted to feeling logy and decided the remedy would be a quick swim in the relatively warm waters of Lake Glen Severn, a shallow freshwater pond on the other side of the island. He and the children jogged two miles to the lake, splashed around in the tepid water, and topped it off with an icy dip in the Bay of Fundy. Franklin was disappointed that he did not get "the glow I'd expected." They trotted back to the cottage, and by then FDR was totally exhausted. The mail had arrived, and he sat down in his wet bathing suit to read it, "too tired even to dress. I'd never quite felt that way before."[4]

About an hour later Roosevelt felt a sudden chill. He told Eleanor he thought he was catching a cold and had better not risk infecting the children. He would go straight to bed. Eleanor sent up a tray of food, but he was not hungry. He had trouble sleeping that night and continued to tremble despite two heavy woolen blankets.

The next morning he was worse. When he swung his legs out of bed and attempted to stand, his left leg buckled beneath him. He managed to get up and shave and assumed the problem would pass. "I tried to persuade myself that the trouble with my leg was muscular, that it would disappear as I used it. But presently it refused to work, and then the other collapsed as well."[5] FDR dragged himself back to bed, and when Eleanor took his temperature it was 102.

There was no telephone in the house, so Eleanor dispatched a runner to fetch their family physician, Dr. E. H. Bennett, from Lubec. Dr. Bennett was an elderly country doctor, well suited to delivering babies and setting broken bones but not especially qualified for complex diagnoses. He examined Franklin and thought he was suffering from a bad cold; he said he would return in the morning to see how his patient was doing.

Roosevelt knew he did not have a cold. The next morning, Friday, August 12, he could not stand, and by evening he had lost the power to move his legs. They were numb, yet extremely sensitive. He ached all over and was paralyzed from the chest down. His thumb muscles had become so weak he could not write.[6]

On Saturday Eleanor and Dr. Bennett decided to seek a second opinion. Louis Howe canvassed the nearby resorts and discovered that the eminent Philadelphia surgeon Dr. William Keen was staying at Bar Harbor. Keen had once operated secretly on President Grover Cleveland and had successfully removed a cancer from the roof of the president's mouth.[7] He was a man of discretion, which Howe appreciated, but he was now eighty-four and his experience had been in surgery, not orthopedics. Dr. Keen examined Franklin thoroughly and decided his paralysis was due to a blood clot in the lower spinal cord. He prescribed heavy massages and predicted that Roosevelt would recover, "but it may take some months."[8]

Dr. Keen was as far off target as Dr. Bennett, and his prescription of vigorous massages exacerbated the problem.* FDR's condition worsened daily. Soon his hands and arms were paralyzed as well as his legs. His fever soared,

---

* For his services, Dr. Keen sent ER a bill for $600, which, converted to today's dollars, would be the equivalent of $6,000. ER to James Roosevelt Roosevelt, August 18, 1921. 2 *The Roosevelt Letters* 414, Elliott Roosevelt, ed. (London: George G. Harrap, 1950).

and he lost control of his bodily functions. For a short time his eyesight seemed threatened. Eleanor slept on a couch in Franklin's room and with the help of Louis Howe managed to move him, bathe him, and turn him over at regular intervals. She administered catheters and enemas, massaged his legs, brushed his teeth, and waited on his every need. "It required a certain amount of skilled nursing," Eleanor remembered, "and I was very thankful for every bit of training which Miss Spring [the children's nurse] had given me."[9]

Slowly, Roosevelt's temperature subsided. He was still in constant pain, but the feeling of panic diminished. "I think he is getting back his grip and a better mental attitude," Eleanor wrote Franklin's half brother, Rosy, on August 18. "We thought yesterday he moved his toes on one foot a little better which is encouraging."[10]

Dr. Keen, for his part, marveled at Eleanor's devotion. "You have been a rare wife and have borne your heavy burden most bravely," he wrote in late August. "You will surely break down if you do not have immediate relief. Even when the catheter has to be used your sleep must be broken at least once a night. I hope that by having his urine drawn the last thing at night, he will be able to wait until morning."[11]

It was Louis Howe who first suspected Franklin had been misdiagnosed. A confirmed cynic and partial hypochondriac, Howe was skeptical of expert opinion in general and the medical profession in particular. He wrote detailed letters to Sara's brother Frederic A. Delano (Uncle Fred), the head of the family in New York, describing Franklin's symptoms and requesting that the information be relayed to orthopedic specialists for their opinion. Uncle Fred saw the point immediately. "All doctors seem to know Dr. Keen," he wrote Eleanor. "He is a fine old chap, but he is a surgeon and not a connoisseur of this malady. I think it would be very unwise to trust his opinion."[12] After making soundings in New York, Uncle Fred went to Boston to consult "the great Dr. Lovett"—Dr. Robert Williamson Lovett, professor of orthopedic surgery at Harvard and the nation's leading authority on infantile paralysis.[13] Lovett was summering in Newport, but his associates at the Harvard Infantile Paralysis Commission agreed that FDR's symptoms were unquestionably those of infantile paralysis.

"On Uncle Fred's urgent advice," Eleanor wrote Rosy, "which I feel I must follow on Mama's account, I have asked Dr. Keen to try to get Dr. Lovett here for a consultation to determine if it is I.P. or not. Dr. Keen thinks *not* but the treatment at this stage differs in one particular and no matter what it costs I feel and I am sure Mama would feel we must leave no stone unturned to accomplish the best results."[14]*

Dr. Lovett arrived at Campobello August 25 and found Franklin paralyzed from the waist down, running a temperature of 100 degrees. His back muscles and arms were weak and the leg muscles even weaker. He could not sit up without assistance. Lovett pronounced the verdict crisply: It was "perfectly clear" that FDR had poliomyelitis.[15]

Eleanor was stunned. Were the children in any danger? she asked. Lovett thought not. If any were going to be ill, it would have happened already. As for Franklin, he ordered the massages discontinued immediately, believing that overtiring the weak muscles might damage them further. A complete recovery was possible, said Lovett. There was nothing to do but wait. "I told them frankly that no one could tell where they stood, that the case was evidently not of the severest type. . . . [I]t looked to me as if some of the important muscles might be on the edge where they could be influenced either way—toward recovery, or turn into completely paralyzed muscles."[16]

Franklin appeared relieved to know the worst. "He looked very strained and very tired," said Eleanor. "But he was completely calm. His reaction to any great event was always to be completely calm. If it was something that was bad, he just became almost like an iceberg, and there was never the slightest emotion that was allowed to show."[17]

As the days wore on, FDR's composure deteriorated. His condition was not improving, and he worried that stopping the massages had been a mistake. At the end of August, Dr. Bennett wired Lovett for help: "Atrophy increasing, power lessening, causing patient much anxiety. Attributed by him to discontinuance of massage. Can you recommend anything to keep up his courage?"[18]

---

* Writing in the *Journal of Medical Biography* in October 2003, Dr. Armond Goldman of the University of Texas Medical Branch at Galveston suggested that FDR might have suffered from Guillian-Barré syndrome (also known as acute ascending polyneuritis), not polio. "No one can be absolutely sure of the cause of Roosevelt's paralysis because relevant laboratory diagnostic studies were not performed or were not available at the time of his illness," Goldman said. Whatever the diagnosis, it would have made no difference since there were no effective treatments for either disease in 1921. Armond S. Goldman, Elisabeth J. Schmalstieg, Daniel H. Freeman, Jr., Daniel A. Goldman, and Frank C. Schmalstieg, Jr., "What Was the Cause of Franklin Delano Roosevelt's Paralytic Illness?" 11 *Journal of Medical Biography* 232–240 (2003).

Dr. Lovett replied instantly. "There is nothing that can be added to the treatment," he wrote. "This is one of the hardest things to make the family understand."

Drugs I believe are of little or no value. . . . Bromide for sleeplessness may be useful. Massage will prolong hyperesthesia and tenderness. . . . The use of hot baths should I think now be considered again, as it is really helpful and will encourage the patient, as he can do so much more under water with his legs. . . . I should have him sit up in a chair as soon as it can be done without discomfort.[19]

In mid-September it was decided to take Franklin back to New York, where he could be treated at Presbyterian Hospital by Dr. George Draper, a Harvard classmate who was a protégé of Dr. Lovett. Uncle Fred arranged for a private railroad car to be dispatched to Eastport, and Howe ensured that FDR was smuggled aboard out of range of inquisitive reporters. Thus far the press had reported only that Roosevelt was ill and was recovering. Polio had not been mentioned.

The news of Franklin's malady first appeared on the front page of *The New York Times* the morning of September 16:

F.D. ROOSEVELT ILL OF POLIOMYELITIS
BROUGHT ON SPECIAL CAR FROM CAMPOBELLO, BAY OF FUNDY,
TO HOSPITAL HERE

The accompanying article quoted Dr. Draper to the effect that although Franklin had lost the use of both legs below the knee, "he definitely will not be crippled. No one need have any fear of any permanent injury from this attack."[20]

FDR's hopes soared. That afternoon he dictated a note to his friend Adolph S. Ochs, publisher of the *Times:*

While the doctors were unanimous in telling me that the attack was very mild and that I was not going to suffer any permanent effects from it, I had, of course, the usual dark suspicion that they were just saying nice things to make me feel good. But now that I have seen the same statement officially made in *The New York Times* I feel immensely relieved because I know of course it must be true.[21]

Wishful thinking. The fact was, FDR was not improving. His fever refused to abate, and his legs continued to atrophy. "There is a marked falling away of the muscle masses on either side of the spine in the lower lumbar region," Draper warned Dr. Lovett in late September. "The lower extremities present a most depressing picture. There is little motion in the long extensors of the toes of each foot." Draper believed the psychological factor would be decisive. "He has such courage, such ambition, and yet at the same time such an extraordinarily sensitive emotional mechanism, that it will take all the skill we can muster to lead him successfully to a recognition of what he really faces without utterly crushing him."[22]

Slowly Franklin improved. By early October he was well enough for Missy LeHand to be admitted an hour or so each morning to take dictation. Eleanor and Louis Howe kept up with his affairs, and the brief dictation sessions worked wonders on FDR's morale. But what Roosevelt craved most was personal contact. Close friends were now allowed into his hospital room for brief visits. Interviewed by the journalist Ernest K. Lindley ten years later, many still recalled their visits with awe. "Roosevelt gaily brushed aside every hint of condolence and sent them away more cheerful than when they arrived. None of them has ever heard him utter a complaint or a regret or even acknowledge that he had had so much as a bit of bad luck."[23]

FDR saw it as his duty not only to appear in the best of spirits but to bolster the spirits of those about him. Despite the grim reality of his condition, he persisted in seeing the bright side. "I am sure you will be glad to learn that the doctors are most encouraging," he disingenuously wrote Josephus Daniels in mid-October. "Your surmise regarding the stern determination of my 'missus' not to let me proceed too rapidly is absolutely correct. In fact, I already suspect that she has entered into an alliance with the doctors to keep me in the idle class long after it is really necessary."[24]

Franklin's arms and back muscles recovered first. "I was delighted to find that he had much more power in the back muscles than I had thought," said Draper in early October.[25] Dr. Lovett came down from Boston to see the patient on October 15. FDR was now able to sit up. "He is cheerful and doing an hour or so of business each day. He has been in a chair once and I recommended pushing him around, and letting him go home when he wanted to."[26]

On October 28, 1921, Roosevelt was discharged from hospital and taken home to East Sixty-fifth Street. He was now able to pull himself up by a strap and, with some assistance, swing himself into a wheelchair. "The patient is doing very well," Dr. Draper noted on November 19. "He navigates about successfully in a wheel chair. He is exceedingly ambitious and anxious to get to the point where he can try the crutches, but I am not encouraging him."[27]

In December, FDR began a carefully constructed exercise regimen with Mrs. Kathleen Lake, a trained physiotherapist. The tendons behind his knees had tightened to the point that it was terribly painful to stretch his legs. Mrs. Lake had him exercise on a board. Some paralytics found this so stressful they could endure it just three days a week. FDR insisted that Mrs. Lake come every day. "Mrs. Lake works so long now every a.m.," Eleanor reported to Sara, "that F. does not get up till after noon at least, except on Sundays when she doesn't come."[28]

Progress was slow. In mid-December Mrs. Lake reported to Dr. Lovett that Franklin

> feels his legs growing stronger all the time. He is perfectly satisfied to remain as he is now and not get up on crutches as he says he has plenty of occupations for his mind, everything is going well in the city, and he would rather strengthen his legs this way than try to get up too soon.
>
> He is a wonderful patient, very cheerful, and works awfully hard and tries every suggestion one makes. He has certainly improved since he started the board which he insists on calling "the morgue!"[29]

FDR did his utmost to reassure his children, displaying his withered legs and reciting the anatomical names of the muscles affected. "How we loved to talk about Pa's *gluteus maximus*," James recalled.[30] When Christmas came, Franklin presided as always, carving the turkey and reading Dickens's *Christmas Carol*. He could no longer trim the tree himself but supervised every detail. "Father was a perfectionist," said one of the children. "Though fear of fire was his only phobia, [he] insisted on decorating the tree with candles rather than electric bulbs. . . . I still don't know how he did it, but Father kept us completely at ease. He cushioned the shock for us. He made it possible to participate in various festivities that Christmas without feeling any depression or guilt."[31]

As was usually the case with the Roosevelts, the double town house on East Sixty-fifth Street was jammed to capacity. Franklin was ensconced in the large back bedroom on the second floor, the quietest in the house. Louis Howe, who had committed himself irrevocably to FDR's fortunes, took the big front room, while the children filled the fourth floor and spilled over into Sara's adjoining house. Live-in servants occupied the rooms on the fifth and sixth floors under the roof. Eleanor slept on a cot in young Elliott's room and dressed in her husband's bathroom. "In the daytime I was too busy to need a room for myself," she recalled.[32]

By this time, Eleanor had become fiercely attached to Louis Howe. "She had called for help and Louis came," said Frances Perkins. "I know that Mrs. Roosevelt loved Louis Howe. She loved him the way you love a person who has stood by you in the midst of the valley of the shadow and not been afraid of anything."[33]

Howe was downtown at Fidelity & Deposit most of the day attending to Franklin's business. But he took breakfast with the family and spent most of his time at the table reading the dozen or so newspapers he consumed daily. "He read more newspapers than any human being I've ever known," Eleanor said.[34]

From the beginning, ER and Howe agreed that insofar as possible Franklin should not be treated as an invalid. Louis maintained that FDR's political future was bright and downplayed the seriousness of his illness. He planted optimistic stories with the press and wrote cheery letters to Roosevelt's wide circle of correspondents.

"Do you really believe that Franklin has a political future?" asked Eleanor.

"I believe someday Franklin will be President," Howe replied.[35]

Eleanor supported Howe in every way. She ushered a continuous stream of visitors in to see Franklin and soon undertook speaking engagements on his behalf. She joined Howe in urging FDR to persevere in his exercises—perhaps a little more sternly than Roosevelt might have desired. Howe was better at cajoling Franklin because he had a lighter touch, interspersing gossipy anecdotes among his exhortations to get on with the job.

Sara took a different view. Instead of resuming public life, she felt Franklin should retire to the pastoral comfort of Hyde Park and settle into the graceful life of an invalid country squire, much as Mr. James had done. There was no need to earn a living—Sara's share of the Delano fortune ensured that—and Franklin could pursue the hobbies and bucolic interests of which he was so fond.

A struggle of wills ensued. "This was the most trying winter of my entire life," Eleanor remembered.[36] She and Howe worked to keep Franklin focused on recovery; Sara just as resolutely decried their efforts and sought to convince her son to follow the path his father had chosen. "My mother-in-law thought we were tiring my husband and that he should be kept completely quiet. This made the discussions about his care somewhat acrimonious on occasion."[37]

Dr. Draper sided with Eleanor and Howe and thought it best for FDR to make every effort to resume a normal life.* Most important, so too did Franklin. As Sara noted laconically, "Franklin had no intention of conforming to my quiet ideas for his future existence."[38] Out of courtesy he offered to resign as vice president of Fidelity & Deposit, but Van Lear Black refused to consider it. Howe kept on top of the work for FDR, and Black was far more interested in retaining the Roosevelt name and the connections associated with it than in Franklin's physical presence at the office. FDR retained his position on the boards of various charitable organizations, including the Cathedral Church of St. John the Divine and the Boy Scouts, and with the help of Howe and Missy LeHand kept up a constant correspondence with Democratic leaders about the party's future.

In March FDR was fitted with steel braces that weighed fourteen pounds and ran from his heels to above his hips. After seven months in bed, Franklin's ability to balance had vanished, and it required the assistance of all hands just to get him to his feet. Since his hips were paralyzed, he was incapable of moving his legs individually and was taught to pivot forward on his crutches, using his head and upper body for leverage. Despite the constant danger of falling, FDR rejoiced at being on his feet and able to move under his own power. "I am indeed delighted to hear you are getting well so fast and so confidently," Woodrow Wilson wrote on April 30. "I shall try and be generous enough not to envy you," said the former president, now confined to a wheelchair at his S Street home in Washington.[39]

---

* Years later, Dr. Draper told his sister, Alice Carter, that if it had not been for Eleanor and Louis Howe, FDR "would have really become an invalid." Joseph P. Lash, interview with Alice Carter, cited in Lash, *Eleanor and Franklin* 276 (New York: W. W. Norton, 1971).

Dr. Draper's progress report to Dr. Lovett was guarded. Franklin "was walking quite successfully and seems to be gaining power in the hip muscles. The quadriceps are coming back a little, but they are nothing to brag of yet. Below the knee I must say it looks rather hopeless." When Dr. Draper said FDR was walking, he simply meant he was capable of moving forward on crutches wearing his braces. There was no suggestion that he would ever walk normally.[40]

When summer came, Franklin was moved to Hyde Park, where it was cooler and he would have easier access to the outdoors. Sara installed ramps ("inclined planes," she called them) and removed all the thresholds so her son's wheelchair could roll smoothly.* The old trunk elevator, operated by rope pulleys and designed to move heavy trunks to the attic, made it possible for FDR to move easily from floor to floor. He resisted having it electrified, believing a power failure would leave him trapped, whereas he could always manipulate the ropes manually. "Mr. Roosevelt seems to be cheerful and I should say that he has gained considerably in the tricks of handling himself," Dr. Draper reported. "There is no question but that the change of scene has had a very ben eficial effect . . . and I look forward to the continued stretch of quiet at Hyde Park with great hopefulness."[41]

FDR's routine rarely varied. He slept late, breakfasted on a tray sent to his room, and worked out on a set of rings mounted over his bed. Three days a week Mrs. Lake came to oversee his exercises, after which he went downstairs and was pushed out onto the porch, where he read and worked on his stamp collection. He swam in Vincent Astor's heated pool in Rhinebeck and exercised with parallel bars on the lawn. Progress remained slow. "I think it is very important for you to do all the walking that you can within your limit of fatigue," wrote Dr. Lovett on August 14. "Walking on crutches is not a gift, but an art, acquired by constant practice just as any other game, and you will have to put in quite a little time before you get about satisfactorily."[42] Franklin devoted his afternoons to struggling up the gravel driveway to the Albany Post Road, awkwardly pushing his braces, his hips swiveling, his crutches working, as he inched ahead, a little farther each day until he reached the brownstone

---

* FDR soon designed his own wheelchair: an armless kitchen chair that was easy to slide onto, mounted on wheels, with a holder attached for his ashtray. He used this simple expedient for the remainder of his life.

gateposts a quarter mile away. At the end of the summer he reported to Dr. Lovett, "I have faithfully followed out the walking and am really getting so that both legs take it quite naturally, and I can stay on my feet for an hour without feeling tired."[43]

Franklin saw the bright side. His daughter, Anna, back from a summer in Europe, was aghast at the effort FDR put in. "It's a bit traumatic," she noted, "to see your father, who took long walks with you, sailed with you, could out-jump you, and suddenly you look up and you see him walking on crutches—trying, struggling in heavy steel braces. And you see the sweat pouring down his face, and you hear him saying, 'I must get down the driveway today—all the way down the driveway.' "[44]

As FDR convalesced, the New York Democratic party once again found itself in disarray. The GOP occupied the governor's mansion, and all bets for the November election were off. William Randolph Hearst, the flamboyant publisher of the *New York American* and *Evening Journal,* had begun corralling delegates for the Democratic nomination and appeared to have a clear track unless Al Smith could be coaxed back from private life. Following his defeat in 1920, Smith had found safe haven as chairman of the United States Trucking Corporation, a largely symbolic position that paid the princely salary of $50,000 a year. That, plus the sizable fees he earned as a director of other firms, made Smith reluctant to run again. But Smith loathed Hearst. He soon agreed with party leaders that the maverick publisher did not have a chance of prevailing in the general election and would likely pull the entire ticket down with him. To save the party, Smith privately agreed to run. And to get the ball rolling he asked Franklin, as the most prominent upstate Democrat, to issue a public appeal for him to do so.

Delighted to be called on, if only to play a symbolic role, FDR wrote a "Dear Al" open letter on August 13. "The Democratic party must put its best foot forward," he told Smith. "I am taking it upon myself to appeal to you in the name of countless citizens of upstate New York. You represent the type of citizen the voters of this state want to vote for for Governor. We realize that years of public service make it most desirable that you think now of your family's needs. I am in the same boat myself—yet this call for further service must come first."[45]

The letter was front-page news throughout the state. So too was Smith's "Dear Frank" reply. The former governor agreed to accept the party's call. Hearst saw the handwriting on the wall and immediately withdrew.[46]

AL NOMINATED WITH GREAT ENTHUSIASM, Howe wired FDR from the Democratic convention in Syracuse. MORGENTHAU [Henry Morgenthau, Jr.] AND YOUR MISSUS LED THE DUTCHESS DELEGATION WITH THE BANNER THREE TIMES AROUND THE HALL.[47]

Smith shared Howe's elation. "Everything went along first rate," he wrote Franklin. "I had quite a session with our lady politicians as Mrs. Roosevelt no doubt told you. I was delighted to see her taking an active part and I am really sorry that you could not be there, but take care of yourself—there is another day coming."[48]

Eleanor was now committed to the Democratic party. At Louis Howe's urging, she had broadened her nonpartisan attachment to the League of Women Voters to include active participation in mainstream politics. As Howe put it, Eleanor "had to become actively involved in Democratic politics in order to keep alive Franklin's interest in the party and the party's interest in him."[49] In June 1922, when Nancy Cook of the New York State Democratic Committee asked her to address a fund-raising luncheon, she dutifully accepted despite her terror of speaking in public. "I trembled so that I did not know whether I could stand up," Eleanor wrote later. "I am quite sure my voice could not be heard."[50] Evidently ER exceeded her expectations: she was immediately asked to chair the finance committee of the Women's Division of the party and later edited the *Women's Democratic News*.

Nancy Cook and Eleanor became fast friends almost immediately, and through Nancy, ER soon met Marion Dickerman, the first woman to run for legislative office in New York. Cook and Miss Dickerman had been partners since their days as graduate students at Syracuse in 1909 and shared an apartment in Greenwich Village. Ardent feminists and committed pacifists, they had served as Red Cross volunteers at a London hospital during the war. After the war ended, Cook managed Dickerman's campaign for the legislature.[51]

Cook was short, athletic, and excitable, with close-cropped hair and expressive brown eyes. One biographer described her as "dashing and roguish, flirtatious and irreverent." Dickerman, by contrast, was tall, calm, steady, and soft-spoken—a woman of "rhythmic regularity."[52] When ER met them, Dickerman was dean of New Jersey State College in Trenton and taught English at Bryn Mawr during the summer; Cook was assistant director of the women's division of and an indefatigable organizer for the New York Democratic party. Eleanor, who sometimes lamented her lack of a university education, rejoiced in the company of these professional women. During the next dozen years, she, Nancy, and Marion would become almost inseparable.[53]

At Franklin's urging, Eleanor devoted as much time to Dutchess County politics as to her work with the state committee. FDR recognized that an upstate Democrat had to secure his base if he were to be effective statewide. He also believed that the dismal showing of the Democratic party upstate was the result of poor organization and neglect.[54] Franklin directed the local effort from his sitting room at Hyde Park, and Eleanor and Howe became his eager lieutenants.* ER recruited several friends and set out to organize and register the women in the county. She spoke frequently to various civic groups. Initially, Howe accompanied her, sat in the back of the hall, and monitored her performance. When her hands shook, he told her to grip the lectern; when she felt nervous, he told her to breathe deeply. Howe was especially critical of ER's penchant to giggle inappropriately. It sent the wrong message. His advice was terse: "Have something to say. Say it. And sit down."[55]

In the autumn, Franklin returned to the city. "I am just back in New York after a very successful summer at Hyde Park," he wrote defeated presidential candidate James Cox, now titular head of the Democratic party. "The combination of warm weather, fresh air and swimming has done me a world of good." To his friend and sometime hunting companion Richard E. Byrd he wrote, "By next autumn I will be ready to chase the nimble moose with you." To General Leonard Wood he boasted that his leg muscles "were all coming back."[56]

ON OCTOBER 9, after an absence of fifteen months, FDR returned to the offices of Fidelity & Deposit on Lower Broadway. Franklin was determined to walk from the car across the sidewalk, in the front door, and through the lobby to the bank of elevators at the far end. As he heaved himself across the sidewalk, his chauffeur at his side, a crowd of passersby gathered to watch. Some-

---

* The Democrats swept New York in 1922. Smith polled 55.2 percent of the vote—the largest plurality a gubernatorial candidate had ever received in the state—and carried the entire ticket to victory. In contrast to past years, the Democrats ran surprisingly well upstate. FDR called it "the reawakening of the Rip Van Winkle of upstate Democracy." FDR to Smith, December 3, 1922, FDRL.

one opened the door. Others stood aside to let him through. Drenched in sweat, Roosevelt began to crutch himself across the highly polished floor of the marble lobby. Suddenly his left foot gave way and he began to fall. The chauffeur reached out but was unable to hold him. Franklin crashed flat on the marble, his crutches clattering down beside him. Onlookers rushed in, then drew back, uncertain what to do.

With an enormous effort Roosevelt wrestled himself into a sitting position. He laughed reassuringly. "There's nothing to worry about," he told anxious spectators. "We'll get out of this all right. Give me a hand there." Two muscular young men stepped forward and with the help of the chauffeur lifted Franklin to his feet. His crutches were restored and his hat was replaced on his head. "Let's go," he said. The spectators opened a path and watched breathlessly as FDR hauled himself across the marble floor, smiling and nodding, one laborious step after another, his knuckles white on the handles of his crutches.[57]

Describing the day to his friend Livingston Davis, Franklin said only that he'd had a "Grand reception at 120 Broadway where I lunched and spent 4–5 hours."[58] In the future, FDR allowed himself to be whisked in by wheelchair. He initially came two days a week, then three, then four. But Roosevelt did not return to his law firm. "The partners are dear, delightful people," he wrote Van Lear Black, "but their type of law business is mostly estates, wills, etc., all of which bore me to death." Instead, Franklin decided to organize a new firm "with my name at the head instead of at the tail as it is now."* This, he told Black, would benefit F & D, "as our connections would be the type of corporations which would help in the bonding end of the game."[59]

One of the men who helped pull Franklin to his feet in the lobby at 120 Broadway was Basil O'Connor, a young red-haired attorney whose office was next door to Fidelity & Deposit. A live-wire graduate of Dartmouth (voted "most likely to succeed" by his classmates) and the Harvard Law School, O'Connor was exactly the type of energetic partner FDR was looking for. He had

---

* FDR's former firm, Marvin, Hooker, & Roosevelt, had been established in 1911 with offices at 52 Wall Street. Other partners included Grenville Emmett and Albert de Roode, a classmate of FDR at Harvard. Franklin's responsibility, as at Fidelity & Deposit, was to bring clients to the firm, but, as he told Black, "I get not one red cent out of my connection with them." Remarkably, FDR's withdrawal from the firm did not damage his friendship with any of the partners. "He was a very devoted and real friend," said Langdon Marvin many years later. Langdon Marvin interview, Columbia Oral History Project, Columbia University.

developed a successful one-man practice handling a variety of international clients in the oil and gas industry and thought nothing of working fifteen-hour days for weeks at a time.

The two men hit it off instantly. Franklin respected O'Connor's aggressiveness and dedication; O'Connor admired the way Roosevelt handled his affliction—his grace under pressure—and saw the advantages that would flow from identifying himself with so illustrious a name. They agreed to form a partnership. The firm would be called "Roosevelt & O'Connor."[60] FDR would be the front man and provide "general legal advice" at a salary of $10,000 a year. O'Connor would do the work.

As with Louis Howe, it was a case of opposites attracting each other. O'Connor's father had been an impoverished tinsmith in Taunton, Massachusetts, and Basil had worked his way through Dartmouth playing violin in a dance orchestra. He and FDR became lifelong friends, and their partnership endured until Roosevelt's death. The president often used O'Connor to transmit messages he did not wish to entrust to political associates—a confidential conduit he knew he could rely on. The fact that during the 1920s their law office was adjacent to Fidelity & Deposit made it easy for Franklin to dovetail both callings.

FDR kept close watch on the Democratic political scene. In December 1922 he counseled against the search for a charismatic figure to lead the party out of the wilderness. "Personal candidacies so rarely develop into anything tangible," he wrote Byron R. Newton of the *New York Herald*. "In our own Party for the last 50 or 60 years the nomination for the Presidency has been nearly every time a matter of luck, or some eleventh hour opportunity boldly seized upon." What was important, said Roosevelt, was "to make the nation understand again that Republican rule means government by selfish interests and powerfully entrenched individuals."[61]

Friends and acquaintances bombarded FDR with home remedies. In February 1923 an old friend in England sent a new elixir that she was certain would effect a cure. "It may be monkey glands or perhaps it is made out of the dried eyes of the extinct three-toed rhinoceros," Franklin wrote Dr. Draper. "You doctors have sure got imaginations. Have any of you thought of distilling the remains of King Tut-Ankh-Amen? The serum might put new life into some of our mutual friends. In the meantime, I am going to Florida to let nature take its course—nothing like Old Mother Nature anyway."[62]

Roosevelt rented a sixty-foot houseboat, the *Weona II*, for $1,500 and planned to spend several months cruising off the Florida Keys. Eleanor accompanied him for the first few days but did not enjoy herself and returned to New York. "I had never considered holidays in winter or escape from cold weather an essential part of living," she remembered. "I tried fishing but had no skill and no luck. When we anchored at night and the wind blew, it all seemed eerie and menacing to me."[63]

Franklin, on the other hand, had a rollicking good time. Old friends came down to visit—Livingston Davis; Lewis Cass Ledyard, Jr., and his wife, Ruth; Henry and Frances De Rahm; and John Lawrence and his wife, Lucy. Ledyard had been an intimate friend of FDR since their clerkship days at Carter, Ledyard & Milburn; De Rahm was a Harvard classmate, and Frances, née Dana, had been one of Franklin's early heartthrobs; Lawrence, another classmate, was now a prosperous New England wool manufacturer.

Except for Franklin, the men began each day with a swim *au naturel*. Frances De Rahm evidently went skinny-dipping too on occasion. As she jauntily wrote in the ship's log:

A female went swimming —she was far from a peach.
She was as the Lord made her, so what could she do
But call herself, gaily, a true 32.

Louis Howe brought down some paperwork that needed FDR's attention and spent a few days on board. Like Eleanor, he had little luck fishing; unlike ER, he gladly took refuge in the illicit rum that flowed freely. As Howe put it:

Colder, colder grew the night,
    we really suffered pain.
We'd sat and sat with rod and reel
    and fished and fished in vain.
And that we thought was reason fair
    to take to rum again.

In Miami, former presidential candidate James Cox came aboard for a visit. "Jim's eyes filled with tears when he saw me," FDR recalled years later. "I gathered from his conversation that he was dead certain that I had had a stroke and that another one would completely remove me. From that day on Jim always shook his head when my name was mentioned and said in sorrow that I was a hopeless invalid."[64]

Cox to the contrary, the voyage worked wonders for Franklin's morale. "I am sure this warmth and exercise is doing lots of good," he wrote his mother on March 15. "I am sunburned and in fine shape. My friends have been dear and look after me all the time. They are great fun to have on board in this somewhat negligée existence. All wander round in pyjamas, nighties and bathing suits."[65] When the cruise ended at the end of March, FDR felt that his legs had improved so markedly that he might soon walk simply with a cane or crutches. "Except for the braces, I've never felt better in my life," he wrote Virginia senator Carter Glass.[66]

Kathleen Lake, Franklin's physical therapist, examined him shortly after he returned and found him "immensely improved, looking at least ten years younger." But the improvement was short-lived. The hectic pace of FDR's life in New York soon wiped out the gains from the Florida trip. "If only his wife could be persuaded that he does not need urging on all day and entertaining all evening," Mrs. Lake wrote Dr. Lovett. "He himself begins to understand how the city affects him . . . but he is so surrounded by family, all giving him advice and ordering him round that he gets quite desperate."[67]

In May 1923 FDR traveled to Boston for a final examination by Dr. Lovett. The doctor told Eleanor he was satisfied that Franklin "handles himself better than he ever had" but there was no improvement in his condition. His arms and neck were normal. So were his bowel, bladder, and sexual functions. Yet he remained paralyzed from the waist down. He was unable to flex his hips; there was no motion in his hamstrings and very little in his toes.[68] Six months later Dr. Draper confirmed Lovett's diagnosis. "I am very much disheartened about his ultimate recovery," wrote Draper. "I cannot help feeling that he has almost reached the limit of his possibilities. I only hope that I may be wrong on this."[69] FDR refused to accept the medical judgments as final. He continued to search for miracle cures, devoting himself increasingly to swimming and exercise, but other than improving his ability to get around, his efforts effected no change in his condition.

Roosevelt believed that cruising the warm waters of the Florida Keys held the secret to recovery. "The water got me into this fix," he was fond of saying, "and the water will get me out."[70] Shortly after returning from his 1923 trip, he convinced John Lawrence to join him in purchasing a secondhand house-boat, the *Roamer,* for which they paid $3,750. They renamed it the *Larooco*—a contraction of Lawrence, Roosevelt, and Company—and planned to sail off the Florida coast each winter.

FDR went aboard for the first time on February 11, 1924. The *Larooco* was seventy-one feet long and according to John Lawrence looked like a floating tenement. The paint was peeling, the bulkheads leaked when it rained, and power was provided by two recalcitrant 35-horsepower engines that looked as though they might have been invented by Robert Fulton. "A great little packet," Roosevelt proclaimed, believing that the boat simply suffered from "lots of bad luck."[71]

Franklin's stateroom, with an adjacent bath, was on the port side. Across a narrow passageway were two smaller cabins for guests, each with two beds. On the deck above was a large stateroom that doubled as wheelhouse. Above that was a broad deck, shaded by a ragged canopy. The ship's crew consisted of an elderly couple from Connecticut, Robert and Dora Morris, who were paid $125 a month. Robert Morris sailed the ship; Dora did the cooking and house-keeping. They were assisted by George Dyer, a young mechanic who labored to keep the engines running.[72]

Before FDR went south, Louis Howe presented him with an elegant black leather logbook embossed in gold letters: "Log of the Houseboat *Larooco,* Being a More or Less Truthful Account of What Happened (Expurgated for the Very Young)." It was dedicated to St. Ananias and St. Sapphira, "the patron saints of liars and fishermen." Not to be outdone, Livingston Davis sent Franklin his old ensign as assistant secretary of the Navy. "A million thanks for the old astnav flag," Roosevelt replied. "I will take it south with me and some day . . . 'hist' the old rag to the mast-head and salute it with 17 rum swizzles."[73]*

Franklin was accompanied on that first voyage by his Negro valet, LeRoy Jones, and Missy LeHand. Jones played a vital but unsung role in FDR's life. He woke him in the morning, bathed him, dressed him, and took care of his most basic needs—a gentle caregiver without whom Roosevelt could not have func-

---

* Bermuda rum swizzles were a popular hot-weather drink in FDR's time, Prohibition notwithstanding: two ounces dark rum, one ounce lime juice, one ounce pineapple juice, one ounce orange juice, and a generous dash of falernum. Shake with ice. Strain into a high-ball glass filled with ice. Garnish with a slice of orange and a cherry.

tioned. Missy was FDR's personal secretary and already a member of the family. She was totally devoted to the Roosevelts and they to her.

Marguerite A. LeHand, twenty-five in the winter of 1924, stood five feet, seven inches tall. She was warm and attractive, with ink-blue eyes, black hair already turning gray, and an engaging, throaty voice. She was also modest, well mannered, exceptionally capable, and thoroughly organized—"a compound of cunning and innocence forever baffling," in the words of the author and editor Fulton Oursler. A native of Potsdam, New York, Missy had grown up in Somerville, Massachusetts, the third child of an Irish gardener. It was at Eleanor's suggestion in 1921 that she left her employment with the Democratic National Committee to work full-time for FDR, clearing up his correspondence after the vice presidential race. In the three years since, she had become indispensable, not only managing Roosevelt's office, screening his visitors, and keeping track of his varied interests but doing so with such charm and courtesy that even those turned away felt placated. In New York, she stayed with a relative on the East Side so she could reach the Roosevelt home at any hour and became almost as ubiquitous as Louis Howe.[74]

Missy often accompanied FDR to Hyde Park for working weekends, and over the years she allowed her life to be taken over by his, assuming his likes and dislikes, his favorite drinks and games, even his turns of phrase. She called him "F.D."—a name no one else dared use—and, like Louis Howe, she always leveled with him and said exactly what she thought. "She was one of the very, very few people who was not a yes-man," remembered Supreme Court justice Felix Frankfurter. "She told [the president] not what she knew he wanted to hear, but what were, in fact, her true views and convictions."[75]

What is most remarkable is that Eleanor was completely supportive and solicitous of Missy. As her friend and biographer, Joseph Lash, noted, ER "was grateful to the young woman. She knew that lack of mobility made the daily routines of life cumbersome and difficult for Franklin, and Missy's presence freed him from housekeeping anxieties and enabled him to stay in touch with the political world through a vast political correspondence, while it eased Eleanor's sense of guilt because she was unable to do more for him."[76]

Aboard the *Larooco*, Missy served as combination hostess and secretary, doing her utmost to ensure Franklin enjoyed himself. That was not always easy. "There were days on the *Larooco* when it was noon before he could pull himself out of depression and greet his guests wearing his lighthearted façade," she tearfully told Frances Perkins many years later.[77] Missy entertained graciously, encouraged FDR to tell his favorite stories, went fishing with him—though she sunburned easily—and was accepted naturally by Roosevelt's many acquaintances. Once that spring she was called away suddenly by the death of her father and was gone almost two weeks. When Missy returned, Eleanor wrote Franklin, "I haven't told Mama that Missy is back because she has more peace of mind when she doesn't know such things."[78]

It was a unique arrangement.* Franklin, Missy, and LeRoy Jones went back again to the *Larooco* in the spring of 1925 and again in 1926, after which FDR decided he had had enough. "The sharks make it impossible to play around in the deep water for any length of time, and the sand beaches are few and far between."[79] After the 1926 cruise, *Larooco* was laid up at the Pilkington Yacht Basin on the Fort Lauderdale River while Roosevelt and Lawrence attempted to sell her. A September hurricane swept the boat upriver, where it came to rest high and dry at the edge of a pine forest, a mile from the nearest water. FDR tried to sell the boat as a hunting lodge, but there were no takers, and in 1927 *Larooco* was scrapped. "So ended a good craft with a personality," he wrote Sara.[80]

Franklin went back to New York toward the end of April 1924. The presidential campaign was heating up, and Al Smith, fresh from his overwhelming reelection as governor, was angling for the Democratic nomination. His principal opponent was Woodrow Wilson's son-in-law (and former secretary of the Treasury) William Gibbs McAdoo. McAdoo was dry, Protestant, and old-stock American. Because of his support for Prohibition he enjoyed the support of Bryan and the rural wing of the party and had become the darling of the Ku Klux Klan, a potent force in national politics following the Red Scare of 1919–20.† Smith was none of the above. Almost by default he became the candidate of the urban, progressive wing of the party, and FDR announced his

---

* During the four-year period from 1925 to 1928, FDR spent 116 of 208 weeks away from home trying to regain his health. According to one biographer, "Eleanor was with him for four of those weeks, Sara for two, and Missy LeHand for 110. Thus Missy is the sole adult 'member of the family' to share an aggregate of more than two years of the most trying and self-searching four years of Roosevelt's life." Bernard Asbell, *The F.D.R. Memoirs* 244 (New York: Doubleday, 1973).

† In an early showdown between McAdoo and Smith supporters, the 1924 Democratic convention narrowly rejected (542 7/20–543 3/20) a plank in the platform that would have condemned the Klan. It also rejected (353½–742½) a plank that called for immediate membership in the League of Nations and participation in the World Court.

support early on. "I have always supposed that if I went to the next Convention I would, in common with the rest of the [New York] delegation, be for Al," he told the *New York Post* in January.

The 1924 convention would be held in New York City—a powerful advantage for Smith—and Charles Murphy was calling the shots for the campaign, another advantage given Tammany's preeminence among the big-city organizations in the Democratic party. But on April 25, 1924, Murphy suffered a fatal heart attack, leaving the Smith campaign leaderless. "New York has lost its most powerful and wisest leader," said FDR in a prepared statement released to the press by Louis Howe.[81]

Two days later, two of Al Smith's closest advisers, Belle Moskowitz and New York Supreme Court justice Joseph Proskauer, called on Roosevelt at East Sixty-fifth Street. The Smith campaign needed a chairman, they said: someone with national standing, preferably Protestant, preferably dry (or at least not publicly identified as wet) who could appeal to the rural, dry, Protestant element in the party. FDR, they said, would be ideal. Would he take the job?

Roosevelt initially demurred. His disability would prevent him from dashing about from meeting to meeting as might be expected of a campaign chairman. Moskowitz and Proskauer assured him that would not be necessary. They would do the work for him. What they wanted was Franklin's name and support.

Roosevelt accepted the position on those terms. Press coverage was generous. "What the campaign lost in practical political ability through the death of Murphy, it has now compensated for in prestige and principles," wrote the *New York Herald Tribune.*[82]

Back in the political spotlight, FDR worked diligently on Smith's behalf. In so doing he helped eradicate the taint of anti-Catholicism that had clung to him since his fight against Blue-Eyed Billy Sheehan. As one historian put it, Roosevelt's new list of political correspondents "read like a sampling of the Dublin telephone directory."[83] FDR attempted to lessen the bitterness between Smith and McAdoo supporters but with little success. Smith was demonized by McAdoo's backers because of his religion and opposition to Prohibition; McAdoo was castigated for his dependence on the Ku Klux Klan. As Franklin saw it, the personal vilification obscured the basic differences between Democrats and Republicans and virtually assured that Coolidge would be reelected in November.

Roosevelt sought support for Smith among Florida fishermen, middle western farmers, and Pennsylvania coal miners. Even Babe Ruth was mobilized in the cause. "Sure, I'm for Al Smith," the Bambino wrote FDR.

> There is one thing about your letter, Mr. Roosevelt, that went across with me good and strong—that was the take about the humble beginning of Governor Smith.
>
> Maybe you know I wasn't fed with a gold spoon when I was a kid. No poor boy can go any too high in this world to suit me.[84]

The death of Charles Murphy had allowed FDR to reenter public life as chairman of the Smith campaign. And it was the death of a second Tammany stalwart that catapulted Franklin to the center of the political stage. Smith had originally counted upon Bourke Cockran, the legendary Irish orator who had nominated him at San Francisco four years earlier, to do the job again. But Cockran had died the year before, and Smith had yet to name a replacement. On the eve of the convention, the governor asked Judge Proskauer for advice. "Who ought to put me in nomination?"

Proskauer reflected a moment and said, "Frank Roosevelt."

"For God's sake why?" Smith asked.

"Because you're a Bowery mick and he's a Protestant patrician and he'd take some of the curse off you."[85]

Smith nodded his head, and the two men walked over to see FDR at campaign headquarters. "Joe and I have been talking this over, and I've come here to ask you to make the nominating speech," Smith said.

"Oh, Al, I'd love to do it, but I'm so busy here working with delegates I have no time to write a speech." Could Joe write it? Roosevelt asked. The fact was, Proskauer had already prepared a draft, concluding with a paraphrase of William Wordsworth's encomium to the "Happy Warrior." FDR thought the reference too poetic for the ordinary delegate on the floor but under the pressure of time agreed to deliver it. "It will probably be a flop," he told Proskauer.[86]

The Democratic convention convened in Stanford White's Madison Square Garden on June 24, 1924, for what would prove the longest convention on record. With 1,098 delegates, and 732 votes required to nominate under the party's two-thirds rule, the Democrats met for an unprecedented seventeen days and required 103 ballots before settling on West Virginia's John W. Davis, a prominent Wall Street lawyer, as the most viable compromise between Smith and McAdoo. The 1924 convention was also the first covered by national radio and broadcast live across the country.[87]

FDR was in his seat as chairman of the New York delegation when the opening gavel fell on June 24, and he attended every session thereafter. His arrival each day was carefully planned. He was driven to a side entrance of the Garden and wheeled inside by his sixteen-year-old son, James. When they reached the door to the hall closest to the New York delegation, James would lock his father's braces and pull him to a standing position so he could enter the convention floor on his feet. FDR would then grasp his son's upper arm with his left hand, place most of his weight on the crutch under his right arm, and ratchet himself forward one halting step at a time.

To make the passage up the aisle as easy as possible, the Roosevelts arrived early and left late. "So as not to scare everyone to death," as FDR put it, he and James joked and bantered as they made their way along. "The process of getting into his seat was an ordeal for Father," James recalled. "We practiced the awkward business standing together by a chair, with me supporting him and taking his crutch as he lowered himself into his chair. Once he was seated, it was my task to stand by, run errands, deliver messages, and help Father off the floor when he wanted to leave."[88]

The galleries, stuffed with Tammany supporters, recognized FDR and regularly broke into applause as he made his perilous way down the aisle each day. Over the radio, a national audience could hear the applause as the announcer intoned, "I don't know what it is, but I rather imagine Franklin D. Roosevelt is coming in. He always gets a hand for the gallant fight he is making. . . . Yes, it is. There he comes slowly down the aisle on his crutches."[89]

Roosevelt was scheduled to speak at twelve noon on Thursday, June 26. Waiting expectantly in the gallery were Sara, Eleanor, and the four other children, plus Nancy Cook and Marion Dickerman, who joined the family for the occasion. Dickerman recalled how carefully Franklin had prepared himself: "Nobody knows how that man worked. They measured off in the library of the Sixty-fifth Street house the distance to the podium, and he practiced getting across that distance. Oh, he struggled."[90]

Shortly before noon Franklin and James left their seats on the floor and made their slow, awkward way up the aisle. "Outwardly, [Father] was beaming, seemingly confident and unconcerned, but I could sense his inner tenseness,"

James recalled. "His fingers dug into my arms like pincers. His face was covered with perspiration."[91]

Finally, they reached the platform. As FDR was introduced, he called out in a stage whisper to Pennsylvania's Joseph Guffey, who stood nearby: "Joe, shake the rostrum." Guffey evidently did not understand, and Roosevelt repeated his request: he wanted to be certain the speaker's stand would support him when he leaned against it. Guffey tested and reported it was firm.

Then came the moment when FDR would have to walk alone: the moment he had been practicing for. James handed him his second crutch, and he began moving slowly toward the podium unassisted. Marion Dickerman held her breath and prayed. "It seemed like an hour," she remembered. Frances Perkins, sitting near the platform, recalled that no one in the Garden seemed to breathe. Eight thousand delegates, alternates, and spectators watched spell-bound as FDR fought his way across the stage, the personification of courage, defying pain with every forward thrust of his heavily braced legs.

When he finally reached the podium, unable to wave for fear of falling but flashing that famous smile, head thrown back, shoulders high, the Garden erupted with a thunderous ovation. Delegates rose to their feet and cheered for three minutes, admiration tinged with awe at the dramatic performance they had witnessed.

Roosevelt spoke for thirty-four minutes. His resonant tenor rang through the Garden with a new and telling passion, interrupted frequently by sustained cheering and applause. When he reached his peroration, his lilting cadence very nearly sang the phrases:

He has a power to strike at error and wrongdoing that makes his adversaries quail before him.

He has a personality that carries to every hearer not only the sincerity but the righteousness of what he says.

He is the "Happy Warrior" of the political battlefield.—Alfred E. Smith[92]

Pandemonium. "The crowd just went crazy," said Marion Dickerman. "It was stupendous, really stupendous."[93] *The New York Times* called FDR the outstanding personality of the convention. The *Herald Tribune* hailed him as "the foremost figure on floor or platform." Tom Pendergast, the no-nonsense head of the Missouri delegation, thought that if Franklin "had been physically able to withstand the campaign, he would have been nominated by acclamation."[94]

Roosevelt's speech set off a demonstration that lasted more than an hour, delegates parading, galleries cheering, the Garden reverberating with chorus after chorus of Smith's anthem, "The Sidewalks of New York."

Franklin remained on his feet, glued to the rostrum. No one had considered how he was to exit. "I saw all around him all those fat slob politicians," said Frances Perkins, "and I knew they wouldn't think of it." She enlisted the woman beside her, and they rushed onstage to stand in front of FDR and shield him from view as he turned to leave. As the cheering continued, Roosevelt finally permitted James to bring his wheelchair to the rear of the platform so that he could ease himself into it and be wheeled offstage.[95]

That evening the Roosevelts gave a reception for the New York delegation at their Sixty-fifth Street home. Marion Dickerman went early to see if she could help Eleanor with the preparations. When she arrived, the butler told her Mr. Roosevelt was upstairs and wished to see her. "He was sitting upright in his bed and obviously was very tired. But his face lit up and he held out his arms."

"Marion," he said, "I did it."[96]

ELEVEN

GOVERNOR

Now what follows is really private. *In case of your election*
I know your salary is smaller than the one you get now.
I am prepared to make up the difference to you.
—SARA TO FRANKLIN, OCTOBER 2, 1928

FROM 1925 TO 1928 Franklin and Eleanor were together infrequently.[1] The children were away, at either boarding school or university; Eleanor had begun her career teaching at the Todhunter School with Marion Dickerman; and FDR was in the South, either on the *Larooco* or at Warm Springs, Georgia, hoping to regain the use of his legs. Both remained in close contact with Democratic politics. Eleanor edited the newsletter of the Women's Division (*Women's Democratic News*), while Franklin continued his voluminous correspondence with party officials all over the country. In many respects ER operated as Roosevelt's surrogate, but it was not always a frictionless relationship. "One of the great quarrels Eleanor had with her lot," said Frances Perkins, "is that Franklin didn't listen to her. . . . He liked her as a reporter, but when most men would have asked their wives what they thought, he didn't."[2]

FDR was genuinely fond of Eleanor's friends Nancy Cook and Marion Dickerman—whom he called "our gang"—and often assumed the role of a gracious and generous paterfamilias.[3] They, in turn, were devoted to promoting his career and enjoyed the bonds of friendship established through Eleanor. It was Franklin, in fact, who originated the idea of a home for the three women on Val-Kill at Hyde Park, donated the land, and supervised the construction.

Dickerman remembered a wonderful Saturday afternoon in the late summer of 1924 when she, Eleanor, Nan Cook, and FDR were picnicking on the wooded banks of Val-Kill, two miles east of the Roosevelt house. ER noted that it was likely their last picnic of the year because Sara would soon close the estate for the winter.

"But aren't you girls silly?" said Franklin. "This isn't mother's land. I bought this acreage myself. And why shouldn't you three have a cottage here of your own, so you could come and go as you please? If you'll mark out the land you want, I'll give you a life interest in it, with the understanding that it reverts to my estate upon the death of the last survivor."[4]

A deed was drawn up and witnessed by Louis Howe, and on August 5 FDR wrote a contractor friend of his, "My missus and some of her female political friends want to build a shack on a stream in the back woods and want, instead of a beautiful marble bath, to have the stream dug out so as to form an old-fashioned swimming hole."[5] The resulting retreat was far from a shack in the backwoods. It was agreed that the cottage should be built of fieldstone in the traditional Hudson River Dutch style. Franklin handled the design, paid for a proper swimming pool, and added a big gray stucco building at the rear in which Eleanor and her friends hoped to establish a furniture workshop.

FDR christened the finished house "The Honeymoon Cottage," which was not far off the mark. Initially Eleanor, Marion, and Nancy slept together in a single, loftlike dormitory bedroom. Much of the furniture, made by Nancy Cook and her assistants, bore the women's initials: E. M. N. Eleanor embroidered towels and linens for the cottage, likewise emblazoned E. M. N., and the three women received housewarming gifts of silver, crystal, and china engraved with their initials intertwined. Franklin frequently gave Eleanor presents for the cottage, especially plantings and picnic accessories. He inscribed a children's book, *Little Marion's Pilgrimage,* to Dickerman: "For my little Pilgrim, whose progress is always upward and onward, to the Things of Beauty and the Thoughts of Love, and of Light, from her affectionate Uncle Franklin."[6] He autographed a favorite speech, "Another first edition for the library of the Three Graces of the Val Kill."[7]

The cottage became the focus of the women's lives. Nancy and Marion retained their Greenwich Village apartment, but it was merely a place to stay during the week until they could go home to Val-Kill. For Eleanor, the life she now led came close to re-creating the rebellious feminism she had enjoyed under the tutelage of Mlle. Marie Souvestre at Allenwood. The swimming pool was always open to Franklin and his friends, and there was a special barbecue pit where he could grill his hamburgers, but Val-Kill was a woman's world, a place where shared confidences became the rule, where Eleanor's earnest sense of duty yielded to spontaneous and casual pleasures.

Sara accepted the arrangement with remarkable grace. "Eleanor is so happy over there that she looks well and plump, don't tell her so," she wrote FDR soon after Val-Kill opened.[8] When she saw that her daughter-in-law was fully committed to her new life, Sara became an ardent supporter. She appeared with Eleanor at political luncheons and dinners, and became a patron of almost all of ER's activities, whether they advanced Franklin's political career or not.[9]

On one such occasion Sara hosted a luncheon Eleanor was giving for thirty-five board members of the National Council for Women in the double dining room on East Sixty-fifth Street. Among the guests was Mary McLeod Bethune, president of the National Council of Negro Women. "I can still see the twinkle in Mrs. James Roosevelt's eyes," Bethune remembered,

> as she noted the apprehensive glances cast my way by the Southern women who had come to the affair.
>
> Then she did a remarkable thing. Very deliberately, she took my arm and seated me to the right of Eleanor Roosevelt, the guest of honor! I can remember too, how the faces of the Negro servants lit up with pride. From that moment on, my heart went out to Mrs. James Roosevelt. I visited her at her home many times subsequently, and our friendship became one of the most treasured of my life.[10]

While Eleanor settled in at Val-Kill, Franklin pursued his quest for a cure at Warm Springs, Georgia. He learned of the therapeutic effect of the thermal waters at the hill country resort during the Democratic convention in 1924. The Wall Street banker George Foster Peabody, a member of the New York delegation who wintered in Columbus, Georgia, told Franklin of the wondrous cures wrought by the warm mineral waters that bubbled from the earth. Peabody had recently bought the Merriweather Inn, a genteel ruin of a hotel that bordered the spring, and urged Franklin to go down and try the waters for himself.

FDR was initially unimpressed by the prospect, but during the summer of 1924 Peabody directed a stream of testimonials to Franklin that eventually piqued his interest. In October, he, Eleanor, and Missy went down to see for themselves. Eleanor stayed for a day, found the rigid segregation and tumble-down poverty not to her liking, and returned to New York to assist in the final days of Al Smith's gubernatorial campaign. Franklin and Missy remained three more weeks.[11]

Roosevelt found the magnesium-laced waters astonishingly buoyant. Swimming in the warm Merriweather pool, he found that his unbraced legs would hold him upright and that by thrashing his powerful arms and shoulders he could move himself back and forth across the water. In his three weeks at Warm Springs he felt that he had made more progress than in the preceding three years. For the first time since August 1921 he thought he felt life in his toes and rejoiced at being able to stay in the water two hours at a time without becoming fatigued.[12]*

When Franklin returned to New York, he laid plans to purchase Warm Springs and convert it into an aftercare facility for polio victims. "I feel that a great 'cure' for infantile paralysis and kindred diseases could be established," he told Sara.[13] Eleanor fretted that Franklin was squandering his resources and lacked the patience to succeed at so ambitious an undertaking; Basil O'Connor was concerned that Franklin was overcommitting himself; and George Peabody was asking $200,000 for the property—roughly twice what he had paid for it a few years earlier. But Louis Howe was supportive and immediately set about raising funds for the project; Missy never questioned the effort; and, most important, Sara added her backing.[14]

For FDR, Warm Springs offered the opportunity to be in complete charge of a significant undertaking—a means of reestablishing his self-esteem. Warm Springs would be his alone, a haven much like Val-Kill was for Eleanor: a place where he could do as he pleased, when he pleased, free from the formality of Hyde Park and East Sixty-fifth Street. More to the point, it provided an opportunity to participate in the fight against polio. Roosevelt had no special training in physiotherapy, but he became an authentic pioneer in its application. His infectious enthusiasm galvanized polio victims hitherto without hope. By instinct and example he infused others with his own unconquerable spirit as

---

* The waters at Warm Springs have been traced to rain that falls on Pine Mountain, several miles away, runs down 3,800 feet into a vast pocket of rock, where it is warmed by the inner earth, and returns to the surface at a temperature of 88° at a rate of 800 gallons per minute. Editor's note, 2 *The Roosevelt Letters,* 448 Elliott Roosevelt, ed. (London: George G. Harrap, 1950).

he led exercises at the pool or lolled in the sun, chatting happily with anyone who passed by. He called himself "Old Doctor Roosevelt" and took a genuine interest in those who came to Warm Springs to exercise under his care.

In April 1926 FDR completed his negotiations with Peabody and purchased the Merriweather Inn, its cottages and pools, plus 1,200 acres of undeveloped land for $201,667.83—approximately two thirds of his fortune.[15] Shortly afterward he bought an additional 1,750 acres. With the help of Sara—who organized exclusive dinners for potential donors—and the indefatigable Louis Howe, Roosevelt organized the Warm Springs Foundation (later the National Foundation for Infantile Paralysis) with a panel of distinguished backers, including Wall Street bankers George Foster Peabody and Russell Leffingwell; businessmen Herbert Straus and William H. Woodin; his friends Henry Morgenthau, Jr., and Basil O'Connor; and John Jakob Raskob of General Motors.* Edsel Ford personally contributed $25,000 to provide a glass enclosure for the swimming pool.[16]

Warm Springs provided a challenge, and Roosevelt threw himself into every detail. He persuaded Dr. LeRoy Hubbard, a respected orthopedic surgeon who supervised rehabilitation care for the New York State Department of Health, to come down and take charge of the patients' treatment. Hubbard brought with him a trained nurse and physiotherapist, Miss Helena Mahoney, who hired a dozen young phys ed graduates from Peabody College in Nashville to work with the patients in the pool. "Our rate is $42 a week," FDR wrote Paul Hasbrouck, a polio victim in Poughkeepsie. "This includes board, lodging, medical and therapeutic treatment, pool charges, etc.—in fact, everything except your traveling expenses and cigarette money."[17] But no one was turned away for lack of money. Indigent patients were supported by a Patients' Aid Fund that Roosevelt established, and when that was depleted, he asked that the bills be sent to him personally at Hyde Park.[18]

From the fall of 1926 until the autumn of 1928, FDR spent well over half of his time at Warm Springs. He ordered a cottage built for himself, all on one level with a driveway designed so he could enter the house directly at grade

---

* William H. Woodin, the president of American Car and Foundry and a registered Republican, became FDR's first secretary of the Treasury in 1933 but resigned because of ill health a year later. He was succeeded by Henry Morgenthau, Jr., who served for the remainder of the Roosevelt administration.

level. He also engineered an ingenious set of hand controls for an automobile to drive through the Georgia countryside. A local mechanic converted an old Model T Ford to Roosevelt's specifications, and by the end of 1926 Franklin was whizzing about Warm Springs at twenty-five miles an hour. Roosevelt was a confident driver and controlled the car with ease. And after five years of being dependent upon others, nothing gave him greater pleasure. He became as familiar to the people along the dusty roads of Merriweather County as the rural mail carrier—except, one resident remembered, "the mail carrier did take Sunday off."[19]

Roosevelt became the leading citizen of Merriweather County, thrilled at his exposure to the life of ordinary people in rural Georgia. When he ran for president, he carried the county by margins ranging from 50 to 1 in 1932 to 16 to 1 in 1944—a result significantly different from Hyde Park and Dutchess County, which he never managed to win.[20] Georgians were open and friendly, FDR liked to say. He remembered their names and considered many of them his friends. He often ventured out alone in his Model T, pulling into farmyards to talk crops and cattle, parking in front of the drugstore, honking his horn and ordering a Coke, nosing into a hollow to buy corn liquor from the local bootlegger. "He was a man that could talk to you," a farmer remembered. "He had sense enough to talk to a man who didn't have any education, and he had sense enough to talk to the best educated man in the world; and he was easy to talk to. He could talk about *anything.*"[21]

Roosevelt also listened. The stories of low farm prices, failed banks, and rural poverty stayed with him into the White House. From the poor people of Merriweather County, Franklin learned what it meant to be without electricity and running water; for children to be without shoes and adequate clothing; for a simple grade school education to be beyond the reach of many who lived in the hardscrabble backwoods. Merriweather County raised corn and short-staple cotton, but drought, falling prices, and the boll weevil made it all but impossible to turn a profit. Farms were small, plowing was done by mules, not tractors, and mortgage indebtedness increased annually. FDR tried his hand at farming and experimented with cattle and timber, but without success. "It pleased him because it offered a challenge," New Dealer Rexford Tugwell remembered. "But there was never a more dismal prospect than was offered by farming that ridge at Pine Mountain."[22]

Warm Springs, on the other hand, more or less held its own. "You needn't worry about my losing a fortune," Franklin assured Sara. "Every step is being planned either to pay for itself or to make a profit."[23] The American Orthopedic Association approved Dr. Hubbard's treatment program, and by the end of 1927 seventy-one patients had visited the resort. The number grew to eighty in 1928—as many as the facilities could accommodate—and the staff totaled 110.[24] Warm Springs would not be free of financial worry, however, until FDR became president and the March of Dimes was organized, first to raise money for the foundation, then to aid polio research nationally.*

While Franklin toiled at Warm Springs, Eleanor found herself fully engaged teaching history, English, and current affairs at the Todhunter School for Girls on East Eightieth Street, just off Park Avenue. In 1927 ER, Marion Dickerman, and Nancy Cook purchased Todhunter—an elite private school for daughters of wealthy New Yorkers—from its founder, Winifred Todhunter, who was returning to England. Dickerman became principal and Eleanor associate principal. Todhunter resembled Allenwood in its commitment to female achievement, and, like Marie Souvestre, Eleanor set the tone for the school.[25] A naturally gifted teacher, she urged her students to challenge authority and, consciously or unconsciously, proselytized relentlessly for the social ideals of the Democratic party. "I am very anxious to send a class which has been studying with me . . . to see the various types of tenements in New York City," she wrote her friend Jane Hoey, who directed the city's Welfare Council. "I would like them to see the worst type of old time tenement. They need to know what bad housing conditions mean."[26]

Eleanor became a role model for many of her students and urged them to assume responsibility for their lives. "In the future," she said, "there will be

---

* The "March of Dimes" (the name suggested by the comedian Eddie Cantor) was the principal fund-raising arm of the National Foundation for Infantile Paralysis, which FDR organized in 1938 and which the historian David Oshinsky called "the gold standard for private charities, the largest voluntary health organization of all time." The pioneering research of Dr. Jonas Salk was supported in large measure by the foundation. His discovery of a vaccine against polio was announced by Basil O'Connor, chairman of the foundation, on April 12, 1955, the tenth anniversary of FDR's death. David M. Oshinsky, *Polio: An American Story* 53–55 (New York: Oxford University Press, 2005); also see Richard Carter, *Breakthrough: The Saga of Jonas Salk* 268 ff. (New York: Trident Press, 1966).

nothing which is closed to women because of their sex."[27] For Eleanor herself, teaching at Todhunter represented enormous personal fulfillment. "I like it better than anything else I do," she told *The New York Times* in 1932.[28]*

While FDR exercised at Warm Springs and Eleanor taught at Todhunter, a great deal of the responsibility for the children fell to Sara. When James was confirmed at St. James' Episcopal Church in Hyde Park, it was Sara who stood in for his parents, just as it was she and Cousin Susie Parish who chaperoned Anna's social debut. Twice Sara took Anna and James to Europe, and Elliott, unhappy at Groton, asked permission to live with his grandmother and attend high school at Hyde Park. (Permission refused.) Anna and the two younger boys, Franklin Jr., and John, who were at school in New York City, usually spent each weekend at Hyde Park.[29] "Looking back on this period," said James, "I must say in all honesty that neither Anna, my brothers, nor I had the guidance and training that I think father would have given us had he not been involved in his own struggle to re-establish a useful life for himself."[30]

That struggle was going remarkably well. By 1926 FDR had learned to walk short distances with a cane in his right hand and a crutch under his left arm. But the difference in height between the cane and crutch made him appear distressingly awkward. He also tried walking with two canes, but the lateral lurch that entailed was equally disconcerting and the slightest nudge could knock him to the ground. Neither method resembled normal walking, and neither would convince an audience that Roosevelt was on the road to recovery. Working closely with Miss Mahoney, FDR developed a technique of walking with a cane in one hand while tightly gripping the arm of a companion with the other. In 1924 he had made his way up the aisle at the Democratic convention leaning on a crutch while holding fiercely to James. By substituting a cane for the crutch the effort looked more natural, and it became Franklin's chosen method of locomotion at public events.

Politics was never far from FDR's mind at Warm Springs. In 1926 he came north to give the keynote address at the New York Democratic convention and successfully fended off well-wishers who sought to nominate him for the U.S. Senate. "Please try to look pallid and worn and weary," counseled Louis Howe,

---

* Eleanor remained active at Todhunter until 1938, although she did not teach after FDR was elected president. In 1939 the school was absorbed by the Dalton School.

"so it will not be too exceedingly difficult to get by with the statement that your health will not permit you to run for anything for 2 more years."[31]

Al Smith was reelected overwhelmingly in 1926 and immediately became the front-runner for the party's nomination for president.[32] After the blood-letting in 1924, the rural and urban wings of the party papered over their differences, McAdoo chose not to run again, and, in a reciprocal gesture of party unity, the Smith forces accepted Houston, Texas, as the convention site—the first time since 1860 that the party would meet in a southern city. Once again Smith asked FDR to deliver the nominating speech at the convention. For Roosevelt, it was another turn in the spotlight and the opportunity to demonstrate to the delegates how far he had come since 1924. "I'm telling everyone you are going to Houston without crutches," Eleanor wrote Franklin at Warm Springs, "so mind you stick at it."[33]*

FDR left Warm Springs early for the convention, traveling by train through the Middle West, speaking at whistle-stops on Smith's behalf, and practicing with his son Elliott the cane-and-arm technique of walking to the rostrum. Franklin cautioned Elliott to appear jovial regardless of the tension he felt. No one should perceive the difficulty their effort entailed.

As in 1924, FDR was floor manager of Smith's campaign. Except for a scattering of favorite sons from the South, there was no serious opposition, and Roosevelt tailored his nominating speech to the 15 million or so who would be listening on the radio. "I tried the experiment of writing and delivering my speech wholly for the benefit of the radio audience and the press," Franklin wrote Walter Lippmann. "Smith had the votes anyway and it seemed to me more important to reach out for the republicans and independents throughout the country."[34] FDR recognized the challenge of writing for the new

* On the eve of the convention, FDR laid out the Democrats' foreign policy in an article in *Foreign Affairs*. Scathingly critical of the GOP's go-it-alone isolationism, Roosevelt urged greater cooperation with the League of Nations and membership in the World Court: "We Democrats do not believe in the possibility or the desirability of an isolated national experience or a national development heedless of the welfare, prosperity and peace of the other peoples of the world. The American people would never be willing consciously to handicap the League in its efforts to maintain peace. Yet since the war, our attitude is that we do not need friends, and that the public opinion of the world is of no importance." Franklin D. Roosevelt, "Our Foreign Policy: A Democratic View," 4 *Foreign Affairs* 573, 582 (July 1928).

medium, which required a significant departure from the forensic flourishes of traditional campaign oratory. In the years ahead, Roosevelt would master the technique of projecting his personality over the air better than any other American politician of the twentieth century.*

FDR was in top form at the convention. As he and Elliott made their way to the platform, without the crutches that had been so evident in 1924, the 15,000 delegates and spectators roared their approval. Franklin's healthy appearance and evident high spirits belied any impression that he was an invalid. At the podium he seemed perfectly relaxed, perfectly natural, nodding left and right, looking up at the galleries, waving with his right hand to acknowledge the applause.

The speech was one of Roosevelt's finest. Again and again he described the qualities Smith brought to the race, culminating with what in retrospect seems an almost autobiographical refrain. To be a great president, said FDR, required "the quality of soul which makes a man loved by little children, by dumb animals, that quality of soul which makes him a strong help to those in sorrow or trouble, that quality which makes him not merely admired but loved by all the people—the quality of sympathetic understanding of the human heart, of real interest in one's fellow man."

The Roosevelt who delivered those lines was a far different man from the callow young assistant secretary of the Navy who had run for vice president in 1920. His concluding remarks invoking the image of the Happy Warrior brought the delegates to their feet in a remarkable display of party unity.[35] Smith was nominated on the first ballot with 849 votes.† Senate Minority Leader Joseph T. Robinson of Arkansas accepted the nomination for vice president, and the convention adjourned ready to take on Herbert Hoover and Charles Curtis in November.

The convention bluster faded quickly. Except for the nation's farmers, the United States basked in unprecedented prosperity. The GOP hold on the House and Senate seemed secure, and Herbert Hoover, dour though he might

---

* *The New York Times* called FDR's speech "a model of its kind. It is seldom that a political speech attains this kind of eloquence. It was not fitted to provoke frenzied applause, but could not be heard or read without prompting to serious thought and sincere emotion." *The New York Times,* June 28, 1928.

† The remaining 251 votes were divided among twelve candidates, Congressman Cordell Hull of Tennessee leading the pack with 71. *Congressional Quarterly's Guide to U.S. Elections* 157 (Washington, D.C.: Congressional Quarterly, 1975).

be, appeared positively scintillating compared to Calvin Coolidge, who had chosen not to run. Even worse for the Democrats, Smith's candidacy found little resonance outside the cities of the East Coast. Catholic and wet, he alienated much of rural, fundamentalist America while his ties to big business did little to energize the party's working-class base. On the stump, Smith proved even more parochial than his city slicker image suggested. As the acerbic Baltimore *Sun* columnist H. L. Mencken noted, "Al Smith's world begins at Coney Island and ends at Buffalo."[36]

FDR declined Smith's offer to become chairman of the Democratic National Committee and continued to resist efforts to nominate him for governor.[37] Both he and Howe recognized that 1928 would not be a good year for Democrats, and Franklin wished to concentrate on regaining the use of his legs so that he might seek the governorship in 1932 and perhaps run for president in 1936. (Roosevelt and Howe assumed that Hoover would be reelected in 1932).[38] When the New York State Democratic convention met in Rochester at the end of September, FDR was ensconced at Warm Springs determined not to be drawn into the fray.

By this time, party leaders recognized that Smith's campaign was in trouble. Unless he could carry New York, with its forty-five electoral votes, he could not hope to win the presidency. And if Smith lost New York, he would likely take the entire ticket down with him. The Republicans had just nominated the state's crusading attorney general, Albert Ottinger, for governor. Ottinger not only had amassed a superb record fighting price racketeers and stock manipulators but was also of working-class Jewish origin, up from the sidewalks of New York. A formidable campaigner, he would cut deeply into the traditional Democratic vote in the five boroughs. The unanimous consensus of the county chairmen who gathered at Rochester was that the only Democrat who stood a chance of beating Ottinger was Franklin D. Roosevelt. And Roosevelt, they believed, would add another 200,000 upstate votes to the ticket.

FDR was unmoved. On the eve of the gubernatorial nomination he sent a public telegram to Smith restating his decision not to run: AS I AM ONLY FORTY-SIX I OWE IT TO MY FAMILY AND MYSELF TO GIVE THE PRESENT CONSTANT IMPROVEMENT A CHANCE TO CONTINUE.[39]

Smith was content to take FDR at his word, but Tammany and the upstate leaders refused to accept a substitute candidate. Roosevelt had no enemies within the party and only Roosevelt could rescue the ticket, they said. At the

insistence of James A. Farley of Rockland County, secretary of the State Democratic Committee, Smith put in another call to FDR at Warm Springs. The
call found Franklin at poolside but he declined to take it, saying "Tell the governor I've gone on a picnic and will not be back all day."[40]

That evening, with the vote for governor scheduled the next day, Smith
sought out Eleanor and implored her to get Franklin on the phone: "He won't
take my calls." ER told Smith that it was her husband's decision and she would
not attempt to influence him, but she agreed to get him on the phone. Eleanor
eventually tracked FDR down, handed the receiver to Smith, and rushed from
the room to catch the last train to New York, where she had to teach at Todhunter the next morning. She would not learn what transpired until she read
the newspapers next day.

First, Smith put John Jakob Raskob on the phone. Raskob had taken the
post of chairman of the National Committee and was one of the party's principal contributors. (Smith's campaign headquarters were in the General Motors Building in New York.) Raskob pleaded with Franklin to run on behalf of
the national party. FDR replied that he had too much invested in Warm
Springs to make that feasible.

"Damn Warm Springs!" Raskob shouted. "We'll take care of it for you."
Raskob said he would personally underwrite Roosevelt's losses.* Then he
handed the phone to Smith.

The governor bore down: "Take the nomination, Frank. You can make a
couple of radio speeches and you'll be elected. Then you can go back to Warm
Springs. After you have made your inaugural speech and sent your message to
the Legislature you can go back there again for a couple of months."

"Don't give me that baloney," said FDR.

Herbert Lehman, a senior partner in Lehman Brothers investment bankers,
an experienced labor negotiator and one of the most respected figures in the
party, came on the phone. If Franklin would take the nomination, he would
accept the nomination for lieutenant governor and fill in whenever needed.

Smith came back on. "Frank, I told you I wasn't going to put this on a per-

---

* Raskob immediately sent FDR a check for $250,000, which Roosevelt returned with his
thanks. It was sufficient to know that Raskob was willing to underwrite him, he said. From 1928
to 1932, Raskob was one of the principal benefactors of Warm Springs, donating more than
$100,000. Frank Freidel, *Franklin D. Roosevelt: The Ordeal* 255 (Boston: Little, Brown, 1954).

sonal basis, but I've got to. As a personal favor, can I put your name before the convention?" Again Roosevelt declined. His health, Warm Springs, the need to regain the use of his legs, whatever reason he could think of.

The governor heard him out. "Frank, just one more question. If those fellows nominate you tomorrow and adjourn, will you refuse to run?"

FDR hesitated.

"Thanks, Frank. I won't ask you any more questions." Smith handed the telephone to Lehman, and in another minute the deal was done.[41]

Egbert Curtis, the Merriweather Inn manager, drove FDR back to his cottage that evening. Was he going to run? Curtis asked.

"Curt," said Roosevelt, "when you're in politics you've got to play the game."[42]

The following afternoon, Mayor Jimmy Walker of New York placed Roosevelt's name in nomination. The vote was pro forma. There was no opposition, and FDR was chosen by acclamation. Eleanor telegraphed her condolences. REGRET THAT YOU HAD TO ACCEPT BUT KNOW THAT YOU FELT IT OBLIGATORY.[43] Louis Howe smelled disaster. MESS IS NO NAME FOR IT, he wired Franklin. FOR ONCE I HAVE NO ADVICE TO GIVE.[44]

New York Republicans, taken aback by FDR's nomination, immediately focused on the health issue. "There is something both pathetic and pitiless in the 'drafting' of Franklin D. Roosevelt," asserted the New York Post. The Herald Tribune said, "The nomination is unfair to Mr. Roosevelt. It is equally unfair to the people of the state."[45] The Democrats were primed and ready. "A Governor doesn't have to be an acrobat," Smith replied. "The work of the governorship is brainwork. Frank Roosevelt is mentally as good as he ever was in his life."[46] FDR joked that most people ran for governor. "I am counting on my friends all over the state to make it possible for me to walk in."[47]

Despite his misgivings, Louis Howe set the campaign in motion, establishing headquarters at the Biltmore and organizing a statewide Independent Committee for Roosevelt and Lehman. Working hand in glove with Howe was Edward J. Flynn, the Democratic boss of the Bronx, who had detached himself from the national campaign to work exclusively on the gubernatorial race. An enlightened protégé of Charles Murphy, Flynn hailed from a prosperous Irish background, had graduated from Fordham Law School, and detested the backslapping and glad-handing endemic to the political fraternity. Courteous and cultivated in social relations, Flynn sought to keep his own machine honest and responsive. He hit it off instantly with both FDR and Howe. "Politics has never been my vocation," Flynn once said, "but it's been an avocation. I've had a lot of fun with politics but I've always been in the position where, if anything happened, it wouldn't make a damned bit of difference to me."[48]

FDR was joined on the campaign trail by Frances Perkins and Sam Rosenman, a young member of the New York legislature assigned to bring Roosevelt up to date on state issues. Like Howe and Missy LeHand, Rosenman would become a permanent fixture of Roosevelt's entourage, a walking file cabinet of legislative detail.* For his part, Rosenman, who had been initially skeptical of FDR's patrician origins, was immediately impressed by his uncanny ability to go to the heart of an issue. Rosenman reported that he "had never seen anybody who could grasp the facts of a complicated problem as quickly and as thoroughly as Roosevelt."[49] Frances Perkins, who had not been thrilled by

---

* After observing Rosenman for three days, FDR asked him to prepare a draft for a speech he was to give the next evening. It was a speechwriting relationship that would endure for the next seventeen years. "I get to know people quickly," said Roosevelt. "Sometimes that is better than a long and careful investigation."

Rosenman remembers that the campaign

> was a difficult one. After the first two days by train, Roosevelt decided that he would continue the rest of the trip by automobile. This would enable him to make speeches at scores of crossroads and villages all through the state. . . . Two large buses accompanied the automobiles. One was used by the newsmen who were covering Roosevelt. In the other bus were the stenographers, mimeograph machine operators and their equipment. The speeches had to be typed and mimeographed as the bus was speeding along.
>
> After a speech had been delivered in one city, I sat up and prepared a draft of the speech for the next night. It had to be ready for the candidate to look at the next morning during his breakfast when we would go over it together.
>
> After breakfast the cavalcade of cars and buses would start the journey to the next city. I would get into the bus where the typewriters were, and, with Roosevelt's corrections and suggestions, would work on the draft. Every once in a while the procession stopped at the center of some small village, where Roosevelt would make a short talk to the crowd. I would get into his car at one of these stops, and, after we started up again, we would discuss some of the changes to the draft. Sometimes he stopped his car at roadside and did some writing on the draft, or sent for one of the stenographers and dictated some new material. . . .
>
> It was not easy for a crippled man to carry on this kind of campaign. He could not climb stairs, and often we had to carry him up some backstairs to a hall and down again. He always went through this harrowing experience smiling. He never got ruffled. Having been set down, he would adjust his coat, smile, and proceed calmly to the platform for his speech.

Samuel I. Rosenman, *Working with Roosevelt* 21–22, 31 (New York: Harper & Brothers, 1952).

Franklin as a state senator, was also impressed by what she saw now. She was awed by FDR's stamina and pleasantly surprised by his good humor. "If you can't use your legs and they bring you milk when you wanted orange juice," Franklin told her, "You learn to say 'that's all right' and drink it."[50]

For four weeks FDR barnstormed the state, sometimes speaking as often as fourteen times a day. Rosenman marveled at his strength and courage, noting that merely to stand up and sit down was, for Roosevelt, "more exercise than the ordinary man takes during an entire day."[51] In Troy on October 26 Franklin delighted a cheering audience with a reference to the effort he was putting forth. He reminded his listeners of the "sob stuff" Republican editorial writers had published about his physical condition: "Too bad about that unfortunate sick man, isn't it."[52] When he spoke in many upstate cities, the turnout was twice as large as the number of registered Democrats. Initially, bookmakers favored Ottinger 2 to 1. By the end of October the odds had reversed. "I am horribly afraid you are going to be elected," Howe told Franklin a week before the election.[53] FDR ended the campaign in Poughkeepsie, where some 20,000 people paraded down Main Street in his honor.

On the morning of November 6, Roosevelt voted at Hyde Park and then went to campaign headquarters at the Biltmore to listen to the returns. By nine o'clock it was clear that the Democrats were going down, and as the evening wore on the avalanche accelerated. Even the Solid South, which Cox and Roosevelt had managed to hang on to in 1920, had split, Virginia, North Carolina, Florida, Tennessee, and Texas going Republican for the first time since Reconstruction.* In New York, Smith trailed Hoover by 100,000 votes. FDR was running ahead of the ticket but was still 25,000 votes behind Ottinger, with much

---

* It is easy to overestimate the magnitude of Smith's defeat. Though he did dismally in rural America, his candidacy solidified the urban, immigrant vote for the Democratic party. For the first time since the Civil War the Democrats carried Massachusetts and Rhode Island and won a plurality in the nation's twelve largest cities. All told, Smith polled more than 15 million votes, virtually as many as Calvin Coolidge's winning total in 1924 and almost twice as many as any previous Democratic candidate. In that sense, it can be argued that Smith's candidacy established the basis of the Roosevelt coalition and paved the way for FDR's victory in 1932. Samuel Lubell, *The Future of American Politics* 28–41 (New York: Harper & Brothers., 1952); Kristi Anderson, *The Creation of a Democratic Majority: 1928–1936* 2–11 (Chicago: University of Chicago Press, 1979); and especially V. O. Key, "A Theory of Critical Elections," 17 *Journal of Politics* 4 (1955); Congressional Quarterly, *Guide to U.S. Elections* 265–288 (Washington, D.C.: Congressional Quarterly, 1975).

of the normally Republican upstate vote still to come in. Shortly after midnight the morning papers appeared, trumpeting a GOP sweep. Franklin browsed through them, took the loss philosophically, and said he was going home to East Sixty-fifth Street to get some sleep. Newsmen and campaign workers drifted away, and the big ballroom in which the Democrats had planned a victory celebration went dark.

One room stayed open. The pros continued to keep watch. Louis Howe, Jim Farley, and Ed Flynn, together with a team of tally clerks and telephone operators, kept a vigil over the late returns. Sitting quietly on a couch in the corner was Frances Perkins, determined to stay until the last vote was counted, hoping her presence might change the result. Beside her sat an elderly woman who was equally determined. "I'll stay with you," said Sara. "It's not over by a long shot."[54]

The two women sat quietly, watching the professionals tabulate the results. At 1 A.M. Ed Flynn detected a stronger than expected showing from the returns trickling in from upstate. He telephoned Roosevelt to say there was a glimmer of hope. FDR was running far ahead of Smith and might squeak through. Franklin didn't believe it. Flynn was "crazy to wake him up," he said.[55]

At two o'clock the mood in the room lightened. Flynn could recognize a trend as well as any politician in the country. But he worried about the slow count. It was an article of faith among Democratic politicians that the GOP bosses upstate delayed reporting their results until they knew how many votes they needed. Flynn issued a statement to the press threatening to dispatch a thousand lawyers upstate to prevent the Republicans from stealing the election. The threat evidently had the desired effect, and the laggard upstate counties began to report more rapidly. Sara and Miss Perkins listened as the men kept count. "Forty votes here, one hundred votes there, seventy-five votes somewhere else. They mounted up."[56]

By 4 A.M. FDR had pulled ahead. The Democrats would hold the governor's mansion. The final results gave Roosevelt 2,130,238 votes to Ottinger's 2,104,630—a majority of 25,608 out of more than 4 million votes cast. Sara and Frances Perkins joined the men in a toast. Then, as Miss Perkins recalled, she shared a taxi with Sara to East Sixty-fifth Street. The seventy-four-year-old matriarch bounded up the steps, eager to get inside and inform her son of his triumph.[57]

TWELVE

ALBANY REDUX

Oh, Franklin, Franklin Roosevelt,
Is there something in a name?
When you tire of being Governor,
Will you look for bigger game?
Will you wish for something higher
When at Albany you're through?
When you weary of the State House
Will the White House beckon you?
—GRIDIRON DINNER DITTY, 1929

WHEN ROOSEVELT TOOK the oath as governor of New York on January 1, 1929, the road to the White House lay open. "It is too early to select the new leader of the Democratic Party or to predict nominations for a date so remote as 1932," declared *The New York Times*. "Yet by a most extraordinary combination of qualities, political fortunes and diversified associations, Governor-elect Roosevelt is within reach of the elements of party leadership."[1] *The Atlanta Constitution*, smitten with the state's adopted son, said, "It is difficult to convey in cold type the fervor of the devotion of Georgians to Governor-elect Roosevelt."[2]

With its forty-five electoral votes (more than three times as many as California), New York was a major player in presidential politics. In the sixteen presidential elections since the Civil War, a New Yorker had led the Democratic ticket eight times.* Add TR and Charles Evans Hughes for the Republicans,

---

* The Democrats nominated Horatio Seymour in 1868; Horace Greeley in 1872; Samuel Tilden in 1876; Grover Cleveland in 1884, 1888, and 1892; Alton B. Parker in 1904; and Al Smith in 1928.

and a majority of the post–Civil War nominees had been from New York. Roosevelt and Howe understood the odds. But it would be a mistake to announce too early. When reporters asked FDR about the Roosevelt-in-'32 predictions, he replied emphatically, "I want to step on any talk of that kind with both feet."[3] For a man who was paralyzed it was a peculiar metaphor, but Franklin peppered his conversation with jokes about walking, running, and jumping. One of his favorite expressions was "Funny as a crutch."

Roosevelt's first priority was to secure his place as governor. Al Smith had not anticipated losing the presidential race and, after spending eight of the last ten years as governor of the Empire State, suddenly found himself with no place to go. He was reluctant to relinquish his hold on the state government to someone he considered as politically inexperienced as FDR and believed he could call the plays from the sidelines. The fact that Smith had leased a suite at Albany's DeWitt Clinton Hotel in order to be nearby confirmed for Roosevelt the problem he faced.[4]

Outwardly, relations between the two men were cordial. "God bless you and keep you, Frank," said Smith as FDR and Eleanor drove up to the ornate portico of the governor's mansion on December 31. "We've got the home fires burning and you'll find this a fine place to live." Roosevelt returned the sentiment, telling Eleanor, "I only wish Al were going to be right here for the next two years. We are certainly going to miss him."[5]

But there was considerable tension beneath the surface. In mid-December Smith had called on FDR at East Sixty-fifth Street to discuss the transition. To provide for continuity and to ensure that Roosevelt would not be out of his depth in Albany, the governor suggested that Franklin retain two of Smith's closest collaborators: the hard-driving Robert Moses as secretary of state and the formidable Belle Moskowitz as his executive secretary, speechwriter, and strategist. The abrasive Moses was an exemplary public servant and an empire builder of great virtuosity. His loyalty to Smith was exceeded only by his loyalty to himself.* Mrs. Moskowitz was even more loyal to Smith. She had handled public relations for him since 1918 and was the den mother of the governor's Albany circle. "I think [Al] suggested this in completely good faith,"

---

* In 1934 Moses departed the party of his patron to run for governor as a Republican. He was trounced by Herbert Lehman, 2,201,727–1,393,744. Congressional Quarterly, *Guide to U.S. Elections* 423 (Washington, D.C.: Congressional Quarterly, 1975).

said FDR many years later, "but at the same time with the rather definite thought that he himself would continue to run the Governorship."[6]

There was little love lost between Robert Moses and FDR. They had clashed frequently over funding for the Taconic State Parkway, of which Roosevelt was the unsalaried chairman from 1925 to 1928, and those disputes had turned ugly. According to Robert A. Caro, Moses's Pulitzer Prize–winning biographer, Moses had hoped Smith would tap him for governor in 1928 and was bitterly disappointed when FDR was nominated.[7] He spewed out his venom to one and all, telling Frances Perkins among others that Franklin was a "pretty poor excuse for a man" and "not quite bright." His characterizations of ER were equally vicious.[8] Franklin inevitably learned of the gossip and wanted no part of Moses. "No," he told Smith. "He rubs me the wrong way."[9] To soften the rejection, Roosevelt agreed to retain Moses as chairman of the State Council for Parks and the Long Island Parks Commission—posts where his demonstrated ability could flourish without direct contact.

With Belle Moskowitz, Roosevelt was circumspect. No one in Albany was closer to Al Smith than Mrs. Moskowitz, and no one had been more influential in shaping the policies of the Smith administration. Smith told FDR that Belle was drafting his inaugural address as well as his initial message to the legislature laying out his program. Roosevelt graciously noted that he was writing the speeches himself but would be happy to show them to Mrs. Moskowitz when he finished. He acknowledged her skill and competence and said her understanding of the issues facing the state was unparalleled. FDR left Smith with the impression that Mrs. Moskowitz would be kept on. Yet he never showed her the speeches and never met with her. "My recollection is that I did not find an opportunity to do so, though I really meant to at the time."[10] In the end, Roosevelt retained sixteen of the eighteen department heads who had served under Smith, but he did not retain Mrs. Moskowitz. He never confronted her, but his decision soon became apparent. As he told Sam Rosenman, "I do not expect to call on these people whom Al has been using."[11]*

---

* For her part, Eleanor Roosevelt distrusted both Belle Moskowitz and Robert Moses, whom she considered stalking horses for Smith. One week after the election she wrote FDR, "By all signs I think Belle and Bob Moses mean to cling to you and you will wake up and find R. M. Secretary of State and B.M. running Democratic Publicity at her old stand unless you take a firm stand. Gosh, the race has nerves of iron and tentacles of steel."

FDR did not feel beholden to Smith, except to recognize that he had been an extraordinarily effective governor and would be a tough act to follow. During his eight-year tenure Smith had reduced state government from a hodge-podge of 187 semi-independent agencies to 18 departments, all but 2 responsible to the governor. He had pushed through a constitutional amendment giving the governor authority over the state budget, laid the basis for significant social reform, and cut taxes while funding public works through the sale of state bonds. Roosevelt had run for governor reluctantly, pressured into doing so to aid the national ticket. He had run well ahead of Smith in New York and withstood the Republican tide. As a result, he did not feel he owed his election to anyone but himself. Smith did not see it that way, and relations between the two men, never close, cooled precipitously.

Roosevelt moved quickly to establish his own cadre in Albany. Ed Flynn, the astute leader of the Bronx, was called back from a European vacation to succeed Robert Moses as secretary of state. Flynn became the principal dispenser of state patronage and FDR's link to Tammany Hall and other city organizations. Sam Rosenman was named counsel to the governor and moved into a spare room in the executive mansion. Missy LeHand lived there too, joined by Grace Tully, who became FDR's second secretary, always on call, twenty-four hours a day, seven days a week. Roosevelt passed Belle Moskowitz's duties as social welfare adviser to Frances Perkins, whom he also named industrial commissioner and a member of the governor's cabinet, the first woman to serve in that capacity. "It is my firm belief that had women had an equal share in making laws in years past," said FDR, "the unspeakable conditions in crowded tenements, the neglect of the poor, the unwillingness to spend money for hospitals and sanitariums . . . would never have come about."[12]*

Later, ER told Franklin, "You have to decide . . . whether you are going to be Governor of this state or whether Mrs. Moskowitz is . . . If Mrs. Moskowitz is your secretary, she will run you. It won't hurt you. It won't give you any pain. She will run you in such a way that you don't know that you are being run. . . . That's the way she works. That is the kind of person she is. She doesn't do it in any spirit of ill will. It's simply that her competence is so much greater than anyone else's."

ER to FDR, November 13, 1928, FDRL; Frances Perkins Interview, Columbia Oral History Project, Columbia University.

* Al Smith warned FDR against appointing Miss Perkins to a cabinet post. "Men will take advice from a woman," said Smith, "but it is hard for them to take orders from a woman."

Henry Morgenthau, Jr., Roosevelt's Dutchess County neighbor and editor of *American Agriculturist,* became chairman of the Agricultural Advisory Commission and later commissioner of conservation. Basil O'Connor, Franklin's law partner, settled in as one of the governor's political intimates while continuing to head the firm in New York City. Also remaining in New York were Jim Farley and Louis Howe. Farley, at Roosevelt's insistence, assumed control of the state Democratic party and cleared the deck for the 1930 election. Howe continued as FDR's political chief of staff, the only person who had access to him night and day on any problem he wished. Howe's major responsibility was to chart Roosevelt's course for the 1932 nomination, and this could be managed more discreetly in New York than in Albany. Howe continued to live in Roosevelt's town house on East Sixty-fifth Street and handled whatever business the governor had in the city. He went to Albany at least once a week and, like Rosenman and Missy, had his own room in the executive mansion.[13]

For the Roosevelts, life in Albany set a pattern that would endure for the remainder of Franklin's life. The executive mansion—still outfitted with furniture from Grover Cleveland's time—took on the informality of an expansive country estate. "It looked more like a home than like the property of the State of New York," Miss Perkins remembered.[14] The nine guest rooms were continually occupied, books and papers littered every available space, while secretaries came and went with important papers for the governor to sign. Meals were uproarious affairs, with everyone talking at once. Family, secretaries, newsmen, friends, state troopers, and distinguished guests often sat elbow to elbow, with no one ever quite sure how many would be sitting down for the evening meal. "Really serious talk at the table was avoided if Roosevelt could manage it," Rexford Tugwell recalled. "But Eleanor, so humorless and so weighted down with responsibility, made this difficult."[15]

Meanwhile, the children were growing up. Anna, now twenty-two, had married and was living in Manhattan with her stockbroker husband but had deposited Chief, her German shepherd, with Eleanor and Franklin. The four

Miss Perkins remembered FDR's chuckle as he related the conversation: "You see, Al's a good progressive fellow but I'm willing to take more chances. I've got more nerve about women and their status in the world than Al has." Frances Perkins, *The Roosevelt I Knew* 55 (New York: Viking Press, 1946).

Roosevelt boys were in and out of the house. James, in his last year at Harvard, was engaged to Betsey Cushing, one of three vivacious daughters of a prominent Boston surgeon.[16]* In future years, both Anna and Betsey would serve as White House hostess during Eleanor's absence. Elliott (18), Franklin, Jr. (14), and John (12) were in the care of the Reverend Endicott Peabody at Groton, experiencing the usual prep school traumas. "Elliott is about to have an operation, Franklin, Jr., has a doubly broken nose and John has just had a cartilage taken out of his knee," FDR wrote a friend in March 1929. "Eleanor is teaching school two and a half days a week in New York, and I am in one continuous, glorious fight with the Republican legislative leaders."[17]

Roosevelt's work habits rarely varied. He had breakfast in bed about eight, during which he read the papers, conferred with Missy and Rosenman (and Howe when he was in town), handled his personal correspondence, and set the schedule for the day. At ten he left for the Capitol, where he worked through until five, taking lunch at his desk. Then home for a swim, followed by tea, frequently with friends and official visitors. During the White House years, with Prohibition repealed, teatime became the "children's hour" and the president mixed martinis for his guests. Dinner was at seven-thirty and, unlike lunch, was seldom taken alone. After dinner, Franklin was wheeled into his study, where he continued to work until bedtime. Before turning out the light, he conferred again with Missy and Rosenman and read the evening papers.[18]

An exception to the daily routine was on movie nights. FDR was addicted to motion pictures, but going to the theater was difficult for him. And so at least once a week an informal theater would be set up in a third-floor hallway and a new release would be shown. Bill and Caroline Phillips, old friends from Washington (Phillips later served as FDR's ambassador to Italy), visited the Roosevelts and reported watching John and Lionel Barrymore in *Arsène Lupin.* "All the servants, black and white, seventeen in all, sat behind the house party and enjoyed the show with us," wrote Caroline.[19]

---

* The Roosevelt children were unlucky in marriage. Anna was married three times, James four, Elliott five, Franklin, Jr., five, and John twice. Among them they had twenty-seven children. Samuel Rosenman, who lived in the executive mansion and had an opportunity to observe firsthand, attributed the children's lack of marital success to an inadequate family life. FDR was pursuing his career, Eleanor had separate interests, and the children were left high and dry. Samuel I. Rosenman interview, Columbia Oral History Project, Columbia University.

The mansion was altered to assist Roosevelt's movements. In place of the greenhouse, a swimming pool was built for his use. An elevator was installed, and ramps were placed over unavoidable steps. FDR retained the services of Sergeant Gus Gennerich, a New York City policeman who had been detailed to protect him during the campaign. Gennerich had little formal education and was proud to be a New York cop. His affable manner made him a friend and companion for Roosevelt. So too Sergeant Earl Miller of the New York State Police, a strikingly handsome officer who was assigned to protect the governor. Gennerich and Miller were big, muscular men and provided solid support for FDR when he walked. They knew how to lift him out of cars and devised a technique for carrying him up long flights of stairs. The two men would each grasp an elbow and lift Roosevelt up the steps in a standing position. Those watching from a distance could well believe Franklin was climbing the stairs himself.[20]

Roosevelt relished informality. He treated employees as friends, enjoyed shirtsleeve poker sessions with journalists, and insisted on calling people by their first names as soon as he met them.* As president he made a point of addressing royalty by their given names: the king and queen of England were "George" and "Elizabeth"; the crown princess of the Netherlands was "Juliana." Yet they always called him "Mr. President," and it was clear that Roosevelt was never one of the boys.[21] There was an unspoken dignity, an impenetrable reserve that protected him against undue familiarity. Aside from relatives, old friends from college, and senior statesmen whom he had known—men like Josephus Daniels and Al Smith—Louis Howe was the only person to call him Franklin.

For Eleanor, FDR's election was a mixed blessing. When asked by reporters shortly afterward how she felt about her husband's victory, she said she was not excited. "I don't care. What difference can it make to me? If the rest of the ticket doesn't get in, what does it matter?"[22] ER's petulant response reflected her unhappiness at Al Smith's defeat. She had worked night and day for the

---

* Dean Acheson, a fellow Grotonian who served on and off as a sub–cabinet officer in the Roosevelt administration, was one of the few who took umbrage at FDR's first-name familiarity. Considered more than a bit pompous himself, Acheson felt Roosevelt was condescending, calling the president's style the Hudson Valley equivalent of the royal prerogative. "His was the royalty of the Tudors and Stuarts and Bourbons and Hapsburgs. . . . So when he called me 'Dean' on the first meeting, I did not like it." Acheson to William D. Hassett, Hassett Papers, FDRL. Also see Acheson, *Morning and Noon* 165 (Boston: Houghton Mifflin, 1965).

past nine months on Smith's campaign, and she hated to lose. It was not merely a personal loss but the defeat at the national level of the social programs she supported.

Then too, she had not participated in FDR's campaign. In retrospect, she wondered if she had really wanted Franklin to run. "I imagine I accepted his nomination and later his election as I had accepted most of the things that had happened in life thus far: one did whatever seemed necessary and adjusted one's personal life to the developments in other people's lives."[23]

Even more important was ER's reluctance to forsake the public life she had staked out for herself. Eleanor had no desire to become a ceremonial first lady, relegated to serving in her husband's shadow. She had grown accustomed to a different role: teacher, writer, and political activist in her own right. She was associated with an ongoing effort to build reproduction furniture at Val-Kill and was teaching full-time at Todhunter.*

Eleanor and Franklin reached an implicit understanding: she would be the governor's wife, preside over the executive mansion, and pursue her own agenda at the same time.[24] "Mrs. Roosevelt Takes on Another Task," bannered *The New York Times Magazine* in its lead article on December 2, 1928.

A woman who teaches school, runs a factory, edits a journal, and is a member of a half dozen civic organizations would appear to have her hands full. Yet to these activities Mrs. Franklin D. Roosevelt will add one more when she takes up the task of the First Lady of Albany on Jan. 1.[25]

Eleanor organized her teaching schedule at Todhunter for Monday, Tuesday, and a half day on Wednesday. She left Albany Sunday evening and returned late Wednesday afternoon. "I like to read on trains," she told the *Times.* "Most of my reading is done on trains. It's one place where reading is sure to be uninterrupted." Eleanor said the work at Val-Kill would occupy her part-time and she would continue to serve on a few committees and boards of directors. Would housekeeping at the executive mansion be a formidable task? asked the *Times.* "I rarely devote more than fifteen minutes a day to it," said Eleanor.[26]

---

* Eleanor's income tax returns for the period indicate a professional income averaging slightly more than $25,000 annually—roughly the same as FDR's salary as governor. FDRL.

For Franklin and Eleanor this was the beginning of a remarkable partnership. FDR did not insist his wife drop anything she cared about to become first lady, and Eleanor undertook to support her husband's public career in every way possible. They would have different priorities and different interests. They would often disagree. Their personal lives would be separate. But they shared a mutual respect that eventually resolved most differences.

From his first day in office FDR operated as though he had been governor for many years. He said there had been so few changes in Albany since he had left the State Senate in 1913 that it was like renewing an acquaintance with an old friend.[27] Roosevelt knew instinctively how to handle the controls of government, an intuitive "feel" that could not be explained rationally. Like all true artists he made what he did look easy. Sam Rosenman was amazed that FDR never seemed to worry. "He would think a problem through very carefully. Having come to a decision, he would dismiss it from his mind as finished business. He never went back to it to worry about whether his decision was right."[28] Frances Perkins said, "Roosevelt was a walking American history book." There were no isolated events for FDR. Everything that happened in politics, every crisis, every decision taken, was part of a larger American tapestry, part of an experiment in government still being worked out.[29]

The state machinery Roosevelt inherited from Al Smith was in good working order. Rather than fix what was not broken, Franklin moved forward in new directions of his own, first in public power, agriculture, and conservation, and then, after the Depression started, in relief and social security.

FDR's concern for electric power dated from his service in the state senate and had continued without interruption. He often spoke of harnessing the high tides of Passamaquoddy Bay, near Campobello, for hydroelectric purposes, and he was an early advocate of dual-purpose flood control dams on the tributaries of major rivers: dams that could be used both to store water and to generate electricity. As Roosevelt saw it, cheaper electric power required greater generating capacity as well as more effective regulation of public utility companies. In March 1929 he asked the legislature for authority to construct a series of hydroelectric plants on the Saint Lawrence and to sell the power to private companies at cost. Roosevelt also sought tighter regulation of existing utilities and suggested that publicly generated power serve "as a yardstick with which to measure the cost of producing and transmitting electricity."[30] The "yardstick" metaphor would later become a staple of New Deal rhetoric.

Roosevelt's interest in agriculture was also of long standing, a natural product of his avocation of gentleman farmer at Hyde Park and Warm Springs. Whereas Al Smith had written off New York's farmers as inherently Republican ("I never made any impression on any considerable number of them"[31]), FDR made farm relief the centerpiece of his legislative program. "If the farming population does not have sufficient purchasing power to buy new shoes, new clothes, new automobiles, the manufacturing centers must suffer."[32] Not only did Roosevelt's interest revitalize the Democratic party upstate, it also helped him balance between the urban and rural wings of the party at the national level.[33]

FDR's agriculture program was scarcely radical. But because the plight of the farmer was so dismal in the late twenties, anything that offered succor attracted national attention. Roosevelt proposed to shift much of the rural tax burden to the state by raising gasoline taxes. The increased revenue would pay for an expanded network of farm-to-market roads and underwrite local school construction. For dairy farmers he proposed the creation of the New York Milk Shed, a marketing cooperative that would fix the price of milk in the Empire State. He also advocated tax relief for small farmers, accelerated rural electrification, significant subsidies for agricultural research, and the conversion of marginal cropland to timber production—a means of reducing agricultural surpluses and easing the problems of flood control.[34]

In the spring of 1929 FDR held the first in a long series of fireside chats, bypassing the Republican legislature and speaking directly to New Yorkers over the radio. Roosevelt was a master at simplifying complicated issues and bringing people into his confidence. His cultivated delivery and easy manner made the audience feel they were participating directly at the highest level of government. Usually Roosevelt spoke on Sunday night, when the radio audience was largest. His remarks were painstakingly crafted to achieve the desired informality. Sometimes Rosenman prepared the first draft; more often it was FDR himself. A flood of letters would deluge the legislature after each talk, and Roosevelt would usually get close to what he asked for from the Assembly.*

---

* Miss Perkins, who was sometimes present in the executive mansion when FDR spoke, said his voice and facial expression were that of an intimate friend. "As he talked his head would nod and his hands would move in simple, natural, comfortable gestures. His face would smile and light up as though he were actually sitting on the front porch or in the parlor with them." Frances Perkins, *The Roosevelt I Knew* 72 (New York: Viking Press, 1946).

In April 1929, after the legislature adjourned, FDR stopped off in Washington on his way to Warm Springs. He had been invited by the capital's newsmen to address their annual Gridiron Dinner, where he, not Al Smith, would represent the Democratic party. The other two speakers were President Hoover and Chief Justice Taft. Roosevelt's remarks were off the record, but from his reception it was clear the Washington press corps considered him a prime contender for the Democratic nomination.*

That summer FDR undertook a round of speaking engagements that kept his name before the public. He was awarded honorary degrees by Hobart College, Dartmouth, Fordham, and Harvard. His commencement remarks stressed the importance of social consciousness and gently decried "the unlikely alliance between big business and big government." At Harvard, where he attended his twenty-fifth reunion—the high point for Ivy League alumni—he was made chief marshal of the graduation exercises and an honorary member of Phi Beta Kappa. "It certainly is grand," FDR wrote his old friend Livingston Davis. "I as sure you that being governor is nothing in comparison."[35]

On July 4 Roosevelt presided at the dedication of Tammany Hall's new headquarters off Union Square. Charles Murphy was gone, succeeded by lesser men, but the wigwam remained the focus of Democratic politics in the city. The fifteen hundred Tammany braves in attendance cheered Roosevelt as "the next president of the United States." FDR rose to the occasion. Unencumbered by academic propriety, he lashed out at the oligarchs of economic feudalism. If the American people wished to preserve their freedom, they should don liberty caps like their Revolutionary forebears and resist the concentration of economic power, said FDR. This time the struggle would be fought with ballots rather than muskets. And unless they were successful, "all property would be concentrated in the hands of a few, and the overwhelming majority would become serfs."[36]

This was fire-and-brimstone populist oratory, and Roosevelt struck a responsive chord. His remarks made banner headlines across the country. Will Rogers, the cowboy humorist, then at the height of his popularity, wrote in his syndicated *New York Times* column that the speech "just about" ensured that Roosevelt would be "the next Democratic candidate."[37†]

---

* The ditty sung by the newsmen to greet FDR is the chapter epigraph.
† Born in the Indian Territory (now Oklahoma) in 1879, Rogers delighted the nation with his homespun wisdom. "I don't belong to an organized political party," he once quipped.

Having made their point, Roosevelt and Howe decided it was time to re-trench. They had lit a spark, but it would be unwise to trigger a premature con-flagration. FDR drafted a statement for the press: "It is probably because of the warm weather and the lack of real news that my young gentlemen friends of the Press are inventing Arabian night tales about presidential possibilities and candidacies for the far distant date of 1932. . . . I am in no sense a candidate for President of the United States."[38]

By the summer of 1929, America's unprecedented prosperity began to look blotchy. Agriculture, which had been in the doldrums for years (per capita farm income was one quarter that of non-farmworkers), was joined by con-sumer durables and residential housing, both of which turned down sharply. Business inventories, always an economic barometer, had almost quadrupled in less than twelve months. Concurrently, the rate of consumer spending, which had risen at a rate of 7.4 percent in 1927–28, slowed to a snaillike pace of 1.4 percent.[39] These developments were reflected in production and price indices. Industrial production hit a high in June and dropped off in July. Em-ployment fell as well, along with wholesale commodity prices. The Federal Re-serve Board compounded the deflationary pressure by raising interest rates a full percentage point in August, hiking the discount rate to 6 percent.

Wall Street appeared oblivious to the downturn. Stock prices, which had doubled in 1928, continued their upward spiral, fueled by margin (credit) pur-chases sometimes as great as 95 percent. As prices rose, investors clamored for more, pushing the market to a record high on September 3. Technology stocks led the climb. Shares of General Electric zoomed from $129 to $396; those of its competitor Westinghouse from $92 to $313; those of RCA from $93 to a breathtaking $505. Giddy commentators proclaimed the old laws of econom-ics had been repealed: what went up did not necessarily have to come down.

In late September the market wobbled but recovered. For the next three weeks prices moved sideways on heavy volume. In retrospect it appears that knowledgeable investors were getting out. The break came Thursday, October 24. Panic selling pushed prices down 4 percent in two hours with a record 12.9 million shares changing hands. The market stabilized Friday and Saturday, but

"I'm a Democrat." Quoted in David M. Kennedy, *Freedom from Fear* 31 (New York: Oxford University Press, 1999).

on Monday, October 28, the wave of selling resumed and the market dropped another 5 percent on volume of 10 million shares. That set the scene for what historians call Black Tuesday, October 29, 1929. The New York Stock Exchange opened down, and three million shares traded in the first half hour. Brokers sold positions for whatever they could get, and for a few ghastly minutes the exchange saw stocks for sale for which there were no buyers at any price. When the carnage ended, the market had lost one fifth of its value on an unprecedented 16.4 million sales—a record that stood for thirty-nine years. The decline continued off and on for the next three years. By mid-1932, the total value of the American stock market stood at 17 percent of its peak in September 1929.

The severity of the depression caught everyone by surprise. In the beginning, most believed the crash was a useful stock market correction. John D. Rockefeller called it a buying opportunity. Charles Schwab of Bethlehem Steel said, "Never before has American business been as firmly entrenched for prosperity as it is today." President Hoover maintained that "the fundamental business of the country—that is, the production and distribution of goods and services—is on a sound and prosperous basis."[40]

Rarely, if ever, have the nation's economic spokesmen been more wrong. The crash may not have caused the Great Depression (economists agree that the causes were manifold), but it surely precipitated it. Farm prices, already depressed, fell by 53 percent from 1929 to 1932; net farm income by 70 percent. A cow that sold for $83 in 1929 now brought $28. Cotton sold for six cents a pound. Corn in Nebraska brought thirty-one cents a bushel, Kansas wheat thirty-eight cents. By early 1933, 45 percent of all farm mortgages were delinquent and facing foreclosure.[41]

In the same period, automobile production fell by 65 percent and steel by 59 percent. The nation's gross domestic product declined from $104 billion to $74 billion. The money supply shrank by 25 percent, and four out of every ten home mortgages were in default. Unemployment soared above 30 percent, with 11.8 million unemployed.[42]

FDR shared the prevailing consensus that the market's correction would be brief. "The little flurry downtown," as he called it, seemed just retribution for speculators who had artificially inflated stock prices.[43] "Black Tuesday" did not figure in New York's legislative elections the following week, and Democratic gains were slight. The party picked up three seats in the Assembly, but the GOP retained control of both houses. Roosevelt claimed victory, although the best that could be said is that the voters did not punish the governor for the crash.

By December the extent of the economic downturn was beginning to dawn. The 1932 election might be winnable after all. On December 10 FDR as much as threw his hat in the ring with a spectacular appearance in Chicago where he delivered three speeches in one day—a performance that could not be misunderstood. Speaking seriatim to the state Democratic committee, the American Farm Bureau Federation, and the Chicago Commercial Club, Roosevelt rose above New York politics and wrapped himself in the mantle of western agrarianism: "If the farmer starves today, we will all starve tomorrow."[44] He predicted that the Democrats would recapture the House of Representatives in 1930, and his remarks generated headlines from coast to coast.

FDR was among the first state governors to recognize the seriousness of the Depression. When Hoover announced in late January that employment was rebounding, Frances Perkins took the president to task, citing Labor Department statistics to prove the situation was getting worse. "Bully for you," said FDR. "That was a fine statement and I'm glad you made it."[45] By March 1930, although the reality of the Depression still was not acknowledged in Washington, Roosevelt established a commission to stabilize employment in New York—the first state commission of its kind in the United States. "The situation is serious," said FDR, "and the time has come for us to face this unpleasant fact dispassionately."[46] Shortly thereafter Roosevelt became the first state chief executive to endorse the idea of unemployment insurance—a radical concept that had been kicking around university economics departments for years but had yet to make its debut in the public arena. First at an ad hoc meeting of New England governors that he convened, then at the National Governors Association Annual Meeting at Salt Lake City, FDR came flat out for a contributory scheme in which employees, employers, and the government would share the risks of future unemployment.

FDR was choosing the ground on which to oppose Hoover two years hence. When the president advised the U.S. Chamber of Commerce on May 1, 1930, that the worst was over and recovery at hand, Roosevelt told Democrats that Hoover had apparently repealed the laws of supply and demand.[47] Speaking to the annual Jefferson Day dinner of the National Democratic Club at New York's Commodore Hotel, FDR castigated financial circles in the East, who he suggested were unresponsive to the nation's distress. "If Thomas Jefferson were alive he would be the first to question this concentration of economic power."[48]

Roosevelt was followed on the dais by Senator Burton K. Wheeler of Montana, who would give the keynote address. Six years earlier Wheeler had run for vice president on the Progressive ticket with Wisconsin's Robert La Follette. He was back in the Democratic fold, a powerful spokesman for the grassroots populism of the high plains. There was no advance text of Wheeler's speech, and he had given no warning of what he intended to say. But his remarks were carried live on a nationwide hookup by NBC, and the assembled Democrats soon heard a clarion call for new leadership. "As I look about for a general to lead the Democratic party, I ask to whom we can go. I say that, if the Democratic party of New York will re-elect Franklin Roosevelt governor, the West will demand his nomination for president and the whole country will elect him."[49]

Wheeler's endorsement created a sensation. He was the first Democrat of national stature to announce for Roosevelt, and his speech had been totally unexpected. FDR, in fact, had departed the dinner before Wheeler spoke. Later, Franklin wrote his cousin Nicholas that he was not concerned about 1932. "Why can't reporters, editorial writers and the politicians let a poor devil alone to do the best he can with a very current job?"[50] Franklin was doubtless sincere about wishing to get on with the job of governor—he was up for re-election in November—but when Governor L. G. Hardman of Georgia announced his support of Roosevelt for president several weeks later, FDR made no move to rein him in. "It was very good of Governor Hardman to say what he did," Franklin wrote his old friend Hollins Randolph.[51]

The gubernatorial campaign occupied FDR completely in the summer and fall of 1930. The Republicans nominated Charles H. Tuttle, the racket-busting U.S. attorney for the Southern District of New York, and focused the campaign on Tammany corruption. Roosevelt chose to run against Washington, stressing the need for farm relief, full employment, and public power. "Never let your opponent pick the battleground on which to fight," FDR told Sam Rosenman. "If he picks one, stay out of it and let him fight all by himself."[52]*

---

* To allay concern about Roosevelt's health, Louis Howe arranged for FDR to be examined by a battery of insurance company physicians at his Sixty-fifth Street home shortly after he received the Democratic nomination. Their report was made public on October 18, 1930, and Roosevelt was issued a life insurance policy for $560,000 (roughly $6 million today)

After Charles Murphy's death, Tammany had returned to its old ways of doing business, and corruption was rampant in New York City. But Roosevelt relied on the votes of Tammany Democrats in the legislature to enact his program, and he was reluctant to call the organization to task. And so he avoided the issue during the campaign. The more Tuttle talked about Tammany corruption, the more FDR talked about unemployment insurance and old-age pensions.

In the closing weeks of the campaign Washington dispatched three high-ranking cabinet officers to New York on Tuttle's behalf. The Hoover administration evidently decided that the best way to stop Roosevelt in 1932 would be to defeat him for governor in 1930. Secretary of State Henry L. Stimson, Secretary of War Patrick J. Hurley, and Ogden Mills, the undersecretary (later secretary) of the Treasury spoke repeatedly to audiences throughout the Empire State, lambasting FDR for his failure to repudiate Tammany.

Roosevelt ignored the charges until his final rally at Carnegie Hall on November 1. His response was brief but complete. If there were corrupt officeholders, he said, they would be removed. "They shall be removed by constitutional means, not by inquisition; not by trial in the press, but by trial as provided by law.

"If there is corruption in our courts I will use every rightful power of the office of Governor to drive it out, and I will do this regardless of whether it affects any Democratic or Republican organization in any one of the five counties of New York City, or in any one of the fifty-seven other counties of the State. That is clear. That is unequivocal. That is honesty. That is justice. That is American. That is right." And that was enough. Roosevelt waited until

---

with the Warm Springs Foundation as the beneficiary. On behalf of the examining physicians, Dr. Edgar W. Beckwith, medical director of the Equitable Life Assurance Company, told newsmen that to issue a policy of that magnitude was highly unusual. It required that the insured be in perfect health, which he said Roosevelt was. Except for his withered legs, said Dr. Beckwith, FDR's physical condition was comparable to that of a man of thirty. His chest expansion was 5½ inches, weight 182 pounds, height six feet, one and a half inches, blood pressure 128/80—"a little better than gilt-edged for a man of forty-eight." Privately, Dr. Beckwith wrote FDR: "Frankly, I have never before observed such a complete recovery in organic function and such a remarkable degree of recovery of muscles and limbs in an individual who had passed through an attack of infantile paralysis such as yours." Dr. Beckwith to FDR, October 21, 1930, Howe Papers, FDRL.

the last day of the race to rebut the charges of corruption, and he did so effectively. Tuttle had waged a one-issue campaign, and it had backfired.

Roosevelt also used his final appearance to ridicule the intervention of
Stimson, Hurley, and Mills.* What qualified "these three estimable gentlemen"
to instruct the people of New York? FDR asked. Hurley, he pointed out, was a
carpetbagger from Oklahoma and knew nothing about the state. The other
two, Stimson and Mills, had both run for governor of New York and been defeated. "The people did not believe in them or their issues then, and they will
not believe in them or their issues now." Roosevelt said the three cabinet officers should return to Washington as soon as possible and address the problems
confronting the nation. "Rest assured that we of the Empire State can take care
of ourselves."[53]

Roosevelt left Carnegie Hall with the rafters ringing. Three days later the
Tammany organization demonstrated its electoral effectiveness. In New York
City a record 91.1 percent of the registered voters went to the polls. Overall,
FDR swamped Tuttle by 725,000 votes, the largest plurality won by any gubernatorial candidate in New York history.[54] Upstate, Roosevelt carried forty-
three counties to Tuttle's fourteen. In every upstate county, FDR's vote total
exceeded the number of registered Democrats in that county. He carried
precincts, wards, districts that had not gone Democratic in living memory.
Times were hard, and voters wanted a change. But the magnitude of the victory reflected not only Roosevelt's determination to revive the Democratic
party upstate but Jim Farley's ability to put an organization on the ground that
could actually do so. The Democrats recaptured both houses of the legislature
and all statewide offices. In Washington, the Democrats won control of the
House of Representatives and came within one seat of taking the Senate. For
all practical purposes, the alliance between Democrats and progressive Republicans in the Senate gave them effective control of that body as well.

Eleanor, who set strategy for the Women's Division of the State Democratic
Committee, did everything possible to ensure Franklin's reelection. Campaign

---

* FDR's response to Stimson, Hurley, and Mills was much like his reply to Martin, Barton,
and Fish in the 1940 presidential campaign, when he worked Democratic crowds into
paroxysms of partisan enthusiasm by invoking the names of the isolationist congressmen
Joseph Martin of Massachusetts, Bruce Barton of New York, and Hamilton Fish of New
York. "Martin, Barton, and Fish" rolled off FDR's tongue in rhythmic cadence and was zest-
fully picked up and chanted by Democratic audiences, to their mutual delight.

aides jocularly referred to the 1930 gubernatorial contest as the "waffle iron election" because of the publicity ER generated comparing the cost of operating various kitchen appliances in New York as opposed to the cost in Ontario. Jim Farley credited Eleanor with adding 10 to 20 percent to the Democratic vote in those counties where her women's organization was active. This time ER savored the victory as much as Franklin. "Much love and a world of congratulations," she penciled in a note left on her husband's pillow on election night. "It is a triumph in so many ways, dear, and so well earned. Bless you and good luck these next two years.—ER."[55]

The fact is, Eleanor relished her role in Albany. She often served as FDR's proxy, speaking on his behalf, inspecting state institutions, reporting back with a thoroughness that increased with time and experience. Roosevelt encouraged state officials to believe that he and "the Missus" were a team. "I do not often go to the big places," Eleanor told the progressive historian and journalist Ida Tarbell, "but often to the little places where they have difficulty securing speakers. I don't do it as well as I wish I did, but after all what they want is to see the Governor's wife."[56]

Throughout the Albany years, Eleanor was accompanied on her inspection tours by New York State Police sergeant Earl Miller. ER refused to be driven in an official limousine and insisted on driving herself. This made Franklin uneasy, and he assigned Miller as her bodyguard. Miller had been Al Smith's personal bodyguard, and he and Franklin were acquainted from World War I, when Miller, the Navy's middleweight boxing champion, had kept watch over FDR during his trip to France in 1918. Miller was a first-rate athlete and had been a member of the U.S. Olympic squad at the Antwerp games in 1920. He was an award-winning swimmer, expert marksman, and trick rider at state fairs, and had once worked as a circus acrobat. He was also a warm and affectionate man, and he and Eleanor hit it off from the beginning.

For Eleanor, Miller provided encouragement and support. He was unfailingly attentive and chivalrous. He protected and defended her and reintroduced her to sports and activities she had long forgotten. He taught her to shoot a pistol, coached her tennis game, and built her a deck tennis court at Val-Kill for daily practice. He gave her riding lessons and eventually bought a horse for her, a chestnut mare named Dot, which ER rode regularly at Hyde Park and later in Washington. He improved her swimming and taught her to dive, a goal that required years to accomplish but something Eleanor was keen to do.

For Miller, Eleanor provided stability and accomplishment and gave his life a purpose. She was forty-four when they met; he was thirty-two. He became her unofficial escort, companion, and manager. One biographer compared their relationship to that of the legendary Scotsman John Brown and Queen Victoria.[57] Earl Miller and Eleanor laughed together, journeyed for weekends through the countryside, and thoroughly enjoyed each other's company. In the evenings Miller sang and played piano, while Eleanor frequently read aloud and listened to his tales of a world she had never known. Their leisure time was filled with pranks and surprises, with home movies like "The Pirate and the Lady," in which Miller, dressed as a pirate, kidnapped ER (by then the nation's First Lady), bound her wrists, tied a blindfold around her eyes, and carried her off into the sunset.

Eleanor always kept a room for Earl at Val-Kill and later in her apartment in Greenwich Village. Whether they were more than good friends is open to conjecture. Marion Dickerman and Nancy Cook were distressed at their public display of affection.[58] Joseph Lash records their love ("He interested her physically") but doubts if it were more than an emotional attachment.[59] Blanche Wiesen Cook calls Miller ER's "first romantic involvement" of her middle years but declines to speculate further. "Whatever rules they agreed upon, they were two mutually consenting adults who were engaged in a discreet relationship. . . . [T]hey did whatever they agreed to do."[60] James Roosevelt, who may have had the best opportunity to judge, believed that Lash was overly protective of ER's reputation. "I believe this is a disservice to her, a suggestion that because of her hang-ups she was never able to be a complete woman." According to James:

Mother was self-conscious about Miller's youth, but he did not seem bothered by the difference in years. He encouraged her to take pride in herself, to be herself, to be unafraid of facing the world. He did a lot of good for her. She seemed to draw strength from him when he was by her side, and she came to rely on him. When she had problems, she sought his help. . . . He became part of the family, too, and gave her a great deal of what her husband and we, her sons, failed to give her. Above all, he made her feel that she was a woman. . . . From my observations, I personally believe they were more than friends.[61]

This remarkable relationship, which commenced in 1929, continued until Eleanor's death in 1962. Yet the trail is largely unmarked.[62] There are photographs and a few home movies, but no diaries or letters despite the fact that she and Earl are believed to have corresponded almost daily.[63] Rumors persist that shortly after Eleanor's death the letters were anonymously purchased and destroyed, or purchased and locked away. To date, not a single letter from ER to Earl Miller has surfaced.[64]*

Eleanor's friendship with Miller paralleled Franklin's relationship with Missy LeHand. Just as Missy provided FDR with the adoration and love his wife could not, so Miller made up for what Franklin could not give. Remarkably, both ER and Franklin recognized, accepted, and encouraged the arrangement. Missy and Earl became members of the family. Eleanor gave Missy the larger bedroom near FDR's in Albany while she took a smaller one down the hall, and Franklin was equally attentive to Earl's requirements. Eleanor and Franklin were strong-willed people who cared greatly for each other's happiness but realized their own inability to provide for it.

* Miller was married three times, briefly and unsuccessfully. In 1932 and again in 1941 he is said to have married to quell rumors about himself and ER. After 1929 he and Eleanor had become constant companions in Albany, and gossip abounded. "That's why I got married in 1932 with plenty of publicity. I got married with someone I wasn't in love with. Same with the second marriage. But I was never successful in killing the gossip."

In 1947, during divorce proceedings initiated by his third wife, Simone, it was alleged that Miller was conducting an adulterous affair with ER and a packet of her letters to him was introduced into the proceedings. The trial judge awarded Mrs. Miller a considerable but undisclosed settlement and custody of their two children and ordered the letters sealed. (Eleanor was godmother to both children.) There was minimum publicity, although New York *Daily News* columnist Ed Sullivan wrote, "Navy Commander's wife will rock the country if she names the co-respondent in her divorce action!!!" Eleanor's FBI file also contains a reference to the proceedings in *Miller v. Miller.* On October 4, 1947, the New York field office informed Clyde Tolson, J. Edgar Hoover's deputy, that Mrs. Miller "is planning to sue her husband for divorce and she will name Eleanor Roosevelt as correspondent." (Microfilm, FDRL.) In 1984, Joseph Lash reported that Eleanor was devastated by the proceedings, "especially because of their possible impact on her children." Joseph P. Lash, interview with Earl Miller, reprinted in *Love, Eleanor* 119 (New York: Doubleday, 1982); Lash, *A World of Love* 296–297 (New York: Doubleday, 1984); New York *Daily News,* January 13, 1947.

THIRTEEN

NOMINATION

I pledge you, I pledge myself,
to a New Deal for the American people.
—FRANKLIN D. ROOSEVELT, JULY 2, 1932

THE DAY AFTER FDR's reelection, James Farley, at Louis Howe's instigation, threw the governor's hat into the presidential ring. "I do not see how Mr. Roosevelt can escape becoming the next presidential nominee of his party," Farley told a hastily assembled press conference, "even if no one should raise a finger to bring it about."[1] Neither Howe nor Farley had cleared the announcement with FDR. Both were convinced it was time to strike, taking the tide of victory at the flood. If Roosevelt disagreed, he could repudiate them.

"I was in doubt as to how he would take it," Farley recalled. But the worry proved groundless. When he reached FDR by phone in Albany, the governor laughed. "Whatever you said, Jim, is all right with me."[2] Roosevelt immediately called reporters into his office and issued his own statement: "I am giving no consideration or thought or time to anything except the duties of Governorship. You can add that this applies to any candidacy, national or otherwise in 1932."[3] It was vintage Roosevelt. Publicly, Farley was disavowed; privately, he and Howe had been flashed a green light to proceed. Roosevelt was committed. "Eddie," he confided to Bronx chieftain Edward J. Flynn, "I believe I can be nominated for the Presidency in 1932 on the Democratic ticket."[4]

Roosevelt left day-to-day management of the campaign to Howe and Farley. Howe was FDR's alter ego. He had little need to consult "the Boss" because after working with Franklin for twenty years he knew precisely what moves to make and when to make them. He was a backroom man without equal in Democratic politics, and his loyalty to Roosevelt was legendary. As Farley noted, "Louis Howe thought of nothing else during his waking hours other than how to secure the party's nomination for the Governor."[5] For his part, Farley was the perfect complement, the outside man to Howe's inside. A tall, jovial Irishman whose smooth skin and bald head made him resemble a peeled egg, Farley was a joiner, a mixer, and a glad-hander who never met a ward heeler he could not charm—and whose name he never forgot.[6] Like Howe, he was unencumbered by ideology, other than partisan attachment to the Democratic party. Unlike Howe, he could work with anyone and was a master at grassroots political organization. They not only made a remarkable team, they liked each other. Farley, seventeen years younger, did not encroach on Howe's role as FDR's deputy, and Howe recognized the skill Farley brought to the effort.

While Howe and Farley busied themselves launching a letter-writing campaign on FDR's behalf, Roosevelt focused on the economic crisis. By the winter of 1930–31, the nation and the State of New York had fallen into the trough of the Depression. Unemployment, which stood at 4 million in March 1930, zoomed to 8 million in March 1931. Desperate men selling apples appeared on urban street corners, breadlines stretched block after block, community soup kitchens ladled out thin porridge, and "Hoovervilles"—little settlements of tin shacks, abandoned autos, and discarded packing crates—were springing up in the dumps and railroad yards of big cities to house the dispossessed. Every week, every day, more workers joined the ranks of despair. Hoover responded in February 1931 by urging Americans to embrace the principles of local responsibility and mutual self-help. If we depart from those principles, said the president, we "have struck at the roots of self-government."[7]

Confronted with the reluctance of federal authorities to take action, FDR summoned the New York legislature into special session. Breaking with the tradition of what economic historians call the "night watchman state," Roosevelt asked the legislature to immediately appropriate $20 million to provide useful work where possible and, where such work could not be found, to provide the needy "with food against starvation and with clothing and shelter against suffering."

In broad terms I assert that modern society, acting through its government, owes the definite obligation to prevent the starvation or dire want of any of its fellow men and women who try to maintain themselves but cannot. . . . To these unfortunate citizens aid must be extended by government—not as a matter of charity but as a matter of social duty.[8]

Roosevelt's speech to the legislature on August 28, 1931, marked the genesis of the New Deal. The term was not used: that would come in FDR's acceptance speech the following year. But the idea that government had the definite responsibility—a "social duty"—to use the resources of the state to prevent distress and to promote the general welfare was first suggested at that time. The speech was written at Hyde Park by FDR and Sam Rosenman, and reflected how Roosevelt's thinking had evolved.[9] In addition to the $20 million relief package, the governor sought the establishment of a new state agency, the Temporary Emergency Relief Administration (TERA), to distribute the funds. He also asked the legislature to raise personal income taxes by 50 percent to pay for the relief effort.* New York was the first state to establish a relief agency, and TERA immediately became a model for other states—New Jersey, Rhode Island, Illinois—as well as a prototype for the Federal Emergency Relief Administration, created by FDR in 1933.

To head TERA, Roosevelt obtained the services of Jesse Straus, president of R. H. Macy department stores, a lifelong Democrat and one of the most respected businessmen in the state. (Straus would later serve as FDR's ambassador to France.) Straus was given a free hand to organize the agency. He chose as his executive director a forty-two-year-old social worker originally from Iowa, Harry L. Hopkins, who at the time was unknown to Roosevelt or to any of Roosevelt's advisers. Hopkins was an inspired choice. A gifted administrator who proved he could deliver aid swiftly with a minimum of overhead, Hopkins gave the relief effort an intensity that propelled him to Roosevelt's attention. When Straus resigned in the spring of 1932, FDR named Hopkins to succeed him. In the next six years TERA assisted some 5 million people—40 percent of the population of New York State—at a cost of $1.155 billion. At the end of that period, 70 percent of those helped had returned to the workforce.[10]

Roosevelt's first skirmish for the presidential nomination erupted unexpectedly with the ultraconservative, Al Smith–appointed leadership of the Democratic National Committee. Acting on Smith's behalf, party chairman

---

* When Roosevelt spoke, only 300,000 New Yorkers paid state income tax and the graduated rate reached a maximum of 2.33 percent for incomes above $100,000 (in current dollars, that would be an income of $1.2 million). For a single person earning $5,000 in 1931, the increase FDR requested would amount to $12.50. For a head of family with two dependents, the increase would be $1. New York State Tax Commission figures, cited in *1931 Public Papers of Governor Franklin D. Roosevelt* 178–179 (Albany, N.Y.: J. B. Lyon, 1937).

John Jakob Raskob and his deputy, former Treasury assistant secretary Jouett
Shouse, sought to preempt the 1932 Democratic platform by having the National Committee commit the party to the repeal of Prohibition and support
for the hyperprotectionist Smoot-Hawley Tariff Act of 1930.* Aside from stak-
ing out the ground to facilitate Smith's renomination (Smith had already endorsed the tariff[11]), Raskob and Shouse hoped to embarrass Roosevelt and
drive a wedge between him and the rural wing of the party. Neither the chairman nor his deputy believed that FDR, as governor of New York, would dare
break with Smith.[12] And to support the proposed platform, even to acquiesce
and remain silent, would surely alienate those southern and western Democrats who were flirting with Franklin—men like Cordell Hull, Burton K.
Wheeler, and Harry F. Byrd of Virginia—all of whom were militantly dry and
even more vehemently antitariff.[13]

Raskob proved too clever by half. Instead of splitting Roosevelt from his potential southern and western supporters, the party chairman gave FDR the opportunity to consolidate his coalition. When news of Raskob's preemptive plan
leaked from Washington, Roosevelt placed himself at the head of the opposition. Hull feared that Raskob wanted to align the Democratic party with the
economic policies of Herbert Hoover. Byrd was incensed at Smith's power
grab. Traditionally, party platforms are drafted at the national convention, and
both Hull and Byrd asked Roosevelt to intervene. "I am appealing to you to
prevent an action which I understand is contemplated by the National Democratic Committee," wrote Byrd. "The Democratic Committee has no right to
make a platform for the party," he said. Byrd told Roosevelt the move would
divide Democrats and pave the way for Hoover's reelection. "I know you have
the interests of the party at heart just as much as I have, and I feel you under-

---

* The Smoot-Hawley Tariff Act (46 Stat. 590 (1930)) almost doubled the already high
American duties on imports and is widely credited with accelerating the decline in world
trade and exacerbating the Depression as other nations quickly raised tariffs in response.
President Hoover ceremoniously signed the act with six golden pens and, despite the almost
unanimous opinion of the nation's economists to the contrary, proclaimed it a significant
advance in protecting American jobs. 1 *State Papers of Herbert Hoover* 314–318, W. W.
Myers, ed. (New York: Doubleday, Doran, 1934). Also see Douglas A. Irwin, "From Smoot-
Hawley to Reciprocal Trade Agreements," in Michael D. Bondo, Claudia Goldin, and Eugene N. White, eds., *The Defining Moment: The Great Depression and the American Economy
in the Twentieth Century* 325–344 (Chicago: University of Chicago Press, 1998).

stand our Southern condition better than many other leaders. Prompt action on your part will be necessary."[14]

Once again Roosevelt had been handed a golden opportunity. "You are absolutely right," he wrote Byrd. "The Democratic National Committee has no authority, in any shape, manner or form, to pass on or recommend national issues or policies."[15]

Before breaking with Smith, Roosevelt asked the party's former nominee to rein Raskob in. "I do not know what the plans for next Thursday's meeting of the National Committee are," FDR wrote, "but the more I hear from different parts of the country, the more certain I am that it would be very contrary to the established powers and precedents of the National Committee, were they to pass resolutions *of any kind* affecting party policies at this time."[16] Smith did not reply but two days later held a press conference at which he declared he could see no objection to the National Committee expressing whatever opinion it wished.[17]

The battle lines were drawn. Having observed the amenities, Roosevelt opened fire. He instructed Farley to convene a special meeting of the New York State Democratic Committee in Albany on March 2. That morning, at a breakfast meeting in FDR's bedroom, Louis Howe, Ed Flynn, and Farley drafted a resolution endorsing Roosevelt's position that the National Committee had no authority to commit the party on any issue arising between conventions. The resolution was introduced by Flynn that afternoon and carried unanimously.[18]

With three days remaining before the National Committee would meet, Roosevelt, Farley, and Howe worked the phones, lining up proxies from committeemen who would not be present. When Farley took the train to Washington on March 4, he held enough proxies to defeat Raskob's motions 2 to 1. Raskob recognized the inevitable, withdrew his proposals before a vote, and hunkered down before an onslaught of southern righteousness. Farley, seated next to Hull at the meeting to make a point, lay back and said nothing. "I think on the whole the meeting did no harm," Roosevelt wrote Buffalo's Norman Mack afterward. "The thing we must work for now is the avoidance of harsh words and no sulking in tents."[19]

For Roosevelt, Raskob's ill-fated maneuver proved a godsend. From that time on, Hull wrote in his *Memoirs,* the southern leaders took Roosevelt seriously and rallied round him as the one candidate who could deliver them from the Smith-Raskob alliance.[20] FDR shared the antitariff sentiments of the

South and West, and on Prohibition he was damp: neither wet nor dry but in favor of leaving the question to the states. That was satisfactory to most southerners.[21]

While Farley dealt with the National Committee in Washington, Louis Howe worked to raise money for the fledgling campaign. FDR had not yet announced, but already contributions were flowing in. Old friends were first off the mark. In March 1931, Henry Morgenthau, Sr., William H. Woodin, and Frank C. Walker, a New York attorney, got the ball rolling with gifts of $5,000 [$60,000 currently] each. Herbert Lehman, Basil O'Connor, Jesse Straus, Ed Flynn, and Joseph P. Kennedy quickly followed suit. Sara chipped in her share, as did publisher Robert W. Bingham of the Louisville *Courier-Journal* (later FDR's ambassador to Great Britain).* The entertainment industry, represented by the moviemaker Harry M. Warner and Broadway impresario Eddie Dowling, did its share as well. James W. Gerard, who had defeated FDR for the Democratic senatorial nomination in 1914, was a particularly generous contributor, always ready to open his checkbook when a campaign payroll came due. Colonel Edward M. House, whose New York apartment was across the street from the Roosevelt home on East Sixty-fifth, was also an early contributor.[22]

At the end of March, Jesse Straus commissioned a presidential poll of delegates and alternates who had attended the 1928 Democratic convention. Purportedly, Straus conducted the poll without FDR's knowledge.[23] Opinion polling was in its infancy in 1931, and the results garnered front-page coverage throughout the country. Roosevelt was the undisputed front-runner. Of the forty-four states that responded, FDR led in thirty-nine.[24] Smith led in three (Massachusetts, Connecticut, and Delaware); Governor Albert C. Ritchie was Maryland's favorite son, as was Senator Joseph T. Robinson in Arkansas. Among the 844 delegates who responded, Roosevelt was favored by 478; Smith by 125; the industrialist Owen D. Young of General Electric by 75; Ritchie by 39; Robinson by 38; and Newton D. Baker of Ohio, Woodrow Wilson's secretary of war, by 35.[25]

Straus commissioned four more polls that spring among Democratic busi-

* "I have given Mr. Howe a check for $5,000 out of *principal* [not income]," Sara wrote Franklin on May 9, 1932. "If you are not nominated, I should not *weep,* but it would be money thrown away." FDRL. (Sara's emphasis).

nessmen, bank presidents, and corporate directors. All showed Roosevelt well ahead—surprising, given FDR's identification with the rural, progressive wing of the party and the conservative, probusiness stance of both Smith and Young. A nationwide survey by twenty-five Scripps-Howard newspapers that summer indicated that Roosevelt was not only the Democratic front-runner, but would defeat President Hoover in the general election.[26]

Buoyed by Straus's polls, Roosevelt decided it was time to troll for delegates. He asked Ed Flynn to be his emissary and undertake a cross-country tour to confer with party leaders. Flynn demurred. "I realized my own limitations. I was not an easy mixer. I was no greeter or hand-shaker. I felt I could do nothing effective by merely going into a state in which I knew no one."[27] At Flynn's suggestion, FDR turned to Farley. A born salesman and political drummer, Farley was the best possible delegate hunter Roosevelt could have chosen.*

At the end of June 1931 Farley embarked on a whirlwind tour of eighteen states west of the Mississippi. The trip coincided with the annual convention of the Benevolent and Protective Order of Elks, which was meeting that year in Seattle. Farley was an enthusiastic Elk, and the convention provided plausible cover for the journey. His itinerary was plotted by Roosevelt on a Rand-McNally map of the United States, and Howe provided the necessary introductions to national committeemen and state chairmen. The trip, Farley wrote later, "did more than anything else to give me a grip on national politics. I always look back upon it as a sort of graduation from the political minor league."[28]

In nineteen days, Farley met more than eleven hundred local Democratic leaders. The message he heard everywhere was the same: Democrats wanted a winner. Farley found a smattering of support for Young and Ritchie and a few ardent Catholics for Smith, but Roosevelt was the overwhelming favorite. "Farley," said William Howes, the Democratic committeeman in South Dakota, "I'm damned tired of backing losers. In my opinion Roosevelt can sweep the country, and I'm going to support him."[29]

---

* Charles Michelson, the publicity director of the DNC and no friend of the Roosevelt campaign, later described Farley's journey with awe: "The hard-boiled, Tammany-tainted politician they expected to find in the West turned out to be a genial, personable fellow who neither drank nor smoked, who carried along pictures of his wife and children, who attended church with regularity, and who never obtruded his abstentions on those convivially inclined." Michelson, *The Ghost Talks* 135 (New York: G. P. Putnam's Sons, 1944).

Farley passed the good news to Roosevelt. "I am satisfied, Governor, that the leaders want to be on the bandwagon. I have also discovered that there are a lot of Democratic candidates for Governor and state offices who believe there is a real chance of winning with you as the nominee, and they feel absolutely no hope if anyone else is named; so these potential candidates are your strongest boosters."[30]

While Farley cultivated Democrats in the West, FDR courted the South. That summer he hosted visiting delegations from Alabama, Mississippi, and Tennessee at Warm Springs and met repeatedly with Georgia's governor, the young Richard Russell. "As far as the South goes," said Senator William J. Harris of the Peach State, "it is all Roosevelt."[31] By the fall of 1931, Roosevelt had secured the support of Senators Pat Harrison of Mississippi, James Byrnes of South Carolina, and Cordell Hull of Tennessee. Georgia, which considered FDR an adopted son, was solid for Roosevelt, and the Democratic organization in Alabama leaned that way as well. "The situation is very odd and my friends in the South and West strongly advise me to let things drift," FDR wrote his friend James Hoey in September, "as the great majority of States through their regular organizations are showing every friendliness towards me."[32]

If there was an Achilles heel in the Roosevelt campaign, it was the health issue. Already FDR's opponents were circulating unfounded gossip concerning his condition. In April 1931 *Time* magazine joined the chorus, repeating the rumor that while Roosevelt might be mentally qualified for the presidency, he was "utterly unfit physically."[33] FDR was jolted. He had undergone a rigorous physical examination by a bevy of insurance doctors six months before, and his health was excellent. Yet the whispering campaign continued. "I find that there is a deliberate attempt to create the impression that my health is such as would make it impossible for me to fulfill the duties of President," he complained to his old friend Hamilton Miles. "I shall appreciate whatever my friends may have to say in their personal correspondence to dispel this perfectly silly piece of propaganda."[34]

Again, events played into Roosevelt's hands. Earle Looker, a respected national journalist who just happened to be a Republican, challenged FDR to undergo a medical examination to prove "you are sufficiently recovered to assure your supporters that you could stand the strain of the Presidency."[35] Roosevelt accepted the challenge immediately.[36] Dr. Lindsay R. Williams, director of the New York Academy of Medicine, was asked to select a panel of

eminent physicians, including a brain specialist, to conduct the examination.*
In addition, Looker was invited to visit Albany unannounced and observe the
governor whenever he wished and as often as he wished.

The panel examined Roosevelt at his East Sixty-fifth Street town house on
April 29, 1931. "We have today carefully examined Governor Roosevelt," they
wired Looker. "We believe that his health and powers of endurance are such as
to allow him to meet any demand of private and public life. We find that his
organs and functions are sound in all respects. There is no anemia. The chest
is exceptionally well developed, and the spinal column is absolutely normal; all
its segments are in perfect alignment and free from disease. He has neither
pain nor ache at any time. . . . Governor Roosevelt can walk all necessary distances and can maintain a standing position without fatigue."[37]

Looker's personal observations coincided with the specialists' findings.
Three times he called on FDR unannounced and spent the day and part of the
evening with him. "I observed him working and resting," Looker wrote. "I
noted the alertness of his movements, the sparkle of his eyes, the vigor of his
gestures. I saw his strength under the strain of long working periods. Insofar as
I had observed him, I came to the conclusion that he seemed able to take more
punishment than many men ten years younger. Merely his knees were not
much good to him."[38]†

During one of his unannounced visits Looker asked Eleanor if she thought
FDR could stand the strain of the presidency.

---

* The blue-ribbon panel appointed by Williams was composed of Dr. Samuel W. Lambert,
former dean of the College of Physicians and Surgeons at Columbia University; Dr. Russell
A. Hibbs, surgeon in chief of the New York Orthopedic Hospital; and Dr. Foster Kennedy,
professor of neurology at Cornell University Medical College and president of the New York
Neurological Society.

† Looker offers an insight into an era of different standards:

> When Roosevelt first came to Albany as governor the newspaper correspondents
> were confronted with the necessity of deciding whether or not to comment on his
> walking. They decided that no comment was required. It was a gentleman's agree-
> ment among themselves which soon included the news photographers in Albany. As
> happens with all public men, the cameras have sometimes caught the governor in an
> awkward pose. Without suggestion from anyone interested, the plates have been de-
> stroyed by the photographers themselves. They have done this because they feel that
> the awkward pictures do not give a true impression of the governor.

Earle Looker, *This Man Roosevelt* 146–147 (New York: Brewer, Warren & Putnam, 1932).

"If the infantile paralysis didn't kill him, the Presidency won't," ER replied.[39]

Looker published the medical findings in *Liberty* magazine. At five cents a copy, *Liberty* was the nation's leading mass-circulation journal, with Theodore Dreiser, Ernest Hemingway, and William Faulkner occasionally gracing its weekly pages. "From the specialist examination, as well as from my own observation," wrote Looker, "I am able to say unhesitatingly that every rumor of Franklin Roosevelt's physical incapacity can be unqualifiedly defined as false."[40] For the Roosevelt campaign, Looker's article could not have been more opportune. Howe ordered 200,000 reprints, sending a copy to every name on the numerous mailing lists Farley had assembled.

Throughout the autumn of 1931 Farley and Howe continued their canvassing for delegates; FDR rested briefly at Warm Springs; and Raskob and Shouse took another run at the platform. At the end of November the party chairman announced he was polling the 90,000 contributors to the 1928 campaign on the question of Prohibition preparatory to the next meeting of the Democratic National Committee on January 9, 1932.[41] It was a rerun of the March 5 battle, with Farley scurrying for proxies and forcing Raskob to back down once again. With Roosevelt's southern and western allies in firm control of the National Committee, Chicago was selected as the site of the 1932 convention.* In an even more impressive display of muscle, Robert Jackson of New Hampshire, a staunch Roosevelt supporter, was elected to the vacant position of national secretary—Farley's first but very obvious move to wrest control of the party machinery from Raskob.[42]

On Saturday, January 23, 1932, FDR announced his candidacy—carefully timed to gain maximum coverage in the nation's Sunday-morning newspapers.[43] The announcement coincided with the Democratic Territorial Convention in Alaska, which had just instructed its six delegates to the National

---

* Four cities had been in contention for the convention: Atlantic City, Chicago, Kansas City, and San Francisco. FDR preferred Kansas City, where Tom Pendergast's organization could pack the galleries, but settled for Chicago to avoid Atlantic City and San Francisco. An Atlantic City convention would have fallen under the control of New Jersey boss Frank Hague, a Smith stalwart, and in San Francisco newspaper mogul William Randolph Hearst would have held sway. Roosevelt and Hearst shared a long-standing antipathy. "I take it we shall be able to prevent the Convention from going to Atlantic City or San Francisco," FDR wrote a friend on the eve of the National Committee vote. Steve Neal, *Happy Days Are Here Again* 12–14 (New York: HarperCollins, 2004).

Convention to vote for Roosevelt under the unit rule.[44] Alaska was the first jurisdiction to select delegates in 1932, and Farley had taken pains to ensure the Roosevelt campaign launched on a high note.[45] The following week, county caucuses met in Washington State and instructed delegates to the state convention to back Roosevelt, who won all sixteen votes.

Roosevelt's quick success energized the opposition. Al Smith announced his availability on February 6. He would not campaign for the nomination, said Smith, but "If the Democratic National Convention, after careful consideration, should decide it wants me to lead I will make the fight."[46] Raskob and Shouse, heading their own Stop Roosevelt movement, encouraged states to send uninstructed delegations to Chicago or to back favorite sons. There was no way to defeat Roosevelt before the convention, but it might be possible to deny him the two-thirds vote necessary for nomination. When Farley announced Roosevelt's candidacy on January 23, he claimed that FDR had the solid support of 678 delegates a thumping majority but still 92 short of the 770 that would be required.[47] If the anti-Roosevelt forces could prevent a first-ballot victory, they might deadlock the Convention and force a compromise choice. The logic of the Stop Roosevelt movement carried a built-in incentive for favorite sons to join the race. If the Convention deadlocked, any one of them might emerge as the nominee.

For Roosevelt it was a question of momentum: Could he roll up delegates fast enough to prevent favorite sons from sprouting in the hinterland? In 1932 seventeen states chose delegates through presidential primaries; the others used various forms of conventions. After Washington, the next state to choose was Oklahoma, which in convention instructed its twenty-two delegates to vote for its governor, "Alfalfa Bill" Murray, a rustic Plains populist—Will Rogers without the humor—who had no chance of winning the nomination but who might eat into FDR's strength in the West.

The first primary state was New Hampshire, on March 6, where Roosevelt and Smith went head to head. The Northeast was considered Al Smith country, and the Happy Warrior anticipated an easy victory.[48] Instead, it was a landslide for Roosevelt—with all the attendant publicity. Howe and Farley, aiming for a knockout, spent more money in New Hampshire than any other state. Roosevelt was supported by the state Democratic organization and cruised to victory with 61.7 percent of the vote, taking all eight delegates. FDR's margin of victory might have been even larger had not a late-winter blizzard in the northern part of the state reduced voter turnout. Four days after the sweep in New Hampshire, FDR carried the Minnesota convention, winning all twenty-four delegates and prompting Smith's supporters to storm out, hold a rump session, and pick a rival delegation. This was little concern to Farley and Howe since Roosevelt would have a clear majority in Chicago, and when push came to shove the Roosevelt Minnesota delegation would be seated.[49]

North Dakota voted next. Smith was not on the ballot (his campaign manager failed to file the necessary petitions), but Governor Murray had qualified and Alfalfa Bill was expected to do well, his plainspoken appeal falling on receptive farm belt ears. "Roosevelt may have the politicians," Murray told his brother George, a North Dakota farmer, "but I will have the people."[50]

This was the first face-off between Roosevelt and Murray, and FDR went all out. He dragooned Senator Burton K. Wheeler from nearby Montana to spearhead his campaign,[51] relied on the state organization to turn out the vote, and vowed to provide emergency relief for western farmers if elected. Like New Hampshire, North Dakota was another landslide. Roosevelt polled 62.1 percent of the vote and won nine of the state's ten delegates. Equally significant, voter turnout was three times greater than expected, suggesting that large numbers of Republicans had crossed over to vote in the Democratic primary.[52] The size of FDR's victories in New Hampshire and North Dakota reflected not only his attractiveness as a candidate but the finely crafted campaign organization Howe and Farley had put together. They did not miss filing deadlines, they worked closely with Democratic leaders in states that were friendly, and they did not forget the precinct workers in the trenches.* Roosevelt faced Murray again in Nebraska, West Virginia, Oregon, and Florida and won by increasingly lopsided margins.

FDR's momentum continued. The week after North Dakota went to the polls, Georgia gave Roosevelt a resounding 8-to-1 victory against a stand-in favorite son.[53] FDR captured all twenty-eight delegates and carried Warm Springs 218–1. The following week Iowa and Maine met in convention. The

* Long before FDR announced his candidacy, Farley had collected the names and addresses of all Democratic precinct captains in the United States—roughly 140,000. When Roosevelt announced on January 23, he sent each one a letter and Farley followed up with several more, always signed in his trademark green ink. Rarely has a primary campaign been more meticulously organized. Roy V. Peel and Thomas C. Donnelly, *The 1932 Campaign: An Analysis* 68–69 (New York: Farrar & Rinehart, 1935).

Stop Roosevelt forces had been active in both states, and there was substantial support for sending uncommitted delegations to Chicago. Farley made a special trip to Davenport to keep the Iowans in line, and Robert Jackson intervened in Maine.[54] Both states voted to send delegations to Chicago pledged to Roosevelt.

"We always looked back upon March 29 as a red-letter day for the Roosevelt candidacy, if not the turning point of the entire campaign," wrote Farley. "Iowa gave us twenty-six votes and Maine twelve. Those two states are far apart on the map—their people have little in common politically. When they took similar action on the same day, it demonstrated to us and to the country that Roosevelt had nationwide appeal."[55]

Missouri and Maryland also met in convention at the end of March. As expected, Missouri voted to send its thirty-six delegates to Chicago pledged to its favorite son, former senator James M. Reed. In 1928, Missouri had supported Reed down the line, but this time he was a stalking horse for the real boss of Missouri politics, Tom Pendergast. "Pendergast assured me," a Roosevelt scout wrote Howe, "that he informed Senator Reed that he might have the Missouri delegation as a complimentary vote until it was needed by Roosevelt." At that time Pendergast said he would cast Missouri's vote as a unit for FDR.[56]

Maryland, also as expected, chose to support its favorite son, Governor Albert C. Ritchie. Unlike Reed, or Murray for that matter, Ritchie was a serious candidate who was hoping for a convention deadlock. A probusiness Democrat, Ritchie had been governor of Maryland since 1920. He opposed government intervention in the economy ("Let natural forces take their course, as free and untrammeled as possible") and was the beau ideal of the party's conservatives.[57] As The New York Times reported, "Governor Ritchie is looked upon as the candidate to whom the anti-Roosevelt forces may rally if they can delay Governor Roosevelt's nomination."[58]

Maryland was the first state to defect from the Roosevelt column. But the loss was offset the following day, when Arkansas senator Joseph T. Robinson withdrew from the race. Robinson told supporters he did not wish to contribute to another deadlocked convention. Left without its favorite son, Arkansas chose an uninstructed delegation, which gave Roosevelt all eighteen votes under the unit rule.

With the campaign unfolding as planned—actually, better than planned—Roosevelt considered the future. Howe and Farley were unexcelled as political managers but had little interest in policy. That deficiency would become a problem unless it was fixed. Sam Rosenman suggested that FDR tap the universities. "You have been having good experiences with college professors. If we can get a small group together willing to give us some time, they can prepare memoranda for you. You'll want to talk with them yourself, and maybe out of all the talk some concrete ideas will come."[59]

Roosevelt was intrigued. Did Rosenman have anyone in mind? he asked. Rosenman suggested Raymond Moley at Columbia. "He believes in your social philosophy and objectives, and he has a clear and forceful style of writing." Roosevelt agreed. "We'll have to keep this whole thing pretty quiet," he told Rosenman. "Do you think these professors can be trusted not to talk about it on the outside? If it gets into the papers too soon it might be bad."[60]

Roosevelt thought it over while Rosenman wheeled him into his bedroom for the night. FDR shifted himself from his wheelchair to his bed. "Well," he said, "we'll just have to take our chances on that."[61]

Raymond Moley was a Columbia political science professor who specialized in criminal justice. FDR had appointed him to the Governor's Commission on the Administration of Justice, and from time to time Moley had drafted policy statements for Roosevelt on judicial reform. In that capacity he had worked with Rosenman, and it was natural that Rosenman should have suggested him. Among academics, Moley was an organizer and manager, not a scholar, and he became, in Arthur Schlesinger's words, a "ringmaster of the experts," a middleman for their ideas.[62] When approached by Rosenman, Moley not only accepted but recommended a number of his colleagues who might be willing to contribute. Two who made the cut were Rexford G. Tugwell and Adolf A. Berle.* Tugwell's specialty was agriculture, and he was highly regarded as an articulate, original thinker who liked to shock his audience and often succeeded. Berle had been a child prodigy, graduating from Harvard Law School at twenty-one. He was now thirty-seven and a star at Columbia's law

---

* Two Columbia faculty members who did not work out were the distinguished political scientist Lindsay Rogers and the equally distinguished economist James W. Angell. Rogers committed the unpardonable error of submitting the same tariff memorandum to Roosevelt and Al Smith, while Angell proved unable to provide the crisp answers FDR wanted, unencumbered by academic hedging. Raymond Moley, *After Seven Years* 15–17 (New York: Harper & Brothers, 1939); Adolf A. Berle interview, Columbia Oral History Project, Columbia University.

school, where he was the resident expert on corporate finance.[63] Joining the group were FDR's law partner Basil "Doc" O'Connor and Rosenman. Roosevelt called the group his privy council. James Kieran, writing in *The New York Times*, referred to it as "FDR's brains trust."[64] That name, shortened to "brain trust," stuck. Roosevelt did not use the brain trust, or privy council, to provide him with new ideas. He engaged its members to flesh out, articulate, and refine the position he had come to embrace: a readiness to use the power of government to redress the economic ills from which the nation suffered.[65]

The first product of the brain trust was Roosevelt's "forgotten man" speech of April 7, 1932. Roosevelt was scheduled to speak for ten minutes coast to coast on NBC's *Lucky Strike Hour,* sponsored by the American Tobacco Company. He told Moley he wanted something that would address the economic problems confronting the nation. Written jointly by FDR, Moley, and Rosenman at the executive mansion, the speech was a shot across the bow of the nation's economic conservatives.[66] Roosevelt excoriated the Hoover administration for attacking the symptoms of the Depression, not the cause. "It has sought temporary relief from the top down rather than permanent relief from the bottom up. These unhappy times call for the building of plans that put their faith once more in the forgotten man at the bottom of the economic pyramid."[67]

The following week Roosevelt carried the message to the Democratic party's Jefferson Day dinner in Saint Paul, Minnesota. The economic problem was national in scope, said FDR, and required "imaginative and purposeful planning."[68] Roosevelt's final speech before the convention was delivered at Oglethorpe University in Georgia on May 22, 1932.* "Must the country remain hungry and jobless while raw materials stand unused and factories idle?" he asked. "The country needs, the country demands, bold, persistent experimentation. Take a method and try it. If it fails admit it frankly and try another. But above all, try something."[69]

When the convention met on June 27, Roosevelt was still about 100 votes

---

* Roosevelt's Oglethorpe University speech was drafted by Ernest K. Lindley of the *New York Herald Tribune.* Lindley was one of the pool of reporters covering FDR and had teased Roosevelt about the quality of his previous speeches. FDR jokingly dared Lindley to do better, and Lindley, with the assistance of other members of the pool, drafted the speech. Roosevelt made only minor changes. Ernest K. Lindley, interview with Earland Irving Carlson, in *Franklin D. Roosevelt's Fight for the Presidential Nomination, 1928–1932* 417n (Ph.D. dissertation, University of Illinois, 1955).

short of the 770 needed for the nomination. Except for the Yankee Kingdom (Maine, New Hampshire, and Vermont), he had lost the Northeast to Smith; the delegations from New York and Pennsylvania were split; and in Virginia, Harry F. Byrd, anticipating that lightning might strike, had emerged as a favorite son. In the heartland, Ohio's 52 votes were locked in behind its governor, George White—presumably a stand-in for Newton D. Baker; Illinois, with 58 votes, was backing its favorite son, Senator J. Hamilton Lewis; and Indiana's delegation (30 votes) was uncommitted. The biggest obstacle—also the biggest surprise—lay in the West, where Texas and California (a total of 90 votes) were bound to House Speaker John Nance Garner.* Add Ritchie in Maryland and Murray in Oklahoma, and the recipe for a deadlocked convention seemed at hand. The key, as Roosevelt confided to Josephus Daniels, lay in the votes committed to Garner. If he could secure them, said FDR, that "would cinch the matter."[70]

"The brethren sniff the scent of battle," H. L. Mencken wrote as the delegates descended on Chicago. "The air will be full of hair and ears within twenty-four hours. God save the Republic."[71] The new Chicago Stadium, where the convention would meet, dwarfed Madison Square Garden and was the first indoor arena to provide an unobstructed view from every seat. Twenty-five thousand people could be accommodated in the galleries and another six thousand on the floor. And the stadium was air-conditioned—not necessarily a good omen to those who traditionally counted on the summer heat to break a convention deadlock.[72]

Farley and Ed Flynn went to Chicago a week early to set up Roosevelt headquarters, stroke delegates as they arrived, and keep watch over the three principal committees of the convention: Rules, Credentials, and the Platform. Given their overall majority, the Roosevelt forces controlled all three, but there were any number of problems that might arise. "I was aware that the national political field was a new one for me and that one bad slip might prove my undoing," said Farley.[73]

---

* On May 3 Garner had won an unexpected victory against FDR and Smith in the California primary. Supported by the Hearst newspaper chain, California drys, and the hundred thousand members of the Texas Society of California, Garner polled 216,000 votes to FDR's 170,000 and Smith's 138,000, despite the fact that Roosevelt had the backing of the state party organization. Howe and Farley can perhaps be forgiven for not anticipating that the hard-drinking John Garner should win on the votes of California drys.

Flynn said, "We were green at national politics. When Farley and I set off for Chicago we confessed to each other that we felt pretty new at this game."[74]

Their inexperience showed quickly. On Thursday, June 23, Farley convened a strategy session attended by sixty or so leaders in the Roosevelt camp. "Almost before we realized what was taking place," Farley later recalled, "the meeting was stampeded into taking hasty and ill-advised action." Prodded by Senators Huey Long, Burton K. Wheeler, and Cordell Hull, with Josephus Daniels putting in his oar, the conclave voted unanimously to seek abolition of the two-thirds rule—that sacrosanct principle of Democratic conventions since Andrew Jackson first called the party together in 1832.[75] "The incident hit me like a blow on the nose," Farley confessed.[76]

Pro-Roosevelt delegates from the cotton belt were apoplectic. Senator Josiah W. Bailey of North Carolina told Farley that FDR had put his entire southern support at risk. Pat Harrison, who was holding Mississippi for Roosevelt by a single vote, called the proposal "foolhardy and asinine." John Sharp Williams, the grand old man of Southern Democracy, waded in from Yazoo City: "The two-thirds rule has been for a century the South's defense," he telegraphed friends at the convention. "It would be idiotic on her part to surrender it."[77]

With his coalition in danger of falling apart, Roosevelt threw in the towel. In a statement that Farley released to the convention, FDR said he thought the two-thirds rule was undemocratic and should be abolished. "Nevertheless, the issue was not raised until after the delegates to the Convention had been selected, and I decline to permit either myself or my friends to be open to the accusation of poor sportsmanship.... I am accordingly asking my friends in Chicago to cease their activities to secure the adoption of the majority nominating rule."[78]

The first day of the convention was sawdust and sideshow. Senator Alben Barkley of Kentucky, the temporary chairman, treated delegates to a two-hour stemwinder—one of the longest keynote addresses on record. "It had to be a long speech," Will Rogers quipped. "When you start enumerating the things the Republicans have got away with in the last twelve years you have cut yourself out a job."[79] The initial test of strength came on day two, when the convention considered the report of the Credentials Committee and chose a permanent chairman. The credentials of the Louisiana, Minnesota, and Puerto Rico delegations were being challenged by the Stop Roosevelt forces. To lose would not only deprive FDR of the fifty votes involved; it would shift the momentum of the Convention against him.[80]

In all three instances the Credentials Committee had voted to seat the pro-Roosevelt delegations. But a floor fight loomed. Louisiana was first. Long, often predisposed to buffoonery, played it straight and delivered a masterly presentation. Clarence Darrow, Chicago's renowned trial lawyer, said it was "one of the greatest summaries of fact and evidence" he had ever heard.[81] A hush settled over Chicago Stadium as the clerk called the roll of the states. Alabama, Arizona, and Arkansas cast forty-eight votes for Long. California answered with forty-four against. The count seesawed until Michigan, Minnesota, and Mississippi put Long ahead. Roosevelt's lines were holding. The final tally was 638¾–514¼ to seat the Long delegation. Farley later called it "the most vital moment of the Convention."[82] The Minnesota and Puerto Rico delegations were seated in due course by even larger margins.[83]

When it came time to choose a permanent chairman, the Roosevelt forces were in firm control. The organization candidate for the post was Raskob's deputy, Jouett Shouse—whose opposition to Roosevelt was a matter of record. Senator Wheeler had warned FDR several months before the convention that if Shouse became the permanent chairman, "You will never be nominated." Farley said, "Mr. Shouse had permitted his zeal in opposing the Governor to bias his actions."[84] As an alternative the Roosevelt camp chose to support Senator Thomas J. Walsh of Montana. Walsh had chaired the marathon 1924 convention with remarkable evenhandedness and had become a Democratic idol for his role spearheading the Senate's Teapot Dome investigation. The vote was tight, but Roosevelt's ranks held. When Michigan was called, Walsh took the lead and ultimately defeated Shouse 626–528. "It was a fight to the death," Ed Flynn recalled. "Moreover, we had the moral advantage because every delegate in the hall knew that Walsh would be eminently fair. His decisions certainly could not, (and, in fact, were not) called into question."[85]

On day three the convention turned to the platform. The issue was Prohibition. Since the Civil War, no question had been more divisive for Democrats. The struggle between wets and drys had sent the convention of 1924 into 103 ballots, had helped defeat Al Smith in 1928, and now loomed ominously before Roosevelt. The Republicans (who also met in Chicago) had straddled the issue by endorsing state option. "It is not a plank," jeered Barkley in his keynote. "It is a promiscuous agglomeration of scrap lumber."[86]

The mood of the country had changed, influenced perhaps by the Depression. A popular poll by *Literary Digest* found majorities for the repeal of Prohibition in every state except Kansas and North Carolina.[87] In Democratic primaries, dry candidates were falling in droves before wet challengers. Even John D. Rockefeller, a lifelong teetotaler who had funded the Anti-Saloon League, called for repeal. "It is my profound conviction that the benefits of the Eighteenth Amendment are more than outweighed by the evils that have developed and flourished since its adoption," said Rockefeller.[88]

For the Stop Roosevelt forces, the repeal of Prohibition seemed tailor-made to embarrass FDR. Much of Roosevelt's support came from traditionally dry areas in the South and West. With the country shouting for repeal, would he buck the tide and side with his dry supporters? Alternatively, would he back repeal and offend them? The issue before the convention was the plank recommended by the Platform Committee that called for outright repeal, versus the minority plank passing the question to the states.

FDR refused to be drawn in. "Vote as you wish," Farley instructed the Roosevelt delegations. FDR said he would be happy to run on whatever platform the convention adopted. In the free vote that followed, Democrats voted for repeal 934–213. "Early this morning," Arthur Krock reported in *The New York Times*, "the Democratic party went as wet as the seven seas."[89]*

For Al Smith and Governor Ritchie, the vote on repeal rekindled their cam-

---

* Aside from Prohibition, the 1932 Democratic platform was a remarkably harmonious document, drafted by A. Mitchell Palmer and Cordell Hull in Washington and brought to Chicago with FDR's endorsement. Totaling fewer than 1,500 words, it was the shortest platform of any major party in American history. The Depression was blamed on the disastrous economic policies pursued by the Republicans: "They have ruined our foreign trade; destroyed the values of our commodities and products, crippled our banking system, robbed millions of our people of their life savings and thrown millions out of work, produced widespread poverty and brought the government to a state of financial distress unprecedented in time of peace."

Proclaiming the platform "a covenant with the people," the Democrats pledged to reduce federal expenditures, balance the budget, and maintain a sound currency. Yet the core of the document shouted for aggressive government action: an income tax based on the ability to pay, reciprocal tariff agreements, unemployment relief, extensive public works, flood control, aid to agriculture, mortgage assistance, regulation of the securities industry, protection for bank deposits, campaign finance reform, independence for the Philippines, and statehood for Puerto Rico. For the text, see *Proceedings of the 1932 Democratic National Convention* 146–148. (Washington, D.C.: Democratic National Committee, 1932).

paigns. Both had departed from convention tradition to appear at the rostrum and urge adoption of the majority plank. The tumultuous demonstration for Smith—heartfelt and genuine—surprised even the most hardened old pols. Whether the Happy Warrior could convert that sentiment into delegates' votes was on everyone's mind as they left the stadium, eager for the afternoon session when the nominations would begin.

As the convention unfolded, Roosevelt stayed close by the telephone in Albany. Howe and Flynn kept in constant contact with FDR over a direct line in Howe's hotel suite, while Farley marshaled the forces on the floor. From time to time Farley would bring delegates in to talk to Roosevelt. "These conversations were carried on at all hours of the day and night," Flynn recalled. Occasionally a rudimentary speakerphone was rigged up and FDR would talk to an entire state delegation ("My friends from Nebraska . . ."). There was no question who was calling the shots for the campaign. All major decisions were made in Albany. "In most matters," said Flynn, "we found it wise to get Roosevelt's judgment. We did nothing without first consulting him."[90]

The nominating session convened at 3 P.M. Thursday, June 30. More than three thousand delegates and alternates crammed the convention floor, waiting for the oratory to begin. Since Farley's team dominated the Arrangements Committee, the Roosevelt delegations enjoyed prime seating. "We put California behind New York and both of them a half mile away from Texas," said Roosevelt floor leader Arthur Mullen. The galleries, on the other hand, were controlled by Chicago mayor Anton Cermak, who packed them with anyone-but-Roosevelt partisans. FDR's supporters received only one hundred of the twenty-five thousand passes available.[91]

When the clerk called the roll, Alabama yielded to New York, and Judge John E. Mack of Poughkeepsie, FDR's old political mentor, made his way to the podium to nominate Roosevelt. When he concluded, thirty-four state delegations and six of seven territories flooded the aisles, standards aloft, chanting for Roosevelt. Giant FDR banners unfurled from the rafters, and the organist broke into "Anchors Aweigh," Roosevelt's theme song. "Sounds like a funeral march to me," said Ed Flynn, who was in Howe's suite listening to the demonstration. "Why don't we get something peppy for them to play, like 'Happy Days Are Here Again'?" Howe agreed and sent word to the stadium.[92]

From that moment on, "Happy Days" would forever be identified with Franklin Roosevelt and the New Deal. Written by Jack Yellen and Milton Ager for the 1929 Hollywood musical *Chasing Rainbows*, it captured the robust optimism that Roosevelt exuded. As delegates sang and danced, James Roosevelt, FDR's oldest son, grabbed the New York standard and joined the parade, "charging down the aisles like a sophomore storming the goal posts of a rival college after his team had won," said Raymond Daniell in *The New York Times*.[93]

Garner was nominated by Senator Tom Connally, and the organist belted out "The Eyes of Texas" and "California, Here I Come" as the Texas and California delegations trooped the hall. Then Al Smith, "The Sidewalks of New York," and another emotional demonstration as the convention paid homage to its former standard-bearer. "The Smith demonstration was the realest thing in the convention," wrote Kansas City editor William Allen White.[94]

After Smith was nominated, the convention took a three-hour dinner break. On his way back to the convention after the recess, Farley paid a goodwill visit to Garner headquarters and spoke with Sam Rayburn, the Speaker's manager in Chicago. It was not the first time they had talked. Farley had dangled the vice presidency before, and now made the offer "This is the time," he told Rayburn. "I know positively that we can bring about his [Garner's] nomination."

Rayburn asked Farley what would be necessary.

"Have the Texas delegation record its vote for Garner on the first ballot, and then before the result is announced switch to Roosevelt."

Rayburn declined. "We've got a lot of people up here from Texas who've never been to a convention before, and they've got to vote for Garner a few times. How many ballots can you hold your lines without breaking?"

"Three ballots," said Farley. "Four, maybe five."

"Well," Rayburn replied, "we must let the convention go on for a while, even if we are interested in the Vice-Presidency, and I'm not saying that we are."[95]

When the convention resumed, six favorite sons were placed in nomination, concluding at 3 A.M. with Alfalfa Bill Murray and a fourteen-minute demonstration led by the Girls Kiltie Band of Ardmore, Oklahoma. Seconding speeches followed, the anti-Roosevelt forces stretching the festivities out as long as possible. For Farley, whose majority gave him the whip hand, the question was whether to adjourn or go directly to the balloting. He placed a call to Albany. "Go to it, Jim," FDR replied.

"The sound of his strong, reassuring voice was like a tonic for jangled nerves," Farley recalled.[96] At 4:28 A.M. the convention clerk stepped to the microphone and began to call the roll. At this point, both sides welcomed the showdown. Smith believed that Roosevelt's support was skin deep and that after the first ballot his delegates would bolt. Farley thought FDR would win on the first ballot as state delegations, recognizing how close Roosevelt was, would jump on the bandwagon.

Roosevelt listened to the balloting from his sitting room in Albany. "We presented a strange picture," Sam Rosenman remembered. Eleanor and Sara were there.* Young Elliott, his ear next to the radio, was sound asleep. Missy and Grace Tully were also asleep. Mrs. Rosenman was sitting on the floor dozing. But FDR was wide awake. From time to time he would look at the accep-

---

* Eleanor was unenthusiastic about FDR's nomination. "From a personal standpoint, I did not want my husband to be president. I realized, however, that it was impossible to keep a man out of public service if that was what he wanted and was undoubtedly well equipped for. It was pure selfishness on my part, and I never mentioned my feelings on the subject to him."

What ER did was confide her doubts to Nancy Cook and Marion Dickerman. On the eve of FDR's nomination she wrote to Cook, who was in Chicago with the campaign. Cook shared the letter with Dickerman and then with Louis Howe. According to Dickerman's account, ER's tone was almost "hysterical." She could not "bear to become First Lady!" She did not wish to be "a prisoner in the White House, forced onto a narrow treadmill of formal receptions, 'openings,' dedications, teas, official dinners." Howe's face darkened as he read the letter. When he finished, he tore it into shreds and dropped the pieces into his wastebasket. "You are not to breathe a word of this to anyone, understand? Not to *anyone*."

In her 1970s interviews with the historian Kenneth S. Davis, Marion Dickerman went on to say that ER wrote that she intended to file suit for divorce and run away with Earl Miller. Because the information was privileged and confidential, Davis chose not to report it until after Dickerman's death. Blanche Wiesen Cook appears to accept Dickerman's version, and Earl Miller's denial, reported by Joseph Lash, is less than categorical. What we know for certain is that after the election FDR took Sergeant Gus Gennerich to the White House but Miller remained in Albany, where he was appointed personnel director of the New York State Department of Corrections.

Eleanor Roosevelt, *This I Remember* 69 (New York: Harper & Brothers, 1949); Kenneth S. Davis, *FDR: The New York Years, 1928–1933* 330–331 (New York: Random House, 1979); Blanche Wiesen Cook, 1 *Eleanor Roosevelt* 445–447 (New York: Viking Penguin, 1992); Joseph Lash, *Love, Eleanor* 119–120 (New York: Doubleday, 1982). Writing later, Doris Kearns Goodwin and Conrad Black report ER's unhappiness at the prospect of becoming first lady but exclude the reference to Earl Miller. Goodwin, *No Ordinary Time* 90 (New York: Simon & Schuster, 1994); Black, *Franklin Delano Roosevelt* 239–240 (New York: PublicAffairs, 2003). David B. Roosevelt, ER's grandson, reports Eleanor's romance with Miller but makes no mention of divorce. *Grandmère: A Personal History of Eleanor Roosevelt* 139–141 (New York: Warner Books, 2002).

tance speech he and Rosenman were working on but could not concentrate. Rosenman left the room at one point to try drafting the peroration. "When I handed him the scrap of paper on which the few paragraphs had been written he said he thought they were all right." Neither considered the words especially memorable.[97]

The first ballot went quickly enough. Roosevelt's support held firm, and the opposition remained scattered. The final tally showed FDR with 666 votes—more than three times as many as his nearest rival but 104 short of victory. Smith ran second with 201, Garner third with 90, followed by the six favorite sons, who split the remainder. The count was almost exactly what Farley had anticipated. What he did not anticipate was that no delegation switched before the result was announced. "I sat there fully expecting that some state would switch and announce its support for the majority candidate. But nothing happened. I was bitterly disappointed."[98]

The second ballot began at 5:17 A.M. and was not completed until 8:05—the longest ballot on record at any Democratic convention as various state delegations asked to be polled individually. Roosevelt's total crept up to 677, Smith's fell back to 194, but still there was no break. Arthur Mullen, Farley's deputy on the floor, moved adjournment. But the opposition sensed that FDR had peaked and pressed for a third ballot. A voice vote on the motion to adjourn was inconclusive. Walsh told Mullen that if he put the motion to a roll call, it would likely lose and the momentum would shift against Roosevelt.[99] Mullen withdrew the motion, and the convention settled in for the third ballot.

"Watch this one closely," Farley told New Hampshire's Robert Jackson. "It will show whether I can ever go back to New York or not."[100]

For FDR, the third ballot was crucial. Farley had told Rayburn that the Roosevelt lines would hold for three ballots, but there was no way of knowing. Any decline would be fatal. Already the delegations from Iowa and Minnesota were restive, and the shift of a few votes under the unit rule could cost Roosevelt those states. The greatest worry was the South, especially Mississippi, where the conservative establishment, led by Governor Sennet Conner, much preferred Newton D. Baker to FDR. Senator Pat Harrison, an old blue blood himself, was holding the Magnolia State for Roosevelt by the slender margin of 10½ to 9½. If Mississippi defected, there was no question that Arkansas would follow.

"We got in touch with Huey Long," said Ed Flynn. "We put the entire responsibility on Long to see to it that there was no break in these two tottering states."[101] Long stormed into the midst of the Mississippi delegation. He threatened. He cajoled. He bullied. He shook his fist in Governor Conner's face: "If you break the unit rule, you sonofabitch, I'll go into Mississippi and break you."[102] There was no doubt in anyone's mind that the Kingfish not only could but would do so.* Mississippi and Arkansas held fast on the third ballot, Roosevelt picked up five more votes, Garner gained eleven, and Smith dropped four. At 9:15 on Friday morning the convention adjourned until evening. "There is no question in my mind," Flynn wrote afterward, "but that without Long's work Roosevelt might not have been nominated."[103]

The convention was on the verge of deadlock. Roosevelt's ranks were holding, Smith was in until the bitter end, and the favorite sons believed they were sitting pretty. The key to breaking the stalemate lay in the ninety votes pledged to Garner. The principal players were now Sam Rayburn and the powerful chairman of the California delegation, William Gibbs McAdoo.

At Farley's request, Pat Harrison tracked Rayburn down and arranged a meeting in Harrison's suite. Harrison and Rayburn were friends of long standing in Washington.

"What shall we offer them?" asked Farley.

"Anything they want," Harrison replied.[104]

Rayburn brought Silliman Evans, the manager of Garner's headquarters, with him to the meeting. "Without wasting much time shadow boxing, we got down to business," Farley recalled. "Once again I stated my opinion we could swing the vice-presidential nomination for Speaker Garner if Texas threw in their lot in with us." Pat Harrison urged Rayburn to accept. "Neither Sam nor Silliman needed much convincing," said Farley. The conference lasted only a few moments.

---

* Shortly after the convention adjourned, Long went into neighboring Arkansas to support the Senate candidacy of Hattie Caraway against the conservative Democratic establishment. Mrs. Caraway was the widow of Senator Thaddeus Caraway and was serving out his unexpired term when she decided to run for the full six-year term. No one gave her a chance. Long barnstormed the state for ten days, and when the votes were counted Mrs. Caraway carried sixty-one of Arkansas's seventy-five counties and her popular vote equaled the total of her six opponents'. Mrs. Caraway was the first woman elected to the U.S. Senate. T. Harry Williams, *Huey Long* 583–593 (New York: Knopf, 1969).

"We'll see what can be done," said Rayburn as he stood to leave. No explicit commitment was made, but Farley and Harrison both recognized that a deal had been struck. "I was elated," Farley wrote. "There wasn't a doubt in the world that they intended to release their delegates and swing the convention for Governor Roosevelt."[105]

At the same time Farley was meeting with Rayburn, Cordell Hull and Daniel Roper of South Carolina were calling on McAdoo, another old friend. "We felt that if we could win California's support for Roosevelt the victory would be gained," said Hull.[106] Roper, who had been commissioner of internal revenue when McAdoo was secretary of the Treasury, asked the Californian whether he would be interested in returning to Washington as secretary of state? Roper was freelancing and had no authority from Farley or anyone else to make such an offer. Fortunately, McAdoo was not interested. No, he told his guests, he did not wish anything for himself. But he was not averse to switching horses. The last thing McAdoo wanted was another deadlocked convention. If Roosevelt would name Garner as his running mate and give McAdoo veto power over who was to be secretary of state and secretary of the Treasury, he would shift California's vote behind FDR on the fourth ballot. He did not wish to suggest anyone for those places, said McAdoo, but he did want to ensure that they were filled with progressives.[107]

McAdoo insisted that Roper put the terms directly to FDR in Albany. "I'll do this only upon certain assurances that he [Roosevelt] must give through you and no one else." Roper reported back to Howe, who placed the call to FDR. "I took the telephone and explained the conditions," said Roper. "Governor Roosevelt gave me the required assurances over the telephone."[108]

At 3 P.M. Chicago time Garner called Rayburn from Washington and made it official. "Sam," he said, "I think it is time to break this thing up. Roosevelt is the choice of the Convention. He has had a majority on three ballots. We don't want to be responsible for wrecking the party's chances. The nomination ought to be made on the next roll call."[109]

Both Rayburn and McAdoo ran into considerable roughhouse when they caucused their delegations. Diehards in the Texas delegation wanted to continue the fight. Rayburn eventually forced a vote and carried the motion to support Roosevelt 54–51, leaving some important Texas noses out of joint. McAdoo found even tougher going when he called the California delegation together. He too eventually prevailed, but never put the question to a vote.[110]

McAdoo graciously suggested to Rayburn that when the roll was called, California yield to Texas and allow the Lone Star State to lead the switch. Rayburn said that would cause even more hard feelings in his delegation and told McAdoo to announce the decision.[111]

Unaware of these developments, the Stop Roosevelt forces looked to the balloting with increasing confidence. Mississippi seemed to have crumbled despite Huey Long's efforts, and there were rumors of defection in North Carolina and Iowa. There was increasing talk of Baker, the compromise candidate waiting in the wings. Some of Roosevelt's closest associates had not been told of Garner's switch. Rexford Tugwell and Harry Hopkins, who shared a cab to the stadium, looked as if they were going to a funeral.[112]

Shortly after eight o'clock Friday evening, July 1, 1932, the clerk began to call the roll for the fourth ballot. "Alabama, 24 votes for Roosevelt." Arizona, Arkansas, the ranks were holding. Then California. McAdoo asked Chairman Tom Walsh for permission to explain the California vote. An eerie silence settled over Chicago Stadium as McAdoo made his way to the platform. "California came here to nominate a President of the United States," he said. "She did not come here to deadlock this Convention." Roosevelt delegates went wild. The organ struck up "Happy Days Are Here Again" followed by "California, Here I Come." The Texas standard joined the parade. When order was eventually restored, McAdoo resumed: "The great state of Texas and the great state of California [sustained cheering] are acting in accordance with what we believe is best for America and best for the Democratic party. California casts its forty-four votes for Franklin D. Roosevelt."[113]

Listening to the radio in Albany, FDR leaned back and grinned: "Good old McAdoo!" By announcing that Texas would also be making the switch, McAdoo had broken the deadlock. The bandwagon rush began. When Illinois was called, Mayor Cermak announced the combined strength of Illinois and Indiana—eighty-eight votes—"for the next President of the United States, Franklin D. Roosevelt." Governor Ritchie personally announced Maryland's switch to FDR. Missouri, Ohio, and Oklahoma came on board. As the alphabet neared the end, Governor Byrd came to the podium to announce Virginia's switch.

At 10:32 P.M., Walsh announced the final tally: 945 votes for Roosevelt, 190 for Smith, who refused to concede. "Franklin D. Roosevelt having received more than two-thirds of all the delegates voting, I proclaim him the nominee of this Convention."[114]

Walsh's next announcement stunned the stadium. It was a telegram from Roosevelt saying he wished to fly to Chicago the next day to accept the nomination.[115] When the cheering subsided, the organist sent the delegates back to their hotels to the tune of "Onward Christian Soldiers"—a tune not heard at Democratic conventions since the heyday of William Jennings Bryan.

"Mr. Roosevelt enters the campaign with a burden on each shoulder," H. L. Mencken wrote in the Baltimore *Evening Sun*. "The first is the burden of his own limitations. He is one of the most charming of men, but like many another very charming man he leaves on the beholder the impression that he is also somewhat shallow and futile. The burden on his other shoulder is even heavier. It is the burden of party disharmony." Mencken said Chicago bookies were offering 5-to-1 odds that Governor Ritchie, if nominated, would beat Hoover. When FDR got the nomination, they offered 5 to 1 that Hoover would win.[116]

Roosevelt's decision to fly to Chicago electrified the nation.[117] Tradition held that the Democratic and Republican nominees be formally notified in their hometowns by a delegation of party notables a month or so after the convention. By smashing precedent and going to Chicago, Roosevelt was demonstrating a spirit of urgency that a dispirited country could embrace. He was also demonstrating remarkable physical courage and stamina. In 1932, air travel was still considered hazardous. Knute Rockne, the nation's most celebrated football coach, had recently died in a plane crash. Navigation aids were rudimentary, planes were primitively underpowered, and pilots had little to fall back on if they encountered heavy weather. In statistical terms, people flying in 1932 were two hundred times more likely to be killed than passengers forty years later.[118]

American Airlines had but one flight a day out of Albany, and it went to Cleveland. To accommodate Roosevelt, the airline pulled a Ford 5-AT Tri-Motor plane from the Dallas to Los Angeles run.* As an American spokesman

---

* The Ford 5-AT Tri-Motor, often referred to as the "Tin Goose," had a top speed of 110 miles an hour. Built with a corrugated aluminum exterior, the plane had a seventy-seven-foot wingspan, was almost fifty feet long, and weighed 13,000 pounds. It had three propellers, low-pressure tires for landing on rough surfaces, and a swiveling rear wheel with a shock absorber. "With its fixed landing gear, exposed air-cooled engines, and boxy shape, it exemplified the problems of drag that designers were trying to identify and fix in the late 1920s," wrote the aviation historian R. G. Grant. *Flight: 100 Years of Aviation* 140–141 (New York: D. K. Publishing, 2002).

said, "People were afraid to fly. To get a governor on a plane might help spread a little confidence. That's why we were willing to go to so much trouble."[119]

Roosevelt's party, an unlucky thirteen, included Eleanor, sons Elliott and John, Missy LeHand, Grace Tully, Earl Miller, Gus Gennerich, and Sam Rosenman, plus pilots and crew. "There were storms all around us," said one of the pilots. "Flying up against the prevailing winds at that low altitude was rough, and that Ford was like a balloon." The pilots prepared for an emergency landing in Rochester, but the weather broke slightly and they pressed on, refueling in Buffalo and Cleveland. At 4:30 the little plane landed at Chicago's Municipal Airport, eight hours on the button after its departure from Albany. In the interim, John Garner had been nominated by acclamation for vice president, Farley bringing the Roosevelt delegations into line without a murmur.

Shortly after 6 P.M. Chairman Walsh introduced Roosevelt amidst a thunderous ovation. FDR was wearing a blue suit with a rose in his lapel, his eyes shining, his head thrown back, as the organist broke into another spirited rendering of "Happy Days Are Here Again." The crowd of 30,000 was on its feet as Roosevelt began. "I regret that I am late, but I have no control over the winds of heaven and could only be thankful for my Navy training. The appearance before a national convention of its nominee for President before being formally notified of his selection is unprecedented, but these are unprecedented times." The audience roared its approval.

With the nation listening—many in the audience were hearing Roosevelt for the first time—he rolled out the sentences in that confident, cultured voice so familiar to radio audiences in New York: "I have started out on the tasks that lie ahead by breaking the absurd tradition that the candidate should remain in professed ignorance of what has happened until he is formally notified many weeks later. Let it be from now on the task of our party to break foolish traditions and leave it to the Republican leadership, far more skilled in that art, to break promises."

Roosevelt served notice on the economic conservatives in the party who wanted to stand pat: "I warn those nominal Democrats who squint at the future with their faces turned to the past, and who feel no responsibility to the demands of the new time, that they are out of step with their Party." (Raucous cheers and applause.) "Ours must be a party of liberal thought, of planned action, of enlightened international outlook, and the greatest good to the greatest number of our citizens."

He reached out to progressives across the political spectrum: "Here and now I invite those nominal Republicans who find that their conscience cannot be squared with the groping and failure of their party leaders to join hands with us." FDR promised aggressive government action to tackle the root causes of the Depression and provide effective distress relief. He recited a litany of programs long overdue: securities regulation, public works, tariff reduction, wages and hours legislation, home mortgage guarantees, farm relief, and the repeal of Prohibition.

To those listening, both at home and in Chicago Stadium, Roosevelt's voice appeared to gain resonance as he approached his conclusion: "On the farms, in the large metropolitan areas, in the smaller cities and in the villages, millions of our citizens cherish the hope that their old standards of living and thought have not gone forever. Those millions cannot and shall not hope in vain."

And then that remarkable close: "I pledge you, I pledge myself, to a New Deal for the American people."[120]

FOURTEEN

NOTHING TO FEAR

Let me assert my firm belief that
the only thing we have to fear
is fear itself.
—FRANKLIN D. ROOSEVELT, MARCH 4, 1933

"THE MOST IMPORTANT thing in a political campaign is to make as few mistakes as possible," wrote Ed Flynn, and the 1932 Democratic presidential campaign was nearly flawless. Roosevelt "seemed to have a sixth sense that enabled him to do the right thing at the right time."[1] Add Farley's meticulous organization, Louis Howe's encyclopedic knowledge of the nation's political byways, and the well-adapted speeches flowing from Moley's brain trust, throw in the ineptitude of the Hoover campaign, and FDR would probably have won even if the country had not been gripped by economic despair. As Brooklyn's Democratic boss, John H. McCooey, noted, "Roosevelt could have spent the entire summer and fall in Europe and been elected just the same."[2]

So it seemed in retrospect. FDR captured the initiative with his dramatic flight to Chicago and his rousing acceptance speech, and never looked back. Before Roosevelt left the platform that evening he had received the endorsement of Nebraska's senior senator, George W. Norris, the grand old man of American progressivism, followed quickly by Norris's fellow Republicans Hiram Johnson of California, Robert La Follette of Wisconsin, and Bronson Cutting of New Mexico. The wheels were coming off the Republican wagon.

With his progressive flank secure, FDR turned right to repair the breach in his own party. Following his acceptance speech, Roosevelt dined with the ninety-six members of the Democratic National Committee at the Congress Hotel. Raskob presided for the last time, and FDR devoted the bulk of his remarks to soothing old wounds, going far out of his way to praise "my very good and old friend, John Raskob" and "my old friend Jouett Shouse." He thanked his former adversaries for their service to the party and invited their help in the coming campaign.[3]

Al Smith posed another problem. He had left Chicago in a huff, and the campaign worried that he would blast FDR when he arrived in New York. His train was intercepted at Harmon-on-Hudson by mutual friends, and the Happy Warrior was persuaded to hold his peace. When the dust settled, Smith rallied to the ticket. He and Roosevelt forced the gubernatorial nomination of Herbert Lehman over Tammany's objections and, to the delight of onlookers, made up publicly on the floor of the state Democratic convention in Albany. "Hello, you old potato," shouted Smith as he pumped FDR's hand. "Hello, Al, I'm glad to see you too—and that's from the heart." Farley remembers the pair grinning like schoolboys, "with hands clasped together, while the excited photographers took picture after picture."[4]

Perhaps only Roosevelt could have launched his campaign by sailing with three of his sons—James, Franklin, Jr., and John—in a battered thirty-seven-foot yawl three hundred miles from Port Jefferson, Long Island, to Portsmouth, New Hampshire. "My son Jimmy has rented a yawl for $150," FDR told his first postconvention press conference. "It was cheap and that's why we could afford it. We are going to do our own navigating, cooking, and washing. I'm going to do the navigating."[5]*

On July 11, 1932, nine days after accepting the Democratic nomination, FDR set sail across Long Island Sound into the New England waters he knew so well. Because the yawl had no engine, a wharf boat towed it from the dock into the harbor and the stiff breeze whipping across the water. "Get out of my wind," Roosevelt jokingly called out to reporters aboard the press boat following behind.[6] The drama of Roosevelt and his sons sailing a choppy sea captured the public's imagination. Daily press and newsreel accounts showed a robust blue-water sailor, muscular and self-confident, beaming and laughing

---

* The Roosevelts were accompanied by FDR's old sailing companion George Briggs and FDR's cousin Bobby Delano, son of Sara's brother Lyman. The boat, *Myth II*, was owned by Mr. and Mrs. Prescott Butler Huntington of St. James, New York, and was described by Mrs. Huntington as "ancient." "It was an old boat. It leaked, and everybody knew it leaked." James said, "I was nervous the whole trip because if heavy weather came out we might lose both a father and a presidential candidate." Robert F. Cross, *Sailor in the White House: The Seafaring Life of FDR* 58 (Annapolis, Md.: Naval Institute Press, 2003).

with a remarkable zest for life—a stark contrast to the starchy, buttoned-up demeanor of Herbert Hoover in the White House. "I think [grandfather] instinctively knew there would be a general sense of admiration for someone who could sail a boat with his sons that distance," said FDR's grandson Curtis Roosevelt.[7]

Aside from putting to rest questions about FDR's health, the sail allowed him to mend fences with Smith's supporters in New England. When his boat anchored in Stonington, Connecticut, and again in Marblehead, Massachusetts, Roosevelt played host to visiting state delegations. In Swampscott he charmed Massachusetts governor Joseph B. Ely, a Smith loyalist who had delivered the Bay State to the Happy Warrior in the primary. At the conclusion of the voyage FDR motored to Hampton Beach, New Hampshire, to deliver his first speech of the campaign to a throng of 50,000 persons gathered at the fairgrounds.[8]

The final disaffected organization brought into line was that of Frank Hague in New Jersey.[9] Like most old-line bosses, Hague was a Democrat first and foremost. Candidates come and go, platforms wax and wane, but the party survives. Hague had opposed Roosevelt fiercely at Chicago but had no problem extending an olive branch. If FDR would come to New Jersey early in the campaign, he told Farley, he would provide the largest political rally ever held in the United States. Roosevelt agreed, and Hague kept his word. In early August FDR went to Sea Girt, New Jersey, to address a summer crowd bused in from across the state estimated at 115,000 persons. "If it wasn't the biggest rally in history, it must have been very close to it," Farley recalled.[10]

Throughout the campaign Farley relied on the regular state organizations, whether they had supported FDR before the convention or not.[11] This brought muted protest from Roosevelt backers, but Farley remained adamant. A united party was central to FDR's campaign, and that meant keeping the regulars on board. When Hull complained that Roosevelt's early supporters in Texas were being sidetracked, Farley showed little sympathy: "To be very frank with you, Senator, I think we will make a terrible mistake if we fail to carry out the campaign through the regular organization in Texas. If we do otherwise we are going to be in trouble."[12]

The fact is, Farley was centralizing the party structure to a degree unprecedented in American politics, and it was more effective to work with organizations already in place than to create something new. At Howe's suggestion, the various state chairmen were called to campaign headquarters in small groups for several days of conferences with Farley and others and were forcefully impressed with the fact that they were solely responsible for the campaign in their territory. "The success of this radical experiment was instantaneous," Howe recalled. "Every state chairman went back feeling he was a person of real importance, of real responsibility, and determined to work as he had never worked before for the success of the Democratic party."[13]

At the same time, Farley accelerated his practice of corresponding individually with each of the 140,000 or so precinct captains throughout the country. Altogether, almost 3 million letters were mailed out from Roosevelt's headquarters, a significant percentage signed personally by Farley. "The fellow out in Kokomo, Indiana, who is pulling doorbells night after night respectfully asking his neighbors to vote the straight Democratic ticket, gets a real thrill if he receives a letter on campaigning postmarked Washington or New York; and we made sure that this pleasure was not denied him."[14]*

Farley and Howe, assisted by Ed Flynn, directed the campaign like field marshals deploying their troops in battle. Politics, organization, and turnout were their responsibility. Policy was handled by the brain trust. They were the staff officers of the campaign, preparing speeches and memoranda for the candidate. Roosevelt made twenty-seven major addresses between August and November, each devoted to a single subject. He spoke briefly on thirty-two additional occasions, usually at whistle-stops or impromptu gatherings to which he was invited. Hoover, by contrast, made only ten speeches, all of which were delivered during the closing weeks of the campaign.[15]

The Democratic campaign's distinction between politics and policy was pure Roosevelt. He worked seamlessly with Howe, Farley, and Flynn on strategy and dealt directly with Moley's team on substance. Campaign headquarters was at New York's Biltmore Hotel; the brain trusters were billeted at the Roosevelt. "The relations between our organization and Moley's brain

---

* Farley signed his mail in the evening, sometimes devoting six hours to the task. "I have been asked if my hand gets cramped or tired from steady letter-signing. On occasion it does, but not often. When that happens, I hold it under the cold water for a few moments, then flex the fingers back and forth, repeating each process until the circulation returns. After five or ten minutes it is usually possible for me to resume without any ill effects. If there were no interruptions, I have been able to sign very close to 2,000 letters an hour." James A. Farley, *Behind the Ballots* 195 (New York: Harcourt, Brace and Co., 1938).

trust were always pleasant," Flynn recalled, "for we attempted to keep a strict differentiation between the job of organization and that of policy-making as reflected in the speeches the candidate was to make."[16] Brain truster Sam Rosenman saw it the same way. "We did not attempt to participate in their political activity, and they scrupulously refrained from interfering with us in any way."[17]

Campaign finances were a problem initially, but as Roosevelt developed momentum the money poured in. The Democrats, who began the race still in the hole after 1928, raised a total of $2.4 million versus the Republicans' $2.6 million.[18]* Expenditures followed roughly the same ratio, with both parties spending slightly more than they took in. Radio was the largest cost item. An hour of prime-time broadcasting over the combined CBS and NBC networks in 1932 cost $35,000.[19] The Republicans spent $551,972 for airtime; the Democrats $343,415. Reflecting the nation's depressed economy, the 1932 campaign was the least expensive in the twentieth century. The final figures filed by each party indicate that the Democrats and Republicans spent an average of thirteen cents for each vote cast.[20] In 2004, the two major parties spent $547,966,644 and 115 million voters went to the polls; that translates into $4.76 per vote.

Events broke for Roosevelt. Throughout the late spring and early summer of 1932, unemployed veterans from World War I flocked to Washington to petition Congress for early payment of wartime bonuses that were due in 1945.[21] They set up a shantytown on the banks of the Anacostia River in southeast Washington and, when space there ran out, occupied several vacant government buildings on Pennsylvania Avenue. At its height, the Bonus Army, as it was called, numbered more than 20,000. When the Senate rejected their petition, most went home, but many others, homeless and jobless, remained in the capital.

Washington officials coped as best they could. Police Chief Pelham Glassford did his utmost to provide tents and bedding for the veterans, furnished medicine, and assisted with food and sanitation. Maintaining order was never a problem. The men were camped illegally, but Glassford (who had been the youngest brigadier general with the AEF in France) chose to treat them simply

---

* To convert 1932 dollars, multiply by 14. Robert C. Sahr, "Currency Conversion Factors, 1700 to estimated 2012," Oregon State University, Corvallis, Oregon.

as old soldiers who had fallen on hard times. He resisted efforts to use force to dislodge them.[22]

Hoover did not share Glassford's equanimity. The specter of Bolsheviks storming the Winter Palace soon dominated administration thinking. The president refused to meet with the leaders of the Bonus Army, ordered the gates to the White House chained shut, and reinforced the guard to contain any demonstration. Secretary of War Patrick J. Hurley, convinced that the nation faced a Communist uprising of vast proportions, lamented that the veterans had been so orderly and longed for an incident that might justify the imposition of martial law.[23]

On July 28, under prodding from the White House, the District of Columbia commissioners ordered Glassford to clear the abandoned buildings along Pennsylvania Avenue in which the veterans were squatting. Brief resistance followed, shots rang out, two veterans were killed, and Hurley had his incident. The commissioners asked the White House for federal troops to maintain order. Hoover passed the request to Hurley, who ordered Army chief of staff General Douglas MacArthur to take the appropriate action.[24] That was at 2:55 P.M. Within the hour troopers from the 3rd Cavalry Regiment, led by their forty-seven-year-old executive officer, Major George S. Patton, clattered across Memorial Bridge into Washington. They were joined by elements of the 16th Infantry from Fort Washington, supported by tanks and machine guns.[25] MacArthur, who normally wore mufti to the War Department, changed into Class A uniform (replete with Sam Browne belt, medals, and decorations) and took command. At his side was his aide-de-camp and military secretary, Major Dwight D. Eisenhower, also in Class A.*

By five o'clock Army units had surrounded the buildings in downtown Washington occupied by the veterans. Cavalrymen drew sabers and cleared the streets while infantry with fixed bayonets emptied the buildings. The air was saturated with tear gas. Prodded by horses and tanks the veterans fell back to their encampment on the Anacostia Flats. As evening fell, the Army troops

---

* In fairness to Ike, he urged MacArthur to remain at the War Department and leave the operation to the troop commanders but was overruled. "MacArthur has decided to go into active command in the field," the chief of staff replied, speaking as he often did in the third person. "There is incipient revolution in the air." William Manchester, *American Caesar: Douglas MacArthur, 1880–1964* 150 (Boston: Little, Brown, 1978). Also see Dwight D. Eisenhower, *At Ease: Stories I Tell to Friends* 216 (New York: Doubleday, 1967).

paused to allow women and children to be evacuated. At 10:14 P.M. MacArthur gave the order to advance. After a tear gas barrage the cavalry swept the camp, followed by infantrymen, who systematically set fire to the veterans' tents and shanties lest anyone return. Coughing, choking, and vomiting, the veterans and their families fled up Good Hope Road into Maryland and safety. "Had President Hoover not acted when he did," said MacArthur at a War Department news conference afterward, "he would have been faced with a very serious situation." The "mob," as MacArthur saw it, was animated by the "essence of revolution."[26]

The nation's press bannered the eviction across its front pages. A few, citing Cleveland's suppression of the Pullman strike in 1895, praised Hoover for acting decisively; most lambasted the administration for excessive force. "What a pitiful spectacle," said the normally Republican Washington *Daily News*. "The mightiest government in the world chasing unarmed men, women and children with Army tanks. If the Army must be called out to make war on unarmed citizens, this is no longer America."[27] *The New York Times* devoted its first three pages to the coverage, including a full page of photographs. In the months ahead, the torching of the veterans' camp on the Anacostia Flats came to symbolize the insensitivity of the Hoover administration to the plight of the unemployed.

Rexford Tugwell, who was in Albany on a speechwriting chore, recalls entering FDR's bedroom at breakfast and finding the morning newspapers spread all around. Pointing to the pictures in the *Times*, Roosevelt said they were "scenes from a nightmare." He pointed to soldiers hauling resisters, still weeping from tear gas, through the wreckage to police wagons, while women and children, incredibly disheveled and weary, waited for some sort of rescue.

Roosevelt told Tugwell he regretted having recommended Hoover for president in 1920. "There is nothing inside the man but jelly; maybe there never had been anything." FDR said he might feel sorry for Hoover if he didn't feel sorrier for the people who had been burned out, eleven thousand of them, according to the *Times*. "They must be camping right now alongside the roads out of Washington. And some of them have families. It is a wonder there isn't more resentment, more radicalism, when people are treated that way."

"What Hoover should have done," Roosevelt said, "was to meet with the leaders of the Bonus Army when they asked for an interview. When two hundred or so marched up to the White House, Hoover should have sent out coffee and sandwiches and asked a delegation in. Instead, he let Pat Hurley and Doug MacArthur do their thing." "MacArthur," said FDR, "has just prevented Hoover's reelection."[28]

At lunch that day Roosevelt took a phone call from Huey Long, who berated FDR for playing up to the party's right wing. Roosevelt placated the Kingfish as best he could and promised to bring him into the campaign. "Keep your shirt on. It'll be all right." When he hung up, FDR turned to Tugwell.

"You know, that's the second most dangerous man in this country. Huey's a whiz on the radio. He screams at people and they love it. He makes them think they belong to some kind of church. He knows there is a promised land and he'll lead 'em to it."*

Tugwell could not resist. "You said Huey was the second most dangerous person."

"You heard right," smiled Roosevelt. "Huey is only second. The first is Douglas MacArthur. You saw how he strutted down Pennsylvania Avenue. You saw that picture of him in the *Times* after the troops chased all those vets out with tear gas and burned their shelters. Did you ever see anyone more self-satisfied? There's a potential Mussolini for you. Right here at home."[29]

Roosevelt approached the campaign with his usual optimism, and his enthusiasm was contagious. "We had one tremendous advantage, even at the very beginning of the 1932 campaign," wrote Farley. "This was the genuine conviction shared by Governor Roosevelt himself and those connected with him that his election to the Presidency was a foregone conclusion."[30] Farley said FDR had an incredible capacity for making people feel at ease and convincing them their work was important. "He was one of the most alive men I have ever met. He never gave me the impression he was tired or bored. His ability to discuss political issues in short, simple sentences made a powerful impression. There was a touch of destiny about the man. He would have been a great actor."[31]

By contrast, Hoover was pessimistic and bitter. He exuded defeat. Not hangdog, whipped-puppy defeat but the vanquishment of the proud, done in

* "We underrated Long's ability to grip the masses," wrote Farley after the election. "He put on a great show and everywhere he went we got the most glowing reports of what he had accomplished for the Democratic cause. . . . If we had sent Huey into the thickly populated cities of the Pennsylvania mining districts, the electoral vote of the Keystone State would have gone to the Roosevelt-Garner ticket by a comfortable margin." Farley, *Behind the Ballots* 171.

by hubris and conceit. Secretary of State Henry L. Stimson deplored Hoover's preference "for seeing the dark side first." To be in the same room with the president, said Stimson, "was like sitting in a bath of ink."[32] Gutzon Borglum, the sculptor of Mount Rushmore, observed that "if you put a rose in Hoover's hand it would wilt."[33]

When Hoover asked Stimson to take to the hustings and attack FDR, the secretary of state declined. Stimson admired Hoover and believed his great intellectual gifts were not sufficiently appreciated. But he thought even more strongly that foreign affairs should be above partisan politics. "To use the great office of Secretary of State to launch a purely personal attack on Roosevelt is quite inconsistent with my dignity and that of the office," wrote Stimson. "Two years ago I was dragged into an attack on Roosevelt in the [New York gubernatorial] campaign, and I have regretted it ever since."[34]

Colonel Stimson (as he liked to be called[35]) went not to Groton and Harvard but to Andover and Yale. Yet Endicott Peabody would have given him high marks for character. It is not surprising that he was venerated by a younger generation looking for heroes: men as varied as McGeorge Bundy, Lucius D. Clay, and George Herbert Walker Bush. Hoover never forgave Stimson for not participating in the campaign.[36] Roosevelt never forgot. When war clouds gathered in 1940 and bipartisanship became essential, FDR reached out to Stimson and asked him to become secretary of war for a second time.*

As the campaign progressed, Roosevelt demonstrated an uncanny ability to say the right thing at the right time to the right audience. Hoover, in a rare turn of phrase, called him "a chameleon on Scotch plaid."[37] Roosevelt traveled more than thirteen thousand miles, speaking to ever-increasing crowds. The rhetorical high point occurred in Baltimore on October 25, when Roosevelt castigated the Four Horsemen of the Republican apocalypse: Destruction, Delay, Deceit, and Despair.[38]

Hoover's voice found little resonance. He was so unpopular that it was unsafe for him to appear in public without heavy police escort.[39] Isolated and out of touch, he came across as a master of malapropism. "Nobody is actually

* Stimson served as secretary of war under Taft from 1911 to 1913 and as secretary of state under Hoover, 1929–1933. He was FDR's secretary of war (and then President Truman's) from 1940 to 1945.

starving," he told the Washington journalist Raymond Clapper. "The hobos, for example, are better fed than they have ever been."[40] It was difficult to credit a candidate who attributed the high unemployment rate to the fact that "many people have left their jobs for the more profitable one of selling apples."[41] Or who asserted, as Hoover did on October 31 at Madison Square Garden, that if the sky-high rates of the Smoot-Hawley tariff were reduced, "the grass will grow in the streets of a hundred cities, a thousand towns; the weeds will over-run the fields of a million farms. Their churches and school houses will decay."[42]

The message of fear was all that remained. As Hoover would have it, Roosevelt was the precursor of revolution. Speaking in Saint Paul three days before the election, an exhausted Hoover equated the Democratic party with "the same philosophy of government which has poisoned all of Europe . . . the fumes of the witch's cauldron which boiled in Russia." He accused the Democrats of being "the party of the mob." When he added, "Thank God, we still have a government in Washington that knows how to deal with the mob," an angry murmur rolled through the audience.[43] Ashen and shaken, Hoover swayed on the platform. "Why don't they make him quit?" a prominent Republican asked White House security chief, Colonel E. W. Starling. "He's not doing himself or the party any good."[44]

On election day FDR and Eleanor voted at Hyde Park and then went into the city, where Eleanor hosted a buffet supper for family and friends at East Sixty-fifth Street. Early in the evening Sam Rosenman noticed two unidentified men in dark suits enter the house unobtrusively and take up positions near Roosevelt. When Rosenman inquired, he was told they were from the Secret Service.[45]

The outcome was never in doubt. The turnout, almost 40 million, was the greatest in American history. The GOP suffered a crushing defeat. Roosevelt received 22,825,016 votes to Hoover's 15,758,397 and carried forty-two states with 472 electors.[46] The result was as much a repudiation of Hoover as it was a triumph for FDR. The president received 6 million fewer votes than he had in 1928 and carried only six states, all in the Northeast. The Democrats gained an unprecedented ninety seats in the House to give them a virtual 3-to-1 majority (310–117) and won control of the Senate, 60–36.

At campaign headquarters in the Biltmore Hotel the celebration began early. Hoover, at his home in Palo Alto, conceded shortly after midnight. After receiving Hoover's message Roosevelt made his way to the Biltmore's grand ballroom, where he spoke briefly to hundreds of jubilant campaign workers. He singled out Louis Howe and James Farley as the "two people in the United States, more than anybody else, who are responsible for this great victory."[47]

Howe did not hear FDR's tribute. Unwilling to be seen in public on election night, he tabulated the results at his hideaway office on Madison Avenue. Eleanor and Farley joined him shortly after eleven, only to find him, in Farley's words, poring over the returns "like a miser inspecting his gold." They tried to persuade him to come back to the main celebration at the Biltmore, but he declined. He extracted an ancient bottle of Madeira from his desk that he had put away after the fight against Blue-eyed Billy Sheehan in 1911. It was not to be opened until FDR was elected president. Carefully Howe filled the glasses and raised his own: "To the next President of the United States."[48] At the age of fifty, Franklin Roosevelt had become president. He would remain president for the remainder of his life.

Eleanor, who did not work directly in the presidential campaign, continued to have mixed feelings about FDR's election:

> I was happy for my husband, of course, because I knew that in many ways it would make up for the blow that fate had dealt him when he was stricken with infantile paralysis; and I had implicit confidence in his ability to help the country in crisis. . . . But for myself, I was probably more deeply troubled than even [*Chicago Tribune* reporter] John Boettiger realized.* As I saw it, this meant the end of any personal life of my own. I knew what traditionally should lie before me; I had watched Mrs. Theodore Roosevelt and had seen what it meant to be the wife of the president, and I cannot say that I was pleased at the prospect. By earning my own money, I had recently enjoyed a certain amount of financial independence, and had been able to do things in which I was personally interested. The turmoil in my heart and mind was rather great that night, and the next few months were not to make any clearer what the road ahead would be.[49]

---

* In January 1935 John Boettiger married Franklin and Eleanor's daughter, Anna, following her divorce from Curtis Dall.

Roosevelt was elected on November 8. Inauguration was not until March 4.*
That four-month hiatus, coinciding with the fourth winter of the Depression,
proved the most harrowing in American memory. Three years of hard times
had cut national income in half. Five thousand bank failures had wiped out 9
million savings accounts. By the end of 1932, 15 million workers, one out of
every three, had lost their jobs. U.S. Steel's payroll of full-time workers fell
from 225,000 in 1929 to zero in early 1933.[50] When the Soviet Union's trade
office in New York issued a call for six thousand skilled workers to go to Russia, more than one hundred thousand applied. "No one can live and work in
New York this winter," noted Tugwell, "without a profound sense of uneasi-
ness. Never in modern times has there been so widespread unemployment and
such moving distress from sheer hunger and cold."[51] From Chicago, the critic
Edmund Wilson wrote, "There is not a garbage dump in the city which is not
diligently haunted by the hungry."[52]

The situation in the countryside was equally bad. Gross farm income had
declined from $12 billion in 1929 to $5 billion in 1932. At the same time, agricultural surpluses—crops and livestock that farmers could not sell—rotted
on farms or were plowed under. Wheat for December delivery dropped to
twenty-three cents a bushel, the lowest since the reign of Queen Elizabeth I
three hundred years earlier. In Iowa, a bushel of corn was worth less than a
package of chewing gum. In the South, thousands of acres of fine, long-staple
cotton stood in the field unpicked, the cost of ginning exceeding any possible
return.[53]

Children went hungry in every corner of the land. In the coal-mining areas
of West Virginia and Kentucky, more than 90 percent of the inhabitants were
suffering from malnutrition. In the nation's major cities, only one out of four
unemployed workers was receiving any relief whatever. In Philadelphia, those
fortunate enough to be on the relief rolls received $4.23 per week for a family
of four. Many state and local governments, including the city of Chicago, ran
out of money to pay their teachers. In Alabama, 81 percent of the children in
rural areas went schoolless. Georgia closed more than a thousand schools with
a combined enrollment of more than 170,000.[54] Homeowners were being

---

* The Twentieth ("Lame Duck") Amendment, changing inauguration day from March 4 to
January 20, was not added to the Constitution until January 23, 1933, and did not become
effective until 1937.

foreclosed at a rate of well over one thousand a day. Farmers lost their land because they could not pay taxes or meet mortgage payments. On a single day in April 1932, one fourth of the entire state of Mississippi went under the hammer of auctioneers at foreclosure sales.[55]

Violence simmered beneath the surface. In Iowa, farmers declared a farm holiday, blocked highways with logs and telephone poles, smashed headlights, and punctured tires with their pitchforks. When authorities in Council Bluffs arrested fifty-five demonstrators, more than a thousand angry farmers threatened to storm the jail unless they were released. Wisconsin dairy farmers dumped milk on the roadsides and fought pitched battles with deputy sheriffs. In Nebraska, farm holiday leaders warned that unless the legislature took beneficial action, "200,000 of us are coming to Lincoln and we'll tear that new State Capitol Building to pieces." In Idaho and Minnesota, the governors declared moratoriums on mortgage foreclosures until state legislatures could enact debt relief measures. In North Dakota, Governor William Langer mobilized the National Guard to halt farm foreclosures.[56]

Hoover's doctrinaire attachment to the free market precluded government intervention. Even more serious in terms of long-term recovery, the president did his utmost to inveigle FDR into endorsing the administration's policy. "I am convinced," Hoover wrote Roosevelt, "that an early statement by you will help restore confidence." What Hoover had in mind was that FDR pledge to retain the gold standard, adopt a balanced budget, and impose additional taxes rather than raise money through government borrowing.[57] Roosevelt should also disavow any effort to insure home mortgages, rule out loans to states and municipalities for public works, disclaim proposals for government development of hydroelectric power in the Tennessee Valley, and desist in his opposition to a national sales tax. "I realize that if these declarations be made by the President-elect," Hoover wrote Senator David A. Reed of Pennsylvania a few days later, "he will have ratified the whole major program of the Republican Administration; that is, it means the abandonment of 90% of the so-called new deal."[58]

Roosevelt refused to be drawn in. He delayed ten days replying to Hoover's "cheeky" letter and then brushed the president's request aside. "I am equally concerned with you in regard to the gravity of the present banking situation, but my thought is that it is so very deep-seated that the fire is bound to spread in spite of anything that is done by way of mere statements."[59]

An exception to FDR's refusal to bail the Republicans out was in foreign policy. During the campaign Roosevelt virtually ignored international affairs—"I think Hoover's foreign policy is about right," he told Raymond Moley—and he chose not to make an issue of it after the election.[60] At FDR's invitation, Secretary of State Stimson visited Hyde Park on January 9, 1933, a cold, blustery Monday morning with rain turning to sleet and then to snow. Stimson was closeted with Roosevelt from eleven in the morning until five-thirty in the afternoon and later said he was "touched, overwhelmed by the kindness he showed me. . . . We both spoke with the utmost freedom and informality." Roosevelt endorsed the administration's efforts to embargo the shipment of arms to belligerents,* remained lukewarm to a world economic conference, and raised a number of questions about Latin America. Most important, he agreed fully with the most controversial aspect of Republican foreign policy, the so-called Stimson Doctrine, by which the United States refused to recognize the fruits of military aggression, specifically the Japanese conquest of Manchuria. "I had never had a talk with him before," Stimson confided to his diary that evening, "but had no difficulty getting on. . . . I was much impressed with his disability and the brave way in which he paid no attention to it whatever."[61]

Roosevelt's endorsement of the Stimson Doctrine created a tizzy among his advisers. Moley and Tugwell told FDR his commitment might trigger war with Japan. The president-elect was unmoved. War might indeed occur, he allowed. In fact, it might be inevitable, given Japan's imperial ambitions. And if that were the case, "it might be better to have it now than later."[62] Roosevelt said he had taken to speaking with Stimson daily over the telephone and that he intended to see the policy through. As Moley remembered the meeting, "Roo-

---

* One of FDR's first acts upon assuming office was to ask Congress for authorization to impose an embargo on the shipment of weapons to Bolivia and Paraguay, then engaged in a war for control of the headwaters of the Chaco River. Congress complied; Roosevelt proclaimed the embargo; and Curtiss-Wright Corporation violated it by attempting to ship sixteen machine guns to Bolivia, setting the stage for one of the landmark decisions of the Supreme Court pertaining to the nature of foreign affairs and the scope of executive authority, *United States v. Curtiss-Wright*, 299 U.S. 304 (1936). Justice George Sutherland, speaking for the Court, held that the authority to conduct foreign affairs was inherent in the national government and did not depend upon express grants in the Constitution. Sutherland's dictum that the president is the "sole organ" of American foreign relations is often quoted, frequently out of context.

sevelt put an end to the discussion by looking up and recalling that his Delano ancestors used to trade with China. 'I have always had the deepest sympathy for the Chinese. How could you expect me not to go along with Stimson on Japan?' "[63]

Roosevelt used the four months between November and March to prepare for the presidency. The brain trust continued to work on policy, while FDR concentrated on putting his team together. Howe would be going to Washington, of course, as chief of staff to the president (the post was called secretary to the president in those days), as would Farley as postmaster general—the traditional post for the dispenser of party patronage, with a hundred thousand jobs at his disposal. Missy LeHand and Grace Tully would take over the White House secretarial duties, joined by Louise Hackmeister as chief telephone operator.* Hacky, as she was called, had manned the switchboard in all of Roosevelt's campaigns and had a legendary feel for who should speak to the Boss and who should not. Rounding out the presidential office were Marvin McIntyre as appointments secretary and Steve Early as press secretary, charter members of the Cuff Links Club dating from FDR's run for the vice presidency in 1920.

The cabinet proved more complicated. For the senior positions at State and Treasury, Roosevelt turned to two old Wilsonians, Cordell Hull and Carter Glass. Hull in many ways epitomized the up-from-poverty yearnings of the New Deal. The son of a hardscrabble dirt farmer from the mountains of southern Appalachia, Hull had served in the Spanish-American War as a captain of Tennessee volunteers and been elected to Congress in 1906 and to the U.S. Senate in 1930. For more than a generation he had led the liberal cause in the South. He had been for Wilson before Baltimore and for Roosevelt before Chicago. Except for a lifelong devotion to free trade, his knowledge of foreign

* FDR was the first president to use the telephone extensively. Wilson had a telephone installed at the White House, but it was not in his office. Hoover was the first to have one on his desk, but he rarely used it. Perhaps because of his immobility, Roosevelt had learned the advantages of telephoning and was a master at the instrument. He had the entire White House wired and by his own testimony spent about a third of each day on the phone. Roughly a hundred people had direct access to FDR, and Hackmeister put them through without reference to Missy or Howe. Charles Hurd, *When the New Deal Was Young and Gay* 117 (New York: Hawthorn Books, 1965); John Gunther, *Roosevelt in Retrospect* 125 (New York: Harper & Brothers, 1950).

affairs was limited and his administrative skills were untested. But Roosevelt genuinely admired Hull's idealism and personal dignity.* And he had a political base FDR could not ignore. "Cordell Hull is the only member of the Cabinet who brings me any political strength that I don't have in my own right."[64]

For Treasury, Carter Glass of Virginia had no competition. The architect of the Federal Reserve Act while a member of the House, secretary of the Treasury under Wilson, and now ranking Democrat on the Senate Appropriations Committee, the seventy-four-year-old Glass had been the party's senior spokesman on public finance so long as anyone could remember. This was the one cabinet post on which Roosevelt had no wiggle room, and he made the offer to Glass at the same time he approached Hull. Both FDR and Glass were apprehensive. Glass was committed to hard currency, fiscal restraint, and a sound dollar. He deplored deficit spending. Roosevelt, on the other hand, was pragmatic: "We're not going to throw ideas out of the window simply because they are labeled inflation."[65] When Glass declined because of ill health, the Roosevelt camp breathed a sigh of relief. To head Treasury, FDR immediately turned to Republican William H. Woodin, a respected New York industrialist who had helped bankroll each of Roosevelt's campaigns. Woodin, too, was reluctant, but Basil O'Connor convinced him to take the post during an hour-and-a-half cab ride circling through Central Park. Like Glass, Woodin was uneasy about inflation, but he was not obsessive about it, and his personal loyalty to FDR was absolute. Like Hull, he would be easy to work with.[66]

When Glass decided to remain on the sidelines, Roosevelt turned to his senior senatorial colleague, Claude A. Swanson, to head the Navy Department. Swanson, dapper in frock coats and winged collars, had chaired the Naval Affairs Committee when FDR had been assistant secretary, and he shared Roosevelt's love for the service. His appointment not only ensured that the admirals would remain in charge but cleared a Virginia Senate seat for Roosevelt's old friend Governor Harry F. Byrd.

For the War Department, Roosevelt selected Governor George Dern of Utah. FDR was indebted to Dern for his preconvention campaigning in the West and had originally slated him for Interior. When conservationists objected, he moved Dern to War. One of the few non-Mormons to hold elective

---

* When five Democratic senators suggested to Raymond Moley that Hull was too idealistic and might not be up to the job of secretary of state, Roosevelt dismissed their concern out

office in Utah, Dern knew little about the Army, but in those days of small budgets and international isolation it seemed of little consequence.

When Dern proved unacceptable at Interior, Roosevelt turned first to Senator Hiram Johnson of California, then to his Republican colleague Bronson Cutting of New Mexico. Both declined. At the last moment Roosevelt asked Harold Ickes of Chicago, whom he did not know but who was recommended by Johnson and Cutting. Ickes had originally hoped to be appointed commissioner of Indian affairs but was elevated to the secretaryship almost by default. "Well," Louis Howe quipped, "that's the first break the Indians have had in a hundred years."[67]

For attorney general Roosevelt went again to the Senate and named Thomas J. Walsh of Montana, who had chaired both the 1924 and 1932 Democratic conventions. Walsh had devoted much of his public life to investigating corporate malfeasance, and his appointment sent a clear signal that special interests were no longer immune. Another septuagenarian, Walsh led an active social life and suffered a fatal heart attack on March 2—two days before the inauguration—having just courted and married a much younger Cuban sugar heiress in Havana. He was replaced by Homer Cummings of Connecticut, whom FDR had planned to name governor-general of the Philippines.

For Commerce FDR had intended to appoint Jesse Straus of R. H. Macy, a position Straus's uncle had occupied in TR's cabinet. But old party hands like Daniels, McAdoo, and Colonel House insisted that Daniel Roper of South Carolina be given a cabinet post, and Commerce seemed the best fit. As a consolation prize, Straus drew the embassy in Paris. Henry Morgenthau, Jr., sought to be appointed secretary of agriculture, but when farm organizations objected he was posted to the Farm Board, soon to become the centerpiece of the New Deal's Farm Credit Administration. For Agriculture, Roosevelt settled on Iowa publisher and crop experimenter Henry A. Wallace. Like Ickes, Wallace was a nominal Republican; also like Ickes, he was unknown to the president-elect before his appointment. For the final cabinet post, secretary of labor, there was no question. From the beginning FDR wanted to appoint a woman, and Frances Perkins was a shoo-in. Organized labor filed a ritual reclama, but Miss Perkins had demonstrated her ability as a member of Roo-

of hand. "You tell the senators I'll be glad to have some fine idealism in the State Department." Raymond Moley, *After Seven Years* 114 (New York: Harper & Brothers, 1939).

sevelt's cabinet in New York, and she was as much a part of FDR's political family as Farley or Flynn.

As Roosevelt described it, the cabinet was "slightly to the left of center." Three members (Hull, Swanson, and Roper) were old Wilsonians. Three were Republicans: either Republican-progressive (Ickes and Wallace) or Republican-conservative (Woodin). Two had served in the Senate (three, counting Walsh), and one (Dern) was a governor. There were two Catholics (Farley and Walsh), and for the first time a woman joined the ranks. All regions of the country were represented, and all the appointees had been FRBC—For Roosevelt Before Chicago. FDR had a fingertip feel for political nuance. He was also the most calculating and hard-nosed politician of his generation. His pre-convention rivals, Al Smith and Newton D. Baker, were not consulted about, let alone appointed to, any position in the administration, nor were their supporters. The same was true of Maryland's governor, Albert C. Ritchie. FDR's former antagonists on the National Committee, John Raskob and Jouett Shouse, were consigned to outer darkness. Roosevelt reached out to Republican progressives and independents, but he snuffed out rivals in his own party.

FDR's hostility was political, not personal. Baker, Raskob, Ritchie, and Smith represented the probusiness wing of the party: a conservative, hard-money tradition dating at least to the era of Grover Cleveland. Roosevelt, standing far to the left, had put together a remarkable coalition of western populists, white southerners, ethnic minorities, and big-city machines. He was not about to share the victory with his rivals nor to divert the Democratic party from the progressive path he had staked out. In 1874 Ulysses S. Grant, with his veto of the inflation bill, had weaned the Republican party from its agrarian, antislavery roots and converted it into the political vehicle of American business. In 1932 FDR broke the conservatives' hold on the Democratic party and made it the instrument of liberal reform.

Eleanor remained at loose ends and speculated what role she might play in the new administration. "I tentatively suggested to my husband that perhaps merely being hostess at the necessary formal functions would not take all my time and he might like me to do a real job and take over some of his mail. He looked at me quizzically and said he did not think that would do; that Missy, who had been handling his mail for a long time, would feel I was interfering. I knew he was right and that it would not work," Eleanor wrote, but FDR's rebuff did little to improve her spirits as the inauguration approached.[68]

On February 4 FDR departed for an eleven-day Caribbean cruise aboard his friend Vincent Astor's sleek 263-foot yacht, *Nourmahal.*[69] It would be Roosevelt's final relaxation before assuming his responsibilities as president—an escape back to the world of Groton and Harvard, of Fly Club and the *Crimson.* Astor, the founder and owner of *Newsweek,* was a Hyde Park neighbor and the nephew of FDR's late half-brother, Rosy.* Joining them were four familiar faces from New York society pages: Kermit Roosevelt, a son of TR and the only one of the Oyster Bay clan to speak kindly of FDR; William Rhinelander Stewart, the wealthy scion of a Four Hundred family and generous contributor to Republican causes; George Baker St. George of Tuxedo Park, another wealthy Republican; and Justice Frederic Kernochan, also of Tuxedo Park, a patrician Democrat, but at least a Democrat. They were all Harvard men, shared the same exclusive clubs, traveled in the same circles, and enjoyed one another's company. "The Hasty Pudding Club puts out to sea," Ed Flynn joked as *Nourmahal* sailed from Jacksonville's Commodore Point. Less kindly was the *New York Sun:*

> *They were just good friends with no selfish ends*
> *To serve as they paced the decks;*
> *There were George and Fred and the son of Ted*
> *And Vincent (he signed the checks);*
> *On the splendid yacht in a climate hot*
> *To tropical seas they ran,*
> *Among those behind they dismissed from mind*
> *Was the well-known Forgotten Man!*[70]

After two days at sea FDR wrote Sara that he was "getting a marvelous rest—lots of air and sun. Vincent is a dear and perfect host. George and Kermit and Freddie are excellent companions. When we land on the 15th I shall be full of health and vigor—the last holiday for many months."[71]

In the early evening of February 15, *Nourmahal* docked at Miami and Roosevelt hurried to Bay Front Park, where he was scheduled to address the annual encampment of the American Legion. Some 20,000 legionnaires crammed the

---

* James Roosevelt Roosevelt ("Rosy"), who died in 1927, had been married to Helen Astor, the daughter of *the* Mrs. Astor, the fabled arbiter of New York society.

brightly lit park to greet the president-elect. Roosevelt spoke briefly, perched on top of the backseat of his open car. When he finished, he slid back into his seat and chatted amiably with Chicago mayor Anton Cermak, who was standing alongside, having made the pilgrimage to Miami to eat political crow.* Suddenly, from a distance no more than forty feet away, five shots rang out in quick succession. Blood spurted from the hand of a nearby Secret Service agent, Mayor Cermak crumpled to the ground, a woman standing behind FDR was hit twice in the abdomen, and two other people were wounded. Roosevelt sat immobile and unflinching, his jaw set, ready for what might follow. He had been spared by inches. At the critical moment an alert spectator, Mrs. Lillian Cross, had hit the assassin's arm with her handbag and spoiled his aim.[72]

"I heard what I thought was a firecracker; then several more," Roosevelt wrote later.

> The chauffeur started the car. I looked around and saw Mayor Cermak doubled up. . . . I called to the chauffeur to stop. He did—about fifteen feet from where we started. The Secret Service man shouted to him to get out of the crowd and he started forward again. I stopped him a second time [and] motioned to have [Mayor Cermak] put in the back of the car, which would be first out. He was alive but I didn't think he was going to last. I put my left arm around him and my hand on his pulse, but I couldn't find any pulse. . . . For three blocks I believed his heart had stopped. I held him all the way to the hospital and his pulse constantly improved. I remember I said: "Tony, keep quiet—don't move. It won't hurt if you keep quiet."[73]

The assassin, an unemployed thirty-two-year-old Italian bricklayer, Giuseppe Zangara, acted alone. He had bought his revolver at a pawnshop on North Miami Avenue for eight dollars. "I have always hated the rich and powerful," he told police. "I do not hate Mr. Roosevelt personally. I hate all

---

* Cermak had stacked the galleries at Chicago Stadium with Smith supporters and needed forgiveness. Chicago's schoolteachers were working without salary, and Cermak was desperately seeking federal assistance. Farley wrote later that Cermak would not have had to go to Miami "if he had jumped on our bandwagon" after the first ballot. James A. Farley, *The Jim Farley Story* 21–22 (New York: Whittlesey House, 1948).

presidents, no matter from what country they come." After Cermak died on March 6, Zangara was tried, convicted, and executed for murder.[74]

After the shooting Roosevelt remained at Jackson Memorial Hospital until Cermak was brought out of the emergency room. He spoke with him for several minutes and then visited the other shooting victims. About 11:15 he returned to the *Nourmahal*. If he had been unnerved, it did not show. "All of us were prepared, sympathetically, for any reaction that might come from Roosevelt now that the tension was over and he was alone with us," wrote Moley.

> There was nothing. Not so much as the twitching of a muscle to indicate that it wasn't any other evening in any other place. Roosevelt was simply himself—easy, confident, poised, to all appearances unmoved.

> FDR had talked to me once or twice during the campaign about the possibility that someone would try to assassinate him. But it is one thing to talk philosophically about assassination and another thing to face it. I confess that I have never in my life seen anything more magnificent than Roosevelt's calm that night on the *Nourmahal*.[75]

Roosevelt's matter-of-fact reaction to his brush with death, his cheerful contempt for danger, brought forth a national surge of confidence. It was abundantly clear that FDR lacked physical fear, and his courage rallied the country behind him. It provided a tonic on the eve of the inauguration; a vital pickup for a nation grappling with unprecedented unemployment, widespread hunger and need, and a banking system that teetered on the brink of collapse.

As Roosevelt's train tracked northward, the nation was deluged with news of bank failures. Already 389 banks had shut their doors since the beginning of the year. The real panic had begun in Detroit when two of Michigan's largest banks, Union Guardian Trust and First National, could not meet their obligations. On February 14, Governor William Comstock declared an eight-day bank holiday, freezing the funds of 900,000 customers and tying up $1.5 billion in deposits. From Michigan the panic spread like wildfire, triggering a rapid fall in stock prices and the flight of gold to Europe. On February 24, following a run on Baltimore banks, Governor Ritchie declared a three-day bank holiday. By the end of the month, banks in every section of the country were in trouble. People stood in long lines clutching satchels and paper bags, determined to take their money and stash it safely at home. Thomas W. Lamont, now chairman of J. P. Morgan, wrote Roosevelt that the situation "could not be worse."[76] Piece by piece the nation's credit structure was falling apart.

At Hyde Park FDR worked over his inaugural address. Moley arrived on February 27 with a draft he had prepared from notes taken on the train. Roosevelt rewrote the draft in longhand on yellow legal pads, reading the sentences aloud, cutting here, adding there, committing the words to memory. At 1:30 on the morning of February 28 the draft was complete, save for the reference to fear, which FDR added the next day.* The final paragraph, invoking God's guidance, was written by Roosevelt after his arrival in Washington.[77]

On March 1, the president-elect left Hyde Park for New York City, where he spent the night. That day the governors of Kentucky and Tennessee declared bank holidays, followed in the evening by California, Louisiana, Alabama, and Oklahoma. By March 4, thirty-eight states, including New York and Illinois, had closed their banks. The New York Stock Exchange suspended trading on March 4, as did the Chicago Board of Trade.

Roosevelt's response to the crisis was similar to his reaction in Miami: serene and confident, unruffled and unafraid. His outward demeanor betrayed no sign of worry. Franklin is not a worrier, Sara told Jim Farley. "His disposition is such that he can accept responsibilities and not let them wear him down."[78] Roosevelt declined to make any public comment or take any action until he had the constitutional authority to do so. In his view, Hoover, as president, should do as he thought best. FDR would act when the time came. In the meantime he refused to make any joint statement and declined to give blanket approval to whatever action the Hoover administration might take. That was less of a problem than it might appear because Hoover still clung to his restricted view of executive power. On March 2 and again on March 3 he rejected the advice of his secretary of the Treasury and the chairman of the Federal Re-

---

* Louis Howe's draft introduction, which Roosevelt received on February 28, contained the sentence "The only thing we have to fear is fear itself." FDR added the sentence and embellished it. Some have noted the resemblance to Henry David Thoreau's "nothing is so much to be feared as fear," but Moley, who was with Roosevelt when the speech was put in final form, discounts the link. Raymond Moley, *The First New Deal* 96–124 (New York: Harcourt, Brace, 1966). And the fact is, the concept has a lengthy history. Francis Bacon said essentially the same thing in *De Argumentis Scientiarum*, Book VI, chapter III, early in the seventeenth century: "*Nil terrible nisi ipse timor.*" 2 *The Works of Francis Bacon* 476, James Spedding, Robert Leslie Ellis, and Douglas Denon Heath, eds. (New York: Hurd and Houghton, 1872).

serve Board that he invoke the emergency powers given the president under World War I's Trading with the Enemy Act (which was still on the books[79]) and issue a proclamation closing the nation's banks, embargo the shipment of gold abroad, and limit the exchange of dollars into foreign currency.

Saturday, March 4, dawned dull and dreary in Washington, the sky overcast with the final days of winter. Homeless men, disheveled and threadbare, wandered the deserted streets in search of a breakfast handout. Under the leafless trees the flags flew at half-mast in honor of Senator Walsh. It was as if the nation's gloom had settled over the city. Roosevelt began the day at 10 A.M. with a precedent-setting prayer service at St. John's Episcopal Church, directly across Lafayette Square from the White House.* He was joined by his family and personal staff, plus the members of the cabinet and their families, some hundred people altogether. At FDR's request, the Reverend Endicott Peabody, still paterfamilias to a growing legion of Groton old boys, presided over the brief service. After reading the appropriate selections from the Book of Common Prayer, the elderly Peabody offered a special request, asking God "Thy favor to behold and bless Thy servant, Franklin, chosen to be President of the United States." Roosevelt selected the hymns and psalms and joined in heartily as the choir led the small congregation in "Faith of Our Fathers" and "O God, Our Help in Ages Past." When the service ended, FDR remained on his knees for some time, his face cupped in his hands, in private prayer, his thoughts to himself.

Shortly before eleven, Roosevelt, in striped pants, cutaway, and silk hat, arrived at the porticoed north entrance to the White House. Breaking with custom again, FDR remained in the car while the presidential party assembled in the East Room. Soon President Hoover joined him, sitting to his right as protocol required. Eleanor rode in the second car with Mrs. Hoover. The seven-car procession, escorted by a troop of cavalry, began its two-mile journey up Pennsylvania Avenue to the Capitol. Roosevelt attempted to make conversation, but except for a brief exchange in which Hoover asked FDR if he might provide a position for the president's administrative assistant, the two sat in si-

---

* Roosevelt laid on the service at the last moment. "I think a thought to God is the right way to start off my administration," he told Jim Farley. "A proper attitude toward religion, and belief in God, will in the end be the salvation of all peoples. For ourselves it will be the means of bringing us out of the depths of despair into which so many have apparently fallen." *Jim Farley's Story* 36. Also see Farley, *Behind the Ballots* 208.

lence.[80] Happily, the ride was a short one. After the inaugural ceremonies they never saw each other again, although they were often in the same city. Hoover, the scapegoat from central casting, retired into domestic exile only to reappear every four years at Republican conventions, much to the delight of Democratic carnivores.

As required by statute, the vice president was sworn in first. Standing in the well of the Senate chamber, Vice President Charles Curtis, president of the Senate, swore in John Nance Garner as his successor. He then declared the Senate of the Seventy-second Congress adjourned *sine die*. Garner called the Seventy-third Senate to order and then recessed it until two o'clock, when it would reconvene to consider FDR's cabinet nominees. When the ceremony ended, there was a rush to the inaugural stand at the east front of the Capitol. When the thousand or so guests were seated, a bugle sounded, followed by ruffles and flourishes, and the Marine Band, resplendent in scarlet and gold, broke into the "President's March." Franklin Roosevelt, braced on the arm of his eldest son, James, began his laborious walk to the rostrum, 146 feet away. Watching the scene, the veteran broadcaster Ed Hill observed that if this man had the courage to lift himself by sheer willpower from the bed of invalidism, had the determination and patience to make himself walk, then he must have within him the qualities to lead the nation to recovery.[81]

Charles Evans Hughes, chief justice of the United States, wearing the black robes of office, stood at the center of the platform to meet him. On the table beside Hughes rested the Dutch family Bible brought to the New World by Claes van Rosenvelt in the 1650s—upon which Roosevelt had twice taken the oath as governor of New York. It was opened to the thirteenth verse of the thirteenth chapter of Paul's First Epistle to the Corinthians: "And now abideth faith, hope, charity, all three; but the greatest of these is charity." FDR had proposed, and Hughes agreed, that he should repeat the oath word for word rather than simply say "I do."[82] As Hughes intoned the constitutional text, Roosevelt recited after him: "I, Franklin Delano Roosevelt, do solemnly swear that I will faithfully execute the office of President of the United States and will, to the best of my ability, preserve, protect, and defend the Constitution of the United States." The chief justice ritually added the words "So help me God," which Roosevelt repeated.[83]

Roosevelt shook hands with Hughes, then pivoted to face the audience drawn up in front of the inaugural stand: 150,000 people spread over forty acres facing the Capitol. In the background, the howitzers of the 5th Field Artillery fired a twenty-one-gun salute. As the cannons boomed, the sun briefly broke through the clouds, and the new president was on cue. "This is a day of national consecration," said FDR, invoking divine guidance as he would throughout the speech. The vast crowd stilled, sensing the destiny of the moment. Roosevelt's voice was firm and reassuring, instilling confidence by tone and example. "This great Nation will endure as it has endured, will revive and will prosper. So, first of all, let me assert my firm belief that the only thing we have to fear is fear itself—nameless, unreasoning, unjustified terror which paralyzes needed efforts to convert retreat into advance."

Roosevelt spoke for fifteen minutes—brief as inaugural addresses go, but the words were memorable, exceeding even Lincoln's magnificent second inaugural in their immediate impact. The most pressing problem was to put people to work, said FDR, and the government must take the lead. "We must act and act quickly." After briefly laying out his program, Roosevelt said he would recommend to Congress "the measures that a stricken Nation in the midst of a stricken world may require." Should Congress fail to act, "I shall not evade the clear course of duty that will then confront me. I shall ask the Congress for the one remaining instrument to meet the crisis—broad Executive power to wage a war against the emergency, as great as the power that would be given me if we were in fact invaded by a foreign foe." For a nation desperate for leadership, Roosevelt had assumed the burden. He closed by asking God's blessing: "May He protect each and every one of us. May He guide me in the days to come."[84]

Frances Perkins said the scene was like a revival meeting.[85] Roosevelt understood the spiritual need of the people, the need for hope, not despair, and he provided it. FDR did not wear his religion on his sleeve. Neither did he believe he was the instrument of God's will. His beliefs, while deeply held, were basically very simple.* And he never hesitated to share them with his audience.

---

* Frances Perkins, who observed FDR at close range for many years, said "he had no doubts. He just believed with a certainty and simplicity that gave him no pangs or struggles. The problems of the higher criticism, of the application of scientific discoveries to the traditional teachings of the Christian faith and the Biblical record, bothered him not in the least. He knew what religion was and he followed it. It was more than a code of ethics for him. It was a real relationship of man to God, and he felt as certain of it as of the reality of his life." *The Roosevelt I Knew* 141 (New York: Viking Press, 1946).

The effect of the speech was electrifying, the praise all but unanimous. The dreary years of Hoover's excuses passed into oblivion. No one doubted that a new era had begun. Myron C. Taylor, the chairman of United States Steel Corporation, said "I hasten to re-enlist to fight the depression to its end." Frederic E. Williamson, president of the New York Central, liked the speech's brevity and force: "I feel that its directness presages immediate and forceful action." Francis H. Sisson, head of the American Bankers Association, said, "I regard the message as a very courageous and inspiring appeal to the American people for their cooperation and confidence." Newspaper and congressional support was overwhelming. Raymond Moley boasted, "He's taken the ship of state and turned it around." Eleanor said simply, "It was very solemn and a little terrifying."[86]

After a brief buffet luncheon at the White House, Roosevelt took his place on the reviewing stand, a replica of the portico of Andrew Jackson's "Hermitage" in Nashville. For partisan Democrats, the fighting spirit of Old Hickory (not the intellectual reflections of Thomas Jefferson) was the lifeblood of the party, and no effort was spared to cast FDR in Jackson's image. Roosevelt loved parades, and the inaugural procession of 1933—six miles in length, with forty marching bands and delegations from every state—was one of the largest on record. FDR had wanted General John J. Pershing to be grand marshal, but the elderly Pershing was ill in Arizona and General Douglas MacArthur acted in his stead. For almost three hours Roosevelt and MacArthur stood side by side reviewing the passing contingents. The State of New York was represented by the braves of Tammany Hall in full regalia, led by Al Smith striding along on foot. He waved his famous brown derby at the reviewing stand and Roosevelt wagged his silk hat in return. The sharpest political statement was made by a well-rehearsed troupe of African Americans pushing whirring lawn mowers down Pennsylvania Avenue—a parody of Hoover's prediction that grass would grow in the streets following Roosevelt's victory.

At dusk the president left the reviewing stand and returned to the White House, where a reception for several thousand guests was in progress. Roosevelt avoided the throng and slipped upstairs to the Lincoln Study, where the members of his cabinet, confirmed that afternoon, had assembled. He then presided over a joint swearing-in of the entire cabinet as Supreme Court justice Benjamin Cardozo administered the oaths in order, beginning with Secretary of State Hull. "No Cabinet has ever been sworn in before in this way," said FDR. "I am glad all of you were confirmed without opposition."[87]

From the study Roosevelt rushed back downstairs to greet thirteen children on crutches who had come at his invitation from Warm Springs to attend the inauguration. That evening the president and Eleanor dined with seventy-two Roosevelts and their kin in the State Dining Room. Cousin Alice called it "a riot of pleasure. I went with great alacrity and enthusiasm and had a lovely, malicious time."[88] Afterward Eleanor took five carloads of relatives to the inaugural ball, a massive gala at the Washington Auditorium attended by eight thousand guests who had paid the equivalent of $150 a couple, the money donated to charity.*

Roosevelt did not attend. After dinner he returned upstairs to the Lincoln Study, where he and Louis Howe talked over the events of the day. They had waited for this day for twenty-two years, and the two old fighters reminisced. At 10:30 the president turned out the lights and went to bed.

---

* The 1933 inaugural ball was the first since William Howard Taft's in 1909. Wilson was too sanctimonious to permit such indulgence, and Harding apparently lacked the self-confidence to resume the practice. In 1925 and 1929 the Republican National Committee organized unofficial celebrations, but Coolidge and Hoover ostentatiously stayed away and there was no formal ball as such.

FIFTEEN

ONE HUNDRED DAYS

I think this would be a good time for a beer.
—FRANKLIN D. ROOSEVELT, MARCH 12, 1933

ANALOGIES BETWEEN MILITARY and political campaigns are often overdrawn, but what FDR did in rescuing the country in the first hundred days bears comparison with what General Ulysses S. Grant did in preserving the Union. Both men accepted responsibility, delegated freely, and radiated a confidence that inspired their subordinates to do their best. Roosevelt's decisive action to save the banking system during the week following his inauguration resembles Grant's steadfast resolution in the face of impending disaster on the battlefield. At Donelson, Shiloh, and the Wilderness, federal forces had been soundly whipped, and caution dictated a Union withdrawal. Grant counterattacked and carried the day. In March 1933 the nation's financial structure was in chaos and disarray. Roosevelt kept his head, quietly took charge, and gave marching orders to his subordinates. "This Nation asks for action, and action now," he said, and he was as good as his word.[1]

Roosevelt came to Washington armed with two proclamations: one calling Congress back to the capital for a special session;[2] the other declaring a bank holiday under the dormant provisions of the wartime Trading with the Enemy Act. On the morning of the inauguration, FDR asked incoming attorney general Homer Cummings to determine whether the act remained in force. At the same time he requested Treasury secretary Woodin to draft emergency legislation that would permit the banks to reopen in an orderly manner. Those tasks assigned, Roosevelt settled back to enjoy the inaugural festivities. Cummings spent the day at the Department of Justice reading the legislative history of the Trading with the Enemy Act, while Woodin, with Raymond Moley in tow, repaired to the Treasury, where Hoover's team still held forth. When the cabinet was sworn in early Saturday evening, Cummings told FDR he was satisfied that the act remained in effect. Woodin said he could produce a bill for Congress by Thursday.

Roosevelt took both reports at face value. The shape of Woodin's bill was unclear, but FDR was content to leave the drafting to the secretary. As Sara had told Jim Farley, Franklin did not worry about details. Sunday afternoon, after services at St. Thomas' Church,* Roosevelt convened the cabinet to review the situation. "The President outlined more coherently than I had heard it outlined before, just what this banking crisis was and what the legal problems were," Frances Perkins remembered.[3] Armed with Cummings's opinion, FDR said he would issue a proclamation that evening that would declare a four-day bank holiday, embargo the transfer of gold and silver, and prohibit the exchange of dollars into foreign currency. The purpose of the bank holiday, he informed the cabinet, was to prevent further runs on the banks and allow Woodin time to draft the necessary legislation. Roosevelt said he would recall Congress on March 9 so Woodin's bill could be acted upon as soon as it was ready.[4]

That evening FDR met with congressional leaders in the White House. In addition, he invited Senator Glass and Representative Henry B. Steagall of Alabama, chairmen of the respective committees that would report the legislation. Later in the evening he met with House minority leader Bertrand H. Snell of New York and Republican senator Hiram Johnson of California. The most remarkable thing, said Johnson afterward, was Roosevelt's "readiness to assume responsibility and his taking that responsibility with a smile."[5] After eight years as assistant secretary of the Navy, working with Josephus Daniels and observing his easy relations with Capitol Hill, Roosevelt had an unparalleled understanding of how to deal with Congress. He knew how to stroke the members, how to play to their vanity, and how to accommodate their needs. "No president ever approached the prerogatives of the legislative body with more scrupulous attention to detail," said John Gunther, one of Washington's most astute observers.[6]

---

* The Roosevelts sat in their old pew, the one they had used when FDR was assistant secretary of the Navy, eight rows from the front on the left. Because it was Communion Day the service was especially long, and Roosevelt did not get back to the White House until 1:30. *The New York Times*, March 6, 1933.

At 11 P.M. Sunday, after FDR was satisfied that the congressional leadership would be supportive, the White House issued the president's proclamation recalling Congress at noon on Thursday, March 9. Three hours later, Roosevelt's proclamation declaring a bank holiday was released, the delay occasioned by doubts expressed by several directors of the Federal Reserve that the president had the authority to close their banks. At 2 A.M., Woodin, supported by outgoing Treasury secretary Ogden Mills and Fed chairman Eugene Meyer, overrode the directors' objections and ordered the banks closed.*

Monday morning, FDR met with the governors of the forty-eight states in the East Room of the White House. Most were in town to attend the inauguration, and the president had intended to spend the day with them discussing common problems. But the banking crisis took priority. "I have been so occupied that I have not had a chance to prepare any formal remarks," Roosevelt told the governors. He spoke impromptu for ten minutes, explained why he had closed the banks, pledged to provide unemployment relief, and said the national government must find a way to prevent the continued foreclosure of farm and home mortgages.[7] He was given a prolonged standing ovation, and in a pledge of support those present stated, "Without regard to our political affiliations we Governors of the States . . . hereby express our confidence and faith in our President and urge the Congress and all the people of our united country to cooperate with him. . . . He is ready to lead if we are ready to follow."[8]

Roosevelt was riding a tidal wave of support. First reaching out to the leaders of Congress, then appealing to the governors were the instinctive acts of a consummate politician. FDR needed no focus groups or opinion polls; he did not require staff direction or an array of political consultants. He was the quarterback calling the plays, and the people responded by giving him their confidence.†

* FDR's proclamation closing the banks reflected extraordinary input from leading members of the Hoover administration. Woodin was without staff support when he took office, and Secretary Mills, Undersecretary Arthur A. Ballantine (a Harvard classmate of FDR's), Comptroller of the Currency Gloyd Awalt, and Walter Wyatt, general counsel of the Federal Reserve Board, helped put the proclamation into final form. "Mills, Woodin, Ballantine, Awalt, and I had forgotten to be Republicans or Democrats," wrote Raymond Moley. "We were just a bunch of men trying to save the banking system." *After Seven Years* 148 (New York: Harper & Brothers, 1939).

† FDR relished the "quarterback" metaphor. As he described his role calling plays to his press conference on April 13, 1933: "It is a little bit like a football team that has a general

Monday afternoon, Senate Democrats took the unprecedented step of agreeing to bind themselves to support the president whenever a majority of the caucus voted to do so.[9] Since the Democrats controlled the Senate 60–35, that ensured quick passage of whatever emergency measures Roosevelt chose to send up.* Three Democrats, including Huey Long, voted against the resolution, but it is unlikely that any caucus vote would have bound the Kingfish.[10]

Secretary Woodin, meanwhile, had run into difficulty. Drafting comprehensive banking legislation on the spur of the moment was not as simple as it had first appeared. Bankers summoned to Washington on Sunday gave conflicting advice, and Treasury officials were uncertain how best to reopen the banks and ensure an adequate supply of currency after so much had been withdrawn. After forty-eight hours of nonstop discussions at the Treasury, Woodin broke off the talks and went to bed. "I'll be damned if I [will] go back into those meetings until I get my head cleared," he told Moley.[11]

Monday night Woodin dozed a little, strummed his guitar a little, and thought through the various proposals to restore the nation's money supply. He rejected the idea of issuing temporary scrip as the government had done during the panic of 1907, and settled on the Federal Reserve's proposal to issue new currency under the Federal Reserve Act. "It won't look like stage money," he told Moley Tuesday morning. "It'll be money that looks like money. And it won't frighten people."[12]†

---

game plan against the other side. Now the captain and the quarterback of that team know pretty well what the next play is going to be and they know the general strategy of the team; but they cannot tell you what the play after the next play is going to be until the next play is run off. If the play makes ten yards, the succeeding play will be different from what it would have been if they had been thrown for a loss. I think that is the easiest way to explain it."
2 *The Public Papers and Addresses of Franklin D. Roosevelt* 139, Samuel I. Rosenman, ed. (New York: Random House, 1938).

* FDR's working majority in the Senate was far greater than 60–35, since Farmer-Labor Senator Henrik Shipstead of Minnesota and four Republicans—Hiram Johnson of California, George Norris of Nebraska, Robert La Follette of Wisconsin, and Bronson Cutting of New Mexico—were solidly behind the president. In future years, when Shipstead, Johnson, Norris, La Follette, and Cutting faced reelection, FDR did his utmost to ensure that there was no serious Democratic opposition.

† Woodin's decision to issue federal reserve notes backed by the assets of the nation's banking system is the basis of American currency today. A quick look at a bill in one's pocketbook will show the words "FEDERAL RESERVE NOTE" clearly printed on the front. The usage dates from the emergency banking legislation of March 1933.

Relying largely on intuition and common sense, Woodin had cut through a fog of financial advice and adopted the simplest of all possible solutions: the government would simply print new money. It would be backed not by gold or silver but by the assets of the banks in the Federal Reserve system. Woodin laid the plan before Roosevelt at ten o'clock Tuesday morning and in twenty minutes had FDR's approval. With the currency issue decided, the rest of the banking bill fell into place, although putting the provisions into statutory language by noon Thursday proved a near-run thing.[13]

On Wednesday morning, at the height of the banking crisis, FDR held his first press conference in the White House. Coolidge had met the press regularly, but his comments had always been off the record. Hoover had held weekly news conferences but the sessions had been brief and exceedingly formal, the president standing behind a podium in the East Room of the White House. Both Coolidge and Hoover had required that the questions be submitted in writing beforehand and answered only those they wished to. Roosevelt received reporters sitting at his desk in the Oval Office. He met them every Wednesday and Friday and answered off the cuff. Correspondents could ask whatever they wished.[14] Nearly 125 members of the White House press corps crowded into FDR's office at ten o'clock March 8 for a remarkable give-and-take with a president who clearly enjoyed every minute. After shaking hands with each reporter, Roosevelt set the ground rules. He would not answer "iffy" questions or those "which for various reasons I do not wish to discuss, or am not ready to discuss, or I do not know anything about." He said he did not wish to be quoted directly unless Press Secretary Steve Early provided the quotation in writing. Straight news should be attributed to the White House. Some of his remarks would provide background information that could be used but not attributed. And then there would be confidential off-the-record material, which was not to be divulged to anyone.[15] Nearly all of FDR's comments that morning were for background or off the record. The one item of hard news was that he would send his banking bill to Congress the next day and his message would be brief. For forty minutes the president bantered with reporters, answered candidly, and gave them almost nothing they could use directly. "Mr. Roosevelt looked fresh and fit," reported *The New York Times*. "There was little sign of the strain he has undergone—and is still under—since he became President."[16]

It was a virtuoso performance. When Francis Stephenson of the Associated Press intoned the traditional "Thank you, Mr. President," hard-bitten Washington reporters broke into spontaneous applause. Every correspondent in the room had a sense that he or she was participating in the new administration, being confided in by the president and treated as a partner. "We were antagonists," wrote Richard Lee Strout of *The Christian Science Monitor*, "but we liked each other and we laughed and had a perfect understanding of what each was trying to do and there was a certain degree of affection."[17]*

After his press conference Roosevelt met with Harvard's Felix Frankfurter, hoping to entice him into becoming solicitor general—the number two post in the Justice Department and the government's primary advocate before the Supreme Court. Frankfurter declined but in the course of the conversation told FDR he was planning to call on retired Supreme Court justice Oliver Wendell Holmes, who was celebrating his ninety-second birthday. Roosevelt, who knew Holmes from the Wilson years, was intrigued and told Frankfurter he would like to pay his respects as well. That afternoon, breaking with protocol,† the president took time off from the banking crisis to visit Justice Holmes at his I Street home. Negotiating the front steps was difficult for Roosevelt, but he found Holmes in a convivial mood, slightly tipsy on bootleg champagne. They chatted amiably about old times, including prizefighters they had known, and when it was time to leave FDR asked the old justice for his advice. Holmes, who friends said had never been psychologically mustered out of the Union Army after the Civil War, drew himself slowly to attention and said, "Mr. President, you are in a war. Form your battalions and fight."[18]

When FDR came out on the street, hundreds of citizens cheered and clapped uproariously. "Gosh, it sounds good to hear that again," whispered Richard Jervis, chief of the White House Secret Service detail, who had served four years under Hoover.[19]

---

* As one reporter noted, "Mr. Roosevelt's features expressed amazement, curiosity, sympathy, decision, playfulness, dignity, and surpassing charm. Yet he *said* almost nothing. Questions were deflected, diverted, diluted. Answers—when they did come—were concise and clear. But I never met anyone who showed greater capacity for avoiding a direct answer while giving the questioner a feeling it *had* been answered." Quoted in Bernard Asbell, *The F.D.R. Memoirs* 58 (New York: Doubleday, 1973).

† The day before the inauguration, a testy Herbert Hoover told FDR, "Mr. Roosevelt, when you are in Washington as long as I have been, you will learn that the President of the United States calls on nobody." Quoted in Arthur M. Schlesinger, Jr., *The Coming of the New Deal* 14 (Boston: Houghton Mifflin, 1959).

Roosevelt's decision to visit Holmes was purely personal. "Your kind thoughtfulness in coming sets me free to express my congratulations and good wishes," wrote Holmes afterward. "They are very sincere, and follow what seems to me a most fortunate beginning of the term."[20] Holmes is alleged to have observed that Roosevelt had a second-class intellect but a first-class temperament. The story was propagated principally by the literary critic Alexander Woollcott but is as apocryphal as Andrew Jackson's supposed comment after the Supreme Court's 1832 decision in *Worcester v. Georgia:* "John Marshall has made his decision, now let him enforce it." There is absolutely no basis for the statement attributed to Jackson nor any reason for him to have made it.[21] The words were put into Old Hickory's mouth by Horace Greeley in 1864, nineteen years after Jackson's death, just as the Holmes quote was put into the justice's mouth by journalists intent on good copy.[22]*

Wednesday evening, Roosevelt called congressional leaders of both parties to the White House to brief them on the banking bill he would submit when Congress convened the next day. Earlier he had met separately with Huey Long and California's newly elected Democratic senator, William Gibbs McAdoo. Both would be key players Thursday: Long, a perennial loose cannon, and McAdoo, who had been Wilson's longtime secretary of the Treasury. Either could cause trouble, and Roosevelt flattered them with a half hour's personal attention.

The text of the bill was not yet in final form, but FDR, flanked by Woodin and Attorney General Cummings, carefully reviewed a draft with the legislative leaders. As Roosevelt explained it, the bill would confirm his actions under the Trading with the Enemy Act, give the president added powers to regulate gold and foreign exchange, provide for the issuance of Federal Reserve notes to restore the nation's currency supply, authorize the secretary of the Treasury to review and reopen all banks found to be solvent, and reorganize those in trouble so they too could eventually reopen. The meeting lasted from 8:30 until shortly before 1 A.M. Drafters at the Treasury were still working on the statu-

---

* Two years later to the day, on what would have been his ninety-fourth birthday, Holmes was buried with full military honors at Arlington National Cemetery. Roosevelt was among the mourners at the graveside. A soft spring rain was falling, but, as one of Holmes's admirers said, "Soldiers don't mind the rain." Liva Baker, *The Justice from Beacon Hill* 643 (New York: HarperCollins, 1991).

tory language, but from his presentation it was clear that Roosevelt had decided to preserve the banking system more or less as it was rather than take advantage of the crisis to nationalize it.

The House of Representatives convened as scheduled at noon, Thursday, March 9. Congress would remain in session until June 15, exactly one hundred days, the most productive legislative session in history. As soon as the members were sworn in and officers elected, the president's banking message was read: "I cannot too strongly urge upon the Congress the clear necessity for immediate action."[23] At 2:55 P.M. House majority leader Joseph Byrns of Tennessee introduced the legislation (H.R. 1491) under a closed rule that permitted no amendments. Debate was limited to forty minutes. Minority Leader Snell asked Republican support: "Give the President what he says is necessary."[24] The printed bill was not yet available, and Chairman Steagall of the Banking and Currency Committee read aloud from a typewritten copy. Before he finished, shouts of "Vote! Vote!" echoed through the chamber. There was no debate. There had been no hearings, no committee consideration, no action by either caucus. Members took on faith what the leadership presented, and the leadership took on faith what FDR requested. Shortly before four o'clock Speaker Henry T. Rainey of Illinois asked for the yeas and nays. The bill passed with a unanimous whoop of approval. There was no request for a roll call. *The New York Times* reported that the members appeared like poker players "who throw in their last chips in the belief they will win."[25]*

By the time the Senate turned to the bill, printed copies were on hand and the debate was less perfunctory. Huey Long sought greater aid for the "little banks at the forks of the creeks," while western populists, led by Robert La Follette, wanted FDR to nationalize all the banks. The amendments were shouted down, and just before seven-thirty the Senate passed the bill 73–7, the opposition coming primarily from Progressives, who believed the bill did not go far enough in asserting federal control.[26] An hour later the measure was at the White House. FDR whipped out a dime-store pen Nancy Cook had given him

---

* Eleanor Roosevelt observed the proceedings from the House gallery. When ER was recognized, she was given a standing ovation. "The House rose as one man," said *The New York Times.* "The informality of the new occupants of the White House was never more forcefully evident. Not only did [ER] wear no hat, but she knitted almost constantly." March 10, 1933.

and quickly added his signature. The entire legislative process, from the bill's introduction in the House to the president's signature, took less than six hours. After signing the bill into law Roosevelt extended the bank holiday. Originally, he hoped some banks might reopen Friday. But officials at Treasury and the Federal Reserve needed more time to separate the sound banks from those that needed help.

Under regulations promulgated by the president, banks wishing to reopen required a license from the secretary of the Treasury. Reviewing assets and liabilities was a time-consuming process, but within a month, eight out of every ten banks were open again. By and large this was a bureaucratic process. The exception was the Bank of America, A. P. Giannini's West Coast goliath, with 410 branches in California and more than a million depositors. Woodin and Comptroller of the Currency F. Gloyd Awalt, a Hoover holdover, believed the giant bank was no worse off than any other California bank and to keep it closed could cause enormous distress with ramifications throughout the country. Lined up on the other side was the Federal Reserve Bank in San Francisco, headed by John U. Calkins, an old-line banker with strong ties to California's economic and social elite. The clubby West Coast banking community, of which Calkins was a charter member, despised and feared Giannini, an upstart Italian immigrant whose vigorous expansion threatened their supremacy. Calkins was adamant in his opinion that the Bank of America was insolvent, although the evidence was mixed.

Woodin and Awalt took the case to the president. Roosevelt's handling of the situation was masterly. He declined to take direct action and order Giannini's bank reopened. Instead, he shifted the decision to Calkins. FDR instructed Woodin to call the San Francisco director and either convince him to agree to the bank's opening or require him to take personal responsibility for keeping it closed. "The conversation was punctuated by some pretty strong language on Woodin's end," Moley recalled. When Woodin asked point-blank if Calkins would accept responsibility for keeping the Bank of America closed, he declined. "Well then," said Woodin, "the bank will open."[27] Giannini was personally grateful to FDR and became a staunch supporter of the New Deal. Roosevelt, for his part, enjoyed taking personal credit, though his hand had been hidden. "It was the same old crowd trying to destroy competition," he told California lawyer J.F.T. O'Connor.[28]

As soon as FDR signed the Emergency Banking Act, he moved to consolidate his conservative support. Just as he did after winning the nomination in Chicago, Roosevelt turned right before he turned left. Within the hour he summoned congressional leaders back to the White House to inform them he wanted authority to reduce government spending across the board.* Roosevelt sought to put the government's house in order: to balance the federal budget before undertaking emergency relief. The two biggest culprits, in FDR's eyes, were government salaries and bloated veterans' benefits. He told the legislators he wanted to cut all government workers' salaries by at least 15 percent to bring them into line with the reduced cost of living since 1928 and scale back the elaborate array of entitlements enacted for veterans since World War I—currently consuming roughly one quarter of the federal budget.[29] Under Roosevelt's proposal, for example, congressional pay would be reduced from $10,000 to $8,500 and his own salary would fall from $90,000 to $75,000. Shortly after midnight the leaders departed—some stunned, some enthusiastic, and a few, such as the populist John Rankin of Mississippi and progressive Robert La Follette, very angry at what the president proposed.

Roosevelt was undeterred. The following day, Friday, March 10, he sent a special message to Congress: "For three long years the Federal Government has been on the road to bankruptcy." The growing deficit, he said, had increased economic stagnation, multiplied the unemployed, and contributed to the banking collapse. National recovery required the government's credit to rest on a solid foundation, and that required that the budget be balanced. Roosevelt asked for broad authority to effect the economies he deemed necessary. "If the Congress chooses to vest me with this responsibility it will be exercised in a spirit of justice to all, of sympathy to those who are in need and of maintaining inviolate the basic welfare of the United States."[30] Attached to the message was "A Bill to Maintain the Credit of the United States" drafted by the Bureau of the Budget.[31]

Congress was incredulous, and for a moment the president's control hung in the balance. Although conservatives such as Carter Glass and Mississippi's

---

* Congressional leaders attending included Speaker Rainey and House minority leader Snell; Senate majority leader Robinson; Congressmen John McDuffie of Alabama, chairman of the House Economy Committee; Sam Rayburn (D., Tex.); John Rankin (D., Miss.); William Connery (D., Mass.); and Senators Glass, La Follette, Wagner, Edward Costigan (D., Colo.), and James Byrnes (D., S.C.). Also in attendance were Secretaries Ickes, Wallace, and Dern, plus Director of the Budget Lewis Douglas. *The New York Times*, March 10, 1933.

Pat Harrison offered unstinting praise, liberal Democrats felt betrayed. The last thing the country needed at this time was more deflation, and FDR's proposal was surely deflationary. In the House, Majority Leader Byrns refused to introduce the bill. When Speaker Rainey assembled the Democratic caucus Saturday morning, he failed to get the necessary two-thirds vote that would have bound the party to support the president. That afternoon the bill was introduced on the floor by Representative John McDuffie of Alabama, a skilled parliamentarian and rock-hard conservative who had been narrowly defeated for the speakership.[32] After two hours of fierce debate, the bill passed 266–138. Ninety-two Democrats and five Farmer-Labor members voted against, but 69 Republicans led by the ultraconservative John Taber of New York crossed the aisle to support the president.* At the same time the House was acting, the Senate Finance Committee, chaired by Pat Harrison, reported the bill favorably, setting the stage for action by the full Senate on Monday. "I am for giving the President whatever he wants in the way of power," said Senator Arthur Capper, a Kansas Republican. "This is an emergency situation."[33]

Sunday evening, at the conclusion of his first week in the White House, FDR gave his first fireside chat. The banks were scheduled to reopen Monday, and Roosevelt wanted to avoid a panic. In simple language he analyzed the banking crisis and spelled out what had been done. "I do not promise you that every bank will be reopened or that individual losses will not be suffered, but there will be no losses that possibly could be avoided."[34] Will Rogers said the president had explained the banking situation so well that even the bankers understood it.[35]

Public response was overwhelming. "When millions of people can hear the President speak to them directly in their own homes, we get a new meaning for the old phrase about a public man 'going to the country,' " said *The New York Times*. When the banks reopened Monday, reassured depositors returned much of the money they had withdrawn. Not only was there no run on the banks, but the Federal Reserve reported that deposits exceeded withdrawals by more than two to one despite the cash-starved existence most had led the past week. The banking crisis was over. On foreign exchanges the dollar soared.

---

* "This is not a Democratic bill and it is not a Republican bill," said Mary Norton of New Jersey. "It is a bill to maintain the credit of the United States, and I shall support it." *The New York Times*, March 12, 1933.

Raymond Moley proclaimed, "Capitalism was saved in eight days."[36] When the New York Stock Exchange reopened March 15 (it had been closed since March 3), stock prices rose by a whopping 15 percent—the greatest one-day rise in living memory.

Conservatives vied with liberals in shouting Roosevelt's praise. "The new Administration in Washington has superbly risen to the occasion," said *The Wall Street Journal*. Henry Stimson wrote FDR, "I am delighted with the progress of your first week and send you my heartiest congratulations." Newton D. Baker called Roosevelt "a providential person at a providential moment." William Randolph Hearst said, "I guess at your next election we will make it unanimous."[37]

Roosevelt stayed on the offensive. At dinner the evening he delivered his fireside chat, the president told guests with a twinkle in his eye, "I think this would be a good time for a beer."[38] That sent Louis Howe scurrying for a copy of the Democratic platform. When FDR finished his radio address, he wrote a seventy-two-word message to Congress quoting word for word the Democratic pledge to amend the Volstead Act and permit the sale of beer and light wine.[39]* The message, perhaps the shortest on record, went to the House at noon Monday. Divided Democrats rallied back to the president's side. The Ways and Means Committee drafted the requisite legislation within five hours of FDR's request. On Tuesday, the House of Representatives, ignoring the pleas of the Anti-Saloon League and the Women's Christian Temperance Union, voted for beer, 316–97. On Wednesday the Senate passed FDR's economy measure 62–13, and on Thursday it voted to amend the Volstead Act 43–30. Roosevelt signed the Economy Act on March 20 and the Beer-Wine Revenue Act two days later. The administration was three for three, and the Democratic ranks were now more solid than ever.

Originally FDR had assumed that Congress would remain in session only so long as necessary to deal with the banking crisis. But with the legislative tide running so strongly in favor of the administration, he decided to hold it in

---

* The lame-duck Seventy-second Congress had voted on February 20, 1933, to repeal the Eighteenth (Prohibition) Amendment, but the proposal, which subsequently became the Twenty-first Amendment to the Constitution, did not become effective until ratified by the thirty-sixth state (Utah) on December 5, 1933. Amending the Volstead Act provided interim relief.

Washington until the bulk of the New Deal program could be enacted. Public confidence had recovered, but the economy remained in the doldrums. Freight car loadings, electric power, and steel production continued to slide, employment had drifted downward, and there was as yet no glimmer of relief for farmers or those without work. "I haven't any real news," Roosevelt told his press conference on Wednesday, March 15. And after that casual disclaimer he broke the story that he was going to move immediately to assist the nation's farmers and the unemployed. The banking bill, the economy measure, and the amendment of the Volstead Act had done nothing constructive for the economy, he said. What was needed was a definite effort to put people to work and a program to raise farm prices. FDR said he could not go into detail because the measures were still being worked out. But he made it clear that he planned no letup.[40]

Congress was ready to respond. A full third of the House (144 of 435 members) were new to Washington, swept into office on FDR's coattails. In the Senate, with fourteen new members, Democrats were in control for the first time since the election of 1916. Both houses turned to the president for leadership. And Roosevelt took no chances. Holding almost one hundred thousand full- and part time jobs not subject to civil service rules, FDR let it be known that he would make no patronage appointments until the end of the session. John McDuffie drove the point home when he demanded a roll-call vote on the economy act. "When the *Congressional Record* goes to President Roosevelt's desk in the morning he will look over the roll call we are about to take, and I warn you new Democrats to be careful where your names are found."[41]*

On Thursday, March 16, FDR sent the first genuine New Deal measure to Congress, an agriculture bill intended to raise farm income by reducing agricultural surpluses through a system of domestic allotments. Farmers would be paid directly by the government not to produce crops beyond an allotment set by the secretary of agriculture. Funding for the allotment payments would be

---

* Roosevelt was true to his word. At the end of the session *Time* reported that of the hundred thousand appointments available, FDR had made only 272, all at the highest level. The remaining jobs were being held in limbo by Postmaster General James A. Farley—whom *Time* called the party's chief patronage dispenser. Farley had a "white list" of Democrats who had consistently supported the president and a "sinners' roll" of party members who had deserted on crucial roll calls. The constituents of those on the "sinners' roll" could expect slim pickings. June 26, 1933.

provided by processing taxes levied on millers, canners, packers, textile manu-facturers, and commodity brokers. Farmers would derive immediate income through the allotment payments, and when the surpluses were reduced the price of farm products was expected to rise proportionately. It was a radical departure, providing unheard-of government control of agricultural produc-tion, historically the most individualistic segment of the economy. "I tell you frankly that it is a new and untried path," Roosevelt told Congress, "but I tell you with equal frankness that an unprecedented condition calls for the trial of new means to rescue agriculture."[42] The measure, eventually known as the Agricultural Adjustment Act, was drafted by Secretary Wallace and Rexford Tugwell following a week of breakneck discussions with farm leaders through-out the country. The bill was followed three weeks later by Roosevelt's request for legislation to provide federal funding to refinance farm mortgages threat-ened with foreclosure.[43] Like the emergency banking legislation and the econ-omy bill, the agricultural adjustment bill was considered by the House under a closed rule prohibiting amendments. Debate was limited to four hours. On March 22, less than a week after it had been received, the measure passed the House 315–98, all but 24 Democrats voting in favor.

The bill ran into trouble in the Senate. Food and fiber processors had time to mobilize against the processing levy, and a knock-down, drag-out fight en-sued. Wallace and Tugwell urged the president to force the bill through with-out amendments, but FDR was not ready to risk his coalition on an issue so fundamental as farm relief. He instructed Majority Leader Robinson to accept whatever changes were necessary. If a senator's support could be obtained by adding his amendment, he said, add it. The resulting bill, said one Washington observer, "sought to legalize almost anything anybody could think up."[44] The final sweetener came when Roosevelt agreed that all jobs created to administer the Agricultural Adjustment Act would be outside the civil service—a vast reservoir for legislative patronage. After five weeks of debate, the Senate ap-proved the measure 64–20, having added the president's mortgage protection plan to the bill. It was signed into law by FDR on May 12.[45]

Roosevelt saw the farm program as the centerpiece of the New Deal. Not only was agriculture the most perennially depressed sector of the economy, but ever since his experience as a state senator, FDR (who had chaired the Agriculture Committee in Albany) had stressed the relationship between farm prosperity and the well-being of the rest of the country. If farmers had no money to buy what industry produced, the cities suffered as well. The lopsided majority that eventually voted for the bill reflected Roosevelt's skill in handling the Senate, almost on a man-to-man basis. The food processors were routed, and the New Deal coalition was solidified.* In that sense the passage of the Agricultural Adjustment Act had a significance considerably beyond its impact on America's farms.

The legislative floodgates were open. The week after FDR sent his farm bill to Congress, he asked for quick authorization to establish a civilian conservation corps, which would employ young men in reforestation and flood control; requested $500 million in federal funds to provide direct relief for the unemployed; and urged the necessity of a public works program to put people to work. These were quickly followed by requests for regulation of the securities market, mortgage relief for home owners, establishment of a Tennessee Valley Authority, and the rehabilitation of the nation's railroads.[46] There was no particular order in which the bills were submitted. Roosevelt was still operating with only a handful of his own appointees. As soon as they were able to get on top of the situation and draft the necessary legislation, FDR sent it forward.

The Civilian Conservation Corps became one of the New Deal's most popular programs. By the time the United States entered World War II, the CCC had put more than 3 million young men to work for $30 a month ($25 of which they were required to send home to their families) planting trees, thinning saplings, cutting firebreaks, building bridges, digging reservoirs—the gamut of vigorous outdoor activity to protect, enhance, and reclaim the nation's natural resources.

The CCC was Roosevelt's personal idea. Throughout his life FDR had an

---

* The processors eventually had their day in court and temporarily prevailed when the Supreme Court, speaking through Justice Owen Roberts, overturned the Agricultural Adjustment Act in *United States v. Butler*, 297 U.S. 1 (1936). The decision is well known to constitutional scholars for Roberts's remarkable description of constitutional adjudication. The Court's duty, as Roberts would have it, was simply "to lay the Article of the Constitution which is invoked beside the statute which is challenged and to decide whether the latter squares with the former." The decision in *Butler* was explicitly overruled in *Mulford v. Smith*, 307 U.S. 38 (1939), and *Wickard v. Filburn*, 317 U.S. 111 (1942). Of more than passing interest, the decision in *Mulford v. Smith* reversing *Butler* was also written by Justice Roberts, who apparently found a new set of carpenter's tools.

abiding interest in conservation, and reforestation ranked high on his list of personal priorities. At Hyde Park he sometimes planted 20,000 to 50,000 trees a year on his estate.[47] As governor of New York when the Depression hit, he had initiated a work program that by 1932 employed 10,000 men planting trees throughout the state. In his acceptance speech at Chicago, he promised to put a million men to work fighting soil erosion and reforesting the land-scape.[48] And during his first week of office, when he was grappling with the banking crisis, he found time to draft a bill that would provide employment for 500,000 men in the nation's forests.

On Thursday, March 9, the day Congress convened and the banking bill was passed, FDR explained his proposal to secretaries Ickes and Dern, gave them a one-page summary, and instructed them to draft the necessary legislation by nine that evening. After signing the banking bill, Roosevelt read over the draft, made a few changes, and invited Miss Perkins and Secretary Wallace to comment. During the next week the program was scaled back to an initial 250,000 men, but the basic structure of Roosevelt's plan remained intact. The men, ages eighteen to twenty-five, would live in government-built camps, food and clothing would be provided, and the pay would be a dollar a day. Enlistment would be for six months, with possible renewals up to two years. The Labor Department would recruit the men, the Army would run the camps, and the Forestry Service would supervise the work.

"I think I will go ahead with this," FDR told Moley, "—the way I did with beer."[49] At his press conference on March 15, Roosevelt revealed his plan on background, explaining in remarkable detail the ins and outs of forest management.[50] The following week he sent his proposal to Congress. "I estimate that 250,000 men can be given temporary employment by early summer if you give me authority to proceed within the next two weeks."[51] Organized labor voiced misgivings: first at the dollar-a-day pay, which, they argued, would depress wages throughout the country; then at the regimentation of camp living. "It smacks of fascism, of Hitlerism, of a form of sovietism," said William Green, president of the American Federation of Labor.[52]

Roosevelt moved quickly to douse the criticism. Yes, the pay was only a dollar a day, he told reporters on March 22, but it cost the government another dollar a day to feed and house the men. "Two dollars a day would probably be higher than what labor is being paid in a great many places." As for the charge of militarization, FDR called it utter rubbish. "The camps will be run just like those in any big project—Boulder Dam or anything like that. Obviously, you can't allow a man in a dormitory to get up in the middle of the night and blow a bugle. You have to have order—just perfectly normal order."[53]

Stung by labor's opposition, FDR made it clear he was not backing down. That evening he invited all members of the House and Senate Labor Committees to the White House to discuss the measure and to emphasize the need for speed. Flattered by the president's solicitation, the legislators agreed to expedite the bill's passage by holding joint hearings of the two committees—an extraordinary procedure reserved for emergency situations. After two days of hearings dominated by administration spokesmen, the CCC bill was reported favorably. Two days later it was passed in the Senate by voice vote without a roll call. The House acted on March 30, again by voice vote, and Roosevelt signed the act on March 31.

In retrospect it seems incredible, but in less than a month, and aside from rescuing the banking system, FDR had taken on and defeated three of the most powerful special interests in the nation: veterans (with the economy bill), temperance (with the beer bill), and organized labor (with the CCC).

Neither FDR nor the union leadership could afford a permanent estrangement, and the fence-mending began immediately. To head the Civilian Conservation Corps, Roosevelt selected Robert Fechner, a vice president of the AFL who had worked with FDR and Howe on labor matters during World War I. A rough-at-the-edges trade unionist with remarkable administrative skills, Fechner proved to be an inspired choice and headed the CCC throughout its existence. And William Green was not neglected. When FDR made his first inspection tour of CCC camps in Shenandoah National Park in August 1933, he invited Green to accompany him. Green was thrilled with the invitation and later wrote Roosevelt that he "could not help but view the whole project in a most sympathetic way."[54] From that point on the CCC aroused no serious opposition from organized labor.

The CCC did more than reclaim natural resources. It literally gave 3 million young men a new lease on life. The money they sent home supported many times their numbers, and the funds spent on constructing and running the camps were a constant source of revenue for the communities in which they were located. Ultimately almost 2,500 camps were established, most west of the Mississippi. The Army provided the organizing talent, and its contribution was enthusiastic and effective.* Many officers associated with the CCC (such as Colonel George C. Marshall, who organized nineteen camps in Georgia and Florida) developed strong ties to the Roosevelt administration and, while not overtly political (most officers in the regular Army never voted), came to understand and sympathize with the aims of the New Deal.[55]

Roosevelt's two other pump-priming initiatives, emergency relief and public works, sailed through Congress as well. On March 30 the Senate approved (55–17) FDR's request for $500 million for grants-in-aid to assist the states in their relief efforts. Three weeks later the House concurred, 326–42.[56] The act established a Federal Emergency Relief Agency to administer the grants, and Roosevelt immediately named Harry Hopkins, who had led relief efforts in New York, to head it. Speed was important, and Hopkins knew it. Before nightfall on his first day in office he had cabled funds to the governors of Colorado, Illinois, Iowa, Michigan, Mississippi, Ohio, and Texas.[57] At the end of its first year, FERA had assisted 17 million people and disbursed $1.5 billion.† All of this with a staff of 121 persons and a monthly payroll of $22,000.[58] As Roosevelt knew from working with Hopkins in New York, money would flow swiftly to where it was needed, and overhead would be kept to a minimum.

Passing the public works bill required more time. Assigned to Miss Perkins and the Department of Labor, the original draft included a wish list of projects that totaled $5 billion—roughly $400 million more than the entire federal budget in 1932–33.[59] Roosevelt reviewed the proposal with his principal cabinet officers on Saturday afternoon, April 29, and pared it to $1 billion. According to Charles Wyzanski, the Labor Department solicitor who had drafted the bill, FDR took the New York projects one by one "and showed a remarkable

---

* After the economy measure was passed in March 1933, FDR and the Bureau of the Budget zeroed in on the Army to absorb a significant portion of the cuts. The 1934 military budget was to be slashed by $80 million, roughly 51 percent. But the necessity to get the CCC up and running placed a premium on military experience. Not only was the Army budget spared, but many reserve officers were recalled to active duty to manage the camps. William Manchester, *American Caesar: Douglas MacArthur* 154–156 (Boston: Little, Brown, 1978); Forrest C. Pogue, *George C. Marshall: Education of a General* 276–280 (New York: Viking Press, 1963).

† In current dollars the $1.5 billion disbursed would amount to roughly $21 billion, given a conversion factor of 13.89.

knowledge of every single item. It was a masterly demonstration, and he convinced everyone how unsound most of the projects were."[60] By the time the bill was presented to Congress in May, the cost of the projects included had risen to $3.3 billion, a figure the Bureau of the Budget thought was sustainable. It was passed in the early morning hours of June 16, 1933, the final piece of legislation enacted during the hundred days.[61]*

At the end of March, as the relief measures took shape, Roosevelt shifted the administration's focus to Wall Street. Reflecting public demand for reform of the stock market, the Democratic platform had pledged legislative action to require full disclosure of all pertinent financial information whenever stocks and bonds were issued.[62] On March 29 FDR sent the securities legislation forward. "This proposal," he said, "adds to the ancient rule of *caveat emptor*, the further doctrine 'let the seller also beware.'" Roosevelt told Congress that the bill put the burden of truth on the seller. "It should give impetus to honest dealing in securities and thereby bring back public confidence."[63] As with the Agricultural Adjustment Act and the CCC, the proposal for federal regulation of securities broke new ground. The bill required that complete information on new stock issues be filed with the Federal Trade Commission, which was empowered to stop the sale if the data were found defective. Company officials were made personally responsible, subject to both criminal and civil penalties. The legislation was put into final form for FDR by Felix Frankfurter and shepherded through Congress by Sam Rayburn, chairman of the Interstate Commerce Committee. Roosevelt signed it into law May 27, 1933. "If the country is to flourish," said FDR, "capital must be invested in enterprise. But those who seek to draw upon other people's money must be wholly candid regarding the facts on which the investor's judgment is asked."[64]

Two weeks after sending the securities bill to Congress, FDR shifted gears by

---

* The act established the Federal Emergency Administration of Public Works, commonly known as the Public Works Administration, and on July 8, 1933, FDR appointed Interior Secretary Harold Ickes to be the administrator. Between July 1933 and March 1939, the PWA financed the construction of more than 34,000 projects at a cost of more than $6 billion. Projects ran the gamut from lighthouses and battleships to municipal sewer systems. Approximately 1.2 million men were employed on site under the program. The PWA was dissolved in June 1941. 2 *Public Papers and Addresses of Franklin D. Roosevelt* 270–271. For the Public Works Administration generally, see *America Builds: The Record of the PWA* (Washington, D.C.: U.S. Government Printing Office, 1939).

asking for the creation of a Tennessee Valley Authority to develop the economic potential of one of the nation's great river basins—and one of the most poverty-stricken regions of the country. The Tennessee River and its tributaries, spilling into seven southern states,* drained an area of 640,000 square miles. Flooded might be more precise. The once-fertile bottomland was sadly depleted; the forests were cut over; the thin soil of the uplands was eroded, crisscrossed with gullies, barren of serious vegetation, and unable to contain the annual runoff from devastating spring rains. Income in the region was less than half the national average. Only two out of every hundred farms had electricity. Infant mortality was four times greater than elsewhere, pellagra and tuberculosis were endemic, medical care was sparse, and sanitation was primitive. There was no industry to speak of, little commercial life, and few prospects other than further descent into squalor.[65]

It was a scene Roosevelt knew well from his exposure to similar rural poverty at Warm Springs. But the Tennessee valley had resources lacking in southern Georgia: specifically, the giant hydroelectric dam on the Tennessee at Muscle Shoals, Alabama, constructed by the federal government during World War I to produce power for the manufacture of munitions. Since the war, the great productive capacity had remained idle, water falling uselessly through its spillways. Twice progressives in Congress, led by George Norris of Nebraska, had passed legislation authorizing the government to operate the dam to produce electric power for the region, but both Coolidge (in 1928) and Hoover (in 1931) had vetoed the bills. For the government to produce electricity, said Hoover, would be "the negation of the ideals upon which our civilization has been based."[66]

The dam at Muscle Shoals was the focus of FDR's proposal. In January 1933 Roosevelt had taken time from Warm Springs to visit Muscle Shoals with his daughter, Anna, accompanied by Norris and an imposing delegation of power experts and congressional leaders.[67] "It is at least twice as big as I ever had any conception of it being," he told Norris. Later that evening, speaking impromptu to a large crowd from the portico of the state capitol in Montgomery, Roosevelt said he was determined to do two things: "The first is to put Muscle Shoals to work. The second is to make of Muscle Shoals a part of an even greater development that will take in all of that magnificent Tennessee River

* Tennessee, Alabama, Mississippi, Kentucky, Georgia, North Carolina, and Virginia.

from the mountains of Virginia down to the Ohio. . . . We have an opportunity of setting an example of planning, tying in industry and agriculture and forestry and flood prevention, tying them all into a unified whole over a distance of a thousand miles."[68]

On April 10 FDR asked Congress for authorizing legislation. The brief message, which he wrote in his own hand, forcefully restated Roosevelt's commitment to use the power of government for the general welfare. The Tennessee Valley Authority, he said, involves "the future lives and welfare of millions. It touches and gives life to all forms of human concerns."[69]

Norris called Roosevelt's message "the most wonderful and far-reaching humanitarian document that has ever come from the White House." In the House of Representatives, Mississippi's John Rankin said, "The power that can be generated at Muscle Shoals now exceeds the physical strength of all the slaves freed by the Civil War."[70] Norris introduced the bill in the Senate, where it passed 63–20. Rankin led the administration forces in the House, where opposition was stiffer. Joseph Martin of Massachusetts spearheaded the Republican attack, asserting that the TVA was "patterned closely after one of the soviet dreams"—a theme embellished by New Jersey's Charles Eaton, who charged that the scheme "is simply an attempt to graft onto our American system the Russian idea." Even *The New York Times* expressed alarm: "Enactment of any such bill at this time would mark the 'low' of Congressional folly."[71] But the Democrats were riding high, the leadership was in firm control, and the House voted its approval, 306–91. Roosevelt signed the Tennessee Valley Authority Act the afternoon of May 18, 1933.[72] At a stroke FDR had solidified his support among the two most disparate elements of his coalition: traditional southern Democrats and Republican progressives. He had also taken a massive step toward modernizing the South.[73]*

From Wall Street and the TVA Roosevelt turned his attention to the plight of home owners beset by mortgages and taxes they could not pay. In 1932, 273,000 home mortgages had been foreclosed—almost four times the normal

---

* Utility shareholders quickly challenged the constitutionality of the TVA but lost in a powerful decision written for an all-but-unanimous Court (8–1) by Chief Justice Hughes. The Court upheld the act based on Congress's authority to provide for national defense and to regulate interstate commerce. The sale of electricity—a by-product—was authorized by Article IV, section 3 of the Constitution, granting the federal government power to sell property it acquires lawfully. *Ashwander v. TVA*, 297 U.S. 288 (1936).

rate—and in early 1933 the rate had doubled yet again. Increased foreclosures not only caused enormous personal hardship but further endangered the assets of hard-pressed banks, savings and loan associations, and insurance companies. House prices plummeted, and the entire real estate market was threatened with collapse. New-home construction shrank to 10 percent of its 1929 level. Even home owners and prospective purchasers who had money found it difficult to negotiate new mortgages or renew old ones.[74] The impact on the nation's morale was devastating. The decline in home values, combined with the threat of foreclosure, struck at the roots of the American dream.

On April 13 FDR asked Congress for legislation to protect individual home owners from foreclosure. Home ownership was a guarantee of social and economic stability, said Roosevelt, and to protect home owners from "inequitable enforced liquidation at a time of general distress is a proper concern of the Government."[75] The resulting legislation, which marched swiftly through Congress, was patterned on the farm mortgage bill. It established a Home Owners' Loan Corporation to refinance the mortgages of distressed home owners, provide money for taxes and repairs, and set repayment schedules over a long term at a relatively low (5 percent) interest rate. To ensure that the act benefited only small home owners, the ceiling for HOLC loans was $20,000.[76]

The act was not only a lifesaver for millions of Americans, it initiated a housing boom that has continued to this day. New loan criteria, longer amortization periods, and lower interest rates made home ownership readily accessible for the first time in American history. The HOLC assumed one sixth of all urban mortgages in the United States. When its loan authority expired in 1936, it had made more than one million loans totaling $3.1 billion.[77] Like the TVA, which brought southern Democrats and northern progressives together, nothing solidified FDR's support among the American middle class as the HOLC.[78]

After six weeks in office, Roosevelt could relish his accomplishments. The banking crisis had been ameliorated, the government's budget pruned, and the heavy hand of mandatory temperance overturned. The farm crisis, if not under control, was being dealt with; young men were being mobilized in the cause of conservation; and relief was flowing to embattled home owners and the unemployed. A significant public works program was in the making, the administration had undertaken to tame Wall Street, and a breathtaking experiment in government planning—the Tennessee Valley Authority—had been approved. FDR was at the top of his game. He was improvising from crisis to crisis and savoring every minute. The legislation passed and the initiatives undertaken shaped the New Deal and decisively altered the nation's course. Yet each measure represented Roosevelt's nimble response to circumstance rather than any grand design. "To look upon these policies as the result of a unified plan," wrote Raymond Moley afterward, is "to believe that the accumulation of stuffed snakes, baseball pictures, school flags, old tennis shoes, carpenter's tools, geometry books, and chemistry sets in a boy's bedroom could have been put there by an interior decorator."[79]

Nothing better illustrates FDR's response to circumstance than his decision on April 18 to take the United States off the gold standard. At issue was whether to inflate the nation's currency and hope that commodity prices would rise in the aftermath. Advice was divided. Traditional economists and the Bureau of the Budget believed that prosperity would return only when government expenditures were brought under control. Adherence to the gold standard ensured a sound dollar and generous protection for creditors and bondholders. Most of Wall Street agreed. Bernard Baruch, an oracle of orthodoxy, ridiculed the idea that to inflate the currency might help restore prices. "People who talk about gradually inflating might as well talk about firing a gun off gradually. . . . Money cannot go back to work in an atmosphere filled with a threat to destroy its value."[80]

Those favoring inflation included most members of Congress, particularly those from the farm states, brain trusters like Moley and Tugwell, and, surprisingly, the House of Morgan. Rising above conventional wisdom, J. P. Morgan and his partners, Thomas Lamont and Russell Leffingwell, worried about the unrest that continued to sweep the farm belt and believed a rise in commodity prices was essential to ensure the nation's political stability.* The fastest way to achieve that was to go off the gold standard and let the market set the value of the dollar. A cheaper dollar would make American farm products more attractive to foreign buyers, and the increased demand would raise domestic prices.

---

* In a scene reminiscent of Shays' Rebellion in 1787, U.S. District Court judge Charles C. Bradley was dragged from the bench in Le Mars, Iowa, by angry farmers, beaten, thrown into a truck, and driven out of town, where he was nearly lynched for refusing to suspend mortgage foreclosures. Six counties in Iowa were placed under martial law, and Governor Clyde L. Herring called out the National Guard to maintain order. The unrest in Iowa was the tip of the iceberg.

Morgan and his partners were not idle spectators. They made whatever overtures they could to the administration through Treasury secretary Woodin and enlisted Walter Lippmann, the nation's premier political analyst, in the cause. "Walter," said Leffingwell over lunch in New York, "you've got to explain to the people why we can no longer afford to chain ourselves to the gold standard. Then maybe Roosevelt, who I am sure agrees, will be able to act."[81]

Roosevelt may or may not have agreed. On monetary matters FDR was agnostic. He was amused at the doctrinal intensity of the gold bugs but wary of unleashing a runaway inflation such as the one that had helped destroy the Weimar Republic in Germany. Eventually he came to the conclusion that if the nation was to recover, inflation was inevitable. The gold standard would have to go. Lippmann's article may have helped. On April 18 Lippmann wrote that the United States faced a choice between keeping up prices at home and defending the gold content of the dollar abroad. "No nation has been able to do both." If Washington stayed with the gold standard, it would be unable to fund the ambitious relief and public works programs the New Deal had initiated. In Lippmann's view, there was no question what the president should do.[82]

That evening Roosevelt summoned his financial advisers to the White House.[83] Normally such conclaves began with considerable jocularity and small talk. This time Roosevelt got right to the point. "Congratulate me," he said. "We are off the gold standard."[84] FDR had made the decision. He wasn't asking advice. Woodin and Moley had been informed beforehand, but for everyone else the news was a shock. "All hell broke loose," Moley remembered.[85] For two hours the discussion raged, much to Roosevelt's amusement. James Warburg, then an adviser to the president, called the plan "harebrained and irresponsible."[86] Budget Director Lewis Douglas wailed, "This is the end of Western civilization."[87] FDR was unmoved. The following day he announced the decision to the press. He had come down with a cold overnight and received reporters in his quarters upstairs in the White House. "I have gotten to the point where even a cigarette tastes bad," he said. After sparring a few rounds with correspondents, FDR broke the news: the United States was off gold. "The whole problem before us is to raise commodity prices. Let the dollar take care of itself. If you want to know the reason why, I think the best exposition of it was by Walter Lippmann yesterday morning."[88] Congress quickly endorsed FDR's action and enacted legislation abrogating the clauses written into public and private contracts stipulating payment in gold—the so-called gold clauses.* The day after Roosevelt's announcement, stock prices soared on record volume. In a rare public statement, J. P. Morgan called the retreat from the gold standard "the best possible course under existing circumstances." Russell Leffingwell wrote FDR, "Your action in going off gold saved the country from complete collapse. It was vitally necessary and the most important of all the helpful things you have done."[89]

On May 9, as the legislative calendar moved forward, the first contingent of Bonus Marchers descended on Washington for another attempt to secure early payment of their insurance policies. They also wanted to protest FDR's Economy Act, which had reduced veterans' benefits substantially. By the end of the month more than three thousand were on hand. Alerted in advance to the veterans' arrival, FDR had quarters prepared for them at Fort Hunt, an old Army post across the Potomac near where the Pentagon stands today. Tents, latrines, showers, mess halls, and a large convention tent were ready and waiting when the veterans arrived. The Army provided a never-ending supply of coffee and three hot meals a day; the Medical Corps treated their ills; service dentists fixed their teeth; and the Navy Band played daily concerts. Louis Howe took personal charge of the arrangements. He met regularly with the leaders, arranged conferences for them with senior congressmen and senators, and took them to the White House to meet FDR. Roosevelt was dead set against yielding to the veterans' demands, but he was determined to give them a full hearing. The breaking point came in late May when Howe took Eleanor to Fort Hunt, unannounced and unaccompanied by the Secret Service or anyone else.

> Although Louis often asked me to take him for a drive in the afternoon, I was rather surprised one day when he insisted that I drive him out to the veterans' camp just off Potomac Drive. It did not take long to get there. When we arrived he announced he was going to sit in the car but that I was to walk around among the veterans and see just how things were. Very hesitatingly I got out and walked over to where I saw a line-up

---

* The legislation was challenged repeatedly and came before the Supreme Court in the "gold clause cases" of 1935: *Norman v. Baltimore & Ohio Railroad,* 294 U.S. 240; *Nortz v. United States* 294 U.S. 317; and *Perry v. United States* 294 U.S. 330. Speaking for a sharply divided Court (5–4), Chief Justice Hughes upheld the power of Congress to regulate the monetary system, including the power to override private contracts if they conflicted with that authority. "This is Nero at his worst," chided Justice James McReynolds in dissent.

of men waiting for food. They looked at me curiously and one of them asked my name and what I wanted. When I said I just wanted to see how they were getting on, they asked me to join them.[90]

At first, the men could not believe the first lady was among them. Mrs. Roosevelt spent more than an hour at the camp. She sloshed through the mud, inspected mess facilities and living quarters, and reminisced about her experience in wartime Washington serving coffee, making sandwiches, and visiting the wounded. In the large convention tent she led the veterans in singing old Army songs and spoke briefly: "I never want to see another war. I would like to see fair consideration for everyone, and I shall always be grateful to those who served their country."[91]

When Mrs. Roosevelt returned to her car, she found Louis Howe fast asleep. It was a boffo performance. "Hoover sent the Army," said one veteran. "Roosevelt sent his wife."[92]* Several days later the Bonus Army voted to disband. FDR waived the age rules (most of the veterans were in their forties), and some twenty-six hundred enlisted in the CCC. The remaining four hundred or so were given free rail transportation home.

The capstone of the one hundred days was the passage by Congress of the National Industrial Recovery Act on the last day of the session. The NIRA was the most inclusive, most ambitious legislation of the hundred days, yet, like FDR's decision to go off gold, it was a response to circumstance. On April 6 the Senate, acting on its own initiative, passed a bill (53–30) introduced by Senator Hugo Black of Alabama that would bar from interstate commerce goods produced in plants where employees worked more than five days a week or six hours a day. By limiting the workweek to thirty hours, Black and his supporters claimed, the bill would create 6 million new jobs.

---

* Unaccompanied forays such as the one to Fort Hunt drove the Secret Service to despair. After the visit to the veterans, the White House detail gave Louis Howe two pistols: one for himself and one for ER. Eleanor carried hers dutifully, but Howe couldn't be bothered, though he enjoyed waving it in the face of startled visitors in his office. Alfred E. Rollins, Jr., *Roosevelt and Howe* 386–387 (New York: Alfred A. Knopf, 1962). Eleanor had been taught to shoot during the Albany years by Sergeant Earl Miller. For ER's refusal to accept Secret Service or police protection, see Joseph P. Lash, *Eleanor and Franklin* 367–368 (New York: W. W. Norton, 1971).

FDR was caught off guard. He believed the Black bill was unconstitutional,* that it was inflexible, and that it would retard recovery by forcing employers into a straitjacket.[93] But with the vigorous support of organized labor, the bill appeared unstoppable. Rather than buck the tide, Roosevelt diverted the flow. Working with Moley, Frances Perkins, and Secretary of War Dern, he expanded the Black bill into an omnibus proposal governing the whole range of industrial recovery. On May 17 FDR sent a new bill to Congress that had something for everyone. Title I, based loosely on the experience of the War Industries Board during World War I, authorized business to establish production codes controlling prices and output in each industry, free from antitrust regulation. Section 7(a) of the bill, modeled on War Labor Board practices, guaranteed labor's right to bargain collectively and stipulated that the industry codes should set minimum wages and maximum hours. Title II contained Roosevelt's public works proposal, $3.3 billion in government spending parceled for the maximum legislative support.[94] The House roared its approval, 325–76. The Senate was more narrowly divided. Progressives like Norris and La Follette objected to the blank check given business to set prices and production levels; conservatives like Carter Glass objected to the collective bargaining provisions for labor. But the center held, and as the clock ticked down on the closing minutes of the first session of the Seventy-third Congress, the Senate added its concurrence 46–39, 15 Democrats voting against.[95]

Earlier in the day Congress had enacted legislation establishing the Farm Credit Administration to consolidate agricultural credit programs, passed the Railroad Coordination Act FDR requested to reorganize the nation's railroads, approved the Glass-Steagall Act divesting investment houses of their banking functions, and voted the largest peacetime appropriation bill in the nation's history. Of the four, the Glass-Steagall Act had the most far-reaching implica-

---

* In 1918 the Supreme Court had overturned the Keating-Owen Federal Child Labor Act, which forbade the interstate shipment of the products of factories, mines, and quarries that employed children under the age of fourteen or where children between the ages of fourteen and sixteen worked more than eight hours a day. "If Congress can thus regulate matters . . . by prohibition of the movement of commodities in interstate commerce, all freedom of commerce will be at an end," said Justice William Day, speaking for the Court. *Hammer v. Dagenhart*, 247 U.S. 251 (1918). FDR believed that Justice Day's reasoning would apply with equal force to the Black bill.

tions. In addition to decreeing that those who sold securities could no longer handle the bank accounts of those who bought them, the act gave the Federal Reserve Board authority to set interest rates and established a Federal Deposit Insurance Corporation to guarantee bank deposits up to $2,500—in effect more than 95 percent of all individual accounts in 1933.[96] FDR had initially opposed the deposit guarantee because he believed it would encourage bankers to be reckless; the weak banks, as he put it, would bring down the strong.[97] But congressional support for deposit insurance was overwhelming. Roosevelt threatened to veto the measure, but when it became clear his veto would be overridden, he gave way. Ironically, federal deposit insurance, a New Deal stepchild, so to speak, became the most successful of the many successful programs launched during the hundred days. The peril of bank failure was almost totally eliminated, and even when a bank did fail—which was rare after 1933—a depositor's funds remained secure.

When the hundred days ended in the early morning hours of June 16, Congress had shattered all precedent for legislative activity. Roosevelt had sent fifteen messages to the Hill, and Congress had responded with fifteen historic pieces of legislation.* FDR's mastery of the legislative process was complete. He compromised when compromise was necessary, zigzagged when required, but in the end saw his program through. "It's more than a New Deal," said Interior secretary Harold Ickes. "It's a new world."[98]

---

* The Emergency Banking Act was passed March 9, 1933; revision of the Volstead Act, March 16; the Economy Act, March 20; Civilian Conservation Corps, March 31; Federal Emergency Relief Act, May 12; Agricultural Adjustment Act, May 12; Emergency Farm Mortgage Act, May 12; Tennessee Valley Authority, May 18; Truth-in-Securities Act, May 27; abrogation of gold clauses in public and private contracts, June 5; Home Owners' Loan Act, June 13; Glass-Steagall Banking Act, June 15; Farm Credit Act, June 15; Railroad Coordination Act, June 15; National Industrial Recovery Act, June 16, 1933.

Franklin H. Delano, 1882, Sara's "Uncle Frank," for whom FDR was named.

Sara Delano Roosevelt in Rome, on her honeymoon, in 1881.

Franklin, six years old, with a Campobello playmate, at the wheel of *Half Moon*, his father's yacht.

At seven years old, on his pony "Debby."

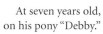

Above: Age fifteen, at the Delano estate in Fairhaven, Massachusetts.

Above right: Franklin and Sara in 1893.

Right: James, Franklin, and Sara in 1899, one year before James's death.

Springwood, the home of James and Sara in Hyde Park, as it appeared in 1885,

The Roosevelt twin town houses at 47–49 East Sixty-fifth Street in New York City. FDR and Eleanor occupied number 49 (*right*), Sara number 47. Note the common entry and the Roosevelt family crest between the third and fourth floors.

Algonac, the home of the Delano family in Newburgh, New York, where Sara was raised.

The Roosevelt home in Hyde Park as it appeared after Sara and FDR's 1916–1917 renovations.

Left: Groton first and second football teams. FDR (without school letter) is seated second from the left in the first row.

Center: Reverend Peabody frowned on too much privacy for his charges.

Below: The Harvard Crimson, 1904. Roosevelt (*center*) was president of the *Crimson* during his final year at Harvard—an incredibly important and prestigious position, the significance of which is best appreciated by Harvard grads.

Above: Eleanor, as she appeared in Saint-Moritz in 1898.

Above right: Young marrieds at Hyde Park in 1905. In a reversal of roles, Franklin is knitting while Eleanor holds a cocktail glass.

Right: Campobello, 1914, FDR's thirty-four room "cottage," given to him by Sara in 1909.

FDR and Eleanor with Elliott, James, and Anna, 1912.

FDR greeting Dutchess County
voters during his first political
campaign, running for the New
York State Senate in 1910.

Flag Day, 1914. *Left
to right:* Secretary of
State William
Jennings Bryan,
Secretary of the Navy
Josephus Daniels,
President Woodrow
Wilson, Assistant
Secretaries of State
Breckinridge Long
and William Phillips,
and FDR.

Assistant Secretary Roosevelt leads the Washington Senators in a
demonstration of patriotic solidarity, May 14, 1917.

FDR and Josephus Daniels standing on the balcony outside their offices in May 1918, gazing at the White House. "You are smiling," said Daniels, "because you are from New York and you know that someday you might live there."

FDR assisted from a seaplane following an aerial inspection of naval facilities in Pauillac, France, August 14, 1918.

FDR accompanies Daniels and the Prince of Wales (later Edward VIII) to inspect the brigade of midshipmen at Annapolis, November 1919.

Democratic presidential candidate James Cox named FDR as his running mate in 1920. They are shown here greeting voters at a Democratic parade in Dayton, Ohio.

Roosevelt and his political entourage relax after a day of campaigning in Billings, Montana. *Left to right:* Louis Howe, Thomas Lynch, FDR, Marvin McIntyre.

This family photo from July 27, 1920, was taken shortly after Franklin's romance with Lucy Mercer was discovered. Sara seems to console Eleanor with her hand on Eleanor's knee. Children, *left to right:* Elliott, FDR, Jr., John, Anna, James. Chief is in the foreground.

Boy Scout encampment, Palisades Park, New York, July 27, 1921. FDR contracted the polio virus here. This is the last photograph to show Roosevelt walking unassisted.

Above: Roosevelt spent the years from 1923 to 1926 in Florida attempting to regain his health, much of the time aboard the *Larooco,* a seventy-one-foot houseboat described by co-owner John Lawrence as "a floating tenement."

Right: On the beach in Florida with Frances (Dana) De Rahm. Aside from his slender legs, it would be difficult to recognize that FDR was paralyzed.

FDR posing on
horseback in Warm
Springs, Georgia,
with Missy LeHand
and Sergeant Earl
Miller of the New
York State Police.

FDR with Democratic
presidential nominee
John W. Davis and
New York governor
Al Smith at Hyde Park,
August 7, 1924.

Franklin and Eleanor with
Anna and her husband,
Curtis Dall, at Hyde Park,
June 1926.

Eleanor poses for a snapshot with her friends Nancy Cook and Marion Dickerman at Val-Kill, July 1926. The depth of their friendship continues to be a subject of speculation.

Eleanor developed a lasting relationship with New York State Police sergeant Earl Miller that continued throughout her life. This photo is from 1930.

Governor Roosevelt rides with Missy LeHand and Eleanor from the governor's mansion to the state capitol.

Roosevelt read four newspapers daily and scanned a dozen others. Here, he is checking the *Times* at Warm Springs in 1931.

FDR sailing with his sons. *Left to right:* John, Elliott, James, and FDR, Jr., off Campobello, September 15, 1931. Roosevelt enjoyed blue-water sailing and used his nautical ability with telling effect in the early 1930s to discount rumors of his invalidism.

Strategy session with vice presidential nominee John Nance Garner at Hyde Park. On the decisive fourth ballot at Chicago, Garner had thrown his support to Roosevelt, ensuring FDR's nomination.

Presidential candidate Roosevelt attending the third game of the 1932 World Series in Chicago. Chicago Cubs manager Charlie Grimm and the Yankees' Joe McCarthy are in the foreground. Chicago mayor Anton Cermak is behind McCarthy. Eleanor is behind Franklin.

Campaigning in Seattle, FDR greets fellow polio victim Melidy Bresina, September 22, 1932. (The young boy is unidentified.)

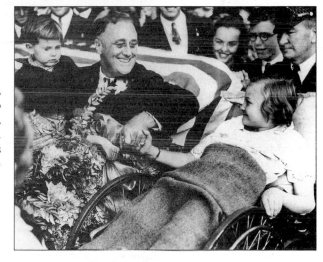

Despite the opposition of UMW president John L. Lewis, FDR carried the coal fields of West Virginia overwhelmingly. He is shown here greeting Zeno Santello in Elm Grove, West Virginia, October 19, 1932.

FDR reviews final election returns with a jubilant James Farley and Louis Howe. Howe's tepid smile is the closest he came to expressing genuine pleasure.

January 23, 1933. President-elect Roosevelt poses with Anna outside his residence at Warm Springs before departing to inspect the giant hydroelectric dam at Muscle Shoals, Alabama.

FDR spoke briefly to American Legionnaires at Bay Front Park in Miami the evening of February 15, 1933. Chicago mayor Anton Cermak was shot moments later when an assassin's bullet aimed at Roosevelt misfired.

SIXTEEN

NEW DEAL ASCENDANT

No president . . . has had a sharper sense of personal
power, a sense of what it is and where it comes from;
none has had more hunger for it, few have had
more use for it, and only one or two could match
his faith in his own competence to use it.

—RICHARD E. NEUSTADT, *PRESIDENTIAL POWER*

UNDER FDR THE WHITE HOUSE, like the governor's mansion in Albany, resembled the Grand Hotel. There were overnight accommodations for twenty-
one, and there was never a vacancy. Franklin and Eleanor continued to move
in separate circles. "The White House had two kinds of visitors," Chief Usher
J. B. West said. "There were the President's people, and then there were Mrs.
Roosevelt's people." According to West, the Roosevelts lived entirely apart. "We
never saw Eleanor and Franklin Roosevelt in the same room alone together."
When she met with him, which was not that often, "she always brought a sheaf
of papers, a bundle of ideas. His secretary, Grace Tully, was usually there, or
hers, Malvina Thompson."[1]

FDR's schedule in the White House differed little from his routine in Albany. He awoke around eight and breakfasted in bed, usually scrambled eggs,
toast, orange juice, and coffee. While eating he scanned the morning press: *The
New York Times* and *Herald Tribune, The Washington Post,* the Baltimore *Sun,*
and one of the McCormick-Patterson papers, either the *Chicago Tribune* or the
Washington Herald. He also leafed through the clipping file prepared by Louis
Howe—jokingly referred to as the *Daily Bugle.* With breakfast FDR lit his first
cigarette of the two packs of Camels he smoked daily, always through a long-
stemmed ivory cigarette holder. While eating, shaving, and dressing, he held a
leisurely, freewheeling staff conference. Louis Howe and Missy LeHand were

always there, Moley when he was not teaching in New York, and in the beginning Lewis Douglas, the former congressman from Arizona whom Roosevelt had named director of the budget. About ten they would be joined by Marvin McIntyre and Steve Early to review the day's calendar.[2]

Roosevelt's bedroom was on the second floor of the White House, next to the Oval Study, facing south, and like his bedrooms at Hyde Park and Warm Springs it was primitively furnished, cluttered with memorabilia, and austerely comfortable in the simple way that seemed to suit old money. Frances Perkins called it too large to be cozy but not large enough to be impressive.

I have a photographic impression of that room. A Victorian mantelpiece held a collection of miniature pigs. Snapshots of children were propped up in back of the pigs. There was an old bureau between the windows, with a plain white towel on top and things men need for their dressing arrangements. There was an old-fashioned rocking chair, often with a piece of clothing thrown over it. Then there was the bed—not the kind you expect a President of the United States to have. Roosevelt used a small, narrow white iron bedstead, the kind one sees in the boy's room of many an American house. It had a thin, hard-looking mattress, a couple of pillows, and an ordinary white seersucker spread. An old grey sweater, much the worse for wear, lay close at hand. He wore it over night clothes to keep his shoulders warm. A white painted table, the kind one often sees in bathrooms, stood beside the bed, with a towel over it and with aspirin, nose drops, a glass of water, stubs of pencils, bits of paper, a couple of books, a worn old prayer book, a watch, a package of cigarettes, an ash tray, a couple of telephones, all cluttered together. And over the door at the opposite end of the room hung a horse's tail. When asked what that was, he would say, "Why, that's Gloster's tail."[3]

As in Albany, Roosevelt worked with an extended family—staff, servants, and even cabinet officers treated as old friends. Louis Howe lived in the White House, as did Missy and Eleanor's reporter friend Lorena Hickok. So too did the Roosevelts' daughter, Anna, and her two children, Sisty and Buzzy. Anna was separated from her husband, Curtis Dall, and would soon marry John Boettiger, a reporter for the *Chicago Tribune* whom she had met during the 1932 campaign. The elfin Howe was assigned the Lincoln Bedroom but before moving in insisted that President Lincoln's nine-foot bed be replaced with something less imposing.[4]

At 10:30 Roosevelt was wheeled downstairs to the Oval Office in the west wing of the White House, where he remained until about six. His appointments were set at fifteen-minute intervals, but he often ran behind. He used the telephone frequently and often placed calls himself. Members of the cabinet, agency heads, congressional leaders, and several dozen others could phone him directly. He ate a light lunch at his desk, often joined by someone from the Hill, a visiting publisher or journalist or simply a person he wished to talk to, such as Henry Stimson or Ed Flynn when they were in town.[5] Twice a week he met the press and on Thursday afternoon the cabinet. Unlike a parliamentary system or even earlier presidencies, FDR's cabinet was not a decision-making body. "Our cabinet meetings are pleasant affairs," Harold Ickes observed, "but we only skim the surface of routine affairs."* Between two and three Roosevelt handled his correspondence, dictating replies to either Missy or Grace Tully. The White House received upward of five thousand letters a day, and his staff had become expert at sorting out those items that required his attention. At six or so FDR would break off for a swim in the new White House pool (donated by New York City schoolchildren) and have a massage and perhaps a session with the White House physician, Navy admiral Ross T. McIntire.[6] He liked nothing better than to play hooky and go for an occasional afternoon drive through Rock Creek Park or the surrounding countryside.

At seven, Roosevelt adjourned to the family quarters for the "children's hour," where he would play host to Louis and Missy, his military aide, Colonel Edwin "Pa" Watson, Grace Tully, and whoever else was on hand. Eleanor did not approve of FDR's penchant for cocktail conviviality, never attended, and, as best one can tell, was never invited. With ice and glasses laid out in front of him, FDR merrily stirred classic martinis (heavy on the vermouth) or mixed old-fashioneds for his guests. "He mixed the ingredients with the deliberation of an alchemist," his speechwriter Robert Sherwood recalled, "but with what

---

* "The cold fact is that on important matters we are seldom called upon for advice," said Ickes. "We never discuss exhaustively any policy of government or question of political strategy. The President makes all of his own decisions and so far as the Cabinet is concerned, without taking counsel with a group of advisors." 1 *The Secret Diary of Harold L. Ickes* 308 (New York: Simon & Schuster, 1953).

appeared to be a certain lack of precision since he carried on a steady conversation while doing it."[7]*

For Mrs. Roosevelt, afternoon tea took the place of the "children's hour." Every day at five o'clock ER poured tea for friends and guests in her second-floor sitting room. She also hosted tea service for female reporters at her press conferences. Presiding over the tea table was for Eleanor, a teetotaler, the psychic equivalent of mixing martinis in the Oval Study at seven.

FDR took dinner at eight, often with his cocktail guests, in the Oval Study. Formal dinners were held in the State Dining Room on the first floor. Unless it was a formal occasion, FDR did not change for dinner. Eleanor had dinner in the Private Dining Room on the first floor with a separate guest list. The men wore black tie. The Hoovers had dressed formally every night and always ate in the State Dining Room, even when they dined alone. President Hoover and his wife enjoyed eating well, and during the Hoover administration the White House fare was excellent. Under the Roosevelts, it was dreadful. Ernest Hemingway, a confirmed trencherman, called the White House food "the worst I've ever eaten. We had rainwater soup followed by rubber squab, a nice wilted salad and a cake some admirer had sent in. An enthusiastic but unskilled admirer." Tallulah Bankhead, equally at home in the world of tasty cuisine, confessed to always eating a full meal before attending a White House dinner.[8] Members of FDR's official family were equally caustic. "I am not very fussy about my food," wrote Harold Ickes, "but it does seem a little out of proportion to use a solid-gold knife and fork on ordinary roast mutton."[9] Grace Tully, almost a regular at the dinner table in the Oval Study, complained that it was like a boardinghouse: One could tell the day of the week by what was set out for dinner—tongue with caper sauce on Mondays, boiled beef without any sauce on Tuesday, and so on.[10]

Running the White House was exclusively Eleanor's domain, part of the balance of power she and FDR had achieved. And given her extensive public

---

* Roosevelt was not a heavy drinker. Except on formal occasions he never drank wine with dinner and rarely had anything afterward. He enjoyed the social aspects of the "children's hour" and spent most of his time mixing drinks for others. Usually he had only one, two at the most, drinks himself. John Gunther, a frequent guest at the "children's hour," complained that FDR used inferior Argentine vermouth and a substandard gin in his martinis, though it was rumored he stocked a better quality for favored guests. John Gunther, *Roosevelt in Retrospect* 95 (New York: Harper & Brothers, 1950).

commitments, she was determined to have someone assist her who was loyal and trustworthy. Social awareness, an ability to cook, even a knowledge of food and wine were secondary. The assistant she chose was Henrietta Nesbitt, a fifty-nine-year-old Hyde Park matron active in the League of Women Voters. Mrs. Nesbitt did some home baking that Eleanor enjoyed, and in late 1932, just before Christmas, ER invited her to take charge of running the White House. "I don't want a professional housekeeper. I want someone I know. I want you, Mrs. Nesbitt."[11]

Blanche Wiesen Cook called it Eleanor's revenge. Mrs. Nesbitt, who had never been gainfully employed and had no supervisory experience, assumed the direction of a White House staff of twenty-six, including cooks, butlers, maids, pantry help, and waiters. "The housekeeper was one expression of her passive-aggressive behavior in a marriage of remarkable and labyrinthine complexity."[12] Mrs. Nesbitt believed in plain food, plainly prepared.[13] "Some of the dishes I served regularly were corned-beef hash, poached eggs, and creamed chipped beef. Sometimes, if the food was too simple, the President made wisecracks, and I'd have to stir myself and think up something fancy."[14] James Roosevelt called her "the worst cook I've ever encountered."[15] Actually, Mrs. Nesbitt did little cooking. But as one firsthand observer noted, "she stood over the cooks, making sure that each dish was overcooked or undercooked or ruined in one way or another."[16] Mrs. Nesbitt was devoted to ER. She displayed contempt for the president's desires. When FDR complained of being served liver and beans three days in a row, Mrs. Nesbitt dismissed it. "Well, he was supposed to have them!"[17] If he ordered something special, she ignored it.[18] When the King and Queen of England wanted coffee, Mrs. Nesbitt sent iced tea. "It was better for them."[19]*

Roosevelt partially remedied the situation in 1941, after Sara died, when he brought her excellent cook, Mary Campbell, down from Hyde Park and installed her in the family kitchen on the third floor.[20] During the presidential campaign in 1944, FDR confided to his daughter, Anna, and Grace Tully, not

---

* Mrs. Nesbitt was equally capricious in her role as chief housekeeper. One day preparing for the arrival of a Latin American head of state, presumably President Getúlio Vargas of Brazil, she told the staff, "Don't bother to put the good linen sheets on the beds for these people." Lillian Rogers Parks and Frances S. Leighton, *The Roosevelts: A Family in Turmoil* 31–32 (Englewood Cliffs, N.J.: Prentice-Hall, 1981).

entirely in jest, that the real reason he wanted to be elected to a fourth term was "so I can fire Mrs. Nesbitt."[21] That privilege fell to President Harry Truman shortly after he assumed office. Mrs. Truman had been asked to bring a stick of butter for the potluck luncheon of the Senate wives' bridge club. When Mrs. Nesbitt refused to give her one—the White House was rationed, she said—President Truman sent her packing that afternoon.[22]

FDR's immediate staff was totally devoted to him and militantly nonideological. Their loyalty was personal. They avoided policy debates and would have followed the president in whatever direction he chose. Howe, Missy, and Grace Tully had been with him throughout the Albany years. Early, McIntyre, and Pa Watson were old Washington hands. All three were southerners: Early, the grandson of Confederate general Jubal Early, was from Virginia, McIntyre from Kentucky, and Watson from Alabama. Early and McIntyre, both former newsmen, handled the foibles of the press and members of Congress with unflappable aplomb. Watson, a much-decorated Army officer, had been an aide to Woodrow Wilson at Versailles and was a man with an eternally sunny outlook. "I have never known anyone just like him," Ickes wrote. "He simply bubbles with good humor. He was great fun fishing and he was equally great fun playing poker. He could be relied upon to keep us all in a mellow humor, and this without any effort on his part, but simply by being himself."[23]

Poker and fishing were two of FDR's diversions in the White House. Missy arranged the poker sessions, often at Harold Ickes's suburban Maryland estate, where the food was certain to be good and the company congenial. In addition to Watson, Early, and McIntyre, the group usually included Harry Hopkins and Henry Morgenthau. Later, the lawyers William Douglas, Tommy Corcoran, and Robert H. Jackson joined the round—Corcoran with his accordion and Irish charm. Like the "children's hour," Roosevelt relished the convivial aspects of poker and played for penny-ante stakes. Vice President Garner, who took his poker as seriously as his bourbon, dismissed FDR's sessions as "just for conversation."[24]

In the evening after dinner Roosevelt read, watched a movie (two or three times a week), or worked on his stamp collection. His reading ran toward history and biography; among movies, he wanted something cheerful and not overly long. *Mickey Mouse* shorts were always on the bill.[25] But it was his stamp collection that absorbed him. FDR took infinite pleasure in perusing philatelic catalogues and placing orders for obscure issues. By the time he entered the

White House, his childhood collection had grown to more than 25,000 stamps in some forty albums. Sometime in the twenties he had begun to specialize, focusing on stamps from the Western Hemisphere and Hong Kong. Roosevelt asked the clerks in the White House mail room to be on the lookout for unusual stamps and literally spent hours alone in his upstairs study with tweezers and hinges, mounting new arrivals in his albums. Shortly before midnight he was wheeled into his bedroom and went to sleep—reportedly within five minutes from the time he was undressed. Unlike other presidents, Roosevelt instructed the Secret Service not to lock the doors of his room at night.[26] He also removed the interior guards in the White House (Hoover had stationed two on each floor) and assigned the Secret Service to a post in the usher's office off the north portico. Both FDR and Eleanor had no fear for their personal safety.

When Congress adjourned June 16, FDR departed for a two-week vacation sailing the New England coast. His son James had chartered a forty-five-foot schooner, *Amberjack II,* and the president planned to sail from Buzzard's Bay, Massachusetts, around Cape Cod, four hundred miles to Campobello—his first trip to the island since he had been stricken twelve years before.[27] "I am having a bang-up good time, and I do not intend to go ashore anywhere along the coast," Roosevelt told newsmen his third day out. "This is my vacation and I am going to stay aboard this boat the whole two weeks."[28]

FDR's crew was the same that had sailed with him to Portsmouth, New Hampshire, after the Democratic convention. But instead of making the trip solo, *Amberjack II* was accompanied by two destroyers (USS *Ellis* and USS *Bernadou*), three Coast Guard cutters, two press boats, and the Navy's newly commissioned heavy cruiser, USS *Indianapolis.** Roosevelt knew the coast thoroughly and put his small craft into places where the naval flotilla could not follow. He had no radio and for three days was stranded by heavy fog in Lakeman Bay, off the Maine coast. FDR savored every moment. He navigated through dangerously rough seas and heavy squalls that terrified the Secret Service.[29] In the treacherous shoal-ridden waters off Gloucester, where more than ten thousand seamen had perished, the accompanying naval vessels plowed

---

* Reporters accompanying FDR invariably datelined their dispatches "At Sea with President Roosevelt." Charles Hurd, *When the New Deal Was Young and Gay* 154 (New York: Hawthorn Books, 1965).

cautiously along behind *Amberjack II,* trusting FDR's navigational judgment.[30] Except for charts and a compass, Roosevelt had no navigation aids and relied on memory and intuition to know where he should go. He sailed by dead reckoning, a skill not unlike that he had recently displayed in Washington.

On the afternoon of June 29, 1933, after almost ten hours of coping with fearsome tides and currents, FDR sailed through the Lubec narrows into Passamaquoddy Bay. James hoisted the presidential pennant to the masthead, and FDR tacked effortlessly around Friar's Head to the dock at Welchpool, on Campobello Island. As *Amberjack II* crossed the bow of the *Indianapolis,* the warship rendered honors, ship's complement manning the rails while the guns boomed a twenty-one-gun salute. When Roosevelt was helped ashore, it marked the first time he had left the schooner since the trip had begun on June 18. He was the first American president to visit Canada while in office, and the outpouring of affection from the islanders, many of whom had known the Roosevelts for two and three generations, was overwhelming. "I was figuring this morning on the passage of time," said FDR in his arrival remarks, "and I remembered that I was brought here because I was teething forty-nine years ago. I was thinking also, as I came through the Narrows and saw the line of fishing boats and the people on the wharves, both here at Welchpool and also at Eastport [Maine], that this reception here is probably the finest example of friendship between nations—permanent friendship between nations—that we can possibly have."[31]

Roosevelt remained at Campobello four days. While there he took advantage of his absence from Washington to launch a torpedo that ultimately sank the World Monetary and Economic Conference meeting in London. At the behest of Britain and France, with reluctant U.S. support, representatives of sixty-six nations had convened in the British capital on June 20 to stabilize world currencies. FDR had studied and reflected on the matter during his cruise northward and by the time he arrived at Campobello had concluded that it was not in America's interest to stabilize the dollar. It would be preferable for the U.S. economy to allow the dollar to float.

On the afternoon of June 30 FDR invited the newsmen who had accompanied him for a buffet lunch at the family cottage. After lunch and a few hands of bridge, the president pushed back his wheelchair and said, "I think it might be more interesting to talk for a while." According to Charles Hurd of *The New*

York Times, FDR "looked at his watch, and added, 'You'll want to go back to your dock with the tide, which gives us about an hour.' (We were amazed that Roosevelt, then probably the busiest man in the world, could take time to keep up with the tide variations in Campobello.)"

FDR ranged over a variety of topics but soon focused on the London conference. "Etiquette forbade us to take notes," Hurd said. "We listened." Roosevelt made clear that while he was much in favor of international accommodation, "the United States was not going to be pushed around." He would not agree to any pegging of the dollar that would benefit foreign countries at American expense. The newsmen—all hardened veterans who had covered the White House for years—were stunned.

"Is that for publication, Mr. President?" asked one reporter.

"No, it is off the record. . . . Of course, if you were simply discussing this on your own, would you not possibly reach the same conclusion?"

"Mr. President, you know very well that no one cares a whit what we think; we don't make the policy."

"Well, how you handle anything you write is up to you," said FDR. "But isn't a Campobello dateline a pretty good hedge?"[32]

The following day, July 1, 1933, *The New York Times* broke Hurd's story on page one. Diplomatic notes dribbled back and forth across the Atlantic for the next two weeks, but for all practical purposes the London conference was dead. Raymond Moley, who had been appointed assistant secretary of state and who ramrodded American efforts in London, felt undercut by FDR and soon resigned from the administration. Secretary of State Hull, always uncomfortable with Moley as assistant secretary, shed no tear, and Roosevelt never had a second thought about torpedoing the conference. "I'm prouder of that than anything I ever did," he told Arthur Krock in 1937.[33]

An equally serious foreign policy issue involved diplomatic recognition of the Soviet Union. In 1933, the United States was the only major power that had not established formal relations with Moscow. The USSR had been a full participant in the London Economic Conference, it had become a vigorous trading partner for the nations of Europe, and it was abundantly clear that the Soviet regime would remain the government of Russia for the foreseeable future.

Under the Constitution the power of diplomatic recognition is entrusted exclusively to the president.* And by the fall of 1933 Roosevelt had come to the conclusion that continued nonrecognition served no useful purpose. The furor of 1920s anti-Bolshevism had subsided, American business looked favorably on increasing trade, and the traditional rivalry between Russia and Japan in the Far East made the Soviet Union a reliable buffer against Japanese expansionism. A survey of 1,139 newspapers in September indicated that fewer than 27 percent opposed recognition. "I think the menace of Bolshevism in the United States is about as great as the menace of sunstroke in Greenland or chilblains in the Sahara," said Roy Howard, head of the Scripps-Howard chain.[34]

Opposition centered in the hierarchy of the Roman Catholic Church, the leadership of the AFL, and conservative patriotic groups such as the Daughters of the American Revolution. FDR could safely ignore the DAR and Bill Green, but the Church required attention. Roosevelt turned on the charm. On September 4 he invited Father Edmund A. Walsh, the dean of Georgetown University's School of Foreign Service, to the White House for a chat. Walsh was one of the most outspoken critics of recognition, and his anti-Soviet public lectures at Washington's Smithsonian Institution drew overflow crowds. An hour after meeting Roosevelt, Walsh told reporters he thought the president should be trusted to do what he thought was right.[35]

Because the career diplomats in the State Department—many of whom had spent the last fifteen years hobnobbing with White Russian émigrés—were still imbued with nostalgia for the czarist past, Roosevelt handled the negotiations himself, first through Henry Morgenthau, then through William C. Bullitt.[36] Morgenthau, as head of the Farm Credit Administration, dealt with the Soviet trade organization Amtorg; Bullitt with Boris Skvirsky, the senior Russian commercial representative in the United States. As a result of these covert discussions, FDR invited Soviet foreign minister Maxim Litvinov to Washington for direct negotiations in early November.[37] The ostensible outstanding is-

---

* The cryptic words of Article II that the president shall send and receive ambassadors provide the textual basis for the president's recognition authority. "In every case the question of recognition was determined solely by the Executive," wrote John Bassett Moore, the dean of international law scholars, after reciting an exhaustive survey of precedent. 3 *International Law Digest* 243–244 (1906). Also see *Goldwater v. Carter,* 444 U.S. 996 (1979), pertaining to President Carter's 1978 decision to withdraw diplomatic recognition from the Republic of China.

sues involved freedom of religion for Americans in Russia and the continued agitation for world revolution mounted by the Comintern. The real sticking point was restitution of American property seized by the Soviet government in its nationalization decree of 1919.* Roosevelt and Litvinov compromised. The agreement is known as the Litvinov Assignment. The Soviet government assigned to the United States its claim to all Russian property in the United States that antedated the Revolution. The United States agreed to seize the property on behalf of the Soviet Union, thus giving effect to the Soviet nationalization decree, and use the proceeds to pay the claims of Americans whose property in Russia had been confiscated. The constitutionality of the assignment was twice challenged before the Supreme Court, but in both instances it was upheld, the "taking clause" of the Constitution notwithstanding.[38†]

Shortly after midnight on the morning of November 17, FDR and Litvinov signed the documents restoring diplomatic relations. At a farewell dinner for the Soviet foreign minister at New York's Waldorf-Astoria, business titans from J. P. Morgan, Chase, and other firms eager to do business with the USSR toasted the new era of recognition. Thomas Watson of IBM asked Americans to "refrain from making any criticism of the present form of government adopted by Russia."[39]

Meanwhile, the National Industrial Recovery Act was having birthing problems. Enacted the last day of the session, the act established two complementary agencies: the National Recovery Administration (NRA) to coordinate economic recovery, and the Public Works Administration (PWA), authorized to spend $3.3 billion in pump-priming construction projects. NRA and PWA, as one historian has written, "were to be like two lungs, each necessary for breathing life into the moribund industrial sector."[40] But FDR made the fatal error of dividing responsibility. To head the NRA, Roosevelt brought in former brigadier general Hugh "Iron Pants" Johnson, a flamboyant protégé of Bernard Baruch, renowned for his can-do military spirit and robust invective. Hard drinking and hard living, Johnson said of his appointment, "It will be red

---

* The issue was not unlike the claim for the restitution of Tory property asserted by Great Britain after the American Revolution and dealt with in the Treaty of Paris of 1783 and the Jay Treaty of 1794.
† The "taking clause" of the Constitution, contained in the Fifth Amendment, provides: "nor shall private property be taken for public use without just compensation."

fire at first and dead cats afterward"—evidently an old Army expression.[41] For PWA, the president turned to Harold Ickes. No two appointees could have been more dissimilar, and no two less likely to cooperate. For Johnson, an old cavalryman, every undertaking was a hell-for-leather charge into the face of the enemy. Ickes, on the other hand, was pathologically prudent. As he saw it, the problem of the public works program was not to spend money quickly but to spend it wisely. Obsessively tightfisted, personally examining every project in minute detail, Ickes spent a minuscule $110 million of PWA money in 1933.[42]

The failure of the Public Works Administration to provide economic stimulus doomed NRA's recovery efforts from the start. Without a significant infusion of construction money, the NRA could not expand the economy. Johnson labored mightily to create industry codes that would control production, fix prices, and regulate working conditions. But without money to prime the pump, he was simply redistributing scarcity. When that became apparent, the brief spurt of popularity NRA enjoyed evaporated. Enforcing industry codes became impossible, and in early 1935 the Supreme Court administered the coup de grâce when it struck down the National Industrial Recovery Act as unconstitutional.[43] Chief Justice Hughes, speaking for a unanimous Court, held that the code-making authority given to the president constituted an impermissible delegation of legislative authority to the executive branch. In a concurring opinion, Justice Benjamin Cardozo, normally in sympathy with the New Deal, called the NIRA "delegation running riot."[44] FDR soon castigated the horse-and-buggy mentality of the Court, and its decision to overturn the NIRA later contributed to his desire to restructure the judicial branch.[45] But the day the decision came down, Roosevelt was relieved.* The Court had

---

* Justice Robert H. Jackson, then general counsel of the Treasury's revenue arm, was in the Oval Office with FDR when he received a phone call from Donald Richberg of the NRA telling him of the *Schechter* decision. According to Jackson, "The conversation at the President's end of the line ran something like this: 'You mean it was unanimous against us? Where was old Isaiah?' This was a favorite characterization of Justice Brandeis. He then asked, 'What about Ben Cardozo?' He then told us that the decision had gone against the government by all members of the Court. It was this feature that shocked him most. . . . We suggested to him that perhaps he had been relieved by the Court of a serious problem. He seemed inclined to agree with that view of it and I was somewhat surprised to read some days later of his [May 31, 1935] press conference remarks." Robert H. Jackson, *That Man: An Insider's Portrait of Franklin D. Roosevelt* 66, John Q. Barrett, ed. (New York: Oxford University Press, 2003).

bailed him out of a program that was increasingly unpopular and unsuccessful. "You know the whole thing has been a mess," FDR told Frances Perkins.

"It has been an awful headache," said Roosevelt. "Some of the things they have done in NRA are pretty wrong. . . . I don't want to impose a system on this country that will set aside the anti-trust laws on any permanent basis. So let's give the NRA a certain amount of time to liquidate. Have a history of it written, and then it will be over."[46]

As the winter of 1933–34 approached, Roosevelt recognized that Ickes's caution in spending PWA money was creating few jobs and doing little to ease the suffering of the destitute. Faced with the critical need to tide people over the winter, FDR turned to Hopkins. Could he provide temporary jobs for 4 million people? Hopkins said he could if he had the money. Roosevelt mentally computed the cost—he assumed it would require an additional $400 million—and decided to tap Ickes's underused Public Works budget for the funds. He delegated Hopkins, Frances Perkins, and Henry Wallace to break the news to Ickes and on November 9, 1933, issued an executive order establishing the Civil Works Administration with Hopkins as director.[47]

As Roosevelt anticipated, Hopkins moved quickly. He shifted staff from FERA to the CWA, raided Army warehouses for tools and equipment, and dragooned the Veterans Administration—the one federal agency with a national disbursement system in place—into becoming the CWA's paymaster.[48] Unlike relief programs, the Civil Works Administration provided jobs. Within ten days Hopkins had put more than 800,000 people to work, 2.6 million by mid-December, and by early January he was well over the 4 million mark. The CWA paid the prevailing minimum wage for unskilled labor, and the work was seasonal. When it went out of existence in April 1934, the CWA had pumped close to $1 billion into the ailing economy. Eighty percent of that had gone directly into workers' wages, with the bulk of the remainder paid out for equipment and material.[49] Less than 2 percent went for administrative overhead—another Hopkins hallmark.

In the bitter winter of 1933–34, with record low temperatures gripping the nation, the CWA laid 12 million feet of sewer pipe and built or upgraded 500,000 miles of secondary roads, 40,000 schools, 3,700 recreation areas, and nearly a thousand airports. It employed 50,000 teachers to keep rural schools open and to provide adult education in the cities. It hired 3,000 artists and writers—and they worked as artists and writers. "Hell," said Hopkins, "they've got to eat like other people."[50] The CWA did more than provide an overdue cash infusion to the economy; it restored a nation's self-respect. "We aren't on relief any more," said a proud woman in Iowa. "My husband is working for the government."[51]

Lieutenant Colonel John C. H. Lee, detailed by the Army to study the CWA, watched with astonishment as Hopkins put people to work in every county and every town in the country in less than two months. In World War I it had taken the Army a year and a half to muster as many men, said Lee, and, unlike the Army, Hopkins paid his people weekly. Lee, whose personal style ran heavily along authoritarian lines,* expressed unaccustomed admiration for Hopkins's informality with his youthful staff. "These assistants address Mr. Hopkins fondly as 'Harry.' There is no rigidity or formality, yet he holds their respect, confidence and whole-souled cooperation."[52]

The second session of the Seventy-third Congress convened on January 3, 1934. FDR was still the quarterback calling plays, but the opposition had begun to coalesce. Republicans were recovering from their postelection shell shock, and in the Democratic party both the far left and the extreme right were in incipient revolt. Roosevelt held the high ground, and at his recommendation Congress enacted legislation establishing the Securities and Exchange Commission to regulate the investment industry and the Federal Communications Commission to control the airwaves.[53] But the majorities behind the bills were smaller, and in the case of the SEC, passage required the president's personal intervention.† Congress also enacted the Railroad Retirement Act to provide mandatory pension coverage in the rail industry and agreed to fix the price of gold at $35 an ounce.[54] After allowing the dollar to float for a year,

---

* In World War II, General Lee performed with distinction as Eisenhower's supply chief in Europe, although his high-handed style, combined with his religious ardor, led him to be dubbed (based on his JCH initials) "Jesus Christ Himself" Lee. The moniker was used freely by both Lee's admirers and detractors, which makes his 1934 comments about Hopkins's style all the more pertinent. For Lee, see Jean Edward Smith, *Lucius D. Clay: An American Life* 181 (New York: Henry Holt, 1990).

† To head the Securities and Exchange Commission, FDR named Joseph P. Kennedy, an early supporter who had been disappointed he was passed over for the Treasury. When the press slammed the appointment because of Kennedy's long record as a stock manipulator, Roosevelt beamed his delight. "Set a thief to catch a thief," he grinned, effectively ending the discussion. Kenneth S. Davis, *Invincible Summer: An Intimate Portrait of the Roosevelts Based on the Recollections of Marion Dickerman* 128–129 (New York: Atheneum, 1974).

Roosevelt decided to devalue it permanently at 59 percent of its previous worth.[55] When the Seventy-third Congress adjourned *sine die* on June 18, FDR wrote Speaker Rainey, "It's been a grand session—the best in all our history."[56]

Two weeks later, Roosevelt went to the people. In his first fireside chat of 1934, FDR asked Americans to judge the progress of recovery for themselves. "Are you better off today than you were last year? Are your debts less burdensome? Is your bank account more secure?" Roosevelt mocked "the Doubting Thomases" who decried the loss of liberty. "Answer this question also out of the facts of your own life. Have you lost any of your rights or liberty or constitutional freedom of action and choice?" It was a powerful performance—as powerful as any speech Roosevelt had given.[57]

On July 1, 1934, the president boarded the USS *Houston,* a sister ship of the *Indianapolis,* for a 14,000-mile trip to the Hawaiian Islands via the Panama Canal—his favorite form of relaxation. The second session of the Seventy-third Congress had not been the bed of roses FDR's letter to Rainey suggested. Roosevelt's rivals for control of the party did not take their exclusion lightly. "It is difficult today," wrote the conservative pundit Frank Kent, "to name any outstanding Democratic leader of the pre–New Deal period who is in sympathy with the Roosevelt policy."[58] Passage of the Securities Exchange Act confirmed the schism. Al Smith, John W. Davis, Newton D. Baker, and the remnants of the Raskob-Shouse organization joined ranks in an attempt to return the party to its pre-Roosevelt, probusiness moorings. "Who is Ickes?" asked Al Smith rhetorically. "Who is Hopkins? And in the name of all that's holy, who is Tugwell? Is La Guardia a Democrat?* If he is, then I am a Chinaman with a haircut."[59]

In August 1934, with generous financial backing from the du Ponts, General Motors, Sun Oil, and Montgomery Ward, the dissidents formed the American Liberty League, with Jouett Shouse as president. The League's avowed objectives were to teach respect for the rights of property and require government to encourage private enterprise. Asked about the formation of the League at his press conference shortly afterward, Roosevelt was withering: "When you define American principles you want to go whole hog. An organization that

---

* Former Republican congressman Fiorello La Guardia had crossed party lines and was running for mayor of New York City as a Fusion candidate representing a coalition of disaffected Democrats, Republicans, reformers, and socialists.

only advocates two or three out of the Ten Commandments may be a perfectly good organization, but it would have certain shortcomings in having failed to advocate the other seven or eight."[60] To William Bullitt, now the U.S. ambassador in Moscow, FDR wrote, "All the big guns have started shooting. Their organization has already been labeled the '*I Can't Take It Club.*' "[61]

In 1934 Roosevelt did not worry about defections on the right. What concerned him were the critics on the left. Huey Long had burst the confines of the Bayou State and was barnstorming the nation to make "every man a king." FDR had worked diligently to keep Long inside the administration tent pissing out, but the Kingfish was now outside pissing in. Long's Share Our Wealth clubs claimed a mailing list of 7.5 million persons. The program was blindingly simple. Long proposed to confiscate large personal fortunes, levy steeply progressive income taxes, and redistribute the revenue to every American family so they could buy a home, a car, and a radio. In addition, each family would receive a guaranteed annual wage of $2,500—roughly double the median family income at the time. The elderly would receive pensions, the young would be provided college educations, and veterans would receive their bonuses. Long meant trouble, and FDR did not underestimate his appeal.*

Marching almost in lockstep with Long was Father Charles Coughlin, a parish priest in Royal Oak, Michigan, whose weekly radio sermons drew a national audience estimated as high as 40 million.[62] Like Long, Coughlin initially supported FDR. But as the New Deal took shape, he became increasingly critical. The Radio Priest, as he was called, railed against the power of "international money," lauded silver as the "gentile" metal, and was soon accusing Roosevelt of having out-Hoovered Hoover. By the fall of 1934 Coughlin was calling for a political realignment. "The old parties are all but dead," he told his Sunday audience. They should "relinquish the skeletons of their putrefying carcasses to the halls of a historical museum."[63] Because he had been born in Canada, Coughlin was not a rival for the presidency like Long. But his National Union for Social Justice, formed in November 1934, was another wild card of which Roosevelt had to beware.

---

* James Farley believed that Long might poll 6 million votes. "I always laughed Huey off," he told Harold Ickes after Long's assassination in 1935. "But I did not feel that way about him." And then Farley reeled off the states FDR would have lost had Long run against him. 1 *The Secret Diary of Harold L. Ickes* 462.

The most benign, yet in some ways the most serious, threat was headed by Dr. Francis Everett Townsend, an unemployed physician in Long Beach, California. Townsend proposed to pay a monthly pension of $200 (roughly $2,600 currently) to every citizen over sixty, on the condition that he or she retire and promise to spend the sum within the coming month. Pensions would be financed by a business transaction tax of 2 percent. Advocates argued that this would reduce unemployment because older workers would yield their jobs to younger people who had none. And the mandatory spending of pension checks would produce a demand for goods and services that would create still more jobs.[64] The Townsend Plan was far from radical. It appealed to heavily Protestant rural America, proclaimed traditional values, and promised to preserve the profit system free from alien collectivism, socialism, and godless communism. As Townsend put it, the movement embraced people "who believe in the Bible, believe in God, cheer when the flag passes by, the Bible Belt solid Americans."[65] It was a movement FDR dared not ignore.

The congressional elections in November 1934 provided the first political test of Roosevelt's policies. Cognizant of the midterm tradition, in which the president's party normally suffers a decline, Vice President Garner predicted the Republicans would pick up *only* thirty-seven seats in the House, a gain so small it could be regarded as "a complete victory" for the administration.[66] Farley thought the party would hold its own and the results would be "about even"—a forecast FDR thought recklessly optimistic.[67] Farley was closer than Garner, but both underestimated the strength of Roosevelt's appeal. Contrary to the predictions of the most seasoned political pros, the Democrats won an additional twelve seats in the House of Representatives and gained nine in the Senate.*

In the House, the Democratic majority increased from 310 to 322 (against 103 Republicans), and in the Senate the Democrats held 69 seats—5 more than a two-thirds majority.[68] Never in the history of the Republican party had its percentage in either House been so low. In the statehouses and governor's mansions across the nation the rout was equally great. When the dust settled from the 1934 election, the GOP retained only seven governorships, as op-

* The only time prior to 1934 the party in power gained seats in the House during an off-year election was in 1902, when the Republicans, under TR, gained eleven seats. *Congressional Quarterly's Guide to U.S. Elections* 928–929 (Washington, D.C.: Congressional Quarterly, 1975).

posed to thirty-nine for the Democrats and one each for the Progressives and
Farmer-Laborites.

In *The New York Times*, Arthur Krock said the New Deal had won "the most
overwhelming victory in the history of American politics." William Allen
White proclaimed that FDR had been "all but crowned by the people." William
Randolph Hearst said simply, "The forgotten man does not forget."[69]

At the end of 1934 the recovery had yet to gain traction. The nation's GDP
registered a 17 percent increase over the dismal figures for 1932 and 1933, but
national income was still little better than half of what it had been in 1929. And
while more than 2 million persons had found jobs, the unemployment rate remained at an uncomfortable 21.7 percent.[70] Yet as the November election results
showed, the mood of the country was on the upswing. Broadway, which had
dimmed its lights in 1933, had its best season in five years.[71] Sixteen new plays
(plus six new musicals) opened on the Great White Way, featuring a who's who
of theatrical talent: James Stewart, Henry Fonda, Jean Arthur, Walter Huston,
Melvyn Douglas, Tallulah Bankhead, Judith Anderson, Claude Rains, and Ethel
Merman. Clark Gable sent men's underwear sales plunging when he removed
his shirt and revealed a bare chest in *It Happened One Night*—for which he,
Claudette Colbert, and director Frank Capra all won Academy Awards. Albert
Einstein made his musical debut, playing second violin (Bach's "Concerto for
Two Violins") in a benefit performance for displaced scientists in Nazi Berlin. In
California, Ernest and Julio Gallo invested $5,900 to enter the wine business, and
Sears, Roebuck commenced carrying contraceptive devices in its catalog.[72]

The Seventy-fourth Congress, swept into office on an enormous wave of
support for the New Deal, was more than ready to follow Roosevelt's lead. First
on the president's agenda was a comprehensive social insurance program that
would provide unemployment compensation and old-age and survivor benefits, as well as aid for dependent children and the handicapped. In June 1934,
FDR had announced his intention to provide for social security but said he
would wait until the new Congress convened before sending up a specific proposal.[73] To draft that proposal, he appointed a special cabinet committee
chaired by Secretary of Labor Perkins.* "Keep it simple," Roosevelt told

---

* The cabinet Committee on Economic Security was composed of Frances Perkins, chairman, Henry Wallace (Agriculture), Henry Morgenthau (Treasury), Attorney General
Homer Cummings, and Relief Administrator Harry Hopkins.

Perkins. "So simple that everybody will understand it." The basic concept was universal coverage. "I see no reason why every child, from the day he is born, shouldn't be a member of the social security system," said FDR.

> When he begins to grow up, he should know he will have old-age bene-
> fits direct from the insurance system to which he will belong all his life.
> If he is out of work, he gets a benefit. If he is sick or crippled, he gets a
> benefit. . . . Cradle to the grave—from the cradle to the grave everyone
> ought to be in the social security system.[74]

Frances Perkins said Roosevelt looked on social security as his personal project, and he knew that if it were going to be enacted he had to move quickly during the early days of the session. Members of Congress were spooked by the Townsend Plan, and FDR had to steal the march or be overwhelmed.

The cabinet committee submitted its report to FDR on January 15, 1935, and two days later he sent the draft bill for social security to Congress.[75] Roosevelt took no chances. The principal congressional advocates of social security were Robert Wagner in the Senate and David Lewis of Maryland in the House. But because the bill would go through the normal committee process, FDR insisted that the legislation be known as the Harrison-Doughton bill—for Mississippi's Pat Harrison, who chaired the Senate Finance Committee, and Robert L. Doughton of North Carolina, who chaired the Ways and Means Committee in the House. Frances Perkins drew the unenviable task of reconciling Wagner and Lewis to Roosevelt's decision.[76]

From the beginning the scheme was self-funding, the contributions to be paid jointly by employers and employees. That was at FDR's insistence. He instructed Perkins to ensure that no government contribution would be required. The plan must be actuarially sound. "It is almost dishonest," said Roosevelt, "to build up an accumulated deficit for the Congress of the United States to meet in 1980. We can't do that. We can't sell the United States short in 1980 any more than in 1935."[77] Benefits would be proportional to a person's earnings. In effect—and contrary to the rule in most modern countries, where governments provide the major funding for pension plans—America's social security system would be freestanding: a property right, not a civil right.[78] The downside of FDR's insistence that social security pay its own way was the immediate adverse effect on the economy. To build the reserve fund from which to pay benefits required withdrawing money from workers' wages—money that otherwise would be spent. Roosevelt understood that the payroll tax would be deflationary. But he was more concerned about what he called "legislative habits and prejudices." "Those taxes were never a matter of economics," FDR said later. "They are politics all the way through. We put those payroll contributions there so as to give the contributors a legal, moral, and political right to collect their pensions and their unemployment benefits. With those taxes in there, no damn politician can ever scrap my social security program."[79]

Roosevelt's concern for the legislative pecking order paid quick dividends. Harrison and Doughton shepherded the legislation through their committees, and the floor fight was led by Wagner in the Senate and Lewis in the House. Opposition was strongest in the business community. "The dangers are manifest," said Alfred Sloan, the president of General Motors. "With unemployment insurance no one will work; with old age and survivor benefits no one will save; the result will be moral decay and financial bankruptcy." "Never in the history of the world," said Representative John Taber of New York, "has any measure been brought in here so insidiously designed as to prevent business recovery, to enslave workers, and to prevent any possibility of the employers providing work for the people."[80] In the procedural motions that preceded final passage, House Republicans voted almost unanimously against social security. But when the final up-or-down vote came on April 19, fewer than half were prepared to go on record against. The final vote in the House of Representatives was a lopsided 371–33.

The debate in the Senate played along similar lines. In both Houses concern focused on old-age pensions rather than unemployment compensation. The administration's proposal "would take all the romance out of life," said New Jersey's A. Harry Moore. "We might as well take a child from the nursery, give him a nurse, and protect him from every experience life affords."[81] When Daniel Hastings of Delaware moved to delete pension coverage from the bill, 12 of the 19 Republicans voted in favor. They were tilting at windmills. When the Senate voted on June 19, social security sailed through, 76–6. Roosevelt signed the measure into law in an elaborate White House ceremony on August 14, 1935.[82] Commemorative pens were presented to Harrison, Wagner, Doughton, Lewis, and Frances Perkins. FDR always regarded the Social Security Act as the cornerstone of the New Deal, said Miss Perkins. "I think he took greater satisfaction from it than from anything else he achieved on the domestic front."[83]

The Social Security Act of 1935 was far from perfect. Despite Roosevelt's desire for universal coverage, only 60 percent of the labor force was initially insured. Farm laborers and domestics—two categories of workers who needed security most—were not covered, nor were teachers, nurses, and those who worked in firms employing fewer than ten people.* Benefits for other programs, such as unemployment compensation, aid to the handicapped, and support for dependent children, varied substantially from state to state.[84] And the provisions for health care and housing that FDR had originally requested proved impossible to obtain. Nevertheless, passage of the act marked a watershed in American history. The responsibility of the nation toward its citizens was redefined. "If, as our Constitution tells us, our Federal Government was established among other things 'to promote the general welfare,' " said FDR, "it is our plain duty to provide for that security upon which welfare depends."[85]

The second item on Roosevelt's 1935 agenda was to curtail relief and find jobs for the unemployed. In his State of the Union message on January 4, FDR recommended "the orderly liquidation" of existing relief agencies and the adoption of a national plan to provide work for 3.5 million people currently on the dole. "The Federal Government," said the president, "is the only governmental agency with sufficient power and credit to meet this situation."[86] Congress responded on April 8 with the largest appropriation in American history: $4.8 billion for Roosevelt to spend largely as he saw fit.[87]

With the money in hand, the question for FDR was how to organize work relief. The choice was whether to rely on Harold Ickes and a monumental pro-

---

* FDR's initial proposal, as recommended by his cabinet committee, included all categories. But in testimony before the House Ways and Means Committee, Secretary Morgenthau broke ranks. Because of the difficulties the Treasury would encounter collecting payments, Morgenthau recommended that farm laborers, domestics, and firms with fewer than ten employees be excluded from coverage. "This was a blow," Frances Perkins reported. "The matter had been discussed in the [Cabinet] Committee on Economic Security and universal coverage had been agreed upon almost from the outset. . . . The Ways and Means Committee members, impressed by the size of the project . . . nodded their heads to Secretary Morgenthau's proposal of limitations. There was nothing for me to do but accept." Frances Perkins, *The Roosevelt I Knew* 297–298 (New York: Harper & Row, 1946).

gram of public works or turn to Hopkins who surely knew how to put money in circulation. The rivalry between Hopkins and Ickes to be top dog spending the $4.8 billion was intense. Ickes claimed Hopkins wanted to prime the pump with a fire hose; Hopkins called Ickes stubborn and self-righteous.[88]* Ultimately FDR turned to Hopkins. "Ickes is a good administrator," the president told Donald Richberg (who had succeeded Hugh Johnson at the NRA), "but often too slow. Harry gets things done. I am going to give this job to Harry."[89] Roosevelt hived off about a quarter of the appropriation for Ickes, gave a small amount to Agriculture secretary Wallace, but awarded the bulk to Hopkins. On May 6, 1935, the president issued an executive order establishing the Works Progress Administration (WPA), "which shall be responsible to the President for the honest, efficient, speedy, and coordinated execution of the work relief program as a whole, and for the execution of that program in such manner as to move from the relief rolls to work on such projects or in private employment the maximum number of persons in the shortest time possible."[90] Hopkins was appointed director; his mandate was to put people to work.

For Hopkins, administering an ongoing work relief effort proved far more complicated than managing the spurt of seasonal jobs provided during the winter of 1933. Federal contracting regulations intervened, paperwork increased exponentially, and on-site supervision became exceedingly time-consuming. Hopkins's small but dedicated staff was initially overwhelmed. Assistance came out of the blue from an unlikely source: the U.S. Army Corps of Engineers.

"Mr. Hopkins was having a great difficulty getting underway," said General Lucius D. Clay, later military governor of Germany. "And I went over with General [Edward M.] Markham [chief of engineers] to see Mr. Hopkins, and said, 'We would like to lend to you, in each of your regions, a capable, compe-

---

* Despite their rivalry Ickes and Hopkins shared a genuine affection for each other. "Harry was an agreeable scoundrel when he wanted to be," said Ickes, who described his liking for Hopkins as "the liking of a man who had grown up under Scotch-Presbyterian restraint for the happy-go-lucky type who can bet his last cent, even if it be a borrowed one, on a horse race." The fact is, both men were pragmatists and shared a common goal. The tension between them may have forced each to excel and produce results beyond what they might have achieved otherwise. Robert E. Sherwood, *Roosevelt and Hopkins* 93 (New York: Harper & Brothers, 1948). Also see Arthur M. Schlesinger, Jr., *The Coming of the New Deal* 347 (Boston: Houghton Mifflin, 1960).

tent Engineer officer who would bring with him a capable and competent chief clerk who knows how to disperse and set up public funds, just to get you going.'"

Clay said Hopkins was very suspicious at first but accepted the offer, and the Corps sent many of its best officers to assist the WPA: Colonel Brehon Somervell, who would later head the Army's entire logistical effort in World War II, took over the troubled WPA district in New York; Colonel Francis Harrington became Hopkins's own deputy; Colonel Donald Connolly headed the program in Los Angeles. "All around the country we provided the basic, experienced staff in knowing how to put government money to work under the proper controls, to let Mr. Hopkins get underway."*

The Corps of Engineers' support for WPA was scarcely disinterested. Just as the CCC program brought many Army officers into contact with the New Deal, the WPA gave a fresh lease on life to the Corps in its battle with Secretary Ickes for control of the nation's rivers and harbors. "You've got to remember that you're always fighting for position," said Clay. "It seemed to me that the best way we could establish ourselves was to make ourselves helpful. Frankly, I would have to admit that if we hadn't felt that Mr. Ickes was trying to give us trouble, we might not have thought of going to Mr. Hopkins." And as Clay—whose father had been a three-term U.S. senator from Georgia—knew very well, in Washington one hand washes the other. "In our subsequent conflicts with Mr. Ickes over flood control, Mr. Hopkins was definitely on our side."[91]

In the first year of its existence the WPA put more than 3 million people to work, and over a span of eight years it employed upward of 8.5 million while pumping some $11 billion into the economy. Projects ranged from make-work undertakings of little lasting value to the construction of schools (5,900), hospitals (2,500), parks (8,000), playgrounds (13,000), and highways (572,000 miles). The WPA restored the Dock Street Theater in Charleston, constructed Timberline Lodge on the slopes of Mount Hood, and ran a pack-horse library

---

* "I had great sympathy for Mr. Hopkins," said Clay. "We knew what his task was. We felt that a public works program was not going to provide the necessary employment in itself, but Mr. Ickes did have a going organization and Mr. Hopkins did not. So we provided the basic elements of an organization for him, and a great many of the men we assigned to him became his lifelong friends." Smith, *Lucius D. Clay* 63. (When Hopkins resigned as WPA director in December 1938 to become secretary of commerce, he was succeeded by Colonel Harrington.)

in the hills of Kentucky.[92] Hopkins funneled money into the arts and entertainment as well. The Federal Music Project sponsored dozens of symphony orchestras, jazz groups, and native ensembles. The Federal Theatre Project brought plays, vaudeville acts, and puppet shows to many who had never seen a stage production. In four years WPA-supported theater played to audiences that totaled more than 30 million. The Federal Art Project employed at one time or another some 9,000 of the 40,000 registered artists and craftsmen in the country to teach their trade, restore objects of art, and paint murals (often controversial) in public buildings. "Some of it was good," said FDR, "some of it not so good, but all of it native, human, eager, and alive: All of it painted in their own country, and painted about things that they know and look at often and have touched and loved."[93] Many of the artists had little talent, but the program also gave a helping hand to some who would achieve international renown, such as Willem de Kooning and Jackson Pollock. Perhaps the most successful cultural endeavor was the Federal Writers Project, which put writers to work preparing the American Guide Series, an encyclopedic and still useful set of guidebooks to each of the states and major cities. The writers included Conrad Aiken, John Cheever, and Richard Wright, whose "Uncle Tom's Children" won *Story* magazine's first prize for a story by an FWP writer.[94] The outpouring of literature under the sponsorship of the WPA was "one of the most remarkable phenomena of the era of crisis," wrote the critic Alfred Kazin. "Whatever form this literature took . . . it testified to an extraordinary national self-scrutinizing. . . . Never before did a nation seem so hungry for news of itself."[95]

Throughout its existence the WPA was a lightning rod for criticism. As director of the Federal Emergency Relief Administration and CWA, Hopkins, the former social worker, had been remarkably nonpartisan. But a national work relief program with an initial $4.8 billion budget inevitably fell victim to party politics. When Congress amended the Work Relief Bill to require senatorial confirmation for appointees earning more than $5,000, Hopkins realized his apolitical days were over. "They told me I had to be part non-political and part political. I found that was impossible, at least for me. I finally realized there was nothing for it but to be all political."[96] Republicans complained that the WPA was a gigantic patronage boondoggle operated for the benefit of the Democratic party.[97] Critics on the left, led by *The Nation*, bellyached the WPA

was a misguided attempt to aid America's "crippled capitalist system" by forcing workers to settle for "depressed wages in a federal work gang."[98] Conservative southerners bridled at what they perceived to be the breakdown of
white supremacy and a mixing of the races in various WPA programs. Hopkins, whom Joseph E. Davies once described as a combination of Saint Francis
of Assisi and a racetrack tout, took the criticism as a badge of honor.[99] "I
haven't a thing to apologize about," he told an audience in Los Angeles. "If we
have made mistakes we have made them in the interests of the people that were
broke."[100]

The two final accomplishments of the New Deal in 1935 were the creation
of the Rural Electrification Administration and the passage of the Wagner
Labor Relations Act. FDR established the REA by executive order on May 11,
1935.[101] Nothing has done more to eliminate rural poverty than bringing electricity to the countryside. In 1935 only 11 percent of American farms had electricity; in Mississippi, less than 1 percent. Under REA, nonprofit rural
cooperatives were organized to build power lines and distribute electricity, financed by long-term federal loans at low (3 percent) interest rates. In the
South, power came primarily from the Tennessee Valley Authority. In the
Northwest, from Bonneville and Grand Coulee; from Boulder (Hoover) Dam
on the Colorado and Fort Peck on the Missouri. By the end of 1941, almost 50
percent of the nation's farms had been electrified. World War II interrupted
the construction of power lines for four years, but by the end of the 1940s
there was virtually no farm without electricity.* Families that had lit their
homes with coal oil lamps; families who had no washing machines, refrigerators, or vacuum cleaners; dairy farms that milked by hand—all now shared the
growing prosperity of a modernizing America. With the possible exception of
the establishment of the Federal Deposit Insurance Corporation, no single action by the New Deal had a greater impact on daily life in the American countryside than rural electrification.[102]

FDR was the prime mover behind rural electrification. The Wagner Labor
Relations Act, which recognized the right of workers to organize and bargain

---

* I vividly recall how my mother's relatives living in northern Chickasaw County, Mississippi, received electricity in the spring of 1941, while our farm in the southern part of the
county did not obtain it until 1946.

collectively, owed its passage almost entirely to the unstinting efforts of Senator Robert Wagner of New York. In the early days of the New Deal, Roosevelt saw himself as a neutral arbiter between labor and management. He shied away from endorsing legislation that would enshrine collective bargaining and in fact had prevailed upon Wagner not to introduce his bill before the 1934 elections. But when the Seventy-fourth Congress convened, Wagner was quick off the mark pressing labor's right to organize and the establishment of a National Labor Relations Board to guarantee it. Reflecting his German trade union heritage (Wagner's father had been a printer in Wiesbaden), Wagner was one of the few Democrats who identified with the union movement. His long legislative career, in both Albany and Washington, had been dedicated to supporting labor's cause. In the Senate he acquired a reputation as a peerless legislative craftsman, and unlike many other progressives he did not bloviate at the drop of a hat. Wagner played by the rules of the Senate club and was respected by his colleagues for it. By 1935 he was recognized as the Senate's resident expert on labor matters. After lengthy hearings in March and April in which industry spokesmen lambasted the bill (even the columnist Walter Lippmann called it "one of the most reactionary measures of our time"), the Senate Labor Committee reported it unanimously on May 2.[103] Two weeks later, after only two days of debate, the Senate added its approval 63–12, with four conservative Democrats and eight Republicans voting against. It was a remarkable achievement, for which Wagner deserved the credit.

Roosevelt still declined to take a stand. The act would be divisive, and FDR wanted to remain above the fray. Even the possibility of a veto could not be ruled out. "It seems almost inevitable that the Administration would have much to lose in public support" if the bill became law, Commerce secretary Daniel Roper told FDR on May 22.[104] But the following week the Supreme Court struck down the NIRA and in the process gutted the nascent collective bargaining provisions contained in the act.[105] The public outcry convinced FDR that the time for Wagner's bill had come. He placed himself at the head of the parade, and the measure whipped through the House of Representatives without a roll call. It was signed into law on July 5, 1935.[106]

In November, FDR resumed his practice of spending Thanksgiving at Warm Springs. On the twenty-ninth he journeyed to Atlanta, where he was received at a massive homecoming rally at the Georgia Tech football stadium. Roosevelt was at his rhetorical best:

You cannot borrow your way out of debt, but you can invest your way into a sounder future. . . . Over three years ago, realizing that we were not doing a perfect thing but that we were doing a necessary thing, we appropriated money for direct relief. But just as quickly as possible we turned to the job of providing actual work for those in need.

I realize that gentlemen in well-warmed and well-stocked clubs will discourse on the expenses of Government and the suffering that they are going through because their Government is spending money on work relief. Some of these same gentlemen tell me that a dole would be more economical than work relief. That is true. But the men who tell me that have, unfortunately, too little contact with the true America to realize that . . . most Americans want to give something for what they get. That something, which in this case is honest work, is the saving barrier between them and moral degradation. I propose to build that barrier high and keep it high.[107]

SEVENTEEN

HUBRIS

I propose that hereafter,
when a Judge reaches the age of seventy,
a new and younger Judge shall be added to
the Court automatically.
—FRANKLIN D. ROOSEVELT, MARCH 9, 1937

FDR KICKED OFF the 1936 campaign early. "We began the first of the year and never let up until the polls closed ten months later," said Jim Farley.[1] Roosevelt told Farley to organize a sponsorship committee of twelve prominent Americans. "I would like to have five clergymen. I think we should have a Catholic priest, a Baptist minister, an Episcopalian minister, a Presbyterian minister, and a rabbi."

"What about the Methodists?" asked Farley.

"Well, we could leave out the Jews," FDR replied. "No, there are more of them than there are Episcopalians. Take the Jews and leave out the Episcopalians."[2]

Roosevelt saw the election as a referendum. "There is one issue in this campaign. It is myself, and the people must be either for me or against me."[3] In FDR's eyes the outcome was never in doubt. "We will win easily," he told his cabinet, "but we are going to make it a crusade."[4]

Roosevelt had good reason for optimism. By almost any measure the economic surge since 1932 had been remarkable. National income had risen by more than 50 percent, 6 million new jobs had been created, and unemployment had dropped by more than a third. Of the 8 million still unemployed, more than 70 percent worked at least part of the year for the WPA or were enrolled in the CCC. Industrial production had doubled, stock prices were up 80 percent from their 1933 lows, farmers' cash income—which had fallen below

$4 billion in 1932—rose to almost $7 billion in 1935, and corporate profits, deep in negative territory when Roosevelt took office, had zoomed to nearly $6 billion.[5]

Statistics told only part of the story. The banking system had been rescued, depositors enjoyed a federal guarantee of their savings, most farm mortgages had been refinanced, and the Home Owners' Loan Corporation had bailed out more than 3 million debt-ridden home owners. Social Security, rural electrification, and the massive public works program now under way were changing the face of the nation. A *Fortune* magazine poll in June 1936 indicated that 53 percent of the nation thought the Depression was over and that 60 percent or more supported the president.[6]

On the political front, Roosevelt's opponents were in disarray. With Huey Long's assassination in September 1935 (Long was forty-two years old), the Share Our Wealth movement imploded. The Reverend Gerald L. K. Smith, a rabble-rousing fundamentalist from Shreveport, had seized the reins and the mailing lists, but without the Kingfish the effort floundered. The remnants of Long's political organization made peace with the administration—critics called it the Second Louisiana Purchase—and Smith was shunted into the rhetorical wilderness.[7] Father Coughlin, for his part, appeared to be concentrating on congressional elections, and the Townsend forces had been undermined by passage of the Social Security Act. To the Democrats' delight, Herbert Hoover had emerged from domestic exile, traveling widely around the country, seeking vindication for what he believed had been a singularly successful four years in the White House. Napoleon said that after the French Revolution the Bourbons had learned nothing and forgotten nothing. The same might be said of Herbert Hoover. His message of retrenchment, the gold standard, and a balanced budget fell on deaf ears. Most Republican politicians shunned the former president's embrace, certain it meant electoral defeat come November.

Roosevelt launched his campaign with a fighting State of the Union message on January 3. At Louis Howe's urging, the president converted what is normally a request for legislation into an election keynote. "Let 'em have it," said Howe. "They'll lap it up."[8]

Roosevelt spoke to Congress in a special evening session—the first president to do so—and to the delight of wildly cheering Democrats pulled every partisan plug. A vast radio audience heard FDR lambaste the "resplendent economic autocracy" that threatened to retard the nation's recovery. "We have earned the hatred of entrenched greed," said FDR with evident relish. Now these sinister forces were conspiring to recapture power. "Autocrats in small things, they seek autocracy in bigger things. . . . Give them their way and they will take the course of every aristocracy of the past—power for themselves, enslavement for the public."[9] It was the language of class war that Long might have used. Speaking to the party's annual Jackson Day celebration several days later, FDR identified with Old Hickory, who like himself had

> an overwhelming proportion of the material wealth of the Nation arrayed against him.
>
> The great media . . . fought him. Haughty and sterile intellectualism opposed him. Musty reaction disapproved him. Hollow and outworn traditionalism shook a trembling finger at him. It seemed sometimes that all were against him—all but the people of the United States. . . . History so often repeats itself.[10]

On January 25, 1936, Roosevelt's autocrats of privilege made their rebuttal. Two thousand guests decked out in formal evening attire gathered at Washington's Mayflower Hotel for the Liberty League's annual dinner. *The New York Times* reported that the audience "represented, either through principals or attorneys, a large portion of the capital wealth of the country."[11] John W. Davis and Governor Albert Ritchie of Maryland were there, as were Newton D. Baker, Winthrop Aldrich, and assorted du Ponts, Mellons, and Vanderbilts. The keynote speech was given by Al Smith, in white tie and tails, who assailed the New Deal and FDR for more than an hour. Smith said that if Roosevelt was nominated, he planned to take a walk in November. "It is all right with me if they want to disguise themselves as Norman Thomas or Karl Marx or Lenin . . . but let me give one solemn warning: There can be only one capital, Washington or Moscow. There can be only one atmosphere of government, the clean, pure, fresh air of free America, or the foul breath of communistic Russia."[12]

Smith's audience went giddy with delight. "It was perfect," crowed Pierre S. du Pont.[13] But as a political effort, the night proved a disaster—"one of the major tactical blunders of modern politics," in the words of Jim Farley.[14] Senate majority leader Joe Robinson of Arkansas, who had been Al Smith's running mate in 1928, gave the administration's response. His voice dripping with sarcasm, Robinson told a national radio audience, "It was the swellest party ever given by the du Ponts." Smith, "the unhappy warrior," had turned his back on the sidewalks of New York. "Now his gaze rests fondly upon the gilded towers and palaces of Park Avenue."[15] Roosevelt's popularity soared. The Liberty League bubble collapsed so completely that by June the GOP was frantically trying to disown it.

A pall was cast over the campaign in April, when Louis Howe died. Howe had been ailing more than usual for the past year and in August 1935 had been moved from the White House to the U.S. Naval Hospital where he died peacefully in his sleep a little before midnight, April 18. "Franklin is on his own now," Howe confided to a visitor shortly before his death.[16] Roosevelt and Eleanor had visited the little man almost daily during his confinement, and his death was a heavy blow. For ER it meant the loss of a dear friend and mentor, an ally who had continued to mediate the differences between her and Franklin. After Howe's death "communication grew harder for each of them," wrote Blanche Wiesen Cook, "and for their work together."[17] For FDR it meant the loss of his most intimate friend and adviser—the only person except for Missy who spoke frankly regardless of the consequences. "For one reason or another, no one quite filled the void," said Eleanor many years later. "There are not many men in this world whose personal ambition is to accomplish things for someone else, and it was some time before a friendship with Harry Hopkins . . . again brought Franklin some of the satisfaction he had known with Louis Howe."[18]

FDR handled the funeral arrangements himself: formal services in the East Room of the White House; flags at half-staff; interment in the Episcopal cemetery at Fall River, Massachusetts. The president and his sons stood bareheaded on the snow-covered ground as Howe's body was carried gently from the hearse to the gravesite.[19] *The New York Times* reported that Roosevelt "appeared oblivious to everything around him, both during the service and when he returned to his car."[20] Later, FDR appointed Howe's widow postmaster of Fall River. Admiral Richard E. Byrd, a family friend, named a peak in Antarctica "Mount Louis McHenry Howe."[21] As one historian has written, Howe's influence will always remain hidden. He talked to FDR daily, but no one knows what they said. "His major service was relentless criticism. He was the 'no' man from whom the Boss could never quite escape."[22]*

Howe's death marked the departure of the last of Roosevelt's original advisers. As FDR veered left, one after another of the early brain trusters fell by the wayside: first Lewis Douglas, then James Warburg, then Moley himself. A new set of acolytes took their places—a changing of the guard that inaugurated a new direction of march. There was the former journalist Stanley High, once editor of the *Christian Herald,* an easy-to-get-along-with speechwriter with a gift for memorable expressions. Sam Rosenman called him the best phrasemaker he ever worked with, and it was High who gave Roosevelt's 1936 campaign speeches their remarkable polish.[23] There were Thomas Corcoran and Benjamin Cohen, gifted legal technicians who had come to Washington under Felix Frankfurter's aegis. The garrulous Corcoran was Mr. Outside to Cohen's Mr. Inside—a remarkable team that not only provided Roosevelt in-house expertise in legislative drafting (sadly lacking in 1933) but was equally adept at lobbying the bills through Congress. Additional legal and economic talent was provided by Robert Jackson, William O. Douglas, and Isador Lubin, who weaved in and out of the White House.

The Republican National Convention convened in Cleveland on June 10, 1936. Caught between self-styled constitutionalists who wanted to repeal the New Deal and progressives like William E. Borah, Hiram Johnson, and Gifford Pinchot, the Grand Old Party turned to Governor Alfred M. Landon of Kansas. A former Bull Moose who had deserted the party in 1924 to vote for La Follette instead of Coolidge, Landon had survived Democratic tidal waves in 1932 and 1934, balanced the state budget, and, aside from an ingrained fiscal conservatism, was regarded as far more liberal than the party's mainstream on social issues and civil rights. "America bids fair to join the procession of nations of the world in the march toward a new social and economic philosophy," he said in his 1935 Topeka inaugural. "Some say this will lead to socialism, some communism, others fascism. For myself I am convinced that the ultimate goal will be a modified form of individual rights and ownership

---

* "Oh, hell, it's no trick to make a President," Howe once said. "Give me a man who stays reasonably sober, shaves, and wears a clean shirt every day and I can make him President." Lela Stiles, *The Man Behind Roosevelt: The Story of Louis McHenry Howe* 251 (Cleveland: World, 1954).

of property out of which will come a wider spread of prosperity and opportunity."[24]

Landon's greatest advantage was that he was not Herbert Hoover. His liability (aside from Roosevelt's immense popularity) was his blandness. For better or worse, Landon personified Kansas: honest, decent, self-contained, hard-working, and dull. After listening to Landon on the radio, Harold Ickes said, "the Democratic Campaign Committee ought to spend all the money it can raise to send him out and make speeches."[25] Unlike the GOP platform, Landon did not seek to dismantle the New Deal and generally refrained from attacking FDR personally.[26] He deplored the Liberty League and vainly sought labor's support. As his running mate he chose the affable Chicago publisher Frank Knox, another Bull Moose, who had charged up San Juan Hill with Theodore Roosevelt. In World War I Knox had enlisted as a private at the age of forty-three, seen combat in France, and ended the war as a colonel of field artillery. He was more energetic and more stridently nationalist than Landon, and still looked on TR as his political idol. What the nation needed, he told an audience in 1935, was "fewer and better Roosevelts."[27]

Three days after Landon was nominated, Gerald L. K. Smith announced from Chicago that he, Father Coughlin, and Dr. Townsend were joining hands to form a new political party—the Union party—dedicated to defeating Franklin Roosevelt and "the communistic philosophy of Frankfurter, Ickes, Hopkins, and Wallace." Smith claimed more than 20 million adherents ready to join forces and elect two-term North Dakota congressman William Lemke, a weathered agrarian populist who had devoted his brief legislative career to rescuing the nation's farmers from mortgage indebtedness. "I look upon Roosevelt," said Lemke, "as a bewildered Kerensky of a provisional government. He doesn't know where he came from or where he is going. As for Landon he represents the dying shadow of a past civilization."[28] Added together, Lemke's farm constituency, Coughlin's urban Catholic base, Townsend's following among the elderly, and the remnants of the Share Our Wealth movement made the Union party, at least on paper, a formidable opponent.

If Roosevelt was concerned, he did not show it. The Democrats met in Philadelphia on June 23. The first order of business was repeal of the two-thirds rule, which had given the South a veto over presidential nominees since the days of Andrew Jackson. "Now that the party is in power and there is no question about my renomination," FDR told Farley, "we should clear up the situation for all time."[29] Roosevelt gave notice to the party well in advance of the convention that he sought a rule change, and Farley entrusted the task to Senator Bennett Champ Clark of Missouri, whose father had fallen victim to the two-thirds rule in 1912.[30] Clark was selected to chair the convention's committee on rules and resolutions and, as South Carolina's James Byrnes said afterward, pursued his goal "with all the energy of an avenging fury."[31] The committee voted 36–13 to abrogate the two-thirds rule, and the committee report was accepted by acclamation. To mollify the South (and with Roosevelt's blessing), a provision was included that in future conventions a state's Democratic voting record would be considered in the allocation of delegates. The significance of the repeal of the two-thirds rule—virtually without a contest—is difficult to overstate. Not only did the power of the South in the Democratic party diminish, but without repeal it is open to question whether FDR could have been renominated in 1940.

The 1936 Democratic National Convention was the most placid on record. There was no fight over the platform, no contested delegations, and, for the first time since 1840, no roll calls. Senator Alben Barkley of Kentucky treated the delegates to another spellbinding keynote and brought down the house with a slam at the Supreme Court. The trouble lay not with the Constitution, said Barkley, but with the men who interpreted it. The Democratic party wanted the Court to treat the Constitution "as a life-giving charter, rather than an object of curiosity on the shelf of a museum." When he asked rhetorically whether the Court was too sacred to be criticized, the convention roared its dissent.[32] Both Roosevelt and Garner were renominated by acclamation, but it required a full day to do so. The president's nomination was seconded by a delegate from every state and territory—fifty-five in all—and more than seventeen delegates spoke on behalf of Garner.

The high point came Saturday night, June 27, when Roosevelt addressed the convention. A crowd of more than 100,000 crammed into the University of Pennsylvania's Franklin Field to hear the president while millions more tuned in their radios to listen. A light drizzle had fallen but the sky had cleared, and a pale half-moon rose overhead. Instead of the usual brass bands, the Philadelphia Symphony Orchestra under Leopold Stokowski played Tchaikovsky. When the incomparable coloratura soprano Lily Pons sang "Song of the Lark" from *The Seasons*, even reporters were on their feet cheering. "Something had happened to that audience," wrote the Washington journalist Raymond Clapper. "It had been lifted, not to a cheap political emotional pitch, but to something finer. It was ready for Roosevelt."[33]

Shortly before 10 P.M.—seven o'clock on the West Coast—the president's limousine entered the stadium, circled the field, and stopped near the platform from which Roosevelt was to speak. As FDR was helped to his feet and began his laborious walk to the lectern on the arm of his son James, Stokowski led the orchestra in a stirring "Hail to the Chief" while a dozen spotlights illuminated the president's progress. The stadium shook with applause. Smiling broadly and shaking hands as he went, Roosevelt made his way to the stage. He recognized the unmistakable white beard of the elderly poet Edwin Markham, whose "Man with a Hoe" had been a battle cry for the forgotten man during TR's time.[34] As Roosevelt reached out to greet Markham, he was jostled and lost his balance. The brace on his right leg came open and FDR went down, the pages of his speech spilling into the crowd. Mike Reilly of the Secret Service dived and got his shoulder underneath the president before he hit the ground. Farley and others clustered around to hide the scene, while Gus Gennerich knelt down and snapped FDR's brace back into place.

Roosevelt was pale and shaken as he was helped to his feet. "Clean me up," he ordered. "And keep your feet off those damned sheets." While Farley and Gennerich brushed the dirt from the president's clothes and straightened his tie, James retrieved the manuscript. "I was the damnedest, maddest white man at that moment you ever saw," said Roosevelt. "It was the most frightful five minutes of my life."[35] When everything was in order, FDR said "Let's go." He started toward the platform, but, catching sight of Markham, who was quietly sobbing, the president stopped again, smiled, and took the old man's hand in his for a moment.

When Roosevelt reached the platform, he was greeted with another thunderous ovation. He had regained his composure and stood waving and smiling as he unobtrusively reassembled his speech and put the crumpled pages in order. When the applause died down, the president struck a bipartisan pose: "I come not only as a leader of a party, not only as a candidate for high office, but as one upon whom many critical hours have imposed and still impose a grave responsibility." He thanked the members of all parties who had put partisanship aside to help defeat the Depression.

"In those days we feared fear. That is why we fought fear. And today, my friends, we have won against the most dangerous of our foes. We have conquered fear."

Roosevelt reminded the audience that political tyranny had been wiped out at Philadelphia on July 4, 1776. But new tyrannies had arisen to threaten American liberty.

Liberty requires opportunity to make a living—a living which gives man not only enough to live by, but something to live for.

For too many of us the political equality we once had won was meaningless in the face of economic inequality. A small group had concentrated into their own hands an almost complete control over other people's property, other people's money, other people's labor—other people's lives.

These economic royalists complain that we seek to overthrow the institutions of America. What they really complain of is that we seek to take away their power. In vain they seek to hide behind the Flag and the Constitution.

Roosevelt's voice rose and fell as he lifted the audience through the rhythmic cadences:

Governments can err. Presidents do make mistakes. But the immortal Dante tells us that divine justice weighs the sins of the cold-blooded and the sins of the warm-hearted in different scales.

Better the occasional faults of a Government that lives in a spirit of charity than the consistent omissions of a Government frozen in the ice of its own indifference.

The vast audience gave Roosevelt another tumultuous ovation. When quiet settled over the stadium, the president lowered his voice and continued, reciting the sermon's lesson, as it were:

There is a mysterious cycle in human events. To some generations much is given. Of other generations much is asked. This generation of Americans has a rendezvous with destiny.

Another thundering ovation. FDR looked up, acknowledged the response, smiled, and threw his head back. He had reached his conclusion. "I accept the commission you . . ."[36] But the cheers and applause that cascaded through the stadium drowned his last words. For ten minutes the shouting continued. FDR raised his hands over his head like a boxer. Then he raised Garner's. They were joined on the podium by Sara and the president's family. The Philadelphia Symphony Orchestra played "Auld Lang Syne." Roosevelt requested another chorus, began singing himself, and soon the whole stadium joined in. Soon the president returned to his car. With the top down, FDR took two victory laps around the track to an intense ovation. Even after he left the stadium the crowd remained, mesmerized by the evening's events.[37]

As he had done after winning the nomination in 1932, Roosevelt left after the convention for a two-week sailing vacation, this time on the *Sewanna*, a fifty-six-foot schooner owned by New York lawyer Harrison Tweed. Once again James, John, and Franklin, Jr., crewed for the president, joined by two professional seamen provided by Mr. Tweed. "I haven't the faintest idea where I'm going except to work to the east'ard," FDR told reporters on July 14 as he set sail from Maine's Pulpit Harbor.[38] Instead of heading immediately to Campobello, Roosevelt sailed across the Gulf of Maine and the mouth of the Bay of Fundy to the southern tip of Nova Scotia. He made the 108-mile crossing in thirty hours and, when the weather turned heavy, personally took the 9 P.M. and 3 A.M. watches.[39] For twelve days FDR sailed in and out of the small coves on Nova Scotia's south shore before recrossing the Bay of Fundy for Campobello. "His seamanship was tested by the sail in rough, white-capped seas," reported *The New York Times*. "The decks were awash in a run before a stiff southeast wind. The president, at the wheel, clad in oilskin, brought the *Sewanna* through the treacherous Grand passage between Digby Neck and Brier Island, where high seas and cross-currents make navigation hazardous."[40] James said later that one of the escort destroyers had attempted to follow them, hoping to pick up survivors, but "thanks to Pa's elegant navigating we soon lost her."[41] Roosevelt spent a day and a night at Campobello and then returned to Hyde Park by train, stopping for a weekend visit in Quebec City at the invitation of Canada's governor-general, Lord Tweedsmuir.[42]

When the campaign began in earnest on Labor Day, FDR left nothing to chance. He whistle-stopped across the country, delivering more than two hundred speeches in sixty days.* Roosevelt concentrated on the heartland. He was confident of carrying the Solid South and the big cities of the North but was determined to deny the farm belt to Landon and Lemke. He spent three days in Iowa, two in the Dakotas, two each in Nebraska and Wyoming, two in Colorado, and two in Kansas. Roosevelt spoke seven times in Landon's home state before moving on to Missouri, Illinois, Michigan, and Ohio.[43] Wherever he went, jubilant crowds reached out to touch him. They waved and cheered and shouted thanks for saving a farm or getting a factory reopened. Even the weather cooperated. Rain began to fall on the parched Middle West as Roosevelt moved through. The president never mentioned his opponent by name. He touted the accomplishments of the New Deal, contrasted the do-nothing years of Herbert Hoover, and did not let his audiences forget the opposition of the "economic royalists" of the Liberty League.[44]

Roosevelt was a natural on the campaign trail because he enjoyed it. "He rode for hours in the 1936 campaign in motor processions, waving constantly to people along the roadsides, shaking hands with hundreds, and delivering often ten to fifteen speeches a day," said Farley. "He never gave the impression of working hard; on the contrary he was stimulated and exhilarated."[45] Who else would join with an American Legion chorus in Syracuse to sing "Pack Up Your Troubles in Your Old Kit Bag" or playfully invite hostile editors to the platform as FDR did with William Allen White in Emporia, Kansas?

The only glitch in the Democratic campaign came early on, when Farley, addressing a gathering of party faithful in Michigan, referred to Landon as the governor of "a typical prairie state."

"Never use the word 'typical,' " chided FDR. "If the sentence had read, 'One of those splendid Prairie States', no one could have picked up on it. But the word 'typical' coming from a New Yorker is meat for the opposition."[46]

Landon recognized he had an uphill fight. He waged a low-key campaign, showed the Republican colors to advantage, and remained on good terms with FDR.† That was shrewd politics. Landon's advisers calculated that rabid Roo-

---

* Roosevelt traveled by train, which was exceedingly time-consuming since he preferred to go at no more than thirty miles an hour. That enabled him to move about more easily when the train was in motion, and he also enjoyed looking at the scenery. No presidential candidate had seen more of the United States than FDR, and none had a better appreciation of regional differences. His slow travel by train reinforced that understanding.

† In early September Roosevelt and Landon met at a midwest governors' conference in Des

sevelt haters would vote Republican in any case and the campaign should aim at the ordinary citizen who liked the New Deal's goals but disapproved of its methods. "None of my campaign speeches will be merely an attack upon the opposition," Landon wrote Idaho's senator William E. Borah in August. "I cannot criticize everything that has been done in the past three years and do it sincerely. Neither do I believe that such an attack is good politics."[47]

If Landon took the high road, Gerald L. K. Smith, Father Coughlin, and the Union party took the low. Alarmed at Lemke's failure to gain traction, Union party rhetoric escalated to a level of vituperation seldom seen in American public life. "I'll teach them how to hate," Smith boasted. "Religion and patriotism, keep going on that. It's the only way you can get them really 'het up.' "[48] For Coughlin, teaching how to hate came naturally. Determined to outdo Smith, Coughlin not only attacked FDR as a liar, a double-crosser, and a Communist but placed much of the blame on the Jewish advisers who surrounded him. Called to task by the Church, Coughlin apologized for calling Roosevelt a liar but was soon at it again. In New York he declared the difference between Roosevelt and Landon a choice "between carbolic acid and rat poison." In New Bedford, he called Roosevelt "the dumbest man ever to occupy the White House." In Cincinnati on September 25 he described FDR as the "anti-God" and implied that bullets would be permissible to dispose of an "upstart dictator in the United States . . . when the ballot is useless."[49]

With that remark Coughlin stepped over the line. The Vatican summoned Coughlin's bishop, Michael Gallagher, to Rome; L'Osservatore Romano accused Coughlin of provoking disrespect for authority; and, at the apparent suggestion of George Cardinal Mundelein of Chicago, a not-so-covert supporter of FDR, the papal secretary of state, Cardinal Eugenio Pacelli (later Pope Pius XII), embarked on a two-month vacation in the United States and remained through the election.*

Moines. "Governor, however this comes out, we'll see more of each other," said FDR. "Either you come to see me [in the White House] or I'll come to see you." "I certainly shall," Landon replied. "And Governor, don't work too hard," Roosevelt joked.

"Harmony dripped so steadily from every rafter," Senator Arthur Capper, a Kansas Republican, noted, "that I fully expected one of the candidates to withdraw." Quoted in Arthur M. Schlesinger, Jr., The Politics of Upheaval 610 (Boston: Houghton Mifflin, 1960).

* Two days after the election, Cardinal Pacelli very publicly visited Hyde Park for lunch with the president. Pacelli's party included Joseph P. Kennedy, Frank C. Walker, and the then

Roosevelt closed the campaign with a massive rally at Madison Square Garden on October 31. With the wind in his sails and well ahead in all opinion polls save one,* FDR all but proclaimed victory. "I prefer to remember this campaign not as bitter but as hard-fought. There should be no bitterness or hate where the sole thought is the welfare of the United States of America. No man can occupy the office of President without realizing that he is President of all the people."

That said, Roosevelt did not disappoint the partisan crowd. After vigorously defending Social Security—"Only desperate men with their backs to the wall would descend so far below the level of decent citizenship" to suggest that the funds collected from workers would not be available when they retired—the president recited a litany of Republican abuse:

For twelve years this Nation was afflicted with hear-nothing, see-nothing, do-nothing Government. The nation looked to Government but Government looked away.

Nine mocking years with the golden calf and three long years with the scourge!

Nine mocking years at the ticker and three long years in the breadlines!

Nine mad years of mirage and three long years of despair!

The applause, reported *The New York Times,* came in "roars which rose and fell like the sound of waves pounding in the surf."[50] FDR savored every moment. "Powerful influences," he continued, "strive today to restore that kind of government with its doctrine that Government is best which is most indiffer-

---

auxiliary bishop of Boston, Francis J. Spellman, who was the cardinal's interlocutor in the United States. "I was very anxious to meet the President of the United States," Pacelli told newsmen afterward. "I am very happy to have had the opportunity of seeing him and congratulating him. I enjoyed my visit very much." *The New York Times,* November 6, 1936.

* *Literary Digest,* which had correctly called the 1932 election, predicted that Landon would carry 32 states with 370 electoral votes against 16 states with 161 electoral votes for Roosevelt. By contrast, the Gallup and Roper organizations forecast that FDR would win in a landslide. Unlike Gallup and Roper, *Literary Digest* polled only persons whose names appeared in telephone books and automobile registration lists, which in 1936 skewed the sample toward more affluent voters. Peverill Squire, "Why the 1936 Literary Digest Poll Failed," 52 *Public Opinion* 125–133 (1988).

ent. Never before in all our history have these forces been so united against one candidate as they stand today. They are unanimous in their hate for me—and I welcome their hatred."

Absolute pandemonium. The vast audience in the Garden rose and cheered and then cheered some more. Roosevelt lowered his voice. "I should like to have it said of my first Administration that in it the forces of selfishness and of lust for power met their match." More sustained cheering and applause, then: "I should like to have it said of my second Administration that in it these forces met their master."[51]

On Monday, November 2, the day before the election, Farley provided Roosevelt a detailed assessment of the party's chances. New Hampshire and Connecticut would be close. Also Michigan and Kansas. But he thought FDR would carry them. "I am still definitely of the opinion that you will carry every state but two—Maine and Vermont."[52] Since Maine had already voted, that meant a virtual clean sweep on election day.*

Roosevelt was incredulous. Participating as he always did in a preelection poll among the newsmen who covered his campaign, FDR put his electoral vote total at 360 to Landon's 171. That was about two thirds the number Farley had given him. As the early returns came in Tuesday night, Roosevelt continued to be skeptical. When New Haven was reported to have gone Democratic by 15,000 votes, the president said it must be a mistake. "It couldn't be that large." He asked Missy to have the figures checked. She was back in two minutes. The figures were accurate. Roosevelt leaned back in his chair, blew a smoke ring in the air, and said, "Wow!" Farley had been right.[53]

When the ballots were tabulated, Roosevelt had won an unprecedented 60.79 percent of the popular vote.† He beat Landon 27,747,636 to 16,679,543—a margin 4 million votes larger than the Democratic landslide in

* Because of the chance of early snow, Maine historically voted early. In 1936 the state went to the polls on September 14 and gave Landon 55.6 percent of the vote to Roosevelt's 41.6 percent.

† In 1964 Lyndon Johnson defeated Barry Goldwater 61.05 percent to 38.47 percent, but Goldwater's percentage was slightly higher than that of Landon, who won only 36.54 percent. Congressional Quarterly, *Guide to U.S. Elections* 290, 297 (Washington, D.C.: Congressional Quarterly, 1975).

1932. Lemke polled a mere 892,492 votes nationwide, and Norman Thomas, running under the Socialist banner for the third time, received 187,785.[54] That was 700,000 votes fewer than Thomas had received in 1932. The Socialist program was indeed being carried out by the New Deal, quipped Thomas: "On a stretcher."[55] In the electoral college, Roosevelt won forty-six states with 523 votes to Landon's 8—a majority not seen since James Monroe cruised to an all-but-unanimous victory during the Era of Good Feelings in 1820.[56]

Roosevelt's confidence about the one-party South proved out. He carried South Carolina with 98.6 percent of the vote, Mississippi with 98.0, and Georgia with 87.1. "Who are the fourteen persons who voted against you in Warm Springs?" asked Farley. "You ought to raise hell with them."[57] Roosevelt's top-heavy majority in Congress increased further. In the House, the Democrats gained eleven additional seats, giving them a 331–89 majority. In the Senate, Democrats outnumbered Republicans 76–16, with four independents who were solidly behind the president: Henrik Shipstead and Ernest Lundeen of Minnesota, Robert La Follette of Wisconsin, and George Norris of Nebraska. Norris had represented Nebraska in the Senate since 1913 but because of his support for the New Deal had been denied the GOP nomination in 1936 and was running as an independent. Roosevelt was particularly concerned about Norris, and the last thing he did before going to bed election night was to call Nebraska to inquire about the Senate race. "Of all the results on November third," he wrote Norris later, "your re-election gave me the greatest happiness."[58]

The 1936 election marked the birth of the Roosevelt coalition—a unique alliance of big-city bosses, the white South, farmers and workers, Jews and Irish Catholics, ethnic minorities, and African Americans that would dominate American politics for the next generation. Gone from the Democratic party was the old hard-money, probusiness crowd: men like John Raskob and Jouett Shouse; John W. Davis and Newton D. Baker; and the checkbooks of the du Ponts and General Motors. In their stead were organized labor, led by John L. Lewis and Sidney Hillman; disaffected businessmen like A. P. Giannini of the Bank of America, who feuded with the financial establishment; and leaders of new industries, typified by Thomas Watson of IBM. Lewis, a lifelong Republican who had supported Hoover in 1932, marshaled the battalions of the CIO behind Roosevelt and contributed $770,000 (roughly $10 million currently) to the president's campaign.[59] Labor's votes helped swing Ohio, Illinois, and Indiana behind FDR. Pennsylvania went Democratic for the first time since James Buchanan. African Americans deserted the party of Lincoln; for the first time since Emancipation, blacks voted Democratic.[60] Not because FDR was in the forefront of the fight for civil rights. He was not. But no segment of American society had suffered more severely from the Depression, and the New Deal provided relief.

Roosevelt made no changes in his administration for the second term. Hull remained at State, Morgenthau at the Treasury, and Homer Cummings continued as attorney general. Frances Perkins, Harold Ickes, and Henry Wallace, the three most ardent New Dealers, stayed at their posts, as did Daniel Roper at Commerce and the elderly Claude Swanson at Navy. James Farley continued to wear two hats—postmaster general and party chairman—and at the War Department former Kansas governor Harry Woodring had succeeded George Dern, who had died in August.* In the White House, Louis Howe was gone, but otherwise FDR's personal staff, essentially an extended family, remained intact. Missy and Grace Tully ran the office seamlessly; Hackmeister handled the phones; Pa Watson, Steve Early, and Marvin McIntyre did the president's bidding; and Admiral Ross McIntire looked after his health. On Capitol Hill, Joe Robinson of Arkansas continued as Senate majority leader, William Bankhead of Alabama was now speaker, and Sam Rayburn had become House majority leader. The chairmen of the principal committees in both houses—from Appropriations to Ways and Means—once again were uniformly from the South.

Across the Capitol grounds to the east, the Supreme Court reflected similar continuity. The Court's membership had not changed since Oliver Wendell Holmes had stepped down five years earlier. Willis Van Devanter, the senior justice, had been appointed by William Howard Taft in 1910. Two justices, James McReynolds and Louis Brandeis, had been appointed by Wilson. Harding had appointed two, Coolidge one, and Hoover three.† Brandeis, the oldest,

---

* FDR was superstitious about making changes, and he had a personal distaste for firing people. The only two cabinet changes since 1933 were because of the deaths of the incumbents: Morgenthau replaced William Woodin at Treasury, and Woodring replaced George Dern at the War Department.

† George Sutherland was appointed to the Court by Harding in 1922; Pierce Butler by Harding in 1923. Coolidge appointed Harlan F. Stone in 1925. Hoover appointed Chief Justice Hughes (1930), Owen Roberts (1930), and Benjamin Cardozo (1932).

was eighty. Five were in their seventies, and Owen Roberts, the youngest, was sixty-one. FDR was the first president since James Monroe (1817–21) to serve four years without making a single appointment to the Court.

Roosevelt was inaugurated on January 20, 1937—the first president to take office under the Twentieth Amendment. The weather was abysmal. An unforgiving January rain pummeled the stands and parade route. Capitol Plaza appeared roofed with umbrellas as more than 40,000 people gathered to watch the ceremony. The inaugural platform was fully open to the storm. Rain swept across the plaza, splattered against the president's winged collar, trickled down his bare head, and blotted his speech. Twice FDR paused during his address to brush water from his face.

With an unprecedented popular mandate, Roosevelt was on the offensive from the beginning. His inaugural address was a call to battle on behalf of those still denied the fruits of the American dream:

The test of our progress is not whether we add more to the abundance of those who have much; it is whether we provide enough for those who have too little.

I see millions of families trying to live on incomes so meager that the pall of family disaster hangs over them day by day.

I see millions denied education, recreation, and the opportunity to better their lot and the lot of their children.

I see millions lacking the means to buy the products of farm and factory and by their poverty denying work and productiveness to many other millions.

I see one-third of a nation ill-housed, ill-clad, ill-nourished.[61]

When the ceremony concluded, Roosevelt ordered an open car. Eleanor joined him, and the two rode slowly back to the White House, waving to the rain-soaked spectators who lined the route. Mrs. Roosevelt's inaugural dress and hat were ruined, her fur coat sopping wet. FDR looked as though he had fallen into a swimming pool with his clothes on. At the end of the fifteen-minute ride the Roosevelts changed clothes hastily to watch the inaugural parade, again from a replica of Andrew Jackson's Hermitage. That too, at FDR's insistence, was open to the weather.[62]

ROOSEVELT DID NOT mention the Supreme Court in his inaugural address. But with Congress cooperative and Democrats or independents in control of forty-two of the nation's governor's mansions, he now took on the Court.[63] As a lawyer he should have known better; as a politician he should have been more cautious; as president he should have had a firmer grasp of the constitutional separation of powers.

Since 1933 the Supreme Court had declared six pieces of New Deal legislation unconstitutional.* It had denied the president the authority to remove members of independent regulatory commissions[64] and in June 1936 had struck down New York State's minimum-wage law for women and children.[65] Four of these decisions had been unanimous or almost so.[66]

At the same time the Court had upheld emergency legislation in Minnesota declaring a mortgage moratorium and had validated similar Depression-based legislation in New York fixing the price of milk.[67] It upheld Congress's authority to abrogate the gold clauses in private contracts,[68] sustained the Tennessee Valley Authority's right to sell electric power,[69] and on December 21, 1936, a month before FDR's inaugural, upheld the broad power of the president to conduct foreign relations: "In this vast external realm, with its important, complicated, delicate and manifold problems, the President alone has the power to speak or listen as a representative of the nation."[70]

The problem in 1937 was not the Court but the law, compounded by the hasty drafting of early New Deal legislation. Both the NIRA and the Frazier-Lemke Farm Mortgage Act (and to a lesser extent the Agricultural Adjustment Act) were loosely drawn and excessively broad, and made little effort to navi-

---

* The so-called Hot Oil act, section 9c of the National Industrial Recovery Act, was overturned by the Court (8–1) in *Panama Refining Co. v. Ryan*, 293 U.S. 388 (1935). In *Schechter Poultry Corp. v. United States*, 295 U.S. 553 (1935), and *Louisville Joint Stock Land Bank v. Radford*, 295 U.S. 595 (1935), unanimous Courts struck down the entire NIRA and the Frazier-Lemke Farm Mortgage Act. The Railroad Retirement Act was declared unconstitutional (5–4) in *Railroad Retirement Board v. Alton Railroad Co.*, 295 U.S. 330 (1935). In *United States v. Butler*, 297 U.S. 1 (1936) the Court (6–3) overturned the Agricultural Adjustment Act, and in *Carter v. Carter Coal Co.*, 298 U.S. 238 (1936) a sharply divided Court (5–4) declared the Guffey Bituminous Coal Act unconstitutional.

gate the shoals of constitutional precedent. Conventional wisdom considers the 1930s Supreme Court hidebound and reactionary. Yet under Hughes's effective leadership the Court had become the nation's principal protector of civil liberties. It had reversed a hundred years of precedent to hold the First Amendment's guarantee of a free press applicable to the states;[71] it had overturned the rape convictions of nine young black men in Scottsboro, Alabama, and made the Sixth Amendment's right to counsel applicable to the states in capital cases.[72] When the young men were tried again and convicted by an all-white jury, a unanimous Court overturned that conviction as well.[73] The Hughes Court declared California's statute making it unlawful to fly a red flag an unconstitutional denial of free speech.[74] And in an equally important decision rendered on January 7, 1937, the justices unanimously reversed the conviction of a Communist activist in Oregon for organizing a political meeting and distributing party literature. "Peaceable assembly for lawful discussion cannot be made a crime," said Hughes for the Court.[75] Each of these decisions was a milestone in the growth of American civil liberty, and the Supreme Court was in the forefront of that growth.

This was not a reactionary Court.[76] But the constitutional law of the last forty years was stacked against the New Deal, and the Roosevelt administration had been cavalier in its approach to the problem. When the early legislation was struck down, it came as no surprise to most informed observers. What was surprising was that FDR chose to attack the Court and not the law: that he zeroed in on the elderly justices and not the questionable precedents they were adhering to.*

* Early New Deal legislation relied on the commerce clause of the Constitution (Article I, section 8), which authorized Congress to regulate interstate and foreign commerce. As originally interpreted by the Marshall Court in the landmark case of *Gibbons v. Ogden,* 9 Wheaton (22 U.S.) 1 (1824), that would have sufficed. But in 1895 the Court, speaking through Chief Justice Melville Fuller, narrowed the scope of the commerce clause to exclude mining, manufacturing, and agriculture. Such activities, said Fuller, had only an "indirect effect" on commerce. *United States v. E. C. Knight,* 156 U.S. 1. That restrictive interpretation was emphatically affirmed in 1918, when the Court rejected Congress's attempt to regulate child labor under the commerce clause. *Hammer v. Dagenhart,* 247 U.S. 251.

In addition to the commerce clause decisions, another line of precedent invoked the due process clauses of the Fifth and Fourteenth Amendments to prevent governments from regulating wages and hours. Beginning with *Lochner v. New York* in 1905 (198 U.S. 45), the Court held such regulation to be a denial of an individual's "liberty of contract." This too

Roosevelt plotted his attack in secret. That was a tactical error. Military commanders going into battle take care to conceal their plans, but they are not dealing with Congress and the Court. For four years Roosevelt had handled Congress masterfully. On every piece of New Deal legislation he worked closely with the members involved: cajoling, co-opting, listening to their contributions. His failure to consult when it came to the Supreme Court—his refusal to include the congressional leadership in the planning stages of his proposal to alter the Court's membership—denied him the support he needed when opposition crystallized.

The genesis of FDR's Court-packing plan traces to a meeting in the Oval Office in January 1935 when the "Gold Clause Cases" were before the Court. Anticipating that the justices might rule against the government, Roosevelt asked what could be done should that occur. Robert H. Jackson, then the general counsel of the Treasury's revenue arm, mentioned that when the "Legal Tender Cases" had been pending in 1870, President Grant had appointed two additional justices, causing the Court to reverse itself and validate the greenbacks that had been circulating since the Civil War.* Roosevelt was intrigued

---

had been recently reaffirmed. "Freedom of contract is the general rule and restraint the exception," said Justice Sutherland in *Adkins v. Children's Hospital*, 261 U.S. 525, 546 (1923).

These two lines of precedent were formidable, but in each of the four cases there had been powerful dissents. *Hammer* and *Lochner* were 5–4, and *Adkins* 5–3 (Brandeis not participating). More important, standing opposed to the contemporary commerce clause rulings was no less a figure than John Marshall, whose expansive definition of commerce in *Gibbons* was a judicial classic.

A wild card in the Court's anti–New Deal holdings was the legal maxim that delegated power could not be redelegated, *delegatus non potest delegare.* The origin of that concept is unclear, and its application has been erratic. It has been employed only three times to invalidate legislation (*Panama Refining v. Ryan, Schechter Poultry Corp. v. United States,* and *Carter v. Carter Coal Co.*). It was rejected by the Hughes Court in *Curtiss-Wright* and buried in *Yakus v. United States,* 321 U.S. 414 (1944). Also see *Morrison v. Olson,* 487 U.S. 654 (1988). When the Court decided to change course in 1937, the maxim did not pose an obstacle.

* In 1862 Congress, confronted with the need to finance the war, passed the Legal Tender Act, authorizing paper money as a substitute for gold. After the war the act was challenged, and in *Hepburn v. Griswold,* 75 U.S. 603 (1870), the Court (4–3) ruled it unconstitutional. The government asked that the case be reargued; Congress increased the size of the Court from eight to nine; and one justice (Robert Grier) died, giving Grant two vacancies to fill. Grant appointed two stalwart Republicans, William Strong of Pennsylvania and Joseph

and instructed Attorney General Cummings to look into the matter.[77] He emphasized to Cummings the need to be discreet. For the next two years Cummings, Solicitor General Stanley Reed, and two of Cummings's assistants reviewed precedent and laid plans. No one on the White House staff was informed. Except for Cummings, no one in the cabinet knew what was afoot. None of FDR's advisers, men like Sam Rosenman, Felix Frankfurter, Tommy Corcoran, and Ben Cohen, were made privy. And Congress was kept in the dark.[78]

Unfortunately for the president, Cummings and Reed were not the sharpest knives in the legal drawer. Cummings's skills were primarily political. He was a former chairman of the Democratic National Committee and had been a floor leader for FDR at the 1932 convention. Originally scheduled to become governor-general of the Philippines, he was tapped as attorney general to fill the vacancy caused by the sudden death of Senator Thomas Walsh two days before the 1933 inauguration. At the time it was assumed the appointment was temporary and that the president would make a high-profile legal appointment, yet he never did. As attorney general, Cummings concentrated on the law enforcement role of the Department of Justice and did an excellent job supervising the reform of federal crime legislation. But constitutional law was not his bent.[79] Much the same could be said for Stanley Reed, a small-town Kentucky lawyer whose interest in tobacco legislation had brought him to Washington during the Hoover administration. Roosevelt had originally offered the solicitor general post to Felix Frankfurter. When Frankfurter declined, he apparently lost interest in the position. Reed was an effective administrator but like Cummings had little experience in constitutional litigation.[80]

Cummings met often with FDR. The president rejected the idea of a constitutional amendment to expand the commerce clause. That was the recommendation of the Democratic platform,[81] and it had been employed three

---

Bradley of New Jersey. When the case was reargued, *Hepburn* was overruled 5–4 and the Legal Tender Act sustained. The decision was written by Justice Strong. *Knox v. Lee,* 79 U.S. 457 (1871).

Jackson wrote FDR a memorandum to this effect on January 12, 1935. Robert H. Jackson, *That Man: An Insider's Portrait of Franklin D. Roosevelt* 65–66 (New York: Oxford University Press, 2003).

times in the past to reverse Supreme Court decisions.* Roosevelt believed the amendment process too cumbersome. Even if he could get the necessary two-thirds majorities in each House, it would still require ratification by three quarters of the states. Thirteen could block adoption. "Give me ten million dollars and I can prevent any amendment to the Constitution from being ratified by the necessary number of states," said FDR.[82]

Roosevelt also rejected the straight-on approach of increasing the Court's membership. The size of the Supreme Court is not constitutionally ordained but is set by Congress, and there was abundant precedent to support changing the number of justices. In addition to the "Legal Tender" appointments under Grant, Congress had altered the size of the Court six times, often for blatantly political purposes.† Roosevelt also dismissed Senator Henry Ashurst's suggestion that he wait the Court out.[83] "Justice [James C.] McReynolds will still be on the bench when he is a hundred and five years old," said FDR.[84] A fourth approach would have been to restrict the appellate jurisdiction of the Court, as a radical Republican Congress had done after the Civil War, when it feared the Reconstruction Acts might be overturned.[85] That too had been ruled out, primarily because of objections raised by lawyers on Cummings's staff.[86]

The convoluted scheme Cummings and Reed came up with purported to improve judicial efficiency and was, on its face, nonpartisan. It was also sufficiently oblique to kindle FDR's enthusiasm—"The answer to a maiden's

---

* The Eleventh Amendment, adopted in 1795, reversed the decision of the Supreme Court in *Chisholm v. Georgia*, 2 Dallas (2 U.S.) 419 (1793), and redefined the jurisdiction of the federal judiciary to exclude suits brought against a state by citizens of another state. The Fourteenth Amendment (1868), by granting citizenship to "all persons born or naturalized in the United States," overruled the Court's definition of citizenship in the Dred Scott case (*Scott v. Sandford*, 19 Howard (60 U.S.) 393 (1857)). Similarly, the Sixteenth Amendment, ratified in 1913, made the income tax constitutional, nullifying the Court's decision in *Pollock v. Farmers' Loan and Trust*, 158 U.S. 601 (1895).

† In 1801 the outgoing Federalist Congress reduced the size of the Supreme Court from six justices to five, hoping to deprive Jefferson of an appointment. The new Democratic Congress promptly restored the number to six and increased it to seven in 1807, giving Jefferson an additional appointment. Jacksonian Democrats added two more justices in 1837, bringing the number to nine. In the Civil War, confronted with a potential proslavery majority, Congress increased the Court to ten. When Democrat Andrew Johnson succeeded Lincoln, a Republican Congress reduced the number of justices to seven to deprive Johnson of any appointments. That reduction was achieved by attrition. The Court was restored to nine in 1870 under Grant.

prayer," he told Cummings.[87] Deep in the files of the Department of Justice, Cummings and Reed discovered a proposal made by the Wilson administration in 1913 that would allow the president, with the advice and consent of the Senate, to appoint a new judge for every one with ten years of service who reached the age of seventy and failed to retire. "This will insure at all times the presence of a judge sufficiently active to discharge promptly and adequately the duties of the court."[88] The fact that the proposal had been made by none other than James C. McReynolds, then Wilson's attorney general and now, at seventy-five, the president's most intransigent judicial opponent, gave Roosevelt particular delight.[89]

With FDR's blessing, Cummings and Reed put the proposal into legislative language. In its final form the Bill to Reorganize the Judicial Branch of Government provided for a maximum of fifty additional federal judges, one for each sitting jurist above the age of seventy. The Supreme Court was included. Since six of the Court's justices were over seventy, that would give FDR six additional appointments. Sam Rosenman and Donald Richberg were called in to draft a statement for the president, and at the last minute Tom Corcoran was added to the team. But the secret was held tightly.

On February 2 FDR hosted the annual dinner for the Supreme Court at the White House. The guest list of eighty included all of the justices except Brandeis, who did not attend evening functions, and Stone, who was ill. Roosevelt was at his convivial best. After the meal, when the ladies retired, Hughes and Van Devanter moved their chairs next to the president. For the next hour or so they joked and reminisced over brandy and cigars.[90] The chief justice and the president always addressed each other as "Governor" and despite their differences enjoyed cordial personal relations. Both hailed from upstate New York (Hughes was born in Glens Falls), both had begun their careers as law clerks for Wall Street firms, and both had survived the rigors of winter in Albany.[91] Van Devanter, the most genial of the justices, was always good company. FDR said nothing of what he planned for the Court or the imminence of his attack. Washington journalists likened the dinner to the ball given by the duchess of Richmond on the eve of the Battle of Waterloo.[92]

Three days later, Roosevelt struck. At 10 A.M. on February 5 he convened an emergency meeting of the cabinet at which he divulged his proposal. At eleven he met the press. At noon the president's message was read on Capitol Hill. Rarely has a political attack of such magnitude been more tightly timed. And rarely has the nation been more surprised. The Court was in session when news of the bill was announced. Hughes ordered copies distributed to the justices on the bench, who read the president's proposal in stoic silence: the quiet vortex of a gathering storm.

Roosevelt was confident he would prevail. "The people are with me," he told Jim Farley.[93] Initially that was true. But as the debate dragged on, and as it became apparent that FDR sought a fundamental change in the constitutional order, that support eroded.

The president's strategy was too clever by half. Rather than address the issue directly, Roosevelt maintained that the elderly justices were no longer up to the job and needed new blood to assist them. The irony was that Louis Brandeis, the only octogenarian on the Court, was the most consistent supporter of the New Deal. FDR asserted that the Court was behind in its workload.[94] Of 803 cases submitted for review, the justices had agreed to hear only 108. "Can it be said that full justice is achieved when a court is forced by the sheer necessity of keeping up with its business to decline, without an explanation, to hear 87 percent of the cases presented to it?"[95]

The claim was absurd, and Roosevelt should have known better. And if he did not, his attorney general should have. In 1937, just as now, there was no automatic right of appeal to the Supreme Court,* The justices heard only those cases they deemed important. And 108 out of 803 was a remarkable percentage. In 2000–1, the Rehnquist Court, with nine thousand requests for review, heard only 87 cases. In the 2003–4 term, it heard only 73 (of 8,883 requests). Rather than being behind in its workload, the Hughes Court was dealing with more cases than any Supreme Court in the previous decade.

On Capitol Hill members listened in stunned silence as reading clerks intoned the president's message. In the House, Speaker Bankhead resented the fact that he had not been consulted beforehand.[96] Majority Leader Sam Ray-

---

* The Judges Bill of 1925, enacted on the recommendation of Chief Justice Taft, gave the Supreme Court almost complete control of its docket. A litigant who wished to appeal to the Court filed a request for a writ of certiorari—a discretionary writ—to allow the case to come forward. Rule 10 of the Rules of the Supreme Court states, "A review on a writ of certiorari is not a matter of right, but of judicial discretion, and will be granted only when there are special and important reasons therefor." It requires the agreement of four justices for the writ to be issued. When the Court denies the writ, as it did in 87 percent of the cases in 1936–37, it customarily does not state the reason why.

burn said nothing, leaving it to Judiciary Chairman Hatton Sumners to fire the first shot. "Boys, here's where I cash in my chips," he told the leadership. Sumners refused to bring the legislation before his committee. That meant the Senate would have to consider the bill first.

In the upper chamber the reaction was mixed. Vice President Garner, whose support FDR needed, held his nose and turned his thumb down as the message was read.[97] Majority Leader Joe Robinson had no enthusiasm for the plan but believed it his duty to support the president. The same was true of Judiciary Committee chairman Henry Ashurst, who just weeks before had denounced any attempt to enlarge the Court as a "prelude to tyranny."[98]

On the other hand, Roosevelt stalwarts such as Joseph Guffey of Pennsylvania, Alabama's Hugo Black, James Byrnes of South Carolina, and Key Pittman of Nevada rallied round the bill. As usual, the center of gravity lay with Senate veterans, who were torn between their respect for constitutional tradition and their loyalty to FDR. What was most surprising was the defection of the Senate's progressives from the president's cause. "I am not in favor of any plan to enlarge the Supreme Court," declared George Norris hours after the bill was introduced.[99] "The issue seems to be plain," said California's Hiram Johnson. "Shall the Congress make the Supreme Court subservient to the Presidency?"[100] Burton K. Wheeler of Montana, the first member of the Senate to endorse FDR in 1932, was scathing. "The court plan is not liberal," said Wheeler. "A liberal cause was never won by stacking a deck of cards, by stuffing a ballot box, or by packing a court."[101]

Wheeler emerged as the consensus choice to lead the opposition. William E. Borah of Idaho, the ranking member on the Judiciary Committee, called the shots for the Republicans. Keep your heads down, he advised his colleagues. Don't make this a partisan issue. Let Wheeler take charge. That suited conservative Democrats as well—men like Millard Tydings of Maryland, Guy Gillette from Iowa, South Carolina's "Cotton Ed" Smith, and Walter George of Georgia. Far better to have a certified liberal like Wheeler take on the White House than someone whose New Deal credentials might be suspect.

The Senate leadership afforded Wheeler plenty of leeway. Ashurst delayed hearings until March, and by then the nation's bar associations had weighed in against the plan. Senators were deluged with mail from their constituents, which ran 9 to 1 against, while the press, almost without exception, condemned the president. "Cleverness and adroitness in dealing with the

Supreme Court are not qualities which sober-minded citizens will approve," said *The New York Times*. "Surely Mr. Roosevelt's mandate was to function as the President, not as *Der Fuehrer*," wrote the gentle William Allen White of *The Emporia Gazette*. Walter Lippmann was "sick at heart"; Mark Sullivan said, "We are going down the road to fascism"; David Lawrence asserted that if the Supreme Court went, "all other institutions will begin to crumble one by one."[102]

Roosevelt went all out. Senators were invited to the White House singly and in groups for the full presidential treatment. FDR held three news conferences on the Court, delivered two major speeches, and spoke to the nation in a fireside chat.[103] "Hold up judicial appointments in states where the delegation is not going along," he told Farley. "And all other appointments as well. I'll keep in close contact with the leaders."[104]

Hearings commenced March 10, and the administration held forth for ten days. Few minds were changed, and if anything the critics on the committee had the better of it. Wheeler was slated to lead off for the opposition on Monday, March 21. On Saturday afternoon Justice Brandeis asked Wheeler to stop by his apartment. The Brandeises and Wheelers were old friends, and Mrs. Brandeis and Mrs. Wheeler were especially close.

"The chief justice would like to see you," said Brandeis. "He will give you a letter. Call him up."

"I can't call him," said Wheeler, who had vigorously opposed Hughes's appointment as chief justice in 1930. "I don't know him."

"But he knows you," Brandeis replied.

The elderly justice took Wheeler by the hand, led him to the telephone, and made the call himself. Hughes, he said, would like to see him immediately.

It was 5:30 when Wheeler called on Hughes at his home at 2223 R Street. "The imposing Chief Justice greeted me warmly," Wheeler recalled. "I told him Brandeis said he would give me a letter."

"Did Brandeis tell you that?"

"Yes."

"When do you want it?"

"Monday morning," said Wheeler. He wanted it when he testified.

Hughes had already marshaled his arguments and had his facts at hand. Sunday afternoon, the chief justice called Wheeler and invited him to return. Hughes had written a seven-page letter, shown it to Brandeis and Van Devanter, and obtained their approval. He handed it to Wheeler. "The baby is born," said the chief justice.

Wheeler read the letter in awe.

"Does that answer your question?" asked Hughes.

"It certainly does," Wheeler replied.

As the Montana senator started to leave, Hughes asked him to sit down. "I am not interested in who are to be the members of the Court," said the chief justice.

I am interested in the Court as an institution. And this proposed bill would destroy the Court as an institution.

If we had an Attorney General in whom the President had confidence, and in whom the Court had confidence, and in whom the people had confidence, the story might have been different. But the laws have been poorly drafted, the briefs have been badly drawn and the arguments have been poorly presented. We've had to be not only the Court but we've had to do the work that should have been done by the Attorney General.[105]

At ten Monday morning Wheeler appeared before a capacity audience in the ornate Senate Caucus Room. He began by matter-of-factly acknowledging his reluctance to oppose the president, turned gradually to the administration's charge of judicial delay, and withdrew from his inside coat pocket a sheaf of papers. "I have here a letter from the Chief Justice of the United States, Mr. Charles Evans Hughes, dated March 21, 1937, written by him and approved by Mr. Justice Brandeis and Mr. Justice Van Devanter."[106]

Consternation gripped the Caucus Room. History was being made. Not since John Marshall had taken up his pen to defend the Court's decision in *McCulloch v. Maryland* in 1819 had a chief justice taken an active role in a public controversy.[107] Stunned senators listened intently as Wheeler began to read. Factually and unemotionally Hughes struck down one by one each of the arguments advanced by FDR and Cummings that the Court was unable to keep up with its workload. "There is no congestion of cases upon our calendar. When we rose on March 15 (for the current recess) we had heard argument in cases in which certiorari had been granted only four weeks before." Hughes presented a detailed statistical analysis of the last six terms, demolishing any allegation that the Court had failed to keep abreast. The addition of more judges would simply mean "more judges to hear, more judges to confer, more judges to discuss, more judges to be convinced and to decide."[108]

Despite its dispassionate tone, the letter hit like a bombshell. The following week, Hughes struck again. On March 29, in a tense, packed courtroom, the chief justice read the Supreme Court's decision upholding the State of Washington's minimum wage law, which was almost identical to the New York law it had overturned six months earlier.[109] Again the vote was 5–4, Justice Roberts providing the margin of victory. Roberts's switch was immediately dubbed "the switch in time that saves nine," but the fact is that the Court had voted 4–4 in December to uphold the Washington statute with Roberts in the affirmative.[110] Justice Stone, who was ill, had missed the vote, and Hughes had waited for his return to announce the decision. Speaking for the Court, Hughes not only sustained the Washington law but explicitly overruled the line of precedent known as substantive due process that for the last thirty years had prevented government from regulating wages and hours.[111] When Hughes finished reading his opinion, the Court went on to uphold three recent pieces of New Deal legislation, all by unanimous vote.*

Two weeks later, in the most eagerly anticipated ruling of the term, the Court, speaking again through Hughes, upheld the Wagner Labor Relations Act—the most ambitious undertaking of the New Deal since the NRA, and the most controversial.[112] Hughes rejected the distinction between direct and indirect effects on commerce that had governed the Court's approach since 1895, restored the commerce clause to the full sweep of John Marshall's expansive definition in *Gibbons v. Ogden*,[113] and dismissed the recent holdings *Schechter Poultry Corp. v. United States* and *Carter v. Carter Coal Co.* "These cases are not controlling here," said Hughes majestically.[114]

When the Court subsequently sustained the Social Security Act (7–2), even the most rabid New Dealer recognized that whatever rationale there was behind FDR's Court-packing scheme had evaporated.[115] On May 18 the Senate

---

* *Sonzinsky v. United States,* 300 U.S. 506 (Stone for the Court), upholding the National Firearms Act; *Wright v. Vinton,* 300 U.S. 440 (Brandeis), sustaining a revised version of the Frazier-Lemke Farm Mortgage Act; and *Virginia Railway Co. v. Federation,* 300 U.S. 515 (Stone), upholding the collective bargaining provisions of the Railway Labor Act.

Judiciary Committee voted 10–8 to report the Judicial Reform Bill unfavorably: "It is a measure which should be so emphatically rejected that its parallel will never again be presented to the free representatives of the free people of America."[116] That same day Justice Van Devanter submitted his resignation to the president. With Van Devanter's retirement and the Court following Hughes's lead, FDR might have declared victory and called off the fight. That was Garner's advice. When Roosevelt refused, the vice president gave up and returned to his ranch in Texas. He would be AWOL during the crucial Senate debate.

FDR refused to compromise. Despite the oppressive heat of an un-air-conditioned Washington summer, he insisted that Congress remain in session. To regain the initiative, he invited Speaker Bankhead and Sam Rayburn to the White House. Would they organize a discharge petition (which required the signatures of 218 members) to pry the bill out of Sumners's committee and bring it to the House floor? Both refused.[117] Back in the Senate, defections continued daily. Majority Leader Joe Robinson battled to stem the tide, but it was a hopeless struggle. FDR could have gotten half a loaf earlier, but it was now too late. His opponents smelled victory. Wilting under the pressure, Robinson collapsed. On the morning of July 14 he was found dead in his apartment in the Methodist Building, across the street from the Capitol, the victim of a heart attack.

Roosevelt declined to attend Robinson's Arkansas funeral—a final, tragic error. As one historian suggests, FDR reacted to the news of Robinson's death with bitterness, identifying the majority leader with the loss of his Court plan.[118] Robinson was beloved by his Senate colleagues and died in harness fighting for a proposal in which he did not fully believe. The president's failure to go to Little Rock was a slap in the face few senators could forgive. Roosevelt's popularity plummeted. Vice President Garner—who attended the funeral—brought the bad news: "You are beat, Cap'n. You haven't got the votes."[119] On July 22 the Senate rejected the bill, 20 in favor, 70 against.[120]

Historians are fond of saying Roosevelt lost the battle and won the war. But the war was won when Roberts joined Hughes, Brandeis, Cardozo, and Stone in December 1936. In the year after the bill's defeat, Roosevelt would appoint three justices to the Court. Ultimately he would appoint eight.[121] But more important than the justices was the law. In sustaining the Washington minimum-wage statute, Hughes overruled the line of precedent that had hamstrung attempts to regulate working conditions since 1905. Those discarded precedents would not reappear. In upholding the Wagner Act, he nullified the exceptions that had shackled the commerce clause since 1895. Mining, manufacturing, and agriculture were no longer out of bounds. The victory in the Court fight of 1937 belonged not to Roosevelt but to Hughes, to the constitutional separation of powers, an independent judiciary, and the law.

EIGHTEEN

LOW TIDE

_Nothing is ever gained by trying
to seek revenge in politics._

—JAMES A. FARLEY

FDR OVERPLAYED HIS HAND. To attack the Court was wrongheaded. To persist after the cause was won was petulant. Roosevelt paid dearly. Not only did he squander public support, but the Court fracas ruptured the Democratic party. Conservative Democrats and Republicans who made common cause to thwart FDR's Court-packing plan found it easy to work together against other White House initiatives. The New Deal ceased to be a synonym for the Democratic party. From 1937 on, it was merely a movement within the party. Not all southerners were conservative, and not all conservative Democrats were from the South. But there were enough to give the anti–New Deal coalition a Dixie twang.

FDR's legislative program was the first casualty. "Must" bills considered certain of passage at inauguration encountered heavy opposition. When the Court plan was defeated in July, five administration measures awaited action: wages and hours legislation, low-cost housing, reorganization of the executive branch, a revised farm program, and the creation of seven additional TVA-type regional authorities. When Congress adjourned at the end of August, only the Wagner Housing Bill had been enacted—a tribute more to Senator Wagner's legislative skill than to White House support. Roosevelt recalled Congress into special session in November with a demand that action be taken, but the session proved a disaster. Despite unprecedented Democratic majorities in both Houses, not one additional piece of legislation was enacted. Only a year after his overwhelming election victory, FDR had lost control of the party.*

Roosevelt stubbed his toe when Senate Democrats chose a leader to replace the revered Joe Robinson. The candidates were Mississippi's Pat Harrison, chairman of the Finance Committee, and Alben Barkley of Kentucky, the assistant leader. Harrison was a fixture in Mississippi's Democratic establishment, Barkley in the populist ranks of Kentucky. On policy issues there was little daylight separating the two. Both backed the New Deal, and both had supported FDR in the Court fight. Both had been for Roosevelt before Chicago. Barkley had given the keynote addresses at the 1932 and 1936 conventions; Harrison had given the keynote in 1924 and played a vital role keeping Mississippi in Roosevelt's column on the crucial third ballot at Chicago in 1932. Harrison, one of the Senate's Big Four, was considered a shoo-in.[1][†] Roosevelt promised not to intervene, as did party chairman Farley and Vice President Garner.[2]

As the senators prepared to vote, Roosevelt changed his mind. He liked Barkley more than Harrison and believed he would be easier to work with. "My dear Alben," the president wrote in a lengthy letter the White House released, making clear where his sympathies lay.[3] FDR used all the power at his disposal to influence the outcome. He placed a late-night call to Farley telling him to telephone Mayor Edward J. Kelly of Chicago to instruct Illinois senator William Dieterich to vote for Barkley. When Farley refused, Roosevelt got Hopkins to make the call, and Dieterich, who was pledged to Harrison, switched sides. The White House also asked Kansas City's Tom Pendergast to pressure freshman senator Harry Truman, and Pendergast dutifully made the

---

* Led by Senator Josiah Bailey of North Carolina—an early Roosevelt supporter—conservative Democrats used the special session to reach out to the GOP and draft a bipartisan ten-point "Conservative Manifesto" that denounced sit-down strikes, demanded lower taxes and a balanced federal budget, championed states' rights, and defended private enterprise against government encroachment. As one historian has written, "The manifesto constituted a kind of founding charter for modern American conservatism." David M. Kennedy, *Freedom from Fear: The American People in Depression and War, 1929–1945* 340 (New York: Oxford University Press, 1999).

† The other three were Vice President Garner, Joseph Robinson, and James Byrnes of South Carolina. See Kevin J. McMahon, *Reconsidering Roosevelt on Race* 79 ff. (Chicago: University of Chicago Press, 2004).

call: "No, Tom," said Truman, "I can't. . . . I've made up my mind to vote for Pat Harrison and I'm going to do it."[4] A third waverer was Harrison's fellow Mississippian, Theodore G. Bilbo. The Mississippi Democratic party was really two parties, one patrician, the other redneck, and Harrison and Bilbo represented opposing factions. The common denominator was white supremacy: both hated the party of Lincoln more than each other. Bilbo said he would vote for Harrison if Harrison would ask him. "Tell the son of a bitch I wouldn't speak to him if it meant the Presidency of the United States," said Harrison.[5] Bilbo voted for Barkley. When the ballots were counted, Barkley beat Harrison by one vote, 38–37.

White House pressure had prevailed. But it was an empty victory. Roosevelt's intervention reinforced the image of the president as deceitful and untrustworthy. Many on Capitol Hill resented FDR's meddling in what was seen as a purely congressional matter—another example of executive overreach. "It is an encroachment on the prerogatives of the members of the legislative branch no President ought to engage in," said Garner.[6] Tactically, the move hurt Roosevelt. If he had remained neutral, most senators believed, Harrison would have won easily and FDR could have persuaded him, as he had Joe Robinson, to support most New Deal measures out of party loyalty.[7] With Harrison now estranged from the administration, his position as chairman of the Finance Committee provided a powerful vantage point from which to derail or delay White House legislation. Barkley, for his part, would henceforth be known to Washington as "Dear Alben," a creature of the president.

In the House, the situation was little better. Members, some of whom had come to Washington when the city's streetcars were pulled by horses, resented the high-handedness of New Deal appointees as well as their intellectual arrogance. "Unless one can murder the broad 'a' and present a Harvard sheepskin he is definitely out," grumbled Michigan congressman John Dingell.[8] When Hatton Sumners, speaking to a crowded chamber, called on House Democrats to establish a new party leadership—implicitly reading Roosevelt out of the party—no one rose in the president's defense. Not Sam Rayburn, who listened mutely to his fellow Texan's rant; not Speaker Bankhead, who sat sphinxlike on the dais; not even Maury Maverick, the unofficial cheerleader for New Dealers in the House. "Nothing quite like it had occurred in that body for a long time," observed The New Republic.[9]

Roosevelt was equally unforgiving. "The Supreme Court fight lived on in the President's memory," said Farley. "His attitude was that he had been double-crossed and let down by men who should have rallied loyally to his support. For weeks and months afterward I found him fuming against the members of his own party. Outwardly he was as gay and debonair as ever; inwardly he was seething."[10]*

FDR twitted Congress. He relished inviting members to the White House, cryptically suggesting that those who crossed him should be on guard. "I've got them on the run," he told Farley. "They have no idea what's going to happen and are beginning to worry. They'll be sorry yet."[11]

Amid mutual recriminations between the White House and Capitol Hill, the country, as John Garner would have said, was going to hell in a handbasket. A rash of sit-down strikes in the spring and summer of 1937 polarized the political scene further. To some extent the strikes were the natural outgrowth of the Wagner Labor Relations Act, which afforded workers the right to join a union. Labor zeroed in on steel and auto production—the "Hindenburg Line" of American industry, in the words of CIO founder John L. Lewis—and the sit-down strike proved an effective organizing weapon. By seizing control of one plant that made a crucial part, striking workers could paralyze an entire company. In the case of General Motors, that plant was at Flint, Michigan. In 1937, General Motors was the world's largest manufacturing corporation. With more than a quarter of a million employees, it produced half of all cars made in America. Yet the only set of dies for every GM model was on the floor at Flint. When workers there laid down their tools and refused to leave the plant, General Motors production slowed to a trickle. A company that built 50,000 cars in December 1936 produced only 125 during the first week of February 1937.[12]

Roosevelt was as surprised as anyone but refused to use force against the strikers. As he told Frances Perkins, "Well, it is illegal, but what law are they breaking? The law of trespass, and that is about the only law that could be invoked. And what do you do when a man trespasses on your property? You can

---

* FDR's bitterness was directed at Congress, not the Court. "Hughes is the best politician in the country," he told SEC head William O. Douglas with undisguised admiration. By 1938 whatever animosity there may have been between the president and the chief justice had been dissipated, and they continued to enjoy cordial personal relations. William O. Douglas, *Go East, Young Man* 327 (New York: Random House, 1974).

order him off. You can get the sheriff to order him off. . . . But shooting it out and killing a lot of people because they have violated the law of trespass somehow offends me. I just don't see that as the answer. The punishment doesn't fit the crime. Why can't these fellows in General Motors meet with the committee of workers? Talk it out. It wouldn't be so terrible."[13]

Michigan governor Frank Murphy saw it the same way. "I'm not going down in history as Bloody Murphy," he told a friend. "If I send soldiers in on the [strikers] there'd be no telling how many would be killed."[14] Murphy also authorized state relief payments for the families of the strikers. When Garner pressed FDR about Murphy's refusal to take action, Roosevelt held his ground. "It was the hottest argument we ever had," said Garner.[15]

With the strike in its seventh week and with both federal and state authorities unwilling to use force, General Motors looked for a way out. Chrysler and Ford had boosted production to take advantage of GM's shutdown, and Walter Chrysler had stolen the march by recognizing the United Auto Workers. "Leave General Motors guessing again," he told Labor secretary Perkins.[16]

At Frances Perkins's suggestion, FDR picked up the phone and called William Knudsen, the president of General Motors. A call from the White House, she said, would give Knudsen an excuse if he wanted to settle. Roosevelt had never met Knudsen but agreed to the gambit and laid on the charm: "Is that you, Bill?" he asked.

"I know you've been through a lot, Bill, and I want to tell you that I feel sorry for you, but Miss Perkins has told me about the situation you are discussing and I have just called up to say I hope very much that you will go through with this and that your people will meet with the [workers'] committee."[17]

With FDR's encouragement General Motors recognized the United Auto Workers as labor's bargaining agent at its sixty factories in fourteen states. Other issues remained unresolved, but the central point had been won: General Motors recognized the union.

Big Steel followed close behind. The United States Steel Corporation ("Big Steel"), with 220,000 employees, produced more steel annually than Germany, the world's second largest steel-producing country.[18] For fifty years U.S. Steel and its predecessors had militantly resisted unionization. The Homestead massacre of 1892, in which ten Pennsylvania steelworkers were killed, was emblematic of the violence that beset the industry. The lesson of the General Motors strike at Flint was not lost on Big Steel. Anxious to avoid a repeat, Myron C. Taylor, the firm's chairman, and John L. Lewis quickly came to an agreement that not only recognized the steelworkers' union but granted a pay hike, a forty-hour workweek, and time and a half for overtime.

Lewis and the leaders of organized labor assumed "Little Steel" (Bethlehem, Republic, Youngstown, and the small firms throughout the country) would fall into line. But Tom Girdler, the gruff, union-busting head of Republic Steel, decided otherwise. Led by Girdler, Little Steel fought a determined rearguard action against unionization. The worst violence in modern labor history erupted on Memorial Day 1937, when South Chicago police opened fire on marchers at the Republic steel works, killing ten and wounding thirty others, including a woman and three children. Violence spread quickly. Two steelworkers were shot and killed in Youngstown, Ohio, on June 19, three in Massillon, eighteen in all during the summer of 1937, and Little Steel refused to budge. Emboldened by Girdler's example, International Harvester, Westinghouse, Maytag, Allis-Chalmers, and the Big Four meatpackers refused to bargain with labor. Ford held out until 1941.

Much of public opinion soured on union tactics. When the organizational drive began, the majority of Americans were sympathetic. But the wave of violence that accompanied labor's rising militancy caused many to draw back. Middle-class businessmen and professionals in particular were terrified by the sit-ins and demanded that government take action. A nonbinding Congressional resolution that declared the sit-down strike illegal cleared the Senate 75–3.[19] Roosevelt was caught in the middle. Asked at his press conference on June 29 to comment on the fight between Little Steel and the CIO, the president repeated Mercutio's line in *Romeo and Juliet:* "A plague on both your houses."[20] FDR's refusal to provide support drove John L. Lewis off the New Deal reservation: "It ill behooves one who has supped at labor's table . . . to curse with equal fervor . . . both labor and its adversaries when they become locked in deadly embrace."[21] At the same time Lewis was castigating the administration, Roosevelt's refusal to take sides alienated those who believed the president was implicitly condoning sit-down strikes and the accompanying assaults on private property. FDR could not win. He was damned if he did and damned if he didn't.

Labor unrest contributed to the economy's sudden collapse in 1937. But it was FDR's misplaced decision to reduce federal spending that triggered the crisis. In the spring of 1937 American production pulled above pre-Depression levels for the first time. The *New York Times*' Weekly Business Index reported output at 110—10 percent higher than in the corresponding week in 1929. Payrolls showed solid gains, and the steel industry was working at 80 percent of capacity. The Dow Jones Industrial Average, which had stood at 34 in 1933, had risen almost sixfold, to 190. Unemployment shrank to 12 percent, barely a third of the March 1933 percentage. Subtract the young men in the Civilian Conservation Corps together with those at work in the job creation programs of the PWA and WPA, and the unemployment figure stood at 4 percent.[22]*

In June 1937 Roosevelt assumed that the economic battle had been won and slashed spending drastically. WPA activities were sharply reduced, farm subsidies curtailed, and public works pump priming eliminated. At the same time, Washington siphoned off some $2 billion in purchasing power in new Social Security taxes, and the Federal Reserve Board raised its reserve requirements for member banks by 50 percent, further reducing liquidity. FDR, a thrifty Dutchman at heart, believed it was time to balance the budget. The federal deficit for 1936 had been $4.3 billion. Roosevelt's 1937 budget reduced that figure to $2.7 billion. Spending projections for 1938 showed the deficit at a mere $740 million, and by fiscal 1939 the budget would be balanced.[23]

Such massive contraction was more than the recovering economy could sustain. On October 19 the New York Stock Exchange suffered its worst day since 1929. Waves of selling hit the market, pushing stocks to new lows. By the end of October the Dow Jones stood at 115, down 40 percent from its August high. Industrial activity declined more abruptly than at any other time in the nation's history. By the end of 1937 steel production was down to 19 percent

---

* In his 2003 biography of FDR, Conrad Black took issue with the school of historiography that asserts that recovery in the United States lagged behind that of other industrial countries. As Lord Black points out, American unemployment figures did not distinguish between those who had no job whatever and those working for the WPA, in the public works program, or enrolled in the CCC. All were lumped together as "unemployed." When the relief workers are factored in, American unemployment totals drop by almost 60 percent. "None of the other Western democracies," writes Black, "provided so much or such original emergency relief employment as the United States did." Conrad Black, *Franklin Delano Roosevelt: Champion of Freedom* 430 (New York: PublicAffairs, 2003). Also see Black's review article "No Bleeding Heart," 5 *Claremont Review of Books* 27–29 (Spring 2005).

of capacity. The *New York Times'* Business Index plunged to 85, wiping out all of the gains since 1935. Nightclubs and restaurants in New York failed; new autos clogged showrooms; gold fled the country.[24] Between Labor Day and Christmas, more than 2 million people lost their jobs, and another 2 million in the first three months of 1938. If the rate of decline continued through the year, the United States would lose almost two thirds of the gains since 1933.[25]

The "depression within a depression" precipitated a sharp split within the administration. Morgenthau, Farley, and Commerce secretary Dan Roper urged FDR to stay the course, balance the budget, and adopt a more conciliatory stance toward business. As Morgenthau put it, the time had come "to strip off the bandages, throw away the crutches" and let the economy see if "it could stand on its own feet."[26] Opposed were Hopkins, Ickes, Perkins, and Wallace, aided by Marriner Eccles of the Federal Reserve, who urged vigorous resumption of government spending. The downturn had occurred when federal expenditures had been reduced; it figured that a sharp increase in spending would reverse the momentum.

Just as in the struggle between the CIO and Little Steel, Roosevelt was caught in the middle. "It is clear that he is greatly disturbed . . . and doesn't know which way to turn," wrote Ickes after a cabinet meeting on November 6, 1937. "He is plainly worried."[27]

Like Hoover in 1930, Roosevelt temporized. "Everything will work out all right if we just sit tight and keep quiet."[28] When Congress reconvened in January 1938, FDR did not mention the economic downturn. "As I see it," said Morgenthau, "you are just treading water."[29]

"Absolutely," said Roosevelt, who was always flippant when confronted with economic issues he did not fully comprehend. As James MacGregor Burns expressed it, "Roosevelt's deficiencies as an economist were as striking as his triumphs as a politician."[30]

"The old Roosevelt magic has lost its kick," chortled Hugh Johnson to the National Press Club. "The diverse elements in his Falstaffian army can no longer be kept together and led by a melodious whinny and a winning smile."[31]

Meanwhile, the economy continued to deteriorate. On March 25, 1938, the stock market broke again, and virtually every economic index continued south. The price of farm products, which had held up well through 1937, joined the rout. Roosevelt was bailed out of his indecision by Harry Hopkins, who descended on the vacationing president at Warm Springs on April 2, armed with specific proposals for a massive spending program. Stung by continued press reference to the "Roosevelt recession," FDR reluctantly jettisoned the balanced budget approach. "They have stampeded him," Morgenthau lamented to aides at Treasury. "They have stampeded him just like cattle."[32]

On April 14 Roosevelt asked Congress for a special appropriation of $3.4 billion to revive the flagging economy. Hopkins would receive a $1.4 billion infusion for the WPA; Ickes, whose PWA had been liquidated some months before, would receive $1 billion for public works; and additional sums were allocated for slum clearance and low-cost housing, farm subsidies, and a small naval construction program. By the end of 1938 the United States had regained half the lost ground. Employment rose by 2 million, factory payrolls by 26 percent, and steel production by 127 percent. The downturn had been induced by the cutback in government spending FDR had ordered, and the recovery was delayed by his procrastination. When Roosevelt sought to pack the Supreme Court, he shot himself in the foot. When he prematurely curtailed federal spending in 1937, he shot the country in the foot.

Into FDR's sea of troubles Senator Robert Wagner introduced antilynching legislation that was certain to create havoc in what remained of the New Deal coalition in Congress. James Byrnes called it "a bill to destroy the Democratic party."[33] Richard Russell of Georgia said it was a piece of legislation designed "to lynch the last remaining evidence of States' rights and sovereignty."[34] As southern senators rose in opposition, Roosevelt ran for cover.

The lynching of African Americans by white southerners, if not a way of life, occurred with such disturbing frequency as to stain the fabric of the nation. Since 1933, eighty-three blacks—roughly seventeen a year—had been viciously put to death in the South. Lynchings were not merely public hangings but community ceremonies where frenzied men, women, and children inflicted unspeakable cruelty on their helpless victims—a shocking reversion to primitive brutality.[35]

To satisfy states' rights concerns, the Wagner bill did not make lynching a federal crime but would hold local law enforcement officials accountable. If a lynching went unprosecuted for thirty days, federal authorities could intervene and bring charges against the local officials responsible for the delay. Fines ranged up to $5,000 with possible imprisonment for five years.[36] Except for racist peckerwoods like Mississippi's Theodore G. Bilbo, most southerners on Capitol Hill shared the nation's shame and deplored the depravity lynchings entailed. For them the issue turned on states' rights and the intrusion, even if one step removed, of federal law enforcement in what was seen as a purely local matter. Shades of Reconstruction colored that view—a festering memory kept alive by a steady stream of popular and scholarly writing, abetted by films such as D. W. Griffith's *Birth of a Nation*.* White supremacy went to the core of the issue, and no Washington incumbent from below the Mason-Dixon Line wanted to be "outniggered" in a Democratic primary.

Wagner had initially introduced his bill in January 1934, but the rush of New Deal legislation prevented it from being considered. In 1935 the threat of a southern filibuster kept it off the floor. Nineteen thirty-six was an election year, and the last thing Democrats wanted was a split in party ranks before November. When the Seventy-fifth Congress convened in January 1937, the bill seemed to have a fighting chance. Aside from unprecedented Democratic majorities in both houses (including many new members from outside the South), recent Gallup polls suggested that more than 70 percent of the public favored an antilynching law. Southerners were 65 to 35 percent in favor.[37] A ghastly double lynching in Duck Hill, Mississippi, in April in which two hand-cuffed black prisoners were chained to a tree, mutilated with blowtorches, doused with gasoline, and set afire underscored the urgency of the legislation. In the House, the southern leadership kept the bill buried in committee but a discharge petition (signed by 218 members) brought it to the floor, and on April 15 the bill passed 277–120, Speaker Bankhead and Majority Leader Rayburn voting against. In the Senate, the Judiciary Committee reported the bill favorably in June, too late for consideration at that session but at the top of the agenda come January.

Roosevelt stayed on the sidelines. "I did not choose the tools with which I must work," he told Walter White, the secretary of the National Association for Advancement of Colored People. "Had I been permitted to choose them I would have selected quite different ones. But I've got to get legislation passed to save America. The Southerners by reason of the seniority rule in Congress

---

* The history of Reconstruction became the life work of the historian William A. Dunning and the graduate students who studied with him at Columbia University. Their factually dubious but influential writing championing white supremacy determined the way many Americans see Reconstruction even today. For a critique of the "Dunning School," see Jean Edward Smith, *Grant* 699–700 (New York: Simon & Schuster, 2001).

are chairmen or occupy strategic places in most of the Senate and House committees. If I come out for the anti-lynching bill now, they will block every bill I ask Congress to pass. . . . I just can't take that risk."[38]*

At his press conference in October 1934, FDR declined to endorse Wagner's bill.[39] In 1935, when the bill faced a Senate filibuster, he refused to comment.[40] When Eleanor was invited to address an NAACP protest rally, Roosevelt counseled caution. "President says this is dynamite," wrote Missy in longhand in the margin of the invitation. Eleanor did not go.[41] In 1935 ER was invited to attend the closing session of the twenty-sixth annual convention of the NAACP in St. Louis. "FDR should I go?" she asked. Missy replied for the president that it would be best if she did not.[42] In private conversation FDR said he thought the antilynching bill was unconstitutional,† but the fact is he did not want to endanger what remained of his ties to the white South—especially to the southern oligarchs who controlled Congress.

Senator Wagner's bill came before the Senate on January 6, 1938. For the next six weeks the upper chamber was immobilized, snarled in a southern filibuster, senators spelling one another round the clock. Twice Wagner moved for cloture to end the debate, and twice he was defeated. Roosevelt kept his hands off. At his press conference on January 14 he was asked whether he favored the bill. "I have not referred to it at all," said FDR. "I should say there was enough discussion going on in the Senate."[43] If Roosevelt had intervened decisively—perhaps if he had simply offered a word of encouragement—cloture could have been obtained and the bill passed. Yet he declined. To some it looked as if the filibuster had White House sanction. Roy Wilkins of the

---

* Thomas Corcoran put it more succinctly: political calculus took precedence over moral outrage; antilynching was too hot for FDR to touch. "He does his best with it, but he ain't gonna lose his votes for it." Corcoran, interview with Nancy J. Weiss, May 23, 1977, cited in Weiss, *Farewell to the Party of Lincoln: Black Politics in the Age of FDR* 119 (Princeton, N.J.: Princeton University Press, 1983).

† Roosevelt's concern about the constitutionality of Wagner's bill was not entirely misplaced. In *United States v. Cruikshank,* 92 U.S. 542 (1876), the Reconstruction-era Supreme Court invalidated the operative sections of the Enforcement Act of 1870, which made it a federal crime to deprive any citizen of his or her constitutional rights. "The power of Congress to legislate does not extend to the passage of laws for the suppression of ordinary crimes within the States," said Chief Justice Morrison Waite. Whether the Hughes Court, which was pacesetting in matters of civil rights, would have invoked, overruled, or distinguished *Cruikshank* is a matter for speculation.

NAACP charged that there was a gentleman's agreement to let the bill be talked to death. Most senators really did not want antilynching legislation "but would have to vote for it if it came up."[44] On February 21, 1938, Senator Wagner withdrew the bill so the Senate could move on. In 1939, when the Seventy-sixth Congress convened, the bill was introduced again but failed to make it to the floor in either chamber. In 1940 it passed the House but was not taken up by the Senate. Then came the war.*

During the twelve years FDR was president not one piece of civil rights legislation became law. No federal effort was made to abolish the white primary in the South or overturn the poll tax.[45] Roosevelt's closest aides—Stephen Early, Marvin McIntyre, and Pa Watson—were southerners who shared the prejudice of the times. To the best of their ability they smothered controversial issues that might offend voters in the South. No effort was made to use the bully pulpit of the White House to advance the cause of racial justice.

That does not mean the Roosevelt administration was insensitive to the needs of African Americans. The segregation of government employees introduced by Woodrow Wilson was quietly set aside; blacks were employed in increasing numbers and at significantly higher levels of federal service—including the appointment of William H. Hastie as district judge for the Virgin Islands, the first African American to sit on the federal bench.[46]

But it was at the symbolic level where the greatest strides were taken, and they were taken by Mrs. Roosevelt, not the president. When ER rose to fetch a glass of water for Mary McLeod Bethune, history was made.† When Eleanor demonstratively placed her chair in the aisle between the white and black sections at a segregated conference in Birmingham, she rallied the spirits of African Americans throughout the country. "You would have to have lived in that era to know what kind of impact this had," recalled the civil rights activist

---

* On June 13, 2005, the Senate, by voice vote, formally apologized for its failure to enact antilynching legislation in the 1930s. "The Senate failed . . . our nation," said Senator Mary L. Landrieu of Louisiana, the chief Democratic sponsor of the resolution. *The New York Times*, June 14, 2005.

† The incident occurred when Miss Bethune's voice cracked while speaking at a benefit for Bethune-Cookman College. ER was on the platform and procured the water for Miss Bethune. "This is democracy in action," said a black policeman at the event. "The wife of the President of the United States pouring a glass of ice water for a Negro woman who's real black—she's black as a black shoe." Quoted in Weiss, *Farewell to the Party of Lincoln* 255.

Pauli Murray.[47] When ER resigned from the Daughters of the American Revolution to protest their refusal to allow world-famous contralto Marian Anderson to sing at Washington's Constitution Hall, shock waves echoed through the country.

No incident did more to advance the cause of racial tolerance than the concert Marian Anderson performed on the steps of the Lincoln Memorial on Easter Sunday, 1939. When the DAR refused to make Constitution Hall available, Sol Hurok, Miss Anderson's manager, conceived the idea of an open-air concert at the shrine of the Great Emancipator. Secretary Ickes signed on, and FDR gave his approval. "Tell Oscar [Chapman, assistant secretary of the interior] he has my permission to have Marian sing from the top of the Washington Monument if he wants it."[48] The Roosevelts were in Hyde Park that Sunday, but an integrated throng that stretched as far as the eye could see gathered to hear the great artist. Washington's *Afro-American* called it "one of those rare occasions when caste is forgotten, when dignitaries rub elbows with street urchins, and when milady and her servant meet in the same social sphere."[49] When Miss Anderson lifted her voice to sing "America," democracy was redeemed. "It was more than a concert for me," she said later. "It was a dedication. When I sang that day, I was singing to the entire nation."[50] Six weeks later, at the invitation of the president, Marian Anderson performed at the White House dinner given for King George VI and Queen Elizabeth.

FRANKLIN AND ELEANOR continued to move in separate circles.* ER was considerably ahead of the president in racial matters and equal rights for women, and was not always an asset in FDR's struggles with Congress. "She is not doing the President any good," wrote Harold Ickes, who could scarcely be described as unsympathetic to the New Deal. "She is becoming altogether too active in public affairs and I think she is harmful rather than helpful."[51]

Roosevelt was tolerant if not supportive. "I can always say, 'Well, that's my wife; I can't do anything about her.' "[52] For her part, Eleanor made the best of

---

* "I realize more and more that FDR is a great man," Eleanor wrote to her friend Lorena Hickok in October 1936. "[H]e is nice to me but as a person I'm a stranger and I don't want to be anything else." Quoted in Doris Faber, *The Life of Lorena Hickok* 221 (New York: Morrow, 1980).

it: "He might have been happier with a wife who was completely uncritical. That I was never able to be. . . . Nevertheless, I think I sometimes acted as a spur, even though the spurring was not always wanted or welcomed. I was one of those who served his purposes."[53]

FDR's relations with his children were another cause for concern. "One of the worst things in the world is being the child of a President," he once said.[54] Anna, now married to the newsman John Boettiger, lived in Seattle and rarely came to Washington. Boettiger had resigned from the stridently anti-Roosevelt *Chicago Tribune* to avoid embarrassing the president, and he and Anna had been given a sweetheart deal by the media mogul William Randolph Hearst. Hearst and FDR disliked each other personally, yet they often needed each other and Hearst relished doing favors for the First Family. Boettiger was made publisher of the *Seattle Post-Intelligencer* at a salary of $30,000 a year plus a share of the profits, and Anna became editor of the women's page at $10,000. The salaries were far in excess of prevailing pay scales but Hearst was buying White House goodwill. Various associates of FDR were disgusted at the arrangement, but neither Roosevelt nor Eleanor seemed concerned. "I shall miss them," ER wrote Franklin, "but it does seem a grand opportunity."[55]

James, the president's eldest son, and his wife, Betsey, lived in Boston, where James was in the insurance business. In 1936, evidently feeling the need for companionship, FDR summoned the couple to Washington and made James his naval aide with the rank of a lieutenant colonel in the Marine Corps. That was the rank FDR deemed appropriate, despite James's lack of military experience. Eleanor disapproved. "Is James a 2nd Lieut. or Lieut. Colonel?" she asked.[56] When Louis Howe died, James became the president's executive assistant and moved into the adjoining office. James was utterly unequipped to fill Howe's role. Roosevelt got loyalty, but his son lacked judgment and experience. He made commitments in the president's name without FDR's knowledge and brazenly used his position for personal gain. William O. Douglas, then head of the Securities and Exchange Commission, reported a visit by James on behalf of a client with business before the SEC.[57] Douglas was so shocked that he went to the White House with his resignation. According to Douglas, FDR cradled his head on his arm and cried like a child for several minutes.[58]

Public criticism of James became so shrill that he was forced to release his income tax returns. They disclosed nothing illegal, but media pressure was sufficiently intense that in mid-1938 the president's son checked into Rochester's Mayo Clinic with a perforated ulcer. A large portion of his stomach was removed, and James chose not to return to the White House. His marriage to Betsey Cushing was also on the rocks. FDR, who was very fond of his daughter-in-law (Betsey often served as White House hostess during ER's travels), sent Harry Hopkins to dissuade James from getting a divorce, but to no avail. "I was hurt that Father had sent him instead of taking it up with me himself," wrote James. "In retrospect, however, I have come to realize that Father felt he could not broach it to me—all his life, he had told us that he would advise us, if asked, but that our personal decisions were our own to make."[59]

After his recovery James married his nurse at the Mayo Clinic and moved to California, where he was hired by Samuel Goldwyn as a movie vice president, first at $25,000, then $40,000 a year. Hollywood buzz had it that James had been given a leaf-raking job by Goldwyn so he could boast to friends that the president's son was on the payroll.[60]* The fact is that Goldwyn was being sued by the Department of Justice for antitrust violations related to film distribution and saw James as a sheet anchor. "How can you do this with a suit pending?" FDR asked his son in December 1938. James said it was only a civil suit. "What is the difference between a civil and a criminal suit?" Roosevelt replied. "All I know is that you are working for a man who is fighting the United States Government."[61]

Number two son, Elliott, was even more of a problem. A natural rebel, he objected to attending Groton, resisted confirmation in the Episcopal Church, and turned in a blank college entrance examination to avoid going to Harvard. Instead of college Elliott found a job with a New York advertising agency and earned enough to support himself but just barely. In 1932, at the age of twenty-one, he married Elizabeth "Betty" Donner, the attractive heiress to a Pennsylvania steel fortune. Betty's father, a pillar in the Republican establishment, bankrolled the couple, provided them with a Park Avenue apartment, and invited Elliott into the family business as a vice president. "I saw my life laid out

---

* "You and I know the average outsider does not receive such an offer," wrote James many years later. "I was willing to take advantage of the fact that I was not the average outsider. I have always felt that, even if I accepted undeserved opportunity, if I worked hard to make the most of it on my own, any success I had would be deserved." James Roosevelt, *My Parents: A Differing View* 252 (Chicago: Playboy Press, 1976).

ahead of me," he said later.[62] Like his maternal grandfather and namesake, Elliott was restless. He and Betty and their infant son attended FDR's 1933 inaugural, and four days later Elliott abandoned them and drove west. "He simply dumped them at the White House," said an upstairs employee. Elliott told ER he needed to think things through. He had a job offer from a start-up airline in California. If it worked out, he might send for his family later.[63]

Elliott ran out of money in Little Rock and placed a collect call to his father. FDR explained that he had closed the banks and suggested to Elliott that he find a prosperous-looking farm where he might earn enough to continue his trip.

"What road are you following?" FDR asked.

"Dallas, El Paso, Tucson," said Elliott.

"Just go as far as you can," Roosevelt replied.[64] Evidently FDR informed Jesse Jones, the Texas banker who headed the Reconstruction Finance Corporation, and Jones in turn alerted the Dallas business establishment. When Elliott arrived in the city, he was feted by the legendary C. R. Smith, the head of American Airlines, introduced to the moneybags of the Texas oil industry, Sid Richardson and Clint Murchison, and made grand marshal of the Fat Stock Show in Fort Worth. "I was vaguely aware that I was being sized up," said Elliott.[65] He also met and immediately fell in love with Ruth Googins, the daughter of a wealthy meatpacking family.

Elliott continued to California. The fledgling airline for which he hoped to work went out of business shortly after his arrival, and he too was rescued by William Randolph Hearst, who engaged Elliott as aviation editor of the *Los Angeles Examiner* at the princely salary of $30,000. Two years later Hearst put him in charge of the company's radio operations at $50,000.* With Hearst's offer on the horizon, Elliott decided to divorce Betty and marry Ruth. The easy way out was to break the news by telephone from the West Coast. The Donners were distraught; Franklin and Eleanor were appalled; and Anna was dispatched to counsel Elliott against the move. "See if you can't keep him from rushing into it," FDR instructed his daughter.[66] When Anna failed, Eleanor flew out to Los Angeles but had no better luck. Elliott divorced Betty in Reno in July 1933, and married Ruth Googins five days later.

---

* In contemporary figures, Elliott's 1933 and 1935 salaries would be equivalent to $417,000 and $658,000, respectively. Considering the low tax rate of the period, the buying power would have been much greater.

Like James—perhaps even more than James—Elliott was always on the lookout for easy money, invariably trading on the family name. In 1934, while working as Hearst's aviation columnist, he engineered a deal with the Dutch airplane designer Anthony Fokker to sell fifty Lockheed transports to the Soviet Union. Fokker was to convert the planes to bombers, and Elliott was to receive a $500,000 commission. The deal ultimately fell through (Elliott received $5,000), and the Nye Committee investigating the arms industry had a field day, particularly since Elliott had failed to report the $5,000 on his tax return.[67]

By 1937 Elliott had assembled five radio stations for Hearst in the Southwest. When Hearst decided to sell the stations, Elliott was eager to buy them. To raise money, he reached out to old friends, business associates, and casual acquaintances, one of whom was John A. Hartford, president of the Great Atlantic & Pacific Tea Company (A&P). Elliott telephoned his father from Hartford's office and then handed the phone to Hartford.

"Hello, John," said FDR with his customary bonhomie. "While any business you have with my son must stand on its own merits, I will appreciate anything you do for him. And the next time you're in Washington come and see me."[68] Hartford was facing an antitrust suit filed by the Federal Trade Commission, and the president's invitation was too good to pass up. He invested $200,000 and took Elliott's personal note as collateral. Several years later, when Elliott's radio empire ran into hard times, FDR asked then commerce secretary Jesse Jones for help. Jones interceded with Hartford, who agreed to settle the note for $4,000. Hartford told Jones he would do whatever the president asked. "Candidly, I would rather not have Elliott Roosevelt's note in my estate after I am dead."[69]

FDR, Jr., son number three, was nineteen when his father became president. He graduated from Harvard in 1937 and promptly married Ethel du Pont, the stunning daughter of Eugene du Pont of Greenville, Delaware, a founding member of the Liberty League and a bitter opponent of the New Deal. Franklin, Jr.—known to the family as "Brud"—bore the strongest resemblance to his father and possessed the same charm and assurance. "He's a good egg," allowed Ethel's father, "but it would be better if he had a different last name."[70] FDR, Jr.'s, marriage to Ethel, the union of Roosevelts and du Ponts, was portrayed by the press as the wedding of the decade. The Army Corps of Engineers set up a field kitchen on the du Pont property, three companies of soldiers were deployed to provide security, and the receiving line required five hours to pass through. Among the guests of the du Ponts were the relief impresario Harry Hopkins, the feminist secretary of labor Frances Perkins, and the Jewish secretary of the Treasury Henry Morgenthau. FDR enjoyed every minute and, according to James, kissed all the bridesmaids. "It doesn't really matter what you do," cautioned Eleanor, "so long as you don't steal the show."[71]

In the autumn of 1937 Franklin, Jr., entered law school at the University of Virginia. Late in his first year, some fraternity jokers decided it would be a good idea to place a transatlantic telephone call to Premier Édouard Daladier of France, person to person from Franklin Delano Roosevelt. M. Daladier was not amused. After the French Foreign Ministry and the State Department finished exchanging notes, Roosevelt wrote his son:

> As you know, there was a somewhat serious international flurry over the call that was put in from the Fraternity House on May 21st to Prime Minister Daladier. . . . It was, of course, purely a prank but I think it would do no harm for you to let them know at the Fraternity House that that kind of prank can have serious results![72]

John Aspinwall Roosevelt, Franklin and Eleanor's youngest son, proved to be the tallest (at six feet, five inches), the most stable, and the most conservative. Unlike his brothers, he never ran for elective office and did not rely on his father's influence for personal advancement. His marriage to the North Shore socialite Anne Lindsay Clark—they were married during John's senior year at Harvard—lasted twenty-seven years, a record for the Roosevelt siblings, and he married only twice, another record. After finishing Harvard in 1938 he went to work as a clerk at Filene's department store in Boston, earning $18 a week. John flourished in the retail trade and later owned and operated his own department store in Los Angeles. In 1953 he entered the investment banking business, where he prospered as well. Because FDR came down with polio when John was a toddler and was absent from the family much of the time, John had less emotional attachment to his parents and their political views than the other children. A closet Republican, he waited until after FDR's death to announce his affiliation. He contributed generously to GOP candidates, publicly endorsed both Eisenhower and Richard Nixon, and when his brother FDR, Jr., ran for New York attorney general in 1954, John backed his Republican opponent, Jacob Javits.

In college during the 1930s, John attracted his share of attention. Visiting Cannes with classmates in the summer after his junior year, he and his friends joined the annual "Battle of Flowers," when decorated floats competed for prizes. By the time their flower-bedecked carriage reached the reviewing stand in front of the Hotel Carlton, they had been drinking vintage Moët & Chandon for three hours and were snockered. When the mayor of Cannes, Pierre Nouveau, advanced to present the coach with a bouquet of flowers, John took a bottle of champagne from an ice bucket on the carriage floor and squirted him in the face with the contents. The incident generated wide press coverage, riled Franco-American relations, and required high-level diplomatic intervention to repair the damage.[73] John provided a ritual denial, and Ambassador William C. Bullitt offered what support he could. Franklin and Eleanor accepted John's version, and ER met him at the dock in New York when he returned. As she put it:

> If it had been one of my other boys I would have felt the incident was more than probable, for they have great exuberance of spirit. It just happens that John is extremely quiet, and, even if he had been under the influence of champagne, I doubt if he would have reacted in this manner.[74]

The Roosevelt sons sought no special favors in World War II. James fought with Carlson's Raiders (the Marines' famous 2nd Raider Battalion) at Guadalcanal, Tarawa, and the Solomon Islands, later commanded the Fourth Raiders, and earned the Navy Cross and a Silver Star. Elliott enlisted in the Army Air Force in 1940, flew three hundred photoreconnaissance missions, was wounded twice, and rose to command the 325th Photographic Reconnaissance Wing during the D-Day invasion. FDR, Jr., after graduating from the University of Virginia Law School, served in the Navy, commanded the destroyer *Ulvert M. Moore*, and won the Navy Cross, the Legion of Merit, and a Purple Heart. John, who was the last to enlist, saw combat as a lieutenant (later lieutenant commander) on the aircraft carrier USS *Wasp* in the Pacific, and earned a Bronze Star.

THE SECOND SESSION of the Seventy-fifth Congress was little more productive than the first. When members departed Washington *sine die* on June 16, 1938, only one significant piece of legislation had been enacted: the Fair Labor

Standards Act, better known as the wages and hours bill. And it had been an uphill struggle. Introduced by liberal Alabama senator Hugo Black, the bill passed the Senate in July 1937. But a combination of conservative Republicans and southern Democrats (who feared the racial equality implications) kept the measure bottled up in the House Rules Committee until a discharge petition brought it to the floor in May 1938. After twelve hours of stormy debate and numerous amendments the bill passed with a lopsided majority of 314–7, only to run into the obstacle course of a House-Senate conference committee that sought to reconcile the newer House version with the bill the Senate had passed the year before. The final bill, reflecting the Hughes Court's latitudinarian interpretation of the commerce clause, banned the employment of child labor and established a minimum wage of forty cents an hour, a forty-hour workweek, and time and a half for overtime.[75] It was passed by both houses on June 14—two days before adjournment—and the president signed it on June 24. "That's that," said FDR, with more finality than he intended. The Fair Labor Standards Act, one of the most important measures ever passed by Congress, would be the last significant New Deal initiative to become law.

Roosevelt's frustration with the Seventy-fifth Congress led him to his third serious mistake. The Court-packing fiasco was the first; the premature cutback in federal spending the second; and his 1938 attempt to purge the Democratic party of dissident members of Congress was the third. Hard-core Republican opposition on Capitol Hill was taken for granted. What FDR could not forgive was the defection of conservative Democrats. The remedy he embarked upon was to oppose the renomination of key members of the House and Senate in upcoming Democratic primaries. It was a breathtaking departure from American tradition. No president since Andrew Johnson had intervened directly in individual congressional contests, and none since Wilson had made an off-year election a referendum on the presidency. Given the unhappy results in both instances, Roosevelt should have been forewarned.

FDR's interest was piqued by the landslide victory in January of New Deal congressman Lister Hill, running for the Alabama Senate seat vacated by Hugo Black.* Hill ran as an out-and-out supporter of the president, much as Black

---

* Black was nominated by FDR on August 12, 1937 to replace retiring Supreme Court justice Willis Van Devanter. He was confirmed (63–16) on August 17 and took the oath of office on August 19. Black was the first of Roosevelt's eight appointees to the Court.

had been. His primary opponent was former senator Tom Heflin, an unrepentant racist from the red clay hills of eastern Alabama who had once shot a black man on a Washington streetcar.[76] Heflin had deserted the party over Al Smith's Catholicism in 1928 and despite his populist, rabble-rousing past was backed by a significant portion of the state's financial establishment. Hill beat Heflin 90,000 to 50,000—almost 2 to 1.[77]

Initially FDR pursued the purge by proxy. As primary season approached, the White House asked Farley to draft a statement defining the administration's position. Farley prepared the customary disclaimer proclaiming the Democratic National Committee's neutrality: "As individuals, the members of the National Committee may have their favorites, but as a body the organization's hands are off. These nominations are entirely the affair of the States or the Congressional districts, and however these early battles may result, the National Committee will be behind the candidate that the people themselves choose. This goes for every state and every Congressional district."[78]

Ten minutes after Farley's draft statement arrived at the White House, James Roosevelt was on the phone. "Father has struck the last two sentences out," he told Farley. The decision was made by the president on the spot. He was not lured into the purge by ideologue advisers; Hopkins's thumbprints were not on it, nor had Corcoran hoodwinked FDR. The decision to intervene in the upcoming Democratic primaries was made by Roosevelt, and it was made in January 1938. "An albatross, not of my own shooting, was hung from my neck," wrote Farley. "From that time on I knew no political peace."[79]

First up was Florida, where pro–New Deal senator Claude Pepper faced an uphill primary fight against Congressman J. Mark Wilcox of West Palm Beach, an ultraconservative member of the Florida business establishment who made opposition to the wages and hours bill the centerpiece of his campaign. Wilcox was a marvel on the stump, and prognosticators gave Pepper little chance. In the colorful rhetoric of the Sunshine State, Wilcox titillated backcountry audiences with rumors that Pepper had been guilty of celibacy before marriage and addicted to monogamy ever since.[80]* On February 6, 1938, James held a press conference in Palm Beach, where he announced the White House's support

---

* In 1950 Pepper was defeated for reelection by Congressman George Smathers, who informed Florida voters that Pepper's actress sister was "a practicing thespian living in New York's Greenwich Village."

for Pepper in the primary. Thomas Corcoran, a Harvard Law School classmate of Pepper, funneled funds from private donors into the campaign, and on May 3 Pepper won an upset victory, beating Wilcox by 65,000 votes. Alabama and Florida made it two for two for the administration.

The next primary was in Iowa on June 7, 1938. FDR was determined to defeat incumbent senator Guy Gillette, a leading spokesman for midwestern farm interests who had made the cardinal error of opposing the president's Court-packing plan. The fifty-nine-year-old Gillette, who had represented Iowa in the House before moving to the Senate in 1936, had supported most New Deal measures.[81] But for Roosevelt the litmus test of party loyalty was the Court battle, and Gillette had been on the wrong side. Hopkins, an Iowa native, became the president's surrogate. He convinced Congressman Otha Wearin to challenge Gillette in the primary, publicly endorsed Wearin (as did James Roosevelt), and mobilized whatever federal employees he could on Wearin's behalf. All to no avail. Gillette enjoyed the support of the state organization; Agriculture secretary Henry Wallace—the most prominent Iowan in Washington—declined to support Wearin; and Gillette's Senate colleagues rallied to his side. Taking aim at Hopkins's role, Montana's Burton K. Wheeler declared that "Congress in appropriating for the relief of the underprivileged never intended that these funds should be utilized to slaughter a member of this body."[82] Gillette won in a landslide, receiving more votes than his three primary opponents combined. "I will not," he told Iowa voters, "be a rubber stamp member of Congress."[83]

Stung by Gillette's victory, Roosevelt entered the fight himself. On Friday, June 24, having just signed the Fair Labor Standards Act, FDR devoted his second fireside chat of the year to an attack on the "Copperheads" in the Democratic party who resisted change.* "We all know that progress may be blocked by outspoken reactionaries," said Roosevelt. But those who posed as progressives and then voted against change were a more serious threat. "As head of the Democratic party . . . charged with the responsibility of carrying out the definitely liberal declaration of principles set forth in the 1936 Democratic plat-

* "You will remember," FDR told his radio audience, "that it was the Copperheads who . . . tried their best to make Lincoln and his Congress give up the fight, let the nation remain split in two and return to peace—peace at any price." 7 *Public Papers and Addresses of Franklin D. Roosevelt* 395, Samuel I. Rosenman, ed. (New York: Macmillan, 1941).

form, I feel that I have every right to speak in those few instances where there may be a clear issue between candidates for a Democratic nomination involving these principles."[84]

Roosevelt's first stop was Kentucky, where Alben Barkley was in the fight of his life against the popular governor, Albert B. "Happy" Chandler (later commissioner of baseball). Farley advised hands off. "I am fond of both Barkley and Chandler," he told FDR. "I wish they could both win."[85] But the president was determined that Barkley be returned. Speaking to voters in Covington, Kentucky, on July 8, he devoted his entire address to praising Barkley's liberal outlook and legislative experience. "I have no doubt whatsoever that Governor Chandler would make a good Senator," said FDR. "But I think my good friend, the Governor, would be the first to acknowledge that as a very junior member of the United States Senate, it would take him many, many years to match the national knowledge, the experience and the acknowledged leadership in the affairs of the Nation of that son of Kentucky, of whom the whole Nation is proud, Alben Barkley."[86]

At the direction of the White House, Hopkins unlimbered the administrative apparatus of the WPA on Barkley's behalf, and on primary day Barkley defeated Chandler easily.[87] The blatant involvement of the WPA (as well as Chandler's use of state workers) triggered a senatorial investigation that culminated in the passage of the 1939 Hatch Act, barring political participation by federal employees. "These facts [in Kentucky] should arouse the conscience of the country," said Senator Morris Sheppard of Texas, who chaired the investigation. "They imperil the right of the people to a free and unpolluted ballot."[88]

FDR identified ten senators he hoped to purge in the primaries. Gillette, the first to face the voters, won handily. Four were ultimately deemed too secure to challenge.* One, George L. Berry of Tennessee, had gotten crossways of Memphis boss Ed Crump, and the Shelby County organization rendered the coup

---

* Alva Adams of Colorado; Pat McCarran of Nevada; Bennett Champ Clark of Missouri; and Augustine Lonergan of Connecticut. Clark had voted against the administration 42 percent of the time, Adams 36 percent, McCarran 35 percent, and Lonergan 21 percent. James T. Patterson, *Congressional Conservatism and the New Deal* 348–349 (Lexington: University of Kentucky Press, 1967).

de grâce. Frederick Van Nuys of Indiana outmaneuvered his opponents and was renominated by acclamation at the Indiana Democratic convention on July 12. That left three in the president's sights: Walter George of Georgia, "Cotton Ed" Smith of South Carolina, and Millard Tydings of Maryland. George had voted against the New Deal one third of the time since 1933; Smith almost half; and Tydings a whopping 77 percent—an opposition record among Democrats exceeded only by the eighty-year-old Carter Glass of Virginia, who was not up for reelection.[89] In the House, Roosevelt focused on the Rules Committee and targeted three members for defeat: John J. O'Connor of New York, Howard Smith of Virginia, and Eugene Cox of Georgia.[90]

On August 11 FDR journeyed to tiny Barnesville, Georgia (1930 population 5,392) to dedicate a new rural electrification project. The little hamlet was jammed with more than 50,000 people who had come by car and wagon and pickup truck to see and hear their Warm Springs neighbor, the president of the United States. On the platform of notables with FDR were Senator George and his two primary opponents: Lawrence Camp, the young U.S. attorney from Atlanta who was the administration's candidate; and the gallus-snapping, race-baiting Eugene Talmadge, the state's former governor. Roosevelt wasted little time before he jumped into the primary fight. As an adopted son of Georgia, the president said, he felt "no hesitation in telling you what I would do if I could vote here next month." The issue was liberal versus conservative. Senator George "is a gentleman and a scholar. He will always be my personal friend. [But he] cannot possibly in my judgment be classified as belonging to the liberal school of thought." Roosevelt said he had known former governor Talmadge for many years. "I am very certain in my own mind that his election would contribute very little to practical progress in government." FDR said his candidate was Lawrence Camp: "a man who honestly believes that many things must be done and done now to improve the economic and social conditions of the country."[91] When Roosevelt finished, he and George shook hands. "Mr. President," said the courtly senator, "I regret that you have taken the occasion to question my Democracy and to attack my record. I want you to know that I accept the challenge."[92]

For the next month Walter George, a charter member of the Senate's inner club, carried the fight to every crossroads and creek bottom in the state. Roosevelt's intervention was "a second march through Georgia," he told rapt audiences from Valdosta to Mountain City.[93] When the votes were counted, George won easily, with 141,235 to Talmadge's 103,075. FDR's candidate finished a distant third, with 76,778.[94]

In South Carolina the race turned ugly. Smith was the Senate's senior Democrat, elected when Taft beat Bryan in 1908. As longtime chairman of the Agriculture Committee, he had earned the sobriquet "Cotton Ed" for the solicitous care he bestowed on the South's plantation economy. The political scientist V. O. Key, Jr., once said of Smith that he was "unrivaled as a critic of the New Deal, unmatched as an exponent of white supremacy, and without peer as a defender of southern womanhood."[95] But Smith was long in the tooth and suffered from Potomac Fever—the disease endemic to legislators who spend too much time in Washington. Of all those earmarked by FDR for defeat, he seemed the most vulnerable. To challenge Smith, the administration convinced Governor Olin D. Johnston to make the race. Johnston announced his candidacy from the steps of the White House, and that gave Smith a tailor-made issue to excite the unreconstructed sentiments of his South Carolina constituents: Washington can't tell the people of the Palmetto State how to vote! Arguing states' rights and "New Deal Reconstruction," Smith resorted to one of the most vicious racist campaigns in South Carolina history and beat Johnston by 10 percentage points.[96] Smith was asked after the election if Roosevelt was not his own worst enemy. "Not as long as I am alive," he snapped.[97]

FDR intervened most vigorously in Maryland. Of all those the president sought to purge, Millard Tydings was the most guilty of party disloyalty. Congressman David Lewis, the House sponsor of Social Security, was persuaded to contest the seat, and Roosevelt barnstormed the state over the Labor Day weekend with Lewis at his side. He spoke six times, never mentioning Tydings by name but making it clear that he considered Maryland's senior senator a political turncoat. "Any man—any political party—has a right to be honestly 'conservative' or 'liberal.' But the Nation cannot stand for the confusion of having him pretend to be one and act like the other."[98] Tydings, like George and Smith, made White House intervention the principal issue in the campaign. When the ballots were tabulated on September 13, Tydings defeated Lewis by 60,000 votes.

Roosevelt had taken on four senior Democratic senators and lost four times. In the House, both Eugene Cox from Georgia's second district and Judge Howard W. Smith, who represented northern Virginia, were returned easily. FDR's only victory in the 1938 purge campaign was the toppling of Rules Committee chairman John J. O'Connor in New York.* Roosevelt put the best face on it. "Harvard," he said, "lost the schedule but won the Yale game," meaning that O'Connor's removal from his powerful post more than compensated for the New Deal's other defeats.[99]

FDR's intrusion into the primaries eroded his standing in Congress and further divided the Democratic party. Having put his prestige on the line and lost, Roosevelt placed New Deal candidates in jeopardy come November. Congressman Maury Maverick lost in Texas and Governor Frank Murphy went down in Michigan, as did George Earle in Pennsylvania. In New York the ticket won, but Governor Lehman's margin of victory over Manhattan district attorney Thomas E. Dewey was less than 1 percent. Republicans picked up eighty-one seats in the House, took eight more in the Senate, and won thirteen governorships. Roosevelt was stunned. He told Farley he had expected to lose one seat in the Senate and perhaps sixteen in the House.[100] The Democrats retained control of Congress, but it was no longer the party FDR had led for the last six years. "We have a large majority," said Garner, "but it is not a *New Deal* majority."[101]

Roosevelt was a lame duck. Farley and Garner were taking presidential soundings, Hull was restless, and liberals scanned the horizon for a possible successor. If the downward momentum continued, the Republicans had their best shot at the White House since 1928. "Clearly," wrote Washington newsman Raymond Clapper, "President Roosevelt could not run for a third term even if he so desired."[102]

* O'Connor, ironically, was the brother of FDR's former law partner and confidant Basil O'Connor. In 1923 he succeeded to the House seat (the so-called silk-stocking district on the Upper East Side) formerly held by the legendary Bourke Cochran. After losing the Democratic primary in 1938, he contested the seat as a Republican (New York's cross-filing provision permitted that) and in November was narrowly defeated for a second time.

NINETEEN

ON THE BRINK

*What America does or fails to do in the next few years
has a far greater bearing and influence on the history
of the whole human race for centuries to come than
most of us who are here today can ever conceive.*
—FRANKLIN D. ROOSEVELT, DECEMBER 5, 1938

REPUBLICAN VICTORIES IN 1938 did not represent a return to Hooverism or a repudiation of the achievements of the New Deal. As the country had changed, so had the GOP. New leaders like Thomas Dewey in New York, Harold Stassen in Minnesota, even Robert Taft in Ohio did not advocate turning the clock back. It was time to digest and assimilate: a period of thermidor after six years of upheaval. "We have now passed the period of internal conflict in the launching of our program of social reform," Roosevelt told Congress in his annual message on January 4, 1939. "Our full energies may now be released to invigorate the process of recovery in order to preserve our reforms."[1]

FDR had sought to refashion the Democratic party into a permanent progressive force. But the resistance proved overwhelming. Southern Democracy remained the ball and chain that hobbled the party's move to the left.[2] The purge failed. And in the curious way of American politics, it would be those same disaffected Southern Democrats who would provide the president bedrock support to resist aggression and prepare the nation for war.

Until 1939 Roosevelt's involvement in foreign affairs had been sporadic. In 1936, when Germany reoccupied the Rhineland, the president was running for reelection. When Japan invaded China in 1937, FDR was consumed by the Court-packing fight. When Hitler annexed Austria in March 1938, it was the "Roosevelt recession" on the front burner. The Czech crisis in September played out against the backdrop of the purge. And during the Spanish Civil

War—which commenced in 1936 and would ultimately cost the lives of 650,000 combatants—the United States stood on the sidelines.[3]

Roosevelt's approach to foreign policy was similar to his conduct of domestic affairs: intuitive, idiosyncratic, and highly personalized. Just as he divided the New Deal's relief effort between Ickes and Hopkins, he split diplomacy between Cordell Hull and Sumner Welles. As secretary of state, Hull had titular responsibility. As undersecretary, Welles exercised operational control. Like Ickes and Hopkins, they competed for FDR's attention. Unlike Ickes and Hopkins, they shared an abiding dislike. In the War Department Roosevelt presided over a similar rivalry. Secretary Harry Woodring and Assistant Secretary Louis Johnson detested each other. Woodring, a low-wattage Kansas banker, was cautious, provincial, and strongly isolationist. Johnson, a former commander of the American Legion, was a glad-handing ball of fire, vigorously internationalist in outlook. The Navy did not require a division of authority because FDR, to the extent he wished, ran it directly through the chief of naval operations, Admiral William D. Leahy. In each case—State, War, and Navy—Roosevelt kept the reins in his own hands. The method was not what textbooks teach, but neither Hull nor Welles, nor Woodring or Johnson, for that matter, could presume to act without clearance from FDR.

Roosevelt distrusted the career diplomats in the State Department. The seven hundred members of the foreign service, primarily prep school progeny with Ivy League pedigrees, were predisposed to political conservatism. Prone to the prejudices of their wealthy WASP backgrounds, they were anti-immigrant, anti-Semitic, antiblack, and anti–New Deal. For the most part FDR ignored them. When he recognized the Soviet Union in 1933, the State Department was fenced out of the negotiations. By the same token, Roosevelt's principal ambassadorial appointments reflected measured contempt for the striped-pants set. To Mexico he sent his old mentor Josephus Daniels—whom he still addressed as "Chief." To Russia he dispatched William Bullitt and then Joseph E. Davies, both sympathetic to the Soviet Union. Joseph P. Kennedy, an unapologetic Irish Catholic, went to the Court of St. James; Jesse Isidor Straus, a Jew (shades of the Dreyfus Affair), was sent to Paris; and Professor William E. Dodd, an outspoken anti-Nazi, to Berlin. Each of these ambassadors enjoyed direct access to FDR. That minimized State Department input and ensured that the president's views would be accurately represented. When war came, the State Department was shunted to a siding. Roosevelt's cable communications with foreign leaders were handled by the Navy; Hopkins and other special emissaries undertook delicate diplomatic missions; and the department was absent from major wartime conferences.

During the 1930s Americans concentrated on domestic recovery. The problems of Europe and Asia appeared remote: of little more than passing interest when a third of the nation was "ill-housed, ill-clad, ill-nourished." Much as they may have sympathized with victims of aggression, Americans had no desire to repeat their entry into World War I. Influenced by an isolationist press, revisionist historians, and the much-ballyhooed revelations of the Nye Committee, which had investigated the role of munitions makers in fomenting war, they eschewed involvement in foreign affairs. Mussolini's 1935 subjugation of Ethiopia caused scarcely a ripple. "The policy of the United States is to remain untangled and free," Walter Lippmann wrote in January 1936. "Let us follow that policy. Let us make no alliances. Let us make no commitments."[4]*

Roosevelt swam with the isolationist tide. He acquiesced in the passage of a series of neutrality acts that denied American arms to aggressors and their victims alike, kept the Army on a starvation budget, and, like Britain and France, refused assistance to the duly elected republican government in Spain.[5] In his speeches and letters during the mid-1930s he repeated his belief that the United States should avoid being drawn into another war. At Chautauqua in August 1936 he revealed the depth of his feeling. "I have seen war," he said. "I have seen war on land and sea. I have seen blood running from the wounded. I have seen men coughing out their gassed lungs. I have seen the dead in the mud. I have seen cities destroyed. . . . I have seen children starving. I have seen the agony of mothers and wives. I hate war."[6]

Japan's incursion into China in the summer of 1937 caused FDR to hesitate. Like most Americans he favored China (the historic ties of the Delano family ensured FDR's sympathy),[7] and he refused to invoke the Neutrality Act on the somewhat specious grounds that neither side had actually declared war. That benefited China, which needed weapons more than Japan did. On October 5, with the Japanese war machine advancing full tilt, Roosevelt tested the water. Speaking in Chicago, the heartland of American isolationism, he sounded the

* A *Fortune* magazine poll taken at the time Lippmann wrote indicated that fewer than 25 percent of the respondents would be willing to go to war to defend the Philippines if they were attacked. "The *Fortune* Survey," *Fortune* 46–47 (January 1936).

first notes of a still uncertain trumpet. "Innocent peoples, innocent nations, are being cruelly sacrificed to a greed for power which is devoid of all sense of justice," he said.

> When an epidemic of physical disease starts to spread, the community approves and joins in a quarantine of the patients in order to protect the health of the community against the spread of the disease.
>
> War is a contagion. . . . The peace of the world is today being threatened. . . . We are determined to keep out of war, yet we cannot insure ourselves against the disastrous effects of war and the dangers of involvement.[8]

Reaction was mixed. "Stop Foreign Meddling; America Wants Peace," bellowed *The Wall Street Journal*.[9] The *Chicago Tribune* and the Hearst press were equally caustic. But *The New York Times*, *The Washington Post*, and most national chains were supportive. A press survey by *Time* reported "more words of approval . . . than have greeted any Roosevelt step in many a month."[10] Overseas reaction was enthusiastic (save in Tokyo and Berlin), and White House mail ran 4 to 1 in favor of the president's remarks. But on Capitol Hill it was a different story. While isolationist members rushed to the barricades, Democrats hunkered down and said nothing. Fearful of a fickle electorate, the president's supporters passed up the opportunity to place themselves on the record. "It's a terrible thing," FDR told Sam Rosenman, "to look over your shoulder when you are trying to lead—and to find no one there."[11]

At his press conference the following day Roosevelt pulled back. "Do you care to amplify your remarks at Chicago, especially where you referred to a possible quarantine?" the president was asked.

"No," he replied dismissively.

Ernest K. Lindley of the *Herald Tribune*, who had covered FDR for years, persisted. "I think it would be very valuable if you would answer a few questions or else talk for background."

Roosevelt demurred. "All off the record."

> q: Is anything contemplated?
> FDR: No, just the speech itself.
> q: Doesn't [quarantine] mean economic sanctions?

FDR: No. "Sanctions" is a terrible word to use. They are out the window.

Q: Is there a likelihood that there will be a conference of the peace-loving nations?

FDR: No; conferences are out the window.[12]

The president sparred with reporters for another ten minutes, and it was clear he had no new policy in mind. "Mr. Roosevelt was defining an attitude and not a program," reported *The Times* of London.[13] Isolationism remained the order of the day. FDR had commenced the laborious process of changing the nation's course. In typical fashion he had taken two steps forward and one step back. "I am fighting against a public psychology of long standing," he wrote Rector Endicott Peabody at Groton. "A psychology which comes very close to saying, 'Peace at any price.' "[14]

The nation's calm was shattered on Sunday, December 12, 1937, when Japanese warplanes bombed, strafed, and sank the gunboat USS *Panay*, lying at anchor in the Yangtze River, twenty miles above Nanking. With the *Panay* were three Standard Oil Company tankers, which were also sunk. The attack lasted more than an hour. Shore batteries joined in, and at one point Japanese soldiers boarded the vessels. Three persons were killed and fifty injured, including *Panay*'s captain, Lieutenant Commander James Hughes.[15]

The attack bore every earmark of being premeditated. The *Panay*, which had been on station since its construction in Shanghai in 1928, was part of the Asiatic Fleet's Yangtze Patrol, assigned to protect American commercial and missionary interests.* It was plainly marked with abundant insignia, including two large American flags, eighteen feet by fourteen feet, painted horizontally across the canvas shading her top deck. The flags were clearly visible from the air at any angle. The attack occurred shortly after twelve noon; the day was bright and clear, the visibility unlimited. A Universal Pictures newsreel photographer who happened to be on board during the attack filmed the incident

---

* U.S. forces were in China under the provisions of the Sino-American Treaty of 1858. In 1937 the Yangtze Patrol consisted of thirteen vessels (nine of which were gunboats), 129 officers, and 1,671 enlisted men. In addition, 814 soldiers from the 15th Infantry were stationed in Tientsien; 528 marines in Peking; and another 2,555 marines in Shanghai. Secretary Hull to Vice President Garner, January 8, 1938, 83 *Congressional Record* 261, 75th Congress, 3rd session (Washington, D.C.: U.S. Government Printing Office, 1938).

showing the planes strafing the vessel at masthead level: so low the pilots' faces could be seen clearly.[16] The American flags could not have been overlooked or mistaken, and when *Panay* returned fire it would have been abundantly clear what was at stake.

At a meeting of the cabinet immediately afterward, Secretary of the Navy Claude Swanson, supported by Vice President Garner and Harold Ickes, clamored for war. "Certainly war with Japan is inevitable sooner or later," Ickes noted. "If we have to fight her, isn't this the best possible time?"[17] Roosevelt steadied the ship. The Navy was not ready for war, and the country was not prepared. "The gunboat *Panay* is not the battleship *Maine*," chided *The Christian Science Monitor*.[18] Arizona senator Henry Ashurst told FDR that a declaration of war would not win one vote on Capitol Hill.[19] Senator Henrik Shipstead of Minnesota spoke for many when he asked that all American forces in China be withdrawn. "How long are we going to sit there and let these fellows kill American soldiers and sailors and sink our battleships?"[20]

Roosevelt directed Hull to demand an apology from the Japanese government, secure full compensation, and obtain a guarantee against a repetition of the attack.[21] He instructed Morgenthau to prepare to seize Japanese assets in the United States if Tokyo did not pay and mused about the possibility of an Anglo-American economic blockade. The day after FDR's demand, Japan's foreign minister, Kiki Hirota, patently embarrassed by the military's action, tendered the official apologies of his government and promised full restitution for the losses sustained. Ten days later Hirota informed Washington that orders had been issued to ensure the future safety of American vessels in Chinese waters and that the commander of the force that had launched the attack had been relieved. On April 22, 1938, the Japanese government provided a check for $2,214,007.36, paying in full the claim submitted by the United States.[22]

The *Panay* incident ended agreeably. But it energized isolationist efforts to keep America out of war. In 1935, when Mussolini invaded Ethiopia, Representative Louis Ludlow, a five-term Democrat from Indianapolis, introduced a constitutional amendment in the House that would require a national referendum before the United States could go to war.[23*] It was referred to the Judi-

---

* The operative portion of what came to be known as the Ludlow Amendment provided:

Except in the event of an invasion of the United States or its Territorial possessions and attack upon the citizens residing therein, the authority of Congress to declare

ciary Committee, where the chairman, Hatton Sumners of Texas—who had "cashed in his chips" over FDR's Court-packing scheme—loyally kept it off the committee's agenda. By 1937 a discharge petition to bring the amendment to the House floor had obtained 205 of the necessary 218 signatures. Twenty-four hours after the attack on the *Panay,* an additional thirteen members signed on. A Gallup Poll recorded that 73 percent of Americans approved of the amendment.[24] "You can cast your ballot for a constable or a dogcatcher," Ludlow told a national radio audience, "but you have absolutely nothing to say about a declaration of war."[25]

With the discharge petition in place, Ludlow's resolution to bring the amendment to the floor became the first order of business when the House reconvened in January 1938. The administration pulled out all the stops. Farley called every Democrat in the chamber, party whips visited each member in his or her office, and FDR wrote a personal letter to Speaker Bankhead.[26] "The proposed amendment would be impracticable in its application and incompatible with our representative form of government," said Roosevelt. It "would cripple any President in his conduct of any foreign relations, and it would encourage other nations to believe that they could violate American rights with impunity."[27] Alf Landon and his 1936 running mate, Frank Knox, weighed in against the amendment, and former secretary of state Henry L. Stimson, speaking for the East Coast Republican establishment, attacked the proposal in a lengthy letter to *The New York Times.*[28]

Debate began January 10, 1938. The Rules Committee allotted twenty minutes. Speaker Bankhead, departing from custom, left the chair to lead the opposition. After Bankhead spoke, Majority Leader Sam Rayburn made one of his rare appearances in the well of the House. He was followed by Republican congresswoman Edith Nourse Rogers of Massachusetts, the ranking member of the Committee on Veterans' Legislation. "This is the gravest question that has been submitted to the Congress of the United States since I became a

---

war shall not become effective until confirmed by a majority of all votes cast thereon in a Nationwide referendum.

The amendment also provided that Congress, by joint resolution, could refer the question of war or peace to the electorate "when it deems a national crisis to exist." 75th Congress, 1st Session, House Joint Resolution 199. See Jean Edward Smith, *The Constitution and American Foreign Policy* 245 (St. Paul, Minn.: West Publishing Co., 1989).

Member of it more than twenty years ago," said Bankhead.[29] Speaking on behalf of the resolution were Ludlow; Hamilton Fish of New York, the ranking
Republican on Foreign Affairs; and Democrat Caroline O'Day of New York, an
old friend of Franklin and Eleanor. When the yeas and nays were called, Ludlow lost, 188–209. The vote, like the debate, crossed party lines. Democrats
split 188–111 against the resolution; Republicans were 64–21 in favor. Support
for the resolution was strongest among members from the Middle West and
the Plains states. All thirteen Progressives and Farmer-Laborite members—
who usually went down the line for FDR—voted with Ludlow. Southern Democrats, a majority of whom were now aligned against the New Deal, backed the
president 74–14.[30]*

Shortly after the defeat of the Ludlow Amendment, the international picture darkened. On March 11, 1938, Hitler annexed Austria, not only overturn-
ing a key element of the post–World War I treaty structure but unleashing a
virulent strain of pan-Germanism not seen in Europe since well before the
time of Bismarck.[31]† The Nazi slogan used to justify the Anschluss—"*Ein Volk,
ein Reich, ein Führer*"—would provide the kindling that would bring the world
to the brink of war. France, which was without a government when the German Army crossed the Austrian frontier, said nothing.[32] Mussolini, who had
rushed four divisions to the Brenner Pass in 1934 to prevent Austria's incorpo-
ration into Germany, this time acquiesced.[33] The Neville Chamberlain government in Great Britain continued to look upon Hitler as an important bulwark
against communism and chose not to make an issue of the takeover.[34] The

* The 188 votes Ludlow received were for his resolution to bring the amendment to the
floor, not for the amendment itself. Even if those 188 members were to vote for the amendment (which was not guaranteed), it would have fallen 102 votes shy of the 290 (two thirds
of 435) required for passage.

† In a plebiscite on April 10 Austrians voted 99.75 percent for union with Germany. Historians of the Third Reich have often noted that Hitler took advantage of the euphoria sur-
rounding the Anschluss to consolidate his hold on the German Army. Field Marshal Werner
von Blomberg was relieved as war minister (Hitler himself assumed the office), General
Freiherr von Fritsch was replaced as commander in chief, sixteen older generals (including
Gerd von Rundstedt) were retired, and forty-four were transferred to less sensitive posts.
Gordon A. Craig, *The Politics of the Prussian Army, 1640–1945* 489 ff. (New York: Oxford
University Press, 1955); John W. Wheeler-Bennett, *The Nemesis of Power: The German Army
in Politics, 1918–1945* 365–368 (London: Macmillan, 1961); Joachim C. Fest, *Hitler* 542–550
(New York: Harcourt Brace Jovanovich, 1974).

League of Nations, which had treaty responsibility to protect Austria's independence, did not even hold a meeting on the question, and the Catholic Church, represented by Theodor Cardinal Innitzer in Vienna, gave its blessing to the Anschluss.[35] Since those closest to the annexation accepted it as a fait accompli, Roosevelt felt nothing could be gained by stirring up domestic opinion in a lost cause. At his press conference on March 11 he was noncommittal.[36] Privately he deplored Chamberlain's eagerness to appease Hitler. "If a Chief of Police makes a deal with the leading gangsters and the deal results in no more hold-ups, that Chief of Police will be called a great man—but if the gangsters do not live up to their word the Chief of Police will go to jail."[37]

In April the president's mood soured when Great Britain gave formal recognition to Italy's conquest of Ethiopia. As Chamberlain explained it, by appeasing Mussolini, Italy might become sated, the Mediterranean pacified, and Britain's Suez gateway to India secured. To Roosevelt, such recognition merely rewarded aggression and would have a ruinous effect on the situation in the Far East "and upon the nature of the peace terms Japan may demand of China." To Winston Churchill, watching events in political exile at his Chartwell estate, Chamberlain and the British cabinet were "feeding the crocodiles."[38]

Scarcely before Austria was digested, Hitler turned his attention to Czechoslovakia. Three million ethnic Germans lived adjacent to the Bavarian border in the Sudetenland, an old Bohemian enclave folded into Czechoslovakia after World War I. The führer demanded that they be added to the Reich. What Clemenceau had once called the anarchic principle of national self-determination had come home to roost. When Hitler threatened military action to effect the union, Czechoslovakia's guarantors capitulated. The Russians refused to act without the French, the French refused to act without the British, and the British were feckless and indifferent. It was a replay of August 1914 with the film running in reverse. Determined to avoid the thoughtless mistakes that had led to World War I, the powers of the old Triple Entente erred on the side of caution. As Neville Chamberlain phrased it, "How horrible, fantastic, incredible, it is that we should be digging trenches and trying on gas masks because of a quarrel in a far away country between people of whom we know nothing."[39] At Munich on September 29, 1938, Chamberlain, Daladier, Hitler, and Mussolini signed the Four Power Agreement, ceding the

Sudetenland to Germany. Hitler avowed no further territorial ambition; Chamberlain proclaimed "peace in our time"; Mussolini boasted that "democracies exist to swallow toads." Churchill, from the Tory backbench, said simply, "The Government had to choose between shame and war. They chose shame and will get war."[40]

As a result of the Munich Agreement, Czechoslovakia lost one third of its population, 29 percent of its territory, its most important industrial area, and the most formidable defense line in Europe. Roosevelt viewed Munich with mixed feelings. He appreciated that war had been avoided but lamented the price that had been paid. England and France, he told Ickes, "will wash the blood from their Judas Iscariot hands."[41] As the Czech crisis played itself out, Roosevelt had urged Hitler and Chamberlain to find a peaceful solution. He tried to bolster British resolve but had little to offer in the way of tangible support. With an army of 185,000 men—ranked eighteenth in the world—the United States was essentially unarmed.[42] It was diplomatically isolated, still in the throes of the Roosevelt recession, and divided over its role in the world. As more than one historian has noted, America's lack of involvement was the handmaiden of European appeasement.[43]

Roosevelt and, to a lesser degree, Hull and Stimson worked to reshape American opinion. Speaking at Queen's University in Kingston, Ontario, on August 18, 1938, FDR pledged American support if Canada were attacked. "We are no longer a far away continent to which the eddies of controversies beyond the seas could bring no harm. The Dominion of Canada is part of the sisterhood of the British Empire. I give to you assurance that the people of the United States will not stand idly by if domination of Canadian soil is threatened by any other Empire."[44]

After Munich, Roosevelt ratcheted the rhetoric higher. "No one who lived through the grave hours of last month," he told a national audience, "could doubt the need for an enduring peace."

> But peace by fear has no higher or more enduring quality than peace by the sword.
>
> We in the United States do not seek to impose on any other people either our way of life or our internal form of government. But we are determined to maintain and protect that way of life and form of government for ourselves.[45]

American public opinion was moving, and perhaps faster than Roosevelt anticipated. A Gallup Poll in October 1938 indicated that 92 percent of Americans doubted Hitler's assurances that he had no further territorial ambitions. Seventy-seven percent believed his demand for the Sudetenland unjustified; 60 percent thought the Munich Agreement was more likely to lead to war than peace.[46]

Crystal Night (Kristallnacht) in Germany, November 10, 1938, helped solidify American opinion against Hitler. On November 7, Herschel Grynszpan, a seventeen-year-old Polish Jewish refugee, shot and mortally wounded the third secretary of the German Embassy in Paris, Ernst vom Rath. Grynszpan was protesting the summary expulsion from Germany of ten thousand long-resident Polish Jews, without notice and without legal recourse. He had intended to assassinate the German ambassador to France and shot Rath by mistake. In response to Rath's death, the Nazi leadership ordered a night of vengeance. Storm troopers burned synagogues, smashed Jewish businesses, and vandalized private homes. *The New York Times* correspondent in Berlin called it "A wave of destruction, looting, and incendiarism unparalleled in Germany since the Thirty Years' War."[47] Nearly 200 synagogues were burned, 7,500 shops broken into and looted, countless houses destroyed. Twenty thousand Jews were arrested and sent to concentration camps. By government decree German insurance companies were absolved of liability; the nation's Jewish community was fined $400 million to atone for Rath's death; and all Jewish retail establishments were shuttered and closed. Jews were barred from attending schools and universities, denied admission to concerts and theaters, and prohibited from driving automobiles.[48]

"I myself could scarcely believe that such things could occur in a twentieth century civilization," said FDR.[49] The American press was unanimous in condemning Nazi brutality. Herbert Hoover, Alf Landon, Harold Ickes, and various religious leaders spoke to express their horror. Roosevelt summoned Hugh Wilson, the American ambassador in Berlin, home for consultation. The United States did not sever diplomatic relations, but Ambassador Wilson never returned to Germany.

At his press conference on November 15, 1938, Roosevelt was asked whether he had given any thought to where Jewish refugees from Hitler might be resettled. "I have given a great deal of thought to it," said FDR.

Q: Can you tell us any place particularly desirable?

FDR: No, the time is not ripe.

Q: Would you recommend a relaxation of our immigration restrictions?

FDR: That is not in contemplation; we have the quota system.[50]

Roosevelt was referring to the 1924 National Origins Act, passed in a fit of American exclusivity after World War I, which effectively closed the nation's borders. The act imposed a ceiling of 150,000 immigrants a year, with quotas allocated by country based on that country's proportional presence in the United States in the 1920 census. Great Britain, the most significant country of origin, was granted 65,721 places; Germany was accorded 25,957; Austria 1,413. Quotas were not transferable: for example, an unfilled British quota could not be transferred to Germany. Nor could a country's future quotas be tapped in the current year. Immigration regulations also forbade issuing visas to persons "likely to become a public charge" and made no provision for offering asylum to victims of religious or political persecution.[51] Since Jews fleeing Germany and Austria were stripped of their assets, few could qualify for the limited number of visas available. Unless Congress amended the law or, at a minimum, provided for refugee status, Roosevelt's hands were tied.

The economic situation made congressional action unlikely. Persistent unemployment, exacerbated by the Roosevelt recession, presented an insurmountable obstacle to raising immigrant quotas, regardless of the country of origin. Roosevelt was also at the nadir of his popularity. The recession, combined with the Court-packing fiasco and the attempted purge of congressional Democrats, left him little political capital to expend on what in all probability would be a losing effort. A *Fortune* survey in 1938 indicated that less than 5 percent of Americans were willing to raise immigration quotas to accommodate more refugees.[52] When Senator Robert Wagner and Representative Edith Nourse Rogers cosponsored legislation to admit 20,000 German children in 1939, two thirds of the respondents in a Gallup Poll reported themselves opposed.[53] Anti-Semitism lurked beneath the surface. A Roper Poll in July 1939 indicated that only 39 percent of Americans believed Jews should be accorded equal rights. Thirty-two percent thought they should be restricted economically, 11 percent favored social segregation, and 10 percent advocated deportation.[54]

Roosevelt did what he could. After the Anschluss he stretched executive authority and unilaterally ordered the merging of German and Austrian immigration quotas and the expediting of Jewish visa applications, measures that permitted an additional 50,000 Jews to escape.[55] He modified immigration regulations to permit American residents to guarantee the support of relatives seeking visas and extended that to permit orphaned and handicapped children to enter under the sponsorship of Jewish charitable organizations.[56] One week after Kristallnacht he advised his press conference that all German and Austrian citizens in the United States on visitor permits—as many as fifteen thousand—would be allowed to stay after their permits expired. "I don't know, from the point of view of humanity, that we have a right to put them on a ship and send them back to Germany under the present conditions." Roosevelt said that under the law the secretary of labor could grant six-month extensions.

> Q: Do you understand that you may at the end of the first six
>   months, extend for another period of six months?
> FDR: Yes.
> Q: And on and on?
> FDR: I think so. . . . I have no doubt Congress will not compel us to
>   send these people back to Germany.[57]

Roosevelt believed that Hitler could be contained through airpower. It was a presidential *idée fixe* that would bedevil military planners for the next three years. Air supremacy was vital. But without supporting ground and naval forces, without the thousands of ancillary items that modern war entailed, airplanes alone could not ensure victory. On November 14, 1938, four days after Kristallnacht, FDR convened a high-level meeting in the Oval Office to launch his plan for a massive expansion of American airpower.[58] "Hitler would not have dared to take the stand he did . . . if the United States had five thousand warplanes and the capacity to produce ten thousand more within the next few months," said the president.[59] According to Roosevelt, the Western Hemisphere was in grave danger. To defend it, America needed an air force of 20,000 planes. Since it was unlikely that Congress would appropriate the money, FDR said he would settle for half that number together with a substantial expansion of production capacity. "Hopkins could build these plants without cost to the

Treasury because it would be work relief."[60] Roosevelt was jawboning to impart a sense of urgency. He did not intend for his figures to be taken literally. When the military followed through with a supplemental budget request for $1.8 billion, FDR slashed it to $525 million.[61]

Roosevelt became consumed with defense and foreign policy. The economy was perking along, on five cylinders if not six, and the social revolution had receded in importance. As the president's attention shifted, a new coalition formed on Capitol Hill. Southern Democrats and Wall Street Republicans rallied to FDR's side. Isolationist progressives and western populists—men like Hiram Johnson, Burton K. Wheeler, and Robert La Follette—fell away. After almost two years of uninterrupted reverses, Roosevelt was back on his game. At Chapel Hill on December 5 he moved adroitly to soothe domestic critics, the avuncular Dutch uncle once again taking the nation into his confidence:

> You undergraduates who see me for the first time have read and heard that I am at the very least, an ogre—a consorter with Communists, a destroyer of the rich, a breaker of our ancient traditions. . . . You have heard for six years that I was about to plunge the nation into war; that you and your little brothers would be sent to the bloody fields of battle in Europe; that I was driving the nation into bankruptcy; and that I breakfasted every morning on 'grilled millionaire.'
>
> Actually, I am an exceedingly mild mannered person—a practitioner of peace, both domestic and foreign, a believer in the capitalist system, and for my breakfast a devotee of scrambled eggs.[62]

In late December, after six years in office, FDR undertook a cabinet shake-up. Homer Cummings was the first to walk the plank. At Roosevelt's request, Cummings submitted his resignation so that he might "return to private practice." He was replaced as attorney general by Michigan governor Frank Murphy, a longtime New Deal favorite who had been narrowly defeated in his bid for reelection. The second casualty was seventy-one-year-old Daniel Roper at Commerce, who graciously made way for the long-anticipated elevation of Hopkins to the cabinet. A lightning rod for Republican opposition, Hopkins was confirmed in a straight-party-line vote, 58–27. The departure of Cummings and the elevation of Hopkins strengthened Roosevelt's cabinet significantly. The War and Navy departments were ripe for change, but FDR chose to move slowly. Woodring was informed that the president would accept his resignation but was placed under no immediate pressure. At Navy, Claude Swanson, another septuagenarian, was in poor health and had become increasingly feeble. His time was growing short, and Roosevelt did not have the heart to force him out.

By the end of 1938 Hopkins had succeeded to the place in Roosevelt's confidence that Louis Howe had occupied. Like Howe, he was one of the president's few intimates who moved confidently between Franklin and Eleanor, and ER was the guardian of Hopkins's young daughter, Diana.* Frequently Hopkins would join FDR at Warm Springs, where he and Missy were the president's only companions. Roosevelt's routine had changed remarkably little. According to Hopkins:

> The President wakes up about eight-thirty—breakfasts in bed—reads the morning papers and if left alone will spend a half hour or so reading a detective story. I would go in about nine-thirty—usually much talk about European affairs—Kennedy and Bullitt our ambassadors in London and Paris would telephone—Hull and Welles from the State Department so we had the latest news of Hitler's moves in the international checkerboard. . . .
>
> Lunch has usually been F.D.R. with Missy and me—these are the pleasantest because he is under no restraint and personal and public business is discussed with the utmost frankness. The service incidentally is as bad as the food. . . .
>
> He will sleep a bit after lunch—visit his farm—look at the tree plantings—back around four thirty for an hour's dictation. Dinner at seven. The ceremonial cocktail with the President doing the honors. He makes a first rate "old fashioned" and a fair martini. . . .
>
> After dinner the President retreats to his stamps—magazines and evening paper. Missy and I will play Chinese checkers. George Fox comes in to give him a rub down and the President is in bed by ten.[63]

---

* Hopkins's second wife, Barbara, Diana's mother, died of cancer in the summer of 1937, when Diana was five years old. Until Hopkins remarried in July 1942, he and Diana lived off and on in the White House, where ER supervised Diana's activities. Robert Sherwood, *Roosevelt and Hopkins* 106–107 (New York: Harper & Brothers, 1948).

FDR sought to deter Hitler without tipping his hand. Nevertheless, his air-power program encountered turbulence shortly after takeoff. One of Roosevelt's goals was to lay the groundwork for a rapid expansion of aircraft production should an emergency arise. Another was to provide planes immediately for Britain and France. Because those nations were at peace, the restrictions of the Neutrality Act did not apply. But Secretary of War Woodring and the Army general staff opposed the sale of weapons abroad. Woodring, an ardent isolationist, was against American overseas involvement in any context. The Army staff resisted because they wanted the material to equip American forces. Roosevelt bypassed the opposition by assigning responsibility for foreign arms sales to Morgenthau and the Treasury. Just as the State Department had been shut out of FDR's decision to recognize the Soviet Union, the War Department was overridden in order to provide planes for America's potential allies. In both instances Roosevelt called the shots, and the details were closely guarded.[64]

The president's cover was blown in January 1939, when an experimental Douglas A-20 bomber crashed in California with a French purchasing agent aboard. Asked about it at his press conference on January 27, Roosevelt dissembled. The plane was not really an American military plane, he said, but a private model that Douglas was trying to peddle. French purchases would provide a shot in the arm for the aircraft industry, and the Treasury was involved because it wished to promote American exports.[65]

When the firestorm did not abate, Roosevelt invited the members of the Senate Military Affairs Committee to the White House. "I cannot overemphasize the seriousness of the situation," he told the senators. All of Europe was threatened. If England and France went down, the other countries "would drop into the basket of their own accord." Africa and South America would follow. The United States would be encircled. "This is not a pipe dream. Would any of you have said six years ago, when this man Hitler came into the control of the German Government, Germany busted, Germany a complete and utter failure, a nation that owed everybody, disorganized, not worth considering as a force in the world, would any of you have said that in six years Germany would dominate Europe, completely and absolutely?"[66]

Roosevelt told the senators it didn't matter whether Treasury or the War Department authorized the bomber sale. "I am frankly hoping that the French will be able to get the fastest pursuit planes we can turn out. I hope they will get the best heavy and medium bombers they can buy in this country. And I hope to God they get the planes and get them fast. . . . That is the foreign policy of the United States."[67]

Gallup Polls taken at the time indicated that 65 percent of the respondents supported the sale of warplanes to Britain and France, while 44 percent favored legislation prohibiting such sales to Germany. In the event of war in Europe, 69 percent advocated providing the Allies all the aid possible short of entering the conflict. When Gallup asked whether the United States would be next on Hitler's list, 62 percent answered yes; 38 percent said no.[68]

With every month the possibility of war heightened. On March 15, 1939, Hitler annexed the remainder of Czechoslovakia, not only breaking the pledge he had made at Munich but negating the principle of self-determination. The Czechs and Slovaks, unlike the residents of the Sudetenland, were not German. The rationale—*Ein Volk, ein Reich, ein Führer*—regardless of how self-serving it had been, did not apply. When German troops marched into Prague, Hitler destroyed the last remaining illusion that his ambitions were limited. One week later, on March 23, the government of Lithuania surrendered the port city of Memel to Germany. Hitler arrived on the battleship *Deutschland* to preside at the takeover. Within the month, Mussolini occupied Albania, General Francisco Franco captured Madrid, and Japan claimed sovereignty over the Spratly Islands, seven hundred miles southwest of Manila.

Roosevelt moved to meet the crisis on two fronts: revision of the Neutrality Act to permit the sale of war materiel to Britain and France in case of war and a long overdue change of command in the Army. General Malin Craig, whose four-year term as chief of staff was about to expire, had served the administration faithfully but was eager to retire, a spent force worn down by incessant feuding between Woodring and Johnson.[69] To replace Craig, FDR turned to Brigadier General George C. Marshall, thirty-fourth on the Army seniority list, former chief of war plans at the War Department and Craig's deputy since October.* Marshall, who had attended Virginia Military Institute, not West Point,

---

* Though Marshall ranked thirty-fourth, the rule that no one be appointed chief of staff who could not complete the four-year term before reaching the mandatory retirement age of sixty-five ruled out all but four general officers senior to Marshall. Of those, the odds-on favorite of military prognosticators was Major General Hugh A. Drum, commander of the First Army at Governors Island and the senior officer on active duty.

was a meticulously organized, self-controlled, no-nonsense soldier with a well-established reputation for generously rewarding success and ruthlessly punishing failure—exactly the leader the Army needed on the threshold of war. Frosty to the point of incivility in personal relations (only Mrs. Marshall called him "George"—and there were some who doubted that even she did), Marshall enjoyed the support of both Harry Hopkins and General Pershing, the nation's hero from World War I. Of the two, Marshall believed that Hopkins had the greater influence in his selection.[70] He assumed office on July 1, 1939.

Roosevelt fared less well in his effort to repeal the Neutrality Act. The administration bill, introduced by Congressman Sol Bloom of New York, chairman of the Foreign Affairs Committee, passed the House 200–188, but with a crippling isolationist amendment that would continue the embargo on "arms and ammunition" while permitting the sale of airplanes and other war materiel.[71] In the Senate, the Foreign Relations Committee, despite frantic ad ministration efforts, voted 12–11 to delay consideration of the House bill until the next session of Congress, which would not convene until January 1940. Purge survivors Walter F. George of Georgia and Guy Gillette of Iowa, who normally would have supported repeal, George especially, voted against the president.

The highlight of the Washington summer was the visit of King George VI and Queen Elizabeth. In September 1938, at the height of the Munich crisis, FDR invited the King to Washington as a goodwill gesture to cement Anglo-American relations. "You would, of course, stay with us at the White House. You and I are fully aware of the demands of the Protocol people, but, having had much experience with them, I am inclined to think you and Her Majesty should do very much as you personally want to do—and I will see to it that your decision becomes the right decision."[72]

The King and Queen arrived in the United States June 7, 1939. After a ceremonial reception in Washington,* the Roosevelts and Windsors adjourned for

---

* As a child of seven I was privileged to watch from the window of my mother's eighth-floor office in the Farm Credit Administration the parade escorting President Roosevelt and the King from Union Station to the White House. The crowd lining the parade route, estimated at 750,000, was the largest ever assembled in Washington. Will Swift, *The Roosevelts and the Royals: Franklin and Eleanor, The King and Queen of England, and the Friendship That Changed History* 113–114 (Hoboken, N.J.: John Wiley & Sons, 2004).

a summer weekend at Hyde Park. FDR, who personally planned every detail of the trip, treated the King as a fellow head of state: no bowing, no curtsies to the Queen, hot dogs on the lawn at Top Cottage, informal dinner at Springwood. Sara had urged Franklin to dispense with the usual cocktail hour. "My mother says we should have tea," Roosevelt told the King. "My mother would have said the same thing," His Majesty replied—at which point FDR reached for the martini shaker. After dinner the King and the president talked privately well into the night. About one-thirty FDR placed a fatherly hand on the King's knee. "Young man, it's time for you to go to bed." Not only had Roosevelt covered the gamut of world affairs, but his combination of charm, respect, and paternal guidance won George's admiration. "Why don't my Ministers talk to me as the President did tonight?" he asked Canadian prime minister Mackenzie King before retiring. "I feel exactly as though a father were giving me his most careful and wise advice."[73]

The King's visit provided a momentary distraction from the deteriorating situation in Europe. After incorporating the Baltic port of Memel into East Prussia, Hitler turned his attention to Danzig and the Polish Corridor. The Treaty of Versailles, in the process of creating an independent Poland, had not only stripped a large slice of Silesia from Germany but granted landlocked Poland access to the sea by establishing a corridor along the Vistula River terminating in the port city of Danzig. Danzig, one of the four principal cities of the Hanseatic League and demonstrably German since the Middle Ages, was made a Free City tied economically to Poland. Even more onerous, the Vistula corridor split East Prussia from the rest of Germany. Hitler demanded the immediate return of Danzig and an extraterritorial road and rail link across the Corridor. Paradoxically, these demands were among the least unreasonable Hitler had made. When Poland refused, war became inevitable.

On August 23, 1939, Hitler achieved his final diplomatic triumph—a surprise Nonaggression Pact with the Soviet Union. A secret protocol provided for the partition of Poland and the liquidation of the Baltic states of Finland, Estonia, Latvia, and Lithuania.[74] At first light on the morning of September 1, forty-two German divisions, including ten armored divisions, stormed across the Polish frontier.[75] Roosevelt was awakened at 2:50 A.M. Washington time by a phone call from Ambassador Bullitt in Paris relaying a message from Anthony Drexel Biddle in Warsaw that war had begun. "Well, Bill, it has come at last," said the president. "God help us all."[76]

TWENTY

STAB IN THE BACK

On this tenth day of June, 1940,
the hand that held the dagger has struck it
into the back of its neighbor.
—FRANKLIN D. ROOSEVELT, JUNE 10, 1940

WITH GERMAN ARMOR slicing through Poland's defenses, Roosevelt met the press in the Oval Office shortly before noon on September 1. "Can we stay out of this?" he was asked. "I not only sincerely hope so," FDR replied, "but I believe we can and every effort will be made by this Administration so to do."[1] Later Roosevelt told the cabinet that his World War I experience was eerily familiar. The president said he felt he was picking up an interrupted routine. "Unless some miracle beyond our present grasp changes the hearts of men the days ahead will be crowded days—crowded with the same problems, the same anxieties that filled to the brim those September days of 1914. For history does in fact repeat."[2]

In London, Chamberlain spoke feebly to Parliament, a waffling, self-pitying address that gave no indication Britain intended to stand by its commitment to the Poles. When Arthur Greenwood, the acting leader of the Labour opposition, rose to reply, Leo Amery, one of many prominent Conservatives appalled at Chamberlain's limp response, shouted, "Speak for England, Arthur." The House erupted with a mighty cheer, and Greenwood gave a brief, stirring speech that reflected the mood of the country: "I wonder how long we are prepared to vacillate . . . when Britain, and all Britain stands for, and human civilization are in peril."[3] A thunderous, prolonged ovation greeted Greenwood's remarks. As one member noted, "A puff would have brought the Government down."[4] With Parliament in revolt the cabinet recovered its lost courage. At 8 A.M. Sunday, September 3, the British government informed Berlin that unless it received assurances within three hours that Germany would begin an immediate withdrawal of its forces from Poland, Great Britain would declare war. At 11:15, with no response, a dispirited Chamberlain informed a radio audience and later Parliament, "This country is now at war." Five hours later France followed suit.*

Roosevelt addressed the nation Sunday night in a fireside chat. "This nation will remain a neutral nation," said the president, "but I cannot ask that every American remain neutral in thought as well. Even a neutral has a right to take account of facts. Even a neutral cannot be asked to close his mind or his conscience."[5]

FDR's first order of business was repeal of the Neutrality Act. So long as the act remained on the books, the United States was precluded from providing aid to any of the belligerents, even if they paid cash on the barrelhead. Congress had adjourned for its annual recess, and the members were spread across the country. On Wednesday, September 13, after touching base with the leadership of the House and Senate, Roosevelt summoned the legislators into special session the following Thursday.[6] "My own personal opinion," he wrote Judge Walton Moore, counselor of the State Department, "is that we can get the votes in the House and Senate but that the principal difficulty will be to prevent a filibuster in the latter."[7]

Isolationist opposition mobilized quickly. The following evening Senator William E. Borah of Idaho, the ranking Republican on the Foreign Relations Committee and the Senate's longest-serving member, delivered a blistering attack over a national radio hookup. European wars, said the aged Borah, were "wars brought on through the unconscionable schemes of remorseless rulers." If the United States sold European countries arms, "we would be taking sides, and that would be the first step to active intervention."[8] Borah's speech resonated strongly among those determined to keep the United States out of war.

Roosevelt recruited the Republican leadership to respond. Alf Landon, Frank Knox, and Henry L. Stimson waded into the fray to support immediate

---

* As a sop to the increasingly bellicose Tory rank and file, Chamberlain recalled Winston Churchill from the political wilderness to reassume his World War I responsibilities as first lord of the Admiralty. "Churchill in the Cabinet," exclaimed Reichsmarshal Hermann Göring. "That means the war is really on." Albert Speer, *Inside the Third Reich* 165 (New York: Macmillan, 1970).

repeal. The academic establishment joined the fight. President Nicholas Murray Butler of Columbia, James B. Conant of Harvard, and Karl Compton of MIT, together with the presidents of Princeton and Yale, mobilized the nation's educators to support repeal. The Kansas editor William Allen White organized a wide array of notables through the Non-Partisan Committee for Peace Through Revision of the Neutrality Act.*

The battle escalated on September 15, when Charles A. Lindbergh, one of the country's sentimental heroes, addressed a national audience at least as large as that which had listened to FDR's fireside chat twelve days before. "This is not a question of banding together to defend the white race against foreign invasion. This is simply one of those age-old struggles within our own family of nations—a quarrel arising from the errors of the last war—from the failure of the victors to follow a consistent policy either of fairness or force."[9] Lindbergh, who had received Germany's second highest decoration from Hermann Göring shortly after Munich,† tapped into a vast reservoir of antiwar sentiment. Midwestern progressives, old-line socialists and Communists, Christian pacifists, cryptofascists such as Father Coughlin, and the German-American Bund launched an avalanche of letters, postcards, and telegrams to representatives and senators demanding retention of the arms embargo. Legislators previously disposed in favor of repeal began to waiver. One Republican congressman reported receiving 1,800 messages after Lindbergh's speech, only 76 of which supported repeal.[10]

When FDR met with the congressional leadership on September 20, the day before Congress would convene, it was clear that outright repeal of the Neutrality Act was beyond reach. "The trouble is," said Senate Republican leader Charles McNary of Oregon, "if we repealed the whole Neutrality Act people

---

* The committee's leadership included Henry R. Luce, the publisher of *Time, Life,* and *Fortune;* New York mayor Fiorello La Guardia; the investment bankers Thomas Lamont and Henry I. Harriman; Thomas Watson of IBM; the department store tycoon Marshall Field; the Protestant theologian Reinhold Niebuhr; the film actors Helen Hayes and Melvyn Douglas; the cultural historian Lewis Mumford; and the rising Democratic politicians J. William Fulbright and Adlai E. Stevenson.

† At a dinner in his honor at the U.S. Embassy in Berlin on October 19, 1938, Lindbergh was presented with the Service Cross of the German Eagle with Star "by order of the Führer." Kenneth S. Davis, *The Hero: Charles A. Lindbergh and the American Dream* 380–382 (New York: Doubleday, 1959).

would think we were repealing our neutrality."[11] Roosevelt reached a bipartisan compromise: repeal the arms embargo, but put the sale of weapons on a "cash-and-carry" basis. No sales on credit; no U.S. funding; no bank loans; no American transport.

To emphasize the urgency of repeal, FDR chose to address Congress directly. Roosevelt always delivered his annual message in person, but not since Warren Harding in 1923 had a president spoken to Congress during the session.[12] Recognizing the bad blood that had accumulated during the past two years, the president was at his conciliatory best. "These perilous days demand cooperation among us without a trace of partisanship. Our acts must be guided by one single hard-headed thought—keeping America out of war." To avoid offending Anglophobic midwesterners and Irish Catholics, Roosevelt downplayed aid to Britain and France while emphasizing that repeal of the embargo would aid the cause of peace. The "cash-and-carry" requirement would avoid economic entanglement and keep American vessels out of the war zone.

"In a period when it is sometimes said that free discussion is no longer compatible with national safety, may you by your deeds show the world that we of the United States are one people, of one mind, one spirit, one clear resolution, walking before God in the light of the living."[13]

Public approval was overwhelming. The White House mail room was inundated with messages of support. Even Senator Borah thought it was a good speech and said privately that he favored "cash and carry."[14] A Gallup poll immediately following the president's speech indicated that 60 percent of Americans now supported repeal and 84 percent favored an Allied victory.[15] On September 28 the Senate Foreign Relations Committee voted 16–7 to send the bill to the floor. This time Senators George and Gillette voted with the president.[16]

On the same day the Foreign Relations Committee reported the "cash-and-carry" bill, the beleaguered Polish garrison in Warsaw capitulated. Organized resistance ended. The Soviet Union, pursuant to the deal Stalin had struck with Hitler, intervened on September 17, and from that point on Poland's fate was sealed. Germany and the USSR proclaimed a Boundary and Friendship Treaty defining Poland's division. The Soviets acquired nearly half of Poland's territory and one third its population. Germany gained the remainder. Like Austria and Czechoslovakia, Poland disappeared from the map of Europe. The

Poles had fought bravely; their losses in battle totaled 70,000 killed, 133,000 wounded, and 700,000 captured. The Nazi war machine did not go unscathed, however; the final figures from Berlin listed 10,572 killed, 30,322 wounded, and 3,400 missing. The first great battle of World War II had ended in total defeat for the Allied powers.

With Poland's collapse the momentum to repeal the arms embargo accelerated. Isolationist stalwarts Styles Bridges of New Hampshire and Robert Taft of Ohio endorsed "cash and carry." On October 5, Henry L. Stimson put the fox among the chickens when he departed from White House strategy and bluntly warned the country that "Britain and France are now fighting a battle which, in the event of their losing, will become our battle." Hull had tried to get Stimson to delete the reference to Britain and France, but Stimson, characteristically, refused. To the administration's surprise, Stimson's speech was well received—so well that tens of thousands of copies were printed for national distribution.[17] Bishop Bernard Sheil of Chicago delivered a powerful radio address supporting repeal, as did Al Smith, both designed to overcome Irish Catholic opposition. Senator Millard Tydings of Maryland, back in the fold, told his colleagues, "Civilization demands that we give all the aid we can to a nation attacked, and not run like cowards until our turn comes."[18]

Roosevelt kept a low profile. These were tense times for the president. "I am almost literally walking on eggs" he wrote Canada's Lord Tweedsmuir.[19] For relaxation the president turned to poker, usually on Saturday evenings. Ickes, Robert Jackson, Pa Watson, Admiral Ross McIntire, FDR's doctor, and Steve Early usually filled the places at the table. "We played until half past twelve," Ickes reported after one such session. "We broke up because the President was tired, having had his sleep interrupted for two or three nights by flash news from Europe." Roosevelt enjoyed wild-card games, especially "Woolworth's," a seven-card hand with fives and tens wild. "We were playing dollar limit," said Ickes. "I won $53.50. The President was the heaviest loser. The game cost him about $35. One thing about playing with the President, we do not have to curry favor by letting him win."[20]

At least once a month, more often if possible, Roosevelt took a cruise to nowhere on the presidential yacht *Potomac*. Downriver, sometimes as far as Point Lookout, the president lolled about and slept late. Missy, Pa Watson, Doc McIntire, and, when he was up to it, Harry Hopkins usually accompanied him. At the White House, FDR averaged fifteen appointments a day, dictated two dozen or so letters to Missy and Grace Tully, and continued to meet the press twice a week. Briefings from the State Department and the military consumed more and more time, cables and state papers streamed across his desk, and there was always the weekly cabinet meeting. He swam less often now, perhaps three times a week, and his blood pressure had climbed to 179/102, which Dr. McIntire dismissed as normal for a man of fifty-eight.[21]

Lindbergh spoke again on October 13, but the wind was gone from his sails. His overtly racist remarks fell flat. "Our bond with Europe is a bond of race and not political ideology. . . . Racial strength is vital—politics a luxury. If the white race is ever seriously threatened, it may then be time for us to take our part for its protection, to fight side by side with the English, French, and Germans. But not with one against the other for our mutual destruction."[22]*

On the eve of the Senate vote, Roosevelt broke his self-imposed public silence to dispel whatever popular fears remained. Speaking to the *Herald Tribune* Forum on October 26, FDR lambasted those "orators and commentators beating their breasts and proclaiming against sending the boys of American mothers to fight on battlefields of Europe." That was "one of the worst fakes in current history," said Roosevelt. "The simple truth is that no person in any responsible place . . . has ever suggested the remotest possibility of sending the boys of American mothers to fight on the battlefields of Europe. That is why I label that argument a shameless and dishonest fake."[23]

Roosevelt worked both sides of the street. He held out repeal of the arms embargo as a step toward peace, while the purpose of the repeal was to aid the Allies. The implicit logic was that by helping Britain and France defeat Hitler, the United States would not have to fight.

The following day, after four weeks of debate, the Senate voted to repeal the arms embargo, 63–30. Southern Democrats supported the president down the line. Eight of twenty-three Republicans voted for repeal. Except for Independent George Norris of Nebraska, western progressives and populists voted

---

* Lindbergh expanded on his views a few days later in an article in the November *Reader's Digest*. "It is time to turn from our quarrels and to build our White ramparts again. . . . Our civilization depends on a united strength among ourselves; . . . on a Western Wall or race and arms which can hold back either a Genghis Khan or the infiltration of inferior blood." Charles A. Lindbergh, "Aviation, Geography, and Race," *Reader's Digest* 64–67 (1939).

against. On November 2, 1939, the House fell in line, 243–181. The voting pattern was similar: southerners supporting FDR, progressives against.

With Europe at war all eyes turned to Roosevelt. Was a third term in the offing? The president kept his own counsel. He did nothing to indicate that he was a candidate, but, more significantly, he did nothing to suggest he was not. Garner, who worked closely with the White House to secure passage of the "cash and carry" bill, believed Roosevelt would run. "He didn't talk like a man who was coming to the end of his term. He didn't say that war was inevitable, but he gave the impression that if there was one he intended to run it."[24]

The idea of a third term was a political bugbear. No presidential incumbent had ever sought one. Roosevelt sometimes joked about the possibility, but never in such a way that would tip his hand. "The country is sick and tired of Roosevelts," he told Ed Flynn, recalling what "Uncle Ted" had said when third-term speculation arose: "They are sick of looking at my grin, and they are sick of hearing what Alice had for breakfast."[25]

As speculation increased, FDR encouraged and exploited it. He relished the backdrop at the annual Gridiron Dinner of Washington journalists in December 1939—a giant sphinx with Roosevelt's face complete with pince-nez and the cigarette holder at a jaunty angle. The chances are that FDR had not made up his mind. The fieldstone library at Hyde Park he had designed to house his papers and memorabilia—the nation's first presidential library—was nearing completion, as was his hilltop dreamhouse above Val-Kill. The three-bedroom cottage was built to FDR's specifications, with extra-wide doors and no thresholds so that his wheelchair could roll easily, and he and Missy had gradually furnished it to his liking. "It's perfect, just perfect," he would often say.[26]

There was also the question of his health. Roosevelt was fifty-eight, but twelve years in Albany and Washington had taken their toll. "No, Dan, I just can't do it," he told Teamster president Daniel Tobin just after Christmas. "I am tired. I really am. I can't be president again. I have to get over this sinus. I have to have a rest. I want to go home to Hyde Park. I want to take care of my trees. I want to make the farm pay. I want to write history. No, I just can't do it."[27]

In January 1940 Roosevelt signed a contract with *Collier's* magazine to become a contributing editor at $75,000, a year commencing after he left office in 1941. *Collier's* had offered substantially more, but FDR considered it inappropriate to earn a greater salary as editor than he had as president of the

United States. The contract ran for three years, several editorial assistants were provided, and Roosevelt would write twenty-six articles annually.[28] His mind was apparently made up. "I definitely know what I want to do," he told Henry Morgenthau. "I do not want to run unless between now and the [Democratic] convention things get very, very much worse in Europe."[29]

When the elderly George Norris visited the White House in February to urge FDR to run for a third term, he said much the same thing: "George, I am chained to this chair from morning till night. People come in here day after day, most of them trying to get something from me, most of them things I can't give them, and wouldn't if I could. You sit in your chair in your office too, but if something goes wrong or you get irritated or tired, you can get up and walk around, or you can go into another room. But I can't. I am tied down to this chair day after day, week after week, month after month. And I can't stand it any longer. I can't go on with it."[30]

William Bullitt, paying a quick visit to Washington from his post in Paris, reports having dinner at the White House with FDR and Missy in late February. Roosevelt collapsed and fell unconscious at the table. Admiral McIntire was summoned and after examining the president said he had suffered a "very slight heart attack." FDR was put to bed, and nothing further was said. McIntire evidently thought it was nothing out of the ordinary.[31]

Meanwhile, anxious contenders edged toward the starting gate. On December 18, 1939, Vice President Garner announced his candidacy. "I see that the vice president has thrown his bottle—I mean his hat—into the ring," Roosevelt quipped at cabinet.[32] Garner's candidacy was a protest against the New Deal, FDR, and a third term rolled into one. He had little chance. John L. Lewis's classic put-down of the vice president as a "labor-baiting, poker-playing, whiskey-drinking, evil old man" rang true among too many of the party's rank and file.*

James Farley also eyed the office. An energetic fifty-one, Farley was immensely popular with the party's professional politicians. But his Catholicism

---

* Lewis's remarks were made in testimony before the House Labor Committee in July 1939. "Yes, I made a personal attack on Mr. Garner," said Lewis, "because Garner's knife is searching for the quivering, pulsating heart of labor." When the Texas congressional delegation prepared a rebuttal denying that Garner did any of the things Lewis charged, one member refused to sign: the second-term congressman from Texas's tenth district, Lyndon Baines Johnson. *The New York Times,* July 28, 1939.

was a handicap, and his lack of familiarity with policy issues was dumbfounding. Ignorance of economics and foreign affairs has never been a bar to high office, but in 1940 the nation required more than Farley could offer. Chicago's Cardinal Mundelein, the Democratic party's unofficial prelate, attempted to talk Farley out of running, but to no avail. "I will not let myself be kicked around by Roosevelt or anyone else," said Farley.[33]

Cordell Hull played his cards closer to his chest. He was betting that Roosevelt would not run and that he would be the natural fallback. FDR encouraged Hull to believe as much. At a cabinet dinner in early 1940, Mrs. Hull sat next to the president and told him her husband did not like to make speeches. "Well, tell him he had better get used to it," Roosevelt replied. "He'll have a lot of it to do soon."[34] Hull considered it incompatible with his position as secretary of state to campaign for the nomination. Knowing that Roosevelt's support was all he needed, he chose to wait.[35] "I believe the world is going straight to hell," he told FDR, "and I think I can be of greater service in the State Department."[36]

Other potentials faded early. Harry Hopkins, with whom the president felt most comfortable, was literally at death's door, hospitalized first at the Mayo Clinic, then at the Naval Hospital in Washington, with an as-yet-undiagnosed digestive ailment. Paul V. McNutt, the former governor of Indiana, whom Roosevelt appointed to head the newly established Federal Security Agency, was new to the ways of Washington and mistook the president's hearty welcome for political support. Henry Wallace, Securities and Exchange Commission head William O. Douglas, and Attorney General Robert H. Jackson all had the presidential urge, but with little professional support their candidacies failed to materialize.

In Europe, meanwhile, the military situation was shrouded in fog. After Poland's defeat, both sides settled into a period of watchful waiting. Troops deployed with theatrical precision, but no shots were fired. The Germans, taking advantage of their recent battlefield experience, honed their maneuver tactics and air-to-ground coordination. The French, whose tactical doctrine traced to World War I, assiduously dug fortifications. The British, equally confident that the home-front hardships induced by the Allied economic blockade would bring Germany to its senses, dithered and did little. "The accumulation of evidence that an attack is imminent is formidable," Chamberlain wrote his sister, "and yet I cannot conceive myself that it is coming." On April 5, 1940, the prime minister gloated to the National Conservative Union meeting in London, "Hitler has missed the bus"—a gaffe second only to his "Peace in our time" proclamation after Munich.[37]

In Berlin, witty Germans who looked west spoke of Sitzkrieg. The French called it *le drôle de guerre*. Ironically, it was Senator Borah who baptized the situation with a name when in December 1939 he spoke of the "phony war" on the western front. If the stalemate in Europe had continued, FDR would likely have retired. "I think my husband was torn," said Eleanor years later. "He would often talk about the reasons against a third term, but there was a great sense of responsibility for what was happening."[38]

FDR did not ask Eleanor's advice, nor did she offer it. "I never questioned Franklin about his political intentions. The fact that I myself never wanted him to be in Washington made me doubly careful not to intimate that I had the slightest preference."[39]

The calm in Europe was shattered on April 9, 1940, at precisely 4:20 A.M., an hour before dawn, when German troops moved unopposed across Schleswig-Holstein's unfortified border with Denmark. Simultaneously, combat-ready Nazi landing parties went ashore all along the Norwegian coast from Oslo to Narvik. The British and French were caught flat-footed. Danish independence was snuffed out by the time most Danes finished breakfast. Norway resisted for two weeks. In strategic terms the occupation of Denmark gave Germany a stranglehold on the Baltic. The audacious defeat of Norway provided Hitler a valuable psychological victory. But the long-term military impact was questionable. Norway's ports proved less useful than the Kriegsmarine had anticipated; iron ore from Lorraine later diminished the importance of Swedish sources, and for the remainder of the war the occupation of Norway consumed vast numbers of German soldiers who could have been better deployed elsewhere.[40]

Norway's defeat became Chamberlain's. On May 10, rather than face the inevitable vote of no confidence in the House, Chamberlain resigned.* He was

* Parliament's great debate on war policy took place May 7–8, 1940. Leo Amery from the Tory backbench launched the missile that brought Chamberlain down, quoting Cromwell's injunction to the Long Parliament, "You have sat too long here for any good you have been doing. Depart, I say, and let us have done with you. In the name of God, go." On the second

succeeded by Winston Churchill. "I felt as if I were walking with Destiny and that all my past life had been but a preparation for this hour and for this trial," wrote Churchill.[41] Roosevelt was less sanguine. "I suppose Churchill was the best man England had," he told his cabinet, "even if he was drunk half of his time."[42]

That same day, German forces stormed across the Belgian and Dutch frontiers. In the north, Field Marshal Fedor von Bock's Army Group B smashed through Holland's defenses, paratroopers seized bridges, and motorized infantry followed on, while the Luftwaffe paralyzed Dutch resistance. The main German thrust was mounted by von Rundstedt's Army Group A in the Ardennes. Rundstedt would repeat the maneuver in December 1944 at the Battle of the Bulge. In 1940 the Ardennes forest was the pivot between the Maginot Line to the south and the bulk of the French Army strung out along the Belgian border; in 1944 it was the hinge between Field Marshal Bernard Law Montgomery's British and Canadian force in the north and General Omar Bradley's American army group in the south. Because of the hilly, heavily wooded terrain, the Allies deemed it impenetrable to enemy armor and it was lightly held. Three German panzer corps, some two thousand tanks, slashed through in five days, opened a fifty-mile gap in the French lines, and were streaking toward the English Channel. At seven-thirty in the morning of May 15, French premier Paul Reynaud telephoned Churchill with the bad news. Speaking in English, Reynaud said, "We are defeated. We have lost the battle."[43]

Later that day, Churchill cabled Roosevelt, his first message to the president since becoming prime minister: "The scene has darkened swiftly. The small countries are simply smashed up, one by one, like matchwood. We expect to be attacked ourselves in the near future. If necessary, we shall continue the war

---

day of the debate Lloyd George gave the last great speech of his career, in the course of which he defended Churchill who as first lord of the Admiralty had taken responsibility for Norway's fall: "The right honorable gentleman must not allow himself to be converted into an air raid shelter to keep the splinters from hitting his colleagues." When the House divided on the evening of May 8, forty-one dissident Conservatives voted with the Labour opposition and sixty more abstained. Chamberlain recognized the inevitable and submitted his resignation. Roy Jenkins, *Churchill: A Biography* 576–588 (New York: Farrar, Straus and Giroux, 2001).

alone. . . . But I trust you realize, Mr. President, that the voice and force of the United States may count for nothing if they are withheld too long."

Churchill proceeded to ask Roosevelt for immediate assistance: "forty or fifty of your older destroyers," several hundred late-model aircraft, antiaircraft weapons, and ammunition, plus steel and other raw materials.[44] The following day FDR made a dramatic appearance before a joint session of Congress to ask for a supplemental defense appropriation of $1.2 billion. The proposal had been in the works for some time, but the news from France gave it increased urgency. Roosevelt's face was drawn, his knuckles white as he gripped the lectern. His voice was resolute. "The brutal force of modern offensive war has been loosed in all its horror. No old defense is so strong that it requires no further strengthening and no attack is so unlikely that it may be ignored."

The United States was currently producing 6,000 airplanes a year. Roosevelt asked for 50,000. He requested funds for modernizing the Army and Navy, as well as to increase production facilities for everything that was needed. Recognizing the power of the America First lobby, he also asked Congress to take no action that would hamper delivery of U.S. planes to the Allies.[45] At the end of the month, with the war in France going badly, Roosevelt asked for another $1.9 billion.[46] By May 1941, one year later, Congress had appropriated a total of $37.3 billion for defense—a figure roughly four times the entire federal budget in 1939.[47]

The day after receiving Churchill's request, Roosevelt responded. Airplanes, antiaircraft weapons, ammunition, and steel, said the president, would be provided. But the destroyers were unavailable. "As you know a step of that kind could not be taken except with the specific authorization of Congress and I am not certain that it would be wise for that suggestion to be made to the Congress at this moment."[48]

Churchill was sympathetic. "We are determined to persevere to the very end whatever the result of the great battle in France may be. But if American assistance is to play any part it must be available."[49]

As events unfolded in Europe, the nation's Democratic primaries passed almost unnoticed. Oregon voters went to the polls on May 17 and voted 9 to 1 for Roosevelt over Garner. In Nebraska, Pennsylvania, and New Jersey, Roosevelt slates were unopposed. In Wisconsin, FDR took twenty-one delegates to Garner's three. In Illinois he swept all fifty-eight. In California, which Garner carried in 1932, Roosevelt won all but one delegate. Even Texas chose a pro-

Roosevelt delegation.[50] FDR made no public reference to the primaries and did not campaign, but he did not prevent supporters from filing slates on his behalf.*

In France the war proceeded with the inevitability of a Greek tragedy. On May 20 German armor reached the Channel coast at Abbeville, slicing France in two. On the twenty-second the panzers wheeled north pinning the French First Army, the 350,000 men of the British Expeditionary Force, and the Belgian Army against the sea. The Belgians surrendered on May 28, and the bulk of the BEF, together with some 100,000 French troops, were evacuated from Dunkirk between May 29 and June 2.[51] Left behind was the equipment of the British Army, including all of its artillery, small arms, 7,000 tons of ammunition, and 120,000 vehicles. "Never has a nation been so naked before her foes," wrote Churchill.[52]

The British losses at Dunkirk created an even greater need for American assistance, but Churchill's request for weapons had been pigeonholed by the War Department. Secretary Woodring opposed providing anything, General Hap Arnold stressed the prior needs of the Army Air Corps, and the general staff worried about hemispheric defense. General Marshall cut through the resistance. Recognizing that the president wanted to provide everything possible, Marshall ordered Army supply depots inventoried, redefined American requirements, and declared surplus more or less what the British needed. Working closely with Treasury secretary Morgenthau, Marshall arranged for the equipment to be sold directly to two U.S. corporations, Curtiss-Wright and United States Steel, which resold it to the British at cost. Solicitor General Francis Biddle sprinkled legal holy water over the transaction, and by June 5 some 22,000 .30-caliber machine guns, 25,000 Browning automatic rifles, 900 75 mm howitzers, 58,000 antiaircraft weapons, 500,000 Enfield rifles left over from World War I, and 130 million rounds of ammunition were on their way to Britain. "I am delighted to have that list of surplus material which is 'ready to roll,' " Roosevelt wrote Morgenthau. "Give it an extra push every morning

---

* Illinois primary law required a sworn statement from a potential candidate that he was indeed seeking the office before his name could be placed on the ballot. Garner complied, but Roosevelt was at sea on the USS *Houston* when the deadline expired. Illinois election officials nonetheless placed his name on the ballot. Bascom N. Timmons, *Garner of Texas* 269–270 (New York: Harper & Brothers, 1948).

and every night until it is on board ship."[53] Except for tanks, which were in short supply, the British Army was substantially rearmed within six weeks after returning from Dunkirk.*

In France, the military situation turned hopeless. The French had lost thirty of their best divisions, the Belgians and Dutch were out of the war, and the BEF had been evacuated. On June 5 the Germans turned south. Panzers crashed through the French line on the Somme, the defense collapsed in confusion, and the Germans crossed the Seine virtually unopposed four days later. Paris was declared an open city, the government fled first to Tours and then to Bordeaux, and General Maxime Weygand, the French commander in chief, urged Reynaud to ask for an armistice. "I am obliged to say that a cessation of hostilities is compulsory."[54]

On Monday, June 10, Roosevelt headed for Charlottesville, Virginia. FDR, Jr., was graduating from law school, and the president had been invited to give the commencement address. As Roosevelt boarded the train, he received word that Italy had declared war on France, launching thirty-two divisions against the lightly held Alpine passes and the Côte d'Azur. Whatever doubts FDR held about his future course vanished with Mussolini's attack. That night, disregarding State Department objections, he went full out. In a voice dripping with scorn, the president told the university's graduands, "On this tenth day of June, 1940, the hand that held the dagger has struck it into the back of its neighbor."

To believe that the United States could exist as "a lone island in a world dominated by the philosophy of force," said Roosevelt, was "an obvious delusion." America's duty was clear: "We will extend to the opponents of force the material resources of this nation; and at the same time, we will harness and speed up the use of those resources in order that we ourselves may have equip-

---

* "When the ships from America approached our shores with their priceless arms," wrote Churchill, "special trains were waiting in all the ports to receive their cargo. The Home Guard in every county, in every town, in every village, sat up all through the nights to receive them. By the end of July we were an armed nation. . . .

"All of this reads easily now, but at that time it was a supreme act of faith and leadership for the United States to deprive themselves of this very considerable mass of arms for the sake of a country which many deemed already beaten." Winston S. Churchill, *Their Finest Hour* 143, 272 (Boston: Houghton Mifflin, 1949).

ment and training equal to the task. Signs and signals call for speed—full speed ahead."[55]

Roosevelt's "stab-in-the-back" speech marked the decisive turning point in American policy. Though polls indicated that only 30 percent of the nation believed an Allied victory possible, FDR unequivocally placed himself shoulder to shoulder with Britain and France.[56] Listening to the president on the radio, Churchill could scarcely contain his enthusiasm. "We all listened to you last night and were fortified by the grand scope of your declaration. Your statement that the material aid of the United States will be given to the Allies in their struggle is a strong encouragement in a dark but not unhopeful hour. Everything must be done to keep France in the fight. The hope with which you inspired them may give them the strength to persevere. . . . I send you my heartfelt thanks and those of my colleagues for all you are doing and seeking to do for what we may now indeed call a common cause."[57]

Despite Churchill's hopes, the weight of the Nazi offensive proved too much for the embattled Third Republic. On June 14 the Germans entered Paris. On the sixteenth Reynaud resigned and was succeeded by Marshal Henri-Philippe Pétain, the aged hero of World War I's Battle of Verdun. Two hours later Pétain sued for peace. On Saturday, June 22, in the Forest of Compiègne, in the very same railway car in which the 1918 armistice had been signed, Hitler personally presided over France's surrender.

When Roosevelt returned from Charlottesville, he reorganized his cabinet for action. Charles Edison was eased out as secretary of the Navy, and Harry Woodring was dumped from the War Department. FDR prevailed upon the New Jersey Democratic organization to nominate Edison for governor (he won the post in November); Woodring, who continued to drag his feet on rearming the British, was cut adrift.[58]

On June 19, 1940, less than a week before the Republican nominating convention in Philadelphia, Roosevelt announced that Colonel Frank Knox, the publisher of the *Chicago Daily News*, the old Rough Rider who had been Alf Landon's running mate in 1936, would succeed Edison at the Navy Department. Joining Knox at the War Department would be Colonel Henry L. Stimson of New York, the principal foreign policy spokesman for the eastern establishment, Hoover's former secretary of state, and Taft's secretary of war.

Knox, whose appointment had been in the works for some time, cleared it with Landon before accepting.* To make the public aware of the gravity of the international situation, he insisted that a Republican join him at the War Department. The war cabinet, so to speak, must be bipartisan. Roosevelt initially thought of his old Columbia Law School classmate William Donovan for the post but at the suggestion of Justice Felix Frankfurter turned to Stimson.[59] Knox also requested that the appointments be deferred until after the Republican convention. Roosevelt declined. It was important to stress the bipartisan nature of the defense effort, he told Knox. Even more important, if the GOP nominated an isolationist candidate, Knox and Stimson would be deemed guilty of bad sportsmanship in joining FDR's team afterward.[60] Stimson, whom Roosevelt surprised with a telephone call to his apartment at New York's Pierre Hotel on the morning of the nineteenth offering the appointment, had his own conditions. Fully aware of the internecine struggle between Woodring and Undersecretary Louis Johnson, he wanted a free hand to name his own assistants. FDR agreed, and Stimson brought to Washington a remarkable team that remained throughout the war: Judge Robert P. Patterson of the U.S. Court of Appeals as undersecretary, John J. McCloy as assistant secretary, and Robert A. Lovett as assistant secretary for air. Knox brought New York investment banker James V. Forrestal to Washington as undersecretary. With the exception of Forrestal, none of these appointees supported the New Deal and none had ever voted for FDR. Patterson had been appointed to the federal bench by Herbert Hoover in 1931; McCloy was the managing partner of Cravath, Swaine, and Moore;† Forrestal was president of Dillon, Reed; and Lovett was a senior partner at Brown Brothers, Harriman. Nevertheless, they proved devoted administrators who rendered superb service to the president and the nation.[61]

Roosevelt not only undercut the isolationist opposition on the eve of the Republican convention, he added two of the most powerful GOP foreign pol-

---

* After meeting with Landon, Knox wrote Roosevelt, "In the light of events which almost hourly show greater implications for us and for the world, our thinking was animated solely by our desire to promote national unity in the face of grave national peril." Knox to FDR, May 21, 1940, FDRL.

† As managing partner of Cravath, Swaine, and Moore, McCloy had supervised the preparation of the Supreme Court brief for the Schechter Brothers challenging the constitutionality of the New Deal's National Industrial Recovery Act. *Schechter Poultry Corp. v. United States*, 295 U.S. 495 (1935). Kai Bird, *The Chairman: John J. McCloy, The Making of the American Establishment* 101 (New York: Simon & Schuster, 1992).

icy voices to the cabinet. On June 18, prior to their appointments, both men had delivered speeches on national defense. In Detroit, Knox had called for compulsory military training, a million-man Army, the most powerful air force in the world, and unstinting aid to Great Britain. Stimson, speaking at the Yale commencement in New Haven, had asked for repeal of the Neutrality Act in its entirety, reinstitution of the draft, and the use of the U.S. Navy to convoy supplies to Britain.* By advocating a peacetime draft, Knox and Stimson prepared the way for the president to follow.[62]

The appointment of Knox and Stimson cast a pall over the Republican convention. Roosevelt had not only upstaged the event but exposed the deep fissure in the GOP over foreign policy. Not since Bull Moosers and Old Guard fought it out in 1912 had the party been so divided. The isolationist wing, stung to the quick by Knox and Stimson's defection, proceeded to read them out of the party—a mean-spirited response that did the Republicans no good with an electorate increasingly concerned about national defense. Keynote speaker Harold Stassen, striking a more responsive chord, noted that the appointment of two distinguished Republicans merely reflected the lack of talent among the Democrats. His only regret, said Stassen, was that the Grand Old Party was not replacing the rest of Roosevelt's "New Deal incompetents."[63]

Four candidates vied for the nomination. Thomas E. Dewey, New York City's thirty-seven-year-old racketbusting district attorney, was the front runner. A forceful public speaker, Dewey started like a house afire, claiming 67 percent of the Republican vote in a May 9 Gallup poll. But with Hitler's invasion of the Low Countries and France's defeat, Dewey's lead diminished. His youth and inexperience worked against him, and his too-clever-by-half ambiguity concerning Nazi aggression satisfied no one.† The more voters saw of

---

* That same week, Stimson also gave the commencement address at Andover. Unaware of FDR's impending call, the seventy-three-year-old Stimson told his young listeners that he envied them because they had the opportunity to choose between "right and wrong," to stand up for good against evil. "I wish to God that I was young enough to face it with you." Among the audience that day was sixteen-year-old George Herbert Walker Bush, for whom Colonel Stimson became a lifelong hero. Godfrey Hodgson, *The Colonel: The Life and Times of Henry Stimson, 1867–1950* 214 (New York: Knopf, 1990); Jean Edward Smith, *George Bush's War* 136–137 (New York: Henry Holt, 1992).

† Dewey's biographer Richard Norton Smith called him "the first American casualty of the Second World War." A novice in foreign affairs, Dewey turned for advice to John Foster

Dewey, the less they liked him: "Cold as a February iceberg," in the words of one of his most ardent supporters.[64]

Senator Arthur H. Vandenberg of Michigan was a distant second. A Senate fixture since his arrival in 1928, the courteous and fair-minded Vandenberg mistook approval by his colleagues for electoral support. He disdained primaries—"Why should I kill myself to carry Vermont?"—and soon found himself trailing badly.[65] Running neck and neck with Vandenberg was freshman Ohio senator Robert A. Taft, son of the former president and chief justice. In the Senate little more than a year, Taft's sense of entitlement left few doubts that he was ready to take on the presidency. Vandenberg and Taft appealed to the same constituency: the isolationist hard core of the GOP who had never forgiven FDR for defeating Hoover in 1932. Vandenberg's campaign was low-key and understated; Taft's strident and self-righteous. "There is a good deal more danger of the infiltration of totalitarian ideas from the New Deal circles in Washington than there ever will be from activities of the Communists or the Nazis."[66]

The convention dark horse was Wendell L. Willkie, the folksy, forty-eight-year-old Hoosier lawyer who had risen to become president and chief executive officer of Commonwealth and Southern, the nation's largest utility holding company. An outsider to politics, Willkie's huggy-bear good looks made him what David Halberstam called "the rarest thing in those days, a Republican with sex appeal." John Gunther called him "one of the most loveable, most gallant, most zealous, and most forward-looking Americans of this—or any—time."[67] The fact is, Willkie was a lifelong Democrat, from a family of lifelong Democrats, who turned Republican in early 1940.[68] He had gained prominence as a progressive, independently minded businessman who could hold his own in public forums with the nation's leading intellectuals. He wrote for *The Atlantic Monthly, The Saturday Evening Post, Fortune, Reader's Digest,* and *The New Republic*—where he defended the free speech rights of Nazis and Communists.[69] He charmed the nation's radio audience with an April 1940

Dulles, a senior partner at Sullivan and Cromwell, who was then in a pro-German phase. As Dewey later expressed it, Foster believed that "Hitler was a passing phenomenon who would disappear." America's proper role was "to stand aside and hopefully wait until a stalemate would occur and then exercise our weight to bring about a peace." Smith, *Thomas E. Dewey and His Times* 302–303 (New York: Simon & Schuster, 1982).

guest appearance on the phenomenally popular *Information Please* program hosted by *The New Yorker*'s Clifton Fadiman[*] and routed the New Deal's Robert H. Jackson in a widely listened to policy debate on *Town Meeting of the Air.*

Politically, Willkie supported virtually all of the accomplishments of the New Deal except the TVA.[70] He had an established record of fighting the Klan in Indiana, and was a firm friend of civil liberties. In foreign policy he supported Woodrow Wilson's League of Nations, advocated American membership in the World Court, and backed unlimited aid to the Allies. "England and France constitute our first line of defense against Hitler," he told the Akron, Ohio, post of the American Legion in May. "If anyone is going to stop Hitler, they are the ones to do it. It must therefore be in our advantage to help them every way we can, short of declaring war."[71]

Willkie had become a Republican because he disliked and distrusted FDR. Personal ambition was part of it. He had lost Commonwealth and Southern's struggle with TVA over electric rates and had failed to prevent passage of the Public Utilities Holding Act, which severely crimped its power. He believed that Roosevelt had steered the Democratic party away from its liberal ideals and converted it into the party of centralized bureaucracy and big government. Still dedicated to the social goals of the New Deal, including national health care, Willkie saw Roosevelt as a threat to individual liberty. The possibility of a third term was a manifestation of that threat.

Willkie was a political outsider in the sense of not being a career politician. But he was very much an establishment insider, a director of the Morgan Bank, and a member of every important club in New York. Harold Ickes accurately described him as "a simple barefoot lawyer from Wall Street." Alice Roosevelt Longworth said that of course Willkie's candidacy sprang from the grass roots—"the grass roots of a thousand country clubs."[72]

Willkie was supported by thousands of We Want Willkie clubs that had sprouted up across America. He was the candidate of media moguls such as Helen and Ogden Reid of the *New York Herald Tribune*, Roy Howard of the Scripps-Howard chain, John and Gardner Cowles of *The Des Moines Register*,

---

[*] In addition to Fadiman, the program's regulars included the columnist Franklin P. Adams of the *New York Post,* the composer and pianist Oscar Levant, Charles Kieran of *The New York Times,* and the sportswriter Heywood Hale Broun.

Minneapolis Star, and *Look* magazine, and Henry and Clare Boothe Luce of *Time, Life, Fortune,* and *Vanity Fair.* "A vote for Taft is a vote for the Republican party," said *Life* on May 13, 1940. "A vote for Willkie is a vote for the best man to lead the country in a crisis." Willkie charmed reporters who covered the campaign. At his press conference on the third day of the convention, hard-bitten journalists gave him a prolonged standing ovation—a scene that could have come straight from Frank Capra's *Mr. Smith Goes to Washington.*

To his Republican rivals Willkie's campaign appeared hopelessly amateurish. Yet the advertising was handled by Bruce Barton and John Young, the heads of two of the most powerful advertising firms in America; the chairman of the convention committee on arrangements (with absolute control over tickets to the gallery) was one of Willkie's earliest supporters; keynote speaker Stassen became Willkie's floor manager; and presiding officer Joe Martin of Massachusetts, the House minority leader, favored Willkie. Martin was a solid anti–New Deal isolationist, but he recognized that Willkie was the only candidate who might topple FDR.[73]

The Republican platform sidestepped a confrontation between the party's isolationist and internationalist wings. The foreign policy plank, said H. L. Mencken, was "so written that it will fit both the triumph of democracy and the collapse of democracy."[74] Connoisseurs of political hara-kiri thrilled when the GOP unveiled Herbert Hoover for a prime-time radio address to a national audience. Democratic strategists regarded Hoover's quadrennial appearances at Republican conventions as electoral reinsurance for victory in November.

On Thursday morning, June 27, with balloting scheduled to begin that afternoon, the *Herald Tribune* leaked (two days early) the results of the most recent Gallup Poll, showing Willkie out in front with 44 percent to Dewey's 29 percent and Taft's 13 percent. The impact was immediate. When the roll of the states was called, Dewey, as expected, led with 360 votes, Taft polled 189, and Vandenberg 76, but Willkie had 105—substantially more than had been expected.* The second ballot followed immediately. Willkie gained 66, Taft 14,

---

* A majority of the convention, 501 votes, was required to nominate. On the first ballot 730 votes were cast for the four front runners. The remaining 270 were split among nine favorite sons. Congressional Quarterly, *Guide to U.S. Elections* 161 (Washington, D.C.: Congressional Quarterly, 1975).

Vandenberg held firm, but Dewey's support began to erode. On the third ballot Willkie moved into second place, ahead of Taft. On the fourth Dewey's strength collapsed and it was now a two-way race between Willkie and Taft, with Willkie leading 306–254.

Chants of "We want Willkie" from the packed gallery threatened to drown out the proceedings on the floor. The Republicans had not gone past the first ballot at any convention since 1920 (when Harding was nominated on the tenth ballot), and Convention Hall was pure pandemonium. Chairman Joe Martin gaveled down efforts by Dewey and Taft supporters to adjourn, and Willkie's momentum accelerated. On the fifth ballot Alf Landon switched the Kansas delegation to Willkie, and on the sixth ballot it was all over. Willkie defeated Taft 655–318, Governor John Bricker of Ohio moved to make the vote unanimous, and at 1:30 A.M. Friday the convention adjourned.

The following day Willkie named Senate Republican leader Charles McNary of Oregon as his running mate. McNary was from the West, isolationist, pro–public power, and far more conservative on most issues than Willkie. But he was well liked in Washington by his colleagues on both sides of the aisle, and Roosevelt found him easy to work with. "I have the general opinion that the Republicans have nominated their strongest possible ticket," said FDR at cabinet the next day.[75]*

For Roosevelt, Willkie's nomination was a mixed blessing. His internationalism removed the question of aid to Britain from the election agenda, but of the four potential Republican candidates he would be the most difficult to defeat. Unlike Taft, Vandenberg, and Dewey, Willkie appealed to the middle-of-the-road voters FDR needed most. Of the four, only he had a chance of cracking the Roosevelt coalition.

---

* Not all Republicans agreed. Former Indiana senator James E. Watson, referring to Willkie's Democratic roots, complained, "If a whore repented and wanted to join the church I'd personally welcome her and lead her up the aisle to a pew. But I'd not ask her to lead the choir the first night." Mary Earhart Dillon, *Wendell Willkie* 143 (Philadelphia: Lippincott, 1952).

TWENTY-ONE

FOUR MORE YEARS

I have said this before, but I shall say it again
and again and again: Your boys are not going
to be sent into any foreign wars.
—FRANKLIN D. ROOSEVELT, OCTOBER 30, 1940

WITH WILLKIE'S NOMINATION and the appointment of Knox and Stimson, the fight over foreign policy shifted to Capitol Hill. On June 28, 1940, at the behest of Senator David I. Walsh of Massachusetts, chairman of the Naval Affairs Committee, Congress amended the defense appropriations bill to prohibit the sale of military equipment to any foreign power unless the chief of staff of the Army and the chief of naval operations certified it to be nonessential to national defense. Walsh, who was passionately isolationist, shared the anti-British sentiments of many of his Irish constituents and was determined to head off the delivery of twenty new torpedo boats to Great Britain.[1]

The act placed enormous pressure on General Marshall and Admiral Harold R. Stark, the chief of naval operations, both of whom worried increasingly about the denuded state of America's defenses. "If we were required to mobilize after having released this equipment and were found short," Major Walter Bedell Smith of the general staff warned Marshall and Morgenthau, "everyone who was a party to the deal might hope to be hanging from a lamp post."[2] FDR called off the torpedo boat transfer but continued to press the military for increased aid to Britain.

The isolationist sentiment on Capitol Hill removed the last doubts Roosevelt had about seeking a third term. FDR now saw himself more as commander in chief than president and recognized the necessity to prepare the nation for war.[3] When the delegates to the Democratic National Convention convened in Chicago on July 15, 1940, there was no serious doubt he would accept renomination. If anything, Willkie's selection by the GOP made his candidacy all the more likely because no other Democrat stood a chance of winning in November.

Roosevelt refused to tip his hand. By not doing so he dominated events in Chicago. He selected the site because he believed Mayor Kelly would control the galleries. He sent Hopkins (now partially recovered) to set up shop in the Blackstone Hotel—not a campaign headquarters but a communications post.* And he asked Judge Samuel Rosenman to come to the White House: a personal visit that could have no purpose other than to prepare his acceptance speech. FDR wanted to be drafted but declined to say so. That frustrated the delegates on the floor, who were awaiting their marching orders, and the president relished the suspense.

The script did not play out as Roosevelt intended. On Monday, the first day, the proceedings were listless. The *Chicago Daily News* reported that the delegates were drafting Roosevelt "with the enthusiasm of a chain gang."[4] The president wanted to be renominated by acclamation, but Garner would not cooperate and neither would Farley. When FDR telephoned to suggest ever so obliquely that an actual ballot might be dispensed with, Farley rejected the proposal out of hand. "That's perfectly silly," he told the president.[5] Even worse for Roosevelt, Farley as national chairman, not Mayor Kelly, controlled the tickets to the gallery. When FDR's name was mentioned by the mayor in his welcoming remarks, the convention's response was tepid. Farley, on the other hand, received a prolonged ovation even though the massive pipe organ— which was to have sounded "When Irish Eyes Are Smiling"—remained mysteriously silent. "Power failure," snapped Mayor Kelly.[6]

Tuesday began badly for the president as well. Hopkins, often condescending when dealing with politicians but now even more abrasive because of his illness, was probably the last man in Washington who should have been entrusted with managing a campaign. Delegates were infuriated by his assumed power over the convention and resentful at the way he exercised it.† "Harry

---

* Hopkins found himself ensconced in the Blackstone's suite 308/309, the same suite with "the smoke-filled room" in which Warren G. Harding had been selected to be the Republican nominee in 1920. Hopkins was connected to the White House with a direct line—the phone mounted in the bathroom to ensure privacy. Charles Peters, *Five Days in Philadelphia* 136 (New York: PublicAffairs, 2005).

† Hopkins was not a delegate to the convention and got onto the floor only by courtesy of

seems to be making all his usual mistakes," Eleanor told friends at Val-Kill, where she listened to the proceedings over the radio. "He doesn't seem to know how to make people happy."[7]

Even the platform miscarried. A sizable group of isolationists led by Senators Wheeler and Walsh insisted on including a plank aimed at blocking any intervention abroad: "We will not participate in foreign wars and we will not send our army or navy or air force to fight in foreign lands outside of the Americas." Roosevelt salvaged the plank at the last moment by adding the words "except in case of attack," which Walsh and Wheeler grudgingly accepted.[8]

At a strategy session attended by Senator James Byrnes and Attorney General Robert Jackson Tuesday morning in Hopkins's suite at the Blackstone, Harold Ickes said that "if the Republicans had been running the convention in the interests of Willkie, they could not have done a better job than we were doing."[9] Hopkins took offense, and Ickes put the case directly to the president. He sent a telegram rather than telephone. "It is too easy to divert a telephone conversation and the President is adept at that." Ickes wrote to FDR at length, but his message boiled down to one sentence: "This convention is bleeding to death and your reputation and prestige may bleed to death with it." Ickes asked Roosevelt to come to Chicago and take charge. "There are more than nine hundred leaderless delegates milling about like worried sheep waiting for the inspiration of leadership that only you can give them."[10]

Frances Perkins, attending her sixth Democratic convention, agreed. She had known FDR more than thirty years and was much closer to him than Ickes. She chose to telephone. ("He was always easy to get on the phone and willing to interrupt whatever he was doing to talk to one of his associates.") He would be renominated, Perkins told the president, but "the situation is just as sour as it can be." Like Ickes, she urged him to come to Chicago.

"No, no, I have given it full consideration," Roosevelt replied. "I thought it all through both ways. I know I am right, Frances. It will be worse if I go. People will get promises out of me that I ought not to make. If I don't make

---

a badge from Mayor Kelly designating him a deputy sergeant at arms. Robert E. Sherwood, *Roosevelt and Hopkins* 179 (New York: Harper & Brothers, 1948).

promises, I'll make new enemies. If I do make promises, they'll be mistakes. I'll be pinned down on things I just don't want to be pinned down on, *yet*. I am sure that it is better not to go."

"What can we do?" asked Perkins.

"How would it be if Eleanor came?" said FDR. "I think she would make an excellent impression. You know, Eleanor always makes people feel right."

Perkins agreed. "Call her," the president said. "I'll speak to her too, but you tell her so that she will know I am not sending her on my own hunch."[11]

When Perkins called Eleanor, she found her reluctant. "I thought it utter nonsense," ER wrote later.[12] She was also concerned about Farley. Both Eleanor and Frances Perkins were very fond of the chairman and regretted that he and Franklin were now rivals. Finally, ER said she would go only if Farley invited her. "I am not going to add to the hard feelings," she told Perkins.[13]

Eleanor put in a call to Farley in Chicago, who was so overcome by the first lady's gesture he could barely speak.[14]

"I don't want to appear before the convention unless you think it is all right," said Eleanor

"It's perfectly all right with me," Farley replied when he regained his composure.

"Please, don't say so unless you really mean it."

"I do mean it and I am not trying to be polite. Frankly, the situation is not good. Equally frankly, your coming will not affect my situation one way or the other. From the President's point of view I think it desirable, if not essential, that you come."[15]

Eleanor made arrangements to fly to Chicago Wednesday. Rather than use government transportation, she called C. R. Smith, the head of American Airlines and an old friend, who put his personal plane at her disposal.

Tuesday evening the clouds parted and the convention came to life. Mayor Kelly regained control. Farley might command the tickets to the gallery, but the Chicago police determined access to the convention site. By the time the delegates were called to order, Chicago Stadium was packed with Cook County regulars waiting for the mayor's signal. The principal address would be given by Senator Alben Barkley upon assumption of his duties as permanent chairman. Nominating speeches would follow. Twice, in 1932 and 1936, Barkley had brought the delegates to a partisan frenzy with his stem-winding keynotes, and in 1948 he would exceed even those performances with a keynote speech that galvanized a fractured and dispirited Democratic party to press on to victory. In 1940 he was at his rhetorical best. As the audience stomped and cheered, Barkley delivered a litany of New Deal accomplishments and Republican failures. Thirteen minutes into the oration he casually mentioned the president's name, igniting the pent-up emotion on the floor and precipitating an unplanned demonstration that lasted almost an hour. When order was restored, Barkley continued another thirty minutes. At the conclusion he announced the magic words the delegates were waiting for: a message from the president of the United States:

> The President has never had and has not today any desire or purpose to continue in the office of President, to be a candidate for that office, or to be nominated by the convention for that office. He wishes in all conviction and sincerity to make it clear that all of the delegates at this convention are free to vote for any candidate.
>
> That is the message which I bear to you tonight from the President.[16]

The vast crowd in Chicago Stadium was speechless for a moment. What did Roosevelt mean? The statement said neither yes nor no. Five, ten, fifteen seconds, and then bedlam broke loose.[17] From loudspeakers all over convention hall a powerful voice boomed out "We want Roosevelt," "We want Roosevelt," over and over. Delegates joined in, the galleries emptied onto the floor, state standards crowded into the aisles, the Chicago police band marched in playing "Happy Days Are Here Again," the city firemen tooted "Franklin D. Roosevelt Jones," and this time there was no power failure as the giant electric organ joined the celebration. It was pure pandemonium, and through it all that deep penetrating voice could be heard above the noise that filled the arena: "We want Roosevelt," "Everybody wants Roosevelt," "The world needs Roosevelt." In a tiny office in the stadium basement, his mouth inches away from a microphone, belting out the message, sat Chicago's leather-lunged superintendent of sewers, fifty-four-year-old Thomas D. Garry, who would gain convention immortality as "the voice from the sewers."[18]

The balloting Wednesday was pro forma. Roosevelt swept the field with 946 votes, Farley received 72, Garner 61, Senator Millard Tydings of Maryland 9, and Cordell Hull, whose name had not been placed in nomination, 5. Shortly

after midnight, the roll call complete, Farley moved to make the vote unanimous.

Equally pro forma was FDR's call to Hull that night offering him the vice
presidential nomination.[19] When Hull again declined—he had turned Roosevelt down three times in the two past weeks—the president called Hopkins
and said he wanted Wallace to be the nominee—Secretary of Agriculture
Henry A. Wallace, a choice that jolted party leaders no less than TR's selection
by the Republican convention in 1900.[20]* Roosevelt wanted Wallace because
he was concerned about carrying the farm belt against a transplanted Hoosier
like Willkie; he wanted a liberal to carry on the New Deal tradition should that
be necessary; and he wanted someone whose antifascist credentials were impeccable. Wallace had done an outstanding job at Agriculture, his revolutionary work as a scientist to develop hybrid corn was transforming the face of
American farming, and unlike the crusty, embittered Garner, Roosevelt found
him likable and loyal. On the negative side, Wallace had never run for elective
office. He was regarded by many as a mystic fascinated by the occult, a crack-
pot quality that professional politicos found difficult to comprehend.[21] And
his loyalty to the Democratic party appeared uncertain. His father had been
secretary of agriculture under Harding and Coolidge, and Wallace had not
registered as a Democrat until the 1936 election. "Just because the Republicans
have nominated an apostate Democrat," shouted one leader, "let us not for
God's sake nominate an apostate Republican."[22]

Other candidates were off and running. Hopkins urged FDR to take
Supreme Court Justice William O. Douglas. Speaker Bankhead believed
FDR had promised the post to him. Paul McNutt wanted it, and so did
the RFC's Jesse Jones. Wallace had no tangible base of support. He would
have to be forced down the throat of a convention already aggrieved and
bitter. Jimmy Byrnes (who also wanted the job) suggested Jones or Alben
Barkley; Farley suggested anyone but Wallace—preferably Jones, Bankhead,
or McNutt in that order. Eleanor concurred. "I've been talking to Jim Farley
and I agree with him. Henry Wallace won't do," she told FDR. "Jesse Jones

---

* "Don't any of you realize that there is only one life between this madman and the presidency?" thundered party chairman Mark Hanna—an observation that would not have been
out of place in 1940. Edmund Morris, *The Rise of Theodore Roosevelt* 763 (New York: Coward, McCann & Geoghegan, 1979).

would bolster the ticket, win it business support and get the party contributions."[23]

When Roosevelt remained adamant, Hopkins and Byrnes fell into line and began to work the convention on Wallace's behalf. Jones bowed to presidential pressure and withdrew. (When Hopkins resigned as secretary of commerce on August 22, 1940, FDR named Jones to replace him.) That left Bankhead, McNutt, and Wallace. Nominations were scheduled for Thursday evening. After his name was placed before the convention, McNutt withdrew. "Franklin Roosevelt is my leader and I am here to support his choice for vice president."[24] That left Bankhead and Wallace. Before the voting began, and with the outcome very much in doubt, FDR received a crucial assist. Escorted by party chairman Farley, Eleanor Roosevelt made her way to the platform. The entire convention rose to its feet in a rousing burst of applause. The obvious affection ER and Farley shared provided a healing effect. The bitterness on the floor subsided. Eleanor began her speech with a tribute to Farley: "I think nobody could appreciate more what he has done for the party and I want to give him here my thanks and devotion." Mrs. Roosevelt hit the right note. The convention that had booed Wallace's name when the nominations were made listened with rapt attention as she moved on. "This is no ordinary time," said ER. "No time for weighing anything except what we can best do for the country as a whole." Without mentioning Wallace by name, she asked the delegates to support her husband's choice. "No man who is a candidate or who is President can carry this situation alone. This is only carried by a united people who love their country and who will live for it . . . to the fullest of their ability."[25]

When she finished, Chicago Stadium was absolutely still. "The hot and weary delegates caught her mood and gravity and fell silent," reported the United Press. "She has done more to soothe the convention bruises than all the efforts of astute Senators," said the New York *Daily News.*[26] When Barkley asked the clerk to call the roll of the states, tempers had subsided. Without ER's intervention, it is not clear that Wallace would have won.

What is clear is that if he had not won, Roosevelt would not have run for a third term. In the White House, FDR listened to the proceedings in the upstairs study, playing solitaire. "His face was grim," Sam Rosenman remembered. As the vote tally seesawed, Roosevelt asked Missy for pad and pencil and began writing. He gave the draft to Rosenman. "Sam, take this inside and go to work on it. Smooth it out and get it ready for delivery. I may have to deliver it very quickly, so please hurry it up." Should Wallace lose, FDR would decline the nomination.* "If I ever saw him with his mind made up it was that night," said Rosenman.[27]

On the floor of Chicago Stadium, South Carolina's James Byrnes moved rapidly from delegation to delegation. "For God's sake, do you want a president or vice president."[28] The vote continued nip and tuck. Eight states, including Ohio and Pennsylvania, passed. When Wyoming was called at the end of the roll, Bankhead held a two-vote lead. The states that passed clamored for attention. Barkley recognized Mayor David Lawrence of Pittsburgh, who cast 68 of Pennsylvania's 72 votes for Wallace. Ohio (52), New Jersey (32), and Michigan (38) followed. Wallace was over the top. Other delegations shifted. The final tally gave Wallace 627 of the convention's 1,100 delegates, a tribute to the muscle of the White House rather than Wallace's support. After Speaker Bankhead's brother, Senator John Bankhead of Alabama, offered the traditional motion to make Wallace's nomination unanimous, the "no"s out-shouted the "aye"s by a considerable margin.[29] As Wallace moved toward the podium to deliver his acceptance speech, Byrnes intercepted him.

"Don't do it, Henry. Don't go out there. You'll ruin the party if you do."[30]

Crestfallen, Wallace walked away. The convention adjourned. For Roosevelt, it was an expensive victory. Farley resigned as national chairman, southerners felt slighted at the treatment Bankhead received, the organization bosses despised Wallace, and the rank-and-file delegates felt bullied by the president. "Everyone got out of Chicago as fast as he could," wrote Ickes. "What could have been a convention of enthusiasm ended almost like a wake."[31] Roosevelt's determination to force Wallace on the convention resembled the obstinacy he had displayed during the 1937 Court-packing fight and the congressional purge in 1938. Commander in chief or not, he had not lost his capacity to shoot himself in the foot.

In Europe the situation was grim. With the defeat of France, the Battle of

---

* Roosevelt wrote in his draft that the Democratic Party could not continue to be divided between liberals and conservatives. "It would be best not to straddle ideals. It would be best for America to have the fight out. Therefore, I give the Democratic party the opportunity to make that historic decision by declining the honor of the nomination for the presidency." For the full text, see Samuel I. Rosenman, *Working with Roosevelt* 216–218 (New York: Harper & Brothers, 1952).

Britain began. Willkie's nomination had removed the questions of preparedness and aid to Britain from the campaign agenda, and the election would
not be waged on those issues. Nevertheless, sizable segments in both parties
continued to fight a rearguard action to ensure American neutrality. The two
principal issues involved Churchill's May 15 request for fifty older American
destroyers and the need for peacetime conscription. Public opinion hung in
the balance. Gallup Polls in June and July 1940 indicated that 61 percent of
Americans believed the most important task for the United States was to stay
out of the war. At the same time, 73 percent favored all possible aid to Britain
short of war. On the question of whether the United States should send airplanes to England "even though it might delay our own national defense program," respondents divided 49 percent in favor, 44 percent against.[32]

Bipartisan legislation for a peacetime draft, the first in American history,
was introduced in the Senate on June 20 by Nebraska Democrat Edward R.
Burke and in the House the next day by New York Republican James W.
Wadsworth. This was not an administration measure. Burke was an anti–New
Deal Democrat who vigorously opposed FDR's Court-packing plan and had
earned the president's ill will. Wadsworth, who had served two terms in the
U.S. Senate (1915–1927), was an upstate Republican from Livingston County
and an old friend of Roosevelt but scarcely in the liberal wing of the party.[33]

The bill was framed by a private citizens group headed by Grenville Clark,
Stimson's former law partner, and was accorded little chance of passage.* James

---

* Clark, a senior partner in the firm of Root, Clark, Buckner, and Ballantine, was a 1906
Harvard Law School classmate of Felix Frankfurter, and had clerked with FDR at Carter,
Ledyard, and Milburn from 1907 to 1910. It was he who suggested to Frankfurter, who conveyed the suggestion to FDR, that Stimson be appointed secretary of war. In May 1940, at a
series of small meetings of elite lawyers and businessmen in New York City's Harvard Club,
he organized the 2nd Corps of the Military Training Camp Association, a nostalgic reminder of the Plattsburg Movement organized at the Harvard Club after the sinking of the
Lusitania in 1915. Among those present were Langdon Marvin, Roosevelt's old law partner;
Julius Ochs Adler of *The New York Times;* Henry L. Stimson; Frank Knox; William J. Donovan; Lewis Douglas, who had been FDR's first budget director; and Judge Robert P. Patterson of the U.S. Court of Appeals. The group issued a series of manifestos advocating
military conscription and established a national network (the MTCA) to press the cause.
General Marshall cooperated covertly with the group and in early June dispatched three officers, including Major Lewis B. Hershey, to New York to assist Clark's organization in drafting a selective service bill. This was the measure Burke and Wadsworth introduced. Hershey
subsequently became the first head of selective service. J. Gary Clifford and Samuel R.

Byrnes, the Democratic whip, said there was "not a Chinaman's chance."[34] Labor's William Green called voluntary enlistments, not the draft, "the American way."[35] John L. Lewis, with his gift for invective, denounced the proposal as "a fantastic suggestion from a mind in full intellectual retreat."[36] Religious leaders such as the Reverend Harry Emerson Fosdick, an internationalist on many issues, vigorously opposed the plan.[37] The Progressive George Norris, who continued to support the president, was convinced that conscription would end in military dictatorship. Isolationists had a field day. "The idea of letting the boys sit around for a year playing stud poker and blackjack is poppycock," said Senator Guy Gillette of Iowa.[38] "The only emergency in this country is the one conjured up by those who want to send our boys to Europe or Asia," proclaimed North Dakota's Gerald Nye. "Militarism repugnant to every American instinct and institution," announced Bennett Champ Clark of Missouri. "If this bill passes," said Montana's Burton K. Wheeler, "it will slit the throat of the last great democracy still living. It will accord to Hitler his greatest and cheapest victory. On the headstone of American Democracy he will inscribe: 'Here lies the foremost victim of the war of nerves.' "[39]

Roosevelt initially kept the bill at arm's length. It was an election year, and he did not wish to move too far ahead of public opinion. "Governments such as ours cannot swing so far so quickly," he wrote his old friend Helen Rogers Reid, the wife of the publisher of the *Herald Tribune,* an old childhood neighbor and playmate. "They can only move in keeping with the thought and will of the great majority of our people. Were it otherwise the very fabric of our democracy—which after all is government by public opinion—would be in danger of disintegration."[40]

Privately he encouraged Grenville Clark and his allies to press forward but suggested they downplay the compulsory aspect. With FDR's blessing, Stimson and Marshall testified repeatedly on Capitol Hill in favor of the Burke-Wadsworth bill. "Selective service was the only fair, efficient, and democratic way to raise an army," Stimson told the House Military Affairs Committee.[41] Marshall said there was "no conceivable way" to secure the men necessary for the nation's defense "except by the draft."[42] Public opinion lurched forward. At the time of France's surrender, slightly more than half of Americans polled fa-

Spencer, *The First Peacetime Draft* 14–26 (Lawrence: University Press of Kansas, 1986); Forrest C. Pogue, *George C. Marshall: Ordeal and Hope* 57–58 (New York: Viking Press, 1966).

vored selective service. On July 20, less than a month later, the figure stood at 69 percent, and by late August it was 86 percent.[43]

The combination of Clark's public relations effort, the testimony of Stimson and Marshall, plus the intrepid stand Britain was making against the Luftwaffe's assault paid dividends. On July 24, 1940, the Senate Military Affairs Committee reported the Burke-Wadsworth bill favorably. Five days later Roosevelt asked Congress for authority to call the National Guard and the Reserve Officers Corps to active duty.[44] On August 2 FDR fired his first public shot in favor of the draft. Meeting the press for the 666th time since assuming office, Roosevelt said he was distinctly in favor of a selective training bill and considered it essential for national defense.[45] Willkie added his endorsement on August 17. Echoing Stimson's remarks, Willkie said that selective service "is the only democratic way in which to assure the trained and competent manpower we need in our national defense." When a reporter told Willkie that if he wanted to win the election he would come out against the draft, Willkie shot back, "I would rather not win the election than do that."[46]

Willkie's support for the draft "broke the back" of the opposition, said California's isolationist senator Hiram Johnson.[47] The democratic aspect of selective service carried the day. On August 28 the Senate passed the Burke-Wadsworth bill 69–16, a majority of Republicans voting in favor. In the House, New York's Hamilton Fish, the ranking member of the Foreign Affairs Committee, introduced a crippling amendment to delay selective service registration until after the election and limit the size of the draft to 400,000 men. Fish's amendment carried narrowly; Stimson, FDR, and Willkie protested vigorously; and the provision was stripped from the final conference report that reconciled the House and Senate versions. On September 14 the bill, essentially as the Clark group had prepared it originally, passed the Senate 47–25 and the House 232–124. Roosevelt signed it into law two days later, and on October 16, 1940, more than 16 million men between the ages of twenty-one and thirty-five registered for the country's first peacetime draft.

Thirteen days later a blindfolded Secretary Stimson dipped a ladle carved from a beam taken from Philadelphia's Independence Hall into a huge fishbowl filled to the brim with bright blue celluloid capsules, each of which contained a number that would determine the order in which men would be called up. Stimson gave the first capsule to FDR, who opened it and announced, "One hundred fifty-eight."[48] At the end of October, the first 16,000 inductees reported for duty. Over the next year, at the rate of 50,000 a month, 600,000 men would be called to active duty. The draftees, together with 500,000 regular Army troops and 270,000 from the National Guard, would form eleven full-strength divisions, an air force of 5,000 planes, and all the support personnel a force of that size required. The Army, which numbered 189,839 men at the end of 1939, would top 1.4 million by mid-1941.[49]

Britain's need for destroyers grew ever more pressing. Three times in June, Churchill repeated his request.[50] Britain was down to its last sixty-eight vessels, with which it had to defend not only its trade routes against German U-boats but patrol the Channel against possible invasion. "We must ask therefore as a matter of life and death to be reinforced with these destroyers. We will carry out the struggle whatever the odds but it may be beyond our resources unless we receive reinforcement."[51] On June 26 King George VI, who unlike his brother David (Edward VIII) stood resolute against Nazi aggression, departed from protocol to add his personal plea for the destroyers. "I well understand your difficulties," he wrote Roosevelt, "and I am certain that you will do your best to procure them for us before it is too late."[52]

FDR's first impulse was to ask Congress for authorization. The United States had 200 four-funnel destroyers from World War I, and in late 1939 172 of the vessels had been refitted and returned to service. Fifty of them could probably be spared.[53] But with the selective service bill pending on Capitol Hill there was a danger of legislative overload, and it was possible both measures might fail. Also, the destroyer deal would fall squarely in the bailiwick of Naval Affairs Committee chairman David I. Walsh, possibly the most intransigent opponent of the transaction in the Senate. To pry the bill loose would not be easy.

Without congressional authorization the road seemed barred. To lease the vessels to a belligerent ran afoul of international law; the Walsh amendment to the 1940 Defense Appropriations Act required the chief of naval operations to sign off on the vessels, and Admiral Stark had recently testified to their usefulness when he had obtained the funds to have them refitted; and above all, the Espionage Act of 1917 made it a criminal offense to deliver naval vessels to a country at war.[54]

On July 19 Benjamin Cohen, who had moved from the White House to become general counsel of Ickes's public works domain, provided Ickes with a skillfully argued memorandum suggesting that the president could release the destroyers to Britain on his own authority as commander in chief. Ickes forwarded the memorandum to the White House but was not convinced.[55] Neither was Roosevelt. "This memorandum from Ben Cohen is worth reading," he told Navy secretary Frank Knox, "but I frankly doubt it will stand up. Also I fear Congress is in no mood at the present time to allow any form of sale." FDR told Knox it might be possible at a later date to get Congress to permit the sale of the destroyers to Canada for hemisphere defense, but at present there was nothing that could be done.[56]

Just when it appeared that the administration's efforts had run aground, Roosevelt received an unexpected assist. On July 11, 1940, at a dinner at New York's prestigious Century Club hosted by Lewis Douglas, thirty distinguished and influential Americans from across the political spectrum formed themselves into a loose alliance to arouse the country to the danger the defeat of Britain would pose and the need to do everything possible to prevent it. Among the guests were *Time*'s Henry Luce; Admiral William Standley, the former chief of naval operations; Ivy League presidents James Conant of Harvard and Ernest Hopkins of Dartmouth; Henry Sloan Coffin and Henry Van Dusen of the Union Theological Seminary; lawyers Dean Acheson, Charles Burlingham, Allen Dulles, and Thomas Thacher; journalists Herbert Agar, Joseph Alsop, Elmer Davis, and Walter Millis; and Francis Pickens Miller of the Council on Foreign Relations, who became executive director of what became known as the "Century Group."

The group discussed a number of proposals that evening, but the one that hit home was the suggestion that the United States provide Britain with the fifty destroyers it needed in exchange for naval bases in the Western Hemisphere.[57] That is the first proposal to trade destroyers for bases on record, which is a surprise since the isolationist press had long favored the acquisition of naval installations in the Americas in exchange for cancellation of Britain's war debts. At the direction of the Century Group, Alsop took the proposal to Lord Lothian, the British ambassador in Washington, who listened with interest but gave no commitment. (Lothian, as Philip Henry Kerr, had been a member of the Century Club since 1938 and was well acquainted with Alsop.) Luce, for his part, put the proposal to FDR on July 25 and met with a similar cautious response. "Harry, I can't come out in favor of such a deal without the support of the entire *Time-Life* organization," said Roosevelt.[58]

Encouraged by reports from Lothian of possible American support, Churchill renewed his plea for the vessels on July 31. "It is some time since I

ventured to cable personally to you," he told FDR. "In the past ten days we have
had eleven destroyers sunk or damaged," said Churchill.

> Destroyers are frightfully vulnerable to air-bombing, and yet they must
> be held in the air-bombing area to prevent sea-borne invasion. We could
> not keep up the present rate of casualties for long, and if we cannot get a
> substantial reinforcement the whole fate of the war may be decided by
> this minor and easily remediable factor.
>
> This is a frank account of our present situation, and I am confident
> that you will leave nothing undone to ensure that fifty or sixty of your
> oldest destroyers are sent to me at once. . . .
>
> Mr. President, with great respect I must tell you that in the long his-
> tory of the world this is a thing to do *now*.[59]

Lothian followed up Churchill's cable with a lengthy late-night meeting
with Secretary Knox on August 1. Both agreed the destroyers were vital. Knox
asked point-blank if the British had considered trading base sites in the Western Hemisphere for the vessels. Lothian conceded they had not. Knox agreed
to raise the issue at cabinet the next day, and Lothian volunteered to query his
government.[60]

The cabinet convened on August 2 in crisis mode. Stimson, who could remember tense sessions under Taft and Hoover, called it "one of the most serious and important debates that I have ever had in a cabinet meeting."[61] Knox
recounted his conversation with Lothian and suggested the destroyers be
traded for bases in the West Indies. Hull questioned whether the acquisition of
British territory might not violate Inter-American agreements. FDR said it
might, but the bases could be leased instead of transferred, which would not
pose a problem.

There were two sticking points. It was unanimously agreed that congressional
authorization would be required, and FDR worried about the political fallout.
Without Willkie's support, Republicans on Capitol Hill would not go along.
Wallace, Attorney General Robert Jackson, and Ickes thought it would be risky
to consult him. He might refuse and leave the administration holding the bag.
Knox, Stimson, and Hull disagreed. Everyone in the room turned to Farley,
whose political judgment weighed heavily with his colleagues. "Consult him,"
said Farley. "It is good for the country, and what is good for the country is good

politics."[62] FDR agreed. That evening he called Kansas editor William Allen White, a mutual friend of the two candidates, who was vacationing near Willkie in Colorado. White thought Willkie would agree and said he would give it a try.[63]

On August 3 Churchill replied to Lothian. His Majesty's Government would agree to swap bases for destroyers but would prefer to lease the facilities to the United States rather than transfer title. That dovetailed with FDR's desire. "It is vital to settle quickly," Churchill told Lothian. "Now is the time when we want the destroyers. Go ahead on these lines full steam."[64]

The Century Group, meanwhile, stepped up its public pressure. On August 4, at the group's behest, General of the Armies John J. Pershing, the nation's most revered military hero, spoke to the country over a national radio hookup from his home in Washington's Carlton Hotel. "The British Navy needs destroyers to convoy merchant ships and to repel invasion. The most critical time is the next few weeks and months. Today may be the last time when, by measures short of war, we can still prevent war."[65]

Pershing's address kicked off a national campaign to make it politically possible for Roosevelt to act. On August 5, 1940, *Time* bannered Britain's need for destroyers. *The New York Times* and the *Herald Tribune* followed suit. The Century Group scored another coup on August 11, when the *Times* published a long and closely reasoned letter from Dean Acheson and three other prominent lawyers arguing that the president could transfer the destroyers to Britain on his own authority without additional legislation.[66] "At the time my friend and classmate Charles Merz had charge of the editorial page of *The New York Times*," wrote Acheson. "I showed him the opinion and suggested putting it forth as a letter to the *Times,* to be prominently displayed on the editorial page in the Sunday edition. He approved of this and published it."[67] Acheson's letter was a reworking and expansion of Ben Cohen's original memo, and it found a responsive audience. Stimson thought the prospect of getting Congress to act was poor, but Acheson's "carefully worked out paper . . . adds a speck of light on the situation."[68]

Until Acheson's letter appeared, no one at the upper levels of the administration contemplated bypassing Congress. But Frankfurter supported the idea, and on August 15 Stimson called FDR. "He said he felt very, very much encouraged," the secretary recorded in his diary. Roosevelt told Stimson he "would talk it over with the Attorney General tomorrow morning and is evidently ready to push it ahead."[69]

Negotiations with Willkie were not going as well. While White and members of the Century Group urged the GOP nominee to speak out forthrightly, Herbert Hoover and other figures in the party advised him to avoid any commitment. The upshot was that Willkie remained silent. "It's not as bad as it seems," White telegraphed FDR. "I have talked with both of you on this subject and I know there is not two bits worth of difference between the two of you."[70] When Willkie officially announced his candidacy on August 17, he came tantalizingly close to backing the swap without explicitly endorsing it. He proclaimed his "wholehearted support for the president in whatever action he might take to give the opponents of force the material resources of the nation," adding that "the loss of the British fleet would greatly weaken our defense."[71]

Armed with Acheson's letter to the *Times,* Jackson provided FDR with an official Opinion of the Attorney General supporting the president's authority to trade the destroyers for bases under his authority as commander in chief.[72] Jackson said the intervening statutes, such as the Espionage Act of 1917, were not intended to apply to such transactions.* With the green light from the Justice Department, the details fell into place. The United States agreed to deliver the fifty destroyers in parcels of eight to Halifax, Nova Scotia, where British crews would be waiting to take possession. In return, Great Britain would provide the United States with ninety-nine-year leases to bases in Newfoundland, Bermuda, the Bahamas, Jamaica, Antigua, Saint Lucia, Trinidad, and British Guiana—a total of eight. To satisfy British pride (Churchill had also to consider public opinion) and to avoid any appearance that His Majesty's Government had been outbargained, it was agreed that the bases in Newfoundland and Bermuda would be a free gift to the United States from Great Britain, the other six provided in return for the destroyers.[73] General Marshall and Admiral Stark had no trouble signing off—the bases provided far more security than fifty World War I destroyers—and on August 30, 1940, Stark ordered the Commander Destroyers Atlantic Squadron to proceed to Boston with the first eight destroyers. D-Day for the transfer would be September 6.[74]

---

* For Jackson's view of the swap, see his *That Man: An Insider's Portrait of Franklin D. Roosevelt* 86–103, John Q. Barrett, ed. (New York: Oxford University Press, 2003). Jackson's Opinion was harshly criticized by Professors Herbert W. Briggs and Edwin Borchard in "Neglected Aspects of the Destroyer Deal," 34 *American Journal of International Law* 569–587, 690–697 (1940). For support, see Quincy Wright, "The Transfer of Destroyers to Great Britain," 34 *AJIL* 680–689 (1940).

Roosevelt announced the deal while on a war plant inspection tour in Charleston, West Virginia. "This is the most important action in the reinforcement of our national defense since the Louisiana Purchase," he said to newsmen traveling with him.[75] Churchill told Parliament that the affairs of the United States and Great Britain henceforth would be "somewhat mixed up together. I do not view the process with any misgiving. I could not stop it if I wished; no one can stop it. Like the Mississippi, it just keeps rolling along."[76] Willkie said "the country will undoubtedly approve," but regretted "the President did not deem it necessary to secure the approval of Congress."[77]

Public reaction was overwhelmingly favorable. On Capitol Hill criticism was muted. The transaction was so manifestly to America's advantage that even the most ardent isolationists found it difficult to find footing. Litigation brought by individual citizens to challenge the constitutionality of FDR's action was routinely dismissed by federal district courts because the plaintiffs lacked standing to sue.[78]

The destroyer deal jump-started Roosevelt's reelection campaign. A Gallup Poll in late August showed FDR and Willkie in a virtual dead heat, the president leading 51 to 49 percent. By mid-September Roosevelt had opened a ten-point gap.[79] Willkie had failed to find a winning issue or to breach the New Deal coalition. Despite his endorsement by John L. Lewis, American workers remained staunchly Democratic. Willkie was booed from factory windows in Detroit, he was egged in Pontiac, and a rock was hurled through his train window in Grand Rapids.[80] Stories circulated about his German ancestry, about signs in his Indiana hometown reading "Nigger, don't let the sun go down on you."[81] Willkie's unpolished campaign style was both an asset and a liability. Voters responded favorably to his openness and unaffected sincerity, but his inexperience on the stump led to more than the usual number of foot-in-mouth encounters. Speaking to a labor audience in Pittsburgh he announced he would appoint a secretary of labor directly from the ranks of organized labor—a slam at Frances Perkins that drew raucous cheers. Hoping to get another big hand he added gratuitously, "And it will not be a woman either."

"Why didn't he have sense enough to leave well enough alone?" FDR asked Frances Perkins. "He was going good. Why did he have to insult every woman in the United States? It will make them mad, it will lose him votes." Which apparently it did.[82]

The campaign bristled with the customary ad hominem, but it was directed at the candidates' stance on public issues. The private lives of public figures were strictly private in 1940. The press respected that, politicians were more tolerant, and neither party sought to exploit personal lapses on the other side. The Democrats had two potential problems: Henry Wallace's mysticism and Undersecretary of State Sumner Welles's homosexuality. In late August the Republican National Committee obtained a packet of letters Wallace had written in 1933 and 1934 to a White Russian émigré and cult leader, Nicholas Roerich. Wallace had engaged Roerich in 1933 to undertake an analysis of drought-resistant grasses in Mongolia and had evidently fallen under his spell. The letters, addressed "Dear Guru," resonated with occult speculation sufficient to call into question Wallace's emotional stability. At Willkie's specific direction the Republicans did not make use of the material.[83] Similarly, Welles's sexual orientation did not enter the campaign even though senior executives of the Southern Railroad possessed affidavits from Pullman car porters attesting to the undersecretary's overtures. Returning to Washington from Speaker Bankhead's Alabama funeral on September 22, 1940,* Welles, who had been drinking heavily, propositioned each of the porters working in his car for oral sex. They refused and afterward reported the incident to their employers. The affair became a matter of Washington gossip but attracted no public notice.[84]

For the Republicans the problem involved Willkie's long-standing extra-marital relationship with Irita Van Doren, editor of the book review section of the *Herald Tribune,* the former wife of Columbia's renowned historian Carl Van Doren, and one of the nation's most influential literary figures. The granddaughter of a Confederate general and one year older than Willkie, she and the GOP standard-bearer had become companions in the late thirties. Irita introduced Willkie to New York's literary world and became his cultural mentor. Among those who gathered under her roof were Carl Sandburg, Rebecca West, Virginia Woolf, André Maurois, James Thurber, Sinclair Lewis,

---

* Speaker Bankhead, campaigning for the national ticket in Maryland, suffered a fatal hemorrhage and died at Washington's Naval Hospital on September 15, 1940. Cognizant of his error at the time of Senator Joseph Robinson's death, FDR not only attended the funeral in Jasper, Alabama, but instructed his entire cabinet to attend. The Southern Railroad laid on two special trains, one for the congressional delegation, another for the president's party. Hull was detained in Washington, and Welles substituted for him at the funeral. Irwin Gellman, *Secret Affairs: FDR, Cordell Hull, and Sumner Welles* 219–220 (New York: Enigma Books, 1995).

Dorothy Thompson, John Gunther, and William L. Shirer. Irita helped write Willkie's speeches and articles and, as one of Wendell's friends observed, was largely responsible for his "acceptance of himself as a political leader with original and important ideas."[85]

Irita was tall and slender, with dark eyes and a mass of pretty curls. "She was not pretty, but she was beautiful," said Shirer. "The kind of woman I like to look at," wrote Harold Ickes. "Physically well set up, but intelligent."[86] Hiram Hayden of the *American Scholar* thought "her graciousness was innate. It came from a sweetness deep within her."[87] FDR, who thrived on such gossip, said he understood she was "an awful nice gal."[88] During the campaign Irita remained in the background and Edith Willkie, the candidate's wife, traveled with her husband. "Politics makes strange bedfellows," Edith joked to reporters.[89] Like FDR's relationship with Eleanor, the Willkie marriage was one of residual affection and political expediency. "At the time I felt like [my mother] might be getting the short end of the stick," recalled Irita's daughter Barbara, "but that wasn't the case. She was wise enough to know that she had everything except the title. They were endlessly and happily in love."[90] The Democrats made no issue of the arrangement and did nothing to spread stories even by word of mouth.* It was their ace-in-the-hole should the Republicans go after Wallace.

Willkie campaigned tenaciously. The candidate, his staff, and seventy-five reporters spent seven weeks on a campaign train crisscrossing America. Willkie traveled 18,785 miles, visited 31 states, and delivered 560 speeches.[91] Roosevelt stayed close to the White House, making the occasional visit to a war plant or defense installation, all the while retaining the pose of commander in chief, the statesman above the fray. And with marked success. The more Willkie campaigned, the farther he fell behind. A Gallup Poll taken in late September indicated that Roosevelt's lead had increased to twelve points. When voters were asked who they thought would win in November, 68 percent said FDR.[92]

Willkie found himself without a cause. The third-term issue fizzled. "I would

---

* Willkie deplored the hypocrisy of politics and insisted that his private life was his own. Several times during the campaign he scheduled press conferences at Van Doren's apartment. "Everybody knows about us—all the newspapermen in New York," Willkie told his friends. "If somebody should come along to threaten me or embarrass me about Irita, I would say, 'Go right ahead. There is not a reporter in New York who does not know about her.'" Steve Neal, *Dark Horse: A Biography of Wendell Willkie* 43–44 (Lawrence: University Press of Kansas, 1984).

rather have FDR with all his known faults than Willkie with his unknown qualities," said New York's independent mayor Fiorello La Guardia.[93] On domestic
matters Willkie supported the accomplishments of the New Deal. Unemployment provided a talking point, but the war boom had begun, workers were
streaming back to factories, steel mills were humming with new orders, and the
construction industry was working at full capacity. On foreign policy Willkie
supported aid to Britain, selective service, and rearmament. It was a "me too"
campaign which except for Willkie's winning personality provided the voter
few reasons to change. Roosevelt was "not a perfect man," Carl Sandburg told a
national radio audience, yet he was "more precious than fine gold."[94]

With his campaign in danger of imploding, Willkie shifted gears. Pressed by
his Republican handlers to become more aggressive, Willkie reversed course
on foreign policy. At first he moved cautiously. In Boston on October 11 he
promised an enormous crowd, including many traditional Democrats of Irish
and Italian extraction, "We shall not undertake to fight anybody else's war. Our
boys shall stay out of European wars."[95] As Willkie's poll numbers crept up, he
intensified his attack. He became the peace candidate and FDR the warmon-
ger. "If [Roosevelt's] promise to keep our boys out of foreign wars is no better
than his promise to balance the budget, they're already almost on the transports."[96] Excess begat excess. Willkie hinted that secret agreements were in
place to take the United States to war. "On the basis of [Roosevelt's] past performance, you may expect war by April, 1941, if he is elected," he told an audience in Baltimore.[97]

By mid-October Willkie's attacks were sending tremors through Democratic ranks. Ed Flynn, who had succeeded Farley as national chairman, sent
dire warnings of the defection of Italian voters in the Bronx and of Germans,
who could turn the tide in the Midwest. The Irish vote in Massachusetts was in
play, and Senator Walsh, up for reelection, was campaigning on an anti-
Roosevelt, isolationist platform.[98] A Gallup Poll taken the second week in October showed that if there were no war in Europe, Willkie would defeat
Roosevelt 53 to 47 percent.[99]

Roosevelt surveyed the damage and decided it was time to respond. "I'm
fighting mad," he told Harold Ickes on October 17.[100] The following day the
White House announced that the president would make five campaign
speeches in the final two weeks leading up to the election, ostensibly to correct
Republican misstatements.[101]

FDR opened the campaign at a mass rally in Philadelphia the night of October 23. "I consider it a public duty to answer falsifications with facts," he told the cheering crowd. "I will not pretend that I find this an unpleasant duty. I am an old campaigner, and I love a good fight."[102] Roosevelt had never been better. His timing was flawless. "He's all the Barrymores rolled into one," a reporter exclaimed.[103]

Roosevelt said the Republicans (he never mentioned Willkie by name) charged that there were secret agreements to take the country to war.

I give to you and to the people of this country this most solemn assurance:

There is no secret treaty, no secret obligation, no secret commitment, no secret understanding in any shape or form, direct or indirect, with any other Government, to involve this nation in any war or for any other purpose.[104]

Five nights later, after a fourteen-hour day touring New York City's five boroughs in an open car—the crowds estimated at more than 2 million—Roosevelt gave another bang-up speech at Madison Square Garden. Mussolini had invaded Greece hours before, and the president expressed his sorrow. No "stab-in-the-back" accusation, simply his concern for "the Italian people and the Grecian people, that they should have been involved together in conflict."

The speech was a slashing attack on the Republican leadership, everyone but Willkie, whom the president again did not mention. FDR was in a rhetorical groove, and the crowd roared its approval—especially after the tag line "Martin, Barton, and Fish" rolled off his tongue in rhythmic cadence. "Great Britain and a lot of other nations would never have received one ounce of help from us—if the decision had been left to Martin, Barton, and Fish."* Several

---

* The reference, following FDR's castigation of Republican Senators McNary, Vandenberg, Nye, and Johnson, was to Representatives Joseph W. Martin, Bruce Barton, and Hamilton Fish. Martin was House minority leader and had been named by Willkie to be Republican National Chairman; Barton, chairman of the board of the New York advertising firm Batten, Barton, Durstine & Osborn, represented New York's Seventeenth District on the fashionable Upper East Side; and Fish, Roosevelt's Dutchess County neighbor and longtime nemesis, was the ranking member on Foreign Affairs.

paragraphs later Roosevelt repeated the refrain, and the audience chanted it with him fortissimo.[105]

Roosevelt's assault stunned the Republicans. With two speeches FDR had regained the initiative. Willkie responded with increased invective, and Roosevelt reciprocated. Two days later in Boston he ended the debate with a blockbuster: "I have said before, but I shall say it again and again and again. Your boys are not going to be sent into any foreign wars."[106]

"That hypocritical son of a bitch," said Willkie, who was listening to the speech with his brother. "This is going to beat me."[107]

On the train to Boston, Roosevelt had put the finishing touches on the speech. In past talks he had always added the words "except in case of attack," just as the Democratic platform put it. When Sam Rosenman pointed that out, FDR dismissed it. "It's not necessary. If we're attacked it's no longer a foreign war."[108] When all is said and done, Franklin Roosevelt was the most unforgiving of politicians. When the stakes were highest he was at his most ruthless. Farley and Bankhead learned that in Chicago. Willkie learned it when FDR spoke in Boston.

Roosevelt closed the campaign with a speech in Cleveland on November 2. Rosenman, who heard FDR deliver speeches for seventeen years, thought the 1940 Cleveland speech was his finest.

> Although it was a campaign speech, it was pitched on a level far above the political battle. It expressed the President's hopes, philosophy and aspirations; it laid out a blueprint for the America of the future. As an example of what the President could do in preparing a speech under great pressure of time and circumstance it was unequaled.
>
> His delivery in this speech was better than in any other speech I have ever heard him make. It is difficult to analyze the oratory of a speaker to see what it is that makes his delivery of speeches effective and moving. Over the years I watched Roosevelt with ever-growing wonderment and admiration as he made speeches of all kinds with exactly the right effect. There were the homey fireside chats, the stirring campaign speeches of attack, the argumentative and persuasive addresses to the Congress, the extemporaneous informal remarks on the rear platform of a train, at a Thanksgiving dinner in Warm Springs, to a group of newspaper editors

calling on him at the White House. Each speech seemed perfectly attuned to the audience and to the occasion.

Though FDR had a team of speechwriters, including Rosenman and the playwright Robert Sherwood, he did the final drafts himself, always in longhand. One of Roosevelt's great advantages, said Rosenman, was that he knew the speech thoroughly from beginning to end. "He had worked so hard and continuously on it that he knew it almost by heart. He knew the development of the theme, he knew always what was coming next, and the result was that his delivery progressed in solid logical fashion from one point to another, making it easy to follow and understand him. He could look away from the manuscript so much that many people did not even know he was reading."[109]

The most moving passages of the Cleveland speech painted FDR's vision of what lay ahead:

I see an America where factory workers are not discarded after they reach their prime, where there is no endless chain of poverty from generation to generation, where impoverished farmers and farm hands do not become homeless wanderers, where monopoly does not make youth a beggar for a job.

I see an America whose rivers and valleys and lakes—hills and streams and plains—the mountains over our land and nature's wealth deep under the earth—are protected as the rightful heritage of all the people.

I see an America where small business really has a chance to flourish and grow.

I see an America of great cultural and educational opportunity for all its people.

I see an America where the income from the land shall be implemented and protected by a Government determined to guarantee to those who hoe it a fair share in the national income.

An America where the wheels of trade and private industry continue to turn to make the goods for America.

I see an America with peace in the ranks of labor.

An America where the workers are really free. Where the dignity and security of the working man and woman are guaranteed by their own strength and fortified by the safeguards of law.

An America where those who have reached the evening of life shall live out their years in peace and security. Where pensions and insurance for these aged shall be given as a matter of right to those who through a long life of labor have served their families and their nation as well.

I see an America devoted to our freedom—unified by tolerance and by religious faith—a people consecrated to peace, a people confident in strength because their body and their spirit are secure and unafraid.[110]

On November 5, 1940, 50 million Americans went to the polls, the largest number ever. The final Gallup polls showed Roosevelt leading by a slim 52 to 48 percent. More worrisome was the state-by-state breakout. In addition to rock-ribbed Republican strongholds, Willkie held slim leads in Illinois, Michigan, Ohio, New York, and Pennsylvania—industrial states with large electoral vote totals the Democrats could ill afford to lose.[111] FDR anticipated a cliffhanger. His entry in the traditional preelection poll taken by the White House press pool showed him with 315 electoral votes to Willkie's 216.

On Tuesday evening FDR settled in with friends and staff at Hyde Park to take the returns. The early reports from New York and New Jersey were glum. As Ed Flynn had warned, Italian precincts were going heavily for Willkie and the Irish less so. Upstate, Democrats were running behind. In the city, only the Jewish vote was holding firm. Roosevelt asked to be left alone. With Mike Reilly of the Secret Service manning the dining room door, FDR tabulated the returns for the next hour by himself. The voter turnout (62.5 percent) was the greatest in more than three decades, and gradually the tide turned.[112] By nine it was clear that the great industrial states in the East and Middle West would fall in behind the president.

The dining room doors were flung open, and the celebration began. By midnight the magnitude of the victory was clear. Roosevelt received 27,263,448 votes to Willkie's 22,336,260. In the electoral college, FDR took 449 votes and Willkie won 82. Except for Maine, Vermont, and six farm states in the great plains, Willkie carried only Michigan and his native Indiana. Roosevelt won every large city in the country except Cincinnati. Labor and blacks remained in the Democratic column. A strong showing among Polish Americans helped offset the losses in the Italian community. German Americans for the most part voted Republican.[113] The Democrats picked up six seats in the House, giving them a 268–162 majority, and lost three in the Senate, which they still controlled by well over 2 to 1.

The hostility between Roosevelt and Willkie faded quickly. Willkie conceded gracefully and called upon the nation to cast bitterness aside and give the president the support and respect he deserved. FDR invited Willkie to the White House and took an immediate liking to him. "You know, he's a very good fellow," Roosevelt told Frances Perkins. "He has lots of talent. I want to use him somehow. I want him to do something where the effort is nonpolitical but important. But I'd like to use him, and I think it would be a good thing for the country, it would help us to a feeling of unity."[114]

TWENTY-TWO

ARSENAL OF DEMOCRACY

---

*The decision as to how much shall be sent abroad
and how much shall remain at home must be made
on the basis of our over-all military necessities. . . .
We must be the great arsenal of democracy.*
—FRANKLIN D. ROOSEVELT, DECEMBER 29, 1940

THE THURSDAY AFTER the election, Roosevelt boarded the presidential train in Hyde Park for the long, slow journey back to Washington. At Union Station Vice President–elect Henry Wallace welcomed him along with a swarm of jubilant Democrats. Two hundred thousand cheering spectators lined Pennsylvania Avenue. FDR repeatedly doffed his battered campaign fedora as the open limousine made its way to the White House. Thousands of well-wishers followed the car through the open gates of the Executive Mansion chanting "We Want Roosevelt" until the president and Eleanor appeared on the north portico.[1]

Waiting for Roosevelt was a congratulatory message from Churchill. "I did not think it right for me as a Foreigner to express my opinion upon American politics while the Election was on," said the prime minister, "but now I feel you will not mind my saying that I prayed for your success."[2] Bismarck had said that the most important geopolitical fact of the modern era was that the Americans spoke English, and Churchill exploited that fact shamelessly.[3] "Things are afoot which will be remembered as long as the English language is spoken in any quarter of the globe," he told Roosevelt. "In expressing the comfort I feel that the people of the United States have once again cast these great burdens upon you, I must avow my faith that the lights by which we steer will bring us all safely to anchor."[4]

As Churchill wrote out that message, the Battle of Britain approached a climax. The Luftwaffe had failed to gain air superiority over the Channel; Operation Sea Lion—the German invasion plan for the British Isles—had been shelved, yet air attacks against civilian targets accelerated. For fifty-seven consecutive nights the Nazis bombed London: ten thousand were dead, more than fifty thousand injured.[5] On November 14 three hundred German bombers hit Coventry, kindling a firestorm that claimed 568 civilian casualties and destroyed the city's center.* Five nights later, 1,353 people were killed in a massive raid on Birmingham.[6] At sea, the battle hung in the balance. More than five hundred British merchant ships had been sunk by German U-boats and surface raiders—a total of more than 2 million tons of lost shipping that was difficult to replace. Most serious of all, Britain was on the verge of bankruptcy. The "cash-and-carry" provision of the Neutrality Act had drained the British Treasury of its dollar reserves.

Roosevelt appeared in little hurry to offer assistance. No one was better at laying a smoke screen to cloak his intentions than FDR, and he masked his plans for aid to Britain in postelection euphoria. In late November, Lord Lothian, who had just returned from London, called on the president to explain Britain's plight. At his press conference on November 26 Roosevelt was asked:

Q: Mr. President, did the British Ambassador present any specific requests for additional help?

FDR: Nothing was mentioned in that regard at all, not one single thing—ships or sealing wax or anything else.[7]

Roosevelt's cavalier denial concealed the intense planning that was under way in Washington. On Tuesday, December 3, Hull, Stimson, Knox, Commerce secretary Jesse Jones, and General Marshall met with Morgenthau at the Treasury to review Britain's financial situation. As Treasury officials scrawled figures across a blackboard, the inescapable conclusion was that the British would exhaust their gold and dollar reserves within the month just to pay for

---

* Over the years allegations have been made that Churchill declined to order preparatory air defense measures for Coventry so as not to reveal that the British were able to decrypt (code name Ultra) German radio signals. To the contrary, the Air Ministry took prompt defensive action. Fighters were scrambled, bombers dispatched to hit the fields from which the German planes departed, and the antiaircraft barrage that night over Coventry was greater than any yet put up and succeeded in keeping the attacking aircraft at very high levels. Martin Gilbert, *Churchill: A Life* 683–684 (New York: Henry Holt, 1991).

the orders already placed with American industry. The money to pay for future orders was nowhere in sight. "What are we going to do?" asked Morgenthau. "Are we going to let them place more orders?"

"Got to," said Knox. "No choice about it."[8]

Roosevelt took the problem with him when he departed Washington the next day for a Caribbean cruise on the USS *Tuscaloosa* accompanied only by Hopkins and his immediate staff—Pa Watson, Dr. McIntire, and Navy captain Daniel Callaghan. The White House proclaimed the purpose of the cruise was to inspect base sites in the West Indies, but FDR wanted time at sea to refresh and regroup.* Aside from meeting local dignitaries, including the Duke of Windsor, Roosevelt spent his days fishing, basking in the sun, and spoofing with cronies. Evenings were devoted to poker and movies. When Ernest Hemingway sent word that many big fish had been caught on a stretch of the Mona Passage between the Dominican Republic and Puerto Rico, FDR trawled there for several hours using a feathered hook baited with a piece of pork rind as Hemingway suggested but failed to get a strike.[9]

Roosevelt seemed carefree and relaxed, almost indifferent to the calamity facing Britain. "I didn't know for quite a while what he was thinking about, if anything," said Hopkins. "But then—I began to get the idea he was refueling, the way he so often does when he seems to be resting and carefree." There were no substantive discussions on board, Roosevelt did not consult or ask advice, he did not study briefing documents or background papers, but it soon became clear he was pondering Britain's problem and plotting his response.[10]

On December 9 Roosevelt's thoughts were stimulated when a Navy seaplane set down alongside *Tuscaloosa*, lying at anchor off Antigua. In the mail pouch was a historic letter from Churchill, a four-thousand-word cable that

---

* "I try to get away a couple of times a year on these short trips on salt water," said Roosevelt in his 1941 Jackson Day message to the Democratic faithful. "In Washington the working day of the President averages about fifteen hours. But at sea the radio messages and the occasional pouch of mail reduce official work to not more than two or three hours a day.

"So there is a chance for a bit of sunshine or a wetted line, or a biography or detective story or a nap after lunch. Above all there is the opportunity for thinking things through— for differentiating between principles and methods, between the really big things of life and those other things of the moment which may seem all-important today and are forgotten in a month." 10 *Public Papers and Addresses of Franklin D. Roosevelt* 82–83, Samuel I. Rosenman, ed. (New York: Harper & Brothers, 1950).

the prime minister considered "one of the most important of my life" and that historians describe as "the most carefully drafted and re-drafted message in the entire Churchill-Roosevelt correspondence."[11]

The letter was Churchill at his best: articulate, comprehensive, well argued, dignified yet deferential. The prime minister began with a masterly restatement of the military situation. He traced the war in minute detail from the North Sea to Gibraltar to Suez to Singapore. "The danger of Great Britain being destroyed by a swift, overwhelming blow has for the time being very greatly receded. In its place there is a long, gradually maturing danger, less sudden and less spectacular, but equally deadly." Churchill reviewed the problems of war production and sea tonnage, both imperiled by persistent attacks by German bombers and U-boats. But the most serious problem Britain faced was financial:

> The moment approaches when we shall no longer be able to pay cash for shipping and other supplies. While we will do our utmost, and shrink from no proper sacrifice to make payments across the Exchange, I believe you will agree that it would be wrong in principle and mutually disadvantageous in effect if at the height of this struggle Great Britain were to be divested of all saleable assets, so that after the victory was won with our blood, civilization saved, and the time gained for the United States to be fully armed against all eventualities, we should stand stripped to the bone.[12]

Hopkins recalled that Roosevelt read and reread Churchill's letter as he sat alone in his deck chair, and for two days he did not seem to reach any conclusion. "He was plunged in intense thought, and brooded silently."[13] Then one evening it all came out: the program the world would know as Lend-Lease. "He didn't seem to have any clear idea how it could be done legally. But there wasn't a doubt in his mind that he'd find a way to do it."[14] Essentially, the president's plan was that the United States would lend Britain whatever it needed, at no cost, and the British would repay the United States by giving back what it had borrowed, or in some other tangible manner, when it could.[15] Like a creative artist, FDR had devoted his time on the cruise to evolving his conceptual idea. Once he saw it clearly, he moved decisively.[16]

Back in Washington a week later, tanned and rested from his cruise, Roosevelt unveiled his masterpiece—"one of the greatest efforts of all his years in office," said Morgenthau.[17] Meeting the press the afternoon of December 17, he broke the news. There had been no staff studies, no diplomatic discussions, no touching of political bases. It was pure Roosevelt. The president took the initiative himself.[18] The working press, especially the White House press corps, was always FDR's greatest ally, and he initiated the debate with a homey analogy:

> Suppose my neighbor's home catches fire, and I have a length of garden hose four or five hundred feet away. If he can take my garden hose and connect it up with his hydrant, I may help him to put out his fire. Now what do I do? I don't say to him, "Neighbor, my garden hose cost me fifteen dollars; you have to pay me fifteen dollars for it." No! I don't want fifteen dollars. I want my garden hose back after the fire is over.

"What I am trying to do is eliminate the dollar sign," he continued. "Get rid of the silly, foolish, old dollar sign." Weapons and war materiel would be of greater service if they were used in Great Britain rather than kept in storage. After the war the United States would be repaid in kind, thereby "leaving out the dollar mark and substituting for it a gentleman's obligation in kind. I think you all get it."[19] Churchill, who had no prior knowledge of the president's plan, was stunned. When he digested the proposal he told Parliament that Lend-Lease was "the most unsordid act in the history of any nation."[20]

With Congress adjourned until the new year, Roosevelt carried his idea directly to the country. On Sunday, December 29, 1940, he delivered one of his most famous fireside chats, the "arsenal of democracy" speech. He called it a talk on national security, coining an expression that would permeate American debate for generations.[21] Movie theaters, restaurants, and other public places emptied as nine o'clock Eastern Standard time approached. CBS, NBC, and the Mutual network carried the address live, and a record 75 percent of Americans would either listen to or read the president's remarks.[22] In the White House, Clark Gable and his wife, Carole Lombard, joined Eleanor, Sara, and members of the cabinet to watch FDR declare that there was no hope of a negotiated peace with Hitler. "No man can tame a tiger into a kitten by stroking it. There can be no appeasement with ruthlessness. There can be no reasoning with an incendiary bomb."

Roosevelt told his listeners, "If Britain goes down, the Axis powers will control the continents of Europe, Asia, Africa, Australasia, and the high seas—and they will be in a position to bring enormous military and naval resources against this hemisphere." The United States must prepare for the danger ahead. "But we well know that we cannot escape danger, or the fear of danger, by crawling into bed and pulling the covers over our heads."

The answer for Roosevelt was unstinting support for Britain's resistance:

The people of Europe who are defending themselves do not ask us to do their fighting. They ask us for the implements of war, the planes, the tanks, the guns which will enable them to fight for their liberty and for our security. Emphatically we must get these weapons to them in sufficient volume and quickly enough, so that we and our children will be saved the agony and suffering of war.

We must be the great arsenal of democracy. For this is an emergency as serious as war itself. We must apply ourselves to our task with the same resolution, the same sense of urgency, the same spirit of patriotism and sacrifice as we would show were we at war.[23]*

At one point in the fireside chat Roosevelt spoke of German fifth columnists operating in the Western Hemisphere. Then followed the sentence "There are also American citizens, many of them in high places, who, unwittingly in most cases, are aiding and abetting the work of these agents."

When the speech had been submitted to the State Department, the draft came back with the words "many of them in high places" crossed out in red pencil. FDR, who had little affection for the nation's career diplomats, was appalled. "Leave it in," he instructed Rosenman. "In fact, I'm very much tempted to say, 'many of them in high places, *especially in the State Department.*' "[24]

---

* The phrase "arsenal of democracy" was first used by Jean Monnet, a representative of the French government in Washington, in a conversation with Justice Felix Frankfurter in late 1940. Frankfurter was struck by the phrase and suggested to Monnet that he desist using it until Roosevelt could make it his own. Assistant Secretary of War John J. McCloy also came upon the phrase (Monnet and McCloy were very close friends), and it was contained in a speech draft submitted to the White House by the War Department. When he saw it, Roosevelt said, "I love it," and included it. Samuel I. Rosenman, *Working with Roosevelt* 260–261 (New York: Harper & Brothers, 1952); Kai Bird, *The Chairman: John J. McCloy and the Making of the American Establishment* 121 (New York: Simon & Schuster, 1992).

In much the way that Churchill galvanized British resistance, Roosevelt's speeches and press conferences in December 1940 and January 1941 deepened America's understanding of what was at stake.[25] Buoyed by his unprecedented third-term mandate, FDR assumed command of public opinion as he had done during the hundred days in 1933. Letters and telegrams to the White House after his fireside chat ran 100 to 1 in the president's favor. A Gallup Poll in early January showed 68 percent of Americans in favor of Lend-Lease and only 26 percent opposed.[26] In Britain and throughout the Commonwealth the public was thrilled by Roosevelt's stirring affirmation of American purpose. Churchill wrote that it was his duty "on behalf of the British Government and indeed the whole British Empire to tell you, Mr. President, how lively is our sense of gratitude and admiration for the memorable declaration which you made to the American people and to the lovers of Freedom in all continents on last Sunday."[27]

On January 6 Roosevelt went to Capitol Hill to deliver his ninth State of the Union message. The bulk of the president's speech was devoted to preparedness, defense production, and the necessity for Lend-Lease. "Let us say to the democracies: 'We Americans are vitally concerned in your defense of freedom. We are putting forth our energies, our resources and our organizing powers to give you the strength to regain and maintain a free world. We shall send you, in ever increasing numbers, ships, planes, tanks, guns. This is our purpose and our pledge.' "

But the address is remembered for Roosevelt's peroration:

In future days, which we seek to make secure, we look forward to a world founded upon four essential human freedoms.

The first is freedom of speech and expression. . . .

The second is freedom of every person to worship God in his own way. . . .

The third is freedom from want. . . .

The fourth is freedom from fear. . . .[28]

Like Lend-Lease, the Four Freedoms were Roosevelt's idea. "Nobody ghost-wrote those words," said Robert Sherwood.[29] Sitting in his upstairs study two nights before the speech was to be delivered, going over the third draft with Rosenman, Sherwood, and Hopkins, FDR said he had an idea for the peroration. "We waited as he leaned far back in his swivel chair with his gaze on the ceiling," Rosenman remembered. "It was a long pause—so long that it began to be uncomfortable." Then he began dictating. "The words seemed to roll off his tongue as though he had rehearsed them many times to himself.* A comparison with the final speech will show that his dictation was changed by only a word here and there, so perfect had been the formulation in his own mind."[30]

Shortly after the State of the Union, Wendell Willkie paid a courtesy call at the White House preparatory to a goodwill visit to England.† When he was announced, FDR was closeted in the Cabinet Room with Rosenman and Sherwood working on his January 20 inaugural address. The president shifted himself onto his wheelchair and moved into the Oval Office to greet Willkie, only to discover that his desk was clear of papers. He turned back to the Cabinet Room and told Rosenman and Sherwood to give him some papers.

"Which particular papers do you want, Mr. President?" asked Rosenman.

"Oh, it doesn't matter," said FDR. "Just give me a handful to strew around on my desk so I will look very busy when Willkie comes in."[31]

Roosevelt and Willkie spent more than an hour together. "At regular intervals great bursts of laughter could be heard coming through the closed doors," James Roosevelt reported.[32] At one point Willkie asked Roosevelt why he retained Harry Hopkins as an intimate adviser in view of Hopkins's general unpopularity. "Someday you may well be sitting here where I am now," FDR replied. "And when you are, you'll realize what a lonely job it is, and you'll dis-

---

* At his press conference on July 5, 1940, Roosevelt gave an offhand answer to a question about his long-range peace objectives in which he casually alluded to five freedoms, two of them falling under the heading "freedom of speech." The fifth freedom, freedom from want, was suggested by Richard L. Harkness, then with *The Philadelphia Inquirer,* later with NBC News. "I had that in mind but forgot it," said FDR. "That is the fifth, very definitely." Press Conference 658, July 5, 1940. 16 *Complete Presidential Press Conferences of Franklin D. Roosevelt* 21–22 (New York: Da Capo Press, 1972).

† Willkie's visit to England was the product of a December 1940 meeting between the chief British intelligence agent in the United States, William Stephenson, and Roosevelt. When FDR asked how he could make a gesture to hearten the British, Stephenson suggested sending Willkie. Roosevelt liked the idea, and at a New Year's Eve party Justice Frankfurter, evidently speaking on the president's behalf, broached the idea to Irita Van Doren. Van Doren passed it on to Willkie, who was receptive. Final arrangements were made at a January 15, 1941, dinner at Van Doren's Upper West Side apartment attended by Willkie, Frankfurter, the publisher Harold Guinzburg, and the writer Dorothy Thompson. Steve Neal, *Dark Horse: A Biography of Wendell Willkie* 188–190 (New York: Doubleday, 1984).

cover the need for somebody like Harry Hopkins who asks for nothing except to serve you."[33]

As Willkie prepared to leave, Roosevelt took a sheet of his personal stationery and commenced writing:

> Dear Churchill,
>   Wendell Willkie will give you this. He is truly helping to keep politics out over here.

Then from memory FDR wrote out a passage from Henry Wadsworth Longfellow's "Building of the Ship," which he had learned as a schoolboy at Groton:

> Thou, too, sail on, O Ship of State!
> Sail on, O Union, strong and great!
> Humanity with all its fears,
> With all the hope of future years
> Is hanging breathless on thy fate.[34]

On January 10, 1941, the Lend-Lease bill (H.R. 1776) was introduced by Majority Leader John W. McCormack of Massachusetts in the House and Alben Barkley in the Senate. Isolationist opponents had a brief field day. The *Chicago Tribune* called H.R. 1776 "a dictator bill" designed to destroy the Republic. New York's Thomas E. Dewey said it meant "an end to free government in the United States." Senator Burton K. Wheeler claimed it "will plough under every fourth American boy." Senator Vandenberg asserted that the bill gave FDR the authority "to make war on any country he pleases any time he pleases." The best line was delivered by Senator Robert Taft of Ohio: "Lending war equipment is a good deal like lending chewing gum. You don't want it back."[35]

The isolationists had the headlines, but Roosevelt had the votes. Polls consistently showed three quarters of Americans supported the president and Lend-Lease.[36] On February 8 the bill cleared the House 260–165, largely along party lines. The following day Wendell Willkie, back from Britain, testified before the Senate Foreign Relations Committee. Nearly 1,200 people crammed into the splendorous Caucus Room (more than twice its rated capacity) to hear the former GOP nominee. They were not disappointed. Breaking with his party's congressional leadership, Willkie endorsed Lend-Lease down the line. The most dramatic segment of Willkie's testimony came when he was questioned about his remarks during the campaign that Roosevelt would lead the nation into war. Willkie said he saw no constructive purpose in discussing old campaign speeches. "I struggled as hard as I could to beat Franklin Roosevelt and I tried to keep from pulling my punches. He was elected president. He is my president now."

Thunderous applause shook the Caucus Room. Nevertheless, Senator Gerald Nye persisted. He quoted Willkie's Baltimore statement that the United States would be at war by April 1941 if Roosevelt was reelected.

"You ask me if I said that." Willkie grinned. The Caucus Room erupted.

When the laughter died down, Nye continued: "Do you still agree that might be the case?"

"It might be. It was a bit of campaign oratory." More laughter. "I'm very glad you read my speeches because the president said he did not."[37] Howls of laughter and sustained, foot-stomping applause.

For practical purposes the debate was over. Willkie's good nature and obvious sincerity carried the day. Just as with selective service, his support for Lend-Lease broke the back of the opposition.

The following day Senator George of Georgia, the new chairman of Foreign Relations, pushed the bill through committee 15–8. On March 8 the full Senate added its approval 60–31, and three days later the House accepted the Senate version by a lopsided 317–71. Roosevelt's preparedness coalition was in full control. Unrepentant Southern Democrats—men like Carter Glass, Pat Harrison, "Cotton Ed" Smith, and Walter George—joined big-city liberals and Republican internationalists to put the president's program across. FDR signed the bill into law thirty minutes after its final passage. The next day Congress appropriated $7 billion to fund the first shipments to Great Britain, the largest single appropriation in American history.* "This decision is the end of any attempts at appeasement," said FDR. "The end of urging us to get along with dictators; the end of compromise with tyranny and the forces of oppression."[38]

Passage of Lend-Lease repealed the "cash" provision of the Neutrality Act.

* The Defense Aid Supplemental Appropriations Act passed the House 336–55 and the Senate 67–9. Among the items included in the first consignment to Great Britain were 900,000 feet of fire hose. Samuel I. Rosenman, *Working with Roosevelt* 272 (New York: Harper & Brothers, 1952).

The "carry" requirement remained in effect. Whatever aid America supplied had to be carried in British bottoms. That posed a serious problem. There was little point providing $7 billion for military aid if it ended up on the ocean floor. In the three months leading up to Lend-Lease, 142 vessels, roughly 800,000 tons of shipping, had been sunk. German U-boats were sinking British ships three times faster than shipyards could replace them. In Churchill's words, the Battle of Britain had become the Battle of the Atlantic.[39]

Roosevelt responded on April 10 by announcing that the United States had concluded an agreement with the Danish government in exile permitting U.S. forces to occupy Greenland and establish bases there.[40] The following day he advised Churchill he was extending the American security zone in the Atlantic to 25 degrees west longitude, roughly midway between the westernmost bulge of Africa and the easternmost bulge of Brazil. The Navy would patrol that zone and inform the British of all enemy vessels sighted. "It is important for domestic political reasons . . . that this action be taken by us unilaterally," Roosevelt told Churchill. "When this new policy is adopted here no statement [should] be issued on your end."[41]*

At his press conference on April 25 the president was asked to distinguish between a patrol and a convoy. Was the United States planning to convoy British merchant vessels? "No," said Roosevelt. The difference between a patrol and a convoy was similar to the difference between a horse and a cow. "You can't turn a cow into a horse by calling it something else. It is still a cow. This is a patrol."

Q: Could you define its functions?

FDR: Protection of the American hemisphere.

Q: By belligerent means?

FDR: Protection of the American hemisphere.

Q: Mr. President, if this patrol should discover some apparently aggressive ships headed toward the Western Hemisphere, what would it do about it?

FDR: Let me know. (*Loud laughter.*)[42]

---

* At cabinet Roosevelt said the patrols were a step forward. "Keep on walking, Mr. President," replied Stimson. "Keep on walking." Stimson diary (MS), April 25, 1941.

Roosevelt's elliptical response reflected his determination not to get too far in front of public opinion. Gallup Polls in April showed overwhelming support for all-out aid to Britain, and FDR's approval rating stood at 73 percent. But the country was evenly divided on whether the Navy should be placed on convoy duty, and a whopping 81 percent opposed America's entry into war.[43] Roosevelt's caution rankled the hawks in the administration. "The President is loath to get into this war," noted Morgenthau. "He would rather follow public opinion than lead it."[44] Stimson, Knox, and Ickes concurred. Even the military chimed in. "How much a part of our Democratic way of life will be handled by Mr. Gallup is a pure guess," Admiral Stark complained to the commander of the Pacific Fleet.[45] A more understanding assessment was offered by King George VI, who watched Roosevelt's helmsmanship with undisguised admiration. "I have been so struck" he wrote the president, "by the way you have led public opinion by allowing it to get ahead of you."[46] Roosevelt's stance involved more than public relations. Like Lincoln before Fort Sumter or Wilson prior to World War I, FDR told his cabinet he was "not willing to fire the first shot." If the United States went to war, it would be because it was attacked.[47]

Despite the expanded American patrol zone in the Atlantic, British losses continued to mount. In the first three weeks of May, twenty merchant vessels were lost to German submarines in the area Roosevelt had staked out.[48] The war was going badly elsewhere as well. In the Balkans, German troops swept through Yugoslavia and expelled the British army from Greece. In North Africa, the Wehrmacht had superseded the Italian Army in Libya and pushed eastward to the Egyptian border. Crete was about to fall, Syria and Iraq were in danger, and the neutral nations—Spain, Portugal, and Turkey—were threatening to jump on the German bandwagon. On May 3 a despondent Churchill asked Roosevelt to intervene. "Mr. President, I am sure you will not misunderstand me if I speak to you exactly what is on my mind. The one decisive counterweight I can see . . . would be if the United States were immediately to range herself with us as a belligerent power. If this were possible I have little doubt that we could hold the situation in the Mediterranean until the weight of your munitions gained the day."[49]

Roosevelt responded on May 10. He ignored Churchill's plea for the United States to enter the war and reassured him that aid was on the way. "Thirty ships are now being loaded to go to the Middle East. I know your determination to win on that front and we shall do everything that we possibly can to help you do it." The president reminded Churchill, "this struggle is going to be decided in the Atlantic. Unless Hitler can win there he cannot win anywhere in the world."[50]

On May 27 Roosevelt notched public awareness a step higher with his first fireside chat of the year. The speech, as Assistant Secretary of State Adolf A. Berle observed, was "calculated to scare the daylights out of everyone."[51] The president spoke from the East Room of the White House to a worldwide audience of some 85 million. After laying out the threat posed by Nazi Germany, he announced his intention to ensure the delivery of needed supplies to Britain by whatever means were necessary. "I say that this can be done; it must be done; and it will be done." That was followed by a "proclamation of unlimited national emergency."[52] Roosevelt did not ask for repeal of the Neutrality Act, he did not request new statutory authority, nor did he suggest the Navy undertake convoy responsibility. Nevertheless, by declaring an unlimited national emergency he prepared public opinion for the prospect that hostilities might follow. "I hope you will like the speech," FDR cabled Churchill. "It goes further than I thought it was possible to go even two weeks ago."[53]

Public response was overwhelmingly favorable. Ninety-five percent of the telegrams to the White House supported the president.[54] A Gallup Poll in early June showed a clear majority of Americans now favored armed convoys to protect vessels carrying goods to Britain. In the South, 75 percent were in favor.[55] "I hope that we will protect every dollar's worth of stuff that we send to Great Britain," said Senator Carter Glass of Virginia, "and that we will shoot the hell out of anybody who interferes."[56]

As May melded into June, Roosevelt confronted one of the most serious racial issues of his presidency. The nation's black leaders were concerned that qualified Negro workers were being passed over by defense contractors and not receiving their share of jobs. Led by A. Philip Randolph, the beloved and powerful head of the Brotherhood of Sleeping Car Porters, they organized a protest march on Washington and scheduled it for July 1. FDR sought to head them off. A black march in segregated Washington could easily provoke violence and at the very least would antagonize the southern leadership of his preparedness coalition. He asked Eleanor and New York mayor La Guardia to meet with Randolph and his colleagues and dissuade them. When that failed, Roosevelt invited the black leaders to the White House.

The meeting took place Wednesday afternoon, June 18. In addition to Randolph and NAACP head Walter White, the president invited Stimson, Knox, and La Guardia. When Randolph asked FDR if he would issue an executive order making it mandatory for the defense industry to hire black workers, Roosevelt declined. "If I issue an executive order for you," he told Randolph, "there will be no end of other groups coming in here and asking me to issue orders for them. In any event, I can't do anything unless you call off this march of yours."

"I'm sorry, Mr. President, the march cannot be called off."

"How many people do you plan to bring?"

"One hundred thousand, Mr. President."

Thinking that Randolph was bluffing, FDR turned to White. "Walter, how many people will really march?"

"One hundred thousand, Mr. President."

Roosevelt recalled the 1919 Washington race riots, when he had been assistant secretary of the Navy. "You can't bring 100,000 Negroes to Washington. Someone might get killed." Randolph held firm, and Roosevelt continued to resist. Finally, La Guardia broke the impasse: "Gentlemen, it is clear that Mr. Randolph is not going to call off the march. I suggest we all begin to seek a formula."[57] FDR at length agreed and asked the group to adjourn to the Cabinet Room to hammer out an appropriate executive order. Negotiations over the precise wording required another week, and on June 25 the president signed Executive Order 8802, banning discrimination in the defense industry and the federal government because of "race, creed, color, or national origin."

Randolph canceled the march, and Roosevelt's action was an important civil rights breakthrough. For the first time since Reconstruction the U.S. government acted to guarantee equal opportunity for blacks. Roosevelt was not the prime mover; it was Randolph who had called the shots. But FDR was wise enough to recognize a just cause and flexible enough to acquiesce when it became necessary. If Lincoln's Emancipation Proclamation freed blacks from physical slavery, wrote the Amsterdam News, Roosevelt's executive order liberated them from economic captivity.[58]

It was about this time in the spring of 1941 that Missy's health began to fail. She was forty-three. For twenty years she had been at FDR's side—his secretary, companion, and confidante—but the strain of long hours with little respite had taken its toll. "The president would work night after night, and she was always there working with him," her friend Barbara Curtis remembered. "He could take it, but I think her strength just didn't hold out."[59]

After dinner with the president, Hopkins, Grace Tully, and Pa Watson on

June 4, Missy collapsed and fell to the floor unconscious. White House physicians initially diagnosed it as a slight heart attack brought on by overwork. In fact, it was a small stroke, a precursor of a massive stroke two weeks later that paralyzed her right side and rendered her unable to speak coherently. Missy was transferred from the White House to Doctors Hospital in Georgetown, where Franklin and Eleanor visited her frequently. As Doris Kearns Goodwin reports, the visits were unbearable for FDR. "All his life, he had steeled himself to ignore illness and unpleasantness of any kind." For Eleanor the visits were easier to handle. More accustomed to vulnerability and loss, she kept up a steady flow of flowers, fruit, presents, and letters.[60]

Grace Tully assumed Missy's secretarial duties, but she was not a companion for FDR. That void was never filled. And in his own way, quietly and with no outward emotion, Roosevelt grieved for Missy. While she was in the hospital he ordered round-the-clock nursing care, paid every expense, and wrote each of her doctors personal notes expressing his gratitude. Aware that Missy might never recover, FDR worried what would happen if he should die and there was no one to pay for her care. Five months after her stroke he changed his will, directing that half of the income from his estate (which was eventually probated at more than $3 million) be left to Eleanor and the remaining half "for the account of my friend Marguerite LeHand" to cover all expenses for "medical care and treatment during her lifetime." Upon Missy's death, the income would go to Eleanor, with the principal eventually divided equally among his five children.[61] "I owed her that much," Franklin told his son James. "She served me so well for so long and asked for so little in return."[62]*

On June 22, 1941, the war took a decisive turn. Without warning Hitler launched Operation Barbarossa, an invasion of his recent ally, the Soviet Union. At 0330 hours German forces poured across the Russian frontier from the Baltic to the Black Sea. One hundred and eighty divisions, 3.8 million men, supported by thousands of planes, tanks, and artillery pieces surged forward in

---

* Missy died in July 1944 without knowing the president had provided for her in his will. After her death, Roosevelt's son James, whom FDR had appointed his executor, suggested to his father that he might wish to change his will. Roosevelt refused. "If it embarrasses mother, I'm sorry. It shouldn't, but it may. But the clause is written so that in the event of Missy's death, that half reverts to mother, too, so she gets it all. Missy didn't make it, her half already has reverted to mother, and so the clause is inoperative. I don't have to change it, so I won't." James Roosevelt, *My Parents: A Differing View* 108 (Chicago: Playboy Press, 1976).

three parallel thrusts. In the north, Field Marshal Ritter von Leeb pressed toward Leningrad; in the center, Marshal von Bock drove on Smolensk and Moscow; in the south, von Rundstedt barreled through the Ukraine toward Kiev. Russian resistance crumbled. In four days German panzers were 200 miles deep in Soviet territory. Two Russian armies had been destroyed and three badly mauled, and 600,000 prisoners were in German captivity. In the air, the Russians lost 1,800 aircraft on the first day of fighting, 800 on the second, 557 on the third, and 351 on the fourth.[63]

Churchill responded with immediate support for the Soviet Union. "No one has been a more consistent opponent of Communism than I have for the last twenty-five years," he told a British radio audience the evening of June 22. "I will unsay no word that I have spoken about it. But all this fades away before the spectacle which is now unfolding. . . . Any man or state who fights on against Nazidom will have our aid. It follows, therefore, that we shall give whatever help we can to Russia and the Russian people."[64]*

Roosevelt followed Churchill's lead, gingerly at first, then with increasing vigor. On June 23, at the president's direction, the State Department issued a cautiously drafted statement affirming Hitler as the nation's number one enemy and proclaiming America's sympathy for any who opposed him "from whatever source." The Soviet Union was not mentioned.[65] Roosevelt may have been testing the waters, or the State Department may have resisted going further. In any event, at his press conference the following day the president came flat out: "Of course we are going to give all the aid that we possibly can to Russia." Roosevelt said he had no idea what the Russians needed and had not yet received any request from Moscow.

Q: Will any priorities on airplanes be assigned to Russia?

FDR: I don't know.

Q: Does any aid we could give come under Lend-Lease?

FDR: I don't know. . . . We will not cross that bridge until we come to it.[66]

* Shortly before the speech was delivered, Churchill's private secretary, J. R. Colville, noted the irony in WSC's warm support of the Soviet Union given his strong anti-Communist stance. "If Hitler invaded Hell," Churchill retorted, "I would at least make a favorable reference to the Devil in the House of Commons." Winston S. Churchill, *The Grand Alliance* 370 (Boston: Houghton Mifflin, 1951).

For Roosevelt there was no question that the Soviets should receive what they needed. He was no more fond of communism than Churchill was. But much of his political life was premised on the doctrine that the enemy of my enemy is my friend, and he saw no reason not to measure Stalin by that standard. The Soviet Union was scarcely engaged in fomenting world revolution and had not been since the mid-1920s. Even if it were, the universalist appeal of communism was far less reprehensible than the genocidal racism of Nazism. And although Russia had attacked Finland and absorbed the Baltic states, it displayed none of the aggressive imperialism of Germany and Italy.[67] But the American administration was divided. Career foreign service officers remained hostile to the Soviet Union; the military advised the White House that the Germans would sweep across Russia in one month, three at the most; and Stimson and Knox worried that supplies sent to the Soviets might fall into Hitler's hands. Together with Ickes, they urged that the breathing space provided by Hitler's invasion be utilized to win the war in the Atlantic.

There was also a political minefield to navigate. "The victory of Communism would be far more dangerous to the United States than a victory of Fascism," said Senator Robert Taft. "It's a case of dog eat dog," allowed Missouri's Bennett Champ Clark. "I don't think we should help either one." The isolationist press, led by the *Chicago Tribune* and the *New York Journal-American,* was predictably opposed to aid to Russia. More serious was the potential opposition of the Catholic Church. Many Catholics felt bound by the 1937 Encyclical of Pius XI, *Divini redemptoris,* which stated categorically, "Communism is intrinsically wrong and no one who would save Christian civilization may give it assistance in any undertaking whatsoever."[68]*

To short-circuit the hostility of the foreign service, Roosevelt sent Hopkins to meet Stalin and observe the situation firsthand. As in 1933, relations with Russia would be handled in the Oval Office. The diplomats would be relegated to the sidelines as interpreters and note takers. Hopkins was impressed by the Soviet resolve. When he returned to Washington, Roosevelt brushed aside the

* From the Vatican, Harold H. Tittman, the president's acting representative to the Holy See, advised Washington that in the Curia "the militant atheism of Communist Russia is still regarded as more obnoxious than the modern paganism of Nazi Germany." Tittman to State Department, June 30, 1941. Quoted in William L. Langer and S. Everett Gleason, *The Undeclared War* 547 (New York: Harper & Row, 1953).

War Department's military estimate; rejected the advice of Knox, Stimson, and Ickes to concentrate on the Battle of the Atlantic; and invited the Soviet ambassador in Washington, Constantine Ourmansky, to present a list of items the United States might supply to the Red Army. Within a week the Soviets submitted a detailed request totaling $1.8 billion.

As Russian resistance stiffened, Roosevelt pressed the military to step up deliveries. He fumed at the cabinet for its foot-dragging: "I am sick and tired of hearing [the Russians] are going to get this and they are going to get that." He wanted a hundred or more fighters delivered to the Soviet Union immediately. "Get the planes right off with a bang," he told Stimson, even if they had to be taken from the U.S. Army.[69] Public opinion rallied to the president's side. A July Gallup Poll indicated that 72 percent of Americans favored a Russian victory. Only 4 percent were opposed.[70] In the fall FDR instructed General Marshall to give precedence to delivery of supplies to Russia. Shortly thereafter he formally declared the defense of the Soviet Union "vital to the defense of the United States," making Russia eligible for aid under the Lend-Lease Act.[71]

Three weeks after Hitler's invasion of Russia, Roosevelt dispatched 4,400 marines to relieve the British garrison in Iceland. The move had been planned for several months, but the White House kept its fingers crossed. Admiral Stark wrote Hopkins that what the Navy was being asked to do was "practically an act of war" and wanted the president's explicit approval. "O.K., FDR," Roosevelt scribbled on the bottom of Stark's request.[72] Marines were deployed initially because it was unclear whether Iceland was in the Western Hemisphere, and the Selective Service Act prohibited the use of draftees if it were not. After the marines were in place the State Department redefined the hemisphere to include Iceland, and FDR pressed the American patrol zone one degree of longitude eastward.

It was at FDR's instigation that he and Churchill met off Newfoundland in early August. "I've just got to see Churchill myself in order to explain things to him," the president told Morgenthau.[73] The arrangements were entrusted to Hopkins. Confidentiality was essential. Churchill would have to cross the U-boat-infested Atlantic coming and going, and Roosevelt for his part wanted to avoid provoking his isolationist critics until after the conference took place. Initially FDR envisaged a private one-on-one meeting, but Churchill pressed to have the senior military staffs included, and Roosevelt agreed.

Churchill boarded the battleship HMS *Prince of Wales* at Scapa Flow on August 4 and sailed with the tide. During his absence, Labour party leader Clement Attlee, who was deputy prime minister in the war cabinet, stood in for Churchill in the House of Commons. Attlee was under firm instructions to answer no questions concerning the prime minister's whereabouts. On the second day out the sea was so rough the *Prince of Wales'* destroyer escort could not maintain the pace. Admiral Sir Dudley Pound, the first sea lord, who was traveling with Churchill, gave the order for the destroyers to drop away. The big battleship plunged on at high speed alone, zigzagging to avoid possible U-boats and maintaining radio silence to avoid detection.[74] It seems mind-boggling in retrospect that Great Britain's prime minister, the chief of the imperial general staff, the first sea lord, and the air vice chief of staff—that nation's highest political and military leadership—should be traveling together on a single warship in the North Atlantic, fully aware of the U-boat menace they faced.* Two days later, when *Prince of Wales* crossed the twenty-fifth meridian, a squadron of Canadian destroyers took up screening positions and escorted the mighty vessel to the American fleet lying at anchor in the deep waters of Placentia Bay, off Argentia Harbor—one of the locations acquired by the United States in the Destroyers for Bases deal.

For his own route to Argentia, Roosevelt organized an elaborate charade. On Sunday evening, August 3, he boarded the presidential yacht *Potomac* at New London, Connecticut, for what was announced as a ten-day fishing vacation off the New England coast. The following day he hosted members of the Danish and Norwegian royal families on board, and that evening, under cover of darkness, rendezvoused with vessels of the Atlantic Fleet off Martha's Vineyard. The *Potomac* returned to Massachusetts waters still flying the presidential pennant and for the next week cruised leisurely around Cape Cod, giving every evidence that FDR was still present.†

---

* The journalist H. V. Morton, traveling with Churchill, grimly recalled the fate of Field Marshal Lord Kitchener, chief of the imperial general staff, who was lost at sea when the vessel he was traveling in to Russia was torpedoed off the coast of Hoy in 1916. Morton, *Atlantic Meeting* 33 (New York: Dodd, Mead, 1943).
† A crewman dressed as FDR, complete with pince-nez and cigarette holder, sat prominently on deck fishing while the ship sent regular bulletins ashore that all was well and the president was enjoying himself. Neither Grace Tully nor Eleanor was aware of Roosevelt's deception; the cabinet was not informed; and the press was kept at a distance. Even the Secret Service was bamboozled, the White House detail avidly attending the *Potomac* from the

Roosevelt, however, had boarded the heavy cruiser *Augusta,* flagship of the Atlantic Fleet, and set sail for Newfoundland. Waiting for the president on ship were General Marshall, Admiral Stark, and General Hap Arnold, each of whom had taken his own circuitous route to the rendezvous. Accompanying the *Augusta* was her sister ship, the 9,000-ton *Tuscaloosa,* and five destroyers. The little flotilla sped along at a steady twenty-one knots and arrived off Argentia the morning of August 7. There they were joined by the venerable *Arkansas,* the 1912 dowager empress of the battleship fleet, and a dozen more destroyers from the Atlantic patrol.[75] *Prince of Wales,* with her Canadian escort, steamed slowly into the magnificent harbor precisely at 9 A.M. on August 9. As the huge battleship made its way through the line of American ships, crews in dress whites stood mustered at the rails—a dazzling panorama on a bright, sunny day.

At eleven o'clock Churchill, dressed in the Navy-like uniform of Warden of the Cinque Ports, crossed the bay to the *Augusta.* On deck, just below the bridge, Roosevelt waited. He stood erect, holding his son Elliott's arm. "The Boss insisted on standing," said presidential bodyguard Mike Reilly. "He hated and mistrusted those braces, but it was a historic occasion and he meant to play his part as much as his limbs would permit. Even the slight pitch of the *Augusta* meant pain and possibly a humiliating fall."[76]

"At last we have gotten together," said Roosevelt.

"We have," Churchill replied as they shook hands.[77]

BY THE TIME lunch was finished, they were "Franklin" and "Winston."[78]* "I like him," FDR wrote his cousin Daisy Suckley, "and lunching alone broke the ice both ways. He is a tremendously vital person and in many ways is an English

---

shore. Jon Meacham, *Franklin and Winston* 105–106 (New York: Random House, 2003); Grace Tully, *F.D.R.: My Boss* 246–248 (New York: Charles Scribner's Sons, 1949).

* Roosevelt and Churchill dined alone with Harry Hopkins. The British commanders—Pound; Field Marshal Sir John Dill, CIGS; Air Vice Marshal Sir Wilfred Freeman; and Sir Alexander Cadogan of the Foreign Office—dined with their American counterparts at a "very good fork lunch" provided by Admiral Ernest J. King, Commander of the Atlantic Fleet. To their dismay the lunch was "entirely dry," save for tea and a "cup of Joe"—Navy lingo for coffee—a derisive reference to Josephus Daniels, who removed alcohol from Navy wardrooms in 1914. (FDR and WSC were not bound by that regulation.) Theodore A. Wilson, *The First Summit: Roosevelt and Churchill at Placentia Bay, 1941* 85 (Boston: Houghton Mifflin, 1969).

Mayor La Guardia."[79] Churchill said, "I formed a very strong affection, which grew with our years of comradeship. We talked of nothing but business, and reached a great measure of agreement on many points, both large and small."[80] For Hopkins, who played interlocutor at lunch, the friendship was preordained. "They were two men in the same line of business—politico-military leadership on a global scale—and theirs was a very limited field and the few who achieve it seldom have opportunities for getting together with fellow craftsmen in the same trade to compare notes and talk shop. They established an easy intimacy, a joking informality and a moratorium on pomposity and cant—and also a degree of frankness which, if not quite complete, was remarkably close to it."[81]

In their working habits Churchill and Roosevelt could not have been more different. Roosevelt always worked in a setting of tranquillity, where outside pressures rarely penetrated. Churchill, on the other hand, "always seemed to be at his command post on a precarious beachhead, the conversational guns continually blazing." Roosevelt retired early; Churchill did not work up a full head of steam until about ten in the evening and often stayed up until three or four. He slept late and always took a nap after lunch. Roosevelt worked straight through from morning to evening and usually took lunch at his desk. Churchill had an unquenchable thirst for champagne, cognac, and Scotch whiskey and fortified himself at regular intervals through most of his working hours. FDR enjoyed a martini, two at the most, during the "children's hour" at seven but otherwise abstained.[82]

The emotional high point of the Argentia meeting was the Sunday religious service on the deck of the *Prince of Wales*. Roosevelt and Churchill sat side by side under a turret of fourteen-inch guns with their military chiefs standing behind them. American and British sailors mingled in the foreground, the flags of the two countries draped the altar, and British and American chaplains shared the prayers and readings. Churchill, who was not an observant Christian, relished the pageantry of the Church. (He sometimes said he was a "buttress" of the Church of England rather than a "pillar" because he supported it from outside.[83]) As host for the ceremony, the prime minister chose the hymns: "O God, Our Help in Ages Past," "Onward, Christian Soldiers," and the Navy hymn "For Those in Peril on the Sea." "Every word seemed to stir the heart," Churchill wrote later, "and none who took part in it will forget the spectacle presented. It was a great hour to live."[84] Roosevelt, who had insisted on walking the length of the ship to his seat on the fantail, called the service the "keynote" of the conference. "If nothing else had happened while we were here," he told his son Elliott, "that would have cemented us. 'Onward Christian Soldiers.' We are, and we will go on, with God's help."[85]*

Several times during the conference Churchill pressed Roosevelt for a declaration of war. "I would rather have a declaration of war now and no supplies for six months than double the supplies and no declaration," he was quoted as saying.[86] Roosevelt replied that he was skating on thin ice with Congress and they would debate a declaration of war for three months. As Churchill later explained to the war cabinet, "The President said he would become more and more provocative. If the Germans did not like it, they could attack the American forces."[87] Roosevelt agreed to provide armed escorts for British convoys as far as Iceland; expedite the shipment of planes and tanks; and request another $5 billion for Lend-Lease. Together they sent a joint message to Stalin pledging further assistance, and, in the event of war in the Pacific, agreed to a "Hitler first" strategy.[88]

The most enduring result of the conference was the Atlantic Charter: a stirring declaration of principles for world peace adopted by Churchill and Roosevelt on August 12. The Charter renounced territorial aggrandizement, supported self-determination, favored a loosening of trade restrictions, reaffirmed the desire to seek a world free from fear and want, and proclaimed the freedom of the seas. In cautious words it advocated a permanent system of international security, a reduction of armaments, and abandonment of the use of force.[89] "The profound and far-reaching importance of this Joint Declaration was apparent," wrote Churchill. "The fact alone of the United States, still technically neutral, joining with a belligerent Power in making such a declaration was astonishing."[90]

While Roosevelt and Churchill met off Newfoundland, Congress grappled with an extension of the draft. The Selective Service Act of 1940 required inductees to serve for twelve months. For many their service commitment was about to expire. If they returned home, the battle-worthiness of almost every Army unit would be severely weakened. It was a crisis not unlike that faced by

---

* "We live by symbols and we can't too often recall them," Felix Frankfurter wrote Roosevelt when photographs of the service were published. "And you two in that ocean, in the setting of that Sunday service, gave meaning to the conflict between civilization and arrogant, brute challenge; and gave promise more powerful and binding than any formal treaty could, that civilization has brains and resources that tyranny will not be able to overcome." *Roosevelt and Frankfurter Correspondence, 1928–1945* 612–613, Max Freedman, ed. (Boston: Little, Brown, 1967).

Union commanders during the Civil War when their soldiers' term of enlistment expired. Roosevelt put the problem to Congress on July 21. Rather than
submit a specific request, he left it to Congress to find a solution. "Time
counts. The responsibility rests solely with the Congress."[91]

Marshall and Stimson carried the fight. At their urging the military affairs
committees of the House and Senate drafted legislation to extend the term of
service by up to eighteen months at the discretion of the president. That would
provide the Army with a sufficient manpower cushion to rotate men in and
out without damaging combat efficiency. The measure carried the Senate easily, 45–30. But in the House opposition was fierce. With all members facing reelection in 1942 there was little enthusiasm for taking action that would be
unpopular with a vast swath of the electorate. An August 6 Gallup Poll indicated that 45 percent of Americans opposed an extension. Between the Ap-
palachians and the Rockies, 54 percent were opposed.[92]

Speaker Rayburn and Majority Leader McCormack worked the corridors
and cloakrooms assiduously but were unable to determine the outcome with
any degree of certainty. More than sixty Democrats indicated they would vote
against the bill. That meant the administration needed at least twenty Republicans to offset their defection. As the House reading clerk called the roll, tension on the floor mounted. The final tally showed 203 in favor, 202 against.
Twenty-one Republicans had joined 182 Democrats to put the measure across.
Rayburn banged his gavel and announced the results. A recapitulation was requested. Rayburn yielded, and the review showed the tally to be correct.
"There is no correction of the vote," he announced. "The vote stands, and the
bill is passed. Without objection, a motion to reconsider is laid on the table."
His gavel came down and that was it. Despite vehement Republican objections
Rayburn had gaveled the measure through. There would be no vote on a motion to reconsider. Passage of the draft extension act prevented the dismantle-
ment of the Army on the threshold of war. Rayburn had pushed the Speaker's
power to the limit and had prevailed.[93]*

* A twelve-month extension would have passed with less difficulty, but Rayburn and
McCormack chose to go for the full eighteen months Marshall and Stimson requested. The
bill passed by the Senate differed slightly from the House version, and rather than go to conference and face another vote in the House, the Senate simply adopted the House version
(37–19) on August 14, 1941 (50 Stat. 886).

After Argentia, Roosevelt moved quickly to protect British shipping. When a German submarine fired torpedoes at the American destroyer USS *Greer* in early September, he seized on the incident to invoke a "shoot-on-sight" policy. "When you see a rattlesnake poised to strike, you do not wait until he has struck before you crush him." The president said, "from now on, if German or Italian vessels of war enter the waters, the protection of which is necessary for American defense, they do so at their own peril."[94]* Later in the month, off Newfoundland, the Canadian Navy turned over a fifty-ship convoy out of Halifax to five American destroyers, which safely shepherded the vessels across the North Atlantic into the hands of the Royal Navy just south of Iceland.[95]

FDR always took the political stance of the Catholic Church seriously, and he worried about possible criticism of Lend-Lease aid to Russia. On September 3, at the suggestion of two American prelates who supported the administration, the president appealed directly to Pope Pius XII.[96] "I believe that the survival of Russia is less dangerous to religion, to the church as such, and to humanity in general than would be the survival of the German form of dictatorship," he wrote.

> Furthermore, it is my belief that the leaders of all churches in the United States [including the Catholic Church] should recognize these facts clearly and should not close their eyes to these basic questions and by their present attitude on this question directly assist Germany in her present objectives.[97]

Considering the president was writing to the Pope, his tone was as sharp as diplomatic practice permitted. Whether Pius XII was convinced is doubtful. His response on September 20 skirted the issue.[98] But the Pope, who as Cardi-

---

* The *Greer* "incident" was ambiguous. While on a mail run to Iceland, *Greer* was notified by a British patrol plane of a U-boat in the area. *Greer* shadowed the submarine using sonar but did not fire. She reported the sub's location to the British plane, which dropped four depth charges but missed. The German U-boat commander could easily have assumed it was the *Greer* that had fired. He might also have assumed from *Greer*'s profile that it was one of the destroyers transferred to the British Navy by the United States. In any event, the U-boat fired two torpedoes at the *Greer*, both of which missed. *Greer* returned fire and loosed nineteen depth charges, which also missed. There was "no positive evidence that submarine knew nationality of ship at which it was firing," the Navy told FDR. Robert Dallek, *Franklin D. Roosevelt and American Foreign Policy, 1932–1945* 287 (New York: Oxford University Press, 1979).

nal Eugenio Pacelli had lunched with Roosevelt at Hyde Park immediately after the 1936 election, chose not to take issue with the president. At the end of September he wrote the apostolic delegate in Washington calling his attention to an often-overlooked paragraph in the encyclical *Divini redemptoris* that distinguished between the Communist government of the Soviet Union and the Russian people, "For whom We cherish the warmest paternal affection."[99] By implication, aid to the Russian people was permissible—a position that was made explicit in a pastoral letter by Archbishop John Timothy McNicholas of Cincinnati in October.[100]

Roosevelt was hammered by personal tragedy in 1941. First Missy, then, on September 7, two weeks before her eighty-seventh birthday, Sara died. During the summer at Campobello her health began to fail. Eleanor assisted her return to Hyde Park and on Friday, September 5, called Franklin at the White House and suggested that the end was near. Roosevelt immediately left by train and arrived at Hyde Park the morning of the sixth. He spent the day sitting with Sara, describing his shipboard meetings with Churchill, filling her in on Washington gossip, talking of old times. That evening at dinner she seemed better. But at 9:30 she lost consciousness. A blood clot had lodged in her lung, and her circulatory system collapsed. Roosevelt sat with her through the night and most of the next morning. Just before noon her breathing stopped. Her son was at her bedside.[101]

Sara was buried next to her husband in the small cemetery behind Hyde Park's St. James' Episcopal Church. The eight men who had worked longest for the estate—including her chauffeur and butler—carried her coffin to the grave. The Secret Service watched from a distance. "I don't think we belong in there," said Mike Reilly, "even if Congress says we do."[102]

Roosevelt remained at Hyde Park several days, sorting Sara's things. He wore a black armband on the left sleeve of his jacket and would continue to do so for well over a year. Late one afternoon Grace Tully brought him a box he had never seen. She untied the twine that held it closed, and together, she and the president looked inside. They found a number of bundles wrapped in tissue, each carefully labeled in Sara's firm hand. One held the gloves she had worn at her wedding. Another contained Franklin's first pair of shoes. Others held his baby toys, his christening dress, a lock of his baby hair. Beneath the bundles were his boyhood letters written from Groton and Harvard. Roosevelt's eyes filled with tears. He told Tully he would like to be alone. She hurried from the room. No one on the White House staff had ever seen the president weep.[103]

TWENTY-THREE

DAY OF INFAMY

*Yesterday, December 7, 1941—a date which
will live in infamy—the United States of America
was suddenly and deliberately attacked by
naval and air forces of the Empire of Japan.*
—FRANKLIN D. ROOSEVELT, DECEMBER 8, 1941

ROOSEVELT WAS CONSUMED by the war in Europe: his relations with
Churchill, Lend-Lease, aid to Russia, and the struggle in the Atlantic. The military leadership—Stimson and Knox, Marshall and Stark—shared the president's concern. As a consequence the deteriorating situation in the Pacific
received less attention. Discussions with Japan were handled by the State Department, and subordinate commanders saw little sense of urgency. Vessels of
the Pacific Fleet routinely put in at Pearl Harbor every Friday so officers could
spend weekends with their families; the Army parked its airplanes wingtip to
wingtip to minimize the number of sentries required; antiaircraft guns remained limbered so as not to alarm Hawaii's tourists; and the island's radar
operated three hours a day. Military intelligence cracked the Japanese diplomatic code in August 1940 (MAGIC), but the Army and Navy initially assigned
it such a low priority that it often required two weeks to translate the intercepts
and occasionally as long as two months. "The island of Oahu, due to its forti-
fication, its garrison, and its physical characteristics, is believed to be the
strongest fortress in the world," General Marshall assured Roosevelt in April
1941. "With the force available [to defend it], a major attack against Oahu is
considered impractical."[1]

American relations with Japan had been on a downward spiral ever since
the Grant administration. President Grant had spent a month in the country

during his world tour in 1879. "My visit to Japan has been the most pleasant of all my travels," the former chief executive wrote from Tokyo. "The country is beautifully cultivated and the people, from the highest to the lowest, the most kindly and the most cleanly in the world. . . . The progress they have made in the last twelve years is incredible. . . . This is marvelous when the treatment of their people—and all eastern people—receive at the hands of the average foreigner is considered."[2] Grant was so captivated that one of the reasons he considered accepting a third term in 1880 was to improve American relations with China and Japan.[3]

Grant lost the Republican nomination to James A. Garfield, and without his contribution Japanese-American relations deteriorated. Rather than accept Japan as a legitimate imperial power in Asia—such as the United States had become with its annexation of the Philippines in 1898—American policy, often colored with an ugly tincture of racism, became gratuitously condescending.[4] After the Japanese victory over the Russian fleet at the Tsushima Strait in 1905, President Theodore Roosevelt, who arbitrated the Russo-Japanese peace settlement at Portsmouth, New Hampshire, denied Tokyo's claim for indemnity and ruled out significant Russian territorial concessions in Manchuria. As the Japanese saw it, the United States denied them the fruits of victory.[5] The so-called Gentlemen's Agreement of 1908 closing off immigration from Japan fueled that resentment.* In 1913 the United States summarily dismissed Japan's protest against California legislation forbidding Japanese citizens to own land in the

---

* The "Gentlemen's Agreement" of 1908 arose in response to action by the San Francisco Board of Education, which in 1906 decreed that Japanese students must attend a segregated Oriental school lest they overwhelm the city's white students. Since there were only ninety-three Japanese students involved, overcrowding was scarcely the issue. As the *San Francisco Examiner* crowed, "Californians do not want their growing daughters to be intimate in daily school contact with Japanese young men."

TR intervened, called the San Francisco action a "wicked absurdity," and invited the school board to Washington, where a compromise was worked out. Tokyo agreed not to issue passports to Japanese citizens who wished to settle in the United States, thus choking off immigration, and the San Francisco school board agreed to allow properly prepared Japanese students to enroll in the same classes with whites. The arrangement was spelled out in a series of notes between the Japanese government and the State Department and is summarized in 2 *Foreign Relations of the United States 1924* 370–371 (Washington, D.C.: U.S. Government Printing Office, 1939).

state. In 1919 Woodrow Wilson rejected a Japanese proposal to include a declaration of racial equality in the League of Nations Covenant. And in 1924 Congress permanently barred Japanese immigration to the United States.[6] But the
most unforgivable action (in Japanese eyes) was American refusal to recognize
Japan's acquisition of Manchuria in 1932.

The Japanese takeover was scarcely unexpected or without precedent. As
early as the Root-Takahira agreement of 1908, the United States recognized
Japanese hegemony over Manchuria.[7] Japan controlled the province's economy, owned its principal railroad, and managed its seaports. And the fact is,
there was little armed resistance (and certainly no atrocities) when the Japanese Army finally took complete control. The League of Nations formally condemned the action, however, prompting Japan to quit the League, and the
United States responded with the Stimson Doctrine, promulgated by high-
minded Henry L. Stimson, who was then Hoover's secretary of state. The
Stimson Doctrine declared that the United States would not recognize any territorial arrangements imposed on China by force. "The Western powers taught
Japan the game of poker," lamented the Japanese diplomat Yosuke Matsuoka,
"but after it acquired most of the chips they pronounced the game immoral
and took up contract bridge."[8]

The Japanese saw themselves as colonizers rather than conquerors—like the
Dutch in the East Indies, the French in Indochina, the British in Burma and
Malaya, and yes, the Americans in the Philippines. They invested heavily in
Manchuria, installed the boy emperor of China (who had been deposed in
1912) as sovereign, renamed the territory Manchukuo, and immediately dis-
patched half a million citizens to settle there, with another 5 million slated to
join them. Between 1932 and 1941 Japanese public and private investment in
Manchuria totaled $3.3 billion (roughly $45 billion in today's currency.)[9]

Nevertheless, the Stimson Doctrine suited America's sense of righteousness. It reflected the influence of generations of American missionaries in
China as well as latent public support for Chinese independence. Yet it ignored
strategic reality in the Far East, overlooked the needs of the growing Japanese
economy, and underestimated the advantages of modernization that accompanied Japanese colonization.

Roosevelt embraced the Stimson Doctrine wholeheartedly. Despite warnings in 1932 by brain trusters Raymond Moley and Rexford Tugwell that
America's interests lay with Japan, FDR, as president-elect, backed Stimson

down the line. "How could you expect me to do otherwise, given my Delano ancestors?" he asked.[10] Roosevelt's comment was flippant. Yet it determined American policy for the next decade.

As Moley and Tugwell had warned, the Stimson Doctrine curdled U.S. relations with Japan but had little effect on the situation in the Far East. As a policy, it was purely rhetorical: "an attitude rather than a program" in the words of historian Herbert Feis.[11] When Japan stepped over the line with its assault on China in 1937, the United States took few tangible steps to oppose it. Roosevelt condemned Tokyo's action and provided some token aid to Chiang Kaishek but did nothing to curtail American exports to Japan, including the strategic materials and petroleum that fueled the Japanese war machine. The United States championed Chinese sovereignty verbally but resisted committing substantial resources to defend it.

By 1940 Japan's wrongful incursion into China was three years old, with no conceivable end in sight. Japanese troops had won significant victories and occupied China's most productive coastal regions but had not been able to subdue Chinese resistance. In a word, China had become a quagmire. The impatience of the military to end the stalemate brought down Japan's government in July 1940 (the third government to fall in less than two years) and installed an Army-dominated regime pledged to expedite the war and solve Japan's dependence on foreign imports, particularly those from the United States.[12] The Roosevelt administration was not complicit in the fall of the government, but a more conciliatory stance toward Manchuria—as was urged by the American embassy in Tokyo—would have provided Japanese politicians more leverage to withstand the military.*

Until 1940 the Sino-Japanese conflict was a purely regional affair. It convulsed Asia but remained an isolated event unconnected with the accelerating pace of aggression in Europe.[13] With a new government in Tokyo, that

---

* By statute, Japanese ministers of war and Navy were chosen from the senior ranks of the services. By refusing to nominate a candidate or withdrawing its officer from the cabinet, either service could topple a government. The Army, moreover, reserved the right to appeal directly to the emperor, bypassing the civilian government altogether. The system was patterned on Germany before World War I, an infelicitous choice similar to General P. G. T. Beauregard's decision to base the Confederate battle plan at Shiloh on Napoleon's tactics at Waterloo. David M. Kennedy, *Freedom from Fear* 503–504 (New York: Oxford University Press, 1999).

changed quickly. Encouraged by Hitler's conquest of France and the Netherlands, as well as the onset of the Battle of Britain, Japan's promilitary government turned its eye to the colonial outposts in Southeast Asia: the oil fields of the Dutch East Indies, the rubber plantations of British Malaya, and the tin mines and rice paddies of French Indochina. "We should not miss the present opportunity or we shall be blamed by posterity," said Japan's new war minister, General Hideki Tojo.[14]

With Britain under German attack, Tokyo prevailed upon London to close the Burma Road for three months (cutting China's principal supply route) and to withdraw the British garrison from Shanghai. A more concerted move against the French and Dutch colonies appeared imminent. The path to a world war lay open. Roosevelt responded on July 26 with an embargo banning the export of high-octane aviation gasoline and premium grades of iron and steel scrap to Japan. It was a slap on the wrist, but Washington hoped it would send a message to Tokyo and deter further moves against Southeast Asia. "We are not going to get into any war by forcing Japan into a position where she is going to fight for some reason or another," FDR told the State Department.[15]

Roosevelt's limited embargo produced the opposite effect to what he intended. It riled the Japanese but did nothing to restrain them. Indeed, it convinced Tokyo that its American supply line was in jeopardy and should be replaced as soon as possible. On September 23, with the reluctant acquiescence of Vichy France, Japan occupied the northern portion of Indochina, adjacent to the Chinese province of Yunnan. Roosevelt responded the following day with a complete embargo on all types of iron and steel intended for Japan and on September 25 announced a $100 million loan to China through the Export-Import Bank.[16] An implacable tit for tat had begun. The United States and Japan settled into a rhythm that would characterize their relations for the next year. Each undertook a series of escalating moves that provoked but failed to restrain the other. Japan gambled on the action it could take without precipitating open conflict with the United States. The Roosevelt administration—which did not give its full attention to the matter—reckoned it could pressure Tokyo by economic means without driving the Japanese to war.[17]

Two days after Roosevelt announced the loan to China, Japan joined the Berlin-Rome axis. The move caught Washington by surprise. Japan recognized the leadership of Germany and Italy in Europe; Germany and Italy recognized Japanese hegemony in Greater East Asia. All three agreed to come to the aid of one another if attacked by a third party that was then at peace. Since the treaty explicitly excluded the Soviet Union, it was unmistakably clear that the pact was aimed at the United States. In effect, events in Europe and Asia were now joined. By threatening Washington with a two-front war, each of the contracting parties hoped to prevent American intervention.[18]

Japan had raised the ante, and Roosevelt began to have misgivings about a confrontation in the Pacific. In early October 1940 Churchill requested the United States send a naval squadron ("the bigger the better") to visit Singapore—a bit of saber rattling he thought would intimidate the Japanese.[19] General Marshall and Admiral Stark thought the move unnecessarily provocative, and FDR agreed. With the election a month away, the president simply ignored Churchill's request and sent no reply.

Throughout the winter and spring of 1940–41 Roosevelt received conflicting advice. The hawks in the administration—Stimson, Knox, Morgenthau, Ickes, and Harry Hopkins—urged the president to tighten the screws on Japan and embargo the shipment of the oil it so desperately needed. (Eighty percent of Japanese petroleum came from the United States.) Secretary of State Hull and the military urged FDR to go slow. Hull favored continued negotiations; Marshall and Stark argued that if Japan's oil supply were closed off she would be forced to seek other sources. The Dutch East Indies, Burma, Malaya, and even the Philippines would be threatened. Not only was the United States unprepared, but a military confrontation against Japan in Southeast Asia would undermine efforts to support Britain in the Atlantic. "Every day that we are able to maintain peace and still support the British is valuable time gained," said Stark. Marshall agreed. This was "as unfavorable a moment as you could choose for provoking trouble," the chief of staff told the president, and he urged that the Marine garrison in Shanghai be withdrawn to avoid a possible incident.[20]

With the Battle of the Atlantic raging full tilt, Japanese policy remained a secondary issue for Roosevelt. But he was not dismayed by the split among his advisers. The president liked to keep his saddlebags balanced. When Justice James McReynolds of Tennessee resigned from the Supreme Court in February 1941, Morgenthau suggested FDR appoint Cordell Hull (another Tennessean) to the vacancy and make Stimson secretary of state. As Morgenthau saw it, that would remove the principal advocate of negotiations from the cabinet and put the more bellicose Stimson in charge. Roosevelt refused to be stampeded. It was a bad suggestion, he told Morgenthau. In retrospect, said the president, he wasn't at all sure Stimson had been right about Manchuria in 1932 and that Hull's tactics of negotiation might have been the better course for the United States to pursue. "The president's comments certainly surprised me," wrote Morgenthau.[21]

Policymakers in Tokyo were equally divided. According to longtime ambassador Joseph C. Grew—a schoolmate of FDR at Groton and Harvard who sometimes wrote "Dear Frank" letters to the president—the Emperor, the premier, and a majority of the cabinet, as well as most of the Japanese Navy, favored continued negotiation with the United States. The Army, desperate for victory in China, pressed for war, as did Foreign Minister Matsuoka, but thus far they had been unable to convince their colleagues.[22]*

On April 13, 1941, Matsuoka scored an important diplomatic victory when Japan and the Soviet Union announced the conclusion of a neutrality pact between the two nations. Again Washington was caught flat-footed. Russia recognized the independence of Manchukuo and implicit Japanese control; Japan reciprocated with respect to Outer Mongolia, a Soviet satellite similarly detached from China. The pact represented a significant strategic breakthrough. By resolving the smoldering colonial tensions along Manchukuo's border, it freed both nations to shift their military focus elsewhere.

While Matsuoka prepared the way for war, the peace faction in the Japanese government moved to repair the breach with Washington. In early 1941 Tokyo replaced its ambassador to the United States with Admiral Kichisaburo Nomura, a former foreign minister who had served as naval attaché in Washington during World War I and was acquainted with Roosevelt from that time. As foreign minister, Nomura had shown a keen interest in improving relations with the United States.[23] He feared the drift to war and undertook the Washington posting at the urging of naval colleagues to help prevent it.[24] Roosevelt received Nomura cordially. He recalled their earlier friendship, said he intended to call him "Admiral" rather than "Ambassador," and proposed they

---

* Ambassador Grew was married to Alice de Vermandois Perry, the granddaughter of Commodore Oliver Hazard Perry, the victor of the Battle of Lake Erie and brother of Commodore Matthew Perry, who opened Japan to the West in 1853. Her father, Thomas Sergeant Perry, held the chair in English literature at Keio University. Alice had spent her youth in Japan and had developed a wide network of contacts who gave her husband remarkable access to the Japanese leadership. Joseph C. Grew, 1 *Turbulent Era: The Diplomatic Record of Forty Years, 1904–1945* 9 (Boston: Houghton Mifflin, 1952).

talk candidly. "There is plenty of room in the Pacific area for everybody," said the president. "It would not do this country any good nor Japan any good, but both of them harm to get into war," to which Nomura readily assented.[25]

Roosevelt suggested that Nomura might find it useful to sit down with Hull and discuss how relations could be improved. For the next nine months Nomura and Hull met some fifty times, often at the secretary's home in the Wardman Park Hotel. Hull wrote later he credited Nomura "with being honestly sincere in trying to avoid war between his country and mine."[26] Both men worked under severe handicaps. Nomura was out of step with his government in Tokyo, and Hull, who was in poor health, was often excluded from White House strategy sessions.[27]

Hitler's invasion of the Soviet Union in June 1941 took Tokyo by surprise. When he recovered from the shock, Foreign Minister Matsuoka said it provided Japan with a golden opportunity to extinguish for all time the Russian threat in Siberia. "He who would search for pearls must dive deep," he told the cabinet.[28] Despite the recently concluded neutrality agreement with Moscow, Matsuoka maintained that the Tripartite Pact with Germany and Italy took precedence. In his view, which he put directly to the Emperor, Japan should join the war against Russia immediately.[29]

The Army high command agreed that Hitler's attack on the Soviet Union offered an opportunity, but they wanted no part of another northern adventure. In May 1939 the Japanese Kwantung Army had crossed the Khalkhin-Gol River separating Manchukuo from Soviet-controlled Mongolia to attack Red Army troops stationed on the other side. The fighting escalated through the summer, culminating in the humiliating defeat of the Japanese at the end of August. Japan's losses totaled more than 50,000 men killed and wounded; the Russians (under General Georgi Zhukov) lost one-fifth that number.[30]* There was as yet no evidence that Stalin was reducing his Siberian garrison to meet the German invasion, and without overwhelming numerical superiority the Japanese generals had no interest in attacking the Red Army again.[31]

* Zhukov established his military reputation on the Khalkhin-Gol. Given command by Stalin in June, Zhukov revitalized a demoralized army, massed his tanks and artillery contrary to traditional military doctrine, and, in a tactic made famous in World War II, launched a tidal wave of a counterattack on August 20 that swept the Japanese from the field. Otto Preston Chaney, Jr., *Zhukov* 38–59 (Norman: University of Oklahoma Press, 1971).

Instead of going north, the Army advocated a southern strategy. The German attack would keep the Russians at bay, and with its northern flank protected Japan could move south against Burma, Malaya, and the Dutch East Indies. Seizing Southeast Asia would further isolate China, ensuring Chiang's eventual defeat. But above all it would provide continued access to vital raw materials. And the petroleum from the rich oil fields of the East Indies would eliminate Japan's dependence on the United States.

"The Japs are having a real drag-down and knock-out fight trying to decide which way to jump," Roosevelt (who thanks to MAGIC intercepts was privy to the Tokyo debate) told Harold Ickes on July 1. "No one knows what the decision will be, but it is terribly important for the control of the Atlantic for us to keep peace in the Pacific. I simply have not got enough Navy to go round."[32]

At a meeting of the privy council held in the presence of the Emperor on July 2, the Japanese government chose to go south. The Kwantung Army would be reinforced to take advantage of the situation should Russia suddenly collapse, but the principal thrust would be southward. "The Imperial Government will continue its efforts to effect a settlement of the China Incident, and seek to establish a solid basis for the security of the nation. This will involve an advance into the Southern Regions and, depending on future developments, a settlement of the Soviet Question as well." The Emperor and the Navy hoped the southern strategy could be pursued peacefully but were under no illusions. "The Imperial Government will carry out the above program no matter what obstacles may be encountered. . . . In case the diplomatic negotiations break down, preparations for war with England and America will also be carried forward."[33]

On July 23 Japanese troops, already garrisoned in northern Indochina, moved into the southern portion of the country. Under a new protocol signed with Vichy, Japan acquired the use of eight airfields including Da Nang and Bienhoa, the naval bases at Saigon and Cam Ranh Bay, and the right to station an unspecified number of troops in the south. This provided the Japanese with a forward vantage point from which not only to interdict the remaining supply routes into China but to threaten Malaya, Singapore, the Dutch East Indies, and the Philippines.

Cables from Ambassador William Leahy in Vichy as well as MAGIC intercepts alerted Roosevelt as early as July 14 that the Japanese planned to move into southern Indochina.* At cabinet on the eighteenth Morgenthau pressed the president for a response: "What are you going to do on the economic front against Japan if she makes this move?"

"Well, to my surprise [wrote Morgenthau] the President gave us quite a lecture why we should not make any move because if we did, if we stopped all oil, it would simply drive the Japanese down to the Dutch East Indies, and it would mean war in the Pacific."[34]

FDR's caution dovetailed with the military's assessment. On July 21, 1941, Admiral Stark forwarded to the president a Navy Department memorandum emphasizing the paramount importance of the Battle of the Atlantic and suggesting that the Japanese were unlikely to move beyond Indochina unless the United States cut off the flow of oil. "An embargo would probably result in a fairly early attack by Japan on Malaya and the Netherlands East Indies, and possibly would involve the United States in an early war in the Pacific." Stark added a handwritten postscript noting his concurrence.[35] Marshall told Stimson essentially the same. "Collapse in the Atlantic would be fatal; collapse in the Far East would be serious but not fatal."[36]

When Roosevelt met with his cabinet on July 24, the day after the Japanese occupation of southern Indochina, he spent much of the time whiplashing his subordinates to expedite aid shipments to the Soviet Union. He was annoyed by the Japanese move but had not changed his view that the United States should not overreact. "Notwithstanding that Japan was boldly making this hostile move," wrote Ickes that evening, "the President was still unwilling to draw the noose tight. He thought it might be better to slip the noose around Japan's neck and give it a jerk now and then."[37]

The noose Roosevelt envisaged was a freeze on Japanese assets in the United States. That would require specific government approval before funds could be released to pay for exports to Japan. It would not embargo trade but would add a modicum of inconvenience and uncertainty. The Japanese would have to

---

* After the fall of France and the establishment of the Vichy regime with Marshal Henri-Philippe Pétain as head of state, FDR appointed Admiral William D. Leahy as U.S. ambassador. Leahy had retired as chief of naval operations in 1939 and was then serving as governor of Puerto Rico. Roosevelt believed a military man would enjoy greater prestige in Vichy.

apply for an export license before each shipment. Much to the disappointment of the hawks in the administration, FDR said the United States would continue to ship oil and gasoline. Asked specifically by acting Treasury secretary Daniel Bell (Morgenthau was on vacation) how Japanese requests for petroleum should be handled, FDR said he was "inclined to grant the licenses for shipment as the applications are presented."[38]

Roosevelt was more explicit later that day when speaking extemporaneously to volunteers from the Office of Civilian Defense. People are asked to conserve gasoline, he said. Why should they do so when we are shipping all of this gasoline to Japan?

> Now the answer is a very simple one. There is a world war going on, and there has been for some time. One of our efforts, from the very beginning, was to prevent the spread of that world war in certain areas where it hadn't started. One of those areas is a place called the Pacific Ocean. It was very essential from our own selfish point of view of defense to prevent a war from starting in the South Pacific. . . .
>
> All right. And now here is this Nation called Japan. Whether they had aggressive purposes to enlarge their empire southward, they did not have any oil of their own. Now, if we had cut the oil off, they probably would have gone down to the Dutch East Indies a year ago, and you would have had war. Therefore, there was—you might call—a method in letting this oil go to Japan, with the hope—and it has worked for two years—of keeping war out of the South Pacific for our own good, for the good of the defense of Great Britain, and the freedom of the seas.[39]

Roosevelt announced the freeze of Japanese assets on July 26. It was coupled with a freeze on Chinese assets and a military order placing the Philippine armed forces under American command.[40] Later that afternoon the War Department announced that General Douglas MacArthur had been recalled to active duty to command U.S. forces in the Philippines.* "If there is going to be

---

* Following his retirement as Army chief of staff in 1935, MacArthur went to Manila as commanding general (field marshal) of the Philippine Army. His headquarters were separate and distinct from the U.S. Army in the Philippines, which was commanded by Major General George Grunert. With MacArthur for a time were Lieutenant Colonel Dwight D.

trouble in the Far East," Roosevelt told his military aide, Pa Watson, "I want Douglas to be in charge."

The chain of circumstances leading to MacArthur's recall is unclear. What little documentation exists suggests MacArthur took the initiative with a letter to FDR's press secretary Steve Early (an old friend) on March 21, 1941, offering his services to the president. "Isn't that fine? It is just what I would expect Douglas MacArthur to do," said Roosevelt. Pa Watson, the president's military aide, thereupon wrote MacArthur that Roosevelt "wants you in your military capacity rather than any other." MacArthur replied, "This would naturally be my choice and I am gratified beyond words that this is his decision."

The War Department was less enthusiastic about MacArthur's recall than FDR was. By the end of May 1941 MacArthur had heard nothing from Washington and dispatched another letter to Early stating he had booked passage back to the United States and planned to settle in San Antonio. There is no paper trail of what happened next, but apparently FDR made his wishes known to Stimson and Marshall. Early wired MacArthur to sit tight, and on June 20, 1941, Marshall wrote that he and Stimson agreed that "your outstanding qualifications and vast experience in the Philippines make you the logical selection for the Army in the Far East should the situation approach a crisis."[41]

After the order freezing Japanese assets was announced, FDR departed Washington for Hyde Park, and four days later he left for New London and the trip to Newfoundland to meet Churchill. There is no doubt about his intentions. The freeze was designed to disconcert the Japanese, but the flow of oil was to continue. Daniel Bell at Treasury was aware of that; Ickes, who had been named petroleum coordinator, was aware; and so was the State Department. "The President's chief objective in the Pacific for the time being," Sumner Welles told his British counterpart, Sir Alexander Cadogan, at Argentia, "is the avoidance of war with Japan."[42]

The export licenses Japan required fell under the jurisdiction of the interdepartmental Foreign Funds Control Committee, a subcabinet body chaired by Assistant Secretary of State Dean Acheson. The committee had the sole au-

---

Eisenhower as his executive officer and Captain Lucius D. Clay as his engineer. For a snapshot of the organization of MacArthur's headquarters and its relation to the U.S. Army in the Philippines, see Clay's comments in Jean Edward Smith, *Lucius D. Clay: An American Life* 76–82 (New York: Henry Holt, 1990).

thority to release the frozen funds. As fate would have it, Acheson was one of the leading hawks in the administration, who had long favored a full embargo of oil shipments to Japan. With Roosevelt and Welles out of the country and Hull taking the waters at the Greenbrier in White Sulfur Springs, West Virginia, Acheson asserted that the freeze order was imprecise and refused to thaw Japanese funds for any purchases whatever. With the breathtaking arrogance that became his hallmark, the future secretary of state maintained his action could not possibly provoke war in the Pacific since "no rational Japanese could believe that an attack on us could result in anything but disaster for his country."[43]* Despite protests from the State Department's Far Eastern Division and the Treasury, Acheson refused to make any Japanese funds available—a de facto embargo that snuffed out Japan's access to petroleum. "Whether or not we had a policy, we had a state of affairs," gloated Acheson in his memoirs.[44]

FDR learned of the freeze only upon his return from Newfoundland in early September, and by then to reverse the policy and issue the export licenses would have been perceived by many as appeasement. Public opinion polls in early August indicated that 51 percent of Americans believed America should risk war rather than allow Japan to become more powerful. By September that number had risen to 67 percent.[45] In that context Roosevelt allowed Acheson's decision to stand. Contrary to his original intention, all American trade with Japan was now cut off.[46] In Tokyo, Ambassador Grew brooded about the effect: "The vicious circle of reprisals and counter reprisals is on. *Facilis descensus Averni est.* [The descent into Hell is easy.] Unless radical surprises occur, it is difficult to see how the momentum of the down-grade movement can be arrested, or how far it will go. The obvious conclusion is eventual war."[47]

The embargo stunned Tokyo. Japan consumed an estimated 12,000 tons of oil each day and had less than a two-year supply on hand. As one Japanese leader put it, the nation was "like a fish in a pond from which the water was gradually being drained away."[48] Added to the worry about petroleum was the balance of naval power in the Pacific. In the summer of 1941 the Imperial Navy

---

* Dean Acheson's record for anticipating the likelihood of war in the Far East sets a standard for error that few statesmen would wish to emulate. Not only did he make the wrong call in July 1941, but his speech to the National Press Club as President Truman's secretary of state on January 12, 1950, placing South Korea outside the American defensive perimeter in the Pacific, contributed significantly to the North Koreans' decision to cross the 38th parallel in June 1950. For the text of Acheson's speech, see 22 *Department of State Bulletin* 116 (January 23, 1950).

enjoyed numerical superiority against the combined fleets of the United States, Great Britain, and the Netherlands. But the naval buildup Congress authorized after the fall of France in 1940 would eliminate that advantage by 1942. If Japan was to act, the window of opportunity was closing rapidly.

On September 6, 1941, the Japanese government met with the Emperor. Prime Minister Prince Fumimaro Konoye, who desperately sought to prevent war, was given a month to negotiate a settlement with the United States. If an agreement to lift the embargo could not be reached by October 10, the armed forces would prepare to move south. Emperor Hirohito, who rarely intervened in such ceremonial conferences, reminded the government of the risks ahead. When the military appeared to equivocate on the desirability of a diplomatic settlement, he reached into his robe, drew out a piece of paper, and read a poem by his grandfather, the great Emperor Meiji:

Throughout the world
Everywhere we are brothers
Why then do the winds and waves rage so turbulently?

After a stunned silence, Admiral Osami Nagano, chief of the Navy general staff, promised that diplomacy would take precedence. "War would be chosen only as an unavoidable last resort."[49]*

On the evening of September 6, after the conference adjourned, Prime Min-

---

* At a separate audience with the heads of the Army and Navy on September 5, Emperor Hirohito pressed the chiefs as to the probable length of hostilities in case of war with the United States. According to the record kept by Prince Konoye, the Army chief of staff, General Sugiyama, said that operations in the South Pacific could be disposed of in about three months. "The Emperor recalled that the General had been Minister of War at the time of the outbreak of the China Incident, and that he had informed the Throne that the incident would be disposed of in about one month. He pointed out that despite the General's assurance, the incident was not yet concluded after four long years of fighting. In trepidation the Chief of Staff went to great lengths to explain that the extensive hinterland of China prevented the consummation of operations according to the scheduled plan. At this the Emperor raised his voice and said if the Chinese hinterland was extensive, the Pacific was boundless. He asked how the General could be certain of his three months calculation. The Chief of Staff hung his head unable to reply." "Konoye Memoirs," quoted in Herbert Feis, *The Road to Pearl Harbor* 266 (Princeton, N.J.: Princeton University Press, 1950). For a more critical assessment of Hirohito's role, see Herbert P. Bix, *Hirohito and the Making of Modern Japan* 387–437 (New York: HarperCollins, 2000).

ister Konoye invited Ambassador Grew for a private dinner. Traditionally in Japan the prime minister had no contact with foreign envoys, and Konoye took elaborate precautions to keep the meeting secret.[50] They dined in the home of a mutual friend, Baron Ito; automobile license plates were altered to avoid identification; servants were sent home before the guests arrived, and the meal was served by Baron Ito's daughter. For three hours Konoye pressed Grew for a personal meeting with FDR, perhaps in Hawaii. "Time is of the essence," said the prime minister.[51] He told Grew that his government believed the four principles for reconciliation previously announced by Secretary Hull provided a satisfactory basis for resolving all differences: the territorial integrity of all nations; noninterference in the internal affairs of other nations; the open door for trade; and the preservation of the status quo except for change by peaceful means.[52] Konoye assured Grew that if he and Roosevelt could agree on the principles, the details would fall into place. "The Prime Minister is cognizant of the fact that certain points may need clarification and more precise formulation, and *he is confident that the divergences in view can be reconciled to our mutual satisfaction*" (Grew's emphasis). Konoye said the ship waiting to take him and his party to meet the president was equipped with powerful radio equipment that would allow him to communicate directly with Tokyo. When he reported to the Emperor that an agreement had been reached, "the Emperor would immediately issue a rescript ordering the suspension forthwith of all hostile operations."[53]

Grew said, "I returned to the Embassy from that historic meeting with the firm conviction that we had been dealing with a man of unquestioned sincerity, a point which need not be labored when one considers the high traditions of Prince Konoye's background and family, extending back to the dim ages of Japanese history."[54]

Grew immediately informed Washington of his talk with Konoye: "the most important cable to go from his hand since the start of his diplomatic career."[55] In numerous follow-up messages, including a personal letter to FDR on September 22, he warned that time was short.* Above all, he cautioned against the

---

* "Dear Frank," wrote Grew on September 22. "As you know from my telegrams, I am in close touch with Prince Konoye who in the face of bitter antagonism from extremist and pro-Axis elements is courageously working for an improvement in Japan's relations with the United States. . . . I am convinced that he now means business and will go as far as is

State Department's tendency to insist on detailed, ironclad commitments before the meeting. It was not the Japanese way. The conciliation process was evolutionary. Konoye, with the Emperor's backing, was taking the first step. The alternative, Grew warned, was replacement of the Konoye government by a military dictatorship and a steady drift toward war.[56]

Washington disregarded Grew's advice. The hawks in the cabinet—Stimson, Knox, Ickes, and Morgenthau—were not interested in a settlement short of Japan's capitulation. "I approve of stringing out negotiations," Stimson told Morgenthau, but "they should not be allowed to ripen into a personal conference between the President and the Prime Minister. I greatly fear that such a conference if actually held would produce concessions which would be highly dangerous to our vitally important relations with China."[57] Hull and the Far Eastern Division of the State Department shared Stimson's concern. When alerted to the possibility of a Roosevelt-Konoye meeting, the division warned Hull of the consequences, believing that FDR might be too accommodating. It insisted that prior to any summit meeting Japan announce its intention to withdraw from the Tripartite Pact with Germany and Italy; agree to remove its troops from China; clarify its stand on the open door; and resolve whatever ambiguities there were concerning Hull's four principles for reconciliation.[58]

Hull needed no prodding. Weaned on the fundamentalist pessimism of southern Appalachia, the secretary wanted every i dotted before agreeing to a meeting with the Japanese prime minister. He was also concerned about the public effect of such a conference coming so soon after FDR's dramatic meeting with Churchill off Newfoundland. "I was thoroughly satisfied that a meeting with Konoye, without an advance agreement, could only result in another Munich or in nothing at all. I was opposed to the first Munich and still more opposed to a second Munich."[59]

In his *Memoirs* Hull wrote, "President Roosevelt would have relished a meeting with Konoye, and at first was excited at the prospect. But he instantly

---

possible, without incurring open rebellion in Japan, to reach a reasonable understanding with us. It seems to me highly unlikely that this chance will come again or that any Japanese statesman other than Prince Konoye could succeed in controlling the military extremists in carrying through a policy which they, in their ignorance of international affairs and economic laws, resent and oppose." 4 *Foreign Relations of the United States, 1941* 468–469 (Washington, D.C.: U.S. Government Printing Office, 1956).

agreed that it would be disastrous to hold the meeting without first arriving at a satisfactory agreement."[60] As Hull would have it, the State Department should control negotiations with Japan, and only when it was satisfied should FDR meet with Konoye to ratify what the diplomats had agreed to. Hull's account appears unlikely. For someone who placed as much faith in his ability to improvise extemporaneous solutions as Roosevelt did, and who thrived in unstructured negotiations, it is difficult to believe that he would have "instantly" passed up the opportunity to meet with Konoye.* A more plausible explanation is that FDR, consumed by the war in Europe, had given the deteriorating situation in the Far East too little attention. Deeply engaged with the battle against German U-boats in the Atlantic, anxious to expedite aid to the Soviet Union, and troubled by the great battle shaping up before Moscow, he had left negotiations with Japan in Hull's hands too long to overrule him now. And so when Hull and the State Department, plus Stimson, Morgenthau, and Hopkins, argued against such a meeting, Roosevelt acquiesced. Whether a meeting between the president and Konoye in autumn 1941 would have averted war is one of history's imponderables. But it did not take place.[61†]

If Hull, the State Department, and the hawks in the cabinet feared a Roosevelt-Konoye meeting, ultranationalists in Tokyo were enraged at the possibility. Konoye narrowly averted assassination on September 18, 1941, when four young men armed with ceremonial daggers charged the vehicle in which he was riding from his home to his office. They were repulsed by plainclothes policemen, but the climate of assassination in Tokyo surely gave increased urgency to the negotiations.[62]

Yet nothing happened. Traditional historiography argues that Japan's refusal to withdraw from China was the sticking point, and to some extent that

* On September 10, 1941, Eleanor wrote to her daughter, Anna, who was living in Seattle, "Father told me this morning to tell you that there are still negotiations going on and he might go to Alaska [FDR thought Hawaii too far] to meet the Japs. You and John [Boettiger] are not to mention this to anyone. If he goes he would leave about Oct. 10 and be returning via Seattle about Oct. 21st." Anna Halstead Papers, FDRL.
† On his return from Japan in 1942, Grew asked Hull why Konoye's proposal to meet with FDR had not been accepted. Grew said he thought it might have brought peace. "If you thought so strongly," Hull replied, "why didn't you board a plane and come tell us?" Grew reminded the secretary of his daily telegrams expressing his feeling about the situation. Later Grew wondered if Hull had read them. Joseph C. Grew, 2 *Turbulent Era* 1330.

is true. But the reverse is also true. Stimson, Morgenthau, and Hull feared that if Japan did withdraw from China it would free the Japanese Army to attack Russia in Siberia, which no one in Washington wanted. Accordingly, the best strategy was to keep the talks with Tokyo going but agree to nothing. On October 16, unable to lift the embargo or secure a summit with FDR, Konoye resigned. The Emperor, who still hoped for a peaceful resolution, turned to his war minister, General Hideki Tojo, to form a new government. Intervening directly in the process and wholly without precedent, Hirohito explicitly requested Tojo not to feel bound by the decision of September 6 to prepare for war but to review all issues anew: to start with a clean slate. Shaken by his new responsibility, Tojo accepted the Emperor's request without question.[63] In some respects, Hirohito's action in picking Tojo was similar to Hindenburg's selection of Hitler as chancellor of the Weimar Republic in January 1933: both hoped to resolve the crisis facing their nation by turning to the strongest player on the board.

On the day Konoye resigned, Roosevelt penned longhand notes to Churchill and King George VI. "I am a bit worried over the Japanese situation," he told the King. "The Emperor is for peace, I think, but the Jingoes are trying to force his hand." To Churchill he said, "The Jap situation is definitely worse and I think they are headed north—however in spite of this you and I have two months of respite in the Far East" (FDR's supposition was that Japan would not move south until Russia was defeated).[64]

The following day, Roosevelt met with Hull and his military advisers. At the president's direction Admiral Stark flashed a warning to commanders in the Pacific that hostilities between Japan and Russia were a strong possibility. An attack on U.S. and British forces could not be ruled out. "In view of these possibilities you will take due precautions."[65] Neither Stark nor General Marshall considered the Japanese threat imminent. The next day, October 17, 1941, Stark assured Admiral Husband E. Kimmel, the Pacific Fleet commander, that he did "not believe the Japs are going to sail into us. In fact, I tempered the [alert] message I was given considerably. Perhaps I am wrong, but I hope not. In any case after long pow-wows in the White House it was felt we should be on guard."[66] General Marshall, for his part, informed General Walter C. Short in Hawaii and MacArthur in the Philippines: "No abrupt change in Japanese foreign policy appears imminent."[67]

In Tokyo the "clean slate" debate within the Tojo government continued through the first week in November. Grew advised Washington that the hopes for a settlement were fading fast. The economic pressure Washington had applied, particularly the oil embargo, had been a mistake, said Grew. In a lengthy cable on November 3, 1941, and a shorter follow-up the next day, Grew warned that if negotiations failed "Japan may go all-out in a do-or-die effort to render herself invulnerable to foreign economic pressure, even to the extent of committing national hara-kiri. Those of us who are in direct touch with the atmosphere from day to day realize that this is not only possible *but probable*" (Grew's emphasis).

Grew said Japan's standards of logic "cannot be gauged by any Western measuring rod. It would be hazardous to base our national policy on the belief, held in certain quarters, that our economic pressure will not drive Japan to war." If war came, Grew noted, it "may come *with dangerous and dramatic suddenness*" (Grew's emphasis).[68]

Grew understood the situation better than most. On the afternoon of November 5, 1941, the Japanese privy council, again meeting in the presence of the Emperor, made the decision to prepare for war. "To adopt a policy of patience and perseverance," said Prime Minister Tojo, "was tantamount to self-annihilation. Rather than await extinction, it was better to face death by breaking through the encircling ring and find a way for existence."[69] At the insistence of Foreign Minister Shigenori Togo, negotiations with Washington would continue. But if an agreement could not be reached by November 25, the final decision for war would be placed before the Emperor. Warning orders to prepare for combat were flashed to the military services, and Ambassador Nomura was instructed to make a final approach to Hull. Said Togo, "The success or failure of the pending discussions will have an immense effect on the destiny of the Japanese Empire. In fact, we gambled the fate of our land on the throw of this die."[70]

At the same time the privy council was meeting in Tokyo, the Joint Board of the Army and Navy—a precursor of the Joint Chiefs of Staff—met in Washington to review the situation. After reaffirming the primary objective of American policy to be the defeat of Germany, the Board explicitly advised FDR, "War between the United States and Japan should be avoided." Such a war, said Marshall and Stark, "would greatly weaken the combined effort in the Atlantic against Germany," and the United States simply was not prepared. To emphasize the need for peace in the Pacific, the chiefs stated categorically that further Japanese advances in China or into Thailand or an attack on Russia "would not justify intervention by the United States against Japan."[71]

Inauguration, March 4, 1933. Except for exchanging pleasantries, President Hoover and Roosevelt rode in silence to the ceremony at the Capitol. They did not see each other again.

First press conference, March 6, 1933. FDR met the press twice a week—a total of 998 times— usually in the Oval Office, and always unrehearsed. Roosevelt enjoyed the sessions as much as the reporters. John Gunther, a frequent attendee, said that in forty minutes FDR "expressed amazement, curiosity, sympathy, decision, playfulness, dignity, and surpassing charm."

Fireside chat. Whenever FDR sought to rally public opinion, he took to the airwaves, usually Sunday nights, to speak directly to the people. By explaining the issues in simple language that everyone could understand, whether it was the banking crisis, Lend-Lease, or the menace of fascism, Roosevelt changed the nature of presidential leadership forever.

Roosevelt was the first president inaugurated under the Twentieth (lame-duck) Amendment, which moved the date from March 4 to January 20. A blinding rainstorm failed to put a damper on the 1937 ceremony as FDR proclaimed "one-third of a nation ill-housed, ill-clad, ill-nourished." Courtesy of the Library of Congress

New York's Mayor Fiorello La Guardia takes a break from the 1938 campaign at Hyde Park. Mrs. La Guardia is at left, Congresswoman Caroline O'Day sits on the rear seat, Eleanor stands at right.

Right: Roosevelt flashes his identification as a member of the volunteer fire department of Hyde Park. *Below:* FDR's devoted secretary and confidant Missy LeHand and the president in the Oval Office, September 6, 1938. Justice Felix Frankfurter called LeHand the fifth most powerful person in the country.

FDR observing naval exercises from the deck of the USS *Indianapolis*, May 3, 1934. Navy secretary Claude Swanson is at left, former secretary Josephus Daniels at right.

Sara entertained the King and Queen at Hyde Park with simple dignity. When she suggested her son forego pre-dinner cocktails, the president demurred, supported by the King. "My mother would have said the same," George VI observed.

"I was never so frightened in my life," said Queen Elizabeth after riding with FDR along woodland trails to Top Cottage at Hyde Park. Betsey Cushing Roosevelt (James's wife) sits beside the King.

Anna and FDR watch an impromptu baseball game between newscaster Lowell Thomas's "Nine Old Men" and White House correspondents at Pawling, New York, August 31, 1938.

Roosevelt liked nothing better than to inaugurate the major league baseball season each year at Washington's Griffith Stadium. The cast changed little from 1934 to 1940: James Farley, Harry Hopkins, Clark Griffith, "Bucky" Harris, Joe McCarthy, Joe Cronin, and Connie Mack. The 1937 All-Star game was played in Washington, and Mel Ott of the New York Giants joined the festivities.

Opening day, 1937.

Above: FDR watches as Secretary of War Henry L. Stimson draws the initial number for the nation's first peacetime draft, October 29, 1940.

Left: Roosevelt salutes the Atlantic Fleet from the bridge of the USS *Houston.*

Churchill, meeting Roosevelt off Newfoundland, presents the president a letter from King George VI on August 9, 1941. FDR grips Elliott's arm; son John stands behind Churchill.

Joint Sunday service on the fantail of the *Prince of Wales*. Roosevelt and Churchill are seated at top left. FDR insisted on walking the length of the ship to take his seat.

FDR and Churchill, shown here at service, became fast friends and were always able to resolve differences between their staffs. *Left to right:* Admiral Ernest J. King, Averell Harriman, General George C. Marshall, Field Marshal Sir John Dill, Admiral Harold R. Stark.

FDR and Churchill hold a joint press conference sitting behind Roosevelt's desk in the Oval Office, December 21, 1941. The president wore a black armband to commemorate Sara's death.

The president bestows the Medal of Honor on Brig. Gen. James Doolittle following his daring 1942 raid on Tokyo. *Left to right:* General Henry H. "Hap" Arnold, FDR, Mrs. Doolittle, Doolittle, General Marshall.

FDR enjoys army field mess in Morocco with Harry Hopkins, Lt. Gen. Mark Clark, and Maj. Gen. George Patton. Military censors blanked out Patton's 1st Armored Division shoulder patch.
Courtesy of the National Archives and Records Administration

General Henri Giraud and General Charles de Gaulle pose for the cameras at FDR's insistence. "Roosevelt meant the peace to be an American peace ... and that France ... should recognize him as its savior," de Gaulle wrote later.
Courtesy of the National Archives and Records Administration

Roosevelt, in the presence of a pensive Churchill, announces the doctrine of "unconditional surrender" at Casablanca.

Churchill keeps FDR company as he fishes at Shangri La, May 16, 1942, during a break from the TRIDENT conference.

A healthy and ruddy Roosevelt meets with Canada's governor general, the Earl of Athlone (George VI's uncle), Prime Minister Mackenzie King, and Churchill at Quebec, August 17, 1943.

The Big Three at their first meeting, Teheran, November 30, 1943. Harry Hopkins, Soviet Foreign Minister Vyacheslav Molotov, and Anthony Eden stand directly behind.

FDR preparing to review American troops with Eisenhower at Castelvetrano, Sicily, December 8, 1943. George Patton stands at left.

Roosevelt huddles with the Democratic congressional leadership following his return from Teheran, December 17, 1943. *Left to right:* Senate Majority Leader Alben Barkley, House Majority Leader John McCormack, Vice President Henry Wallace, Speaker Sam Rayburn.

Five-year-old Ruthie Bie was the granddaughter of
Christian Bie, caretaker of Top Cottage. This photo, taken
by Daisy Suckley, is one of only two images known to exist
showing FDR in a wheelchair.

Roosevelt sailed to Hawaii to discuss Pacific strategy with MacArthur and Nimitz, shown here on the deck of the USS *Baltimore,* July 16, 1944. Courtesy of the National Archives and Records Administration

A beaming Churchill greets FDR at Quebec for the OCTAGON conference, September 14, 1944. It was here that Roosevelt and Churchill initially approved the Morgenthau Plan for the pastoralization of Germany. Courtesy of the National Archives and Records Administration

Running mate Senator Harry Truman and Roosevelt at a Rose Garden photo op, August 18, 1944. "I had no idea he was in such a feeble condition," said Truman afterward. "He got more cream in the saucer than he did in the cup."

To allay concerns about his health, FDR barnstormed through New York City for
four hours in pouring rain and near-freezing temperatures, October 21, 1944.
Courtesy of the National Archives and Records Administration

Roosevelt's fourth inauguration, January 20, 1945, was held on the south portico
of the White House rather than at the Capitol, and there was no parade. "Who's
going to march?" asked FDR.

Stalin and FDR confer privately at Yalta (interpreters Pavlov and Bohlen at right). At this meeting Stalin agreed to join the war against Japan three months after Germany's defeat.

FDR and Stalin await Churchill for the formal picture-taking ceremony, February 9, 1945. Secretary of State Edward Stettinius stands behind the empty chair; General Marshall, caught with his hands in his pockets, is behind Roosevelt.

Formal portrait of the Big Three. Air Chief Marshal Sir Charles Portal, Admiral William Leahy, and General Alexei Antonov stand behind the principals.
Courtesy of the Library of Congress

An exhausted Roosevelt reports to Congress on the results of the Yalta conference. This is the first time FDR remained seated when he addressed a joint session.

FDR at his writing table at Warm Springs two days before his death.
The president went to Georgia to regain his health.

Lucy Rutherfurd at Warm Springs, April 11, 1945. After Missy LeHand's stroke in 1941, Lucy and FDR resumed seeing each other, often at the White House or at Shangri La. Lucy was with the president when he died and hers was the last face he saw.

Franklin D. Roosevelt, April 11, 1945. This is the last photograph of the president.

Marshall and Stark's recommendation made sense to Roosevelt. When the cabinet met on November 7, he asked Hull to summarize the situation in the Far East. In his meandering Tennessee vernacular, Hull spoke fifteen minutes. ("If Cordell says, 'Oh Chwrist' again I'm going to scream," FDR whispered to Frances Perkins. "I can't stand profanity with a lisp.")[72] The secretary of state's conclusion was that the situation was critical and that Japan might attack at any time.[73] Roosevelt asked each member of the cabinet for his or her opinion. All agreed that Congress would give the president a declaration of war if he asked for it, but public support would depend on the circumstances. The president turned sharply to Hull. "Do not let the talks [with Nomura] deteriorate. Let us make no more of ill will. Let us do nothing to precipitate a crisis."[74] The split was evident. Hull and the cabinet, temperamentally inclined to support China regardless of the strategic consequences, were ready for war; Roosevelt and the military, determined to avoid a diversion in the Far East, sought to minimize conflict with Japan.

In his talks with Nomura (who was joined on November 15 by Saburo Kurusu, a seasoned diplomat sent by Tokyo to impart a final urgency to the discussions*) Hull was rigid and sanctimonious. White supremacy ran deep in east Tennessee and Hull found it difficult not to be condescending. When the Japanese sought concrete answers, Hull lectured on moral principles. As one scholar wrote, the secretary of state was more "intrusive, altogether more 'preachy,' he flogged the tired old issues again and again."[75]

On November 20, 1941, Nomura and Kurusu presented Japan's final offer—a proposal for a six-month cooling-off period that would allow both sides time to reassess the situation. Essentially it was a return to the status quo before the American embargo. Japan would agree to no further territorial expansion and would withdraw its troops from southern Indochina in return for a relaxation of U.S. trade sanctions.[76] Thanks to MAGIC intercepts, the administration knew this was Tokyo's last stand. "This time we are making our last possible bargain," Foreign Minister Togo informed his Washington representatives. "I hope we can settle all our troubles with the United States peacefully."[77]

* Kurusu had most recently served as Japanese ambassador to Germany, which made him suspect in the eyes of the State Department. But he had also been Japan's consul in Chicago, was married to an American whom he had met there (Alice Little), and spoke English flawlessly, which Nomura did not. In retrospect it appears his assignment was indeed made to move the talks forward.

The Japanese proposal said nothing about China. As a result Hull found it "clearly unacceptable."[78] But Roosevelt saw a glimmer of hope. Fully mindful of Marshall and Stark's admonition to avoid war with Japan, he seized on the idea of a temporary modus vivendi. After learning the details of the Japanese offer, he scribbled a note to Hull as a basis for a conciliatory reply:

6 MONTHS

1. U.S. to resume economic relations—some oil and rice now—more later.
2. Japan to send no more troops to Indochina or Manchurian border or any place South (Dutch. Brit. or Siam).
3. Japan to agree not to invoke tripartite pact even if U.S. gets into European war.
4. U.S. to introduce Japs to Chinese to talk things over but U.S. to take no part in their conversations.

Later on Pacific agreements.[79]

Roosevelt said the United States did not intend to interfere or mediate between Japan and China. "I don't know whether there is such a word in the parlance of diplomats, but the United States' only intention is to become an 'introducer.' "[80] The president dropped earlier American demands that Japan withdraw from China. Later he told Ickes "he was not sure whether or not Japan had a gun up its sleeve." Ickes was convinced war was inevitable, but Roosevelt was not. "It seemed to me," wrote Ickes, "that the President had not yet reached the state of mind where he is willing to be aggressive as to Japan."[81]

Roosevelt's conciliatory stance won quick military support. On November 21 Major General Leonard T. Gerow, chief of the Army's War Plans Division, representing General Marshall, who was spending Thanksgiving in Florida, wrote Hull that the Army considered it a matter of "grave importance to the success of our effort in Europe that we reach a modus vivendi with Japan. . . . [A] temporary peace in the Pacific would permit us to complete defensive preparations in the Philippines and at the same time insure continuance of material assistance to the British—both of which are highly important."[82]

Time was running out. Nomura and Kurusu asked Tokyo for an extension of the November 25 deadline, and Togo gave them until the twenty-ninth. "This time we mean it. The deadline absolutely cannot be changed. After that things are automatically going to happen."[83] MAGIC intercepts delivered the message to FDR and Hull almost as quickly as Nomura received it.

For whatever reasons, Roosevelt's suggestion of a modus vivendi was never presented to the Japanese. Revisionist historians and some conspiracy theorists argue that the Roosevelt administration had given up hope for peace in the Pacific and wanted to lure the Japanese into attacking first.[84] Traditional historians have downplayed the significance of modus vivendi and assert that Japan was bent on war in any event.[85] Hull's rendition of events is meretricious; Stimson's is flawed; and Roosevelt left no record.[86] Professors William L. Langer and S. Everett Gleason, in their magisterial account of prewar diplomacy, call the failure to present the modus vivendi a mystery: "Until and unless additional evidence comes to light, the role of the President as well as of Secretary Hull will remain a subject of speculation."[87]

The sparse record available indicates that FDR's plan encountered heavy going, both from America's allies and in the cabinet. China was outraged, the Australians and the Dutch thought it was a bad idea, and Churchill, who always favored a tough stance toward the Japanese, deftly played the China card. "Of course, it is for you to handle this business and we certainly do not want an additional war," he cabled Roosevelt. "But what about Chiang Kai-shek? Is he not having a very thin diet? If [China] collapses our joint dangers would enormously increase."[88] In the cabinet Stimson and Knox were prepared to play for time but despaired of leaving China in the lurch; Morgenthau was appalled at the prospect; Hull was already on record to that effect; and Ickes (for the umpteenth time) considered resigning. "If this negotiation with Japan had been consummated, I would have promptly resigned from the Cabinet with a ringing statement attacking the arrangement. . . . I believe the President would have lost the country on this issue and that hell would have been to pay generally."[89]

When Roosevelt met with his war council (Hull, Stimson, Knox, Marshall, and Stark) on November 25, 1941, it was agreed that little room for negotiation remained.[90] The discussion focused on what to do should Japan reject a temporary truce. Aware that Tokyo had set a November 29 (Saturday) deadline, Roosevelt said, "We are likely to be attacked perhaps as soon as next Monday because the Japanese are notorious for attacking without warning. The question is how to maneuver them into firing the first shot without too much danger to ourselves."[91] The president was not baiting a trap but, like Lincoln prior to Fort Sumter, wanted Japan to be perceived as

the aggressor.* The consensus was that the Japanese would move from Indochina against Thailand, Malaya, Singapore, and the Dutch East Indies,
rather than the Philippines. It was not a question of whether the Japanese
would attack, but where and when.[92]

Separated by more than sixty years and three generations from events in
1941, it is difficult to appreciate the implicit racial hostility toward Japan that
characterized Roosevelt's discussions with his advisers as war drew near. Sir
Lewis Namier, the eminent British scholar, once observed that historians are inclined to remember the present and forget the past. Dimensions of tolerance are
much greater now than they were then, and, given Japan's current economic and
industrial prowess, we can easily forget how little credibility Westerners assigned
to the Japanese military in 1941. The army had been bogged down in China for
four years; Zhukov had made quick work of the garrison in Manchukuo; and the
Japanese Navy had not been engaged in battle on the high seas since 1905. "The
Japs," as FDR called them, might prevail in Southeast Asia, but they were scarcely
seen as a threat to American forces in the Pacific, certainly not to Pearl Harbor,
which both the Army and the Navy believed to be impregnable. This supercil-
ious dismissal of Japan as a serious military rival allowed the war council to discuss the possibility of war in Southeast Asia with remarkable detachment. The
conflict, if it came, they felt would be a distraction but little more.

Hull met Nomura and Kurusu in the late afternoon of Wednesday, November 26. Instead of presenting FDR's plan for a modus vivendi, he gave the Japanese what they interpreted to be an ultimatum: a ten-point clarification of
American demands for settlement in the Pacific that went far beyond anything
broached previously. Not only was it nonresponsive to the Japanese truce offer,

---

* In his 1946 statement to the Joint Committee on the Investigation of the Pearl Harbor Attack, Secretary Stimson expanded on FDR's remarks. According to Stimson, "If you know
that your enemy is going to strike you, it is not usually wise to wait until he gets the jump
on you by taking the initiative. In spite of the risk involved, however, in letting the Japanese
fire the first shot, we realized that in order to have the full support of the American people
it was desirable to make sure that the Japanese be the ones to do this so that there should remain no doubt in anyone's mind as to who were the aggressors. We discussed at this meeting the basis on which this country's position could be most clearly explained to our own
people and to the world, in case we had to go into the fight quickly because of some sudden
move on the part of the Japanese." Stimson Statement, 11 *Hearings Before the Joint Committee on the Investigation of the Pearl Harbor Attack* 5421–5422 (Washington, D.C.: U.S. Government Printing Office, 1946).

but the United States called for Japan's complete withdrawal from China and Indochina, recognition of the Chungking government of Chiang Kai-shek, renunciation of further expansion in Southeast Asia, and withdrawal from the Tripartite Pact.[93] It was a statement for the record rather than a serious attempt to reach agreement.[94] "I have washed my hands of it," Hull told Stimson afterward. "It is now in the hands of you and Knox—the Army and Navy."[95]

The abrupt shift from modus vivendi to confrontation caught the military by surprise.[96] On November 27, 1941, Admiral Stark alerted Kimmel in Hawaii and Admiral Thomas C. Hart, commanding the Asiatic Fleet, to be on guard. "This dispatch is to be considered a war warning. Negotiations with Japan looking toward stabilization of conditions in the Pacific have ceased and an aggressive move is expected within the next few days. The number and equipment of Japanese troops and the organization of naval task forces indicates an amphibious expedition against either the Philippines, Thai or Kra [Malay] peninsula or possibly Borneo."[97]*

The Army's warning to commanders in the Pacific was less strongly worded but made the same point:

Negotiations with Japan appear to be terminated to all practical purposes, with only the barest possibilities that the Japanese Government might come back and offer to continue. Japanese future action unpredictable but hostile action possible at any moment. If hostilities cannot, repeat cannot, be avoided the United States desires that Japan commit the first overt act. This policy should not be construed as restricting you to a course of action that might jeopardize your defense.[98]

To this day there is no satisfactory explanation of why Hull jettisoned the quest for a cooling-off period with Japan or why FDR supported him. Roosevelt had too much on his plate. There is no doubt he was under great pressure. He had just ordered the Navy to shoot enemy vessels on sight in the Atlantic; he had just finished a bruising battle with Congress over repeal of the

* Accompanying the war warning was a personal letter from Stark to his friend Kimmel. "I held this [letter] up pending a meeting with the President and Mr. Hull today. . . . Neither will be surprised over a Japanese surprise attack. From many angles an attack on the Philippines would be the most embarrassing that could happen to us." Stark to Kimmel, November 27, 1941, 5 *Pearl Harbor Attack* 2301.

Neutrality Act;* and the German Army was thirty miles from Moscow. To press his proposal for a modus vivendi may have been more than Roosevelt wanted to take on. Like the wrongheaded oil embargo in July, events got ahead of him. As for Hull, his official biographer, Julius Pratt, confesses to being baffled: "The President had given Hull a very free reign in dealing with Japan. . . . [I]t seems that his decision to 'kick the whole thing over' (as Stimson records him saying) was a petulant one by a tired and angry man."[99] Whatever the reason, the plan for a temporary truce was discarded, and, as Stanford historian David Kennedy recently observed, "the last flimsy hope of avoiding, or even delaying, war with Japan thus evaporated."[100]

Nomura and Kurusu were dumbfounded at the severity of Hull's ten-point memorandum. Tokyo's reaction was similar. "We felt that clearly the United States had no hope or intention of reaching an agreement for a peaceful settlement," said Foreign Minister Togo, one of the most moderate members of the government,[101] On December 1, at a meeting of the privy council attended by the Emperor, the Japanese government opted for war. "It is now clear that Japan's claims cannot be attained through diplomatic means," said Prime Minister Tojo. The Emperor asked each member of the council for his opinion. The decision was unanimous. Hirohito nodded acceptance. "At this moment," concluded Tojo, "our Empire stands on the threshold of glory or oblivion."[102]

On the morning of December 2 the chiefs of staff of the army and navy went to the Imperial Palace to formally request the Emperor's approval for a war order issued in his name setting the date for attack as December 8 (December 7 in Hawaii and Washington), 1941. That afternoon, following the Imperial assent, powerful radio transmitters in Tokyo flashed the message to the Japanese armed forces:

NIITAKAYAMA NOBORE 1208.
(CLIMB MOUNT NIITAKA ON DECEMBER 8.)[103]†

---

* Repeal of the Neutrality Act carried the Senate 50–37, the smallest majority FDR had won on any foreign policy issue since the war in Europe began. In the House the vote was even closer (212–194), with only Southern Democrats solidly behind the president. Critics who wonder why FDR said so little about racial inequality in the South should consider the source of his foreign policy support in Congress.
† Mount Niitaka (Yu Shan in Chinese), which at 13,113 feet was the largest peak in the Japanese empire, is located in Yu Shan National Park in central Taiwan (Formosa).

As was the case with all great powers at the time, the filing cabinets of the Japanese military bulged with war plans to fit any contingency. A drive to the south had been war-gamed repeatedly, and the consistent finding was that an attack on the Dutch East Indies, Singapore, or Malaya would be at risk so long as the U.S. Asiatic Fleet was intact in the Philippines and the Pacific Fleet in Hawaii. The problem fell squarely into the lap of Admiral Isoroku Yamamoto, commander in chief of the Japanese Combined Fleet since 1939.

Yamamoto was at the summit of his distinguished naval career. Four years younger than MacArthur, Marshall, and Stark (all of whom were born in 1880), he had lost the fore and middle fingers on his left hand as a junior officer at Tsushima. No one in the Japanese Navy knew the United States better than Yamamoto, and no one had wanted war less than he. In the early twenties Yamamoto studied English as a graduate student at Harvard. He hitchhiked across America and understood the vast industrial and agricultural capacity of the country. From 1926 to 1928 he served as naval attaché in Washington. In the tense foreign policy debates in the 1930s he had been a voice of moderation, steeling the Navy against military adventurism and skeptical of the alliance with Nazi Germany and Mussolini's Italy. His life had repeatedly been threatened by nationalist extremists.[104]*

Yamamoto's experience provided a unique perspective on modern warfare. Though not a pilot, he was closely associated with naval aviation, having been executive officer of the Navy's flight school in the mid-1920s, commander of the First Carrier Division in the early 1930s, director of the Aeronautical Department of the Navy from 1935 to 1936, and vice minister from 1936 to 1939. Like Brigadier General William "Billy" Mitchell in the United States, he was a

---

* Yamamoto was to have accompanied Konoye to meet FDR had the conference taken place. He advised the prime minister to approach the talks "as though your life depended on the outcome. Even if the discussions break down, don't get defiant, but leave room for further moves."

Yamamoto was a regular subscriber to *Life* magazine and always left his copy in the wardroom of his flagship. When a junior officer asked him to recommend a biography to improve his English, Yamamoto recommended Carl Sandburg's *Lincoln*. "I like Lincoln. I think he's great not just as an American, but as a human being." The admiral was also very fond of American football. On his way to the London Naval Conference in 1934, he took his staff to see Northwestern play Iowa in Evanston (Iowa 20, Northwestern 7). Hiroyki Agawa, *The Reluctant Admiral: Yamamoto and the Imperial Navy* 21, 24, 53 (Tokyo: Kodansha International, 1979).

champion of airpower; unlike Mitchell, Yamamoto possessed the rank, prestige, and administrative skill to do something about it. In the Navy he was known as a bold, original thinker and an inveterate gambler. He thrived on all-night poker games, testing his opponents' nerves, endurance, and patience—just as he tested himself. "In all games Yamamoto loved to take chances just as he did in naval strategy," explained his administrative aide, Captain Yasuji Watanabe. "He had a gambler's heart."[105]

The war plan Yamamoto inherited in 1939 envisaged a decisive naval battle with the American fleet near the home islands in which land-based planes and submarines would whittle down the U.S. armada until the Imperial Navy took it on in an old-fashioned line-of-battle slugfest. Yamamoto recognized that strategy was inadequate to support an all-out southward thrust against numerous objectives several thousand miles away. The U.S. Navy would have to be destroyed at the outset if the long, exposed Japanese flank were to be secured.[106]

When Yamamoto first thought of attacking Pearl Harbor is unclear. The British victory at Taranto on November 12, 1940, in which twelve carrier-based torpedo planes surprised the Italian fleet lying at anchor and sank three battleships, focused his attention on the possibility.[107] In his own correspondence, Yamamoto suggests that planning began in December 1940, first as a concept, then a plan, finally as an exercise, including repeated mock attacks on a model of Pearl Harbor set up in Japan's Kagoshima Bay. The logistical problems were enormous. To mass the necessary number of planes (Yamamoto estimated 300) would require a task force of at least six carriers, and the 3,500-mile attack route—well beyond the fleet's cruising range—would require tricky refuelings at sea.* But the most difficult problems were tactical: first, to ensure complete surprise; then to launch a torpedo attack in the shallow waters of Pearl Harbor. The Italian anchorage at Taranto, by contrast, was in deep water, and the general view in naval circles was that aerial torpedoes required a depth of at least 12 fathoms (72 feet), otherwise they would hit bottom, lodge in the mud, or explode prematurely. The American Navy was so convinced that was the case that it rejected the use of antitorpedo nets at Pearl

* Because Japan's original war plan anticipated meeting the American fleet near the home islands, the Japanese Navy had neglected to design ships with a long cruising radius. The destroyers escorting the Pearl Harbor task force, for example, had to be refueled daily. Gordon W. Prange, *At Dawn We Slept* 322–323 (New York: Penguin, 1982).

Harbor as unnecessary.[108] By October 1941 the Japanese had developed a finned torpedo that could run in 6 fathoms (36 feet), and by November had perfected a launch technique with pilots flying at 100 knots (roughly 115 mph) and an altitude of 60 feet that guaranteed an 83 percent success rate.[109]

As finally written, Yamamoto's attack plan had eight interlocking components, of which the attack on Pearl Harbor was the centerpiece. Additional formations moved against the American Asiatic Fleet in the Philippines, against the British off Singapore, and the Dutch near Borneo. Invasion forces, some comprised of more than a hundred vessels, steamed independently toward Malaya, Guam, and Luzon, plus a small neutralization force toward Midway. Yamamoto kept the main body of the Combined Fleet—six battleships, two light carriers, two cruisers, and thirteen destroyers—under his personal command in the Inland Sea, ready to move wherever required. The principal task, the attack on Pearl Harbor, was assigned to the newly created First Air Fleet under Vice Admiral Chuichi Nagumo, a battleship sailor who was president of the Naval Staff College in Tokyo when Yamamoto tapped him for the assignment. Described by friends as "a Japanese Bull Halsey"—jaunty, extroverted, supremely self-confident—Nagumo was the senior officer available for the post, and Yamamoto chose to go with rank and tradition rather than specialized carrier expertise.*

By November 29, 1941, each of the Japanese task forces had put to sea. Each was instructed that "in the event an agreement is reached with the United States, the task force will immediately return to Japan." The First Air Fleet was also instructed to turn back if sighted by the enemy before X-Day minus one.[110]

Yamamoto's decision to attack the Pacific Fleet at Pearl Harbor not only was breathtakingly bold but involved a revolutionary, hitherto untried use of naval airpower—an experimental concept untested in the crucible of battle. Taranto had involved twelve planes from a single carrier 170 miles away. The First Air Fleet would assault what was considered the strongest naval base in the world, halfway across the Pacific, with the largest air armada ever assembled at sea. "What a strange position I find myself in," Yamamoto wrote to his friend Rear Admiral Teikichi Hori on the eve of the fleet's departure, "—having to pursue

---

* Naval historians are fond of pointing out that while Nagumo's appointment rested on seniority, Kimmel was a "merit" appointee, selected to command the Pacific Fleet over the heads of six more senior admirals. U.S. Congress, *Report of the Joint Committee on the Investigation of the Pearl Harbor Attack* 75, note 4.

with full determination a course of action which is diametrically opposed to my best judgment and firmest conviction. That, too, perhaps is fate."[111]

When the attack order was given on December 2, 1941, the First Air Fleet had covered about half the distance to Oahu. Nagumo's sprawling task force of nearly three dozen ships moved wedgelike in an easterly direction at a steady fourteen knots: six fast aircraft carriers jacketed by a protective screen of destroyers, cruisers, and battleships, with submarine lookouts fore and aft and a supply train of eight 20,000-ton tankers. On December 4, in heavy seas, First Air Fleet pivoted southeast, roughly nine hundred miles north of Hawaii. Two days later, at precisely 11:30 A.M., Nagumo completed his final refueling, released his slow-moving tankers, swung due south toward Oahu, and increased speed to twenty knots. After hoisting the historic "Z" flag Admiral Togo had flown at Tsushima, Nagumo flashed Yamamoto's Nelson-like message to the fleet: "The rise and fall of the Empire depends upon this battle. Every man will do his duty."[112]

At 5:50 the following morning, December 7, 1941, the First Air Fleet was 220 miles north of Oahu. Nagumo wheeled due east into a brisk wind and increased speed to twenty-four knots, essential for a successful launch. The flat-tops pitched violently, listing between twelve and fifteen degrees, making the first-light takeoffs all the more risky. "I have brought the task force successfully to the point of attack," Nagumo told his air officer, Commander Minoru Genda. "From now on the burden is on your shoulders."[113]

Weather delayed the takeoff twenty minutes. At 6:10 A.M. the launch began: first the fighters, then the horizontal bombers, dive-bombers, and torpedo planes—183 in all. By 6:20 they were in battle formation bound for Oahu. One hour later, Nagumo launched the second attack wave, mostly horizontal bombers and dive-bombers. Within ninety minutes of the first wave's initial takeoff, a formidable fleet of 350 planes was homing in on its targets at Pearl Harbor, Hickam and Wheeler Fields, and Kaneohe Air Station.

Despite widespread knowledge of the worsening political situation in the Pacific and an explicit war warning from Washington, the Japanese attack caught the American military in Hawaii off guard.* In a sense, the defense of

---

* In the two weeks prior to December 7, 1941, the nine military and naval commanders in the Pacific area received repeated warnings of pending hostile action by Japan. Seven of the commanders, including Admiral Hart and General MacArthur in the Philippines, General John L. DeWitt on the West Coast, and General Frank M. Andrews in Panama, put their

Pearl Harbor fell into the void between the Army and the Navy. The Army assumed that the Navy was conducting distant reconnaissance off the islands, as provided for in joint defense plans; the Navy, for its part, believed the Army was continuously manning Oahu's early-warning radar, which was also provided for. Neither proved to be the case. And neither the Army nor the Navy placed their forces on alert.[114] Perhaps it was overconfidence, perhaps sloth—peacetime laziness amid the comforts of Honolulu, perhaps simply a refusal to take Washington's war warning seriously. "I never thought those little yellow sons-of-bitches could pull off such an attack, so far from Japan," Kimmel confessed years later.[115]

General Marshall put the attack into perspective. Pearl Harbor, he said,

> was the only installation we had anywhere that was reasonably well equipped. Therefore we were not worried about it. In our opinion the commanders had been alerted. In our opinion there was nothing more we could give them. . . . In our opinion it was the one place that had enough within itself to put up a reasonable defense. The only place we had any assurance about was Hawaii.[116]*

The Japanese attack lasted little more than two hours. When the last plane winged away at 10 A.M., eighteen U.S. vessels, including eight battleships, had

---

commands on a war footing. Hawaii was the only exception. Neither Admiral Kimmel nor General Short took Washington's war warnings seriously. Mark S. Watson, *Chief of Staff: Prewar Plans and Preparations* 505–512 (Washington, D.C.: U.S. Government Printing Office, 1950).

* The judgment of the Joint Congressional Committee on the Investigation of the Pearl Harbor Attack is scathing with respect to Admiral Kimmel and General Short. After months of hearings and detailed field investigations, the committee concluded:

> The commanders in Hawaii were clearly and unmistakably warned of war with Japan. They were given orders and possessed information that the entire Pacific area was fraught with danger. They failed to carry out these orders and to discharge their basic and ultimate responsibilities. They failed to defend the fortress they commanded—their citadel was taken by surprise. Aside from any responsibilities that may appear to rest in Washington, the ultimate and direct responsibility for failure to engage the Japanese on the morning of December 7 with every weapon at their disposal rests essentially and properly with the Army and Navy commands in Hawaii whose duty it was to meet the enemy against which they had been warned.

Report, Pearl Harbor Attack 238.

been sunk or heavily damaged. More than 175 military aircraft were destroyed on the ground and another 159 crippled. In all, 2,403 servicemen were dead, 1,103 of them entombed on the battleship *Arizona,* which sank almost instantly when a bomb exploded in its forward magazine. Another 1,200 men were wounded. Japan lost twenty-nine planes, mostly dive-bombers, in the second attack wave. "If I am told to fight regardless of the circumstances," Yamamoto had told Konoye the year before, "I shall run wild for the first six months or a year, but I have utterly no confidence for the second or third years."[117]

Roosevelt learned of the attack at 1:40 P.M. Washington time, roughly forty-five minutes after the first wave of Zeros began their strafing run. He was having a late lunch with Harry Hopkins at his desk in the upstairs study when Knox called from the Navy Department. "Mr. President, it looks like the Japanese have attacked Pearl Harbor."[118] A flurry of phone calls followed. At 2:30 Stark called the president with confirmation. "I could hear the shocked unbelief in Admiral Stark's voice," said Grace Tully as she put him through to FDR.[119] Stark said that it was a very severe attack, the fleet had been heavily damaged, and there was considerable loss of life. Roosevelt told Stark to execute the standing orders that were to go into effect in case of war in the Pacific.[120] Official Washington was not surprised by the Japanese attack, but it was stunned that it had come at Pearl Harbor and appalled by the damage.

At three o'clock Roosevelt met his war council. Reports continued to come in, each more terrible than the last. The president handled the telephone personally. He ordered Hull to inform the Latin American governments and secure their cooperation; Knox and Stimson were instructed to draft the necessary orders to put the nation on a war footing. Roosevelt discussed troop deployments at length with General Marshall and ordered military protection for the Japanese Embassy and all Japanese consulates in the United States. His mood was businesslike with no sign of panic. As Sumner Welles reported, FDR was at the center of the action and completely in charge. Eleanor, who went briefly into the study, noted her husband's steadiness.[121]

Churchill called from Chequers, his weekend estate. "Mr. President, what's this about Japan?"

"It's quite true," Roosevelt replied. "They have attacked us at Pearl Harbor. We are all in the same boat now."

"That certainly simplifies things," said Churchill. "God be with you."[122]

Later Churchill wrote, "To have the United States on our side was to me the greatest joy. I thought of a remark [Sir] Edward Grey [the British foreign secretary] had made to me more than thirty years before—that the United States was like 'a gigantic boiler. Once the fire is lighted under it there is no limit to the power it can generate.' Being saturated and satiated with emotion I went to bed and slept the sleep of the saved and thankful."[123]

Shortly before 5 P.M. Roosevelt called Grace Tully to his study. He was alone, Tully remembered, and had just lit a cigarette. "Sit down, Grace. I'm going before Congress tomorrow. I'd like to dictate my message. It will be short."

Roosevelt dictated in the same steady tone in which he answered his correspondence, only more slowly and precisely: "Yesterday comma December seventh comma 1941 dash a date which will live in infamy dash . . ." The entire message ran less than five hundred words—about twice as long as Lincoln's Gettysburg Address. Every word was Roosevelt's own, except for the next-to-last sentence, which was suggested by Hopkins.[124] The president focused on Japanese treachery and catalogued the areas where the enemy had struck. Contrary to Stimson's advice, he did not ask for a declaration of war against Germany. Contrary to Hull's wishes, he kept it short.[125]

Dinner that evening was with Hopkins and Grace Tully in the upstairs study. At 8:30 FDR met the cabinet. He was grim as the members filed in, and there was no small talk.[126] Roosevelt opened on a somber note: "This is the most serious meeting of the Cabinet that has taken place since 1861." By coincidence they were meeting in the same Oval Study in which Lincoln's cabinet had assembled after Fort Sumter.[127] He then recounted what had happened. Frances Perkins recalled that FDR "could hardly bring himself to describe the devastation. His pride in the Navy was so terrific that he was having actual physical difficulty in getting out the words that put him on the record as knowing that the Navy was caught unawares."

Twice FDR asked Knox, "Find out, for God's sake, why the ships were tied up in rows." To Perkins it was obvious that Roosevelt "was having a dreadful time just accepting the idea that the Navy could be caught off guard."[128] As a former assistant secretary of the Navy, FDR never forgave Kimmel and Stark for the lack of readiness at Pearl Harbor. Kimmel was relieved of command, reduced in rank to rear admiral, and forced to retire. Stark was removed as chief of naval operations, shunted to England, and, after a suitable period, also pushed into retirement. Roosevelt chose Chester Nimitz to replace Kimmel and Admiral Ernest W. King, the hard-as-nails commander of the Atlantic Fleet, as chief of naval operations.

At ten the cabinet was joined by the congressional leadership. Roosevelt extended the invitations personally, including the Republican isolationist Hiram Johnson of California (whom he wanted to win over) and excluding the House Foreign Affairs ranking member Hamilton Fish (whom he detested). For all his many virtues FDR had a vindictive streak, and Fish was one of those who experienced it.[129] When Roosevelt recounted what had happened at Pearl Harbor, the legislators were dumbfounded. "They sat in dead silence and even after the recital was over they had very few words," wrote Stimson.[130] Finally Tom Connally of Texas spoke up. "How did it happen that our warships were caught like sitting ducks at Pearl Harbor?" he bellowed. "How did they catch us with our pants down? Where were our patrols? They were all asleep!"[131]

FDR dipped his head. "I don't know, Tom, I just don't know."[132]

Roosevelt asked the leaders when they would be ready to receive him, and it was agreed he would speak to a joint session of Congress at 12:30 the next day. FDR declined to say in advance whether he would ask for a declaration of war, determined to make the announcement to the country himself. "Republicans will go along with whatever is done," said Senate minority leader Charles McNary. GOP House leader Joe Martin (of "Martin, Barton, and Fish") told Roosevelt, "Where the integrity and honor of the Nation is involved there is only one party."[133] The meeting broke up shortly after eleven.

Roosevelt had one last meeting that evening—a personal tête-à-tête over beer and sandwiches with two outsiders: thirty-three-year-old Edward R. Murrow, back from London; and FDR's Columbia classmate William Donovan, who since July had been heading the president's clandestine intelligence operations as the innocuous "coordinator of information." From Murrow he wanted to know how the British were bearing up. From Donovan, a current intelligence assessment. From both he wanted independent judgment on how the American people would react to a declaration of war. And he let his hair down. American planes had been destroyed "on the ground, by God, on the ground," pounding his fist on the table.[134]

At noon Monday, Roosevelt motored down Pennsylvania Avenue to Capitol Hill, deliberately choosing an open car to demonstrate his confidence and resolve. In the second car rode Eleanor and Mrs. Woodrow Wilson, whom FDR had asked to join the presidential party. When he entered the House chamber, the Congress rose as one for a prolonged standing ovation. Twelve times in a speech of only twenty-five sentences the president was interrupted by thunderous applause. He catalogued Japan's Pacific aggression—not only at Pearl Harbor but in Malaya, Hong Kong, Guam, the Philippines, Wake Island, and Midway:

> The facts of yesterday speak for themselves. No matter how long it may take us to overcome this premeditated invasion, the American people in their righteous might will win through to absolute victory.
>
> I ask that the Congress declare that since the unprovoked and dastardly attack by Japan on Sunday, December 7, 1941, a state of war has existed between the United States and the Japanese Empire.[135]

It was a powerful speech, powerfully delivered. Congress acted within thirty-three minutes: unanimously in the Senate, 388–1 in the House, the lone dissenter Congresswoman Jeannette Rankin of Montana—who had also voted against war in 1917.

The United States was at war.

TWENTY-FOUR

COMMANDER IN CHIEF

When the news first came that Japan
had attacked us, my first feeling was
of relief that the indecision was over
and that a crisis had come in a way
which would unite all our people.
—HENRY L. STIMSON, DECEMBER 7, 1941

THE ROOSEVELT ADMINISTRATION, like most of America, seriously underestimated Japan's military capacity. Cartoon caricaturizations of the Japanese as little yellow men with buckteeth and horn-rimmed glasses who were no good at piloting airplanes because of their slanty eyes led to woeful miscalculations up and down the line. Japanese stereotypes of the United States were equally off base, particularly at high levels of government and in the Army. Not only did the Japanese leadership fail to recognize the enormous industrial potential and spiritual strength of the country, they grossly misinterpreted the nature of American society. Because women played no public role in Japan, decision makers had no way of measuring their impact on national policy. As Admiral Shigeyoshi Inoue observed, many Japanese leaders had "a childish notion" that because women had a powerful say in America "it wouldn't be long before they started objecting to the war and demanding a settlement."[1]

Pearl Harbor united Americans as nothing else could. If the Japanese had attacked Singapore, Borneo, or even the Philippines, the nation would have been divided over how to respond. But the attack on Pearl Harbor was so unexpected and so devastating that the nation rallied instantly behind the president. Isolationists were stilled, domestic squabbles receded, and debate adjourned. "We are now in this war," FDR told the country in a fireside chat Tuesday evening, December 9. "We are all in it—all the way. Every single man, woman and child is a partner in the most tremendous undertaking in American history. We must share together the bad news and the good news, the defeats and the victories—the changing fortunes of war."[2]

Initially the news was bad. On December 10 Japanese aircraft sank the British battleships *Repulse* and *Prince of Wales* off Malaya. (*Prince of Wales* had been the site of FDR's Atlantic Charter meeting with Churchill.) Hong Kong, Guam, Wake Island, New Britain, the Gilbert Islands, and the Solomons all fell within weeks of Pearl Harbor. In the Philippines, American and Filipino troops retreated to the Bataan peninsula and the island redoubt of Corregidor. In Burma, Japanese forces advanced almost without opposition. In Malaya, British and Indian forces, despite a two-to-one, sometimes three-to-one, numerical advantage, proved no match for the better-trained, better-led divisions of General Tomoyuki Yamashita. Singapore, with a garrison of 85,000 troops—the "Gibraltar of the Pacific"—fell on February 15, 1942, the most ignominious defeat of British arms on record. If Pearl Harbor represented the nadir of the U.S. Navy, the defeat at Singapore was as much a disaster for the British Army. Twelve days later, in the Battle of the Java Sea, a Japanese naval force of five cruisers and nine destroyers took on an equivalent American-British-Dutch-Australian formation, sinking all five Allied cruisers (including the USS *Houston*) and five of nine destroyers. Fighting ended in the Dutch East Indies on March 12, and another 93,000 troops entered Japanese captivity. Allied propaganda notwithstanding, many in Burma, Malaya, and the East Indies initially welcomed the Japanese as liberators who were freeing Asian peoples from European imperialism.[3]

Roosevelt had not asked Congress to declare war against Germany and Italy. On December 11 Hitler remedied the omission by appearing before the Reichstag to announce that a state of war existed between the United States and the Third Reich. Italy followed two hours later. Neither Hitler (who was at the eastern front) nor Mussolini had been apprised of the attack on Pearl Harbor beforehand. And the strict black-letter text of the Tripartite Pact did not oblige them to follow Japan's lead. But they were overjoyed to do so. Mussolini welcomed the clarification of America's status, and Hitler saw the Japanese attack as a harbinger of victory. "Now it is impossible for us to lose the war," the führer told his generals. "We have an ally who has never been vanquished in three thousand years."[4]

So confident were Hitler and Mussolini of ultimate victory that they did not press Japan for a parallel declaration of war against Russia. Hitler wished to finish off the Soviet Union himself and was content to see the Japanese free the Pacific of American and British influence. Germany's declaration of war against the United States intensified the U-boat campaign in the Atlantic. Hitler removed the restraints under which the German submarine fleet had been operating, and American coastal shipping became a prime target. By late January 1942 more than twenty U-boats were operating in American waters. On January 28, a single submarine standing off New York harbor sank eight ships, including three tankers, in just twelve hours.[5]*

Roosevelt chose not to respond to Hitler by going before Congress. Late on the afternoon of December 11 he sent a written message requesting both houses to acknowledge that the United States and Germany were at war.[6] The House acted instantly by voice vote, the Senate shortly afterward. Both votes were unanimous.

As soon as the Japanese attacked Pearl Harbor, Churchill decided it was essential for him to meet Roosevelt. "I have formed the conviction that it is my duty to visit Washington without delay," he wrote the King on December 8. "The whole plan of Anglo-American defence and attack has to be concerted in light of reality. We have also to be careful that our share of munitions and other aid which we are receiving from the United States does not suffer more than is inevitable."[7]

FDR was initially reluctant. He wished to meet Churchill, but not until the dust from Pearl Harbor had settled. "I would like to suggest delay . . . until early stages of mobilization complete here and situation in Pacific more clarified," the president wrote on December 10. "My first impression is that full discussion would be more useful a few weeks hence than immediately."[8] Evidently Roosevelt spoke directly with Churchill later that day and expressed concern for the prime minister's safety on the long ocean voyage, especially the return trip after his presence in the United States had become known.

Churchill refused to be deterred. "We do not think there is any serious danger about return journey," he replied. "There is however, great danger in our

---

* In January 1942 German U-boats prowling off the East Coast sank 48 ships of 276,795 tons; in February, 73 ships of 429,891 tons; and in March, 95 ships of 534,064 tons. The Navy did not sink its first German submarine until April 1942. Williamson Murray and Allan B. Millett, *A War to Be Won* 250 (Cambridge, Mass.: Harvard University Press, 2000).

not having a full discussion on the highest level about the extreme gravity of the naval position as well as upon all the production and allocation issues involved. . . . I never felt so sure about the final victory, but only concerted action will achieve it."[9]

Roosevelt conceded. "Delighted to have you here at White House," he cabled the evening of December 10. "The news is bad but it will be better."[10]

Three days later Churchill sailed from Scotland on the shakedown cruise of the new battleship *Duke of York* (a sister ship to *Prince of Wales*), accompanied by his military chiefs and Lord Beaverbrook, Britain's Canadian-born minister of supply. It was a stormy crossing with gale force winds and forty-foot waves, and the second day out the great battleship shed its destroyer escort, relying on its 28-knot speed to elude German U-boats. Once again Britain's entire war leadership was making the perilous passage across the Atlantic on a single ship in a hostile sea. Churchill had originally planned to sail up the Chesapeake to the Potomac and then motor to Washington, but the rough weather delayed his arrival. When *Duke of York* reached Hampton Roads on December 22, the prime minister disembarked and boarded a U.S. Navy Lockheed Lodestar, which landed in Washington forty-five minutes later. "On no account come out to meet me," he advised FDR, but when the plane landed Roosevelt stood waiting, his back propped against a White House limousine.

Churchill hit the White House like a cyclone. Eleanor had arranged for his personal staff to be housed there and had cleared the Monroe Room on the second floor for the prime minister's "map room," modeled on his London command post. Churchill would sleep in the Lincoln Bedroom. Or so Eleanor thought. "Won't do," said Winston. "Bed's not right." The prime minister thereupon undertook his own tour of the second floor, trying the beds and examining the storage space in each room, and finally settled on the Rose Bedroom—the same room Sara had occupied on her visits to Washington and in which Queen Elizabeth had stayed in 1939.[11]

Churchill confronted FDR's butler, Alonzo Fields. "Now Fields, we want to leave here as friends, right? So I need you to listen. One, I don't like talking outside my quarters. Two, I hate whistling in the corridors. And three, I must have a tumbler of sherry in my room before breakfast, a couple of glasses of scotch and soda before lunch, and French champagne and well-aged brandy before I go to sleep at night."[12] No one in the White House had ever seen anything like Winston before, said Secret Service chief Mike Reilly. "He ate, and thoroughly enjoyed, more food than any two men or three diplomats; and he consumed brandy and scotch with a grace and enthusiasm that left us all openmouthed in awe. It was not the amount that impressed us, although that was quite impressive, but the complete sobriety that went hand and hand with his drinking."[13] When Eleanor said she feared Churchill was a bad influence on her husband because of his drinking, FDR cut her short with a reminder that it was not his side of the family that had a problem with alcohol.[14]

For his part Churchill felt completely at home: up at eleven, two hot baths a day, a long nap in the late afternoon, bedtime at two-thirty or three. "We live here as a big family," he cabled Deputy Prime Minister Clement Attlee, "in the greatest intimacy and informality,* and I have formed the very highest regard and admiration for the President. His breadth of view, resolution and his loyalty to the common cause are beyond all praise."[15]

The day after his arrival, Churchill joined FDR at one of his twice-weekly press conferences in the Oval Office. The setting and informality were new, but after forty years' experience with question period in the House of Commons, Churchill was in his element. Sitting to Roosevelt's right behind the president's crowded desk, the prime minister parried inquiries with deft aplomb.

Q: Mr. Prime Minister, isn't Singapore [which had not yet fallen] the key to the whole situation out there?

WSC: The key to the whole situation is the resolute manner in which the British and American Democracies are going to throw themselves into the conflict.

Q: Mr. Minister, can you tell us when you think we may lick these boys?

WSC: If we manage it well it will take only half as long as if we manage it badly. [Loud laughter.][16]

Roosevelt beamed as Churchill cast his spell. "The smiling President looked like an old trouper who, on turning impresario, had produced a smash hit,"

---

* One morning FDR wheeled himself into Churchill's bedroom just as the prime minister emerged from his bathroom stark naked and gleaming pink from a hot bath. Roosevelt apologized and turned about, but Churchill protested, "The Prime Minister of Great Britain has nothing to conceal from the President of the United States." Robert Sherwood, *Roosevelt and Hopkins* 442 (New York: Harper & Brothers, 1948).

wrote *Newsweek.* "It was terribly exciting," confirmed Alistair Cooke, who covered the White House for the London *Times.*[17]

On December 26 Churchill addressed a joint session of Congress, the first foreigner accorded the privilege since Lafayette's triumphal visit in 1824. For Churchill it was a signal honor, and a mighty roar greeted the prime minister as he was escorted down the aisle to the House rostrum. Roosevelt remained at the White House and listened to the proceedings over the radio.

Churchill understood the audience and crafted his speech to perfection. "I cannot help reflecting that if my father had been American and my mother British, instead of the other way round, I might have gotten here on my own." The legislators clapped and cheered. Churchill continued confidently:

> In that case this would not have been the first time you would have heard
> my voice. In that case I should not have needed any invitation, but if I
> had, it is hardly likely it would have been unanimous. [Cheers and laugh-
> ter.] So perhaps things are better as they are. I may confess, however, that
> I do not feel quite like a fish out of water in a legislative assembly where
> English is spoken.[18]

More laughter and thunderous applause. Churchill spoke thirty-five minutes. It was magnificent drama, reported *The Washington Post.* As the prime minister left the floor he flashed his "V for victory" sign. The effect was electric. Throughout the chamber hundreds of arms were raised, fingers spread in a return salute: a stunning climax to a speech that the *Post* ranked with Edmund Burke's defense of the American colonies.[19]

Churchill had intended to stay only about a week. But as in *The Man Who Came to Dinner,** the visit lengthened to three and a half weeks, including brief side trips to Ottawa and Pompano Beach, Florida.[20] Christened the ARCADIA conference by Churchill, the meeting produced agreement on the "Germany first" strategy deemed essential by the British. It also (with perceptible Ameri-

---

* Written by George S. Kaufman and Moss Hart, and acted in the title role by Monty Woolley, *The Man Who Came to Dinner* portrays an eccentric, acid-tongued radio critic and lecturer (based loosely on Alexander Woollcott) who arrives as a houseguest for one night and suffers a fall, which confines him to a wheelchair and renders him unable to depart for several weeks. The play was a smash hit on Broadway and in London and was made into a movie in 1941, also starring Monty Woolley.

can misgiving) accepted a British-inspired plan for an Anglo-American invasion of North Africa (GYMNAST) later in the year. At General Marshall's insistence the conference agreed that the war would be waged in each theater
under a single supreme commander, who would control all of the forces in his
area from all countries and from all branches of the service. The first supreme
commander appointed was British General Sir Archibald Wavell for the
Southwest Pacific.

To direct the actions of each supreme commander and to coordinate British
and American military policy, ARCADIA established the Combined Chiefs of
Staff (CCS), a joint British-American undertaking composed of the three
British chiefs—General Sir Alan Brooke (CIGS); Admiral Sir Dudley Pound,
the first sea lord; and Air Chief Marshal Sir Charles Portal—and their American counterparts, Marshall, King, and Arnold. At Roosevelt's insistence the
Combined Chiefs was headquartered in Washington, where its work was directed by Field Marshal Sir John Dill, who became the ranking British chief
and Churchill's personal representative. Dill was joined in July 1942 by Admiral William D. Leahy, whom Roosevelt brought back from Vichy to become
chief of staff to the commander in chief and, in effect, chairman of the American Joint Chiefs of Staff.*

In retrospect, the establishment of the command structure to fight the war
was an unprecedented achievement that reflected the extraordinary ability of
Churchill and Roosevelt to saw off minor differences and find common
ground. Roosevelt, unlike Lincoln, was also well served by his long familiarity
with the Army and Navy and his ability to pick effective military subordinates.
Leahy, Marshall, King, and Arnold were exactly the right men for the job, and
they served in their posts throughout the war. In their own way they were
ruthless taskmasters, loyal to the president, and, when pushed by FDR, worked
effectively with their British counterparts.†

---

* The statutory basis of the Joint Chiefs of Staff (and an independent air force) was not established until the passage of the Defense Reorganization Act of 1947. But the American
side of the CCS, with Leahy as chairman, plus Marshall, King, and Arnold, provided the
model for the act.
† Admiral Leahy had served with Roosevelt since FDR had been assistant secretary of the
Navy and enjoyed the president's complete confidence. Marshall, Roosevelt's personal
choice for chief of staff, brought a single-minded, take-no-prisoners dedication to his
task—combined with a remarkable sensitivity to political nuance at the highest level.

An equal achievement was the creation of the Combined Munitions Assignment Board for the allocation of supplies among the allies. At General Marshall's insistence the Board was made subordinate to the Combined Chiefs of Staff. As Marshall told FDR, he could not plan military operations and carry them through if some other body controlled the allocation of the materiel required for such operations. Roosevelt backed Marshall, the Board was located in Washington, and Harry Hopkins, who had long played go-between for Churchill and FDR, became its chairman.[21] Like the CCS, the Munitions Assignment Board worked with remarkable efficiency. When disputes arose Hopkins resolved them before they festered.[22]

The ARCADIA conference marked the first reference to the United Nations. On New Year's Day 1942 twenty-six nations, led by the United States, Great Britain, the Soviet Union, and China, affixed their signatures to a document drafted initially by FDR pledging cooperation in the defeat of the Axis powers.[23] The term "United Nations" was Roosevelt's choice (rather than "Associated Nations"),* but this was purely a declaration of wartime purpose, not the organization for postwar security that was established at San Francisco three and a half years later.

Arnold, underneath his affable exterior, had a genius for organization urgently required to create an air force virtually from scratch. King, to some extent, was odd man out: fiercely Anglophobic, incredibly stubborn, not as gifted intellectually as his colleagues, but a powerful command presence that the Navy needed after Pearl Harbor. FDR said King shaved with a blowtorch, and it was that fierceness that propelled the Navy, even when King was wrong (as he was in early 1942, when he refused to convoy ships in American waters). For insightful sketches of FDR's subordinates, see Eric Larrabee, *Commander in Chief: Franklin Delano Roosevelt, His Lieutenants and Their War* (Annapolis, Md.: Naval Institute Press, 1987).

* Churchill embraced the term enthusiastically and, to the delight of his White House dinner companions on December 31, recited from memory Lord Byron's "Childe Harold's Pilgrimage":

> Here, where the sword United Nations drew,
>   Our countrymen were warring on that day
> And this is much—and all—which will not pass away.

The quotation is from Canto III, Verse xxxv. *The Complete Poetical Works of Lord Byron* 40 (Boston: Houghton Mifflin, 1905).

Churchill evidently knew Byron's lengthy "Childe Harold" by heart and later recited it to his daughter Sarah on the eighty-five-mile drive from Saki airfield to Yalta in February 1945. Sarah Churchill, *A Thread in the Tapestry* 78 (New York: Dodd, Mead, 1967).

On January 6, 1942, Roosevelt went to Capitol Hill to deliver his tenth State of the Union message. Within a span of little more than a week the Congress heard both Churchill and FDR. Both were captivating speakers, but their styles were distinctly different. Churchill, like Charles de Gaulle—and Hitler and Mussolini, for that matter—spoke to his audience collectively with rhetorical flourishes and stirring cadences that rallied the nation's soul. Roosevelt addressed his remarks to each listener individually, with homey references and simple words that struck a personal note. For Churchill it was an oration; for FDR, a conversation.[24]

Roosevelt was at his best that Tuesday. "The militarists of Berlin and Tokyo started this war. But the massed, angered forces of humanity will finish it." He galvanized the nation with a breathtaking set of production goals for 1942: 60,000 airplanes, 45,000 tanks, 20,000 antiaircraft guns, 6 million tons of merchant shipping. "These figures," the president told a wildly cheering Congress, "will give the Japanese and the Nazis a little idea of just what they accomplished at Pearl Harbor."[25]

Roosevelt's production targets provided inspiration for the nation in the dark days after Pearl Harbor. It was, said Stimson, "the best speech I ever heard him make."[26] But FDR had drawn his figures more or less out of a hat. "Oh, the production people can do it if they really try," he told an incredulous Hopkins the night before the speech.[27]*

For the military, Roosevelt's figures proved a mixed blessing. "Everyone set out to build sixty thousand planes and forty-five thousand tanks," said General Lucius D. Clay, who had been placed in charge of all military procurement. "But we needed balanced forces. We needed ammunition, we needed machine guns, field artillery, anti-tank weapons—the whole range of equipment to fit out the troop formations which were being raised. And we could not afford to expend all our resources meeting the president's goals. It was a hell of a fight. Finally I prepared a chart showing what the Army would have if the President's

---

* Roosevelt relied on the guesswork of Lord Beaverbrook, who cautioned against underestimating U.S. production capacity. Taking the projected Canadian production for 1942 as a base, Beaverbrook estimated that the excess of American resources over Canadian resources should permit the United States to produce fifteen times as much. According to Beaverbrook's calculations, this would mean 45,000 tanks and 60,000 planes—figures that FDR relied on in drafting his speech. Memorandum, Lord Beaverbrook to the President, December 29, 1941, FDRL.

goals were achieved, and what it would lack, especially artillery and anti-tank guns. I gave it to Mr. Hopkins, who quickly saw the point we were making. Mr. Hopkins got the President's personal O.K. (although he never gave it a public O.K.), and Mr. Roosevelt's goals were quietly revised downward."[28]

On February 19, 1942, in one of the shabbiest displays of presidential prerogative in American history, Roosevelt approved Executive Order 9066, authorizing the forcible evacuation of persons of Japanese ancestry from the Pacific coast. The order applied to forty thousand older, first-generation Japanese immigrants (Issei) who were debarred from citizenship by the Immigration Act of 1924, as well as to their children (Nisei), some eighty thousand persons born in the United States and therefore American citizens by birth.* There was no military necessity for the order. J. Edgar Hoover, then in his seventeenth year as director of the FBI, called the evacuation "utterly unwarranted"; Major General "Vinegar Joe" Stilwell, commanding the southern sector of the Western Defense Zone, labeled reports of Japanese sabotage "wild, farcical, and fantastic stuff"; the *Los Angeles Times* initially editorialized against removal; and Attorney General Francis Biddle thought the program "ill-advised, unnecessary, and unnecessarily cruel, taking Japanese who were not suspect, and Japanese-Americans whose rights were disregarded, from their homes and from their businesses to sit idly in the lonely misery of barracks while the war was being fought in the world beyond."[29]

For the first month after Pearl Harbor, little concern was given to the Japanese on the West Coast. But as the magnitude of the Navy's defeat became clear, and as Japan advanced unstopped across the South Pacific, public opinion turned sharply antagonistic. Many Americans could not comprehend or explain the humiliating defeats suffered by Allied forces unless they were betrayed by legions of saboteurs undermining resistance from within. Lieutenant General John De Witt, the overall Army commander on the West Coast (whom FDR had passed over when he named George Marshall chief of staff in 1939), argued in a tortured twist of logic that "the very fact that no sabotage

---

* The Fourteenth Amendment to the Constitution provides that "*All persons born* or naturalized in the United States and subject to the jurisdiction thereof, are, citizens of the United States and of the State wherein they reside" (emphasis added). In the leading case of *Wong Kim Ark v. United States,* 169 U.S. 649 (1898), the Supreme Court held that the Fourteenth Amendment meant exactly what it said and guaranteed American citizenship to all those born in the country regardless of their ethnic heritage or the status of their parents.

has taken place [in California] is a disturbing and confirming indication that such action *will* be taken."[30]

Racism fed fears of sabotage. For fifty years anti-Japanese sentiment had pervaded the social structure of the Pacific Coast. "California was given by God to a white people," said the president of the Native Sons and Daughters of the Golden West, "and with God's strength we want to keep it as he gave it to us."[31] Greed and economic rivalry contributed. Though Japanese farms occupied only 1 percent of the cultivated land in California, they produced nearly 40 percent of the state's crop.[32] As the manager of the Grower-Shipper Vegetable Association told *The Saturday Evening Post:* "We're charged with wanting to get rid of the Japs for selfish reasons. We might as well be honest. We do."[33]

The tipping point for public opinion came on January 24, 1942, when the Roberts Commission, which had been appointed by FDR to investigate the Pearl Harbor attack,* reported that Nagumo's strike force had been aided by Hawaii-based espionage agents, including American citizens of Japanese ancestry.[34] The commission provided no evidence to substantiate the charge, but the remark was sufficient to unleash a torrent of anti-Japanese reaction. The *Los Angeles Times,* which as recently as January 23 had advised moderation, called on January 28 for the relocation of all Japanese living in the State whether they were citizens or not. Politicians jumped on the bandwagon. By the end of January the entire California congressional delegation, as well as Democratic governor Culbert L. Olsen and Republican attorney general Earl Warren, was clamoring for removal of the Japanese.†

---

* The Roberts Commission was created by Executive Order on December 18, 1941. It was composed of Supreme Court justice Owen Roberts as chairman, plus two retired admirals, Joseph M. Reeves and William H. Standley (a former CNO); and two generals, Frank R. McCoy (ret.) and Joseph T. McNarney. The commission took testimony from 127 witnesses, including Admiral Kimmel and General Short. It reported to FDR on January 23, 1942, and the entire report was made public the next day. The principal finding was that Kimmel and Short were guilty of dereliction of duty. For the text of the Roberts Commission Report, see *Hearings Before the Joint Committee on the Investigation of the Pearl Harbor Attack,* Part 39 (Washington, D.C.: U.S. Government Printing Office, 1946).

† In his autobiography Warren confessed he had been wrong. "I have since deeply regretted the removal order and my own testimony advocating it. Whenever I thought of the innocent little children who were torn from home, school friends, and congenial surroundings I was conscience-stricken. It was wrong to act so impulsively . . . even though we had a good motive." *The Memoirs of Earl Warren* 149 (New York: Doubleday, 1977).

The national press took up the cry. On February 12, 1942, following a long interview with General De Witt, Walter Lippmann, the dean of the liberal establishment, bannered his influential column in the *Herald Tribune* "Fifth Column on the West Coast." After declaring the entire Pacific coast a combat zone, Lippmann pronounced judgment: "Nobody's constitutional rights include the right to reside and do business on a battlefield."[35] Lippmann's widely read conservative colleague Westbrook Pegler came to the same conclusion. "The Japanese in California should be under armed guard to the last man and woman right now. And to hell with habeas corpus until the danger is over."[36]

In Washington, Attorney General Biddle found himself and the Justice Department fighting a rearguard action.* Stimson, who was keenly aware of the constitutional difficulties, believed a Japanese invasion of the West Coast to be a distinct possibility.[37] Assistant Secretary John J. McCloy, the War Department's point man for domestic security, shared that concern: "If it is a question of safety of the country or the Constitution of the United States, why the Constitution is just a scrap of paper to me."[38] In mid-February, when General De Witt asked the War Department for permission to evacuate all Japanese from the West Coast, the Army registered its opposition.[39] General Mark Clark, the deputy chief of staff, told Stimson and McCloy that California was not endangered and that the Army was unwilling to allot De Witt any additional troops for evacuation purposes. "I cannot agree with the wisdom of such a mass exodus," wrote Clark. "We must not permit our entire offensive effort to be sabotaged in an effort to protect all establishments from ground sabotage."[40]† At that point Stimson could have turned De Witt down summarily. Instead, he referred the question to FDR.

---

* When Biddle asked for an outside opinion from a trio of New Deal stalwarts (Benjamin Cohen, Joseph L. Rauh, and Oscar Cox), which he hoped would buttress the case against removal, he got instead a seven-page brief that affirmed the constitutionality of removing citizens on a racial basis if necessary for national security. "It is a fact and not a legal theory that Japanese who are American citizens cannot readily be identified and distinguished from Japanese who owe no loyalty to the United States." Cohen, Rauh, and Cox, "The Japanese Situation on the West Coast," in Greg Robinson, *By Order of the President* 104 (Cambridge, Mass.: Harvard University Press, 2001).

† In congressional testimony on February 4, 1942, General Clark and Admiral Stark told legislators that the Pacific states were unduly alarmed. Clark said the chances of invasion were "nil." Admiral Stark said, "it would be impossible for the enemy to engage in a sustained attack on the Pacific Coast at the present time." 77th Cong., 2d Sess., *House Document 1911* 2–3.

Stimson called Roosevelt the afternoon of February 11. Singapore was under siege (it would fall four days later), and the president was preoccupied with military matters. "I took up with him the West Coast matter first," Stimson recorded in his diary. "[I] told him the situation and fortunately found that he was very vigorous about it and told me to go ahead on the line that I thought the best."[41] FDR expressed no opinion on the evacuation and tossed the matter back to Stimson and the War Department. That was sufficient for McCloy. "We have carte blanche to do what we want to as far as the President is concerned," he informed Fourth Army headquarters in San Francisco. "He states there will probably be some repercussions, and it has got to be dictated by military necessity, but as he puts it, 'Be as reasonable as you can.' "[42]

The chain of events is clear: Roosevelt delegated the decision to Stimson, Stimson turned it over to McCloy, and McCloy made the call. "This does not exonerate Roosevelt," wrote McCloy's principal biographer, "but at the very least it was McCloy's job to determine if military necessity justified such draconian measures."[43]

One week later Roosevelt signed the executive order that had been prepared by the civilian leadership in the War Department. It authorized the department to "prescribe military areas . . . from which any and all persons may be excluded." No explicit reference to the Japanese was necessary. When Attorney General Biddle registered a mild objection, FDR said it was a matter of military judgment. Having been blindsided at Pearl Harbor, Roosevelt was unwilling to skimp on what constituted military necessity. "I did not think I should oppose it any further," wrote Biddle.[44]

Japanese evacuees were forced to liquidate their property at fire-sale prices. White scavengers went through Japanese-American neighborhoods buying refrigerators for one dollar and washing machines for a quarter.[45] The U.S. government made no effort to secure fair prices, guarantee land values, or ensure the safety of goods placed in storage. "I am not concerned about that," FDR told Morgenthau on March 5, 1942.[46] Estimates of Japanese property losses exceeded $400 million in 1942 dollars—the current equivalent of almost $5 billion. After the war Congress provided a meager $37 million in reparations. Forty years later another Congress awarded each surviving detainee an additional $20,000.

Though Roosevelt said he later regretted "the burdens of evacuation and detention which military necessity imposed on these people," he showed no concern when he signed the measure on February 19.[47] "I do not think he was much concerned with the gravity or implications of this step," wrote Biddle. "He was never theoretical about things. What must be done to defend the country must be done. The military might be wrong. But they were fighting the war. Nor do I think that the constitutional difficulty plagued him—the Constitution has never greatly bothered any wartime President."[48]*

The news from the Pacific was all bad and getting worse, and Roosevelt recognized American morale needed a pickup. Could the Army bomb Tokyo? he asked General Hap Arnold shortly after Pearl Harbor. Air planners in the War Department went to work but found no Allied airfield within range. The president turned to Admiral King: Could medium-range bombers, B-25s, take off from a Navy carrier? It sounded like a harebrained stunt, but King and Arnold put their staffs to work and by mid-January concluded that it might be possible. Lieutenant Colonel James Doolittle was selected to lead the mission with a force of sixteen B-25s and an all-volunteer crew of airmen.† The B-25s were

* At the request of the War Department, Congress unanimously enacted legislation on March 21, 1942, authorizing the removal of the Japanese from the West Coast (56 Stat. 173). The only objection was raised by Senator Robert Taft of Ohio, who said the bill was constitutionally vague. "I think this is probably the sloppiest criminal law I have ever read or seen anywhere." But Taft did not vote against it. 90 *Congressional Record* 2722–2726 (1942).

In two test cases, *Hirabayashi v. United States,* 320 U.S. 81 (1943), and *Korematsu v. United States,* 323 U.S. 214 (1944), the Supreme Court upheld the curfew and relocation. Said Justice Black, speaking for the Court in *Korematsu:* "We are not unmindful of the hardships imposed upon a large group of American citizens. But hardships are a part of war, and war is an aggregation of hardships." Justice Roberts and two former attorneys general, Frank Murphy and Robert Jackson, dissented vigorously.

In 1984 a federal court, in an unusual coram nobis procedure initiated by the University of California at San Diego professor Peter Irons, voided Fred Korematsu's original conviction because of official misconduct (584 F. Supp. 1406 (N.D. Cal. 1984)). The West Coast military had exaggerated the danger and falsified the evidence. "Fortunately, there are few instances in our judicial history when courts have been called upon to undo such profound and publicly acknowledged injustice," said the court (584 F. Supp. at 1413). In 1998 President Clinton bestowed on Korematsu the nation's highest civilian honor, the Medal of Freedom.

† Lieutenant Colonel James Doolittle was a pioneer in American aviation. In 1922 he made the first transcontinental flight in less than twenty-four hours; in 1929, the first blind instrument-controlled landing; and he won both the Bendix and Thompson trophies for world speed records in 1932. Along the way he picked up a doctorate in aeronautical science from MIT and was an aviation manager for Shell Oil helping to develop aviation fuels when he returned to active duty in 1940.

converted to carry extra fuel, and the pilots were trained to take off at short distances with heavy loads. But it was a gamble—so risky that neither the Army Air Corps nor the Navy dared attempt a practice carrier takeoff beforehand.

In early April the B-25s were lashed to the flight deck of the carrier *Hornet,* which rendezvoused with Vice Admiral William Halsey's Task Force 16 a dozen miles north of Midway Island, some 1,100 miles from Honolulu. The task force, which included the carrier *Enterprise,* four cruisers, eight destroyers, and two tankers, steamed westward through heavy seas to a point 800 miles east of Tokyo, where the *Enterprise*'s radar picked up a Japanese patrol vessel much further from shore than anticipated. Doolittle had set 650 miles as the outside limit for the launch, but rather than risk discovery by continuing on, he ordered the takeoff immediately. With a forty-knot gale splashing water over the bow of *Hornet* and only 467 feet of deck in front of him, Doolittle led his planes into the air without mishap. The squadron arrived over Tokyo shortly after noon, dropped its bombs, and flew on toward prearranged landing fields in China. Because of the premature takeoff, none of the planes made it to its scheduled destination. Pilots flew until they were out of fuel and parachuted into Chinese territory. Some were captured by the Japanese. One died in prison, and three were executed after a show trial in which they were charged with attacking civilian targets. But of the eighty men who had volunteered for the mission, seventy-one survived.[49]

The damage in Tokyo was minimal. But the psychological impact was enormous. FDR was at Hyde Park working on his next fireside chat on April 18 when he received an urgent phone call from Washington. An intercepted Japanese radio broadcast had just reported in a tone of near hysteria that American planes were bombing Tokyo. A grin crossed Roosevelt's face as he put in a call to White House press secretary Steve Early. Anticipating the questions that would be asked and savoring the moment of mystery, the president told Early "the bombers came from a secret base in Shangri-la"—a mythical land in the trackless wastes of Tibet depicted in James Hilton's bestselling novel *Lost Horizon.*[50]

It was the first good news from the Pacific theater. Telegrams of support flooded the White House. Secretary Stimson, who had privately been critical of the president's "pet project," thought the raid had "a very good psychological effect both here and abroad."[51] Colonel Doolittle was awarded the Medal of Honor.

In Tokyo the attack came in the midst of a sharp disagreement between Yamamoto and the Japanese high command over future strategy. The high command wanted to consolidate Japan's success, establish a ribbon of bases from the Bismarck Archipelago to American Samoa, and block the convoy routes from California and the Panama Canal to Australia and New Zealand. Yamamoto and the admirals of the Combined Fleet, intoxicated with victory, insisted it was time to finish the job begun at Pearl Harbor. They wished to seek out the remnants of the U.S. Pacific Fleet and defeat it in a decisive battle. The doctrine of "decisive battle" was a basic tenet of naval theology, and the Japanese admirals believed their opportunity was at hand.

For Yamamoto, Midway Island was the key. Whoever controlled Midway controlled the Pacific. If the island were in Japanese hands, Hawaii would be threatened with invasion. That would provide an important bargaining chip to force the United States to accept a negotiated settlement. If the Americans held Midway, the Japanese home islands would never be secure. Doolittle's raid provided stunning confirmation of that. Yamamoto believed that if the Combined Fleet moved against Midway, the U.S. Navy would be forced to give battle. Final victory appeared one step away.

Rather than choose between the two alternatives, the Japanese government elected to move south and simultaneously attack Midway. That stretched the resources of the Imperial Navy to the limit. At the beginning of May, Vice Admiral Shigeyoshi Inoue led a South Seas invasion task force against Port Moresby on the south coast of New Guinea—a vital step if Australia was to be isolated. To ensure success, the high command added two carriers from the Pearl Harbor attack force. Fortunately, American intelligence had by this time broken the Japanese naval code and knew Inoue's destination. Admiral Nimitz dispatched a two-carrier task force (*Lexington* and *Yorktown*) to intercept the invaders, and on May 4, 1942, battle was joined.

For the next four days the American and Japanese carrier groups engaged in one of the most complex naval actions ever fought. The Battle of the Coral Sea was unique in that the two forces were separated by 175 miles of open water. The warships never came into contact, there was no surface gunnery, and the fight was waged by carrier-based aircraft. Tactically the result was a standoff.

The Japanese sank the *Lexington* and destroyed *Yorktown*'s flight deck; the Americans sank a light carrier and severely damaged one of the large Pearl Harbor carriers. More significantly, the United States lost thirty-three aircraft; the Japanese twice that number. Having lost air superiority, Inoue canceled the invasion and returned to his base at Rabaul. In the strategic sense, with the invasion thwarted, the Battle of the Coral Sea was an undisputed Allied victory.

A more serious setback awaited the Imperial Navy. On May 27, 1942, the anniversary of the Battle of Tsushima Strait, the Combined Fleet sailed triumphantly from the Inland Sea against Midway. With Nagumo's four large carriers in the van, Yamamoto brought eleven battleships, sixteen cruisers, and fifty-three destroyers to attack what was left of the American Pacific Fleet. Yamamoto assumed personal command and sailed aboard his flagship, the 67,000-ton *Yamato,* the largest battleship afloat.* His battle plan was simple enough: Nagumo's carrier vanguard would assault Midway, the American fleet would challenge, and then Yamamoto's battlewagons, lurking in the rear, would move in for the kill.

Once again, as at Pearl Harbor, Yamamoto and Nagumo counted on surprise. But this time the tables were turned. Thanks to code intercepts, it was the American Navy that had advance warning, not the Japanese. With foreknowledge of Yamamoto's intent, and fully aware of the enormous firepower he could bring to bear, Nimitz instructed his task force commanders to seek out Nagumo's carriers but dodge his big guns.

The Japanese invasion force commenced its assault on Midway on June 4. At dawn Nagumo launched his first air strike, unaware that three American carriers—*Enterprise, Hornet,* and a quickly refitted *Yorktown*—stood off to the northeast. Believing his position secure, Nagumo ordered a time-consuming change of armament for his second attack wave just as his first wave returned

---

* With its massive 18-inch guns capable of firing 3,200-pound shells twenty-seven miles, *Yamato* dwarfed American battleships of the *Iowa* class. The length of three football fields with a complement of 2,800 men, it had a cruising range of 7,500 miles and a top speed of twenty-seven knots. With Vickers-hardened steel 16 inches thick in places and triple bottoms, no warship was ever so heavily armored. It was sunk on April 6, 1945, off Okinawa following a massive attack by planes from fourteen American carriers. William E. McMahon, *Dreadnaught Battleships and Battle Cruisers* 215–217 (Washington, D.C.: University Press of America, 1978).

to refuel. At that point, with his flight decks cluttered, American bombers and torpedo planes attacked. But Japanese antiaircraft fire and Zeros kept the attackers at bay, and by 10:24 Nagumo felt he had weathered the storm. None of his ships had been hit.

The next five minutes would change the course of history. Arriving at the precise moment when Nagumo's protective screen of Zeros had been drawn down to refuel, two squadrons of American dive-bombers, one from *Enterprise,* the other from *Yorktown,* poured through the open sky to unload their bombs on the exposed Japanese carriers. Three were sunk and the fourth so heavily damaged the Japanese scuttled it. Deprived of air cover, Yamamoto reversed course and sailed the Combined Fleet back to Japan.

The Battle of Midway proved to be the decisive battle in the Pacific. With the loss of four large carriers, their aircraft and their pilots, Japan never regained naval superiority. In the two years following Midway the Japanese were able to launch only six battlefleet carriers. The United States added seventeen, as well as ten medium carriers and eighty-six smaller escort carriers. As Princeton professor Marius B. Jansen observed, "Technology and materiel may have sealed the ultimate verdict, but the months ahead required grinding determination and immense hardship in battles that produced some of the highest casualty rates in United States history."[52]

Meanwhile, the situation on the Russian front remained grim. Hitler resumed his offensive in the spring of 1942, pressing southeast toward the oil fields of the Caucasus. Von Manstein overran the Crimea, a Soviet counterattack in the Ukraine failed dismally, and two German Army Groups crashed forward to the Don. Russian losses were staggering. By the end of May the Germans had killed or captured an additional 700,000 Red Army troops and destroyed more than 2,000 tanks and 6,000 artillery pieces.[53]

Russian foreign minister Vyacheslav Molotov arrived in Washington May 29 to plead for assistance. Like Churchill, Molotov stayed as FDR's guest in the White House. Unlike Churchill's, the visit remained secret (Molotov bore the code name "Mr. Brown") and the White House press corps scrupulously adhered to Steve Early's request that nothing be published. Unaware of what he might find in Washington, Molotov traveled with basic necessities: black bread, sausage, and a loaded pistol tucked into his luggage, plus a secretarial pool that evidently did more than take dictation.[54]

"I am terribly busy with a visiting fireman from across the water," FDR told his cousin Daisy Suckley. "He comes from Shangri-La and speaks nothing but Mongolian. We speak through interpreters: one, a Russian who speaks perfect English [Vladimir N. Pavlov]; the other, an American who has lived for years in Russia [Harvard professor of Slavic Languages Samuel H. Cross]! Two and two equals four."[55]

Molotov wasted little time on social niceties. As soon as he met FDR in the Oval Office, he put the case for a second front. The balance of forces in Russia was slightly in Hitler's favor, said Molotov. If the United States and Great Britain could mount a cross-Channel attack, it would drain away forty German divisions. These might not be first-line troops, but it would diminish Hitler's margin of superiority. Molotov stressed that a landing in 1942, with the Russian front still intact, would be far easier than in 1943, by which time it might have collapsed. "If you postpone your decision, you will have eventually to bear the brunt of the war, and if Hitler becomes master of the continent, next year will unquestionably be tougher than this one." Molotov requested a straight answer: Was the United States prepared to establish a second front in 1942?[56]

Roosevelt was sympathetic. Before Molotov arrived, the president had sent a memo to Marshall and King noting that "Our principal objective is to help Russia. . . . Russian armies are killing more Germans and destroying more Axis materiel than all 25 United Nations put together."[57] He turned Molotov's question over to General Marshall. "Are developments clear enough so that we could say to Mr. Stalin that we are preparing a second front?" asked the president.

When Marshall said "Yes," Roosevelt authorized Molotov to tell Stalin that "we expect the formation of a second front this year."[58] Roosevelt repeated the promise the following day. But at the urging of Marshall and King, who were uneasy about being tied to a precise time, he added that in order to build up materiel for opening a second front, the United States would have to cut back Lend-Lease supplies to Russia. Molotov bristled. What would happen if the Soviet Union agreed to cut its Lend-Lease requirements and no second front developed?

"You cannot have your cake and eat it too," FDR replied. "Ships cannot be in two places at once. Every ship we shift to the English run means that the second front is so much closer to being realized." Roosevelt then repeated his pledge for a second front in 1942, and Molotov agreed to advise Moscow of the reduction in aid shipments.*

On June 11, 1942, with FDR in Hyde Park and Molotov back in the Soviet Union, Washington and Moscow released a joint statement acknowledging the discussions. "In the course of the conversations full understanding was reached with regard to the urgent tasks of creating a Second Front in Europe in 1942." General Marshall had objected to any specific reference to 1942, but Roosevelt overruled him. The president was concerned about public reaction to Molotov's visit and wanted to strike a positive note. As with the ambitious production targets he had announced earlier, Roosevelt recognized the need to set goals that would keep the nation moving. He also hoped to solidify the coalition. "I am especially anxious that he [Molotov] carry back some real results of his Mission, and that he will give a favorable account to Stalin," Roosevelt wrote Churchill. "I was greatly pleased with the visit. He warmed up far more than I expected and I am sure he has a far better understanding of the situation than when he arrived."[59]

Washington's announcement of a second front in 1942 energized Churchill. The last thing the British government wanted was a premature cross-Channel attack. The enormous battlefield losses of World War I, Churchill's own unfortunate experience with the amphibious landing at Gallipoli in 1915, and an awareness of how ill prepared and unready the Western Allies, particularly the United States, were to take on the Wehrmacht made London doubly cautious about launching an invasion of the Continent.

Scarcely before the ink had dried on the Washington-Moscow communiqué, Churchill was in Hyde Park, determined to dissuade Roosevelt. The bumpy plane ride from Washington and the even bumpier landing at tiny New Hackensack airport disconcerted Churchill, but not nearly so much as careening around the Roosevelt estate in the president's made-over Ford convertible with FDR behind the steering wheel. "I confess that when on several occasions the car poised and backed on the grass verges of the precipices over the Hud-

---

* The Soviet Union had requested 4.1 million tons of assistance in 1942, of which only 1.8 million tons were actual military materiel. Eventually it was agreed to reduce overall shipments to Russia to 2.5 million tons, with no reduction in the volume of military equipment the Red Army could use in actual fighting. Robert Sherwood, *Roosevelt and Hopkins* 574 (New York: Harper & Brothers, 1948).

son I hoped the mechanical devices [by which Roosevelt drove] and brakes would show no defects," he wrote.[60] As at the White House, Churchill made himself at home, walking barefoot, going wherever he chose, whenever he chose. FDR enjoyed the informality. "There was something intimate in their friendship," said Lord Ismay years later. "They used to stroll in and out of each other's rooms as two subalterns occupying adjacent quarters might have done. Both of them had the spirit of eternal youth."[61]

Churchill was alone with Roosevelt at Hyde Park for a day and a half. Except for Hopkins, no aides or advisers were privy to their discussions. Official Washington waited nervously. "I can't help feeling a little bit uneasy about the influence of the Prime Minister," wrote Stimson. "The trouble is WC and FDR are too much alike in their strong points and in their weak points. They are both penetrating in their thoughts but they lack the steadiness of balance that has got to go along with warfare."[62]

Stimson's apprehension was well founded. Churchill presented a masterly case for why a second front in Europe should not be mounted in 1942. Aside from the severe shortage of landing craft—a problem that would plague the Allies for the next two years—America's troops were unready and Britain's too thinly spread. And the time to prepare was too short. "No responsible British military authority has so far been able to make a plan [for a cross-Channel attack in 1942] which has any chance of success unless the Germans become utterly demoralized, of which there is no likelihood," said Churchill. "Have the American Staffs a plan? At what points would they strike? Who is the officer prepared to command such an enterprise? What British forces and assistance are required?"[63]

Churchill recognized that the Allies could not remain idle throughout 1942 and once again proposed an invasion of French North Africa (GYMNAST). "This has all along been in harmony with your ideas," he told FDR. "In fact it is your commanding idea. Here is the true second front of 1942. I have consulted cabinet and defense committees and we all agree. Here is the safest and most fruitful stroke that can be delivered this autumn."[64]

Roosevelt needed little convincing. The risk of a premature landing in Europe was one he did not wish to run, particularly with congressional elections looming in November.* As early as June 17, two days before Churchill's arrival,

* Churchill's skepticism about landing on the Continent in 1942 was more than borne out by the disastrous commando raid at Dieppe in August. Some 5,000 troops, mostly Cana-

he had indicated to the War Department his concern about a cross-Channel attack.[65] Armed with Churchill's reservations, the president cut short his sojourn at Hyde Park and summoned General Marshall and Admiral King to a meeting in the Oval Office on Monday, June 21.

In the course of four White House conferences, the last of which continued well past midnight, Churchill held forth on the advantages of invading North Africa. Marshall and King just as vigorously defended the cross-Channel attack. Marshall argued that GYMNAST was at best an unnecessary diversion that would indefinitely postpone the invasion of Europe. King doubted if the British would ever agree to invade the Continent. Both at one point suggested that if Britain persisted in its opposition to a cross-Channel attack, the United States should abandon the "Germany first" strategy agreed to at ARCADIA, "turn to the Pacific and strike decisively against Japan."[66] Roosevelt came down hard. The chiefs' suggestion, he said, was "a little like taking up your dishes and going away."[67] Later he told Marshall and King, the "defeat of Japan does not defeat Germany. On the other hand . . . defeat of Germany means the defeat of Japan, probably without firing a shot or losing a life."[68]

Over the robust objections of the American joint chiefs, Roosevelt ordered the North African attack. Aside from Britain's reluctance, FDR now recognized that a cross-Channel invasion could not be launched in 1942 and it was imperative that U.S. ground forces be brought into action against Germany as soon as possible. American public opinion was howling for vengeance against the Japanese. To keep the nation's strategic priorities straight, Roosevelt wanted to come to grips somewhere with Hitler. "We failed to see," said Marshall many years later, "that the leader in a democracy has to keep the people entertained. That may sound like the wrong word, but it conveys the thought. The people demand action. We couldn't wait to be completely ready."[69]*

---

dian, landed under hostile fire and suffered horrendous casualties. Nearly 1,000 were killed and another 2,000 taken prisoner. Little damage was inflicted on the Germans. If nothing else, the Dieppe raid demonstrated to Allied planners how difficult it would be to land on a fortified enemy coast. Robin Neillands, *The Dieppe Raid: The Story of the Disastrous 1942 Expedition* (Bloomington: Indiana University Press, 2006).

* In a 1956 interview with Forrest Pogue, Marshall said, "When I went in to see Roosevelt and told him about the planning [for the North African invasion], he held his hands in an attitude of prayer and said, 'Please make it before Election Day.' However, when I found we had to have more time and it came afterward, he never said a word. He was very coura-

Once Roosevelt unequivocally ordered the invasion of North Africa [now code-named TORCH], Marshall and King gave it their complete support. Marshall organized the Army's part of the operation with his usual tenacity, and King set aside his customary Anglophobia. "We are embarked on a risky undertaking," Stimson confided to his diary on September 17, 1942, "but it is not at all hopeless and, the Commander in Chief having made the decision, we must do our best to make it a success."[70] To lead the invasion Churchill diplomatically suggested an American be named, and General Marshall chose Dwight D. Eisenhower, Marshall's former deputy for war plans, who was in England planning the cross-Channel attack.[71]

Roosevelt's biggest problem was breaking the news to Stalin. The Russians had already invited Churchill to Moscow, and FDR chose to let the prime minister explain the change of plans. "It is essential for us to bear in mind our Ally's personality and the very difficult and dangerous situation he confronts," Roosevelt cabled Churchill. "I think we should attempt to put ourselves in his place, for no one whose country has been invaded can be expected to approach the war from a global point of view."[72]

Churchill met with Stalin in the Kremlin for five lengthy sessions between the thirteenth of August and the early morning hours of the sixteenth. The Soviets followed their customary negotiating strategy: rigid intransigence sandwiched between an exceptionally cordial welcome and an uproariously celebratory good-bye.* Stalin said he regretted the Allies' decision but acknowledged that it was not his to make. To Churchill's surprise he instantly saw the advantages of a North African attack. "It would hit Rommel in the back. It would over awe Spain. It would produce fighting between Germans and Frenchmen . . . and it would expose Italy to the whole brunt of the war."[73] Churchill told Roosevelt the meetings had gone well. "I am sure that the disappointing news I brought could not have been imparted except by me personally without leading to really serious drifting apart. Now they know the worst,

---

geous." Forrest C. Pogue, 2 *George C. Marshall* 402 (New York: Viking, 1965). (In the 1942 congressional elections the Democrats lost eight seats in the Senate and fifty in the House, reducing their majorities to twenty-one and ten, respectively.)

* FDR once told the cabinet that the Russians had a habit of sending him "a friendly note on Monday, spitting in his eye on Tuesday, and then being nice again on Wednesday." *The Price of Vision: Diary of Henry A. Wallace, 1942–1946* 245, John Morton Blum, ed. (Boston: Houghton Mifflin, 1973).

and having made their protest are entirely friendly. Moreover, Monsieur Stalin is entirely convinced of the great advantages of TORCH."[74]

Planning for TORCH led to considerable toing and froing between the American and British chiefs of staff that Churchill and Roosevelt ultimately had to resolve. The British wanted to land on the Mediterranean coast of Africa, as far east as possible. That would provide instant support for Montgomery's beleaguered Eighth Army in Egypt. General Marshall, on the other hand, insisted on landing on the Atlantic (west) coast of Morocco. Marshall worried that a landing inside the Mediterranean would require passage through the Strait of Gibraltar. "A single line of communication through the Straits is far too hazardous," he told FDR.[75] Churchill thought Marshall's caution misplaced. Spain was not going to war because of TORCH, he told Roosevelt, and it would take at least two months for Germany to work its way through Spain to Gibraltar. It was essential, said Churchill, to land on the Mediterranean coast. "If TORCH collapses or is cut down as is now proposed, I should feel my position painfully affected."[76]

Roosevelt was sympathetic. Churchill had convinced Stalin of the importance of TORCH, and the president did not wish to leave him in the lurch. He rejected a harsh reply drafted by General Marshall and suggested instead that simultaneous landings be considered.[77] The president and Churchill exchanged several more cables—"we are getting very close together," said FDR on September 4—and eventually a compromise was reached. The United States offered to reduce the size of its landing at Casablanca and provide additional support for the British to land near Algiers. "I am directing all preparation to proceed," Roosevelt told Churchill. "We should settle this thing with finality at once."[78]

"We agree with the military layout as you propose it," Churchill replied. "It is imperative now to drive straight ahead and save every hour."[79] What General Eisenhower referred to as a "transatlantic essay contest" ended with a boisterous exchange of cables.[80]

"Hurray!" said FDR on September 5.

"Okay full blast," Churchill rejoined.[81]

U.S. and British troops went ashore near Casablanca, Oran, and Algiers in the early-morning hours of Sunday, November 8. Resistance was slight. French units offered token resistance but negotiations with local commanders quickly brought the fighting to a close. Many in the United States and Great Britain criticized Allied military authorities for collaborating with Vichy's representatives, but the consequences of not doing so would have been catastrophic. Not only would the casualties have been heavy (there were nearly 120,000 French troops in North Africa), but the specter of American and British forces in pitched battle against the French would have poisoned public opinion in France. By November 12 all of Morocco and Algeria were under Allied control.*

Roosevelt provided direct support. He prerecorded a message to the people of France and North Africa that was broadcast as the troops came ashore. In his accented but elegant French FDR noted his personal familiarity with France ("I know your farms, your villages, your cities"), his admiration for the Republic ("I salute again and reiterate my faith in Liberty, Equality, and Fraternity"), and the historic bonds between France and the United States ("No two nations are more united by friendly ties"). He pledged immediate withdrawal once the Germans were defeated, and evoked the image of French grandeur. *"Vive la France éternelle!"*[82]

To ensure regional support and head off possible intervention by neighboring powers Roosevelt dispatched personal letters to the Sultan of Morocco, the

* Roosevelt, who initially had approved, was subsequently embarrassed when the arrangements Eisenhower had made with Vichy's representatives were heavily criticized in the United States and Great Britain. On November 7 he cabled Ike:

Marshall has shown me your dispatch giving your reasons for placing [Admiral] Darlan in charge of civil administration of North Africa. I want you to know that I appreciate fully the difficulties of your military situation. I am therefore not disposed to in any way question the action you have taken. . . .

However I think you should know and have in mind the following policies of this government:

1. That we do not trust Darlan.
2. That it is impossible to keep a collaborator of Hitler and the one whom we believe to be a fascist in civil power any longer than is absolutely necessary.
3. His movements should be watched carefully and his communications supervised.

Darlan was assassinated by a young Gaullist on December 24, 1942, relieving the embarrassment for the Allies. Few believe he acted independently. The text of FDR's message to Eisenhower was first printed in Robert Sherwood, *Roosevelt and Hopkins* 654 (New York: Harper & Brothers, 1948). For the murky details of Darlan's assassination, see Anthony Verrier, *Assassination in Algiers* 193–252 (New York: W. W. Norton, 1990).

Bey of Tunis, the President of Portugal, and Generalissimo Francisco Franco. FDR had kept the United States neutral during the Spanish Civil War, much to the chagrin and discomfiture of many Americans, and now he collected his IOU. "The presence of American military forces in North Africa presages in no manner whatsoever a move against the people or Government of Spain," he told Franco.[83]

Franco's response relieved whatever fears American military planners may have had of Spanish intervention. "I accept with pleasure and I thank you for the assurances which Your Excellency offers the Government and the people of Spain," said Franco. "I can assure you that Spain knows the value of peace and sincerely desires peace for itself and all other peoples."[84]

Hitler responded to the Allied invasion by seizing what remained of unoccupied France. German mechanized forces quickly overran the southern part of the country, six Italian divisions marched in from the east, and the Luftwaffe set up shop in Tunisia, quickly joined by two panzer divisions. When the Germans attempted to capture the French fleet at Toulon (they had mined the harbor exit to prevent its escape), the Navy scuttled it. The Allies regretted that the French admirals had not sailed to North Africa earlier but could rejoice that the fleet had not fallen into German hands.[85]

In January 1943 Roosevelt and Churchill met again, this time at Casablanca. The tide had turned ever so slightly. Heavy fighting was under way in Tunisia, but Montgomery had broken Rommel's Afrika Korps at El Alamein and was driving westward across Libya; Zhukov, now a Marshal of the Soviet Union, had mounted a massive counterattack at Stalingrad, isolating the German Sixth Army Group and subtracting 350,000 soldiers from the Wehrmacht; in the Pacific the Allies' laborious island-hopping campaign had begun with the capture of Guadalcanal.

Hitler's defeat in Africa was a matter of time. The problem for Churchill and Roosevelt was the next step. As in June, Marshall argued for a cross-Channel attack; Admiral King pressed the Navy's case for the Pacific; and the British insisted on the invasion of Sicily. That would clear the shipping lanes in the Mediterranean, menace Italy, and had the virtue that it could be mounted immediately. The British case was compelling. Even General Marshall recognized that the preconditions for a successful landing on the coast of France did not yet exist. The Battle of the Atlantic had not been won; the Luftwaffe remained formidable; the logistical base to support an invasion was not in place;

and the U.S. Army had still to prove its combat effectiveness.* When Eisenhower, who had firsthand experience landing in North Africa, noted that the forces to invade Europe could not be assembled until 1944, the decision to attack Sicily was settled. Churchill and Roosevelt, who monitored the meetings of the Combined Chiefs but did not attend, formally approved the choice on January 23, 1943.[86]

A second pressing issue at Casablanca was the future of France—or, more precisely, the determination of who was to represent France. The matter was given added urgency by the fall of Algeria and Morocco. These were departments of metropolitan France and could not simply be occupied by the Allies as conquered enemy territory. The problem was exacerbated by the historic division of French society. Neither London nor Washington fully appreciated the extent to which France was at war with itself. Large segments of the French population, much of the officer corps, and central elements of the Church had never accepted the French Revolution or the Republic. Unlike in Great Britain or the United States there was no consensus on the rules of the constitutional game. Since 1789 France had experienced three republics, three monarchies, two Napoleonic empires, two provisional regimes, a Directory, and the Paris Commune. Vichy was not an entirely German import, and Marshal Pétain spoke to and for those who rejected Liberty, Equality, and Fraternity.[87]

Roosevelt's preference was to postpone thinking about postwar France until hostilities were over. In the interim Washington supported General Henri Giraud, a senior but obscure French general whom diplomat Robert Murphy had discovered rusticating in the Loire. Giraud had no following in France or North Africa, no public persona, and little political insight. Simply put, he was an American puppet invented by the State Department to avoid having to deal with the recognized leader of the French resistance, Brigadier General Charles de Gaulle.

The British supported de Gaulle, as did most of antifascist France. Al-

---

* In mid-February 1943 Rommel's panzers clobbered the U.S. II Corps at Kasserine Pass. Eisenhower said afterward that the American commanders lacked battlefield experience. "The divisions involved had not had the benefit of intensive training programs. . . . They were mainly divisions that had been quickly shipped to the United Kingdom. Training was for them a practical impossibility. Commanders and troops showed the effects of this, although there was no lack of gallantry and fortitude." Dwight D. Eisenhower, *Crusade in Europe* 163 (New York: Doubleday, 1948).

though de Gaulle was under a death sentence from Vichy, his Free French movement had become the rallying point of the liberation. His roster read like a who's who of France's future political and military leadership including Jean Monnet, Maurice Schuman, René Pleven, Michel Debré, François Mitterrand, André Malraux, and generals Philippe Leclerc, Alphonse Juin, Pierre Koenig, and Jean de Lattre de Tassigny. The Free French movement spanned the political spectrum from left to right and transcended the division between the Republic and its enemies. The symbol de Gaulle chose, the republican tricolor with the cross of Lorraine superimposed, reflected (for one of the few times in French history) the union of Christianity and the Revolution. Obstinate, difficult, impossible in many respects, de Gaulle personified French independence.

Roosevelt wished to create a power-sharing coalition between de Gaulle and Giraud, but de Gaulle was not interested. He posed for a photograph with Giraud but tore up a press release Robert Murphy had written and composed his own asserting the independence of the Free French movement. Later de Gaulle said, "Roosevelt meant the peace to be an American peace, convinced that he must be the one to dictate its structure, and that France in particular should recognize him as its savior and its arbiter. . . . Like any star performer he was touchy as to the roles that fell to other actors. In short, beneath his patrician mask of courtesy, Roosevelt regarded me without benevolence."[88]

After the picture taking ceremony with de Gaulle and Giraud, Roosevelt and Churchill met the press on the lawn at Casablanca. Roosevelt captured headlines around the world with what appeared to be an offhand comment. After a casual reference to General Grant, FDR said:

The elimination of German, Japanese and Italian war power means the unconditional surrender by Germany, Italy, and Japan. That means a reasonable assurance of future world peace. It does not mean the destruction of the population of Germany, Italy, or Japan, but it does mean the destruction of the philosophies in those countries which are based on conquest and the subjugation of other peoples.[89]

Roosevelt was not shooting from the hip. The doctrine of unconditional surrender had been discussed extensively in Washington in early January, Churchill was apprised of it during informal discussions at Casablanca, and the British war cabinet was informed on January 20.[90] Far from being a spontaneous improvisation on Roosevelt's part, "unconditional surrender" was deliberately announced at Casablanca to aid Allied morale, assure Stalin that there would be no separate peace with Hitler, and confirm that Germany's defeat would be complete—that there would be no "stab-in-the-back" mythology that might lead to the re-creation of a new Third Reich. There is also no evidence that "unconditional surrender" prolonged the war. Hitler refused to admit the possibility of any defeat, and anti-Nazi dissidents accepted unconditional surrender at face value.[91]

When the conference ended, Churchill went to the airport to see Roosevelt off. He helped the president into the plane and returned to his limousine. "Let's go," he told an aide. "I don't like to see them take off. It makes me far too nervous. If anything happened to that man, I couldn't stand it. He is the truest friend; he has the farthest vision; he is the greatest man I have ever known."[92]

TWENTY-FIVE

D-DAY

Almighty God: Our sons this day
have set upon a mighty endeavor.
Lead them straight and true;
give strength to their arms,
stoutness to their hearts,
steadfastness in their faith.

—FRANKLIN D. ROOSEVELT, JUNE 6, 1944

ROOSEVELT'S FLIGHT TO CASABLANCA marked the first time an American president had flown while in office—and FDR had mixed feelings. He much preferred travel by ship, where the slow pace, the roll of the sea, and the fresh air afforded time to rejuvenate. To minimize the distance over open water on the return leg, the president puddle-jumped from Marrakech to Gambia to Liberia; crossed the South Atlantic to Recife, Brazil; then flew north to Trinidad and Miami, where he boarded a train to Washington. "What do you know," he cabled Eleanor en route. "Will be back in the United States Saturday evening [January 30, 1943—FDR's sixty-first birthday]. We should get to Washington by 8 p.m. on Sunday."[1]

ER was not at home when Franklin arrived. She had departed the White House Friday for the weekend in New York. But she penned a note: "Welcome home! I can't be here Sunday night as months ago I agreed to open a series of lectures at Cooper Union but I'll be home for dinner Monday night. . . . I have to be gone again for the day Tuesday but will be back Wednesday a.m. I'm terribly sorry not to be home. . . . Much love and I am so glad you are back."[2]

Roosevelt had been away from Washington three weeks. A new Congress (the Seventy-eighth) was in session and already making mischief. Numerous administration supporters had gone down to defeat in the 1942 off-year elections, and for the first time since FDR had become president the Democrats commanded only a slender (218–208) majority in the House. Republicans had picked up eight seats in Ohio, five in Connecticut, four in Missouri, and three each in Illinois, Pennsylvania, Washington, and West Virginia. That left Roosevelt more dependent than ever on white supremacist votes from the Solid South.

On the home front the alphabet soup of wartime agencies created by FDR had soured and urgently needed attention. The War Manpower Commission (WMC), charged with allotting workers between military and civilian needs, competed with the Selective Service System (SSS) and the National War Labor Board (NWLB), both of which enjoyed independent statutory authority. The Office of Price Administration (OPA), responsible for controlling inflation, shared overlapping authority with the Office of Economic Stabilization (OES). And the War Production Board (WPB), denied power over both labor and prices, floundered under the erratic leadership of Donald Nelson, a former Sears, Roebuck sales executive congenitally incapable of making tough decisions. "It took Lincoln three years to discover Grant," Justice Felix Frankfurter wrote FDR when Nelson was appointed, "and you may not have hit on your production Grant first crack out of the box."[3]

But it was the military situation that was most pressing. The Battle of the Atlantic hung in the balance. In October 1942 German submarines sank 101 Allied merchant ships. In November the total rose to 134. Heavy losses continued through the winter. In January, as Churchill and Roosevelt met at Casablanca, submarines off West Africa demolished a tanker convoy carrying much-needed fuel to Eisenhower's forces. Seven of the nine vessels were sunk in one of the most devastating attacks of the war.

In February and March 1943 merchant sinkings approached an all-time high. The Germans had 212 operational U-boats in the Atlantic (compared to 91 a year earlier) and were adding 17 each month. By contrast, Allied shipping tonnage—despite impressive American production figures—had declined by almost a million tons since the outbreak of war. "The Germans never came so near to disrupting communication between the New World and the Old as in the first twenty days of March, 1943," said the Admiralty in retrospect.[4]

A modest breakthrough occurred in December 1942, when British intelligence officers at Bletchley Park outside London cracked the German naval code, allowing them to read U-boat message traffic. But the German decryption service had previously broken the British convoy cipher, so in effect both sides were reading each other's mail.

The key to control of the Atlantic was airpower. Submarines of World War II vintage were unable to remain submerged for long periods of time, and when surfaced they were extremely vulnerable to air attack. In early 1943 small escort carriers began to arrive from American shipyards. These "baby flattops" carried up to twenty planes and provided some convoys their own air cover. But a vast midocean gap remained in which German U-boats operated with impunity. "Sinkings in the North Atlantic of 17 ships in two days are a final proof that our escorts are stretched too thin," Churchill cabled FDR on March 18. The prime minister recommended the immediate cessation of all convoys to Russia so that aircraft and escort vessels could be shifted to the Atlantic.[5]

"We share your distress over recent sinkings," Roosevelt replied. But he was reluctant to curtail convoys to Russia. Instead, the president suggested that additional long-range aircraft be assigned to the Atlantic theater. "I will provide as many as can be made available and I hope you can augment the number," he told Churchill.[6]

As he had done when he ordered the invasion of North Africa contrary to the recommendation of the Joint Chiefs of Staff, Roosevelt assumed personal responsibility. The Navy had an abundance of long-range aircraft, but Admiral King had sent most of them to Nimitz in Hawaii. Roosevelt gave King a direct order: transfer sixty very-long-range B-24 Liberator bombers from the Pacific to the Atlantic immediately.[7]

Results followed almost overnight. The B-24s, equipped with radar, powerful searchlights, machine guns, and depth charges, could stay aloft eighteen hours and, in the words of military historian John Keegan, "were flying death to a U-boat caught on the surface."[8] In the last week of March the Allies sank eight U-boats; in April, thirty-one; in May, forty-three. Faced with the inevitable destruction of his submarine fleet, Grand Admiral Karl Dönitz called it quits. On May 24, 1943, he ordered German U-boats out of the North Atlantic. In the next four months, sixty-two convoys comprising 3,546 merchant vessels crossed the Atlantic without the loss of a single ship.[9] Churchill gave the good news to the House of Commons on September 21. "This is altogether unprecedented in the whole history of the U-boat struggle, either in this war or in the last."[10]

With the sea-lanes to Britain secure, American industrial production tipped the balance in favor of the Allies. Roosevelt's 1942 production goals appeared puny once the economy converted to war. The figures are staggering. Between 1941 and 1945 the United States produced 300,000 military aircraft. In the peak year of 1944 American factories built 96,318 planes—more than the yearly total of Germany, Japan, Great Britain, and the Soviet Union combined. Henry Ford's enormous Willow Run plant produced a B-24 every sixty-three minutes. By war's end the United States had manufactured 2.4 million trucks, 635,000 jeeps, 88,400 tanks, 5,800 ships, and 40 billion rounds of ammunition.

Quantity was the all-important goal of the war effort. American industry thrived on high-volume output performed on an assembly-line basis. No other industrialized nation had mastered the art of mass production so efficiently. In a sense the United States made a virtue of necessity. With a workforce composed disproportionately of unskilled labor, assembly-line techniques fit American industry like a glove. And they matched the needs of war perfectly. The Germans and Japanese, by contrast, with their highly trained labor pools (at least in the early stages of the war), chose qualitative superiority over mass production and depended on precision-made, flawlessly performing, high-standard weapons for their margin of victory.[11] But as the war dragged on they simply could not produce enough of them. "We never did develop a top tank during the war," said General Lucius D. Clay. "We did all right because we made so many of them. That offset some of their weaknesses. But we never had a tank that equaled the German tank."[12]*

Roosevelt, who had handled the Navy's contracting responsibilities in World War I, was well served by the procurement team Stimson assembled at the War Department. Undersecretary Robert Patterson, General Brehon Somervell, who commanded the supply services, and Clay presided over the greatest military buildup the world has ever known within a time frame few considered possible. Between Pearl Harbor and VJ Day the armed services let contracts that ultimately exceeded $200 billion ($2 trillion currently) with scarcely a breath of scandal. "We were not against industry making a profit," said Clay, "but we were

---

* When Field Marshal von Rundstedt launched his counterattack in the Ardennes in December 1944, his ten panzer divisions possessed a total of 1,241 tanks. By contrast, Eisenhower's order of battle included 7,079 medium tanks alone. As the commander of a German 88 mm gun unit remarked, "The Americans kept sending tanks down the road. We kept knocking them out. Every time they sent a tank we knocked it out. Finally we ran out of ammunition and they didn't run out of tanks." John Ellis, *Brute Force: Allied Strategy and Tactics in the Second World War* 335, 421 (New York: Viking, 1990).

damned sure they were not going to make an excess profit." For the first and only time in American history the military employed a process of mandatory contract renegotiation. Whenever a supplier reaped an excessive profit or the Army no longer needed what it had contracted for, the War Department renegotiated the contract and recaptured the government's money. "I think it was the greatest job we did during the whole war," said Clay years later. "You haven't heard any criticism of excess profits from World War II, and no one else has."[13]*

The conflict in North Africa continued longer than Roosevelt anticipated. The Germans and Italians resisted stiffly in Tunisia, and fighting did not end until May 13. The Allies took upward of 250,000 prisoners—a victory roughly equivalent to the Russian success at Stalingrad, with the added benefit of clearing Africa of Axis forces.

At the time of surrender Churchill was en route to Washington on the Cunard liner *Queen Mary* for another conference with FDR. The giant 80,000-ton vessel and her sister ship, the *Queen Elizabeth,* had been converted to troop transports each capable of carrying 15,000 men, the major part of a division. Their speed, almost thirty knots, provided a margin of safety, and no submarine ever managed to intercept them on their many wartime crossings. With Churchill, in addition to a large staff, were five thousand German prisoners of war destined for American internment camps.

Dubbed TRIDENT by Churchill, the Washington conference of May 1943 wrestled with the problem of what to do after the battle for Sicily. Churchill and the British chiefs sought to press on in the Mediterranean, drive Italy out of the war, and hit Germany from Europe's "soft underbelly." Roosevelt and the American chiefs of staff wanted to go at Hitler directly with a quick cross-Channel attack and minimize efforts in the Mediterranean—which they continued to see as diversionary. After two weeks of sometimes acrimonious staff debate, Roosevelt and Churchill reached a compromise. The British agreed to set the invasion of France (code name OVERLORD) for May 1, 1944. The initial assault would be mounted by nine U.S., British, and Canadian divisions,

* Mandatory contract renegotiation and the recapture of excess profits faced repeated court challenges, but in the end the Supreme Court upheld the Army's authority. Said Justice Harold Burton for the Court, "The constitutionality of the conscription of manpower for military service is beyond question. The constitutional power of Congress to support the armed forces with equipment and supplies is no less clear and sweeping. The mandatory renegotiation of contracts is valid, *a fortiori.*" *Lichter v. United States,* 334 U.S. 742 (1948).

with twenty additional divisions ready to move in once the beachhead was secure. The United States, for its part, agreed to move against Italy provided it be
done with forces already committed to the Mediterranean. The buildup in
Britain for the cross-Channel attack was to be accelerated, and after Sicily had
been conquered seven divisions (four American and three British) were to be
withdrawn from the Mediterranean to fight in France.

Halfway through the TRIDENT conference, FDR invited Churchill for a
quiet weekend at the president's wooded retreat in Maryland's Catoctin
Mountains. As the presidential party motored through Frederick, Churchill
(who had visited the Gettysburg battlefield years before) inquired about the
house that had belonged to Barbara Frietschie, the elderly woman whose
courage in mounting an American flag in her attic window as the Confederate
army marched by inspired John Greenleaf Whittier's 1864 poem "Barbara
Frietchie." The prime minister's inquiry prompted Roosevelt to quote Whittier's famous lines:

> *"Shoot if you must this old grey head,*
> *But spare your country's flag," she said.*

Churchill waited a moment, and when it became clear that no one in the
presidential party was going to finish the quotation he began reciting the
poem from memory:

> *Up from the meadows rich with corn,*
> *Clear in the cool September morn,*
> *The clustered spires of Frederick stand,*
> *Green walled by the hills of Maryland.*

Churchill sailed on, word for word, through the entire poem—which he had
not read for at least thirty years—and then proceeded to entertain his listeners
with a review of Confederate and Union tactics at Gettysburg.[14]*

---

* Churchill repeated the performance in 1959 as he was riding with President Eisenhower
to his farm in Gettysburg. Ike recited the famous "Shoot if you must" lines as they drove
through Frederick, and Churchill again quoted the entire poem from memory. *New York
Herald Tribune*, May 11, 1959.

Roosevelt told Churchill he was looking forward to a few hours with his stamp collection. "I watched him with much interest and in silence for perhaps half an hour as he stuck them in, each in its proper place, and so forgot the cares of State," Churchill wrote later. "My friendship for the President was vastly stimulated. We could not have been on easier terms."[15]

Sunday morning FDR took Churchill fishing in a nearby stream. The president "was placed with great care by the side of a pool and sought to entice the nimble and wily fish," Churchill remembered. "I tried for some time myself in other spots. No fish were caught, but he seemed to enjoy it very much, and was in great spirits for the rest of the day."[16]

Eleanor evidently had her fill of Churchill and left the men to themselves. "Mrs. Roosevelt was away practically all of the time," Winston wrote his wife, Clementine. "[The President] does not tell her the secrets because she is always making speeches and writing articles and he is afraid she might forget what was secret and what was not. No one could have been more friendly than she was during the two or three nights she turned up."[17]

It was during the TRIDENT conference that Roosevelt recognized he could not conduct the war and manage the home front at the same time. As soon as the conference ended and Churchill returned to England, FDR announced the establishment of the Office of War Mobilization with Supreme Court justice James F. Byrnes as director. Byrnes was a consummate Washington insider. A former congressman and senator from South Carolina—and one of the few southerners who consistently supported the New Deal—he stepped down from the Court at Roosevelt's behest to head the mobilization effort. With an office in the east wing of the White House adjacent to Admiral Leahy's, Byrnes became the final arbiter of home-front decision making. "Your decision is my decision," FDR told Byrnes, "and there is no appeal. For all practical purposes you will be assistant President."[18]

On July 10, 1943, Allied forces invaded Sicily in the largest amphibious operation of the war.* Because of the shaky performance of the U.S. II Corps in

---

* Eight divisions (four British, three American, and one Canadian), a total of 175,000 men, hit the beaches the first day. Within two days 478,000 troops were ashore. At Normandy, by contrast, and despite earlier projections, the Allies landed only five divisions plus three British armored brigades, a total of 150,000 men, on D-Day. B. H. Liddell Hart, *History of the Second World War* 440 (London: Cassell, 1970); Williamson Murray and Allan R. Millett, *A War to Be Won* 420 (Cambridge, Mass.: Harvard University Press, 2000).

North Africa, the principal task was assigned to General Montgomery's veteran Eighth Army, which was to attack northward along Sicily's east coast and seal the island exit across the Strait of Messina to the Italian mainland. Patton's Seventh Army would cover Montgomery's left flank. But when Montgomery bogged down sixty miles short of Messina, Patton seized the initiative, sliced through western Sicily, and captured the city of Palermo on July 22. The Seventh Army then wheeled east along Sicily's north coast and after heavy fighting arrived at Messina August 17, shortly before Montgomery. The Seventh Army's relentless offensive resolved whatever doubts military planners had about the combat-worthiness of American troops. But it arrived too late in Messina to prevent the Germans and Italians from evacuating some one hundred thousand troops, together with most of their vehicles and equipment.

Three days after Patton took Palermo, King Victor Emmanuel III of Italy triggered a coup in Rome, dismissed Mussolini as prime minister, and ordered him into custody. To replace Il Duce the King appointed Marshal Pietro Badoglio, the ranking member of the Italian armed forces, a Darlan-like figure fully prepared to fight or parley, whichever course seemed more advantageous. While assuring Hitler that Italy remained loyal to the Axis, Badoglio opened secret negotiations with the Allies in Lisbon.

Roosevelt paid lip service to unconditional surrender. "Our terms to Italy are still the same," he told the nation in a fireside chat on July 28, 1943. "We will have no truck with Fascism in any way, in any shape or manner."[19] Privately he told Churchill, "we should come as close to unconditional surrender as we can, followed by good treatment of the Italian populace."[20]

Like Victor Emmanuel and Badoglio, Roosevelt was ready to cut a deal. He not only wished to end the fighting but recognized the need to accommodate the nation's large Italian-American community. Asked at his press conference on July 30 whether the United States would negotiate with Italy's new government, the president ignored his previous insistence on unconditional surrender. "I don't care who we deal with in Italy so long as it isn't a definite member of the Fascist government, so long as they get them to lay down their arms, and so long as we don't have anarchy. Now his name may be a King, or a present prime minister, or a Mayor of a town or a village."

Q: Mr. President, you wouldn't consider General Badoglio as a Fascist, then?

FDR: I am not discussing personalities.[21]

Churchill was equally eager to negotiate. Separating Italy from Germany had been a goal of British diplomacy for at least a decade, and Winston had no qualms. "I will deal with any Italian authority which can deliver the goods," he cabled Roosevelt. "I am not in the least afraid of seeming to recognize the House of Savoy [Victor Emmanuel] or Badoglio, providing they are the ones who can make the Italians do what we need for our war purposes. Those purposes would certainly be hindered by chaos, bolshevism, or civil war."[22] In effect, Roosevelt and Churchill were ready to conclude a separate peace with Italy, the doctrine of unconditional surrender notwithstanding.

Badoglio prolonged negotiations until an Allied ultimatum at the end of August forced his hand. Italy surrendered on September 3, 1943, switched sides, and declared war against Germany. Hitler responded by rushing sixteen battle-tested divisions down the boot of Italy. Rome was occupied, the Italian Army disarmed, and Mussolini restored to office.* When American and British forces landed near Salerno in early September, they were met by well-positioned German forces determined to contest every kilometer of Italian soil. So much for Europe's "soft underbelly."

Roosevelt and Churchill met for their fourth wartime conference (QUADRANT) at Quebec City on August 17, 1943. Once again Churchill traveled on the *Queen Mary,* this time bringing Clementine and their daughter Mary. The British party arrived in Halifax, Nova Scotia, a week early, and Churchill took advantage of the interval to spend time privately with FDR at Hyde Park. "You know," he told Eleanor, "one works better when one has a chance to enjoy a little leisure now and then. The old proverb all work and no play makes Jack a dull boy holds good for all of us."[23] Churchill wore a ten-gallon Stetson to pro-

---

* Under German tutelage Mussolini proclaimed the "Italian Socialist Republic" with its headquarters at Salò on the banks of Lake Garda in northern Italy. Badoglio and King Victor Emmanuel fled safely to the Adriatic resort city of Brindisi, where they were protected by British forces. The Italian Navy, including four battleships, sailed to Malta, where it ceremoniously surrendered to the British.

tect his head from the sun, sipped Scotch chilled in a wine cooler, and downed the obligatory hot dogs at a picnic hosted by ER at Val-Kill. Cousin Daisy Suckley, a guest for the weekend, believed Churchill "adored the president, loves him, looks up to him, defers to him, leans on him." In Churchill's presence FDR was "relaxed and cheerful in the midst of the deepest problems."[24]

During the weekend Churchill proposed that the command of OVER-LORD, the cross-Channel invasion, be entrusted to an American. Churchill and FDR had previously agreed that whichever country furnished the preponderance of forces should command the operation, and it was becoming increasingly clear that the United States would do so. Both Churchill and Roosevelt assumed General Marshall would be tapped for the assignment.[25]

The Quebec conference focused on the projected Normandy landing, particularly the logistics of crossing the Channel—landing craft, temporary harbors, fuel pipelines, and the mountains of equipment that would have to be off-loaded. Roosevelt and Churchill were absorbed in the details. "I'm nearly dead," the president confided to Frances Perkins. "I have to talk to the P.M. all night, and he gets bright ideas in the middle of the night and comes pattering down to my bedroom. They are probably good ideas, but I have to have my sleep."[26]

Roosevelt raised the question of Germany's surrender. Had the military staffs prepared for Hitler's sudden collapse? According to General Marshall, the president "recognized the importance of capturing Berlin as both a political and psychological factor. He felt that it was a question of prestige and ability to carry out the reorganization of Europe on an equal status with the Soviet Union." General Alan Brooke, the British chief of staff, assured FDR that plans were in place for a prompt Allied entry into German-occupied territory should the opportunity arise.[27]

Churchill and the president also discussed the atomic bomb. Following receipt of a letter from Albert Einstein in October 1939, Roosevelt had authorized preliminary research on a nuclear bomb.* Einstein and FDR shared

---

* Einstein's letter, dated August 2, 1939, was drafted initially by the Hungarian émigré physicist Leo Szilard and delivered personally to FDR by New Deal businessman Alexander Sachs, then with Lehman Brothers and an old friend of the president. Sachs recounted to Roosevelt Napoleon's error when he rejected Robert Fulton and Robert R. Livingston's offer to build a fleet of steamships and suggested that Einstein's letter represented a similar technological breakthrough. According to Sachs, Roosevelt's interest was piqued and he ordered

a long history. When the scientist arrived in the United States in 1933, the president invited him and his wife to spend a night at the White House. They dined with the Roosevelts and conversed at length in German, which Einstein later recalled FDR spoke very well.[28] It is likely that no other physicist could have captured the president's attention, and when Einstein warned of the potential destructive capacity of nuclear fission, Roosevelt listened. When he said evidence suggested the Germans were already at work on a nuclear weapon, the president took action. At FDR's direction an Advisory Committee on Uranium was established to explore a weapons program. The uranium committee was annexed by the National Defense Research Council and then in May 1941 melded into the Office of Scientific Research and Development, headed by Vannevar Bush. But its initial work was unpromising. The expense of isotope separation plus the uncertainty of whether a controlled chain reaction was even possible appeared to rule out a bomb-making program.

Meanwhile, British scientists, working independently, concluded that a deliverable bomb could be constructed using as little as twenty-five pounds of fissionable material and that if sufficient resources were devoted to the project the first weapon could be ready by the end of 1943.[29] Churchill gave the go-ahead at the end of August 1941, and on September 3 the British chiefs of staff concurred. "Although personally I am quite content with existing explosives," wrote Churchill, "I feel we must not stand in the path of improvement."[30]

After reviewing the British findings, Vannevar Bush recommended to Roosevelt that the United States expedite its research for an atomic bomb. That was October 9, 1941. The project, Bush warned, would require a vast industrial plant "costing many times as much as a major oil refinery"—an estimate woefully short of what the project would ultimately entail.[31] The president pigeonholed Bush's recommendation. Then came Pearl Harbor. On January 19, 1942,

---

an authentic bottle of Napoleon brandy to be brought out—a Roosevelt family heirloom. FDR poured two glasses, gave one to Sachs, and sat back to listen as Sachs summarized Einstein's presentation. Roosevelt comprehended its import instantly. "Alex, what you are after is to see that the Nazis don't blow us up." "Precisely," Sachs replied. Richard Rhodes, *The Making of the Atomic Bomb* 313–314 (New York: Simon & Schuster, 1985). For the text of Einstein's 1939 letter, see Ronald W. Clark, *Einstein: The Life and Times* 556–557 (New York: World Publishing, 1971).

he returned the memo to Bush with a terse reply handwritten on White House stationery:

> V.B.
>
> OK—returned—I think you had best keep this in your own safe.
>
> —FDR[32]

Roosevelt's "OK" galvanized American efforts. Secretary of War Stimson went to Capitol Hill for the money—"I don't want to know why," said Sam Rayburn, who arranged with Appropriations Committee chairman Clarence Cannon to conceal the funds in the War Department budget.[33] Robert Oppenheimer of the University of California assembled physicists to work on bomb design; General Leslie R. Groves of the Corps of Engineers, fresh from building the Pentagon, assumed direction of the "Manhattan Project," named for a mythical Manhattan engineering district; and in December 1942 Enrico Fermi, an Italian Nobel laureate who had fled to the United States with his Jewish wife after Italy enacted Nazi-like racial laws, attained a sustained chain reaction in his Chicago laboratory, establishing the reality of what until then had been merely a theoretical prospect. Curiously, while the United States and Britain were moving ahead, Germany dropped out of the race. In the autumn of 1942 Albert Speer, the Third Reich's armaments minister, after conferring with scientists Otto Hahn and Werner Heisenberg, decided the construction of an atomic bomb was too uncertain and too expensive. "It would have meant giving up all other projects." The decision to cancel the effort came easily for Speer. Hitler was uninterested in an atomic weapon and disparaged nuclear science as "Jewish physics."[34]* Japan also discontinued its efforts in 1943, scientists telling the government that neither the United States nor Germany could possibly develop a weapon that would be usable in the current war.[35]

From the beginning Churchill and Roosevelt agreed to cooperate. In October 1941, shortly after their meeting off Newfoundland, FDR wrote Churchill suggesting that American and British nuclear efforts be coordinated "or even jointly conducted."[36] Churchill followed up during his visit to Hyde Park in

---

* "If I had known that the Germans would not succeed in constructing the atom bomb, I would have never lifted a finger," said Einstein years later. Quoted in Michael Walzer, *Just and Unjust War* 263 (New York: Basic Books, 1977).

June 1942. At the prime minister's suggestion it was agreed that the programs be combined and that future research and development be conducted in the United States. Churchill believed continued German air attacks made it unwise to locate the massive facilities needed to construct a bomb in Great Britain.[37] This momentous decision to share the development of an atomic weapon was made on the spot by Roosevelt and Churchill. Neither had his scientific advisers with him at Hyde Park—although Hopkins was sitting in a corner when the deal was struck—and there was no written record of the agreement. The president and Churchill felt sufficiently self-confident to plunge ahead on their own.[38]

As work on the atomic bomb progressed, American officials charged with the bomb's development grew reluctant to share secrets with the British. Churchill raised the matter with FDR at the TRIDENT conference in May 1943, and Roosevelt once more agreed that the enterprise was a joint one "to which both countries would contribute their best endeavors."[39] The president instructed Vannevar Bush to be fully forthcoming with the British, but evidently there was sand in the gearbox. British scientists continued to believe the Americans were holding back. To resolve the problem, Churchill asked FDR for a written commitment, to which the president quickly agreed. The final version, typed out on stationery from the Quebec Citadel, where both were staying, promised to share the results of the Manhattan Project, keep it secret, and not use the weapon against each other, or against anyone else without mutual consent.[40]

On the day before they signed the atomic accord, Roosevelt and Churchill cabled Stalin a joint invitation for a personal meeting sometime later in Alaska, where they could "survey the whole scene in common" at this "crucial point in the war."[41] Roosevelt had not met Stalin and was eager to negotiate postwar matters, preferably one on one, but with Churchill if necessary. Stalin sidestepped the invitation—he neither accepted nor rejected it—and suggested that the foreign ministers of the three nations meet to discuss matters. FDR and Churchill embraced the idea, and on September 4, 1943—the day after Italy surrendered—the president again wrote Stalin to suggest they get together, perhaps in Cairo. Four days later, with U.S. and British troops pouring ashore in Italy, Stalin agreed. The Soviet leader said that because of his command responsibilities he could not travel as far as North Africa, but he recommended Teheran sometime in November or December. As a preliminary, Stalin suggested the foreign ministers meet in Moscow in October. FDR agreed. "I really feel that the three of us are making real headway," he told Stalin. Churchill was equally pleased. "On this meeting may depend not only the best and shortest method for finishing the war, but also those good arrangements for the future of the world which will enable the British and American and Russian nations to render a lasting service to humanity."[42]

It was during the Quebec conference that the feud between Cordell Hull and Sumner Welles at the State Department reached a climax. Hull had chafed for years that FDR often dealt directly with Welles; that he bypassed Hull and excluded him from major foreign policy decisions. It was Welles, not Hull, who attended wartime conferences with Churchill, who carried the mail for the president on special missions abroad, and with whom foreign ambassadors preferred to deal after paying routine courtesy calls on the secretary. Yet Hull knew Welles was vulnerable. His homosexual advances to Pullman car porters at the time of Speaker William Bankhead's Alabama funeral in 1940 were a matter of record.

Roosevelt chose to ignore the incident, believing it was a momentary lapse triggered by alcohol and fatigue, and felt confident the episode would soon be forgotten.[43] Hull was less forgiving and over the years amassed evidence pertaining to the encounter. When J. Edgar Hoover and the Department of Justice declined to provide Hull access to Welles's file, he sought out FDR's former confidant William Bullitt, who had been the original source of the information. With Bullitt's aid Hull leaked the story to Maine's Republican junior senator, Owen Brewster (who later made headlines pursuing Howard Hughes).*

---

* When Republicans regained control of Congress in 1947, Brewster became chairman of the Special Senate Committee Investigating the National Defense Program—the old "Truman Committee." Brewster's first target was Howard Hughes, whose Hughes Aircraft Company had been awarded a multimillion-dollar contract to develop an enormous transport plane made of plywood (the "spruce goose"). Critics charged that Brewster—"the kept senator of Pan American Airways"—was pursuing Hughes because TWA, which Hughes owned, was challenging Pan Am's dominance of transatlantic travel. After five days of hilarious hearings in the Senate Caucus Room, Hughes demolished Brewster and made the committee look foolish. When Hughes successfully flew the plane during a test in November 1947, the committee abruptly closed the investigation. (One of the highlights of my life as a teenager growing up in Washington, D.C., was to attend the hearings and witness Hughes's aplomb before the committee.) The Hughes flying boat remains the largest plane ever built, with a wingspan of 320 feet (compared to the Boeing 747's 195 feet) and a weight of 400,000 pounds (versus 378,000.) Donald L. Barlett and James B. Steele, *Empire: The Life, Legend and Madness of Howard Hughes* 145–160 (New York: W. W. Norton, 1979).

When Brewster threatened a Senate probe, Hull had what he wanted. Lunching with FDR on August 15, 1943, he demanded Welles's scalp. Either Welles went or he would resign, said Hull.[44]

Roosevelt had no choice. A Senate investigation of the incident, particularly as to why the president had kept Welles on the job for almost three years afterward, would deal a blow to Democratic chances in 1944. Of more immediate concern, Roosevelt needed Hull to ensure continued support in Congress—where his majority (at least in the House) was paper thin. Many Southern Democrats idolized Hull, and Roosevelt could not afford to cut him loose. Shortly after meeting with Hull on August 15, FDR sent for Welles and requested his resignation. To soften the blow, he offered Welles a roving ambassadorship to Latin America, which Welles refused. Roosevelt may have hoped he could find a way to retain Welles, because he did not announce his resignation until September 25. The press suggested that differences with Hull were the cause. No mention was made of Welles's sexual preference.

Roosevelt took the loss bitterly. When Bullitt called at the White House soon afterward and asked to be appointed undersecretary in Welles's place, the president exploded. "I remember coming back to the White House one day and finding Franklin shaking with anger," said Eleanor. "He was white with wrath." According to ER, the president told Bullitt:

> Bill, if I were St. Peter and you and Sumner came before me, I would say to Sumner, "No matter what you have done, you have hurt no one but yourself. I recognize human frailties. Come in." But to you I would say, "You have not only hurt another human being, you have deprived your country of the services of a good citizen; and for that you can go straight to Hell."[45]

FDR was bitter not only at Bullitt. After Welles's departure the State Department found itself shunted into diplomatic limbo. Hull attended the Moscow conference of foreign ministers in October, but after that the diplomats were relegated to the sidelines. Except for providing interpreters and note takers, no one from Hull's State Department attended a major wartime conference, and the correspondence that passed between FDR and Churchill and Stalin was rarely seen in Foggy Bottom.

With the tide of battle shifting in favor of the Allies, Roosevelt turned briefly to the domestic scene. Mobilization brought unprecedented prosperity to America, and FDR looked to the future. Speaking to the nation in a fireside chat in late summer, the president addressed the problem of reconversion. "While concentrating on military victory," said Roosevelt, we must not neglect planning for things to come, particularly "the return to civilian life of our gallant men and women in the armed forces. They must not be demobilized into an environment of inflation and unemployment, to a place on a bread line, or on a corner selling apples."[46]

That autumn, in a domestic initiative such as the United States had not seen since the hundred days, Roosevelt asked Congress for a massive program of education and training for returning servicemen—soon to be known as the G.I. Bill of Rights. Ever since his early visits to Warm Springs, Georgia, in the 1920s, FDR had been disturbed by the poor quality of education in many parts of the country. As Sam Rosenman noted, "he often made it clear in private conversation that he felt strongly that there was no reason why a child born in some county too poor to sustain a good school system should have to start life in competition with children from sections of the country that had fine schools."[47] Roosevelt saw the returning veterans as a way to level the playing field—a means of introducing a federal aid to education that was politically irresistible.

The president's message to Congress requested federal support for college and vocational training for every returning veteran for up to four years, with increased stipends for those who were married and had dependents. "Lack of money," said Roosevelt, "should not prevent any veteran of this war from equipping himself for the most useful employment for which his aptitudes and willingness qualify him. . . . I believe the Nation is morally obligated to provide this training and education and the necessary financial assistance by which they can be secured."[48]

In the months that followed Roosevelt tapped into the support of veterans' and patriotic organizations to expand benefits for returning servicemen: generous unemployment insurance, job counseling, and enhanced medical care, as well as guaranteed low-cost loans for buying homes and farms and covering business costs. Despite the anti–New Deal complexion of the Seventy-eighth Congress, the G.I. Bill of Rights passed both Houses unanimously. Roosevelt signed it into law June 22, 1944. "While further study and experience may suggest some changes and improvements, Congress is to be congratulated on the prompt action it has taken."[49]

The G.I. Bill changed the face of America. Not only did it make colleges and universities accessible, it overturned the states' rights taboo against federal funding for education. Until World War II, less than 5 percent of the nation's college-age population attended universities. The cost of a year in college was roughly equal to the average annual wage, and there were few scholarships. Higher education was a privileged enclave for the children of the well-to-do. Under the G.I. Bill more than a million former servicemen and women attended universities at government expense in the immediate postwar years.[50] In the peak year of 1947, veterans accounted for 49 percent of total college enrollment. And of the 15 million who served in the armed forces during World War II, more than half took advantage of the schooling opportunities provided by the G.I. Bill.[51] The educational level of the nation rose dramatically. So did the country's self-esteem. As Stanford historian David Kennedy observed, FDR's veterans legislation "aimed not at restructuring the economy but at empowering individuals. It roared on after 1945 as a kind of afterburner to the engines of social change and upward mobility that the war had ignited, propelling an entire generation along an ascending curve of achievement and affluence that their parents could not have dreamed."[52]

On the evening of Armistice Day, Saturday, November 11, 1943, Roosevelt and his immediate White House staff—Hopkins, Admiral Leahy, Doc McIntire, and Pa Watson—drove to the Marine Base at Quantico, Virginia, where they boarded the presidential yacht *Potomac* on the first leg of the journey to Teheran. The departure was nothing out of the ordinary—another weekend fishing trip like so many in the past. Sunday morning, just off Cherry Point, Virginia, at the confluence of the Potomac River and Chesapeake Bay, the presidential craft pulled alongside the USS *Iowa*, the latest of a new class of battleships, for the long ocean crossing.[53] "Everything is very comfortable," Franklin wrote Eleanor. "Weather good and warm enough to sit with only a sweater over an old pair of trousers and a fishing shirt. . . . It is a relief to have no newspapers."[54]

In addition to Hopkins and the president's personal staff, the *Iowa*'s passengers included General Marshall, Admiral King, General Arnold, and a full complement of military planners. Notably absent was any senior official from the State Department. The long voyage across the Atlantic allowed Roosevelt time to discuss major strategic issues with his military advisers before meeting Churchill and Stalin. The subject of postwar Europe was considered in detail.

When General Marshall asked about zones of occupation, FDR reached for a National Geographic Society map of Germany and penciled in demarcation lines. "There is going to be a race for Berlin," said the president, "and the United States should have Berlin."[55]

In Roosevelt's sketch the American and Russian occupation zones met at Berlin. The large American Zone comprised northwest Germany, including the ports of Hamburg, Bremerhaven, Lübeck, and Rostock; the Russians would hold a smaller zone in the East, and the British were relegated to Bavaria and the Black Forest. The president told Marshall that perhaps a million U.S. troops would remain in Germany "for at least one year and possibly two."[56] General Marshall assumed the occupation of Germany was a military problem. The commander in chief had provided definitive guidance, and insofar as Marshall was concerned the matter was closed. Roosevelt's map was filed away, and the meeting adjourned.[57]*

Steaming at twenty-five knots and Condition of Readiness Three, which required one third of her crew at battle stations at all times, the *Iowa* arrived at the port city of Oran in French Algeria the morning of November 20, eight days after leaving Chesapeake Bay. Waiting for Roosevelt when he came ashore were General Eisenhower and the president's sons Elliott and Franklin, Jr., who were stationed nearby. "The sea voyage had done father good," Elliott recalled. "He looked fit and he was filled with excited anticipation of the days ahead."[58] The president inspected the ruins at Carthage and that evening dined with Ike, Kay Summersby, Admiral Leahy, Air Chief Marshal Sir Arthur

---

* It is unfortunate that no one from the State Department attended FDR's meeting with the military chiefs on the *Iowa* or was privy to his views on zonal boundaries. The Teheran conference placed the matter in the hands of a newly created European Advisory Commission based in London. The United States was represented by Ambassador John G. Winant and his deputy, George Kennan, but neither was familiar with Roosevelt's wishes and the commission quickly adopted a proposal framed by the British cabinet that established the demarcation between east and west more or less on the Elbe River, with Berlin located 110 miles inside the Russian zone.

The fumbled decision on zonal boundaries in Germany plagued the Western powers throughout the Cold War and can be attributed in no small measure to FDR's exclusion of the State Department from administration planning following Welles's resignation. The War Department's failure to inform State of the president's position is equally inexcusable. Of course, if Hull had not vindictively pursued Welles and forced his resignation, the problem would not have arisen. Had Winant and Kennan been familiar with Roosevelt's design, it is certainly conceivable that different demarcation lines would have been drawn.

Tedder, Elliott, and Franklin, Jr., at Eisenhower's villa overlooking the Gulf of Tunis.[59]

From Tunis Roosevelt flew to Cairo, where he met with Churchill and Chiang Kai-shek. Churchill insisted on meeting the president before they saw Stalin, but FDR was reluctant to appear to be caucusing. He agreed to the meeting only if China were invited and spent much of his time in Cairo with Chiang and his wife. Roosevelt was concerned about China's postwar role in the Pacific. "I really feel that it is a triumph to have got the four hundred and twenty-five million Chinese in on the Allied side," he wrote. "This will be very useful 25 or 50 years hence, even though China cannot contribute much military or naval support for the moment."[60] Churchill took a more jaundiced view. "Our talks," he said, "were sadly distracted by the Chinese story, which was lengthy, complicated, and minor."[61]

The high point of the four days in Cairo was Thanksgiving dinner at the residence of the American minister on November 25. "Let's make it a family affair," said FDR as he carved two enormous turkeys for the nineteen British and American guests. "This took a long time," Churchill remembered, "and those of us who were helped first had finished before the President had cut anything for himself. As I watched the huge platefuls he distributed I feared that he might be left with nothing at all. But he had calculated to a nicety, and I was relieved when at last the two skeletons were removed to see him set about his own share."[62]

After dinner Hopkins unearthed an ancient gramophone and began to play dance music. Churchill's actress daughter Sarah was the only woman present and was in great demand. Never one to be outdone, the prime minister asked Pa Watson, the president's big, jovial military aide to dance, much to the amusement of FDR, who roared with laughter as the two fox-trotted to the tunes of Glenn Miller, Benny Goodman, and Harry James. "For a couple of hours we cast care aside," wrote Churchill. "I had never seen the President more gay."[63]

Roosevelt landed in Teheran Saturday afternoon, November 27, 1943, following a six-and-a-half-hour, 1,300-mile flight from Cairo. Initially the president planned to stay at the American legation, but the distance between the legation and the British and Soviet embassies was such that after one night he accepted Marshal Stalin's invitation to stay at the guest house in the Russian compound. Driving through the narrow, crowded streets of Teheran posed a security risk for each of the Big Three, and by staying close to one another the need to do so was eliminated.

Roosevelt was eager to meet Stalin. The president had come to Teheran determined to strike up a working relationship with the Soviet leader, and as Hopkins told Lord Moran, "he is not going to allow anything to interfere with that purpose. After all," said Hopkins, "he has spent his life managing men, and Stalin at bottom could not be so very different from other people." To FDR, Stalin was "Uncle Joe" ("U.J." in his cables to Churchill), and he was confident that even if he could not convert him into a good democrat, he could at least establish a personal bond.[64]

Nevertheless, Roosevelt did not know quite what to expect. Churchill told him that Stalin was remarkably astute, with a startling capacity for "swift and complete mastery of a problem hitherto novel to him."[65] Averell Harriman, FDR's ambassador in Moscow, considered the Soviet dictator "the most inscrutable and contradictory character I have ever known—a baffling man of high intelligence and fantastic grasp of detail." Later Harriman wrote that Stalin was "better informed than Roosevelt, more realistic than Churchill, and in some ways the most effective of the war leaders. At the same time he was, of course, a murderous tyrant."[66] Hopkins warned Stalin was strictly business. "He does not repeat himself. There is no waste of word, gesture, or mannerism. . . . He's built close to the ground, like a football coach's dream of a tackle. His hands are huge, as hard as his mind. His voice is harsh [Stalin, like Roosevelt, was a chain-smoker], but ever under control. What he says is all the accent and inflection his words need."[67]

Roosevelt was not burdened at Teheran by briefing books and position papers. The issues he wanted to discuss with Stalin were political, and the president steered his own course. "He did not like any rules or regulations to bind him," remembered Charles Bohlen, who as a young foreign service officer served as FDR's interpreter.* "He preferred to act by improvisation rather than by plan."[68]

---

* Harvard professor Samuel Cross, who served as interpreter when Roosevelt met Molotov, did an excellent job, but he blotted his copybook by entertaining dinner parties in Cambridge with stories of what Molotov had said to the president and what the president had said in reply. When he heard of it, Roosevelt was furious and instructed Hopkins to find someone in government service who could keep his mouth shut. After an extensive search Hopkins chose Bohlen. Charles E. Bohlen, *Witness to History* 132–133 (New York: W. W. Norton, 1973).

Scarcely had the president settled into his quarters in the Soviet compound than Marshal Stalin walked over to meet him. "Stalin sort of ambled across the room toward Roosevelt grinning," Mike Reilly of the Secret Service recalled.[69] He wore a simple khaki tunic with the star of the Order of Lenin on his chest. As Roosevelt and Stalin shook hands, the president said, "I am glad to see you. I have tried for a long time to bring this about." Stalin, after expressing his pleasure, accepted blame for the delay because he had been "very occupied with military matters."[70] The two chatted informally for almost an hour—half an hour, actually, because of the translation required. When Roosevelt spoke, Bohlen translated; when Stalin spoke, the duty fell to Vladimir Pavlov. To ease translation, each spoke for short periods, allowing the interpreter to intervene before continuing. According to Bohlen, Roosevelt and Stalin were very good at this. "Churchill was much too carried away by his own eloquence to pay much attention."[71] Each of the Big Three spoke through his own interpreter. Presumably that person would better understand what his leader was trying to say and would be more familiar with the country's idiom.

The first formal conference of the Big Three convened at 4 P.M. Sunday in the conference room of the Soviet Embassy, which had been especially fitted with a large round table to preempt any question of who would sit at the head. Each country had four seats. Ambassador Harriman sat to FDR's right, Bohlen at his left, and Hopkins next to Bohlen. With Stalin were Molotov, Pavlov, and Marshal Kliment Voroshilov, an old sidekick of Stalin's from the Revolution. Churchill brought Anthony Eden, Lord Ismay, and his interpreter, Major Arthur Birse. Soviet secret police stood guard. As the only head of state, Roosevelt was asked to preside at the first session, and at FDR's insistence there was no formal agenda. In fact, there was no agenda for any of the plenary sessions.[72]

Informality prevailed. "Everything was so relaxed it did not seem possible that the three most powerful men in the world were about to make decisions involving the lives and fortunes of millions of people," said Bohlen.[73] Roosevelt opened on a light note: as the youngest member present, he wished to welcome his elders. Churchill pointed out that they held the future of mankind in their hands. Stalin, as host, welcomed his guests. "History," he said, "has given us a great opportunity. Now let us get down to business."[74]

After a *tour d'horizon* the discussion turned to Germany. During the plenary session and at dinner that evening, conversation focused on the postwar period. Roosevelt several times suggested that Hitler was mentally unbalanced and had led the German people astray. Stalin demurred. Hitler was a very able man, he thought. "Not basically intelligent, lacking in culture, and with a primitive approach to political problems, [but] only a very able man could accomplish what Hitler had done in solidifying the German people whatever we thought of the methods."[75]

Stalin believed Germany should be dismembered. The Germans, he said, were a very talented people and could easily revive within fifteen or twenty years. Disarmament was insufficient. Furniture and watch factories could make airplanes and shell fuses. He preferred dismemberment—"as Richelieu had done three hundred years ago."[76]

Churchill said he was primarily interested in seeing Prussia—"the evil core of German militarism"—separated from the rest of Germany.[77] Roosevelt proposed the division of Germany into five parts, plus two regions, Hamburg and the Ruhr, placed under international control. Stalin said he preferred the president's plan to Mr. Churchill's, but "if Germany is to be dismembered, it should really be dismembered."

"Germany had been less dangerous to civilization when divided into 107 provinces," Roosevelt responded.

"I would have hoped for larger units," said Churchill.[78]

At one point Stalin wryly suggested that 50,000 officers of the German general staff should be summarily executed at the end of the war. Bohlen saw that Stalin was smiling sardonically as he spoke, and so did FDR. "Not fifty thousand, but perhaps forty-nine thousand," the president shot back. Churchill was not amused. He did not perceive that Stalin was goading him and rose to the bait. Britain would never tolerate such an outrage, he passionately responded. "I would rather be taken out in the garden here and be shot myself rather than sully my own and my country's honor by such infamy."[79]

Dinner the first evening was hosted by Roosevelt. As during "children's hour" at the White House, the president commenced proceedings by mixing martinis for his guests. Over the years FDR's martinis had become increasingly heavy on the vermouth, often both sweet and dry. Stalin accepted a glass and drank without comment until Roosevelt asked him how he liked it. "Well, all right, but it is cold on the stomach."[80] Bohlen noted that Stalin was not a heavy drinker. He took vodka sparingly and much preferred wines from his native Georgia. Roosevelt was much impressed. Stalin is a very interesting man, he told Frances Perkins. "They say he is a peasant from one of the least progressive parts of Russia. But let me tell you he had an elegance of manner that none of the rest of us had."[81]

After dinner Churchill raised the question of Poland. "It would be very valuable if here at Teheran the representatives of the three governments could work out some agreed understanding on the question of Polish frontiers." Stalin said he did not feel any necessity to discuss the Polish question just yet but was curious what the prime minister had in mind. Churchill said that Great Britain had gone to war with Germany in 1939 because Poland had been invaded. The British government was committed to the reestablishment of a strong Polish state—"an instrument needed in the orchestra of Europe"—but was not attached to any specific frontiers. He suggested moving Poland west. The Soviet Union would retain what it took in 1939, and Poland would be compensated by shifting its border westward to the Oder, taking the German provinces East Prussia, Silesia, and Pomerania. To illustrate his point, Churchill placed three matchsticks representing Germany, Poland, and the Soviet Union on the table. He then moved them east to west "like soldiers at drill executing 'two steps left, close.' "[82]

Roosevelt, who had retired earlier, took no part in the discussion. Later he met privately with Stalin to discuss the Polish issue. He said he did not object to moving the Polish border westward to the Oder, but for political reasons he could not yet endorse it. A presidential election was coming up in 1944, and although he did not wish to run again, he might have to if the war was still going on. "There are from six to seven million Americans of Polish extraction in the United States and as a practical man I do not wish to lose their vote."[83] Having alienated many Italian-American voters with his stab-in-the-back speech in 1940, FDR did not want to antagonize the Poles as well.

Stalin replied that he now understood the president's dilemma and would not complicate the problem for him. Later he told Churchill that he earnestly wanted Roosevelt reelected and believed it would be much to the world's advantage if he were.[84] FDR's mention of the 1944 election to Stalin at Teheran is the first indication the president gave that he might seek a fourth term.

Roosevelt also alluded to the Baltic states. There were a number of people in the United States of Lithuanian, Latvian, and Estonian origin. The United States was not going to war with the Soviet Union to protect the independence of the three Baltic states, he joked, but he hoped Stalin would permit some type of plebiscite to express the will of the people. The right of self-determination was a moral issue for most Americans. Stalin said there would be abundant opportunity under the Soviet constitution for the Baltic people to express themselves. Roosevelt replied that it would be very helpful to him personally if some public declaration of future elections could be made.[85]

The principal issue at Teheran was the second front. At the first plenary session of the Big Three, Stalin, in an almost matter-of-fact tone, confirmed that Russia would join the war against Japan once Germany was defeated. Soviet forces in Siberia would be reinforced and then take the offensive.[86] This was a significant Russian commitment and drastically reduced the importance of China to the Pacific war effort.[87] But the Soviet Union expected a quid pro quo. When were the Allies going to land in France?

Roosevelt believed that at Quebec he had received Churchill's absolute assurance for a cross-Channel invasion no later than May 1, 1944. But Churchill evidently had reservations. Employing his vast reservoir of rhetoric, the prime minister dissembled. He spoke at length about the virtues of alternative approaches—Italy, Turkey, the island of Rhodes, the Balkans—and the shortage of landing craft for an invasion of France.

Stalin replied bluntly. From the Russian point of view Turkey, Rhodes, Yugoslavia, and even the capture of Rome were irrelevant. "If we are here to discuss military matters, Russia is only interested in OVERLORD."[88] Roosevelt came down hard on Stalin's side. "We are all agreed that OVERLORD is the dominating operation, and that any operation which might delay OVERLORD cannot be considered by us."[89] The president said he favored sticking to the original date set at Quebec, namely the first part of May.[90]

For all practical purposes the issue was settled. As Hopkins recalled, Stalin looked at Churchill as if to say, "Well, what about that?"[91] He then pressed on: "I do not care if it is the 1st of May, or the 15th, or the 20th. But a definite date is important."

He turned to Roosevelt. "Who will command OVERLORD?" The president was caught off guard.* It was widely assumed that General Marshall would be

---

* Admiral Leahy, who was sitting next to FDR at the meeting, said the president leaned over and whispered, "That old Bolshevik is trying to force me to give him the name of our Supreme Commander. I just can't tell him because I haven't made up my mind." Admiral William D. Leahy, *I Was There* 208 (New York: Whittlesey House, 1950).

named, but FDR apparently had second thoughts. He told Stalin no decision had been made. "Then nothing will come out of these operations," said Stalin. The Soviet Union had learned that in military matters decisions could not be made by committee. "One man must be responsible and one man must make decisions."[92]

Churchill fought a rearguard action. The Mediterranean ought not be neglected. Once again he argued the case from every conceivable angle. Stalin allowed that such operations might have value but were diversions. "Do the British really believe in OVERLORD or are they only saying so to make us feel better?"[93]

Churchill glowered, chomped on his cigar, and suggested that his Mediterranean proposals be considered by the military staffs. "Why do that?" asked Stalin. "We are the chiefs of government. We know what we want to do. Why turn the matter over to subordinates to advise us?"[94]

With the mood at the table turning testy, Roosevelt adjourned the meeting for dinner. That evening Hopkins called on Churchill at the British Embassy. Whether FDR sent him is unclear. Hopkins told Churchill he was fighting a losing battle. Roosevelt was determined to hold to the May date for the cross-Channel attack, and the Russian view was equally firm. Hopkins told Churchill there was little he could do to prevent it, and he advised the prime minister to yield gracefully.[95]

The effect of Hopkins's visit cannot be measured for certain. But the next day the British announced their agreement to OVERLORD. The Combined Chiefs set the invasion date for May 1944 in conjunction with supporting landings in southern France (ANVIL). Stalin pledged a simultaneous Soviet offensive to pin the Germans down and prevent the transfer of any divisions to the West. Churchill suggested they needed a cover plan to confuse and deceive the enemy. "The truth," he said, "deserves a bodyguard of lies."[96]

"I thank the Lord Stalin was there," wrote Stimson when he learned of the discussion at Teheran. "He saved the day. He was direct and strong and he brushed away the diversionary attempts of the Prime Minister with a vigor which rejoiced my soul."[97]

November 30, 1943, the third day of the conference, was Churchill's sixty-ninth birthday, and dinner that evening at the British Embassy was a gala celebration. "This was a memorable occasion in my life," wrote Churchill. "On my right sat the President of the United States, and on my left the master of

Russia. Together we controlled practically all the naval and three-quarters of all the air forces in the world, and could direct armies of nearly twenty millions of men, engaged in the most terrible of wars that had yet occurred in human history."[98]

Bohlen reports that the table was set with British elegance. The crystal and silver sparkled in the candlelight.[99] "The speeches started directly we sat down and continued without interruption until we got up," Lord Ismay recalled.[100] Churchill praised Roosevelt, whose courage and foresight had "prevented a revolution in the United States in 1933," and followed with a toast to Stalin, "who would be ranked with the great heroes of Russian history."

Stalin responded that the honors heaped upon him belonged to the Russian people. "The Red Army has fought heroically, but the Russian people would have tolerated nothing less. Persons of medium courage and even cowards become heroes in Russia. Those who do not are shot. It is dangerous to be a coward in Russia."[101]

The conviviality continued all evening. "I felt that there was a greater sense of solidarity and good-comradeship than we had ever reached before," wrote Churchill.[102] "Uncle Joe enjoyed himself as much as anybody," said the prime minister's secretary, John Martin.[103]

At one point Churchill remarked, "England is getting pinker."

"It is a sign of good health," Stalin responded.

"I drink to the proletarian masses," said Churchill.

"I drink to the Conservative Party," replied Stalin.

"I believe that God is on our side," said Churchill. "At least I have done my best to make him a faithful ally."

"And the devil is on my side," Stalin, a former seminary student, rejoined. "Everyone knows the devil is a Communist—and God, no doubt, is a good Conservative."[104]

As Churchill raised his glass for the concluding toast, Stalin requested the privilege of proposing one more toast—to the president and people of the United States:

> I want to tell you, from the Russian point of view, what the President and the United States have done to win the war. The most important thing in this war are machines. The United States has proven it can turn out 10,000 airplanes a month. Russia can turn out, at most, 3,000 airplanes a

month. The United States is a country of machines. Without the use of those machines, through Lend-Lease, we would lose this war.[105]

Stalin's generous and unexpected tribute to American aid prompted Roosevelt to request the last word. He compared the Grand Alliance to a rainbow of many colors, "each individualistic, but blending into one glorious whole. Thus with our nations, we have differing customs and philosophies and ways of life. But we have proved here at Tehran that the varying ideas of our nations can come together in a harmonious whole, moving unitedly for the common good of ourselves and of the world."[106]

Roosevelt had been concerned at Teheran to break through to Stalin. "For the first three days I made absolutely no progress," he told Frances Perkins. On the final day

> I began to tease Churchill about his Britishness. [FDR had forewarned the PM.] It began to register on Stalin. Winston got red and scowled, and the more he did so the more Stalin smiled. Finally Stalin broke into a deep, hearty guffaw, and for the first time in three days I saw light. I kept it up until Stalin was laughing with me, and it was then I called him "Uncle Joe." He would have thought me fresh the day before, but that day he laughed and came over and shook my hand. The ice was broken and we talked like men and brothers.[107]

The president need not have tried so hard. Stalin had bugged FDR's suite and knew the details of every conversation. The eavesdropping was entrusted to Sergo Beria, the nineteen-year-old son of secret police head Lavrenti Beria. (Sergo and Stalin's daughter Svetlana were the same age and as children had often played together.) "I want to entrust you with a mission that is delicate and morally reprehensible," Stalin told the young Beria on the eve of the conference. "You are going to listen to the conversations that Roosevelt will have with Churchill, with the other British, and with his own circle. I must know everything in detail, be aware of all shades of meaning."

"I have never done anything with such enthusiasm," Sergo confessed. He briefed Stalin at eight every morning. "It's bizarre," said the Soviet dictator. "They say everything in the fullest detail. Do you think they know we are listening to them?" Beria doubted it. The microphones were so well hidden that his own team could not spot them. "I was able to establish from my eavesdropping that Roosevelt felt great respect and sympathy for Stalin. Admiral Leahy tried several times to persuade him to be firmer with the Soviet leader. Every time he received the reply: 'That doesn't matter. Do you think you can see further than I can? I am pursuing this policy because I think it is more advantageous. We are not going to pull the chestnuts out of the fire for the British.' "[108]*

Roosevelt departed Teheran for Cairo in the early-morning hours of Thursday, December 2, 1943. The president had promised Stalin and Churchill to name a commander for OVERLORD within a week but had not reached a decision. Originally Roosevelt had planned to name Marshall. "I want George to have the big Command," he told Eisenhower in Tunis. "He is entitled to establish his place in history as a great general."[109] Hopkins and Stimson backed the choice of Marshall vigorously, and both Churchill and Stalin believed he would get the nod. Marshall may have assumed so as well. Although he refused to express any views on the appointment, Mrs. Marshall had quietly begun moving the family's personal belongings out of Quarters One at Fort Myer to Lexington, Virginia, and there were stories that Marshall had crated his large Pentagon desk that once belonged to General Philip Sheridan for shipment to London.[110]

Yet there was good reason for Roosevelt to hesitate. General John J. Pershing, who knew both Marshall and Eisenhower, wrote the president from his bed at Walter Reed Hospital to caution against transferring Marshall to Europe. Both the command structure in Washington and the command structure in Europe were working well, said Pershing. "It would be a fundamental and very grave error in our military policy to break up working relationships at both levels."[111]

Marshall's colleagues on the Joint Chiefs also voiced concern. Leahy, King, and Arnold believed it essential to retain Marshall as a member of the Combined Chiefs of Staff, where he could fight for American concepts of Allied strategy.[112] "None of us, least of all myself, wanted to deny Marshall the thing

---

* "Nobody thanked me for my services," wrote Beria. "I was rewarded solely with a Swiss watch. According to my father, Stalin was satisfied with the results of the conference and considered he had won the game. I am sure my summaries must survive somewhere in the archives. Perhaps the recordings too have been preserved." Sergo Beria, *Beria, My Father* 94 (London: Duckworth, 2001).

he wanted most," wrote Leahy. "On the other hand, he was a tower of strength to Roosevelt and to the high command."[113]

Roosevelt was also concerned about the carping of the conservative press in the United States, some of which saw Marshall's transfer to Europe as a left-wing plot to elevate General Brehon Somervell or Eisenhower to chief of staff. That could make them possible running mates if FDR sought a fourth term. Somervell, who headed the WPA in New York under Hopkins, was considered an ardent New Dealer (which surely would have astonished Somervell), and Eisenhower was believed to be a closet Democrat. Above all, however, there was the problem of dealing with the fractious Seventy-eighth Congress. As far as most members of Congress were concerned, George Marshall could do no wrong, and Roosevelt wondered if a new chief of staff would enjoy similar credibility.

On the other side of the ledger, Roosevelt had taken Eisenhower's measure during the two days he spent in Tunis and liked what he saw. Ike had proved his ability to command large multinational coalitions in battle, had defeated the Germans in North Africa and Sicily, and had successful working relationships with Montgomery, Bradley, and Patton, who would likely command the forces on the ground in France. He worked well with the British high command—General Sir Harold Alexander, Air Marshal Tedder, and Admiral Cunningham were unanimous in their praise—and he had demonstrated a unique ability to underplay American special interests for the benefit of the common cause—an essential ability that George Marshall may not have possessed, or that may have been substantially eroded after two years of making the case for the United States on the Combined Chiefs of Staff. Said differently, Roosevelt had come to believe that Eisenhower might actually be a better fit to head the cross-Channel attack, although the job was Marshall's if he wanted it.

In Cairo, Roosevelt delegated Hopkins to determine what Marshall preferred. "I shall accept any decision the President would make," said Marshall.[114] The chief of staff realized that FDR was wavering. The following day, Sunday, December 5, the president sent for Marshall shortly before lunch. "I was determined," Marshall said later, "that I should not embarrass the President one way or the other—that he must be able to deal in this matter with a perfectly free hand in whatever he felt was the best interests of the country."[115]

As Marshall recalled, Roosevelt beat around the bush for a while "and then asked what I wanted to do. Evidently it was left up to me." Again Marshall replied that it was the president's decision to make. His own feelings did not matter. "I would cheerfully go whatever way he wanted me to go and I didn't express any desire one way or the other."

"Then it will be Eisenhower," said Roosevelt. "I don't think I could sleep at night if you were out of Washington."[116] The president dictated to Marshall a message for Stalin:

> *The immediate appointment of General Eisenhower to command of OVERLORD operation has been decided upon.*
>
> *—Roosevelt*[117]*

The selection of Eisenhower as supreme commander in Europe was the last major military decision Roosevelt was required to make. FDR did not second-guess or micromanage the military. More than any president before or since, he was uniquely able to select outstanding military leaders and give them sufficient discretion to do their jobs. Leahy, Marshall, King, and Arnold made a cohesive team at the highest level, and they handled their individual service responsibilities superbly. In the Pacific, Roosevelt turned to MacArthur over War Department objections, and he named Nimitz to command the fleet despite the lukewarm enthusiasm of more senior admirals. Eisenhower ranked 252nd on the Army list when Marshall chose him to head the North African invasion, and he was still well down when FDR tapped him as supreme commander.

Roosevelt's stance toward the military differed substantially from his approach to domestic matters. Unlike the professional accomplishment he sought from the admirals and generals, his civilian appointments reflected the demands of politics. Hull, Ickes, Wallace, and Frances Perkins spoke for particular constituencies whose support the president needed. They symbolized his political coalition, but they were not free to set policy in their individual bailiwicks. Roosevelt did not hesitate to dip down to resolve departmental issues, often structured competing lines of authority, and had no hesitation in

---

* The message was handwritten by Marshall and signed by Roosevelt. Afterward Marshall passed it along to Eisenhower with the message: "Dear Eisenhower: I thought you would like to have this memento. It was written very hurriedly by me . . . the President signing it immediately. G.C.M." Reproduced in Dwight D. Eisenhower, *Crusade in Europe* 229 (New York: Doubleday, 1948).

second-guessing decisions his subordinates had made. Cabinet officers were kept on a short leash; the military were free to roam the reservation.

Like FDR's other military choices, Eisenhower rose to the occasion. The planning for D-Day, inter-Allied cooperation, and the logistical backup left little to be desired. At the crucial moment, with a brief break in the weather, Eisenhower made the decision to land on June 6, 1944, entirely on his own authority. Washington and London were informed but not consulted. The bravery, conditioning, and discipline of the troops who hit the beaches carried the day against determined German resistance. Three million men organized into thirty-nine divisions—twenty American, fourteen British, three Canadian, one Polish, and one French—constituted the invasion force. They were supported by 12,000 aircraft and the largest naval armada ever assembled. At the last moment Churchill decided he wanted to participate. Eisenhower could not dissuade him. George VI finally intervened. If his prime minister was going to take part in the landing, so would he. Except for the air raids on London, said the King, he had not been under fire since the Battle of Jutland, and he eagerly welcomed the prospect of renewing the experiences of his youth.[118] At that point Churchill saw the problem: Britain could not risk losing the King or a prime minister. He yielded to Eisenhower's wishes.

TWENTY-SIX

LAST POST

I can't talk about my opponent the way I would like to sometimes, because I try to think that I am a Christian.

—FRANKLIN D. ROOSEVELT, NOVEMBER 4, 1944

ROOSEVELT APPEARED TO BE in excellent health at Teheran. Bohlen said he was "clearly the dominating figure at the conference, never showing any signs of fatigue and holding his magnificent leonine head high."[1] Lord Ismay thought he "looked the picture of health and was at his best . . . wise, conciliatory, and paternal."[2] Stimson, greeting the president on his return to Washington on December 17, 1943, noted that he looked very well. "He was at his best [and] greeted all of us with very great cheeriness and good humor and kindness."[3]

Franklin and Eleanor spent Christmas at Hyde Park—the first time since 1932 that the family gathered at Springwood. Anna was there from Seattle, and the two younger boys, FDR, Jr., and John, had secured leave from their units. For Anna, whose husband was with the Army's press contingent in North Africa, it was a special reunion. The president was lonely. Missy, his companion for twenty years, languished stroke-ridden at her sister's home in Massachusetts; Louis Howe had been gone for a decade; Marvin McIntyre, FDR's longtime appointments secretary, had died while the president was in Teheran; and Hopkins had moved out of the White House on December 21.* Anna

---

* Hopkins and his young daughter, Diana, had lived in the Lincoln Suite down the hall from FDR since the death of Hopkins's wife in May 1940. When Hopkins remarried in July 1942, his new wife, Louise Macy, joined them. But the inevitable friction that developed between Mrs. Roosevelt and Mrs. Hopkins in such close quarters caused Hopkins to seek other accommodations, and in December 1943 he, Louise, and Diana moved to a town house near 33rd and N Streets in Georgetown.

filled the void. She gossiped with her father as Missy had done, shared breakfast with him in the morning, sat beside him in his study as he worked, and
joined him for cocktails before dinner. "It was the beginning of a new intimacy
in their relationship," wrote Doris Kearns Goodwin.[4]

Anna had intended to return to her job at the *Seattle Post-Intelligencer* after
Christmas, but Roosevelt asked her to stay on. Would she consider coming to
work for him? he asked. "Father could relax more easily with Anna than with
Mother," Elliott observed. "He could enjoy his drink without feeling guilty."[5]
Anna agreed to the change immediately. "With no preliminary talks or discussions," she recalled, "I found myself trying to take over little chores that I felt
would relieve Father of some of the pressure under which he was constantly
working."[6] Anna was never given an official title or paid a salary, but she became as much a part of FDR's daily routine as Missy had been. "It was immaterial to me whether my job was helping to plan the 1944 campaign, pouring
tea for General de Gaulle, or filling Father's empty cigarette case."[7] She rented
out her house in Seattle, moved with her children into the Lincoln Suite, which
Hopkins had vacated, and settled into the White House for the duration of
the war.

Roosevelt met the press for the 929th time on December 28, 1943. He was
asked about the New Deal: Was the term still appropriate to describe his administration? FDR thought not. "How did the New Deal come into existence?"
he asked. "It was because there was an awfully sick patient called the United
States of America, and it was suffering from grave internal disorder. And they
sent for the doctor."

"Old Doctor New Deal" prescribed a number of remedies, said Roosevelt.
"He saved the banks of the United States and set up a sound banking system.
One of the old doctor's remedies was Federal Deposit Insurance to guarantee
bank deposits. Another remedy was saving homes from foreclosure, through
the H.O.L.C. [Home Owners' Loan Corporation]; saving farms from foreclosure by the Farm Credit Administration; rescuing agriculture from disaster
through the Triple A [Agricultural Adjustment Administration] and Soil Conservation; protecting stock investors through the S.E.C. [Securities and Exchange Commission]." The president ticked off a list of prescriptions Doctor
New Deal had written: Social Security; unemployment insurance; aid to the
handicapped and infirm; minimum-wage and maximum-hours legislation;
abolition of child labor; rural electrification; flood control; the public works

program; the TVA; the Civilian Conservation Corps; the WPA; and the National Youth Administration. "And I probably left out half of them," he added.

"But two years ago after the patient had recovered, he had a very bad accident. Two years ago on the seventh of December he was in a pretty bad smashup—broke his hip, broke his leg in two or three places, broke a wrist and an arm, and some ribs, and they didn't think he would live for a while. Old Doctor New Deal didn't know 'nothing' about legs and arms. He knew a great deal about internal medicine but nothing about surgery. So he got his partner, who was an orthopedic surgeon, Dr. Win-the-War, to take care of the fellow who was in this bad accident. And the result is that the patient is back on his feet. He has given up his crutches. He isn't wholly well yet, and he won't be until he wins the war."

Q: Does all that add up to a fourth term declaration? (Laughter.)
FDR: Oh now—we are not talking about things like that now.[8]

The deterioration of Roosevelt's health became evident in the late winter and early spring of 1944. For years his blood pressure had been rising, and he had given up his daily dips in the White House pool sometime in 1940.[9] Grace Tully noticed that the president was slowing down: the dark circles under his eyes grew darker, his shoulders slumped, his hands shook more than ever as he lit his cigarette. The year before he had ordered a coffee cup twice as large so he could hold it to his lips without spilling it. These were normal signs of aging, Tully thought, intensified by the relentless pressure under which Roosevelt worked.[10]

But in February and March 1944 the signs grew worse. FDR seemed unusually tired even in the morning hours; he occasionally nodded off while reading his mail and several times fell asleep while dictating. "He would grin in slight embarrassment as he caught himself," Tully recalled. Once he blanked out halfway through signing his name to a letter, leaving a long, illegible scrawl.[11]

Anna was stunned at her father's failing health. She mentioned it to Eleanor, but her mother dismissed it. "I don't think she saw it," Anna told the writer Bernard Asbell. "She simply wasn't interested in physiology."[12] In the last week of March Roosevelt's temperature reached 104 degrees. He canceled all appointments and confined himself to his bedroom. Anna stayed beside him and grew increasingly worried. After consulting with Grace Tully, she confronted Admiral Ross T. McIntire, the president's personal physician.[13] (McIntire wore a second hat as the Navy's surgeon general, and in retrospect the two jobs may have been more than he could handle.)[14] What was happening to her father? Anna asked. McIntire, originally an ear, nose, and throat specialist, saw no reason to worry. The president was recovering from his usual winter bout with influenza, he said. A week or two in the sun, and he would be fine. "I didn't think he really knew what he was talking about," Anna said later.

"Do you ever take his blood pressure?" she asked.

"When I think it necessary," McIntire testily replied.[15]*

At Anna's insistence, Admiral McIntire reluctantly scheduled a checkup for the president at Bethesda Naval Hospital on March 27, 1944. "I feel like hell!" Roosevelt told White House aide William Hassett as he entered his limousine.[16] Anna rode with FDR up Wisconsin Avenue to Bethesda. When they reached the hospital grounds, the president pointed to the tall tower that dominated the facility. "I designed that one," he said proudly. And it was true. While campaigning in the Midwest during the 1936 election, Roosevelt had been struck by the design of the Nebraska state capitol in Lincoln—a twenty-two-story skyscraper rising out of the prairie. Like President Grant many years earlier, FDR deplored the pedestrian style of federal architecture. "Therefore, I personally designed a new Naval Hospital with a large central tower of sufficient square footage and height to make it an integral and interesting part of the hospital itself, and at the same time present something new," he wrote his

---

* According to FDR's medical history, as reported by Dr. Howard G. Bruenn, the president had not had his blood pressure checked since February 27, 1941—three years previously—when it had measured 188/105. By current standards Admiral McIntire would be considered guilty of egregious neglect for failing to consult a cardiologist and recommend remedial treatment at that time. But in the 1940s—and indeed, even into the 1960s—a majority of physicians believed that rising blood pressure was a necessary physiological response by an aging body to force blood through hardened arteries.

According to Dr. Daniel Levy, the director of the Framingham Heart Study, "Leading physicians believed that it was dangerous and irresponsible to lower high blood pressure. That position grew out of scientific dogma from the nineteenth century which suggested that with normal aging elevated blood pressure was necessary . . . to supply enough blood to organs, especially the kidneys." Dr. Daniel Levy and Susan Brink, *A Change of Heart* 45 (New York: Alfred A. Knopf, 2005); Howard G. Bruenn, "Critical Notes on the Illness and Death of President Franklin D. Roosevelt," 72 *Annals of Internal Medicine* 580 (1970). Also see Ray W. Gifford, Jr., "FDR and Hypertension: If We'd Only Known Then What We Know Now," 51 *Geriatrics* 29–32 (1996).

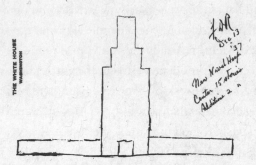

FDR's sketch of Bethesda Naval Hospital

uncle Frederic Delano.[17] Roosevelt laid the cornerstone for the hospital on Armistice Day 1940 and spoke at its dedication in 1942.

Waiting for FDR inside the hospital was Lieutenant Commander Howard G. Bruenn of the Naval Reserve, the staff consultant in cardiology from Columbia-Presbyterian Medical Center in New York. McIntire had instructed Bruenn to examine Roosevelt, report his findings directly to him (McIntire), and say nothing to the patient.[18] "I suspected something was terribly wrong as soon as I looked at the president," Bruenn recalled. "His face was pallid and there was a bluish discoloration of his skin, lips and nail beds. When the hemoglobin is fully oxygenated it is red. When it is impaired it has a bluish tint. The bluish tint meant the tissues were not being supplied with adequate oxygen."[19]

Bruenn noted Roosevelt was having difficulty breathing. With his stethoscope he listened to FDR's heart. "It was worse than I feared," said Bruenn. X-rays and an electrocardiogram revealed that the apex of the heart was much further to the left than it should have been, indicating a grossly enlarged heart. Blood pouring through the atrium to the left ventricle of the heart was meeting resistance. Bruenn heard a blowing sound—a systolic murmur, which indicated the mitral valve was not closing properly. When he asked the president to take a deep breath and hold it as long as he could, Roosevelt expelled it after only thirty-five seconds.[20] His blood pressure was 186 over 108. Bruenn could not understand why McIntire had not reacted earlier. The conclusion seemed obvious: Roosevelt was suffering from congestive heart failure. His heart was no longer able to pump blood effectively. If it continued untreated, the president was unlikely to survive for more than a year.[21]

Roosevelt chatted amiably with Dr. Bruenn throughout the examination but did not inquire about his condition, nor did Bruenn (in keeping with his instructions from McIntire) volunteer any information. But the young cardiologist recognized that the situation was critical. He immediately reported the findings to Admiral McIntire, along with his recommendations: bed rest with nursing care for one to two weeks; digitalis; a light, easily digestible diet with reduced sodium intake; codeine (½ grain) for his cough; and sedation in the evening to ensure a good night's sleep.[22] McIntire was appalled. He doubted that Roosevelt had a heart condition, and he did not want to worry the president or upset his routine. "The president can't take time off to go to bed," he told Bruenn. "You can't simply say to him, Do this or that. This is the president of the United States."[23]

When Roosevelt's condition failed to improve, McIntire convened a team of senior consultants to review Bruenn's findings. They unanimously rejected his diagnosis. After all, someone said, Admiral McIntire had been treating the president for years and it was impossible to imagine that FDR had become so ill overnight.[24]

"I was only a lieutenant commander," Bruenn remembered. "McIntire was an admiral. But I knew I was right, so I held my ground."[25] Finally McIntire agreed to let two outside consultants, Dr. James Paullin of Atlanta and Dr. Frank Lahey of Boston, examine the president. Afterward, both agreed that Bruenn was correct. Lahey believed Roosevelt's condition was sufficiently serious that he should be informed of "the full facts of the case in order to insure his full cooperation."[26] McIntire rejected the suggestion. He preferred not to tell the president of the diagnosis. The conference agreed on a scaled-down version of Dr. Bruenn's original recommendations. Low doses of digitalis would be administered, callers would be held to a minimum at lunch and dinner, and Roosevelt would be asked to cut his consumption of cigarettes, limit his cocktails in the evening, and try to obtain ten hours of sleep.[27]

In addition to keeping Roosevelt in the dark about his condition, McIntire also misled the public. Speaking to the press on April 3, he blithely reported the president was fine; FDR had come through his medical checkup with flying colors. "When we got through we decided that for a man of sixty-two we had very little to argue about, with the exception that we have had to combat the influenza plus respiratory complications that came along afterwards."

McIntire made no mention of the president's heart condition or the treatment that had been prescribed.[28]*

Roosevelt responded quickly to his new regimen. X-rays taken two weeks after treatment began showed a definite decrease in the size of the heart and a notable clearing of the lungs. His blood chemistries were normal, and an EKG revealed marked improvement in the heart's rhythm. Dr. Bruenn was reassigned from Bethesda to the White House and examined FDR almost daily. "At no time did the President ever comment on the frequency of these visits," said Bruenn, "or question the reason for the electrocardiograms and other laboratory tests that were performed from time to time. Nor did he ever have any questions as to the type and variety of medications that were used."[29]

On April 19 Roosevelt, accompanied by Bruenn, McIntire, Pa Watson, and Admiral Leahy, departed Washington for what was planned as a two-week stay at Bernard Baruch's secluded South Carolina plantation, Hobcaw Barony, but which stretched into almost a month. "The whole period was very pleasant," Bruenn recalled. "The president thrived on the simple routine. I had never known anyone so full of charm. At lunch and dinner alike he animated the conversation, telling wonderful stories, reminiscing with Baruch, talking of current events, pulling everyone in. He was a master raconteur."[30] According to Bruenn, Roosevelt displayed no cardiac symptoms, although his blood pressure remained elevated, ranging from 240/130 after breakfast to 194/96 in the evening.[31]

Returning to Washington in early May, Roosevelt wrote to Hopkins, who was recovering at White Sulphur Springs from abdominal surgery complicated by a bout of jaundice. "It is a good thing to connect up the plumbing and put your sewerage into operating condition," he told Hopkins. "You have got to lead not the life of an invalid but the life of common sense. I, too, over one hundred years older than you are, have come to the same realization and have cut my drinks down to one and a half cocktails per evening and nothing else—not one complimentary highball or night cap. Also, I have cut my cigarettes down from twenty or thirty a day to five or six a day. Luckily they still taste rotten but it can be done. . . . I had really a grand time down at Bernie's—slept

---

* Roosevelt's medical file, including all clinical notes and test results, was kept in the safe at Bethesda Naval Hospital. It disappeared immediately after the president's death. Supposition holds that the file was removed by Admiral McIntire and later destroyed.

twelve hours out of the twenty-four, sat in the sun, never lost my temper, and decided to let the world go hang. The interesting thing is the world didn't hang. I have a terrific pile in my basket but most of the stuff has answered itself anyway."[32]

One of the pressing issues Roosevelt returned to confront was the crisis of European Jewry. Hitler's campaign of genocide was now in full swing. Few as yet grasped the extent to which mass extermination was being conducted in specially constructed death camps, but it was becoming increasingly clear that the problem Washington faced was not so much providing asylum for several hundred thousand refugees but rescuing an entire population caught in the Nazi death machine.[33]

From the beginning of his presidency Roosevelt had been sympathetic to the plight of the Jews.* Yet he faced insurmountable obstacles. The Immigration Act of 1924 was unyielding, and the Seventy-eighth Congress was in no mood to consider changes. Public opinion, always susceptible to nativist appeals, was at best indifferent. Church leaders for the most part remained silent, and the intellectual community, with few exceptions, took little notice. The State Department's striped-pants set (particularly those charged with immigration matters) was permeated with genteel anti-Semitism. The War Department—from Stimson and McCloy to Marshall and Eisenhower—resisted any diversion of military resources from the central effort to defeat Germany. And at that time the American Jewish community itself was divided. Members of the old-school Jewish establishment, primarily German in origin—men close to FDR, such as Felix Frankfurter, Sam Rosenman, Herbert Lehman, and the publishers of *The New York Times*—were lukewarm about mounting any special effort to rescue the Jewish populations of eastern Europe, fearing its effect on efforts to assimilate.

Hitler's "final solution" had been launched with the utmost secrecy on January 20, 1942, at what historians call the Wannsee Conference—a meeting of top government officials on the outskirts of Berlin. By the summer of '42 reports of death camps began to filter west. How much Roosevelt knew is uncer-

---

* American anti-Semites, of whom there were many, often referred to FDR as "Rosenfeld" and the New Deal as the "Jew Deal." Some to this day continue to believe that Franklin Delano Roosevelt was Jewish, and the limericks that circulated about his and ER's racial attitude, particularly during the 1940 election, were truly revolting.

tain. The State Department initially suppressed the information because of its "fantastic nature." Career foreign service officers, remembering the atrocity stories manufactured during World War I, characterized the reports as having "the earmarks of war rumors inspired by fear" and declined to send them forward.[34] When Rabbi Stephen Wise, the head of the American Jewish Congress (and a longtime friend of FDR*) provided Sumner Welles with irrefutable documentation in September 1942, Welles asserted the State Department had authoritative confirmation that the Jews were being transported eastward to construct roads and fortifications on the Russian front.[35] Throughout the autumn of 1942 the evidence mounted, including a report from Myron C. Taylor, the president's personal representative to the Vatican.† Welles soon confirmed the reports—"There is no exaggeration," he told Wise—and on December 2 the rabbi appealed directly to FDR:

> *Dear Boss,*
> *I do not want to add an atom to the awful burden you are bearing . . . but you do know that the most overwhelming disaster of Jewish history has befallen Jews in the form of the Hitler mass-massacres.*

Wise asked Roosevelt to meet as soon as possible with him and other Jewish leaders to discuss a course of action. "As your old friend I beg you somehow to arrange this."[36]

Roosevelt responded immediately. Wise was invited to the White House December 8 and brought with him the heads of four major Jewish organiza-

---

* Dr. Stephen S. Wise, a Reform rabbi and longtime Zionist, was the foremost Jewish spokesman in the 1930s and 1940s. A longtime leader of the interfaith social justice movement, Wise was a crusader for political change and in that capacity strongly endorsed FDR for governor in 1928 against Albert Ottinger, New York's Jewish attorney general. Roosevelt's narrow victory was no doubt assisted by Jewish voters influenced by Wise. Wise believed in FDR and trusted him, and Roosevelt for his part respected Wise and always appreciated his political assistance. Many writers on the holocaust, particularly the noted scholar David S. Wyman of the University of Massachusetts (Amherst), are critical of Wise for placing so much faith in FDR. David S. Wyman, *The Abandonment of the Jews* 69–70 (New York: Pantheon Books, 1984).

† The United States did not establish official diplomatic relations with the Holy See until January 10, 1984, during the administration of Ronald Reagan.

tions.[37] FDR received the delegation cordially. Wise made a brief oral presentation and presented the president with a twenty-page summary of the extermination data. He asked Roosevelt "to warn the Nazis that they will be held to strict accountability for their crimes."[38] Roosevelt agreed without hesitation and requested Wise and his colleagues to draft a statement for him condemning the atrocities. He said he would endorse it sight unseen.

Roosevelt acknowledged that the government was now aware that Wise's information had been correct. "We have received confirmation from many sources." The president asked for concrete recommendations as to what might be done. The group, which was apparently taken by surprise, had none to suggest other than a public statement. FDR said he understood. "We are dealing with an insane man. Hitler and the group around him represent . . . a national psychopathic case. We cannot act toward them by normal means. That is why the problem is very difficult."[39] When the meeting ended, Roosevelt assured his visitors, "we shall do all in our power to be of service to your people in this tragic moment."[40]

Nine days after meeting with Wise, Roosevelt induced Churchill and Stalin to join with him in a Declaration on Jewish Massacres, which denounced "in the strongest possible terms this bestial policy of cold-blooded extermination"; condemned the German government's "intention to exterminate the Jewish people in Europe"; and announced their joint determination to try as "war criminals" all those responsible—the origin of the war crimes trials that later convened in Nuremberg.[41] Given that U.S. and British troops had yet to land on the continent of Europe, the declaration nevertheless represented a powerful statement of Allied purpose.[42]* It received wide publicity in the American and British press and committed the United States, Great Britain, and the Soviet Union to prosecute war crimes against European Jewry.[43]

But the fact is that little tangible could be done. An Anglo-American confer-

---

* In issuing the statement Roosevelt overrode the objections of the State Department, which believed it too strong and too definite. "In the first place, these reports are unconfirmed," wrote R. Borden Reams, a specialist on Jewish matters in the Division of European Affairs. "The way will then be open for further pressure from interested groups for action that might affect the war effort." Reams to [John D.] Hickerson and [Ray] Atherton, December 8, 1942. For background, see Kenneth S. Davis, *F.D.R.: The War President* 739–740 (New York: Random House, 2000).

ence on refugees convened in Bermuda in April 1943 but foundered on Britain's refusal to discuss Palestine as a possible destination for whatever Jews might be liberated from Hitler's grasp.[44] In June Roosevelt met with Zionist leader Chaim Weizmann, who pressed the Jewish case for a Palestinian homeland. "The attitude of Mr. Roosevelt was completely affirmative," wrote Weizmann.[45] The president said the Arabs had not been helpful in the war and had not developed their vast territories. He thought they could be bought off and suggested that Weizmann meet with Saudi Arabia's Ibn Saud.[46] Later FDR authorized Rabbi Wise and Rabbi Abba H. Silver to announce on his behalf that "full justice will be done to those who seek a Jewish National Home." The United States, Roosevelt was quoted as saying, had never approved Britain's 1939 white paper restricting immigration. As Wise and Silver put it, "The President was happy that the doors of Palestine are today open to Jewish refugees."[47]*

In the summer of 1943 the Treasury Department pressed plans to ransom 70,000 Jews from Romania at a cost of $170,000. The money would be deposited in Switzerland for Romanian officials to collect after the war. Roosevelt approved the arrangement, but because of State Department foot-dragging nothing came of it.[48] Similarly, when Rabbi Wise came to FDR in July with a Swiss proposal to rescue Jewish children hiding in France, Roosevelt immediately agreed. "Stephen, why don't you go ahead and do it," the president said. When Wise suggested that Morgenthau and the Treasury Department might not cooperate, Roosevelt picked up the phone. "Henry, this is a very fair proposal which Stephen makes about ransoming Jews." Treasury thereupon approved the plan, but again diplomats at State scuttled it.[49]

By the end of 1943 it had become evident that the European Affairs Division of the Department of State was determined to block any rescue effort. Officials at Treasury (most of whom were not Jewish) were incensed. Led by

* Roosevelt's views about Palestine were revealed to Henry Morgenthau in December 1942. According to Morgenthau's diary entry, the president said he "would call Palestine a religious country . . . leave Jerusalem the way it is and have it run by the Orthodox Greek Catholic Church, the Protestants, and the Jews—have a joint committee run it. [He] would put a barbed wire around Palestine . . . begin to move the Arabs out" and "provide land for the Arabs in some other part of the Middle East. Each time we move out an Arab we would bring in another Jewish family. Palestine would be 90 percent Jewish and an independent nation." Morgenthau Diary, MS, December 3, 1942, FDRL.

General Counsel Randolph Paul, Foreign Funds Control Chief John Pehle, and Assistant Counsel Josiah DuBois, the Treasury staff prepared a confidential report for Morgenthau documenting State Department obstructionism entitled "Report to the Secretary on the Acquiescence of This Government in the Murder of the Jews." It charged that the State Department was "guilty not only of gross procrastination and willful failure to act, but even of willful attempts to prevent action from being taken to rescue Jews from Hitler."[50]

Morgenthau retitled the memorandum "A Personal Report to the President" and met with FDR on January 16, 1944. Accompanying the secretary were Paul and Pehle. Morgenthau summarized the findings of the report and urged the president to establish a cabinet-level rescue commission that would strip the State Department of its refugee responsibility. Roosevelt needed little convincing. On January 22, 1944, he signed Executive Order 9417, establishing a War Refugee Board (WRB) consisting of Morgenthau, Hull, and Stimson, with Treasury's John Pehle as director. "It is the policy of this government to take all measures within its power to rescue victims of enemy oppression in imminent danger of death" and to provide "relief and assistance consistent with the successful prosecution of the war," the order stated.[51] Three days after the WRB was established, New York congressman Emanuel Celler wrote Roosevelt, "Your glorious action has cleared the atmosphere. It is like a bolt of lightning dispelling the storm."[52]

Under John Pehle's aggressive leadership, the WRB moved swiftly to provide whatever relief was possible. "The board," Morgenthau wrote later, "was made up of crusaders, passionately persuaded of the need for speed and action."[53] When Hitler occupied Hungary in March 1944 and ordered the deportation of 700,000 Jews—the largest intact Jewish community in Europe—the WRB dispatched the Swedish diplomat Raoul Wallenberg to Budapest under diplomatic cover. With a combination of bluff and bribery, using funds funneled through the WRB, Wallenberg saved thousands of Jews. The board also arranged for air-leaflet drops warning of war crimes prosecutions and induced New York's Francis Cardinal Spellman, the ranking Catholic prelate in the United States, to record a radio broadcast reminding Hungarian Catholics that persecution of the Jews was in direct contradiction of Church doctrine.[54]

Roosevelt addressed the issue again on March 24, 1944. Stung by Morgenthau's report of State Department malfeasance, FDR took pains to clarify the government's intention to provide succor. "In one of the blackest crimes of all history," said the president, "the wholesale systematic murder of the Jews of Europe goes on unabated every hour." The Jews of Hungary were now threatened. "That these innocent people, who have already survived a decade of Hitler's fury, should perish on the very eve of triumph over the barbarism which their persecution symbolized, would be a major tragedy." FDR promised swift retribution. "This applies not only to the leaders but also to their functionaries and subordinates in Germany and in the satellite countries. All who knowingly take part in the deportation of Jews to their death . . . are equally guilty with the executioner. All who share the guilt shall share the punishment."

Roosevelt pledged to persevere in the effort to rescue the victims of Nazi brutality. "Insofar as the necessity of military operations permit, this Government will use all the means at its command to aid the escape of all intended victims of the Nazi and Jap executioner. . . . We shall find havens of refuge for them, and we shall find the means for their maintenance and support until the tyrant is driven from their homelands and they may return."[55]

The president's statement received front-page treatment. "Roosevelt Warns Germans on Jews," bannered *The New York Times*. It was broadcast by the BBC and translated into many languages throughout Europe, and copies were dropped behind enemy lines. Rarely has there been a more explicit announcement of American intentions. And rarely was there so little the United States could do.

In postwar years the question has often been raised whether the United States should have bombed the death camps or at least the rail lines running to them. There is no evidence that Roosevelt was ever approached about the matter.[56] When John Pehle raised the issue with the War Department in the summer of 1944, John J. McCloy rejected the proposal as impractical.[57] The U.S. Strategic Air Force in Europe concurred.[58] General Marshall firmly opposed any operation not aimed specifically at enemy forces, and Eisenhower, who had his hands full moving against the Siegfried Line, resisted any diversion from the main effort.[59] If Roosevelt had been consulted, there is no question that he would have backed the military. Aside from the fact that the president never intervened in tactical matters, he firmly believed that the most effective way to save the Jews from Hitler was to defeat Germany as quickly as possible.*

Harvard's Alan Dershowitz put the matter into perspective:

> Roosevelt was a man with considerable, but certainly not unlimited, power to influence the course of events in Europe. And he prioritized the use of that power in what he believed was the most effective manner: win the war as quickly as possible and save as many Jews as was consistent with the first priority and the political realities that limited his power.
>
> Reasonable people can debate specific decisions, indecisions, actions and inactions. . . . But no one should question Roosevelt's motives or good will toward the Jewish victims of the world's worst human atrocity.[60]

A second pressing matter Roosevelt faced was the status of General Charles de Gaulle and his Free French movement. With D-Day the issue became acute. Were those portions of France that were liberated to be governed by Eisenhower and the SHAEF general staff as occupied territory, or would the provisional regime of de Gaulle—the French Committee of National Liberation (FCNL)—hold sway? Eisenhower, who had lived in Paris for two years (1928–1929) and knew France well, unequivocally favored de Gaulle.[61] He wanted the military cooperation of the French resistance, which was inextricably linked to the FCNL, and above all wanted a civil authority to govern France, freeing his headquarters of the administrative burden. So too did Churchill. "It is very difficult to cut the French out of the liberation of France," he told Roosevelt on May 26, 1944.[62] But FDR resisted. Abetted by State Department man-

---

* Leonard Dinnerstein, in his careful study *Antisemitism in America,* notes that "Roosevelt always dealt with the Jews as an issue in the context of a broader agenda. His primary goal was to end the war as quickly as possible, his British allies were pressuring him to do nothing to help Jews escape from Europe, and he wanted to retain Congressional good will to insure support for a United National organization after the war. . . . The country had elected an extremely conservative group of men and women to the House of Representatives in 1942. When he sought permission from Congress to permit him to allow people into the country who would not qualify under existing legislation, the members emphatically rejected his request." *Antisemitism in America* 143–144 (New York: Oxford University Press, 1994).

darins enthralled by Vichy's rollback of the social excesses of the Third Republic and fortified daily by the anti–de Gaulle rants of Admiral Leahy, his former
ambassador to Pétain, the president petulantly refused to recognize the FCNL
as the legitimate or even provisional government of France.[63]

The best that can be said for Roosevelt's intransigence is that the president
wished to delay recognizing any French government until the people of France
could make a free choice after the war. "We have no right to color their views
or to give any group the sole right to impose one side of a case on them," he
told Eisenhower on May 13, 1944.[64] But the fact is that by 1944 de Gaulle had
established his government in exile as the legitimate successor to the Third Republic. He had swept the competitors from the field, leaving only Vichy as an
alternative—which the Allies under no circumstances could accept. In seeking
an alternative to de Gaulle, Roosevelt was flogging a dead horse. The president's attitude, as the general presciently observed, "seemed on the same order
as Alice's Adventures in Wonderland."[65]

At Roosevelt's insistence, de Gaulle (who was in Algeria at the time) was not
informed of the invasion until two days before D-Day. At Eisenhower's urging,
he was brought to England, taken to Ike's headquarters, and given a complete
briefing. Afterward Eisenhower sheepishly gave him the copy of a speech
SHAEF wished him to deliver to the French people after the troops had
landed.[66] De Gaulle refused. Aside from the limp military prose (which would
have been reason enough to decline), de Gaulle rejected categorically the idea
that as head of the provisional government of the French Republic his words
should be dictated by the Allies. Churchill intervened and eventually brokered
an arrangement for de Gaulle to write his own message.[67] "It's a girls' school,"
lamented Sir Alexander Cadogan, permanent undersecretary in the British
Foreign Office. "Roosevelt, P.M. and—it must be admitted deG.—all behave
like girls approaching the age of puberty."[68]*

The problem of who would govern liberated France resolved itself. On

---

* An important collateral issue pertained to the currency Allied forces would use in France.
In January 1944 Morgenthau and McCloy met with Roosevelt and suggested that the bills
(which were to be printed by the Bureau of Engraving) be emblazoned "Répulic
Française." FDR overruled them. "How do you know what kind of a government you will
have after the war is over?" he asked. "De Gaulle is on the wane." At the president's insistence
the new currency proclaimed "La France," with the Tricolor supported on either side by
British and American flags. The FCNL objected strenuously. "*Allez, faites la guerre avec votre*

June 14, with Eisenhower's acquiescence, de Gaulle landed at Bayeux with members of the provisional government. His reception exceeded all expectations. Local officials appointed by Vichy pledged their allegiance, and the provisional government assumed control. Ike gave his military blessing to the arrangement, calling it essential to secure his rear areas. Civil affairs officers deferred to de Gaulle's appointees. Whether the United States recognized him or not, de Gaulle was now de facto the chief executive of liberated France.[69]

Roosevelt adjusted to military reality.[70] He invited de Gaulle to Washington but insisted it was not a state visit, and the customary honors were not rendered. De Gaulle stayed in the capital from July 6 to July 9 and then touched down briefly in New York and Canada, where he addressed the Houses of Parliament. Wherever he went, the reception was enthusiastic. FDR might be unwilling to recognize de Gaulle, but it had little effect on the warmth with which he was welcomed.

Aside from the usual round of luncheons and dinners, Roosevelt and de Gaulle met twice privately for extended discussions. De Gaulle also met with Hull ("who acquitted himself of his crushing task with great conscientiousness and distinction of spirit"); Morgenthau ("a great friend of our cause, in charge of a treasury which, for being inexhaustible, was no less subject to his scrupulous ordering"); Marshall ("a bold organizer but a reserved interlocutor, the animating spirit of a war effort and military strategy of global dimensions"); and Leahy ("astonished by the events that had defied his counsels of conformity, surprised to see me there, but persisting in his prejudice").[71]

Roosevelt's discussions with de Gaulle dealt primarily with global matters. The president laid out his plans for a four-power (Britain, China, Russia, and the United States) directorate to settle the world's postwar problems. "His will to power cloaked itself in idealism," de Gaulle wrote afterward. "The President, moreover, did not explain matters as a professor setting down principles, nor

---

fausse monnaie [Go make war with your counterfeit money]," said de Gaulle contemptuously. The issue was not resolved until de Gaulle's visit to Washington in July, when it was agreed that only the government of the Republic of France could issue currency. Charles de Gaulle, 3 *The War Memoirs of Charles de Gaulle* 253, 275 (New York: Simon & Schuster, 1959); G. E. Maguire, *Anglo-American Policy Towards the Free French* 133–135 (London: Macmillan, 1995); Ted Morgan, *FDR: A Biography* 717–719 (New York: Simon & Schuster, 1985); McCloy to FDR, June 10, 1944, FDRL.

as a politician who flatters passions and interests. It was by light touches that he sketched his notions, so skillfully that it was difficult to contradict this artist, this seducer, in any categorical way."

De Gaulle countered by stressing the primacy of Western Europe. "It is the West that must be restored. If it regains its balance, the rest of the world will take it for an example. If it declines, barbarianism will ultimately sweep everything away." The exchanges were civil, but there was no meeting of minds and little warmth. De Gaulle resented Roosevelt's reluctance to recognize his government, and Roosevelt did not hide his skepticism about the future of France. "The American President's remarks ultimately proved to me," wrote de Gaulle, "that in foreign affairs, logic and sentiment do not weigh heavily in comparison with the realities of power. To regain her place, France must count only on herself."[72]

The encounter had one practical consequence: on July 11, while de Gaulle was addressing Parliament in Ottawa, Roosevelt announced he was granting de facto recognition to the FCNL, which, he said, "is qualified to exercise the administration of France."[73] Formal recognition, however, was months away. In mid-August, the Allies landed in southern France, assisted by seven divisions of the French First Army, and still de Gaulle was not recognized. On August 25 de Gaulle entered Paris to a tumultuous welcome and was not recognized. On September 17, Hull, now firmly in de Gaulle's camp, recommended recognition, but again FDR refused. "The Provisional Government has no direct authority from the people," he told Hull. "It is best to let things go along as they are for a moment."[74] By mid-October Eisenhower, the Joint Chiefs, the State Department, and Churchill were all urging recognition.[75] Roosevelt realized he was completely isolated on the question and on October 23 gave way. Britain, the Soviet Union, and the United States officially recognized the FCNL as the provisional government of France. De Gaulle said drolly, "The French Government is satisfied to be called by its name."[76] Diplomatic recognition is a presidential prerogative. FDR's pique against de Gaulle poisoned the well of Franco-American relations, the legacy of which continues to this day.

De Gaulle's visit to Washington coincided with the run-up to the Democratic National Convention. In June the Republicans, meeting in Chicago, acclaimed Thomas E. Dewey ("Boy Orator of the Platitude") as the party's nominee on the first ballot.* Photogenic governor John Bricker of Ohio ("an honest Harding" in the words of William Allen White) was chosen as his running mate.[77] Unlike 1940 (when Willkie ran) it was scarcely a compelling ticket. But after twelve years of Democratic rule perhaps it did not matter. Even though there was a war on, the midterm elections in 1942 had indicated the country was ready for a change—and FDR's failing health was difficult to conceal.

In 1940 Roosevelt did not announce his decision to run for a third term until the convention voting was about to begin. This time he put his cards on the table early. In a message to party chairman Robert E. Hannegan of Missouri on July 11, well over a week before the delegates would assemble, the president said that although he did not wish to run, his duty compelled him to do so. "Reluctantly, but as a good soldier, I will accept and serve in this office, if I am ordered to do so by the Commander in Chief of us all—the sovereign people of the United States."[78]

Roosevelt's renomination was never in doubt. Three southern delegations— Louisiana, Mississippi, and Virginia—defected to Senator Harry F. Byrd, but the president won easily on the first ballot, 1,086–89.[79] The fight was over the vice presidency. Wallace, who still mystified Democratic politicians, was a drag on the ticket. Ickes claimed he would cost 3 million votes. And FDR's health could not be ignored. "If something happened to you, I certainly wouldn't want Wallace to be president," Morgenthau told Roosevelt two weeks before the convention.[80]

Roosevelt recognized the problem Wallace posed. In June he invited Bronx boss Edward J. Flynn and his wife to spend a weekend at the White House. FDR genuinely enjoyed Flynn's company, who as national chairman in 1940 had organized the president's third-term campaign. With Farley out of the picture, no one had a better grasp of electoral mechanics than Flynn, and Roosevelt valued his judgment.

Flynn and his wife were astonished at how FDR's health had deteriorated. "We were both very unhappy about his condition and sat up for two hours dis-

---

* Dewey received 1,056 of the 1,059 votes, two delegates being absent and one from Wisconsin voting for Douglas MacArthur. The allusion is to Nebraska's William Jennings Bryan, known at the inception of his career as the Boy Orator of the Platte.

cussing it." When the question of a fourth term came up, Flynn urged the president not to consider it. He also spoke with Mrs. Roosevelt and begged her to use whatever influence she had to keep him from running again. "I felt that he would never survive the term."[81]

Both Roosevelt and Eleanor dismissed Flynn's concern. FDR believed it was his duty to run, and ER thought her husband's victory was essential for the good of the country. "If elected, he'll do his job well," she wrote her son James. "And I think he can be kept well to do it."[82] Roosevelt asked Flynn to take the party's pulse. The Solid South was taken for granted, but it was imperative to carry New York, Pennsylvania, Illinois, New Jersey, and California. Would Wallace help or hurt the ticket?

Flynn, who personally admired Wallace, took soundings across the country. He told Roosevelt that notwithstanding the vice president's strong support from organized labor, he would drive independents and middle-of-the-road voters to Dewey. There was no hope of carrying the key electoral states if Wallace remained on the ticket.[83] FDR accepted Flynn's analysis. The two men thereupon reviewed alternatives. FDR thought James Byrnes was the strongest candidate, but Flynn said he would not do. Born and raised a Catholic, Byrnes had left the Church when he married; labor opposed him because of his decisions as director of war mobilization; and he was an outspoken segregationist. Catholics, labor, and African-American voters in the North were three constituencies the Democratic party could not afford to offend. Sam Rayburn was ruled out because he was from Texas, and if FDR could not have Byrnes, he did not want another southerner. That also eliminated Alben Barkley. "We went over every man in the Senate," said Flynn,

> and Truman was the only one who fitted. His record as head of the Senate Committee to investigate the National Defense Program was excellent; his labor votes in the Senate were good; on the other hand he seemed to represent to some degree the conservatives in the party, he came from a border state, and he had never made any "racial" remarks. He just dropped into the slot.

In Flynn's words, "It was agreed that Truman was the man who would hurt [the president] least."[84]

Roosevelt left the mechanics to Flynn. Remembering the repercussions when he had forced Wallace on the convention in 1940, the president did not want to repeat the episode. For that reason he consistently denied he had made any commitment. That encouraged both Wallace and Byrnes to believe they would get the nod. "While I cannot put it just that way in public," Roosevelt told the vice president after a private luncheon meeting on July 13, "I hope it will be the same old team."[85] To Byrnes he said, "You are the best qualified man in the whole outfit and you must not get out of the race. If you stay in, you are sure to win."[86] Flynn did not believe FDR was being duplicitous. "I did not think President Roosevelt enjoyed the physical strength and mental vigor he had in the past. He had aged considerably. I believe that in order to rid himself of distress or strife and rather than argue, he permitted all aspirants for the nomination to believe it would be an open convention."[87]

Wallace and Byrnes both went to Chicago confident they had the president's support. Byrnes was told of Roosevelt's decision the night before the voting and withdrew "in deference to the wishes of the President."[88] Wallace remained in the race. The final session of the convention on Friday, July 21, lasted nine hours. National committee chairman Hannegan controlled tickets to the gallery, and Mayor Kelly's Chicago police ensured that Wallace supporters did not crash the gate. Nevertheless, Wallace's delegate strength was formidable. Flynn aimed to prevent a first-ballot victory for the vice president, then stampede the delegates to Truman. Sixteen names, including fourteen favorite sons, were placed in nomination. When the roll call concluded, Wallace led with 429 votes—far short of the 589 required; Truman had 319; and the remaining 428 votes were scattered. A second ballot commenced immediately. By prearrangement Alabama's favorite son, Senator John Bankhead, withdrew in favor of Truman, and the rout began. State after state switched from favorite son to Truman. Massachusetts put Truman over the top when Senator David I. Walsh withdrew in favor of his Missouri colleague. The final count was Truman 1,031, Wallace 105. Truman's acceptance speech, one of the shortest in American political history, lasted less than a minute. As David McCullough and others have written, Truman did virtually nothing to secure the nomination. Party leaders from Flynn down recognized that they were choosing a president, not a vice president. They were determined to dump Wallace, and Truman fit the bill.[89]

Roosevelt did not attend the 1944 convention. When his nomination was announced, he was in San Diego making ready to embark on the cruiser USS

Baltimore for Pearl Harbor, where he would confer on Pacific strategy with Nimitz and MacArthur. "His mind was on the war," said his son James, who was stationed nearby at Camp Pendleton. "The fourth-term race was simply a job that had to be accomplished, and his attitude toward the coming political campaign was one of 'let's get on with it.' "[90]

While the balloting was under way at Chicago, Roosevelt was scheduled to review an amphibious-landing exercise staged by the 5th Marine Division, a dress rehearsal for its next Pacific operation. Just as he was about to leave for the exercise he suffered a sudden seizure. The president turned deathly white, with a look of agony in his face. "Jimmy, I don't know if I can make it—I have horrible pains." Roosevelt struggled to speak. James wanted to call a doctor, but FDR resisted. "Both of us thought he was suffering from some sort of acute digestive upset—Father himself was positive it had nothing to do with his heart." James helped him lie flat on the floor of his railroad car and watched in terrified silence for ten minutes or so as his father recovered. "Never in all my life had I felt so alone with him—and so helpless." Gradually color returned to the president's face and he opened his eyes. "Help me up now, Jimmy. I feel better." Minutes later Roosevelt was seated in an open car, smiling jauntily and waving to spectators as he headed out to watch the marines hit the beach.[91]

FDR sailed for Pearl Harbor July 21, 1944, accompanied by Leahy, Sam Rosenman, and his dog, Fala. The crossing was uneventful, save for Rosenman having to intervene to protect Fala's pelt from young seamen who wished to clip a souvenir lock of the famous dog's hair. "The poor dog was in danger of being completely shorn."[92] At 3 P.M., Wednesday, July 26, the *Baltimore* docked in Honolulu to the cheers of an immense crowd of Hawaiians alerted to Roosevelt's arrival. Nimitz and some forty flag officers sprinted up the gangway to greet the president on the quarterdeck. One commander was conspicuously absent. "Where's Douglas?" FDR asked Nimitz. An embarrassed silence followed. As the presidential party prepared to debark, the scream of police sirens shattered the calm. Onto the dock roared a motorcycle phalanx of Honolulu's finest, followed by what Rosenman remembered as "the longest open car I have ever seen."[93] In front was a military driver in starched khaki; in back—MacArthur.

"Hello, Doug," said the president. "What are you doing with that leather jacket on? It's darn hot today."

"Well, I've just landed from Australia," MacArthur replied. "It's pretty cold up there."[94]

Between strategy sessions Roosevelt toured the island's installations, driving in an open car through the streets of Honolulu flanked by MacArthur and Nimitz, with Leahy riding shotgun beside the driver. Visiting a military hospital, Roosevelt asked a Secret Service man to wheel him slowly through the amputee wards occupied by patients who had lost one or both legs. The president stopped at one bed after another, chatting briefly. He wanted to show his useless legs to those who would face the same affliction.* "I never saw Roosevelt with tears in his eyes," Rosenman recalled. "That day as he was wheeled out of the hospital he was close to them."[95]

The strategy issue Roosevelt faced was simple enough. The Joint Chiefs—Admiral King, General Arnold, and to a lesser extent General Marshall—wanted to bypass the Philippines, land on Formosa, and take the fight quickly to the Japanese home islands. "Bypassing the Philippines is not synonymous with abandoning them," Marshall reminded MacArthur at the beginning of July.[96]

MacArthur insisted that the Philippines be liberated first. It was as much a moral issue as a military one. Filipinos looked on the United States as their "mother country." To leave them at the mercy of a Japanese army of occupation, said MacArthur, would be "a blot on American honor."[97]

MacArthur made a masterly presentation, speaking as he customarily did without notes, and concluded with a strictly military analysis: Luzon was more important than Formosa because with it went control of the South China Sea. Japan's lines of communication to its southern outposts would be cut; the Filipinos, unlike the Formosans, would provide powerful guerrilla support; and bypassing Luzon would expose American forces to crippling attacks from Japanese bombers stationed there. Nimitz, less eloquent, made King's case for Formosa first, but, as Leahy perceived, he did not disagree with MacArthur. Pressed by Roosevelt, Nimitz said he could support either operation.[98]

FDR had assumed he was going to Hawaii to referee a knock-down, drag-

---

* Roosevelt normally was seen in public either standing with his braces locked, or seated in an open car. On only one other occasion did he allow strangers to witness his infirmity. That was in 1936, when he dedicated a new building at Washington's Howard University. Howard's president, Dr. Mordecai Johnson, asked Roosevelt if the students could see that he was crippled. They had been so crippled because of their race, said Johnson, the president's example would inspire them. "Roosevelt agreed. He let himself be lifted from his car and set down in public view, and then he proceeded to walk slowly and painfully to the platform." Doris Kearns Goodwin, *No Ordinary Time* 532–533 (New York: Simon & Schuster, 1994).

out fight between the Army and the Navy. Instead, consensus arrived quickly. MacArthur and Nimitz agreed that the Philippines should be recovered with the forces available in the western Pacific and that, contrary to the view of the Joint Chiefs, Japan could be forced to surrender without invading the Japanese homeland. "It was highly pleasing and unusual to find two commanders who were not demanding reinforcements," wrote Leahy.[99]

MacArthur had expected the worst but was pleasantly surprised at the outcome. The president, he said, had conducted himself as a "chairman" and had remained "entirely neutral," while Nimitz displayed a "fine sense of fair play."[100]* Leahy thought FDR was "at his best as he tactfully steered the discussion from one point to another and narrowed down the areas of disagreement between MacArthur and Nimitz."[101] The only discordant note was Roosevelt's health. "He is just a shell of the man I knew," MacArthur told his wife, Jean. "In six months he will be in his grave."[102]

From Pearl Harbor, Roosevelt sailed to Alaska. On July 31, while under way, he received a cable from the White House that Missy LeHand had died of a cerebral embolism earlier that day. She had never recovered from her stroke three years earlier. Eleanor, along with James Farley and Joseph Kennedy, attended her Cambridge funeral, presided over by Bishop (later Cardinal) Richard Cushing. FDR issued a moving personal statement.[103] Writing in *The New York Times,* Arthur Krock noted that Roosevelt had now lost two of his most trusted advisers, Louis Howe and Missy LeHand.[104] Rosenman said, "She was one of the most important people of the Roosevelt era. . . . She was the frankest of the President's associates, never hesitating to tell him unpleasant truths or to express an unfavorable opinion about his work or about any proposed action or policy. I feel that had she lived she could have so lightened his wartime burden that his own life would have been prolonged."[105]

Roosevelt mourned silently, but Missy's death took its toll. He spoke informally to the troops at Adak, Alaska, on August 3, and then suffered an attack of angina a week later while delivering a speech to Navy Yard workers at Bremerton, Washington. FDR had been out of the country twenty-nine days and had traveled 10,000 miles by ship, a voyage that in past years would have restored him.

---

* "You know, the President is a man of great vision—once things are explained to him," MacArthur is alleged to have told the newspaper correspondent Clark Lee. William Manchester, *American Caesar: Douglas MacArthur, 1880–1964* 370 (Boston: Little, Brown, 1978).

But the Bremerton speech sent shock waves through the country. Roosevelt had intended the speech to be an informal report to the American people on his travels together with some reassurances on the progress of the war in the Pacific. He had written it two days before delivery and had not bothered to polish it—a surprising lapse since the speech was to be broadcast nationally and would be his first opportunity to address the country since the Democratic convention. He spoke from the fantail of a destroyer, facing a brisk wind, standing on braces he had not worn in almost a year. The heavy rocking of the ship forced him to hold on to the lectern with both hands, making it difficult to turn the pages. All of this affected Roosevelt's delivery, which was rambling, halting, and indecisive.[106]

Ten minutes into the speech, the president experienced excruciating chest pains that extended to both shoulders. Despite the pain he gamely persevered with the speech, sweating profusely for the next fifteen minutes, until the discomfort subsided. When he finished speaking, he returned to the destroyer captain's cabin and collapsed into a chair. Dr. Bruenn cleared everyone out, administered an electrocardiogram, and took a white blood count, but found no abnormalities.[107]

Rosenman, listening to Roosevelt's speech over the radio, thought it was "a dismal failure." That, together with the president's gaunt appearance—he had lost nineteen pounds—caused many to write Roosevelt off. "It looks like the old master has lost his touch," *The Washington Post* concluded. "His campaigning days must be over. It's going to look mighty sad when he begins to trade punches with young Dewey."[108]

Roosevelt arrived back in Washington on August 15 and less than a month later left for Quebec, where he would meet again with Churchill and the Combined Chiefs of Staff (OCTAGON). Because postwar monetary issues were on the agenda, the president was accompanied by Secretary Morgenthau, and it was at Quebec that he and Churchill endorsed the Morgenthau Plan for the pastoralization of Germany. Churchill was initially aghast. "I am all for disarming Germany, but we ought not prevent her living decently. There are bonds between the working classes of all countries, and the English people will not stand for the policy you are advocating. . . . You cannot indict a whole nation."[109] But when Morgenthau agreed to write off Britain's Lend-Lease debt and proposed a $3 billion postwar loan for the British economy, Churchill relented. "When I have to choose between my people and the German people, I am going to choose my people," he told an incredulous Eden.[110]

The Morgenthau Plan had a short shelf life. Back in Washington the responsible cabinet officers heaped scorn on the proposal. "I have yet to meet a man who is not horrified at the 'Carthaginian' attitude of the Treasury," said Stimson. "It is Semitism gone wild for vengeance and will lay the seeds for another war in the next generation." In Stimson's view, the industrial capacity of the Ruhr and the Saar were essential for the recovery of Europe.[111] Hull told Roosevelt it would lead to last-ditch, bitter-end German resistance that would cost thousands of American lives.[112] When the Republicans appeared ready to make the Morgenthau Plan a campaign issue, FDR backed off. "Henry Morgenthau pulled a boner," he told Stimson on October 3. The president said he was frankly staggered by the plan to convert Germany into an agricultural and pastoral country and "had no idea how he could have initialed this."[113]

That Roosevelt did not remember may have been his way of dissociating from an unpopular position. It may also have been a sign of his flagging health. Churchill sought out Admiral McIntire at Quebec to inquire about FDR's wan appearance. McIntire assured him that the president was fine. "With all my heart I hope so," Churchill replied. "We cannot have anything happen to that man."[114] Lord Moran, for his part, wondered how far Roosevelt's health impaired his judgment. "You could have put your fist between his neck and his collar—and I said to myself then that men at his time of life do not go thin all of a sudden just for nothing."[115]

Harry Truman, who called at the White House for a symbolic picture-taking session with the president, shared Moran's worry. "You know, I am concerned about the president's health," he told his legislative assistant, Major Harry H. Vaughan. "I had no idea he was in such a feeble condition. In pouring cream in his tea, he got more cream in the saucer than he did in the cup. There doesn't seem to be any mental lapse, but physically he's just going to pieces. I'm very much concerned about him."[116]

Like an old fire horse responding to the station's alarm bell, Roosevelt rallied for the campaign. This was America's first wartime election since 1864, and, like Lincoln, FDR made the most of his role as commander in chief. While Dewey toured the country, racking up short-term gains with attacks on the "tired old men" who were running the government and outrageous charges of Communist influence (FDR had pardoned Earl Browder, leader of the American Communist Party), the president held his fire until September 23, when he kicked off the Democratic campaign with a speech to the Teamsters Union at the Statler Hotel in Washington, D.C. This would be FDR's first speech to the nation since the debacle at Bremerton, and the party leadership worried about the outcome. "Do you think Pa will put it over?" Anna whispered to Sam Rosenman. "It's the kind of speech which depends almost entirely on delivery. If the delivery isn't just right, it'll be an awful flop."[117]

Roosevelt not only rose to the occasion but gave what many believe to be the greatest speech of his political career. Mindful of his problems at Bremerton, the president delivered the speech seated and honed the text through dozens of drafts. He began with a humorous reference to his age: "Well, here we are together again—after four years—and what years they have been. You know, I am actually four years older, which is a fact that seems to annoy some people." The audience loved it. As they warmed to the president, Roosevelt proceeded with a voice that purred softly and then struck hard, taunting his opponents for their reactionary record and ridiculing Republicans for their quadrennial efforts to pose as friends of labor and the working class. "The whole purpose of Republican oratory these days seems to be to switch labels. The object is to persuade the American people that the Democratic party was responsible for the 1929 crash and the depression. . . . If I were a Republican leader speaking to a mixed audience, the last word in the whole dictionary that I would use is that word 'depression.' "[118]

Waves of thunderous applause cascaded through the Statler's giant ballroom. The outpouring of affection from the audience startled even those who had seen Roosevelt on the campaign trail in many past elections. "The Old Master still had it," a reporter from *Time* observed. "He was like a veteran virtuoso playing a piece he has loved for years, who fingers his way through it with a delicate fire, a perfection of timing and tone, and an assurance that no young player, no matter how gifted, can equal."[119]

The climax came when Roosevelt delivered his facetious rebuttal to Republican charges about Fala. "These Republican leaders have not been content with attacks on me, or my wife, or my sons. No, they now include my little dog, Fala. Well, of course, I don't resent attacks, and my family doesn't resent attacks, but Fala *does* resent them." The audience howled its delight, and Roosevelt continued with deadpan seriousness:

You know, Fala is Scotch, and being a Scottie, as soon as he learned that the Republican fiction writers in Congress and out had concocted a story that I had left him behind on an Aleutian Island and had sent a destroyer back to find him—at a cost to the taxpayers of two or three, or eight or twenty million dollars—his Scotch soul was furious. He has not been the same dog since. I am accustomed to hearing malicious falsehoods about myself . . . but I think I have a right to resent, to object to libelous statements about my dog.[120]

The Dewey campaign suffered a body blow from which it never recovered. "The campaign of 1944 was the easiest in which I ever participated," wrote Harry Truman afterward. "The Republican candidates never had a chance."[121] Thomas E. Dewey, a humorless, self-important young prosecutor propelled by his own ambition—the groom on the wedding cake, in Alice Longworth's dismissive phrase—was an easy man for Democrats to despise and for Roosevelt to hate. The only remaining hurdle to victory in November was the question of the president's health, and FDR chose to address it head-on. On Saturday, October 21, he undertook a grinding tour of New York City's four largest boroughs—Brooklyn, Queens, the Bronx, and Manhattan—riding in an open White House limousine. Roosevelt wanted to make a point, and the weather could not have been more opportune. It was forty degrees and raining heavily when he started out at Brooklyn Army Terminal, pouring when he addressed 10,000 spectators at Ebbets Field on behalf of Senator Robert Wagner, and coming down in bucketsful by the time he reached Times Square. Roosevelt was soaked almost as soon as he got under way, often riding bareheaded and without his cape, waving and flashing his famous smile for four hours as the procession wound its way fifty-one miles through the city. In 1944, 7 percent of American voters lived in New York City, and Roosevelt was seen by an estimated 3 million persons. Two and a half inches of rain fell on New York that day, the tail end of a hurricane lingering off the Atlantic coast, and Roosevelt's bravura performance temporarily stilled speculation that his health was not up to the demands of another four years in the White House.

That evening, after resting at ER's Washington Square apartment (his first visit there), Roosevelt gave a powerful internationalist address to the two thousand members of the Foreign Policy Association at the Waldorf-Astoria. "Peace, like war," said the president, "can succeed only when there is a will to enforce it, and where there is available power to enforce it. The Council of the

United Nations must have the power to act quickly and decisively to keep the peace by force if necessary."[122]

In late October MacArthur landed in the Philippines; the Navy sent most of what remained of the Japanese fleet to the bottom of the Pacific in the Battle of Leyte Gulf (four carriers, three battleships, ten cruisers, and nine destroyers); and the campaign turned into a rerun of 1864 after Sherman captured Atlanta. Roosevelt repeated his New York appearance in Philadelphia on October 27, riding another four hours in an open car despite intermittent rain and near-freezing temperatures. In Chicago he spoke to the largest crowd in the city's history, 125,000 persons shoehorned into Soldier Field plus another 150,000 outside, and closed out the campaign with a swing through New England and a final address to a packed house at Fenway Park, where Frank Sinatra sang the national anthem. "Religious intolerance, social intolerance, and political intolerance have no place in American life," said Roosevelt in Boston.

> I reminded a genealogical society—I think they are called 'ancestor worshippers'*—I said to them that they knew that all our people—except the pure-blooded Indians—are immigrants or descendants of immigrants, including even those who came over here on the Mayflower. . . .
> It is our duty to make sure that, big as our country is, there is no room in it for racial or religious intolerance—and that there is no room for snobbery.[123]

When the campaign ended, Dr. Bruenn examined the president and was pleasantly surprised. Roosevelt, he said, "really enjoyed the 'hustings' and his B[lood] P[ressure] levels, if anything, were lower than before. He is eating somewhat better, and despite prolonged periods of exposure, he has not contracted any upper respiratory infections. The patient appears to be well stabilized on his digitalis regime."[124]

As was his habit, FDR awaited the returns on election night in the dining room at Hyde Park—AP and UP news tickers in the corner and the radio on. He tabulated the results on long tally sheets, placing a call to Democratic Na-

---

* The reference is to FDR's 1937 speech to the Daughters of the American Revolution. 5 *Public Papers and Addresses of Franklin D. Roosevelt* 214–217, Samuel I. Rosenman, ed. (New York: Macmillian, 1939).

tional Headquarters at the Biltmore from time to time, and by 10 P.M. the
trend was clear. The president put down his pencil and turned to Admiral
Leahy. "It's all over, Bill. What's the use of putting down the figures."[125] Roosevelt defeated Dewey 25.6 million to 22 million and carried thirty-six states
with 432 electoral votes. Dewey took twelve states with 99 electoral votes. He
carried Wisconsin, Wyoming, and Ohio, which Willkie had not, but lost
Michigan, which returned to the Democratic column. In the House, the Democrats gained 24 seats, giving them a comfortable 242–190 majority, and lost 2
in the Senate, where they retained control 56–38. The icing on the cake for
Roosevelt was the defeat of his neighbor and bitter political opponent Hamilton Fish in New York's Twenty-ninth Congressional District, and the isolationist Senator Gerald P. Nye in North Dakota.[126]

Roosevelt's health took a decided downturn after the election. His appetite
was poor, and he lost more weight. Dr. Bruenn reported that his blood pressure climbed to 260/150, although an electrocardiogram showed no change
and there was no evidence of digitalis toxicity.[127] After a two-hour cabinet
meeting on January 19, Frances Perkins noted the president's fatigue and
thought he had the pallor of a man who had long been ill. "He looked like an
invalid who had been allowed to see guests for the first time and the guests had
stayed too long."[128]

Though his health was obviously failing, Roosevelt's spirit appeared un-
daunted. He resumed his twice-weekly press conferences in the Oval Office,
and his bantering with newsmen continued unabated. Asked by Tom Reynolds
of the *Chicago Sun* to reflect on his presidential years, FDR replied, "The first
twelve were the hardest." That moved May Craig to inquire whether "the word
first" had any significance.[129]

Inauguration day, Saturday, January 20, 1945, dawned bitterly cold, an inch
of snow blanketing the capital. Because of the war Roosevelt dispensed with
the traditional parade ("Who's going to march?"), and shifted the scene from
the Capitol steps to the south portico of the White House. Leaning once again
on the arm of his son James, the president, hatless and coatless, made his way
laboriously to the lectern, repeated the oath after Chief Justice Harlan Stone,
and delivered a brief, five-hundred-word address before several thousand people assembled in the snow. This was the first time since Bremerton that Roosevelt had worn his leg braces and the last time he would deliver a speech
standing. "We have learned that we cannot live alone at peace, that our own

well-being is dependent on the well-being of other Nations far away. We have learned to be citizens of the world. We have learned, as Emerson said, 'The only way to have a friend is to be one.' "[130]

Rosenman recalled the simple majesty of the scene.[131] John Gunther called it something from Brueghel, "with sharply colored figures etched on the loose snow, the throng of tall men in dark clothes above, and the fluid, informal movement of the listeners."[132] Roosevelt was chilled to the bone and afterward felt the same kind of angina attack he had experienced at San Diego. He rested briefly in the Green Room with his son James before heading into the reception that had been laid on in the State Dining Room. "Jimmy, I can't take this unless you give me a stiff drink. You'd better make it straight." His son brought him half a tumbler of scotch, which Roosevelt downed virtually in one gulp, after which he went off to the reception.[133] Dr. Bruenn, evidently unaware of the president's seizure, reported that Roosevelt seemed in excellent spirits.[134] The New York Times said, "the President appears in good shape to carry on his job" and noted that "he looks as well as he did several years ago."[135]

Others who had not seen Roosevelt recently were shocked by his appearance. Gunther, who attended the ceremony with Orson Welles and Mark Van Doren, said he was terrified. "I felt certain he was going to die. All the light had gone out under the skin. It was like a parchment shade on a bulb that had been dimmed."[136] Mrs. Woodrow Wilson whispered to Frances Perkins, "He looks exactly as my husband did when he went into his decline."[137]

Two days after the inauguration Roosevelt departed for Norfolk, Virginia, where he boarded the cruiser *Quincy* (sister ship of the *Baltimore*), bound for the Mediterranean island of Malta. There he rendezvoused with Churchill before proceeding seven hours by air to Yalta, a Soviet resort town on the Black Sea, where Stalin waited. The meeting of the Big Three was intended to review current military matters and reach agreement on the structure of the postwar world. Roosevelt's primary concern was not to keep the Soviets out of Eastern Europe, where the presence of the Red Army was an accomplished fact, but to secure early Russian entry in the war against Japan. The atomic bomb had yet to be tested, and whether it would be available was problematic. If the Japanese home islands had to be invaded, the Joint Chiefs estimated the fighting would continue through 1946 and cost perhaps a million American casualties.[138]

The Crimea conference (ARGONAUT) convened in the Livadiya Palace, the vacation residence of the Romanovs, on February 4, 1945. Roosevelt was billeted in the czar's bedroom suite; Marshall and King in the quarters of the czarina. Sergo Beria was on hand once more, this time armed with newly developed directional microphones that could pick up conversations two hundred yards away.[139] Churchill thought Roosevelt looked frail and ill. Stalin told the Politburo, "Let's hope nothing happens to him." Lord Moran assumed that the president was suffering from an advanced case of arterial sclerosis. "I give him only six months to live."[140]

On the other hand, the American delegation saw no problem. Edward R. Stettinius, who had succeeded Hull as secretary of state in December, thought Roosevelt had recovered significantly since the inauguration and appeared to be "cheerful, calm, and quite rested."[141] Leahy felt the president conducted the meetings with great skill. "His personality dominated the discussions. He looked fatigued when we left, but so did we all."[142] Charles Bohlen, again serving as FDR's translator, saw no loss in the president's acumen at Yalta: "While his physical state was not up to normal, his mental and psychological state was certainly not affected. Our leader was ill, but he was effective."[143] Harriman said Roosevelt carried on the negotiations "with his usual skill and perception."[144] Dr. Bruenn, who was best placed to observe, told Anna the president had a "serious ticker situation" but did not appear overly concerned.[145] In his notes Bruenn recorded that throughout the conference, with one exception, Roosevelt's blood pressure and electrocardiogram remained unchanged.* "His mood was excellent. His appetite was excellent, and he appeared to enjoy Russian food and cooking."[146]

The Big Three met eight times in eight days, usually for three to four hours. As had become customary, FDR presided. Additional discussions took place over lunch and dinner. The conference began with a review of the military situation. On the eastern front, Red Army troops had taken Warsaw, enveloped Budapest, driven the Germans out of Yugoslavia, occupied East Prussia, and were poised on the Oder, fifty miles from Berlin. In the West, the Allies had recovered from the Battle of the Bulge, expelled Nazi forces from Belgium,

---

* The exception came after a particularly stressful session on February 8 when Poland was discussed. Bruenn reported that the president suffered *pulsus alternans* (alternating strong and weak beats) that night but soon recovered. Howard G. Bruenn, "Clinical Notes on the Illness and Death of President Franklin D. Roosevelt," 72 *Annals of Internal Medicine* 589 (1970). Also see Jay Kenneth Herman, "The President's Cardiologist," 82 *Navy Medicine* 6–13 (1990).

cracked the Siegfried Line, and were closing on the Rhine. Slowly the war in Europe was winding down.

The conference reached quick agreement on the occupation of Germany. The country would not be dismembered (as had been suggested at Teheran), and France would be added as an occupying power. The divisive issue of reparations was papered over. It was agreed to take the figure of $20 billion as a basis of discussion, with the Russians entitled to 50 percent, but the matter was referred to a tripartite commission for final action. Arrangements for the trial of major war criminals was handed off to the three foreign ministers. In a major breakthrough, Stalin accepted FDR's proposal for voting procedures on the United Nations Security Council.[147] Each member of the Council would have one vote, but all major decisions would require the unanimous agreement of the permanent members. The Soviets also agreed to Roosevelt's suggestion that a conference to organize the United Nations convene shortly in San Francisco.

The issue of postwar Poland proved the most contentious, although, as Harriman observed, "events were in the saddle." The Red Army occupied the entire country and had already installed a pro-Soviet government in Warsaw. "It would have taken a great deal more leverage than Roosevelt and Churchill in fact possessed," Harriman observed, "in order to alter the situation fundamentally."[148] Stalin wanted a Communist Poland for security reasons. "It was a matter of life and death."[149] Roosevelt wanted face-saving cover to protect his standing among Polish Americans. The result was the Declaration on Liberated Europe. It pledged free elections in liberated countries and governments that were "broadly representative of all democratic elements."[150] The formula was so elastic, Leahy complained to FDR, that "the Russians can stretch it all the way from Yalta to Washington without ever technically breaking it."

"I know, Bill—I know it," Roosevelt replied. "But it's the best I can do for Poland at this time."[151] And there is no doubt he was correct. When Yalta convened, the war had progressed to such a point that political decisions could do little more than ratify military reality.[152]

With the Polish issue in place, Roosevelt met privately with Stalin to arrange Russia's entry into the war against Japan. Agreement came quickly. Stalin pledged to move against the Japanese within two or three months of Germany's surrender. For his part, Roosevelt agreed to recognize the status quo in Soviet-controlled Outer Mongolia; return the southern portion of

Sakhalin Island to the Soviet Union (Japan had acquired it in the 1904 Russo-Japanese War); also return the Kurile Islands (ceded to Japan in 1875); and lease Port Arthur to the Soviets as a naval base. Dairen would become a free port, and the Soviet lease on Manchurian railroads would be revived.[153] Roosevelt made these commitments without consulting the Chinese, but his overriding concern was to secure quick Soviet participation in the war against Japan, with which, incidentally, Russia had a nonaggression pact. FDR saw Stalin's agreement as a major victory. "This makes the trip worthwhile," Leahy was quoted as saying.[154]

The Americans and British left Yalta feeling they had done well. Stalin had wanted a firm commitment on German reparations and had not gotten it. The Soviets had wanted to exclude France from the control machinery in postwar Germany, but France had been included. They had wanted to exclude governments in exile from Eastern Europe, but the door had been left open. The framework for the United Nations was in place, and Russia had agreed to join the war against Japan. Even on Poland, which was overrun by the Red Army, the agreement on free elections represented a significant Soviet concession.[155] Churchill wrote Clementine, "We have covered a great deal of ground and I am very pleased with the decisions we have gained."[156] Roosevelt advised Daisy Suckley that the conference "turned out better than he dared hope for." Later he told Adolf Berle, "I didn't say the result was good. I said it was the best I could do."[157]

On March 1, 1945, Roosevelt made a dramatic appearance before a joint session of Congress. The House chamber was packed to overflowing as the president made his way down the aisle in his wheelchair, the simple Hyde Park kitchen chair with no arms that he had designed two decades earlier. This was the first time FDR had not walked to the well of the House on the arm of an aide or associate, and he was greeted with a thunderous ovation. "I hope you will pardon me for this unusual posture of sitting down during the presentation, but I know that you will realize that it makes it a lot easier for me not to have to carry about ten pounds of steel around on the bottom of my legs."[158] Another prolonged ovation.

"It was the first reference he had ever made to his incapacity," Frances Perkins recalled. "He did it with such a casual, debonair manner, without self-pity or strain that the episode lost any grim quality and left everybody quite comfortable." Perkins thought Roosevelt had recovered substantially from his earlier exhaustion. "His face was gay, his eyes were bright, his skin was a good color again. His speech was good. His delivery and appearance were those of a man in good health."[159]

The president relished the occasion. "It has been a long journey. I hope you will also agree that it has been a fruitful one. I returned from the trip refreshed and inspired. The Roosevelts are not, as you may suspect, averse to travel. [Howls of laughter.] We seem to thrive on it." [Laughter and sustained applause.]

Roosevelt spoke for almost an hour. At times he rambled, but his message was clear:

The Crimea Conference was a successful effort by the three leading Nations to find a common ground for peace. It ought to spell the end of the system of unilateral action, the exclusive alliances , , . the balances of power, and all other expedients that have been tried for centuries—and have always failed.

    This time we are not making the mistake of waiting until the end of the war to set up the machinery of peace. This time, as we fight together to win the war finally, we work together to keep it from happening again.[160]

Roosevelt's address to Congress was his last major public appearance. On Saint Patrick's Day he and Eleanor celebrated their fortieth wedding anniversary with a small formal dinner in the State Dining Room. The guests included Crown Princess Juliana of the Netherlands, Justice and Mrs. Robert Jackson, and the Nelson Rockefellers. "Thus another milestone is passed in the career of an extraordinary man and wife," reported White House aide William Hassett.[161]

Roosevelt had exerted himself to the utmost during the campaign, the trip to Yalta, and his address to the joint session. His health was spent. And he had resumed a taxing schedule. According to Dr. Bruenn, Roosevelt was again working too hard, seeing too many people, and working too late in the evenings. "His appetite had become poor, and although he had not been weighed, it appeared that he had lost more weight. He complained of not being able to taste his food."[162] On Saturday, March 24, the president and Eleanor left for several days' rest at Hyde Park. ER noticed that for the first time

Franklin did not wish to drive himself. He let her drive, and he let her mix the drinks before dinner, something that ordinarily would have been inconceivable.[163]

Roosevelt returned to Washington briefly on March 29, before leaving for Warm Springs that evening. Grace Tully, who saw FDR upon his arrival, was distressed at his appearance. "Did you get any rest at Hyde Park, Mr. President?" she asked.

"Yes child, but not nearly enough. I shall be glad to get down South."[164]

Roosevelt's last appointment in the White House was with General Lucius D. Clay, who had just been named to head the military government in Germany. Clay was then deputy director of war mobilization, and he was escorted into the Oval Office by James Byrnes. FDR reminisced about his boyhood in Germany and stressed the need for a giant power development in Central Europe, something along the line of the TVA. He never gave Clay a chance to get a word in. "Two or three times Steve Early tried to break it up," Clay recalled, "but without success. Finally we left, and when we got out, Mr. Byrnes sort of teasingly said, 'Lucius, you didn't answer any questions. You didn't say very much.'

"I said, 'No, I didn't. The President didn't ask me any questions, but I am glad that he didn't. Because I was so shocked watching him that I don't think I could have made a sensible reply. We've been talking to a dying man.' "[165]

Roosevelt arrived in Warm Springs in the early afternoon of March 30, 1945. Mike Reilly of the Secret Service found it difficult to transfer the president to his car—"he was absolutely dead weight"—but once seated behind the wheel FDR appeared to revive and drove from the station to the Little White House joking with his cousins Laura Delano and Daisy Suckley.[166]

"He is steadily losing weight," William Hassett wrote in his diary. "Told me he has lost 25 pounds—no strength—no appetite—tires so easily. . . . The old zest was going." That evening Hassett told Dr. Bruenn, "He is slipping away from us and no earthly power can keep him here." Bruenn admitted the president was in a precarious condition but thought the situation was not hopeless. He told Hassett that Roosevelt could be saved "if measures were adopted to rescue him from certain mental strains and emotional influences." Hassett did not believe Bruenn's conditions could be met. "This confirmed my conviction that the Boss is leaving us."[167]

The weather in Warm Springs was ideal, and Roosevelt seemed to recover.

"Within a week," Bruenn recorded, "there was a decided and obvious improvement in his appearance and sense of well-being. He had begun to eat with appetite, rested beautifully, and was in excellent spirits. He began to go out every afternoon for short motor trips, which he clearly enjoyed. The physical examination was unchanged except for the blood pressure, the level of which had become extremely wide, ranging from 170/88 to 240/130."[168]

On one afternoon outing Roosevelt encountered Merriman Smith, the White House pool reporter from United Press, riding a horse he had hired at the village drugstore. "As I reined in the horse," Smith remembered, the president "bowed majestically to me. His voice was wonderful and resonant. It sounded like the Roosevelt of old. In tones that must have been audible blocks away, FDR hailed me with 'Heigh Ho, Silver!.' "[169]

On Monday, April 9, Lucy Rutherfurd arrived from Aiken, South Carolina, with her friend the society portraitist Elizabeth Shoumatoff, whom she had commissioned to paint a portrait of the president. Doris Kearns Goodwin reports that presidential phone logs reveal that in the days leading up to her visit, FDR called Lucy almost daily from Warm Springs.[170] Dinner that evening was festive. Shoumatoff reported that the president was "full of jokes" and seemed constantly to address himself to Lucy in a wide-ranging conversation that moved from Churchill to Stalin to food.[171]

On April 11 Roosevelt worked on his Jefferson Day address for the Democratic faithful. He penned the peroration in his own hand:

The only limit to our realization of tomorrow will be our doubts of today. Let us move forward with strong and active faith.[172]

That evening Henry Morgenthau came to dinner. He was shocked at the president's appearance. "I found he had aged terrifically and looked very haggard. His hands shook so that he started to knock over the glasses. I had to hold each glass as he poured out the cocktail. . . . I found his memory bad and he was constantly confusing names. I have never seen him have so much difficulty transferring himself from his wheelchair to a regular chair, and I was in agony watching him."[173]

The following day, Thursday, April 12, 1945, Roosevelt sat in the living room of the Little White House while Elizabeth Shoumatoff painted. She was struck how much better the president looked. The "gray look" had disappeared, and he had "exceptionally good color." Later Shoumatoff learned from doctors that Roosevelt's flushed appearance was a warning sign of an approaching cerebral hemorrhage.[174]

Shortly before one o'clock the butler came in to set the table for lunch. FDR glanced at his watch and said, "We have fifteen minutes more to work." Then suddenly, he put his hand to his head in a quick jerky manner. "I have a terrific pain in the back of my head," he said.[175] Roosevelt slumped forward and collapsed. He never regained consciousness. At 3:35 P.M. Dr. Bruenn pronounced the president dead.

The world mourned. "I was overpowered by a sense of deep and irrefutable loss," wrote Churchill.[176] In Moscow, Averell Harriman drove to the Kremlin to inform Stalin. The Soviet leader was "deeply distressed" and held Harriman's hand for perhaps thirty seconds before asking him to sit down. "President Roosevelt has died but his cause must live on," he told Harriman and then agreed to send Molotov to represent the Soviet Union at the upcoming United Nations conference in San Francisco.[177] Senator Robert Taft, long in opposition, captured the moment. "The President's death," he said, "removed the greatest figure of our time at the very climax of his career, and shocks the world to which his words and actions were more important than those of any other man. He dies a hero of the war, for he literally worked himself to death in the service of the American people."[178]

On a soggy country road behind enemy lines near Pffeffenhausen, Germany, a band of American prisoners of war was being marched to a new enclosure, presumably to prevent their liberation by advancing Allied forces. From the German guards they learned that President Roosevelt was dead. At noon the ranking American officer climbed a nearby hill, accompanied by a bugler. He turned and addressed his fellow prisoners: "I have been told that President Roosevelt died yesterday, April the 12th. The sergeant will now play *Taps*, then we will have a moment of silence."

"It was the saddest *Taps* I had ever heard," remembered Bill Livingstone, who had been captured by the Germans after bailing out of his damaged B-17 in 1944. "Tears ran down my face, as they did on the faces of the rest of the group. When the sergeant finished playing, we all stood silently, with our heads bowed. Then we marched on."[179]

Notes

THE INITIAL EPIGRAPH is from Mario Cuomo's keynote address to the Democratic National Convention in 1984. The Preface is written without endnotes. The quotations appear elsewhere in the text and are fully cited at that point. I am indebted to Michael Barone for the final observation concerning FDR.

ONE | Heritage

The epigraph is from Michael Teague, *Mrs. L: Conversations with Alice Roosevelt Longworth* 18–19 (New York: Doubleday, 1981). As governor and later as president, Franklin enjoyed teasing his mother about the family's forebears. According to FDR's son James, when important people were dining at Hyde Park, the president would often hint that "old Claes left Holland because he was a horse thief or worse . . . or would take off on the subject of the Delanos who went into the China trade, implying that they smuggled everything from opium to immigrants. Sometimes he sounded as if he were taking his text, chapter and verse, from the columnist Westbrook Pegler." James Roosevelt and Sidney Shalett, *Affectionately, F.D.R.* 18 (New York: Harcourt, Brace, 1959).

1. The most accessible sources for the history of the Roosevelt family are Kenneth S. Davis, *FDR: The Beckoning of Destiny, 1882–1928* 17–26 (New York: Putnam, 1972); Frank Freidel, *Franklin D. Roosevelt: The Apprenticeship* 5–9 (Boston: Little, Brown, 1952); Geoffrey C. Ward, *Before the Trumpet: Young Franklin Roosevelt, 1882–1905* 13–60 (New York: Harper & Row, 1985). Also see Karl Schriftgiesser, *The Amazing Roosevelt Family: 1613–1942* (New York: W. Funk, 1942); Nathan Miller, *The Roosevelt Chronicles* (New York: Doubleday, 1979); Alvin Page Johnson, *Franklin D. Roosevelt's Colonial Ancestors* (Boston: Lothrop, Lee & Shepard, 1933); Allen Churchill, *The Roosevelts: American Aristocrats* (New York: Harper & Row, 1965); Bellamy Partridge, *The Roosevelt Family in America* (New York: Hillman-Curl, 1936). The *Herald Tribune* quotation is by Gerald W. Johnson. A more disparaging observation is by Mrs. Schuyler van Rensselaer, who in her *History of New York in the Seventeenth Century* noted that "at no pre-Revolutionary period was the Roosevelt family conspicuous nor did any member of it attain distinction."

2. Theodore Roosevelt, *Autobiography* 1 (New York: Macmillan, 1913). TR's emphasis.

3. Clara and Hardy Steeholm, *The House at Hyde Park* 38–39 (New York: Viking, 1950).

4. The quotation is from Dr. Isaac's brother-in-law, William Henry Aspinwall, reported in Ward, *Before the Trumpet* 21. Also see Steeholm, *House at Hyde Park* 46.

5. Quoted in Ted Morgan, *FDR: A Biography* 27 (New York: Simon & Schuster, 1985).

6. Steeholm, *House at Hyde Park* 40. John Aspinwall Roosevelt, Dr. Isaac's second and last child, was born in 1840.

7. 3 *FDR: His Personal Letters* 1224, Elliott Roosevelt, ed. (New York: Duell, Sloan and Pearce, 1950). Like many family stories told by FDR, the Garibaldi tale was artfully embellished. Roosevelt records show that James was in Naples in March 1849, but Garibaldi was encamped at the time at Rieti, some forty miles northeast of Rome. The siege of Naples did not begin until 1860. See Christopher Hibbert, *Garibaldi and His Enemies* 275–293 (Boston: Little, Brown, 1966).

8. For Silliman's eminence at the New York bar, see 6 *National Cyclopedia of American Biography* 54–55 (New York: J. T. White & Co., 1879).

9. Steeholm, *House at Hyde Park* 54–55.

10. Anna "Bamie" Roosevelt's reminiscences, quoted in David McCullough, *Mornings on Horseback* 57 (New York: Simon & Schuster, 1981). Also see Edmund Morris, *The Rise of Theodore Roosevelt* 8–10 (New York: Coward, McCann & Geoghegan, 1979). Theodore, Sr., did not serve in the war in deference to his wife, Mittie Bulloch, the daughter of a prominent Georgia family. Indeed, Mittie's brother, James Dunwody Bulloch, was the principal Confederate agent in London, and it was he who arranged for construction of the *Alabama* and other rebel raiders. At the same time, William Henry Aspinwall, Isaac Roosevelt's brother-in-law, was Lincoln's confidential agent in the British capital.

    I am grateful to Professor John Y. Simon, editor of the *Grant Papers,* for alerting me that it was James Roosevelt who first notified the U.S. government of James Bullock's presence in London to arrange for construction of the *Alabama.* On July 10, 1861, Hiram Barney, the collector of customs in New York, advised Secretary of State William Henry Seward, "These vessels will sail from Liverpool under the flag of the Confederacy and will operate upon our merchantmen and navy ships. . . . Of course I know not the grounds of this apprehension, but give it on Mr. Roosevelt's authority exclusively. Mr. Roosevelt is an ardent Union man and would feel bound to denounce a brother probably to save the government, but he does not wish his name used if it can be avoided." 2 *Official Records of the War of the Rebellion* (Series 2) 18. James Bullock was excluded from the general amnesty President Johnson proclaimed at the end of war and lived out his life in Liverpool. He occasionally visited the United States under an assumed name and once asked James Roosevelt to dine with him. The president's father refused, horrified at the thought of dining with a traitor. 2 *Roosevelt Letters* 23n.

11. McClellan graduated from West Point in 1845 and quickly established a reputation as a brilliant engineer and mapmaker. He resigned from the army in 1855 to

become superintendent of the Illinois Central. See Stephen W. Sears, *George B. McClellan: The Young Napoleon* 64–70, 388–390 (New York: Ticknor & Fields, 1988).

12. During his wedding trip abroad in 1853, James briefly worked as Buchanan's private secretary. Buchanan was then American minister in London. He suddenly found himself shorthanded and asked James to pitch in until additional help arrived. James admired Buchanan personally, which may have facilitated his switch to the Democrats. For FDR's version of the episode, see President's Personal File 3012, Franklin D. Roosevelt Library (FDRL).

13. James Roosevelt to John Roosevelt, December 23, 1865, in John Aspinwall Roosevelt's Collection of Roosevelt Family Papers, FDRL.

14. For FDR's notes on Leland Stanford's purchase of Gloster, see his "History of the President's Estate," FDRL.

15. John Gunther, *Roosevelt in Retrospect* 172 (New York: Harper & Brothers, 1950).

16. As quoted in Ward, *Before the Trumpet* 52. James's marriage to Rebecca is lovingly described in Aileen Sutherland Collins's *Rebecca Howland & James Roosevelt: A Story of Cousins*, based on Rebecca's diary, (Virginia Beach, Va.: Parsons Press, 2005).

17. Ibid. 55.

18. With respect to marrying advantageously, the Roosevelts were not unlike the Hapsburgs, of whom it was said:

> *Bella gerant alii! Tu, felix Austria, nube,*
> *Nam quae Mars aliis dat tibi regna Venus.*
> *(Let others make war. Thou, happy Austria, marry,*
> *for Venus gives thee those realms which on others Mars bestows.)*

19. Dollar conversions are from Robert G. Sahr, "Inflation Conversion Factors for Years 1700 to Estimated 2012," Political Science Department, Oregon State University, 2002.

20. Ward, *Before the Trumpet* 59–60, 350–351. Eleanor Roosevelt called Bamie "one of the most interesting women I have ever known. [She] had a mind that worked as a very able man's mind works. She was full of animation, was always the center of any group she was with." Eleanor Roosevelt, *This Is My Story* 57–58 (New York: Harper & Brothers, 1937).

21. Davis, *Beckoning Destiny* 34. Also see Peter Collier with David Horowitz, *The Roosevelts: An American Saga* 53–54 (New York: Simon & Schuster, 1994).

22. "The Delanos," said Eleanor, "were the first people I met who were able to do what they wanted to do without wondering where to obtain the money." *Autobiography of Eleanor Roosevelt* 47 (New York: Harper & Brothers, 1961).

23. Rita Halle Kleeman, *Gracious Lady* 5–6 (New York: D. Appleton–Century, 1935).

24. Daniel W. Delano, Jr., *Franklin Roosevelt and the Delano Influence* 31–33 (Pittsburgh: J. S. Nudi Publications, 1946).

25. Steeholm, *House at Hyde Park* 13; Freidel, *Apprenticeship* 13–14; James MacGregor Burns and Susan Dunn, *The Three Roosevelts* 19 (New York: Grove Press, 2001). Warren Delano's million-dollar fortune would translate into roughly $24 million in 2006. Perhaps a more accurate gauge would be that when John Jacob Astor, the nation's first millionaire, died in 1848 he left an estate valued at somewhat less than $20 million: a sum "as incomprehensible as infinity," according to one obituary writer. Ward, *Before the Trumpet* 130.

26. Colonnade Row was designed in the 1830s by Ithiel Town and Alexander Jackson Davis, noted Greek Revival architects whose work included the New York Customs House and state capitols in Connecticut, Indiana, North Carolina, and Ohio.

27. Within the family, Sara was called "Sallie" to distinguish her from Aunt Sarah, Warren's sister. For simplicity, I have referred to the president's mother as "Sara" throughout.

28. Downing's *Treatise on the Theory and Practice of Landscape Gardening Adapted to North America,* published in 1840, is an American classic. Also see his *The Architecture of Country Houses* (New York: D. Appleton, 1850).

29. Quoted in Kleeman, *Gracious Lady* 35.

30. For an extended treatment of Chinese complicity in the opium trade, see William Travis Hanes and Frank Sanello, *The Opium Wars: The Addiction of One Empire and the Corruption of Another* 42–49 (Naperville, Ill.: Sourcebooks, 2002). Also see John King Fairbank, *Trade and Diplomacy on the China Coast* 65–68 (Stanford, Calif.: Stanford University Press, 1969); William O. Walker III, *Opium and Foreign Policy* 4–14 (Chapel Hill: University of North Carolina Press, 1991); David Edward Owen, *British Opium Policy in China and India* 204 ff. (New Haven, Conn.: Yale University Press, 1934).

31. Warren's letter was written from Canton on April 11, 1839, but the sentiments expressed apply *a fortiori* to his stint in Hong Kong in the 1860s. Warren noted that if the Chinese authorities disapproved of the opium trade, they could easily extinguish it. Quoted in Frederic D. Grant, Jr., "Edward Delano and Warren Delano II: Case Studies in American China Trader Attitudes Toward the Chinese, 1834–1844" (honors thesis, Bates College, 1976) 183–185, 260–261. Also see the lengthy notation concerning Warren Delano and the opium trade in Ward, *Before the Trumpet* 87–88n as well as Daniel Delano, *Franklin Roosevelt and the Delano Influence* 163, which frankly acknowledges, "Warren was now engaged in the opium trade and it paid large and handsome returns." For additional background, see Jacques M. Downs, "American Merchants and the China Opium Trade, 1800–1840," 42 *Business History Review* 418–442 (1968), and the sources citied therein.

32. Quoted in Ward, *Before the Trumpet* 90.

33. R.J.C. Butow, "A Notable Passage to China: Myth and Memory in FDR's Family History," *Prologue,* Fall 1999, 159–160. Also see Kleeman, *Gracious Lady* 43–60.

34. FDR to Felix Frankfurter, April 18, 1942, in *Roosevelt and Frankfurter: Their Correspondence* 656, Max Freedman, ed. (Boston: Little, Brown, 1967).

35. Quoted in Ward, *Before the Trumpet* 95.
36. Kleeman, *Gracious Lady* 65.
37. Suzannah Lessard, *The Architect of Desire: Beauty and Danger in the Stanford White Family* 203 (New York: Dial Press, 1996).
38. Quoted in Steeholm, *House at Hyde Park* 36. Also see Davis, *Beckoning Destiny* 35.
39. Quoted in Kleeman, *Gracious Lady* 111.

TWO | My Son Franklin

The epigraph is from Sara (Mrs. James) Roosevelt, *My Boy Franklin* 7 (New York: Ray Long and Richard R. Smith, 1933).

1. James's handwritten diary entry is displayed in the museum at the Franklin D. Roosevelt Library.
2. The conflict between Sara and James is described in James Roosevelt and Sidney Shalett, *Affectionately, F.D.R.* 34 (New York: Harcourt, Brace, 1959).
3. Warren Delano's comments are from letters to his son Warren III, in the Delano Family Papers, FDRL.
4. Sara Roosevelt diary, March 19, 1882, FDRL. A facsimile of Sara's entry is reproduced in Rita Halle Kleeman, *Gracious Lady* 129 (New York: D. Appleton–Century, 1935).
5. Warren Delano to Warren Delano III, FDRL.
6. Bureau of the Census, U.S. Department of Commerce, *The Statistical History of the United States from Colonial Times to the Present* 7, 23, 57 (Stamford, Conn.: Fairfield Publishers, 1965); B. R. Mitchell, *European Historical Statistics, 1750–1970* 85, 89 (New York: Columbia University Press, 1975).
7. GDP (in millions of 1990 Geary-Khamis dollars):

	1870	1882
France	71,419	89,167
Germany	44,101	55,126
United Kingdom	95,651	122,459
United States	98,418	177,153

   Source: Angus Maddison, *Monitoring the World Economy, 1820–1992* 180, 182 (Paris: Organization for Economic Co-operation and Development, 1995).

8. *Statistical History of the United States* 207, 212, 369, 416–417.
9. Franklin D. Roosevelt, untitled, undated reminiscences dictated at the White House, FDRL.
10. SDR, *My Boy Franklin* 44–46.
11. Mittie Roosevelt to Elliott Roosevelt, June 7, 1882, Eleanor Roosevelt Papers, FDRL. Mittie's emphasis.

12. Rita Halle Kleeman, untitled notes, FDRL.

13. Sara was an indefatigable journal keeper and recorded daily events at Algonac and Springwood with clipped precision. This was a trait bred into the Delanos, who seemed to believe everything that happened to them was noteworthy. Yet for some reason Sara destroyed her journals for the years 1884 to 1887. No one knows why. Various authors suggest that evidence of marital stress might have found its way into the diaries and Sara chose to obliterate it. See Geoffrey C. Ward, *Before the Trumpet* 124–125 (New York: Harper & Row, 1985); also see Nona Ferdon, "Franklin D. Roosevelt: A Psychological Interpretation of His Childhood and Youth" (Ph.D. thesis, University of Hawaii, 1971).

14. SDR, *My Boy Franklin* 6.

15. FDR to Jeanne Rosat-Sandoz, March 31, 1933, FDRL.

16. FDR to SDR, 1888. 1 *The Roosevelt Letters: Being the Personal Correspondence of Franklin Delano Roosevelt* 30, Elliott Roosevelt, ed. (London: George G. Harrap & Co., 1949). A facsimile copy of FDR's letter is reproduced between pages 128 and 129.

17. SDR, *My Boy Franklin* 33.

18. Ibid. 20–21. The president's son Elliott wrote, "In some sense of the word, [FDR] had no father, only a man old enough to be his grandfather, who, no matter how hard he tried, could not keep up with his growing son." Elliott Roosevelt and James Brough, *An Untold Story: The Roosevelts of Hyde Park* 35 (New York: G. P. Putnam's Sons, 1973).

19. FDR to JR, June 7, 1890. 1 *Roosevelt Letters* 32.

20. Ward, *Before the Trumpet* 140.

21. Kleeman, *Gracious Lady* 151–152. *Germanic* was not only the newest but the fastest ship on the North Atlantic run and won the Blue Riband for record transatlantic crossings three times. In February 1899 the vessel sank in New York harbor, covered with 1,800 tons of ice accumulated during a severe North Atlantic storm. She was raised and refitted, sailed under a number of flags, and after seventy-five years of service was scrapped at Messina, Sicily, in October 1950.

22. Kleeman, *Gracious Lady* 144.

23. Ibid. 146.

24. SDR, *My Boy Franklin* 4.

25. Kleeman, *Gracious Lady* 138.

26. *The Philadelphia Record,* April 6, 1913.

27. SDR, *My Boy Franklin* 7. "His father felt that an only son should not choose a profession which would take him so much away from home," said Eleanor. *Autobiography* 47 (New York: Harper & Brothers, 1961).

28. Ernest K. Lindley, *Franklin D. Roosevelt: A Career in Progressive Democracy* 47 (Indianapolis: Bobbs-Merrill, 1931).

29. Admiral Ross T. McIntire, *White House Physician* 78–79 (New York: G. P. Putnam's Sons, 1946). At his death, Roosevelt's stamp collection was appraised at

$79,267. Shortly afterward it sold at auction for $212,847, or roughly $2.5 million in today's currency. That figure neglects the value the collection would have accrued in the intervening fifty-eight years. *The New York Times,* June 7, 1945. For FDR's collection, see Brian C. Baur, *Franklin D. Roosevelt: The Stamp Collecting President* (Sidney, Ohio: Linn's Stamp News, 1999).

30. Lindley, *Franklin D. Roosevelt* 48; SDR, *My Boy Franklin* 27.

31. No detail of the St. James' operation escaped FDR's attention. In 1941, when the church treasurer resigned, the president proposed a candidate of his own. "What would you think of the young man who runs the drug store?" he wrote his neighbor Gerald Morgan. "He seems up and coming. He is a violent Republican!" President's Secretary's File (PSF) 154, FDRL. Also see Ward, *Before the Trumpet* 156–157.

32. Eleanor Roosevelt, *This Is My Story* 149–150 (New York: Harper & Brothers, 1937). After the president's death, Eleanor wrote, "I think he felt that in great crises he was guided by a strength and wisdom higher than his own, for his religious faith, though simple, was unwavering and direct. . . . I have always felt my husband's religion had something to do with his confidence in himself," *This I Remember* 69–70 (New York: Harper & Brothers, 1949).

33. FDR to Muriel and Warren Robbins (Aunt Kassie Delano's children by her first marriage), May 30, 1891. 1 *Roosevelt Letters* 35. FDR remained in contact with the Robbinses for the rest of his life and in 1933 appointed Warren to be U.S. minister to Canada.

34. *The New York Times,* January 17, 1933. Also see Christian Bommersheim to Roosevelt family, July 1, 1891, FDRL.

35. Kleeman, *Gracious Lady* 166. On the eve of World War II, when he was under fire from isolationist critics for being pro-British and pro-French, Roosevelt could not resist alluding to his youthful days in imperial Germany. "I did not know Britain and France as a boy," the president said, "but I did know Germany. If anything, I looked upon the Germany I knew with far more friendliness than I did on Great Britain or France." 3 *Roosevelt Letters* 943.

36. Quoted in Bernard Asbell, *The F.D.R. Memoirs* 24 (New York: Doubleday, 1973).

37. September 18, 1896, 1 *Roosevelt Letters* 47–48.

38. Ibid. 45. Also see Frank D. Ashburn, *Peabody of Groton* 45 (New York: Coward McCann, 1944). "We had a sad shooting affray the other day," Peabody wrote to a friend back east on July 8, 1882. "[A] worthy young deputy sheriff was murdered by a drunken Mexican. They tried to get up enough excitement among the populace to lynch the murderer—but there was no leader. I really think that an example of frontier justice with the next white murderer would be a good thing—for the place is full of desperados who hold the lives of others and themselves very cheap." Ibid. 59.

39. *Statistical History of the United States* 91.

40. Quoted in Arthur M. Schlesinger, Jr., *The Crisis of the Old Order* 321 (Boston: Houghton Mifflin, 1957).

41. Roosevelt was so impressed with the elder Peabody's reading of *A Christmas Carol* that as soon as he had a family of his own he undertook to read a condensed version every year on Christmas Eve, insisting that the assembled family join him in repeating the final words of Tiny Tim, "God bless us every one." James Roosevelt, *Affectionately, F.D.R.* 57. Also see Rexford G. Tugwell, *The Democratic Roosevelt* 510 (New York: Doubleday, 1957).

42. Peabody to Camp, November 23, 1909, reproduced in Ashburn, *Peabody* 195.

43. *The New York Times,* June 3, 1934. Shortly after he became president, FDR wrote Peabody, "I count it among the blessings of my life that it was given to me in my formative years to have the privilege of your guiding hand and the benefit of your inspiring example." Reprinted in Ashburn, *Peabody* 349.

44. Quoted in 1 *Roosevelt Letters* 47. Not all students fared as well as FDR. For example, Peabody considered Dean Acheson [Groton '11] "an undesirable citizen . . . so flippant and unpleasant" that the faculty wanted nothing to do with him. Peabody to Acheson's father, March 13, 1909, Peabody Papers, Houghton Library, Harvard University.

45. FDR to Mama and Papa, May 14, 1897, 1 *Roosevelt Letters* 97.

46. Ibid., June 25, 1900, 356–357.

47. In 1933 FDR ascribed the remark about boyhood ideals to Phillips Brooks, 1933 *Public Papers and Addresses of Franklin D. Roosevelt* 419, Samuel I. Rosenman, ed. (New York: Random House, 1948).

48. Quoted in 1 *Roosevelt Letters* 362. Philosopher William James lamented that the young men who lived in the Yard "seldom or never darken the doors of Pudding or the Porcellian; they hover in background on the days when the crimson color is most in evidence, but they nevertheless are intoxicated and exultant with the nourishment they find there." William James, "The True Harvard," 12 *Harvard Graduates Magazine* 7 (September 1903).

49. Eliot, strongly influenced by the intellectualism of German universities, subscribed to the unity of the quest for knowledge. As he expressed it in his famous address on the aims of higher education, "There is today no difference between the philologist's method of study and the naturalist's, or between the psychologist's method and the physiologist's. Students of history and natural history, of physics and metaphysics, of literature and the fine arts, find that, though their fields of study are different, their method and spirit are the same. This oneness of method characterizes the true university." For criticism, see Samuel Eliot Morison, *Three Centuries of Harvard, 1636–1936* 342–346 (Cambridge, Mass.: Harvard University Press, 1936).

50. 1941 *Public Papers of Franklin D. Roosevelt* 460.

51. Kleeman, *Gracious Lady* 209; Ted Morgan, *FDR: A Biography* 77 (New York: Simon & Schuster, 1985).

52. Kleeman, *Gracious Lady* 218–219; Ward, *Before the Trumpet* 230.

53. 47 *Harvard Alumni Bulletin* 444 (April 28, 1945). Bowie subsequently became pastor of New York City's Grace Church.

54. FDR Diary, October 1, 1903, FDRL.

55. FDR to SDR, October 7, 1903, 1 *Roosevelt Letters* 434–435.

56. Schlesinger, *Crisis of the Old Order* 324. "Perhaps the most useful preparation I had in college for public service was on the Harvard *Crimson*," Roosevelt said many years later. Quoted in Nathan Miller, *FDR: An Intimate History* 39 (New York: Doubleday, 1983).

57. *The Oregonian* (Portland), April 20, 1914.

58. Kleeman, *Gracious Lady* 213.

59. FDR to SDR, January 6, 1902, 1 *Roosevelt Letters* 403.

60. SDR, *My Boy Franklin* 55–56.

61. Quoted in Ward, *Before the Trumpet* 243.

62. To Sara, FDR wrote, "Last week I dined at the Quincy's, the Armory's and the Thayer's, three as high-life places as are to be found in blue-blooded, blue stockinged, bean eating Boston!" January 12, 1904, 1 *Roosevelt Letters* 447.

63. Roosevelt's remark was made to Bamie's son, W. Sheffield Cowles, Jr., who was returning from Europe with President Wilson in 1919. Letter, Cowles to Nathan Miller, March 18, 1980, in *FDR: An Intimate History* 35, 513.

64. Lathrop Brown was elected to Congress from New York as a Democrat in 1912 and later served as joint secretary to President Wilson's Industrial Conference in 1919. His remark was made to Frank Freidel and is reprinted in Ward, *Before the Trumpet* 237. Brown himself was a member of Porcellian.

65. Freidel, *Apprenticeship* 52.

THREE | Keeping the Name in the Family

The epigraph is from James Roosevelt, *My Parents: A Differing View* 17 (Chicago: Playboy Press, 1976). Also see David B. Roosevelt, *Grandmère: A Personal History of Eleanor Roosevelt* 168 (New York: Warner Books, 2002).

1. *The New York Times*, March 18, 1905; *Town Topics*, March 9, 1905.

2. James Roosevelt, *My Parents* 33. Or, as their son Elliott wrote, "If [father] was no more than a boy in terms of his experience with women at the time of their marriage, mother was no more than a child in her knowledge of men." Elliott Roosevelt and James Brough, *An Untold Story: The Roosevelts of Hyde Park* 25 (New York: G. P. Putnam's Sons, 1973).

3. "Who do you think it would be nice to have at Hyde Park with the crowd?" Franklin asked Sara. "You'd better send me a list." Two days later Sara complied: "I send a short list of girls either one of whom you may be pleased to dance with, and you ought to write at once—

Mary Newbold [Hyde Park neighbor]
Mary Soley [cousin]
Muriel [Delano Robbins—cousin]
Helen [Roosevelt—Rosy's daughter and FDR's niece].

As you know very few girls you ought to make haste." FDR to SDR, December 4, 1898; SDR to FDR December 6, 1898, 1 *The Roosevelt Letters* 213–214, Elliott Roosevelt, ed. (London: George G. Harrap, 1949).

4. FDR to SDR, October 16, 1901, ibid. 396.

5. Elliott Roosevelt, *Untold Story* 33–34; James Roosevelt, *My Parents* 18. After the romance disintegrated, Frances Dana married FDR's classmate Henry de Rahm. Roosevelt remained on friendly terms with both and spent much time with them in Florida in the 1920s, when he was recovering from polio.

6. The account of FDR's relationship with Alice Sohier is derived from Geoffrey Ward's original research with the Sohier family and described in detail in *Before the Trumpet: Young Franklin Roosevelt: 1882–1905* 253–255 (New York: Harper & Row, 1985). Alice's 1910 marriage to Herbert Bramwell Shaw, an insurance executive, ended in divorce in 1925. All her life she remained a Republican, professing not to be surprised that FDR was "so careless with the country's money since he had always overspent his allowance as a youth." Alice died in 1972, having made sure that all of FDR's letters to her had been burned. Ibid. 255n.

7. FDR to Robert D. Washburn, August 18, 1928, FDRL. There is no record of FDR traveling to the West or the South in 1902.

8. FDR was an usher at Alice's coming-out ball, January 13, 1904. Thirty years later, Alice's father came across a photograph of the ushers and mailed it to the president. FDR wrote back immediately, "That photograph brings back many delightful memories. I well remember Alice's coming out dance. Of all the debutantes of that year she was the loveliest." FDR to Colonel Sohier, March 21, 1934, FDRL.

9. FDR diary entry, November 17, 1902, FDRL.

10. Corinne Robinson Alsop, unpublished memoir, Alsop Family Papers, Houghton Library, Harvard University.

11. Joseph P. Lash, *Eleanor and Franklin* 101 (New York: W. W. Norton, 1971).

12. Eleanor Roosevelt, *Autobiography* 41 (New York: Harper & Brothers, 1961). Eleanor's first letter to Franklin, or at least the first that survives, was October 3, 1905, a matter-of-fact note that she signed "yours in haste." FDRL.

13. ER, *Autobiography* 41. "It was years later before I understood what being in love or what loving really meant," wrote Eleanor. Ibid.

14. Eleanor Roosevelt Genealogy, FDRL.

15. Philip Livingston (1716–1778) was one of four New York signatories to the Declaration of Independence; Brockholst Livingston, then the nation's leading authority on commercial law, was appointed to the Supreme Court by Thomas Jefferson in 1806 and served until 1823; Robert R. Livingston was the first U.S. secretary of foreign affairs under the Continental Congress, 1781–1783; his brother, Edward, served as Andrew Jackson's secretary of state from 1831 to 1833. William Livingston, who signed the Constitution, served as governor of New Jersey from 1776 to 1790.

16. Anna (1863), Elizabeth, known as "Tissie" (1865), Valentine, Jr. ("Vallie") (1868), Edward (1870), Edith (1873), and Maude (1877).

17. According to Joseph Lash, who examined the medical records, there were reports of epilepsy, "but there is no other record of epilepsy in the family and the seizures . . . were too infrequent to fit such a diagnosis. Some doctors . . . have noted that Elliott's seizures occurred when he was confronted with demands that evidently were too much for him and have suggested that they may have been . . . a form of escape." *Eleanor and Franklin* 8. Also see Ward, *Before the Trumpet* 261; Blanche Wiesen Cook, 1 *Eleanor Roosevelt* 33–35 (New York: Viking Penguin, 1992).

18. Dollar conversion factors are based on the table prepared by Professor Robert G. Sahr of the Political Science Department at Oregon State University.

19. Shandigaff, better known as "shandy," is one-half beer and one-half ginger beer. Theodore Roosevelt Memorial Association Collection, Widener Library, Harvard University, quoted in Lash, *Eleanor and Franklin* 11.

20. Elliott's account of a tiger shoot in Hyderabad and an elephant hunt in Sri Lanka was edited by Eleanor and published by Scribner's in 1933 under the title *Hunting Big Game in the Eighties*.

21. *New York Herald*, *The New York Times*, December 2, 1883. David McCullough and Geoffrey Ward assert that TR was Elliott's best man. Contemporary coverage in the *Herald* and *Times* suggests otherwise. Compare David McCullough, *Mornings on Horseback* 250 (New York: Simon & Schuster, 1981); Ward, *Before the Trumpet* 264.

22. *In Loving Memory of Anna Hall Roosevelt*, FDRL, quoted in Ward, *Before the Trumpet* 265.

23. John Sargeant Wise, *Recollections of Thirteen Presidents* 241–243 (New York: Doubleday, 1906).

24. The quotation is from ER, *Autobiography* 5. Hall's full name was Gracie Hall Roosevelt. James King Gracie was Elliott's uncle, having married his mother's sister, Anna Bulloch.

25. TR's comment is in a letter to Bamie, August 22, 1891.

26. News of the suit was featured in all New York dailies on August 17, 1891. "Wrecked by Liquor and Folly," said the *Herald*. "His Brother Theodore Applies for a Writ of Lunacy," reported the *Sun*.

27. Elliott's letter was reprinted in the New York edition of the *Herald*, August 21, 1891.

28. TR to Bamie, January 21, 1892 (TR's emphasis).

29. Undated letter from TR to Bamie, cited in Edmund Morris, *The Rise of Theodore Roosevelt* 447 (New York: Coward, McCann & Geoghegan, 1979).

30. Cook, 1 *Eleanor Roosevelt* 65n.

31. Mrs. Sherman blamed Anna for Elliott's demise. Blanche Wiesen Cook states the case to the contrary with uncompromising directness. "Throughout the entire

period," she writes, "Anna struggled desperately against medical advice, TR's bullying, and what must have been her own doubts to persuade his family that Elliott was curable. She stood virtually alone in her effort to find an alternative and loving approach to Elliott's treatment. Only when Elliott became uncontrollable and vindictive, did she agree to leave him in [Paris], and consent to TR's suit to establish a trust that would protect her children's financial interest. But she continued to hope for Elliott's recovery, and to worry about his peace of mind." Ibid. 66–67.

32. Eleanor Roosevelt, *This Is My Story* 12–13 (New York: Harper & Brothers, 1937). ER omitted this passage when she republished *This Is My Story* in her *Autobiography* in 1961.

33. *The New York Times,* December 8, 1892.

34. Morris, *Rise of Theodore Roosevelt* 848–849; Ward, *Before the Trumpet* 278.

35. TR to Bamie, July 29, 1894; August 18, 1894.

36. Cook, 1 *Eleanor Roosevelt* 80. For the tension between Eleanor and Anna, see pages 70–72. See also Ward, *Before the Trumpet* 288.

37. Alice Roosevelt Longworth, quoted in Michael Teague, *Mrs. L: Conversations with Alice Roosevelt Longworth* 151 (New York: Doubleday, 1981).

38. ER, *Autobiography* 11–12.

39. Cook, 1 *Eleanor Roosevelt* 95.

40. Teague, *Mrs. L* 154.

41. Ibid. "I had a lot of admiration for her," Alice recalled. "But I did get bored with her type of piety. . . . She always wanted to discuss things like whether contentment was better than happiness and whether they conflicted with one another. Things like that I didn't give a damn about."

42. Norman and Jeanne MacKenzie, eds., 1 *The Diary of Beatrice Webb* 277 (Cambridge, Mass.: Harvard University Press, 1982); also see vol. 2, pp. 340–341.

   Before moving to England, Mlle. Souvestre had founded Les Ruches, a girls school at Fontainebleau, in partnership with another woman. This was the school Bamie attended. After Bamie left, the two women quarreled and the school disbanded. A charged account of the breakup is in *Olivia,* a roman à clef of Les Ruches and Allenwood written by Dorothy Strachey Bussy in 1933 and published under a pseudonym in 1948. Dorothy Strachey Bussy had been a student with Bamie at Les Ruches and taught Eleanor English at Allenwood. In her biography of ER, Blanche Wiesen Cook discusses *Olivia* perceptively: "It is a very simple love story of a young, uncontrollable romance. A lesbian romance. The passions that devastated Olivia did not devastate Eleanor. But she understood the book." 1 *Eleanor Roosevelt* 116–120, 515–517.

43. Quoted in Joseph Lash, *Love, Eleanor* 27 (New York: Doubleday, 1982). From an interview with Helen Gifford by the London *Daily Mail* in 1942.

44. Mlle. Souvestre to Mrs. Hall, 1899, n.d., FDRL.

45. ER, *Autobiography* 29–30.

46. In her memoirs, Eleanor said Auntie Tissie "was always kindness itself to me. . . . She was one of those people whom the word 'exquisite' describes best." Ibid. 20.

47. The comment is by Eleanor's classmate Dorothy Horn, quoted in Lash, *Eleanor and Franklin* 84.

48. Marie Souvestre to Corinne Robinson (ER's cousin). Corinne entered Allenwood during Eleanor's final year. "When I arrived she was 'everything' at the school. She was beloved by everybody. Saturdays we were allowed to sortie into Putney which had stores where you could buy books, flowers. Young girls have crushes and you bought violets or a book and left them in the room of the girl you were idolizing. Eleanor's room every Saturday would be full of flowers because she was so admired." Corinne Robinson Alsop, unpublished memoir, Alsop Family Papers, Harvard University.

49. ER, *Autobiography* 35.

50. Quoted in Ward, *Before the Trumpet* 303.

51. Elliott Roosevelt, *Untold Story* 33.

52. "Eleanor has a very good mind," Franklin told Sara. Quoted in Ward, *Before the Trumpet* 307.

53. Elliott Roosevelt, *Untold Story* 33.

54. ER to FDR, January 4, 1904, FDRL.

55. Cook, 1 *Eleanor Roosevelt* 139.

56. ER's letter is in Lash, *Eleanor and Franklin* 135.

57. Quoted in Ward, *Before the Trumpet* 319. Also see Cook, 1 *Eleanor Roosevelt* 138.

58. ER to FDR, October 12, 1904, quoted in Lash, *Eleanor and Franklin* 136.

59. Corinne Robinson Alsop's unpublished journals, Alsop Family Papers, Harvard University.

60. The congratulatory letters, variously dated, are in the wedding folders, Box 20, FDRL.

61. TR to ER, December 19, 1904; TR to FDR, November 29, 1904, Box 20, FDRL.

62. TR received 7.6 million votes to Parker's 5.1 million. Eugene Debs, the Socialist candidate, received .4 million. Roosevelt carried every state except the Solid South, which went for Parker.

63. January 8, 1938, 1938 *Public Papers and Addresses of Franklin D. Roosevelt* 38, Samuel I. Rosenman, ed. (New York: Random House, 1939).

64. Contrary to popular belief, TR did not mention his trademark "square deal" in his inaugural address. See instead his Labor Day speech to the New York State Fair in Syracuse, September 7, 1903, or his remarks to the veterans of the Civil War in Springfield, Illinois, July 4, 1903.

65. James Roosevelt Roosevelt, FDR's half brother, was in Florida at the time of the wedding and unable to attend.

66. ER, *Autobiography* 50. *The New York Times* noted that Eleanor was "considerably taller than the head of the nation, suggesting to many present her beautiful mother. . . . She has much of that simple grace that characterized her mother."

March 18, 1905. *Town Topics* reported one guest to have said, "the bridegroom had been especially handsome," to which another added, "Surprising for a Roosevelt."

67. Teague, *Mrs. L.* 156.

FOUR | Albany

The epigraph is from a conversation between Ed Perkins, Democratic chairman of Dutchess County, and FDR in September 1910, preparatory to Roosevelt's acceptance of the Democratic nomination for the State Senate. Interview with Ed Perkins, quoted in Ted Morgan, *FDR: A Biography* 112 (New York: Simon & Schuster, 1985).

1. John Gunther, *Roosevelt in Retrospect* 201 (New York: Harper & Brothers, 1950). Donovan, who won the Distinguished Service Cross at Saint-Mihiel, was awarded the Medal of Honor for his action at Landres-et-Saint-Georges, October 14 and 15, 1918. According to the citation: "Lt. Col. Donovan personally led the assaulting wave in an attack upon a very strongly organized position, and when our troops were suffering heavy casualties he encouraged all near him by his example, moving among his men in exposed positions, reorganizing decimated platoons, and accompanying them forward in attacks. When he was wounded in the leg by machine gun bullets, he refused to be evacuated and continued with his unit until it withdrew to a less exposed position." War Department General Order 56, 1922.

2. FDR to SDR, August 22, 1905, 2 *The Roosevelt Letters* 72–73, Elliott Roosevelt, ed. (London: George G. Harrap, 1950). I have used the current term, "civil procedure," rather than "pleading and practice," as it was delineated in FDR's time. For FDR's law school absences, see Morgan, *FDR* 106.

3. Interview with Professor Jackson E. Reynolds (1949), Columbia Oral History Project, Columbia University. Reynolds, a lifelong Republican, was a good friend of Herbert Hoover from their undergraduate days at Stanford. He was also president of the First National Bank of New York and a committed foe of the New Deal. See Geoffrey C. Ward, *A First-Class Temperament* 62n (New York: Harper & Row, 1989).

4. Of the 106 men who entered Columbia Law School with FDR, only 84 remained by third year. Frank Freidel, *Franklin D. Roosevelt: The Apprenticeship* 76 (Boston: Little, Brown, 1952).

5. ER to SDR, August 29, 1905, 2 *Roosevelt Letters* 79.

6. Quoted in Joseph P. Lash, *Eleanor and Franklin* 151 (New York: W. W. Norton, 1971). "You can imagine what a speech on gardening, and the raising of vegetables in general, by your son must have been like," FDR wrote Sara. "I will say nothing more except that my appetite for those damned weeds has since that time departed." FDR to SDR, September 7, 1905, 2 *Roosevelt Letters* 81.

7. FDR to SDR, July 3, 1905, 2 *Roosevelt Letters* 35–36. "We went to two churches or so—San Toy and Santa Claus, and in one of them I drew a picture of the ceiling to be copied in the addition to the Hyde Park house," wrote Franklin.

8. FDR to SDR, July 5, 1905, ibid. 44–45.

9. In 1903, seven years after the death of her first husband, William Howard Forbes, Dora married his younger brother, Paul Forbes, who was also associated with Russell and Company in the China trade. After thirty years' residence in Hong Kong, the Forbeses then moved to Paris, and their spacious Right Bank apartment became the headquarters for the Delano and Roosevelt families in Paris. In 1940, with France at war, Sara returned to escort Dora back to the United States. Sara's interviews with the French press, which she conducted entirely in French, did much to cement Franco-American relations at that critical time. See Geoffrey C. Ward, *Before the Trumpet: Young Franklin Roosevelt, 1882–1905* 61–62 (New York: Harper & Row, 1985).

10. ER to SDR, June 23, 1905, 2 *Roosevelt Letters* 31. Madame Howland was the widow of Rebecca Howland Roosevelt's brother. (Rebecca was James's first wife.) After her husband's death, James became one of the two trustees of Hortense Howland's estate. When the other trustee absconded with all her funds, James drew upon his own resources to provide her with the means to continue her style of life in Paris. Ibid. Madame Howland repaid James's consideration by sending home in Eleanor's luggage a pair of diamond earrings for Sara said to have belonged to Marie Antoinette. Eleanor Roosevelt, *This Is My Story* 132 (New York: Harper & Brothers, 1937).

11. FDR to SDR, August 14, 1905, 2 *Roosevelt Letters* 67–68.

12. ER, *This Is My Story* 131. This passage was omitted by ER when she republished *This Is My Story* in her *Autobiography.*

13. FDR to SDR, June 16, 22, July 8, August 14, 1905, 2 *Roosevelt Letters* 24–25, 29–30, 39, 67–68.

14. FDR to SDR, July 22, 1905, 2 *Roosevelt Letters* 50.

15. ER to SDR, August 1, 1905, ibid. 59. "[We] will be quite happy if the plumbing is good and the paint and papers fresh and new. If there is a telephone please don't let it be taken out and is there a safe in the house?"

16. ER to SDR, August 8, 1905, ibid. 62. "Altogether we feel very jubilant," wrote Eleanor, "and I am looking forward so much to getting it in order with you to help us. I am afraid my unaided efforts would not be very successful." Later, Eleanor asked Sara whether the kitchen and basement could be whitewashed (August 13, 1905).

   I have devoted more space than may be warranted to Sara's renting the Draper house for Franklin and Eleanor because ER in her autobiography implies that she was surprised and put out by Sara's action, which was made to appear the unilateral meddling of an overprotective mother-in-law. Eleanor's letters from Europe suggest otherwise. Compare, Eleanor Roosevelt, *Autobiography* 55 (New York: Harper & Brothers, 1961). Also see Kenneth S. Davis, *FDR: The Beckoning of Destiny* 197 (New York: Putnam, 1972).

17. The houses are at 47–49 East Sixty-fifth Street. Sara's 1908 journal entry indicates that the total price for the two houses, each 17½ feet wide, was $247,345.19

(roughly $5 million currently). The two lots cost $105,284.25; construction, painting, and papering, $134,554.84; and Mr. Platt's architect fee, $7,506.10. Except for a small $26,000 mortgage on her own house at 49 E. Sixty-fifth, Sara paid cash. SDR Journal, 1908. FDRL. Also see James MacGregor Burns and Susan Dunn, *The Three Roosevelts: Patrician Leaders Who Transformed America* 108 (New York: Grove Press, 2001). In 2003, the City University of New York undertook to restore the houses for the Roosevelt House Public Policy Institute, at a cost of $15 million. *The New York Times,* March 18, 2003.

18. ER, *Autobiography* 61. Eleanor was not as divorced from the project as she later suggested. On August 22, 1907, she wrote Sara from Campobello, "Franklin and I have been working over the plans for lighting, bells, and telephones which [Charles A. Platt, the architect] sent us two days ago. All of the arrangements seem very good except in one or two bedrooms where I think he has made a mistake as one would want lights over dressing tables it seems to me and not in the four corners of the room." 2 *Roosevelt Letters* 112.

19. For this early confrontation, I have relied on the treatment of ER's friend and biographer Joseph P. Lash. Mr. Lash was privy to Mrs. Roosevelt's thoughts and offers the most objective appraisal of the episode. See *Eleanor and Franklin* 162.

20. ER, *Autobiography* 61. "I pulled myself together and realized that I was acting like a little fool, but there was a good deal of truth in what I had said, for I was not developing any individual taste or initiative."

21. ER interview with Arnold Michaelis, on the recording "A Recorded Portrait" (1958), FDRL.

22. ER, *This Is My Story* 162–163.

23. Elliott Roosevelt and James Brough, *An Untold Story: The Roosevelts of Hyde Park* 40 (New York: G. P. Putnam's Sons, 1973).

24. Horace Coon, *Columbia: Colossus on the Hudson* 99 (New York: E. P. Dutton, 1947).

25. ER, *Autobiography* 62.

26. Ibid. 57–60. Also see Cook, 1 *Eleanor Roosevelt* 178–180.

27. ER, *This Is My Story* 142–146.

28. James Roosevelt and Sidney Shalett, *Affectionately, F.D.R.* 40 (New York: Harcourt, Brace, 1959).

29. John R. Boettiger, *A Love in Shadow* 62. (New York: W. W. Norton, 1978).

30. Quoted in Lash, *Eleanor and Franklin* 152.

31. 157 U.S. 429 (1894). Carter's argument to the Court made few friends among his corporate clients. Granted, the income tax would fall upon only the nation's wealthiest 2 percent, said Carter. "But that two percent received more than fifty percent of the country's income. The rapid concentration of wealth in the hands of the few creates an inequitable situation that Congress has the right to correct." Carter reminded the Court that its authority was limited and it would transgress those limits if it invalidated an act of Congress simply because the justices disagreed with the economic principles involved. Five justices disagreed, and the

Court overturned the tax. Carter also represented the United States before the Tribunal of Arbitration in Paris in 1893, pertaining to sealing rights on the Pribilof Islands. Once asked by Professor Francis Greenwood Peabody of Harvard why he was so successful at law, Carter replied, "I never take lunch."

32. *United States v. American Tobacco Co.*, 221 U.S. 106 (1911). For Ledyard's role in 1907, see Stanley Jackson, *J. P. Morgan* 272–275 (New York: Stein and Day, 1983); Jean Strouse, *Morgan: American Financier* 584–589 (New York: HarperCollins, 2000).

33. *Standard Oil Co. v. United States*, 221 U.S. 1 (1911). Milburn and Ledyard lost back to-back challenges to the Sherman Antitrust Act in the Supreme Court but then succeeded in reorganizing the two trusts so effectively that the government's dissolution order was rendered nominal. Shareholders suffered no damage, competition remained minimal, and management was barely affected.

34. Grover Cleveland once said of Milburn, "He usually had a lawbook under his arm in the street and I used to wonder if he was trying to absorb the law through his armpits." Francis M. Ellis and Edward F. Clark, Jr., *A Brief History of Carter, Ledyard & Milburn* 30 (Portsmouth, N.H.: Peter E. Randall, 1988).

35. Quoted in Davis, *Beckoning Destiny* 213.

36. Grenville Clark, "Franklin D. Roosevelt, 1882–1945: Five Harvard Men Pay Tribute to His Memory," 47 *Harvard Alumni Bulletin* 452 (April 28, 1945).

37. Cornelius Vanderbilt, Jr., *Farewell to Fifth Avenue* 245 (New York: Simon & Schuster, 1935).

38. Extemporaneous remarks at Vassar College, August 26, 1933, 1 *Public Papers and Addresses of Franklin D. Roosevelt* 338, Samuel I. Rosenman, ed. (New York: Random House, 1938).

39. Interview with Edward E. Perkins, quoted in Morgan, *FDR* 112. Geoffrey Ward suggests that the quote is most likely apocryphal, but compare Allen Churchill, *The Roosevelts: American Aristocrats* 209 (New York: Harper & Row, 1965); Henry Noble MacCracken, *Blithe Dutchess: The Flowering of an American County from 1812* 79 (New York: Hastings House, 1958).

40. FDR to L. J. Magenis, August 15, 1928; also see Campaign Expenditures Account in FDR manuscripts, FDRL.

41. Rita Halle Kleeman, *Gracious Lady* 252 (New York: D. Appleton–Century, 1935).

42. Sara Delano Roosevelt Journal, FDRL.

43. Quoted in Kleeman, *Gracious Lady* 252–253.

44. Cook, 1 *Eleanor Roosevelt* 185.

45. ER, *Autobiography* 63.

46. TR to Bamie (Mrs. Anna Roosevelt Cowles), August 10, 1910, in Theodore Roosevelt, *Letters from Theodore Roosevelt to Anna Roosevelt Cowles* 289 (New York: Charles Scribner's Sons, 1924). As they grew older, Franklin and TR had what amounted to a two-man mutual admiration society. "I'm so fond of that boy, I'd be shot for him," Theodore told Sara shortly before his death. Quoted in Kleeman, *Gracious Lady* 204.

47. In 1884, when Grover Cleveland headed the Democratic ticket, Thomas Jefferson Newbold, a Roosevelt neighbor in Hyde Park, slipped through in a freakish three-man race.

48. *Poughkeepsie Eagle,* October 7, 1910.

49. 1 *Public Papers and Addresses* 339.

50. Reminiscences of Harry Hawkey, in Clara L. Dawson to Eleanor Roosevelt, December 13, 1937, FDRL. Also see Morgan H. Hoyt, "Roosevelt Enters Politics," 1 *F.D.R. Collector* 3–9 (May 1949).

51. Interview with Thomas Leonard, conducted by George Palmer and Fred Rath, National Park Service, FDRL. Leonard was the third member (with Perkins and Judge Mack) of the Dutchess County Democratic Executive Committee and remained a friend of FDR throughout the president's life. Tom Leonard always accompanied FDR to the poll in Hyde Park on election day and in 1944 accompanied him there for the last time. Roosevelt had trouble closing the curtain and said, "Tom, the Goddamned thing won't work." *Time* magazine reported the comment, triggering an avalanche of protests from the nation's clergymen. When asked about the remark, FDR said he had been misquoted. Presidential press conference, November 21, 1944.

52. Interview with Judge John Mack, National Park Service, FDRL.

53. *The New York Times,* September 5, 1932.

54. Judge John Mack interview, FDRL.

55. Speech at Hudson, N.Y., October 27, 1910, speech file, FDRL.

56. FDR to John Anthony, June 11, 1911, FDRL.

57. *Poughkeepsie News-Press,* October 22, 1910.

58. Ibid., October 27, 1910.

59. Quoted in Freidel, *Apprenticeship* 93.

60. Alfred B. Rollins, Jr., *Roosevelt and Howe* 22 (New York: Knopf, 1962).

61. *Poughkeepsie Eagle,* October 28, 1910.

62. FDR to L. J. Magenis, August 15, 1928; Ward, *First-Class Temperament* 120.

63. FDR, address at Hyde Park, November 5, 1910, speech file, FDRL.

64. Cook, 1 *Eleanor Roosevelt* 186.

65. Ward, *First-Class Temperament* 4.

66. Quoted in Ernest K. Lindley, *Franklin D. Roosevelt: A Career in Progressive Democracy* 78 (Indianapolis: Bobbs-Merrill, 1931).

67. ER, *Autobiography* 64.

68. ER to Isabella Ferguson, November 26, 1910, quoted in Cook, 1 *Eleanor Roosevelt* 525.

69. FDR's comment is in a diary he began keeping January 1, 1911. Referring to their New York City town house, Franklin said "it is a comfort to have only three stories instead of six." Sara's comment is quoted in Lash, *Eleanor and Franklin* 170.

70. FDR diary, January 1, 1911, FDRL.

71. Franklin D. Roosevelt, *The Happy Warrior, Alfred E. Smith: A Study of a Public Servant* 4 (Boston: Houghton Mifflin, 1928).

72. Quoted in Lindley, *Roosevelt* 82–83.

73. *New York Herald,* January 18, 1911.

74. *The New York Times,* January 18, 1911.

75. *New York Post,* January 17, 1911.

76. *New York American,* January 18, 1911.

77. *The New York World,* January 17, 1911.

78. *New York Globe,* February 6, 1911.

79. Edmund R. Terry, "The Insurgents at Albany," 71 *The Independent* 538 (September 7, 1911).

80. *The New York Times,* January 22, 1911.

81. ER, *Autobiography* 66.

82. Quoted in Lash, *Eleanor and Franklin* 173.

83. Cook, 1 *Eleanor Roosevelt* 189.

84. Lindley, *Franklin D. Roosevelt* 85.

85. Ibid. 97.

86. *Saratoga Sun,* April 1, 1911.

87. Quoted in Ward, *First-Class Temperament* 150–151.

88. FDR to H. W. Lunger, January 30, 1928.

89. Cleveland *Plain Dealer,* March 30, 1911.

90. Raleigh *News & Observer,* April 1, 1911.

91. TR to FDR, January 29, 1911. "I am delighted with your action and told Woodrow Wilson today how he and you are serving the nation," William Grosvenor, a prominent clergyman, wrote FDR. Quoted in Nathan Miller, *FDR: An Intimate History* 75.

92. *The New York World,* January 26, 1911.

93. Quoted in Jon Margolis, "The Boss Who Out-Daleys Daley," *Chicago Tribune,* April 2, 1976.

94. James A. Farley, *Jim Farley's Story: The Roosevelt Years* 68 (New York: McGraw-Hill, 1948). Said Farley, "Never was I invited to spend a night in the [White House]. Only twice did I ever make a cruise on the presidential yacht. Both were political. Never was I invited to join informal White House gatherings."

95. Quoted in Lindley, *Franklin D. Roosevelt* 101.

96. *The New York Times,* December 25, 1911. The remarks are those of Senate clerk Patrick E. McCabe, who fired both barrels at FDR: "Disloyalty and party treachery is the political cult of a few snobs in our party . . . who are political accidents [and] who come as near being political leaders as a green pea does to a circus tent."

FIVE | Awakening

The epigraph is a remark FDR made to Frances Perkins while he was president. Quoted in Frances Perkins, *The Roosevelt I Knew* 12 (New York: Viking, 1946).

1. For Smith on FDR, see Matthew and Hannah Josephson, *Al Smith: Hero of the Cities* 95 (Boston: Houghton Mifflin, 1969). Wagner's remarks were made while

presiding over the senate as president pro tem, June 1, 1911. *New York Globe,* June 2, 1911. Frank Freidel, *Franklin D. Roosevelt: The Apprenticeship* 118–119 (Boston: Little, Brown, 1952); Perkins, *The Roosevelt I Knew* 11–12.

2. Perkins, *The Roosevelt I Knew* 11–12. Miss Perkins writes with great affection for the self-made men of Tammany. "The warm, human sympathies of these people, less than perfect as I examine their record, gave me insight into a whole stratum of American society I had not known. In contrast with these roughnecks, I don't hesitate to say now, Franklin Roosevelt seemed just an ordinary, respectable, intelligent young man. . . . I was not much impressed by him."

3. *New York Tribune,* March 26, 27; April 6, 1911. For a vivid depiction of the inferno, see David Von Drehle, *Triangle: The Fire That Changed America* 116–170 (New York: Atlantic Monthly Press, 2003). On March 25, 2003, the building that housed the Triangle Shirtwaist factory (the Asch Building) was designated an official city landmark by Mayor Michael Bloomberg. *The New York Times,* March 26, 2003.

4. Perkins, *The Roosevelt I Knew* 31. Von Drehle, *Triangle* 207–208. The quote also appears in Kenneth S. Davis, *FDR: The Beckoning of Destiny* 263 (New York: Putnam, 1972).

5. Quoted in Ted Morgan, *FDR: A Biography* 127 (New York: Simon & Schuster, 1985); also Geoffrey Ward, *A First-Class Temperament* 165 (New York: Harper & Row, 1989).

6. Von Drehle, *Triangle* 216–217; Perkins, *The Roosevelt I Knew* 14. "I seen my sister go out to work when she was fifteen," said Sullivan, "and I know we ought to help these gals by giving 'em a law which will prevent 'em from being broken down while they are still young."

7. Elizabeth Dutcher, "Frances Perkins, Doctor of Politics," *Women Voter* 12–13 (September 1912). The fifty-four-hour bill was reluctantly signed into law by Governor Dix on April 19, 1912. "I don't think it is a good idea," said Dix. "I think it will put women out of work. I think they'll hire men instead. I think women will lose their jobs. Anyhow, it's not good for them not to be fully occupied." Quoted in Morgan, *FDR* 131.

8. Frances Perkins Interview, Columbia Oral History Project, Columbia University; Perkins, *The Roosevelt I Knew* 14.

9. Quoted in Morgan, *FDR* 129.

10. Presidential press conference, August 26, 1938.

11. Louis Howe, "The Winner," *The Saturday Evening Post,* February 25, 1933. The fact is, it was The MacManus who held the floor until the Sullivans arrived. Von Drehle, *Triangle* 217.

12. FDR to Anna G. W. Dayley, February 1, 1911, FDRL.

13. FDR to Frances G. Barlow, May 24, 1911, FDRL.

14. Linda J. Lumsden, *Inez: The Life and Times of Inez Milholland* 75 (Bloomington: Indiana University Press, 2004). "No suffrage parade was complete without Inez Milholland," wrote the *New York Sun,* "for with her tall figure and free step, her

rich brown hair, blue eyes, fair skin and well cut features, she was an ideal figure of the American woman." November 6, 1916. Also see Blanche Wiesen Cook, 1 *Eleanor Roosevelt* 195 (New York: Viking Penguin, 1992); Joseph P. Lash, *Eleanor and Franklin* 173 (New York: W. W. Norton, 1971).

15. Eleanor Roosevelt, *Autobiography* 68 (New York: Harper & Brothers, 1961).

16. "An Advocate of Christian Patriotism," *American Issue* (March 1913).

17. [Ray Thomas Tucker], *The Mirrors of 1932* 85 (New York: Brewer, Warren, Putnam, 1931).

18. FDR to Dexter Blagden, February 21, 1912, FDRL.

19. *Poughkeepsie News-Press,* March 5, 1912 (emphasis added).

20. Freidel, *Apprenticeship* 134–135.

21. Wilson's Ph.D. dissertation on the American system of government is considered a classic and is now in its fifteenth edition as *Congressional Government: A Study in American Politics* (New Brunswick, N.J.: Transaction Publishers, 2002).

22. FDR to Ray Stannard Baker, 3 *The Roosevelt Letters* 467, Elliott Roosevelt, ed. (London: George G. Harrap, 1950).

23. Freidel, *Apprenticeship* 134–139. Wilson had attracted Wall Street's attention while president of Princeton with a series of conservative pronouncements attacking Bryan, who he once suggested should be "knocked into a cocked hat." Led by Colonel George Harvey, an associate of J. P. Morgan, Wall Street had bankrolled Wilson's gubernatorial campaign as a preliminary to running him for president.

24. Champ Clark, like Wilson, was a former college president, having headed Marshall College, now Marshall University, in Huntington, West Virginia, before entering politics in Missouri.

25. The Orange County delegation nominated FDR as an alternate but was pressured by the Murphy forces and "concluded to get out from under and withdraw your name." J. J. Bippus to FDR, April 12, 1912, FDRL.

26. FDR to O'Gorman, June 10, 1912; O'Gorman to FDR, June 15, 1912. FDRL. See especially Ernest K. Lindley, *Franklin D. Roosevelt: A Career in Progressive Democracy* 102–104 (Indianapolis: Bobbs-Merrill, 1931).

27. Josephus Daniels, *The Wilson Era: Years of Peace, 1910–1917* 125 (Chapel Hill: University of North Carolina Press, 1944).

28. Thomas R. Marshall, a dry-as-dust midwestern politico, is best remembered for his observation "What this country needs is a good five-cent cigar!" Quoted in Samuel Eliot Morison, *The Oxford History of the American People* 882 (New York: Oxford University Press, 1965).

29. 2 *Roosevelt Letters* 192.

30. FDR's speech is in the papers of the Empire State Democracy, July–August 1912, FDRL.

31. Henry F. Pringle, *Theodore Roosevelt* 556 (New York: Harcourt, Brace, 1931); William Henry Harbaugh, *Power and Responsibility: The Life and Times of Theodore Roosevelt,* rev. ed. 404–409, 419–420 (New York: Oxford University

Press, 1975). Also see TR to Herbert Spencer Hadley, February 29, 1912, in 7 *The Letters of Theodore Roosevelt* 513, Elting E. Morison, ed. (Cambridge, Mass.: Harvard University Press, 1954).

32. Quoted in Ward, *First-Class Temperament* 187.

33. Arthur Schlesinger, Jr.'s, observation is in *The Vital Center* 23–24 (Boston: Houghton Mifflin, 1949). For the Armageddon and Bull Moose quotes, see Harbaugh, *Life and Times of Theodore Roosevelt* 405–406, 419–420.

34. On November 6, 1912, the day after his election victory, Wilson told his campaign manager that he owed him nothing. "Whether you did little or much, remember that God ordained that I should be the next president of the United States. Neither you nor any other mortal or mortals could have prevented that!" William E. McCombs, *Making Woodrow Wilson President* 208 (New York: Fairview Publishing Company, 1921).

35. *The New York Times,* September 30, 1912.

36. 1 Diary of Edward M. House 1 (September 25, 1912), Yale University Library. One of the best analyses of the New York convention and its impact on the Wilson campaign is in Arthur S. Link, *Wilson: The Road to the White House* 494–497 (Princeton, N.J.: Princeton University Press, 1947).

37. Shortly after he took office, Sulzer refused Murphy's request to appoint Big Jim Gaffney of the New York Contracting and Trucking Company as state highway commissioner. "It will be Gaffney or war," said Murphy. Sulzer again refused, and Murphy pulled the plug. None of Sulzer's legislative program made it out of committee. On May 20, 1913, Murphy upped the ante and told Smith and Wagner that Sulzer would have to be impeached. Smith found the votes in the Assembly, and the articles of impeachment passed, August 13, 1913. Wagner followed through on October 17, and Sulzer was removed from office by a Senate vote of 43–12, the only time a New York governor has been impeached. Characteristically, Murphy made no public comment. Alfred Connable and Edward Silberfarb, *Tigers of Tammany: Nine Men Who Ran New York* 252–255 (New York: Holt, Rinehart and Winston, 1967). Also see M. R. Werner, *Tammany Hall* 529–555 (New York: Greenwood Press, 1968).

38. New York *Evening Post,* October 3, 1912.

39. *The New York Times,* August 25, 1912.

40. Thomas Mott Osborne to Thomas Ewing, Jr., October 17, 1912, Osborne Papers, Auburn, New York.

41. Rudolph W. Chamberlain, *There Is No Truce: A Life of Thomas Mott Osborne* 182–184 (New York: Macmillan, 1935).

42. Freidel, *Apprenticeship* 146–147.

43. ER, *Autobiography* 69–70.

44. Alfred B. Rollins, Jr., *Roosevelt and Howe* 56 (New York: Knopf, 1962).

45. Quoted in Arthur Schlesinger, Jr., *The Crisis of the Old Order* 340 (Boston: Houghton Mifflin, 1957).

46. Howe to FDR, undated (circa August 1, 1912), FDRL.

47. Quoted in Schlesinger, *Crisis of the Old Order* 314.

48. Freidel, *Apprenticeship* 151.

49. Howe to FDR, October 1912, FDRL.

50. ER, *Autobiography* 70–71.

51. Rollins, *Roosevelt and Howe* 60.

52. Quoted in Ward, *First-Class Temperament* 197n.

53. Quoted in Davis, *FDR: Beckoning of Destiny* 296.

54. ER, *Autobiography* 71.

55. Quoted in Ward, *First-Class Temperament* 198.

56. When the votes were tabulated, FDR had 15,590 (virtually identical to the 15,708 he had received in 1910). His Republican opponent, Jacob Southard, a Poughkeepsie banker and utility owner, had 13,889, and George A. Vossler, the Progressive candidate, 2,628. *The New York Red Book* 677 (Albany: New York State, 1913).

57. In addition to 291 Democrats and 127 Republicans, the House of Representatives contained 17 Independents, Progressives, and Socialists. *Guide to U.S. Elections* 928.

58. Walker to FDR, November 7, 1912.

59. FDR to ER, January 1913, Eleanor Roosevelt Papers, FDRL. In addition to Agriculture and Forest, Fish, and Game, Roosevelt was placed on the standing committees on Codes; Railroads; and Military Affairs.

60. FDR to Joseph Tumulty, January 13, 1913, FDRL.

61. Eleanor Roosevelt, interview with Frank Freidel, May 1, 1948, cited in Freidel, *Apprenticeship* 154–155.

62. Garrison summarized his view of his duties in a revealing letter to a friend in 1915: "I have made it a rule ever since I have been in the Department, not to interfere in any way with the ordinary disposition, location of duty, etc., of the officers of the Army. Whenever the commanding officer needs service to be done in a certain place, he, as a matter of routine, selects the proper command to perform the duty, and I of course would know nothing whatever about such matters." Garrison to Ollie M. James, November 17, 1915, Lindley M. Garrison Papers, Princeton University Library.

63. Baker led the unsuccessful fight by Wilson delegates against the unit rule, and his mention of Wilson set off a thirty-minute demonstration when the convention began. See Alice Roosevelt Longworth, *Crowded Hours* 206–207 (New York: Charles Scribner's Sons, 1933).

64. Arthur S. Link, *Wilson: The New Freedom* 117 (Princeton, N.J.: Princeton University Press, 1956).

65. The banquet for Wilson was hosted by eight hundred Princeton alumni. "There are some emotions that are much deeper than a man's vocabulary can reach, and I have a feeling tonight that moves me very much indeed," said Wilson, more choked up than was his wont. Ibid. 57.

66. Daniels, *Wilson Era* 124. "It is singular that I never thought of any other man in that connection," Daniels noted in his diary on March 15, 1913.

67. Josephus Daniels, *The Cabinet Diaries of Josephus Daniels, 1913–1921* 10, E. David Cronon, ed. (Lincoln: University of Nebraska Press, 1963).

68. TR to FDR, March 18, 1913, FDRL. "When I see Eleanor," the former president continued, "I shall say to her that I do hope she will be particularly nice to the naval officers wives. They have a pretty hard time, with very little money to get along on, and yet a position to keep up, and everything that can properly be done to make things pleasant for them should be done."

69. *New York Herald*, March 10, 1913.

70. Daniels, *Cabinet Diaries* 4; *Wilson Era* 124–129.

71. Wagner's satisfaction at FDR's departure from Albany was attested by his son, Robert F. Wagner, Jr., in an ABC documentary, "FDR and His Times." Additional evidence suggests that Charles Murphy did his utmost to ensure that FDR joined the Wilson administration in Washington. Some in the Navy Department thought that it was Murphy who actually engineered Roosevelt's appointment. Admiral Frederic Harris, interview with Frank Freidel, Freidel Papers, FDRL.

SIX | Anchors Aweigh

The epigraph is from Frances Perkins, *The Roosevelt I Knew* 20 (New York: Viking Press, 1946), discussing FDR's formative years in Washington.

1. Wilson was a terrible golfer. He almost never broke 100 and sometimes needed fifteen putts to finish a hole. But he played relentlessly. Don Van Natta estimates that Wilson played as many as 1,600 rounds while president, roughly twice as many as Dwight D. Eisenhower. Golf, said Wilson, was "the perfect diversion" from the pressures of the Oval Office. Don Van Natta, Jr., *First Off the Tee* 135–151 (New York: PublicAffairs, 2003).

   Bryan announced the no-alcohol policy at an April 21, 1913, farewell dinner he hosted for Lord Bryce, who was retiring as British ambassador. Bryan told the guests that when Wilson asked him to be secretary of state, he had asked whether that would necessitate serving liquor and had been told to use his own judgment. "We have always been teetotalers," said Bryan, and "could not depart from this custom without contradicting our past." William Jennings Bryan and Mary Baird, *The Memoirs of William Jennings Bryan* 351 (Philadelphia: John C. Winston, 1925).

2. The term "New Freedom" derives from a collection of Wilson's campaign speeches, arranged and edited by William Bayard Hale and published by Doubleday in early 1913. In retrospect, writers rarely distinguish between TR's New Nationalism and Woodrow Wilson's New Freedom and lump the two together as manifestations of the progressive wave that swept the country in the early twentieth century. In fact, the election of 1912 turned on the difference. Both movements sought to benefit the common man, but each reflected a different stream of thought. Theodore Roosevelt's New Nationalism embraced the Hamiltonian tradition of a strong central government, dominated by executive

power, that intervened vigorously in the economy on behalf of the many. Taken literally, it exhorted voters to put national needs ahead of sectional or individual advantage. Wilson's New Freedom, by contrast, hewed more closely to Jeffersonian states' rights, minimized the role of the federal government, and sought to achieve prosperity purely through regulation of the market place. It stressed individual liberty rather than collective action. Once in office, Wilson gradually accepted a greater role for the national government than he had originally espoused. FDR's New Deal was much closer to TR's New Nationalism than to Wilson's New Freedom. See Arthur S. Link, *Wilson: The New Freedom* 242–243 (Princeton: Princeton University Press, 1956), and the sources cited therein.

3. Josephus Daniels dates the decision to segregate the federal government to a cabinet meeting on April 11, 1913. According to Daniels, Postmaster General Albert S. Burleson, a former Texas congressman who helped swing the Lone Star State behind Wilson at Baltimore, raised the issue, complaining of the distaste white mail clerks felt at working with blacks: "It is very unpleasant for them to work in a [railway mail] car with Negroes where it is almost impossible to have different drinking vessels and different towels, or places to wash and he was anxious to segregate white and Negro employees in all Departments of the Government. The President said he made no promises in particular to Negroes, except to do them justice, and he wished the matter adjusted in a way to make the least friction." No member of the cabinet objected, then or later. With Wilson's approval, cabinet officers immediately began to segregate their departments, though no formal executive order was ever issued. *The Cabinet Diaries of Josephus Daniels* 32–33, E. David Cronon, ed. (Lincoln: University of Nebraska Press, 1963). Also see Kathleen Wolgemuth, "Woodrow Wilson and Federal Segregation," *Journal of Negro History* 158–173 (April 1959); Nancy J. Weiss, "The Negro and the New Freedom: Fighting Wilsonian Segregation," *Political Science Quarterly* 61–79 (March 1968).

4. W. E. B. DuBois, "An Open Letter to Woodrow Wilson," *The Crisis*, September, 1913. Booker T. Washington, who had not supported Wilson, expressed a similar sentiment to the journalist Oswald Garrison Villard on August 10, 1913: "I have recently spent several days in Washington, and I have never seen colored people so discouraged and bitter as they are at the present time." For Washington's view of the 1912 election, see Louis R. Harlan, *Booker T. Washington: Wizard of Tuskegee, 1901–1915* 353–355 (New York: Oxford University Press, 1983). When Washington attended Wilson's 1901 inauguration as president of Princeton, he was the only honored invitee who was not accommodated in a faculty house.

5. Josephus Daniels, who ran Wilson's publicity organization in the South during the campaign, made the party's position crystal clear in an editorial in his Raleigh *News & Observer* a month before the election. The South, he said, was solidly Democratic because of "the realization that the subjugation of the negro, politically, and the separation of the negro, socially, are paramount to all other

considerations in the South short of the preservation of the Republic itself. And we shall recognize no emancipation, nor shall we proclaim any deliverer, that falls short of these essentials to the peace and welfare of our part of the country." Raleigh *News & Observer,* October 1, 1912.

6. The newly empowered Southern Democrats demanded that Washington's street-cars be segregated, that Congress enact a miscegenation statute for the District of Columbia, and that all black appointees be dismissed, especially those in a position "to boss white girls." As the newly appointed collector of internal revenue in Atlanta asserted, "There is no Government position for negroes in the South. A negro's place is in the cornfield." *Atlanta Georgian and News,* October 7, 1913.

7. FDR to ER, March 17, 1913, FDRL. Eleanor wired to congratulate Franklin. "I ordered your 17th of March present as we couldn't do anything else together." FDRL.

8. The State, War, and Navy Building, now refurbished as the Eisenhower Executive Office Building, is the finest remaining example of what architectural historians call "General Grant style," a reference to the monumental federal buildings constructed during Grant's presidency, most of which were designed by Alfred B. Mullett. For an assessment, see Elsa M. Santoyo, ed., *Creating an American Masterpiece: Architectural Drawings of the Old Executive Office Building, 1871–1888* (Washington, D.C.: Executive Office of the President, 1988); Donald H. Lehman, *Executive Office Building* (Washington, D.C.: General Services Administration, 1964). For an iconoclastic view, see Dean Acheson, *Present at the Creation* 9 (New York: W. W. Norton, 1969). Mr. Acheson's criticism stems from his service as assistant secretary of state under FDR in the 1940s.

9. FDR and Daniels posed for a picture on that balcony shortly after they took office (see illustrations). FDR was caught smiling broadly, and Daniels noted his expression. "We were both looking on the White House," said the secretary, "and you are saying to yourself, being a New Yorker, 'some day I will be living in that house'—while I, being from the South, know I must be satisfied with no such ambition." Josephus Daniels, *The Wilson Era: Years of Peace, 1910–1917* 129 (Chapel Hill: University of North Carolina Press, 1944).

10. FDR to SDR, March 17, 1913; SDR to FDR, March 18, 1913, 2 *The Roosevelt Letters* 170–171, Elliott Roosevelt, ed. (London: George G. Harrap. 1950).

11. Navy Department, *Ships' Data: U.S. Naval Vessels* 6–14 (Washington, D.C.: U.S. Government Printing Office, 1914); Bureau of the Census, *Statistical History of the United States from Colonial Times to the Present* 711, 736 (Stamford, Conn.: Fairfield Publishers, 1965). To convert 1913 dollars, multiply by 18. Thus, $144 million would equal $2.592 billion in 2006.

12. 19 *Encyclopedia Britannica,* 11th ed. 310–311 (Cambridge, England: Cambridge University Press, 1911). The United States's first two modern battleships, the *Nevada* and *Oklahoma,* were laid down at the end of TR's presidency but were not launched until 1914 and not commissioned until 1916. They and their sister ships *Pennsylvania* and *Arizona,* obsolescent but serviceable, continued on active

service until Pearl Harbor in 1941. The *Arizona* and *Oklahoma* were sunk, the *Nevada* was run aground, and the *Pennsylvania*, in dry dock, was heavily damaged. Edward L. Beach, *The United States Navy: 200 Years* 429–430 (New York: Henry Holt, 1986).

13. Testifying before the Select Committee on the Budget of the House of Representatives in 1919, FDR said, "We feel that the present bureau system concentrates too much dog-in-the-manger policy on the part of each bureau as against every other bureau, that they are not all working sufficiently for the common end of the Navy Department, and that they are working too much for the particular good of their own particular bureau." Transcript, October 1, 1919, FDRL.

14. Daniels steadfastly resisted all efforts to make the bureaus responsible to the chief of naval operations, believing that would "Prussianize" the Navy. As Daniels saw it, such a reorganization would make the secretary of the Navy a figurehead sitting on top of the Washington Monument without a telephone. "I would be ashamed to draw the salary, and I would go home," said Daniels. FDR did not share Daniels's view. Daniels, *Wilson Era: Years of Peace* 241–243.

15. Edmund Morris, *The Rise of Theodore Roosevelt* 606 (New York: Coward, McCann & Geoghegan, 1979).

16. Transcript, October 1, 1919, House of Representatives Select Committee on the Budget, FDRL. Following the attack on Pearl Harbor, FDR preempted traditional congressional support for the bureaus with a masterly two-step maneuver. On December 20, 1941, he appointed Admiral Ernest J. King to the newly established post of commander in chief, U.S. Fleet (COMINCH), and placed the bureaus under him (Executive Order 8984). In March 1942, Roosevelt named King to be chief of naval operations (CNO) as well, in effect combining the two posts (Executive Order 9096). That gave King command of the entire Navy, similar to the authority General Marshall exercised as Army chief of staff. It was wartime, and no one on Capitol Hill questioned the president's decision. And in the Navy no one dared question King—a hard-drinking, self-styled sonofabitch who gave no quarter. For King's discussion of the transition, see Ernest J. King and Walter Muir Whitehill, *Fleet Admiral King: A Naval Record* 349–359 (New York: W. W. Norton, 1952).

17. Paragraph 2 (1) of section 415 of the Revised Statutes of the United States provided that there be "an Assistant Secretary of the Navy . . . and he will perform such duties as may be prescribed by the Secretary."

18. Josephus Daniels, *The Wilson Era: Years of War and After* 253 (Chapel Hill: University of North Carolina Press, 1946).

19. As acting secretary of the Navy on February 25, 1898, TR cabled Dewey:

> ORDER THE SQUADRON, EXCEPT THE MONOCACY, TO HONG KONG.
> KEEP FULL OF COAL. IN THE EVENT OF DECLARATION OF WAR
> SPAIN, YOUR DUTY WILL BE TO SEE THAT THE SPANISH
> SQUADRON DOES NOT LEAVE THE ASIATIC COAST, THEN OFFEN-

SIVE OPERATIONS IN THE PHILIPPINE ISLANDS. KEEP OLYMPIA
UNTIL FURTHER ORDERS.

ROOSEVELT

20. *New York Sun,* March 19, 1913. Beginning with TR, five Roosevelts (Theodore, 1897–1898; Franklin, 1913–1920; TR, Jr., 1921–1924; Theodore Douglas Robinson [son of Corinne Roosevelt, TR's sister], 1924–1929; Henry L., 1933–1936) have served as assistant secretary of the Navy. TR's birthday, January 27, was officially celebrated as Navy Day from 1922 until the unification of the services in 1949.

21. "He was young then and made some mistakes," Daniels wrote many years later. "Upon reflection, although I was older, I made mistakes too." Daniels, *Wilson Era: Years of Peace* 129.

22. On November 9, 1932, Daniels, who had always written to FDR as "Dear Franklin," posted a letter to the president-elect with the salutation "My dear Chief." Roosevelt would not hear of it. "My dear Chief," he replied. "That title still stands! And I am still Franklin to you." And so it continued until Daniels's death. Quoted in Joseph L. Morrison, *Josephus Daniels: The Small-d Democrat* 167 (Chapel Hill: University of North Carolina Press, 1966). The extensive twenty-two-year correspondence between FDR and Daniels was collected and edited by Carroll Kilpatrick and published by the University of North Carolina Press in 1952 under the title *Roosevelt and Daniels: A Friendship in Politics.*

23. Rex Tugwell, an early brain truster, remembers the deference FDR exhibited toward Daniels on the train carrying the president-elect's party from Albany to Washington for the inauguration in 1933. "Rex, this is the man who taught me a lot that I needed to know," said Roosevelt as he introduced Daniels to Tugwell. Rexford G. Tugwell, *The Democratic Roosevelt* 105 (New York: Doubleday, 1957). For Daniels's contribution as ambassador to Mexico, see E. David Cronon, *Josephus Daniels in Mexico* (Madison: University of Wisconsin Press, 1960).

24. Daniels, *Wilson Era: Years of Peace* 124.

25. When FDR first met Daniels at the 1912 Baltimore convention, he thought he was the "funniest looking hillbilly I ever saw." William D. Hassett, "The President Was My Boss," *The Saturday Evening Post* 38–39 (October 31, 1953).

26. Ernest K. Lindley, *Franklin D. Roosevelt: A Career in Progressive Democracy* 117 (Indianapolis: Bobbs-Merrill, 1931).

27. Daniels, *Wilson Era: Years of Peace* 290–292. Also see Brian Johnson, *Fly Navy: The History of Maritime Aviation* 25 (London: David & Charles, 1981).

28. TR to California governor Hiram Johnson, November 16, 1914. This was TR's famous "speak softly and carry a big stick" letter in which he said, among other things, that Bryan and Daniels were "the two most wretched creatures we have ever seen at the head of those great departments [State and Navy]." 8 *The Letters of Theodore Roosevelt* 846, Elting E. Morison, ed. (Cambridge, Mass.: Harvard University Press, 1954).

29. Daniels shared the racism of the Wilson administration; the enlisted men he was concerned about were white. Shortly after assuming office, he wrote that there was no discrimination in the Navy: "All Negroes are messmen." Later he expressed surprise to Eleanor that the Roosevelts employed white servants and suggested they be replaced by blacks. Daniels's views changed over the years, and by the time the New Deal came to power he and Eleanor stood shoulder to shoulder in the struggle for black equality. Daniels to J. J. Adkins, May 27, 1913, Daniels Papers, Library of Congress; Jonathan Daniels, *The End of Innocence* 79–80 (Philadelphia: J. B. Lippincott, 1954). Also see Blanche Wiesen Cook, 1 *Eleanor Roosevelt* 204 (New York: Viking Penguin, 1992).

30. Stimson's reference is to Admiral Alfred Thayer Mahan (1840–1914), whose book *The Influence of Sea Power upon History, 1660–1783* became the Bible for advocates of naval expansion. Quoted in Beach, *United States Navy* 421.

31. "I soon observed as I voyaged on the Navy ships," Daniels wrote, "that sailors and marines had spare time that was not employed. I also learned that many of them were lacking in elementary education. Some did not even have knowledge of the three R's. . . . I determined to strengthen the Navy as an educational institution with schools on every ship. . . . Opposition did not deter me, and I issued instructions that schools should be open to every enlisted man and marine, that attendance should be compulsory, and that young officers should do the teaching (General Order 53, issued October 1, 1913). I followed it up with detailed instructions [General Order 63, December 16, 1913] and a magazine article entitled: 'The Navy's Universities Afloat.' " Daniels, *Wilson Era: Years of Peace* 253–254.

32. The rum ration for sailors was abolished under Andrew Jackson, and in 1899 John D. Long, McKinley's secretary of the Navy, prohibited the sale or issue of all alcoholic beverages to enlisted men. In the first years of the twentieth century, prohibitionist sentiment was such that battleships named for dry states (e.g., *Mississippi*) were christened with lemonade rather than champagne.

33. Quoted in Ted Morgan, *FDR: A Biography* 148 (New York: Simon & Schuster, 1985). I was unable to find the text of Daniels's condom order in the archives of the Navy Department but did locate an October 10, 1917, letter from Raymond A. Fosdick, chairman of the Navy's civilian advisory panel, to Daniels in which Fosdick referred to the secretary's order banning the distribution of "Individual Prophylactic Packets." Fosdick complained that Commander Berryhill, chief medical officer at the Mare Island Naval Station in California, was critical of Daniels's order. Berryhill, said Fosdick, believed "men were animals and needed sexual activities, and the only sensible way was to have a red light district with the women examined periodically." Fosdick recommended that Berryhill be transferred, and Daniels complied the following week. Daniels to Fosdick, October 17, 1917. Both letters in the Daniels Papers, Library of Congress.

34. FDR to Louis Howe, April 9, 1914, Howe Personal Papers, quoted in Alfred B. Rollins, Jr., *Roosevelt and Howe* 118 (New York: Alfred A. Knopf, 1962). Many

years later, FDR could not resist taking credit for the order. "The Chief took the blame, but he didn't formulate the order at all," Roosevelt told press secretary William Hassett. "I did it." If FDR did formulate the order, the evidence is elusive. Jonathan Daniels, *The End of Innocence* 129 (Philadelphia: J. B. Lippincott, 1954).

35. The sobriquet derives from a Tillman speech in 1896 in which he proposed to stick a pitchfork in the broad posterior of Grover Cleveland. Daniels accumulated a unique record as secretary of the Navy: during his eight-year tenure, Congress approved every request he made except for the large construction program he submitted after the armistice in 1918. Paolo E. Coletta, "Josephus Daniels," in Coletta (ed.), 2 *American Secretaries of the Navy* 530 (Annapolis, Md.: Naval Institute Press, 1980).

36. Wilson and Daniels remained close throughout their eight years in Washington. Professor Arthur Link, Wilson's principal biographer, attributes it to the fact that "Daniels was willing to give friendship on Wilson's terms. There was nothing calculated about the North Carolinian's devotion and loyalty; he simply loved the President and supported him without question. Wilson returned Daniels's love and trust with an affection equally warm . . . and the more Daniels's critics raged, the stronger Wilson's affections grew." *Wilson: The New Freedom* 125.

37. In 1923 the Supreme Court upheld the California statute, holding that the right of Japanese aliens to own land was not secured by treaty. *Terrace v. Thompson*, 263 U.S. 197 (1923). But twenty-five years later, in *Oyama v. California*, 332 U.S. 633 (1948), the Court found the law in conflict with the equal protection clause of the Fourteenth Amendment, a view subsequently adopted by the California Supreme Court in *Sei Fujii v. State*, 242 P. 2d 617 (1952).

38. *The New York Times*, May 16, 1913; *The New York World*, May 16, 1913.

39. Daniels, *Wilson Era: Years of Peace* 163–167. Also see Daniels, *Cabinet Diaries* 48–68; Link, *Wilson: New Freedom* 289–304. FDR supported Daniels vigorously. There was "no Japanese scare," he told the press, since "Japan doesn't want war and neither does this country. It is a California question purely." But Roosevelt was always his own best revisionist. Writing to Admiral Mahan a year later (June 16, 1914), he said, "I did all in my power to have the ships return nearer their base. . . . Orders were sent against my protest to Admiral Nicholson, telling him not to move out of the Yangtze River." Watertown (Mass.) *Standard*, May 29, 1913; FDR to Mahan, FDRL.

40. Daniels was not content with simply driving the price down. The Navy, he thought, should have its own plant for making armor plate, and in 1914 he cajoled Congress into passing authorizing legislation. The general board of the Navy recommended that for security reasons the plant be located at least 100 miles inland, and Daniels selected Charleston, West Virginia, for the site. The plant was begun in 1917 but not completed in time to produce armor plate for the war. After the war it produced shells for the Navy, but the Harding adminis-

tration chose not to complete the armor plate facilities. "Monopoly won when it put Harding in the White House," said Daniels. *Wilson Era: Years of Peace* 355–363.

41. Roosevelt paid approximately $2,000 annually in club dues, roughly 40 percent of his $5,000 salary as assistant secretary. His checkbook stubs are among his personal papers at the FDRL.

42. Henry B. Wilson to FDR, July 7, 1913.

43. William F. Halsey and J. Bryan III, *Admiral Halsey's Story* 18 (New York: McGraw-Hill, 1947).

44. Quoted in Geoffrey C. Ward, *A First-Class Temperament* 205 (New York: Harper & Row, 1989).

45. ER to FDR, July 1913, FDRL.

46. FDR to Charles A. Munn, March 26, 1913, FDRL.

47. Elliott Roosevelt and James Brough, *An Untold Story: The Roosevelts of Hyde Park* 24 (New York: G. P. Putnam's Sons, 1973).

48. Quoted in Arthur Schlesinger, Jr., *The Crisis of the Old Order* 352 (Boston: Houghton Mifflin, 1957).

49. Quoted in Jonathan Daniels, *Washington Quadrille* 88–89 (New York: Doubleday, 1968).

50. Camp to FDR, July 25, 1917, FDRL.

51. In 1912 Longworth became the victim of his father-in-law's presidential candidacy and lost a three-way race for his congressional seat in Cincinnati by 101 votes. Longworth, running as a Republican, received 22,229 votes; Stanley Bowdle, his Democratic opponent, received 22,330; and Millard Andrew, the Progressive candidate, 5,771. In 1914 Longworth defeated Bowdle 29,822 to 24,054, essentially the margin Andrew had siphoned off in 1912. Longworth was elected House majority leader in 1923, and became Speaker on December 7, 1925, a post he held until just before his death in 1931.

52. FDR to ER, July 14, 1914, 2 *Roosevelt Letters* 192–193.

53. Don Van Natta, Jr., *First Off the Tee* 101–111. FDR loved golf and regularly shot in the low eighties. He had been taught the game by his father at Campobello and in 1904 won the island championship. After he was paralyzed FDR no longer played, but he did design a special nine-hole course for polio victims at Warm Springs, Georgia—the only president to design a golf course. Not surprisingly, Roosevelt did more than any president to democratize the game. During his administration, the WPA built more than 250 municipal golf courses, making golf accessible to hundreds of thousands of new players. As Eleanor said, golf was "the game that he enjoyed above all others."

54. James Roosevelt and Sidney Shalett, *Affectionately, F.D.R.* 71–72 (New York: Harcourt, Brace, 1959). James reports that he often caddied for his father at Chevy Chase for twenty-five cents a week but that the bigger benefit was that "I, too, got to skip church occasionally in favor of the golf course."

55. Quoted in Ward, *First-Class Temperament* 210.

56. The house at 1733 N Street was demolished in the 1950s to make way for the Canterbury Apartments, which were subsequently converted to the Topaz Hotel. The R Street house, still in good repair but painted white, is now the residence of the ambassador from Mali.

57. FDR's federal tax returns are filed among his personal papers at Hyde Park. His 1915 return, typical for the period, shows a gross income of $22,845, of which $9,256 came from dividends (untaxed) and $4,177 from interest. The New York town house was valued conservatively at $84,150 ($1.5 million in today's dollars), which he depreciated at 1% annually. State and local taxes totaled $257.92.

58. FDR to Howe, March 19, 1913, FDRL.

59. Howe to FDR, March 23, 1913, FDRL.

60. Elliott Roosevelt, *Untold Story* 22.

61. Lela Stiles, *The Man Behind Roosevelt: The Story of Louis McHenry Howe* 42 (Cleveland: World, 1954).

62. Kenneth C. Davis, *FDR: The Beckoning of Destiny, 1882–1928* 311 (New York: Putnam, 1971).

63. ER, interview with Louis Eisner, FDRL. Also see ER's "Foreward" in Stiles, *Man Behind Roosevelt* vii.

64. John Gunther, *Roosevelt in Retrospect* 84 (New York: Harper & Brothers, 1950).

65. Daniels, *Wilson Era: Years of Peace* 128.

66. FDR to Howe, n.d., Howe Personal Papers.

67. Perkins, *The Roosevelt I Knew* 12.

68. Quoted in Davis, *FDR: Beckoning of Destiny* 313.

69. Stiles, *Man Behind Roosevelt* 49, 40.

70. *The Washington Post*, April 30, 1913.

71. Quoted in Ward, *First-Class Temperament* 234.

72. Speaking in Butte, Montana, August 18, 1920, FDR, running for vice president, claimed credit for the Navy's exemplary labor relations. The only exception was at the Norfolk Navy Yard, where there was ongoing friction, attributable mainly to dangerous and unsanitary working conditions. See Frank Freidel, *Franklin D. Roosevelt: The Apprenticeship* 203 (Boston: Little, Brown, 1952).

73. Quoted in Ward, *First-Class Temperament* 234.

74. Lodge to FDR, August 1, 1913; FDR to Lodge, August 2, September 15, 1913. Afterward, Lodge's son-in-law, Representative Augustus P. Gardner, wrote that Lodge thought FDR "the promptest and most efficient Assistant Secretary in any Department with whom we have dealt." Gardner to FDR, June 25, 1913, FDRL.

75. Perkins, *The Roosevelt I Knew* 20.

76. Lindley, *Franklin D. Roosevelt* 115–116; Freidel, *Apprenticeship* 237–238n.

77. Daniels, *Wilson Era: Years of Peace* 179.

78. For the text of the Convention on the Rights and Duties of States promulgated at Montevideo, see Charles I. Bevans, ed., 3 *Treaties and Other International*

Agreements of the United States, 1776–1949 145 (Washington, D.C.: U.S. Government Printing Office, 1969). [*TIAS.*]

79. The Platt Amendment, named for Connecticut senator Orville H. Platt, gave ultimate control of Cuba's finances and foreign relations to the United States, permitted the U.S. to intervene to maintain law and order, and provided for a long-term lease for a naval station on Guantánamo Bay. It was added as an appendix to the Cuban constitution and became part of the May 22, 1903, treaty between the United States and Cuba. [6 *TIAS* 1116.]

SEVEN | War

The epigraph appears in a letter written by FDR to Eleanor on Sunday, August 2, 1914. 2 *The Roosevelt Letters* 199, Elliott Roosevelt, ed. (London: George G. Harrap, 1950).

1. *New York Sun,* December 10, 1913. Inspired by Howe, the *Sun* suggested that if Governor Glynn did not establish his independence from Tammany, the Wilson administration would throw its support behind Roosevelt. As with many of Howe's planted stories, the article was moonshine. Also see *New York Post,* January 15, 1914; *New York Herald,* February 10, 1914; *New York Times,* February 10, 1914.

2. FDR to WW (handwritten), circa March 31, 1914, Wilson Papers, Library of Congress. The message was handed to Wilson by Secretary Daniels after Cabinet on the thirty-first.

3. Wilson to FDR, April 1, 1914. Wilson Papers.

4. George Mowry, *Theodore Roosevelt and the Progressive Movement* 300–301 (Madison: University of Wisconsin Press, 1946). FDR had ingratiated himself with TR earlier by announcing he would not seek the Democratic nomination if Theodore ran for governor on the Progressive ticket. "Blood is thicker than water," FDR told the press. TR was apparently unmoved and did not reciprocate. Quoted in Ernest K. Lindley, *Franklin D. Roosevelt: A Career in Progressive Democracy* 301 (Indianapolis: Bobbs-Merrill, 1931).

5. *The New York Times,* July 23, 1914.

6. Ibid., July 24, 1914.

7. FDR to ER, July 19, 1914, 2 *Roosevelt Letters* 192.

8. *The New York Times,* July 24, 1914.

9. Philip C. Jessup, 2 *Elihu Root* 238–242 (New York: Dodd, Mead & Co., 1938). Also see *The New York Times,* May 20, 1914.

10. FDR to ER, July 19, 1914, 2 *Roosevelt Letters* 192.

11. The archduke was in Sarajevo in conjunction with the annual summer maneuvers of the Austro-Hungarian Army, which in 1914 were conducted nearby. His party of six open-top vehicles (Franz Ferdinand and his wife rode in the third car) was returning from a reception at City Hall when the column slowed to make a difficult right-angle turn. The car in which the archduke was riding

came to an almost complete stop in front of Princip, who stepped from the crowd, approached the vehicle, and fired two shots at point-blank range from a large-caliber military pistol. The first bullet struck the duchess in the abdomen; the second hit the archduke near the heart. Both died instantly. Princip and his collaborators were tried in open court and convicted. Because of his youth, Princip avoided the death penalty and was sentenced to twenty years' imprisonment. He died of tuberculosis in prison at Theresienstadt on April 28, 1918. Vladimir Dedijer, *The Road to Sarajevo* 285–323 (New York: Simon & Schuster, 1966). For Serbian complicity, see Sidney B. Fay's magisterial *The Origins of the World War,* 2 vols. (New York: Macmillian, 1930), particularly volume 2, pages 53–166.

12. Bismarck's quote, often cited, was repeated by Albert Ballin to Winston Churchill in July 1914, when Ballin was sent by William II to London in an effort to persuade Britain to remain neutral. Winston Churchill, 1 *The World Crisis* 112 (New York: Scribner, 1928).

13. David Fromkin, *Europe's Last War: Who Started the Great War in 1914?* 307–316 (New York: Knopf, 2004). For the text of Austria's ultimatum and Serbia's reply, see the World War I documentary Web site maintained by Brigham Young University at www.lib.byu.edu.

14. Russia commenced hostilities with 114 divisions, roughly 2.4 million men, and soon built up to a peak strength of 6 million. Germany called 2 million men to the colors, and by the end of the first week in August fielded 87 divisions of 18,000 men each. Three quarters of these were in the West, one quarter in the East. Between August 2 and 18, France placed 3.8 million men under military orders, two thirds of whom were reservists. Austria initially mobilized 500,000 men and would eventually muster 2.7 million. S.L.A. Marshall, *The American Heritage History of World War I* 35–36 (New York: Simon & Schuster, 1964).

15. Princess Evelyn Blücher, *An English Wife in Berlin* 137 (London: Constable, 1920).

16. Viscount Edward Grey of Falloden, 2 *Twenty-Five Years* 20 (London: Hodder & Stoughton, 1925).

17. Frederich E. Smith, Earl of Birkenhead, 1 *Points of View* 22 (London: Hodder & Stoughton, 1922).

18. FDR to ER, August 1, 1914, 2 *Roosevelt Letters* 195.

19. Ellen Wilson died on August 6, 1914. "It is too horrible about Mrs. Wilson," FDR wrote Eleanor the next day. "We knew on Wednesday [August 5] that there was little hope and the end came last night. The President has been truly wonderful and I dread a breakdown. The funeral is Monday at the White House. I don't yet know whether Assistant Secretaries will be expected to go or not. The interment will be private." Ibid. 204.

20. FDR to ER, August 2, 1914, ibid. 198–199 (FDR's emphasis).

21. Ibid.

22. ER to FDR, August 7, 1914, FDRL.

23. Department of State, *Foreign Relations of the United States, 1914, Supplement* 547–551 (Washington, D.C.: U.S. Government Printing Office, 1928). Americans must be "neutral in fact as well as in name," said Wilson, "impartial in thought as well as action."

24. Wilson to Daniels, August 6, 1914. Wilson Papers.

25. 2 *Roosevelt Letters* 204 (FDR's emphasis).

26. FDR to ER, August 5, 1914, ibid. 202 (FDR's emphasis).

27. Lindley, *Franklin D. Roosevelt* 132.

28. FDR to Howe, August 13, 1914. Howe Papers, FDRL.

29. Josephus Daniels, *The Wilson Era: Years of Peace* 131 (Chapel Hill: University of North Carolina Press, 1944).

30. FDR to Montgomery Hare, August 31, 1914, FDRL.

31. FDR to Howe, August 22, 1914. Howe Papers. For Hearst's refusal, see *New York American*, August 27, 1914.

32. Howe to FDR, August 24, 1914, FDRL.

33. Gerard cabled the State Department on September 10 that he would accept the nomination only if the president and Secretary Bryan approved. Bryan passed the query on to Wilson:

    > Asst. Sec. Roosevelt is as you know a candidate and has, as I understand, the endorsement of Secs. McAdoo and [William C.] Redfield [Secretary of Commerce]. I have also felt Roosevelt would be the best man—having the advantage of being actively progressive and an upstate man. Gerard could not of course leave Berlin in the near future. What do you wish said to Gerard? He will do as you wish.

    Wilson declined to intervene, and Gerard took the president's silence as approval. Bryan to Wilson, n.d., Wilson Papers.

34. Walton *Chronicle*, September 23, 1914.

35. SDR to FDR, September 30, 1914, FDRL.

36. 2 *Roosevelt Letters* 212.

37. FDR to Langdon P. Marvin, October 19, 1914, FDRL. Ernest K. Lindley, writing one of the earliest Roosevelt biographies, accepted FDR's version of the election, which then became gospel until after the president's death when biographers checked the facts. See Lindley, *Franklin D. Roosevelt* 133.

38. Daniels, *Wilson Era: Years of Peace* 132.

39. Arthur M. Schlesinger, Jr., *The Crisis of the Old Order* 347 (Boston: Houghton Mifflin, 1957). For Sara and Franklin's half brother, Rosy, FDR's embrace of Tammany required considerable adjustment. "Rosy was in town yesterday," Sara wrote her son a few days later, "and says 'they all feel quite upset at [your] T. Club appearance as T. is working against [John P.] Mitchel [the reform candidate for mayor] and Franklin's speaking strengthens Tammany.' Uncle Warren [Delano] says one of the papers has pictures of you and *Murphy* side by side—All of this

rather upsets me I confess." Quoted in Geoffrey C. Ward, *A First-Class Tempera-ment: The Emergence of Franklin Roosevelt* 376–368 (New York: Harper & Row, 1989).

40. Lindley, *Franklin D. Roosevelt* 133–134.

41. The House letter is in the collection of the Franklin and Eleanor Roosevelt Insti-tute, FDRL. On October 11, 1914, Thomas D. McCarthy, Gerard's campaign manager, wrote FDR asking for an endorsement. "I do not know any one thing that would have a greater influence on the vote that Ambassador Gerard will re-ceive on Election Day than your support of his candidacy during this cam-paign," wrote McCarthy. FDR did not reply. FDRL.

42. James A. Farley, *Jim Farley's Story* 56 (New York: McGraw-Hill, 1948). Gerard told Farley that FDR "would never forget the defeat he suffered . . . in the Demo-cratic senatorial primary of 1914."

43. Evidently at Eleanor's suggestion, Gerard prepared a six-page summary of his services to the Democratic party and the promises he believed had been made to him and then broken. ER sent the memo to Franklin with a penciled comment: "F.D.R. read the end. He is very bitter. E.R." FDRL.

   In his autobiography, Gerard does not mention the 1914 primary but notes that in 1932 he "contributed money whenever [FDR] needed it for his [cam-paign] payroll, giving it to Louis Howe, Roosevelt's grand vizier," and suggests he had been promised the embassy in either London or Rome. James W. Gerard, *My First Eighty-Three Years in America* 324 (New York: Doubleday, 1951).

44. *The New York Times,* October 22, 1914.

45. FDR to ER, October [22?] 1914, 2 *Roosevelt Letters* 212.

46. FDR, Memorandum for the Press, November 14, 1914, FDRL.

47. The text of Wilson's 1914 State of the Union message is most easily accessible online at http://janda.org/politxts/State%20of%20Union%20Addresses/1913=1920%20Wilson/wilson.1914.html.

48. U.S. Congress, House, Committee on Naval Affairs, *Hearings, 1915* 571–572, 586 (Washington, D.C.: U.S. Government Printing Office, 1915).

49. Ibid. 921.

50. Ibid. 921–995.

51. *New York Herald,* December 16, 1914; *New York Sun,* December 17, 1914. The extensive *New York Times* coverage of FDR's testimony is reprinted in 2 *Roosevelt Letters* 216–218.

52. FDR to SDR, December 17, 1914, 2 *Roosevelt Letters* 215.

53. ER to Isabella Ferguson, December 19, 1914, FDRL.

54. William Graham Greene, permanent undersecretary, to Commander Powers Symington, U.S. naval attaché, December 19, 1914. Symington forwarded Greene's note to FDR with the following message: "I regret to tell you that the Admiralty would find it very inconvenient for you to come over here for the pur-pose of studying the war organization of the British Navy. . . . I am afraid that at this time it is hardly worthwhile to send any more officers over as observers. The

lid is down tight and we get almost nothing." Symington to FDR, December 23, 1914, FDRL.

55. For a report of the London dinner, held at Gray's Inn, see Jon Meacham, *Franklin and Winston: An Intimate Portrait of an Epic Friendship* 3–5 (New York: Random House, 2003). "I always disliked [Churchill]," FDR told Joseph P. Kennedy in 1939. "At a dinner I attended he acted like a stinker." Quoted in Amanda Smith, ed., *Hostage to Fortune: The Letters of Joseph P. Kennedy* 411 (New York: Viking, 2001).

56. Francis L. Loewenheim, Harold D. Langley, and Manfred Jones (eds.), *Roosevelt and Churchill: Their Secret Wartime Correspondence* 5–6 (New York: E. P. Dutton & Co., 1975).

57. For the text of the German proclamation, see "Memorandum of the German Government," February 4, 1914, *Foreign Relations, 1915, Supplement* 96–97.

58. British Ambassador to Secretary of State, March 1, 1915, ibid. 127–128. Also see *The New York Times*, March 2, 1915.

59. Arthur S. Link, *Wilson: The Struggle for Neutrality* 321–323 (Princeton, N.J.: Princeton University Press, 1960). For the complete text of the U.S. note, see *Foreign Relations, 1915, Supplement* 98–100.

60. March 30, 1915, ibid. 152–156.

61. Wilson's remarks were made to an audience of four thousand newly naturalized citizens at Convention Hall in Philadelphia, May 10, 1915. For text, see *The New York Times*, May 11, 1915. For the American note to Berlin, see *Foreign Relations, 1915, Supplement* 393–396.

62. "Resting Our Case," *The New Republic* 57 (May 22, 1915). A survey of newspaper opinion is reprinted in *Literary Digest* 1197–1199 (May 22, 1915). Also see *The New York Times*, May 15, 1915. Not surprisingly, TR had nothing but contempt for Wilson's effort to avoid war, which he alleged was supported "by all the hyphenated Americans . . . [by] every soft creature, every coward and weakling, every man who can't look more than six inches ahead, every man whose god is money, or pleasure, or ease." TR to his son Archibald, May 19, 1915. Theodore Roosevelt Papers.

63. German foreign minister Gottlieb von Jagow told *The New York Times*, "The issues involved are of such importance, and the views in regard to the *Lusitania* show such variance, that the German Government believed it essential to attempt to establish a common basis of fact before entering into a discussion of the issues involved." May 31, 1915.

64. To allay German public opinion, military and naval authorities were explicitly instructed to keep the emperor's order secret. Grand Admiral Alfred von Tirpitz, the Navy's head, and Admiral Gustav Bachmann, the emperor's naval aide, immediately submitted their resignations, which William II refused. "My order stands. If there are political consequences, the Imperial Chancellor carries the responsibility." Quoted in Link, *Wilson: Struggle for Neutrality* 409.

65. The text of the American note, June 9, 1915, is in *Foreign Relations, 1915, Supplement* 436–438.

66. WJB to WW, June 3, 1915, 1 *The Lansing Papers* 419–421. Library of Congress. For the text of Bryan's resignation and Wilson's reply, see Link, *Wilson: Struggle for Neutrality* 422–423.

67. FDR to ER, June 10, 1915, 2 *Roosevelt Letters* 222. Numerous biographers, eager to put daylight between FDR and Daniels, suggest that Roosevelt was disappointed Daniels was not quitting as well. Nothing supports that assertion. To the contrary, Daniels did not believe Wilson's note to Germany meant war, tried to dissuade Bryan from resigning, and was determined to remain loyal to the president, whom he adored. Taken in context of the Washington furor, FDR's italicized comment that J. D. would *not* resign was a commendation of his boss. See Daniels, *Wilson Era: Years of Peace* 424–435.

68. FDR to WW, June 9, 1915, Wilson Papers.

69. WW to FDR, June 14, 1915, Wilson Papers.

70. WW to Garrison, July 21, 1915; WW to Daniels, July 21, 1915, cited in Link, *Wilson: Struggle for Neutrality* 591–594. Professor Link provides an extensive analysis of why Wilson changed his mind, which I have summarized.

71. Daniels, *Wilson Era: Years of Peace* 327–328.

72. FDR to ER, August 28, 1915, 2 *Roosevelt Letters* 235–236.

73. The council was composed of six members of cabinet, chaired by the secretary of war, plus a nonpartisan advisory panel made up of leaders of industry, labor, and science. Ibid. For the council's operation, see Daniels, *Wilson Era: Years of Peace* 586–590.

74. Samuel I. Rosenman, ed., 8 *The Public Papers and Addresses of Franklin D. Roosevelt* 205, 243 (New York: Random House, 1950). This was the National Defense Advisory Commission (NDAC). See David M. Kennedy, *Freedom from Fear* 478 (New York: Oxford University Press, 1999).

75. FDR to Daniels, February 16, 1916, Daniels Papers.

76. *The New York Times,* September 3, 1916.

77. FDR to ER, September 2, 1916, 2 *Roosevelt Letters* 237–238.

78. Quoted in Kenneth S. Davis, *FDR: The Beckoning of Destiny* 425–426 (New York: G. P. Putnam's Sons, 1971).

79. Elihu Root dutifully contested the nomination as a conservative alternative and trailed Hughes 253–103 on the first ballot. Hughes won the nomination 328–98 on the second ballot, and the third ballot made it unanimous. Congressional Quarterly, *Guide to U.S. Elections* 151 (Washington, D.C.: Congressional Quarterly, Inc., 1975).

80. FDR to ER, June 15, 1916, FDRL.

81. Washington *Evening Star,* June 15, 1916; *New York Sun,* rotogravure, June 25, 1916.

82. FDR to the Navy League Convention, April 13, 1916, FDRL.

83. 1940 *Public Papers and Address* 606–615.

84. William Henry Harbaugh, *Power and Responsibility: The Life and Times of Theodore Roosevelt* 491 (New York: Oxford University Press, 1975).

85. FDR to ER, November 8, 1916, 2 *Roosevelt Letters* 273.

86. FDR to ER, November 9, 1916, ibid. 273–274.

87. The reference is to Theodore Roosevelt's *The Winning of the West* in *The Works of Theodore Roosevelt,* Hermann Hagedorn, ed. (New York: Charles Scribner's Sons, 1926). FDR to ER, November 9, 1916, 2 *Roosevelt Letters* 273–274.

88. Quoted in Marshall, *History of World War I* 204; also see Josephus Daniels, *The Wilson Era and After* 18 (Chapel Hill: University of North Carolina Press, 1946). The Zimmermann telegram did not come entirely out of the blue. In 1913–14 the German government had supplied arms to the Huerta regime in Mexico, which the United States refused to recognize. The telegram was drafted by Dr. Klaus von Kemnitz, the Latin American specialist in the German Foreign Office. Whether it was approved beforehand by Chancellor Theobald von Bethmann-Hollweg and the Supreme Command is unclear, but both were in sympathy with its contents. Friedrich Katz, *Deutschland, Dias, und die mexikanische Revolution: die deutsche Politik in Mexiko, 1870–1920* 337–473 (Berlin: Deutscher Verlag des Wissenschaften, 1964).

89. *Housatonic,* sunk off the Scilly Islands, was carrying contraband and was a legitimate target. But the German U-boat fired without warning, which became the basis of the American complaint. All twenty-five members of the crew were rescued. *The New York Times,* February 4, 1917.

90. Daniels's message, in a private code he and FDR used, stated, "Because of political situation please return to Washington at once. Am sending ship to meet you and party at Puerto Plata tomorrow morning." FDR, "Trip to Haiti and Santa Domingo, 1917," FDRL.

91. Ibid.

92. Harrison J. Thornton, "The Two Roosevelts at Chautauqua," 28 *New York History* 55 (January 1947).

93. Daniels autobiography, Daniels Papers; also see *Wilson Era: Years of War* 23.

94. Washington *Evening Star,* March 10, 1917. The Chicago *Post* urged Daniels's replacement by his "virile-minded, hard-fisted, civilian assistant. Uncuriously enough his name is Roosevelt." Chicago *Post,* March 20, 1917.

95. FDR to Edwyn Johnstone, November 22, 1916, FDRL.

96. Daniels, *Wilson Era: Years of War* 23.

97. Wilson was the first president since John Adams to address Congress in person, and the Supreme Court, respecting the separation of powers, normally did not attend when the president's State of the Union message was read. It departed from tradition in 1917 under Chief Justice White's leadership to show its support for Wilson and war. Daniels, *Wilson Era: Years of War* 31–33.

98. For the text of Wilson's speech, see *The New York Times,* April 3, 1917. Martin Luther's words were "*Ich kann nicht anders* [I can do no other.]," refusing to recant in 1518.

99. Diary of Thomas W. Brahany, chief clerk, White House executive office, entry for April 2, 1917. Typescript at FDRL.

100. FDR, press statement, April 3, 1917, FDRL.
101. Eleanor Roosevelt, *Autobiography* 87 (New York: Harper & Brothers, 1961).
102. Daniels, *Wilson Era: Years of War* 34.

EIGHT | Lucy

The epigraph is from a letter FDR wrote to Eleanor from Washington in the summer
of 1917. The emphasis is FDR's. 2 *The Roosevelt Letters* 280, Elliott Roosevelt, ed. (London: George G. Harrap, 1950).

1. The vote for war was 82–6 in the Senate and 375–50 in the House. La Follette,
   Norris, and Vardaman were joined by Senators A. J. Gronna of North Dakota,
   William Stone of Missouri, and Harry Lane of Oregon in voting against the war.
   La Follette, Norris, and Gronna were Republicans; Vardaman, Stone, and Lane,
   Democrats. In the House, Representative Jeannette Rankin of Montana voted
   against war, as she would do again on December 8, 1941.
2. A key element of Elihu Root's 1903 military reforms provided for the equipping
   and training of the various state militias by the federal government. Under the
   National Defense Act of 1916, the militias were reconstituted as the National
   Guard and made to conform organizationally to the regular Army. The guard
   expanded rapidly in 1917–18 and ultimately provided seventeen divisions
   (Twenty-sixth through Forty-second) to the AEF.

   The 1916 act also provided for a Reserve Officers Training Corps, but there
   were no organized reserve units until the act was amended in 1920, and even
   then they were largely paper formations. Department of the Army, *The Army Almanac* 308–310, 323–324 (Washington, D.C.: U.S. Government Printing Office,
   1950).
3. Bureau of the Census, *Statistical History of the United States from Colonial Times
   to the Present* 736 (Stamford, Conn.: Fairfield Publishers, 1965).
4. Robert William Love, 1 *History of the U.S. Navy* 512–513 (Harrisburg, Pa.: Stackpole Books, 1992).
5. The Navy lost 48 vessels in World War I: 14 to German U-boats, 5 to mines, 16
   to collisions, and 13 to other causes generally associated with poor seamanship.
   The largest vessel lost, the *Cyclops,* a 19,000-ton collier, "mysteriously disappeared" on April 21, 1918, with the loss of all 293 aboard. For a list of the vessels
   lost, see *The Army Almanac* 188.2.
6. "It is perfectly true that I took the chance of authorizing certain large expenditures before Congress had actually appropriated money," said FDR in 1920. "I
   felt confident that Congress would pass the emergency appropriations for which
   we asked." Ernest K. Lindley, *Franklin D. Roosevelt: A Career in Progressive
   Democracy* 140 (Indianapolis: Bobbs-Merrill, 1931).
7. *Time,* May 28, 1923.
8. FDR related the incident to Ernest Lindley while he was governor of New York.

Given Roosevelt's penchant for hyperbole, one should approach the quote with caution. Lindley, *Franklin D. Roosevelt* 140.

9. Josephus Daniels recalled that "Around the [Navy] Department it was said that inasmuch as his cousin Theodore left the position of Assistant Secretary to become a Rough Rider . . . Franklin actually thought fighting in the war was the necessary step toward reaching the White House." Daniels, *The Wilson Era: Years of Peace* 130 (Chapel Hill: University of North Carolina Press, 1944).

10. Quoted in Kenneth S. Davis, *FDR: The Beckoning of Destiny, 1882–1928* 429 (New York: G. P. Putnam's Sons, 1971). All four of TR's sons volunteered for service as enlisted men, but Pershing chose to allow them to serve in the AEF as officers. "It's rather up to us to practice what father preaches," said Quentin, the youngest, who became a pilot and was killed in aerial combat. TR, Jr., won the Distinguished Service Cross and twenty-six years later led the First Division ashore at Normandy. Both he and Archie were wounded in the First World War. Kermit, who served in the British Army, won the Military Cross for gallantry.

11. Daniels, *Years of Peace* 130.

12. Quoted in Davis, *Beckoning of Destiny* 460.

13. Cited in Langdon Marvin to FDR, July 17, 1917, FDRL.

14. Arthur J. Marder, 4 *From Dreadnought to Scapa Flow* 142–143 (New York: Oxford University Press, 1961); Love, *History of the U.S. Navy* 484.

15. Jellicoe's comment was made to U.S. Rear Admiral William Sims, who had been designated by Daniels to head the American naval efforts in Europe. William S. Sims, *The Victory at Sea* 9 (New York: Doubleday, 1920).

16. Arthur Marder, the leading historian of naval warfare in the early twentieth century, reported that a "strange dogma had emerged [in the Royal Navy] that to provide warship escorts to merchant ships was to act essentially 'defensively' (because it protected ships from attack), which was *ipso facto* bad, and that to use naval forces to patrol trade routes, however futile the result, was to act 'offensively' against the warships of the enemy, and this was good." Marder, 4 *From Dreadnought to Scapa Flow* 157–158.

17. Elting E. Morison, *Admiral Sims and the Modern American Navy* 355 (Boston: Houghton Mifflin, 1942).

18. It is Navy lore that Commander Joseph K. Taussig, commanding the destroyer squadron, was asked upon his arrival at Queenstown when his ships would be fit for duty. "We are ready now, sir," Taussig is supposed to have replied, although a witness recalled Taussig as saying, "Ready when fueled." Love, 1 *History of U.S. Navy* 487.

19. FDR to Livingston Davis, April 28, 1917, FDRL. Also see FDR to Daniels, February 25, 1921, in Carroll Kilpatrick, *Roosevelt and Daniels: A Friendship in Politics* 72–74 (Chapel Hill: University of North Carolina Press, 1952). The head of the French mission was former premier René Viviani, but it was Marshal Joffre who attracted the most attention.

20. Love, *History of the U.S. Navy* 498–500.

21. James Roosevelt and Sidney Shalett, *Affectionately, F.D.R.* 79–80 (New York: Harcourt, Brace, 1959); Roosevelt Family Papers, FDRL.

22. Quoted in Lindley, *Franklin D. Roosevelt* 160–161. "Certainly my own interest in the project was due to [Roosevelt's] enthusiasm and encouragement," said Harris.

23. Josephus Daniels, *The Wilson Era: Years of War and After* 83 (Chapel Hill: University of North Carolina Press, 1946).

24. Wilson vented his displeasure to officers in the ward room of the *Pennsylvania* on August 11, 1917. "Every time we have suggested anything to the British Admiralty the reply has come back that it had never been done that way, and I felt like saying, 'Well nothing was ever done so systematically as nothing is being done now.'" Quoted in Kenneth S. Davis, *FDR: The Beckoning of Destiny* 474.

25. FDR, Memorandum on Submarine Situation, 1917, FDRL.

26. The mines were laid by eight specially equipped vessels built with three decks to hold the mines and modified railroad tracks so that as the ships traveled at full speed the mines could be put on the rails and dropped at twelve-second intervals. Each mine contained 300 pounds of TNT and was fitted with an anchor and a buoy that deployed automatically when it hit the water. The mines were set at 300-foot intervals in three tiers, the first at 45 feet, the second at 160 feet, and the third at 240 feet. The barrier was many miles wide, requiring several hours for a submarine to traverse it. Lindley, *Franklin D. Roosevelt* 158–159. Also see Morison, *Admiral Sims* 414–417.

27. Lindley, *Franklin D. Roosevelt* 158–159.

28. Sims, *Victory at Sea* 308.

29. Michael R. Beschloss, *Kennedy and Roosevelt: An Uneasy Alliance* 45–46 (New York: W. W. Norton, 1980).

30. FDR to John J. Fitzgerald, September 3, 1915; Fitzgerald to FDR, September 8, 1915, FDRL.

31. Frank Freidel, interview with John J. Fitzgerald, June 17, 1948, FDRL.

32. Quoted in Ted Morgan, *FDR: A Biography* 193 (New York: Simon & Schuster, 1985).

33. *New York Tribune,* February 11, 1918. For a contemporaneous report of the celebration, see *The New York Times,* July 5, 1917.

34. James J. Walker to FDR, November 30, 1917, FDRL.

35. *New York Tribune,* May 28, 1918.

36. FDR to Fred J. Sisson, May 7, 1918. The letter contains the notation "unsent." FDRL.

37. *The Cabinet Diaries of Josephus Daniels,* June 18, 1918, E. David Cronon, ed. (Lincoln: University of Nebraska Press, 1963).

38. FDR to Wilson, July 8, 1918. Also see FDR to John Mack, June 18, 1918, FDRL.

39. With more than 2 million votes cast in the 1918 gubernatorial election, Smith defeated Whitman by fewer than 15,000 votes. Smith received 1,009,936 to

Whitman's 995,094. Charles W. Ervin, running on the Socialist ticket, received 121,705.

40. Quoted in Lindley, *Franklin D. Roosevelt* 165. "I feel confident that you would bring to the governorship not only an unsurpassed knowledge of the administration of State affairs, but a single-minded purpose to carry on these affairs for the liberal and progressive good of the State as a whole." FDR to Al Smith, November 5, 1918. FDRL.

41. Eleanor's role as a Red Cross volunteer during World War I is described by Joseph P. Lash in *Eleanor and Franklin* 208–219 (New York: W. W. Norton, 1971) and in ER's *This Is My Story* 250–263 (New York: Harper & Brothers, 1937).

42. ER to SDR, January 14, 1918; January 16, 1918, FDRL.

43. ER to SDR, May 12, 1918.

44. Maurice Low, *Woodrow Wilson: An Interpretation* (Boston: Little, Brown, 1918). Quoted in Geoffrey C. Ward, *A First-Class Temperament: The Emergence of Franklin Roosevelt* (New York: Harper & Row, 1989).

45. Blanche Wiesen Cook, 2 *Eleanor Roosevelt* 317 (New York: Viking, 1999). ER's friendship with Baruch began when they sailed for Europe on the same ship in November 1918. Throughout the 1920s Baruch supported Eleanor's concerns financially, and by the 1930s ER was referring to him as "one of the wisest and most generous people I have ever known." Eleanor Roosevelt, *This I Remember* 256 (New York: Harper & Brothers, 1949).

46. Roosevelt Family Papers, FDRL, quoted in Ward, *First-Class Temperament* 251n.

47. Thomas A. Krueger and William Glidden, "The New Deal Intellectual Elite," in *The Rich, the Well Born, and the Powerful* 344, Fred Cople Jaher, ed. (Urbana: University of Illinois Press, 1973).

48. FDR to Philip Slomovitz, March 7, 1935, FDRL.

49. The Comstock Act, passed by Congress on March 3, 1873, was primarily an anti-obscenity measure that closed the mails to "obscene, lewd, and/or lascivious" printed matter. It also made it a crime to disseminate information or devices relating to birth control. Its birth control provisions were challenged by Margaret Sanger following her arrest for opening the nation's first birth control clinic in 1916 (*People v. Sanger*, 118 N.E. 637 [N.Y. 1918]), and was not completely overturned until *United States v. One Package of Japanese Pessaries* in 1936.

50. ER uttered these words to her daughter, Anna, at the time of Anna's marriage in June 1926. They were repeated by Anna to her daughter, Eleanor Seagraves, who confirmed them to Blanche Wiesen Cook. 1 *Eleanor Roosevelt* 536 (New York: Viking Penguin, 1992).

51. James Roosevelt with Bill Libby, *My Parents: A Differing View* 97 (Chicago: Playboy Press, 1976).

52. Elliott Roosevelt and James Brough, *An Untold Story: The Roosevelts of Hyde Park* 81 (New York: G. P. Putnam's Sons, 1973). Sleeping arrangements at Hyde Park would confirm the children's assessment. When the house was redone in 1916, there were three new bedrooms above the mammoth first-floor library.

Sara occupied the large one facing the Albany Post Road, Franklin had another large one facing the river, and Eleanor had a small one in between. On June 14, 1918, Sara wrote Franklin about buying a new desk for "her" [ER's] room; a year later Sara wrote her son about the two big rooms, "yours" and "mine." Roosevelt Family Papers, FDRL. Compare Eleanor Roosevelt, "I Remember Hyde Park," *McCall's* (February 1963).

53. "Standards were different in those days," recalled Robert Donovan of the Associated Press. "I'm sure there were some reporters, friends of the White House, who knew about Lucy. But none of them ever thought about exposing the situation. The newspaper business in those days was not so damn serious as it is today. It was a hell of a lot more fun." Quoted in Doris Kearns Goodwin, *No Ordinary Time* 518 (New York: Simon & Schuster, 1994).

54. Arthur Schlesinger, Jr., in Ellen Feldman, *Lucy: A Novel* 1 (New York: W. W. Norton, 2003).

55. Elliott Roosevelt, *An Untold Story* 73. "Though she was a paid employee . . . she was a lady to her fingertips."

56. Michael Teague, *Mrs. L: Conversations with Alice Roosevelt Longworth* 157–158 (New York: Doubleday, 1981). "I think their relationship [FDR's and Lucy's] was very much a lonely-boy-meets-girl thing. The rose behind the ear, the snipped-off lock of hair. That kind of thing."

57. Quoted in Bernard Asbell, *The F.D.R. Memoirs* 229 (New York: Doubleday, 1973).

58. Letter, Captain Lyman B. Cotton, Jr., USN, to Jonathan Daniels, January 29, 1967, quoted in Daniels, *Washington Quadrille: The Dance Beside the Documents* 157 (New York: Doubleday, 1968).

59. Davis, *FDR: The Beckoning of Destiny* 488. Olive Clapper, *Washington Tapestry* (New York: Whittlesey House, 1946).

60. Roy Jenkins, *Franklin Delano Roosevelt* 35–36 (New York: Times Books/Henry Holt, 2003).

61. FDR was the youngest of the fifteen assistant secretaries who served between 1860 (when the position was established) and 1936. He was thirty-one when he assumed office; the average age was forty-eight. He also served longest: seven years and five months. Arthur W. Macmahon and John D. Millett, *Federal Administrators* 247 (New York: Ames Press, 1967). Reprint.

62. Arthur C. Murray, *At Close Quarters* 85 (London: John Murray, 1946).

63. Admiral W. Sheffield Cowles to FDR, August 17, 1917, FDRL.

64. Quoted in John Gunther, *Roosevelt in Retrospect* 214 (New York: Harper & Brothers, 1950).

65. The dowager was the famed Washington socialite Margot Oxford. *Ibid.*

66. Jenkins, *Franklin Delano Roosevelt* 36.

67. Michael Teague, *Mrs. L* 157–158. Joseph P. Lash quotes Mrs. Longworth in a similar manner, based on his own interview with her. *Eleanor and Franklin* 226.

68. Elliott Roosevelt, *An Untold Story* 82.

69. Henry Brandon, "A Talk with an 83-year-old Enfant-Terrible [ARL]," *The New York Times Magazine,* August 6, 1967.

70. Levi Morton, the son of a Vermont preacher, made a fortune in New York banking, ranking with the Drexels and Morgans in post–Civil War American finance. His firm, Morton Trust Company, later became the foundation of the Guaranty Trust Company. Morton served in Congress and was vice president under Benjamin Harrison and later governor of New York. Ellerslie, his great country house on the Hudson, was near Hyde Park. The Roosevelts and Mortons made several Atlantic crossings together and often went to the Adirondacks for winter sports with Franklin and the Morton daughters in tow. Jonathan Daniels, *Washington Quadrille* 163–164.

71. In his edited collection of his father's letters, Elliott noted that "during the war years F.D.R. frequently spent the evenings with the Eustis family," 2 *The Roosevelt Letters* 227n.

72. Eleanor Roosevelt, *Autobiography* 86 (New York: Harper & Brothers, 1961). The quote originally appeared in ER's *This Is My Story,* published in 1937. Also see Lash, *Eleanor and Franklin* 222–223.

73. Elliott Roosevelt, *An Untold Story* 83.

74. Ibid. 86.

75. FDR to ER, July 16, 1917, 2 *Roosevelt Letters* 280 (FDR's emphasis).

76. *The New York Times,* July 17, 1917. The text of the *Times* article is reprinted in 2 *Roosevelt Letters* 282–283n.

77. FDR to ER, July 18, 1917, ibid. 282.

78. ER to FDR, July 20, 1917, ibid. 283n.

79. According to Elliott, "Mother arrived with a long list of complaints to make. She was lonely for his presence in Campobello. . . . She was tired of the string of excuses he had been making for not leaving Washington. He did not even bother to read the letters she sent 'for you never answer a question and nothing I ask appears.' She even chided him for neglecting Granny by not taking the trouble to go to Hyde Park." *An Untold Story* 89.

80. ER to FDR, August 15, 1917, FDRL (ER's emphasis).

81. Morgan, *FDR: A Biography* 205. Ward, *First-Class Temperament* 369.

82. Elliott Roosevelt, *An Untold Story* 89.

83. Cook, 1 *Eleanor Roosevelt* 224.

84. Jonathan Daniels, *Washington Quadrille* 148.

85. Mrs. Daniels was close friends with Mary Patten, ER's Red Cross co-worker, and Mrs. Thomas R. Marshall, both of whom spread stories about Franklin and Lucy that autumn. Letter, Mrs. Charles Sumner Hamlin to Jonathan Daniels, February 19, 1955, ibid. 132.

86. ER to Lorena Hickok, October 1932, Hickok Papers, FDRL.

87. ER to SDR, January 22, 1918, FDRL.

88. ER to SDR, March 18, 1918, FDRL.

89. Daniels gave FDR a carte blanche. His instructions were to (1) inspect U.S. naval forces with particular attention to administrative and business organization; (2) to coordinate with other branches in order to coordinate naval activities with their enterprises; (3) gather information pertaining to general conditions abroad and their applicability to naval affairs; and (4) investigate any other matters he deemed advisable. 2 *Roosevelt Letters* 301.

90. FDR's extensive diary entries for his crossing on the *Dyer* and his stay in Europe are reproduced in ibid. 301–316.

91. Ibid. 327–328.

92. Ibid 326. FDR's Aunt Dora, Sara's older sister, had refused to leave her Paris apartment even when the city's fall appeared imminent. A quarter of a century later she would do the same. While most Americans in Paris fled home after war began in 1939, Dora would not budge. When asked by newsmen what the president's aunt intended to do, a spokesman for her responded:

> Madame is determined to remain in her Avenue George V home so long as it is tenable. She has lived in Paris forty years. All the friends of her whole life are here. . . . Madame is in excellent health and in excellent spirits. She is not uncomfortable . . . and is not making any emergency plans.

Sara made a special trip to Paris to try to extract Dora but was unable to change her mind. Eventually Dora left on one of the last ships to depart France, her fiftieth crossing of the Atlantic. She died at Algonac on July 20, 1940, at the age of ninety-three.

93. Unpublished memoir of Captain Edward McCauley, quoted in Ward, *First-Class Temperament* 399.

94. 2 *Roosevelt Letters* 333–336.

95. The remark is that of Admiral Paolo Thaon di Revel, quoted by FDR, ibid. 346.

96. FDR to ER, August 20, 1918, ibid. 350–351.

97. ER, *Autobiography* 96.

98. I am indebted to Geoffrey Ward for this insight. *First-Class Temperament* 410n.

99. ER to Joseph P. Lash, October 25, 1943, quoted in Lash, *Eleanor and Franklin* 220. "Mother spent the first seven years of her marriage constantly pregnant, and my father went through World War I being busier and busier and busier," Elliott remembered. "And my mother was such an insecure person during those first few years that I think it became a tremendous blow to her to realize what was going on. I don't think she had any inkling that such a thing was possible between two people who had said their vows, and so it was horribly upsetting to her." Elliott Roosevelt, oral interview, June 20, 1975, FDRL.

100. The oft-repeated Roosevelt version was set forth by Alice Longworth in her interview with Henry Brandon for *The New York Times Magazine,* August 6, 1967.

"I remember one day I was having fun with Auntie Corinne [Mrs. Douglas Robinson, TR's youngest sister] . . . I was doing imitations of Eleanor, and Auntie Corinne looked at me and said, 'Never forget, Alice, Eleanor offered Franklin his freedom.' And I said, 'But darling, that's what I've wanted to know about all these years. Tell.' And so she said, 'Yes, there was a family conclave and they talked it over and finally they decided it affected the children and there was Lucy Mercer, a Catholic, and so it was called off.' "

Also see Elliott Roosevelt, *An Untold Story* 95; David B. Roosevelt, *Grandmère: A Personal History of Eleanor Roosevelt* 112 (New York: Warner Books, 2002); Linda Donn, *The Roosevelt Cousins* 158 (New York: Knopf, 2001); and especially Joseph Alsop, *FDR: A Centenary Remembrance* 68–71. (New York: Viking, 1982).

101. Letters of Mrs. Lyman Cotton and Miss Mary Henderson (Lucy's North Carolina cousins) to Jonathan Daniels, quoted in *Washington Quadrille* 145–146.

102. Cook, 1 *Eleanor Roosevelt* 228.

103. Alsop, *FDR* 70.

104. Cook, 1 *Eleanor Roosevelt* 231.

105. Quoted in Jonathan Daniels, *Washington Quadrille* 145.

106. ER, *Autobiography* 93.

107. Quoted in Lash, *Eleanor and Franklin* 227. Blanche Wiesen Cook reports that it was during the Lucy Mercer years that Eleanor lost her appetite and that "when she did eat she could not keep her food down. . . . We now know that one of the results of frequent vomiting is a deterioration of the teeth and gums. During this period Eleanor's teeth loosened, spread, and protruded more than ever." 1 *Eleanor Roosevelt* 235.

108. Quoted in Lois Scharf, *Eleanor Roosevelt: First Lady of American Liberalism* 56 (Boston: Twayne Publishers, 1987); Alsop, *FDR: A Centenary Remembrance* 73–74.

109. The first veiled reference to appear in print came in 1946, when Olive Clapper, wife of the famous Washington reporter Raymond Clapper, alluded to "a persistent rumor" in her book *Washington Tapestry*. Mrs. Clapper wrote, "Mrs. Roosevelt was supposed to have called her husband and the enamored woman to a conference, at which she offered to give her husband a divorce if the woman wished to marry him. A Catholic, the woman could not marry a divorced man. When she expressed these sentiments, Mrs. Roosevelt issued an ultimatum that they must stop seeing each other—to which they promptly acquiesced." Lucy Mercer was not mentioned by name, and only her Catholicism links her with the story. Ibid. 238.

Also see John Gunther, *Roosevelt in Retrospect* 73 (New York: Harper & Brothers, 1950). Gunther cites Mrs. Clapper and also does not name Lucy Mercer.

110. Frank Freidel, *Franklin D. Roosevelt: The Apprenticeship* 320n. (Boston: Little, Brown, 1952).

111. James MacGregor Burns, *Roosevelt: The Lion and the Fox* 67–68 (New York: Harcourt, Brace & World, 1956). Rexford Tugwell in *The Democratic Roosevelt,* published the next year, makes no mention of the rumor or of Lucy Mercer. (New York: Doubleday, 1957).

    In 2001, James MacGregor Burns provided an excellent summary account of the romance in *The Three Roosevelts* 155–156, with Susan Dunn (New York: Grove Press, 2001).

112. Arthur Schlesinger, Jr., *The Crisis of the Old Order* 354–355 (Boston: Houghton Mifflin, 1957). Writing in *Ladies' Home Journal* in 1966, Professor Schlesinger thought the story of FDR and Lucy had been exaggerated in the Washington rumor mill but conceded that they had been "emotionally involved." "No doubt Franklin began to show a delight in Lucy; no doubt this worried Eleanor, as it would any wife." *Ladies' Home Journal,* November 1966.

113. Jonathan Daniels, *The End of Innocence* (Philadelphia: J. B. Lippincott, 1954); *Washington Quadrille: The Dance Beside the Documents* (New York: Doubleday, 1968).

114. Joseph P. Lash, *Eleanor and Franklin* (New York: W. W. Norton, 1971); *Love, Eleanor: Eleanor Roosevelt and Her Friends* (New York: Doubleday, 1982). More recently the story has been treated effectively by Geoffrey Ward in his perceptive *A First-Class Temperament* 361–374, 411–417. Another fine account is provided by Blanche Wiesen Cook in volume one of her biography of Mrs. Roosevelt, pages 216–232.

115. Consuelo's front-page marriage to the duke, which cost the Vanderbilts an estimated $10 million to arrange, ended in separation in 1908 and annulment in 1926. At the hearings before the Rota in the Vatican, Ava Vanderbilt Belmont (Consuelo's mother) testified, "I have always had absolute power over my daughter. . . . I ordered her to marry the Duke."

    At the time of Consuelo's marriage, a New York society writer chirped, "Winty was outclassed. Six feet two in his golf stockings, he was no match for five feet six in a coronet." Elizabeth Eliot, *Heiresses and Coronets* 188 (New York: McDowell, Obolensky, 1959); Cleveland Amory, *Who Killed Society?* 233–234 (New York: Harper & Brothers, 1960).

116. Elizabeth Shoumatoff, *FDR's Unfinished Portrait* 76–77 (Pittsburgh: University of Pittsburgh Press, 1990).

117. Jonathan Daniels, *Washington Quadrille* 250–251.

118. The president's official schedule for April 5, 1941, indicates that FDR returned from the Oval Office to his White House study "accompanied by Mrs. Johnson." The time given is 1555–1740. Cited in Ellen Feldman, "FDR and His Women," *American Heritage* 53, 55 (February–March 2003).

119. Interview, Geoffrey Ward with Franklin D. Roosevelt, Jr., cited in Ward, *First-Class Temperament* 777n.

120. Quoted Goodwin, *No Ordinary Time* 591–592.

121. Feldman, "FDR and His Women" 59.

122. "Thank you so much," wrote Lucy. "You must know it will be treasured always. I have wanted to write you for a long time to tell you that I had seen Franklin and of his great kindness to my husband when he was desperately ill in Washington. . . . I think of your sorrow—you—whom I have always felt to be the most blessed and privileged of women must now feel immeasurable grief and pain and they must be almost unbearable." Lucy Rutherfurd to Eleanor Roosevelt, May 2, 1945, FDRL.

123. Lucy Rutherfurd to Anna Roosevelt Boettiger, May 9, 1945, FDRL. Franklin's early letters to Lucy have not been located. Lucy claimed to have burned them, but writers such as Ellen Feldman doubt that is the case.

124. John R. Boettiger, Jr., *A Love in Shadow* 261 (New York: W. W. Norton, 1978). Additional insight into Franklin's deep affection for Lucy can be found in Resa Willis's *FDR and Lucy: Lovers and Friends* (New York: Routledge, 2004).

NINE | The Campaign of 1920

The epigraph is from a letter by FDR, November 9, 1920. Quoted in Alfred Steinberg, *Mrs. R.: The Life of Eleanor Roosevelt* 121 (New York: G. P. Putnam's Sons, 1958).

1. The *George Washington* was built as a passenger liner for North German Lloyd by A. G. Vulcan at Stettin in 1908. Displacing 33,000 tons, with a cruising speed of 18 knots, it was one of the largest liners afloat, accommodating 568 passengers in first class; 433 in second class; 152 in third class; and 1,226 in steerage. When war began in 1914, *George Washington* sought refuge in New York, a neutral port, where it remained berthed until the United States entered the war in 1917. It was thereupon seized by the United States government, converted to a troopship, and made eighteen round-trips to France during the war, transporting 48,000 troops.

  Under the peace settlement, *George Washington* became the property of the United States and was reconverted to passenger service, where it sailed on the transatlantic run under the flag of the United States Lines until 1931. Laid up by the Depression, it was reacquired by the Navy in 1941 and served again as a troopship until taken out of service in 1947. Damaged by fire at her mooring in Baltimore, *George Washington* was scrapped in 1951. Arnold Kludas, 1 *Die grossen Passagierschiffe der Welt*, 2 ed. 122–123, (Oldenburg/Hamburg: Gerhard Stalling, 1972).

2. ER to Isabella Ferguson, July 11, 1919. Greenway Collection, Arizona Historical Society, Tucson.

3. Among the papers at Eleanor's bedside when she died was a sonnet by Ambassador Cecil Spring-Rice extolling the statue:

   > *O steadfast, deep, inexorable eyes*
   > *Set look inscrutable, nor smile nor frown!*
   > *O tranquil eyes that look so calmly down*
   > *Upon a world of passion and of lies . . .*

Quoted in Joseph P. Lash, *Eleanor and Franklin* 237 (New York: W. W. Norton, 1971).

4. Elizabeth Cameron was the daughter of Senator John Sherman of Ohio and the favorite niece of General William Tecumseh Sherman. See Blanche Wiesen Cook, 1 *Eleanor Roosevelt* 235, 245–247, 539 (New York: Viking Penguin, 1992); Eugenia Kaledin, *The Education of Mrs. Henry Adams* 183, 245 (Philadelphia: Temple University Press, 1981). Also see Otto Friedrich, *Clover* 330–331 (New York: Simon & Schuster, 1979), and Arline Boucher Tehan, *Henry Adams in Love* 86–90 (New York: Universe Books, 1983).

5. ER to SDR, January 3, 1919, 2 *The Roosevelt Letters* 355, Elliott Roosevelt, ed. (London: George G. Harrap, 1950).

6. Joseph L. Gardner, *Departing Glory: Theodore Roosevelt as Ex-President* 394 (New York: Charles Scribner's Sons, 1973).

7. Ibid. 400.

8. FDR to Daniels, January 9, 1919, Daniels Papers, Library of Congress.

9. ER to SDR, January 9, 1919, 2 *Roosevelt Letters* 355.

10. ER to SDR, January 11, 20, February 11, 1919, ibid. 359, 361, 373.

11. Orlando bitterly withdrew from the conference on April 24, 1919, protesting the refusal of Wilson to grant Italy the former Austrian city of Fiume and the province of Dalmatia on the Adriatic. "Now President Wilson, after ignoring and violating his own Fourteen Points, wants to restore their virginity by applying them vigorously where they refer to Italy." Following his withdrawal, Orlando's government won a whopping 382–40 vote of confidence in the Italian Parliament. Aldrovandi Marescotti, *Guerra Diplomatica* 262 (Milan: Mondadori, 1946).

12. Wilson, like Lloyd George, spoke only English. Perhaps because he had been the president of Princeton, conventional wisdom has considered Woodrow Wilson an intellectual. Professor Arthur Link, his biographer and the longtime editor of *The Wilson Papers,* disputes this. According to Link, Wilson "had little command of foreign languages and almost no interest in political developments abroad before he entered the White House; he was indifferent to the great scientific developments that were transforming the philosophy and technology of the age; he knew virtually nothing about serious art and music. His reading in the field of literature was desultory, spasmodic, and erratic. . . . Even in his own specialties of political science, constitutional law, and English and American history, Wilson was surprisingly poorly read. . . . His thinking was pragmatic rather than philosophical, he had little interest in pure speculation and . . . he was rarely an original thinker."

John Maynard Keynes, who worked closely with Wilson and Lloyd George in Paris, decided the president was essentially a Nonconformist minister. "His thought and temperament essentially theological, not intellectual." J. M. Keynes, "When the Big Four Met," *The New Republic,* December 24, 1919. Arthur S. Link, *Wilson: The Road to the White House* 62–63 (Princeton, N.J.: Princeton University Press, 1947).

13. Margaret MacMillan, *Paris, 1919* 54 (New York: Random House, 2001).

14. "The return of a Republican majority to either House of Congress," said Wilson, "would certainly be interpreted on the other side of the water as a repudiation of my leadership." Quoted in Joseph P. Tumulty, *Woodrow Wilson as I Knew Him* 331 (New York: Doubleday & Page, 1921), with a facsimile of the statement as typed by Wilson.

15. The Republicans gained 30 seats in the House and 7 in the Senate. As a result, they controlled the Sixty-sixth Congress, 240–190 in the House and 49–47 in the Senate.

16. In June 1915 Lodge delivered a commencement address at Union College endorsing a league of nations. See *The New York Times,* June 9, 1915. Later, on May 27, 1916, he told the League to Enforce Peace that George Washington's warning against entangling alliances was never meant to exclude the United States from joining other nations in "a method . . . to diminish war and encourage peace." Quoted in Samuel Eliot Morison, *Oxford History of the American People* 881 (New York: Oxford University Press, 1965).

17. In 1915 Taft, Root, and Harvard president A. Lawrence Lowell organized the League to Enforce Peace. In May 1918 Taft, Lowell, and Hughes addressed the Win-the-War for Permanent Peace Convention in Philadelphia and spoke positively about a league of nations. Ibid. Also see *The New York Times,* November 11, 1917.

18. Colonel House likened the discussions in Paris to a meeting of the board of Aldermen in his home town of Austin, Texas. "There are the same jealousies, rivalries, and personal problems to be adjusted, and if you lost sight of the bigger issue at Paris I could almost think I was back in Austin debating which street should be paved first." Quoted in Josephus Daniels, *The Wilson Era: Years of War and After* 533 (Chapel Hill: University of North Carolina Press, 1946).

19. Francesco Nitti, *Rivelazioni: dramatis personae* 95 (Naples: Edizioni Scientifiche Italiani, 1948).

20. Geoffrey C. Ward, *A First-Class Temperament: The Emergence of Franklin Roosevelt* 424 (New York: Harper & Row, 1989).

21. Letter, Nigel Law to Jonathan Daniels, quoted in *Washington Quadrille: The Dance Beside the Documents* 155 (New York: Doubleday, 1968).

22. ER to SDR, January 14, 1919, 2 *Roosevelt Letters* 361.

23. The term of the lame-duck Sixty-fifth Congress expired on March 3, 1919. The Republican-controlled Sixty-sixth Congress would not convene until May 19, 1919.

24. Robert Cecil, *A Great Experiment: An Autobiography* 59 (New York: Oxford University Press, 1941). The final draft of the covenant of the League of Nations, including textual recognition of the Monroe Doctrine, was approved by the peace conference on April 28, 1919.

25. Eleanor Roosevelt, *This Is My Story* 289–290 (New York: Harper & Brothers, 1937).

26. Ibid.
27. Quoted in Arthur Krock, *Memoirs: Sixty Years on the Firing Line* 156 (New York: Funk and Wagnall's, 1968). Also see Josephus Daniels, *The Wilson Era: Years of War and After* 256 (Chapel Hill: University of North Carolina Press, 1946); Ray Stannard Baker, *American Chronicle* 470 (New York: Charles Scribner's Sons, 1946). This was one episode FDR did not have to embellish. According to a contemporaneous report in *The Boston Traveler* (February 24, 1919),

> The weather was thick at the time and the President's ship and her escort were running on dead reckoning. . . . When the wind shifted and the fog lifted, one of the officers perched on the upper deck sang out:

> "Thatcher's Island dead ahead."

> Assistant Secretary Roosevelt, who took the bridge immediately with Captain [Edward] McCauley, had yachted in the waters in which the *Washington* lay and gave it as his guess just before the fog lifted that the ship and her escort were in the vicinity of Marblehead. It turned out that the secretary was very nearly accurate in his guess.

28. Quoted in Ward, *First-Class Temperament* 436.
29. Daniels to FDR, March 13, 14, 1919, Daniels Papers, Library of Congress.
30. FDR to Daniels, April 3, 1919, ibid.
31. FDR to John McIlhenny, May 23, 1919, FDRL.
32. James Roosevelt and Sidney Shalett, *Affectionately, F.D.R.* 60 (New York: Harcourt, Brace, 1959).
33. ER to SDR, June 3, 1919, FDRL.
34. FDR to ER, July 23, 1919, 2 *Roosevelt Letters* 381 (FDR's emphasis). The riot, one of twenty-five that broke out in the nation that year, was triggered by rumors that a white woman, the wife of a naval officer, had been jostled by blacks. A mob of several hundred white servicemen, supported by an estimated thousand civilians, retaliated by rampaging through black neighborhoods, shooting into apartments, and beating up men and women encountered on the street. Blacks armed themselves and fought back. The *Washington Herald* subsequently declared the capital "the most lawless city in the Union."
35. The tenor of hysteria is reflected in the numerous articles written during this period by the attorney general. One such appeared in *The Forum* in February 1920, in which Palmer warned of the dangers of the Red menace: "Like a prairie fire, the blaze of revolution" would devour "every American institution. It was eating its way into the homes of the American workman, its sharp tongues of revolu-

tionary heat were licking at the alter of churches, leaping into the belfry of the school bells, crawling into the sacred corners of American homes, seeking to re-place the marriage vows with libertine laws, burning up the foundations of our society." A. Mitchell Palmer, "The Case Against the Reds," *The Forum* 19 (February 1920).

36. Morison, *History of the American People* 883.

37. The 1918 results from the Fifth Congressional District of Wisconsin show Berger, the Socialist candidate, with 17,920 votes; Joseph P. Carney, Democrat, 12,450; and William H. Stafford, Republican, 10,678. Following the refusal of the House to seat him, Berger was indicted in U.S. District Court for sedition, tried, convicted, and sentenced to twenty years in prison by Judge Kenesaw Mountain Landis. The conviction was reversed by the Supreme Court in 1921, *Berger v. United States,* 255 U.S. 22, after which the government withdrew all charges. Berger stood for election to Congress again in 1922 as a Socialist and was over-whelmingly elected. This time he was seated, and he served in Congress from March 4, 1923 until his death in 1929. See Blanche Wiesen Cook, "The Socialist Party Convention," in *Crystal Eastman on Women and Revolution* 349–356 (New York: Oxford University Press, 1978).

38. FDR to Rear Admiral Samuel S. Robinson, December 30, 1919, FDRL.

39. Paul Tuckerman to FDR, FDRL.

40. ER to Isabella Ferguson, September 16, 1919, Arizona Historical Society, Tucson.

41. Eleanor Roosevelt, *You Learn by Living* 29–30 (New York: Harper & Brothers, 1960).

42. Eleanor Roosevelt, *This Is My Story* 257–258.

43. ER to SDR, October 28, 1919, FDRL.

44. Eleanor Roosevelt, *This Is My Story* 304.

45. Albert Fried, ed., *A Day of Dedication: The Essential Writings and Speeches of Woodrow Wilson* 395 (New York: Macmillan, 1965).

46. To mock Wilson's Fourteen Points, Lodge introduced fourteen reservations, the most serious of which merely reasserted the constitutional power of Congress to declare war. Later, in a bow to his Irish constituents in Massachusetts, Lodge added a fifteenth reservation urging the independence of Ireland. David Hunter Miller, legal adviser to the American delegation in Paris, noted that the reserva-tions would have no effect upon the League's structure or function and urged that they be accepted. The text of the Lodge reservations can be found in most diplomatic histories, e.g., Samuel Flagg Bemis, *A Diplomatic History of the United States* 653 (New York: Holt, Rinehart and Winston, 1963). The Hunter Miller comment is in Herbert Hoover, *The Ordeal of Woodrow Wilson* 284 (New York: McGraw-Hill, 1958). The best analysis of the Senate debate remains Thomas A. Bailey, *Woodrow Wilson and the Great Betrayal* (Chicago: Quadran-gle Books, 1945). Also see John Milton Cooper, *Breaking the Heart of the World* 234 ff. (New York: Cambridge University Press, 2001).

47. Transcript, FDR to New York Bar Association, March 8, 1919, FDRL.

48. Transcript, FDR address at Worcester Polytechnic Institute, June 25, 1919, FDRL.

49. FDR speech in Atlantic City, June 21, 1919, in 2 *Roosevelt Letters* 379–380.

50. Cook, 1 *Eleanor Roosevelt* 261; Ward, *First-Class Temperament* 482; Kenneth S. Davis, *FDR: The Beckoning of Destiny* 591 (New York: G. P. Putnam's Sons, 1972).

51. FDR to Judge Henry M. Heymann, December 2, 1919, FDRL.

52. Quoted in Ted Morgan, *FDR: A Biography* 219 (New York: Simon & Schuster, 1985).

53. The Nineteenth Amendment, proposed by Congress on June 4, 1919, became part of the Constitution on August 18, 1920, when it was approved by Tennessee, the thirty-sixth state to do so. As for his support among women, Hoover was endorsed by such household staples as *Ladies' Home Journal* and *The Saturday Evening Post* as well as *The New Republic,* which called him a "Providential gift to the American people for the office of pilot during the treacherous navigation of the next few years."

54. Louis B. Wehle, *Hidden Threads of History: Wilson Through Roosevelt* 81–82 (New York: Macmillan, 1953).

55. FDR to Hugh Gibson, January 2, 1920, FDRL.

56. Wehle, *Hidden Threads of History* 82.

57. Ibid.

58. ER to SDR, March 7, 1920, FDRL.

59. Herbert Hoover to Frank Freidel, October 11, 1951, quoted in Freidel, *Franklin D. Roosevelt: The Ordeal* 57 (Boston: Little, Brown, 1954).

60. James K. Libbey, *Dear Alben: Mr. Barkley of Kentucky* 99 (Lexington: University of Kentucky Press, 1979).

61. Elliot A. Rosen, "Not Worth a Pitcher of Warm Piss," in *At the President's Side: The Vice Presidency in the Twentieth Century,* Timothy Walch, ed., 45 (Columbia: University of Missouri Press, 1997).

62. FDR's friend Tom Lynch somehow got hold of the battered New York standard and in 1932 presented it, suitably inscribed, to FDR, who proudly hung it in his study at Hyde Park where it remains. Interview with John E. Mack, FDRL.

63. Edward George Hoffman, *Official Report of the Proceedings of the Democratic National Convention* 140–141 (Indianapolis: Bookwalter, Ball, 1920).

64. Grenville Emmett to Langdon Marvin, July 8, 1920. Frances Perkins, *The Roosevelt I Knew* 27 (New York: Viking, 1946).

65. James Cox, *Journey Through My Years* 232 (New York: Simon & Schuster, 1946).

66. Ibid.

67. *Proceedings of the Democratic National Convention* 420–450.

68. Josephus Daniels, *Wilson Era: Years of War and After* 554–555.

69. Lippmann to FDR, July 8, 1920; Hoover to FDR, July 13, 1920; Lane to FDR, July 15, 1920, FDRL.

70. "This is not goodbye," Franklin wrote Daniels. "That will always be impossible after these years of the closest association. All my life I shall look back—not only to the *work* of the place—but mostly on the wonderful way in which you and I have gone through these nearly eight years *together.* You have taught me so wisely and kept my feet on the ground when I was about to skyrocket—and in it all there has never been a real dispute or antagonism or distrust."

Daniels's reply was equally heartfelt: "Love at first sight is rare with men, but sometimes I flatter myself in believing that I have some of woman's intuition, and on the day the President asked me to become Secretary of the Navy I told my wife I would recommend your appointment as Assistant Secretary. . . . [W]ith mutual regard and mutual consecration, we have spent seven and a half years in the service of our country. We little thought then of the great responsibility we were assuming. . . . I always counted on your zeal, your enthusiasm, your devoted patriotism, and efficient and able service. . . . [W]e will be brothers in all things that make for the good of our country." FDR to Daniels, August 6, 1920 (FDR's emphasis); Daniels to FDR, August 7, 1920. 2 *Roosevelt Letters* 388–389.

71. Ibid. 402.

72. FDR speech at Waukegan, Illinois, August 12, 1920, FDRL.

73. Theodore Roosevelt, Jr., joined the GOP attack. "Franklin is a maverick. He does not wear the brand of our family," the president's son told a band of former Rough Riders at Sheridan, Wyoming, September 16, 1920. *The New York Times,* September 19, 1920.

74. Quoted in Cook, 1 *Eleanor Roosevelt* 278.

75. Harold L. Ickes, 1 *The Secret Diary of Harold L. Ickes* 699 (New York: Simon & Schuster, 1953).

76. Press releases, FDR addresses at Helena, Montana, and Butte, Montana, August 18, 1920. Stenographic transcript, speech at San Francisco, August 23, 1920, FDRL.

77. *The New York Times,* August 19, 1920. Harding added that this was "the first official admission of the rape of Haiti and Santo Domingo by the present Administration. To my mind, moreover, it is the most shocking assertion that ever emanated from a responsible member of the government of the United States." Ibid., September 18, 1920.

78. Ibid., September 3, 1920; *New York Telegraph,* August 28, 1920.

79. Cox and Roosevelt received 781,238 votes in New York to Harding's 1,871,167. By contrast, and thanks to Tammany's efforts in New York City, Al Smith polled 1,261,812 versus 1,335,878 for his Republican opponent. The Democratic national ticket did even worse in California (24.3%), Illinois (25.5%), Iowa (25.5%), Minnesota (19.4%), North Dakota (18.3%), South Dakota (19.8%) Washington (21.1%), and Wisconsin (16.2%). Congressional Quarterly, *Guide to U.S. Elections* 286 (Washington, D.C.: Congressional Quarterly, Inc., 1975).

80. Robert H. Jackson, *That Man: An Insider's Portrait of Franklin D. Roosevelt* 6 (New York: Oxford University Press, 2003).

81. "It's becoming almost impossible to stop F. when he begins to speak," Eleanor wrote Sara. "Ten minutes is always 20, 30 is always 45, and the evening speeches are now about 2 hours! The men all get out and wave at him and when nothing succeeds I yank his coat tails! Everyone is getting tired but on the whole the car is still pretty good natured." ER to SDR, October 19, 1920, FDRL.

82. Eleanor Roosevelt, *Autobiography* 110.

83. Ibid., 109–110.

84. Cook, 1 *Eleanor Roosevelt* 285.

85. Lash, *Eleanor and Franklin* 258.

86. FDR to Cox, November 6, 1920; FDR to Mathew Hale, November 6, 1920; FDR to Willard Saulsbury, December 9, 1920; FDR to Early, December 21, 1920. FDRL. In 1933 Roosevelt appointed Cox a delegate to the World Monetary Conference in London. Thereafter he offered him various government appointments, all of which Cox graciously declined.

87. ER to FDR, April 11, 1921, FDRL.

TEN | Polio

The epigraph is from the "Character of the Happy Warrior" written by William Wordsworth in 1806. *Wordsworth's Poems in Two Volumes (1807): A Facsimile* (London: British Library, 1984).

1. Missy to ER, August 5, 1921, quoted in Joseph P. Lash, *Eleanor and Franklin* 267 (New York: W. W. Norton, 1971).

2. SDR to ER, July 20, 1921, FDRL. Franklin and Eleanor were appalled when they learned of Sara's flight. "Don't do it again," FDR cabled. But Rosy and his wife were delighted. "We put her up to it before she left," he wrote. "I knew Franklin would have a fit!! I think it a splendid thing for her to have done and will make her feel years younger." James Roosevelt Roosevelt Papers, FDRL.

3. Quoted in Earle Looker, *This Man Roosevelt* 111 (New York: Brewer, Warren & Putnam, 1932).

4. Ibid.

5. Ibid.

6. Anna Roosevelt, "How Polio Helped Father," *Woman* 54 (July 1949); Ross T. McIntire, *White House Physician* 31 (New York: G. P. Putnam's Sons, 1946).

7. John Stuart Martin, "When the President Disappeared," *American Heritage* (October 1957). For Dr. Keen's account, see W. W. Keen, *The Surgical Operations on President Cleveland in 1893* (Philadelphia: J. B. Lippincott, 1928).

8. ER to James Roosevelt Roosevelt, August 14, 1921, 2 *The Roosevelt Letters* 412–413, Elliott Roosevelt, ed. (London: George G. Harrap, 1950).

9. Eleanor Roosevelt, *This Is My Story* 328–329 (New York: Harper & Brothers, 1937).

10. ER to James Roosevelt Roosevelt, August 18, 1921, 2 *Roosevelt Letters* 413–414.

11. Dr. William W. Keen to ER, August 26, 1921, FDRL.

12. Frederic A. Delano to ER, August 20, 1921, FDRL.

13. Dr. Lovett's groundbreaking study, *The Treatment of Infantile Paralysis,* was published in Philadelphia in 1916 by Blakiston. For the history of polio in the United States, and the cure inspired by FDR, see David M. Oshinsky, *Polio: An American Story* (New York: Oxford University Press, 2005).

14. ER to James Roosevelt Roosevelt, August 23, 1921, 2 *Roosevelt Letters* 414–415 (ER's emphasis).

15. Quoted in Geoffrey C. Ward, *A First-Class Temperament* 590 (New York: Harper & Row, 1989).

16. Lovett Papers, Francis A. Countway Library of Medicine, Boston.

17. Quoted in Ward, *First-Class Temperament* 591.

18. Dr. Bennett to Dr. Lovett, August 31, 1921, Lovett Papers.

19. 2 *The Roosevelt Letters* 415–416.

20. *The New York Times,* September 16, 1921.

21. FDR to Ochs, September 16, 1921, FDRL.

22. Dr. Draper to Dr. Lovett, September 24, 1921, Lovett Papers.

23. Ernest K. Lindley, *Franklin D. Roosevelt: A Career in Progressive Democracy* 204 (Indianapolis: Bobbs-Merrill, 1931).

24. FDR to Daniels, October 6, 1921. FDRL.

25. Dr. Draper to Dr. Lovett, October 11, 1921, Lovett Papers.

26. Lovett notes, October 15, 1921, Ibid.

27. Dr. Draper to Dr. Lovett, November 19, 1921, Lovett Papers.

28. ER to SDR, December 15, 1921, FDRL.

29. Mrs. Lake to Dr. Lovett, December 17, 1921, Lovett Papers.

30. James Roosevelt and Sidney Shalett, *Affectionately, F.D.R.* 147 (New York: Harcourt, Brace, 1959).

31. Ibid. 58, 146–147.

32. Eleanor Roosevelt, *Autobiography* 118 (New York: Harper & Brothers, 1961).

33. Interview, Frances Perkins, Columbia Oral History Project, Columbia University.

34. Quoted in Ward, *First-Class Temperament* 616.

35. Ibid. 616–617.

36. ER, *Autobiography* 117.

37. Ibid. 117–118.

38. Mrs. James [Sara] Roosevelt, *My Boy Franklin* 101 (New York: Ray Long & Richard R. Smith, 1933).

39. WW to FDR, April 30, 1922, FDRL.

40. Dr. Draper to Dr. Lovett, March 30, 1922, Lovett Papers.

41. Ibid., July 10, 1922.

42. Dr. Lovett to FDR, August 14, 1922, FDRL.

43. FDR to Dr. Lovett, September 28, 1922, FDRL.

44. Anna Roosevelt Interview, Columbia Oral History Project, Columbia University.

45. FDR to Smith, August 13, 1922, FDRL. "I had quite a tussle in New York to keep our friend Hearst off the ticket and to get Al Smith to run, but the thing went through in fine shape," FDR wrote his friend Joseph E. Davies shortly after the election. FDR to Davies, November 18, 1922, FDRL.

46. Smith to FDR, August 15, 1922, FDRL.

47. Howe to FDR, September 29, 1922, FDRL.

48. Smith to FDR, October 9, 1922, FDRL.

49. Joseph P. Lash, *Eleanor and Franklin* 277 (New York: W. W. Norton, 1971). Eleanor's recollection differs slightly: "I was pushed into the women's division of the Democratic State Committee, not because Louis cared so much about my activities, but because he felt that they would make it possible for me to bring into the house people who would keep Franklin interested in state politics." Eleanor Roosevelt, *This I Remember* 30 (New York: Harper & Brothers, 1949).

50. Blanche Wiesen Cook, 1 *Eleanor Roosevelt* 319–320 (New York: Viking Penguin, 1992).

51. Dickerman ran a strong second against the conservative Speaker of the Assembly, Thaddeus C. Sweet, and effectively eliminated him as a potential gubernatorial candidate. Marion Dickerman interview, Columbia Oral History Project, Columbia University.

52. Cook, 1 *Eleanor Roosevelt* 320–321.

53. Because most of the correspondence between ER and Cook and Dickerman has disappeared, it is impossible to reconstruct the precise dimensions of their friendship. Blanche Wiesen Cook tackled the task with gusto, and her account should be a starting point for any who wish to untangle the relationship. Ibid. 319–328 and the notes pertaining thereto.

54. Roosevelt was particularly concerned to organize the distaff vote. "Get the right kind of woman in every election district," he wrote Caroline O'Day of the Women's Division. "There are thousands of election districts upstate where it is not only unfashionable to be a Democrat, but even where Democrats are rather looked down upon. It is absolutely necessary for us to restore in the country districts . . . the prestige of the party. Democratic women have too often in the past been rather apologetic for calling themselves Democrats. This should end, and they should let the world and their neighbors know that they take great pride in their Party." FDR to Caroline O'Day, January 28, 1922, FDRL.

55. ER, *This I Remember* 32.

56. FDR to Cox, December 8, 1922; FDR to Byrd, November 21, 1921; FDR to Wood, May 22, 1922. FDRL.

57. Turnley Walker, *Roosevelt and the Warm Springs Story* 7–9 (New York: A. A. Wyn, 1953). Walker's account is based on the eyewitness recollection of Basil O'Connor.

58. FDR to Livingston Davis, October 11, 1922.

59. FDR to Black, September 24, 1924.

60. Roosevelt and O'Connor began working together in early 1923 but did not formally announce their partnership until January 1, 1925. See O'Connor to FDR, December 8, 1924, FDRL.

61. FDR to Byron R. Newton, December 20, 1922, FDRL.

62. FDR to Dr. Draper, February 13, 1923, FDRL.

63. ER, *This Is My Story* 345–346.

64. Quoted in Ward, *First-Class Temperament* 662.

65. FDR to SDR, March 15, 1923, FDRL.

66. FDR to Carter Glass, March 27, 1923, FDRL.

67. Kathleen Lake to Dr. Lovett, March 30, 1923, Lovett Papers.

68. Lovett examination, May 28, 1923, Lovett Papers.

69. Dr. Draper to Dr. Lovett, February 11, 1924, Lovett Papers.

70. Louis Depew interview, January 5, 1948, FDRL.

71. FDR to John Lawrence, April 30, 1925, FDRL.

72. The most complete depiction of life aboard the *Larooco* is provided by Donald S. Carmichael, "An Introduction to the Log of the *Larooco*," 1 *The Franklin D. Roosevelt Collector* 1–37 (November 1948).

73. FDR to Davis, February, 1924.

74. Franklin, Jr., once told a friend that it was Missy, not Louis Howe, whom he most resented as a youth. He especially resented the time she spent with FDR. "Are you always so agreeable?" he once asked her. "Don't you ever get mad and flare up? Do you always smile?"

    "Missy looked as if she would burst into tears," he remembered. Joseph P. Lash, *Eleanor Roosevelt: A Friend's Memoir* 210 (New York: Doubleday, 1964).

75. Felix Frankfurter, *From the Diaries of Felix Frankfurter,* Joseph P. Lash, ed., January 18, 1943 (New York: W. W. Norton, 1975). Judge Samuel Rosenman, FDR's speechwriter, told Frankfurter that he "always regarded Missy as one of the five most important people in the U.S. during the Roosevelt Administration." Ibid.

76. Lash, *Eleanor and Franklin* 294.

77. Frank Freidel, interview with Frances Perkins, May 1953, FDRL.

78. ER to FDR, February 24, 1924, FDRL.

79. FDR to John Lawrence, April 25, 1925, FDRL.

80. FDR to SDR, postscript to letter originally written March 26, 1926, 2 *Roosevelt Letters* 479–480.

81. Typewritten copy of statement, FDRL.

82. *New York Herald Tribune,* April 29, 1924.

83. Frank Freidel, *Franklin D. Roosevelt: The Ordeal* 170 (Boston: Little, Brown, 1954).

84. George Herman Ruth to FDR, June 13, 1924, FDRL.

85. Judge Joseph Proskauer interview, Columbia Oral History Project, Columbia University.

86. Ibid.

87. David Burner, "The Election of 1924," in 2 *Running for President: Candidates and Their Images, 1900–1992* 125, Arthur M. Schlesinger, Jr., ed. (New York: Simon & Schuster, 1994).

88. Roosevelt and Shalett, *Affectionately, F.D.R.* 205.

89. Morgan Hoyt interview, FDRL.

90. Kenneth S. Davis, *Invincible Summer: An Intimate Portrait of the Roosevelts Based on the Recollection of Marion Dickerman* 30 (New York: Atheneum, 1974).

91. Roosevelt and Shalett, *Affectionately, F.D.R.* 205.

92. Franklin D. Roosevelt, *The Happy Warrior* 18 (Boston: Houghton Mifflin, 1928).

93. Davis, *Invincible Summer* 31.

94. *The New York Times,* July 10, 1924; *New York Herald Tribune,* July 1, 1924; Pendergast's comment is quoted in Ike B. Dunlap to FDR, July 10, 1924. Pendergast predicted Roosevelt would be the nominee in 1928. FDRL.

95. Frances Perkins interview, Columbia Oral History Project, Columbia University.

96. Davis, *Invincible Summer* 31.

ELEVEN | Governor

The epigraph is from a letter Sara wrote FDR after learning of his decision to run for governor. "Eleanor telephoned me before I got my papers that you have to 'run' for governorship," said Sara. "If you do run, I want you not to be defeated." SDR to FDR, October 2, 1928, FDRL (Sara's emphasis).

1. Blanche Wiesen Cook, 1 *Eleanor Roosevelt* 316 (New York: Viking Penguin, 1992).

2. Frances Perkins interview, Columbia Oral History Project, Columbia University.

3. Geoffrey C. Ward, *A First-Class Temperament* 631 (New York: Harper & Row, 1989).

4. Kenneth S. Davis, *Invincible Summer: An Intimate Portrait of the Roosevelts Based on the Recollections of Marion Dickerman* 35 (New York: Atheneum, 1974).

5. FDR to Elliott Brown, August 5, 1924, FDRL.

6. Quoted in Davis, *Invincible Summer* 50.

7. Quoted in Cook, 1 *Eleanor Roosevelt* 325.

8. Quoted in Ward, *First-Class Temperament* 740.

9. Cook, 1 *Eleanor Roosevelt* 334.

10. Mary McLeod Bethune, "My Secret Talks with FDR," *Ebony* (April 1949).

11. FDR to SDR, October, 1924, 2 *The Roosevelt Letters* 445, Elliott Roosevelt, ed. (London: George G. Harrap, 1950).

12. Editor's note, ibid. 447–448.

13. FDR to SDR, October 1924, 2 *Roosevelt Letters* 447.

14. Alfred B. Rollins, Jr., *Roosevelt and Howe* 203–205 (New York: Knopf, 1962). Blanche Wiesen Cook suggests Howe and Sara opposed the Warm Springs venture but offers no evidence. Cf. 1 *Eleanor Roosevelt* 336.

15. FDR lent the $201,677.83 to the Warm Springs Foundation and in return received a demand note for that amount, dated February 29, 1928. The money was gradually repaid over the years, the last installment after the president's death. The repayment history is printed in Eleanor Roosevelt, *This I Remember* 367–368 (New York: Harper & Brothers, 1949).

16. "Mrs. Ford and I are deeply impressed with the wonderful work which is being carried out at Warm Springs," Ford wrote FDR on March 15, 1928. "I am sending herewith a check for twenty-five thousand dollars which I hope you will accept for the Foundation with our best wishes for its complete success." 2 *Roosevelt Letters* 500n.

17. FDR to Paul Hasbrouck, Hasbrouck papers, FDRL.

18. Ward, *First-Class Temperament* 770.

19. Ibid. 758.

20. Roosevelt received 97.8 percent of the votes in Merriweather County in 1932; 94.6 percent in 1936; 93.7 percent in 1940; and 92.0 percent in 1944. His Dutchess County totals were 43.5 percent (1932); 45.0 percent (1936); 44.1 percent (1940); and 40.8 percent (1944). *America at the Polls: A Handbook of American Presidential Election Statistics* 100–106, 313–317, Richard M. Scammon, ed. (Pittsburgh: Governmental Affairs Institute, 1965).

21. Ward, *First-Class Temperament* 765 (italics in original).

22. Rexford Tugwell papers, FDRL.

23. FDR to SDR, October 13, 1926, 2 *Roosevelt Letters* 486.

24. Editor's note, ibid. 492.

25. Cook, 1 *Eleanor Roosevelt* 398–408.

26. ER to Jane Hoey, April 9, 1930, FDRL.

27. *The New York Times,* October 10, 1929.

28. *The New York Times Magazine,* December 4, 1932.

29. Jan Pottker, *Sara and Eleanor* 230–232 (New York: St. Martin's Press, 2004).

30. James Roosevelt and Sidney Shalett, *Affectionately, F.D.R.* 161 (New York: Harcourt, Brace, 1959).

31. Howe to FDR, n.d. (summer 1926), FDRL.

32. In a two-man race, Smith received 1,523,813 votes to Republican Ogden Mills's 1,276,137. Mills, a sitting member of Congress, was a Harvard classmate and Dutchess County neighbor of FDR and later served as Herbert Hoover's secretary of the Treasury.

33. ER to FDR, June 15, 1928, FDRL.

34. FDR to Lippmann, August 6, 1928, FDRL.

35. Franklin D. Roosevelt, *The Happy Warrior: Alfred E. Smith* (Boston: Houghton Mifflin, 1928). Louis Howe, for one, was not taken in by the public display of affection for Smith. "Al's enemies will nominate him, then knife him at the polls," he told FDR. Rollins, *Roosevelt and Howe* 227.

36. Quoted in Ted Morgan, *FDR: A Biography* 289 (New York: Simon & Schuster, 1985).

37. FDR to SDR, July 14, 1928, 2 *Roosevelt Letters* 504. Eleanor accepted the co-chairmanship, along with former Wyoming governor Nellie Tayloe Ross, of the Women's Division of the national Democratic party and worked arduously on Smith's behalf.

38. "Strictly between ourselves," FDR wrote Josephus Daniels, "I am very doubtful whether any Democrat can win in 1928." FDR to Daniels, June 23, 1927, FDRL. Also see Rollins, *Roosevelt and Howe* 226–234.

39. FDR to Smith, September 30, 1928, FDRL.

40. Ernest K. Lindley, *Franklin D. Roosevelt: A Career in Progressive Democracy* 12 (Indianapolis: Bobbs-Merrill, 1931). Also see James A. Farley, *Behind the Ballots* 79 (New York: Harcourt, Brace, 1938).

41. Quoted in Frank Freidel, *Franklin D. Roosevelt: The Ordeal* 254–255 (Boston: Little, Brown, 1954).

42. Quoted in Ward, *First-Class Temperament* 794. Later, FDR wrote to his uncle Frederic Delano that he "would not allow the use of my name before the convention, but . . . if, in the final analysis the convention insisted on nominating me, I should feel under definite obligation to accept the nomination." FDR to Frederic A. Delano, October 8, 1928, FDRL.

43. ER to FDR, October 2, 1928, FDRL. Interviewed later at Democratic National Headquarters, Eleanor said she was "very proud" FDR had accepted the nomination, though she "did not want him to do it. In the end you have to do what your friends want you to do. There comes to every man, if he is wanted, the feeling that there is almost an obligation to return the confidence shown in him." Kenneth S. Davis, *FDR: The New York Years. 1928–1933* 29 (New York: Random House, 1985).

44. Howe to FDR, October 2, 1928, FDRL.

45. *New York Post,* October 2, 1928; *New York Herald Tribune,* October 3, 1928.

46. Lindley, *Franklin D. Roosevelt* 21.

47. *New York Herald Tribune,* October 9, 1928.

48. "So long as we have a two-party system of government," Flynn wrote, "we will have machines. Whether they are good or bad depends upon the interest of citizens in their party government." Edward J. Flynn, *You're the Boss* 231 (New York: Viking Press, 1947).

49. Samuel I. Rosenman, *Working with Roosevelt* 21 (New York: Harper & Brothers, 1952).

50. Frances Perkins interview, Columbia Oral History Project, Columbia University.

51. Rosenman, *Working with Roosevelt* 22.

52. 1 *Public Papers and Addresses of Franklin D. Roosevelt* 53–54, Samuel I. Rosenman, ed. (New York: Random House, 1938).

53. *New York Herald Tribune,* October 25, 1928.

54. Francis Perkins interview, Columbia Oral History Project, Columbia University.

55. Flynn, *You're the Boss* 71–72.

56. Frances Perkins interview, Columbia Oral History Project, Columbia University.

57. Ibid.

TWELVE | Albany Redux

FDR was one of three speakers (and the only Democrat) to address the Washington newsmen's Gridiron Dinner in 1929. The epigraph is from the song sung by the newsmen to greet FDR. *The New York Times,* April 14, 1929.

1. *The New York Times,* November 13, 1928.

2. Quoted ibid., December 5, 1928.

3. Ibid., November 12, 1928. Samuel Rosenman, who accompanied FDR to Warm Springs after the election, reports that "strangely" no one speculated about the presidency, so busy were they planning for the governorship. Samuel I. Rosenman, *Working with Roosevelt* 28 (New York: Harper & Brothers, 1952).

4. FDR to Adolphus Ragan (unsent), 3 *F.D.R.: His Personal Letters* 772–773, Elliott Roosevelt, ed. (New York: Duell, Sloane & Pearce, 1950). "No man," said FDR, "ever willingly gives up public life—no man who has ever tasted it."

5. *The New York Times,* January 1, 1929.

6. FDR to Adolphus Ragan, 3 *Personal Letters* 772–773. Also see Frances Perkins, *The Roosevelt I Knew* 49–53 (New York: Viking Press, 1946).

7. Robert A. Caro, *The Power Broker: Robert Moses and the Fall of New York* 291 (New York: Knopf, 1974).

8. Frances Perkins interview, Columbia Oral History Project, Columbia University. Caro cites a confidential source for Moses's characterization of ER and reports that Adolf A. Berle, professor of law at Columbia at the time, said Moses "always talked badly about Eleanor Roosevelt." *The Power Broker* 1194.

9. Emily Smith Warner and Hawthorne Daniel, *The Happy Warrior: A Biography of My Father, Alfred E. Smith* 240 (New York: Doubleday, 1956).

10. FDR to Adolphus Ragan, 3 *Personal Letters* 772–773.

11. Rosenman, *Working with Roosevelt* 30. Mrs. Moskowitz complained bitterly to Frances Perkins about being replaced. "Franklin Roosevelt can never run that show. It's going to be terrible. He's got that dreadful Louis Howe up there. Louis Howe will poison his mind about everything. Howe hates Smith. He's that kind of sour person. It's going to be very bad." Elisabeth Israels Perry, *Belle Moskowitz: Feminine Politics and the Exercise of Power in the Age of Alfred E. Smith* 207 (New York: Oxford University Press, 1987).

12. Franklin D. Roosevelt, "Women's Field in Politics," *Women's City Club Quarterly* (1928).

13. Alfred B. Rollins, Jr., *Roosevelt and Howe* 259 (New York: Knopf, 1962).

14. Perkins, *The Roosevelt I Knew* 62.

15. As Tugwell remembers dinners in Albany, Sam Rosenman and Basil O'Connor "were so disillusioned with the cuisine and so prone to be annoyed with

Eleanor's well-meant probing that they often turned up after dinner rather than before. [Sam] could stand it as long as Missy LeHand was there. Her presence was like a quiet blessing on any company she graced," Rexford G. Tugwell, *The Brains Trust* 53–54 (New York: Viking Press, 1968).

16. Betsey was the eldest daughter of the famous brain surgeon Dr. Harvey Cushing. Dr. Cushing had recently won the Pulitzer Prize for his 1925 biography of Sir William Osler, physician in chief at Johns Hopkins Hospital (1889–1905) and regius professor of medicine at Oxford University (1905–19).

    When ER learned of the engagement, she wrote Franklin that Betsey was "a nice child, family excellent, nothing to be said against it. . . . Perhaps it will be a good influence and in any case we can do nothing about it." ER to FDR, November 22, 1928, FDRL.

17. FDR, 3 *Personal Letters* 43.

18. Rosenman, *Working with Roosevelt* 38.

19. Quoted in Joseph P. Lash, *Eleanor and Franklin* 326 (New York: W. W. Norton, 1971).

20. Hugh Gregory Gallagher, *FDR's Splendid Deception* 76–77 (New York: Dodd, Mead, 1985).

21. For background, see Will Swift, *The Roosevelts and the Royals,* especially 108–151 (Hoboken, N.J.: John Wiley & Sons, 2004).

22. *New York Evening Post,* November 8, 1928.

23. Eleanor Roosevelt, *This I Remember* 46 (New York: Harper & Brothers, 1949).

24. Blanche Wiesen Cook, 1 *Eleanor Roosevelt* 381 (New York: Viking Penguin, 1992).

25. *The New York Times,* December 2, 1928.

26. Ibid.

27. Nathan Miller, *FDR: An Intimate History* 229–230 (New York: Doubleday, 1983).

28. Rosenman, *Working with Roosevelt* 36. Rosenman quotes FDR: "Once you've made a decision, there's no use worrying about whether you were right or wrong. Events will prove whether you were right or wrong, and if there is still time you can change your decision. You and I know people who wear out the carpets walking up and down worrying whether they have decided something correctly. Do the very best you can in making up your mind, but once your mind is made up go ahead."

29. Frances Perkins interview, Columbia Oral History Project, Columbia University.

30. Senator George Norris of Nebraska, the national champion of public power, called Roosevelt's speech to the legislature "a very brave step in the right direction." He also pointed out that across the Saint Lawrence both Ontario and Quebec were providing electric power to the consumer at cost. *The New York Times,* March 15, 1929. Also see S. I. Rosenman, "Governor Roosevelt's Power Program," *Nation,* September 18, 1929.

31. Alfred E. Smith, *Up to Now* 314 (New York: Viking Press, 1929).

32. *Public Papers of Franklin D. Roosevelt: Forty-eighth Governor of the State of New York: 1929* 40 (Albany, N.Y.: J. B. Lyon Co., 1930).

33. "I am not an 'Urban leader,' " FDR wrote the editor of the Mitchell, South Dakota, *Republican* in April 1931. "I was born and brought up and have always made my home on a farm in Dutchess County." FDRL.

34. For an extensive review of FDR's agricultural program, see the chapter "Parity for the Farmer," in Bernard Belluch, *Franklin D. Roosevelt as Governor of New York* 76–102 (New York: Columbia University Press, 1955).

35. FDR, 3 *Personal Letters* 24.

36. *The New York Times,* July 5, 1929.

37. Ibid. July 8, 1929.

38. Howe deleted the persiflage before the statement was released to the press. The final version stated simply that FDR was not a candidate. 3 *Personal Letters* 40–41.

39. Thomas Wilson, *Fluctuations in Income and Employment: With Special Reference to Recent American Experience* 118 (New York: Pitman Publishing Corporation, 1948). Also see David M. Kennedy, *Freedom from Fear* 34–42 (New York: Oxford University Press, 1999).

40. *The New York Times,* October 26 (Hoover), November 22 (Rockefeller), December 11 (Schwab), 1929. John Edgerton, president of the National Association of Manufacturers, said, "I can observe little on the horizon today to give us undue or great concern." For a compilation of business predictions, see *Review of Reviews* (January 1930).

41. Department of Commerce, Bureau of the Census, *Statistical History of the United States* 283, 292 295 (Stamford, Conn.: Fairfield Publishers, 1965).

42. Ibid. 140–141.

43. FDR to Howe, December 1, 1929, 3 *Personal Letters* 92. The day after the market dipped on October 23, Roosevelt wired *The New York Times* from Warm Springs: "Do not know detailed conditions but firmly believe fundamental industrial and trade conditions are sound." FDRL.

44. *The New York Times,* December 11, 1929.

45. "All the evidences," said Hoover, "indicated that the worst effects of the crash upon employment will have been past during the next sixty days." *The New York Times,* January 21, 1930; Perkins, *The Roosevelt I Knew* 95–96.

46. FDR statement, March 29, 1930, *Public Papers of Franklin D. Roosevelt, Forty-eighth Governor of the State of New York, 1930* 506 (Albany, N.Y.: J. B. Lyon Co., 1934).

47. "I am convinced we have now passed the worst and with continued unity of effort we shall rapidly recover," said Hoover. Herbert Hoover, 1 *State Papers and Other Public Writings* 289–296, William Starr Myers, ed. (New York: Doubleday, Doran, 1934).

48. *The New York Times,* April 27, 1930.

49. Ibid.

50. FDR to Nicholas Roosevelt, May 19, 1930, FDRL.

51. FDR to Hollins N. Randolph, July 16, 1930, FDRL.

52. Rosenman, *Working with Roosevelt* 45.

53. *Public Papers of Governor Roosevelt 1930* 835–837; *The New York Times,* November 2, 1930.

54. FDR received 1,770,342 (59.1%) votes to Tuttle's 1,045,231 (34.9%). Professor Robert Paris Carroll of Syracuse University, running on the Prohibitionist ticket, received 181,000 (6.0%) votes.

55. Quoted in Lash, *Eleanor and Franklin* 336.

56. Ida Tarbell, in the *Delineator* (October 1931).

57. Roy Jenkins, *Franklin Delano Roosevelt* 61 (New York: Henry Holt, 2003).

58. Marion Dickerman interview, Columbia Oral History Project, Columbia University.

59. Joseph P. Lash, *Love, Eleanor* 111–123 (New York: Doubleday, 1982). Also see Lash, *Eleanor and Franklin* 340–343. In *A World of Love,* published in 1984, Lash concedes, "There may have been an affair" (New York: Doubleday, 297n).

60. Cook, 1 *Eleanor Roosevelt* 429, 442.

61. James Roosevelt with Bill Libby, *My Parents: A Differing View* 110–111 (Chicago: Playboy Press, 1976). David B. Roosevelt, ER's grandson and the author of *Grandmere: A Personal History of Eleanor Roosevelt,* accepts James's judgment. (New York: Warner Books, 2002, 139–141).

62. Cook, 1 *Eleanor Roosevelt* 435. In 1937, when ER published *This Is My Story,* the first volume of her memoirs, she ordered four leather-bound copies. They were for FDR; her daughter, Anna; her longtime personal secretary, Malvina Thompson; and Earl Miller. Lash, *Love, Eleanor* 508–509.

63. Miller later became chief inspector of prison guards in New York State. Lash reports that ER "wrote him faithfully, letters full of warmth and affection," which suggests that Lash may have seen them. *Eleanor and Franklin* 481. In *Love, Eleanor,* published twenty years after ER's death, Lash referred to "Eleanor's many letters to Earl, which have disappeared" (page 116).

64. Cook, 1 *Eleanor Roosevelt* 436, 438.

THIRTEEN | Nomination

The epigraph is from FDR's acceptance speech to the Democratic National Convention, July 2, 1932. *Official Report of the Proceedings of the 1932 Democratic National Convention* 374 (Washington, D.C.: Democratic National Committee, 1932).

1. James A. Farley, *Behind the Ballots* 62 (New York: Harcourt, Brace and Company, 1938).

2. Ibid.

3. *The New York World,* November 6, 1930; *The New York Times,* November 8, 1930. The *Times,* apparently taken in, reported that Farley's announcement came as an unwelcome surprise to Roosevelt.

4. Edward J. Flynn, *You're the Boss* 82 (New York: Viking, 1947).

5. Farley, *Behind the Ballots* 67.

6. Professor Raymond Moley of Columbia University, one of FDR's original brain trusters, said that "Farley possessed and cultivated, more than any man of his generation, the primary talent of a politician mentally to catalogue names and faces, to learn and retain the facts of association among people, to know who is related to whom by blood, business or politics, to labor with meticulous diligence by mail or otherwise to make and retain contacts." 27 *Masters of Politics* 107 (New York: Funk & Wagnalls, 1949).

7. Herbert Hoover, 3 *Memoirs* 55–56 (New York: Macmillan, 1952).

8. State of New York, *1931 Public Papers of Governor Franklin D. Roosevelt* 173 (Albany, N.Y.: J. B. Lyon, 1937).

9. Roosevelt first broached the necessity for "social consciousness" on the part of government in his June 17, 1929, commencement address to Phi Beta Kappa at Harvard. "A century and a half ago our forefathers spoke in theoretical terms of equality, meaning thereby the equality of right. Much later came the ideal of the equality of opportunity." FDRL.

10. Frank Freidel, *Franklin D. Roosevelt: The Triumph* 223 (Boston: Little, Brown, 1956).

11. Immediately after the November 1930 election, Raskob composed a conciliatory open letter to President Hoover promising bipartisan support for the administration's economic policies, including the historically high levels of the Smoot-Hawley tariff. The letter was signed by the last three Democratic presidential nominees, James Cox, John W. Davis, and Al Smith, as well as Senator Joseph T. Robinson, the Democratic leader of the Senate, and the incoming Speaker of the House, John Nance Garner of Texas. *The New York Times*, November 8, 1930.

12. For background on the Raskob-Shouse strategy, see Charles Michelson, *The Ghost Talks* 135–137 (New York: Putnam, 1944). Michelson was publicity director for the DNC at the time and a co-conspirator with Raskob and Shouse.

13. Hull and Roosevelt had met at the 1912 Democratic National Convention in Baltimore and remained in contact. Wheeler had been the first prominent Democrat to endorse Roosevelt for president. Byrd was acquainted with FDR through his brother, Admiral Richard Byrd, who had been an intimate friend and hunting companion of Franklin's since FDR's stint as assistant secretary of the Navy. In June 1930, Admiral Byrd stayed with the Roosevelts at Hyde Park following his flight to the South Pole and later was decorated by FDR with the Distinguished Service Medal of the State of New York. For Admiral Byrd's medal ceremony, see 1930 *Public Papers of Governor Franklin D. Roosevelt* 745 (Albany, N.Y.: J. B. Lyon, 1931).

14. Harry F. Byrd to FDR, February 27, 1931, Virginia preconvention file (1932), DNC. Hull also warned FDR: "I am thoroughly confirmed in the belief that the paramount purpose of the meeting thus far has been to make a wet recommendation to the next national convention and to write all those seeking important

special privileges from the government to join the Democratic party on a wet issue alone, by virtually merging the two parties on economics, including special privileges." February 22, 1931, FDRL.

15. FDR to Harry F. Byrd, March 2, 1931, ibid.
16. FDR to Al Smith, February 28, 1931. 3 *The Roosevelt Letters* 67, Elliott Roosevelt, ed. (London: George G. Harrap, 1952) (FDR's emphasis).
17. *The New York Times*, March 3, 1931.
18. Ibid.
19. FDR to Norman E. Mack, March 9, 1931. Mack was New York's national committeeman and had accompanied Farley to the meeting. FDRL. Also see Farley, *Behind the Ballots* 73–76.
20. Cordell Hull, 1 *The Memoirs of Cordell Hull* 143–145 (New York: Macmillan, 1948).
21. Farley, *Behind the Ballots* 73.
22. Other early contributors included William A. Julian of Ohio, Laurence Steinhardt, Guy Helvering, Dave Hennen Morris, Eugene Lorton, and E. J. Machette, all of New York. Steinhardt later served as FDR's ambassador to Peru (1937–39), the Soviet Union (1939–41), Turkey (1941–44), and Czechoslovakia (1944–48). Julian became treasurer of the United States; Helvering, commissioner of internal revenue; Morris, ambassador to Belgium; and Lorton a member of the International Joint Commission.
23. *The New York Times*, March 30, 1931. Also see Freidel, *Franklin D. Roosevelt: The Triumph* 205.
24. There were no replies from Oregon, Wisconsin, and Wyoming. Straus did not poll New York, ostensibly because he thought it safe for Governor Roosevelt. More likely, he recognized it would spell trouble, given Tammany's long affection for Smith. See Steve Neal, *Happy Days Are Here Again* 24 (New York: HarperCollins, 2004).
25. *The New York Times*, March 30, 31, 1931. The remaining votes were scattered among thirteen favorite sons, of whom ex-senator Reed of Missouri led with 15.
26. Roy V. Peel and Thomas C. Donnelly, *The 1932 Campaign: An Analysis* 60–61 (New York: Farrar & Rinehart, 1935).
27. Flynn, *You're the Boss* 84.
28. Farley, *Behind the Ballots* 82.
29. Ibid. 83.
30. Ibid. 85.
31. "I've just come back from New England," Harris added, "and I found there as much enthusiasm for Governor Roosevelt as I have found in the South. There is no question that Governor Roosevelt is the most popular man . . . in the country." *The New York Times*, October 14, 1931.
32. FDR to James J. Hoey, September 11, 1931, 3 *Roosevelt Letters* 73.
33. *Time*, April 27, 1931. The comment was made by Mrs. Jesse W. Nicholson, president of the National Women's Democratic Law Enforcement League.

34. FDR to Hamilton V. Miles, May 4, 1931, FDRL.

35. Looker to FDR, February 23, 1931. Reprinted in Earle Looker, *This Man Roosevelt* 134–135 (New York: Brewer, Warren & Putnam, 1932).

36. "Being assured of your integrity," Roosevelt wrote Looker, "I am prepared to permit you to make an investigation of my physical fitness, to give you every facility for thoroughly making it, and authority for you to publish its results without censorship from me." Ibid. 135.

37. Ibid. 156–157. The technical portion of the report, which was not reprinted in Looker, was first published by John Gunther in *Roosevelt in Retrospect* 267 (New York: Harper & Brothers, 1950). It states:

> *Heart:* regular; rate, 80; no increased cardiac dullness; no murmurs; aortic dullness is not widened. Blood pressure 140/100.
>
> *Pulse:* Regular 80—after examination by three physicians rate is 84, returning to 80 after 3 minutes. Electrocardiogram—left preponderance. Inverted T_3. PR and QRS intervals normal.
>
> *Lungs:* No dullness, no changes in respiratory murmurs, no extraneous sounds or rales; no abnormalities in voice sounds or fremitus. Chest expansion good.
>
> *Abdomen:* Liver and spleen, not enlarged, no pain, no masses. Abdominal muscles show slight bulging on left. No hernia. Umbilical excursion upward.
>
> No evidence of columnar degeneration of spinal cord. Both optic nerves normal. A false Babinski reflex is present on both sides (old "polio" symptom). Right knee jerk absent. Left shows responses in upper and outer portion of quadriceps extensor.
>
> Some coldness of feet below knees; cocktail makes them right. The lower erector spinae are slightly affected. Gluteus medius partial R. and L.
>
> Wassermann—negative with both alcoholic and cholesterinized antigen.
>
> No symptoms of *impotentia coeundi.*

38. Looker, *This Man Roosevelt* 154–155.

39. Ibid. 140.

40. Earle Looker, "Is Franklin D. Roosevelt Fit to Be President?" *Liberty* 7–8, July 25, 1931.

41. *The New York Times,* November 22, 24, 1931.

42. Farley, *Behind the Ballots* 93.

43. Roosevelt's announcement was made in a handwritten letter to Fred W. McLean, secretary of the Democratic State Committee of North Dakota, authorizing McLean to enter FDR's name in the upcoming North Dakota primary. "I willingly give my consent, with full appreciation of the honor that has been done

me." The letter was dated January 22, 1932, but not released until the twenty-third. 1 *Public Papers and Addresses of Franklin D. Roosevelt* 623–624, Samuel I. Rosenman, ed. (New York: Random House, 1938).

44. In 1932, U.S. territories and possessions enjoyed thirty-eight votes at the Democratic National Convention, the same number as Michigan. The territorial vote was divided among Alaska, the Canal Zone, District of Columbia, Hawaii, the Philippines, and Puerto Rico, each of which had six, and the Virgin Islands, which had two. Thanks to the labors of Farley and Howe, Roosevelt won all the territorial vote save for the Philippines, which voted for Smith.

45. Farley, *Behind the Ballots* 94.

46. *The New York Times*, February 8, 1932.

47. Ibid., January 24, 1932. There were 1,154 delegates to the 1932 Democratic Convention, 54 more than in 1928, the increase (reflecting the 1930 census) coming principally in California (+18), New York (+4), Ohio (+4), and Texas (+6). With the two-thirds rule in place, it required 770 to nominate.

48. Robert Jackson memorandum of meeting with Al Smith, January 26, 1932. James A. Farley Papers, Library of Congress.

49. When the Minnesota credentials fight went to the floor of the convention, the Roosevelt delegation was seated 658¼ to 492¾, a clear indication of FDR's strength. The vote for Roosevelt was very close to Farley's January 23 prediction.

50. *The New York Times*, March 4, 1932.

51. Wheeler spoke the argot of embattled plainsmen. "Murray was a good man," he told radio listeners in North Dakota, "but he was being used by a corrupt gang in the East, which for want of better name might be called the 'Wall Street Crowd.' " Quoted in Keith L. Bryant, Jr., *Alfalfa Bill Murray* 229 (Norman: University of Oklahoma Press, 1968).

52. FDR defeated Murray 52,634 to 32,036, with almost 85,000 votes cast. That contrasts to the 11,000 votes cast in the 1928 Democratic primary. Contemporary reports from North Dakota suggest at least 70,000 Republicans crossed over—apparently identifying Hoover with the Depression and wishing to vote for change. *Bismarck Tribune*, Valley City *Times-Record*, March 17, 1932. Also see *The New York Times*, March 16, 17, 1932.

53. Against the advice of party elders, including Sam Rayburn, Judge G. H. Howard of Atlanta filed as a proxy candidate for Speaker of the House John Garner. Roosevelt carried all 159 counties and defeated Howard roughly 60,000 to 8,000.

54. "It would have been absolutely impossible to have gotten an instructed delegation if Mr. James A. Farley had not come to Davenport," Iowa Democrat John T. Sullivan wrote FDR. "As soon as Mr. Farley appeared, the opposition melted away."

55. Farley, *Behind the Ballots* 99.

56. William Crawford to Howe, January 29, 1932, Howe Papers, FDRL.

57. Albert C. Ritchie, "Give Us Democracy," *North American Review* (October 1930). Also see *The New York Times*, January 8, 1932.

58. *The New York Times,* June 28, 1932.

59. Sam Rosenman, *Working with Roosevelt* 56–57 (New York: Harper & Brothers, 1952).

60. Ibid. 58.

61. Ibid.

62. Arthur M. Schlesinger, Jr., *The Crisis of the Old Order* 400 (Boston: Houghton Mifflin, 1957).

63. In the summer of 1932, Berle, together with economist Gardiner C. Means, published the groundbreaking study *The Modern Corporation and Private Property.* (New York: Harcourt, Brace & World, 1968; reprint).

64. *The New York Times,* April 27, 1932.

65. Ernest K. Lindley, *The Roosevelt Revolution—First Phase* 7 (New York: Viking Press, 1933).

66. Moley, *After Seven Years* 5, 10–11.

67. For the text of the "forgotten man" speech, see 1932 *Public Papers of Governor Franklin D. Roosevelt* 572–573 (Albany, N.Y.: J. B. Lyon, 1937). The term "forgotten man" was supplied by Moley and is taken from an 1883 essay by Yale economist William Graham Sumner. Sumner was referring to the middle class. *The Forgotten Man and Other Essays* 465–498 (New Haven, Conn.: Yale University Press, 1918).

   Probusiness Democrats were aghast at FDR's rhetoric. "I will take off my coat and fight to the end against any candidate who persists in any demagogic appeal to the masses of the working people of this country to destroy themselves by setting class against class and rich against poor," rasped Al Smith, who had become the party's principal spokesman for an alliance with big business. *The New York Times,* April 14, 1932.

68. *The New York Times,* April 19, 1932; 1932 *Public Papers* 577–583.

69. Ibid. 588–591.

70. Quoted in Freidel, *Franklin D. Roosevelt: The Triumph* 290. Garner was a reluctant candidate at best. On the eve of the convention he confided to his manager, Sam Rayburn, that he did not want a deadlocked convention. "I want to live long enough to see a Democrat in the White House. So we must make certain we don't have a deadlock in Chicago. Sam, you and I both know that I am not going to be nominated for President. But a lot of these people who are pushing me are loyal friends, and . . . I couldn't very well say no." D. B. Hardeman and Donald C. Bacon, *Rayburn: A Biography* 137–138 (Austin: Texas Monthly Press, 1987).

71. H. L. Mencken, *Making a President: A Footnote to the Saga of Democracy* 117 (New York: Knopf, 1932).

72. Don Hayner and Tom McNamee, *The Stadium* 19 (Chicago: Performance Media, 1993).

73. Farley, *Behind the Ballots* 114.

74. Flynn, *You're the Boss* 89.

75. The two-thirds rule was adopted at the Democratic party's first convention, which was held in Baltimore in 1832. "A nomination made by two-thirds of the

whole body would show a more general concurrence of sentiment in favor of a particular individual, would carry with it a greater moral weight and be more favorably received than one made by a smaller number," wrote Senator William R. King of Alabama, a member of the committee that drafted the rule. Frank R. Kent, *The Democratic Party: A History* 116–119 (New York: Century, 1928).

76. Farley, *Behind the Ballots* 117.

77. Williams's telegram was to his former Senate colleague James Reed of Missouri. Reed released it to *The New York Times,* June 26, 1932.

78. FDR to Farley, June 27, 1932. Farley, *Behind the Ballots* 119.

79. Alben W. Barkley, *That Reminds Me* 141 (New York: Doubleday, 1954).

80. Farley said afterward that the contesting Louisiana delegation, headed by former governor Jared Y. Sanders, had agreed to support Roosevelt if they were seated, but the Roosevelt camp believed Long's claim to the seats to be superior. Farley, *Behind the Ballots* 124.

81. T. Harry Williams, *Huey Long: A Biography* 580 (New York: Knopf, 1969). Ed Flynn said, "Never in all my experience have I listened to a finer or more logical argument than [Long] presented for the seating of his delegation. *You're the Boss* 96. For the text of Long's presentation see *Official Proceedings of the 1932 Democratic Convention* 61–64 (Washington, D.C.: Democratic National Committee, 1932).

82. Farley Convention Diary, Farley Papers, Library of Congress.

83. Iowa and North Carolina, which had jumped the traces to vote against Long, returned to the Roosevelt stable. Considering that Boston mayor James Michael Curley headed the Roosevelt Puerto Rico delegation, its status was surely questionable.

84. The Wheeler quotation is from Neal, *Happy Days Are Here Again* 179; Farley, *Behind the Ballots* 105.

85. Flynn, *You're the Boss* 99. On the first ballot Walsh rendered three important rulings that assisted Roosevelt: he dismissed a request from Smith's supporters that the Iowa delegation be polled; rejected Ritchie's challenge to the unit rule in the District of Columbia; and denied a request that the Minnesota delegation be polled, holding that they had been instructed by the state convention. *Proceedings of the 1932 Democratic National Convention* 289–292, 297–300.

86. Barkley had a remarkable capacity to ridicule: "Dr. [Nicholas Murray] Butler condemns [the Republican plank] because it is dry; Senator Borah because it is wet, and the American people condemn it because it is neither." (Ironically, Barkley had been one of the chief sponsors of the Eighteenth Amendment.) For the text of Barkley's keynote see the *Proceedings of the 1932 Democratic National Convention* 17–39.

87. "The Great Prohibition Poll's Final Report," *Literary Digest,* April 30, 1932.

88. *New York Herald Tribune,* June 7, 1932.

89. *The New York Times,* June 10, 1932. Of the 934 votes for repeal, 499½ came from Roosevelt delegates. For the roll-call vote, see *Proceedings of the 1932 Democratic*

National Convention 188–189. Also see Peel and Donnelly, *The 1932 Campaign* 100.

90. Flynn, *You're the Boss* 90, 93.

91. Arthur Mullen, *Western Democrat* 268 (New York: Wilfred Funk, 1940).

92. Flynn, *You're the Boss* 100.

93. *The New York Times,* July 1, 1932.

94. William Allen White, column, *The New York Times,* July 1, 1932.

95. Farley, *Behind the Ballots* 138.

96. Ibid. 140.

97. Rosenman, *Working with Roosevelt* 70–71.

98. Ibid. 142.

99. Mullen, *Western Democrat* 275–276.

100. Farley, *Behind the Ballots* 143.

101. Flynn, *You're the Boss* 101.

102. Flynn reports that Long shook his fist at Pat Harrison, but Farley credits Harrison with a yeoman effort to hold Mississippi for FDR. No one doubts that Long shook his fist, but it is more likely that the face into which it was shaken belonged to Conner. Flynn, *You're the Boss* 101; compare Farley, *Behind the Ballots* 143.

103. Flynn, *You're the Boss* 101.

104. George E. Allen, *Presidents Who Have Known Me* 55–56 (New York: Simon & Schuster, 1950).

105. Farley, *Behind the Ballots* 144–145.

106. Hull, 1 *Memoirs* 153–154.

107. Brice Clagett, Memorandum, Personal and Confidential, February 22, 1933. Mr. Clagett, McAdoo's law partner and son-in-law, was staying with McAdoo in his penthouse suite at Sherman House and was privy to the McAdoo-Roper discussion.

108. Daniel Roper, *Fifty Years in Public Life* 259–260 (Durham, N.C.: Duke University Press, 1941).

109. Bascom N. Timmons, *Garner of Texas* 165–166 (New York: Harper & Brothers, 1948).

110. Thomas M. Storke, *California Editor* 321–325 (Los Angeles: Westernlore Press, 1958).

111. Farley, *Behind the Ballots* 151.

112. Moley, *After Seven Years* 30.

113. *Proceedings of the 1932 Democratic National Convention* 325–327.

114. Ibid. 329.

115. Ibid. 332.

116. Baltimore *Evening Sun,* July 5, 1932. The journalist Elmer Davis, writing in *Harper's,* believed the Democrats had nominated "the man who would probably make the weakest President of the dozen aspirants." Veteran Washington correspondent Charles Willis Thompson quipped, "The Democrats have nominated

nobody quite like him since Franklin Pierce." Davis, "The Collapse of Politics," 165 *Harper's* 388; Thompson, "Wanted: Political Courage," ibid. 726–727 (1932).

117. FDR was the first American candidate to utilize the airplane, but not the first on the world stage. In April 1932, in his runoff presidential campaign against Field Marshal Paul von Hindenburg, Adolf Hitler barnstormed Germany in a Junkers trimotor plane, very similar to the one in which FDR flew to Chicago. Hitler's campaign (*"Hitler über Deutschland"*) was reported extensively in the American press, and it is inconceivable that FDR was unaware of it. (See *The New York Times,* April 3, 7, 1932.) Hitler lost to Hindenburg, 13.4 million–19.4 million, but following parliamentary elections in November was asked by Hindenburg to form a government (January 30, 1933). Joachim C. Fest, *Hitler* 320 (New York: Harcourt Brace Jovanovich, 1973).

118. Thomas Petzinger, Jr., *Hard Landing* 8 (New York: Random House, 1995).

119. Interview with Goodrich Murphy, cited in Neal, *Happy Days* 296.

120. *Proceedings of the 1932 Democratic National Convention* 372–383.

FOURTEEN | Nothing to Fear

The epigraph is from Roosevelt's inaugural address, March 4, 1933. 2 *Public Papers and Addresses of Franklin D. Roosevelt* 11–16, Samuel I. Rosenman, ed. (New York: Random House, 1938).

1. Edward J. Flynn, *You're the Boss* 122 (New York: Viking Press, 1947).

2. Quoted in Roy V. Peel and Thomas C. Donnelly, *The 1932 Campaign: An Analysis* 107 (New York: Farrar & Rinehart, 1935).

3. *Proceedings of the 1932 Democratic National Convention* 596–597 (Washington, D.C.: Democratic National Committee, 1932).

4. James A. Farley, *Behind the Ballots* 176–177 (New York: Harcourt, Brace and Co., 1938). Also see Frank Freidel, *Franklin D. Roosevelt: The Triumph* 337 (Boston: Little, Brown, 1956).

5. *The New York Times,* July 6, 1932. For details of the trip, see Robert F. Cross, *Sailor in the White House: The Seafaring Life of FDR* 57–63 (Annapolis, Md.: Naval Institute Press, 2003).

6. *The New York Times,* July 12, 1932.

7. Robert F. Cross interview with Curtis Roosevelt, October 15, 1994, in Cross, *Sailor in the White House* 64.

8. *The New York Times,* July 13, 16, 17, 18, 1932.

9. Farley took it upon himself to repair relations with Tammany. Immediately following the convention, the new party chairman ventured into the wigwam on Seventeenth Street to "smoke the pipe of peace with the Tammany leaders," as he put it. The occasion was the annual Fourth of July celebration, and Farley, uninvited, made the most of the meeting. "They were friendly enough, and I got the impression that it helped considerably to have me extend the olive branch first. A news writer in describing the incident said the good will of the Tammany

Sachems was won over when I remarked, 'Aren't we all Democrats?' It was a great line and I certainly would have used it if it had occurred to me." Farley, *Behind the Ballots* 157.

10. Ibid. 158.

11. As Louis Howe put it, "It was determined that the state organizations themselves, not only theoretically but in reality, were to be entirely responsible for the campaign in their respective territories." Louis McHenry Howe, North American Newspaper Alliance article, December 1932, quoted in Peel and Donnelly, *1932 Campaign* 113–116.

12. Hull to Farley, July 14, 1932; Farley to Hull, July 15, 1932. Democratic National Committee manuscripts, 1932. FDRL.

13. Howe, North American Newspaper Alliance article.

14. Farley, *Behind the Ballots* 159–160, 194.

15. For the text of Hoover's campaign speeches, see 2 *State Papers and Other Public Writings of Herbert Hoover* 289–487, William Starr Myers, ed. (New York: Doubleday, Doran, 1934).

16. Flynn, *You're the Boss* 120.

17. Samuel I. Rosenman, *Working with Roosevelt* 80 (New York: Harper & Brothers, 1952).

18. The 1932 election expenses are based on figures filed by the two parties with the Clerk of the House of Representatives, as required by the Corrupt Practices Act of 1925 (43 Stat. 1070). For a detailed analysis, see Louise Overacker, "Campaign Funds in a Depression Year," *American Political Science Review* 769–783 (October 1933). Also see Louise Overacker, *Money in Elections* (New York: Macmillan, 1932).

19. Peel and Donnelly, *1932 Campaign* 116.

20. Aggregate expenses for both parties in 1932 totaled $5,146,027. With 39,816,522 votes cast, the cost per vote was 12.9 cents.

21. In 1924, Congress passed the Adjusted Compensation Act (43 Stat. 121) to pay former servicemen for the time spent away from home in World War I. Each veteran would receive a life insurance policy in 1925, which could be cashed after twenty years for $500 plus interest. These were the bonuses at issue. The story of the Bonus Army is told most effectively by Paul Dickson and Thomas B. Allen in their carefully researched and eminently readable *The Bonus Army: An American Epic* (New York: Walker and Company, 2004).

22. Fleta Campbell Springer, "Glassford and the Siege of Washington," 145 *Harper's* 641–655 (1932). Also see John Dos Passos, "The Veterans Come Home to Roost," 71 *The New Republic* 177 (1932); Donald J. Lisio, *The President and Protest: Hoover, Conspiracy, and the Bonus Riot* (Columbia: University of Missouri Press, 1974). When food ran out, Glassford brought nearly a thousand dollars' worth with his own money. "Why some of those boys soldiered for me; they're my boys." Quoted in Arthur M. Schlesinger, Jr., *The Crisis of the Old Order* 260 (Boston: Houghton Mifflin, 1956).

23.	Schlesinger, *Crisis of the Old Order* 262.

24.	The text of Hurley's order to MacArthur, reprinted in *The New York Times*, July 29, 1932, reads as follows:

> TO: General Douglas MacArthur, Chief of Staff, U.S. Army.
>
> The President has just informed me that the civil government of the District of Columbia has reported to him that it is unable to maintain law and order in the District.
>
> You will have United States troops proceed immediately to the scene of disorder. Cooperate fully with the District of Columbia police force which is now in charge. Surround the affected area and clear it without delay.
>
> Turn over all prisoners to the civil authorities.
>
> In your orders insist that any women and children who may be in the affected area be accorded every consideration and kindness. Use all humanity consistent with the due execution of this order.
>
> > Patrick J. Hurley
> > Secretary of War

25.	Martin Blumenson, *Patton: The Man Behind the Legend* 133–135 (New York: William Morrow, 1985).

26.	*The New York Times*, July 29, 1932.

27.	Washington *Daily News*, July 29, 1932.

28.	Rexford G. Tugwell, *The Brains Trust* 357–359 (New York: Viking Press, 1968).

29.	Ibid. 427–434. "I've known Doug for years," FDR told Tugwell. "You've never heard him talk, but I have. He has the most pretentious style of anyone I know. He talks in a voice that might come from the oracle's cave. He never doubts and never argues or suggests; he makes pronouncements. What he thinks is final. Besides, he's intelligent, a brilliant soldier like his father before him. He got to be a brigadier general in France. I thought he was the youngest until I read that Glassford was. There could be times that Doug would exactly fit. We've just had a preview."

30.	Farley, *Behind the Ballots* 160–161.

31.	Ibid. 65, 155.

32.	Henry L. Stimson, MS diary, June 18, 1931, Yale University. When the campaign began, Stimson worried that Hoover and his advisers had underestimated Roosevelt. That, plus the economy, "gives us an uphill fight. Also, there is no split in the Democratic party as there was in 1896, and there is no Mark Hanna in the Republican party." Ibid., July 5, 1932.

33.	Grace Tully, *F.D.R.: My Boss* 60 (New York: Charles Scribner's Sons, 1949).

34.	Stimson, MS diary, September 6, 1932. The White House continued to pressure Stimson, but he refused to comply. "I think that to attack a presidential candidate who is a cripple and who has a pleasant appearance, particularly when the attack comes from a close advisor of the President, is about the most dangerous thing that the President and his foolish advisors can settle on, and I hate to be the goat." Ibid., September 22, 1932.

35. In 1917, Stimson, at the age of forty-nine, volunteered for active duty and was assigned as first a major, then a lieutenant colonel, to the 305th Field Artillery Battalion of the 77th Division. Promoted to colonel, he commanded the 31st Artillery Regiment at war's end. Stimson's battalion was the first American unit to fire at the enemy in France, and he was the first secretary of war to serve on active duty afterward. (At FDR's request, Patrick J. Hurley returned to the Army as a major general in World War II.) Henry L. Stimson and McGeorge Bundy, *On Active Service in Peace and War* 91–100 (New York: Harper & Brothers, 1947).

36. Herbert Hoover, 3 *Memoirs* 233 (New York: Macmillan, 1952).

37. Quoted in Kenneth S. Davis, *FDR: The New York Years* 362 (New York: Random House, 1979), and many others. See FDR's remarkable speech to the Republicans for Roosevelt League at the Metropolitan Opera House, November 3, 1932, in which FDR managed to find many good words for Calvin Coolidge, "a great figure in our national life and a great Republican." For text, see 1932 *Public Papers of Franklin D. Roosevelt, Forty-eighth Governor of the State of New York* 662–665 (Albany, N.Y.: J. B. Lyon, 1939).

38. The Horseman of Destruction, said Roosevelt, was "the embodiment of governmental policies so unsound, so inimical to true progress that it left behind in its trail economic paralysis, industrial chaos, poverty and suffering." The Horseman of Delay reflected the Republicans' do-nothing attitude. "When they say 'don't change horses while crossing the stream,' what they mean is 'don't run the risk of crossing the stream at all.' " The Horseman of Deceit intended "to cover the trail of the Horsemen of Destruction and Delay." "Bringing up the rear is the Horseman of Despair. He tells you economic conditions must work themselves out. He tries to close the door of hope in your face." For full text, see 1 *Public Papers and Addresses of Franklin D. Roosevelt* 831–842.

39. For a firsthand description of Hoover's hostile reception in Detroit, see Thomas L. Stokes, *Chip off My Shoulder* 304–305 (Princeton, N.J.: Princeton University Press, 1940).

40. Clapper's forty-minute interview with Hoover was on February 27, 1931. Olive E. Clapper, *Washington Tapestry* 3–4 (New York: Whittlesey House, 1946).

41. Hoover, 3 *Memoirs* 195.

42. *The New York Times*, November 1, 1932. For complete text, see 2 *State Papers of Herbert Hoover* 408–428. The quotation is at page 418.

43. *The New York Times*, November 6, 1932; *New York Herald Tribune*, November 6, 1932. For the complete text of Hoover's speech, see 2 *State Papers* 449–466.

44. E. W. Starling, *Starling of the White House* 300 (New York: Simon & Schuster, 1946).

45. Rosenman, *Working with Roosevelt* 87.

46. Socialist candidate Norman Thomas received 883,990 votes and the Communist William Z. Foster 102,221. A sprinkling of ten other candidates, including Pro-

hibitionist William David Upshaw and the Liberty Party's William Hope Harvey, received a total of 128,758. Roosevelt's overall percentage was 57.42 to Hoover's 39.64. *Congressional Quarterly's Guide to U.S. Elections* 289, 304–305 (Washington, D.C.: Congressional Quarterly, 1975).

47. *The New York Times,* November 9, 1932.

48. Lela Stiles, *The Man Behind Roosevelt: The Story of Louis McHenry Howe* 216 (Cleveland: World, 1954); Farley, *Behind the Ballots* 186.

49. Eleanor Roosevelt, *This I Remember* 74–75 (New York: Harper & Brothers, 1949).

50. Irving Bernstein, *The Lean Years* 506–507 (Boston: Houghton Mifflin, 1960).

51. Rexford Tugwell, "Notes from a New Deal Diary," December 24, 1932, FDRL.

52. Edmund Wilson, "Hull House in 1933: III," *The New Republic* 320 (February 1, 1933).

53. 113 *Literary Digest* 6 (November 12, 1932).

54. Avis Carlson, "Deflating the Schools," 167 *Harper's* 705–715 (1933).

55. 113 *Literary Digest* 10 (May 7, 1932).

56. *The New York Times,* January 22, 1933; *The Denver Post,* February 12, 1933; A. William Hoglund, "Wisconsin Dairy Farmers on Strike," 35 *Agricultural History* 24–34 (1961). Also see Theodore Saloutos and John D. Hicks, *Agricultural Discontent in the Middle West: 1900–1939* 435–448 (Madison: University of Wisconsin Press, 1951).

57. Hoover to FDR, February 17, 1933, in W. S. Myers and W. H. Newton, *The Hoover Administration: A Documented Narrative* 338–341 (New York: Charles Scribner's Sons, 1936).

58. Hoover to D. A. Reed, February 20, 1933, ibid. 351.

59. FDR to Hoover, March 1, 1933, ibid. 344–345.

60. Nathan Miller, *FDR: An Intimate History* 292 (New York: Doubleday, 1983).

61. Stimson, MS diary, January 9, 1933. Also see Stimson and Bundy, *On Active Service* 292–293.

62. Tugwell, MS diary, January 17 [?], 1933, FDRL.

63. Raymond Moley, *After Seven Years* 95 (New York: Harper & Brothers, 1939).

64. Quoted in Ted Morgan, *FDR: A Biography* 371 (New York: Simon & Schuster, 1985). Hull was initially reluctant to take the post because he could not afford the expected social expenses. FDR relieved him of the social burden by appointing an old (and wealthy) friend, William Phillips, as undersecretary. Phillips later served as Roosevelt's ambassador to Italy.

65. Moley, *After Seven Years* 121.

66. In addition to successfully running American Car and Foundry, the world's largest producer of railroad rolling stock, Woodin was a skilled musician and composer whose published works included *The Covered Wagon Suite, The Oriental Suite,* and "The Franklin Delano Roosevelt March," written for the inauguration.

67. Morgan, *FDR* 372, citing Alfred B. Rollins, *Roosevelt and Howe* 374 (New York: Alfred A. Knopf, 1962).

68. Eleanor Roosevelt, *This I Remember* 76. Also see Joseph P. Lash, *Eleanor and Franklin* 357–358 (New York: W. W. Norton, 1971). "My zest for life is rather gone for the time being," ER wrote to Lorena Hickok. "I get like this sometimes. It makes me feel like a dead weight and my mind goes round and round like a squirrel in a cage. I want to run and I can't, and I despise myself." ER to Lorena Hickok, in Joseph P. Lash, *Love, Eleanor* 159 (New York: Doubleday, 1982).

69. *Nourmahal,* the flagship of the New York Yacht Club, was built in Germany for Astor in 1928. It was described by *The New York Times* as "an ocean liner in miniature . . . the biggest and fastest ocean-going motor yacht ever built." It had a cruising range of 19,000 miles and a top speed of sixteen knots. In 1934, FDR would return to *Nourmahal* to watch the America's Cup race from her decks. James Roosevelt and Sidney Shalett, *Affectionately, F.D.R.* 275–278 (New York: Harcourt, Brace, 1959).

70. Vincent Astor, a nominal Republican, contributed $25,000 to FDR's campaign in 1932, making him one of the ten largest contributors. The verse is quoted in James Roosevelt, *Affectionately, F.D.R.* 278.

71. FDR to SDR, February 6, 1933, 3 *The Roosevelt Letters* 100–101, Elliott Roosevelt, ed. (London: George G. Harrap, 1952).

72. FDR was quick to express his gratitude to Mrs. Cross. From his train returning to New York he wired, "How much greater and sadder a tragedy was averted by your unselfish courage and quick thinking of course no one can estimate. It now appears that by Divine Providence the lives of all the victims of the assassin's disturbed aim will be spared." *The New York Times,* February 20, 1933. Roosevelt spoke too soon. Both Mayor Cermak and Mrs. Joseph H. Gill, the wife of the president of Florida Light and Power Company, the woman shot in the abdomen, perished from infection.

73. Roosevelt gave the statement to the press immediately afterward. *The New York Times,* February 17, 1933. Jackson Memorial Hospital is 2.6 miles from Bay Front Park.

74. Some have speculated that Zangara had intended to kill Cermak all along. That is not supported by the evidence. Zangara had never been in Chicago and had no ties with the Mob. Asked at his trial if he knew Mayor Cermak, Zangara replied, "No, not at all. I just went there to kill the president. The capitalists killed my life. I suffer, always suffer. I make it 50-50—someone else must suffer."

> Q: Do you want to live?
> A: No. Put me in the electric chair.
> Q: Are you sorry only because you tried to kill Mr. Roosevelt?
> A: No. I am sorry because I failed.

The courtroom examination was reported in *The New York Times,* March 10, 11, 21, 1933. Zangara's life is treated in some detail by Kenneth S. Davis in *FDR: The New York Years* 432–434.

75. Moley, *After Seven Years* 139.

76. Thomas W. Lamont to FDR, February 27, 1933, FDRL. Lamont had rented Roosevelt's East Sixty-fifth Street town house for the seven years FDR was assistant secretary of the Navy and remained on intimate terms with the president-elect.

77. Raymond Moley, *The First New Deal* 96–124 (New York: Harcourt, Brace, 1966).

78. James A. Farley, *Jim Farley's Story* 36 (New York: Whittlesey House, 1948).

79. The original Trading with the Enemy Act was enacted October 6, 1917, chap. 106, 40 Stat. 411, and has been recodified more than a dozen times, most recently on March 10, 1939, chap. 75, 46 Stat. 84.

80. Hoover was concerned about the fate of Walter H. Newton, a longtime Republican congressman from Minnesota who had resigned his House seat in 1929 to become the president's administrative assistant. Newton had no outside source of income, and in his final days Hoover had nominated him to a federal judgeship but the Senate had blocked his confirmation. FDR happily agreed to take care of Newton and two weeks later appointed him to the Federal Home Loan Bank Board. Frank Freidel, *Franklin D. Roosevelt: Launching the New Deal* 200–201 (Boston: Little, Brown, 1973). Also see ER, *This I Remember* 77, and Grace Tully, *FDR: My Boss* 68.

81. Ed Hill transcript, FDRL.

82. See the correspondence between Charles E. Cropley, clerk of the court, and FDR, February 20, 25, 1933, and Chief Justice Hughes's reply of February 28, 1933. "I am glad to have the suggestion that you repeat the oath in full instead of saying simply 'I do,' " wrote Hughes. "I think the repetition is the more dignified and appropriate course." 3 *Roosevelt Letters* 102–105.

83. The text of the presidential oath, reproduced above, is found in Article II, section 1, of the Constitution.

84. Roosevelt, 2 *Public Papers and Addresses* 11–16.

85. Frances Perkins interview, Columbia Oral History Project, Columbia University.

86. Lorena Hickok, *Eleanor Roosevelt: Reluctant First Lady* 104–105 (New York: Dodd, Mead, 1980).

87. In the confusion following the inauguration FDR's family Bible was misplaced, and there was some difficulty finding one for Justice Cardozo. Eventually Chief Usher Ike Hoover located one in the locker of Charles S. Baum, a White House policeman, and it was used to administer the cabinet oaths. *The New York Times*, March 5, 7, 1933. It required less than thirty minutes for the Senate to unanimously confirm all of Roosevelt's appointees. No hearings were held.

88. Michael Teague, *Mrs. L: Conversations with Alice Roosevelt Longworth* 171, 161 (New York: Doubleday, 1981).

FIFTEEN | One Hundred Days

The epigraph is a remark FDR made at dinner in the White House, March 12, 1933, prior to sending his message to Congress requesting that the Volstead Act (48 Stat. 305) be amended to permit the sale of beer and light wine. Ernest K. Lindley, *The Roosevelt Revolution* 91 (New York: Viking, 1933).

1. Inaugural address, March 4, 1933. 2 *Public Papers and Address of Franklin D. Roosevelt* 12, Samuel I. Rosenman, ed. (New York: Random House, 1938).
2. Prior to adoption of the Twentieth (Lame Duck) Amendment in 1933, the new Congress did not convene until late in the year following its election (variably set by statute). The Twentieth Amendment set January 4 as the date for Congress to meet, but it was not yet in effect. The Senate, of course, is a continuing body and is always in session, which explains the confirmation of FDR's cabinet appointees on March 4.
3. Frances Perkins interview, Columbia Oral History Project, Columbia University.
4. For the texts of Roosevelt's proclamations declaring a bank holiday (No. 2039) and the recall of Congress (No. 2038), see 2 *Public Papers and Addresses* 24–26, 17.
5. Hiram Johnson to his sons, March 12, 1933, Johnson Papers, Bancroft Library, University of California, Berkeley.
6. John Gunther, *Roosevelt in Retrospect* 278 (New York: Harper & Brothers, 1950).
7. Address before the Governors' Conference at the White House, March 6, 1933. 2 *Public Papers and Addresses* 18–21.
8. Pledge of Support to the President by the Governors' Conference, March 6, 1933. Ibid. 21–24.
9. The caucus resolution gave Majority Leader Joseph Robinson authority to convene the caucus "for the purpose of considering any measure recommended by the President and that all Democratic senators shall be bound by vote of the majority of the conference." *The New York Times*, March 7, 1933. The prior caucus rule had required a two-thirds vote. In the House of Representatives, it continued to require a two-thirds vote to bind the Democratic caucus.
10. In addition to Huey Long, Senators George McGill of Kansas and Edward Costigan of Colorado voted against. Ibid.
11. Raymond Moley, *After Seven Years* 151 (New York: Harper & Brothers, 1939).
12. Ibid. 152. The bills were copies of the national banknote series of 1929 and printed from the same plates. They carried the phrase "National Currency—secured by United States bonds deposited with the Treasurer of the United States of America or by like deposit of other securities." *The New York Times*, March 14, 1933.
13. The drafting was largely the work of Walter Wyatt, general counsel of the Federal Reserve Board. Moley, *After Seven Years* 152.
14. FDR held 337 press conferences during his first term. He scheduled his conferences for 10:00 A.M. Wednesday, and—to give the morning papers a break—4:00 P.M. on Friday. Attendance was limited to the White House press corps. Editors and visiting journalists saw the president separately. Frank Freidel, *Franklin D. Roosevelt: Launching the New Deal* 224n (Boston: Little, Brown, 1973).
15. First Press Conference, March 8, 1933, 2 *Public Papers and Addresses* 30–38.
16. *The New York Times*, March 9, 1933.

17. Graham J. White, *FDR and the Press* 7; Richard Lee Strout, in Katie Louchheim, ed., *The Making of the New Deal: The Insiders Speak* 13 (Cambridge, Mass.: Harvard University Press, 1983). In addition to writing for *The Christian Science Monitor*, Strout wrote the weekly "TRB" column in *The New Republic*. Also see Theodore G. Joslin, "President Meets the Press," *Sunday Star* (Washington, D.C.), March 4, 1934, reprinted in 2 *Public Papers and Addresses* 40–45.

18. Liva Baker, *The Justice from Beacon Hill* 641 (New York: HarperCollins, 1991); Catherine Drinker Bowen, *Yankee from Olympus* 414 (Boston: Little, Brown, 1945). Holmes served as a captain of the 20th Massachusetts Infantry, fought at Balls Bluff, Fair Oaks, Malvern Hill, and Antietam, and was wounded three times, twice so seriously that he was given up for dead.

19. *Time*, March 20, 1933.

20. Holmes to FDR, March 16, 1933, FDRL.

21. Jean Edward Smith, *John Marshall: Definer of the Constitution* 517–518 (New York: Henry Holt, 1996). Also see Charles Warren, 1 *The Supreme Court in United States History* 758–760 (Boston: Little, Brown, 1926).

22. *Worcester v. Georgia*, 6 Peters (31 U.S.) 515 (1832). Horace Greeley's gratuitous attribution first appears in volume 1 of his *The American Conflict* 106 (Hartford, Conn.: O. D. Case, 1864).

23. "Recommendation to the Congress for Legislation to Control Resumption of Banking," March 9, 1933, 2 *Public Papers and Addresses* 45–47.

24. *The New York Times*, March 10, 1933.

25. Ibid.

26. The seven senators to vote against the Emergency Banking Act were William E. Borah (Idaho); Robert Carey (Wyoming); Porter Dale (Vermont); Robert La Follette (Wisconsin); Gerald Nye (North Dakota); Edward Costigan (Colorado); and Henrik Shipstead (Minnesota).

27. Moley, *After Seven Years* 154. "I shall never forget the look of joy on the faces of [California senators] Hiram Johnson and William McAdoo when I stepped out of Woodin's office to give them the news," wrote Moley.

28. The comment was made by FDR to J.F.T. O'Connor, a California lawyer, when he appointed O'Connor comptroller of the currency in May 1933. O'Connor, diary, May 29, 1933.

29. Lindley, *Roosevelt Revolution* 87–89.

30. The text of FDR's message is in 2 *Public Papers and Addresses* 49–51.

31. Enacted March 20, 1933, 48 Stat. 8.

32. Roosevelt acknowledged his debt to McDuffie by appointing him to the U.S. District Court in Alabama the following year.

33. *The New York Times*, March 11, 1933.

34. "The First Fireside Chat," March 12, 1933, 2 *Public Papers and Addresses* 61–66. The initial draft was prepared by Charles Michelson of the Democratic National Committee and was vetted by Hoover's undersecretary of the Treasury, Arthur Ballantine. FDR took the vetted draft and rewrote it Sunday afternoon, dictating

to Grace Tully and putting it into language easily comprehensible to the average citizen. Arthur M. Schlesinger, Jr., *The Coming of the New Deal* 12–13 (Boston: Houghton Mifflin, 1958).

35. Will Rogers, *Sanity Is Where You Find It* 167, Donald Day, ed. (Boston: Houghton Mifflin, 1955).

36. Moley, *After Seven Years* 155. Moley gives credit to Treasury secretary Woodin, whose "imagination and sturdiness and common sense" carried the day.

37. *The Wall Street Journal,* March 13, 1933; Stimson to FDR, March 14, 1933; Hearst to FDR, n.d. FDRL. The Baker quote is in *The New York Times,* March 19, 1933.

38. Lindley, *Roosevelt Revolution* 91.

39. "I recommend to the Congress the passage of legislation for the immediate modification of the Volstead Act, in order to legalize the manufacture and sale of beer and other beverages of such alcoholic content as is permissible under the Constitution; and to provide under such manufacture and sale, by substantial taxes, a proper and much needed revenue for the government.

    "I deem action at this time to be of the highest importance." 2 *Public Papers and Addresses* 66–67.

40. Third Press Conference, March 15, 1933, ibid. 67–73.

41. *The New York Times,* March 12, 1933. McDuffie's decision to demand a roll call was crucial to the passage of the economy act. In caucus (where the proceedings were secret) a majority of Democrats deserted FDR, but when threatened with having to take a public stand against the president most returned to the fold. Ibid. The quotation is from McDuffie's ally, Congressman Clifton Woodrum of Virginia. *Congressional Record* 214, 73d Cong., 1st Sess.

42. FDR, "New Measures to Rescue Agriculture," March 16, 1933. 2 *Public Papers and Addresses* 74.

43. "I seek an end to the threatened loss of homes and productive capacity now faced by hundreds of thousands of American farm families." "A Message Asking for Legislation to Save Farm Mortgages from Foreclosure," April 3, 1933. Ibid. 100–101.

44. Russell Lord, *The Wallaces of Iowa* 330 (Boston: Houghton Mifflin, 1947).

45. 48 Stat. 31. The Emergency Farm Mortgage Act was Title II of the Agricultural Adjustment Act (48 Stat. 31, 41).

46. FDR's message to Congress on the Civilian Conservation Corps, the Federal Emergency Relief Agency, and the Public Works Administration was March 21, 1933. The securities regulation message was March 29; TVA, April 10; home mortgages, April 13; emergency railroad legislation, May 4, 1933. 2 *Public Papers and Addresses* 80–83, 93, 122–128, 135, 153–154.

47. Schlesinger, *Coming of the New Deal* 336.

48. *Proceedings of the 1932 Democratic National Convention* 372–383 (Washington, D.C.: Democratic National Committee, 1932).

49. Moley, *After Seven Years* 174.

50. Press Conference, March 15, 1933, 2 *Public Papers and Addresses* 70.

51. FDR, message to Congress, March 21, 1933, ibid. 81.

52. Senate Education and Labor Committee, House Labor Committee, Unemployment Relief: Joint Hearings 46, 69, 73rd Cong., 1st Sess. (Washington, D.C.: U.S. Government Printing Office, 1933).

53. Press Conference, March 22, 1933, 1 *Press Conference Transcripts* 64–66, FDRL.

54. Green to FDR, September 18, 1933, FDRL.

55. Forrest C. Pogue, *George C. Marshall: Education of a General* 276–280 (New York: Viking Press, 1963).

56. Federal Emergency Relief Act of 1933, Public Law 15, 73d Congress, May 12, 1933.

57. "The half-billion dollars for direct relief of States won't last a month if Harry L. Hopkins, the new relief administrator, maintains the pace he set yesterday in disbursing more than $5,000,000 during his first two hours in office," said *The Washington Post*. Quoted in Robert E. Sherwood, *Roosevelt and Hopkins: An Intimate History* 44 (New York: Harper & Brothers, 1948).

58. Ibid. 48. Hopkins's salary as administrator was $8,000 annually. In New York he earned $15,000.

59. Federal expenditures in FY 1932–33 amounted to $4.6 billion, receipts totaled $1.9 billion, leaving a deficit of $2.7 billion. Bureau of the Census, *Statistical History of the United States* 711 (Stamford, Conn.: Fairfield Publishers, 1965).

60. Charles Wyzanski to his parents, April 29, 1933. Wyzanski MSS., reproduced in Freidel, *Launching the New Deal* 431. On loan from the Department of Labor to the Justice Department, Wyzanski successfully defended the constitutionality of the National Labor Relations Act and the Social Security Act before the Supreme Court in 1937. *NLRB v. Jones Laughlin* 301 U.S. 1 (1937); *Steward Machine Co. v. Davis*, 301 U.S. 548 (1937). He was appointed to the U.S. District Court in Massachusetts by FDR in 1941.

61. The public works program was Title II of the National Industrial Recovery Act of 1933. Public Law 77, 73rd Congress.

62. The 1932 Democratic platform stated, "We advocate protection of the investing public by requiring to be filed with the Government, and carried in advertisements, of all offerings of foreign and domestic stocks and bonds, true information as to bonuses, commissions, principal invested, and interests of the sellers."

63. Message to Congress, "Recommendation for Federal Supervision of Investment Securities in Interstate Commerce," March 29, 1932, 2 *Public Papers and Addresses* 93–94. The White House public statement concerning the legislation is ibid. 94.

64. Securities Act of 1933, 48 Stat. 74, Public Law 22, 73rd Congress. For FDR's statement when he signed the act, as well as figures pertaining to the act's effectiveness, see 2 *Public Papers and Addresses* 213–215. The most useful description of the law's passage remains James M. Landis, "The Legislative History of the Securities Act of 1933," 28 *George Washington Law Review* 33 ff. (October 1959).

65. Schlesinger, *Coming of the New Deal* 320–321.

66. Hoover, 1 *The State Papers of Herbert Hoover* 526–527, William Starr Myers, ed. (New York: Doubleday, Doran, 1934).

67. The date of FDR's visit to Muscle Shoals was January 21, 1933. In addition to Norris, the delegation included Senators Clarence C. Dill, Cordell Hull, Kenneth McKellar, Hugo Black, and John H. Bankhead; Congressmen John Rankin, Luther Lister Hill, and John J. McSwain; plus Frank P. McNitch of the Federal Power Commission, Frank P. Walsh of the New York Power Authority, and E. F. Scattergood of the Los Angeles power system.

68. *The New York Times,* January 22, 1933.

69. Message to Congress, "A Suggestion for Legislation to Create the Tennessee Valley Authority," April 10, 1933, 2 *Public Papers and Addresses* 122–123.

70. Rankin's comment was to the House Military Affairs Committee, quoted in Schlesinger, *Coming of the New Deal* 324–325.

71. *Congressional Record* 2178–2179, 73rd Cong., 1st Sess.; *The New York Times,* April 26, 1933.

72. 48 Stat. 58; Public Law 17, 73rd Congress.

73. David M. Kennedy, *Freedom from Fear* 148–149 (New York: Oxford University Press, 1999).

74. 2 *Public Papers and Addresses* 136n.

75. "A Message Asking for Legislation to Save Small Home Mortgages from Foreclosure," April 13, 1933, ibid. 135 136.

76. Home Owners Loan Corporation Act, 48 Stat. 128; Public Law 43, 73rd Congress. The $20,000 ceiling in 1933 would be the rough equivalent of $280,000 in 2006.

77. 2 *Public Papers and Addresses* 233–237n.

78. Schlesinger, *Coming of the New Deal* 298.

79. Moley, *After Seven Years* 369–370.

80. William Lindsay White, *Bernard Baruch* 82 (New York: Harcourt, Brace, 1950).

81. Ronald Steel, *Walter Lippmann and the American Century* 302–303 (Boston: Little, Brown, 1980).

82. Walter Lippmann, "Today and Tomorrow," *New York Herald Tribune,* April 18, 1933.

83. Those in attendance included Secretaries Hull and Woodin, Budget Director Lewis Douglas, Moley, James Warburg, Charles Tausig, Herbert Feis, William Bullitt, and Senator Key Pittman of Nevada, chairman of the Foreign Relations Committee.

84. Warburg diary, April 18, 1933, quoted in Freidel, *Launching the New Deal* 333.

85. Moley, *After Seven Years* 159.

86. Quoted in Schlesinger, *Coming of the New Deal* 200.

87. Moley, *After Seven Years.*

88. Thirteenth Press Conference, April 19, 1933, *Complete Presidential Press Conferences* 153 (New York: Da Capo Press, 1972). FDR's reference to Lippmann appears in the original official transcript. It was deleted when Judge Rosenman

republished the transcript in Roosevelt's *Public Papers*. Cf. 2 *Public Papers and Addresses* 137–141.

89. Schlesinger, *Coming of the New Deal* 202; Leffingwell to FDR, October 2, 1933, FDRL.

90. Eleanor Roosevelt, *This I Remember* 112–113 (New York: Harper & Brothers, 1949).

91. "It was as comfortable as a camp can be," Eleanor told her press conference afterward. "Remarkably clean and orderly, grand-looking boys, a fine spirit. There was no kind of disturbance, nothing but the most courteous behavior." Quoted in Blanche Wiesen Cook, 2 *Eleanor Roosevelt* 46 (New York: Viking, 1999).

92. Schlesinger, *Coming of the New Deal* 15.

93. For a firsthand account of FDR's surprised response to the Black bill, see Frances Perkins, *The Roosevelt I Knew* 192–195 (New York: Viking Press, 1946).

94. "A Recommendation to the Congress to Enact the National Industrial Recovery Act to Put People to Work," May 17, 1933, 2 *Public Papers and Addresses* 202–206.

95. 48 Stat. 195, Public Law 67, 73rd Congress.

96. Using a conversion factor of 13.89, that would amount to roughly $35,000 currently.

97. Press Conference, March 8, 1933, 2 *Public Papers and Addresses* 37.

98. Quoted in Ray Tucker, "Ickes—and No Fooling," *Collier's*, September 30, 1933. Jonathan Alter's lively *The Defining Moment: FDR's Hundred Days and the Triumph of Hope* (New York: Simon & Schuster, 2006) appeared too late to be helpful, but see especially pages 207–318.

SIXTEEN | New Deal Ascendant

The epigraph is from Richard E. Neustadt, *Presidential Power* 229 (New York: New American Library, 1960).

1. J. B. West with Mary Lynn Kotz, *Upstairs at the White House* 18, 23 (New York: Coward, McCann & Geoghegan, 1973).

2. FDR's daily schedule is discussed by Arthur Schlesinger, Jr., *The Coming of the New Deal* 511–515 (Boston: Houghton Mifflin, 1959); Kenneth S. Davis, *FDR: The New Deal Years* 201–205 (New York: Random House, 1979); Frank Freidel, *Franklin D. Roosevelt: Launching the New Deal* 267–288 (Boston: Little, Brown, 1973); and Conrad Black, *Franklin Delano Roosevelt: Champion of Freedom* 284 (New York: PublicAffairs, 2003). I am indebted to each.

3. Frances Perkins, *The Roosevelt I Knew* 65–66. Gloster, a champion trotter, was raised by FDR's father, sold to Leland Stanford, and killed in a train wreck on the West Coast. See chapter 1.

4. *Time*, March 20, 1933.

5. Eleanor lunched daily in the Private Dining Room, adjacent to the State Dining Room, on the first floor. Chief Usher West reports these were formal lunches for at least twelve and that ER often wrote the place cards herself. West, *Upstairs at*

the White House 19. For Stimson's luncheons with FDR, see Henry L. Stimson and McGeorge Bundy, *On Active Service in Peace and War* 300–301 (New York: Harper & Brothers, 1948). For Flynn's visits, see Edward J. Flynn, *You're the Boss* 161–168 (New York: Viking Press, 1947).

6. Admiral McIntire was an ear, nose, and throat specialist. His main concern was FDR's sinus problems and head colds. See Ross McIntire, *White House Physician* (New York: Putnam, 1946).

7. Robert Sherwood, *Roosevelt and Hopkins* 214 (New York: Harper & Brothers, 1948).

8. Hemingway's comments are in a letter to his second wife, Pauline Pfeiffer, from the Bahamas, August 2, 1937. "Martha Gellhorn, the girl who fixed it up for Joris Ivens and I to go there [Hemingway married Ms. Gellhorn in 1940] ate three sandwiches in the Newark airport before we flew to Washington. We thought she was crazy at the time but she said the food was always uneatable and everybody ate before they went there for dinner." *Ernest Hemingway Selected Letters* 470, Carlos Baker, ed. (New York: Charles Scribner's Sons, 1981).

9. Ickes's comments were written after the annual dinner the Roosevelts gave for the cabinet on December 18, 1934. "Wine was served for the first time since prohibition went into effect. Mrs. Roosevelt had announced she would serve one glass each of two domestic wines and she kept her word. The sherry was passable but the champagne was undrinkable.... I am bound to say that probably on only one other occasion have I ever tasted worse champagne, and it does seem to me that if decent champagne can't be made in the United States, it ought to be permissible, even for the White House, to serve imported champagne." 1 *The Secret Diary of Harold L. Ickes* 248–249 (New York: Simon & Schuster, 1953).

10. John Gunther, *Roosevelt in Retrospect* 93 (New York: Harper & Brothers, 1950).

11. Henrietta Nesbitt, *White House Diary* 19–20 (New York: Doubleday, 1948).

12. Blanche Wiesen Cook, 2 *Eleanor Roosevelt* (New York: Viking Penguin, 1999).

13. Grace Tully, *F.D.R.: My Boss* 115 (New York: Charles Scribner's Sons, 1949).

14. Nesbitt, *White House Diary* 66.

15. James Roosevelt with Bill Libby, *My Parents: A Differing View* 213 (Chicago: Playboy Press, 1976). ER chided James for his criticism of Mrs. Nesbitt. If the president did not like the food or the menus, it was her responsibility since she approved them, wrote Eleanor. ER to James Roosevelt, July 30, 1959, quoted in Joseph P. Lash, *Eleanor and Franklin* 501 (New York: W. W. Norton, 1971).

16. Lillian Rogers Parks and Frances S. Leighton, *The Roosevelts: A Family in Turmoil* 69–70 (Englewood Cliffs, N.J.: Prentice-Hall, 1981). The observation is by Ms. Parks.

17. Nesbitt, *White House Diary* 185.

18. Parks, *The Roosevelts* 30–31.

19. Ibid. 170.

20. "Mary was devoted heart and soul to the Boss and warred with the rest of the White House management to see to it that he got what he wanted," wrote Grace

Tully. "From the time of her arrival the fare in the family kitchen, at least, took a decided turn for the better." *F.D.R.: My Boss* 117–118.

21. Ibid.

22. West, *Upstairs at the White House* 78.

23. Ickes, 1 *Secret Diary* 461.

24. John Garner interview, *U.S. News & World Report*, March 8, 1957.

25. Eleanor Roosevelt, *This I Remember* 117 (New York: Harper & Brothers, 1949).

26. Schlesinger, *Coming of the New Deal* 513, 580–581.

27. *Amberjack II*, built in 1931 by George Lawley and Son of Neponset, Massachusetts, was owned by Paul Drummond Rust, Jr., a college friend of James. Seaworthy and easy to handle, the two-masted vessel had finished third the year before in Fastnet, the grueling 3,000-mile transatlantic race to England, though it was the smallest vessel competing. If not luxurious, it was well appointed and had a 40-horsepower gasoline auxiliary engine. Robert F. Cross, *Sailor in the White House: The Seafaring Life of FDR* 9 (Annapolis, Md.: Naval Institute Press, 2003).

28. Nantucket *Inquirer and Mirror*, June 24, 1933.

29. Edmund W. Starling and Thomas Sugrue, *Starling of the White House* 308–311 (New York: Simon & Schuster, 1946).

30. Cross, *Sailor in the White House* 13.

31. *The New York Times*, June 30, 1933.

32. Charles Hurd, *When the New Deal Was Young and Gay* 165–170 (New York: Hawthorn Books, 1965).

33. Arthur Krock interview, Columbia Oral History Project, Columbia University.

34. Quoted in William E. Leuchtenburg, *Franklin D. Roosevelt and the New Deal* 205 (New York: Harper & Row, 1963).

35. Davis, *FDR: New Deal Years* 339. In 1922, Walsh served as director-general of the Papal Relief Mission to the USSR and also as the Vatican's representative to the Soviet government.

36. For the State Department's attitude, see Daniel Yergin, *Shattered Peace* 17–22 (Boston: Houghton Mifflin, 1977). Morgenthau's role is discussed extensively in John Morton Blum, *From the Morgenthau Diaries* 54 ff. (Boston: Houghton Mifflin, 1959).

37. When a newsman asked FDR who was going to conduct the negotiations with Litvinov, the president pointed to himself and said, "This man here." Undersecretary of State William Phillips tried to persuade FDR to say publicly that the State Department was not being cut out, but Roosevelt refused. Martin Weil, *A Pretty Good Club: The Founding Fathers of the U.S. Foreign Service* 87–88 (New York: W. W. Norton, 1978), quoting Caroline Phillips's journal, October 27, 1933.

38. Cf., *United States v. Belmont*, 301 U.S. 324 (1937); *United States v. Pink*, 315 U.S. 203 (1942), emphasizing the sovereign power of the U.S. government to conduct foreign relations. "We take judicial notice of the fact that coincident with the assignment, the President recognized the Soviet Government, and normal diplo-

matic relations were established," said Justice George Sutherland for a unanimous Supreme Court in *Belmont.* "The effect of this was to validate, so far as this country is concerned, all acts of the Soviet Government here involved. . . . [As for the taking clause] our constitution, laws and policies have no extraterritorial operation, unless in respect of our own citizens." Justice Sutherland, it should be noted, was the intellectual leader of the conservative bloc on the Supreme Court in the 1930s.

For the text of the Litvinov Assignment, see 2 *Public Papers and Addresses of Franklin D. Roosevelt* 484–486, Samuel I. Rosenman, ed. (New York: Random House, 1938).

39. Quoted in Leuchtenburg, *Franklin Roosevelt and the New Deal* 207.

40. David M. Kennedy, *Freedom from Fear* 178 (New York: Oxford University Press, 1999).

41. Hugh S. Johnson, *The Blue Eagle from Egg to Earth* 208 (New York: Doubleday, 1935)..

42. Kennedy, *Freedom from Fear* 178.

43. On January 7, 1935, in *Panama Refining Co. v. Ryan,* 293 U.S. 388, the Court, speaking through Chief Justice Hughes, struck down the "hot oil" provisions (Section 9) of the NIRA (Cardozo dissenting). Four and a half months later, in *Schechter Poultry Corp. v. United States,* 295 U.S. 495 (1935), a unanimous Court completed the process and held all code provisions in the NIRA unconstitutional.

44. 295 U.S. at 501.

45. Press conference remarks, May 31, 1935, 4 *Public Papers and Addresses* 205.

46. Perkins, *The Roosevelt I Knew* 252–253. Marion Dickerman, a houseguest in the White House when the decision was announced, reports that she dreaded going down to dinner that evening. But FDR showed "no sign of dismay or even minor perturbation. The Supreme Court was not so much as mentioned!" When Marion went to Roosevelt's bedroom to say good night, "He was sitting up in bed with his old sweater on, working on his stamps. To all appearances he was perfectly happy and at peace with the world." Kenneth S. Davis, *Invincible Summer* 134–135 (New York: Atheneum, 1974). The NRA was terminated by Executive Order 7252, December 21, 1935. 4 *Public Papers and Addresses* 503.

47. Executive Order 6420B, Creation of Civil Works Administration, 2 *Public Papers and Addresses* 456–457. Ickes proved surprisingly cooperative. "This would put a serious crimp in the balance of the public works fund," he confided to his diary, "but we all thought it ought to be done." November 6, 1933. 1 *Secret Diary of Harold Ickes* 116.

48. Kennedy, *Freedom from Fear* 175.

49. The final total was $933 million, of which $740 million went for wages. 2 *Public Papers and Addresses* 457–458.

50. Quoted in Schlesinger, *Coming of the New Deal* 220.

51. Quoted in Harry Hopkins, *Spending to Save* 114 (New York: Norton, 1936).

52. Lieutenant Colonel John C. H. Lee, "The Federal Civil Works Administration: A Study Covering Its Organization and Operation," Hopkins Papers, FDRL.

53. For FDR's message requesting the SEC, February 9, 1934, see 3 *Public Papers and Addresses* 90–91. The act was signed into law on June 6, 1934. 73rd Congress, Public Law 291; 48 Stat. 881. The FCC message was sent to the Hill on February 26, 1934, and the act was signed June 19, 1934. 73rd Congress, Public Law 416; 48 Stat. 1064. 3 *Public Papers and Addresses* 107–108.

54. The Railroad Retirement Act was signed into law June 30, 1934. It was declared unconstitutional by the Supreme Court May 6, 1935, Justice Roberts speaking for a sharply divided (5–4) Court. *Alton Railroad Co. v. Railroad Retirement Board,* 295 U.S. 330 (1935).

55. FDR signed the Gold Reserve Act on January 30, 1934. 48 Stat. 337. The following day he issued Executive Order 2072, fixing the gold content of the dollar at "15$\frac{5}{21}$ grains nine-tenths fine," which was 59.06 percent of its former value. 3 *Public Papers and Addresses* 64–76.

56. FDR's letter to Rainey, June 18, 1934, is in the personal collection of Conrad Black and is quoted at page 322 of his *Franklin Delano Roosevelt.*

57. When Roosevelt finished his address he winked at James Farley, one of the invited guests at the White House: "Jim, didn't you think it was a good campaign document?" Farley agreed wholeheartedly, "and we made much use of it." James A. Farley, *Jim Farley's Story* 47 (New York: Whittlesey House, 1948).

58. "None of them have been consulted by the President," wrote Kent. "Most of them have been completely ignored. Yet until two years ago, they were the most conspicuous and respected leaders of the party." Frank Kent, "Which Way Will the Elephant Jump?," *American Magazine* (December 1935); Kent, *Without Grease* 8–10 (New York: William Morrow & Co., 1936).

59. Quoted in Schlesinger, *Coming of the New Deal* 484.

60. "To put it in a Biblical way," FDR continued, "it has been said that there are two great Commandments—one is to love God, and the other to love your neighbor. A gentleman with a rather ribald sense of humor suggested that the two particular tenets of this new organization say you shall love God and then forget your neighbor, and he also raised the question as to whether the other name for their God was not 'property.' " Press Conference 137, August 24, 1934. 4 *Complete Presidential Press Conferences of Franklin D. Roosevelt* 18 (New York: Da Capo Press, 1972).

61. FDR to Bullitt, 3 *Personal Letters* 417.

62. For the impact of Long and Coughlin, see especially Alan Brinkley, *Voices of Protest: Huey Long, Father Coughlin, and the Great Depression* (New York: Knopf, 1982).

63. Quoted in Arthur M. Schlesinger, Jr., *The Politics of Upheaval* 24 (Boston: Houghton Mifflin, 1960).

64. Leuchtenburg, *Franklin Roosevelt and the New Deal* 103–104.

65. Quoted ibid. 105.

66. Garner to FDR, October 1, 1934, FDRL.

67. Farley, *Jim Farley's Story* 47–48.

68. Ten members of the House belonged to minor parties, as did two senators (Shipstead and La Follette).

69. *The New York Times,* November 7, 11, 1934; *Time,* November 19, 1934, quoted in Schlesinger, *Coming of the New Deal* 507.

70. Lois Gordon and Alan Gordon, eds., *American Chronicle: Year by Year Through the Twentieth Century* 315, 324 (New Haven, Conn.: Yale University Press, 1999).

71. Leuchtenburg, *Franklin Roosevelt and the New Deal* 93.

72. Gordon and Gordon, *American Chronicle* 324–332. *It Happened One Night* also won an Oscar for best picture.

73. FDR, "Message to Congress Reviewing the Broad Objectives and Accomplishments of the Administration," June 8, 1934. 3 *Public Papers and Addresses* 287–292.

74. Frances Perkins, *The Roosevelt I Knew* 282–283.

75. "A Greater Future Economic Security for the American People," Message to Congress, January 17, 1935, 4 *Public Papers and Addresses* 43–56.

76. Ibid. 296.

77. Ibid. 294.

78. Kennedy, *Freedom from Fear* 266.

79. Schlesinger, *Coming of the New Deal* 308–309.

80. Ibid. 311.

81. 119 *Literary Digest* (June 29, 1935), quoted in Leuchtenburg, *Franklin D. Roosevelt and the New Deal* 131.

82. 4 *Public Papers and Addresses* 324–326.

83. Frances Perkins, *The Roosevelt I Knew* 301.

84. In 1936, combined federal-state payments to the indigent elderly varied from $3.92 monthly in Mississippi to $31.36 in California. Aid for dependent children ranged from $8.10 in Arkansas to $61.07 in Massachusetts. Kennedy, *Freedom from Fear* 272. (To convert 1936 dollars, multiply by 13.)

85. 3 *Public Papers and Addresses* 291.

86. Annual Message to Congress, January 4, 1935, 4 ibid. 20–22.

87. Emergency Relief Appropriation Act of 1935. Joint Resolution 11, 74th Congress.

88. Schlesinger, *Coming of the New Deal* 346–347.

89. Donald Richberg, *My Hero* 241 (New York: Putnam, 1954).

90. Executive Order 7034, May 6, 1935, 4 *Public Papers and Addresses* 163–168.

91. Jean Edward Smith, *Lucius D. Clay: An American Life* 62–63 (New York: Henry Holt, 1990). Also see Sherwood, *Roosevelt and Hopkins* 75–76.

92. Kennedy, *Freedom from Fear* 252–253.

93. Quoted in Leuchtenburg, *Franklin D. Roosevelt and the New Deal* 128.

94. Ibid. 127.

95. Alfred Kazin, *On Native Ground* 378–379 (New York: Doubleday, 1942).

96. Sherwood, *Roosevelt and Hopkins* 68. Also see Schlesinger, *Coming of the New Deal* 355.

97. Kennedy, *Freedom from Fear* 253.

98. *The Nation,* February 13, 1935.

99. The Davies comparison is reported in Schlesinger, *Politics of Upheaval* 357.

100. Sherwood, *Roosevelt and Hopkins* 84.

101. Executive Order 7037, 4 *Public Papers and Addresses* 172–174. In May 1936 the REA was given a statutory basis when Congress adopted the Norris-Rankin Act. Public Law 605, 74th Congress; 49 Stat. 1363.

102. For a still useful general survey, see Morris Cooke, "Early Days of Rural Electrification," 42 *American Political Science Review* 431–444 (1948). Cooke, whom FDR had placed on the board of the New York Power Authority in 1931, was the first head of the Rural Electrification Administration.

103. Walter Lippmann, *Interpretations: 1933–1935* 154, Allan Nevins, ed. (New York: Macmillan, 1936).

104. Roper to FDR, May 22, 1935, FDRL.

105. *Schechter Poultry Corp. v. United States,* 295 U.S. 495 (1935).

106. Public Law 198, 74th Congress; 49 Stat. 449. For FDR's statement upon signing the bill, see 4 *Public Papers and Addresses* 294–295.

107. Ibid. 470–478. Governor George Earle of Pennsylvania later regaled FDR with the story of four wealthy Philadelphians sipping their whiskey in the posh Rittenhouse Club and damning the president and the New Deal with considerable gusto. At that point a member turned on the club radio and out came Roosevelt's voice ridiculing "gentlemen in well-warmed and well-stocked clubs."

   "My God," exclaimed one of the men. "Do you suppose that sonofabitch could have overheard us?" James MacGregor Burns, *Roosevelt: The Lion and the Fox* 235 (New York: Harcourt, Brace & World, 1956).

SEVENTEEN | Hubris

The epigraph is from FDR's Fireside Chat on Reorganization of the Judiciary, March 9, 1937. 6 *Public Papers and Addresses of Franklin D. Roosevelt* 122–133, Samuel I. Rosenman, ed. (New York: Random House, 1941).

1. James A. Farley, *Jim Farley's Story* 58 (New York: Whittlesey House, 1948).

2. Ibid. 59.

3. Raymond Moley, *After Seven Years* 343 (New York: Harper & Brothers, 1939).

4. Harold L. Ickes, 1 *The Secret Diary of Harold L. Ickes* 465 (New York: Simon & Schuster, 1953).

5. U.S. Department of Commerce, Bureau of the Census, *Statistical History of the United States* 70, 143, 283 (Stamford, Conn.: Fairfield Publishers, 1965). Also see Arthur M. Schlesinger, Jr., *The Politics of Upheaval* 571 (Boston: Houghton Mifflin, 1960); James MacGregor Burns, *Roosevelt: The Lion and the Fox* 266–267 (New York: Harcourt, Brace & World, 1956).

6. Conrad Black, *Franklin Delano Roosevelt* 381–382 (New York: PublicAffairs, 2003).

7. Thomas L. Stokes, *Chip off My Shoulder* 404 (Princeton, N.J.: Princeton University Press, 1940). The "Second Louisiana Purchase" phrase was coined by journalist Westbrook Pegler following the government's quashing of indictments against a number of Long's lieutenants for income tax evasion.

8. Alfred B. Rollins, Jr., *Roosevelt and Howe* 447 (New York: Alfred A. Knopf, 1962).

9. 5 *Public Papers and Addresses* 8–18.

10. Roosevelt spoke to the dinner in Washington on January 8, 1936, but his remarks were broadcast to three thousand similar dinners throughout the nation. Ibid. 38–44.

11. *The New York Times,* January 26, 1936.

12. Ibid.

13. Ibid.

14. James A. Farley, *Behind the Ballots* 293 (New York: Harcourt, Brace and Company, 1938).

15. *The New York Times,* January 29, 1936.

16. The visitor was Fannie Hurst. Black, *Franklin Delano Roosevelt* 376.

17. Blanche Wiesen Cook, 2 *Eleanor Roosevelt* 353 (New York: Viking, 1999).

18. Eleanor Roosevelt, *This I Remember* 145 (New York: Harper & Brothers, 1949).

19. Rollins, *Roosevelt and Howe* 448.

20. *New York Times,* April 23, 1936.

21. Byrd to FDR, November 16, 1940, September 9, 1944, FDRL.

22. Rollins, *Roosevelt and Howe* 453. For a loving portrait of Howe during his illness, see James Farley, *Behind the Ballots* 296–303. "The only tribute I can pay him," wrote Farley, "is to say that, as long as I live, I shall never ask for a better friend than Louis Howe."

23. Samuel I. Rosenman, *Working with Roosevelt* 99 (New York: Harper & Brothers, 1952).

24. Quoted in Schlesinger, *Politics of Upheaval* 533–534.

25. 1 *Secret Diary of Harold L. Ickes* 648–649.

26. The 1936 Republican platform proclaimed, "America is in peril. The welfare of American men and women and the future of our youth are at stake. We dedicate ourselves to the preservation of their political liberty, their individual opportunity and their character as free citizens, which today for the first time is threatened by the Government itself." Landon, by contrast, was generally sympathetic to the New Deal. "From the very first, I advocated granting of unusual powers to the President because of the national emergency." He also found little to object to in New Deal economics. "I do not think there is anything new or revolutionary about the redistribution of wealth theory. Every wise statesman in every period of history has been concerned with the equitable distribution of property in his country." Landon to Raymond Clapper, quoted in Olive Ewing Clapper, *Washington Tapestry* 119 (New York: Whittlesey House, 1946).

27. Schlesinger, *Politics of Upheaval* 529.

28. Ibid. 560.

29. Farley, *Jim Farley's Story* 57.

30. In 1912, House Speaker Champ Clark led the voting for twenty-eight ballots and commanded a majority for eight but ultimately lost the nomination to Woodrow Wilson.

31. James F. Byrnes, *All in One Lifetime* 95 (New York: Harper & Brothers, 1958).

32. Alben Barkley, *That Reminds Me* 152 (New York: Doubleday, 1954).

33. Raymond Clapper, *Watching the World* 86–87 (New York: McGraw-Hill, 1944); *The New York Times,* June 28, 1936.

34. Schlesinger, *Politics of Upheaval* 583.

35. Ibid. 584.

36. "Acceptance of the Renomination for the Presidency," June 27, 1936, 5 *Public Papers and Addresses* 230–236.

37. Schlesinger, *Politics of Upheaval* 585.

38. Charles W. Hurd, "Roosevelt Starts Cruise as Skipper," *The New York Times,* July 15, 1936.

39. Robert F. Cross, *Sailor in the White House* 97 (Annapolis, Md.: Naval Institute Press, 2003).

40. *The New York Times,* July 25, 1936.

41. James Roosevelt and Sidney Shalett, *Affectionately, F.D.R.* 284 (New York: Harcourt, Brace and Company, 1959).

42. Lord Tweedsmuir was the celebrated novelist John Buchan. In his chatty opening remarks, Roosevelt playfully demurred being addressed as a foreign ruler. "I say this because, when I have been in Canada, I have never heard a Canadian refer to an American as a 'foreigner.' He is just an 'American.' And, the same way across the border in the United States, Canadians are not 'foreigners,' they are 'Canadians.' " FDR interlaced his speech with several paragraphs of flawless French, paying homage to the valor and heroism of the Quebecois. (Roosevelt was the only president, Mr. Jefferson and J. Q. Adams included, who spoke French fluently.) 5 *Public Papers and Addresses* 276–279.

43. Roosevelt's 1936 campaign speeches are in ibid. 285–581.

44. Nathan Miller, *FDR: An Intimate History* 384–385 (New York: Doubleday, 1983).

45. Farley, *Behind the Ballots* 305–306.

46. Ibid.

47. Quoted in Schlesinger, *Politics of Upheaval* 603.

48. Ibid. 627. Union party publicists originally touted Lemke as "Liberty Bell" Lemke. Democrats whooped with delight. "Both are cracked," said a party spokesman.

49. *The New York Times,* September 26, 1936.

50. Ibid., November 1, 1936.

51. Campaign Address, October 31, 1936. 5 *Public Papers and Addresses* 566–573.

52. Farley, *Behind the Ballots* 324–325. Farley was correct about New Hampshire,

which FDR carried with a razor-thin margin of 3,818 votes, 49.7 percent to Landon's 48.0 percent. But Kansas went for Roosevelt 54–46 percent; Connecticut 55–40; and Michigan 56–39. Congressional Quarterly, *Guide to U.S. Elections* 290 (Washington, D.C.: Congressional Quarterly, 1975).

53. Rosenman, *Working with Roosevelt* 137.

54. Other minor-party candidates included Earl Browder (Communist) 79,211; David Leigh Colvin (Prohibition) 37,668; and John W. Aiken (Socialist Labor) 12,790. Congressional Quarterly, *Guide to U.S. Elections* 304.

55. Quoted in Kenneth S. Davis, *FDR: The New Deal Years* 647 (New York: Random House, 1979).

56. Monroe received 231 of 235 electoral votes in 1820. One elector each in Mississippi, Pennsylvania, and Tennessee did not vote, and one Democratic elector in New Hampshire voted for John Quincy Adams rather than the party's nominee.

57. Farley, *Jim Farley's Story* 66. Farley spoke with FDR a dozen times on election night. There was never any doubt about the outcome, but it was not until 3:36 A.M. that Roosevelt pulled ahead in New Hampshire.

58. Quoted in Schlesinger, *Politics of Upheaval* 642. The week before the election, FDR wrote Senator Hiram Johnson of California, "I am frankly a little worried about George Norris's chances in Nebraska. It would be a tragedy if he did not come back." 3 *The Roosevelt Letters* 189, Elliott Roosevelt, ed. (London: George G. Harrap, 1952). The 1936 vote count in Nebraska gave Norris 258,700; Robert G. Simmons, his Republican opponent, 223,276; and Democrat Terry Carpenter, 108,391.

59. William E. Leuchtenburg, *Franklin D. Roosevelt and the New Deal* 187–190 (New York: Harper & Row, 1963).

60. In 1932 African-American precincts in Detroit, Chicago, Cincinnati, Cleveland, Philadelphia, and Pittsburgh went down the line for Hoover. FDR carried Chicago handily but won only 23 percent of the black vote. In Cincinnati's heavily black Ward 16, Roosevelt got less than 29 percent. In 1936, every black ward in each of the cities went Democratic; in Cincinnati's Ward 16, FDR took 65 percent, and Pittsburgh's black Third Ward went for Roosevelt 10 to 1. According to a July 1938 *Fortune* poll, 84.7 percent of African Americans considered themselves pro-Roosevelt. Ernest Collins, "Cincinnati Negroes and Presidential Politics," 41 *Journal of Negro History* 132–133 (1956). Also see Leuchtenburg, *Franklin D. Roosevelt* 185–187.

61. 6 *Public Papers and Addresses* 1–6 (emphasis added).

62. At the direction of the Secret Service, the tribune from which the president was to review the parade had been enclosed with bullet-proof glass. When FDR learned that, he ordered the glass removed. *Life,* February 1, 1937.

63. Republicans held the governorships in only six states in 1937: California, Maine, New Hampshire, New Jersey, South Dakota, and Vermont. Three states were held by independents: Minnesota, North Dakota, and Wisconsin. The remaining governors were Democrats. FDR's speechwriters had prepared a draft of the in-

augural address critical of the Court, but Roosevelt chose not to use it. "I'm not quite ready yet," he told Sam Rosenman. *Working with Roosevelt* 141–144.

64. In *Humphrey's Executor v. United States,* 295 U.S. 602 (1935) a unanimous Court, speaking through Justice George Sutherland, held that the president's blanket removal authority (see *Myers v. United States,* 272 U.S. 52 [1926]) did not extend to members of independent regulatory commissions, in this case the Federal Trade Commission.

65. The New York minimum-wage law was overturned in *Morehead v. New York ex rel Tipaldo,* 298 U.S. 587 (1936). Justice Butler, for the Court, held that the freedom of an individual to contract for wages in return for work "is part of the liberty protected by the due process clause [of the Fourteenth Amendment]" (at page 610).

66. The decisions in *Schechter, Radford,* and *Humphrey's Executor* were unanimous. That in *Panama Refining* was 8–1.

67. In *Home Building & Loan Association v. Blaisdell,* 290 U.S. 398 (1934), the Court (5–4) upheld the 1933 Minnesota Mortgage Moratorium Act, authorizing state courts to delay foreclosure proceedings. Said Chief Justice Hughes for the Court, "while emergency does not create power, emergency may furnish the occasion for the exercise of power" (at page 426).

In *Nebbia v. New York,* 291 U.S. 502 (1934), the Court (5–4) upheld that state's Milk Control Act. Justice Roberts (for the Court) said, "a state is free to adopt whatever economic policy may reasonably be deemed to promote public welfare, and to enforce that policy by legislation adapted to its purpose" (at page 537).

68. *Gold Clause Cases,* 294 U.S. 240 (1935). Chief Justice Hughes for the Court (5–4).

69. *Ashwander v. TVA,* 297 U.S. 288 (1936). Hughes for the Court (8–1). *Ashwander* is noteworthy for the concurring opinion of Justice Brandeis laying out the rules for constitutional adjudication.

70. *United States v. Curtiss-Wright,* 299 U.S. 304 (1936). The decision (7–1) was authored by Justice Sutherland, the intellectual powerhouse of the Court's conservatives. As he described the president's powers: "He *makes* treaties with the advice and consent of the Senate; but he alone negotiates. Into the field of negotiation the Senate cannot intrude; and Congress itself is powerless to invade it. As [Chief Justice John] Marshall said in his great argument of March 7, 1800 to the House of Representatives, 'The President is the sole organ of the nation in its external relations, and its sole representative with foreign nations' " (Sutherland's emphasis). Marshall was a representative from Virginia at the time and spokesman for the Adams Federalists in the House.

71. The rule that the Bill of Rights applied only to the national government, not to the states, was first articulated by John Marshall in *Barron v. Baltimore,* 7 Peters (32 U.S.) 243 (1833), and reaffirmed after adoption of the Fourteenth Amendment in *Hurtado v. California,* 110 U.S. 516 (1884). That was the law when the

Court (5–4) changed course in *Near v. Minnesota,* 283 U.S. 697 (1931), and overturned Minnesota's statute, which permitted a trial court judge to enjoin publication of a newspaper he found "obscene, lewd, and lascivious" or "malicious, scandalous, and defamatory." Said Chief Justice Hughes for the Court, "It is no longer open to doubt that the liberty of the press . . . is within the liberty safeguarded by the due process clause of the Fourteenth Amendment from invasion by State action" (at page 706).

72. In *Powell v. Alabama,* 287 U.S. 45 (1932), the Court (7–2), speaking through Justice Sutherland, held that the due process clause of the Fourteenth Amendment required fairness in criminal trials and that the right to counsel was an integral part of the process, particularly in capital cases. This too was a groundbreaking decision, expanded in *Gideon v. Wainwright,* 372 U.S. 335, in 1963 to include all criminal cases.

73. *Norris v. Alabama,* 294 U.S. 587 (1935). "For this long-continued, unvarying, and wholesale exclusion of negroes from jury service we find no justification consistent with the constitutional mandate [of the due process clause]," said Hughes for the Court.

74. During the Red Scare after World War I, California enacted legislation prohibiting the public use or display of a red flag. Yetta Stromberg was convicted for violating the statute at a youth camp in 1929, and the Supreme Court (7–2) reversed. Chief Justice Hughes, for the Court, held the flag to be a symbol of political protest protected by the First Amendment and applicable to the states under the due process clause of the Fourteenth. *Stromberg* is doubly important for its extension of the concept of speech to include symbolic statements as well as those made orally and in writing. *Stromberg v. California,* 283 U.S. 359 (1931).

75. *DeJonge v. Oregon,* 299 U.S. 353 (1937). Dirk DeJonge had been convicted of violating Oregon's criminal syndicalism law, another relic of the Red Scare.

76. Professor G. Edward White of the University of Virginia provides an insightful antidote to traditional historiography in *The Constitution and the New Deal* (Cambridge, Mass.: Harvard University Press, 2000), especially in his chapter "The Canonization and Demonization of Judges." To characterize Justices Van Devanter, McReynolds, Sutherland, and Butler as reactionary is "grossly inaccurate," wrote White. "They repeatedly upheld police powers legislation against due process and Contract Clause challenges. They regularly sustained the taxing and spending powers of the state and federal governments. They voted to sustain several New Deal statutes regulating economic activity. They consistently upheld the powers of administrative agencies against constitutional challenges. And they demonstrated considerable solicitude for civil rights and civil liberties. . . . In short, a comprehensive treatment of the constitutional decisions of each of the Four Horsemen could produce a fair amount of supportive evidence for labeling them 'progressives' or 'liberals' " (at page 295).

77. In the summer of 1933 Roosevelt had instructed Cummings to undertake planning for a general reorganization of the federal judiciary, but the Supreme Court

was not included in that effort. Much of Cummings's planning pertained to the political affiliation of federal judges at the district and appellate levels. "You will note that of 266 judges listed," Cummings wrote Roosevelt on November 8, 1933, "only 28% are Democrats." Quoted in Marian C. McKenna, *Franklin Roosevelt and the Great Constitutional War* 146. Also see Frances Perkins, *The Roosevelt I Knew* 331 (New York: Viking Press, 1946). Cf. William E. Leuchtenburg, *The Supreme Court Reborn* 84–85 (New York: Oxford University Press, 1995).

78. Rosenman, *Working with Roosevelt* 140–156.

79. Shortly after Cummings assumed office, Justice Brandeis and Justice Stone (a former attorney general) informed Roosevelt of their concern over the competence of the government's lawyers in the cases coming before the Court. Frankfurter to Stone, July 12, 1933, in Peter H. Irons, *The New Deal Lawyers* 11 (Princeton, N.J.: Princeton University Press, 1982).

80. Schlesinger, *Politics of Upheaval* 261.

81. The 1936 Democratic platform stated, "We have sought and will continue to seek to meet these problems through legislation within the Constitution.

"If these problems cannot be effectively solved by legislation within the Constitution, we shall seek such clarifying amendment as will assure to the legislatures of the several States and to the Congress of the United States . . . the power to enact those laws which the State and Federal legislatures . . . shall find necessary, in order adequately to regulate commerce, protect public health and safety and safeguard economic security." Oliver A. Quayle, *Official Report of the Proceedings of the Democratic National Convention, 1936* 196 (Philadelphia: Democratic National Committee, 1936).

82. Ickes, 2 *Secret Diary* 65.

83. Age would eventually take its toll, advised Ashurst. Prophetically, the Arizona senator wrote FDR, "It will fall to your lot to nominate more Justices of the Supreme Court than any President since General Washington." Ashurst to FDR, February 19, 1936, quoted in Nathan Miller, *FDR: An Intimate History* 392 (New York: Doubleday, 1983).

84. Ickes, 1 *Secret Diary* 705. Justice McReynolds, for his part, reciprocated the feeling. "I'll never resign as long as that crippled son-of-a-bitch is in the White House." At least the remark was attributed to McReynolds by Drew Pearson and Robert S. Allen in their inflammatory *Nine Old Men at the Crossroads* 2 (New York: Doubleday, 1936).

85. In March 1868, while just such a case was pending, Congress repealed the Court's authority to hear appeals under the Habeas Corpus Act. A unanimous (8–0) Court subsequently dismissed the appeal for lack of jurisdiction. *Ex parte McCardle*, 74 U.S. 506 (1869).

86. Alexander Holtzoff, memorandum, in Cummings to FDR, January 16, 1936, reprinted in McKenna, *Franklin Roosevelt and the Great Constitutional War* 167–168. Also see Leuchtenburg, *Supreme Court Reborn* 99.

87. Quoted in Burns, *Roosevelt: The Lion and the Fox* 296.

88. *Annual Report of the Attorney General, 1913* 5 (Washington, D.C.: U.S. Government Printing Office, 1913).

89. William E. Leuchtenburg, in his authoritative reconstruction of the origins of FDR's Court-packing plan, reports that on December 16, 1936, Edward S. Corwin, McCormick Professor of Jurisprudence at Princeton, wrote Cummings to suggest that legislation be considered that would permit the president to appoint a number of younger justices whenever a majority of the justices were seventy years old or more. This was a week or two before Cummings discovered the McReynolds memorandum. Corwin was considered by many to be the nation's premier scholar of constitutional law, and his suggestion, which apparently originated with Professor Arthur Holcombe of Harvard, signaled to Cummings that he was on the right track. Leuchtenburg, *Supreme Court Reborn* 116–119.

90. Rosenman, *Working with Roosevelt* 154. Senator Borah, seeing the three together, is alleged to have said, "That reminds me of the Roman Emperor who looked around his dinner table and began to laugh when he thought how many of those heads would be rolling on the morrow." *Time*, March 1, 1937.

91. "The Chief Justice had an external severity that contrasted with the President's external urbanity," wrote Justice Robert Jackson. "But Hughes was one of the kindest of men, and no person who saw him preside over the Supreme Court will ever have any other standard of perfection. He was firm and prompt, dignified and kindly. . . . He never used his position on the bench to embarrass counsel or to heckle them, and if counsel were frightened or timid or incompetent, he often went out of his way to make sure their position was fully brought out. He was a model of dignity." Robert H. Jackson, *That Man: An Insider's Portrait of Franklin D. Roosevelt* 67, John Q. Barrett, ed. (New York: Oxford University Press, 2003). For Justice Roberts's similar assessment of Hughes, see Merlo J. Pusey, 2 *Charles Evans Hughes* 675–677 (New York: Macmillan, 1951).

92. Joseph Alsop and Turner Catledge, *The 168 Days* 64 (New York: Doubleday, 1938).

93. Quoted in Pusey, 2 *Charles Evans Hughes* 753. Also see McKenna, *Franklin Roosevelt and the Great Constitutional War* 324.

94. According to Sam Rosenman, who drafted FDR's message to Congress, "It was hard to understand how he expected to make people believe that he was suddenly interested primarily in delayed justice rather than in ending a tortured interpretation of the Constitution; but the cleverness, the too much cleverness, appealed to him." Rosenman, *Working with Roosevelt* 147.

95. FDR, "Message to Congress on Reorganization of the Judiciary," February 5, 1937, 6 *Public Papers* 53.

96. "Wouldn't you have thought that the President would have told his own party leaders what he intended to do?" Bankhead asked North Carolina congressman Lindsay Warren. "He didn't because he knew that hell would break loose." Warren Memorandum, February 7, 1937, quoted in Leuchtenburg, *Franklin D. Roosevelt and the New Deal* 234.

97. *The New York Times,* February 6, 1937.

98. Leuchtenburg, *Supreme Court Reborn* 127.

99. Quoted in Burns, *Roosevelt: The Lion and the Fox* 298.

100. Quoted in McKenna, *Franklin Roosevelt and the Great Constitutional War* 298.

101. Ibid. 319.

102. Professor McKenna provides a useful sampling of press coverage, ibid. 305–311.

103. For texts, see 6 *Public Papers* 35–267.

104. Farley, *Jim Farley's Story* 74.

105. Burton K. Wheeler, *Yankee from the West* 327–329 (New York: Doubleday, 1962).

106. Ibid. 332.

107. *McCulloch v. Maryland,* 4 Wheaton (17 U.S.) 316 (1819). For a discussion of the case and Marshall's defense, see Jean Edward Smith, *John Marshall: Definer of a Nation* 440–454 (New York: Henry Holt, 1996).

108. The full text of the Hughes letter to Wheeler is in the Hughes Papers at the Library of Congress. It also appears as Appendix C of the Adverse Report of the Senate Judiciary Committee on Bill S. 1392, 75th Cong., 1st Sess. (Washington, D.C.: U.S. Government Printing Office, 1937).

109. *West Coast Hotel Co. v. Parrish,* 300 U.S. 379 (1937), reversing *Morehead v. New York ex rel. Tipaldo,* 298 U.S. 587 (1936).

110. The Washington Supreme Court had upheld the statute. A tie vote by the Court would have sustained that holding. For Justice Roberts's shift, see Charles A. Leonard, *A Search for a Judicial Philosophy: Mr. Justice Roberts and the Constitutional Revolution of 1937* (Port Washington, N.Y.: Kennikat Press, 1971).

111. Hughes rejected the idea that "freedom of contract" was constitutionally sacrosanct. "What is this freedom?" he asked. The Constitution protects liberty, but subject to reasonable regulation in the interest of the community. "The community may direct its law-making power to correct the abuse which springs from [employers'] selfish disregard of the public interest. . . . Our conclusion is that the case of *Adkins v. Children's Hospital* [261 U.S. 525 (1923)] should be, and it is, overruled." Hughes's opinion in *Parrish* was fully consistent with his dissent in *Tipaldo,* in which he fired a broadside at the doctrine of freedom of contract.

112. *National Labor Relations Board v. Jones & Laughlin Steel Corp.,* 301 U.S. 1 (1937). This was the most important of five companion cases relating to the Wagner Act that the Court decided on April 12, 1937. "We are asked to shut our eyes to the plainest facts of national life and to deal with the question of direct and indirect effects in an intellectual vacuum," said Hughes. "When industries organize themselves on a national scale, making their relation to interstate commerce the dominant factor in their activities, how can it be maintained that their industrial labor relations constitute a forbidden field into which Congress may not enter when it is necessary to protect interstate commerce from the paralyzing consequences of industrial war?" (at page 41).

113. *Gibbons v. Ogden,* 9 Wheaton (22 U.S.) 1 (1824). "Commerce," said Marshall, "is undoubtedly traffic, but it is something more: it is intercourse. It describes the

commercial intercourse between nations, and parts of nations, in all its branches, and is regulated by prescribing rules for carrying on that intercourse. . . . Commerce among the States cannot stop at the boundary line of each State, but may be introduced into the interior."

114. 301 U.S. 1, 41.

115. *Steward Machine Co. v. Davis,* 301 U.S. 548 (1937), Cardozo for the Court.

116. Quoted in Wheeler, *Yankee from the West* 334.

117. Alfred Steinberg, *Sam Rayburn: A Biography* 144–145 (New York: Hawthorn Books, 1975).

118. McKenna, *Franklin Roosevelt and the Great Constitutional War* 505 ff.

119. Quoted in Bascom N. Timmons, *Garner of Texas* 222–223 (New York: Harper & Brothers, 1948).

120. The vote was taken on the question to recommit the bill to the Judiciary Committee, effectively killing it.

121. Justice Van Devanter was replaced by Hugo Black in August 1937. George Sutherland was replaced by Stanley Reed in January 1938. Cardozo resigned in July 1938 and was replaced by Felix Frankfurter. William O. Douglas replaced Brandeis in 1939. Frank Murphy succeeded Pierce Butler in 1940. James Byrnes replaced McReynolds in 1941. As FDR predicted, McReynolds was the last of the so-called Four Horsemen to step down. Robert Jackson replaced Stone when Stone succeeded Hughes as chief justice in 1941. When Byrnes left the Court in 1942 to become director of war mobilization, he was replaced by Wiley Rutledge.

EIGHTEEN | Low Tide

The epigraph is from James A. Farley, *Behind the Ballots* 375 (New York: Harcourt, Brace & Co., 1938).

1. Nancy J. Weiss, *Farewell to the Party of Lincoln: Black Politics in the Age of FDR* 106 (Princeton, N.J.: Princeton University Press, 1983). For Harrison generally, see Martha H. Swain's excellent biography, *Pat Harrison: The New Deal Years* 33–167 (Jackson: University Press of Mississippi, 1978).

2. James A. Farley, *Jim Farley's Story* 91 (New York: Whittlesey House, 1948); Bascom N. Timmons, *Garner of Texas* 223–224 (New York: Harper & Brothers, 1948).

3. FDR to Senator Alben Barkley, July 15, 1937, 6 *Public Papers and Addresses of Franklin D. Roosevelt* 306–308, Samuel I. Rosenman, ed. (New York: Macmillan, 1941).

4. Farley, *Jim Farley's Story* 92; David McCullough, *Truman* 228 (New York: Simon & Schuster, 1991). "To say No to Tom was one of the hardest things I ever had to do," said Truman afterward.

5. Quoted in Swain, *Pat Harrison* 159–160. Also see Joseph Alsop and Turner Catledge, *The 168 Days* 282–283 (New York: Doubleday, Doran, 1938).

6. Quoted in Timmons, *Garner of Texas* 224.

7. Kevin J. McMahon, *Reconsidering Roosevelt on Race* 95 (Chicago: University of Chicago Press, 2004).

8. Dingell to FDR, June 26, 1937, quoted in William E. Leuchtenburg, *Franklin D. Roosevelt and the New Deal* 253 (New York: Harper & Row, 1963).

9. "Washington Notes," 91 *The New Republic* 313 (1937). In length of service, Hatton Sumners was the fourth-ranking member of the House, having been elected in 1912.

10. Farley, *Jim Farley's Story* 95–96.

11. Ibid. 96.

12. David M. Kennedy, *Freedom from Fear* 313 (New York: Oxford University Press, 1999). Dies for all Chevrolet products were at Fisher Body Plant 2 in Cleveland, but a week after the strike began in Flint, the factory in Cleveland was also shut down by workers.

13. Frances Perkins, *The Roosevelt I Knew* 321–322 (New York: Viking Press, 1946).

14. Quoted in Irving Bernstein, *Turbulent Years: A History of the American Worker, 1933–1941* 541 (Boston: Houghton Mifflin, 1970).

15. Timmons, *Garner of Texas* 216.

16. Perkins, *The Roosevelt I Knew* 323.

17. Ibid. 324.

18. Kennedy, *Freedom from Fear* 303.

19. In *NLRB v. Fansteel Metallurgical Corporation,* 306 U.S. 240 (1939), the Supreme Court ruled the sit-down strike "a high-handed proceeding without a shadow of a legal right."

20. 9 *Complete Press Conferences of Franklin D. Roosevelt* 467 (New York: Da Capo, 1972).

21. Melvyn Dubofsky and Warren Van Tine, *John L. Lewis: A Biography* 327 (New York: Quadrangle/New York Times, 1977).

22. Conrad Black, *Franklin Delano Roosevelt: Champion of Freedom* 429 (New York: PublicAffairs, 2003).

23. Nathan Miller, *FDR: An Intimate History* 407 (New York: Doubleday, 1983).

24. Leuchtenburg, *Franklin D. Roosevelt* 224.

25. Black, *Franklin Delano Roosevelt* 429.

26. "The Morgenthau Diaries," 120 *Collier's* 82 (September 27, 1947). Also see John Morton Blum, *From the Morgenthau Diaries: Years of Crisis, 1928–1938* 387–388 (Boston: Houghton Mifflin, 1959).

27. Harold L. Ickes, 2 *Secret Diary* 240 (New York: Simon & Schuster, 1954).

28. Farley, *Jim Farley's Story* 101.

29. Blum, *Morgenthau Diaries* 415.

30. James MacGregor Burns, *Roosevelt: The Lion and the Fox* 336 (New York: Harcourt, Brace & World, 1956).

31. *Time,* May 16, 1938.

32. Blum, *Morgenthau Diaries* 421.

33. David Robertson, *Sly and Able: A Political Biography of James F. Byrnes* 284 (New York: W. W. Norton, 1994).

34. *Congressional Record* 311 (January 11, 1938).

35. For the grisly details of the lynching of Claude Neal in Marianna, October 26, 1934, see Weiss, *Farewell to the Party of Lincoln* 108. Professor Weiss quotes at length from the extensive NAACP investigation.

36. Blanche Wiesen Cook provides a useful summary of the Wagner bill in 2 *Eleanor Roosevelt* 178 (New York: Viking, 1999).

37. Gallup Poll, January 31, 1937, in George H. Gallup, 1 *The Gallup Poll: Public Opinion, 1935–1971* 48 (New York: Random House, 1972).

38. Walter White, *A Man Called White: The Autobiography of Walter White* 169–170 (New York: Viking, 1948).

39. "You'll have to give me about twenty-four hours," Roosevelt said, "because I will have to check up and see what I did last year. I have forgotten." 4 *Complete Press Conferences* 155–156.

40. "Care to comment on the anti-lynching bill?" FDR was asked. "No." he replied. April 24, 1935, 5 ibid. 243.

41. Joseph P. Lash, *Eleanor and Franklin* 516–517 (New York: W. W. Norton, 1971).

42. Cook, 2 *Eleanor Roosevelt* 247.

43. 11 *Complete Press Conferences* 88.

44. Quoted in Weiss, *Farewell to the Party of Lincoln* 245.

45. It was the Supreme Court, in *Smith v. Allwright*, 321 U.S. 649 (1944), that overturned the white primary. The Justice Department did not file a brief as *amicus curiae* or give any encouragement to the appellants. The poll tax was abolished by adoption of the Twenty-fourth Amendment in 1964.

46. Weiss, *Farewell to the Party of Lincoln* 256.

47. Nancy Weiss, interview with Pauli Murray, ibid.

48. *Chicago Defender,* January 30, 1943, ibid. 260.

49. *Afro-American,* April 15, 1939.

50. Remarks of Marian Anderson, January 6, 1943, quoted in Weiss, *Farewell to the Party of Lincoln* 264. The segregation of the era prevented Ms. Anderson from registering at a Washington hotel. She and her mother were accommodated by Mrs. Gifford Pinchot, who hosted them at her Massachusetts Avenue town house. Olive Ewing Clapper, *Washington Tapestry* 210–212 (New York: Whittlesey House, 1946).

51. Ickes, 1 *Secret Diaries* 285. Cf. Farley, *Behind the Ballots* 353–355.

52. Quoted in Miller, *FDR: An Intimate History* 361.

53. Eleanor Roosevelt, *This I Remember* 349 (New York: Harper & Brothers, 1949).

54. James Roosevelt and Sidney Shalett, *Affectionately, F.D.R.* 264 (New York: Harcourt, Brace & Company, 1959).

55. ER to FDR, November 22, 1936, quoted in Lash, *Eleanor and Franklin* 487.

56. Roosevelt and Shalett, *Affectionately, F.D.R.* 284.

57. "Possibly I should have been sufficiently mature and considerate enough of Father's position to have withdrawn from the insurance business entirely," wrote

James. "But I was young, ambitious, and spoiled so I went right ahead in pursuit of what seemed to me the easiest solution." Ibid. 218.

58. William O. Douglas, *Go East, Young Man* 302 (New York: Random House, 1974). Cf. James Roosevelt, *My Parents: A Differing View* 245–246 (Chicago: Playboy Press, 1976).

59. Roosevelt and Shalett, *Affectionately, F.D.R.* 310–311.

60. Ted Morgan, *FDR: A Biography* 464 (New York: Simon & Schuster, 1985). Also see Lash, *Eleanor and Franklin* 495.

61. Morgenthau Diary, December 6, 8, 1938. FDRL.

62. Elliott Roosevelt interview, cited in Peter Collier with David Horowitz, *The Roosevelts: An American Saga* 371 (New York: Simon & Schuster, 1994).

63. Lillian Rogers Parks, *The Roosevelts: A Family in Turmoil* 142 (Englewood Cliffs, N.J.: Prentice-Hall, 1981).

64. Quoted in Morgan, *FDR* 459.

65. Elliott Roosevelt and James Brough, *A Rendezvous with Destiny: The Roosevelts of the White House* 39 (New York: Putnam, 1975).

66. Joseph P. Lash interview with Anna Halstead, quoted in Lash, *Eleanor and Franklin* 490. "When I called [FDR] from Chicago and told him Elliott was going to marry right away, he was very annoyed, but his annoyance was at Elliott's doing it so quickly."

67. *The New York Times,* October 7, 8, 1936.

68. Ibid.

69. Elliott Roosevelt, *Rendezvous with Destiny* 37 ff.

70. Quoted in Collier, *The Roosevelts* 362.

71. Lash, *Eleanor and Franklin* 489.

72. Roosevelt and Shalett, *Affectionately, F.D.R.* 305.

73. For *The New York Times*' front-page coverage; see August 18 and August 19, 1937.

74. Quoted in Lash, *Eleanor and Franklin* 492. Also see *The New York Times,* August 21, 1937.

75. The act provided for a gradual two-year phase-in and allowed numerous exemptions. See Paul Douglas and Joseph Hackman, "The Fair Labor Standards Act of 1938," 53 *Political Science Quarterly* 491–515 (1938).

76. Michael Barone, *Our Country: The Shaping of America from Roosevelt to Reagan* 117 (New York: Free Press, 1990).

77. Hill received 90,601 votes to Heflin's 50,189. Congressional Quarterly, *Guide to U.S. Elections* 909 (Washington, D.C.: Congressional Quarterly, 1975).

78. For the full text, see Farley, *Jim Farley's Story* 120–121.

79. Ibid. 121.

80. Davis, *FDR: Into the Storm* 239–240.

81. Professor James T. Patterson provides a useful table of the support senators gave the New Deal in the Appendix (pages 348–349) of his *Congressional Conser-*

vatism and the New Deal (Lexington: University of Kentucky Press, 1967). Gillette's voting record indicates he supported the New Deal three quarters of the time. That was better than twenty-three of his Democratic colleagues.

82. Davis, *FDR: Into the Storm* 249.

83. *The Indianapolis Star,* June 6, 1938.

84. 7 *Public Papers and Addresses of Franklin D. Roosevelt* 391–400, Samuel I. Rosenman, ed. (New York: Macmillan, 1941).

85. Farley, *Jim Farley's Story* 125.

86. 7 *Public Papers and Addresses* 432–439, at 438.

87. The unofficial results of the August 9 Kentucky primary showed Barkley with 274,131; Chandler 184,266. Mrs. Chandler, with down-home directness, said she hoped her husband would quit politics. "You know, you can't make any money in politics, especially when you're a psychopathic case of honesty such as Happy is." *Louisville Courier-Journal,* August 9, 1938, quoted in Leuchtenburg, *Franklin D. Roosevelt and the New Deal* 267n.

88. Quoted in Thomas L. Stokes, *Chip off My Shoulder* 536 (Princeton, N.J.: Princeton University Press, 1940). Stokes, a Scripps-Howard syndicated columnist, broke the Kentucky story in a series of eight articles that won the 1939 Pulitzer Prize.

89. Patterson, *Congressional Conservatism* 348–349. Glass voted against the New Deal 81 percent of the time.

90. Farley, *Jim Farley's Story.*

91. 7 *Public Papers and Addresses* 463–471.

92. *Augusta Chronicle,* August 12, 1938.

93. Ibid., August 16, 1938.

94. Congressional Quarterly, *Guide to U.S. Elections* 912.

95. V. O. Key, Jr., *Southern Politics in State and Nation* 139 (New York: Alfred A. Knopf, 1950).

96. Smith received 186,519 votes (55.4%) to Johnston's 150,437 (44.7%). Six years later Johnston defeated Smith 138,440 to 88,045. Ibid. 915.

97. Quoted in Kennedy, *Freedom from Fear* 348.

98. Address at Denton, Maryland, September 5, 1938. FDR also spoke at Morgantown, Berlin, Sharptown, Salisbury, and Annapolis. 7 *Public Papers and Addresses* 512–520, at 515. Some of the most incisive coverage of the Maryland primary is provided by Caroline H. Keith in *"For Hell and a Brown Mule": The Biography of Senator Millard E. Tydings* 329–361 (Lanham, Md.: Madison Books, 1991).

99. FDR to James H. Fay, September 23, 1938, FDRL. O'Connor was succeeded as chairman of the Rules Committee by Adolph J. Sabath of Illinois, the dean of the House and a staunch New Dealer. Under Sabath the Rules Committee was no longer the roadblock it had been, but on the other hand the House itself was no longer under firm New Deal control.

100. Farley, *Jim Farley's Story* 148.

101. Timmons, *Garner of Texas* 239 (Garner's emphasis).

102. Raymond Clapper, "Return of the Two-Party System," 49 *Current History* 14 (December 1938).

NINETEEN | On the Brink

The epigraph is from the address FDR gave at Chapel Hill, December 5, 1938, upon receipt of an honorary degree from the University of North Carolina. 7 *Public Papers and Addresses of Franklin D. Roosevelt* 613–621, Samuel I. Rosenman, ed. (New York: Macmillan, 1941).

1. 8 Ibid. 1–12.
2. Thomas L. Stokes, *Chip off My Shoulder* 505 (Princeton, N.J.: Princeton University Press, 1940).
3. Combatant casualties in the Spanish Civil War are from Melvin Small and J. David Singer, *Resort to Arms: International and Civil Wars, 1816–1980* 229 (Beverly Hills: Sage Publications, 1982).
4. Quoted in Nathan Miller, *FDR: An Intimate History* 421–422 (New York: Doubleday, 1983).
5. On May 9, 1938, FDR told Harold Ickes that to lift the embargo and allow arms to be shipped to the Spanish government "would mean the loss of every Catholic vote next fall and the Democratic members of Congress . . . didn't want it done." The cat was out of the bag, wrote Ickes, "and it is the mangiest, scabbiest cat ever." 2 *Secret Diary of Harold L. Ickes* 389–390 (New York: Simon & Schuster, 1954).
6. Address at Chautauqua, New York, August 14, 1936, 5 *Public Papers and Addresses* 289.
7. A Gallup Poll in late 1937 found that 57 percent of American respondents favored China while only 1 percent backed Japan. Hadley Cantril, *Public Opinion 1935–1946* 1081–1082 (Princeton, N.J.: Princeton University Press, 1951).
8. 6 *Public Papers and Addresses* 406–411.
9. *The Wall Street Journal,* October 8, 1937.
10. *Time,* October 18, 1937.
11. Samuel I. Rosenman, *Working with Roosevelt* 167 (New York: Harper & Brothers, 1952).
12. 10 *Complete Presidential Press Conferences of Franklin D. Roosevelt* 232–252 (New York: Da Capo Press, 1972).
13. *The Times* (London), October 7, 1937.
14. FDR to Peabody, October 16, 1937, 3 *The Roosevelt Letters* 220, Elliott Roosevelt, ed. (London: George G. Harrap, 1952).
15. Manny T. Koginos, *The Panay Incident: Prelude to War* 26–31 (Lafayette, Ind.: Purdue University Studies, 1967).
16. Kenneth S. Davis, *FDR: Into the Storm* 154–155 (New York: Random House, 1993); *The New York Times,* December 13–26, 1937.
17. Ickes, 2 *Secret Diaries* 274. Also see John Morton Blum, *From the Morgenthau Diaries: Years of Crisis, 1928–1938* 485–492 (Boston: Houghton Mifflin, 1959).

18. *The Christian Science Monitor,* December 13, 1937.
19. Robert Dallek, *Franklin D. Roosevelt and American Foreign Policy 1932–1945* 154 (New York: Oxford University Press, 1979).
20. Quoted in William E. Leuchtenburg, *Franklin D. Roosevelt and the New Deal* 229 (New York: Harper & Row, 1963).
21. "Memorandum to the Secretary of State," December 13, 1937, 6 *Public Papers and Addresses* 541–542.
22. Ibid. 542n. In addition to the shipping and personnel losses, the U.S. bill included $74.27 to reimburse the Post Office Department for lost stamps. Koginos, *Panay Incident* 73.
23. United States Congress, 75th Cong., 1st Sess., *Congressional Directory* 33 (Washington, D.C.: U.S. Government Printing Office, 1937).
24. George Gallup, 1 *The Gallup Polls: Public Opinion, 1935–1971* 71 (New York: Random House, 1972).
25. Radio Address by Louis Ludlow, November 29, 1937, Legislative Division, National Archives.
26. Cordell Hull, 1 *The Memoirs of Cordell Hull* 563–564 (New York: Macmillan, 1948).
27. FDR to Bankhead, January 6, 1938, 7 *Public Papers and Addresses* 36–37.
28. In a public telegram to FDR on December 20, 1937, Landon congratulated the president for the uncompromising stand he had taken opposing the amendment. "Many members of Congress from both parties," he said, "seem to have forgotten the basic principle of American politics and wish to create the impression on foreign governments that they do not trust your administration of foreign affairs." Quoted in *The Christian Science Monitor,* December 21, 1937.

    Knox, publisher of the *Chicago Daily News,* called the amendment "an idea that could be harbored only by persons utterly ignorant of the realities of international life and death," *Chicago Daily News,* December 18, 1937. Stimson, whose letter occupied three quarters of the editorial page in the *Times,* and who was also given extensive front-page coverage, said of the proposal that "No more effective engine for the disruption of national unity on the threshold of a national crisis could ingeniously have been devised." *The New York Times,* December 22, 1937.
29. U.S. Congress, *Congressional Record* 276–283 (January 10, 1938).
30. Ibid. In addition to the official 188–209 tally, 10 members were paired, 2 voted present, 23 abstained, and there were 3 vacancies. Bertrand Snell of New York, the Republican leader, voted against the resolution.
31. Article 88 of the Treaty of Saint-Germain, one of the "suburb treaties" negotiated simultaneously with the Treaty of Versailles, proclaimed Austria's independence to be inalienable and made the League of Nations its guarantor.
32. On March 10, 1938, Premier Camille Chautemps and his cabinet resigned, and it was not until the thirteenth of March that a new government under Léon Blum was installed.

33. In his testimony at Nuremberg on August 9, 1946, Field Marshal Erich von Manstein said the chief worry of the military at the time of the Anschluss was whether Italy would intervene because "Italy always sided with Austria and the Hapsburgs." Quoted in William L. Shirer, *The Rise and Fall of the Third Reich* 345n (New York: Simon & Schuster, 1959).

34. "The hard fact is that nothing could have arrested what actually has happened unless this country and other countries had been prepared to use force," Chamberlain told Parliament on March 14, 1938. Ibid. 353.

35. Ibid. 350.

36. 11 *Complete Presidential Press Conferences* 223–226.

37. FDR to John Cudahy (U.S. minister to the Irish Free State), March 9, 1938, 3 *Roosevelt Letters* 232.

38. Quoted in Conrad Black, *Franklin Delano Roosevelt: Champion of Freedom* 449 (New York: PublicAffairs, 2003). Also see Kennedy, *Freedom from Fear* 408–409.

39. Chamberlain's remarks were made September 27, 1938, and reported in all major newspapers the following day.

40. Quoted in Joachim C. Fest, *Hitler* 567, 572 (New York: Harcourt Brace Janovich, 1974); Black, *FDR* 476. Mussolini was the only one of the four at Munich who spoke all four languages. As a result he played a role in the negotiations that was not always appreciated. Note that the Czech government was not represented. That was at Hitler's insistence, to which Britain and France agreed.

41. Ickes, 2 *Secret Diaries* 469. FDR feared that Chamberlain was so eager to appease Hitler that "in the interest of world peace" he might cede Trinidad to Germany and convince France to yield Martinique. If that happened, Roosevelt told Ickes, he would send the U.S. fleet to take both islands. Ibid. 484.

42. The ranking is that of Army chief of staff Malin Craig, in U.S. Department of State, *Peace and War: United States Foreign Policy, 1931–1941* 55 (Washington, D.C.: U.S. Government Printing Office, 1943).

43. Kennedy, *Freedom from Fear* 419, quoting Robert A. Divine, *The Reluctant Belligerent: American Entry into World War II* 55 (New York: John Wiley & Sons, 1969).

44. 7 *Public Papers and Addresses* 491–494. Secretary Hull, with FDR's approval, spoke to the National Press Club on March 17, 1938, stressing the need for rearmament. For Welles, see Cordell Hull, 1 *Memoirs* 576–577 (New York: Macmillan, 1948).

45. Radio Address to the *Herald Tribune* Forum, October 26, 1938. 7 *Public Papers and Addresses* 563–566.

46. Gallup Poll, October 14, 1938. 1 *The Gallup Polls* 121.

47. *The New York Times,* November 11, 1938.

48. Shirer, *Rise and Fall of the Third Reich* 430–434. To preserve their international credit ratings, the insurance companies paid the claims, but the German government confiscated the money and returned most of it to the insurers.

49. Press Conference, November 15, 1938, 7 *Public Papers and Addresses* 596–598.

50. Ibid.

51. Herbert Hoover, 1 *Public Papers of the President . . . Messages, Speeches, and Statements* 36–40 (Washington, D.C.: U.S. Government Printing Office, 1974). Proclamation 1872, "Limiting the Immigration of Aliens into the United States on the Basis of National Origin."

52. Arthur Morse, *While Six Million Died* 288 (New York: Random House, 1968).

53. Cantril, *Public Opinion* 1081.

54. Black, *Franklin Delano Roosevelt* 491.

55. Kennedy, *Freedom from Fear* 414.

56. Frances Perkins, *The Roosevelt I Knew* 348–349 (New York: Viking Press, 1946).

57. Press conference, November 18, 1938, 7 *Public Papers and Addresses* 603–604. Despite widespread public disapproval, Roosevelt assisted some 150,000 refugees to enter the United States between the Anschluss and Pearl Harbor. "I only wish I could do more," he wrote investment banker Robert Lehman in New York. Harry L. Feingold, *The Politics of Rescue: The Roosevelt Administration and the Holocaust, 1938–1945* 24 (New Brunswick, N.J.: Rutgers University Press, 1970).

58. Among those present were Morgenthau; Hopkins; Assistant Secretary of War Louis Johnson; Solicitor General Robert Jackson; Army chief of staff General Malin Craig; Major General Henry H. "Hap" Arnold, chief of the Army Air Corps; and Brigadier General George C. Marshall, deputy chief of staff.

59. John Morton Blum, 2 *From the Morgenthau Diaries* 48–49 (Boston: Houghton Mifflin, 1965).

60. Quoted in David Reynolds, *From Munich to Pearl Harbor* 48 (Chicago: Ivan R. Dee, 2001).

61. "Supplemental Appropriations for National Defense," Message to Congress, January 12, 1939, 8 *Public Papers and Addresses* 70–74.

62. 7 *Public Papers and Addresses* 613–621.

63. Hopkins memorandum, FDRL, quoted in Robert Sherwood, *Roosevelt and Hopkins* 114 (New York: Harper & Brothers, 1948).

64. A useful summary of FDR's role is provided in William L. Langer and S. Everett Gleason, 1 *The Challenge to Isolation: The World Crisis of 1937–1940 and American Foreign Policy* 45–49 (New York: Harper & Brothers, 1952).

65. 13 *Complete Presidential Press Conferences* 91.

66. Transcript, Conference with the Senate Military Affairs Committee, January 31, 1939, Item 1565, 8 *Franklin D. Roosevelt and Foreign Affairs,* Donald B. Schewe, ed. (New York: Garland Publishing Co., 1979). The transcript indicates FDR's statement was met with applause from the senators.

67. Ibid.

68. Gallup Polls, September 29, 1939, 1 *Gallup Polls* 182–183. Also see Kenneth S. Davis, *FDR: Into the Storm* 409 (New York: Random House, 1993).

69. "They have crucified my husband," said Mrs. Craig, speaking of the rivalry between Woodring and Johnson. Quoted in Forrest C. Pogue, 1 *George C. Marshall: Education of a General* 318 (New York: Viking Press, 1963).

70. Ibid. 325–330.
71. The amendment was narrowly adopted 159–157 after many administration sup-
    porters had left the chamber for the night. One of the Democrats voting for the
    amendment was Franklin and Eleanor's close friend Caroline O'Day of New
    York. FDR immediately rebuked her:

    > Dear Caroline:
    >   I think it may interest you to tell you in great confidence that
    > two of our Embassies abroad tell us this afternoon that the action
    > of the House last night has caused dismay in democratic peaceful
    > circles. The anti-war nations believe that a definite stimulus has
    > been given Hitler by the vote of the House, and that if war breaks
    > out in Europe . . . an important part of the responsibility will rest
    > with last night's action.

    FDR to Caroline O'Day, Item 1907, 10 *Franklin D. Roosevelt and Foreign Affairs.*
72. FDR to George VI, September 17, 1938, Item 1282a, 7 Ibid. Roosevelt addressed
    the letter "My dear King George" and concluded it "Faithfully yours." George VI
    posted his acceptance October 8, addressing FDR in longhand "My dear Presi-
    dent Roosevelt" and concluding, also in longhand, "Believe me, yours very sin-
    cerely, George R.I." Ibid, Item 1333.
73. John W. Wheeler-Bennett, *King George VI: His Life and Reign* 389 (London:
    Macmillan, 1958). Also see Will Swift, *The Roosevelts and the Royals: Franklin
    and Eleanor, The King and Queen of England, and the Friendship That Changed
    History* 135–137 (Hoboken, N.J.: John Wiley & Sons, 2004).
74. For the text of the German-Soviet Pact and of the secret additional protocol
    signed in Moscow, August 23, 1939, see U.S. Department of State, 7 *Documents
    on German Foreign Policy* 245–247 (Washington, D.C.: U.S. Government Print-
    ing Office, 1957).
75. The initial assault wave, supported by Stuka dive-bombers, was followed by six-
    teen reserve divisions and two SS divisions. Ultimately 1.3 million men would
    take part in the invasion. To meet the assault, Poland deployed thirty infantry di-
    visions, eleven cavalry brigades, one mountain brigade, and only two armored
    brigades. Field Marshal Erich von Manstein, then chief of staff of Southern
    Army Group (Rundstedt commanding) and one of the most reflective German
    officers, notes that the Poles massed their forces at or near the frontier, deter-
    mined to defend every foot of Polish soil. That facilitated a German break-
    through. Manstein argued that the Poles would have been better served to
    withdraw, mass their forces, and stall for time, particularly since the German
    west wall, facing France, was held only by a light screening force and no armor
    whatever. Erich von Manstein, *Lost Victories* 34–63 (Chicago: Henry Regnery,
    1958).

76. Joseph Alsop and Robert Kintner, *American White Paper* 1, 58–60 (New York: Simon & Schuster, 1940).

TWENTY | Stab in the Back

The epigraph is from FDR's commencement speech at the University of Virginia, June 10, 1940. 9 *Public Papers and Addresses of Franklin D. Roosevelt* 259–264, Samuel I. Rosenman, ed. (New York: Macmillan, 1941).

1. 14 *Complete Presidential Press Conferences of Franklin D. Roosevelt* 130–132 (New York: Da Capo Press, 1972).

2. The record of Roosevelt's remarks to the cabinet was made by acting Navy secretary Charles Edison, who then forwarded it to FDR. "My only reason for sending it is that *somebody* ought to make a record of how you felt after getting the phone call [from Bullitt] and this may serve as notes for—that somebody—." Edison to FDR, September 2, 1939. 2 *FDR: His Personal Letters, 1928–1945* 915–916, Elliott Roosevelt, ed. (New York: Duell, Sloan and Pearce, 1950). Edison's emphasis.

3. Quoted in Donald Cameron Watt, *How War Came: The Immediate Origins of the Second World War, 1938–1939* 579 (New York: Pantheon, 1989). Clement Attlee, the Labour leader, was ill in hospital.

4. Walter Crookshank, diary, quoted in Watt, ibid.

5. 8 *Public Papers and Addresses* 460–464. Roosevelt's statement, made over Hull's objections, provided a deliberate contrast to Woodrow Wilson's 1914 admonition that Americans must be "neutral in fact as well as in name; impartial in thought as well as action." Department of State, *Foreign Relations of the United States, 1914, Supplement* 547–551 (Washington, D.C.: U.S. Government Printing Office, 1928). For Hull's objections, see 1 *The Memoirs of Cordell Hull* 676 (New York: Macmillan, 1948).

6. Presidential Proclamation 2365, September 13, 1939, 8 *Public Papers and Addresses* 510. After an informal head count, Ed Halsey, secretary of the Senate, advised the White House that at least sixty senators would support repeal and twenty-five oppose, a remarkably accurate assessment. Steve Early to FDR, September 7, 1939, 2 *FDR: Personal Letters* 918–919.

7. FDR to Moore, September 11, 1939, ibid. 919.

8. *The New York Times*, September 15, 1939.

9. 5 *Vital Speeches* 751–752.

10. Kenneth S. Davis, *FDR: Into the Storm* 496 (New York: Random House, 1993).

11. Joseph Alsop and Robert Kintner, *American White Paper* 73 ff. (New York: Simon & Schuster, 1940).

12. Harding set a presidential record, addressing joint sessions of Congress six times in two years. His final message, on February 7, 1923, pertained to Britain's war debt to the United States. Neither Coolidge nor Hoover addressed Congress, and

their annual messages were read by the reading clerks. Office of the Clerk, U.S. House of Representatives, "Joint Meetings, Sessions, Inaugurations, 60th to 79th Congress."

13. Message to Congress, September 21, 1939. 8 *Public Papers and Addresses* 512–522.

14. Memo of General Watson to FDR, September 21, 1939, reporting Borah's approval but also the senator's determination "to make some kind of fight." William L. Langer and S. Everett Gleason, 1 *The Challenge to Isolation* 224n (Cambridge, Mass.: Peter Smith, 1970) (reprint).

15. 4 *Public Opinion Quarterly* 102 (1940); Davis, *Into the Storm* 499.

16. For the committee vote, see *The New York Times,* September 29, 1939. Democrat Bennett Champ Clark of Missouri voted against; Republican Wallace White of Maine in favor. Otherwise it was a straight party-line vote.

17. Davis, *FDR: Into the Storm* 500.

18. *The New York Times,* October 27, 1939.

19. FDR to Lord Tweedsmuir, October 5, 1939, 2 *FDR: Personal Letters* 934.

20. 2 *The Secret Diary of Harold L. Ickes* 712–713 (New York: Simon & Schuster, 1954).

21. Daniel Levy and Susan Brink, *A Change of Heart* 13 (New York: Alfred A. Knopf, 2005).

22. 6 *Vital Speeches* 57–59.

23. Radio address to the *New York Herald Tribune* Forum, October 26, 1939. 8 *Public Papers and Addresses* 554–557.

24. Bascom N. Timmons, *Garner of Texas* 265 (New York: Harper & Brothers, 1948).

25. Edward J. Flynn, *You're the Boss* 154 (New York: Viking Press, 1947).

26. Geoffrey C. Ward, *A First-Class Temperament* 740–741n (New York: Harper & Row, 1989); Doris Kearns Goodwin, *No Ordinary Time* 107–108 (New York: Simon & Schuster, 1994).

27. FDR's conversation with Tobin was reported by Frances Perkins, who had accompanied the Teamster president to the Oval Study. Perkins, *The Roosevelt I Knew* 126 (New York: Viking Press, 1946).

28. John Gunther, *Roosevelt in Retrospect* 308–309 (New York: Harper & Brothers, 1950). Also see Paul H. Appleby, "Roosevelt's Third Term Decision," 46 *American Political Science Review* 754–765 (1952).

29. Morgenthau diary, January 24, 1940, FDRL.

30. Quoted in Ted Morgan, *FDR: A Biography* 519–520 (New York: Simon & Schuster, 1985).

31. *For the President: Personal and Secret: The Correspondence Between Franklin D. Roosevelt and William C. Bullitt* 398, Orville H. Bullitt, ed. (Boston: Houghton Mifflin, 1972).

32. Ickes, 3 *Secret Diaries* 95.

33. "James, it is my sincere feeling that a Roman Catholic could not be elected President of the United States at this time or for many years to come," said

Mundelein. "I hope, therefore, that you will do nothing to involve the Catholics of this country in another debacle such as we experienced in 1928." James A. Farley, *Jim Farley's Story* 174–177 (New York: Whittlesey House, 1948).

34. Hull, 1 *Memoirs* 856.

35. James MacGregor Burns, *Roosevelt: The Lion and the Fox* 414 (New York: Harcourt, Brace & World, 1956).

36. Hull, 1 *Memoirs* 856.

37. Quoted in Williamson Murray and Allan R. Millett, *A War to Be Won* 63 (Cambridge, Mass.: Harvard University Press, 2000).

38. Senator Borah's "phony war" remark was made in a Washington press conference on December 18, 1939, and reported in *The New York Times* the following day. Professor Henry Graff, interview with ER, Graff papers, FDRL.

39. Eleanor Roosevelt, *Autobiography* 214 (New York: Harper & Brothers, 1961).

40. When Allied forces landed in France in 1944, there were nearly 500,000 German troops in Norway. When the war ended, there were more than 300,000. Murray and Millett, *A War to Be Won* 66.

41. Winston S. Churchill, *The Gathering Storm* 667 (Boston: Houghton Mifflin, 1948).

42. The remark was recorded by Harold Ickes in his manuscript diary entry of May 12, 1940. When the diaries were published after the war, Ickes deleted "even if he was drunk half of his time." 3 *Secret Diaries* 176.

43. Winston S. Churchill, *Their Finest Hour* 42 (Boston: Houghton Mifflin, 1949).

44. Churchill to FDR, May 15, 1940, *Roosevelt and Churchill: Their Secret Wartime Correspondence* 94–95, Francis L. Loewenheim, Harold D. Langley, and Manfred Jones, eds. (New York: E. P. Dutton, 1975).

45. "Appropriations for National Defense," May 16, 1940, 9 *Public Papers and Addresses* 198–205.

46. "Additional Appropriations for National Defense," May 31, 1940, ibid. 250–253.

47. Ibid. 207; U.S. Department of Commerce, Bureau of the Census, *Statistical History of the United States* 718 (Stamford, Conn.: Fairfield Publishers, 1965).

48. FDR to Churchill, May 16, 1940, *Roosevelt and Churchill* 95–96.

49. Churchill to FDR, May 18, 1940, ibid. 96–97.

50. Congressional Quarterly, *Guide to U.S. Elections* 328–329 (Washington, D.C.: Congressional Quarterly, 1975).

51. One of the best accounts of the German breakthrough and the evacuation at Dunkirk is provided by Churchill in *Their Finest Hour* 74–118. Also see B. H. Liddell Hart, *History of the Second World War* 79–80 (London: Cassell, 1970); Murray and Millett, *A War to Be Won* 80–81.

52. Churchill, *Their Finest Hour* 141–143.

53. FDR to Morgenthau, June 6, 1940. Quoted in John Morton Blum, 2 *From the Morgenthau Diaries: Years of Urgency, 1938–1941* 155 (Boston: Houghton Mifflin, 1965).

54. Quoted in Liddell Hart, *History of the Second World War* 85.

55. Address at the University of Virginia, June 10, 1940, 9 *Public Papers and Addresses* 259–264. Drafts of the speech at the Roosevelt Library show FDR's handwritten inserts stiffening the message. The "stab in the back" reference was ad-libbed by Roosevelt and does not appear in the copy from which he spoke.

56. William E. Leuchtenburg, *Franklin D. Roosevelt and the New Deal* 302–303 (New York: Harper & Row, 1963).

57. Churchill to FDR, June 11, 1940, *Roosevelt and Churchill* 98–99.

58. On June 17, and again on June 18, Woodring challenged presidential authority when he refused to approve the sale of B-17 bombers to Great Britain. On the morning of the nineteenth Roosevelt requested his resignation. FDR offered Woodring a consolation prize of governor of Puerto Rico—a considerable stepdown—which Woodring refused. FDR to Harry Woodring, June 19, June 25, 1940, 2 *FDR: His Personal Letters* 1041–1044.

59. FDR to Knox, December 29, 1939, ibid. 975–977. Also see Grace Tully, *F.D.R.: My Boss* 242–243 (New York: Charles Scribner's Sons, 1949). After his dismissal Woodring told the *Topeka Capital* he had been the victim of "a small clique of international financiers who want the United States to declare war and get into the European mess with everything we have. . . . They don't like me because I am against stripping our own defenses for the sake of trying to stop Hitler 3,000 miles away." Reprinted in *The New York Times,* June 21, 1940.

60. Robert E. Sherwood, *Roosevelt and Hopkins* 163 (New York: Harper and Brothers, 1948).

61. Henry L. Stimson and McGeorge Bundy, *On Active Service in Peace and War* 323–325 (New York: Harper & Brothers, 1948). FDR had promised the post of undersecretary of the Navy to Thomas Corcoran, but Knox rejected him as too political. Robert C. Albion and Robert H. Connery, *Forrestal and the Navy* 1–9 (New York: Columbia University Press, 1962).

62. For the text of the Stimson and Knox speeches, see *The New York Times,* June 19, 1940. The fact that both Knox and Stimson should advocate conscription in their commencement addresses was scarcely coincidental. On May 22, 1940, the two, joined by William Donovan; former budget director Lewis Douglas; Judge Robert Patterson; Julius Ochs Adler of *The New York Times;* Grenville Clark, who had clerked with FDR at Carter, Ledyard, and Milburn; Langdon Marvin, Roosevelt's old law partner; and some ninety other distinguished alumni met at the Harvard Club in New York and agreed to beat the drum for reinstitution of the draft, universal service, and immediate expansion of the regular Army and the National Guard. J. Garry Clifford and Samuel R. Spencer, *The First Peacetime Draft* 14–26 (Lawrence: University of Kansas Press, 1986).

63. *The New York Times,* June 25, 1940.

64. The statement was made by Ruth McCormick Simms, one of Dewey's principal aides at the convention. Charles Peters, *Five Days in Philadelphia* 19 (New York: PublicAffairs, 2005).

65. Ibid. 20.

66. Taft's remarks were in a speech he delivered in St. Louis, May 20, 1940. Taft also said that America's participation in war was "more likely to destroy American democracy than to destroy German dictatorship." James Patterson, *Mr. Republican: A Biography of Robert A. Taft* 217 (New York: Houghton Mifflin, 1973).

67. David Halberstam, *The Powers That Be* 60 (New York: Knopf, 1975); Gunther, *Roosevelt in Retrospect* 310–311.

68. *New York Sun,* January 16, 1940, reported in Peters, *Five Days* 25. In 1920, Willkie, as a young lawyer in Akron, Ohio, introduced James Cox (FDR's running mate) at a Democratic rally. He supported Al Smith at the 1924 Democratic convention, served as an assistant floor manager for Newton D. Baker at the 1932 convention, and voted for Herbert Lehman against Thomas Dewey in the 1938 New York gubernatorial race. Ibid. 30–32.

69. "Fair Trial," *The New Republic* 370 (March 18, 1940). Also see "Political Power: The Tennessee Valley Authority," *The Atlantic Monthly,* August 1937; "Brace Up, America!" *The Atlantic Monthly,* 163 (June 1939): 549–561; "Idle Money—Idle Men," *The Saturday Evening Post,* 211 (June 17, 1939); "The Faith That Is America," *Reader's Digest,* 36 (December 1939): 1–4; "With Malice Toward None," *The Saturday Evening Post,* 212 (December 30, 1939); "We, the People," *Fortune,* 21 (April 1940): 64–65; "New Deal Power," *The New York Times Magazine,* October 31, 1937, p. 6; "Five Minutes to Midnight," *The Saturday Evening Post,* 212 (June 22, 1940).

70. Steve Neal, *Dark Horse: A Biography of Wendell Willkie* 57 (New York: Doubleday, 1984).

71. Quoted in Peters, *Five Days* 41.

72. Neal, *Dark Horse* 99. Ickes's characterization was made in a speech to a Democratic rally in Saint Louis on October 18, 1940. T. H. Watkins, *The Life and Times of Harold L. Ickes, 1874–1952* 694 (New York: Henry Holt, 1990).

73. Joseph W. Martin and Robert J. Donovan, *My First Fifty Years in Politics* 101–108 (New York: McGraw-Hill, 1960). After the convention Willkie named Martin chairman of the Republican National Committee.

74. *Time,* July 1, 1940. The Republican plank stated, "We favor the extension of aid to all people fighting for liberty or whose liberty is threatened as long as such aid is not in violation of international law or inconsistent with the requirements of our national defense." Peters, *Five Days* 91.

75. Ickes, 3 *Secret Diaries* 223. FDR said that he liked McNary and he "deserved the nomination."

TWENTY-ONE | Four More Years

The epigraph is from FDR's campaign speech at Boston, October 30, 1940. 9 *Public Papers and Addresses of Franklin D. Roosevelt* 514–524, Samuel I. Rosenman, ed. (New York: Macmillan, 1941).

1. James MacGregor Burns, *Roosevelt: The Lion and the Fox* 421–422 (New York: Harcourt, Brace & World, 1956). Walsh's rider to the appropriations bill left FDR no choice but to sign.

2. Mark S. Watson, *The United States Army in World War II: Chief of Staff: Prewar Plans and Operations* 312 (Washington, D.C.: U.S. Government Printing Office, 1950).

3. Frank Freidel, *Franklin D. Roosevelt: A Rendezvous with Destiny* 341 (Boston: Little, Brown, 1990).

4. *Chicago Daily News,* July 16, 1940.

5. Roosevelt phoned Farley Monday morning, July 15, and elliptically suggested that Farley withdraw. *Jim Farley's Story* 271–272 (New York: Whittlesey House, 1948).

6. Ibid. 274–275.

7. Quoted in Joseph P. Lash, *Eleanor and Franklin* 619 (New York: W. W. Norton, 1971). Ed Flynn, who had superseded Farley as FDR's principal political adviser, wrote that the Democratic leaders considered Hopkins an amateur. "While they had nothing against him personally, they felt that he, representing the President, directly lowered their prestige." Edward J. Flynn, *You're the Boss* 156 (New York: Viking Press, 1947).

8. Roosevelt wrote the statement in pencil and transmitted it to James Byrnes, who convinced Walsh and Wheeler to go along. 2 *F.D.R.: His Personal Letters* 1048, Elliott Roosevelt, ed. (New York: Duell, Sloan and Pearce, 1950).

9. Harold L. Ickes, 3 *The Secret Diary of Harold L. Ickes* 245 (New York: Simon & Schuster, 1955).

10. The text of Ickes's telegram is ibid. 249–250.

11. Frances Perkins, *The Roosevelt I Knew* 131–132 (New York: Viking, 1946) (FDR's emphasis supplied by Miss Perkins).

12. Eleanor Roosevelt, *This I Remember* 214 (New York: Harper & Brothers, 1949).

13. Ibid. 215.

14. Lash, *Eleanor and Franklin* 620.

15. Farley, *Jim Farley's Story* 283.

16. July 16, 1940, 9 *Personal Papers and Addresses* 292. Roosevelt's disavowal was strikingly similar to the statement of "Uncle Ted" to the Republican convention in 1900 announcing he was not a candidate for the vice presidency (which of course he was):

   In view of the revival of the talk of myself as a Vice-Presidential candidate, I have this to say. It is impossible too deeply to express how touched I am by the attitude of those delegates, who have wished me to take the nomination. . . . I understand the high honor and dignity of the office, an office so high and so honorable that it is well worthy of the ambition of any man in the United States. But while appreciating all this to the full, I nevertheless feel most deeply that the field of my best usefulness to the public and to the party is in New York State; and that, if the party should see fit to renominate me for Governor, I can in that position help the National ticket as in no other way. I very earnestly hope and ask that every friend of mine in this Convention respect my wish and my judgment in this matter.

Edmund Morris, *The Rise of Theodore Roosevelt* 764 (New York: Coward, McCann & Geoghegan, 1979).

17. *Chicago Daily News,* July 17, 1940.

18. "It was a job right up my alley," Garry told *Time.* "I figured out a lot of my own angles. . . . I'm just an ordinary lug who loves the game of politics." Garry's day job involved keeping 3,800 miles of sewers in working order. "First thing when you get up in the morning you come in and see me. You don't know it but that's me you're visiting." *Time,* July 29, 1940. Also see Kenneth S. Davis, *FDR: Into the Storm* 597 (New York: Random House, 1993).

19. For Hull's description of FDR's overtures, see 1 *The Memoirs of Cordell Hull* 860–861 (New York: Macmillan, 1948).

20. Charles Peters, *Five Days in Philadelphia* 145 (New York: PublicAffairs, 2005).

21. "He's not a mystic, he's a philosopher," FDR told a skeptical Farley. "He'll help people think." Farley, *Jim Farley's Story* 294. Also see Samuel I. Rosenman, *Working with Roosevelt* 213 (New York: Harper & Brothers, 1952).

22. Quoted in Robert E. Sherwood, *Roosevelt and Hopkins* 179 (New York: Harper & Brothers, 1948).

23. *Time,* July 29, 1940; Eleanor Roosevelt, *This I Remember* 216.

24. Quoted in Lash, *Eleanor and Franklin* 623.

25. Doris Kearns Goodwin, *No Ordinary Time* 133 (New York: Simon & Schuster, 1994). For the full text of ER's address, see the *Proceedings of the Democratic National Convention, 1940* 238–239 (Washington, D.C.: Democratic National Committee, 1940).

26. *New York Daily News,* July 19, 1940; Lash, *Eleanor and Franklin* 623.

27. Rosenman, *Working with Roosevelt* 215.

28. Farley, *Jim Farley's Story* 302.

29. *The New York Times,* July 19, 1940. *Time* reported that of Wallace's 627 votes, not more than 50 were personal votes for the secretary. *Time,* July 29, 1940.

30. Quoted in Peters, *Five Days* 150.

31. Ickes, 3 *Secret Diaries* 265.

32. Hadley Cantril, "America Faces War: A Study in Public Opinion," 4 *Public Opinion Quarterly* 387–407 (September 1940).

33. As a member of the Senate, Wadsworth had been co-author of the 1920 National Defense Act.

34. Elting E. Morison, *Turmoil and Tradition: A Study of the Life and Times of Henry L. Stimson* 480 (Boston: Houghton Mifflin, 1960).

35. *The New York Times,* August 6, 1940.

36. Ibid., June 20, 1940.

37. "A conscript army is needed only if we are going to send an expeditionary force to conquer Europe or Asia," said Fosdick. "The well-justified suspicion will not down, that behind this hectic haste to force conscription on us is the policy of belligerent interventionists." Radio address, August 7, 1940. Quoted in William L. Langer and S. Everett Gleason, 2 *The Challenge of Isolation* 682 (Gloucester, Mass.: Peter Smith, 1970; reprint).

38. *Time,* August 12, 1940, quoted in William E. Leuchtenburg, *Franklin D. Roosevelt and the New Deal* 308n (New York: Harper & Row, 1963).

39. Quoted in ibid. Senator Wheeler's remarks were in a radio address on August 15, 1940.

40. Quoted in Davis, *FDR: Into the Storm* 564.

41. Henry L. Stimson and McGeorge Bundy, *On Active Service in Peace and War* 346 (New York: Harper & Brothers).

42. Forrest C. Pogue, *George C. Marshall: Ordeal and Hope* 60 (New York: Viking Press, 1966).

43. George H. Gallup, *The Gallup Poll: Public Opinion, 1935–1971* 226 (New York: Random House, 1972).

44. July 29, 1940. 9 *Public Papers and Addresses* 313–314. Congress passed the requested legislation on August 27, 1940, and FDR initiated the Guard call-up on August 31 (Executive Order 8530). Guard members were limited to twelve months' active duty and could be deployed only in the Western Hemisphere.

45. 666th Press Conference, August 2, 1940, ibid. 321.

46. Ellsworth Barnard, *Wendell Willkie: Fighter for Freedom* 204–205 (Marquette: Northern Michigan University Press, 1966).

47. Steve Neal, *Dark Horse: A Biography of Wendell Willkie* 139 (New York: Doubleday, 1984).

48. Ed Cray, *General of the Army: George C. Marshall* 172 (New York: W. W. Norton, 1990).

49. U.S. Department of Commerce, Bureau of the Census, *Statistical History of the United States* 736 (Stamford, Conn.: Fairfield Publishers, 1965).

50. WSC to FDR, June 11, 1940; June 13, 1940; June 15, 1940. *Roosevelt and Churchill: Their Secret Wartime Correspondence* 98–100, 104–106 (New York: E. P. Dutton, 1975).

51. WSC to FDR, June 15, 1940, ibid. 105–106. After reading Churchill's message, Henry Morgenthau told FDR that "unless we do something to give the English additional destroyers, it seems to me it is absolutely hopeless to expect them to keep going." Ibid. 106.

52. George VI to FDR, June 26, 1940, quoted in John W. Wheeler-Bennett, *King George VI: His Life and Reign* 511 (New York: St. Martin's Press, 1958). For a useful summary of David Windsor (Edward VIII)'s flirtation with Nazism, see Joseph E. Persico, *Roosevelt's Secret War* 70–76 (New York: Random House, 2001).

53. Langer and Gleason, 2 *Challenge to Isolation* 745.

54. Section 3 of the act of June 15, 1917 (40 Stat. 217, 222) provides, "During a war in which the United States is a neutral nation, it shall be unlawful to send out of the jurisdiction of the United States any vessel, built, armed, or equipped as a vessel of war, or converted from a private vessel into a vessel of war, with any intent or under any agreement or contract, written or oral, that such vessel shall be delivered to a belligerent nation, or to an agent, officer, or citizen of such nation, or with reasonable cause to believe that the said vessel shall or will be employed in the service of any such belligerent nation after its departure from the jurisdiction of the United States."

55. "I told Ben very frankly, as Tom Corcoran already had, that in view of [the attorney general's opinion prohibiting the delivery of torpedo boats to Great Britain] the President could not now reverse himself. He couldn't get away with it in public opinion." Ickes, 3 *Secret Diaries* 271.

56. FDR to Knox, July 22, 1940, 2 *F.D.R.: His Personal Letters* 1048–1049. For an extract of Cohen's memorandum, see Philip Goodhart, *Fifty Ships That Saved the World* 152 (New York: Doubleday, 1965).

57. Francis P. Miller Papers, record of Century Group meeting July 11, 1940, University of Virginia. The acquisition of American bases in the British possessions in exchange for the cancellation of war debts had long been advocated by the Isolationist press, particularly the *Chicago Tribune*. See Langer and Gleason, 2 *Challenge to Isolation* 746.

58. Quoted in Robert Shogan, *Hard Bargain: How FDR Twisted Churchill's Arm, Evaded the Law, and Changed the Role of the American Presidency* 153 (New York: Charles Scribner's Sons, 1995).

59. WSC to FDR, July 31, 1940, quoted in Churchill, *Their Finest Hour* 401–402 (Boston: Houghton Mifflin, 1949) (Churchill's emphasis).

60. John Morton Blum, 2 *From the Morgenthau Diaries* 177 (Boston: Houghton Mifflin, 1965); Ickes, 3 *Secret Diaries* 283.

61. Stimson diary (MS), August 2, 1940.

62. Ibid. Stimson, who did not know Farley, formed a high opinion of the postmaster general. "I was particularly pleased with the attitude throughout this whole day's debate of Jim Farley, who sat next to me. His suggestions were fair-minded and entirely non-political." Also see 288 Morgenthau Diaries 158 (MS). Morgenthau was not present, but Daniel Bell, who represented Treasury, provided a memo of the session.

63. FDR's memo of the cabinet meeting and his call to White is in 2 *F.D.R. His Personal Letters* 1050–1051.

64. WSC to Lothian, August 3, 1940, quoted in Churchill, *Their Finest Hour* 402–403.

65. *The New York Times*, August 5, 1940.

66. Ibid., August 11, 1940. The other signatories were Charles C. Burlingham, Thomas D. Thacher, and George Rublee.

67. Acheson to Philip Goodhart, quoted in Goodhart, *Fifty Ships* 162. The text of Acheson's letter is reprinted in Appendix A of Goodhart.

68. Stimson diary (MS), August 12, 1940.

69. Ibid., August 15, 1940.

70. Matthew 26:63, quoted in Peters, *Five Days* 165–166.

71. *The New York Times,* August 18, 1940.

72. 39 Ops. Atty. Gen. 484 (1940). The text of Jackson's Opinion is most easily accessible in 9 *Public Papers and Addresses* 394–405 (August 27, 1940).

73. The text of the Hull-Lothian agreement, actually, an exchange of letters between the two, September 2, 1940, is ibid. 392–394.

74. Goodhart, *Fifty Ships* 192–193. For a list of the vessels provided, see Arnold Hague, *Destroyers for Britain: A History of Fifty Town Class Ships Transferred from the United States to Great Britain in 1940 passim* (Annapolis, Md.: Naval Institute Press, 1990).

75. 677th Press Conference, September 3, 1940, 9 *Public Papers and Addresses* 375–390.

76. Churchill, *Their Finest Hour* 408–409.

77. *The New York Times,* September 4, 1940.

78. Under the rule expounded by Justice Sutherland, speaking for a unanimous Court in *Frothingham v. Mellon,* 262 U.S. 447 (1923), an individual lacks standing to sue the federal government over a constitutional issue unless he or she has been seriously injured by the governmental action complained of. An individual taxpayer's injury is "so remote, fluctuating and uncertain, that no basis is afforded for an appeal to the preventive powers of a court of equity." Sutherland said that if every taxpayer could bring suit, every government policy would be challenged in the courts and the Supreme Court would become the ultimate arbiter of all government policy: "an authority which plainly we do not possess." (Cf. *Flast v. Cohen,* 392 U.S. 83 (1968)).

79. *The Gallup Poll* 239, 242. September 3, 1940, reflecting interviews conducted August 24–29; September 20, 1940, reflecting interviews September 5–10, 1940.

80. Leuchtenburg, *Franklin D. Roosevelt* 320.

81. Burns, *Roosevelt: The Lion and the Fox* 442.

82. Perkins, *The Roosevelt I Knew* 117. Secretary Perkins reported receiving hundreds of telegrams afterward, more than half from Republican women, complaining about Willkie's remark.

83. Ted Morgan, *FDR: A Biography* 533 (New York: Simon & Schuster, 1985).

84. The rumors of Welles's behavior eventually filtered back to the Oval Office, and on January 3, 1941, FDR ordered J. Edgar Hoover to conduct "a full and thorough investigation." The FBI deployed its top agents, and on January 29, 1941, Hoover reported to Roosevelt that the accusations were true. No further action was taken until August 1943, when Hull used the incident to force Welles's resignation. Hoover memorandum, January 30, 1941, Sumner Welles Federal Bureau of Investigation O.C. File, quoted in Irwin F. Gellman, *Secret*

Affairs: FDR, Cordell Hull, and Sumner Welles 237 (New York: Enigma Books, 1995). Gellman treats the Hull-Welles relationship with great insight and perception.

85. Joseph Barnes, *Willkie: The Events He Was Part of, the Ideas He Fought For* 156 (New York: Simon & Schuster, 1952).
86. Quoted in Steve Neal, *Dark Horse: A Biography of Wendell Willkie* 29 (New York: Doubleday, 1984).
87. Ibid. 50.
88. FDR's comment was to Lowell Mellett, a presidential aide, and was recorded on the primitive recording system David Sarnoff had installed in the Oval Office for Roosevelt. FDR Tapes, FDRL.
89. Quoted in Neal, *Dark Horse* 144. The film *State of the Union,* starring Spencer Tracy and Katharine Hepburn, is a takeoff on the Willkie campaign, and Hepburn, the candidate's estranged wife, travels with him on the campaign trail.
90. Ibid. 43.
91. Peters, *Five Days* 175.
92. 1940 *The Gallup Poll* 244–245.
93. Quoted in Morgan, *FDR* 540.
94. Ibid.
95. Quoted in Freidel, *A Rendezvous with Destiny* 354.
96. Burns, *The Lion and the Fox* 443.
97. Barnes, *Willkie* 226.
98. Burns, *The Lion and the Fox* 445.
99. 1940 *The Gallup Poll* 247.
100. Ickes, 3 *Secret Diaries* 352.
101. 9 *Public Papers and Addresses* 481.
102. Address at Philadelphia, October 23, 1940. Ibid. 485–495.
103. Burns, *The Lion and the Fox* 447.
104. 9 *Public Papers and Addresses* 488.
105. Address at Madison Square Garden, October 28, 1940. Ibid. 490–510.
106. Address at Boston, Massachusetts, October 30, 1940. Ibid. 514–524.
107. Quoted in Freidel, *Rendezvous with Destiny* 355.
108. Rosenman, *Working with Roosevelt* 242.
109. Ibid. 249.
110. Address at Cleveland, Ohio, October 2, 1940. 9 *Public Papers and Addresses* 544–553.
111. Gallup Poll, November 4, 1940. *The Gallup Poll* 249–250.
112. In 1908 voting turnout was 65.4 percent. Note that American turnout figures are based on the entire voting-age population. In Europe, Canada, and Australia turnout figures are given as a proportion of the registered voters. That explains why turnout figures in those countries are inevitably higher. U.S. Bureau of the Census, *Historical Statistics of the United States* 1071–1072 (Washington, D.C.: U.S. Government Printing Office, 1975).

113. One of the best analyses of the 1940 election remains Samuel Lubell's classic *The Future of American Politics* 51–57 (New York: Harper & Row, 1952).

114. Perkins, *The Roosevelt I Knew* 118.

TWENTY-TWO | Arsenal of Democracy

The epigraph is from FDR's fireside chat, December 29, 1940. 9 *Public Papers and Addresses of Franklin D. Roosevelt* 633–644, Samuel I. Rosenman, ed. (New York: Macmillan, 1941).

1. James MacGregor Burns, *Roosevelt: The Soldier of Freedom* 22 (New York: Harcourt Brace Jovanovich, 1970).

2. WSC to FDR, November 6, 1940, quoted in *Roosevelt and Churchill: Their Secret Wartime Correspondence* 119–120, Francis L. Loewenheim, Harold D. Langley, and Manfred Jonas, eds. (New York: E. P. Dutton, 1975).

3. David M. Kennedy, *Freedom from Fear* 465 (New York: Oxford University Press, 1999).

4. WSC to FDR, November 6, 1940, quoted in *Roosevelt and Churchill* 119.

5. Martin Gilbert, *Churchill: A Life* 679–681 (New York: Henry Holt, 1991); Kennedy, *Freedom from Fear* 632.

6. Roy Jenkins, *Churchill: A Biography* 631n (New York: Farrar, Straus and Giroux, 2001).

7. 16 *Complete Presidential Press Conferences of Franklin D. Roosevelt* 324 (New York: Da Capo Press, 1972); 1 *The Memoirs of Cordell Hull* 871–873 (New York: Macmillan, 1948).

8. William L. Langer and S. Everett Gleason, *Undeclared War* 229 (New York: Harper & Row, 1952). Also see John Morton Blum, 2 *From the Morgenthau Diaries* 201–203 (Boston: Houghton Mifflin, 1965).

9. Robert E. Sherwood, *Roosevelt and Hopkins* 222 (New York: Harper & Brothers, 1948).

10. Ibid. 224.

11. Winston S. Churchill, *Their Finest Hour* 558 (Boston: Houghton Mifflin, 1949); Kennedy, *Freedom from Fear* 467.

12. The full text of Churchill's December 8 message together with earlier drafts is in 1 *Churchill and Roosevelt: The Complete Correspondence* 89–109, Warren F. Kimball, ed. (Princeton, N.J.: Princeton University Press, 1984). Also see Churchill, *Their Finest Hour* 558–567. An abbreviated version appears in *Roosevelt and Churchill* 122–126.

13. Churchill, *Their Finest Hour* 567.

14. Sherwood, *Roosevelt and Hopkins* 224.

15. Conrad Black, *Franklin Delano Roosevelt* 605 (New York: PublicAffairs, 2003).

16. Sherwood, *Roosevelt and Hopkins* 225.

17. Blum, 2 *From the Morgenthau Diaries* 208.

18. A useful summary of FDR's actions is provided by Warren F. Kimball in *The Most Unsordid Act: Lend-Lease, 1939–1941* 119–125 (Baltimore, Md.: Johns Hopkins University Press, 1969).

19. Press Conference, December 17, 1940. 16 *Complete Presidential Press Conferences* 350–355.

20. Churchill, *Their Finest Hour* 569.

21. FDR, "Fireside Chat," December 29, 1940, 9 *Public Papers and Addresses* 633–644.

22. Black, *Franklin Delano Roosevelt* 607.

23. 9 *Public Papers and Addresses* 633–644 (emphasis added).

24. Samuel I. Rosenman, *Working with Roosevelt* 262 (New York: Harper & Brothers, 1952); also see Sherwood, *Roosevelt and Hopkins* 227.

25. Jon Meacham, *Franklin and Winston: An Intimate Portrait of an Epic Relationship* 79 (New York: Random House, 2003).

26. Langer and Gleason, *The Undeclared War* 249; *The Gallup Poll* 262 (interviewing dates January 11–16, 1941).

27. 1 *Churchill and Roosevelt* 120.

28. Annual Message, January 6, 1941, 9 *Public Papers and Addresses* 663–672.

29. Sherwood, *Roosevelt and Hopkins* 231.

30. Rosenman, *Working with Roosevelt* 262–263.

31. Sherwood, *Roosevelt and Hopkins* 233–234.

32. James Roosevelt and Sidney Shalett, *Affectionately, F.D.R.* 325 (New York: Harcourt, Brace & Company, 1959).

33. Sherwood, *Roosevelt and Hopkins* 2–3.

34. 1 *Churchill and Roosevelt* 131. On January 28, 1941, Churchill wrote FDR, "I received Willkie yesterday and was deeply moved by the verse of Longfellow's which you quoted. I shall have it framed as a souvenir of these tremendous days as a mark of our friendly relations." Ibid. 134.

35. Kimball, *Most Unsordid Act* 77–104; Kennedy, *Freedom from Fear* 472–473; Steve Neal, *Dark Horse: A Biography of Wendell Willkie* 187 (New York: Doubleday, 1984).

36. A January 27, 1941, Gallup Poll indicated FDR enjoyed a 71 percent approval rating. On Lend-Lease, respondents were 68 percent in favor on January 22; 69 percent in favor on February 10; 56 percent in favor on February 28; and 76 percent in favor on March 10. George H. Gallup, *The Gallup Poll: Public Opinion, 1935–1971* 262–268 (New York: Random House, 1972).

37. Neal, *Dark Horse* 203–206. Also see *The New York Times*, February 12, 1941.

38. Annual Address to the White House Correspondents Association, March 15, 1941, 10 *Public Papers and Addresses* 63.

39. Winston S. Churchill, *The Grand Alliance* 123–139 (Boston: Houghton Mifflin, 1951).

40. 10 *Public Papers and Addresses* 96–98.

41. FDR to WSC, April 11, 1941, 1 *Churchill & Roosevelt* 166.

42. 738th Press Conference, April 25, 1941, 10 *Public Papers and Addresses* 133–135. An April 23 Gallup Poll indicated that only 41 percent of Americans favored convoying British ships, while 50 percent were opposed. *The Gallup Poll* 275.

43. Gallup Polls, April 7, 18, 23, 28, 1941. Ibid. 273–276.

44. Blum, 2 *From the Morgenthau Diaries* 254. "The President said that public opinion was not yet ready for the United States to convoy ships," Morgenthau wrote after an April 2 conversation with FDR. Ibid. 251.

45. Quoted in Frank Freidel, *Franklin D. Roosevelt: A Rendezvous with Destiny* 370 (Boston: Little, Brown, 1990).

46. George VI to FDR, June 3, 1941, FDRL. "I often think of those talks we had at Hyde Park," wrote the King. "After so many years of anxiety, when what we wanted to happen seemed so far from realisation, it is wonderful to feel that at last our two great countries are getting together for the future betterment of the world. . . . My prime minister, Mr. Churchill, is indefatigable at his work. He is a great man, and has at last come into his own as leader of his country in this fateful time in her history. I have every confidence in him."

   King George, who wrote in beautiful script, asked to write to FDR directly. "So many communications between Heads of State have to go through 'official channels.' " The King signed himself "Believe me Yours very sincerely George R.I. [*Rex Imperator*]."

47. Harold L. Ickes, 3 *The Secret Diaries of Harold L. Ickes* 523 (New York: Simon & Schuster, 1955). After cabinet Stimson lamented, "because the President shows evidence of waiting for the accidental shot of some irresponsible captain on either side to be the occasion of his going to war." Stimson diary (MS), May 23, 1941.

48. For a list of British ships lost in the American patrol zone, see WSC to FDR, May 23, 1941, 1 *Churchill & Roosevelt* 195.

49. WSC to FDR, May 3, 1941, ibid. 181–182.

50. FDR to WSC, May 10, 1941, ibid. 184–185.

51. Berle diaries (MS), May 26, 1941, FDRL.

52. "Fireside Chat Announcing Unlimited National Emergency," May 27, 1941, 10 *Public Papers and Addresses* 181–194. The text of the president's proclamation (No. 2487) is in ibid. 194–195.

53. FDR to WSC, May 27, 1941, 1 *Churchill & Roosevelt* 196–197. "Pray accept my heartfelt thanks," Churchill replied. "It was very kind of you to let me know beforehand of the great advance you found it possible to make." WSC to FDR, May 28, 1941, ibid. 198–199.

54. Sherwood, *Roosevelt and Hopkins* 298.

55. Gallup Poll, June 15, 1941 (polling dates June 9–14), *The Gallup Poll* 284. The opposition to war still ran strong. A similar Gallup Poll published on June 20 reported 56 percent of Americans still favored a national referendum before troops were sent overseas. Ibid. 285.

56. *New York Herald Tribune,* May 29, 1941.

57. Jervis Anderson, *A. Philip Randolph: A Biographical Portrait* 256–258 (New York: Harcourt Brace Jovanovich, 1973).

58. *Amsterdam News,* June 27, 1941.

59. Doris Kearns Goodwin, *No Ordinary Time* 242 (New York: Simon & Schuster, 1994).

60. Ibid. 245.

61. Last Will and Testament of Franklin D. Roosevelt, November 12, 1941, FDRL.

62. James Roosevelt, *My Parents: A Differing View* 108 (Chicago: Playboy Press, 1976).

63. Williamson Murray and Allan B. Millett, *A War to Be Won* 120–123 (Cambridge, Mass.: Harvard University Press, 2000).

64. 6 *Winston S. Churchill: His Complete Speeches* 6427–6431, Robert Rhodes James, ed. (London: Chelsea House, 1974).

65. 3 *Documents on American Foreign Relations* 364–365 (New York: World Peace Foundation, 1942).

66. Press Conference 750, June 24, 1941, 17 *Complete Presidential Press Conferences* 408–411.

67. Black, *Franklin Delano Roosevelt* 640.

68. Langer and Gleason, *Undeclared War* 537–543.

69. Quoted in Burns, *Soldier of Freedom* 115.

70. Gallup Poll, July 14, 1941, *The Gallup Poll* 288.

71. FDR to Lend-Lease Administrator, Lend-Lease to Russia, November 7, 1941, 10 *Public Papers and Addresses* 481. Also see Warren F. Kimball, *The Juggler: Franklin Roosevelt as Wartime Statesman* 37 (Princeton, N.J.: Princeton University Press, 1991).

72. Burns, *Soldier of Freedom* 105.

73. Morgenthau diaries (MS), February 17, 1941, FDRL.

74. Churchill, *Grand Alliance* 429.

75. Theodore A. Wilson, *The First Summit: Roosevelt and Churchill at Placentia Bay, 1941* 61–67 (Boston: Houghton Mifflin, 1969).

76. Michael F. Reilly, as told to William J. Slocum, in *Reilly of the White House* 120 (New York: Simon & Schuster, 1947).

77. Ibid. 120.

78. Elliott Roosevelt, *As He Saw It* 25 (New York: Duell, Sloan & Pearce, 1946).

79. Geoffrey C. Ward, *Closest Companion: The Unknown Story of the Intimate Friendship Between Franklin Roosevelt and Margaret Suckley* 141 (Boston: Houghton Mifflin, 1995).

80. Churchill, *Grand Alliance* 663.

81. Sherwood, *Roosevelt and Hopkins* 363.

82. Ibid. 241.

83. Churchill, *Grand Alliance* 432.

84. Black, *Franklin Delano Roosevelt* 653.

85. Elliott Roosevelt, *As He Saw It* 33.

86. Kennedy, *Freedom from Fear* 496; Gilbert, *Winston S. Churchill* 1173. Also see Robert Dallek, *Franklin D. Roosevelt and American Foreign Policy, 1932–1945* 285 (New York: Oxford University Press, 1979).

87. War cabinet minutes, August 19, 1941, quoted in Joseph P. Lash, *Roosevelt and Churchill, 1931–1941* 402 (New York: W. W. Norton, 1976).

88. Wilson, *First Summit* 210–211. For text, see 1 *Foreign Relations of the United States, 1941* 822–823 (Washington, D.C.: U.S. Government Printing Office, 1948). Also see Maurice Matloff and Edwin M. Snell, *Strategic Planning for Coalition Warfare, 1941–1942* 53–62 (Washington, D.C.: U.S. Government Printing Office, 1953). For the joint message to Stalin, see 10 *Public Papers and Addresses* 317–319.

89. For the text of the Atlantic Charter, see *Foreign Relations of the United States, 1941* 367–369. Also see 10 *Public Papers and Addresses* 314–317.

90. Churchill, *Grand Alliance* 444.

91. FDR, Message to Congress, July 21, 1941, "Extension of Selective Service," 10 *Public Papers and Addresses* 272–277.

92. Gallup Poll, August 6, 1941, *The Gallup Poll* 291–292.

93. D. B. Hardeman and Donald C. Bacon, *Rayburn: A Biography* 262–270 (Austin: Texas Monthly Press, 1987). For the House roll call, see *The New York Times*, August 13, 1941. The Senate roll calls are in ibid., August 8, August 15, 1941.

94. "Fireside Chat," September 11, 1941, 10 *Public Papers and Addresses* 384–392.

95. Kennedy, *Freedom from Fear* 497–498.

96. The advice of the Catholic prelates is in an August 25, 1941, letter from Sumner Welles to FDR. Also see Myron C. Taylor to FDR, August 30, 1941, FDRL.

97. FDR to Pius XII, September 3, 1941, in *Wartime Correspondence Between President Roosevelt and Pope Pius XII* 61–62, Myron C. Taylor, ed. (New York: Macmillan, 1947).

98. Pius XII to FDR, September 20, 1941, ibid. 63–64.

99. Paragraph 24, *Divini redemptoris,* Encyclical of Pope Pius XI on Atheistic Communism.

100. Langer and Gleason, *Undeclared War* 793–797.

101. Goodwin, *No Ordinary Time* 270–273.

102. Reilly and Slocum, *Reilly of the White House* 83–85.

103. Geoffrey C. Ward, *A First-Class Temperament: The Emergence of Franklin Roosevelt* 5–9 (New York: Harper & Row, 1989).

TWENTY-THREE | Day of Infamy

The epigraph is from FDR's address to a Joint Session of Congress, December 8, 1941, requesting a declaration of war against Japan. 10 *Public Papers and Addresses of Franklin D. Roosevelt* 514–515, Samuel I. Rosenman, ed. (New York: Harper & Brothers, 1950).

1. Marshall, memorandum to the President, April 24, 1941, in U.S. Congress, 79th Cong., 2d Sess., 15 *Hearings Before the Joint Committee on the Investigation of the Pearl Harbor Attack* 1635 (Washington, D.C.: U.S. Government Printing Office, 1946). In Marshall's words, "[E]nemy carriers, naval escorts and transports will begin to come under attack at a distance of approximately 750 miles. This attack will increase in intensity until when within 200 miles of the objective, the enemy forces will be subject to attack by all types of bombardment closely supported by our most modern pursuit [planes]."

2. Grant to Adam Badeau, August 1, August 25, 1879, quoted in Badeau, *Grant in Peace: From Appomattox to Mount McGregor* 517–519 (Hartford, Conn.: Scranton, 1887). Grant's reference to twelve years pertains to the overthrow of Japanese feudalism and the Meiji Restoration in 1868.

3. Ibid. 319–321. Also see Jean Edward Smith, *Grant* 612–615 (New York: Simon & Schuster, 2001).

4. David Kennedy, *Freedom from Fear* 500–501 (New York: Oxford University Press, 1999).

5. TR received the Nobel Peace Prize for his efforts. For the text of the Treaty of Portsmouth, August 23, 1905, see 2 *Major Peace Treaties in Modern History, 1648–1967* 1149–1155, Fred L. Israel, ed. (New York: Chelsea House, 1967).

6. The Japanese protest note of May 9, 1913, pertaining to California's land statute was summarily rejected by President Wilson, precipitating a brief war scare (see chapter 6). In 1920 California enacted additional legislation denying Japanese the right to lease agricultural land. More than a dozen states followed California's example. The statutes were upheld by the U.S. Supreme Court in *Terrance v. Thompson*, 263 U.S. 197 (1923).

   Wilson's action at Versailles is more shameful. When on April 11, 1919, the Japanese delegation sought to amend the preamble to the League of Nations Covenant to include a reference to racial equality, a majority of delegations voted in favor. Wilson, who was presiding, ruled the amendment out of order because of the strong opposition it faced. His dubious holding was not appealed by the Japanese. Margaret Macmillan, *Paris 1919* 316–321. Also see David Hunter Miller, 2 *Drafting of the Covenant* 387–393 (New York: G. P. Putnam's Sons, 1928).

   Section 26 of the Immigration Act of 1924, 43 *U.S. Statutes at Large* 153–169, which excluded "aliens not eligible for citizenship" from admission to the United States, was aimed exclusively at the Japanese, since all other Orientals had been excluded by prior legislation. The provision was enacted over the vigorous objection of Secretary of State Charles Evans Hughes.

7. Samuel Flagg Bemis, the late dean of American diplomatic historians, wrote that the Root-Takahira agreement "suggests President [Theodore] Roosevelt was preparing to give Japan a free hand in Manchuria as he had done already in Korea. He had already come to feel that the Philippines were the 'Achilles heel' of the United States, and that the United States could not fight Japan over Manchuria." Bemis, *A Diplomatic History of the United States* 495–496 (New

York: Holt, Rinehart, and Winston, 1963). Elihu Root was TR's secretary of state; Kogoro Takahira was Japan's ambassador in Washington. For the exchange of notes that constitute the agreement, November 30, 1908, see *Foreign Relations of the United States, 1908* 511–512 (Washington, D.C.: U.S. Government Printing Office, 1912). Also see Thomas A. Bailey, "The Root-Takahira Agreement," 9 *Pacific Historical Review* 19–35 (1940).

8. Quoted in Robert H. Ferrell, *American Diplomacy: A History* 540 (New York: W. W. Norton, 1975).

9. Louise Young, *Japan's Total Empire: Manchuria and the Culture of Wartime Imperialism* 214–215 (Berkeley: University of California Press, 1998). I have converted yen to dollars at 3.5 to 1.

10. Raymond Moley, *Seven Years After* 95 (New York: Harper & Brothers, 1939).

11. Quoted in Kennedy, *Freedom from Fear* 501.

12. Herbert Feis, *The Road to Pearl Harbor* 76–87 (Princeton, N.J.: Princeton University Press, 1950).

13. Kennedy, *Freedom from Fear* 504.

14. Quoted in William E. Leuchtenburg, *Franklin D. Roosevelt and the New Deal* 308 (New York: Harper & Row, 1963).

15. Fred L. Israel, ed., *The War Diary of Breckinridge Long* 140 (Lincoln: University of Nebraska Press, 1966).

16. William L. Langer and S. Everett Gleason, *The Undeclared War, 1940–1941* 20–21 (New York: Harper & Row, 1953). The text of the president's order is in *Foreign Relations of the United States 1940, 2 Japan* 222 ff. (Washington, D.C.: U.S. Government Printing Office, 1946).

17. Kennedy, *Freedom from Fear* 506.

18. Japanese foreign minister Yosuke Matsuoka made it explicit that the pact was aimed at the United States. "It is the United States that is encouraging the Chungking Government," he told his cabinet colleagues. "Should a solid coalition come to exist between Japan, Germany, and Italy, it will become the most effective expedient to restrain the United States." *Tokyo War Crimes Documents*, No. 1259. For the text of the Tripartite Pact, see 3 *Documents on American Foreign Relations* 304–305 (New York: World Peace Foundation, 1942).

19. WSC to FDR, October 4, 1940, 1 *Roosevelt & Churchill: The Complete Correspondence* 74–75, Warren F. Kimball, ed. (Princeton, N.J.: Princeton University Press, 1984).

20. Mark S. Watson, *Chief of Staff: Prewar Plans and Preparations* 117 (Washington, D.C.: U.S. Government Printing Office, 1950).

21. John Morton Blum, 2 *From the Morgenthau Diaries* 374–375 (Boston: Houghton Mifflin, 1965). Roosevelt named Senator James Byrnes of South Carolina to replace McReynolds.

22. Grew to Secretary of State, May 13, 1941, *Foreign Relations of the United States, 1941* 4 *The Far East* 187–188 (Washington, D.C.: U.S. Government Printing Office, 1956).

23. Cordell Hull, 1 *Memoirs* 723–725 (New York: Macmillan, 1948). Also see Waldo Heinrichs, *Threshold of War: Franklin D. Roosevelt and America's Entry into World War II* 49–50 (New York: Oxford University Press, 1988).

24. Joseph C. Grew, *Ten Years in Japan* 350–351 (New York: Simon & Schuster, 1944; Frank Freidel, *Franklin D. Roosevelt: Rendezvous with Destiny* 380–381 (Boston: Little, Brown, 1990).

25. Roosevelt and Nomura corresponded occasionally during the interwar period, the latter always congratulating FDR on his electoral victories and the president always responding. On April 6, 1937, Roosevelt wrote, "As I have often told you, I hope the day will come when I can visit Japan. I have much interest in the great accomplishments of the Japanese people and I should much like to see many of my Japanese friends again." FDRL.

    For Secretary Hull's *aide-mémoire* of the Roosevelt-Nomura meeting, see *Foreign Relations of the United States, 1941,* 2 *Japan* 387–389 (Washington, D.C.: U.S. Government Printing Office, 1955).

26. Hull, 2 *Memoirs* 987.

27. Kennedy, *Freedom from Fear* 507.

28. Hosoya Chihiro, "The Japanese-Soviet Neutrality Pact," in J. W. Morley, ed., *The Fateful Choice: Japan's Advance into Southeast Asia, 1939–1941* 97 (New York: Columbia University Press, 1980).

29. Langer and Gleason, *Undeclared War* 627 and the Tokyo War Crimes Documents cited therein.

30. Otto Preston Chaney, Jr., *Zhukov* 57 (Norman: University of Oklahoma Press, 1971).

31. Japanese intelligence estimates counted thirty Russian divisions in the Far East versus the Kwantung Army's twelve, and 2,800 planes versus Japan's 800. Heinrichs, *Threshold of War* 120.

32. Harold L. Ickes, 3 *The Secret Diary of Harold L. Ickes* 567 (New York: Simon & Schuster, 1955).

33. "Konoye Memoirs," in 20 *Pearl Harbor Attack* 4018–4019. Also see "Tojo Memorandum," in *Tokyo War Crimes Documents* 36254–36258.

34. Blum, 2 *Morgenthau Diaries* 377. Stimson called FDR's statement "the same old rot." Handwritten notation on Robert Patterson's memorandum of the cabinet meeting, cited in James MacGregor Burns, *Roosevelt: The Soldier of Freedom, 1940–1945* 109–110 (New York: Harcourt Brace Jovanovich, 1970).

35. 5 *Pearl Harbor Attack* 2382–2384. Also see Herbert Feis, *Road to Pearl Harbor* 231–232.

36. Memo, Chief of Staff to Secretary of War, May 20, 1941, cited in Watson, *Chief of Staff: Prewar Plans and Operations* 347.

37. Ickes, 3 *Secret Diary* 588.

38. Blum, 2 *Morgenthau Diaries* 378–379. Also see Ickes, 3 *Secret Diary* 588.

39. FDR, Extemporaneous remarks to the Volunteer Participation Committee of the Office of Civilian Defense, July 24, 1941. 10 *Public Papers and Addresses* 277–281.

40. Executive Order 8832, July 21, 1941, ibid. 281–283.

41. Mark S. Watson, *Chief of Staff: Prewar Plans and Preparations* 434–438; William Manchester, *American Caesar: Douglas MacArthur, 1880–1964* 188–189 (Boston: Little, Brown, 1978); Eric Larrabee, *Commander in Chief: Franklin Delano Roosevelt, His Lieutenants, and Their War* 314–315 (Annapolis, Md.: Naval Institute Press, 1987); Frazier Hunt, *The Untold Story of Douglas MacArthur* 208 (New York: Devin-Adair, 1954); Forrest C. Pogue, 2 *George C. Marshall* 181, 466 (New York: Viking, 1965).

42. Robert Dallek, *Franklin D. Roosevelt and American Foreign Policy, 1932–1945* 300 (New York: Oxford University Press, 1979).

43. Quoted in Scott D. Sagan, "The Origins of the Pacific War," in *The Origin and Prevention of Major Wars* 336, Robert I. Rotberg and Theodore K. Rabb, eds. (New York: Cambridge University Press, 1989).

44. Dean Acheson, *Present at the Creation: My Years in the State Department* 26 (New York: W. W. Norton, 1969). Robert L. Beisner's well-researched *Dean Acheson: A Life in the Cold War* (New York: Oxford University Press, 2006) deals primarily with the postwar period. His brief treatment of Acheson as assistant secretary of state under FDR (especially pages 14–15) is consistent with my presentation.

45. Hadley Cantril, "Gallup and Fortune Polls," 5 *Public Opinion Quarterly* 687 (Winter 1941); Dallek, *Franklin D. Roosevelt and American Foreign Policy* 302.

46. Sagan, "Origins of the Pacific War" 336.

47. Quoted in Feis, *Road to Pearl Harbor* 248. Also see Jonathan G. Utley, *Going to War with Japan, 1937–1941* 95–101, 126–133, 151–156 (Knoxville: University of Tennessee Press, 1985).

48. Robert J. C. Butow, *Tojo and the Coming of the War* 245 (Princeton, N.J.: Princeton University Press, 1961).

49. Feis, *Road to Pearl Harbor* 266–267; Heinrichs, *Threshold of War* 184–185; Butow, *Tojo* 259; Gordon W. Prange, *At Dawn We Slept* 261 (New York: Penguin, 1981).

50. Joseph C. Grew, 2 *Turbulent Era: A Diplomatic Record of Forty Years, 1904–1945* 1324–1325 (Boston: Houghton Mifflin, 1952).

51. Joseph C. Grew, *Ten Years in Japan* 423–428 (New York: Simon & Schuster, 1944).

52. Ambassador Grew's memorandum of his conversation with Prime Minister Konoye is reprinted in Grew, 2 *Turbulent Era* 1326–1329.

53. Ibid. 1327. Grew believed the potential intervention of the Emperor added great weight to Konoye's proposal. It was the device used in 1945 to accomplish Japan's surrender and was always the government's ace in the hole in dealing with the military.

54. Ibid. 1333.

55. Waldo H. Heinrichs, *American Ambassador: Joseph C. Grew and the Development of United States Diplomatic Tradition* 347 (Boston: Little, Brown, 1966).

56. Heinrichs, *Threshold of War* 186. In particular, see Grew's September 29, 1941, cable from Tokyo. *Foreign Relations of the United States,* 2 *Japan* 645–650.

57. Conversation between Stimson and Morgenthau, September 18, 1941, in 442 *Morgenthau Diaries* (MS) 45 ff. For Ickes view, see 3 *Secret Diary* 610–611.

58. Memo to Hull, August 28, 1941, 20 *Pearl Harbor Attack* 4406 ff.

59. Hull, 2 *Memoirs* 1024.

60. Ibid. 1024–1025.

61. Numerous scholars have speculated about the missed opportunity. One of the best analyses is by F. C. Jones in his authoritative account of Japanese expansionism: *Japan's New Order in East Asia: Its Rise and Fall* 182–183 (New York: Cambridge University Press, 1954). Also see Feis, *Road to Pearl Harbor* 274–277.

62. On August 14, 1941, just one month before the attempt on Konoye's life, Baron Hiranuma, the minister for home affairs and an ardent advocate of peace with the United States, was severely injured in an assassination attempt. Grew, 2 *Turbulent Era* 1332.

63. Langer and Gleason, *Undeclared War* 729.

64. FDR to George VI; FDR to Churchill; both letters dated October 15, 2 *F.D.R.: His Personal Letters* 1223–1224, Elliott Roosevelt, ed. (New York: Duell, Sloan and Pearce, 1950).

65. 14 *Pearl Harbor Attack* 1402. Also see Roberta Wohlstetter, *Pearl Harbor: Warning and Decision* 132–133 (Stanford, Calif.: Stanford University Press, 1962).

66. 16 *Pearl Harbor Attack* 2214 ff.; Wohlstetter, *Pearl Harbor* 146–147.

67. War Department to Short and MacArthur, October 20, 1941, quoted in Watson, *Chief of Staff* 496.

68. Grew, *Ten Years in Japan* 470. Grew's long cable of November 3, 1941, is paraphrased in *Foreign Relations of the United States, 2 Japan* 701–704, and reprinted in full in 14 *Pearl Harbor Attack* 1045–1057.

69. Langer and Gleason, *Undeclared War* 852, quoting "Tojo Memorandum," in *Tokyo War Crimes Documents*. Also see Feis, *Road to Pearl Harbor* 293.

70. Togo to Nomura, November 4, 1941, quoted in Feis, *Road to Pearl Harbor* 296.

71. Memo, Chief of Naval Operations and Chief of Staff for the President, November 5, 1941, 14 *Pearl Harbor Attack* 1061–1062.

72. Frances Perkins interview, Columbia Oral History Project, Columbia University.

73. Hull, 2 *Memoirs* 1058.

74. Stimson diary (MS), November 7, 1941, quoted in Freidel, *Rendezvous with Destiny* 397.

75. Heinrichs, *Threshold of War* 200. Also see Langer and Gleason, *Undeclared War* 865–867; Burns, *Roosevelt: Soldier of Freedom* 155.

76. The text of the Japanese proposal ("Plan B") is reprinted in Feis, *Road to Pearl Harbor* 309. Also see *Foreign Relations of the United States, 2 Japan* 755–756.

77. Togo to Nomura, November 4, 1941, 12 *Pearl Harbor Attack* 92–93. Also see Langer and Gleason, *Undeclared War* 856.

78. In his *Memoirs* Hull wrote that acceptance of the Japanese offer would have meant "condonement by the United States of Japan's past aggressions . . . betrayal of China and Russia, and acceptance of the role of silent partner aiding

and abetting Japan in her effort to create a Japanese hegemony over the western Pacific and eastern Asia . . . [The proposals] were of so preposterous a character that no responsible American official could ever have dreamed of accepting them." 2 *Memoirs* 1069–1070.

    For a skeptical assessment of Hull's ex post facto judgment, see Langer and Gleason, *Undeclared War* 880. The Japanese offer was only an interim, stopgap arrangement to provide further time to negotiate a long-term settlement.

79. 14 *Pearl Harbor Attack* 1109. FDR's note is also reprinted in Langer and Gleason, *Undeclared War* 872, and Freidel, *Rendezvous with Destiny* 398. Langer and Gleason date the note earlier than do others.

80. *Foreign Relations of the United States,* 2 *Japan* 739 ff.

81. Ickes, 3 *Secret Diary* 649–650.

82. Gerow to Hull, November 21, 1941, 14 *Pearl Harbor Attack* 1103–1107.

83. Togo to Nomura, November 22, 1941, 12 *Pearl Harbor Attack* 163–165.

84. The classic revisionist argument is Charles A. Beard's *President Roosevelt and the Coming of the War,* especially 517–569 (New Haven, Conn.: Yale University Press, 1948). Also see Rear Admiral Edwin T. Layton, *And I Was There: Pearl Harbor and Midway, Breaking the Secrets* 198–207 (New York: William Morrow, 1985); William Henry Chamberlain, *America's Second Crusade* 167–168 (Chicago: Henry Regnery, 1950).

85. Robert Dallek, *Franklin D. Roosevelt and American Foreign Policy* 307–308; Robert H. Ferrell, *American Diplomacy* 572–573; Gordon W. Prange, *At Dawn We Slept* 369; Thomas A. Bailey, *A Diplomatic History of the United States* 737 (New York: Appleton-Century-Crofts, 1964); Freidel, *Rendezvous with Destiny* 400; Gordon W. Prange, Donald M. Goldstein, and Katherine V. Dillon, *Pearl Harbor: The Verdict of History* 177–193 (New York: Penguin Books, 1991).

86. For Hull's account, see Hull, 2 *Memoirs* 1081–1082 and the memorandum he dictated pertaining thereto at 14 *Pearl Harbor Attack* 1176–1177. Colonel Stimson's account is in his diary entry of November 26, 1941. The most sustained critique of the accounts provided by Hull and Stimson is not in the works of radical and revisionist historians but in Langer and Gleason, *Undeclared War* 885 ff.—a work sponsored by the Council on Foreign Relations.

87. Ibid. 893.

88. WSC to FDR, November 26, 1941, 1 *Churchill & Roosevelt* 277–278.

89. Ickes, 3 *Secret Diary* 655. For Morgenthau's opposition to negotiating with Japan, see Blum, 2 *Morgenthau Diaries* 389–391.

90. On November 24, 1941, Admiral Stark warned Navy commanders in the Pacific, "There are very doubtful chances of a favorable outcome of negotiations with Japan. This situation coupled with statements of [Japanese] government and movement of their naval and military forces indicate in our opinion that a surprise aggressive movement in any direction, including an attack on the Philippines or Guam, is a possibility. . . . Utmost secrecy is necessary in order not to complicate an already tense situation or precipitate Japanese action." Stark to

CinC Asiatic Fleet and CinC Pacific Fleet, November 24, 1941, 14 *Pearl Harbor Attack* 1405.

91. Stimson diary (MS), November 25, 1941.

92. Ibid.

93. The text of Hull's "Ten Point Offer" is in *Foreign Relations of the United States,* 2 *Japan* 766–770. Also see Langer and Gleason, *Undeclared War* 896–897.

94. Freidel, *Rendezvous with Destiny* 400.

95. Stimson diary (MS), November 27, 1941; 11 *Pearl Harbor Attack* 5422 ff. When Hull met with his advisers on November 27, his hard-line stance was roundly applauded. Stanley Hornbeck, Hull's senior Far East specialist, urged that the president tell the Army and Navy what to do rather than asking them. In a widely quoted memorandum of that date Hornbeck maintained that Japan would advance into Thailand or Yunnan but would avoid conflict with the United States. He bet 5 to 1 there would not be war by December 15; 3 to 1 there would be no war by January 15; and even money there would be no war by March 1. Such was the advice Hull received from his senior specialist. The Hornbeck memorandum is at 20 *Pearl Harbor Attack* 4487.

96. Most scholars are incredulous that Hull acted, apparently with FDR's approval, without informing the War Department and the Navy beforehand. "It was both bad strategy and careless administrative procedure for the civilian leaders of the Government to make the momentous decisions of November 26, 1941, without formal consultation with the responsible military leaders. The argument that by this date no practical difference could have been anticipated does not alter the seriousness of this breach of fundamental rules for achieving sound decisions of national security policy." Langer and Gleason, *Undeclared War* 900.

97. CNO to CinC Pac and CinC AF, November 27, 1941, 14 *Pearl Harbor Attack* 1406.

98. Marshall to CG American forces in the Far East, ibid.

99. Julius W. Pratt, 2 *Cordell Hull* 515 (New York: Cooper Square Publishers, 1964).

100. Kennedy, *Freedom from Fear* 515.

101. Shigenori Togo, testimony, *Tokyo War Crimes Documents,* Document 2927.

102. Nobutake Ike, *Japan's Decision for War: Records of the 1941 Policy Conferences* 265, 283 (Stanford, Calif.: Stanford University Press, 1967).

103. SRN 115376, CinC Combined Fleet to Combined Fleet, December 2, 1941, 1500 hrs., Record Group 457, NSA, National Archives.

104. Hiroyuki Agawa, *The Reluctant Admiral: Yamamoto and the Imperial Navy* 158 (Tokyo: Shincho Sha, 1966).

105. Gordon W. Prange, interview with Capt. Watanabe, February 12, 1949, cited in Prange, *At Dawn We Slept* 13.

106. Yamamoto to Admiral Koshiro Oikawa, January 7, 1941, quoted in ibid. 16–17.

107. For the attack at Taranto, see Don Newton and A. Cecil Hampshire, *Taranto* (London: W. Kimber, 1959).

108. The average depth at Pearl Harbor was forty feet. "We did not give aerial torpedoes a great deal of consideration for that reason," said Admiral Kimmel. 33

Pearl Harbor Attack 1318. Ironically, the Japanese in their training sessions had been unable to penetrate protective torpedo nets, and their pilots were instructed to confine the Pearl Harbor attack to bombing only if they found the American fleet protected by netting. Prange, *At Dawn We Slept* 321.

109. Ibid. 332–333.
110. Ibid. 387, 373.
111. Yamamoto to Hori, November 11, 1941, ibid. 340. Hori, commanding the submarine fleet, put to sea the next day.
112. Ibid. 472.
113. Ibid. 488.
114. Watson, *Chief of Staff: Prewar Plans and Preparations* 511.
115. Gordon W. Prange with Donald M. Goldstein and Katherine V. Dillon, *Pearl Harbor: The Verdict of History* 460 (New York: Penguin, 1991). Kimmel's remarks were made to Edward M. Morgan, chief counsel for the congressional Pearl Harbor investigation.
116. *Pearl Harbor Report* 150–151. General Lucius D. Clay, then in Washington directing the nation's emergency airport construction program (La Guardia, O'Hare, Los Angeles, National) said much the same. Attending a football game at Griffith Stadium on Sunday, December 7, with Commerce Secretary Jesse Jones, Clay was asked by Secretary Jones about the attack. "I immediately proved my great military expertise because I said, 'The Japs would attack Guam or the Philippines, but Pearl Harbor is impregnable. I just can't believe they would attack Pearl Harbor.'" Jean Edward Smith, *Lucius D. Clay: An American Life* 96 (New York: Henry Holt, 1990).
117. According to the diary kept by Konoye, Yamamoto added, "I hope you will endeavor to avoid a Japanese-American war." 2 *Report of General MacArthur: Japanese Operations in the Southeast Pacific Area* 33 (Washington, D.C.: U.S. Government Printing Office, 1966).
118. Richard Ketcham, "Yesterday, December 7, 1941," *American Heritage* 54 (November, 1989).
119. Grace Tully, *F.D.R.: My Boss* 255 (New York: Charles Scribner's Sons, 1949).
120. Robert Sherwood, *Roosevelt and Hopkins* 431 (New York: Harper & Brothers, 1948).
121. ER, interview with Professor Henry Graff, FDRL, quoted in Doris Kearns Goodwin, *No Ordinary Life* 289 (New York: Simon & Schuster, 1994).
122. Winston S. Churchill, *The Grand Alliance* 605 (Boston: Houghton Mifflin, 1951).
123. Ibid. 608–609.
124. Tully, *F.D.R.: My Boss* 256. Hopkins's sentence ran, "With confidence in our armed forces—with the unbounded determination of our people—we will gain the inevitable triumph—so help us God." ("The most platitudinous in the speech," according to Hopkins's biographer Robert Sherwood. *Roosevelt and Hopkins* 436.)

125. Sherwood, *Roosevelt and Hopkins* 436–438.

126. Frances Perkins, *The Roosevelt I Knew* 381 (New York: Harper & Row, 1946).

127. Ickes, 3 *Secret Diaries* 662.

128. Frances Perkins interview, Columbia Oral History Project.

129. The congressional delegation was composed of Senate majority leader Alben Barkley and his Republican opposite, Charles McNary; Tom Connally of Texas, chairman of Foreign Relations; Warren Austin of Vermont, the ranking member of Military Affairs; and Hiram Johnson of California. From the House, Speaker Sam Rayburn, Minority Leader Joe Martin, and Majority Leader John McCormack, plus Sol Bloom of New York and Charles Eaton of New Jersey, the chairman and second-ranking member of Foreign Affairs.

130. Stimson diary (MS), December 7, 1941.

131. *American Heritage* 86, November 1989.

132. Francis Biddle, *In Brief Authority* 206 (New York: Doubleday, 1948).

133. Quoted in Prange, *At Dawn We Slept* 559.

134. Alexander Kendrick, *Prime Time: The Life of Edward R. Murrow* 239–240 (Boston: Little, Brown, 1965). That night Murrow paced his hotel room. "It's the biggest story of my life," he told his wife, Janet, "and I can't make up my mind whether it's my duty to tell it, or to forget it." (FDR had not said "off the record.") In the end, Murrow decided Roosevelt had been using him as a sounding board, thinking out loud, in full confidence. Though technically not bound to confidentiality, Murrow felt that in conscience he could not report the details of his meeting with the president.

135. FDR to Congress, December 8, 1941, 10 *Public Papers and Addresses* 514–515.

TWENTY-FOUR | Commander in Chief

The epigraph is from Secretary Stimson's diary entry of December 7, 1941, Stimson Papers, Yale University.

1. Quoted in Hiroyuki Agawa, *The Reluctant Admiral: Yamamoto and the Imperial Navy* 282 (Tokyo: Shincho Sha, 1966).

2. FDR, Fireside Address, December 9, 1941, 10 *Public Papers and Addresses of Franklin D. Roosevelt* 522–530, Samuel I. Rosenman, ed. (New York: Harper & Brothers, 1950).

3. David M. Kennedy, *Freedom from Fear* 527 (New York: Oxford University Press, 1999); Williamson Murray and Allan R. Millett, *A War to Be Won* 180–188 (Cambridge, Mass.: Harvard University Press, 2000).

4. Quoted in John Keegan, *The Second World War* 240 (New York: Viking, 1989).

5. Kennedy, *Freedom from Fear* 566.

6. FDR, Message to Congress, December 11, 1941, 10 *Public Papers and Addresses* 522.

7. WSC to King George VI, December 8, 1941, 3 *Churchill War Papers, 1941* 1585, Martin Gilbert, ed. (New York: W. W. Norton, 1993).

8. Roosevelt's remarks are in two cables drafted but not sent on December 10, 1941. Their contents were conveyed to Churchill in a subsequent telephone conversation that day. For texts, see *Churchill and Roosevelt: The Complete Correspondence* 285–286, Warren F. Kimball, ed. (Princeton, N.J.: Princeton University Press, 1984).

Separately, Lord Halifax, Britain's ambassador in Washington, told Churchill, "He [Roosevelt] was not sure if your coming here might not be rather too strong medicine in the immediate future for some of his public opinion that he still feels he has to educate up to the complete conviction of the oneness of the struggle against both Germany and Japan." Halifax to Churchill, December 9, 1941, Halifax Papers, Cambridge University.

9. WSC to FDR, December 10, 1941, 3 *Churchill & Roosevelt* 284.

10. FDR to WSC, December 10, 1941, ibid. 286–287.

11. David Bercuson and Holger Herwig, *One Christmas in Washington* 125 (New York: Overlook Press, 2005).

12. Doris Kearns Goodwin, interview with Alonzo Fields, cited in *No Ordinary Time* 302 (New York: Simon & Schuster, 1994).

13. Michael Reilly and William J. Slocum, *Reilly of the White House* 125 (New York: Simon & Schuster, 1947).

14. Lillian Rogers Parks, *The Roosevelts: A Family in Turmoil* 99 (Englewood Cliffs, N.J.: Prentice-Hall, 1981). In addition to her father, Elliott, ER's brother Hall died of acute alcoholism on September 25, 1941.

15. Winston S. Churchill, *The Grand Alliance* 608 (Boston: Houghton Mifflin, 1950).

16. Presidential Press Conference 794, December 23, 1941, 18 *Complete Presidential Press Conferences of Franklin D. Roosevelt* 387–388 (New York: Da Capo, 1972).

17. *Newsweek,* January 5, 1942; Alistair Cooke's comment was made to Curtis Roosevelt in October 1993. Quoted in Jon Meacham, *Franklin and Winston* 142–143 (New York: Random House, 2003).

18. 6 *Winston S. Churchill: His Complete Speeches* 6536–6541, Robert Rhodes James, ed. (New York: Chelsea House, 1974).

19. *The Washington Post,* December 27, 1941.

20. In Ottawa on December 30, 1941, Churchill made his famous "some chicken, some neck" speech to the Canadian Parliament, mocking the words of French general Maxime Weygand, who in June 1940 had told his government that "In three weeks England will have her neck wrung like a chicken." "Some chicken!" Churchill told his Canadian listeners. "Some neck!" 6 *Speeches of Winston Churchill* 6541–6547.

At the invitation of Edward Stettinius, Churchill spent five days at Stettinius's Pompano Beach oceanfront estate. He enjoyed splashing naked in the surf, "half submerged in the water like a hippopotamus in a swamp," in the words of his doctor, Lord Moran. *The Struggle for Survival: The Diaries of Lord Moran* 22 (Boston: Houghton Mifflin, 1966).

21. Robert Sherwood, *Roosevelt and Hopkins* 472–473 (New York: Harper & Brothers, 1948); Forrest C. Pogue, 2 *George C. Marshall* 285–287 (New York: Viking, 1966).

22. For firsthand insight into the operation of the Munitions Assignment Board, see the comments of General Lucius D. Clay, the Army's representative, in Jean Edward Smith, *Lucius D. Clay: An American Life* 134–139 (New York: Henry Holt, 1990).

23. The text is most easily accessible in Kenneth S. Davis, *FDR: The War President* 371–372 (New York: Random House, 2000). Also see 11 *Public Papers and Addresses* 3–4.

24. For this comparison I am indebted to Isaiah Berlin, "Mr. Churchill," *Atlantic Monthly* (September 1949).

25. FDR, Address on the State of the Union, January 6, 1942, 11 *Public Papers and Addresses* 32–42.

26. Stimson diary (MS), January 6, 1942. Yale University.

27. Sherwood, *Roosevelt and Hopkins* 273–274.

28. Smith, *Lucius D. Clay* 119–126. The chart Clay prepared for the president is reproduced on page 125. A transcript of my interviews with General Clay, some one thousand pages, is on file at the Columbia Oral History Project at Columbia University. The tapes themselves are at the George C. Marshall Library at VMI in Lexington, Virginia, along with Clay's papers.

    In place of the original 45,000 tanks, Roosevelt accepted the Army's suggestion for 46,523 tracked vehicles (tanks, armored personal carriers, and self-propelled artillery), "of which 24,700 shall be tanks." The president's goal of 60,000 airplanes was reduced by 25 percent.

29. Hoover to Biddle, February 1, 1942, quoted in Greg Robinson, *By Order of the President* 100 (Cambridge, Mass.: Harvard University Press, 2001). Also see Conrad Black, *Franklin Delano Roosevelt* 721–722 (New York: PublicAffairs, 2003). Stilwell's remark was made on December 19, 1941, in Los Angeles. See Richard N. Current, *Secretary Stimson: A Study in Statecraft* 193 (New Brunswick, N.J.: Rutgers University Press, 1942). *Los Angeles Times*, December 8, 1941; January 23, 1942. Francis Biddle, *In Brief Authority* 213 (Westport, Conn.: Greenwood Press, 1962).

30. De Witt to War Department, February 13, 1942, quoted in Carey McWilliams, *Prejudice: Japanese Americans* 109 (Boston: Little, Brown, 1944).

31. Quoted in Goodwin, *No Ordinary Time* 321.

32. Richard Lingeman, *Don't You Know There's a War On?* 337 (New York: G. P. Putnam's Sons, 1970).

33. Peter Irons, *Justice at War* 39–40 (New York: Oxford University Press, 1983).

34. *The New York Times*, January 25, 1942.

35. *New York Herald Tribune*, February 12, 1942.

36. *Times-Herald* (Washington, D.C.), February 16, 1942.

37. Stimson diary (MS), February 10, 1942, Yale University. "The second generation Japanese can only be evacuated as part of a total evacuation, or by frankly trying

to put them out on the ground that their racial characteristics are such that we cannot understand or trust even the citizen Japanese. This latter is the fact but I am afraid it will make a tremendous hole in our constitutional system."

38. Kai Bird, *The Chairman: John J. McCloy and the Making of the American Establishment* 149–150 (New York: Simon & Schuster, 1992).

39. Said De Witt, "The Japanese race is an enemy race and while many second and third generation Japanese born on United States soil have become Americanized, the racial strain is undiluted." De Witt to War Department, February 14, 1942, in Davis, *F.D.R.: The War President* 423n.

40. Quoted in Irons, *Justice at War* 61. Also see Robinson, *By Order of the President* 105; Bird, *The Chairman* 153.

41. Stimson diary (MS), February 11, 1942, Yale University.

42. Stetson Conn, "The Decision to Evacuate the Japanese from the Pacific Coast," 143, in Kent Roberts Greenfield, ed., *Command Decisions* (Washington, D.C.: U.S. Government Printing Office, 1960).

43. Bird, *The Chairman* 154.

44. Biddle, *In Brief Authority* 219.

45. Frank S. Arnold, Michael C. Barth, and Gilah Langer, "Economic Losses of Ethnic Japanese as a Result of Exclusion and Detention, 1942–1946," quoted in Robinson, *By Order of the President* 144.

46. Morgenthau diaries (MS), March 5, 1942, FDRL.

47. Quoted in Goodwin, *No Ordinary Time* 322.

48. Biddle, *In Brief Authority* 219. The case *contra* is argued by Michelle Malkin, *In Defense of Internment* (Chicago: Regnery, 2004).

49. This narrative is based on General Arnold's letter to Judge Rosenman describing the raid in 11 *Public Papers and Addresses* 214–216. For Admiral King's version, see Ernest J. King and Walter Muir Whitehill, *Fleet Admiral King: A Naval Record* 375–376 (New York: W. W. Norton, 1952). Above all, see Quentin Reynolds's elegant *The Amazing Mr. Doolittle* 168–223 (New York: Arno Press, 1953).

50. Roosevelt liked the term so much that he named the presidential Catoctin Mountain retreat Shangri-la (Eisenhower re-christened it "Camp David" in honor of his grandson), and toward the end of the war a Navy carrier was also named *Shangri-la*.

51. Stimson diary (MS), April 18, 1942.

52. Edmund L. Castillo, *Flat-tops: The Story of Aircraft Carriers* 86 (New York: Random House, 1969); Marius B. Jansen, *The Making of Modern Japan* 648 (Cambridge, Mass.: Harvard University Press, 2000).

53. Murray and Millett, *A War to Be Won* 273–278.

54. For Molotov's travel accoutrements, see Eleanor Roosevelt, *This I Remember* 250–251 (New York: Harper & Brothers, 1949). For Molotov's secretaries, see Sherwood, *Roosevelt and Hopkins* 560. "I went in for a moment to talk to him [before going to bed]' " wrote Hopkins, "and he asked that one of the girls he brought over as secretaries be permitted to come [to his room] and that has been arranged."

55. Geoffrey C. Ward, ed., *Closest Companion: The Unknown Story of the Intimate Friendship Between Franklin Roosevelt and Margaret Suckley* 159 (Boston: Houghton Mifflin, 1995).

56. Memorandum of conversation, May 30, 1942, recorded by Professor Samuel H. Cross, in Sherwood, *Roosevelt and Hopkins* 561–563.

57. FDR to Marshall and King, May 6, 1942, FDRL. Quoted in Goodwin, *No Ordinary Time* 344.

58. Cross memorandum, in Sherwood, *Roosevelt and Hopkins* 563.

59. FDR to WSC, May 31, June 6, 1942, 1 *Churchill and Roosevelt: Their Complete Correspondence* 503–504, 508 (Princeton, N.J.: Princeton University Press, 1984). "The Molotov visit went off well," Hopkins wrote Churchill. "I liked him much better than I did in Moscow. Perhaps it was because he wasn't under the influence of 'Uncle Joe.' At any rate, he and the President had very direct and straightforward conferences." Sherwood, *Roosevelt and Hopkins* 580.

60. Winston S. Churchill, *The Hinge of Fate* 338 (Boston: Houghton Mifflin, 1950).

61. William D. Hassett, *Off the Record with F.D.R.* 67 (New Brunswick, N.J.: Rutgers University Press, 1958); Hastings Ismay, *The Memoirs of General Lord Ismay* 256 (New York: Viking, 1960).

62. Stimson diary (MS), June 20, 1942, Yale University. General Marshall said, "We were largely trying to get the President to stand pat on what he had previously agreed to. The President shifted, particularly when Churchill got hold of him. . . . The President was always willing to do any sideshow and Churchill was always prodding him." Forrest C. Pogue, 2 *George C. Marshall* 329 (New York: Viking, 1965).

63. WSC to FDR, June 20, 1942, quoted in *Hinge of Fate* 381–382.

64. WSC to FDR, July 8, 1942, *Churchill & Roosevelt* 520–521.

65. "It looks as if the President is going to jump the traces," Stimson recorded in his diary on June 17, 1942. "He wants to take up the case of GYMNAST [the North African invasion] again, thinking that he can bring additional pressure to save Russia."

66. Mark A. Stoler, *The Politics of the Second Front: American Military Planning and Diplomacy in Coalition Warfare, 1941–1943* 55 (Westport, Conn.: Greenwood, 1977).

67. Quoted in Henry L. Stimson and McGeorge Bundy, *On Active Service in Peace and War* 425 (New York: Harper and Brothers, 1947).

68. FDR to Hopkins, Marshall, and King, July 16, 1942, in Sherwood, *Roosevelt and Hopkins* 603–605.

69. Forrest Pogue interview with General Marshall, November 15, 1956, quoted in Pogue, 2 *Marshall* 330.

70. Stimson diary (MS), September 17, 1942. Marshall said, "A failure [of a cross-channel attack], for which the public has been adequately prepared, could have been accepted. But failure in TORCH would bring only ridicule and loss of confidence." 38th Mtg, CCS, August 28, 1942, quoted in Pogue, 2 *Marshall* 403.

71. WSC to FDR, July 31, 1942, quoted in Churchill, *Hinge of Fate* 450. Also see B. H. Liddell Hart, *History of the Second World War* 312 (London: Cassell, 1970). Marshall chose Eisenhower ahead of 366 general officers who were more senior.

72. FDR to WSC, July 29, 1942, 1 *Churchill & Roosevelt* 545–546.

73. WSC to FDR, August 13, 1942, ibid. 560–562.

74. WSC to FDR, August 18, 1942, ibid. 571–572.

75. Quoted in Liddell Hart, *Second World War* 314.

76. WSC to FDR, August 27, 1942, 1 *Churchill & Roosevelt* 577–579.

77. Marshall's draft (August 29, 1942) is in ibid. 571–582. FDR's cable of August 30, 1942, ibid. 583–584.

78. FDR to WSC, September 4, 1942, ibid. 590–591.

79. WSC to FDR, September 5, 1942, ibid. 591–592.

80. Eisenhower's remark is quoted in Arthur L. Funk, *The Politics of Torch* 100 (Lawrence: University Press of Kansas, 1974).

81. Churchill's rejoinder was September 6. 1 *Churchill & Roosevelt* 592.

82. FDR, Broadcast to the French People, November 7, 1942, 11 *Public Papers and Addresses* 451–452.

83. Roosevelt's letters to the heads of state were delivered by the respective American ambassadors when the invasion commenced. Ibid. 458–459.

84. Franco's reply, November 13, 1942, is in ibid. 459.

85. For details of the attempted German seizure of the fleet and the French response, see Rear Admiral Paul Auphan and Jacques Mordal, *The French Navy in World War II* 255–271 (Annapolis, Md.: United States Naval Institute, 1959).

86. The cross-Channel attack, Eisenhower told the War Department's Major General Thomas T. Handy, "could not possibly be staged before August of 1944, because our original conception of the strength required was too low." Quoted in Forrest Pogue, 3 *George C. Marshall* 31. For the text of the CCS decision, see Churchill, *Hinge of Fate* 692–693.

87. Under Pétain, "Work, Family, Country" replaced the republican motto "Liberty, Equality, Fraternity" at Vichy. As one leading supporter of Pétain said in 1940, "Parliamentary democracy has lost the war. It must disappear and give place to a hierarchical authoritarian regime, national and social." R. Aron, *Histoire de Vichy, 1940–1944* 130 (Paris: Fayard, 1954).

88. Charles de Gaulle, 2 *War Memoirs* 88–89 (New York: Simon & Schuster, 1956).

89. Transcript of Press Conference, January 24, 1943, U.S. Department of State, *Foreign Relations of the United States, Conferences in Washington and Casablanca* 727 (Washington, D.C.: U.S. Government Printing Office, 1968).

90. Ibid. 635, 726–729, 833–837, 847–849; Churchill, *Hinge of Fate* 595–600; Sherwood, *Roosevelt and Hopkins* 695–696. Churchill's message to the war cabinet is in Premier Files, 3, 1972 Public Records Office, London.

91. Paul Kecskemeti, *Strategic Surrender: The Politics of Victory and Defeat* 122 (Stanford, Calif.: Stanford University Press, 1958). Cf., Anne Armstrong, *Uncon-*

ditional Surrender: The Impact of the Casablanca Policy upon World War II 48–50 (New Brunswick, N.J.: Rutgers University Press, 1961).

92. Kenneth Pender, *Adventure in Diplomacy: Our French Dilemma* 152 (New York: Dodd, Mead, 1945). Pender was American vice consul in Marrakech and accompanied Churchill to the airport.

TWENTY-FIVE | D-Day

The epigraph is from FDR's D-Day prayer delivered to the nation June 6, 1944. 13 *Public Papers and Addresses of Franklin D. Roosevelt,* Samuel I. Rosenman, ed. (New York: Harper & Brothers, 1950).

1. FDR to ER, January 29, 1943, FDRL.
2. ER to FDR, January 28, 1943, FDRL.
3. Frankfurter to FDR, *Roosevelt and Frankfurter: Their Correspondence, 1928–1945* 329 Max Freedman, ed. (Boston: Little, Brown, 1967).
4. Quoted in B. H. Liddell Hart, *History of the Second World War* 388 (London: Cassell, 1970).
5. WSC to FDR, March 18, 1943, 2 *Churchill and Roosevelt: The Complete Correspondence* 158, Warren F. Kimball, ed. (Princeton, N.J.: Princeton University Press, 1984).
6. FDR to WSC, March 20, 1943, ibid. 164–165.
7. David Kennedy, *Freedom from Fear* 589 (New York: Oxford University Press, 1999). Also see Letter, President to COMINCH, 18 March 1943, FDRL.
8. John Keegan, *The Second World War* 120 (New York: Viking, 1989).
9. Kennedy, *Freedom from Fear* 590.
10. 7 *Winston S. Churchill: His Complete Speeches, 1897–1963* 6831, Robert Rhodes James, ed. (London: Chelsea House, 1974).
11. Kennedy, *Freedom from Fear* 648–649.
12. Jean Edward Smith, *Lucius D. Clay: An American Life* 116 (New York: Henry Holt, 1990).
13. Ibid. 156–157.
14. Winston S. Churchill, *The Hinge of Fate* 795–796 (Boston: Houghton Mifflin, 1950); Robert Sherwood, *Roosevelt and Hopkins* 729 (New York: Harper & Brothers, 1948).
15. Churchill, *Hinge of Fate* 797; *Winston and Clementine: The Personal Letters of the Churchills* 483, Mary Soames, ed. (Boston: Houghton Mifflin, 1999).
16. Churchill, *Hinge of Fate* 798.
17. WSC to Clementine Churchill, May 28, 1943, in *Personal Letters of the Churchills* 483.
18. James F. Byrnes, *All in One Lifetime* 155 (New York: Harper & Brothers, 1958).
19. 12 *Public Papers and Addresses of Franklin D. Roosevelt* 327, Samuel I. Rosenman, ed. (New York: Harper & Brothers, 1943).
20. FDR to WSC, July 25, 1943, 2 *Churchill & Roosevelt* 347.

21. Press Conference 912, July 30, 1943, 22 *Complete Presidential Press Conferences of Franklin D. Roosevelt* 50 (New York: Da Capo, 1972).

22. WSC to FDR, July 31, 1943, ibid. 369.

23. Eleanor Roosevelt, "My Day," August 16, 1943.

24. Geoffrey Ward, ed., *Closest Companion* 230–231 (Boston: Houghton Mifflin, 1995).

25. Forrest C. Pogue, 3 *George C. Marshall* 261–262 (New York: Viking, 1973); Sherwood, *Roosevelt and Hopkins* 758; Winston S. Churchill, *Closing the Ring* 85 (Boston: Houghton Mifflin, 1951).

26. Frances Perkins interview, Columbia Oral History Project, Columbia University. "PM's sleeping habits have now become quite promiscuous," wrote British Foreign Office Undersecretary Sir Alexander Cadogan. "He talks with President till 2 am and consequently spends a large part of day hurling himself violently in and out of bed, bathing at unsuitable moments and rushing up and down the corridors in his dressing gown." *Diaries of Sir Alexander Cadogan, 1938–1945* 559, David Dilks, ed. (New York: Putnam, 1972).

27. Pogue, 3 *George C. Marshall* 249; Albert C. Wedemeyer, *Wedemeyer Reports* 245 (New York: Henry Holt, 1958).

28. Einstein felt singularly honored by the president and afterward composed a jingle:

> *In der Haupstadt stolzer Pracht*
> *Wo das Schicksal wird gemacht*
> *Kämpfet froh ein stolzer Mann*
> *Der die Lösung schaffen kann.*

Which, translated loosely, reads:

> *In the Capital's proud glory*
> *Where Destiny unfolds her story,*
> *Fights a man with happy pride*
> *Who solution can provide.*

Ronald W. Clark, *Einstein: The Life and Times* 514 (New York: World, 1971).

29. MAUD Report, July 15, 1941, in Margaret Gowing, *Britain and Atomic Energy, 1939–1945* 394 ff. (New York: Macmillan, 1964).

30. Churchill, *Hinge of Fate* 814.

31. Richard Rhodes, *The Making of the Atomic Bomb* 377 (New York: Simon & Schuster, 1985). Before the war ended, appropriations for the Manhattan Project would exceed $2 billion, and it would employ more than 150,000 persons with plants at Oak Ridge, Tennessee, and Hanford, Washington, aside from the research facility at Los Alamos, New Mexico.

32. A facsimile of FDR's note to Bush is ibid. 388.

33. In the House, Stimson met with Rayburn, Majority Leader John McCormack, and minority leader Joe Martin; in the Senate, with Majority Leader Alban Barkley and Republicans Styles Bridges of New Hampshire and Wallace White of Maine. Henry L. Stimson and McGeorge Bundy, *On Active Service in Peace and War* 614 (New York: Harper & Brothers, 1948). The view expressed by Rayburn was shared by all. "If I don't know a secret," said Rayburn, "I can't let it leak out." None of the legislators ever pressed Stimson for details. David Brinkley, *Washington Goes to War* 211 (New York: Alfred A. Knopf, 1988).

34. Albert Speer, *Inside the Third Reich* 225–229 (New York: Macmillan, 1970).

35. Kennedy, *Freedom from Fear* 667.

36. FDR to WSC, October 11, 1941, 1 *Churchill & Roosevelt* 249–250.

37. Churchill, *Hinge of Fate* 380–381.

38. Ibid. Also see Sherwood, *Roosevelt and Hopkins* 593; Doris Kearns Goodwin, *No Ordinary Time* 346 (New York: Simon & Schuster, 1994).

39. Quoted in Robert Dallek, *Franklin D. Roosevelt and American Foreign Policy, 1932–1945* 417 (New York: Oxford University Press, 1979).

40. For the text of the Quebec atomic agreement, see Rhodes, *Making of the Atomic Bomb* 523.

41. Quoted in Dallek, *Franklin D. Roosevelt* 418.

42. 1 *Correspondence Between the Chairman of the Council of Ministers of the USSR and the Presidents of the USA and the Prime Ministers of Great Britain During the Great Patriotic War* 157–161; vol. 2, 84–94 (Moscow: Foreign Language Publishers, 1957).

43. Ted Morgan, *FDR: A Biography* 677–680 (New York: Simon & Schuster, 1985).

44. Irwin F. Gellman, *Secret Affairs: FDR, Cordell Hull, and Sumner Welles* 312–317 (New York: Enigma Books, 1995); Morgan, *FDR* 682–685; cf. Cordell Hull, 2 *Memoirs* 1230–1231 (New York: Macmillan, 1948).

45. Eleanor Roosevelt, *This I Remember* 63 (New York: Harper & Brothers, 1949). Mrs. Roosevelt deleted the names in her retelling.

46. FDR, Fireside Chat, July 28, 1943, 12 *Public Papers and Addresses* 333.

47. Samuel I. Rosenman, *Working with Roosevelt* 395 (New York: Harper & Brothers, 1952).

48. FDR, Message to Congress, October 27, 1943, 12 *Public Papers and Addresses* 450–451.

49. FDR, June 22, 1944, 13 *Public Papers and Addresses* 180–182.

50. Kennedy, *Freedom from Fear* 787.

51. Department of Veterans Affairs, History of G.I. Bill, www.gibill.va.gov/GI_Bill_Info/history.htm.

52. Kennedy, *Freedom from Fear* 787.

53. The 58,000-ton *Iowa*, sister ship of *New Jersey*, *Wisconsin*, and *Missouri*, was 888 feet in length and had a beam of 108 feet. *Iowa* was armed with nine 16-inch guns, and its power plant was capable of producing 210,000 horsepower and a top speed of 33.5 knots. The ship's complement included 142 officers, 2,394 en-

listed men, and 98 Marines. It was commanded by Captain John L. McCrea, the president's former naval aide.

54. FDR to ER, November 18, 1943, 2 *F.D.R.: His Personal Letters* 1469, Elliott Roosevelt, ed. (New York: Duell, Sloan and Pearce, 1950).

55. Memo of Major General Thomas Handy, November 19, 1943, cited in Maurice Matloff, *Strategic Planning for Coalition Warfare, 1943–1944* 341–342 (Washington, D.C.: U.S. Government Printing Office, 1959). The minutes of the *Iowa* conference are reproduced in *Foreign Relations of the United States, The Conferences at Cairo and Teheran, 1943* 253–261 (Washington, D.C.: U.S. Government Printing Office, 1961).

56. *FRUS, Cairo and Teheran* 256.

57. For a facsimile fold-out copy of FDR's *National Geographic* sketch, see Jean Edward Smith, *The Defense of Berlin* 18–19 (Baltimore: Johns Hopkins Press, 1963).

58. Elliott Roosevelt, *As He Saw It* 133 (New York: Duell, Sloan and Pearce, 1946).

59. *FRUS, Cairo and Teheran* 285–287. Lieutenant Junior Grade William M. Rigdon, who kept the president's log, chastely recorded that Ms. Summersby was a guest of Elliott and FDR, Jr. The following day FDR shared a picnic lunch with Ike and Kay Summersby and subsequently told his daughter, Anna, he believed they were sleeping together. Anna to John Boettiger, December 27, 1943, FDRL.

60. FDR to Lord Louis Mountbatten, November 8, 1943, 2 *F.D.R.: His Personal Letters* 1468.

61. Winston S. Churchill, *Closing the Ring* 328 (Boston: Houghton Mifflin, 1951).

62. Ibid. 341.

63. Ibid.

64. Lord Moran, *Churchill: Taken from the Diaries of Lord Moran* 143 (Boston: Houghton Mifflin, 1966).

65. Churchill, *Hinge of Fate* 434.

66. W. Averell Harriman and Edie Abel, *Special Envoy to Churchill and Stalin, 1941–1946* 536 (New York: Random House, 1975).

67. Sherwood, *Roosevelt and Hopkins* 344.

68. Charles E. Bohlen, *Witness to History: 1929–1969* 136 (New York: W. W. Norton, 1973).

69. Michael F. Reilly and William J. Slocum, *Reilly of the White House* 179 (New York: Simon & Schuster, 1947).

70. *FRUS, Cairo and Teheran* 483. "Bohlen Minutes," Roosevelt-Stalin meeting, 3 P.M., November 28, 1943.

71. Bohlen, *Witness to History* 136.

72. Ibid. 139.

73. Ibid. 142.

74. Combined Chiefs of Staff Minutes, November 28, 1943, in *FRUS, Cairo and Teheran* 497.

75. Bohlen Supplementary Memorandum, November 28, 1943, ibid. 513.

76. In the years before the Treaty of Westphalia (1648), Richelieu aligned France with the numerous German dukes against Hapsburg hegemony. Tripartite Dinner Meeting, November 28, 1943, ibid. 511.
77. Tripartite Political Meeting, December 1, 1943, ibid. 600.
78. Ibid. 602–603.
79. Churchill, *Closing the Ring* 374.
80. Bohlen, *Witness to History* 143.
81. Frances Perkins, *The Roosevelt I Knew* 85 (New York: Viking, 1946.)
82. *FRUS, Cairo and Teheran* 512; Churchill, *Closing the Ring* 362.
83. *FRUS, Cairo and Teheran* 594. Also see Harriman, *Special Envoy* 279.
84. WSC to FDR, October 18, 1944, *FRUS, Cairo and Teheran* 884–885. For the full text of the cable, see 3 *Churchill and Roosevelt* 358–359.
85. *FRUS, Cairo and Teheran* 594–595.
86. *FRUS, Cairo and Teheran* 489.
87. Kennedy, *Freedom from Fear* 681.
88. *FRUS, Cairo and Teheran* 535–537; Sherwood, *Roosevelt and Hopkins* 788–789; Lord Moran, *Churchill* 147.
89. Lord Moran, *Churchill* 147.
90. *FRUS, Cairo and Teheran* 538.
91. Lord Moran, *Churchill* 147.
92. Bohlen, *Witness to History* 148.
93. *FRUS, Cairo and Teheran* 539. Admiral William D. Leahy, *I Was There* 207 (New York: Whittlesey House, 1950).
94. Leahy, *I Was There* 207.
95. Bohlen, *Witness to History* 148.
96. *FRUS, Cairo and Teheran* 578.
97. Stimson diary (MS), December 5, 1943, Yale University.
98. Churchill, *Closing the Ring* 384–385.
99. Bohlen, *Witness to History* 149.
100. Lord Hastings Ismay, *The Memoirs of General Lord Ismay* 340 (New York: Viking, 1960).
101. *FRUS, Cairo and Teheran* 583. Also see Harriman, *Special Envoy* 276; Lord Moran, *Churchill* 154.
102. Churchill, *Closing the Ring* 387.
103. John Martin letter, December 2, 1943, quoted in Martin Gilbert, 7 *Winston S. Churchill* 586 (Boston: Houghton Mifflin, 1986).
104. Stalin spent the years 1894 to 1899 as a student at Tiflis Orthodox Theological Seminary. Anthony Eden, *The Reckoning* 427 (Boston: Houghton Mifflin, 1965).
105. Harriman, *Special Envoy* 277.
106. *FRUS, Cairo and Teheran* 585.
107. Perkins, *The Roosevelt I Knew* 84–85.
108. Sergo Beria, *Beria, My Father* 92–94 (London: Duckworth, 2001).
109. Sherwood, *Roosevelt and Hopkins* 770.

110. David Eisenhower, *Eisenhower at War, 1943–1945* 42–43 (New York: Random House, 1986).

111. The texts of Pershing's letter and Roosevelt's reply are in Katherine Tupper Marshall, *Together* 156–157 (New York: Tupper and Love, 1946).

112. Forrest C. Pogue, *The Supreme Command* 27 (Washington, D.C.: U.S. Government Printing Office, 1954).

113. Leahy, *I Was There* 192.

114. Pogue, *Supreme Command* 32; Sherwood, *Roosevelt and Hopkins* 803.

115. Pogue, 3 *George C. Marshall* 321 (New York: Viking, 1973).

116. Ibid. 321–322.

117. *FRUS, Cairo and Teheran* 819.

118. Churchill, *Closing the Ring* 620.

TWENTY-SIX | Last Post

The epigraph is from FDR's campaign remarks in Bridgeport, Connecticut, November 4, 1944. 13 *Public Papers and Addresses of Franklin D. Roosevelt* 391 Samuel I. Rosenman, ed. (New York: Harper & Brothers, 1950).

1. Charles E. Bohlen, *Witness to History* 137 (New York: W. W. Norton, 1973).

2. Lord Hastings Ismay, *The Memoirs of General Lord Ismay* 338 (New York: Viking, 1960).

3. Stimson diary (MS), December 17, 1943, Yale University.

4. Doris Kearns Goodwin, *No Ordinary Time* 489 (New York: Simon & Schuster, 1994).

5. Goodwin, interview with Elliott Roosevelt, ibid.

6. Quoted in John R. Boettiger, Jr., *A Love in Shadow* 253 (New York: W. W. Norton, 1978).

7. Bernard Asbell, *Mother and Daughter: The Letters of Eleanor and Anna Roosevelt* 176 (New York: Fromm, 1988).

8. 22 *Complete Presidential Press Conferences of Franklin D. Roosevelt* 246–252 (New York: Da Capo Press, 1972).

9. Roosevelt's blood pressure was recorded as follows:

July 30, 1935	136/75
April 22, 1937	162/98
November 30, 1940	178/88
February 27, 1941	188/105
March 27, 1944	186/108

    Dr. Howard G. Bruenn, "Clinical Notes on the Illness and Death of President Franklin D. Roosevelt," 72 *Annals of Internal Medicine* 579–591 (1970).

10. Grace Tully, *F.D.R.: My Boss* 273–274 (New York: Charles Scribner's Sons, 1949); Jim Bishop, *FDR's Last Year* 5 (New York: Morrow, 1974).

11. Tully, *F.D.R.: My Boss* 274; James MacGregor Burns, *Roosevelt: Soldier of Freedom* 448 (New York: Harcourt Brace Jovanovich, 1970).

12. Asbell, *Mother and Daughter* 177.

13. Ibid.

14. As the Navy's wartime surgeon general, a post to which he was appointed in 1938, McIntire had command responsibility for 175,000 doctors, nurses, and other professionals, 52 hospitals, and 278 mobile medical units. Robert H. Ferrell, *The Dying President: Franklin D. Roosevelt, 1944–1945* 8 (Columbia: University of Missouri Press, 1998).

15. Asbell, *Mother and Daughter* 177.

16. Bishop, *FDR's Last Year* 4.

17. FDR to Frederic Delano, chairman of the National Capital Park and Planning Commission, December 1, 1938, FDRL.

18. Bishop, *FDR's Last Year* 4.

19. Doris Kearns Goodwin interview with Dr. Howard Bruenn, in Goodwin, *No Ordinary Time* 494.

20. Bishop, *FDR's Last Year* 6.

21. Goodwin, *No Ordinary Time* 494–495.

22. Bruenn, "Critical Notes" 580.

23. Goodwin interview with Dr. Bruenn, quoted in *No Ordinary Time* 495.

24. Ibid. 496.

25. Ibid.

26. Bruenn, "Clinical Notes" 581.

27. Goodwin, *No Ordinary Time* 496. For Admiral McIntire's highly selective account, see Vice Admiral Ross T. McIntire, *White House Physician* 183–184 (New York: G. P. Putnam's Sons, 1946).

28. Admiral McIntire's press conference remarks are quoted in ibid. 184. Also see *The New York Times*, April 5, 1944. In fairness to McIntire, the medical culture of the time generally observed a lack of candor in discussing serious diseases. As Dr. Hugh E. Evans writes, "Illness or its progress was not customarily discussed with patients. . . . Presidential health matters were assumed to be private, rarely reported frankly or with clinical detail." *The Hidden Campaign: FDR's Health and the 1944 Election* 61 (Armonk, N.Y.: M. E. Sharpe, 2002).

29. Bruenn, "Critical Notes" 583.

30. Goodwin, interview with Dr. Bruenn, quoted in *No Ordinary Time* 498.

31. Bruenn, "Critical Notes" 583–584.

32. FDR to HH, May 18, 1944, FDRL.

33. Kennedy, *Freedom from Fear* 794.

34. The "fantastic nature" comment was that of Elbridge Durbrow of the State Department's Division of European Affairs. The "earmarks" notation was by the American legation in Geneva. Durbrow Memorandum, August 13, 1942; Minister Leland Harrison to State, August 11, 1942. Both are quoted in David S. Wyman, *The Abandonment of the Jews* 43–44 (New York: Pantheon, 1984).

35. Wyman, *Abandonment of the Jews* 43. Also see Kenneth S. Davis, *F.D.R.: The War President* 731 (New York: Random House, 2000).

36. Wise to FDR, December 2, 1942, FDRL.

37. In addition to Wise, the group included Maurice Wertheim of the American Jewish Committee; Henry Monsky of B'nai B'rith; Rabbi Israel Rosenberg (Union of Orthodox Rabbis); and Adolph Held (Jewish Labor Committee).

38. Wyman, *Abandonment of the Jews* 72, quoting Wise, et al., to FDR, December 8, 1942, FDRL.

39. Quoted in Davis, *F.D.R.: War President* 737.

40. Wyman, *Abandonment of the Jews* 73.

41. *Department of State Bulletin,* December 17, 1942; also in *The New York Times,* December 18, 1942.

42. Kennedy, *Freedom from Fear* 794–795.

43. Robert N. Rosen, *Saving the Jews: Franklin D. Roosevelt and the Holocaust* 245–246 (New York: Thunder's Mouth Press, 2006). When the declaration was read in the House of Commons, the members rose and stood in silence for two minutes, a demonstration of sympathy unprecedented in Parliament's history. Wyman, *Abandonment of the Jews* 75.

44. Kennedy, *Freedom from Fear* 795.

45. Chaim Weizmann, *Trial and Error* 435 (New York: Harper & Brothers, 1949).

46. Ted Morgan, *FDR: A Biography* 713 (New York: Simon & Schuster, 1985); Rosen, *Saving the Jews* 290.

47. Cordell Hull, 2 *Memoirs* 1539 (New York: Macmillan, 1948). *The New York Times,* March 10, 1944. Hull incorrectly dates the meeting in 1943.

48. The episode is discussed at length in Wyman, *Abandonment of the Jews* 178–192.

49. Rosen, *Saving the Jews* 289.

50. Morgenthau diaries (MS), January 15, 1944. Also see Wyman, *Abandonment of the Jews* 186–187; Rosen, *Saving the Jews* 338–339.

51. Executive Order 9417, January 22, 1944, 13 *Personal Papers and Addresses* 48–50.

52. Emanuel Celler to FDR, January 25, 1944, FDRL.

53. Henry Morgenthau, "The Refugee Runaround," *Collier's,* November 1, 1947.

54. Kennedy, *Freedom from Fear* 795–796.

55. FDR, Statement on Victims of Nazi Oppression, March 24, 1944, 13 *Public Papers and Addresses* 103–105.

56. Kai Bird, *The Chairman: John J. McCloy and the Making of the American Establishment* 472–476 (New York: Simon & Schuster, 1942); Michael J. Neufeld and Michael Berenbaum, eds., *The Bombing of Auschwitz: Should the Allies Have Attempted It?* 122–124 (New York: St. Martin's Press, 2000); David S. Wyman, *Abandonment of the Jews* 410, note 78. After listing the primary sources he consulted, Wyman stated, "An exhaustive search made in 1983 by *Washington Post* reporter Morton Mintz showed that the bombing proposals almost certainly did not reach Roosevelt and most likely were not discussed at all by OPD [the Operations and Plans Division of the War Department]." Also see Martin Gilbert,

Auschwitz and the Allies: A Devastating Account of How the Allies Responded to the News of Hitler's Mass Murder 299–311 (New York: Henry Holt, 1981).

57. Bird, *The Chairman* 231–222.

58. General Frederick Anderson to War Department, quoted in Neufeld and Berenbaum, *Bombing of Auschwitz* 39.

59. Michael Beschloss in *The Conquerors* maintains that McCloy took the matter of bombing the concentration camps to FDR and that the president rejected it. Beschloss cites an interview the ninety-one-year-old McCloy gave to Henry Morgenthau III in 1986. But, as he notes, that is the sole piece of evidence that FDR was informed. Kai Bird, McCloy's assiduous biographer, who was aware of the interview, states unequivocally that "there is no evidence Roosevelt was ever approached about the matter." Michael Beschloss, *The Conquerors: Roosevelt, Truman and the Destruction of Hitler's Germany, 1941–1945* 64–67 (New York: Simon and Schuster, 2002). Cf., Kai Bird, *The Chairman* 212–223. Also see Robert N. Rosen, *Saving the Jews* 385–406.

60. Alan Dershowitz, "Afterword," in Robert N. Rosen, *Saving the Jews: Franklin D. Roosevelt and the Holocaust* 499–502.

61. Eisenhower's view was consistent and absolute. "I shall need not only the cooperation of your forces, but still more the assistance of your officials and the moral support of the French people," he told de Gaulle on December 30, 1943. "I can assure you that as far as I am concerned and regardless of whatever apparent attitudes are imposed upon me, I will recognize no French power in France other than your own in the practical sphere." (Eisenhower served on Pershing's Battle Monuments Commission in 1928–29 and resided near Pont-Mirabeau on the right bank of the Seine.) Charles de Gaulle, 3 *The War Memoirs of Charles de Gaulle* 241 (New York: Simon & Schuster, 1959). Also see Dwight D. Eisenhower, *Crusade in Europe* 272–273 (New York: Doubleday, 1948); David Eisenhower, *Eisenhower at War: 1943–1945* 230–248 (New York: Random House, 1986); Stephen E. Ambrose, *The Supreme Commander* 377–388 (New York: Doubleday, 1970).

62. WSC to FDR, May 26, 1944, 3 *Churchill and Roosevelt: The Complete Correspondence* 145, Warren F. Kimball, ed. (Princeton, N.J.: Princeton University Press, 1984).

63. Lord Halifax, Britain's ambassador in Washington, told Anthony Eden on the eve of D-Day that Leahy had advised the president that only Pétain could help the Allies in the liberation of France. This Halifax learned from John McCloy. Simon Berthon, *Allies at War* 298 (London: HarperCollins, 2002). Also see Conrad Black, *Franklin Delano Roosevelt: Champion of Freedom* 963–964. Lord Black's critique of Leahy leaves little unresolved.

64. FDR to Eisenhower, May 13, 1944, FDRL. Quoted in Forrest C. Pogue, *The Supreme Command* 148 (Washington, D.C.: U.S. Government Printing Office, 1954).

65. de Gaulle, 3 *War Memoirs* 240.

66. Pogue, *Supreme Command* 148–149. Also see de Gaulle, 3 *War Memoirs* 254–256.

67. De Gaulle spoke with his customary elegance: "The supreme battle has been joined. For the sons of France, wherever they are, whatever they are, the simple and sacred duty is to fight the enemy by every means in their power. . . . The orders given by the French Government [de Gaulle's provisional regime] and its leaders must be followed precisely. . . . From behind the cloud so heavy with our blood and our tears, the sun of our greatness is now reappearing." de Gaulle, 3 *War Memoirs* 256.

68. Alexander Cadogan, *The Cadogan Diaries, 1938–1945* 634–635, David Dilks, ed. (New York: Putnam, 1972). Entry of June 5, 1944.

69. The assumption of political responsibility in France by de Gaulle and the FCNL is handled adroitly by G. E. Maguire in *Anglo-American Policy Towards the Free French* 132–139 (London: Macmillan, 1995).

70. On June 13, 1944, six days after D-Day, the Joint Chiefs of Staff (Marshall, King, and Arnold) advised Roosevelt that for military reasons alone it was essential to recognize de Gaulle. "The situation is serious and the effect on military operations unhappy at best, and may be dangerous in view of possible reactions of the French underground and resistance groups, who have generally expressed their allegiance to General de Gaulle." JCS to FDR, June 13, 1944, FDRL.

71. de Gaulle, 3 *War Memoirs* 267–268.

72. Ibid. 269–270.

73. Claude Fohlen, "De Gaulle and Franklin D. Roosevelt," in *FDR and His Contemporaries* 39, Cornelius A. van Minnen and John E. Sears, eds. (New York: St. Martin's Press, 1992).

74. Quoted in Morgan, *FDR: A Biography* 724.

75. Maguire, *Anglo-American Policy* 143–146; 3 *Churchill & Roosevelt* 338–369. See especially WSC to FDR, October 14, 1944, at 355–356.

76. Quoted in Morgan, *FDR: A Biography* 725.

77. James MacGregor Burns, *Roosevelt: Soldier of Freedom* 502 (New York: Harcourt Brace Jovanovich, 1970); Steven Fraser, "1944," in Arthur M. Schlesinger, Jr., 2 *Running for President: The Candidates and the Images* 219–220 (New York: Simon & Schuster, 1994).

78. FDR to Robert E. Hannegan, July 11, 1944, 13 *Public Papers and Addresses* 197–199.

79. One New York delegate voted for James A. Farley. Congressional Quarterly, *Guide to U.S. Elections* 162 (Washington, D.C.: Congressional Quarterly, 1975).

80. Ickes diary (MS), June 18, 1944, Library of Congress; Morgenthau diary, July 6, 1944, FDRL.

81. Edward J. Flynn, *You're the Boss* 194 (New York: Viking, 1947).

82. Goodwin, *No Ordinary Time* 525; James Roosevelt and Sidney Shalett, *Affectionately, FDR* 353 (New York: Harcourt, Brace, 1959).

83. Flynn, *You're the Boss* 195.

84. Ibid. 195–196.

85. John C. Culver and John Hyde, *American Dreamer: The Life and Times of Henry A. Wallace* 348 (New York: Norton, 2000).

86. James F. Byrnes, *All in One Lifetime* 222 (New York: Harper & Brothers, 1958).

87. Flynn, *You're the Boss* 196–197.

88. David McCullough, *Truman* 312 (New York: Simon & Schuster, 1992).

89. Ibid. 320.

90. Roosevelt and Shalett, *Affectionately, FDR* 351.

91. Ibid. 351–352.

92. Sam Rosenman, *Working with Roosevelt* 456 (New York: Harper & Brothers, 1956).

93. Ibid.

94. Ibid. 457.

95. Ibid. 458–459.

96. Quoted in William Manchester, *American Caesar: Douglas MacArthur, 1880–1964* 364 (Boston: Little, Brown, 1978).

97. Admiral William D. Leahy, *I Was There* 250–251 (New York: Whittlesey House, 1950); D. Clayton James, 2 *The Years of MacArthur* 530 (Boston: Houghton Mifflin, 1975); Douglas MacArthur, *Reminiscences* 197 (New York: McGraw-Hill, 1964).

98. Leahy, *I Was There* 250–251.

99. Ibid. 251.

100. Manchester, *American Caesar* 368.

101. Leahy, *I Was There* 251.

102. Manchester, *American Caesar* 358.

103. 13 *Public Papers and Addresses* 212–213.

104. *The New York Times,* August 1, 1944.

105. Rosenman, *Working with Roosevelt* 459–460.

106. Ibid. 462. For the text of FDR's Bremerton speech, see 13 *Public Papers and Addresses* 216–227.

107. Bruenn, "Clinical Notes" 586.

108. Rosenman, *Working with Roosevelt* 462.

109. Lord Moran, *Churchill: From the Diaries of Lord Moran* 190 (Boston: Houghton Mifflin, 1966).

110. John Morton Blum, 3 *From the Morgenthau Diaries: Years of War, 1941–1945* 371 (Boston: Houghton Mifflin, 1967). Privy Councillor Lord Cherwell, the British government's scientific adviser, also pointed out to Churchill that the destruction of German industry would save Britain from bankruptcy by eliminating a dangerous competitor.

111. Henry L. Stimson and McGeorge Bundy, *On Active Service in Peace and War* 568–582 (New York: Harper & Brothers, 1948).

112. Hull, 2 *Memoirs* 1613–1621.

113. Stimson and Bundy, *On Active Service* 581.

114. McIntire, *White House Physician* 204.

115. Moran, *Diaries* 192.

116. Harry H. Vaughan Oral History, Harry S. Truman Library, quoted in Ferrell, *The Dying President* 89.

117. Rosenman, *Working with Roosevelt* 478.

118. FDR, Teamsters Union Address, September 23, 1944, 13 *Public Papers and Addresses* 284–293.

119. *Time,* October 2, 1944.

120. 13 *Public Papers and Addresses* 290. On September 1, 1944, Admiral Leahy, on behalf of the Navy, officially confirmed to Speaker Rayburn and House Majority Leader John McCormack that "the president's dog was not at any time left behind or sent for." Leahy, *I Was There* 255.

121. Harry S. Truman, *Memoirs: Years of Destiny* 193 (New York: Doubleday, 1956).

122. FDR, Foreign Policy Association Address, October 21, 1944, 13 *Public Papers and Addresses* 342–354.

123. FDR, Campaign Address at Fenway Park, November 4, 1944, ibid. 397–406.

124. Bruenn, "Clinical Notes" 587; Ferrell, *Dying President* 93.

125. Leahy, *I Was There* 278.

126. Fish, the ranking member of the House Rules Committee, was defeated by Augustus W. Bennett, 70,630–62,583. Nye, third most senior Republican in the Senate, lost to John Moses 95,102–69,530. Congressional Quarterly, *Guide to U.S. Elections* 501, 803 (Washington, D.C.: Congressional Quarterly, 1975).

127. Bruenn, "Clinical Notes" 587–588.

128. Frances Perkins, *The Roosevelt I Knew* 393 (New York: Viking Press, 1946).

129. 990th Press Conference, January 19, 1945, 25 *Complete Presidential Press Conferences* 45.

130. FDR, Fourth Inaugural Address, January 20, 1945, 13 *Public Papers and Addresses* 523–525. The quotation is from Emerson's *Essays, First Series, Friendship.*

131. Rosenman, *Working with Roosevelt* 517.

132. John Gunther, *Roosevelt in Retrospect* 29 (New York: Harper & Brothers, 1950).

133. "I'd never seen Father drink in that manner," James wrote. Roosevelt and Shalett, *Affectionately, F.D.R.* 354–355.

134. Bruenn, "Clinical Notes" 588.

135. *The New York Times,* January 21, 1945.

136. Gunther, *Roosevelt in Retrospect* 28.

137. George Martin, *Madam Secretary: Frances Perkins* 461 (Boston: Houghton Mifflin, 1976).

138. Stimson and Bundy, *On Active Service* 619. "Russia's entry at as early a date as possible consistent with her ability to engage in offensive operations is necessary to provide maximum support [for] our main effort against Japan," the Joint Chiefs advised Roosevelt on January 23. "The objective of Russia's military effort against Japan should be defeat of the Japanese forces in Manchuria, air opera-

tions against Japan proper . . . and maximum interference with Japanese sea traffic between Japan and the mainland of Asia."

139. "We foresaw that Roosevelt would have himself wheeled into the park surrounding the palace to take the air, and so we could no longer be satisfied with microphones hidden in the rooms that were assigned to him." Sergo Beria, *Beria: My Father* 104 (London: Duckworth, 2001).

140. Winston S. Churchill, *Triumph and Tragedy* 344 (Boston: Houghton Mifflin, 1953). Beria, *Beria: My Father* 106; Moran, *Diaries* 242.

141. Edward R. Stettinius, *Roosevelt and the Russians: The Yalta Conference* 72 (New York: Doubleday, 1949).

142. Leahy, *I Was There* 321.

143. Bohlen, *Witness to History* 172; also see Bohlen, *The Transformation of American Foreign Policy* 44 (New York: Norton, 1969).

144. W. Averell Harriman and Elie Abel, *Special Envoy to Churchill and Stalin* 389 (New York: Random House, 1973).

145. Anna to John Boettiger, February 6, 1945, FDRL.

146. Bruenn, "Clinical Notes" 589.

147. Without that agreement by the Soviets, wrote Bohlen, "There would hardly have been a United Nations." Bohlen, *Witness to History* 193–195.

148. Harriman and Abel, *Special Envoy* 405.

149. Ibid. 407.

150. For the text of the Declaration of Liberated Europe, see FRUS, *The Conferences at Malta and Yalta, 1945* 977–978 (Washington, D.C.: U.S. Government Printing Office, 1955).

151. Leahy, *I Was There* 315–316.

152. Kennedy, *Freedom from Fear* 802–803.

153. For text, see FRUS, *Conferences at Malta and Yalta* 984. Also see Bohlen, *Witness to History* 196–196; Harriman and Abel, *Special Envoy* 400. Churchill added his signature to the agreement, though he took no part in its negotiation. "To us the problem was remote and secondary."

154. Frank Freidel, *Franklin D. Roosevelt: A Rendezvous with Destiny* 591 (Boston: Little, Brown, 1990); Forrest C. Pogue, 3 *George C. Marshall* 531–539 (New York: Viking, 1973). Cf. Ernest J. King and Walter Muir Whitehill, *Fleet Admiral King: A Naval Record* 591–592 (New York: Norton, 1952).

155. Morgan, *FDR* 755.

156. WSC to Clementine Churchill, February 12, 1945, *Winston and Clementine: The Personal Letters of the Churchills* 515, Mary Soames, ed. (Boston: Houghton Mifflin, 1998).

157. Ward, ed., *Closest Companion* 397; Beatrice Bishop Berle and Travis Beale Jacobs, eds., *Navigating the Rapids: From the Papers of Adolf A. Berle* 477 (New York: Harcourt Brace Jovanovich, 1973).

158. FDR, Address to Congress on Yalta, March 1, 1945, 13 *Public Papers and Addresses* 570–586.

159. Frances Perkins, *The Roosevelt I Knew* 395. Rosenman, who helped draft the speech, was disappointed with Roosevelt's delivery and felt the fire was gone. *Working with Roosevelt* 527–530.

160. 13 *Public Papers and Addresses* 586, 578.

161. Hassett, *Off the Record with FDR* 324–325. "I do not think we will ever see the President alive again," Mrs. Jackson told her husband afterward. Robert H. Jackson, *That Man: An Insider's Portrait of Franklin D. Roosevelt* 154, John Q. Barrett, ed. (New York: Oxford University Press, 2003).

162. Bruenn, "Clinical Notes" 590.

163. Goodwin, *No Ordinary Time* 596.

164. Tully, *F.D.R., My Boss* 356.

165. Jean Edward Smith, *Lucius D. Clay: An American Life* 215–216 (New York: Henry Holt, 1990).

166. Reilly, *Reilly of the White House* 226–227; Hassett, *Off the Record* 327.

167. Hassett, *Off the Record* 327–329. Also see Michael Beschloss, *The Conquerors: Roosevelt, Truman and the Destruction of Hitler's Germany, 1941–1945* 203 (New York: Simon & Schuster, 2002).

    Dr. Bruenn was evidently candid with Hassett about the problem, but in publishing his diary Hassett omitted the details. Years later, Dr. Bruenn, talking to Dr. James Halsted, Anna Roosevelt's third husband, referred to a particularly upsetting phone call from ER to the president "a week or two before his death and talking forty-five minutes urging help for Yugoslavia. This resulted in rise of blood pressure of 50 points. His veins stood out on his forehead. Obviously the necessity to deny her request and the long telephone conversation was a major strain." Dr. Halsted took notes on the conversation, March 8, 1967, and gave a copy to Geoffrey Ward, who passed them to Frank Freidel. See Freidel, *Rendezvous with Destiny* 604, 662.

168. Bruenn, "Clinical Notes" 590.

169. Merriman Smith, *Thank You, Mr. President: A White House Notebook* 186 (New York: Harper & Brothers, 1946).

170. Goodwin, *No Ordinary Time* 600.

171. Elizabeth Shoumatoff, *FDR's Unfinished Portrait* 100 (Pittsburgh: University of Pittsburgh Press, 1990).

172. FDR, Undelivered Jefferson Day (April 13, 1945) Address, 13 *Public Papers and Addresses* 613–616.

173. Blum, 3 *From the Morgenthau Diaries* 416.

174. Shoumatoff, *FDR's Unfinished Portrait* 115.

175. Ibid. 116. Also see Ward, *Closest Companion* 418.

176. Churchill, *Triumph and Tragedy* 471.

177. Harriman and Abel, *Special Envoy* 442.

178. Quoted in Bernard Asbell, *When F.D.R. Died* 117 (New York: Holt, Rinehart & Winston, 1961).

179. Bill Livingstone, "The Day FDR Died," *Senior News* (April 2006).

Bibliography

THE PAPERS OF Franklin and Eleanor, their children, and most members of the Roosevelt administration are at the Franklin D. Roosevelt Library in Hyde Park, New York. So too are the Roosevelt, Delano, and Aspinwall family papers, including the collection of Sara Delano Roosevelt. Others' (Farley, Ickes, Leahy, Hughes, Daniels) are at the Library of Congress. The Stimson and House papers are at Yale; the Alsop, Peabody, and Theodore Roosevelt collections at Harvard; and copies of the Wilson papers at Princeton. All of these I have consulted, plus the extensive oral history collection at Columbia. Whenever that material is used, I have provided a full citation in the text.

The bibliography below includes the books I have referred to. For the sake of brevity I have not included journal and magazine articles or newspaper coverage. These are cited fully in the Notes.

Abbott, Philip. *The Exemplary Presidency: Franklin D. Roosevelt and the American Political Tradition.* Amherst: University of Massachusetts Press, 1990.

Acheson, Dean. *Morning and Noon.* Boston: Houghton Mifflin, 1965.

———. *Present at the Creation: My Years in the State Department.* New York: Norton, 1969.

Adamic, Louis. *Dinner at the White House.* New York: Harper & Brothers, 1946.

Adams, Henry H. *Harry Hopkins: A Biography.* New York: Putnam, 1977.

Aga Rossi, Elena. *Origins of the Bipolar World: Roosevelt's Policy Toward Europe and the Soviet Union: A Reevaluation.* Berkeley: Center for German and European Studies, University of California, 1993.

Agawa, Hiroyuki. *The Reluctant Admiral: Yamamoto and the Imperial Navy.* Tokyo: Shincho Sha, 1966.

Aglion, Raoul. *Roosevelt and de Gaulle: Allies in Conflict, A Personal Memoir.* New York: Free Press, 1988.

Albee, Peggy A. *Home of Franklin D. Roosevelt: Roosevelt-Vanderbilt Sites, Hyde Park, New York.* Lowell, Mass.: Building Conservative Branch, U.S. Dept. of the Interior, 1996.

Albion, Robert G. *Makers of Naval Policy.* Annapolis, Md.: Naval Institute Press, 1980.

Albion, Robert G., and Robert H. Connery. *Forrestal and the Navy.* New York: Columbia University Press, 1962.

Alinsky, Saul. *John L. Lewis: An Unauthorized Biography.* New York: G. P. Putnam's Sons, 1949.

Alldritt, Keith. *The Greatest of Friends: Franklin D. Roosevelt and Winston Churchill 1941–1945.* New York: St. Martin's Press, 1995.

Allen, George E. *Presidents Who Have Known Me.* New York: Simon & Schuster, 1950.

Alsop, Joseph. *FDR, 1882–1945: A Centenary Remembrance.* New York: Viking, 1982.

Alsop, Joseph, and Robert Kintner. *American White Paper: The Story of American Diplomacy and the Second World War.* New York: Simon & Schuster, 1940.

———. *Men Around the President.* New York: Doubleday, 1939.

Alsop, Joseph, and Turner Catledge. *The 168 Days.* New York: Doubleday, 1938.

Alter, Jonathan. *The Defining Moment: FDR's Hundred Days and the Triumph of Hope.* New York: Simon & Schuster, 2006.

Ambrose, Stephen E. *The Supreme Commander: The War Years of General Dwight D. Eisenhower.* New York: Doubleday, 1970.

Amory, Cleveland. *The Last Resorts.* New York: Harper & Brothers, 1952.

———. *Who Killed Society?* New York: Harper & Brothers, 1960.

Anderson, Jervis. *A. Philip Randolph: A Biographical Portrait.* New York: Harcourt Brace Jovanovich, 1973.

Andersen, Kristi. *The Creation of a Democratic Majority, 1928–1936.* Chicago: University of Chicago Press, 1979.

Armstrong, Anne. *Unconditional Surrender: The Impact of the Casablanca Policy Upon World War II.* New Brunswick, N.J.: Rutgers University Press, 1961.

Arnold, General Henry H. *Global Mission.* New York: Harper & Brothers, 1949.

Arnold, Thurman. *The Folklore of Capitalism.* New Haven: Yale University Press, 1937.

Aron, Robert. *Histoire de Vichy, 1940–1944.* Paris: A. Fayard, 1954.

Asbell, Bernard. *The F.D.R. Memoirs.* New York: Doubleday, 1973.

———, ed. *Mother & Daughter: The Letters of Eleanor and Anna Roosevelt.* New York: Coward, McCann & Geoghegan, 1982.

———. *When FDR Died.* New York: Holt, Rinehart & Winston, 1961.

Ashburn, Frank D. *Fifty Years On: Groton School, 1884–1934.* New York: Privately printed, 1934.

———. *Peabody of Groton: A Portrait.* New York: Coward McCann, 1944.

Aspinwall, A. A. *The Aspinwall Genealogy.* Rutland, Vt.: Tuttle Co., 1901.

Atkinson, Rick. *An Army at Dawn: The War in Africa, 1942–1943.* New York: Henry Holt, 2002.

Attlee, Clement R. *As It Happened.* London: Heinemann, 1954.

Auphan, Paul, and Jacques Mordal. *The French Navy in World War II.* Annapolis, Md.: Naval Institute Press, 1959.

Axelrod, Alan. *Nothing to Fear: Lessons in Leadership from FDR, President of the Greatest Generation.* Paramus, N.J.: Prentice Hall Press, 2003.

Badeau, Adam. *Grant in Peace: From Appomattox to Mount McGregor.* Hartford, Conn.: S. S. Scranton & Co., 1887.

Bailey, Thomas A. *A Diplomatic History of the United States.* New York: Appleton-Century-Crofts, 1964.

———. *Woodrow Wilson and the Great Betrayal.* Chicago: Quadrangle Books, 1945.

Bailey, Thomas A., and Paul B. Ryan. *Hitler vs. Roosevelt: The Undeclared Naval War.* New York: Free Press, 1979.

———. *The Lusitania Disaster.* New York: Free Press, 1975.

Baker, Carlos, ed. *Ernest Hemingway Selected Letters.* New York: Charles Scribner's Sons, 1981.

Baker, Leonard. *Roosevelt and Pearl Harbor.* New York: Macmillan, 1970.

Baker, Liva. *The Justice from Beacon Hill: The Life and Times of Oliver Wendell Holmes.* New York: HarperCollins, 1991.

Baker, Paul R. *Stanny: The Gilded Life of Stanford White.* New York: Free Press, 1989.

Baker, Ray Stannard. *American Chronicle: The Autobiography of Ray Stannard Baker.* New York: Charles Scribner's Sons, 1945.

———. *Woodrow Wilson: Life and Letters.* 8 vols. New York: Doubleday, 1927.

Baldwin, Hanson W. *The Crucial Years, 1939–1941: The World at War.* New York: Harper & Row, 1976.

———. *Great Mistakes of the War.* New York: Harper & Brothers, 1950.

Barber, Noel. *The Week France Fell.* New York: Stein & Day, 1976.

Barber, William J. *Designs Within Disorder: Franklin D. Roosevelt, the Economists, and the Shaping of American Economic Policy, 1933–1945.* New York: Cambridge University Press, 1996.

Barkley, Alben W. *That Reminds Me.* New York: Doubleday, 1954.

Barlett, Donald L., and James B. Steele. *Empire: The Life, Legend, and Madness of Howard Hughes.* New York: Norton, 1979.

Barnard, Ellsworth. *Wendell Willkie: Fighter for Freedom.* Marquette: Northern Michigan University Press, 1966.

Barnard, John. *Walter Reuther and the Rise of the Auto Workers.* Boston: Little, Brown, 1983.

Barnes, Joseph. *Willkie: The Events He Was Part Of, the Ideas He Fought For.* New York: Simon & Schuster, 1952.

Barone, Michael. *Our Country: The Shaping of America from Roosevelt to Reagan.* New York: Free Press, 1990.

Barrett, Walter. *The Old Merchants of New York City.* New York: Greenwood Press, 1968.

Baruch, Bernard M. *Baruch: The Public Years.* New York: Holt, Rinehart & Winston, 1960.

Baur, Brian C. *Franklin D. Roosevelt: The Stamp Collecting President.* Sidney, Ohio: Linn's Stamp News, 1999.

———. *Linn's Franklin D. Roosevelt and the Stamps of the United States 1933–45.* Sidney, Ohio: Linn's Stamp News, 1993.

Beach, Edward L. *The United States Navy: 200 Years.* New York: Henry Holt, 1986.

Beale, Howard K. *Theodore Roosevelt and the Rise of America to World Power.* Baltimore: Johns Hopkins University Press, 1956.

Beard, Charles Austin. *American Foreign Policy in the Making, 1932–1940.* New Haven, Conn.: Yale University Press, 1946.

———. *President Roosevelt and the Coming of the War, 1941: A Study of Appearances and Realities.* New Haven, Conn.: Yale University Press, 1948.

Beasley, Maurine H. *Eleanor Roosevelt and the Media: A Public Quest for Self-Fulfillment.* Urbana: University of Illinois Press, 1987.

Beisner, Robert L. *Dean Acheson: A Life in the Cold War.* New York: Oxford University Press, 2006.

Bellush, Bernard. *Franklin D. Roosevelt as Governor of New York.* New York: Columbia University Press, 1955.

Bemis, Samuel Flagg. *A Diplomatic History of the United States.* New York: Holt, Rinehart and Winston, 1965.

Bennett, Edward M. *Franklin D. Roosevelt and the Search for Security: American-Soviet Relations 1933–1939.* Wilmington, Del.: Scholarly Resources, 1997.

———. *Franklin D. Roosevelt and the Search for Victory: American-Soviet Relations 1939–1945.* Wilmington, Del.: Scholarly Resources, 1990.

Bercuson, David, and Holger Herwig. *One Christmas in Washington: The Secret Meeting Between Roosevelt and Churchill That Changed the World.* New York: Overlook Press, 2005.

Berg, Roland H. *The Challenge of Polio: The Crusade Against Infantile Paralysis.* New York: Dial Press, 1946.

Beria, Sergo. *Beria, My Father: Inside Stalin's Kremlin.* London: Duckworth, 2001.

Berle, Adolf A., and Gardiner C. Means. *The Modern Corporation and Private Property.* New York: Harcourt, Brace & World, 1968.

Berle, Beatrice Bishop, and Travis B. Jacobs, eds. *Navigating the Rapids, 1918–1971: From the Papers of Adolf A. Berle.* New York: Harcourt Brace Jovanovich, 1973.

Berlin, Isaiah. *Personal Impressions.* Henry Hardy, ed. New York: Viking, 1981.

Bernstein, Irving. *The Lean Years: A History of the American Worker, 1920–1933.* Boston: Houghton Mifflin, 1960.

———. *Turbulent Years: A History of the American Worker, 1933–1941.* Boston: Houghton Mifflin, 1970.

Berthon, Simon. *Allies at War: The Bitter Rivalry Among Churchill, Roosevelt, and de Gaulle.* London: HarperCollins, 2002.

Beschloss, Michael R. *The Conquerors: Roosevelt, Truman, and the Destruction of Hitler's Germany, 1941–1945.* New York: Simon & Schuster, 2002.

———. *Kennedy and Roosevelt: The Uneasy Alliance.* New York: Norton, 1980.

Best, Gary Dean. *FDR and the Bonus Marchers, 1933–1935.* Westport, Conn.: Praeger, 1992.

———. *Pride, Prejudice, and Politics: Roosevelt Versus Recovery, 1933–1938.* Westport, Conn.: Praeger, 1991.

Biddle, Francis. *In Brief Authority.* New York: Doubleday, 1948.

Binkley, Wilfred E. *President and Congress.* New York: Knopf, 1947.

Bird, Kai. *The Chairman: John J. McCloy and the Making of the American Establishment.* New York: Simon & Schuster, 1992.

Birkenhead, Frederick Edwin Smith, Earl of. *Points of View.* 2 vols. London: Hodder & Stoughton, 1922.

Birkenhead, Frederick Winston Furneaux Smith, Earl of. *Halifax: The Life of Lord Halifax*. Boston: Houghton Mifflin, 1966.

———. *The Prof. in Two Worlds: The Official Life of Professor F. A. Lindemann, Viscount Cherwell*. London: Collins, 1961.

Bishop, Jim. *FDR's Last Year*. New York: Morrow, 1974.

Bix, Herbert P. *Hirohito and the Making of Modern Japan*. New York: HarperCollins, 2000.

Black, Conrad. *Franklin Delano Roosevelt: Champion of Freedom*. New York: PublicAffairs, 2003.

Black, Ruby. *Eleanor Roosevelt: A Biography*. New York: Duell, Sloan and Pearce, 1940.

Black, Theodore Milton. *Democratic Party Publicity in the 1940 Campaign*. New York: Plymouth, 1941.

Blücher, Evelyn. *An English Wife in Berlin*. London: Constable, 1920.

Blum, John Morton. *From the Morgenthau Diaries: Years of Crisis, 1928–1938*. Boston: Houghton Mifflin, 1959.

———. *From the Morgenthau Diaries: Years of Urgency, 1938–1941*. Boston: Houghton Mifflin, 1965.

———. *From the Morgenthau Diaries: Years of War, 1941–1945*. Boston: Houghton Mifflin, 1967.

———. *Joe Tumulty and the Wilson Era*. Boston: Houghton Mifflin, 1951.

———. *The Progressive Presidents*. New York: Norton, 1980.

———. *The Republican Roosevelt*. Cambridge, Mass.: Harvard University Press, 1954.

———. *Roosevelt and Morgenthau*. Boston: Houghton Mifflin, 1970.

———. *V Was for Victory: Politics and American Culture During World War II*. New York: Harcourt Brace Jovanovich, 1976.

Blumenson, Martin. *Patton: The Man Behind the Legend*. New York: Morrow, 1985.

Boettiger, John R. *A Love in Shadow*. New York: Norton, 1978.

Bohlen, Charles E. *The Transformation of American Foreign Policy*. New York: Norton, 1969.

———. *Witness to History, 1929–1969*. New York: Norton, 1973.

Bordo, Michael D., Claudia Goldin, and Eugene N. White. *The Defining Moment: The Great Depression and the American Economy in the Twentieth Century*. Chicago: University of Chicago Press, 1998.

Borg, Dorothy, and Shumpei Okamoto. *Pearl Harbor as History*. New York: Columbia University Press, 1973.

Bosworth, Allan R. *America's Concentration Camps*. New York: Norton, 1967.

Bowen, Catherine Drinker. *Yankee from Olympus*. Boston: Little, Brown, 1945.

Bradford, Sarah. *The Reluctant King: The Life and Reign of George VI, 1895–1952*. New York: St. Martin's Press, 1990.

Bradley, Omar. *A Soldier's Story*. New York: Henry Holt, 1951.

Bradley, Omar, and Clay Blair. *A General's Life*. New York: Simon & Schuster, 1983.

Brandt, Clare. *An American Aristocracy: The Livingstons*. New York: Doubleday, 1986.

Brinkley, Alan. *The End of Reform: New Deal Liberalism in Recession and War.* New York: Knopf, 1995.

———. *Voices of Protest: Huey Long, Father Coughlin, and the Great Depression.* New York: Knopf, 1982.

Brinkley, David. *Washington Goes to War.* New York: Knopf, 1988.

Brinkley, Douglas, ed. *Dean Acheson and the Making of U.S. Foreign Policy.* New York: Macmillan, 1994.

Brinnin, John Malcom. *The Sway of the Grand Saloon: A Social History of the North Atlantic.* New York: Delacorte Press, 1971.

Brogan, D. W. *The Era of Franklin D. Roosevelt.* New Haven, Conn.: Yale University Press, 1951.

Brough, James. *Princess Alice.* Boston: Little, Brown, 1975.

Browder, Robert Paul, and Thomas Smith. *Independent: A Biography of Lewis W. Douglas.* New York: Knopf, 1986.

Brown, Robert J. *Manipulating the Ether: The Power of Broadcast Radio in Thirties America.* Jefferson, N.C.: McFarland & Co., 1998.

Brown, Rollo W. *Harvard Yard in the Golden Age.* New York: Current Books, 1948.

Brownell, Will, and Richard N. Billings. *So Close to Greatness: A Biography of William C. Bullitt.* New York: Macmillan, 1987.

Brownlow, Louis. *The President and the Presidency.* Chicago: Public Administration Service, 1949.

Bryan, William Jennings, and Mary Baird Bryan. *The Memoirs of William Jennings Bryan.* Philadelphia: John C. Winston, 1925.

Bryant, Arthur. *Triumph in the West: A History of the War Years Based on the Diaries of Field Marshal Lord Alanbrooke, Chief of the Imperial General Staff.* New York: Doubleday, 1959.

———. *The Turn of the Tide, A History of the War Years Based on the Diaries of Field Marshal Lord Alanbrooke, Chief of the Imperial General Staff.* New York: Doubleday, 1957.

Bryant, Keith L., Jr. *Alfalfa Bill Murray.* Norman: University of Oklahoma Press, 1968.

Buell, Thomas B. *Master of Sea Power: A Biography of Fleet Admiral Ernest J. King.* Boston: Little, Brown, 1980.

Buhite, Russell. *Decisions at Yalta: An Appraisal of Summit Diplomacy.* Wilmington, Del.: Scholarly Resources, 1986.

Buhite, Russell, and David Levy, eds. *FDR's Fireside Chats.* Norman: University of Oklahoma Press, 1992.

Bullitt, William C. *For the President, Personal and Secret: The Correspondence Between Franklin D. Roosevelt and William C. Bullitt.* Orville H. Bullitt, ed. Boston: Houghton Mifflin, 1972.

Bunker, John. *Liberty Ships: Ugly Ducklings of World War II.* Annapolis, Md.: Naval Institute Press, 1972.

Burgan, Michael. *Franklin D. Roosevelt.* Minneapolis: Compass Point Books, 2002.

Burner, David. *Herbert Hoover: A Public Life*. New York: Knopf, 1979.

———. *The Politics of Provincialism*. New York: Knopf, 1968.

Burns, James MacGregor. *Leadership*. New York: Harper & Row, 1978.

———. *Roosevelt: The Lion and the Fox*. New York: Harcourt, Brace, 1956.

———. *Roosevelt: The Soldier of Freedom*. New York: Harcourt Brace Jovanovich, 1970.

Burns, James MacGregor, and Susan Dunn. *The Three Roosevelts: Patrician Leaders Who Transformed America*. New York: Grove Press, 2001.

Burt, Nathaniel. *First Families*. Boston: Little, Brown, 1970.

Butcher, Harry C. *My Three Years with Eisenhower: The Personal Diary of Captain Harry C. Butcher, USNR, Naval Aide to General Eisenhower, 1942 to 1945*. New York: Simon & Schuster, 1946.

Butow, Robert J. C. *Tojo and the Coming of the War*. Princeton, N.J.: Princeton University Press, 1961.

Butterfield, Roger, Robert D. Graff, and Robert Ginna. *FDR*. New York: Harper & Row, 1963.

Byrnes, James F. *All in One Lifetime*. New York: Harper & Brothers, 1958.

———. *Speaking Frankly*. New York: Harper & Brothers, 1947.

Cadogan, Sir Alexander, *The Diaries of Sir Alexander Cadogan, O.M., 1938–1945*. David Dilks, ed. New York: G. P. Putnam's Sons, 1972.

Cantril, Hadley, ed. *Public Opinion 1935–1946*. Princeton, N.J.: Princeton University Press, 1951.

Carlson, Earland Irving. *Franklin D. Roosevelt's Fight for the Presidential Nomination, 1928–1932*. Ann Arbor: University of Michigan Press, 1956.

Caro, Robert A. *The Power Broker: Robert Moses and the Fall of New York*. New York: Knopf, 1974.

Caroli, Betty Boyd. *The Roosevelt Women*. New York: Basic Books, 1998.

Carter, John F. *The New Dealers*. New York: Literary Guild, 1939.

Carter, Richard. *Breakthrough: The Saga of Jonas Salk*. New York: Trident Press, 1966.

Casey, Steven. *Cautious Crusade: Franklin D. Roosevelt, American Public Opinion, and the War Against Nazi Germany*. New York: Oxford University Press, 2001.

Cashman, Sean Dennis. *America, Roosevelt, and World War II*. New York: New York University Press, 1989.

Castillo, Edmund L. *Flat-tops: The Story of Aircraft Carriers*. New York: Random House, 1969.

Cebula, James E. *James M. Cox: Journalist and Politician*. New York: Garland, 1985.

Cecil, Robert. *A Great Experiment: An Autobiography*. New York: Oxford University Press, 1941.

Chace, James. *1912: Wilson, Roosevelt, Taft & Debs—The Election That Changed the Country*. New York: Simon & Schuster, 2004.

Chamberlain, Rudolph W. *There Is No Truce: A Life of Thomas Mott Osborne*. New York: Macmillan, 1935.

Chamberlin, William H. *America's Second Crusade*. Chicago: Regnery, 1950.

Chambers, Clarke A. *Seedtime of Reform: American Social Service and Social Action, 1918–1933.* Minneapolis: University of Minnesota Press, 1963.

Chaney, Otto Preston, Jr. *Zhukov.* Norman: University of Oklahoma Press, 1971.

Charles, Searle F. *Minister of Relief: Harry Hopkins and the Depression.* Syracuse, N.Y.: Syracuse University Press, 1963.

Childs, Marquis W. *I Write from Washington.* New York: Harper & Brothers, 1942.

———. *They Hate Roosevelt!* New York: Harper & Brothers, 1936.

Churchill, Allen. *The Roosevelts: American Aristocrats.* New York: Harper & Row, 1965.

Churchill, Randolph S., and Martin Gilbert. *Winston S. Churchill.* 8 vols. and 5 companions. Boston: Houghton Mifflin, 1966–1988.

Churchill, Sarah. *A Thread in the Tapestry.* New York: Dodd, Mead, 1967.

Churchill, Winston. *The Churchill War Papers.* Martin Gilbert, ed. 3 vols. New York: Norton, 1993.

———. *The Second World War: The Gathering Storm.* Boston: Houghton Mifflin, 1948.

———. *The Second World War: Their Finest Hour.* Boston: Houghton Mifflin, 1949.

———. *The Second World War: The Grand Alliance.* Boston: Houghton Mifflin, 1950.

———. *The Second World War: The Hinge of Fate.* Boston: Houghton Mifflin, 1950.

———. *The Second World War: Closing the Ring.* Boston: Houghton Mifflin, 1951.

———. *The Second World War: Triumph and Tragedy.* Boston: Houghton Mifflin, 1953.

———. *Winston Churchill: His Complete Speeches.* Robert Rhodes James, ed. 8 vols. London: Chelsea House, 1974.

———. *The World Crisis.* 4 vols. New York: Charles Scribner's Sons, 1928.

Churchill, Winston S., and Franklin D. Roosevelt. *Churchill and Roosevelt: The Complete Correspondence.* Warren F. Kimball, ed. 3 vols. Princeton, N.J.: Princeton University Press, 1984.

Clapper, Olive. *Washington Tapestry.* New York: Whittlesey House, 1946.

Clapper, Raymond. *Watching the World.* New York: McGraw-Hill, 1944.

Clark, James C. *Faded Glory: Presidents out of Power.* New York: Praeger, 1985.

Clark, Ronald W. *Einstein: The Life and Times.* New York: World, 1971.

Clemens, Diane Shaver. *Yalta.* New York: Oxford University Press, 1970.

Clifford, J. Garry, and Samuel Spencer. *The First Peacetime Draft.* Lawrence: University Press of Kansas, 1986.

Cline, R. S. *Washington Command Post: The Operations Division.* Washington, D.C.: U.S. Government Printing Office, 1951.

Coit, Margaret L. *Mr. Baruch.* Boston: Houghton Mifflin, 1957.

Cole, Wayne S. *Charles A. Lindbergh and the Battle Against American Intervention in World War II.* New York: Harcourt Brace Jovanovich, 1974.

———. *Determinism and American Foreign Relations During the Franklin D. Roosevelt Era.* Lanham, Md.: University Press of America, 1994.

———. *Roosevelt and the Isolationists, 1932–1945.* Lincoln: University of Nebraska Press, 1983.

Coletta, Paolo E., ed. *American Secretaries of the Navy.* 2 vols. Annapolis, Md.: Naval Institute Press, 1980.

Coletta, Paul K. *Admiral Bradley A. Fiske and the American Navy.* Lawrence: Regent's Press of Kansas, 1979.

Collier, Peter, and David Horowitz. *The Roosevelts: An American Saga.* New York: Simon & Schuster, 1994.

Collins, Aileen Sutherland, ed. *Rebecca Howland and James Roosevelt: A Story of Cousins.* Virginia Beach, Va.: Parsons Press, 2006.

Commager, Henry Steele. *The American Mind.* New Haven, Conn.: Yale University Press, 1950.

Congressional Quarterly. *Congressional Quarterly's Guide to U.S. Elections.* Washington, D.C.: Congressional Quarterly, 1975.

Conkin, Paul Keith. *The New Deal.* Wheeling, Ill.: Harlan Davidson, 1992.

Connable, Alfred, and Edward Silberfarb. *Tigers of Tammany: Nine Men Who Ran New York.* New York: Holt, Rinehart and Winston, 1967.

Connally, Tom. *My Name Is Tom Connally.* New York: Crowell, 1954.

Cook, Blanche Wiesen, ed. *Crystal Eastman on Women and Revolution.* New York: Oxford University Press, 1978.

———. *Eleanor Roosevelt, 1884–1933.* New York: Viking Press, 1992.

———. *Eleanor Roosevelt, 1933–1938.* New York: Viking Press, 1999.

Coon, Horace. *Columbia: Colossus on the Hudson.* New York: E. P. Dutton, 1947.

Cooper, John Milton. *Breaking the Heart of the World.* New York: Cambridge University Press, 2001.

———. *The Warrior and the Priest: Woodrow Wilson and Theodore Roosevelt.* Cambridge, Mass.: Harvard University Press, 1983.

Cox, James M. *Journey Through My Years.* New York: Simon & Schuster, 1946.

Craig, Gordon A. *Germany: 1866–1945.* New York: Oxford University Press, 1978.

———. *The Politics of the Prussian Army, 1640–1945.* New York: Oxford University Press, 1955.

Cray, Ed. *General of the Army: George C. Marshall, Soldier and Statesman.* New York: Norton, 1990.

Creel, George. *Rebel at Large: Recollections of Fifty Crowded Years.* New York: G. P. Putnam's Sons, 1947.

Croly, Herbert. *The Promise of American Life.* New York: Macmillan, 1909.

Cronon, Edmund David. *Josephus Daniels in Mexico.* Madison: University of Wisconsin Press, 1960.

———, ed. *The Cabinet Diaries of Josephus Daniels, 1913–1921.* Lincoln: University of Nebraska Press, 1963.

Cross, Robert F. *Sailor in the White House: The Seafaring Life of FDR.* Annapolis, Md.: Naval Institute Press, 2003.

Culver, John C., and John Hyde. *American Dreamer: The Life and Times of Henry A. Wallace.* New York: Norton, 2000.

Current, Richard N. *Secretary Stimson: A Study in Statecraft.* New Brunswick, N.J.: Rutgers University Press, 1954.

Dall, Curtis B. *FDR, My Exploited Father-in-Law.* Tulsa, Okla.: Christian Crusade, 1968.

Dallek, Robert. *Franklin D. Roosevelt and American Foreign Policy, 1932–1945.* New York: Oxford University Press, 1979.

Daniels, Jonathan. *The End of Innocence.* Philadelphia: Lippincott, 1954.

———. *The Time Between the Wars.* New York: Doubleday, 1966.

———. *Washington Quadrille: The Dance Beside the Documents.* New York: Doubleday, 1968.

———. *White House Witness, 1942–1945.* New York: Doubleday, 1975.

Daniels, Josephus. *The Wilson Era: Years of Peace, 1910–1917.* Chapel Hill: University of North Carolina Press, 1944.

———. *The Wilson Era: Years of War and After, 1917–1923.* Chapel Hill: University of North Carolina Press, 1946.

Davies, Joseph E. *Mission to Moscow.* New York: Simon & Schuster, 1941.

Davis, Kenneth Sydney. *FDR: The Beckoning of Destiny, 1882–1928: A History.* New York: G. P. Putnam's Sons, 1972.

———. *FDR: Into the Storm, 1937–1940: A History.* New York: Random House, 1993.

———. *FDR: The New Deal Years, 1933–1937: A History.* New York: Random House, 1979.

———. *FDR: The New York Years: 1928–1933.* New York: Random House, 1985.

———. *FDR: The War President, 1940–1943: A History.* New York: Random House, 2000.

———. *The Hero: Charles A. Lindbergh and the American Dream.* New York: Doubleday, 1959.

———. *Invincible Summer: An Intimate Portrait of the Roosevelts, Based on the Recollections of Marion Dickerman.* New York: Atheneum, 1974.

Dawidowicz, Lucy. *The War Against the Jews, 1933–1945.* New York: Holt, Rinehart, and Winston, 1975.

Day, Donald, ed. *Franklin D. Roosevelt's Own Story: Told in His Own Words from His Private and Public Papers.* Boston: Little, Brown, 1951.

Daynes, Byron W., William D. Pederson, and Michael P. Riccards, eds. *The New Deal and Public Policy.* New York: St. Martin's Press, 1998.

Dedijer, Vladimir. *The Road to Sarajevo.* New York: Simon & Schuster, 1966.

de Gaulle, Charles. *War Memoirs.* 5 vols. New York: Simon & Schuster, 1955–1960.

Delano, Daniel W., Jr. *Franklin Roosevelt and the Delano Influence.* Pittsburgh: J. S. Nudi Publications, 1946.

Dickinson, Matthew J. *Bitter Harvest: FDR, Presidential Power, and the Growth of the Presidential Branch.* New York: Cambridge University Press, 1996.

Dickson, Paul, and Thomas B. Allen. *The Bonus Army: An American Epic.* New York: Walker & Company, 2004.

Dillon, Mary Earhart. *Wendell Willkie, 1892–1944.* Philadelphia: Lippincott, 1952.

Divine, Robert A. *The Reluctant Belligerent: American Entry into World War II.* New York: John Wiley & Sons, 1969.

———. *Roosevelt and World War II.* Baltimore: Johns Hopkins University Press, 1969.

Dizikes, John. *Britain, Roosevelt, and the New Deal: British Opinion, 1932–1938.* New York: Garland, 1979.

Documents on American Foreign Relations. New York: World Peace Foundation, 1942.

Documents on German Foreign Policy, 1918–1945, from the Archives of the German Foreign Ministry. Washington, D.C.: Government Printing Office, 1949–1964.

Dodd, William E., ed. *Ambassador Dodd's Diary, 1933–1938.* New York: Harcourt, Brace, 1941.

Donn, Linda. *The Roosevelt Cousins: Growing Up Together, 1882–1924.* New York: Knopf, 2001.

Donovan, Hedley. *Roosevelt to Reagan: A Reporter's Encounter with Nine Presidents.* New York: Harper & Row, 1985.

Donovan, Robert J. *Conflict and Crisis.* New York: Norton, 1977.

Douglas, William O. *Go East, Young Man: The Early Years; The Autobiography of William O. Douglas.* New York: Random House, 1974.

Downing, Andrew Jackson. *The Architecture of Country Houses.* New York: Appleton, 1850.

———. *Treatise on the Theory and Practice of Landscape Gardening Adapted to North America.* New York: Appleton, 1840.

Dows, Olin. *Franklin Roosevelt at Hyde Park: Documented Drawings and Text.* New York: American Artists Group, 1949.

Draper, George. *Acute Poliomyelitis.* Philadelphia: Blakiston, 1917.

Dubofsky, Melvyn, and Warren Van Tine. *John L. Lewis: A Biography.* New York: Quadrangle/New York Times Book Co., 1977.

Duncan, Robert C. *America's Use of Sea Mines.* White Oak, Md.: Naval Research Laboratory, 1962.

Dunn, Dennis J. *Caught Between Roosevelt & Stalin: America's Ambassadors to Moscow.* Lexington: University of Kentucky Press, 1998.

Dunne, Gerald T. *Hugo Black and the Judicial Revolution.* New York: Simon & Schuster, 1977.

Eccles, Marriner. *Beckoning Frontiers: Public and Personal Recollections.* New York: Knopf, 1951.

Eden, Anthony. *The Reckoning: The Memoirs of Anthony Eden, Earl of Avon.* Boston: Houghton Mifflin, 1965.

Edmonds, Robin. *The Big Three: Churchill, Roosevelt, and Stalin in Peace and War.* New York: Norton, 1991.

Einaudi, Mario. *The Roosevelt Revolution.* New York: Harcourt, Brace, 1957.

Einstein, Lewis. *Roosevelt: His Mind in Action.* New York: Houghton Mifflin, 1930.

Eisenhower, David. *Eisenhower at War, 1943–1945.* New York: Random House, 1986.

Eisenhower, Dwight D. *At Ease: Stories I Tell to Friends.* New York: Doubleday, 1967.

———. *Crusade in Europe.* New York: Doubleday, 1948.

Ekirch, Arthur A., Jr. *Ideologies and Utopias: The Impact of the New Deal on American Thought.* Chicago: Quadrangle Books, 1969.

Eliot, Elizabeth. *Heiresses and Coronets: The Story of Lovely Ladies and Noble Men.* New York: McDowell, Obolensky, 1959.

Ellis, Francis M., and Edward F. Clark, Jr. *A Brief History of Carter, Ledyard & Milburn.* Portsmouth, N.H.: Peter E. Randall, 1988.

Ellis, John. *Brute Force: Allied Strategy and Tactics in the Second World War.* New York: Viking Press, 1990.

Evans, Hugh E. *The Hidden Campaign: FDR's Health and the 1944 Election.* Armonk, N.Y.: M. E. Sharpe, 2002.

Faber, Doris. *The Life of Lorena Hickok: E.R.'s Friend.* New York: Morrow, 1980.

Fairbank, John King. *Trade and Diplomacy on the China Coast.* Stanford, Calif.: Stanford University Press, 1969.

Farley, James A. *Behind the Ballots: The Personal History of a Politician.* New York: Harcourt, Brace, 1938.

———. *Jim Farley's Story: The Roosevelt Years.* New York: Whittlesey House, 1948.

Farnham, Barbara. *Roosevelt and the Munich Crisis: A Study of Political Decision Making.* Princeton, N.J.: Princeton University Press, 1997.

Farr, Finis. *FDR.* New Rochelle, N.Y.: Arlington House, 1948.

Faulkner, Harold U. *From Versailles to the New Deal.* New Haven, Conn.: Yale University Press, 1950.

Fay, Sidney B. *Origins of the World War.* 2 vols. New York: Macmillan, 1930.

Feingold, Henry L. *The Politics of Rescue: The Roosevelt Administration and the Holocaust, 1938–1945.* New Brunswick, N.J.: Rutgers University Press, 1970.

Feis, Herbert. *1933: Characters in Crisis.* Boston: Little, Brown, 1966.

———. *Churchill-Roosevelt-Stalin: The War They Waged and the Peace They Sought.* Princeton, N.J.: Princeton University Press, 1957.

———. *The Road to Pearl Harbor.* Princeton, N.J.: Princeton University Press, 1950.

Feldman, Ellen. *Lucy: A Novel.* New York: Norton, 2003.

Felsenthal, Carol. *Alice Roosevelt Longworth.* New York: Putnam, 1988.

Ferrell, Robert H. *American Diplomacy: A History.* New York: Norton, 1975.

———. *Choosing Truman: The Democratic Convention of 1944.* Columbia: University of Missouri Press, 1994.

———. *The Dying President: Franklin D. Roosevelt, 1944–1945.* Columbia: University of Missouri Press, 1998.

Fest, Joachim C. *Hitler.* New York: Harcourt Brace Jovanovich, 1974.

Fischer, Fritz. *Germany's Aims in the First World War.* New York: Norton, 1967.

Fish, Hamilton. *FDR: The Other Side of the Coin.* New York: Vantage Press, 1976.

Flanagan, Hallie. *Arena: The History of the Federal Theatre.* New York: Duell, Sloan and Pearce, 1940.

Fleming, Thomas J. *The New Dealer's War: FDR and the War Within World War II.* New York: Basic Books, 2001.

Flynn, Edward J. *You're the Boss.* New York: Viking Press, 1947.

Flynn, John T. *Country Squire in the White House.* New York: Doubleday, 1940.

Frankfurter, Felix. *From the Diaries of Felix Frankfurter.* Joseph P. Lash, ed. New York: Norton, 1975.

Freedman, Max, ed. *Roosevelt and Frankfurter: Their Correspondence, 1928–1945.* Boston: Little, Brown, 1967.

Freedman, Russell. *Franklin Delano Roosevelt.* New York: Clarion Books, 1990.

Freidel, Frank. *F.D.R. and the South.* Baton Rouge: Louisiana State University Press, 1965.

———. *Franklin D. Roosevelt: The Apprenticeship.* Boston: Little, Brown, 1952.

———. *Franklin D. Roosevelt: The Ordeal.* Boston: Little, Brown, 1954.

———. *Franklin D. Roosevelt: The Triumph.* Boston: Little, Brown, 1956.

———. *Franklin D. Roosevelt: Launching the New Deal.* Boston: Little, Brown, 1973.

———. *Franklin D. Roosevelt: A Rendezvous with Destiny.* Boston: Little, Brown, 1990.

Fried, Albert. *FDR and His Enemies.* New York: St. Martin's Press, 1999.

———, ed. *A Day of Dedication: The Essential Writings and Speeches of Woodrow Wilson.* New York: Macmillan, 1965.

Friedrich, Otto. *Clover.* New York: Simon & Schuster, 1979.

Fromkin, David. *Europe's Last Summer: Who Started the Great War in 1914?* New York: Knopf, 2004.

Funk, Arthur L. *The Politics of TORCH: The Allied Landings and the Algiers Putsch, 1942.* Lawrence: University Press of Kansas, 1974.

Fusfeld, Daniel R. *The Economic Thought of Franklin D. Roosevelt and the Origins of the New Deal.* New York: AMS Press, 1956.

Gable, John A. *The Bull Moose Years: Theodore Roosevelt and the Progressive Party.* Port Washington, N.Y.: Kennikat Press, 1978.

Galbraith, John Kenneth. *The Great Crash.* Boston: Houghton Mifflin, 1955.

Gallagher, Hugh Gregory. *FDR's Splendid Deception.* New York: Dodd, Mead, 1985.

Gallup, George H. *The Gallup Poll: Public Opinion, 1935–1971.* New York: Random House, 1972.

Gardner, Joseph L. *Departing Glory: Theodore Roosevelt as Ex-President.* New York: Charles Scribner's Sons, 1973.

Garson, Robert A., and Stuart S. Kidd. *The Roosevelt Years.* Edinburgh: Edinburgh University Press, 1999.

Geddes, Donald Porter. *Franklin Delano Roosevelt, A Memorial.* New York: Dial Press, 1945.

Gellman, Irwin F. *Good Neighbor Diplomacy: United States Policies in Latin America, 1933–1945.* Baltimore: Johns Hopkins University Press, 1979.

———. *Secret Affairs: Franklin Roosevelt, Cordell Hull, and Sumner Welles.* Baltimore: Johns Hopkins University Press, 1995.

George, Alexander L., and Juliette L. George. *Woodrow Wilson and Colonel House: A Personality Study.* New York: J. Day, 1956.

Gerard, James W. *My First Eighty-three Years in America.* New York: Doubleday, 1951.

Gilbert, Martin. *Auschwitz and the Allies.* New York: Holt, Rinehart, and Winston, 1981.

———. *Churchill: A Life.* New York: Henry Holt, 1991.

Goldberg, Richard Thayer. *The Making of Franklin D. Roosevelt.* Lanham, Md.: National Book Network, 1991.

Goldman, Eric. *Rendezvous with Destiny.* New York: Knopf, 1952.

Goodhart, Philip. *Fifty Ships That Saved the World: The Foundation of the Anglo-American Alliance.* New York: Doubleday, 1965.

Goodwin, Doris Kearns. *No Ordinary Time: Franklin and Eleanor Roosevelt: The Home Front in World War II.* New York: Simon & Schuster, 1994.

Gordon, Lois, and Alan Gordon, eds. *American Chronicle: Year by Year Through the Twentieth Century.* New Haven, Conn.: Yale University Press, 1999.

Gosnell, Harold F. *Champion Campaigner: Franklin D. Roosevelt.* New York: Macmillan, 1952.

Gould, Jean. *A Good Fight: The Story of F.D.R.'s Conquest of Polio.* New York: Dodd, Mead, 1960.

Gowing, Margaret. *Britain and Atomic Energy, 1939–1945.* New York: St. Martin's Press, 1964.

Graebner, Norman A. *Roosevelt and the Search for a European Policy, 1937–1939.* Baton Rouge: Louisiana University Press, 1987.

Grafton, John, ed. *Great Speeches.* Mineola, N.Y.: Dover Publications, 1999.

Graham, Otis L., Jr. *Franklin D. Roosevelt: His Life and Times: An Encyclopedic View.* New York: Da Capo Press, 1991.

———. *Toward a Planned Society.* New York: Oxford University Press, 1976.

Grant, R. G. *Flight: 100 Years of Aviation.* New York: D. K. Publishing, 2002.

Grapes, Bryan J., ed. *Franklin D. Roosevelt.* San Diego: Greenhaven Press, 2000.

Greeley, Horace. *The American Conflict.* Hartford, Conn.: O. D. Case, 1864.

Greenfield, Kent R., ed. *Command Decisions.* Washington, D.C.: Government Printing Office, 1960.

Greer, Thomas H. *What Roosevelt Thought: The Social and Political Ideas of Franklin D. Roosevelt.* East Lansing: Michigan State University Press, 1999.

Grew, Joseph. *Ten Years in Japan: A Contemporary Record Drawn from the Diaries and Private and Official Papers of Joseph C. Grew, United States Ambassador to Japan, 1932–1942.* New York: Simon & Schuster, 1944.

———. *Turbulent Era: A Diplomatic Record of Forty Years, 1904–1945.* 2 vols. Boston: Houghton Mifflin, 1952.

Grey of Falloden, Edward, Viscount. *Twenty-five Years, 1892–1916.* 2 vols. London: Hodder & Stoughton, 1925.

Gunther, John. *Inside U.S.A.* New York: Harper & Brothers, 1947.

———. *Roosevelt in Retrospect: A Profile in History.* New York: Harper & Brothers, 1950.

Hacker, Jeffrey H. *Franklin D. Roosevelt.* Lakeville, Conn.: Grey Castle Press, 1994.

Hagedorn, Hermann. *The Roosevelt Family of Sagamore Hill.* New York: Macmillan, 1954.

Hague, Arnold. *Destroyers for Britain: A History of Fifty Town Class Ships Transferred from the United States to Great Britain in 1940.* Annapolis, Md.: Naval Institute Press, 1990.

Halberstam, David. *The Powers That Be.* New York: Knopf, 1979.

Halsey, William F., and J. Bryan, III. *Admiral Halsey's Story.* New York: McGraw-Hill, 1947.

Hamm, Margherita. *Famous Families of New York.* New York: G. P. Putnam's Sons, 1976.

Handlin, Oscar. *Al Smith and His America.* Boston: Little, Brown, 1958.

Hanes, William Travis and Frank Sanello. *The Opium Wars: The Addiction of One Empire and the Corruption of Another.* Napierville, Ill.: Sourcebooks, 2002.

Harbaugh, William H. *Lawyer's Lawyer: The Life of John W. Davis.* New York: Oxford University Press, 1973.

———. *Power and Responsibility: The Life and Times of Theodore Roosevelt.* New York: Oxford University Press, 1975.

Hardeman, D. B., and Donald C. Bacon. *Rayburn: A Biography.* Austin: Texas Monthly Press, 1987.

Hareven, Tamara. *Eleanor Roosevelt: An American Conscience.* Chicago: Quadrangle, 1968.

Harlan, Louis R. *Booker T. Washington: Wizard of Tuskegee, 1901–1915.* New York: Oxford University Press, 1983.

Harriman, Averell, and Elie Abel. *Special Envoy to Churchill and Stalin, 1941–1946.* New York: Random House, 1975.

Harrity, Richard, and Ralph G. Martin. *The Human Side of FDR.* New York: Duell, Sloan and Pearce, 1960.

Harrod, R. F. *The Life of John Maynard Keynes.* New York: Avon Books, 1971.

Hassett, William D. *Off the Record with FDR, 1942–1945.* New Brunswick, N.J.: Rutgers University Press, 1958.

Hatch, Alden. *Franklin D. Roosevelt.* New York: Henry Holt, 1947.

Hawkins, Hugh. *Between Harvard and America: The Educational Leadership of Charles W. Elliot.* New York: Oxford University Press, 1972.

Hayner, Don, and Tom McNamee. *The Stadium.* Chicago: Performance Media, 1993.

Heale, M. J. *Franklin D. Roosevelt: The New Deal and War.* New York: Routledge, 1999.

Hearden, Patrick J. *Roosevelt Confronts Hitler: America's Entry into World War II.* Dekalb: Northern Illinois University Press, 1987.

Heinrichs, Waldo H. *American Ambassador: Joseph C. Grew and the Development of United States Diplomatic Tradition.* Boston: Little, Brown, 1966.

———. *Threshold of War: Franklin D. Roosevelt and American Entry into World War II.* New York: Oxford University Press, 1988.

Herring, E. Pendleton. *Presidential Leadership: The Political Relations of Congress and the Chief Executive.* New York: Farrar & Rinehart, 1940.

Herzstein, Robert Edwin. *Roosevelt & Hitler: Prelude to War.* New York: J. Wiley, 1994.

Hess, Stephen. *America's Political Dynasties from Adams to Kennedy.* New York: Doubleday, 1966.

Hibbert, Christopher. *Garibaldi and his Enemies.* Boston: Little, Brown, 1966.

Hickok, Lorena. *Eleanor Roosevelt: Reluctant First Lady.* New York: Dodd, Mead, 1980.

———. *The Road to the White House: FDR: The Pre-presidential Years.* New York: Scholastic Book Services, 1962.

Hicks, John D. *The Populist Revolt: A History of the Farmers' Alliance and the People's Party.* Minneapolis: University of Minnesota Press, 1931.

———. *Republican Ascendancy, 1921–1933.* New York: Harper & Row, 1960.

Higgins, Trumbull. *Winston Churchill and the Second Front, 1940–1943.* New York: Oxford University Press, 1957.

High, Stanley. *Roosevelt—And Then?* New York: Harper & Brothers, 1937.

Hodgson, Godfrey. *The Colonel: The Life and Wars of Henry Stimson, 1867–1950.* New York: Knopf, 1990.

Hoehling, A. A., and Mary Duprey Hoehling. *The Last Voyage of the* Lusitania. New York: Henry Holt, 1956.

Hoffman, Edward George. *Official Report of the Proceedings of the Democratic National Convention.* Indianapolis: Bookwalter-Ball, 1920.

Holt, Rackham. *Mary McLeod Bethune.* New York: Doubleday, 1964.

Hoover, Herbert. *Memoirs.* 3 vols. New York: Macmillan, 1951–1952.

———. *The Ordeal of Woodrow Wilson.* New York: McGraw-Hill, 1958.

———. *Public Papers of the President of the United States: Herbert Hoover: Containing the Public Messages, Speeches, and Statements of the President, March 4, 1929 to March 4, 1933.* Washington, D.C.: U.S. Government Printing Office, 1974–1977.

———. *State Papers and Other Public Writings of Herbert Hoover.* William S. Myers, ed. 2 vols. New York: Doubleday, Doran, 1934.

Hoover, Irwin Hood. *Forty-two Years in the White House.* Boston: Houghton Mifflin, 1934.

Hopkins, Harry. *Spending to Save.* New York: Norton, 1936.

Houck, Davis W. and Amos Kiewe. *FDR's Body Politics: The Rhetoric of Disability.* College Station: Texas A&M University Press, 2003.

Houston, David F. *Eight Years with Wilson's Cabinet.* New York: Doubleday, Page & Co., 1926.

Howard, Thomas C., and William D. Pederson, ed. *Franklin D. Roosevelt and the Formation of the Modern World.* Armonk, N.Y.: M. E. Sharpe, 2002.

Hull, Cordell. *The Memoirs of Cordell Hull.* 2 vols. New York: Macmillan, 1948.

Hunt, Frazier. *The Untold Story of Douglas MacArthur.* New York: Devin-Adair, 1954.

Hunt, John G. *The Essential Franklin Delano Roosevelt.* New York: Gramercy Books, 1995.

Hurd, Charles. *When the New Deal Was Young and Gay.* New York: Hawthorn Books, 1965.

Huthmacher, J. Joseph. *Senator Robert F. Wagner and the Rise of Urban Liberalism.* New York: Atheneum, 1968.

Hyman, Sidney. *The American President.* New York: Harper & Brothers, 1954.

Ickes, Harold L. *The Secret Diary of Harold L. Ickes.* 3 vols. New York: Simon & Schuster, 1953–1954.

Ike, Nobutaka. *Japan's Decision for War: Records of the 1941 Policy Conferences.* Stanford, Calif.: Stanford University Press, 1967.

Irons, Peter H. *Justice at War.* New York: Oxford University Press, 1983.

———. *The New Deal Lawyers.* Princeton, N.J.: Princeton University Press, 1982.

Irwin, Will. *Letters to Kermit from Theodore Roosevelt, 1902–1908.* New York: Charles Scribner's Sons, 1946.

Ismay, Lord. *The Memoirs of General Lord Ismay.* New York: Viking, 1960.

Israel, Fred L., ed. *Major Peace Treaties in Modern History, 1648–1967.* New York: Chelsea House, 1967.

Jackson, Robert H. *That Man: An Insider's Portrait of Franklin D. Roosevelt.* John Q. Barrett, ed. New York: Oxford University Press, 2003.

Jackson, Stanley. *J. P. Morgan.* New York: Stein and Day, 1983.

Jaher, Frederic Cople, ed. *The Rich, the Well Born, and the Powerful: Elites and Upper Classes in History.* Urbana: University of Illinois Press, 1973.

James, D. Clayton. *The Years of MacArthur.* 3 vols. Boston: Houghton Mifflin, 1975.

Janeway, Eliot. *The Struggle for Survival.* New Haven, Conn.: Yale University Press, 1950.

Jenkins, Roy. *Churchill: A Biography.* New York: Farrar, Straus and Giroux, 2001.

———. *Franklin Delano Roosevelt.* New York: Times Books, 2003.

Jansen, Marius B. *The Making of Modern Japan.* Cambridge, Mass.: Harvard University Press, 2000.

Jessup, Philip C. *Elihu Root.* 2 vols. New York: Dodd, Mead, 1938.

Johnson, Alvin Page. *Franklin D. Roosevelt's Colonial Ancestors: Their Part in the Making of American History.* Boston: Lothrop, Lee & Shepard, 1933.

Johnson, Brian. *Fly Navy: The History of Maritime Aviation.* Newton Abbot, Devon: David & Charles, 1981.

Johnson, Gerald W. *Roosevelt: An American Study.* London: H. Hamilton, 1942.

———. *Roosevelt: Dictator or Democrat?* New York: Harper & Brothers, 1941.

Johnson, Hugh S. *The Blue Eagle, from Egg to Earth.* New York: Doubleday, 1935.

Jones, F. C. *Japan's New Order in East Asia: Its Rise and Fall.* New York: Cambridge University Press, 1954.

Josephson, Matthew, and Hannah Josephson. *Al Smith: Hero of the Cities; A Political Portrait Drawing on the Papers of Frances Perkins.* Boston: Houghton Mifflin, 1969.

Joslin, Theodore G. *Hoover off the Record.* New York: Doubleday, 1934.

Kaledin, Eugenia. *The Education of Mrs. Henry Adams.* Philadelphia: Temple University Press, 1981.

Kammen, Michael. *Colonial New York: A History.* New York: Charles Scribner's Sons, 1975.

Katz, Friedrich. *Deutschland, Diaz, und die mexikanische Revolution: die deutsche Politik in Mexiko, 1870–1920.* Berlin: Deutscher Verlag des Wissenschaften, 1964.

Kazin, Alfred. *New York Jew*. New York: Knopf, 1978.

———. *On Native Grounds: An Interpretation of Modern American Prose Literature*. New York: Harcourt, Brace & World, 1942.

Kearney, James R. *Anna Eleanor Roosevelt: The Evolution of a Reformer*. Boston: Houghton Mifflin, 1968.

Kecskemeti, Paul. *Strategic Surrender: The Politics of Victory and Defeat*. Stanford, Calif.: Stanford University Press, 1958.

Keegan, John. *The Mask of Command*. New York: Viking Press, 1987.

———. *The Second World War*. New York: Viking Press, 1989.

Keen, William Williams. *The Surgical Operations on President Cleveland in 1893, Together with Six Additional Papers of Reminiscences*. Philadelphia: Lippincott, 1928.

Kendrick, Alexander. *Prime Time: The Life of Edward R. Murrow*. Boston: Little, Brown, 1965.

Kennedy, David M. *Freedom from Fear: The American People in Depression and War, 1929–1945*. New York: Oxford University Press, 1999.

Kennedy, William. *O Albany!* New York: Viking Press, 1983.

Kent, Frank. *The Democratic Party: A History*. New York: Century, 1928.

———. *Without Grease*. New York: Morrow, 1936.

Kessler, Henry H., and Eugene Rachlis. *Peter Stuyvesant and His New York*. New York: Random House, 1959.

Key, V. O., Jr. *Southern Politics in State and Nation*. New York: Knopf, 1950.

Kilpatrick, Carroll, ed. *Roosevelt and Daniels: A Friendship in Politics*. Chapel Hill: University of North Carolina Press, 1952.

Kimball, Warren F. *Forged in War: Roosevelt, Churchill, and the Second World War*. New York: Morrow, 1997.

———. *The Juggler: Franklin Roosevelt as Wartime Statesman*. Princeton, N.J.: Princeton University Press, 1991.

———. *The Most Unsordid Act: Lend-Lease, 1939–1941*. Baltimore: Johns Hopkins University Press, 1969.

King, Ernest J., and Walter M. Whitehill. *Fleet Admiral King: A Naval Record*. New York: Norton, 1952.

Kingdon, Frank. *As FDR Said*. New York: Duell, Sloan and Pearce, 1950.

Kleeman, Rita Halle. *Gracious Lady: The Life of Sara Delano Roosevelt*. New York: D. Appleton–Century, 1935.

———. *Young Franklin Roosevelt*. New York: J. Messner, 1946.

Klein, Jonas. *Beloved Island: Franklin and Eleanor and the Legacy of Campobello*. Forest Dale, Vt.: Paul S. Eriksson, 2000.

Kludas, Arnold. *Die grossen Passagierschiffe der Welt*. Oldenburg/Hamburg: Gerhard Stalling, 1972.

Koenig, Louis W. *Bryan: A Political Biography of William Jennings Bryan*. New York: G. P. Putnam's Sons, 1971.

Koginos, Manny T. *The Panay Incident: Prelude to War*. Lafayette, Ind.: Purdue University Studies, 1967.

Krock, Arthur. *Memoirs: Sixty Years on the Firing Line.* New York: Funk & Wagnalls, 1968.

LaCerra, Charles. *Franklin Delano Roosevelt and Tammany Hall of New York.* Lanham, Md.: University Press of America, 1997.

Langer, William L., and S. Everett Gleason. *The Challenge to Isolation, 1937–1940.* New York: Harper & Brothers, 1952.

———. *The Challenge to Isolation: The World Crisis of 1937–1940 and American Foreign Policy.* Gloucester, Mass.: Peter Smith, 1970. Reprint.

———. *The Undeclared War.* New York: Harper & Brothers, 1953.

Langston, Thomas S. *Ideologues and Presidents: From the New Deal to the Reagan Revolution.* Baltimore: Johns Hopkins University Press, 1992.

Lansing, Robert. *The Lansing Papers, 1914–1920.* 2 vols. Washington, D.C.: U.S. Government Printing Office, 1939.

Laqueur, Walter. *The Terrible Secret.* Boston: Little, Brown, 1980.

Larrabee, Eric. *Commander in Chief: Franklin Delano Roosevelt, His Lieutenants, and Their War.* New York: Harper & Row, 1987.

Larsen, Rebecca. *Franklin D. Roosevelt: Man of Destiny.* Danbury, Conn.: Franklin Watts, 1991.

Lash, Joseph P. *Eleanor and Franklin: The Story of Their Relationship.* New York: Norton, 1971.

———. *Eleanor Roosevelt: A Friend's Memoir.* New York: Doubleday, 1964.

———. *Eleanor: The Years Alone.* New York: Norton, 1972.

———. *Love, Eleanor: Eleanor Roosevelt and Her Friends.* New York: Doubleday, 1982.

———. *Roosevelt and Churchill, 1939–1941: The Partnership That Saved the West.* New York: Norton, 1976.

———. *A World of Love: Eleanor Roosevelt and Her Friends.* New York: Doubleday, 1984.

Laski, H. J. *The American Presidency.* New York: Harper & Brothers, 1940.

Layton, Edwin T. *And I Was There: Pearl Harbor and Midway, Breaking the Secrets.* New York: Morrow, 1985.

Leahy, William D. *I Was There: The Personal Story of the Chief of Staff to Presidents Roosevelt and Truman.* New York: Whittlesey House, 1950.

Lehman, Donald H. *Executive Office Building.* Washington, D.C.: General Services Administration, 1964.

Leitch, Alexander, ed. *A Princeton Companion.* Princeton, N.J.: Princeton University Press, 1978.

Lemons, J. Stanley. *The Woman Citizen: Social Feminism in the 1920s.* Urbana: University of Illinois Press, 1973.

Leonard, Charles A. *A Search for a Judicial Philosophy: Mr. Justice Roberts and the Constitutional Revolution of 1937.* Port Washington, N.Y.: Kennikat Press, 1971.

Lessard, Suzannah. *The Architect of Desire: Beauty and Danger in the Stanford White Family.* New York: Dial Press, 1996.

Lester, DeeGee. *Roosevelt Research: Collections for the Study of Theodore, Franklin, and Eleanor.* Westport, Conn.: Greenwood Press, 1992.

Leuchtenburg, William E. *The FDR Years.* New York: Columbia University Press, 1995.

———. *Franklin D. Roosevelt and the New Deal, 1932–1940.* New York: Harper & Row, 1963.

———. *In the Shadow of FDR: From Harry Truman to George W. Bush.* Ithaca, N.Y.: Cornell University Press, 2001.

———. *The Perils of Prosperity, 1814–1932.* Chicago: University of Chicago Press, 1958.

———. *The Supreme Court Reborn: The Constitutional Revolution in the Age of Roosevelt.* New York: Oxford University Press, 1995.

Levine, Lawrence W. and Cornelia R., eds. *The People and the President: America's Conversation with FDR.* Boston: Beacon Press, 2002.

Levy, Daniel, and Susan Brink. *A Change of Heart.* New York: Knopf, 2005.

Levy, William Turner, and Cynthia Eagle Russett. *The Extraordinary Mrs. R: A Friend Remembers Eleanor Roosevelt.* New York: John Wiley, 1999.

Lewin, Ronald. *The American Magic: Codes, Ciphers and the Defeat of Japan.* New York: Farrar, Straus and Giroux, 1982.

Libbey, James K. *Dear Alben: Mr. Barkley of Kentucky.* Lexington: University of Kentucky Press, 1979.

Liddell Hart, B. H. *History of the Second World War.* London: Cassell, 1970.

Lindbergh, Charles A. *The Wartime Journals of Charles A. Lindbergh.* New York: Harcourt Brace Jovanovich, 1970.

Lindley, Ernest K. *Franklin D. Roosevelt: A Career in Progressive Democracy.* Indianapolis: Bobbs-Merrill, 1931.

———. *Half Way with Roosevelt.* New York: Viking Press, 1937.

———. *The Roosevelt Revolution: First Phase.* New York: Viking Press, 1933.

Lingeman, Richard. *Don't You Know There's a War On? The American Home Front, 1941–1945.* New York: G. P. Putnam's Sons, 1970.

Link, Arthur S. *Wilson: The New Freedom.* Princeton, N.J.: Princeton University Press, 1956.

———. *Wilson: The Road to the White House.* Princeton, N.J.: Princeton University Press, 1947.

———. *Wilson: The Struggle for Neutrality, 1914–1915.* Princeton, N.J.: Princeton University Press, 1960.

Lippman, Theo, Jr. *The Squire of Warm Springs: F.D.R. in Georgia, 1924–1945.* New York: Simon & Schuster, 1977.

Lippmann, Walter. *Interpretations, 1933–1935.* Allan Nevins, ed. New York: Macmillan, 1936.

Lisio, Donald J. *The President and Protest: Hoover, Conspiracy, and the Bonus Riot.* Columbia: University of Missouri Press, 1974.

Long, Breckinridge. *The War Diary of Breckinridge Long: Selections from the Years 1939–1944.* Fred Israel, ed. Lincoln: University of Nebraska Press, 1966.

Longworth, Alice Roosevelt. *Crowded Hours: Reminiscences of Alice Roosevelt Longworth.* New York: Charles Scribner's Sons, 1933.

Looker, Earle. *This Man Roosevelt.* New York: Brewer, Warren & Putnam, 1932.

Lorant, Stefan. *FDR: A Pictorial Biography.* New York: Simon & Schuster, 1950.

———. *The Life and Times of Theodore Roosevelt.* New York: Doubleday, 1959.

Lord, Russell. *The Wallaces of Iowa.* Boston: Houghton Mifflin, 1947.

Louchheim, Katie, ed. *The Making of the New Deal: The Insiders Speak.* Cambridge, Mass.: Harvard University Press, 1983.

Love, William Robert. *History of the U.S. Navy.* Harrisburg, Pa.: Stackpole Books, 1992.

Lovett, Robert Williamson. *The Treatment of Infantile Paralysis.* Philadelphia: P. Blakiston's Son & Co., 1916.

Low, Maurice. *Woodrow Wilson: An Interpretation.* Boston: Little, Brown, 1918.

Lubell, Samuel. *The Future of American Politics.* New York: Harper & Brothers, 1952.

Ludwig, Emil. *Roosevelt: A Study in Fortune and Power.* New York: Viking Press, 1938.

Lumsden, Linda J. *Inez: The Life and Times of Inez Milholland.* Bloomington: Indiana University Press, 2004.

MacArthur, Douglas. *Reminiscences.* New York: McGraw-Hill, 1964.

MacCracken, Henry Noble. *Blithe Dutchess: The Flowering of an American County from 1812.* New York: Hastings House, 1958.

Mackenzie, Compton. *Mr. Roosevelt.* New York: E. P. Dutton, 1944.

MacLeish, Archibald. *The Eleanor Roosevelt Story.* Boston: Houghton Mifflin, 1965.

Macmahon, Arthur W., and John D. Millett. *Federal Administrators: A Biographical Approach to the Problem of Departmental Management.* New York: AMS Press, 1967.

Macmillan, Harold. *The Blast of War, 1939–1945.* New York: Harper & Row, 1968.

MacMillan, Margaret. *Paris, 1919.* New York: Random House, 2001.

Maddison, Angus. *Monitoring the World Economy, 1820–1992.* Paris: Organization for Economic Co-operation and Development, 1995.

Maguire, G. E. *Anglo-American Policy Towards the Free French.* New York: St. Martin's Press, 1995.

Malkin, Michelle. *In Defense of Internment.* Chicago: Regnery, 2004.

Manchester, William. *American Caesar: Douglas MacArthur, 1880–1964.* Boston: Little, Brown, 1978.

Maney, Patrick J. *The Roosevelt Presence: A Biography of Franklin Delano Roosevelt.* New York: Twayne Publishers, 1993.

———. *The Roosevelt Presence: The Life and Legacy of FDR.* Berkeley: University of California Press, 1998.

Mangione, Jerre. *The Dream and the Deal.* Boston: Little, Brown, 1972.

Manstein, Erich von. *Lost Victories.* Chicago: Henry Regnery, 1958.

Marder, Arthur J. *From the Dreadnought to Scapa Flow: The Royal Navy in the Fisher Era, 1904–1919.* New York: Oxford University Press, 1961.

Marescotti, L. Aldrovandi. *Guerra diplomatica: ricordi e frammenti di diario, 1914–1919.* Milan: A. Mondadori, 1936.

Marks, Frederick W., III. *Wind Over Sand: The Diplomacy of Franklin Roosevelt.* Athens: University of Georgia Press, 1990.

Marolda, Edward J. *FDR and the U.S. Navy.* New York: St. Martin's Press, 1998.

Marshall, Katherine Tupper. *Together: Annals of an Army Wife.* New York: Tupper and Love, 1946.

Marshall, S. L. A. *The American Heritage History of World War I.* New York: Simon & Schuster, 1964.

Martin, George. *Madam Secretary: Frances Perkins.* Boston: Houghton Mifflin, 1976.

Martin, Joseph W., and Robert J. Donovan. *My First Fifty Years in Politics.* New York: McGraw-Hill, 1960.

Marx, Rudolph. *The Health of the Presidents.* New York: G. P. Putnam's Sons, 1960.

Matloff, Maurice, and Edwin M. Snell. *Strategic Planning for Coalition Warfare, 1941–1942, 1943–1944.* 2 vols. Washington, D.C.: U.S. Government Printing Office, 1953–1959.

May, Ernest R., ed. *The Ultimate Decision: The President as Commander in Chief.* New York: G. Braziller, 1960.

McAdoo, William Gibbs. *Crowded Years: The Reminiscences of William G. McAdoo.* New York: Houghton Mifflin, 1931.

McCombs, William F. *Making Woodrow Wilson President.* New York: Fairview Publishing, 1921.

McCullough, David. *Character Above All: Doris Kearns Goodwin on Franklin D. Roosevelt.* New York: Simon & Schuster, 1996.

———. *Mornings on Horseback.* New York: Simon & Schuster, 1981.

———. *Truman.* New York: Simon & Schuster, 1991.

McElvaine, Robert S. *Franklin Delano Roosevelt.* Washington, D.C.: CQ Press, 2002.

McIntire, Ross T. *White House Physician.* New York: G. P. Putnam's Sons, 1946.

McJimsey, George T. *Documentary History of the Franklin D. Roosevelt Administration.* Lanham, Md.: University Publications of America, 2000.

———. *The Presidency of Franklin Delano Roosevelt.* Lawrence: University Press of Kansas, 2000.

McKenna, Marian C. *Franklin Roosevelt and the Great Constitutional War: The Court-Packing Crisis of 1937.* New York: Fordham University Press, 2002.

McMahon, Kevin J. *Reconsidering Roosevelt on Race: How the President Paved the Road to* Brown. Chicago: University of Chicago Press, 2004.

McMahon, William E. *Dreadnought Battleships and Battle Cruisers.* Washington, D.C.: University Press of America, 1978.

McWilliams, Carey. *Prejudice; Japanese-Americans: Symbol of Racial Intolerance.* Boston: Little, Brown, 1944.

Meacham, Jon. *Franklin and Winston: An Intimate Portrait of an Epic Friendship.* New York: Random House, 2003.

Mencken, H. L. *Making a President: A Footnote to the Saga of Democracy.* New York: Knopf, 1932.

Michelson, Charles. *The Ghost Talks.* New York: G. P. Putnam's Sons, 1944.

Miller, David Hunter. *The Drafting of the Covenant.* 2 vols. New York: G. P. Putnam's Sons, 1928.

Miller, Nathan. *F.D.R.: An Intimate History.* New York: Doubleday, 1983.

————. *The Roosevelt Chronicles.* New York: Doubleday, 1979.

Mitchell, B. R. *European Historical Statistics, 1750–1970.* New York: Columbia University Press, 1975.

Mitchell, Broadus. *Depression Decade: From New Era Through New Deal, 1929–1941.* New York: Rinehart, 1947.

Moley, Raymond. *After Seven Years.* New York: Harper & Brothers, 1939.

————. *The First New Deal.* New York: Harcourt, Brace & World 1966.

————. *Masters of Politics.* New York: Funk & Wagnalls, 1949.

Monaghan, Frank, and Marvin Lowenthal. *This Was New York, the Nation's Capital in 1789.* New York: Doubleday, Doran & Co., 1943.

Moran, Lord. *Churchill: Taken from the Diaries of Lord Moran; The Struggle for Survival, 1940–1965.* Boston: Houghton Mifflin, 1966.

More, Paul Elmer. *The Complete Poetical Works of Lord Byron.* Boston: Houghton Mifflin, 1905.

Morgan, Ted. *FDR: A Biography.* New York: Simon & Schuster, 1985.

Morison, Elting E. *Admiral Sims and the Modern American Navy.* Boston: Houghton Mifflin, 1942.

————. *Turmoil and Tradition: A Study of the Life and Times of Henry L. Stimson.* Boston: Houghton Mifflin, 1960.

Morison, Samuel Eliot. *The Oxford History of the American People.* New York: Oxford University Press, 1965.

————. *Three Centuries of Harvard, 1636–1936.* Cambridge, Mass.: Harvard University Press, 1936.

Morley, J. W., ed. *The Fateful Choice: Japan's Advance into Southeast Asia, 1939–1941.* New York: Columbia University Press, 1980.

Morris, Edmund. *The Rise of Theodore Roosevelt.* New York: Coward, McCann & Geoghegan, 1979.

————. *Theodore Rex.* New York: Random House, 2001.

Morris, Sylvia Jukes. *Edith Kermit Roosevelt: Portrait of a First Lady.* New York: Coward, McCann & Geoghegan, 1980.

Morrison, Joseph L. *Josephus Daniels: The Small-d Democrat.* Chapel Hill: University of North Carolina Press, 1966.

Morse, Arthur D. *While Six Million Died.* New York: Random House, 1968.

Morton, H. V. *Atlantic Meeting: An Account of Mr. Churchill's Voyage in H.M.S.* Prince of Wales, *in August, 1941, and the Conference with President Roosevelt Which Resulted in the Atlantic Charter.* New York: Dodd, Mead & Company, 1943.

Moscow, Warren. *Politics in the Empire State.* New York: Knopf, 1948.

————. *Roosevelt and Willkie.* Englewood Cliffs, N.J.: Prentice-Hall, 1968.

Mowry, George E. *The Era of Theodore Roosevelt.* New York: Harper & Row, 1958.

————. *Theodore Roosevelt and the Progressive Movement.* Madison: University of Wisconsin Press, 1946.

Mullen, Arthur. *Western Democrat.* New York: W. Funk, 1940.

Murphy, Robert. *Diplomat Among Warriors.* New York: Doubleday, 1964.

Murray, Arthur C. *At Close Quarters.* London: John Murray, 1946.

Murray, Robert K. *The 103rd Ballot: Democrats and the Disaster in Madison Square Garden.* New York: Harper & Row, 1976.

Murray, Williamson, and Allan Millett. *A War to Be Won: Fighting the Second World War.* Cambridge, Mass.: Harvard University Press, 2000.

Myers, Gustavus. *The History of Tammany Hall.* New York: Burt Francis, 1968.

Myers, William S., and Walter H. Newton. *The Hoover Administration: A Documented Narrative.* New York: Charles Scribner's Sons, 1936.

Neal, Steve. *Happy Days Are Here Again.* New York: HarperCollins, 2004.

———. *Dark Horse: A Biography of Wendell Willkie.* New York: Doubleday, 1984.

Neillands, Robin. *The Dieppe Raid: The Story of the Disastrous 1942 Expedition.* Bloomington: Indiana University Press, 2006.

Nesbitt, Henrietta. *White House Diary.* New York: Doubleday, 1948.

Neufeld, Michael J., and Michael Berenbaum, eds. *The Bombing of Auschwitz: Should the Allies Have Attempted It?* New York: St. Martin's Press, 2000.

Neustadt, Richard E. *Presidential Power.* New York: New American Library, 1960.

Nevins, Allan. *The New Deal and World Affairs, 1933–1945.* New Haven, Conn.: Yale University Press, 1950.

Newton, Don, and A. Cecil Hampshire. *Taranto.* London: W. Kimber, 1959.

Newton, Verne W., ed. *FDR and the Holocaust.* New York: St. Martin's Press, 1996.

Nicolson, Harold. *Diaries and Letters, 1930–1939.* New York: Atheneum, 1966.

Nitti, Francesco. *Rivelazioni: dramatis personae.* Naples: Edizioni Scientifiche Italiani, 1948.

Norris, George W. *Fighting Liberal: The Autobiography of George W. Norris.* New York: Macmillan, 1945.

Nourse, Edwin G. *Three Years of the Agricultural Adjustment Administration.* Washington, D.C.: Brookings Institution, 1937.

O'Connor, Harvey. *The Astors.* New York: Knopf, 1941.

O'Connor, Raymond G. *Diplomacy for Victory: FDR and Unconditional Surrender.* New York: Norton, 1971.

O'Connor, Richard. *The First Hurrah, A Biography of Alfred E. Smith.* New York: Putnam, 1970.

Oshinsky, David M. *Polio: An American Story.* New York: Oxford University Press, 2005.

Overacker, Louise. *Money in Elections.* New York: Macmillan, 1932.

Owen, David Edward. *British Opium Policy in China and India.* New Haven, Conn.: Yale University Press, 1934.

Parks, Lillian Rogers, and Frances S. Leighton. *The Roosevelts: A Family in Turmoil.* Englewood Cliffs, N.J.: Prentice-Hall, 1981.

Partridge, Bellamy. *The Roosevelt Family in America: An Imperial Saga.* New York: Hillman-Curl, 1936.

Patterson, James T. *Congressional Conservatism and the New Deal.* Lexington: University of Kentucky Press, 1967.

———. *Mr. Republican: A Biography of Robert A. Taft.* Boston: Houghton Mifflin, 1972.

Paul, John R. *A History of Poliomyelitis.* New Haven, Conn.: Yale University Press, 1971.

Pearson, Drew, and Robert S. Allen. *Nine Old Men at the Crossroads.* New York: Doubleday, 1936.

Peel, Roy V., and Thomas C. Donnelly. *The 1932 Campaign: An Analysis.* New York: Farrar & Rinehart, 1935.

Pendar, Kenneth. *Adventure in Diplomacy: Our French Dilemma.* New York: Dodd, Mead, 1945.

Perkins, Dexter. *The New Age of Franklin Roosevelt.* Chicago: University of Chicago Press, 1957.

Perkins, Frances. *The Roosevelt I Knew.* New York: Viking Press, 1946.

Perlmutter, Amos. *FDR and Stalin: A Not So Grand Alliance, 1943–1945.* Columbia: University of Missouri Press, 1993.

Perras, Galen Roger. *Franklin Roosevelt and the Origins of the Canadian-American Security Alliance, 1933–1945: Necessary but Not Necessary Enough.* Westport, Conn.: Praeger, 1998.

Perry, Elisabeth Israels. *Belle Moskowitz: Feminine Politics and the Exercise of Power in the Age of Alfred E. Smith.* New York: Oxford University Press, 1987.

Persico, Joseph E. *Roosevelt's Secret War: FDR and World War II Espionage.* New York: Random House, 2001.

Peters, Charles. *Five Days in Philadelphia: The Amazing "We Want Willkie!" Convention of 1940 and How It Freed FDR to Save the Western World.* New York: PublicAffairs, 2005.

Picchi, Blaise. *The Five Weeks of Giuseppe Zangara: The Man Who Would Assassinate FDR.* Chicago: Academy Chicago Publishers, 1998.

Pogue, Forrest C. *George C. Marshall: Education of a General, 1880–1939.* New York: Viking Press, 1963.

———. *George C. Marshall: Ordeal and Hope, 1939–1942.* New York: Viking Press, 1966.

———. *George C. Marshall: Organizer of Victory, 1943–1945.* New York: Viking Press, 1973.

———. *The Supreme Command.* Washington, D.C.: U.S. Government Printing Office, 1954.

Pottker, Jan. *Sara and Eleanor.* New York: St. Martin's Press, 2004.

Potts, Steve. *Franklin D. Roosevelt: A Photo Illustrated Biography.* Mankato, Minn.: Bridgestone Books, 1996.

Prange, Gordon W. *At Dawn We Slept: The Untold Story of Pearl Harbor.* New York: McGraw-Hill, 1981.

Prange, Gordon W. with Donald M. Goldstein and Katherine V. Dillon. *Pearl Harbor: The Verdict of History.* New York: Penguin, 1991.

Pratt, Fletcher. *The Navy's War.* New York: Harper & Brothers, 1944.

Pratt, Julius W. *Cordell Hull, 1933–1944.* 2 vols. New York: Cooper Square Publishers, 1964.

Preston, Diana. *Lusitania: An Epic Tragedy.* New York: Walker, 2002.

Pringle, Henry F. *The Life and Times of William Howard Taft.* New York: Farrar & Rinehart, 1939.

———. *Theodore Roosevelt: A Biography.* New York: Harcourt, Brace, 1931.

Pritchett, C. Herman. *The Roosevelt Court: A Study in Judicial Politics and Values, 1937–1947.* New York: Macmillan, 1948.

Proceedings of the 1932 Democratic National Convention. Washington, D.C.: Democratic National Committee, 1932.

Proceedings of the 1936 Democratic National Convention. Washington, D.C.: Democratic National Committee, 1936.

Proceedings of the 1940 Democratic National Convention. Washington, D.C.: Democratic National Committee, 1940.

Proskauer, Joseph M. *A Segment of My Times.* New York: Farrar, Straus, 1950.

Pusey, Merlo J. *Charles Evans Hughes.* 2 vols. New York: Macmillan, 1951.

Putnam, Carleton. *Theodore Roosevelt: The Formative Years.* New York: Charles Scribner's Sons, 1958.

Reilly, Michael F., and William J. Slocum. *Reilly of the White House.* New York: Simon & Schuster, 1947.

Reynolds, David. *From Munich to Pearl Harbor: Roosevelt's America and the Origins of the Second World War.* Chicago: Ivan R. Dee, 2001.

Reynolds, Quentin. *The Amazing Mr. Doolittle: A Biography of Lieutenant General James H. Doolittle.* New York: Arno Press, 1953.

Rhodes, Richard. *The Making of the Atomic Bomb.* New York: Simon & Schuster, 1986.

Richberg, Donald. *My Hero: The Indiscreet Memoirs of an Eventful but Unheroic Life.* New York: G. P. Putnam's Sons, 1954.

———. *The Rainbow: After the Sunshine of Prosperity, the Deluge of the Depression, the Rainbow of the NRA, What Have We Learned? Where Are We Going?* New York: Doubleday, Doran, 1936.

Rixey, Lillian. *Bamie.* New York: McKay, 1963.

Robertson, David. *Sly and Able: A Political Biography of James F. Byrnes.* New York: Norton, 1994.

Robinson, Corinne Roosevelt. *My Brother, Theodore Roosevelt.* New York: Charles Scribner's Sons, 1921.

Robinson, Edgar E. *The Roosevelt Leadership 1933–1945.* Philadelphia: Lippincott, 1955.

Robinson, Greg. *By Order of the President: FDR and the Internment of Japanese Americans.* Cambridge, Mass.: Harvard University Press, 2001.

Rogers, Will. *Sanity Is Where You Find It: An Affectionate History of the United States in the 20's and 30's.* Donald Day, ed. Boston: Houghton Mifflin, 1955.

Rollins, Alfred B., Jr. *Roosevelt and Howe.* New York: Knopf, 1962.

Roosevelt, David B. *Grandmère: A Personal History of Eleanor Roosevelt.* New York: Warner Books, 2002.

Roosevelt, Eleanor. *The Autobiography of Eleanor Roosevelt.* New York: Harper & Brothers, 1961.

———. *Christmas, 1940.* New York: St. Martin's Press, 1986.

———. The *Eleanor Roosevelt Oral History Collection of the Franklin D. Roosevelt Library.* Roger Daniels, ed. 4 vols. Westport, Conn.: Meckler, 1991.

———. *Eleanor Roosevelt's My Day.* 3 vols. New York: Pharos Books, 1989–1991.

———. *It Seems to Me.* New York: Norton, 1954.

———. *This I Remember.* New York: Harper & Brothers, 1949.

———. *This Is My Story.* New York: Harper & Brothers, 1937.

———. *You Learn by Living.* New York: Harper & Brothers, 1960.

Roosevelt, Eleanor, and Lorena Hickok. *Empty Without You: The Intimate Letters of Eleanor Roosevelt and Lorena Hickok.* Roger Streitmatter, ed. New York: Free Press, 1998.

Roosevelt, Elliott. *As He Saw It.* New York: Duell, Sloan, and Pearce, 1946.

———. *Hunting Big Game in the Eighties: The Letters of Elliott Roosevelt, Sportsman.* Eleanor Roosevelt, ed. New York: Charles Scribner's Sons, 1932.

Roosevelt, Elliott, and James Brough. *A Rendezvous with Destiny: The Roosevelts of the White House.* New York: G. P. Putnam's Sons, 1975.

———. *An Untold Story: The Roosevelts of Hyde Park.* New York: G. P. Putnam's Sons, 1973.

Roosevelt, Franklin D. *Complete Presidential Press Conferences of Franklin D. Roosevelt.* 25 vols. New York: Da Capo Press, 1972.

———. *FDR: His Personal Letters.* Elliott Roosevelt, ed. 4 vols. New York: Duell, Sloan, and Pearce, 1947–1950.

———. *F.D.R. Columnist: The Uncollected Columns of Franklin D. Roosevelt.* Donald S. Carmichael, ed. Chicago: Pellegrini & Cudahy, 1947.

———. *The Happy Warrior, Alfred E. Smith: A Study of a Public Servant.* Boston: Houghton Mifflin, 1928.

———. *On Our Way.* New York: John Day, 1934.

———. *Public Papers and Addresses of Franklin D. Roosevelt.* Samuel I. Rosenman, ed. 13 vols. New York: Random House, Macmillan, Harper & Brothers, 1933–1950.

———. *The Public Papers of Franklin D. Roosevelt, Forty-eighth Governor of the State of New York, 1929–1932.* 4 vols. Albany, N.Y.: J. B. Lyon, 1930–1939.

———. *The Roosevelt Letters: Being the Personal Correspondence of Franklin Delano Roosevelt.* Elliott Roosevelt, ed. 3 vols. London: George G. Harrap, 1949–1952.

———. *The Wit and Wisdom of Franklin D. Roosevelt.* Maxwell Meyersohn, ed. Boston: Beacon Press, 1950.

Roosevelt, Franklin D., and Winston Churchill. *Roosevelt and Churchill: Their Secret Wartime Correspondence.* Loewenheim, Francis L., Harold Langley, and Manfred Jonas, eds. New York: Saturday Review Press, 1975.

Roosevelt, Franklin D., and Pope Pius XII. *Wartime Correspondence Between President Roosevelt and Pope Pius XII.* Myron C. Taylor, ed. New York: Macmillan, 1947.

Roosevelt, Hall, with Samuel Duff McCoy. *Odyssey of an American Family: An Account of the Roosevelts and Their Kin as Travelers from 1613–1938.* New York: Harper & Brothers, 1939.

Roosevelt, James, and Sidney Shalett. *Affectionately, F.D.R.: A Son's Story of a Lonely Man.* New York: Harcourt, Brace, 1959.

Roosevelt, James, with Bill Libby. *My Parents: A Differing View.* Chicago: Playboy Press, 1976.

Roosevelt, Mrs. James [Sara Delano]. As told by Isabel Leighton and Gabrielle Forbush. *My Boy Franklin.* New York: R. Long & R. R. Smith, 1933.

Roosevelt, Nicholas. *A Front Row Seat.* Norman: University of Oklahoma Press, 1953.

Roosevelt, Theodore. *Letters from Theodore Roosevelt to Anna Roosevelt Cowles, 1870–1918.* New York: Charles Scribner's Sons, 1924.

———. *The Letters of Theodore Roosevelt.* Elting E. Morison, ed. 8 vols. Cambridge: Harvard University Press, 1954.

———. *Progressive Principles: Selections from Addresses Made During the Presidential Campaign of 1912.* New York: Progressive National Service, 1913.

———. *Theodore Roosevelt: An Autobiography.* New York: Macmillan, 1913.

———. *Theodore Roosevelt's Letters to His Children.* Joseph Bucklin Bishop, ed. New York: Charles Scribner's Sons, 1919.

———. *The Works of Theodore Roosevelt.* Hermann Hagedorn, ed. 24 vols. New York: Charles Scribner's Sons, 1923–1926.

Roosevelt, Theodore, Jr. *All in the Family.* New York: G. P. Putnam's Sons, 1929.

Roper, Daniel C. *Fifty Years of Public Life.* Durham: Duke University Press, 1941.

Rosen, Elliot A. *Hoover, Roosevelt, and the Brains Trust: From Depression to New Deal.* New York: Columbia University Press, 1977.

Rosen, Robert N. *Saving the Jews: Franklin D. Roosevelt and the Holocaust.* New York: Thunder's Mouth Press, 2006.

Rosenman, Samuel I. *Working with Roosevelt.* New York: Harper & Brothers, 1952.

Ross, Leland M., and Allen W. Grobin. *This Democratic Roosevelt: The Life Story of "F.D."; An Authentic Biography.* New York: E. P. Dutton, 1932.

Rossi, Mario. *Roosevelt and the French.* Westport, Conn.: Praeger, 1993.

Rotberg, Robert I., and Theodore K. Rabb, eds. *The Origin and Prevention of Major Wars.* New York: Cambridge University Press, 1989.

Rozell, Mark J., and William D. Pederson, eds. *FDR and the Modern Presidency: Leadership and Legacy.* Westport, Conn.: Praeger, 1997.

Rusbridger, James. *Betrayal at Pearl Harbor: How Churchill Lured Roosevelt into World War II.* New York: Summit Books, 1991.

Sainsbury, Keith. *Churchill and Roosevelt at War: The War They Fought and the Peace They Hoped to Make.* New York: New York University Press, 1994.

Saloutos, Theodore, and John D. Hicks. *Agricultural Discontent in the Middle West, 1900–1939.* Madison: University of Wisconsin Press, 1951.

Sandifer, Irine Reiterman. *Mrs. Roosevelt as We Knew Her.* Silver Spring, Md.: Sandifer, 1975.

Santoyo, Elsa M., ed. *Creating an American Masterpiece: Architectural Drawings of the Old Executive Office Building, 1871–1888.* Washington, D.C.: American Institute of Architects Press, 1988.

Savage, Sean J. *Roosevelt: The Party Leader, 1932–1945.* Lexington: University Press of Kentucky, 1991.

Scammon, Richard M., ed. *America at the Polls: A Handbook of American Presidential Election Statistics.* Pittsburgh: Governmental Affairs Institute, 1965.

Scharf, Lois. *Eleanor Roosevelt: First Lady of American Liberalism.* Boston: Twayne Publishers, 1987.

Schewe, Donald B., ed. *Franklin D. Roosevelt and Foreign Affairs, January 1937–August 1939.* 10 vols. New York: Garland Publishing, 1979.

Schlesinger, Arthur M., Jr. *The Coming of the New Deal.* Boston: Houghton Mifflin, 1958.

———. *The Crisis of the Old Order, 1919 1933.* Boston: Houghton Mifflin, 1957.

———. *The New Deal in Action, 1933–1939.* New York: Macmillan, 1940.

———. *The Politics of Upheaval.* Boston: Houghton Mifflin, 1960.

———. *The Vital Center.* Boston: Houghton Mifflin, 1949.

———, ed. *Running for President: The Candidates and their Images, 1900–1992.* New York: Simon & Schuster, 1994.

Schriftgiesser, Karl. *The Amazing Roosevelt Family, 1613–1942.* New York: W. Funk, 1942.

Sears, Stephen W. *George B. McClellan: The Young Napoleon.* New York: Ticknor & Fields, 1988

Sherwin, Mark, and Chales L. Markmann. *One Week in March.* New York: G. P. Putnam's Sons, 1961.

Sherwood, Robert E. *Roosevelt and Hopkins: An Intimate History.* New York: Harper & Brothers, 1948.

Shirer, William L. *The Rise and Fall of the Third Reich.* New York: Simon & Schuster, 1959.

Shogan, Robert. *Hard Bargain: How FDR Twisted Churchill's Arm, Evaded the Law, and Changed the Role of the American Presidency.* New York: Charles Scribner's Sons, 1995.

Shoumatoff, Elizabeth. *FDR's Unfinished Portrait: A Memoir.* Pittsburgh: University of Pittsburgh Press, 1990.

Sims, William S. *The Victory at Sea.* New York: Doubleday, 1920.

Small, Melvin, and J. David Singer. *Resort to Arms: International and Civil Wars, 1816–1980.* Beverly Hills: Sage Publications, 1982.

Smith, A. Merriman. *Thank You, Mr. President: A White House Notebook.* New York: Harper & Brothers, 1946.

Smith, Alfred E. *Up to Now: An Autobiography.* New York: Viking Press, 1929.

Smith, Amanda. *Hostage to Fortune: The Letters of Joseph P. Kennedy.* New York: Viking Press, 2001.

Smith, Jean Edward. *The Constitution and American Foreign Policy.* St. Paul, Minn.: West Publishing Co., 1989.

———. *The Defense of Berlin.* Baltimore: Johns Hopkins Press, 1963.

———. *George Bush's War.* New York: Henry Holt, 1992.

————. *Grant.* New York: Simon & Schuster, 2001.

————. *John Marshall: Definer of a Nation.* New York: Henry Holt, 1996.

————. *Lucius D. Clay: An American Life.* New York: Henry Holt, 1990.

Smith, Richard Norton. *Thomas E. Dewey and His Times.* New York: Simon & Schuster, 1982.

Soames, Mary, ed. *Winston and Clementine: The Personal Letters of the Churchills.* Boston: Houghton Mifflin, 1999.

Spedding, James, Robert Leslie Ellis, and Douglas Denon Heath, eds. *The Works of Francis Bacon.* 15 vols. New York: Hurd and Houghton, 1872.

Speer, Albert. *Inside the Third Reich: Memoirs.* New York: Macmillan, 1970.

Stafford, David. *Roosevelt and Churchill: Men of Secrets.* Woodstock, N.Y.: Overlook Press, 2000.

Stalin, Joseph, Winston S. Churchill, C. R. Attlee, Franklin D. Roosevelt, and Harry S. Truman. *Correspondence Between the Chairman of the Council of Ministers of the USSR and the Presidents of the USA and the Prime Ministers of Great Britain during the Great Patriotic War of 1941–1945.* 2 vols. Moscow: Progress, 1957.

Starling, Edmund W., and Thomas Sugrue. *Starling of the White House: The Story of the Man Whose Secret Service Detail Guarded Five Presidents from Woodrow Wilson to Franklin D. Roosevelt.* New York: Simon & Schuster, 1946.

Steeholm, Clara and Hardy. *The House at Hyde Park.* New York: Viking Press, 1950.

Steel, Ronald. *Walter Lippmann and the American Century.* Boston: Little, Brown, 1980.

Stein, Leon. *The Triangle Fire.* Philadelphia: Lippincott, 1962.

Steinberg, Alfred. *Mrs. R.: The Life of Eleanor Roosevelt.* New York: G. P. Putnam's Sons, 1958.

————. *Sam Rayburn: A Biography.* New York: Hawthorn Books, 1975.

Stettinius, Edward R. *The Diaries of Edward R. Stettinius, Jr., 1943–1946.* Thomas M. Campbell and George C. Herring, eds. New York: New Viewpoints, 1975.

————. *Roosevelt and the Russians: The Yalta Conference.* New York: Doubleday, 1949.

Stiles, Lela. *The Man Behind Roosevelt: The Story of Louis McHenry Howe.* Cleveland: World, 1954.

Stillwell, Paul. *Air Raid, Pearl Harbor: Recollections of a Day of Infamy.* Annapolis, Md.: Naval Institute Press, 1981.

Stimson, Henry L., and McGeorge Bundy. *On Active Service in Peace and War.* New York: Harper & Brothers, 1948.

Stinnett, Robert B. *Day of Deceit: The Truth About FDR and Pearl Harbor.* New York: Free Press, 1999.

Stokes, Thomas L. *Chip off My Shoulder.* Princeton, N.J.: Princeton University Press, 1940.

Stoler, Mark A. *The Politics of the Second Front: American Military Planning and Diplomacy in Coalition Warfare, 1941–1943.* Westport, Conn.: Greenwood Press, 1977.

Storke, Thomas M. *California Editor.* Los Angeles: Westernlore Press, 1958.

Strouse, Jean. *Morgan: American Financier.* New York: Perenial, 2000.

Sulzberger, C. L. *A Long Row of Candles: Memoirs and Diaries, 1934–1954.* New York: Macmillan, 1969.

Sumner, William Graham. *The Forgotten Man and Other Essays.* New Haven, Conn.: Yale University Press, 1918.

Swain, Martha H. *Pat Harrison: The New Deal Years.* Jackson: University Press of Mississippi, 1978.

Swift, Will. *The Roosevelts and the Royals: Franklin and Eleanor, The King and Queen of England, and the Friendship That Changed History.* Hoboken, N.J.: John Wiley & Sons, 2004.

Tansill, Charles C. *Back Door to War: The Roosevelt Foreign Policy, 1933–1941.* Chicago: Regnery, 1952.

Taylor, Charles Carlisle. *The Life of Admiral Mahan.* New York: George H. Doran, 1920.

Taylor, F. J. *The United States and the Spanish Civil War, 1936–1939.* New York: Bookman Associates, 1956.

Teague, Michael. *Mrs. L: Conversations with Alice Roosevelt Longworth.* New York: Doubleday, 1981.

Tehan, Arline Boucher. *Henry Adams in Love.* New York: Universe Books, 1983.

Teichmann, Howard. *Alice: The Life and Times of Alice Roosevelt Longworth.* Englewood Cliffs, N.J.: Prentice-Hall, 1979.

Thomas, Gordon, and Max Morgan Witts. *The Day the Bubble Burst.* New York: Doubleday, 1979.

Thompson, Robert Smith. *A Time for War: Franklin Delano Roosevelt and the Path to Pearl Harbor.* New York: Prentice-Hall, 1991.

Timmons, Bascom N. *Garner of Texas: A Personal History.* New York: Harper & Brothers, 1948.

———. *Jesse H. Jones: The Man and the Statesman.* New York: Henry Holt, 1956.

Truman, Harry S. *Memoirs.* 2 vols. New York: Doubleday, 1956.

Tuchman, Barbara W. *The Guns of August.* New York: Macmillan, 1962.

———. *The Zimmermann Telegram.* New York: Viking Press, 1958.

Tucker, Ray Thomas. *The Mirrors of 1932.* New York: Brewer, Warren & Putnam, 1931.

Tugwell, Rexford G. *The Brains Trust.* New York: Viking Press, 1968.

———. *The Democratic Roosevelt: A Biography of Franklin D. Roosevelt.* New York: Doubleday, 1957.

———. *In Search of Roosevelt.* Cambridge, Mass.: Harvard University Press, 1972.

———. *Roosevelt's Revolution.* New York: Macmillan, 1977.

Tully, Grace. *F.D.R.: My Boss.* New York: Charles Scribner's Sons, 1949.

Tumulty, Joseph P. *Woodrow Wilson as I Know Him.* New York: Doubleday, Page & Co., 1921.

Underhill, Robert. *FDR and Harry: Unparalleled Lives.* Westport, Conn.: Praeger, 1996.

United States Civilian Production Administration. *Industrial Mobilization for War.* Washington, D.C.: U.S. Government Printing Office, 1947.

United States Congress. *Pearl Harbor Attack: Hearings Before the Joint Committee on the*

Investigation of the Pearl Harbor Attack. 39 vols. Washington, D.C.: U.S. Government Printing Office, 1946.

United States Congress, House, Committee on Naval Affairs. *Hearings, 1915.* Washington, D.C.: U.S. Government Printing Office, 1915.

United States Department of Commerce, Bureau of the Census. *Statistical History of the United States from Colonial Times to the Present.* Stamford, Conn.: Fairfield Publishers, 1965.

United States Department of Justice. *Annual Report of the Attorney General of the United States.* Washington, D.C.: U.S. Department of Justice, 1913.

United States Department of State. *Foreign Relations of the United States, 1908.* Washington, D.C.: U.S. Government Printing Office, 1912.

———. *Foreign Relations of the United States, 1914, Supplement.* Washington, D.C.: U.S. Government Printing Office, 1928.

———. *Foreign Relations of the United States, 1915, Supplement.* Washington, D.C.: U.S. Government Printing Office, 1928.

———. *Foreign Relations of the United States, 1924.* Washington, D.C.: U.S. Government Printing Office, 1939.

———. *Foreign Relations of the United States, 1940.* 5 vols. Washington, D.C.: U.S. Government Printing Office, 1955–1961.

———. *Foreign Relations of the United States, 1941.* 7 vols. Washington, D.C.: U.S. Government Printing Office, 1956–1963.

———. *Foreign Relations of the United States, Conferences at Malta and Yalta, 1945.* Washington, D.C.: U.S. Government Printing Office, 1955.

———. *Foreign Relations of the United States, Conferences at Cairo and Teheran, 1943.* Washington, D.C.: U.S. Government Printing Office, 1961.

———. *Foreign Relations of the United States, Conferences at Washington, 1941–1942, and Casablanca, 1943.* Washington, D.C.: U.S. Government Printing Office, 1968.

———. *Peace and War: United States Foreign Policy, 1931–1941.* Washington, D.C.: U.S. Government Printing Office, 1943.

———. *Treaties and Other International Agreements of the United States, 1776–1949.* Charles I. Bevans, ed. 13 vols. Washington, D.C.: U.S. Government Printing Office, 1968–1976.

United States Department of the Army. *The Army Almanac.* Washington, D.C.: U.S. Government Printing Office, 1950.

United States Department of the Navy. *Ships' Data: U.S. Naval Vessels.* Washington, D.C.: U.S. Government Printing Office, 1914.

United States Federal Writers' Project. *Washington: City and Capital, Federal Writers' Project Works Progress Administration . . . Washington, 1937.* Washington, D.C.: U.S. Government Printing Office, 1937.

United States Public Works Administration. *America Builds: The Record of the PWA.* Washington, D.C.: U.S. Government Printing Office, 1939.

Utley, Jonathan G. *Going to War with Japan, 1937–1941.* Knoxville: University of Tennessee Press, 1985.

Vandenberg, Arthur H., and Joe Alex Morris. *The Private Papers of Senator Vandenberg.* Boston: Houghton Mifflin, 1952.

Vanderbilt, Cornelius, Jr. *Farewell to Fifth Avenue.* New York: Simon & Schuster, 1935.

Van Minnen, Cornelius A., and John F. Sears, eds. *FDR and His Contemporaries: Foreign Perceptions of an American President.* New York: St. Martin's Press, in association with the Roosevelt Study Center, 1992.

Van Natta, Don. *First Off the Tee: Presidential Hackers, Duffers, and Cheaters, from Taft to Bush.* New York: PublicAffairs, 2003.

Verrier, Anthony. *Assassination in Algiers: Churchill, Roosevelt, de Gaulle, and the Murder of Admiral Darlan.* New York: Norton, 1990.

Von Drehle, David. *Triangle: The Fire That Changed America.* New York: Atlantic Monthly Press, 2003.

Waite, John G. *The President as Architect: Franklin D. Roosevelt's Top Cottage.* Albany, N.Y.: Mount Ida Press, 2001.

Walker, Turnley. *Roosevelt and the Warm Springs Story.* New York: A. A. Wyn, 1953.

Walker, William O., III. *Opium and Foreign Policy.* Chapel Hill: University of North Carolina Press, 1991.

Wallace, Henry A. *The Price of Vision: Diary of Henry A. Wallace, 1942–1946.* John Morton Blum, ed. Boston: Houghton Mifflin, 1973.

Walzer, Michael. *Just and Unjust Wars: A Moral Argument with Historical Illustrations.* New York: Basic Books, 1977.

Ward, Geoffrey C. *Before the Trumpet: Young Franklin Roosevelt, 1882–1905.* New York: Harper & Row, 1985.

———. *A First-Class Temperament: The Emergence of Franklin Roosevelt.* New York: Harper & Row, 1989.

———, ed. *Closest Companion: The Unknown Story of the Intimate Friendship Between Franklin Roosevelt and Margaret Suckley.* Boston: Houghton Mifflin, 1995.

Warner, Emily Smith, and Hawthorne Daniel. *The Happy Warrior: A Biography of My Father, Alfred E. Smith.* New York: Doubleday, 1956.

Warren, Charles. *The Supreme Court in United States History.* 2 vols. Boston: Little, Brown, 1926.

Warren, Earl. *The Memoirs of Earl Warren.* New York: Doubleday, 1977.

Warren, Harris Gaylord. *Herbert Hoover and the Great Depression.* New York: Oxford University Press, 1959.

Watkins, T. H. *Righteous Pilgrim: The Life and Times of Harold L. Ickes, 1874–1952.* New York: Henry Holt, 1990.

Watson, Mark S. *The United States Army in World War II: Chief of Staff: Prewar Plans and Preparations.* Washington, D.C.: U.S. Government Printing Office, 1950.

Watt, Donald Cameron. *How War Came: The Immediate Origins of the Second World War, 1938–1939.* New York: Pantheon, 1989.

Webb, Beatrice. *The Diary of Beatrice Webb.* Norman and Jeanne MacKenzie, eds., Cambridge, Mass.: Harvard University Press, 1982–1985.

Wedemeyer, Albert C. *Wedemeyer Reports!* New York: Henry Holt, 1958.

Wehle, Louis B. *Hidden Threads of History, Wilson Through Roosevelt*. New York: Macmillan, 1953.

Weil, Martin. *A Pretty Good Club: The Founding Fathers of the U.S. Foreign Service*. New York: Norton, 1978.

Weiss, Nancy J. *Charles Francis Murphy, 1858–1924: Respectability and Responsibility in Tammany Politics*. Northampton, Mass.: Smith College, 1968.

———. *Farewell to the Party of Lincoln: Black Politics in the Age of FDR*. Princeton, N.J.: Princeton University Press, 1983.

Weizmann, Chaim. *Trial and Error: The Autobiography of Chaim Weizmann*. New York: Harper & Brothers, 1949.

Welles, Sumner. *Seven Decisions That Shaped History*. New York: Harper & Brothers, 1951.

———. *Time for Decision*. New York: Harper & Brothers, 1944.

Werner, M. R. *Bryan*. New York: Harcourt, Brace, 1929.

———. *Tammany Hall*. New York: Greenwood Press, 1968.

West, J. B., with Mary Lynn Kotz. *Upstairs at the White House*. New York: Coward, McCann & Geoghegan, 1973.

Wharton, Don. *The Roosevelt Omnibus*. New York: Knopf, 1934.

Wharton, Edith. *The Age of Innocence*. New York: D. Appleton, 1920.

Wheeler, Burton K. *Yankee from the West*. New York: Doubleday, 1962.

Wheeler-Bennett, John W. *King George VI: His Life and Reign*. New York: St. Martin's Press, 1958.

———. *The Nemesis of Power: The German Army in Politics, 1918–1945*. New York: St. Martin's Press, 1954.

White, G. Edward. *The Constitution and the New Deal*. Cambridge, Mass.: Harvard University Press, 2000.

White, Graham J. *F.D.R. and the Press*. Chicago: University of Chicago Press, 1979.

White, Walter. *A Man Called White: The Autobiography of Walter White*. New York: Viking Press, 1948.

White, William L. *Bernard Baruch*. New York: Harcourt, Brace, 1950.

Whittelsey, Charles B. *The Roosevelt Genealogy, 1649–1902*. Hartford, Conn.: Burr, 1902.

Williams, T. Harry. *Huey Long*. New York: Knopf, 1969.

Willis, Resa. *FDR and Lucy: Lovers and Friends*. New York: Routledge, 2004.

Wilson, Theodore A. *The First Summit: Roosevelt and Churchill at Placentia Bay, 1941*. Boston: Houghton Mifflin, 1969.

Wilson, Woodrow. *Congressional Government: A Study in American Politics*. Boston: Houghton Mifflin, 1885.

Winfield, Betty Houchin. *FDR and the News Media*. New York: Columbia University Press, 1994.

Wise, John Sargeant. *Recollections of Thirteen Presidents*. New York: Doubleday, 1906.

Wohlstetter, Roberta. *Pearl Harbor: Warning and Decision*. Stanford, Calif.: Stanford University Press, 1962.

Wolf, Thomas P., Byron W. Daynes, and William D. Pederson. *Franklin D. Roosevelt and Congress: The New Deal and Its Aftermath.* Armonk, N.Y.: M. E. Sharpe, 2001.

Wordsworth, William. *Wordsworth's Poems in Two Volumes (1807): A Facsimile.* London: British Library, 1984.

Wyman, David. *The Abandonment of the Jews: America and the Holocaust, 1941–1945.* New York: Pantheon, 1984.

Yeager, M. Hildegarde. *The Life of James Roosevelt Bayley.* Washington, D.C.: Catholic University Press, 1947.

Yergin, Daniel. *Shattered Peace.* Boston: Houghton Mifflin, 1977.

Young, Louise. *Japan's Total Empire: Manchuria and the Culture of Wartime Imperialism.* Berkeley: University of California Press, 1998.

Acknowledgments

THIS BOOK COULD not have been written without the assistance of Rhonda Mullins of the Communications Department (President's Office) of Marshall University. I write in longhand with a ballpoint pen on yellow legal pads. Ms. Mullins not only was able to read my writing but translated it to typescript with remarkable efficiency. Over the course of four years and endless drafts, she provided me with finished copy on a daily basis. I am eternally grateful.

Writing contemporary biography requires consulting vast collections of primary documents. I am indebted to the John and Elizabeth Drinko Foundation for providing the assistance that permitted my frequent visits to the Franklin D. Roosevelt Library at Hyde Park; the Manuscript Division of the Library of Congress; the special collections of personal papers at Princeton, Harvard, and Yale; and the Oral History Project at Columbia. John and Elizabeth's contribution to higher education is truly remarkable. Over the last thirty years they have established nine endowed chairs, supported more than a dozen academic programs, and provided the funds for the construction of the Ohio State University Law School, the Marshall University Library, and the Performing Arts Recital Hall at Cleveland State. Neither John nor Elizabeth was a fan of Franklin Roosevelt, but that did not prevent them from providing unstinting support.

To those who have read the manuscript, I am indebted beyond measure. Their suggestions have been invaluable, and I thank them for the time and effort they generously granted. The entire manuscript was read by the "Gang of Thirteen"—old friends, colleagues, and former students, many of whom helped with *Clay, Marshall,* and *Grant:* Thomas Bergquist, Paul Ehrlich, Bennett Feigenbaum, Joanne Feld, Ellen Feldman, Alan Gould, Sanford Lakoff, William Nelson, John Seaman, John Simon, Kelly and David Vaziri, and Frank Williams. Portions of the manuscript were read by George Carter, Michael Donnelly, Harry Moul, Roger Newman, Kent Newmyer, Dan O'Hanlon, and Simon Perry, to whom I am also grateful. My classmates Alan Blumberg and Brice McAdoo Clagett provided valuable assistance pertaining to New York divorce proceedings and the 1932 Democratic National Convention. Dr. Sonya Vaziri of the Harvard Medical School helped me understand the problems of FDR's hypertension.

The bibliography was prepared by Aaron Arthur, Jessica Watkins, and Jarrett Gerlach. The reference librarians at the Franklin D. Roosevelt Library, Mark Renovitch, Virginia Lewick, and Alycia Vivona, were helpful beyond description. The copyediting was done by Lynn Anderson, Dennis Ambrose was the production editor, and Simon Sullivan was the book's designer.

To my agent, Elizabeth Kaplan, I am especially grateful for navigating the tricky shoals of contract negotiation and helping to place this book with Random House. I cannot say too much about the pleasure of working with Vice President and Executive Editor Robert Loomis. Mr. Loomis is justly regarded as the nation's premier editor of nonfiction and is a man of wonderful warmth and diligence. This is his fiftieth year at Random House, and I am pleased that *FDR* has appeared in time to mark the occasion.

Index

JEAN EDWARD SMITH is the author of twelve books, including highly acclaimed biographies of Chief Justice John Marshall, General Lucius D. Clay, and Ulysses S. Grant (a 2002 Pulitzer Prize finalist). A graduate of Princeton University and Columbia, Smith taught at the University of Toronto thirty-five years before joining the faculty at Marshall University, where he is the John Marshall Professor of Political Science.